572214

D1448563

PENGUIN REFERENCE
The Penguin Dictionary of Law

Julian Webb BA, LLM, LLD is Professor of Legal Education at the University of Warwick, and Director of the Higher Education Academy's UK Centre for Legal Education. He has published over 40 journal articles and book chapters and is co-author/editor of five other books, including Holland and Webb's *Learning Legal Rules* (6th edn, Oxford University Press, 2006). He is joint editor of the Routledge-Cavendish *Law, Science and Society* book series, and was a founding editor of the journal *Legal Ethics*. Julian is course director of Warwick Law School's LLM in Legal Education and for seven years taught courses on the theory and practice of dispute resolution on the Westminster LLM in Dispute Prevention and Resolution. He has also taught undergraduate courses on English and comparative legal systems, public law, legal ethics, legal skills and philosophy of law.

The Penguin Dictionary of
LAW

Edited by Julian Webb

PENGUIN BOOKS

PENGUIN BOOKS

Published by the Penguin Group
Penguin Books Ltd, 80 Strand, London WC2R 0RL, England
Penguin Group (USA) Inc., 375 Hudson Street, New York, New York 10014, USA
Penguin Group (Canada), 90 Eglinton Avenue East, Suite 700, Toronto, Ontario, Canada M4P 2Y3
(a division of Pearson Penguin Canada Inc.)
Penguin Ireland, 25 St Stephen's Green, Dublin 2, Ireland (a division of Penguin Books Ltd)
Penguin Group (Australia), 250 Camberwell Road, Camberwell, Victoria 3124, Australia
(a division of Pearson Australia Group Pty Ltd)
Penguin Books India Pvt Ltd, 11 Community Centre, Panchsheel Park, New Delhi – 110 017, India
Penguin Group (NZ), 67 Apollo Drive, Rosedale, North Shore 0632, New Zealand
(a division of Pearson New Zealand Ltd)
Penguin Books (South Africa) (Pty) Ltd, 24 Sturdee Avenue, Rosebank, Johannesburg 2196, South Africa

Penguin Books Ltd, Registered Offices: 80 Strand, London WC2R 0RL, England

www.penguin.com

First published 2009
1

Set in ITC Stone Sans and ITC Stone Serif
Typeset by Data Standards Ltd, Frome, Somerset
Printed in England by Clays Ltd, St Ives plc

ISBN: 978-0-141-02727-2

www.greenpenguin.co.uk

Penguin Books is committed to a sustainable future
for our business, our readers and our planet.
The book in your hands is made from paper
certified by the Forest Stewardship Council.

Contents

Acknowledgements

Inevitably with a project of this scale I have accumulated numerous debts of gratitude which I wish to acknowledge here, though I suspect a number of them may still be called in, with interest, at a later date.

Julian Roskams of Etica Press was responsible for bringing me into this project, and has been a constant support throughout its lengthy gestation. Anna Farmer gallantly and conscientiously took on the role of assistant editor at the eleventh hour, Jane Robertson (copy-editor and part-time Lecturer in Law at the University of Brighton) undertook the copy-editing and final checking of entries with consummate skill and patience, and Moira Bailey-Webb has not only been an enormously tolerant and supportive partner, especially as more of my 'free' time became absorbed by the dictionary, but has also provided substantial editorial and administrative assistance.

Last, and by no means least, is the team of contributors without whom this project really would not have been possible. Thank you to you all.

Julian Webb
Warwick, January 2009

List of Contributors

ALTC Professor Andrew Choo, Professor of Law, University of Warwick

AD   Professor Alison Diduck, Professor of Law, University College, London

AF   Anna Farmer, Graduate Research Fellow, University of Warwick

BF   Ben Fitzpatrick, Senior Lecturer in Law, University of York

CM   Christopher MacArthur, Visiting Lecturer in Law, University College, London

DR   Douglas Rhodes, Trainee Solicitor, Trowers & Hamlins

FK   Felicity Kaganas, Reader in Law, Brunel University

HC   Helen Carr, Senior Lecturer in Law, University of Kent at Canterbury

HJ   Helen James, Senior Lecturer in Law, University of Winchester

IB   Professor Ilias Bantekas, Professor of Public International Law, Brunel University

JP   Dr John Paterson, Reader in Law, University of Aberdeen

JPl   Professor Jill Poole, Professor of Commercial Law, Aston University

JW   Professor Julian Webb, Professor of Legal Education, University of Warwick

MJ   Michael Jefferson, Senior Lecturer in Law, University of Sheffield

MON Dr Maria O'Neill, Senior Lecturer in Law, University of Abertay-Dundee

MS   Dr Maureen Spencer, Principal Lecturer in Law, Middlesex University

PK   Paul Kohler, Senior Lecturer in Law, School of Oriental and African Studies, and Visiting Fellow, Queen Mary University of London

RE   Richard Earle, Senior Lecturer in Law, University of Westminster

SN   Professor Susan Nash, Professor of Law, City University, London

US   Dr Uma Suthersanen, Reader in Intellectual Property Law and Policy, Queen Mary University of London

Introduction

This dictionary has been written to provide a clear but authoritative (within the constraints of the dictionary format) guide to the law: a social institution that most of us will come into contact with at some point in our lives.

The primary focus of this work is on English law, or, more properly, the law of the legal system of England and Wales. Although it is increasingly plausible in some areas to speak of UK law (and this is reflected in the contents that follow), the fact remains that the UK operates as a number of discrete legal systems, and it is not possible to reflect all the different nuances of those systems within a single volume. The text does include extensive treatment of European law, and of both private and public international and humanitarian law, not least because, in an increasingly globalized world, no legal system functions in isolation. In addition, some key concepts of Scots law have been included where these provide useful and likely points of comparison with English law.

We have sought to keep the coverage broad, encompassing not just the core foundations of law (contract, tort, criminal law, public law, equity, land and European law), but also including key concepts from civil and criminal procedure and evidence, and of more specialist areas of interest such as employment law, family, intellectual property, tax and succession. Entries on key thinkers and concepts in the philosophy of law are also included.

So far as possible the law is stated as at 30 November 2008, though it has been possible to include a small number of more recent developments as well.

How to use this book

To achieve clarity and consistency of treatment, each substantive entry adopts broadly the following structure:

- the language derivation and translation (if not English)
- a definition, including reference to primary legal sources, if appropriate
- some explanation (including references to sub-concepts, shown in bold text) and examples
- references to key cases, where appropriate
- relevant website addresses are included, though please be aware these may be subject to change during the life of this edition
- larger key concepts may include references to 'Further reading' at the end
- full cross-referencing to other entries as appropriate, shown in SMALL CAPITALS.

Entries have been organized to support natural language searching wherever possible. They are in strictly alphabetical order, and if you want to find a reference to the Court of Appeal, you will find it under 'Court of Appeal', not 'Appeal, Court of'. Biographical entries are organized by the subject's family name (surname). Entries generally are based on proper terms of art in the field, though some common non-legal or colloquial terms are also included as these may be a more obvious starting point.

Cross-referencing tends to be quite full, to encourage browsing, but some of the more obvious legal terms are not consistently cross-referenced, especially where their everyday meaning is close enough to any technical meaning for a reasonable understanding to be possible. Where concepts have been superseded, or are of historical relevance only, this will be indicated by the word '(obsolete)' at the start of the relevant entry.

Finally, some words of warning. We have not ignored complexity where it matters and some explanations will require some effort of understanding, for which we do not apologize. There is a balance to be struck between simplicity and accuracy. Law is often complex, and understanding the law involves developing a basic level of comfort with that, and with the specialist language that the law uses. We hope this text can help you in that process, whether you are a general reader, law student or professional. At the same time, a dictionary cannot be encyclopaedic. Dictionary-sized explanations are no substitute for a fuller treatment of a topic, as they must include a degree of simplification and generalization. It follows also that this book is no substitute for legal advice where that is required, though it may help clear a path through some of the jargon you could encounter along the way.

THE DICTIONARY

A

a posteriori (Lat. from the later) A proposition is knowable *a posteriori* on the basis of experience. It contrasts with A PRIORI knowledge that is gained, e.g. through the application of 'intuition' or pure logic or other non-experiential sources. *A posteriori* is used in legal reasoning specifically to describe a proposition derived from observed or observable facts, or a conclusion which requires evidence for its support. [JW]

See also ANALOGY; A PRIORI; INDUCTIVE REASONING.

a priori (Lat. from the previous) *A priori* knowledge is that which is known 'before the fact'. It is derived deductively from general principles or pure reasoning without the need for empirical proof. In NATURAL LAW theory, for example, certain fundamental rights are said to exist *a priori* by virtue of their accordance with universal or natural law. [JW]

See also A POSTERIORI; DEDUCTIVE REASONING.

a vinculo matrimonii (Lat. from the bond of marriage) A DIVORCE which changes the parties' legal status; it frees the parties from the MARRIAGE entirely, so that they are able to remarry. Before the Matrimonial Causes Act 1857 this type of divorce could only be granted in England and Wales by parliamentary decree and had to be distin-

guished from a **divorce** *a mensa et thoro* (Lat. from bed and board), which was a decree issued by the ECCLESIASTICAL COURTS, relieving the parties from the obligation to cohabit, but not altering their legal status. [AD]

ab initio (Lat. from the beginning) The phrase *ab initio* is used to distinguish those acts or omissions that have legal significance from the outset from those which only become significant because of some other event or intervening cause. For example, in certain circumstances a contract or a marriage may be described as 'void *ab initio*' where on the true construction of the agreement, or the true facts, that contract or marriage was never capable of having legal validity. [JW]

See also EX POST FACTO.

abatement In the administration of an ESTATE it may happen that there are not sufficient assets to meet all the provisions made in the WILL after payment of all the deceased's debts. The Administration of Estates Act 1925 sets out the order in which assets are to be used to pay debts, and the result will be that some beneficiaries will see their entitlement reduced or even destroyed altogether. When this happens the gift is said to be abated. [CM]

See also BENEFICIARY.

abduction Wrongful removal or kidnap of a person by force or deception. [FK]

See also CHILD ABDUCTION; INTERNATIONAL CHILD ABDUCTION.

abet A word rarely used outside a legal context, meaning to 'encourage'. The word is most closely associated with the phrase to AID AND ABET, which denotes, in part, the *ACTUS REUS* of being an ACCESSORY.
[BF]

ABH *See* ACTUAL BODILY HARM.

abortion The termination of a pregnancy, whether by chemical or surgical means. Under the Abortion Act 1967, s. 1, it is lawful for a pregnancy to be terminated by a registered medical practitioner if two registered medical practitioners are of the opinion, formed in good faith, that, for example, the pregnancy has not exceeded its 24th week and that the continuance of the pregnancy would involve risk, greater than if the pregnancy were terminated, of injury to the physical or mental health of the pregnant woman or any existing children of her family. The 1967 Act prescribes a number of alternative conditions which will render an abortion lawful.

An abortion conducted other than in accordance with the 1967 Act risks falling foul of the criminal law. Thus, it is an offence under the Offences against the Person Act 1861, s. 58, for a pregnant woman to administer any poison or noxious thing to herself with intent to procure her own miscarriage, or for anybody else to administer to her (whether or not she is pregnant) or cause to be taken by her any poison or noxious thing, or to use any instrument or other means with the same intent. Section 59 of the 1861 Act also makes it an offence for a person unlawfully to supply or procure poison or anything else, knowing that it is intended to be unlawfully (i.e. other than in accordance with the 1967 Act) used to procure the miscarriage of any woman (irrespective of whether the woman is actually pregnant). [BF]

See also CHILD DESTRUCTION.

absconding A person who has been released on BAIL in criminal proceedings is guilty of the offence of absconding if they fail without reasonable cause to surrender to custody. [SN]

absent parent A PARENT who does not reside in the same household as his/her CHILD. In the UK, this term has to some extent been supplanted by the term NON-RESIDENT PARENT. [FK]

See also RESIDENCE ORDER.

absolute discharge A sentencing decision whereby a court takes no further action against an offender other than to record the discharge on his or her criminal record. [SN]

absolute owner Someone in whom the full range of ownership rights are vested. This occurs when a legal title is held free from any form of trust. [PK]

absolute privilege A statement cannot be the basis for an action for DEFAMATION where the words used (whether spoken or written) are protected by PARLIAMENTARY PRIVILEGE, or are communicated between certain officers of state, or are used in the ordinary course of legal proceedings, or where (under the Defamation Act 1996, s. 14) they constitute a fair and accurate contemporaneous report of public legal proceedings. [JW]

See also QUALIFIED PRIVILEGE; WAIVER OF PRIVILEGE.

absolute rights Those rights which, under the EUROPEAN CONVENTION ON HUMAN RIGHTS, the STATE cannot limit, withhold or take away. Absolute rights include prohibitions on torture, inhuman and degrading treatment or punishment (Article 3), and freedom of thought, conscience and religion (Article 9). [JW]

See also HUMAN RIGHTS; QUALIFIED RIGHTS.

abstract of title In the CONVEYANCING of REGISTERED LAND, the abstract provides written details of the title deeds and other documents necessary for the vendor to prove their ownership of the property, and should be provided to the purchaser before completion of any sale. The abstract of title comprises OFFICIAL COPIES of entries in the register held by the Land Registry, and details of any other documents that are necessary to prove the owner's TITLE to the legal ESTATE. It will also provide details of any equitable interests over the property that are not overreached.   [DR]

See also EPITOME OF TITLE; OVERREACHING.

abstracting electricity An offence under the Theft Act 1968, s. 13. It is committed by the person who dishonestly uses electricity without due authority, or who dishonestly causes electricity to be wasted or diverted. A typical situation in which the offence would be charged would be where a suspect had allegedly tampered with an electricity meter such as to bypass it, or who had reconnected a disconnected meter without the permission of the electricity company. Electricity is not property within the meaning of the Theft Act 1968, s. 4 and is thus incapable of being stolen; that is to say, it cannot form the subject of a charge of THEFT.   [BF]

abuse of dominant position Unlawful and anti-competitive practices carried out by large businesses, normally defined as those having a share of at least 40 per cent of the market in one or more European Union Member States. Practices such as predatory pricing or refusing to supply an established customer are abuses contrary to Article 82 EC Treaty.   [JW]

See also UNFAIR COMPETITION.

abuse of process 1. A ground for amending, staying or striking out proceedings in the exercise of the discretion of the court because it would be inappropriate to permit them to continue. The discretion applies in both civil and criminal proceedings. In civil proceedings, abuse of process is characterized by the use of a court procedure for an improper purpose, in the sense that it is 'for a purpose or in a way significantly different from its ordinary and proper use' – *per* Lord Bingham CJ in *Attorney General* v. *Barker* [2000] 1 FLR 759. Where the court finds that a procedural act constitutes an abuse of process, it has a wide discretion at COMMON LAW to prevent such a step or action from being taken, or to STRIKE OUT the offending statement or process. The courts' powers to deal with abuse of process also

overlap with express procedural powers under the CPR to deal with frivolous litigation or other improper acts by a party to proceedings. In the criminal context a court will stay proceedings only when:

> to try those proceedings will amount to an abuse of its own process either [i] because it will be impossible (usually by reason of delay) to give the accused a fair trial or [ii] because it offends the court's sense of justice and propriety to be asked to try the accused in the circumstances of a particular case. ... *prima facie* it is the duty of a court to try a person who is charged before it with an offence which the court has power to try and therefore ... the jurisdiction to stay must be exercised carefully and sparingly and only for very compelling reasons. (*R* v. *Horseferry Road Magistrates' Court, ex p Bennett* [1994] 1 AC 42, 74).

2. A TORT grounding an action in damages where a person has suffered loss as a consequence of another using a legal process for an ulterior and improper purpose.

         [ALTC & JW]

See also CONTEMPT OF COURT; VEXATIOUS LITIGATION.

abuse of process estoppel The ground on which a court may use its inherent powers to prevent litigation that is an ABUSE OF PROCESS so as to prevent a party from raising an issue which was or should have been decided in earlier proceedings. This reflects a facet of the principle of public policy, identified in the leading case of *Henderson* v. *Henderson* [1843–60] All ER Rep 378, that, generally, a party must bring his or her entire case before the court in one action, and not subject a defendant to the oppressive effects of successive suits arising from the same circumstances.   [JW]

See also RES JUDICATA.

AC The standard abbreviation for Appeal Cases in the Law Reports. Published by the INCORPORATED COUNCIL OF LAW REPORTING, the Appeal Cases series publishes decisions of the HOUSE OF LORDS and JUDICIAL COMMITTEE OF THE PRIVY COUNCIL.   [JW]

See also LAW REPORTS.

ACAS *See* ADVISORY CONCILIATION AND ARBITRATION SERVICE.

acceleration In land law, the doctrine under which, on the determination of an interest in land, a future interest takes effect in possession sooner than originally intended. This may be as a result of a disclaimer, surrender, merger, lapse or the extinguishing of the preceding interest, among other reasons. For example, where X gives land 'on my death to Y for life, remainder to Z', on X's death Y will have a LIFE INTEREST and Z will have an interest in the REMAINDER. However, if Y dies before X, then on X's death his gift to Y will lapse and Z's interest will be accelerated, taking effect as a FEE SIMPLE ABSOLUTE IN POSSESSION.   [DR]

acceptance **1**. *Of an offer*: in general CONTRACT law, acceptance of an OFFER results in agreement. The acceptance can be made by express words of unconditional assent to the offer terms or may be inferred from conduct where there is clear evidence of such an unqualified intention to assent, e.g. by using goods that have been obtained 'on approval', although it is not generally possible for an offeror to stipulate that the offeree's silence will constitute acceptance. A subjective intention to accept which is not evidenced by words or conduct will not suffice as acceptance of an offer.

In order to constitute a valid acceptance, the 'acceptance' must assent to all the terms of the offer or it will constitute a counter-offer. It must be unconditional, so that an acceptance 'subject to contract' is not a valid acceptance. In addition, the offeree must know of the existence of the offer and accept in response to it, and the offer must be subsisting at the time of assent. An assent must be communicated to the offeror in accordance with the applicable communication requirement, e.g. postal acceptance is binding on dispatch, whereas other acceptances are binding on receipt. However, if the offer requires the performance of an act (see UNILATERAL CONTRACT), the offeror waives the communication requirement and acceptance occurs on performance of that act,

e.g. giving information in response to an offer of reward.

2. *Of a bill of exchange*: acceptance in a written and signed agreement by the drawee of a BILL OF EXCHANGE (i.e. the person on whom a bill of exchange is drawn) from the drawer (i.e. the person who draws the bill on him). On acceptance, the drawee becomes the party primarily liable on the bill.

3. *In contracts for the sale of goods*: once goods are accepted they can no longer be rejected. If goods are delivered to the buyer, and the buyer has not previously examined them, he is not deemed to have accepted the goods until he has had a reasonable opportunity to examine them to ensure that they are in conformity with the contract. A consumer cannot lose this right to a reasonable opportunity to inspect by agreement, WAIVER or other means. A buyer is deemed to have accepted the goods (Sale of Goods Act 1979, s. 35) by intimating acceptance to the seller after a reasonable opportunity to examine them; or following delivery of the goods, performing any act in relation to the goods which is inconsistent with the seller's ownership of them; or after the lapse of a reasonable time, retaining the goods without indicating to the seller that he has rejected them.   [JPL]

See also UNILATERAL CONTRACT.

access Contact between a CHILD and adults and/or children who do not live in the same household. This was originally a legal term that referred to visits ranging from brief contact to overnight stays to periods spanning several days or more. It no longer appears in UK statutes, having been replaced by the wider term 'contact'. It is still in use colloquially and it is used in international instruments such as the Hague Convention on the Civil Aspects of International Child Abduction, 1980. [FK]

See also ABDUCTION; CONTACT ORDER.

accession (to treaty) Accession, adherence or adhesion occurs when a state formally adopts A TREATY that it did not initially sign but which has already been signed by other states. There is no reason why accession cannot take place through notification or the sending of an instrument of ratification to the treaty's depository organ, unless the terms of the treaty specify otherwise. 'Acceptance' and 'approval' are also contemporary means of accession. Accession has the effect of ratification and not merely of signature, unless otherwise specified by the terms of the treaty or by the parties. This is also recognized in Articles 15 and 16 of the 1961 Vienna Convention on the Law of Treaties. [IB]

See also RATIFICATION OF TREATIES; SIGNATURE OF TREATY.

accessory One who assists or encourages another to commit an offence, which is then committed; also known as an **accomplice** or a **secondary party**. Being an accessory is not an offence in itself, but is a mode of participation in a specific offence. Thus, where P robs a bank, having been driven there by A, P commits ROBBERY as a PRINCIPAL offender, and A is an accessory to robbery. The *ACTUS REUS* of being an accessory is to 'aid, ABET, counsel or procure'. Although it has been suggested that each of these words has a distinct meaning (see Lord Widgery CJ in *Attorney General's Reference (No. 1 of 1975)* [1975] 1 QB 773), they amount, collectively, to assistance or encouragement, and all four words can be used together on an indictment or information.

To become an accessory, one must, as a minimum, foresee that the principal offender will commit the principal offence (see *R* v. *Bryce* [2004] EWCA Crim 1231). Thus, I will not be an accessory to your BURGLARY if I lend you a ladder (which you, in the event, use to gain entry to premises) in the honest belief that you are going to use it on a window-cleaning round.

One becomes an accessory at the point at which the principal offence is committed. Consequently, if I lend you a ladder, in the belief that you will use it to commit burglary, I will not become an accessory should you decide not to do so. [BF]

See also AID AND ABET.

accessory liability The criminal liability incurred as a result of being an ACCESSORY. [BF]

accident record book An EMPLOYER is obliged to keep a record of all workplace accidents: the law originated in the Notification of Accidents and Dangerous Occurrences Regulations 1980 (SI 1980/904) and is now found in the Reporting of Injuries, Diseases and Dangerous Occurrences Regulations 1995 ('RIDDOR') (SI 1995/3163). [MJ]

accomplice *See* ACCESSORY.

accord and satisfaction A binding agreement by which one party purchases a release from their obligations under an existing CONTRACT. Technically, the accord is the agreement to discharge the contract or particular contractual obligation, and satisfaction is the CONSIDERATION to support the promise to discharge. In general, this satisfaction must constitute fresh consideration and cannot be the actual performance of the contract or contractual obligation itself. [JPL]

account An equitable action by which a party can apply to court for any monies arising in respect of an equitable or legal right owed to that party by another; for example, a BENEFICIARY under a TRUST might obtain an account from his TRUSTEE, a mortgagor might obtain an account from a mortgagee who has entered into possession, or a PRINCIPAL could obtain an account against his AGENT. Although historically an action to account existed at COMMON LAW this was superseded by equity's more flexible response which, even today, results in there being no definite rule as to when an action to account will be permitted. The general principle is that the jurisdiction will not be exercised where the matter can be fully and conveniently dealt with by means of a legal action. Detailed provisions relating to the taking of accounts are also now to be found in the CIVIL PROCEDURE RULES. [PK]

account of profits A remedy whereby the claimant is able to recover a sum equivalent to the monetary gain made by the defendant as a result of his wrong; for example, a company DIRECTOR may be made liable to account to the COMPANY for profits he has made by taking a corporate opportunity for himself, or gains made as a result of an infringement of COPYRIGHT or PATENT may be the subject of an order to account for profits.

In the contractual context, an account of profits may be available only in very exceptional circumstances (see *Attorney General v. Blake* [2001] 1 AC 268), to enable one party to recover the profits made as a result of the other's breach of contract. [JPL]

accountability of the judiciary *See* JUDICIAL ACCOUNTABILITY.

accretion The gradual and imperceptible addition of land mass (and very rarely water mass) to the existing territory of the STATE. There is no fixed rule in international law as to whether this new land mass creates a sui generis title for the riparian state, or whether title is conferred as a result of effective occupation. [IB]

See also AVULSION.

accumulation A type of TRUST in which the trustees have a power or duty to amass capital and/or income, rather than simply distribute it among the objects of the trust, by managing the property in accordance with the terms of the trust instrument and the trustees' common law and statutory duties; see in particular the Trustee Act 2000. Accumulation and maintenance trusts have a special tax status in that during the accumulation period they are DISCRETIONARY TRUSTS but are not subject to the discretionary trust tax regime. [PK]

accusatorial system *See* ADVERSARIAL SYSTEM.

acknowledgement and undertaking In CONVEYANCING, a promise given by the seller, usually made on the sale of a part of some UNREGISTERED LAND, whereby the seller acknowledges the buyer's right to have the original TITLE DEEDS produced and undertakes to keep those deeds safe.

The reason why this is often necessary is that on the sale of a part of unregistered land (e.g. if part of the land is being sold as a separate plot for building on) the seller usually keeps the original TITLE DEEDS for the retained land on COMPLETION, because they

constitute evidence of TITLE to the retained land. However, because the buyer may need to produce those original deeds to a third party (e.g. in order to prove the position of a boundary), it is standard practice for a conveyance on the sale of a part to include an acknowledgement of that right and an undertaking to keep those deeds safe. Under the Law of Property Act 1925, s. 64, where such an acknowledgement is made, it is for the buyer to pay for the cost of production of the title deeds. [DR]

acknowledgement of service A document issued by the defendant in civil proceedings which acknowledges receipt of the claimant's particulars of CLAIM. An acknowledgement of service is required in proceedings under the CIVIL PROCEDURE RULES (CPR), Part 8 and before the COMMERCIAL COURT. Where it is not required, its use has some advantages, since it will normally give the defendant more time in which to respond to the claim. For example, under CPR 15.4, the defendant has 14 days from receipt of the claim to issue a DEFENCE. If the defendant first serves an acknowledgement, he has a total of 28 days after SERVICE of the particulars of claim in which to serve that defence (CPR 15.4(1)(b)) – i.e. he is allowed up to an extra 14 days. [JW]

See also PART 8 CLAIM.

acquired rights The Acquired Rights Directive 1977/187/EEC (also known as the Business Transfers Directive; now replaced by the Acquired Rights Directive 2001/23/EC) was transposed into UK law by means of the Transfer of Undertakings (Protection of Employment) Regulations 1981 (SI 1981/1794), familiarly known as 'TUPE'. The current Regulations of the same name date from 2006 (SI 2006/246). The Regulations marked a sea-change in the law. Previously when a company had been taken over and a change of ownership had occurred (a situation which does not happen when there is a transfer of shares alone), the employee was deemed to have been dismissed. The 1981 Regulations and now the 2006 ones, however, transfer the employee with almost all of his or her rights to the new employers, the principal exceptions being criminal liabilities and most pension rights. For example, if the employee had a SEX DISCRIMINATION claim against the transferring employer, that claim was, subject to the application of TUPE, transferred to the new employer, also called 'the transferee'. For this to occur, the whole or part of the business transferred must be an economic entity which retains its identity after transfer (see Reg. 3(1)(a)). An economic entity is one which comprises an organized grouping of resources (such as staff or assets or both) which has the object of pursuing an economic activity, whether that activity is central or ancillary (Reg. 3(2)). For whether an entity is transferable under the Directive, see in particular the ECJ cases of *Spijkers* v. *Gebroeders Benedik Abattoir CV* [1986] ECR 1119 and *Aysp Süzen* v. *Zehnacker Gebäudereinigung GmbH Krankenhaus service* [1997] ECR 1-1259. [MJ]

acquis communautaire (Fr. acquisition of the community) The body of law that comprises EUROPEAN COMMUNITY (EC) law. It includes the EUROPEAN COMMUNITY TREATY; all secondary legal tools, including REGULATIONS, DIRECTIVES and DECISIONS currently in force in the EC; and all current rulings of the EC courts and tribunals. [MON]

See also COMMUNITY LAW; COURT OF FIRST INSTANCE; COURT OF JUSTICE OF THE EUROPEAN COMMUNITIES; EUROPEAN COURT OF JUSTICE; TREATY OF ROME.

acquis jurisprudential (Fr. acquisition of jurisprudence) A sub-classification of *ACQUIS COMMUNAUTAIRE*, it refers to the body of EUROPEAN COMMUNITY (EC) law which is contained in all current rulings of the EC courts and tribunals. [MON]

See also COMMUNITY LAW; COURT OF FIRST INSTANCE; COURT OF JUSTICE OF THE EUROPEAN COMMUNITIES; EUROPEAN COURT OF JUSTICE.

acquittal The discharge from prosecution of a defendant following a VERDICT or DIRECTION of not guilty. [SN]

act of God A natural disaster or other unforeseen event arising from natural causes, the consequences of which are so severe that no one could reasonably be expected to have guarded against it. The phrase is used in commercial and insurance contracts as one of a number of factors that might affect performance or liability under the agreement. [JW]

See also FORCE MAJEURE CLAUSE.

Act of Parliament *See* STATUTE.

act of state (doctrine) A principle found in the domestic law of STATES by which domestic courts refuse to assess the validity of sovereign acts of other states, leaving such matters to the executive authority. This reflects a policy consideration by the judiciary, which seeks to avoid judicial interference in matters concerning the state's external relations. The legal effect of the doctrine is to render a matter nonjusticiable. UK courts have more recently taken the view that the doctrine cannot be invoked in every case. In *Attorney General* v. *Nissan* [1970] AC 179, the House of Lords upheld a claim of reparation for damage to the property of a UK national by British troops in Cyprus as a result of an agreement with the government of Cyprus. It is doubtful that the doctrine can be invoked vis-à-vis acts perpetrated by state agents that violate international human rights. [IB]

See also STATE IMMUNITY.

acte clair (Fr. clear act) The term is used in the context of an ARTICLE 234 REFERENCE, also known as a **preliminary ruling**. If a case comes before a national court or tribunal, and an issue of European COMMUNITY LAW arises, the national court or tribunal is not required to make a preliminary reference to the EUROPEAN COURT OF JUSTICE if the EC law in question has already been ruled on by the Court of Justice (*acte éclairé*), or if the law is so clear that there is no lack of clarity as to its meaning: i.e. *acte clair*. The doctrine of *acte clair* was ruled on in Case 283/81, *S.L. CLIFT* v. *Italian Ministry of Health* [1982] ECR 3451. [MON]

action An alternative term for legal proceedings, as in the phrase 'to bring an action [against *X*]'. The origin of this usage lies with the medieval FORMS OF ACTION that were the means by which a complainant could obtain a remedy for injury in the

COMMON LAW courts. Historically, actions were divided into civil ('common pleas') and criminal ('pleas of the Crown') matters. [JW]

action for payment The appropriate action in SCOTS LAW where one party has fulfilled their obligations under a contract (for example, to deliver goods) but the price has not been paid. [JP]

See also SPECIFIC IMPLEMENT.

action plan order Introduced by the Crime and Disorder Act 1998, this order is intended to provide an intensive response to offending behaviour by a child or young person. The offender is required to comply with an action plan, and is supervised by a YOUTH OFFENDING TEAM. Action plan orders also normally include a requirement for reparation, following contact with the VICTIM, where possible. The order may stay in place for up to three months. [JW]

action short of dismissal *See* DETRIMENT.

active euthanasia *See* EUTHANASIA.

active nationality A principle by which a STATE may choose to exercise jurisdiction over criminal acts committed abroad where the offender is a national of that state. The active nationality principle has traditionally been applied by CIVIL LAW countries in Europe because, until the entry into force of the EUROPEAN ARREST WARRANT, it was normally constitutionally forbidden for these countries to extradite their own nationals. [IB]

active trust A TRUST in which the TRUSTEE is required to perform certain duties in respect of the trust property and/or the objects of the trust. [PK]

actual authority *See* AGENCY.

actual bodily harm The Offences against the Person Act 1861, s. 47, provides that ASSAULT occasioning actual bodily harm is an OFFENCE punishable by a maximum of five years' imprisonment. In this context, 'occasioning' means 'causing'. 'Actual' means more than merely trivial (see *R* v. *Chan-Fook* [1994] 2 All ER 552). 'Bodily harm' may include clinically recognizable psychological injuries, but not mere emotional upset (*R* v. *Ireland* [1998] AC 147). It is not necessary that the defendant intend or foresee the actual bodily harm, merely that he or she has the MENS REA for ASSAULT (*Savage* [1992] 1 AC 699). [BF]

See also GRIEVOUS BODILY HARM.

actus non facit reum nisi mens sit rea (Lat. an act is not criminal unless there is also a guilty mind) *See* ACTUS REUS; MENS REA.

actus reus (Lat. guilty act) The term is used by criminal lawyers, in a narrow sense, to refer to the act or acts which one has to perform (or, under certain circumstances, fail to perform) to commit a particular criminal offence. The term can be used in a broader sense to refer to all the elements of a criminal offence except those corresponding to the state of mind required for the offence (itself known as MENS REA). Thus, *actus reus* would correspond to the acts, circumstances and consequences which amount to a criminal offence. According to this broader usage the *actus reus* of, for example, MURDER would be doing an unlawful act under the QUEEN'S PEACE which causes the death of a human being. The *actus reus* of an offence is sometimes known as its physical element or external element.

All criminal offences are capable of being analytically broken down into their constituent elements of *actus reus* and *mens rea*. Of course, what constitutes those elements differs from crime to crime, but the general formula of 'crime = *actus reus* + *mens rea*' is valid. [BF]

See also OMISSION.

ad hoc arbitration An arbitral process which is not administered by any arbitral institution. The rules of procedure for the process are agreed by the parties (with or without the assistance of the ARBITRAL TRIBUNAL) or, in the absence of agreement, provided by the arbitral tribunal. The UNCITRAL ARBITRATION RULES 1976 are often adopted as the procedural rules in ad hoc INTERNATIONAL ARBITRATION, and also in international commercial arbitration conducted ad hoc. One of the sets of Arbitration Rules of the Chartered Institute of Arbitrators is often adopted in ad hoc DOMESTIC ARBITRATION. [RE]

See also ARBITRATION AGREEMENT; INSTITUTIONAL ARBITRATION.

ad idem (Lat. to the same thing) In the contractual context it means, 'of the same mind', i.e. in agreement. [JPL]

See also CONSENSUS AD IDEM.

ad referendum (Lat.) For further consideration. [JW]

address for service The address at which a party to civil proceedings is prepared to receive all formal documents relating to those proceedings. Normally an address for service must be within the jurisdiction of the court, i.e. in England and Wales where the matter is to be heard by an English or Welsh court. In certain circumstances, it may be possible to require service out of the jurisdiction, e.g. where the party is a foreign state, or where the court believes it has jurisdiction as a matter of private international law. [JW]

adduce To introduce EVIDENCE in the course of EXAMINATION-IN-CHIEF or RE-EXAMINATION. [ALTC]

ademption Occurs when property which is the subject of a specific GIFT in the WILL of a TESTATOR either ceases to exist, or is disposed of by the testator before his death. Since the property no longer forms part of the ESTATE of the testator, the gift cannot take effect, and is said to be adeemed. [CM]

adjective law That part of the law which deals with matters of court practice, procedure and evidence. [JW]

See also SUBSTANTIVE LAW.

adjournment Postponement of the hearing of a case until a future date. The power to adjourn may be exercised by all civil and criminal courts and by tribunals, though the scope of the power may vary between different courts and tribunals. [JW]

adjudication 1. The act of deciding a legal case.
2. The decision handed down by a court or TRIBUNAL. [JP]

See also ADJUDICATION THEORY.

adjudication theory A theory which seeks to account for the approach adopted by judges in deciding legal cases.

While there is general agreement with the proposition that judges apply applicable RULES to the proven facts of the case before them, considerable differences may arise when closer attention is paid to any one of the steps within that proposition. AMERICAN REALISM, for example, was sceptical of the ease with which rules could be unambiguously interpreted or facts unambiguously found.

The most significant disagreements arise, however, when the move is made away from clear cases, where an applicable rule is readily identifiable, and towards HARD CASES, where no such rule is available. In this regard, RONALD DWORKIN'S critique of H.L.A. HART represents the most celebrated exchange. Whereas Hart, as a LEGAL POSITIVIST, postulated an account of law based solely on rules, Dworkin contended that the legal system also encompasses **principles**. Accordingly, whereas a judge in Hart's account is left with no guidance when rules run out and may thus look where he or she wishes for an answer, a judge in Dworkin's account turns to legal principles in such circumstances. Whereas rules are understood as applying in an all-or-nothing manner, Dworkin acknowledges that principles do not possess this character. Indeed, competing principles may suggest different answers and it will be a matter for the judge to weigh one against the other to see which is best in terms of coherence and fit with the legal system as a whole, given the circumstances of the case. Accordingly, whereas Hart's approach is characterized as allowing the judge DISCRETION in a strong sense in hard cases, Dworkin insists that even in such cases the judge only has discretion in a weak sense. [JP]

Adjudicator, the An individual who is independent of HM REVENUE AND CUSTOMS (the Revenue), and who is appointed to determine complaints made by taxpayers against the Revenue with regard to the manner of treatment accorded to them by the Revenue. He is one of the persons to whom taxpayers may submit their complaints against the Revenue, another being the Parliamentary Commissioner for Administration.

The Adjudicator is an office holder with power to recommend to the Revenue that one or more remedies should be afforded to taxpayers in respect of the detriment caused to them by the Revenue as a result of the manner in which the taxpayers' affairs have been handled. Examples of possible complaints include personal mistreatment; delay in dealing with issues arising between the Revenue and the taxpayer; and other non-legal errors which may have been perpetrated by the Revenue. It is not a tribunal which imposes a decision on the Revenue (or the taxpayer): the Revenue can ignore the recommendation, but do not usually do so. In particular, the Adjudicator is not a tribunal concerned with the substantive and management laws applying to the taxpayer's affairs: appeals from HM Revenue and Customs on facts and points of law must be made to the GENERAL COMMISSIONERS or to the SPECIAL COMMISSIONERS. [RE]

See also COMMISSIONERS OF REVENUE AND CUSTOMS.

administration of justice A term that has no formal legal meaning but is used generally to encompass the range of functions necessary to make the legal system or, more specifically, the court system, work fairly and efficiently, for example by providing proper access to impartial legal advice, an independent judiciary and a properly resourced court infrastructure. [JW]

administration of poison Under the Offences against the Person Act 1861, s. 23, it is an offence for a person to unlawfully and maliciously administer to or cause to be administered to or taken by any other person any poison or other destructive or noxious thing, so as to endanger that person's life, or so as to inflict GRIEVOUS BODILY HARM upon that person. In the context of s. 23, 'maliciously' means intentionally or recklessly (see *R* v. *Cunningham* [1957] 2 QB 396).

Under s. 24 of the 1861 Act it is a less serious offence for a person to unlawfully and maliciously administer to or cause to be administered to or taken by any other person any poison or other destructive or noxious thing, with intent to injure, aggrieve, or annoy that person. It can be assumed that 'maliciously' has the same meaning as in s. 23. [BF]

See also INTENTION; RECKLESSNESS.

Administrative Court The name given to the DIVISIONAL COURT of the QUEEN'S BENCH DIVISION of the HIGH COURT of justice when hearing an application for JUDICIAL REVIEW under Part 54 of the CPR. Judges have to be nominated by the Lord Chief Justice specifically to sit on administrative cases. There are presently 37 such judges drawn from across all three Divisions of the High Court. [JW]

administrative justice An umbrella term that is increasingly used to describe the rules, values and principles which shape administrative action by state officials and others who deliver public services, and the institutions in which ADMINISTRATIVE LAW is practiced. [JW]

Administrative Justice and Tribunals Council (AJTC) An advisory non-departmental public body established by the Tribunals, Courts and Enforcement Act 2007 as a replacement for the COUNCIL ON TRIBUNALS. The principal functions of the AJTC are to keep the administrative justice system under review, and to keep under review and report on the constitution and working of listed tribunals and statutory inquiries. The Council's work in Scotland and Wales is informed by separate Scottish and Welsh Committees. [JW]

administrative law The law concerning the exercise and control of power by government agencies and public bodies who have been given statutory powers of regulation, administration and decision-making, including certain judicial and quasi-judicial powers. [JW]

See also JUDICIAL REVIEW.

administrative tribunal A body established normally by STATUTE to adjudicate on matters of a regulatory nature that fall outside the jurisdiction of the normal courts, for example matters such as employment rights, access to social security benefits, rights of immigration and asylum, and tax disputes.

Tribunals tend to be distinguishable from courts in terms both of their procedure and membership. Many tribunals were created to be much more informal than courts; the hearing process is often inquisitorial with few explicit evidential or procedural rules, and legal representation is far less common than in the court system. Tribunals are also distinctive in their membership. While some tribunals consist of a lawyer sitting alone, more comprise a lawyer sitting with one or more lay members who may be experts in their field (such as doctors or accountants) or people who have other experience relevant to the work of the tribunal. A few tribunals have no legal members at all.

The UK tribunal system expanded dramatically in the period following World War II as the development of the welfare state increased the scope and reach of state regulation. Much of that expansion was relatively ad hoc and has been criticized for its undue complexity and wasteful duplication of administrative resources across a range of government departments. Concerns have also been raised that some tribunals do not appear to be sufficiently independent of their sponsoring departments.

Following the recommendations of the Leggatt Review of Tribunals (2001), the Tribunals, Courts and Enforcement Act 2007 provides a new unified structure by creating two new tribunals, the **First-tier Tribunal** and the **Upper Tribunal** into which existing tribunal jurisdictions are gradually being transferred. The Upper Tribunal is designed primarily, but not exclusively, to hear appeals from the First-tier Tribunal. As a general rule decisions of the Upper Tribunal may be appealed to a court on a point of law. The Act also provides for the establishment of 'chambers' within the two tribunals so that the many different jurisdictions that are transferred into the

tribunals can be grouped together appropriately. Each chamber is headed by a Chamber President and the tribunals' judiciary as a whole is led by a **Senior President of Tribunals**. Three very significant tribunals are not being transferred into the new structure, and will retain their existing jurisdiction; these are the ASYLUM AND IMMIGRATION TRIBUNAL, the EMPLOYMENT TRIBUNALS and the EMPLOYMENT APPEAL TRIBUNAL. [JW]

See also DOMESTIC TRIBUNAL; TRIBUNAL.

administrator *See* PERSONAL REPRESENTATIVE.

admiralty The distinct body of law governing navigation and shipping, including disputes over damage to cargo, collisions and salvage. Today, admiralty cases are heard within the QUEEN'S BENCH DIVISION of the HIGH COURT, though in some cases the judge will sit with expert **nautical assessors**, who will assist the court, for example, on technical matters of navigation or seamanship. [JW]

See also COURT OF ADMIRALTY.

admissibility Whether certain EVIDENCE is capable of being admitted into proceedings. Inadmissible evidence can never be admitted. A court may have the discretion not to admit admissible evidence. [ALTC]

See also CONDITIONAL ADMISSIBILITY.

admissible Evidence that satisfies the criteria for ADMISSIBILITY and may be received by the court. [JW]

admission 1. A statement by a party to legal proceedings admitting a fact or accepting liability for an event, either wholly or in part; or, in a criminal setting, admitting an offence. Admissions may be **formal** or **informal**, depending on how and where they are made. In civil proceedings, admissions will normally be made formally in writing by a party in a statement of case, for example by the defendant as part of the DEFENCE. A valid admission may also be made informally in other documents, such as a letter, or orally. Under CPR Rule 14.1(2), an oral admission may be relied on as evidence to establish liability, but it cannot be used to enter judgment without trial. In criminal proceedings, a formal admission may be made either before or at a hearing, but if made outside court, it must be in writing and signed by the defendant or his legal representative. The most common formal admission is a GUILTY PLEA. A formal admission may be withdrawn at any stage of the proceedings, with permission of the court. A CONFESSION is considered an informal admission, even when it has been reduced to writing.

2. Admission of evidence The acceptance of evidence by a court, so that it becomes part of the proceedings.

3. Admission to the Roll/admission as a solicitor When a trainee SOLICITOR qualifies, he or she is formally admitted to the register or 'Roll' of Solicitors. [JW]

adoption The process through which legal parentage of a CHILD is irrevocably transferred and he/she permanently becomes a member of a new FAMILY. Usually the transfer is from the birth PARENT(s) to adoptive parent(s). A court order under the Adoption and Children Act 2002 is necessary for an adoption to take place. Adoption normally has the effect of severing the child's legal relationship with the birth family (s. 67) and of vesting PARENTAL RESPONSIBILITY in the adopter(s) (s. 46); however it is possible for a partner of a birth parent to adopt so that the child is treated as the legitimate child of both partners in that relationship. In all other situations, an application to adopt a child may be made by one person or by a couple, whether they are married to each other, in a CIVIL PARTNERSHIP or (whether of different sexes or same sex) living together as partners in an enduring family relationship (s. 144(4)). [FK]

See also ADOPTION AGENCY; ADOPTION CONTACT REGISTER; ADOPTION ORDER; ADOPTION SERVICE; ADOPTION SOCIETY; ADOPTIVE RELATIONSHIP.

adoption agency A LOCAL AUTHORITY or registered ADOPTION SOCIETY (Adoption and Children Act 2002, s. 2). Privately arranged ADOPTIONS are prohibited except where the prospective adopters are PARENTS, relatives or GUARDIANS of the CHILD or the prospective adopter is the partner of a parent of the child. In all other instances, an adoption can be arranged only by an adoption agency or in pursuance of an order of court (Adoption and Children Act 2002, s. 92). This restriction covers activities such as the selection of the adopters and the placement of the child with them; agencies are obliged to set up adoption panels to consider whether a child should be placed for adoption and whether the prospective adopter is suitable. [FK]

See also ADOPTION ORDER; ADOPTION CONTACT REGISTER; ADOPTION SERVICE; ADOPTIVE RELATIONSHIP.

Adoption Contact Register A register maintained at the General Register Office by the Registrar General under the Adoption and Children Act 2002, s. 80. The register is intended to enable adopted persons and their biological or pre-adoption relatives to contact one another if they wish to do so. Adopted persons over 18 who request this can have their details recorded in Part 1 of the register, while details of relatives over 18 who wish to be entered are recorded in Part 2 of the register. The relatives who may be entered on the register are defined as persons who would, but for the adoption, have been related to the adopted person by blood, MARRIAGE or CIVIL PARTNERSHIP (s. 81). The adopted person must provide a name, address and date of birth, together with information about those relatives with whom they want to have contact and those relatives with whom they do not (the Adopted Children and Adoption Contact Registers Regulations 2005, Reg. 6). Relatives can indicate when registering whether or not they wish to have contact with the adopted person named (Reg. 7). The Registrar General must give an adopted person whose name is in Part 1 the name and address of any relative who is registered in Part 2 and who has asked for contact with that adopted person (Reg. 8). [FK]

See also ADOPTION; ADOPTION AGENCY; ADOPTION ORDER; ADOPTION SERVICE.

adoption leave EMPLOYEES are entitled to take adoption leave under the Paternity and Adoption Leave Regulations 2002 (SI 2002/2788) as amended. Adoption leave, which may be taken in respect of children aged under 18 at the time of adoption, is based on the model for MATERNITY LEAVE and currently takes two forms: ordinary adoption leave (OAL) and additional adoption leave (AAL). Both consist of periods of 26 weeks' leave. To qualify for OAL the employee must have been continuously employed for not fewer than 26 weeks; AAL is available to an employee who has completed a period of OAL.   [MJ]

adoption order An order of court giving PARENTAL RESPONSIBILITY for a CHILD to the adopter(s). Except in cases where the partner of a PARENT adopts that parent's child, an adoption order extinguishes, from the moment of the ADOPTION, the parental responsibility vested in any person other than the adopter(s) (Adoption and Children Act 2002, s. 46). The order is irrevocable but an appeal against an order may be allowed in exceptional circumstances. An adoption order cannot be made unless the court is satisfied that it is better for the child to make the order than not to do so, and the decision must be based on the welfare of the child (s. 1(2)). In addition, each parent with parental responsibility or GUARDIAN of the child must consent to the order before it can be made. Alternatively, the court may dispense with consent (s. 47) if the welfare of the child demands this (s. 52(1)). Once the order is made, the adopted person is treated in law as if he/she is the biological child of the adopter(s). An adoption order can be made in relation to a child up to the age of 19, provided he/she has not entered into MARRIAGE or a CIVIL PARTNERSHIP (s. 47(9)).
                                                     [FK]

See also ADOPTION AGENCY; ADOPTION CONTACT REGISTER; ADOPTION SERVICE; ADOPTION SOCIETY; ADOPTIVE RELATIONSHIP; WELFARE PRINCIPLE.

adoption service The service maintained in an area by the local authority (Adoption and Children Act 2002, s. 2) to meet the needs, as regards ADOPTION, of those persons specified in s. 3 of the Act and, to that end, to provide the services listed. The persons specified are children who may be adopted, their PARENTS and GUARDIANS and prospective adopters as well as people who have been adopted and their parents, birth parents

and former guardians. The facilities that must be provided include the making of and participation in arrangements for adoption and also the provision of adoption support services. Adoption support services are defined as 'counselling, advice and information' as well as 'any other services prescribed by regulations' (s. 2(6)). [FK]

See also ADOPTION AGENCY; ADOPTION CONTACT REGISTER; ADOPTION ORDER; ADOPTION SOCIETY; ADOPTIVE RELATIONSHIP.

adoption society 'A body whose functions consist of or include making arrangements for the ADOPTION of children' (Adoption and Children Act 2002, s. 2(5)). Adoption societies are voluntary organizations; they are not public or LOCAL AUTHORITY organizations and they are not 'carried on for profit' (s. 2(5)). A registered adoption society is a voluntary organization that is an adoption society registered under Part 2 of the Care Standards Act 2000 and may be referred to as an ADOPTION AGENCY (s. 2(2)). As such it is authorized to arrange adoptions by adopters outside the FAMILY group of the CHILD (s. 92).   [FK]

See also ADOPTION CONTACT REGISTER; ADOPTION ORDER; ADOPTION SERVICE; ADOPTIVE RELATIONSHIP.

adoptive relationship FAMILY relationship created as a result of an ADOPTION ORDER. An adopted person is treated in law, from the time of the adoption order, as the legitimate child born of the adopter(s) (Adoption and Children Act 2002, s. 67). An adopter may be referred to as an adoptive PARENT or, as appropriate, an adoptive mother or father (s. 68(1)(a)). Any other relative within the adopter's family may be referred to as an adoptive relative of the appropriate degree, e.g. adoptive aunt/uncle (s. 68(1)(b)). An adoptive parent and child are deemed to be related within the prohibited degrees of CONSANGUINITY, so that they may not marry each other or enter into a CIVIL PARTNERSHIP. However, the bar does not affect other adoptive relationships. Conversely, the child may not marry or enter into a civil partnership with any relative who would been regarded as being within the prohibited degrees had the adoption

not taken place (Adoption and Children Act 2002, s. 74(1)(a); Marriage Act 1949; Civil Partnership Act 2004, Schedule 1).
[FK]

See also ADOPTION AGENCY; ADOPTION CONTACT REGISTER; ADOPTION SERVICE; ADOPTION SOCIETY.

ADR *See* ALTERNATIVE DISPUTE RESOLUTION.

ADR order Under Practice Direction 29, 4.10 9, the civil courts have a general power to direct the parties to litigation to consider whether their case is capable of resolution by ALTERNATIVE DISPUTE RESOLUTION (ADR), such as mediation. Note that under the terms of the PRACTICE DIRECTION and CPR Rule 1.4(2), the court cannot *require* the parties to use ADR, but merely to consider whether it should be used. However, the court also has the power to penalize a party in costs if it considers that party has, taking into account all the circumstances of the case, failed or refused to participate in ADR without proper justification. Relevant circumstances in this context include: the nature and merits of the party's case; the relative cost of using ADR; the consequences of ADR in terms of delaying proceedings; and the relative likelihood of ADR succeeding – see *Halsey* v. *Milton Keynes General NHS Trust*; *Steel* v. *Joy* [2004] EWCA Civ 576. [JW]

See also COMPROMISE.

adultery Voluntary sexual intercourse between a married person and another person of the opposite sex, married or unmarried, who is not the other's spouse. Sexual activity without penile–vaginal penetration does not constitute adultery in English law: *Dennis* v. *Dennis* [1955] 2 WLR 187. Adultery, combined with the petitioner's inability to continue to live with the RESPONDENT, is one of the five facts by which the court may hold that the ground for DIVORCE, IRRETRIEVABLE BREAKDOWN of MARRIAGE has been met: see Matrimonial Causes Act 1973, s. 1(2)(a). [AD]

See also CO-RESPONDENT.

advance corporation tax (obsolete) A payment made by a COMPANY to HM REVENUE & CUSTOMS on account of the full amount of tax due by the company for a tax period. It was an approach to the collection of CORPORATION TAX (CT) which was adopted in the United Kingdom between 1973 and 1999. [RE]

advance decision There are circumstances in which a mentally competent adult may wish to leave instructions as to the treatment they receive, should they later become incompetent. The ability of the competent adult to make such advance decisions has been given legislative force by the Mental Capacity Act 2005. An advance decision must be in writing, signed by the patient or in his presence by a representative acting on his instruction and in the presence of a witness who must also sign the document. It must also relate specifically to the proposed treatment. Such decisions will only be binding when criteria are strictly met and where they relate to refusal of treatment. Requests for a specific treatment or type of treatment are not binding. [HJ]

See also EUTHANASIA; LASTING POWER OF ATTORNEY; MENTAL CAPACITY.

advance directive *See* ADVANCE DECISION.

advance information A defendant charged with a triable either way offence is entitled to receive details of the prosecution case before deciding whether to elect in a trial CROWN COURT or to consent to a SUMMARY TRIAL in a magistrates' court. The CRIMINAL PROCEDURE RULES require the prosecution to serve on the defendant or his solicitor the evidence upon which the prosecution proposes to rely or a summary of the evidence. The principle has also been extended to cover summary only cases.
[SN]

advancement 1. A power enabling TRUSTEES to pay capital sums to, or on behalf of, a BENEFICIARY before the date the beneficiary is entitled to demand payment from the trustees under the terms of the TRUST. The power can generally be used both to provide capital sums and to minimize tax liability, although its particular scope is dependent upon the trust instrument and/or the Trustee Act 1925, s. 32. **2.** The **presumption of advancement**

establishes that, in the absence of evidence to the contrary, gratuitous transfers between certain classes of person are not subject to the presumption of a RESULTING TRUST. Thus a transfer from husband to wife or from parent to child (but not in England and Wales from wife to husband, nor child to parent) is presumed to transfer the entire beneficial ownership to the recipient; unlike most gratuitous transfers where, in absence of evidence to the contrary, beneficial ownership results back to the donor. Despite *Pettitt* v. *Pettitt* [1970] AC 777, where a majority of the House of Lords expressed the unambiguous opinion that the presumption was outmoded and more applicable to the 19th rather than the 20th (let alone the 21st) century, it has still been neither abolished nor reformed (unlike in Australia where it now also applies to transfers from wife to husband).   [PK]

adversarial system A legal system is described as adversarial, or sometimes as an 'adversary system', when it displays the following features: (a) 'party autonomy', i.e. the idea that it is the parties, not the judge, that primarily decide the issues on which the case will be heard; (b) a strong reliance on the oral hearing of evidence, rather than written statements; and (c) a strong expectation that the judge will operate as an impartial umpire, i.e. it is not generally the role of the judge to investigate the issues, or to direct the parties (provided that the parties are acting within the parameters allowed by law) as to the procedural steps they should take. Courts within the COMMON LAW tradition tend to operate along adversarial lines, though the introduction of greater judicial CASE MANAGEMENT powers in many such systems, particularly in civil matters, is seen as changing the judicial role and reducing, to a degree, the adversarial character of such systems.   [JW]

See also INQUISITORIAL SYSTEM; OVERRIDING OBJECTIVE.

adversarialism The process of being adversarial. In the Anglo-American tradition of advocacy, adversarialism is said to underpin the duty of the lawyer to put the interests of the client first. This is variously described as the obligation to represent the client 'zealously' or to 'promote and protect fearlessly and by all proper and lawful means' the client's best interests; see, for example, Lord Hobhouse in *Medcalf* v. *Mardell* [2002] 3 All ER 721 at 51. The duty to the client is not absolute, however, and may in some circumstances be defeated by an advocate's overriding duty to the court. For example, it would be inappropriate for an advocate to act on instructions that would require them actively to mislead the court.   [JW]

adverse witness *See* HOSTILE WITNESS.

advertisement In contract law, an advertisement of goods for sale is generally an INVITATION TO TREAT and not an OFFER, and so cannot form the basis of a valid CONTRACT. However, unilateral advertisements are offers and are capable of being accepted by performance of the requested act.   [JPL]

Advisory Committee on Genetic Testing *See* HUMAN GENETICS COMMISSION.

Advisory Conciliation and Arbitration Service (ACAS) An independent body which works with employers and employees, according to its website, 'to improve organizations and working life through better employment relations'. It has a lengthy history, dating back to the Conciliation Act 1896, though its present structure and powers originate in the Employment Protection Act 1975. Its website is www.acas.org.uk, and its helpline is 08457 474747 (a number which receives some 800,000 inquiries per annum). While its focus in the 1980s was on seeking to resolve large-scale industrial action such as the miners' strike of 1984–85, this has now altered with the changing nature of employment relations, so that its primary role today is, through its CONCILIATION OFFICERS, to attempt to resolve individual employment disputes before they reach the EMPLOYMENT TRIBUNALS.   [MJ]

See also CONCILIATION.

advisory jurisdiction Article 65 of the Statute of the INTERNATIONAL COURT OF JUSTICE

(ICJ) provides that the ICJ may give an advisory opinion on any legal question at the request of whatever body may be authorized by, or in accordance with, the Charter of the UNITED NATIONS (UN), to make such a request. Article 96 of the UN Charter provides that the UN General Assembly, the SECURITY COUNCIL or other authorized organs of the UN may request the ICJ to provide an advisory opinion on a legal question. [IB]

advocate **1**. In general terms, one who pleads a case before a court or tribunal on behalf of another.

2. Specifically, a member of the Scottish Bar (the Faculty of Advocates), broadly equivalent to a BARRISTER in England. To become an advocate in Scotland, a candidate must first petition the COURT OF SESSION for admission to the public office of advocate. The Court then passes the matter to the Dean of the Faculty to check the candidate's legal qualifications. If these are in order, the candidate is matriculated as an intrant, that is, someone who is seeking to join the Faculty. The intrant must also meet requirements with regard to professional training, both in a solicitor's office and as a pupil of a practising member of the Faculty. Once these requirements are satisfied, the intrant may apply for admission to the Faculty. The process then returns to the Court of Session, which ultimately effects admission to the public office of advocate. **Queen's Counsel** (senior counsel) have been recognized in Scotland since the end of the 19th century and are appointed by the Queen on the recommendation of the Lord Justice-General.

Instructions to advocates come almost exclusively from solicitors. In addition to litigation, advocates may be asked by solicitors for their opinion on a matter upon which they have a particular expertise.

Until 1993, only advocates were permitted to plead before the superior courts in Scotland. At that point, however, solicitors were granted extended rights of audience provided they had at least five years' experience of court work, underwent further training and passed an examination. These SOLICITOR-ADVOCATES may seek right of audience before the superior criminal courts, the superior civil courts or both.

[JP]

Advocate General An official of the EUROPEAN COURT OF JUSTICE, he is appointed on the same terms and conditions as the judges of the COURT OF JUSTICE OF THE EUROPEAN COMMUNITIES. After the hearing of the case and the written submission, the Advocate General makes a detailed report and opinion on the legal aspects of the case to the judges, the parties and the public in general. The role of the Advocate General is to represent the public interest in the case. The judges have time to reflect on the opinion of the Advocate General, before giving a final ruling, but this opinion is not binding on the judges. [MON]

advowson The right to nominate a member of the clergy to an ecclesiastical living, e.g. as vicar or rector of a parish. The patron (often the lord of the manor within which the living is located) must present the candidate to the appropriate bishop for institution and induction; the nomination may be refused. An advowson is an INCORPOREAL HEREDITAMENT and may be bought, sold or given away by the patron who owns it, or, where it is an advowson appendant, it will pass with ownership of the land to which it is attached. [JW]

affidavit A sworn written statement of evidence which may be used in civil and family proceedings to support an application for certain court orders (such as a search order, for example) or, in some circumstances, as an alternative to oral EVIDENCE.

[JW]

affiliation order An order made under the Affiliation Proceedings Act 1957 (as amended) which identifies the father of an illegitimate CHILD and requires him to pay MAINTENANCE. This Act was repealed by the Family Law Reform Act 1987. [FK]
See also ILLEGITIMACY.

affinity A relationship created by MARRIAGE, such as the relationship between a man and his wife's mother. Historically, marriages between people of relationships of affinity were VOID MARRIAGES or VOIDABLE MARRIAGES in English law, but other countries and other cultures regulate these marriages differently or not at all.

Parts II and III of the First Schedule to the Marriage Act 1949 (as amended) lists the PROHIBITED DEGREES OF RELATIONSHIP by affinity. There is a prohibition on marrying the following people, unless both partners are at least 21 years old at the time of the marriage and the younger partner has never been a child of the marriage in relation to the other partner: daughter of former wife; son of former husband; former wife of father; former husband of mother; former wife of mother's father; former husband of mother's mother; daughter of son of former wife; son of son of former husband; daughter of daughter of former wife; son of daughter of former husband.

Additionally, there is a prohibition on marrying the following people, unless both parties are at least 21 years old at the time of the marriage: mother of former wife (unless both former wife and father of former wife are both deceased); former wife of son (unless both son and mother of son are deceased); father of former husband (unless both former husband and mother of former husband are deceased).

The EUROPEAN COURT OF HUMAN RIGHTS has recently held that the prohibition on parents-in-law marrying their children-in-law while the former partner is still alive violates Article 12 of the EUROPEAN CONVENTION ON HUMAN RIGHTS (*B and L* v. *UK* [2006] 1 FLR 35) and the UK government has agreed to review this provision of the Marriage Act 1949. There are similar provisions regarding entering into a CIVIL PARTNERSHIP within the prohibited degrees of relationship. [AD]

See also CONSANGUINEOUS MARRIAGE; CONSANGUINITY.

affirmation A declaration made by a WITNESS that he or she will tell the truth in court as an alternative to swearing an OATH. An affirmation may be made by saying: 'I solemnly, sincerely and truly declare and affirm that the evidence which I shall give shall be the truth, the whole truth, and nothing but the truth.' [ALTC]

affirmative action Use of the law to advantage one gender, race etc. over another in order to remedy (actual or perceived) past discrimination. The term 'affirmative action' is most commonly used in the US and is rarely permitted in UK or EC employment law. The equivalent concept in UK and EC law is POSITIVE DISCRIMINATION. [MJ]

affirmative resolution A parliamentary procedure for dealing with SECONDARY LEGISLATION. The majority of the 3,000 Statutory Instruments enacted each year are subject to no parliamentary procedure at all. Most of the rest pass into law by negative resolution although they could in theory be overturned by a negative vote in either House of Parliament. A small number are made with the positive approval of both Houses of Parliament under the affirmative resolution procedure. The procedure does not allow for amendment; the resolution must be accepted or rejected in its entirety. Any examination of the content of the Statutory Instrument is usually carried out by a standing committee which recommends whether or not the legislation should be accepted. [MS]

affirmed A term used in relation to the doctrine of PRECEDENT. Where an APPELLATE COURT agrees with the decision of the lower court in the same case, the lower court's decision is said to be 'affirmed'.

[JW]

affray An offence under the Public Order Act 1986, s. 3, which is triable either way. It requires that the defendant use or threaten unlawful violence towards another person, and that the defendant's conduct is such as would cause an (actual or notional) person of reasonable firmness present at the scene to fear for their personal safety. The offence might typically be charged in response to gang fights in public places (although it is not necessary that the behaviour actually occur in a public place). There must be an actual person or persons against whom the unlawful violence is used or threatened. Thus, in *I* v. *DPP* [2001] UKHL 10, where gang A were dispersed by police while carrying primed but unlit petrol bombs and awaiting the arrival, for a fight, of gang B, the offence had not been committed by members of gang A, because there was nobody present towards whom unlawful violence had been used or threatened. The MENS REA of the offence is an intention to use or threaten violence or an awareness that one's conduct may be violent or threaten violence (see Public Order Act 1986, s. 6(2)). [BF]

See also RIOT; VIOLENT DISORDER.

after the event insurance An insurance policy, commonly referred to as an ATE policy, under which insurers agree to pay the insured person's litigation costs, usually up to a maximum amount determined by the premium. ATE insurance has become a normal part of CONDITIONAL FEE AGREEMENTS, which are commonly used to fund civil litigation, especially relatively low-value and low-risk personal injury cases. The ATE policy will take effect should the insured lose their case, and so become liable for costs on the normal principle that the loser pays (see COSTS). If the insured wins, the cost of the ATE premium is usually recoverable from the other side as a litigation expense. In the event that some of the insured's own costs are ruled irrecoverable from the other party, an ATE policy may also meet these. [JW]

AG *See* ATTORNEY GENERAL.

age discrimination DISCRIMINATION on the grounds of age is unlawful under the Employment Equality (Age) Regulations 2006 (SI 2006/1031). Discrimination under the Regulations applies to discrimination on the grounds of age, apparent age and age group (whether a particular age or age range) and protection covers employment, training and education. There are exemptions, in particular genuine occupational requirements (e.g. an actor playing the role of a character of a particular age) or where existing law stipulates an age requirement (e.g. licensing requirements that only persons over 18 are to serve alcohol). The law provides limited protection for people aged over 65, particularly in

areas of recruitment and forced retirement. [MJ]

See also LESS FAVOURABLE TREATMENT.

age of consent The age at which one can give consent, effective at law, to sexual activity. In England and Wales, the age of consent to heterosexual and homosexual activity alike is 16 years. Sexual activity involving persons below that age may involve the commission of SEXUAL OFFENCES. [BF]

agency Generally a FIDUCIARY, and often contractual, relationship, created when one person (the AGENT) is authorized to act on behalf of another (the **principal**) to create a legal relationship between the principal and a third party. An agent thus has the power to bind the principal to agreements made on the principal's behalf, though the extent of that power will depend on the extent and nature of the agent's authority to act. Where a contract is not enforceable against the principal, a third party may have an action against the agent for breach of WARRANTY of authority. An agent's authority may be categorized in the following terms. First, the agent will have **actual authority** based on the express terms of the CONTRACT with the principal, or implied from circumstances that make it reasonably necessary for the person to assume the powers of an agent. Secondly, an agent will also have **implied authority** to undertake any incidental tasks necessary to carry out his express authority. In some situations – particularly professional relationships such as SOLICITOR and client – implied authority may also extend to encompass the **usual authority** of such agents, i.e. to include acts that may not be an express part of this particular agreement, but are within the normal scope of the agent's business (see, for example *Waugh* v. *H.B. Clifford & Sons Ltd* [1982] Ch 374). Lastly, an agent may also acquire **apparent** or **ostensible authority** in circumstances where the principal leads a third party (whether by a positive act or omission) to believe that an agent has authority in circumstances where the agent in fact lacks the actual authority to bind the principal. This is sometimes called agency by ESTOPPEL or **'holding out'**. The most common form of holding out is permitting a director or senior manager in a COMPANY to act in the conduct of that company's business, and this authority is often inferred simply from allowing the agent to use a particular title, such as 'chief financial officer' or 'personnel director' (see *Freeman and Lockyer* v. *Buckhurst Park Properties* [1964] 2 QB 480).   [JW]

agency worker An individual offered paid work with a third party by an employment agency. Until comparatively recently it was thought that agency workers were not employees at all, i.e. they were employed neither by the employment agency nor by the end user (the client). However, this area of law is now uncertain as there are a number of potentially conflicting principles in operation. The Court of Appeal by a 2:1 majority in *Dacas* v. *Brook St Bureau (UK) Ltd* [2004] EWCA Civ 217 said *obiter* that a worker may be an employee of the end user on the basis that there is an implied contract of employment between the two. This dictum was accepted by the Court of Appeal in *Cable & Wireless plc* v. *Muscat* [2006] EWCA Civ 220. Such an implied contract, it was said, will exist where there has been a long-lasting relationship, and the end user has used disciplinary proceedings against the worker. It should be noted that the *Dacas* ruling has come in for much criticism and is inconsistent with earlier authority in *McMeechan* v. *Secretary of State for Employment* [1997] ICR 549 (CA), where the worker was held to be an employee of the agency. There is also a line of authority which emphasizes that a contract of employment requires mutuality of obligations: see, in particular, *Bunce* v. *Postworth Ltd (t/a Skyblue)* [2005] IRLR 557 (CA). In the case where there is no such mutuality, then no implied contract between the end user and the agency worker should arise.   [MJ]

agent The person who acts on behalf of a principal in an AGENCY relationship. Agents can be broadly of two kinds: a **general agent**, who has authority to act for his or her principal in the normal course of the agent's business, or in all the principal's business of a specific kind, or a **special agent** who is authorized to conduct just a single transaction or a specified series of transactions over a limited period of time, where such transactions are not a normal part of the agent's business. The principal of a special agent will not be bound by acts that are outside the authority granted to the agent.

In most circumstances the agent's status as agent will be expressly known or apparent to the third party. However, in some cases an agent may act for an **undisclosed principal.** In such situations, the agent as well as the principal are entitled to the benefits and burdens of any contract with a third party. Moreover, the undisclosed principal will not be entitled to the benefit of such a contract where its terms are inconsistent with the agency relationship, or where the third party can demonstrate that it was his or her intention to contract with the agent personally.   [JW]
See also COMMERCIAL AGENT.

agent provocateur The Royal Commission on Police Powers and Procedure (1929) suggested that an agent provocateur was: 'a person who entices another to commit an express breach of the law which he would not otherwise have committed, and then proceeds or informs against him in respect of such offence'.

It is no defence to a criminal charge to suggest that it would not have been committed but for the actions of an agent provocateur: there is no substantive defence of entrapment. However, depending on the precise role of the agent provocateur, there may be questions as to the fairness of admitting the evidence gathered by his or her activities, which would bring into play the judicial power to stay proceedings as an abuse of process, and/or the DISCRETION TO EXCLUDE EVIDENCE under the Police and Criminal Evidence Act 1984, s. 78.   [BF]

aggravated assault An offence of ASSAULT may be aggravated by the consequences flowing from it. Thus, where ACTUAL BODILY HARM is caused, the offence of assault occasioning actual bodily harm is committed. An assault may also be aggravated by the circumstances surrounding it. Thus, where a defendant commits an assault, and, at the time of, immediately before, or immediately after the assault, demonstrates hostility towards the victim based on the latter's membership of a racial or religious group, the offence is one of racially or religiously aggravated assault (see Crime and Disorder Act 1998 (as amended), ss. 28 and 29). [BF]

aggravated burglary An offence under the Theft Act 1968, s. 10, punishable by life imprisonment. It is committed by the person who commits any BURGLARY, and who, at the time, has with him any firearm or imitation firearm, any explosive, or any weapon of offence. A weapon of offence is any article made or adapted for use to cause injury or incapacitation, or intended to be used for such a purpose.

The requirement that the defendant have the aggravating item at the time of the burglary is significant. If it is alleged that, for the purposes of determining whether the aggravated offence is committed, the underlying burglary is under the Theft Act 1968, s. 9(1)(a), then the defendant must have the item with him at the time of entry, for it is at that moment that the s. 9(1)(a) burglary becomes complete. If, on the other hand, it is sought to build the aggravated offence on a burglary under s. 9(1)(b) of the 1968 Act, then it is necessary that the defendant has the item at the time of committing theft or attempted theft or inflicting or attempting to inflict grievous bodily harm in the building. If the defendant comes into possession of the aggravating item only after having entered, then it is too late for a s. 9(1)(a) burglary to be aggravated. [BF]

aggravated damages DAMAGES awarded in circumstances where the reprehensible acts of the defendant have caused some additional loss to the claimant. Such an award, while leaning toward the punitive, falls short of EXEMPLARY DAMAGES and allows for compensation for the claimant's hurt feelings or loss of dignity. Aggravated awards are more likely to be made in the context of TORTS such as TRESPASS TO THE PERSON or DEFAMATION. [HJ]

aggravated vehicle taking An offence under the Theft Act 1968, s. 12A. It is committed by a person who commits an offence under s. 12 (taking a motor vehicle or other CONVEYANCE without authority, sometimes known as TWOC) in relation to a mechanically propelled vehicle, in circumstances where the vehicle is then driven dangerously on a road or other public place; or where, owing to the driving of the vehicle, an accident occurs in which somebody is injured or some property other than the vehicle is damaged; or the vehicle itself is damaged. [BF]

aggression **1**. The illegal use of armed force by one state against another; see Article 39, UN CHARTER.

2. An international crime imposing personal criminal responsibility under INTERNATIONAL LAW for the person(s) responsible for waging the act of aggression. The international crime of aggression (or **crime against peace**) is currently not settled in customary or treaty law. Its first formulation in Article 6 (a) of the 1945 Nuremberg Statute as encompassing the 'planning, preparation, initiation or waging of a war of aggression' or participation in a common plan or conspiracy to do so, was not followed up by any subsequent treaty, but was the subject of an important UN General Assembly Resolution in 1974. Resolution 3314 determined that the use of armed force against the SOVEREIGNTY, territorial integrity or political independence of another state is an international crime, although it is not clear whether this is tantamount to the Nuremberg formulation of crimes against peace. Article 5 of the 1998 INTERNATIONAL CRIMINAL COURT Statute includes aggression as a crime within the jurisdiction of the Court. [IB]

agréation The practice in diplomatic relations where the appointment of DIPLOMATIC AGENTS and head of mission of the sending STATE must receive the express prior consent of the receiving state. The rule is part of CUSTOMARY INTERNATIONAL LAW and is also reflected in Article 4 of the 1961 Vienna Convention on Diplomatic Relations. Agréation is most typically codified in a subsequent act, called AGRÉMENT, by which the host state formally accepts the proposed diplomatic agents. [IB]

See also DIPLOMATIC MISSION.

agreement for a lease A CONTRACT to enter into a LEASE. This usually contains a copy of the proposed lease. The contract itself has some legal significance even if the lease is not formally granted. It is recognized as an ESTATE CONTRACT which confers on the prospective TENANT an EQUITABLE LEASE. If the agreement is for a lease of longer than three years then the contract must be in writing. [HC & DR]

agrément An agreement, whether written or oral, whereby a host STATE provides its prior approval for the appointment of diplomatic personnel by a sending state, particularly the head of the mission. This rule is reflected both in custom and in Article 4 of the 1961 Vienna Convention on Diplomatic Relations. The official position of the UNITED NATIONS is that no such *agrément* is required with regard to persons accredited as agents of the United Nations organization. [IB]

See also AGRÉATION; DIPLOMATIC AGENT; DIPLOMATIC MISSION.

agricultural holding A tenancy of LAND that is farmed by the agricultural tenant. Limited SECURITY OF TENURE and RENT protection is conferred on the agricultural tenant by the Agricultural Holdings Act 1986. A FIXED TERM TENANCY for two years or more does not terminate at the expiry of the fixed term but continues as a YEARLY TENANCY unless either party serves notice not less than one year nor more than two years before the expiry of the fixed term. No new agricultural holdings can be created following the implementation of the Agricultural Tenancies Act 1995. [HC & DR]

See also ASSURED TENANCY.

aid and abet Part of the definition of the *ACTUS REUS* of being an ACCESSORY. Broadly speaking, the phrase means to assist or encourage. It appears in the Accessories

and Abettors Act 1861, s. 8, which makes a party who 'aid[s], abet[s], counsel[s] or procure[s]' the commission of an INDICTABLE OFFENCE liable to be tried and punished in the same way as the PRINCIPAL offender. The corresponding provision for SUMMARY OFFENCES is the Magistrates' Courts Act 1980, s. 44. [BF]

See also ABET.

airspace All space that is super-adjacent to land or water territory, its outer limit being the boundaries of OUTER SPACE. Airspace is therefore to be considered for all legal purposes as an extension of STATE territory. The customary rule of INNOCENT PASSAGE which applies to the coastal state's territorial sea and other maritime belts (except for internal waters) is inapplicable with regard to airspace. Therefore, states possess SOVEREIGNTY over their airspace and not merely sovereign rights. In order for commercial or military aircraft to fly over national airspace their country of registration must seek permission. With respect to commercial aircraft, this takes place in the context of multilateral treaties under the aegis of the International Civil Aviation Organization (ICAO). [IB]

alcohol Cannot be sold without a licence issued by a LOCAL AUTHORITY under the terms of the Licensing Act 2003. It is a criminal offence under the same Act to sell alcohol, whether for consumption on or off of licensed premises, to a person under the age of 18 (s. 146).

Under the Criminal Justice and Police Act 2001, as amended by the Violent Crime Reduction Act 2006, s. 26, local authorities have the power to introduce a Designated Public Place Order, making it an offence to drink alcohol in a designated public place after being required by a police officer not to do so. The police have the power to require individuals to surrender the alcohol or face a fixed penalty notice for disorder of £50, or arrest and prosecution with the risk of a higher fine on SUMMARY CONVICTION.

Public drunkenness is of itself an offence under the Licensing Act 1872, s. 12, and an individual guilty of disorderly conduct through drink thereby commits an offence under the Criminal Justice Act 1967, s. 91.

[JW]

See also DRUNKEN DRIVING; INTOXICATION.

alibi 'EVIDENCE in support of an alibi is evidence tending to show that by reason of the presence of the accused at a particular place or in a particular area at a particular time he was not, or was unlikely to have been, at the place where the offence is alleged to have been committed at the time of its alleged commission': see s. 6A(3) of the Criminal Procedure and Investigations Act 1996. By s. 6A(2), if an alibi is disclosed in a DEFENCE STATEMENT, the statement must give particulars of the alibi. [ALTC]

alien A person who is not a citizen of the host country in which they are currently residing. Distinctions are made between aliens who are resident, that is, DOMICILED in the host country, and those who are transient, that is, temporarily in the host country on holiday, or on business, studying, etc. At COMMON LAW, friendly resident aliens incur the obligations of subjects, including ALLEGIANCE to the CROWN (*The Angelique* (1801) 3 Ch Rob App 7), whereas enemy aliens resident in the country during a period of hostilities may lawfully be subjected to additional disabilities, consistent with international human rights obligations, such as reporting requirements and restrictions on their movement. The British Nationality Act 1981, s. 50 specifically defines an alien as 'a person who is neither a Commonwealth citizen nor a BRITISH PROTECTED PERSON nor a citizen of the Republic of Ireland'. [JW]

alienation The transfer of property from one person to another. FREEHOLD property is conveyed from one party to another; LEASEHOLD property is assigned. [HC & DR]

See also ASSIGNMENT; CONVEYANCING.

aliment SCOTS LAW term for the support owed by parents to their children under the Family Law (Scotland) Act 1985. Rarely used in situations where the CHILD is living with its parents (married or not), the relevance of the action for aliment in situations where parents have separated is now restricted by child support legislation. The 1985 Act sets no amount for aliment, but rather obliges the provision of such support as is reasonable in the circumstances, including the needs of the child and the resources of the parents.

An action for aliment may be brought by the child (if aged 16 or over), his or her CURATOR BONIS (in the event of incapacity), PARENT or GUARDIAN, or any person with whom the child lives or who is seeking a residence order in respect of the child. [JP]

alimony A payment, either by lump sum or in regular payments, made after SEPARATION or DIVORCE by one spouse or former spouse to the other by way of supporting or maintaining him or her. Alimony was awarded originally by the ECCLESIASTICAL COURTS to separated wives only. MARRIAGE was said to create a lifelong obligation on the husband to support his wife. The obligation persisted after separation if she had not committed a MATRIMONIAL OFFENCE. The term is rarely used now, with courts preferring the terms MAINTENANCE, FINANCIAL PROVISION ORDER or support. [AD]

See also ANCILLARY RELIEF.

All ER The accepted abbreviation for the All England Law Reports series. [JW]

See also LAW REPORTS.

allegiance A duty of fidelity owed by a citizen or subject to the head of STATE or sovereign, in return for their protection. Allegiance is owed by all citizens, whether by birth or NATURALIZATION. A resident ALIEN also owes allegiance to the state in which he or she is resident. Historically, under English COMMON LAW, allegiance to the CROWN could never be lost or resigned, except by STATUTE or by the recognition of the independence or cession to another state of the British territory in which the citizen resided. The Naturalization Act 1870, however, permitted British subjects to renounce both their nationality and their allegiance. [JW]

allocation The process by which a defended claim in civil proceedings is placed on one of three procedural 'tracks' according to its value and/or complexity: see Part 26, CIVIL PROCEDURE RULES. The **small**

claims track is used for claims of up to £5,000 in the COUNTY COURT; such cases tend to be settled informally and without legal representation. Cases valued at between £5,000 and £15,000 and estimated to require a day, or less, in court are allocated to the **fast track** and, normally, will also be tried in the county courts. All higher value as well as more difficult or important cases are allocated to the **multi-track**, and may appear in the county or HIGH COURT. Generally, where a multi-track case is valued at below £50,000 it will be sent to a county court CIVIL TRIAL CENTRE, though there are a number of important exceptions to this rule. Where a claim has no financial value, it will be allocated to the most appropriate track in the circumstances, taking into account factors such as the complexity of the case and the nature of the remedy being sought.   [JW]

See also CASE MANAGEMENT; SMALL CLAIMS TRACK.

allocation decision The process by which the judge allocates a case to its appropriate **track**. Notice of the allocation decision must be sent to the parties together with any DIRECTIONS that the court has given at that stage. A party who is dissatisfied with the allocation decision may apply to have the case reallocated.   [JW]

See also ALLOCATION.

allocation of council housing When LOCAL HOUSING AUTHORITIES decide whom to house, they must give **reasonable preference** in allocating accommodation to people who are homeless, to people who are owed duties under the homelessness provisions of the Housing Act 1996, to helping people move out of seriously substandard or insecure housing, and to people with medical or other problems, or people who need to move to a particular locality in the district of the authority, where failure to meet that need would cause hardship to themselves or to others (s. 167 of the Housing Act 1996). Housing authorities may decide to give **additional preference** to particular categories of people in urgent housing need. Other factors which may be taken into account

when housing authorities are devising an allocation scheme include the financial resources available to a person to meet his housing costs, the behaviour of any person or a member of his household which affects suitability to be a tenant, and any LOCAL CONNECTION which exists between a person and the authority's district. The authority must publish the criteria it uses to decide how it allocates its accommodation, including how it will apply these statutory priorities.   [HC & DR]

See also CHOICE-BASED LETTINGS.

allocation of risk It is important in business matters to determine who will bear the loss under a contract if certain RISKS (accidental loss of cargo, damage to goods in transit, etc.) transpire. The parties may expressly agree the allocation of risk within the CONTRACT terms. In the absence of a contractual allocation of risk, the law provides principles to determine who will bear the loss. For example, in the case of sale of goods contracts, risk generally follows property (ownership), or if the loss is the result of subsequent impossibility, which is not the fault of either party, the doctrine of FRUSTRATION may determine the respective positions of the parties. Where the contract is affected by initial impossibility (COMMON MISTAKE), the contract will be VOID in the absence of a contractual allocation of the risk of this impossibility to one of the parties.   [JPL]

allocation questionnaire A document issued by the court in civil proceedings on the basis of which a 'procedural judge' can allocate a case to the appropriate **track**. Each party is normally required to complete an allocation questionnaire and return it to the court by the date specified within it. The questionnaire requires parties to provide information on factors such as the likely duration of the case, anticipated COSTS, whether the parties seek a stay of proceedings in order to attempt to reach a settlement, their views as to the complexity of the case and the appropriate track, and their compliance with any PRE-ACTION PROTOCOL. The court may sanction a party for failure to complete its questionnaire. [JW]

See also ALLOCATION.

allodial land Land held absolutely by the owner, free of any encumbrances or obligations, and distinguished, therefore, from land held under FEUDAL TENURE. The only example of allodial land in the UK is land subject to UDAL LAW in Orkney and Shetland. [JP]

alternative business structure (ABS) A concept used but not defined in the Legal Services Act 2007. An alternative business structure is a form of business organization that will allow different kinds of lawyers (e.g. SOLICITORS and BARRISTERS) and non-lawyers to work together, and will allow non-lawyers to own, or bring capital into, a law firm. ABSs have been created to overcome traditional restrictions over the ways in which lawyers could join together and work in partnership with non-lawyers to provide legal and other services to clients. ABSs must be licensed in accordance with the detailed rules contained in Part 5 of the 2007 Act which are expected to come fully into force in 2010. [JW]

Alternative Dispute Resolution (ADR) An umbrella term used to describe a range of civil dispute resolution and settlement mechanisms that provide an alternative to taking a case to court. The most widely used form of ADR is MEDIATION. Under Part 1 of the CIVIL PROCEDURE RULES, the parties to a dispute may be encouraged by the court to use ADR, and penalties in COSTS may be imposed if they have unreasonably failed to consider or attempt ADR. [JW]

See also ADR ORDER; FAMILY MEDIATION.

ameliorating waste *See* WASTE.

American Arbitration Association An ARBITRATION institution created in the United States of America in 1926 to provide facilities for the administration of arbitrations pursuant to its own INSTITUTIONAL ARBITRATION rules, including specialist rules for commercial, patent and construction disputes. It also provides facilities for AD HOC ARBITRATION based on the UNCITRAL ARBITRATION RULES

1976. It created the **International Centre for Dispute Resolution** (ICDR), based in New York, in 1996, and a European office of the ICDR in Dublin in 2001. It also provides opportunities for private dispute resolution otherwise than by arbitration. [RE]

American Realism The dominant movement in American legal theory for much of the early 20th century, characterized by a focus upon 'law in action' as opposed to 'law in the books'. Its adherents were concerned in particular with what actually happened in courts rather than with written rules or abstract theorizing about the law. Their exclusive focus on the behaviour of the judiciary may be explained by the presence in the US legal system of an unelected Supreme Court with the power to set aside unconstitutional legislation. It may also be explained as a reaction against the dominant influence in American legal education at the end of the 19th century of Christopher Columbus Langdell (1826–1906), who presented law as an exact science, based on written materials and immune from the fluctuations of society. One of the movement's key foundational texts, *The Path of Law* by OLIVER WENDELL HOLMES, may best be understood in these terms, introducing as it did the BAD MAN PERSPECTIVE on law in place of Langdell's overly simplistic lawyer's view.

While different strands of American Realism may be distinguished, all may be said to agree on certain basic premises, which were set out by another of the movement's key figures, KARL LLEWELLYN, in his 1931 article 'Some Realism about Realism' (*Harvard Law Review*, 44 1222–64). For example, American Realists are united in seeing law as a means to social ends and not an end in itself; they are, as a consequence, concerned with law's effects. That said they insist on a rigorous separation of fact from value when they are engaged in their critical appraisal of law; if what law *is* is not distinguished from what law *ought to be* then perceptions will be coloured by value judgements.

Two principal strands are usually identified within American Realism: RULE SCEPTI-

CISM and FACT SCEPTICISM. Rule sceptics, again drawing on the work of Holmes, are sceptical about the role performed by legal rules. Whereas a traditional view would be that judges apply clearly defined rules to established facts in a syllogistic fashion in order to reach a determination, rule sceptics insist that there will often be other factors at work, which the judge may or may not explicitly acknowledge. For example, a judge's own beliefs or emotional reaction to the facts of a case may actually determine the way he or she interprets the rule. Fact sceptics, notably JEROME FRANK, may be seen to be even more extreme in their scepticism: not only are they sceptical about the role played by rules, but they are also sceptical about the ability of judges to find the facts of a case to which rules are then applied. As Frank puts it, judges are in essence witnesses to witnesses. The decision on which witness to believe is subject to the same prejudices and emotional reactions that had the potential to colour the interpretation of the rule.

A further strand of thought within the American Realist movement was developed by Llewellyn in his later work, namely the idea of LAW-JOBS. This is the suggestion that law exists to perform certain functions that are necessary for the continuation of society: specifically those related to avoiding and resolving disputes and to allocating and implementing state power. As a consequence of the need for these jobs to be done, people develop particular skills, which Llewellyn describes as **law-crafts**. Llewellyn remains sceptical, however, and notes that in any given case the rules only guide the judge's decision but do not determine it. His particular contribution to the study of the role of the judge is the notion of **situation-sense**, the particular way in which the individual judge understands the rules and facts, as well as the interests and policies that are at stake. His advice to lawyers in practice is accordingly to look beyond what a particular court or judge has held and instead to read judgments with a view to understanding what is really going on in the background.

The ramifications of the American Realist movement continue to be felt. It may be said that the political engagement of its adherents paved the way for the idea that law could be an instrument of social change, an idea that came to full fruition during the 20th century in the shape of the welfare state. Furthermore, the interest of the movement in law's effects led it to engage with other social sciences in a way that could not have been countenanced in the era of Langdell, but which is now a significant feature of practically any law school. Finally, American Realism is credited with laying the foundations for the CRITICAL LEGAL STUDIES movement.   [JP]

See also SCANDINAVIAN REALISM.

amnesty Granted at the national level – normally through an executive act as a means of national reconciliation – amnesties excuse the offenders of crimes committed in the past. They do not extinguish the crime, but lift criminal liability by excusing the offender. However, since amnesties are granted under domestic law, their effect and validity remain within the confines of the country that granted them and not with regard to the international community as a whole. The UNITED NATIONS organization has consistently rejected all amnesties concerning serious violations of international human rights and humanitarian law, particularly in the context of national TRUTH AND RECONCILIATION COMMISSIONS and post-civil war peace agreements, as this would in many cases lead to the intentional granting of IMPUNITY.   [IB]

Amsterdam Treaty *See* TREATY OF AMSTERDAM.

analogy A mode of reasoning based on a comparison between specific examples. In legal reasoning, analogy is fundamental to the operation of PRECEDENT. Edward Levi describes precedent as involving a three-step reasoning process. Step one is where the judge sees a relevant factual similarity between an earlier case and the present one. In step two, the judge identifies the legal rule or principle on which the earlier case was based, and in step three he or she applies that rule to the present case. Reasoning by analogy is thus a process of justification: the reasoning in an earlier decision is used to justify the decision in a later one. Reasoning by analogy differs from DEDUCTIVE REASONING precisely because an analogy is not, logically, the only possible solution. This means that there is likely to be a degree of uncertainty about the outcome because, as NIKLAS LUHMANN observes, 'the formulation of a [legal] rule is the result of, and not the condition of, such a way of arguing' (*Law as a Social System*, Oxford: Oxford University Press, 2004, p. 314). Another consequence of this approach is identified by Levi, namely that the rules change as they are applied. [JW]

Further reading: E. Levi, *An Introduction to Legal Reasoning* (Chicago: University of Chicago Press, 1949); Martin P. Golding, *Legal Reasoning* (New York: Knopf, 1984).

analytical jurisprudence The theoretical investigation of law on the basis of any approach that seeks to describe it as it is in terms of its constituent parts, for example, analytical POSITIVISM. Analytical jurisprudence may be compared with NORMATIVE JURISPRUDENCE. [JP]

ancillary relief FINANCIAL RELIEF and/or property adjustment agreed between the parties or ordered by the court in a DIVORCE, ANNULMENT or proceedings for the DISSOLUTION of a CIVIL PARTNERSHIP. So called because these matters are considered to be 'ancillary', i.e. additional, to the divorce (etc.) itself.

[AD]

See also FINANCIAL PROVISION ORDER; MAINTENANCE; PENSION SHARING ORDER; PROPERTY ADJUSTMENT ORDER.

angary The right granted under CUSTOMARY INTERNATIONAL LAW to a belligerent to destroy or seize the moveable and immoveable property of a neutral, subject to compensation, at the close of hostilities. This right constitutes an exception to the normal rule for respect for a state's territorial SOVEREIGNTY. It is also contained in Article 53 of the Regulations attached to the 1907 Hague Convention No. IV, which provides that railways, land telegraphs, telephones, steamships and other ships belonging to neutral companies or private persons may be used for military operations, but 'must be restored and compensation fixed when peace is made'. The rule of angary does not cover neutral shipping on the high seas, nor objects that are outside the immediate sphere of hostilities. [IB]

See also NEUTRALITY.

animus (Lat. the mind) A term commonly used in law to indicate the intention or state of mind of a person or persons. In this context it usually forms part of a stock phrase, such as *animus contrahendi* – an intention to contract; *animus possidendi* – the intentional possession of a thing (as opposed to mere custody of it) and *animus testandi* – testamentary intent. In legal usage it lacks the imputation of dislike or bad faith which the term *animus* carries in ordinary language. [JW]

animus revocandi (Lat. the intention to revoke) See REVOCATION OF WILL.

animus testandi (Lat. the intention to make a testamentary disposition) An intention that the TESTATOR'S expressed wishes shall take effect on his death. If this is not his intention, then the WILL is invalid. In normal situations, where the testator has complied with the formal requirements of a valid will, there is a rebuttable PRESUMPTION of *animus testandi*, since it would be unusual for someone to observe the formalities if he did not have this intention. However, the intention must be the true intention of the testator, and this would not be the case if the testator was subject to coercion, fraud or UNDUE INFLUENCE. In the case of a PRIVILEGED WILL, where no formal requirements are necessary, whether an informal document or conversation is made with *animus testandi* is often much more difficult to decide. [CM]

See also TESTAMENT.

annexation A formal declaration, or other sovereign act, of a STATE by which it is intended to recognize the existence of, or acquire anew, SOVEREIGNTY over land territory or an island. The application of this principle in the modern era is precluded by (a) the existence of the *JUS COGENS* norm contained in Article 2(4) of the UN CHARTER which prohibits any unlawful act through the use, or threat, of armed force, that would violate the territorial integrity or political independence of a state; and (b) the objective fact that there do not exist any more unoccupied and unclaimed (*terra nullii*) lands or islands on the planet. Therefore, annexation of any land through unlawful means does not produce lawful TITLE to such land (for example in the Israeli occupied territories). It is, of course, possible for the annexing state to claim at some point in time historical title through long and effective OCCUPATION of particular land and as a result proclaim the annexation (symbolic annexation), but such title would only be valid if it has not been met by any opposition. [IB]

See also JUS COGENS; USE OF FORCE.

annual exemption An amount of value which each individual taxpayer is entitled to exclude, each tax year, from the computation of his **capital gains**. Other non-corporate taxpayers, such as TRUSTEES and PERSONAL REPRESENTATIVES, are also entitled to a deduction each tax year, but the amounts differ from those allowed to individuals. The amounts are increased each tax year, usually in line with inflation: see http://www.hmrc.gov.uk/ for updates. If the exemption is not used in a tax year, it cannot be carried forward to a later tax year. Deduction of available losses can be adjusted so that the exemption is used in full, leaving the losses or a balance of losses to be carried forward.

A similar deduction is permitted for inheritance tax purposes. The amount for each individual is £3,000 each tax year. If the exemption is not used in a tax year, it can be carried forward into the next tax year, where it may be used once the annual exemption for that following tax year has been used up. If the deduction is not used in the year it is granted or in the next following tax year, it cannot be carried forward to any later year; for example, if a taxpayer does not use his annual exemption in 2007–08 he can carry it forward to 2008–09, giving him a maximum deduc-

tion of £6,000; but he must use the exemption for 2008–09 first, and only then the amount for 2007–08. If he does not use any of the £6,000 in 2008–09, he can carry the exemption for 2008–09 to 2009–10, but the exemption for 2007–08 will no longer be available. It is not necessary to use the whole of the exemption in a tax year. [RE]

See also CAPITAL GAINS TAX; PERSONAL ALLOWANCE.

annual return The method by which a taxpayer provides evidence to HM REVENUE AND CUSTOMS, usually in a prescribed form on paper or by electronic means, on the basis of which the taxpayer is assessed to tax for the year of assessment. The assessment is either by the taxpayer (self-assessment) or by the Revenue.

Annual returns can be required in relation to income tax, CORPORATION TAX, and CAPITAL GAINS TAX. Individuals and other non-corporate taxpayers use one annual return to report required information for income tax and capital gains tax purposes. Companies report their income and capital gains tax information in a single corporation tax return.

A return comprises: (a) all statutorily required information concerning value received by the taxpayer for the year of assessment; (b) claims for allowances, exemptions, reliefs and any other advantages for the same year of assessment; and (c) a declaration that the information and claims are full and accurate. [RE]

See also FISCAL YEAR; TAX RETURN.

annulment A DECREE declaring that a MARRIAGE or CIVIL PARTNERSHIP is void. A **decree of nullity** or an annulment declares that the marriage or civil partnership was not valid and thus that the parties' status has not changed. Annulments of marriage were decreed originally by the ECCLESIASTICAL COURTS but the common law, from the time of Lord Hardwicke's Marriage Act in 1753, also prescribed that certain formalities be observed in contracting a valid marriage, breach of which may render a marriage void or voidable. The Matrimonial Causes Act 1973 and the Marriage

Act 1949 now provide the grounds upon which a decree of nullity of marriage may be granted by the family court, and the Civil Partnership Act 2004 outlines the grounds of nullity of civil partnerships. [AD]

See also VOID MARRIAGE; VOIDABLE MARRIAGE.

annulment proceedings An action before the EUROPEAN COURT OF JUSTICE, under Article 230 EC Treaty, for laws to be cancelled. The EUROPEAN COMMUNITY TREATY is the primary law of the EC. All EC SECONDARY LEGISLATION must comply with this primary law, and implementing laws must comply with the legal framework on which they are based. If laws do not so comply it is possible for a MEMBER STATE, the EUROPEAN PARLIAMENT, the COUNCIL OF MINISTERS or the COMMISSION OF THE EUROPEAN COMMUNITIES to bring annulment proceedings. The COURT OF AUDITORS and the EUROPEAN CENTRAL BANK have limited rights to bring such actions, as does any natural or legal person. The grounds of such actions are 'lack of competence, infringement of an essential procedural requirement, infringement of this Treaty or of any rule of law relating to its application, or misuse of powers' (Article 230 EC Treaty). [MON]

See also INFRINGEMENT PROCEEDINGS.

answer A statement of case served by the respondent to a petition. It is equivalent to the DEFENCE of a claim in ordinary civil proceedings. [JW]

Antarctic, legal regime of All matters relating to the right of TITLE over territory in the ARCTIC regions applies also to the Antarctic region. However, in addition, a special cooperation regime has been established through the 1959 Antarctic Treaty, which sets out the basic rule that the territory is to be used only for scientific and peaceful purposes. The Antarctic Treaty rejects the invocation of territorial claims of whatever nature, whether these are raised by parties to the Treaty or non-parties, although the extension of the Treaty's legal effects upon third parties is obviously problematic. More recent conventions regarding the conservation of the region have also been concluded, such as the 1980 Convention on the Conservation of Antarctic Marine Living Resources and the 1988 Convention on the Regulation of Antarctic Mineral Resource Activities. [IB]

See also SECTOR PRINCIPLE.

ante-nuptial settlement A settlement of property made before MARRIAGE, upon either or both of the parties to a marriage, including by WILL. The Matrimonial Causes Act 1973 gives the court, as part of its jurisdiction in ANCILLARY RELIEF claims, the power to vary any such MARRIAGE SETTLEMENT or extinguish any interest under it. [AD]

See also POST-NUPTIAL SETTLEMENT; PRE-NUPTIAL AGREEMENT.

antecedents A summary of the offender's personal history of offending, including details of previous convictions and cautions. The antecedent history should include dates of release and sentence expiry dates: *R* v. *Egan (Paul), The Times,* 9 March 2004. [SN]

anticipatory breach BREACH OF CONTRACT which occurs when, after the CONTRACT has been made but before the date fixed for its performance, one party makes it clear, by express words or conduct, that it will not perform its obligations under that contract. For example, if A engages B on 1 June to commence a consultancy project from 1 July, but on 15 June A informs B that his services will not be required, A has committed an anticipatory breach of contract. Since this breach is repudiatory (SEE REPUDIATION), B can choose to accept it as terminating the contract and claim DAMAGES for breach from the date of termination, or can affirm and wait until 1 July (the date fixed for performance to commence). [JPL]

anti-dumping In economics, **dumping** refers to any kind of predatory pricing activity. However, the term is now most widely used in the context of international trade law, where dumping is defined as a manufacturer in one country exporting a product to another country at a price which is either below its production cost, or below the price set for the home market.

Opinions vary as to whether or not dumping constitutes UNFAIR COMPETITION. Under the WTO Agreement, dumping is condemned, but not actually prohibited. Article VI of the GENERAL AGREEMENT ON TARIFFS AND TRADE (GATT) allows countries the option of taking anti-dumping (or '**trade defence**') measures, though these too are restricted given that they have the potential to operate as a means of domestic trade protection.

Goods entering the EUROPEAN UNION (EU) may be subject to EU trade defence measures (import duties) where they are being dumped in the EU, or their price is being kept artificially low by state subsidies in the exporting country. At the same time, the EU's COMMON AGRICULTURAL POLICY has also been accused of dumping, though significant reforms were agreed as part of the 1992 Uruguay round of GATT negotiations, and a number of subsequent changes have been introduced. [JW]

See also WORLD TRADE ORGANIZATION.

anti-social behaviour contract A written agreement between a person who has been involved in anti-social behaviour and one or more local agencies, such as the police or local housing department, whose role it is to control such behaviour. The contract identifies the anti-social acts in which the person has been involved and which they agree not to continue. The contract, unlike an ANTI-SOCIAL BEHAVIOUR ORDER, is not legally enforceable. It is most commonly used for young people but may also be adopted for adults. [JW]

anti-social behaviour order A civil order, which can be made by both the criminal and civil courts prohibiting the commission of specific anti-social acts or restricting access to defined areas. If the court considers an offender has acted in a manner that caused or was likely to cause harassment, alarm or distress to a person, it may make an order prohibiting the offender from doing anything described in the order. Anti-social behaviour orders were introduced in England and Wales by s. 1 of the Crime and Disorder Act 1998. The power to impose orders was increased by the Police Reform Act 2002 and the Anti-Social Behaviour Act 2003. [SN]

antitrust *See* COMPETITION LAW.

Anton Pillar order (obsolete) This term was replaced by **search order** after the introduction of the CIVIL PROCEDURE RULES in 1999. [JW]

apparent authority *See* AGENCY.

appeal An application for the re-examination of a decision of a lower court or tribunal by a higher judicial authority.

In civil cases, the system of appeals was extensively restructured by Part IV of the Access to Justice Act 1999 and the Access to Justice Act 1999 (Destination of Appeals) Order 2000; the resulting procedural framework is now contained in the CIVIL PROCEDURE RULES Part 52. Part of the function of these reforms was to restrict the scope for appellate interference to the minimum necessary to avoid injustice. Consequently, as a matter of general principle, appeals are restricted to the review of the lower court's decision, rather than granting a full rehearing of the case, and, with very few exceptions, appeals normally require permission (often referred to as **leave to appeal**) from the appropriate trial or appellate court. In terms of jurisdiction, appeals are generally heard by the next most appropriate level of judge, rather than the next level of court. Thus appeals from the decision of a DISTRICT JUDGE on the SMALL CLAIMS TRACK will be heard by a CIRCUIT JUDGE in the COUNTY COURT; a single HIGH COURT judge may hear appeals from district judges and county court circuit judges, and the COURT OF APPEAL (Civil Division) will hear appeals from the High Court, and, in certain circumstances, from the county court via the so-called leapfrog procedure.

In criminal proceedings, appellate jurisdiction is determined by the nature of the offence. An appeal by the defendant against conviction and/or sentence from a matter tried on INDICTMENT will go to the Court of Appeal (Criminal Division). The ATTORNEY GENERAL may also refer a matter to the Court of Appeal where the sentence is considered to be unduly lenient, or on a point of law following acquittal. Appeals from the magistrates' court will normally be heard by the CROWN COURT, though prosecution or defence may alternatively appeal by way of CASE STATED to the Divisional Court of the QUEEN'S BENCH DIVISION, but on a point of law only.

Appeals to the HOUSE OF LORDS in both civil and criminal matters require leave and will only be permitted where the case raises a point of law of general public importance. Appeals to the House of Lords normally constitute a second and final review of the matter, as the appeal will usually have already been considered in the Court of Appeal. Exceptionally, however, leave may be granted under the leapfrog procedure from the High Court.

(Simplified schematics of both the civil and criminal court systems are contained in the **Appendix**.) [JW]

appeal on a point of law *See* APPEAL.

appearance When a party to a civil or criminal action attends the court, or, in the context of some proceedings, gives the court or tribunal notice of their intention to attend, they are said to 'enter an appearance'. By doing so, a party implicitly accepts the power of the court to try the matter. Persons appearing before a Parliamentary Select Committee are also described as entering an appearance. [JW]

appellant A person who makes an APPEAL to a higher court. [AF]
See also RESPONDENT.

appellant's notice (of appeal) The means by which most appeal procedures are commenced in civil proceedings. The form of appellant's notice is laid down in the CPR. It notifies the respondent and the court of the details of the claim, and of any order appealed, the nature of the decision sought from the appeal court and, in some cases, an estimate of the time required for an appeal hearing. It thus fulfils a similar role to the statements of case pre-trial. A SKELETON ARGUMENT must normally be included with the notice, or filed within 14 days of the notice. [JW]

appellate *See* APPEAL.

Appellate Committee *See* HOUSE OF LORDS.

appellate court Any court with the power to hear APPEALS from inferior courts or tribunals. The following courts are appellate courts in England: the CROWN COURT, which can hear appeals from the magistrates' court on matters of fact and law; the HIGH COURT, which hears appeals on matters of law alone from the magistrates' court or Crown Court (when sitting as an appeal court) by way of 'CASE STATED' and from various TRIBUNALS; the COURT OF APPEAL (Civil Division), which hears appeals from the COUNTY COURTS and the High Court on civil matters; the Court of Appeal (Criminal Division), which hears appeals from the Crown Court when acting in its capacity as a superior court (e.g. sitting as a trial court); and the HOUSE OF LORDS, which can, with leave, hear both criminal and civil appeals from the High Court (when sitting as a Divisional court) and Court of Appeal. The House of Lords is the only appellate court in criminal appeals from the High Court or from the Court of Appeal (Criminal Division). The House of Lords is also the highest appellate court for Scotland and Northern Ireland.

Following the Constitutional Reform Act 2005, a new SUPREME COURT of the United Kingdom is to be created (in 2009). It will take over the appellate jurisdiction of the House of Lords and the devolution jurisdiction of the JUDICIAL COMMITTEE OF THE PRIVY COUNCIL. [AF]

applicable law The substantive law (or *LEX CAUSAE*) of a jurisdiction which will apply to an agreement or transaction. The term 'applicable law' is used in the Rome Convention on the Law Applicable to Contractual Obligations 1980, a EUROPEAN COMMUNITY Convention which forms part of the law of England and Wales by virtue of the Contracts (Applicable Law) Act 1990. The term 'proper law' is used in COMMON LAW contractual contexts. The term 'applicable law' is also used in the Recognition of Trusts Act 1987, and in Part III of the Private International Law (Miscellaneous Provisions)

Act 1995, in the context of the choice of law in TRUSTS and TORT respectively. [RE]
See also CONFLICT OF LAWS.

application In civil litigation, a request to the court by a party, and in some circumstances by a non-party, for a decision. **Interim applications** are the most common kind of application procedure in civil litigation. Interim applications are not designed to determine a final issue in proceedings, but will be used to regulate procedure or to protect certain rights or property in dispute until there can be a final determination of the issues. As a general rule applications must be made **with notice** under CIVIL PROCEDURES RULES, Rule 23.6. An application notice is a document filed with the court in which the applicant states the nature of the order sought and the reasons why it should be made. An **application without notice** may be made where there is not yet another party on which notice could be served (e.g. where the applicant is seeking an extension of time for serving a claim form); where secrecy is necessary because notice to the respondent would risk defeating the very purpose of the application (e.g. this may be necessary where the application is for a FREEZING ORDER or similar INTERIM INJUNCTION); or where the application is so urgent that it is not possible for the applicant to give the normal, or any, notice. [JW]
See also INJUNCTION.

applied A term used in relation to the doctrine of PRECEDENT. Where a court regards itself as bound by the earlier decision of a court of equal or higher status than itself, and has employed the same reasoning in this later decision, it is said that the earlier decision has been applied. [JW]

appointed auditor A statutory appointment made by the AUDIT COMMISSION. Each auditor works to audit the accounts of local government and National Health Service bodies and produce value-for-money reports on the audited bodies, with the intention of helping them to improve their services. The work of district auditors (as they were called) was organized independently of the other activities of the Commission through a service called District Audit. In January 2003, this merged with the Commission's Inspection Service to become the Operations Directorate of the Audit Commission. [JW]

appointed day The date specified in an Act of Parliament (or commencement order) for its coming into operation. [AF]

appointment of trustees A generic term encompassing the various ways in which a TRUSTEE might be appointed. In an EXPRESS TRUST the initial trustees are normally appointed by the settlor or testator in the deed or will creating the trust. Subsequently, new trustees may be appointed in respect of all trusts by: any person given an express power to do so under the terms of the TRUST INSTRUMENT; trustees or their personal representatives under the Trustee Act 1925, s. 36; beneficiaries under the Trusts of Land and Appointment of Trustees Act 1996, s. 19; and even the court itself under the Trustee Act 1925, s. 41. [PK]

appropriate adult A person in the presence of whom a juvenile, or someone who is mentally disordered or mentally vulnerable, is to be interviewed by the police. Provision as to who constitutes an appropriate adult is made in the Police and Criminal Evidence Act 1984 (PACE) Codes of Practice, Code C, para. 1.7. [ALTC]

appropriation 1. The power which a PERSONAL REPRESENTATIVE has to appropriate or allocate any part of the ESTATE in satisfaction of the entitlement of a BENEFICIARY. The Administration of Estates Act 1925, s. 41, confers such a power both on executors appointed under the WILL and to administrators where the deceased died intestate (see INTESTACY), although in some cases consents have to be obtained. Perhaps for this reason, wills often confer a power of appropriation in wider terms than the statutory power.
2. The taking of property. *See* THEFT. [CM]

Appropriation Act A STATUTE passed annually by Parliament to 'authorize the use of resources and the issue of sums out of the CONSOLIDATED FUND towards making good the supply which they have granted to Her Majesty in this Session of Parliament'. The Act gives the government formal authority to spend an overall sum of money and breaks down that sum by government department.   [MS]

approved When a higher court states in its decision that another case in a lower court was correctly decided, that lower court decision is said to be 'approved'. For the purposes of PRECEDENT, this adds weight to the decision of the lower court.   [JW]

approved judgment A court judgment which the presiding judge has determined is the final, official transcript of the judgment. When a judgment handed down in court is not the final corrected version, it must be clearly marked as an 'unapproved judgment' and may not be copied or cited in court.   [JW]

approximation of laws The process of bringing of laws together to some central (approximate) point. An alternative phrase in some contexts is 'harmonization of laws', though the approximation of laws is generally deemed to be a looser interaction of legal systems than harmonization. The phrase 'approximation of laws' is not to be confused with the **unification of laws**, which would be the process of having exactly the same laws throughout the EUROPEAN COMMUNITY (EC). This process is rarely used. Each of these terms (unify, harmonize and approximate) need to be examined in context in order to establish their exact effect.   [MON]

Aquinas, St Thomas (1224–74) The most influential Christian exponent of NATURAL LAW of the medieval period, whose work in this field formed part of his monumental *Summa Theologica*. He divided law into four categories: the *lex aeterna* (eternal law) or divine reason; the *lex divina* (divine law) or God's will as it is revealed in the Scriptures; the *lex naturalis* (natural law) or that part of the *lex aeterna* which is known innately by God's creatures; and the *lex humana* (or human or positive law). This latter is required because Aquinas recognized, first, that the *lex naturalis* cannot answer every question as to how one should act in every situation and, second, that it would be naive to expect the wicked to be guided solely by natural law.

Aquinas developed natural law thinking in that he allowed a stronger role for human or positive law than had been the case in the work of previous Christian natural lawyers, such as St Augustine. This was possible as a result of the rediscovery of Aristotle's work, which was unknown to Augustine. Aquinas's great achievement was to synthesize Christian and Aristotelian philosophy. In particular, he drew on Aristotle's idea that everything has a natural goal or *telos*. While for Aristotle the *telos* of the human was to live as a social individual, for Aquinas it was to live as a Christian social individual. Accordingly, Aquinas was able to say that human law is in accordance with natural law (that is, just) insofar as it allowed humans to achieve this goal.

As regards the question of obedience, where a human law was unjust Aquinas indicated that there were circumstances in which obedience was not required, namely where the human law was contrary to the *lex aeterna*. In circumstances short of that, Aquinas's view (akin to that of Socrates in this regard) was that it was better to obey in order to avoid scandal.

It is also significant that Aquinas was writing at a time when Church and State were vying for the pre-eminent political position. Insofar as temporal rulers who were themselves Christian wanted to resist the authority of the pope, they required a Christian understanding of law that allowed them to govern without falling into sin. Aquinas's version of natural law, according as it did a more significant role to human law, provided such an understanding.

Aquinas's work remains significant, not least for the inspiration it has provided to JOHN FINNIS in his important modern restatement of natural law.   [JP]

Further reading: John Finnis, *Aquinas:*

Moral, Political, and Legal Theory, (Oxford: Oxford University Press, 1998).

arbitrability The suitability of the subject matter of a dispute for submission to ARBITRATION, rather than to litigation. Most business-related disputes can be characterized as suitable for arbitration; for example, a CONTRACT dispute between two companies is almost always suitable for resolution by an ARBITRATOR. In such a case, the public courts of a legal system in which arbitration is an accepted mode of dispute resolution are not concerned that the contract dispute has been submitted to private adjudication. Nevertheless, the courts of the seat of arbitration can, if requested, determine whether or not it is acceptable in law for the dispute, or an issue in the dispute, to be arbitrated rather than litigated by those courts. There are some disputes which, depending on the legal system concerned, are never regarded as being suitable for private adjudication. Thus, the Arbitration Act 1996, s. 81 (1)(a), preserves the COMMON LAW as to those disputes and issues 'which are not capable of settlement by arbitration' where the seat is in England and Wales. They include criminal matters and other cases in which the STATE has an interest, such as those in which the status of parties and the contents of public registers are involved. In these and a few other cases, the dispute or issue should be referred to the courts for adjudication. Section 103(3) of the 1996 Act also authorizes the court to refuse recognition and enforcement of foreign AWARDS if they would not have been arbitrable in England and Wales. [RE]

arbitral award *See* AWARD.

arbitral tribunal A legally recognized body appointed by the parties to an ARBITRATION AGREEMENT, comprising one or more arbitrators. It will have the competence to determine its own jurisdiction; and, subject to that determination, jurisdiction to adjudicate the dispute referred to it by the parties to the arbitration agreement. A tribunal will often comprise only one ARBITRATOR,

and will rarely have more than three arbitrators. [RE]

See also ARBITRATION; KOMPETENZ-KOMPETENZ.

arbitrary detention Article 9 of the UNIVERSAL DECLARATION OF HUMAN RIGHTS, as well as Article 9 (1) of the 1966 INTERNATIONAL COVENANT ON CIVIL AND POLITICAL RIGHTS (ICCPR), states that no one shall be subjected to arbitrary arrest and detention, nor deprived of liberty, except in such cases as prescribed by law. The UN Human Rights Commission in its Resolution 1997/50 and the UN Working Group on Arbitrary Detention define as 'arbitrary' those deprivations of liberty which for one reason or another are contrary to relevant international provisions contained in HUMAN RIGHTS treaties ratified by states. Moreover, according to the Working Group, deprivation of liberty is arbitrary if a case falls into one of the following categories: (a) when it is clearly impossible to invoke any legal basis justifying the deprivation of liberty (as when a person is kept in detention after the completion of his or her sentence, or despite an amnesty law applicable to him or her); (b) when the deprivation of liberty results from the exercise of the rights or freedoms guaranteed by Articles 12, 18, 19, 21, 22, 25, 26 and 27 of the ICCPR and Articles 7, 13, 14, 18, 19, 10 and 21 of the Universal Declaration; and (c) when the total or partial non-observance of the international norms relating to the right to a fair trial, spelled out in the relevant human rights treaties, is of such gravity as to give the deprivation of liberty an arbitrary character. [IB]

See also DEGRADING TREATMENT; FAIR TRIAL; TREATY.

arbitration A process of dispute resolution in which the parties to a dispute, being unable to resolve their dispute by themselves (whether by negotiation, MEDIATION or other peaceful process), submit their dispute to the decision of one or more arbitrators who, if they have jurisdiction, adjudicate the dispute and provide one or more awards to the parties. Subject to challenges to the appropriateness of the AWARD or awards in the courts of the seat of arbitration, the dispute (and each of its substantive and procedural issues) is RES JUDI-CATA (i.e. finally determined) once the award has been issued by the arbitral tribunal. Where arbitration is commenced in accordance with the LEX ARBITRI of the seat of the arbitration, commencement will, in most legal systems, stop time running for limitation purposes.

There is no single kind of arbitration proceedings: arbitration can be fast, inexpensive and successful; but it can be the opposite. Much depends on the correct choice of the seat of arbitration and the ARBITRATOR or arbitrators, and also on the degree of cooperation between the disputing parties and their respective legal advisers. Recent innovations in arbitration include **on-line arbitration** facilities for some types of disputes.

Arbitration is also a private process in which the media and other unconnected persons are excluded. For the most part it is a confidential process, but confidentiality issues must be considered early and carefully.

Arbitration between sovereign STATES is not as common as between non-sovereign parties, but there is a growing demand for arbitration between sovereign states and non-sovereign parties, such as companies.

[RE]

See also DOMESTIC ARBITRATION; INSTITUTIONAL ARBITRATION; INTERNATIONAL ARBITRATION.

Further reading: Sir Michael J. Mustill and Stewart C. Boyd, *Commercial Arbitration*, 2nd revd edn (London: Butterworths, 2001); David Sutton and Judith Gill, *Russell on Arbitration*, 23rd edn (London: Sweet & Maxwell, 2007); Andrew Tweeddale and Keren Tweeddale, *Arbitration of Commercial Disputes – International and English Law and Practice* (Oxford: Oxford University Press, 2007).

arbitration agreement An agreement between two or more parties to submit a legal dispute to ARBITRATION for a binding decision on its merits. It is the means by which parties to legal disputes contract out of litigation in national courts into the private process of arbitration.

The agreement to arbitrate must be recognized as an enforceable CONTRACT: (a) according to its GOVERNING LAW (the *LEX CAUSAE*); (b) according to the *LEX ARBITRI* of the seat of arbitration; and also, in many cases, (c) according to the New York Convention 1958. One of the criteria for enforceability is that agreements to arbitrate must (except in extremely rare circumstances) be in writing.

Where the agreement to arbitrate is an enforceable contract according to its *lex causae* and the *lex arbitri* of the seat of arbitration, the ARBITRAL TRIBUNAL will, in most circumstances, have jurisdiction to determine the merits of the parties' dispute provided that the dispute is of the kind contemplated by the parties when they agreed to arbitration (i.e. the dispute is within the scope of the arbitration agreement).

An arbitration agreement can be either ad hoc or institutional. Where no arbitration institution is referred to in the agreement, as the administering institution, it will be an AD HOC ARBITRATION agreement. Where an arbitration institution is identified as the administering institution it will be an INSTITUTIONAL ARBITRATION agreement.

[RE]

See also ARBITRABILITY; BRUSSELS CONVENTION 1968; BRUSSELS I REGULATION; GOVERNING LAW.

arbitration award *See* AWARD.

arbitration clause A dispute resolution provision comprised within a trade, commercial or other (usually business-related) agreement (the primary agreement), by which the parties consent to submit to the binding determination of arbitrators some or all of the disputes which may arise in the future in the context of the primary agreement. The exact nature of the dispute or disputes which can be submitted to arbitration depends on the scope of the wording of the clause; it is also subject to the dispute or disputes being arbitrable according to the *LEX ARBITRI* of the seat of arbitration.

The arbitration clause is, in most circumstances, treated in law as being a separate agreement (the **doctrine of separability**) from the primary agreement. The effect of this approach is that if the primary agreement is alleged by the respondent party not to be valid according to its GOVERNING LAW, the arbitrators are, nevertheless, able to assume jurisdiction to determine the validity or otherwise of the primary agreement and, therefore, of the arbitration clause. Subject to those decisions, the arbitrators can determine the merits of the dispute or disputes between the parties. The clause should, usually, identify: (a) the agreement of the parties as to the seat of arbitration; (b) the APPLICABLE LAW of the primary agreement; and as a counsel of perfection; (c) the proper law of the arbitration clause. However, in the case of some international commercial transactions, it can be advantageous for the seat of arbitration not to be expressed or implied by the parties in the arbitration clause, but for the seat to be left to the arbitral tribunal to determine once an ARBITRATION has been commenced and the tribunal appointed. But, in such cases, it is necessary to provide directions in the arbitration clause for the commencement of the arbitration process.

Arbitration clauses often incorporate reference to one of the private arbitration institutions. In such cases it is normal to use the draft arbitration clause recommended by the preferred arbitration institution. The recommended clause can usually be accessed on the website of the institution concerned.   [RE]

See also ARBITRABILITY; ARBITRATOR; INSTITUTIONAL ARBITRATION.

arbitration 'club' A loosely connected number of individuals who are appointed – often on the recommendations of each other – to act as lawyers, appear as counsel, or sit as arbitrators in the context of international commercial arbitration. It is not a club in the normal sense of that word, but rather an informal network of interlocking personal contacts between individuals who are regularly engaged in such arbitrations. These contacts are fostered by meetings at institutional gatherings and during arbitration proceedings. The word 'club' is a convenient shorthand (perhaps rarely used by outsiders) to describe the professional links and professional rapport which exists between those engaged in international commercial arbitration; but which might perhaps, on occasion, pose problems for the appearance of independence of arbitrators.   [RE]

See also ARBITRATOR; INSTITUTIONAL ARBITRATION.

Further reading: Yves Dezalay and Bryant Garth, *Dealing in Virtue: International Commercial Arbitration and the Construction of a Transnational Legal Order* Chicago, IL: University of Chicago Press, 1996).

arbitrator An individual who, sitting alone, comprises the whole of an arbitral tribunal, or sitting with one or more other individuals comprises part of an arbitral tribunal in respect of a dispute which the disputing parties have consented to submit to ARBITRATION for binding determination.

Arbitrators are usually appointed by the parties to a dispute; but where the parties cannot agree on the identity of the arbitrator, or arbitrators, the appointment may (depending on the arbitration agreement) be made by an arbitral institution, or by the courts of the seat of arbitration.

Although the relationship between the arbitrators and the parties is based on an agreement to act, the function of arbitrators is quasi-judicial in that they are under a duty to adjudicate disputes submitted to them, and their awards can be – and should be expected to be – enforced as judgments of national courts. It follows that arbitrators must be unbiased and impartial; and, so far as is possible, independent of the parties.

Once appointed, the arbitrator is required to take charge of the arbitral process, to determine procedural issues (such as jurisdiction) and substantive issues (such as whether or not there has been a breach of contract), and to issue one or more orders and awards. The authority of the arbitrator can be terminated prior to the conclusion of the arbitration proceedings where the arbitrator resigns or is removed. Subject to that, the arbitrator's authority continues until the final AWARD has been issued to the parties, at which point the authority ceases: the arbitrator is then FUNCTUS OFFICIO. [RE]

See also ARBITRATION AGREEMENT.

Arches, Court of *See* ECCLESIASTICAL COURTS.

archipelago 'A group of islands, including parts of islands, interconnecting waters and other natural features which are so closely interrelated that such islands, waters and other natural features form an intrinsic geographical, economic and political entity, or which historically have been regarded as such' (Article 46(b) of the UN Convention on the Law of the Sea (UNCLOS)). An example of an archipelagic state is Indonesia. The biggest problem with archipelagic states is establishing the BASELINES on which one can calculate the breadth of their maritime belts taken as a whole, rather than as distinct islands. Precise rules for calculating the baselines of archipelagic states are contained in Article 47 of UNCLOS. [IB]

See also TERRITORIAL WATERS.

Arctic, legal regime of The Arctic region is not composed of a land mass, but rather consists of a frozen sea mass. Questions have arisen as to whether such types of non-land masses on the high seas are susceptible to regulation through the existing international legal regimes pertaining to acquisition of land territory, or whether a *sui generis* regime should instead be adopted. The practice of STATES with regard to the Arctic region is to treat it, for all legal purposes, as a land mass and states have laid claim to their respective sovereign boundaries in accordance with the law of OCCUPATION and discovery. [IB]

See also ANTARCTIC, LEGAL REGIME OF.

area child protection committee Non-statutory committees set up in local areas to promote CHILD protection though inter-agency and multi-disciplinary cooperation. These have been replaced by LOCAL SAFE-GUARDING CHILDREN BOARDS, established under the terms of the Children Act 2004, s. 13. [FK]

arraignment The formal process of put-ting charges to the defendant in the CROWN COURT. The clerk of the house calls the defendant by name and reads the INDICT-MENT, asking whether he or she pleads guilty or not guilty to the charge. [SN]

arrest Lawful detention by a police officer. An arrest is implemented by the use of words, physical seizure or touching of a person with a view to detention. [SN]

arrest warrant *See* WARRANT OF ARREST.

arrestable offence Obsolete since 1 January 2006, offences are no longer classified as arrestable or non-arrestable. Distinctions are now drawn between the power of a police constable to arrest without a WARRANT OF ARREST and the power of other persons to arrest without a warrant. [SN]

arson CRIMINAL DAMAGE caused by fire (see the Criminal Damage Act 1971, s. 1(3)). [BF]

Article 234 reference A procedure established by Article 234 of the TREATY OF ROME (formerly Article 177) whereby any court or tribunal of a MEMBER STATE of the EUROPEAN COMMUNITY (EC) may refer a case to the EURO-PEAN COURT OF JUSTICE (ECJ) on any point of COMMUNITY LAW. An Article 234 reference is not an appeal process. The final decision on the facts of the case remains with the referring court or tribunal, which must determine the issues in the light of the ECJ's ruling on the question of EC law. It is also known as a **preliminary reference procedure**. [MON]

See also ACTE CLAIR.

articles of association Under the Companies Act 2006, s. 18, a registered COMPANY must have articles of association which prescribe regulations for the company. These may be 'model articles' as prescribed by the Secretary of State, or a bespoke set of articles drafted for the company, though in the latter case these must be registered by the company at the COMPANIES REGISTRY. Together with the MEMORANDUM OF ASSOCIATION, the articles provide the framework for governance of the company. [JW]

articles of war Domestic military manuals regulating the conduct of a country's armed forces in time of armed conflict. They are most typically enacted into formal law and thus have the effect of transplanting and implementing international humanitarian law rules into the positive law of the STATE. Articles of war are not merely of a disciplinary/administrative character, but will also have penal consequences. [IB]

See also WAR CRIMES.

artificial person *See* LEGAL PERSON.

artistic work One of the category of works protected by COPYRIGHT. It is defined under s. 4 of the Copyright, Designs and Patents Act 1988 to mean (a) a graphic work, photograph, sculpture or collage, irrespective of artistic quality; (b) a work of architecture being a building or a model for a building; or (c) a work of artistic craftsmanship.

Almost any type of two-dimensional drawing or design would come under the general category of graphic work, irrespective of its artistic merit or style or form. In the past, the courts have generously extended the notion of graphic works to protect simple drawings, navigational charts, architectural plans, functional, technical or engineering drawings, typefaces and packaging labels.

On the other hand, it is extremely difficult for three-dimensional products such as furniture or toys or even clothing to gain copyright protection unless such products are proven either to be sculptures or works of artistic craftsmanship. The latter two categories have been narrowed to works which require artistic intention or merit. Products such as baby rain-capes, modern furniture suites and toys have all been denied protection as these products could not come within the definition of artistic works. Such works are protected under DESIGN law.

Drawings are considered as both artistic works and LITERARY WORKS, especially where such drawings or documentation are accompanied by engineering notation and symbols which can be read by an engineer or skilled person – *Aubrey Max Sandman* v. *Panasonic UK Ltd & Matsushita Electric Industrial Co. Ltd* [1998] FSR 651. [US]

See also COMMUNITY DESIGN RIGHT.

ASBO *See* ANTI-SOCIAL BEHAVIOUR ORDER.

assault In the narrow usage of the term, A assaults B where A intentionally or recklessly causes B to fear the immediate and unlawful application of force. This would contrast with BATTERY which is the (intentional or reckless) *actual* application of such force. Criminal lawyers often use the term 'assault' in a broader sense, to denote both behaviours (see COMMON ASSAULT). While most batteries will be preceded by or accompanied by assaults (in the narrow sense), it is possible to have a battery without an assault, where A approaches B from behind and applies unlawful force to B. Although assault and battery are common law concepts, they form the basis of a number of statutory offences against the person, for example, assault occasioning actual bodily harm under the Offences against the Person Act 1861, s. 47. [BF]

See also AGGRAVATED ASSAULT.

Assembly Measures *See* NATIONAL ASSEMBLY FOR WALES.

Assembly of the European Community (obsolete) The former name for the EUROPEAN PARLIAMENT. The European Parliament is now one of the main institutions of the EUROPEAN COMMUNITY (EC), comprised of directly elected representatives (MEMBERS OF THE EUROPEAN PARLIAMENT) from the MEMBER STATES. The Assembly of the EC was comprised of nominees from Member State governments. [MON]

assent The means by which a PERSONAL REPRESENTATIVE transfers to a BENEFICIARY the property to which he is entitled under a WILL or INTESTACY. This is necessary, because the property of the deceased first devolves upon his personal representatives. The form of the assent differs depending upon whether the property is pure personalty or LAND. So far as pure personalty is concerned, however, the Administration of Estates Act 1925, s. 36 (4), provides that the assent must be in writing in favour of a named beneficiary; it is not required to be in the form of a DEED, and so is one of the few instances where a deed is not required for the transfer of a legal estate in land. [CM]

assent procedure One of the primary law-making procedures in the EUROPEAN COMMUNITY (EC) and EUROPEAN UNION (EU). The assent procedure was introduced by the SINGLE EUROPEAN ACT 1986, and broadened in use by the TREATY ON EUROPEAN UNION (TEU) 1992. Under the TEU, the assent of the EUROPEAN PARLIAMENT is required for deciding on an application of a country for membership of the EU (Article 49 EU Treaty), and in the taking of sanctions by the EU (under Article 7.1 EU) against a MEMBER STATE which is in serious and persistent breach of the basic principles of the EU set out in Article 6 EU. In the EC Treaty, the assent procedure is provided for in a number of different articles, to include the monetary policy provisions of Article 105.6, and the STRUCTURAL FUNDS provisions, Article 161 EC. [MON]

See also CO-DECISION PROCEDURE; COOPERATION PROCEDURE.

assessment of costs The process whereby the COSTS payable by one party to another, or between a client and their solicitor, are determined. Assessments may be summary or detailed. **Summary assessment** is the more common and simpler process and may be used in a range of specified situations – see Costs Practice Direction 13.2. Summary assessment is normally conducted by the trial judge at the end of proceedings or, if necessary, at a further hearing before the same judge. **Detailed assessment**, by comparison, is a highly complex process, commenced by the recipient serving on the paying party a notice of commencement (of assessment) and a BILL OF COSTS. The costs hearing itself is private and relatively informal. [JW]

assessment of parenting Assessment, normally undertaken by CHILD welfare professionals, of the ability of PARENTS to perform their role adequately. Assessment is generally undertaken during the course of investigations or court proceedings in cases where there are concerns about a child's welfare. For example, professionals dealing with children and child protection are required to apply the Framework for the Assessment of Children in Need and their Families. This entails an assessment of the parents' or caregivers' 'capacities to respond appropriately' to the developmental needs of the children in their care. It also necessitates consideration of the wider FAMILY and environmental factors such as the home environment. [FK]

See also CHILD ABUSE; CHILDREN IN NEED.

assessor *See* COURT APPOINTED ASSESSOR.

assets All property, whether real, personal, having a monetary value and owned (or in some circumstances, purely possessed) by a natural or artificial (juristic) legal person. The identification and evaluation of assets is important in a number of areas of law, including valuing companies for the purposes of acquisition; assessing liability for certain taxes, and identifying the composition of a deceased's ESTATE before paying debts and liabilities. [JW]

See also CAPITAL GAINS TAX; EXECUTOR; LEGAL PERSON.

assignment A transfer of property, such as a LEASE or a CHOSE IN ACTION, but can also include assignment of a contractual benefit or liability to a third party. Benefits under a CONTRACT may be assigned by legal assignment, equitable assignment, statute or by operation of the law. However, the general rule is that liabilities under a contract cannot be assigned. Nevertheless, the parties may make a non-personal liability assignable where this has been agreed. [JPL]

assignment of arbitration rights The transmission to a third party, by means of a transfer or by operation of law, of the rights and obligations provided for in an ARBITRATION AGREEMENT. Assignment will normally be permitted provided it is not excluded by the GOVERNING LAW of the arbitration agreement, the *LEX ARBITRI* of the seat of arbitration or the arbitration agreement itself. Where the assignment is effective, the third party (the assignee) becomes entitled to sue and may be sued by reference to the arbitration agreement as if the assignee had been an original party to the arbitration agreement. The assignee also becomes liable to comply with the terms of any subsequent AWARD.

In the event of assignment of a primary agreement, the ARBITRATION CLAUSE can also be assigned. Where one of the parties becomes insolvent, any arbitration rights and obligations of the insolvent party will be transmitted to the liquidator by operation of law. [RE]

assignment of intellectual property Also referred to as the transfer or transmission of intellectual property rights. An assignment of intellectual property is not effective unless it is in writing, signed by or on behalf of the assignor. In relation to COPYRIGHT law, the law recognizes not just the assignment of existing rights but future assignment, i.e. an agreement signed by or on behalf of the prospective owner of the copyright, where the prospective owner assigns the copyright in a work yet to be created. MORAL RIGHTS are not assignable. A PATENT or any application for a patent is considered to be PERSONAL PROPERTY (without being a CHOSE IN ACTION), and as such it can be assigned, transferred or granted. An assignment of a patent or any application or a share in it can confer on the assignee the same right as the assignor to bring proceedings for a previous infringement or for a previous act. [US]

See also PATENT LICENCE.

assisted dying See ASSISTED SUICIDE; EUTHANASIA.

assisted suicide When a patient, usually terminally ill or experiencing unendurable pain and/or suffering, has expressed a wish to die and is assisted in doing so by someone else, often a doctor. This differs from EUTHANASIA in that it is the actions of the patient that directly cause death rather than those of the doctor or other third party; for instance, a doctor may prescribe a lethal dose of drugs but it is the patient who administers them. Assisting a suicide is a criminal offence under the the Suicide Act 1961, s. 2(1) and remains so in light of the judgments of both the HOUSE OF LORDS and the EUROPEAN COURT OF HUMAN RIGHTS in the cases of *R (on the application of Pretty)* v. *DPP* [2002] 1 AC 800 HL and *Pretty* v. *UK* (2002) 35 EHRR 1. [HJ]

assisting an offender This is an offence under the Criminal Law Act 1967, s. 4(1). It is committed by D, in circumstances where another person, P, has committed a relevant offence, and D, knowing or believing P to be guilty of that or another relevant offence, does, without lawful authority or reasonable excuse, any act with intent to impede P's apprehension or prosecution.

The criterion of a 'relevant offence' sets a threshold of seriousness which P's offence must surpass. The term is defined in s. 4(1A) to mean an offence for which the sentence is fixed by law or an offence for which an adult first-time offender may be sentenced to a term of imprisonment of five years. The sentence to which D may be subject is related to the maximum penalty for P's offence.

The consent of the DIRECTOR OF PUBLIC PROSECUTIONS is required before proceedings can be instituted for this offence. [BF]

See also HARBOURING AN OFFENDER; PERVERTING THE COURSE OF JUSTICE.

assizes (obsolete) Courts of civil and criminal jurisdiction which originated with the circuit system introduced into England by the Normans. Judges were authorized by special commission to visit every county in England and Wales to hear cases on assize. Assize courts were conventionally held in the county town of each shire. Despite increasing concerns as to the inefficiencies of the system as populations moved and expanded, the assize system remained in place until abolished by the Courts Act 1971. [JW]

See also CROWN COURT.

assumpsit (obsolete) Literally, an assumpsit means a voluntary promise or undertaking. Before it was abolished by the Judicature Acts 1873–5, assumpsit was a COMMON LAW action for breach of a promise, such as a promise to pay, for example in *Slade's Case* (1602) 4 Co. Rep 91. This form of action had grown out of the action of 'trespass on the case' and had become the primary form of action for enforcing simple CONTRACTS not made under SEAL. [JPI]

assured tenancy A residential TENANCY at

market RENT that offers the tenant SECURITY OF TENURE. To be an assured tenancy, the premises must be valued below a certain rateable value, let as a separate dwelling, and with no part of the dwelling shared with the LANDLORD. A number of other specific kinds of premises or lettings are also excluded from being let as assured tenancies.

The landlord can only regain possession if he has served the tenant with a Notice of Seeking Possession in the prescribed form and can prove one of the 'grounds' for possession listed in the Housing Act 1988. These include non-payment of rent; that the landlord previously occupied the property and requires it again for his own residence; that the TENANT has been a nuisance to a neighbour or has deliberately damaged the property or furniture in the property; or that the landlord was persuaded to enter into the tenancy after the tenant knowingly made a false statement which misled the landlord and resulted in the tenancy being granted. [HC & DR]

asylum A right of refuge or sanctuary granted to an individual who is fleeing from persecution in his or her home STATE or is the subject of EXTRADITION proceedings by a foreign government. In INTERNATIONAL LAW, asylum may be territorial (i.e., refuge granted by a sovereign state on its own territory) or extra-territorial (e.g. refuge in a foreign embassy, also known as **diplomatic asylum**).

Under UK law, a claim for asylum is a claim that it would be contrary to the UK's obligations under the United Nations Convention Relating to the Status of Refugees 1951, or the EUROPEAN CONVENTION ON HUMAN RIGHTS (Article 3), for the claimant to be removed from, or required to leave, the UK (see Immigration and Asylum Act 1999, s. 69). An **asylum seeker** is a person who is not under 18 and has made a claim for asylum which has been recorded by the Secretary of State, but whose claim has not been determined (s. 94(1)). [AF]

See also ASYLUM AND IMMIGRATION TRIBUNAL; REFUGEE.

Asylum and Immigration Tribunal An independent judicial body that hears appeals against decisions made by the Home Secretary and his or her officials in ASYLUM, immigration and nationality matters. Under the Asylum and Immigration (Treatment of Claimants, etc.) Act 2004, the single-tier structure of the AIT was created in 2005 to replace the two-tier structure (i.e. **immigration adjudicators** and IMMIGRATION APPEAL TRIBUNAL) of the Immigration Appellate Authority. The main types of appeal heard are on decisions to refuse a person asylum in the United Kingdom; to refuse a person entry to, or leave to remain in, the UK for permanent settlement; to deport someone already in the UK; and to refuse a person entry to the UK for a family visit. The AIT consists of a President (a HIGH COURT judge), two Deputy Presidents, Senior Immigration Judges, Designated Immigration Judges, Immigration Judges and non-legal members. Appeals are heard by one or more judges (previously, immigration adjudicators) who are sometimes assisted by non-legal members of the tribunal. There is no ordinary right to appeal a decision of the AIT; however, decisions of a single judge of the AIT may be reconsidered by a Senior Immigration Judge by application from the appellant on the grounds there has been an error of law. If the application is refused, the appellant may appeal to the HIGH COURT in England and Wales, and the COURT OF SESSION (Outer House) in Scotland for reconsideration of the original decision. Decisions of the AIT with three members sitting can only be appealed to the COURT OF APPEAL (Civil Division) in England and Wales, and the Court of Session (Inner House) in Scotland. See http://www.ait.gov.uk. [AF]

See also ALIEN; REFUGEE; SPECIAL IMMIGRATION APPEALS COMMISSION.

attachment of earnings A court order instructing a debtor's employer to deduct a regular amount from the debtor's earnings and pay this amount to the court. The amount to be deducted is fixed by the court. [SN]

attempt One of the INCHOATE offences. All criminal attempts are statutory offences:

see Criminal Attempts Act 1981, ss. 1 and 6. For a criminal attempt to be committed, it is necessary that the defendant, with intent to commit an offence, does an act which is more than merely preparatory to the commission of that offence. Section 1(4) of the 1981 Act states that it is only attempts to commit indictable offences which are criminal. The law also does not criminalize an attempt to conspire, or to aid, ABET, counsel or procure the commission of an offence.

Whether the act of a defendant is more than merely preparatory to the commission of an offence is a question of fact. Accordingly, there are apparent tensions in the case law on this point. In *R* v. *Jones* [1990] 1 WLR 1057, J got into V's car with him, pulled out a gun and pointed it at V from close range. It was held that there was sufficient evidence to convict J of attempted murder. In *R* v. *Campbell* (1990) 93 Cr App R 350, C was arrested just outside a post office, carrying an imitation pistol and a threatening note. It was held that there was not sufficient evidence to convict C of attempted robbery.

A person may still be guilty of attempt even if the facts are such as to make the commission of the further offence impossible. Thus, if a defendant puts his hand into the victim's empty pocket, he may still be guilty of attempted theft.   [BF]

attendance centre A young person convicted of a crime may be required to attend an attendance centre as part of their sentence. Attendance centres provide programmes which develop basic skills and an awareness of the impact of offending behaviour.   [BF]

attendance centre order An order of a criminal court requiring a person under the age of 25 to attend a non-residential centre, called an ATTENDANCE CENTRE, outside normal school or working hours, for a period of up to three hours per day, and to a maximum of 36 hours in total. Where the offender is aged 16 or under, an attendance centre order is imposed as a YOUTH COMMUNITY ORDER.   [JW]

attestation The signature of a witness to a WILL or DEED. A will has to be attested by not less than two witnesses. By signing the will as attesting witnesses the witnesses are confirming that the TESTATOR signed the will or acknowledged his signature on the will in their simultaneous presence. This is a statutory requirement contained in the Wills Act 1837, s. 9 (as amended). The section provides that no form of attestation is necessary, which means that the will is valid even if the witnesses simply sign the will without stating that the correct formalities have been observed, but a professionally drawn will contains a clause known as an attestation clause that confirms that the formalities have been met. If no such clause has been included, a court will require some evidence that the correct procedure was followed, normally an AFFIDAVIT of due execution made by one of the witnesses.   [CM]

attorney (obsolete) Historically, a separate branch of the English legal profession that gradually became wholly absorbed, by the late 19th century, into the SOLICITORS' profession. The term still survives in some long-established titles, such as the ATTORNEY GENERAL, and as part of the title used by other specialists in the legal field, e.g. patent attorney, or trade mark attorney. It is retained in the USA as the title given to all practising lawyers on completion of the State Bar examination (properly 'attorney at law').   [JW]

Attorney General The government's principal legal adviser. The Attorney General is a qualified lawyer and usually a Member of Parliament holding ministerial rank in the government. The Attorney General supervises the prosecuting authorities within England, Wales and Northern Ireland. These are the CROWN PROSECUTION SERVICE, the Serious Fraud Office, the Revenue and Customs Prosecutions Office and the Public Prosecution Service for Northern Ireland. The Attorney General also has overall responsibility for the TREASURY SOLICITOR'S department. The Attorney General may sometimes appear as a government advocate in high-profile cases, but may not continue in private practice while holding office. [MS]

See also SOLICITOR GENERAL.

auction A method of sale involving an invitation to others to make competing OFFERS (bids) to buy the goods. The auctioneer acts as the AGENT for the seller and the CONTRACT of sale at an auction is complete 'when the auctioneer announces its completion by the fall of the hammer or in other customary manner' (Sale of Goods Act 1979, s. 57(2)). Until this completion, any bidder can withdraw his bid and the auctioneer may withdraw the goods from sale.

Although generally advertising an auction is not an offer to hold it, if an auction is advertised as being held without a reserve and bids are accepted, the auctioneer will be liable in damages for breach of promise if he either fails to sell the item to the highest bidder, or allows the seller to bid, or withdraws the goods from the sale. [JPL]

auction ring A group of buyers who have agreed not to bid against each other at an auction in order to keep the price low and acquire the goods for less than their market value. The Auction (Bidding Agreements) Acts 1927 and 1969 make it a criminal offence for dealers to participate in auction rings and the seller can set aside a sale where the purchaser was dealing in an auction ring. [JPL]

audi alterem partem (Lat. hear the other side) Together with the rule against BIAS, this is one of the principles of NATURAL JUSTICE. The principle is a broad one and applies not only to strictly legal tribunals, but to every body of persons empowered to adjudicate on matters involving civil consequences to individuals. Lord Reid in *Ridge* v. *Baldwin* [1964] AC 40 observed that 'The principle audi alterem partem goes back many centuries in our law and appears in a multitude of judgments of judges of the highest authority.' The case established that a Watch Committee, in dismissing a chief constable, was obliged to inform the chief constable of the grounds on which they intended to proceed and give him a

proper opportunity to present a defence. The courts have applied the principle flexibly so as to take account of the practical requirements of administration in any particular case. As Lord Lane CJ observed in *R* v. *Commission for Racial Equality, ex parte Cottrell* [1980] 1 WLR 1580, 'there is no doubt that what may be the rules of natural justice in one case may well not be the rules of natural justice in another … all that the rules of natural justice mean is that the proceedings must be conducted in a way which is … fair in all the circumstances.' The principle may entail a right to notice, a right to make written or oral representations, and where there is an oral hearing, a right to comment on evidence and question witnesses. Bodies such as prison boards of visitors may have a discretion whether to allow legal representation, but the discretion must be exercised in accordance with the requirements of fairness. [MS]

See also NEMO JUDEX IN CAUSA SUA; LEGITIMATE EXPECTIONS.

Audit Commission An independent public body responsible for ensuring value for money in local government, housing, health, criminal justice and fire and rescue services. The chair and deputy chair are appointed by the Secretary of State. Commissioners are appointed following consultation by the Department for Communities and Local Government. The Commission publishes an annual review and appoints outside auditors to go through relevant accounts and make reports. Its powers are set out in the Audit Commission Act 1998. A comparable body, **Audit Scotland**, was created for Scotland in 2000. [MS]

Austin, John (1790–1859) English jurist and first Professor of Jurisprudence at the University of London. A disciple of JEREMY BENTHAM, his own work reflected an attenuated version of his master's but was nevertheless for many years more influential as Bentham's writing on law lay largely unknown and unpublished until 1970. Austin's lectures at London were published in 1832 as *The Province of Jurisprudence Determined,* and the book dominated the teaching of the subject in England and much of the common law world until well into the 20th century.

Austin's main concern was to delimit the proper boundaries of jurisprudence, which for him could only be concerned with positive, political laws. Other bodies or systems of rules were of no concern to this field of study. Adopting a legal positivist approach, Austin provided a definition in order that positive, political laws could be identified: 'A law, in the most general and comprehensive acceptation in which the term, in its literal meaning, is employed, may be said to be a rule laid down for the guidance of an intelligent being by an intelligent being having power over him.'

Underlying this definition is a version of COMMAND THEORY that Austin adapted from Bentham's original. For Austin, a command has three components: the wish or desire of one that another should do or not do something; an 'evil' imposed by one on another in the event of non-compliance; an expression of the wish or desire, whether by words or by other signs. This approach allows Austin to produce a list of three types of law 'properly so-called': divine law; political or positive law; laws analogous to those given by parents to children. Jurisprudence for Austin is only concerned with the second. Things which are called laws but which contain no command are accordingly for Austin 'improper' laws and he offers two examples: laws of nature and laws by analogy (such as rules of games, laws of honour, and so on).

Austin's single-minded clarity of thought in respect of the law was immensely attractive, but the simplicity of his approach disguised problems. First, the rigidity of the notion of command produces problems when the situation on the death of a sovereign is analysed. The new sovereign does not re-enact the laws of the old and yet they remain law. Attempts to avoid this problem by focusing on the institution of the sovereign rather than the individual encounter further problems when Austin's insistence on the **will** of the sovereign is recalled. Second, Austin's insistence on the indivisibility of the sovereign was already out of step in his own time with more sophisticated arrangements such as the federal structure in the United States. Third, the focus on the presence of an 'evil' appears too limiting when reasons for obedience are considered. Problems such as these provide the foundation upon which H.L.A. HART built his version of analytical positivism in *The Concept of Law*, the book which replaced Austin's as the most influential in the teaching of jurisprudence in the English-speaking world in the latter half of the 20th century.   [JP]

See also LEGAL POSITIVISM.

author In relation to a COPYRIGHT work, this means the person who creates it. In the following instances, the creator is, subject to any agreement to the contrary, deemed to be: the producer of a sound recording; the producer and principal director of a film; the person making a broadcast; the publisher of a typographical arrangement of a published edition; and in the case of a work which is computer-generated, the person by whom the arrangements necessary for the creation of the work are undertaken (s. 9(1), Copyright, Designs and Patents Act 1988).   [US]

authority The term is used in two ways in legal discourse.

1. 'Authority' in the sense of the 'bindingness' of officially sanctioned sources of law. This can be described as the notion of authority *in* law. For example, we can say that case *X* is 'authority' for a particular legal principle. In the COMMON LAW tradition, the most authoritative statements of law are STATUTES and PRECEDENTS – these are often called **primary sources of law**. Though established textbooks and other statements of academic opinion – **secondary sources** – may also be used in legal argument, conventionally they carry less weight than the primary sources.

2. The 'authority' *of* law as a whole. This is a large issue for both jurisprudence and sociological understandings of law. The question of the authority of law is first and foremost a question of legitimacy – i.e. looking at how and why certain social rules are given the distinctive status of law.

Sociologically this issue tends to be associated with questions of power and who has the authority to make laws, and why. ANALYTICAL JURISPRUDENCE, notably in the work of HART and Raz, on the other hand, tends to try to conceptualize the nature of the rules themselves and the ways in which certain rules provide (in Raz's terms) 'criteria of validity' within a legal system. Thinking about the authority *of* law thus also helps explain why lawmakers and legal theorists are so concerned with questions of authority *in* law. The use of authority *in* law can serve to sustain the authority *of* law, by providing a means of justifying decisions, and by setting limits on the ways in which interpreters can qualify, modify or extend the law.

[JW]

See also STARE DECISIS.

authorized investments The range of real and personal property in which a trustee is permitted to invest under the terms of the trust instrument and/or the Trustee Act 2000, ss. 3–7. [PK]

automatic reservation A RESERVATION contained in declarations lodged under the OPTIONAL CLAUSE of the Statute of the INTERNATIONAL COURT OF JUSTICE, according to which the reserving STATE excludes all disputes that fall within its 'domestic jurisdiction'. The scope of automatic reservations is problematic, since in case of doubt as to whether the ICJ enjoys jurisdiction over a particular legal dispute, it has sole competence to assess its own jurisdiction (so-called Kompetenz-Kompetenz) in accordance with Article 36(6) of its Statute. Thus, whether a matter falls within the domestic jurisdiction of a state is a matter for the Court to decide. The USA submitted such an amendment to its declaration in 1946 (the Connally Amendment). The Court has so far declined to pronounce on the validity of these reservations. [IB]

automatism For a defendant to be guilty of a criminal offence, it is necessary that his or her conduct is voluntary. A defendant who pleads automatism is suggesting that his or her conduct was not voluntary. To act voluntarily in this context is to exercise willed muscular control. Thus, in order for D to be convicted of a driving offence, it must be proved that D was indeed 'driving' the vehicle in question. If D were to suffer a seizure at the wheel then he or she would not necessarily be 'driving' the vehicle and would be entitled to be acquitted (see *Hill* v. *Baxter* [1958] 1 QB 277). Similarly, if D receives a blow to the head, loses control over his or her actions, and assaults V while in that state, he or she may successfully plead automatism.

The aetiology of D's automatic state is significant. For D to successfully plead automatism, it is necessary that the cause of the automatic state is external, such as a blow to the head. If the cause is internal to the defendant, for example a disease, then the more appropriate defence is INSANITY. The law operates a presumption of voluntariness, and therefore a defendant who pleads automatism bears an evidential burden on that issue; D must raise sufficient evidence to make the issue live. It was suggested in *Bratty* v. *Attorney General for Northern Ireland* [1963] AC 386 that D is likely to have to adduce medical evidence to discharge the burden. [BF]

autonomy The principle of self-determination or self-governance. In ethics, and particularly professional ethics, it is regarded as a necessary condition of moral agency. Thus in **medical ethics** it relates to the right of the competent patient (see MENTAL CAPACITY) to make a voluntary and informed decision about his or her medical treatment. In relation to **lawyer's ethics** it tends to arise in the context of theoretical questions concerning (a) the right (or not) of the client to determine the means and/or ends of legal representation and (b) the corresponding – and sometimes conflicting – right of the lawyer to exercise moral autonomy, e.g. in deciding who to represent (cf. the CAB RANK RULE), and in making one's own decisions about the appropriate and lawful means and outcomes of representation.

[HJ & JW]

See also CONSENT TO TREATMENT; GILLICK COMPETENCE; LEGAL ETHICS.

autopoiesis A version of social systems

theory which proposes that society is composed of a series of normatively closed but cognitively open communicative subsystems, such as law, economy, politics, science and religion. The theory was developed especially by NIKLAS LUHMANN on the basis of ideas developed within the field of the biology of cognition. The application of these ideas to society has been controversial and autopoiesis has provoked debate about its implications. As applied to society, the theory proposes that each subsystem reproduces itself on the basis of its own fixed binary code (legal/illegal on the part of law) and steers itself according to its own variable programmes. Each subsystem thus constructs its own environment on the basis of its own code.

This understanding of social subsystems has profound implications for the possibility of communication between them. There is, in short, no opportunity for the straightforward transfer of information; rather, information is constructed internally in each subsystem on the basis of its own code.

The implications for law are particularly severe. Traditional understandings of law assume that it is possible to effect social change via the law. Indeed, such understandings essentially assume a linear causal relationship between the identification of a societal problem, the promulgation of law, its implementation and the achievement of desired societal effects. Autopoiesis calls each step in this process into question and raises the possibility that at each stage the 'signal' being sent by law is being reconstructed in unforeseen and unintended ways. Indeed, the theory raises the possibility that the law may not signify at all in the environment constructed by another subsystem.

Adherents to autopoiesis differ at this point as to whether there is anything that can be done about this situation. On the one hand, Gunther Teubner suggests that law can adopt a new orientation that is able to some extent to come to terms with autopoiesis. This *reflexive law* is essentially law that is aware of its own autopoietic closure and that of the other social subsystems.

Teubner makes no claim that the problem of the internal construction of information is overcome by reflexive law, only that this orientation is the best that can be hoped for in the circumstances and is the one that has the best prospect of achieving societal effects through law in this context. His expectations for the success of regulatory interventions, for example, are considerably more modest that what might be claimed on the basis of other social theories, such as that proposed by JÜRGEN HABERMAS. On the other hand, Luhmann denies that reflexive law is a possibility within the confines of the theory. In essence his objection is premised on the observation that the self-description of law required in order to make a reflexive orientation a reality imposes an unduly heavy burden on the law. In particular, he suggests that such a self-description would bring law face to face with the founding paradox on which it is built; that is, the fact that while law operates on the basis of the code legal/illegal it can never apply that distinction to itself without the risk of negating itself.

[JP]

Further reading: Niklas Luhmann, *Law as a Social System* (Oxford: Oxford University Press, 2004); Gunther Teubner, *Law as an Autopoietic System* (Oxford: Blackwell, 1993).

autopsy A medical investigation to determine the cause of death and to identify and evaluate any disease or injuries that may be present; also known as a **post-mortem** examination. Autopsies may be performed for either legal or medical purposes. When the cause of death is potentially a criminal act, or is simply unknown, the autopsy may be requested by a CORONER. Under the Human Tissue Act 2004, s. 1, all organs and tissue removed during an autopsy must be returned to the body unless the family gives permission for specific organs or tissue to be retained for further investigation.

[JW]

autre vie (Fr. another's life) An ESTATE PUR AUTRE VIE is a freehold estate granted for the life of someone other than the tenant in possession. It may arise either when the owner of a life estate assigns their life interest to another, who thereby acquires an estate limited to the original grantee's life, or via an express grant (e.g. to Eloise for the life of Tamara).   [PK]

autrefois acquit *See* DOUBLE JEOPARDY.

autrefois convict *See* DOUBLE JEOPARDY.

averment (Old Fr. averer, to affirm) A formal statement of facts, pleaded in litigation that the party offering intends to prove. Although obsolete in English procedural law, the term is still used in a number of other COMMON LAW systems.   [JW]

avulsion The process of sudden, forcible and significant natural change in the course of a river. Where the frontier line between STATES is a river boundary, by far the most prevalent opinion is that avulsion does not change the existing frontier line.   [IB]

See also ACCRETION; THALWEG PRINCIPLE.

award The decision of an ARBITRAL TRIBUNAL (usually recorded in writing) in respect of one, or some, or all of the issues in a dispute which have been submitted to the tribunal for determination. The term is used in respect of decisions on substantive issues (i.e. relating to the merits of the dispute) as well as to some procedural issues. In general, the term is used to signify decisions pertaining to the legal rights of the parties (whether substantive or procedural), rather than to decisions which are concerned merely with the conduct of the arbitral process. The latter should, normally, be recorded in orders rather than awards, thus reflecting the *RES JUDICATA* effect of awards.

In most ARBITRATION proceedings there is only a single award at the conclusion of proceedings. But, depending on the *LEX ARBITRI* of the seat of arbitration, awards can also be partial or final. A partial award is normally one which resolves a particular issue or combination of issues in dispute prior to the conclusion of the arbitration proceedings, whereas a final award is one which normally deals with all remaining issues in dispute and which are resolved at the conclusion of the arbitration proceedings.

All awards, whether single, partial or final, are binding on the parties by virtue of their ARBITRATION AGREEMENT. However, if a party is dissatisfied with an award (whether single, partial or final), that party may be able to challenge the award in the courts of the seat of arbitration. Where the seat is in England and Wales or Northern Ireland, the Arbitration Act 1996 gives the court power to entertain challenges on the grounds of: (a) the tribunal's alleged lack of substantive jurisdiction; (b) the tribunal's alleged 'serious irregularity'; and (c) the tribunal's alleged failure in relation to the substantive law. Subject to any challenge, an award will in most cases be capable of being submitted to the courts of the seat of arbitration for enforcement in that COUNTRY. Thus, Part I of the Arbitration Act 1996 gives the courts the power to enforce any award made by the arbitral tribunal as if the award were a judgment of the court.

Awards are often capable of being submitted to the courts of foreign countries for recognition and enforcement (in addition to or instead of enforcement in the courts of the seat), for example, where the New York Convention 1958 applies. Thus, awards can be sent from England and Wales and Northern Ireland to other jurisdictions for recognition and enforcement, pursuant to the provisions of the 1958 Convention (where the receiving state is a party to the Convention), and foreign awards may be recognized and enforced in England and Wales and Northern Ireland under Part III of the 1996 Act (which is based on the provisions of the New York Convention). [RE]

B

bad man perspective The perspective on law introduced by OLIVER WENDELL HOLMES in reaction to the overly simplistic lawyer's view dominating American legal education at the end of the 19th century, which considered law to be an exact science concerned with legal reasoning, deduction and axioms. Holmes insisted that law was best understood from the perspective of the bad man who is concerned simply to know in what circumstances and with what degree of risk he will be subject to the imposition of the will of the state via the mechanism of the courts. [JP]

See also AMERICAN REALISM.

bail The release of a suspect or defendant pending the completion of a criminal investigation or proceedings. The grant of bail in all criminal proceedings is governed by the Bail Act 1976. Release on bail is subject to a duty to surrender at an appointed time and place. Bail is usually granted following the acceptance of conditions, or the provision of a SECURITY, to guarantee the person's attendance at court. There is a statutory right to bail, subject to limited exceptions. [SN]

bailment A COMMON LAW relationship, independent of CONTRACT, involving the transfer of possession of GOODS to a person (the **bailee**) by the owner of the goods (the **bailor**). Agreements for the hire, loan, car-riage or repair of goods commonly involve a bailment of the goods involved. Ownership of the goods remains with the bailor and the bailee's rights of possession are restricted to those consistent with the purpose or purposes of the bailment, i.e. the bailee does not have unrestricted use of the goods. For example, a car repairer could legitimately test-drive the bailor's car as part of the repair process, but he could not use it to go shopping. In some circumstances, the bailee may acquire additional rights over the goods, e.g. where the goods have been abandoned by the bailor, or where the bailee has a LIEN over the goods. [JW]

balance of convenience A test used in deciding an application for an INTERIM INJUNCTION. The essence of the test was summarized by Lord Diplock in the leading case of *American Cyanamid Co.* v. *Ethicon* [1975] AC 396 at 406: 'the plaintiff's need for [interim] protection must be weighed against the corresponding need of the defendant to be protected against injury resulting from his having been prevented from exercising his own legal rights for which he could not be adequately compensated under the plaintiff's undertaking in damages if the uncertainty were resolved in the defendant's favour at the trial.' [JW]

balance of probabilities The STANDARD OF

PROOF that is satisfied if the trier of fact considers that the occurrence of the event in question was more likely than not. This is the standard of proof applicable in civil cases. It also applies to the defence in criminal cases when the defence bears the BURDEN OF PROOF. [ALTC]

bankruptcy A legal status established by order of a court where an individual is insolvent (i.e. cannot meet his debts). Bankruptcy proceedings are commenced by a **bankruptcy petition**; this may be either a debtor's petition, where the individual concerned wishes to declare himself bankrupt, or a creditor's petition, which may be presented by any creditor owed payment on an unsecured debt of more than £750. Where a bankruptcy order is issued, the bankrupt's assets are put in the hands of the Official Receiver and used to pay off creditors. Under the Insolvency Act 1986, as amended, bankrupts who are not reckless and cooperate with the Official Receiver will normally be discharged from their debts and released from any restrictions after a maximum of twelve months. Bankrupts who are adjudged to have been negligent or reckless in the circumstances leading to their bankruptcy may be made subject to a Bankruptcy Restrictions Order that imposes continuing restrictions on their activities for a period of between two and 15 years. Further information about bankruptcy can be found on the Insolvency Service website at http://www.insolvency.gov.uk. [JW]

See also INSOLVENCY.

banns Publication or notification of intent to marry. All MARRIAGES in England and Wales must be preceded by some form of notice of intention of the parties to marry in order to establish the parties' consent to the marriage and the lack of any impediments to it. Parties intending to marry in a CHURCH OF ENGLAND ceremony may proceed to solemnize their marriage if they publish that intent in the form of banns in the parish in which they intend to marry. In England and Wales, the publication of banns is regulated by the Marriage Act 1949, ss. 6 – 12. [AD]

Bar *See* BARRISTER.

bar A legal block or impediment; for example, someone may be barred from taking office, or an action may be said to be **statute-barred**. [JW]

Bar Council The governing body of the barrister's profession in England and Wales. In January 2006 the Bar Council divided its regulatory and representative functions and created a separate regulatory board called the **Bar Standards Board** (BSB). The BSB now takes responsibility for setting professional standards and guidance, and for dealing with complaints and discipline. See www.barcouncil.org.uk and www.barstandardsboard.org.uk respectively. [JW].

bare trust It is commonly understood that a bare trust is one in which the trustees have no active duties and are required to deal with the trust property as directed by the beneficiaries. However, this definition can be criticized on two grounds: first, that the very concept of a TRUST necessarily connotes both passive and active duties; and secondly that, provided the beneficiaries are all *sui juris*, trustees are always required to do as directed by the beneficiaries irrespective of whether the trust is bare or not under the RULE IN SAUNDERS V. VAUTIER. As a consequence, bare trusts are sometimes defined simply as trusts in which the TRUSTEE holds no beneficial interest, although this is not the usual understanding of a term whose meaning inevitably varies from STATUTE to statute. Matters are also complicated by the fact that there seems no logical reason why a trust in which trustees hold property on trust for themselves, as commonly occurs in trusts of land, cannot be a bare trust as is seemingly implied in the Trusts of Land and Appointment of Trustees Act 1996, s. 1(1), 2(a).

A workable generic definition might therefore be simply a trust in which the trustees are under no special duties in respect of the trust property. In recognition of this absence of particular obligation, bare trustees are often described as nominees to indicate they have little to do apart from hold the trust property in their names and deal with it as directed by their beneficiaries. A bare trust is synonymous with a simple or naked trust and any trust that is not bare may be correctly described as a special trust. [PK]

barrister A qualified lawyer who is a member of the English or Welsh **Bar**; that is, they have completed a Bar Vocational Course and been called to the Bar by one of the INNS OF COURT. A barrister in independent (i.e. private) practice must also complete a minimum of 12 months' work-based training called **pupillage** before they can practise on their own account. Once qualified, barristers in independent practice automatically have a right of audience before all courts.

The independent Bar has traditionally operated as a specialist, referral advocacy profession. This means that barristers normally obtain work on referral from a firm of solicitors. However, amendments to the Bar's professional conduct rules have increasingly enabled some other professions to instruct barristers without first retaining a firm of solicitors. This is called the principle of **direct access.**

Barristers in independent practice normally work with other barristers in an unincorporated association, referred to as **Chambers**, or more colloquially as a 'set'. A growing proportion of the Bar now work in employed practice, either as in-house lawyers for business or local or central government, or as employed advocates within solicitors' firms. The introduction of alternative business structures under the Legal Services Act 2007 is likely to bring yet further changes to the organization of legal practice at the Bar. [JW]

baselines Lines drawn on the map on the basis of which we can measure the starting point of the TERRITORIAL WATERS. Given that coastlines are rarely straight and sea water constantly erodes them, a system with greater permanence was devised for this purpose. There are two types of baselines: normal and straight. According to Article 5 of the UNITED NATIONS CONVENTION ON THE LAW OF THE SEA (UNCLOS), normal baselines are drawn on the basis of the low-water line along the coast as marked on large-scale charts officially recognized by the coastal STATE. Where, however, the coast is heavily indented and cut into, or if there is a fringe of islands along the coast in its immediate vicinity, then the method of straight baselines may be employed. In general terms, this method involves drawing straight lines from the outermost edges of the coastline. It is subject to a number of limitations in accordance with Article 7 of UNCLOS. [IB]

See also EXCLUSIVE ECONOMIC ZONE; INTERNAL WATERS.

basic award *See* COMPENSATION.

basic intent A term used in contrast to SPECIFIC INTENT and of principal significance in the context of the defence of INTOXICATION. If a defendant is so intoxicated as to be unable to form the MENS REA for an offence of basic intent then he will nevertheless be liable for the offence. In contrast with an offence of specific intent, the defendant's intoxication provides no defence. Offences of basic intent are, broadly speaking, those with a *mens rea* of something less serious than intention. Thus, for example, rape, criminal damage and malicious wounding under the Offences against the Person Act 1861, s. 20, are offences of basic intent. It has been suggested that a defendant's recklessness in becoming intoxicated becomes the equivalent to *mens rea* for the basic intent offence. However, the rule that intoxication is no defence to a crime of basic intent is principally policy driven, on the basis of the significant proportion of crime committed by intoxicated defendants. For discussion, see *DPP* v. *Majewski* [1977] AC 443. [BF]

battered spouse or cohabitant A spouse or cohabitant who is the victim of DOMESTIC VIOLENCE, usually of a physical nature. [AD]

battered women's syndrome A form of post-traumatic stress disorder suffered by some women who have undergone periods of violent abuse, typically in a domestic context. The condition is precipitated by a repeated cycle of violent behaviour towards the woman, and the development of a state of 'learned helplessness' in which the woman feels unable to remove herself from her situation by conventional means. Although the condition was proposed in 1984 by a feminist psychologist, Dr Lenore Walker, it is now viewed by some as reinforcing stereotypes of women as passive and helpless, and as medicalizing their condition to an unhelpful extent.

The principal significance of the syndrome in the criminal law of England and Wales is in the context of the defences to MURDER of PROVOCATION and DIMINISHED RESPONSIBILITY, which may be relevant in situations where a battered woman kills her abuser. The Court of Appeal in *R* v. *Thornton (No. 2)* [1996] 2 Cr App R 108 suggested that battered women's syndrome was a characteristic which the jury might take into account when considering how the reasonable person might have responded to provoking conduct. However, the decision of the Privy Council in *Attorney General for Jersey* v. *Holley* [2005] UKPC 23 signals a retreat from this position. In the context of diminished responsibility, the question would be whether the syndrome constitutes or contributes to a relevant 'abnormality of mind'. [BF]

battery **1**. A criminal offence where D applies unlawful force to V. The Criminal Justice Act 1988, s. 39, makes battery a SUMMARY OFFENCE. Where battery is alleged, the INFORMATION should allege 'assault by beating' (*DPP* v. *Little* [1992] 1 QB 645). An allegation in an information should not allege ASSAULT and battery as that would be bad for duplicity.

2. A TORT involving the actual, intended (or negligent) and direct use of physical force: *Scott* v. *Shepherd* (1773) 2 WBI 892. It is actionable *per se* and it is not necessary that the force used be significant or that any harm is suffered by the claimant.

[BF & HJ]

See also TRESPASS TO THE PERSON.

battle of forms Where the parties have exchanged their own STANDARD FORM CONTRACT in an effort to ensure that their own terms govern the contract, it may be unclear whose terms govern their contract or even whether a contract has resulted. The courts apply the traditional principles of offer and acceptance so that each conflicting form amounts to a counter-offer which is then available for acceptance by the other party. This may result in no contract between the parties, although both believe they have contracted. Alternatively, the battle of forms may be won by the party who fires the 'last shot' if the other party does something which amounts to express or implied acceptance of that last shot offer, e.g. by returning an acknowledgement slip or supplying the goods covered by the contract (*Butler Machine Tool Co. Ltd* v. *Ex-Cell-O-Corporation (England) Ltd* [1979] 1 WLR 401).

[JPL]

Beddoe order An order issued by the court, granting TRUSTEES leave to sue or defend an action when litigation appears to be *prima facie* proper and in the interests of the TRUST. The order enables trustees to be reimbursed their costs from the trust estate, and protects them from any action by the beneficiaries in respect of the litigation, irrespective of the result. Trustees who omit the precaution of applying for a Beddoe order are still entitled to be reimbursed their costs, provided the action was properly brought or defended on behalf of the trust. The principle was established in *Re Beddoe* [1893] 1 Ch 547. [PK]

bench Judges or MAGISTRATES sitting collectively. Magistrates would normally sit as one of a 'bench' of three magistrates. [SN]

bench book A guide to practice and procedure generally, written for new or relatively inexperienced judges, tribunal chairs and members. In England and Wales, for example, bench books are published by the Judicial Studies Board on civil and family proceedings, for the magistrates' and youth courts, and on equal treatment: see http://www.jsboard.co.uk/index.htm. [JW]

bench warrant A warrant issued by MAGISTRATES or a judge, ordering the immediate arrest of a defendant. This type of warrant is usually issued for persons who have failed to appear before the court. Bench warrants can be issued in either criminal or civil proceedings. [SN]

Bencher The most senior of the three types of membership of an INN OF COURT. Benchers are elected from among the BARRISTER members of the Inn by fellow Benchers. Also known as Masters of the Bench. [JW]

beneficial interest The rights of a beneficiary under a TRUST. For example, where land is held by X on trust for Y, X owns the LEGAL ESTATE, but Y owns the beneficial interest in the land. As beneficial owner of the land, Y is entitled to use and enjoy the land and to receive rents and profits from the land. However, Y must also pay any taxes liable in relation to the land. Beneficial interests in land may be subject to the process of OVERREACHING. [DR]

See also EQUITABLE INTERESTS.

beneficial owner The person in whom the right to enjoy a particular item of property is vested. In the absence of a TRUST, the legal owner is properly described as the beneficial owner, while in a trust setting it is the BENEFICIARY to whom such a description applies. [PK]

beneficiary 1. The person(s) entitled to benefit under a TRUST and to whom the right to enjoy (rather than manage) the trust property belongs. The beneficiary is regarded as owning the equitable title in contrast to the TRUSTEE who owns the legal title. The beneficiary was formerly known as the *cestui que trust*.
2. The person entitled to benefit under a WILL. [PK]

beneficiary principle The requirement that every TRUST must have either a human or legal person as a BENEFICIARY. Charitable trusts and a small category of anomalous private purpose trusts are exempt from a rule the rationale of which is still subject to debate. Some argue doctrinally that a trust without a beneficiary is a contradiction in terms as a trust necessarily involves a separate BENEFICIAL TITLE vested in someone. In contrast, others argue from a more pragmatic perspective that the principle is concerned with identifying someone with *locus standi* to enforce the trustees' duties. The issue is significant in the context of cases such as *Re Denley* [1969] 1 Ch 373 where the court controversially adopted a pragmatic approach in validating a private purpose trust without beneficial owners on the grounds that the trust instrument identified 'indirect beneficiaries' with standing to enforce the trustees' duties and thus complied with the beneficiary principle. [PK]

benevolent purposes A purpose within a TRUST INSTRUMENT that is regarded as being for the public good, although not necessarily charitable. It is likely that the range of benevolent purposes that are not also charitable will be reduced in the wake of the Charities Act 2006. [PK]

Benjamin order An order made by the court to facilitate the distribution of a deceased's ESTATE (from the case, *Re Benjamin* [1902] 1 Ch 723) where it has proved impossible to ascertain certain facts. The order is that distribution can take place 'on the footing that', i.e. on an assumption that, such and such are the case; for example, who is to benefit from an estate might depend on whether a certain person has survived the TESTATOR or not, and it might be impossible to ascertain the truth. In such circumstances an order could be made for distribution to take place 'on the footing that' the person had not survived. Failing such an order, the PERSONAL REPRESENTATIVES might have to retain some or all of the assets to safeguard themselves from a possible future claim. The effect of such an order is not to destroy anyone's entitlement, but simply to protect the personal representatives. Should an order be made that distribution should proceed on the footing that X is dead, and it transpires subsequently that he is not, X might still be able to trace into the hands of other beneficiaries who have received more than they would have done by virtue of the order being made. [CM]

Bentham, Jeremy (1748–1832) English legal philosopher, regarded as the founder of classical LEGAL POSITIVISM and a key figure in the history of UTILITARIANISM. His work was greatly influenced by the times he lived in and in particular by what he perceived, first, to be the complacent belief that English law was in accord with NATURAL LAW despite manifest social abuses, and secondly, the danger inherent in the NATURAL RIGHTS language emerging from the American and French Revolutions. These concerns led to his scathing attack on natural law theories and the development of his own distinctive ideas.

Bentham had both logical and pragmatic objections to natural law and natural rights. Logically, he denied (in language prefiguring HOHFELD) that it made sense to speak of natural rights as these had no discernible correlative duties. Pragmatically, he worried that natural law and natural rights encouraged an unfettered individualism that threatened social order.

Bentham was also influenced by DAVID HUME'S criticism of the naturalistic fallacy, which essentially provided him with this philosophical framework. Taking seriously Hume's insistence on the clear separation between the realms of 'is' and 'ought', he distinguished between two branches of jurisprudence, which he called expositorial and censorial. The first is concerned only with an explanation of what the law is; the second sets out to propose what it ought to be. It is not, therefore, that Bentham is not interested in questions of what the law ought to be. He simply wants to maintain clarity of thought and discussion. It is impossible to discuss what the law ought to be without having a clear picture first of all of what it is, untainted by normative considerations.

As regards the expositorial dimension of Bentham's jurisprudence, his key contribution was to set down a clear definition of law. This is usually rendered as 'the command of a sovereign backed by a sanction', although Bentham's definition was much more sophisticated:

an assemblage of signs declarative of a volition conceived or adopted by the sovereign in the state, concerning the conduct to be observed in a certain case by a certain person or class of persons, who in the case in question are or are supposed to be subject to his power: such volition trusting for its accomplishment to the expectation of certain events which it is intended such declaration should upon occasion be a means of bringing to pass, and the prospect of which it is intended should act as a motive upon those whose conduct is in question.

Bentham was also ahead of his time in postulating a sovereign as divided and partial. Furthermore, he recognized that there may be legal limits on the sovereign and even hints at a notion of JUDICIAL REVIEW. As regards sanctions, he is willing to accept, for example, that laws may be obeyed in situations where the sanctions are not physical or monetary penalties but merely religious or moral in character. Nor is he closed to the idea that a law may also be obeyed on the basis of the expectation of a reward. Bentham's analytical approach was not confined to any very narrow notion of law, such as criminal law. He saw that what is written in statutes is often only part of the picture of law and that accordingly it is necessary to take account of judicial and administrative orders, as well as the orders to which individuals are subject in what we might term domestic circumstances.

While Bentham was vehemently opposed to any notion of natural rights, he was still interested in values such as liberty and equality. He dealt with these, however, in a very particular way within the censorial part of his jurisprudence and specifically under the rubric of utilitarianism.

Remarkably, given Bentham's high profile during his lifetime, the major part of his legal positivist writing was unpublished until 1970. It fell therefore to his less sophisticated disciple JOHN AUSTIN to transmit his ideas on the command theory of law, something which he did with enthusiasm and success, to the extent that his ideas dominated the teaching of jurisprudence in English universities until well into the 20th century.   [JP]

Further reading: Jeremy Bentham, *Of Laws*

in General, edited by H.A.L. Hart (London: Athlone Press, 1970).

bequeath When a testator makes a GIFT of personal property by WILL, he is said to bequeath it. The gift so made is said to be a bequest.   [CM]

bequest *See* BEQUEATH.

Berne Convention The Berne Convention on the Conservation of European Wildlife and Natural Habitats was adopted in 1979 with the purpose of conserving wild flora and fauna and their natural habitats, monitoring and controlling endangered and vulnerable migratory species, helping with the provision of assistance concerning scientific issues and promoting inter-state cooperation. It was adopted under the aegis of the COUNCIL OF EUROPE.

The designation of 'Berne Convention' is also applied to distinguish the 1971 Berne Convention for the Protection of LITERARY and ARTISTIC WORKS.   [IB]

See also STOCKHOLM DECLARATION; SUSTAINABLE DEVELOPMENT.

best-evidence rule The rule under which a party is required to call the best (i.e. most reliable) EVIDENCE to support his or her case. For example, SECONDARY EVIDENCE of a document is not ADMISSIBLE unless the party seeking to adduce the secondary evidence proves that it is not reasonably possible to produce the document itself. The continued existence of such a rule has been doubted in civil cases, and in criminal cases it has been effectively abolished by s. 133 of the Criminal Justice Act 2003.
                                            [ALTC]

best interests of the child A term used synonymously with the 'welfare' of the CHILD'. The term 'best interests' is more frequently used in other jurisdictions such as those situated in the United States of America. It is also used in the UN convention on the Rights of the Child 1989. Article 31. states that '[i]n all concerning children … the best interests of the child shall be a primary consideration.   [FK]

See also WELFARE PRINCIPLE.

best interests (of the patient) Derived

by the courts from the doctrine of NECESSITY. Doctors treating patients lacking the MENTAL CAPACITY, whether permanently or temporarily, to consent to treatment have a duty to act in the best interests of the patient (see *Re F (Mental Patient: Sterilisation)* [1990] 2 AC 1. In determining best interests, a number of factors other than purely medical considerations may be taken into account, including emotional and other general welfare interests (see *Simms* v. *Simms and another* [2003] 1 All ER 669). Where lack of capacity is expected to be of a temporary nature, treatment must be no more extensive than reasonably required for the immediate survival or well-being of the patient (see *Marshall* v. *Curry* [1933] 3 DLR 260 and *Murray* v. *McMurchy* [1949] 2 DLR 442). A modified version of the best interests test has now been embraced by the Mental Capacity Act 2005, s. 6.   [HJ]

See also AUTONOMY; CONSENT TO TREATMENT.

best value The Local Government Act 1999 imposes a duty on LOCAL AUTHORITIES and other designated bodies to achieve 'best value'. The authority must make arrangements to secure a continuous improvement in the way in which its functions are exercised, having regard to a combination of economy, efficiency and effectiveness. Authorities are required to meet performance indicators set by the Secretary of State. Their duty is to be exercised in consultation with representatives of ratepayers, service users and other interested persons. The Act confers wide powers on the Secretary of State to enforce best value requirements.   [MS]

bestiality Intercourse with an animal is an offence under the Sexual Offences Act 2003, s. 169, which replaces the offence of BUGGERY with an animal. It is committed by a person, who intentionally penetrates, with his penis, the vagina or anus of a living animal, where that person knows that or is reckless as to whether that is what is penetrated. It is also committed by a person, who intentionally causes or allows her vagina or his or her anus to be penetrated by the penis of a living animal where that person knows that or is reckless as to whether that is what she or he is being penetrated by. [BF]

Better Regulation Commission (obsolete) An independent expert body set up in January 2006 as the successor to the BETTER REGULATION TASK FORCE. It was replaced in January 2008 by the RISK AND REGULATION ADVISORY COUNCIL. [MS]

Better Regulation Executive This is part of the Department for Business, Enterprise & Regulatory Reform (BERR). Its role is primarily to work with other government departments and regulators to improve the transparency of and accountability for regulation, to ensure that regulatory enforcement is proportionate and RISK-based, and, where possible, to reduce the regulatory burden on businesses, local government and the voluntary sector. [JW]

See also PRINCIPLES OF BETTER REGULATION.

Better Regulation Task Force (obsolete) Established in September 1997 to advise the government on action to improve the effectiveness of government regulation. One of its key achievements was to establish five PRINCIPLES OF BETTER REGULATION which have become widely used as a measure of the quality of regulation. It was replaced in 2006 by the BETTER REGULATION COMMISSION.
[JW]

See also BETTER REGULATION EXECUTIVE; RISK AND REGULATION ADVISORY COUNCIL.

beyond reasonable doubt The STANDARD OF PROOF that is satisfied if the trier of fact is left with no reasonable doubt that the event in question occurred. This is the standard of proof that must be satisfied by the prosecution in a criminal case. [ALTC]

bias A one-sided inclination of the mind, a prejudice. In a legal sense it is usually applied to the attitude of a decision-maker, usually a judge, adjudicator or JUROR. Some prejudices are clearly acceptable – we expect judges to be biased against crime and in favour of accepted moral values, for example. But there is a general requirement that a court or TRIBUNAL should be in a position to deal fairly with the issues that are before it. The test for apparent bias

is whether a fair-minded and informed observer, having considered all the circumstances which have a bearing on the suggestion that the decision-maker was biased, would conclude that there was a real possibility that he was biased: *Porter* v. *Magill* [2001] UKHL 67; [2002] 2 AC 357. Sources of bias do not include the religion, ethnic or national origin, gender, age, class, means or sexual orientation of the judge. But bias might well be thought to arise if there were personal friendship or animosity between the judge and any member of the public involved in the case: *Locabail (UK) Ltd* v. *Bayfield Properties Ltd* [2000] QB 451. Conversely the presence of a serving police officer and an official of the CROWN PROSECUTION SERVICE on a JURY does not render a trial unfair: *R* v. *Abroikov* [2005] EWCA Crim 1986. Where there is a real possibility of bias, a judge may be asked to, or may of his own volition, **recuse** himself – that is, step down from hearing the case. [MS]

See also NATURAL JUSTICE.

bid A contractual OFFER to buy goods for the price contained in that bid at an AUCTION, or an offer in response to an invitation to bid for the award of a particular contract to provide a service. [JPL]

bigamy Going through a ceremony of MARRIAGE with another man or woman while validly married to another. In English law, one can only have one husband or wife at a time; a purported MARRIAGE CEREMONY to another will be invalid and, if contracted with the required intent, may constitute the crime of bigamy. The crime of bigamy is found in the Offences against the Person Act 1861, s. 57, and requires knowledge of the existence of the first marriage. It provides for a maximum punishment of seven years' imprisonment on conviction. [AD]

See also VOID MARRIAGE.

bilateral contract A bilateral contract is also known as a **synallagmatic contract** in that it creates mutual obligations. Each party has made a promise in exchange for the promise of the other, so that both parties are bound from the moment of that

exchange, i.e. the contract is EXECUTORY. [JPL]
See also UNILATERAL CONTRACT.

bilateral discharge Refers to the ending
of EXECUTORY contractual obligations (i.e. yet
to be performed) by both parties agreeing
to a release. Each party supplies consideration for the bilateral discharge agreement
by agreeing to release the other from performance of future existing obligations.
[JPL]

bilateral immunity agreement (BIA) An
inter-state treaty by which the two parties
agree to afford immunity to their respective
nationals from crimes falling within the
jurisdiction of the INTERNATIONAL CRIMINAL
COURT. BIAs were initiated by the USA,
which is not a party to the ICC Statute.
The legality of BIAs vis-à-vis the obligations
of ICC member states is unclear. Although
Article 98(2) of the ICC Statute prohibits
the Court from proceeding with a request
for surrender where this would force the
requested state to act inconsistently with
its obligations under international agreements, the adoption of BIAs subsequent
to entering into the ICC Statute would frustrate to a large degree the object and purpose of the ICC and would seem to be
irreconcilable with the obligation to prosecute offenders contained therein.   [IB]
See also AMNESTY.

Bill A proposal for legislation is known as a
Bill while it is under consideration in Parliament. There are four overlapping types
of Bill: public Bills, private Bills, hybrid Bills
and money Bills. A **public Bill** is of general
application, a **private Bill** affects only a particular individual or body, such as a local
authority. A **hybrid Bill** is a public Bill which
particularly affects certain private interests.
An example is the Crossrail Bill (2005–)
which is a complex piece of legislation
drafted to secure the powers necessary to
integrate the east–west rail network
through two tunnels beneath central London, including powers to compulsorily purchase land in private ownership. The
hybrid Bill procedure includes an extra
stage so that persons affected by the private
aspect of the Bill can petition a select com-

mittee about it. A **money Bill** is one certified
by the SPEAKER to contain nothing but financial measures.

Most Bills are promoted by the government, but each year some MPs are chosen
by ballot to have the opportunity of presenting a Bill on a matter of their choosing.
This is called a **Private Member's Bill**.

Though most Bills begin their life in the
HOUSE OF COMMONS, a Bill may be presented
first in the HOUSE OF LORDS, coming to the
Commons after passage through the
upper house. A Bill presented in the Commons will undergo a **first reading** (where it
is formally presented without debate), followed by a **second reading**, which consists
of a debate on the floor of the Commons
(or, if there is no objection, in a committee
of the House). If the Bill passes this stage, it
goes for clause-by-clause consideration to a
standing committee, selected along party
lines. The committee reports back to the
whole House (**report stage**) and the Bill
proceeds to a largely formal **third reading**.
The Bill then goes to the House of Lords
where it goes through a similar series of
stages. If it survives all these, it will then
receive the ROYAL ASSENT and become law.
[MS]

bill of costs A statement of COSTS prepared
by a solicitor in respect of services rendered
to a client.   [JW]
See also ASSESSMENT OF COSTS; REMUNERATION
CERTIFICATE; RETAINER.

bill of exchange A financial instrument;
an unconditional order addressed by one
person (the **drawer**) to another person or
entity (the **drawee**), requiring the drawee
to pay the amount specified in the bill to
the drawer or any third party (payee)
named in that document on a specified or
determinable future date. A cheque is thus
a simple bill of exchange drawn by an
account holder on their bank and payable
on demand.

Bills of exchange are less significant in
practice than they were, but still serve as
a form of payment in international and
local trade. They have the advantage of
being transferable by endorsement (i.e. by
counter-signature of the payee) and are a

form of negotiable instrument – unlike ordinary contract documents, the right to performance of a bill of exchange is linked (with some exceptions) to the possession of the bill itself. In England and Wales the law on bills of exchange is largely contained in the Bills of Exchange Act 1882 and the Cheques Act 1992. [JW]

bill of indictment A written accusation of a crime issued by an officer of the court, charging a person with an INDICTABLE OFFENCE. A criminal trial in the CROWN COURT cannot start without a valid indictment. [SN]

bill of lading A document issued by a carrier of sea freight (usually a company's shipping department), acknowledging that specified goods have been received as cargo for carriage to a named place for delivery to a recipient (the consignee), who is normally identified. Bills of lading take various forms and can be issued as a receipt for shipment, evidence of the contract of carriage by sea, and, in some forms, as document of TITLE to the goods. The rights and liabilities attached to carriers under a bill of lading are laid down in INTERNATIONAL LAW by the INTERNATIONAL LAW COMMISSION'S 1921 Hague Rules, as amended in 1968. These have been extensively adopted into national (including UK) law. Later, major, revisions to the Hague Rules were introduced in a new treaty, the 1978 Hamburg Rules, but these have not been widely adopted. [JW]

bind over An order of the court requiring a person to carry out a specific act. A person may be bound over to appear in court at a particular time if BAIL has been granted or, most commonly, be bound over not to commit some offence; for example, causing a BREACH OF THE PEACE. [SN]

bind over for sentence A court order requiring the defendant to return to court on an unspecified date for sentencing. Failure to observe this order may result in a forfeit or penalty. [SN]

bioprospecting The search for and possible commercialization of genetic resources found in wild plants, animals and micro-organisms. There are two main outputs from bioprospecting activities. First, bioprospecting can be solely concerned with the harvesting of the tangible, organic material, either for making a product directly or for the chemical, genetic or other information provided by the organic material. Secondly, bioprospecting activities can also extend to extracting and exploiting informational resources, including established gene banks, seed banks, and human-cultivated information concerning the use or maintenance of organic resources – especially indigenous or tribal or cultural knowledge, referred to alternatively as indigenous knowledge, traditional knowledge or ethnobotanical knowledge.

The international law in this area is loosely governed by the Rio de Janeiro Convention on Biological Diversity 1992 which links bioprospecting activities with INTELLECTUAL PROPERTY rights. The concept of 'biological resources' is wide enough to include 'genetic resources, organisms or parts thereof, populations, or any other biotic component of ecosystems with actual or potential use or value for humanity' (Article 2 of the Rio Convention). [US]

biotechnological inventions An increasingly significant commercial area of activity but one that is also controversial. Biotechnological invention, particularly genetic engineering, involves the alteration of existing biological material or processes and the discovery of new ones. Biological material is defined under Council Directive 98/44/EC on the legal protection of biotechnological inventions as 'any material containing genetic information and capable of reproducing itself or being reproduced in a biological system'.

The general consensus is that many such INVENTIONS should not be protected as INTELLECTUAL PROPERTY as this would be contrary to EU and international fundamental principles which safeguard HUMAN DIGNITY and personal integrity. Accordingly the following types of biotechnological inventions are not patentable: (a) the human body, at the various stages of its formation and development, and the simple discovery of one of its elements, including the sequence or partial sequence of a gene; (b) processes for cloning human beings; (c) processes for modifying the germ line genetic identity of human beings; (d) uses of human embryos for industrial or commercial purposes; (e) processes for modifying the genetic identity of animals which are likely to cause them suffering without any substantial medical benefit to man or animal, and also animals resulting from such processes; (f) any variety of animal or plant or any essentially biological process for the production of animals or plants, not being a microbiological process or the product of such a process; (g) inventions where their commercial exploitation would be contrary to *ordre public* or morality, though exploitation is not to be deemed to be contrary merely because it is prohibited by law or regulation.

Permitted biotechnological inventions will be protected under EUROPEAN PATENT and national PATENT laws as long as they fulfil the normal criteria for patent protection, even if such inventions concern a product consisting of, or containing, biological material or a process by means of which biological material is produced, processed or used. [US]

Further reading: Brian Sheridan, *EU Biotechnology Law & Practice* (London: Sweet and Maxwell, 2004); Oliver Mills, *Biotechnological Inventions: Moral Restraints and Patent Law* (Aldershot: Ashgate, 2005).

birth certificate A document issued by an official body (in England and Wales the General Register Office), certifying the REGISTRATION OF BIRTH of an individual. The birth certificate will state the name of the individual, his or her sex and date and place of birth. It is issued after registration of the birth by the CHILD'S parent(s). In certain circumstances, for example if a *Gender Recognition Certificate* has been issued, information on a birth certificate may be changed. [AD]

See also GENDER REASSIGNMENT.

Black Rod An official of the HOUSE OF LORDS appointed by the Crown, his full title is 'Gentleman Usher of the Black Rod'. The office has its origins in the 14th century. Today Black Rod is Sergeant-at-Arms of the House of Lords and acts as the sovereign's personal attendant in the House. He controls the admission of 'strangers' and is responsible for enforcing the orders of the Lords' Speaker. It is his job to carry the ceremonial mace in and out of the chamber. Black Rod summons the Members of the House of Commons to attend the Queen's Speech in the House of Lords. Black Rod also serves as usher and doorkeeper at meetings of the Order of the Garter. The office has also been adopted by a number of Commonwealth parliaments. [MS]

blackmail A person commits blackmail under the Theft Act 1968, s. 21, if, with a view to gain for himself or another or with intent to cause loss to another, he makes any unwarranted **demand with menaces**. A demand with menaces is unwarranted unless the person making the demand does so in the belief that he has reasonable grounds for making the demand and that the use of menaces is a proper means of reinforcing the demand.

Menaces are not limited to threats of violence. It was suggested in *Thorne* v. *Motor Traders Association* [1937] AC 797: that 'the word "menace" is to be liberally construed and not as limited to threats of violence but as including threats of any action detrimental to or unpleasant to the person addressed. It may also include a warning that in certain events such action is intended.'

It is unlikely that menaces comprising the threat of behaviour known by a person to be criminal will support his assertion that he believed the use of such menaces to be 'proper'. As was stated in *R* v. *Harvey* (1980) 72 Cr App R 139, 'The test is not what [D] regards as justified, but what he believes to be proper'. Earlier in the same case, it was observed that 'no assistance is given to any defendant, even a fanatic or a deranged idealist, who knows or suspects that his threat, or the act threatened, is criminal, but believes it to be justified by his end or his peculiar circumstances.' [BF]

Blackstone, Sir William (1723–80) The son of a London silk mercer, Blackstone was educated at Charterhouse School and Pembroke College, Oxford. He subsequently read for the Bar and practised, with only limited success, before the royal courts for a number of years. He returned to Oxford in 1758 as the first Vinerian Professor of English Law. In 1770 Blackstone was knighted and accepted an appointment to the COURT OF COMMON PLEAS, though as a judge his record was little more distinguished than his time at the Bar. His reputation derives almost entirely from the lectures he gave at Oxford, which were first published in four volumes, under the title *Commentaries on the Laws of England,* between 1765 and 1769. Drawing on earlier treatises and on the organizing principles of Roman law, he ordered his *Commentaries* into four books, the first two on the system of rights (of persons and things respectively), with the third and fourth focusing on civil and criminal wrongs and remedies. The *Commentaries* were a significant advance on earlier attempts to systematize the complex and rather chaotic structure of English law, and became hugely influential as one of the most significant sources of law throughout the expanding COMMON LAW world of the late 18th and 19th centuries. Although of largely historical significance today, Blackstone's *Commentaries* are still cited, and remain widely regarded as the most comprehensive single treatment of English law ever attempted. [JW]

blasphemy A rarely prosecuted common law offence, it is committed where a person orally or in writing attacks Christianity in a manner likely to shock and outrage the general body of Christian believers. The offence only applies to Christianity, and not to other religions. It appears to follow from *R* v. *Lemon and Gay News Ltd* [1979] AC 617 that a person need only intentionally utter or publish the words or material in question; it is not necessary that he or she be aware of the tendency of the words or material to shock and outrage Christians.

To that extent, blasphemy might be regarded as a STRICT LIABILITY OFFENCE. [BF]

blight notice A notice issued by a property owner, requiring a local planning authority to purchase his property because its value has been adversely affected by the planning proposals of that authority. A blight notice may be issued where a person claims that he has made reasonable endeavours to sell a property containing BLIGHTED LAND but has been unable to sell the land except at a price substantially lower than that which may have been expected if it did not contain blighted land (Town and Country Planning Act 1990, s. 150(1)).

The relevant public authority then has two months in which to serve a counternotice, if it objects to the blight notice, specifying the grounds of its objections. The property owner may then require the objection to be referred to the Lands Tribunal to be determined. A valid blight notice leaves only the issue of the amount of compensation to be agreed between the parties. [DR]

blighted land Land that is adversely affected by the planning proposals of a local planning authority. The Town and Country Planning Act 1990, Schedule 13, states the circumstances in which land is to be considered blighted land, including land that is allocated for the function of a government department, local authority or statutory undertaker under a DEVELOPMENT PLAN; land declared to be part of a CLEARANCE AREA; land on which a highway is to be constructed; and land which is subject to COMPULSORY PURCHASE. An example of blighted land would be land that is identified in a local planning authority's development plan for a road-widening scheme. [DR]
See also BLIGHT NOTICE.

blockade A military maritime operation whose purpose is to block all entries and exits to a country's ports or harbours. Since the employment of a blockade will give rise either to a simple use of armed force or even an armed attack on the part of the blockading state, its lawful use is restricted as a means of self-defence under

Article 51 of the UN Charter, unless it is authorized by the UN SECURITY COUNCIL under Article 42. The Council has on some occasions authorized such blockades, as in 1990 when it ordered the military blockade of Iraqi and Kuwaiti ports in response to the invasion of Kuwait by Iraq. Enforcement of a blockade cannot take place on the high seas because, in accordance with Article 88 of the UNCLOS, the high seas are reserved only for peaceful purposes. The practice of states, however, is to set blockades on the high seas adjoining the closest coastal maritime belt. Neutral merchant ships may be confiscated if they attempt to break the blockade. Moreover, a right of visit, search and capture exists against neutral ships carrying contraband or helping the enemy. [IB]

blood relationship *See* CONSANGUINITY.

board of inquiry A board convened by one or more of the armed services and charged with investigating incidents such as 'friendly fire' deaths in combat, military aircraft accidents and Royal Navy collisions. There are provisions in QUEEN'S REGULATIONS for commanders to establish such inquiries, which hear evidence, reach conclusions and make recommendations. [MS]

bodily harm *See* ACTUAL BODILY HARM; GRIEVOUS BODILY HARM.

Bolam test The standard of care against which proposed medical treatment is recognized as appropriate by a responsible body of medical opinion skilled in the delivery of that particular treatment. The test is named after *Bolam* v. *Friern Hospital Management Committee* [1957] 2 All ER 11. A doctor treating a patient in accordance with the principles of the test will have satisfied the duty of care and will not be liable in NEGLIGENCE. The test has been criticized for being too reliant upon peer opinion and was modified by the HOUSE OF LORDS in *Bolitho* v. *City and Hackney Health Authority* [1997] 4 All ER 771. The views expressed must now be based on logic and the risks and benefits of competing options considered. [HJ]

See also BEST INTERESTS.

bona vacantia (Lat. vacant property or ownerless property) Under the statutory provisions for the distribution of the assets of a deceased person on INTESTACY (i.e. where assets are not disposed of by WILL), if the deceased was survived by no spouse, no issue and no other specified relatives, then the assets will go to the CROWN as *bona vacantia*. [CM]

border The formal demarcation or delimitation of land territory between two STATES; also called a boundary. Borders may be set up on the basis of bilateral or multilateral border treaties, through title settled by occupation, and if disputed between states, a border may be settled through judicial means (including ARBITRATION). The demarcation of borders, whether on the basis of geography (e.g. rivers or mountain ranges) or ethnic/national divides, or others, depends solely on the parties concerned. In the case of state succession, in the absence of any contrary formal agreement between the relevant states, recent practice has followed the rule that demarcation will be based on the administrative borders prior to secession or decolonization (see *UTI POSSIDETIS*). [IB]

borough Historically, this denotes towns that once operated a certain form of local government called a 'municipal corporation'. As a formal legal status it was abolished by the Local Government Act 1972, except in respect of the metropolitan area of **Greater London**, which still comprises 32 boroughs, in addition to the City of London. The status of borough today carries only ceremonial connotations, including the right to bestow the title 'mayor' on the leader of the council. [MS]

Boundary Commissions Independent, non-political bodies constituted by the Parliamentary Constituencies Act 1986. There are separate Commissions for England, Scotland, Wales and Northern Ireland. Their function is to keep the borders of parliamentary constituencies under continuous review and, every eight to twelve years, conduct a general review of all constituency boundaries and submit to the Secretary of State a report showing the constituencies they recommend. [MS]

See also BOUNDARY COMMITTEE FOR ENGLAND.

Boundary Committee for England Responsible for reviewing the structure, boundaries and electoral arrangements of local government in England, the Boundary Committee is a statutory committee of the ELECTORAL COMMISSION and took over the functions of the former Local Government Commission for England in 2001. Local Government Boundary Commissions for Scotland and Wales perform equivalent roles in each of those nations. [JW]

See also BOUNDARY COMMISSIONS.

breach of close A form of trespass to land, involving the unlawful entry onto enclosed land. [DR]

See also CLOSE.

breach of confidence The relationship between two persons may be of such a quality that the law or equity will impose a duty on one to act in the interests of another, including a duty to treat all or certain information within that relationship as confidential. Such relationships may include that between agent and principal, director and company, employee and employer, husband and wife, lawyer and client, trustee and beneficiary, and partners in a business partnership. Any actual or threatened failure to preserve such confidentiality may be a ground for an action for breach of confidence.

Breach of confidence is a COMMON LAW action. It is of particular significance in protecting commercially sensitive information and TRADE SECRETS. It is a branch of COMPETITION LAW in many CIVIL LAW countries. With the passing of the Human Rights Act 1998, the tort of breach of confidence has been extended, by reference to Article 8 of the EUROPEAN CONVENTION ON HUMAN RIGHTS (respect for privacy and family life), to protect aspects of individual privacy: see *Campbell* v. *Mirror Group Newspapers Ltd* [2004] UKHL 22. Three essential ingredients must be proven for an action to succeed: (a) the information must be confidential in quality; (b) it must be

imparted so as to import an obligation of confidence; and (c) there must be an unauthorized use of that information to the detriment of the party communicating it: see *Coco* v. *A.N.Clark (Engineers) Ltd* (1969) RPC 41.

Where confidential information has already been disclosed, except where that disclosure has itself been under conditions of confidentiality, the courts will not normally grant an INJUNCTION to prevent further breach. Consequently, once the element of secrecy is lost, the information will often fall into the public domain. [US & JW]

See also CONFIDENTIALITY; GOOD FAITH.

breach of contract When one party, without lawful excuse such as intervening impossibility, either refuses or fails to perform an express or implied contractual obligation, or performs it defectively. DAMAGES are available as of right on proof of breach of contract to compensate for losses caused by the breach. However, the CONTRACT will remain in place and both parties' future obligations will need to be performed unless the breach amounts to a repudiatory breach. In some circumstances, the remedy of SPECIFIC PERFORMANCE or an INJUNCTION may be available for breach of contract. If the breach is repudiatory, the injured party will have the option to terminate or affirm the contract in addition to the remedy of damages for the breach. [JPL]

See also REPUDIATION.

breach of privilege *See* PARLIAMENTARY PRIVILEGE.

breach of statutory duty When someone breaks a statutory duty or obligation they will be liable for whatever (criminal) penalty the STATUTE provides. Sometimes a person suffering damage from the breach may also bring a civil action in TORT to obtain compensation, if this is permitted under the Act, for example, under the Consumer Protection Act 1987, or, if the Act is silent, the courts may decide, as a matter of proper construction or public policy, that a civil action should also be allowed. Breach of statutory duty constitutes a separate tort from NEGLIGENCE (see *Thornton* v. *Kirklees Metropolitan Borough Council* [1979] QB 626), though in practice the facts (as in many safety at work contexts) would often also disclose an action in negligence, and both actions may be advanced as alternative grounds of claim (see *West Wiltshire District Council* v. *Garland* [1995] Ch 297).

[JW]

breach of the peace A COMMON LAW offence which occurs 'whenever harm is actually done or is likely to be done to a person or in his presence to his property or a person is in fear of being so harmed through an assault, an affray, a riot, unlawful assembly or other disturbance' – *per* Watkins LJ in *R* v. *Howell* [1982] QB 416 at 427. Anybody, whether or not a constable, may arrest a suspect in respect of an actual breach of the peace or if they reasonably believe that a breach of the peace is about to take place. [BF]

See also CITIZEN'S ARREST.

breach of trust Any act or omission by a TRUSTEE, or other person in a FIDUCIARY position, which fails to comply with the duties imposed by the trust or other fiduciary relationship. The trustee is under a personal liability to make good any loss that occurs (or account for any profits made) irrespective of whether or not the breach was deliberate or dishonest. Despite the somewhat pejorative tone, breach of trust is concerned with compensating the beneficiary for actual or potential loss, rather than punishing the trustee in default. [PK]

breakdown of marriage Where the relationship between parties to a MARRIAGE breaks down to such an extent that they are unable to continue to live with each other or to remain married to each other. The Matrimonial Causes Act 1973, s. 1(1) designates IRRETRIEVABLE BREAKDOWN of marriage as the only ground for DIVORCE in England and Wales. [AD]

breath test A procedure for analysing alcohol concentration in the human body. Breath-testing instruments have been developed to obtain a sample of alveolar breath for analysis. A person who is driving, attempting to drive, or in charge of a motor vehicle on the road or in a public place may be required by a uniformed police officer to provide a specimen of breath to ascertain whether they are over the prescribed limit of alcohol. The police officer must have reasonable cause to suspect that the person has committed, or is committing, a moving traffic offence. A breath test can also be requested if a police officer has reasonable cause to suspect that a person driving or attempting to drive or in charge of a vehicle has consumed alcohol. [SN]

breathalyser A device for measuring the proportion of alcohol in the breath. [BF]

See also DRUNKEN DRIVING.

Brezhnev doctrine Adopted by President Brezhnev of the USSR following the suppression of moves towards democratization in Czechoslovakia in 1968, the Brezhnev doctrine held that socialist states could, if necessary, employ armed force to ensure that other socialist states did not deviate from socialism. This doctrine, much like the relevant provisions in the NATO Agreement, was based on the assumption that a threat to the security of one socialist state was a threat to all socialist states. The doctrine was used to justify the Soviet invasion of Afghanistan in 1980. [IB]

See also USE OF FORCE.

bribery Defined at COMMON LAW as 'the receiving or offering [of] any undue reward by or to any person whatsoever, in a public office, in order to influence his behaviour in office, and incline him to act contrary to the known rules of honesty and integrity' (J. W. C. Turner, *Russell on Crime,* 12th edn, (1964), p. 381). In addition to the common law offence, a number of statutory offences were also created in the late 19th and early 20th centuries, chiefly under the so-called Prevention of Corruption Acts between 1889 and 1916. These created separate offences in respect of the bribery of public officials and of private persons in some commercial settings.

The resulting patchwork of offences has long been criticized as unduly complex and ineffective, and the Organization for Economic Cooperation and Development has been particularly critical of English law for failing to conform to the standards expected under its 1998 Convention on Combating Bribery of Foreign Public Officials in International Business Transactions. Recent attempts by the UK government to reform the law with a draft Corruption Bill have also met with substantial criticism, and as a result the government has passed the issue over to the LAW COMMISSION for further consultation and recommendations: see *Reforming Bribery*, Consultation Paper No. 185 (Law Commission, November 2007). [JW]

See also CORRUPTION.

brief 1. The written instructions to a barrister to appear in a case, together with a summary of the facts of that case. This is properly called the 'brief to counsel'.

2. (slang) A legal representative, usually a solicitor or barrister, as in the phrase 'my brief'. [JW]

brief fee The amount of remuneration agreed between a barrister and his or her professional client. [JW]

British citizenship A category of British nationality introduced by the British Nationality Act 1981, and granted to all former CITIZENS OF THE UK AND COLONIES (CUKCs) who had a right of abode in the United Kingdom on 1 January 1983, that is, the unconditional right to live and work in the UK, the Channel Islands and the Isle of Man. British citizenship is now the only category of British nationality to carry with it a right of abode in the UK. Neither the granting of 'indefinite leave to remain' by the UK immigration authorities, nor the right of residence and free movement given to citizens of the EUROPEAN ECONOMIC AREA constitute a formal right of abode. Commonwealth citizenship (conferred by British citizenship, or the status of British Overseas Territories, British Overseas, or British National (Overseas) citizen, or nationality of a country listed in the British Nationality Act 1981, Schedule 3) also does not provide a right of abode in the UK,

although Commonwealth citizens in the UK are treated for various legal purposes as non-ALIENS.

British citizenship can be obtained in one of five ways: (a) by birth in the UK to a parent who is a British citizen at the time of the birth, or who is settled in the United Kingdom; (b) by descent, where the child is not born in the UK, but one of the parents is themselves a British citizen otherwise than by descent; (c) by NATURALIZATION; (d) by registration, though the rules are complex; in some cases citizenship by registration may be granted as of right, in others it is at the discretion of the Secretary of State; (e) by adoption, though this is only automatic where at least one adoptive parent is a British citizen on the date of the adoption, and the adoption order was made (after a specified date) either by a UK court or in the court of a British Overseas Territory; or it is a so-called 'Convention adoption' under the Hague Convention on Intercountry Adoption 1993 and the adoptive parents are resident in the UK. In other situations an adopted child may only obtain citizenship by registration.

The other main forms of citizenship granted by or after the 1981 Act are: BRITISH OVERSEAS TERRITORIES CITIZENSHIP (between 1981 and 2002 this was called British Dependent Territories citizenship); BRITISH OVERSEAS CITIZENSHIP; BRITISH NATIONAL (OVERSEAS) CITIZENSHIP.

There is also a residual category of British subject which applies chiefly to persons who were British subjects, mostly born in British India and the Republic of Ireland before 1949, but who were not CUKCs or Commonwealth citizens. [JW]

See also BRITISH PROTECTED PERSON; SETTLEMENT.

British Medical Association (BMA) The professional organization established to look after the professional and personal needs of doctors from all branches of medicine in the UK. The Association is an independent trade union that protects the collective and individual interests of practising doctors and medical students. Allied to this is the Association's role in promoting the interests of the medical profession and the achievement of high-quality healthcare. Policies cover a range of issues, including public health, medical ethics, science, the state of the NHS, medical education and doctors' contracts.   [HJ]

British National (Overseas) citizenship (BN(O)) A form of citizenship created by the Hong Kong Act 1985, which enabled Hong Kong residents who held BRITISH OVERSEAS TERRITORIES CITIZENSHIP (then called British Dependent Territories citizenship) to apply to become BN(O)s. Any person who failed to register as a BN(O) by 1 July 1997, and thereby would be rendered stateless, automatically acquired BRITISH OVERSEAS CITIZENSHIP. Holders of BN(O) status do not have an automatic right of abode in the UK, but enjoy a similar status and rights to other Commonwealth citizens in the UK (see BRITISH CITIZENSHIP). Lord Goldsmith's Citizenship Review, *Citizenship – Our Common Bond* (2008) has recommended that the BN(O) status should be converted into full British citizenship.   [JW]

British Overseas citizenship One of the three forms of citizenship introduced by the British Nationality Act 1981. It has served as a residual category for those former citizens of the United Kingdom and Colonies who were not entitled to or did not claim BRITISH CITIZENSHIP or BRITISH OVERSEAS TERRITORIES CITIZENSHIP. British Overseas citizenship was acquired automatically by eligible persons on the passing of the 1981 Act. Subsequent entitlement to the status can only be obtained by registration, and has been confined almost entirely to minors. Holders do not have an automatic right of abode in the UK, but those resident in the UK may obtain British citizenship by registration.   [JW]

See also BRITISH NATIONAL (OVERSEAS) CITIZENSHIP.

British Overseas Territories citizenship (BOTC) A form of citizenship covering all the British Overseas Territories listed in a schedule to the British Nationality Act 1981 (including Bermuda, the Cayman Islands and Gibraltar). The individual overseas territories are not independent territories and so do not have their own nationality status, though they retain the right to make their own immigration laws and award belonger status to those resident within that territory. Without belonger status, BOTC does not give a right to reside in a British Overseas territory. However, the British Overseas Territories Act 2002 has now extended BRITISH CITIZENSHIP to virtually all BOTCs.   [JW]

British protected person Under the British Nationality Act 1981, s. 50, 'a person who is a member of any class of persons declared to be British protected persons by an Order in Council for the time being in force under section 38 [of the British Nationality Act 1981] or is a British protected person by virtue of the Solomon Islands Act 1978'. British protected persons enjoy a *sui generis* legal status which does not give them the full rights of British citizenship (e.g. they cannot vote in UK elections), but does exempt them from the category of ALIENS under UK law. However, since 30 April 2003, British protected persons resident in the UK who hold no other citizenship or nationality, and who have not lost or renounced any other citizenship or nationality after 4 July 2002, may apply to be registered as British citizens (British Nationality Act 1981, s. 4B).   [JW]

brothel 'A house resorted to or used by more than one woman for the purposes of fornication' *per* Lord Parker CJ, in *Gorman* v. *Standen* [1964] 1 QB 294 at 303. 'Woman' should now be read as referring to either gender as appropriate. A number of features of this definition are important: (a) the reference to 'more than one woman' obviously means that a house cannot be a brothel if it is used by only a single prostitute; (b) it does not require that sexual intercourse take place or be offered; and (c) curiously, it does not appear to require that the house is used for prostitution, that is, where sexual services are offered for reward, though this will often be the case in practice. This would explain why it is an offence under the Sexual Offences Act 1956, s. 33, to keep a brothel, or to manage, or act or assist in the management of a brothel, but there is also a separate offence under s. 33A of keeping (etc.) a brothel used for prostitution. [BF]

See also DISORDERLY HOUSE.

Brussels Convention 1968 (largely obsolete) A TREATY entered into between the original MEMBER STATES of the EUROPEAN ECONOMIC COMMUNITY for the purpose of harmonizing the rules applied by their national courts on the issues of (a) taking jurisdiction and (b) recognition and enforcement of judgments made by the courts of other Member States. The scheme of the treaty is to prevent, so far as is possible, the making within the Community of more than one judgment in respect of the same dispute and between the same parties, thus eliminating (or at least greatly minimizing) the possibility of there being competing judgments within the Community.

However, application of the 1968 Convention is restricted to civil and commercial matters, and there are also specific exclusions from the scope of the treaty, for example, in respect of revenue and customs, administrative matters and ARBITRATION.

As regards jurisdiction, where the defendant is domiciled in a Member State, the claimant must commence proceedings against the defendant in the defendant's home courts. There are exceptions to this basic requirement, for example in relation to contracts and torts, so that the claimant can commence proceedings against the defendant in the country in which the contract or tort is juridically located (e.g. the country in which a loan is to be repaid, or in which the performance of contract terms is to take place). The judgments formula requires the receiving court to recognize and enforce judgments made in other Community courts except as provided for by the 1968 Convention.

In 2000, the EU adopted Council Regulation (EC) 44/2001 (BRUSSELS I REGULATION) on jurisdiction and the recognition and enforcement of judgments in civil and commercial disputes, known as the Brussels Regulation. This replaces and modifies the 1968 Brussels Convention in all Member States. In the UK, the EU rules are set out in the Civil Jurisdiction and Judgments Order 2001, as amended by the Civil Jurisdiction and Judgments Regulations 2007. [RE]

See also LEX DOMICILII.

Brussels I Regulation The colloquial name for Council Regulation 44/2001. This is a European Communities instrument intended to ensure continued judicial cooperation in civil and commercial matters as prescribed by Article 65 of the EC Treaty. The Preamble to the Regulation (recital 6) shows that it was introduced because it was thought to be necessary and appropriate for the rules governing jurisdiction and the recognition and enforcement of judgments to be set out in Community legislation, which is binding and directly applicable within the Community. The Regulation originally superseded the BRUSSELS CONVENTION 1968 (the Convention) for all Member States except Denmark, though Denmark is now subject to the Regulation as a result of a separate agreement (Official Journal L120/22).

The Regulation is substantially similar, though not identical, to the Convention. The rules on jurisdiction in civil and commercial proceedings must be 'highly predictable', in general 'based on the defendant's domicile', but with exceptions for certain 'well-defined situations' (recital 11); the possibility of 'concurrent proceedings' must be minimized so as to ensure that there will be no 'irreconcilable judgments' (recital 15); there must be 'mutual trust' between the courts of Member States in the context of the recognition of judgments made in other Member States (recital 16); enforcement in one Member State of judgments made in other Member States must be 'efficient and rapid' (recital 17); and there should be 'continuity' between the Convention and the Regulation (recital 19).

In the UK, the modified EU rules are set out in the Civil Jurisdiction and Judgments Order 2001, as amended, which also provides rules for allocation of jurisdiction within the UK. [RE]

budget The statement made to Parliament by the Chancellor of the Exchequer in Spring each year in which he assesses current general economic conditions, reviews the UK's public finances for the year, provides a forecast of government economic policy; and presents his proposals for adjustments to the legislation concerned with the raising of revenue from taxes.

Changes which are to take effect immediately are given effect by resolutions which have to be confirmed. The effects of the debated resolutions are incorporated into the Finance Bill (usually only one each year) which becomes the Finance Act.

There is also an Autumn Budget in which the Chancellor announces various plans which are taken forward to the Spring Budget. [RE]

See also TAX STATUTE.

buggery (obsolete) At COMMON LAW, 'buggery' referred to anal intercourse by a man with a man or woman, or anal or vaginal intercourse between a man or woman and an animal. It was regulated by the Sexual Offences Acts of 1956 and 1967, the latter of which decriminalized buggery between men, subject to certain conditions, including that the act took place in private. The offence was repealed by the Sexual Offences Act 2003. [BF]

See also BESTIALITY.

bugging Colloquial term for covert ELECTRONIC MONITORING. [BF]

building lease A building lease was a common form of LEASE in the 19th century when there was speculative building of houses. The freeholder sold a lease of the land to a builder. The builder built housing on the land, and then sold individual LONG LEASES of houses to TENANTS. The tenants paid GROUND RENT to the freeholder. Tenants of long leases now have the right to ENFRANCHISEMENT. [HC & DR]

building preservation notice A notice issued by a local planning authority granting a building temporary LISTED BUILDING status. Building preservation notices may be issued if it appears to a local planning authority that a building which is not a listed building is of special architectural or historic interest and is in danger of demolition or alteration in such a way as to affect its character as a building of such interest (Planning (Listed Buildings and Conservation Areas) Act 1990, s. 3).

The effect of the notice is to prohibit the demolition, alteration or extension of the building without the express consent of the local planning authority or Secretary of State. The notice remains effective for six months and may be renewed, but in any event lapses either on the grant of permanent listed building status or on notification by the Secretary of State that he does not intend to grant such status. [DR]

See also CONSERVATION AREA.

building scheme A scheme of development where a property developer sells a variety of FREEHOLD plots from one larger area of LAND. The technical problems associated with the enforcement of RESTRICTIVE COVENANTS are particularly complex in building schemes. The intention is that each purchaser complies with obligations which maintain the character of the development as a whole. However, because the sales are not instantaneous but successive, the imposition of obligations by the transfer cannot, at COMMON LAW, bind those plots of land already sold. EQUITY then intervenes to protect the arrangement because of its characteristic of mutuality of obligation. In order for the technicalities of the common law to be overcome, there has to be an identifiable building scheme and evidence of a mutually understood common intention. [HC & DR]

bundle *See* JURY BUNDLE; TRIAL BUNDLE.

burden of proof The duty of a party to prove a particular fact to the trier of fact by the end of the proceedings. Failure to discharge this burden means that the issue will be decided in favour of the other party. In a criminal case, the prosecution generally bears the burden of proving every issue, subject to two broad exceptions. First, a defendant who raises INSANITY or insane automatism as a defence, or who argues UNFITNESS TO PLEAD, bears the burden of proving it. Secondly, a statutory provision may expressly or impliedly place the burden of proving a particular issue on the defendant. The principle in civil trials is that the party asserting an issue essential to their case bears the burden of proof in relation to that issue. [ALTC]

See also PRESUMPTION OF INNOCENCE.

burglary The name given to two offences under the Theft Act 1968, s. 9. In both offences, the defendant must enter a building or part of a building as a trespasser. According to *R* v. *Collins* [1973] 1 QB 100, a defendant trespasses if his or her presence is without the consent of the proprietor, and he or she knows that there is no consent or is reckless as to the existence of consent.

To commit the offence under s. 9(1)(a) of the Act, the defendant must enter with the intention of committing therein one of the offences identified in s. 9(2): THEFT, inflicting GRIEVOUS BODILY HARM or CRIMINAL DAMAGE. Until the Sexual Offences Act 2003, RAPE was also an offence identified in s. 9(2). However, this situation has been amended by the Sexual Offences Act 2003, s. 63(1), which created the separate offence of trespass with intent to commit a sexual offence.

To commit the offence in s. 9(1)(b) of the Theft Act 1968, the defendant, having entered, must commit theft or attempted theft, or must inflict grievous bodily harm or ATTEMPT to inflict grievous bodily harm, but the section does not state that the infliction of grievous bodily harm must be such as to constitute an offence but that must surely be what was intended. [BF]

See also AGGRAVATED BURGLARY.

business liability Liability which arises from breach of a contractual obligation arising from things done in the course of a business or from occupation of business premises (see the Unfair Contract Terms Act (UCTA) 1977, s. 1(3)). This is defined in s. 14, as including a profession, LOCAL AUTHORITY or government department. UCTA 1977 and the Unfair Terms in Consumer Contracts Regulations (UTCCR) 1999 limit the extent to which it is possible to exclude this business liability. [JPL]

business name For legal purposes, the name used by any person, partnership or company for carrying on business, unless it is identical to their own name. Thus, to trade as 'Sarah Smith Associates' is to trade under a business name, whereas trading simply as 'Sarah Smith' is not. Since 1982 there has been no general legal requirement to register a business name, unless the business is a limited company in which case the COMPANY name must be registered with Companies House. There are some general restrictions on words that can be used and which would require consent from the Secretary of State under the Business Names Act 1985. These include words such as 'bank', 'international', 'royal' and 'trust'. In addition, the adoption of a name and/or visual identity that is very similar to that of an established business may lead to claims for infringement of trade mark, or PASSING OFF. [JW]

See also DOMAIN NAME.

'but for' test *See* NEGLIGENCE.

byelaw A type of DELEGATED LEGISLATION made by a body such as a LOCAL AUTHORITY under an enabling power contained in an Act of Parliament. Examples of such enabling Acts include the Open Spaces Act 1906, which allows local authorities to make byelaws for the regulation of open spaces and burial grounds, and the Airports Act 1986, which allows the British Airports Authority to make byelaws governing matters such as car parking, access to and advertising on airport property.

Byelaws are geographically limited and have legal effect only within the areas to which they apply. Because they tend to create criminal offences, byelaws must be confirmed by the relevant Secretary of State before they can come into force. Byelaws may be challenged in the courts by JUDICIAL REVIEW.

A series of model byelaws developed by the Department for Communities and Local Government is published online at http://www.communities.gov.uk/publications/localgovernment/modelbyelaw [JW]

C

C. *See* COMMAND PAPERS.

CA *See* COURT OF APPEAL.

cab rank rule The ethical principle that barristers in self-employed practice must accept any BRIEF that is offered provided it is within their competence to act and at a proper fee, and act regardless of their opinion of the case or the client's conduct, character, reputation, or guilt or innocence: see paragraphs 602–606, *Code of Conduct of the Bar of England and Wales*, at http://www.barstandardsboard.org.uk/standardsandguidance/codeofconduct/section1codeofconduct/partvi_acceptanceandreturnofinstructions/.   [JW]

Cabinet A body normally composed of 20–22 MEMBERS OF PARLIAMENT and peers who are usually leading figures within the governing political party. The members of the Cabinet hold ministerial rank, and although membership is entirely within the gift of the Prime Minister, the Cabinet includes, by convention, the holders of the great offices of state, including the Chancellor of the Exchequer, the LORD CHANCELLOR and the Home and Defence Secretaries.

The Cabinet serves as the principal executive body of government under the British Constitution. The idea of Cabinet government implies governance by committee, which in turn requires that the Cabinet operates collegially and on principles of collective responsibility for decision-making. However, it has been noted since the early 1960s that the British style of government has become increasingly centralized in the person of the Prime Minister, as that role has attracted or acquired greater power and authority. The reality of Cabinet government today might thus be described as 'a loosely structured collective political executive with strong prime-ministerial direction' (Nevil Johnson, *Reshaping the British Constitution* (Basingstoke: Palgrave Macmillan, 2004) p. 86).   [JW]

See also MINISTERIAL RESPONSIBILITY.

cabotage The ability of a company in one MEMBER STATE to provide transport facilities in another Member State. Originally relevant to cargo shipping, the term now applies to cargo transport generally and is more an industry term rather than a EUROPEAN COMMUNITY (EC) legal term. Cabotage was traditionally very restricted; however the EC is in the process of liberalizing these services and increasing the frequency of cabotage.   [MON]

CAC *See* CENTRAL ARBITRATION COMMITTEE.

Cafcass *See* CHILDREN AND FAMILY COURT ADVISORY AND SUPPORT SERVICE.

Calderbank letter A means whereby one party makes an offer of settlement to the other, normally in circumstances where it is not possible or appropriate to make the offer by paying funds into court. *Calderbank* letters may be used in matters such as family proceedings or cases where the claim is not for damages or the payment of a debt. The effect of a *Calderbank* letter is 'without prejudice except as to costs', that is, it forms a basis for WITHOUT PREJUDICE NEGOTIATIONS while giving the party making the offer some protection from costs should that offer be rejected: see *Calderbank* v. *Calderbank* [1975] 3 All ER 333; *Rush & Tompkins* v. *Greater London Council* [1989] AC 1280. Although the CIVIL PROCEURES RULES have increased the range of offers available within the statutory regime, they have not eliminated the possibility of parties making offers outside the rules and so *Calderbank* offers remain an option in proceedings.

[JW]

See also PART 36 OFFER.

cannabis Now a Class B controlled drug (reclassified in January 2009), specified in the Misuse of Drugs Act 1971, Schedule 2, Part III. Cultivation of cannabis is a specific offence under s. 6 of the 1971 Act. [BF]

cannon-shot rule Used as a method of measurement of the breadth of the TERRITORIAL WATERS in the 17th century. It consisted of a belt over which an imaginary cannon would range if positioned along the entirety of the seafront. The cannon-shot rule was initially employed to set the limit of territorial SOVEREIGNTY at a distance of one marine league or three miles from land. The rule is not widely recognized today, as broader territorial limits have become the norm. [IB]

canon law (From G., kanōn / κανών, a rule, standard or measure) Church law. The term canon law is commonly associated with the laws of the Roman Catholic Church; however, this is a misnomer as it can also properly be used to describe the laws of Anglican and Orthodox communions. [JW]

See also CHURCH OF ENGLAND; ECCLESIASTICAL COURTS.

CAP *See* COMMON AGRICULTURAL POLICY.

capacity to contract In order to enter into a valid CONTRACT, the parties must have the competence in law (LEGAL CAPACITY) to contract. People who have reached 18 and are of sound mind are regarded as having legal capacity to contract. However, agreements made by minors (children under 18) (see CHILDREN'S CONTRACTS) or by those suffering from a mental disorder may not be fully enforceable against them. The capacity of corporations is provided for by STATUTE: under the Companies Act 2006 it is possible to restrict the company's capacity in the ARTICLES OF ASSOCIATION, but acting outside that capacity does not invalidate the company's actions in favour of the other contracting party.

[JPL]

capacity to marry To contract a valid MARRIAGE both parties must have the **legal** and **mental capacity** to marry. To have legal capacity, both parties: (a) must be over the age of 16 years (see the Matrimonial Causes Act 1973, s. 11(a)(ii) and the Marriage Act 1949, s. 2) and, if between 16 and 18 years, they must also have the required consents (see the Marriage Act 1949, s. 3); (b) must be male and female respectively (see the Matrimonial Causes Act 1973, s. 11(c)); (c) must not be within the PROHIBITED DEGREES OF RELATIONSHIP of AFFINITY or CONSANGUINITY (see Matrimonial Causes Act 1973, s. 11(a)(i), and the Marriage Act 1949); and (d) neither party may already be married to another (Matrimonial Causes Act 1973, s. 11(b)). Lack of capacity for any of these reasons renders the marriage void.

Both parties must also possess the mental capacity to marry. Mental capacity means that the person must understand the nature of the marriage contract and be capable of understanding the duties and responsibilities that normally attach to marriage: see *Sheffield City Council* v. *E and S* [2004] EWHC 2808 (Fam). It is likely that this requirement also applies to CIVIL PARTNERSHIPS. [AD]

See also BIGAMY; GENDER REASSIGNMENT; VOID MARRIAGE.

capital allowance A deduction permitted

for the purposes of the income tax legislation in the United Kingdom (UK) in respect of capital outlay made by a business taxpayer. The Capital Allowances Act 2001 (the 2001 Act) authorizes the deduction of some capital value for the purposes of income tax computations. There are a number of categories of capital outlay which can qualify for capital allowances, including expenditure on industrial buildings, research and development, and purchase of patent rights, and perhaps most importantly for plant and machinery. Part 2 of the 2001 Act provides a first-year allowance (FYA) and a writing-down allowance (WDA) where there has been qualifying expenditure, which relates to a qualifying activity, such as the carrying on of a trade or a profession (s. 15). So, for example, where a small business purchases a computerized control system, a FYA at 40 per cent would be claimed in the year of outlay, and WDA would be claimed at 25 per cent thereafter on the reducing balance.

Capital allowances are extremely important to businesses. The 2001 Act reflects this, running to 581 sections and four schedules.

[RE]

See also CORPORATION TAX.

capital gains tax (CGT) The tax payable on the chargeable gains realized or deemed to be realized by a natural or juristic person (the taxpayer) who is resident or ordinarily resident in the UK for a YEAR OF ASSESSMENT in which they make a disposal or deemed disposal of chargeable assets owned by them. Individuals are not required to make returns where the gains do not exceed the annual exempt amount.

Where a person is a chargeable person who disposes of an ASSET which is not exempted, the open market value of the asset at the date of disposal is compared with the open market value of the asset at the date of acquisition. If the difference between the two values shows an increase in value (a gain), that amount is used in the computation of the taxpayer's tax liability. If the difference between the two values shows a reduction (a loss), that amount can be used to set off against gains made

by the taxpayer in the same or future assessment periods. An asset is disposed of when it is sold or given away. There can be a disposal of an asset even where there is no sale or gift, and this is known as a deemed disposal. A deemed disposal arises where, for example, an asset is destroyed. There is an acquisition where a taxpayer buys an asset or receives a gift of an asset.

The tax was introduced by the Finance Act 1965, and consolidated by the Capital Gains Tax Act 1979, and the Taxation of Chargeable Gains Act 1992. The tax is chargeable on disposals after 5 April 1965.

[RE]

See also ANNUAL EXEMPTION; CHARGEABLE ASSET; CORPORATION TAX.

capital money 1. Money which is paid to SETTLED LAND ACT TRUSTEES, resulting from the exercise of the TENANT FOR LIFE'S statutory powers under a SETTLEMENT, governed by the Settled Land Act 1925 (SLA 1925). For example, if a tenant for life exercises his power to raise money by the grant of a LEGAL MORTGAGE, money arising from that transaction is capital money which must be paid to the trustees of the settlement. If capital money is raised for a particular purpose, for example if money raised by granting a mortgage was obtained in order to pay for improvements to the land, the trustees must use the money for that particular purpose. For capital money raised for no particular purpose, the money must be used in one of the ways set out by the Settled Land Act 1925, s. 73, as amended, which includes investment in securities, the purchase of land or any other way set out by the settlement.

2. Money arising from similar transactions as above, but relating to trusts of land, where the money is to be paid to the trustees of that land. In particular, in order to effect the OVERREACHING OF EQUITABLE INTERESTS on the sale of land, capital money is the money that must be paid to at least two trustees of that land.   [DR]

capital punishment Abolished in all circumstances in the United Kingdom, following the ratification by the UK, in October 2003, of Protocol No. 13 to the

EUROPEAN CONVENTION ON HUMAN RIGHTS. The protocol came into force in relation to the UK in February 2004. In June 2004, the Human Rights Act 1998 (Amendment) Order 2004 (SI 2004/1574) came into force, making the 13th Protocol a 'Convention Right' for the purposes of the 1998 Act. The 13th Protocol superseded the 6th Protocol to the Convention, which permitted reintroduction of capital punishment in time of war.

Capital punishment remained available for TREASON (under the Treason Act 1814, s. 1) and for piracy accompanied by attempted MURDER (under the Piracy Act 1837, s. 2) until its removal by the Crime and Disorder Act 1998, s. 36.

Capital punishment for murder was removed by the Murder (Abolition of Death Penalty) Act 1965. The penalty for murder is now a mandatory sentence of life imprisonment. [BF]

capital transfer tax (obsolete) A tax introduced by the Finance Act 1975 to replace ESTATE DUTY. The principal difference between estate duty and capital transfer tax was that the latter included a tax on lifetime transfers. The 1975 Act was consolidated by the Capital Transfer Tax Act 1984. That Act was renamed by the Finance Act 1986, s. 100, as the Inheritance Tax Act 1984, and Capital Transfer Tax was converted into inheritance tax by other provisions of that Finance Act. [RE]

See also LIFETIME TRANSFER.

care and control (obsolete) The responsibility for, and the right to make decisions about, day-to-day matters in relation to a child's upbringing. After divorce, this would be awarded to the PARENT living with the CHILD. It used to be possible for a court to make a SPLIT ORDER, dividing the powers and responsibilities contained in custody: one parent might be given CUSTODY and the other care and control. But there was confusion as to the precise effect of such an order and the concepts of custody and care and control were abandoned. With the enactment of the Children Act 1989,

they were replaced by the concepts of PARENTAL RESPONSIBILITY, residence and contact. [FK]

See also CONTACT ORDER; RESIDENCE ORDER.

care centre A class of COUNTY COURT established under the terms of the Children (Allocation of Proceedings) Order 1991. Care centres are specialist courts, presided over by judges with specialist training. They have jurisdiction to hear cases concerning DIVORCE, CIVIL PARTNERSHIPS, ADOPTION and both public and private law cases concerning children, including CARE PROCEEDINGS and contested residence and contact cases. [FK]

See also CHILDREN AND FAMILY COURT ADVISORY AND SUPPORT SERVICE (CAFCASS); CONTACT ORDERS; INNER LONDON FAMILY PROCEEDINGS COURT; RESIDENCE ORDERS.

care contact order An order directing that a CHILD who is in care should have contact with the person(s) designated (Children Act 1989, s. 34). Such an order can be made on the court's own initiative when making a CARE ORDER or in FAMILY PROCEEDINGS concerning a child who is in care (s. 34(5)). Alternatively, it can make an order on the application of a person specified in s. 34(1) such as the PARENT(s), GUARDIAN, special guardian or person with PARENTAL RESPONSIBILITY. Persons who are not entitled to apply in this way must seek the leave of the court to do so. An application can also be made by a LOCAL AUTHORITY for an order permitting it to refuse to allow contact between the child and a person named in the order (s. 34(4)). There is a presumption that children in care will have reasonable contact with their parents and the local authority must seek a court order if it wishes to limit or terminate such contact. [FK]

care or control Alternative grounds that can be invoked to satisfy the THRESHOLD CRITERIA for a CARE ORDER. A CHILD may be taken into care if he or she is suffering, or likely to suffer, significant harm and that harm is attributable either to the inadequacy of the care the child is receiving or to the

fact that the child is beyond parental control (Children Act 1989, s. 31).   [FK]
See also CHILD ABUSE.

care order An order made under the terms of the Children Act 1989, s. 31, intended to enable local authorities, who are responsible for children in their areas, to take measures to protect children who have been abused or who are at risk. A care order often leads to the removal of the CHILD from his or her home but an order may be granted in some circumstances even where the plan is to leave the child at home. To obtain an order, the LOCAL AUTHORITY must satisfy the court that the child concerned has suffered, or is likely to suffer, significant harm. It must also be shown that the harm is attributable to the fact that the child is not receiving, or is not likely to receive, the standard of care that would reasonably be expected of a PARENT of that child. Care orders can also be granted if the harm can be attributed to the fact that the child is beyond parental control. The order must also be shown to be in the best interests of the child (s. 1). The effect of a care order is to vest PARENTAL RESPONSIBILITY in the local authority which then shares it with those people, such as parents, who had it prior to the order (s. 33(3)). However, the local authority has the power to restrict the exercise of parental responsibility by parents and GUARDIANS.   [FK]
See also CARE PLAN; CHILD ABUSE; THRESHOLD CRITERIA.

care plan A plan, devised by a LOCAL AUTHORITY seeking a CARE ORDER, outlining the CHILD'S needs and explaining how these will be met. The plan should include information on where the child is to live if the order is granted and what arrangements for contact are being made. Before making a care order, the court must be satisfied that to do so would be better for the child than not to do so (Children Act 1989, s. 1(5)). Although courts have required local authorities to provide care plans for some time, the obligation to produce one is now on a statutory footing. In terms of s. 31A, under which an application for a care order

is made, the local authority must produce a plan, within the time specified by the court, for the future care of the child. A care order (as opposed to an interim care order) cannot be made if the court has not considered a care plan (s. 31(3A)). However, if a court is not satisfied with the care plan, it cannot compel the local authority to change it; all the court can do is suggest a change, or, as a last resort, refuse the care order. In addition, the court cannot keep the care plan under review once the care order is made (*Re S (Minors) (Care Order: Implementation of Care Plan); Re W (Minors) (Care Order: Adequacy of Care Plan)* [2002] UKHL 10; [2002] 1 FLR 815.   [FK]
See also CHILD ABUSE; THRESHOLD CRITERIA.

care proceedings Proceedings to consider the granting of a CARE ORDER (Children Act 1989, s. 31) or interim care order (s. 38). The term might also be used to cover other proceedings under Parts IV and V of the Act such as those concerning SUPERVISION ORDERS, EMERGENCY PROTECTION ORDERS and CHILD ASSESSMENT ORDERS. Proceedings should follow the procedures and the timetable set out in *The Public Law Outline. Guide to Case Management in Public Law Proceedings* at http://www.judiciary.gov.uk/docs/public_law_outline.pdf.   [FK]
See also CARE CENTRE; CARE PLAN; CHILD ABUSE; THRESHOLD CRITERIA.

careless driving Under the Road Traffic Act 1988, s. 3, it is an offence to drive a mechanically propelled vehicle on a road or other public place without due care and attention, or without reasonable consideration for other persons using the road or place.   [BF]
See also CAUSING DEATH BY DANGEROUS DRIVING; DANGEROUS DRIVING.

carriage 1. The act of carrying goods or persons (e.g. by air or sea).
2. A generic term still sometimes used to describe any vehicle, motorized or otherwise, used to carry goods or people in transit. As a matter of law, a taxi cab may only ply for hire in the street if it is licensed as a **hackney carriage** under the Town Police

Clauses Act 1847, s. 38, rather than as a private hire car. [JW]

See also MOTOR VEHICLE.

cartel **1**. An agreement or association among independent commercial or industrial enterprises designed to limit competition. Cartels are contrary to COMPETITION LAW. Agreements to limit production or fix prices, collusion on discount rates, credit terms, or distribution networks, and bid-rigging are all anti-competitive practices under both the (UK) Competition Act 1998 and Article 81 of the EC Treaty. EC competition law also operates a leniency policy whereby, if a company in a cartel is the first to denounce the agreement and cooperate with the competition authorities, it is excluded from legal responsibility. This device has significantly increased the detection of cartel agreements in the EU, since they are often hard to identify and prosecute without inside information.

2. A written agreement between belligerent nations, normally governing non-hostile activities such as the exchange of prisoners of war. [JW]

cartel offence Introduced by the Enterprise Act 2002, s.188, the cartel offence imposes criminal liability, including imprisonment of up to five years and/or an unlimited fine, on any person shown to be entering into or involved in so-called 'hard core' CARTEL activity. The offence has two elements: (a) an individual must be shown to have agreed with another person to make or implement (or cause to be made or implemented) an arrangement between at least two undertakings to fix prices, limit supply or production, share customers, share supply or to enter into bid-rigging arrangements; (b) the individual must have entered into the agreement dishonestly.

The cartel offence was introduced primarily because it was believed that criminal sanctions would have a greater deterrent effect on hard-core cartel activity. Before the 2002 Act, although it was technically possible to prosecute cartel activity for the common law offence of CONSPIRACY to defraud, such activity was dealt with primarily by civil sanctions, probably because of the difficulties of obtaining sufficient evidence to prove a criminal conspiracy. [JW]

case **1**. A legal matter or cause that has been decided in a court of law.

2. The factual and legal arguments formally advanced by a party to legal proceedings which support their claim as, for example, in the phrases to 'formulate a case' or 'advance a theory of the case'.

3. (largely obsolete) A FORM OF ACTION in TORT that was developed to supplement the writ of trespass. While trespass required the deliberate invasion of the complainant's property, this was not a condition of bringing an action on the case, which thus enabled the courts to compensate more indirect injuries to the person than those allowed by trespass. An action on the case for wilful injury still exists in some jurisdictions, notably in Australia. [JW]

case management The process by which cases are 'actively managed' by the courts in preparing them for trial. The aim of judicial case management is to avoid delay and wasting the court's time and resources in getting cases ready for trial. The duty to actively manage cases applies to both civil and criminal courts: see generally Rule 1.4 of the CIVIL PROCEDURE RULES and Rule 3.2 of the CRIMINAL PROCEDURE RULES. Moreover, the parties to proceedings are also under a legal duty actively to assist the court in the case management process. The emphasis on 'active' case management deliberately distinguishes the new procedural frameworks from the systems they replaced, involving a relatively passive and non-interventionist style of case management by judges. It is thus seen as setting important limits on party control of the litigation process, which, historically, has been a distinctive feature of the ADVERSARIAL SYSTEM of justice. [JW]

case management conference A pretrial stage in civil proceedings used to review the parties' compliance with allocation directions, to give further directions where necessary and, so far as possible, to reach agreement between the parties as regards the issues for trial and the conduct of the case. [JW]

case stated An appeal to the HIGH COURT against the decision of a magistrates' court on the basis that the decision was wrong in law or in excess of the magistrates' jurisdiction. The higher court may reverse, AFFIRM or amend the decision of the lower court in respect of which the case has been stated, or remit the matter to the lower court with an opinion. [SN]

casus belli (Lat. occasion of war) An act justifying a threat of, or the use of armed force against another STATE on the basis of a perceived provocation which the other state was forewarned against. The only legitimate use of a *casus belli* is in self-defence against an unprovoked attack; in all other cases it constitutes a threat to use armed force, which is strictly prohibited by Article 2(4) of the UN CHARTER. For example, the *casus belli* declared in 1995 by Turkey against Greece in the event that the latter extended its TERRITORIAL WATERS from 6 to 12 nautical miles, as is allowed under the terms of the UNITED NATIONS CONVENTION ON THE LAW OF THE SEA (UNCLOS), is thus a violation of Article 2(4). [IB]

See also USE OF FORCE.

catching bargain *See* UNCONSCIONABLE BARGAIN.

causation (in civil law) Describes the factual relationship between an act and its consequences, and the legal attribution of responsibility for an outcome that constitutes a civil wrong. The question of whether or not something done by D is a factual cause of C's loss is primarily an evidential matter; the question of C's responsibility at law for any losses arising is commonly referred to as a matter of REMOTE-NESS OF DAMAGE. This is sometimes viewed as a separate test, but in reality it is a feature of causation. The importance of the distinction can be illustrated by a simple CONTRACT dispute: even if D's breach of contract is clearly the factual cause of C's loss, C may still not recover damages unless it can be shown that D's breach was also the legal cause, i.e., that C's loss was of a kind that was a natural consequence of the breach, or otherwise was in the reasonable anticipation of the parties at the time.

In TORT, the basic test for establishing causation-as-fact is the 'BUT FOR' TEST, whereby D will be liable only if C's damage would not have occurred 'but for' his negligence. The test of remoteness in tort will be satisfied if it was reasonably foreseeable at the relevant time that D's behaviour would cause loss and damage of that type. Where a third party does something to break the chain of causation, this may, if it is unforeseeable, exonerate the original tortfeasor (i.e., wrongdoer): see *NOVUS ACTUS INTERVENIENS*. In practice, however, concurrent and intervening acts by different tortfeasors are often foreseeable and in such cases will lead only to some apportionment of liability between the tortfeasors, rather than extinguishing the liability of the first.

In contract, the concept of causation, on the whole, has developed much less explicitly, and is largely addressed by other specific doctrines, such as MITIGATION OF LOSS and REMOTENESS OF DAMAGE. This has created difficulties in determining the appropriate test to be used where questions of causation are confused by concurrent or cumulative causes which may break the original chain of causation, or at least reduce the responsibility of a single defendant, (for example, where a court has to determine which of a number of proximate causes should be held responsible for delay in completion of a construction contract). [JW]

causation (in criminal law) Some offences require that the accused causes a particular result; for example, in murder, the accused must cause the death of the victim. Causation requires, first, that but for the person's actions, the other party would not have died in that fashion (this is sometimes referred to as causation in fact). Second, it is also necessary that the person's actions are an 'operating and substantial' cause of the other person's death (see *R* v. *Smith* [1959] 2 QB 35) (this is sometimes referred to as legal causation); this is a requirement that the occurred's act makes a more than minimal contribution to the victim's death. [BF]

cause list The published schedule of court actions (called **causes**) that are to be dealt with ('set down for hearing') before a court. It must be displayed publicly in the precincts of the court. [JW]

cause of action The set of facts that constitutes the basis (or **grounds**) for one person to sue another. [JW]

causing death by dangerous driving Under the Road Traffic Act 1988 (as amended), s. 1, it is an offence to cause the death of another person by driving a mechanically propelled vehicle dangerously on a road or other public place. [BF]
See also DANGEROUS DRIVING.

causing the death of a child *See* FAMILIAL HOMICIDE.

caution 1. A formal warning given to adult offenders where it is in the public interest not to prosecute. The warning is issued by a police officer to an offender who admits guilt. Cautions are classified as either simple or conditional. A **simple caution**, which was previously known as a **formal caution**, is used for less serious crime. A **conditional caution**, which was introduced by the Criminal Justice Act 2003, requires the offender to comply with certain conditions before receiving the caution. Failing to comply with these conditions will result in a prosecution for the original offence. Police consult with the CROWN PROSECUTION SERVICE before administering a conditional caution.
2. The warning given by a police officer to a suspect that they need not say anything but that any statement they do make may be used in evidence. The wording of the caution is: 'You do not have to say anything. But it may harm your defence if you do not mention when questioned something which you later rely on in court. Anything you do say may be given in evidence.' [SN]

caveat (Lat. let him beware) A form of notice given by the court which means that the court will not SEAL or give a GRANT OF REPRESENTATION to the estate of a deceased person without first giving notice to the caveator, who may then wish to oppose the grant. It is useful in a situation where someone feels they may wish to oppose an application for a grant, but has yet to establish some facts or take legal advice. A caveat will normally expire after six months, but it can be renewed.

Where a caveat has been entered, a person wishing to apply for a grant can issue what is known as a warning, requiring the caveator either to enter an appearance or to issue a SUMMONS for directions, in either case within eight days. If either course is followed, the court can adjudicate upon the matter, but if the caveator does neither, then the caveat ceases to be effective. [CM]

caveat emptor (Lat. let the buyer beware) In English law, a duty is placed on the buyer to ensure that he or she finds out as much as possible about the property to be purchased, since there is generally no duty of disclosure. The seller will only be legally bound where he or she made express or implied promises relating to the subject matter or specific statements of fact to induce the buyer to purchase. The Sale of Goods Act 1979 contains implied promises relating to the goods (ss. 12–15), i.e. that the seller has TITLE, correspondence with description, satisfactory quality, FITNESS FOR PURPOSE and correspondence with sample. In the absence of promises or such representations, English law will not generally excuse or protect a buyer when the goods are not as envisaged, i.e. the risk as to quality will rest with the buyer. [JPL]

Cd. *See* COMMAND PAPERS.

Central Arbitration Committee (CAC) A permanent independent body with powers under STATUTE to adjudicate applications regarding the statutory RECOGNITION and DERECOGNITION of TRADE UNIONS; to determine disputes between EMPLOYERS and trade unions over the DISCLOSURE OF INFORMATION for COLLECTIVE BARGAINING; and to resolve applications and complaints in matters relating to, for example, EUROPEAN WORKS COUNCILS. The CAC consists of a chair, 11 deputy chairs, 29 members experienced as representatives of employers, and 27 members experienced as representatives of EMPLOYEES. The committee is appointed by the Secretary of State for Trade and Industry after consulting ACAS. See further at http://www.cac.gov.uk. [MJ]

Central Criminal Court The name given to the CROWN COURT sitting in central London, known also as the 'Old Bailey'. It was established by the Central Criminal Court Act 1824 which provided it with criminal jurisdiction for the Greater London area. Although the Courts Act 1971 established a single Crown Court to replace the system of ASSIZE and QUARTER SESSIONS, the Crown Court, when sitting in central London, is still known as the Central Criminal Court. [SN]

certainty *See* UNCERTAINTY OF CONTRACT TERMS.

certainty of intention *See* THREE CERTAINTIES.

certainty of objects *See* THREE CERTAINTIES.

certainty of persons *See* THREE CERTAINTIES.

certainty of subject matter *See* THREE CERTAINTIES.

certainty of words *See* THREE CERTAINTIES.

certificate of incorporation A document issued by the COMPANIES REGISTRY on first incorporation of a COMPANY and on any change of name. Incorporation is the process by which the company is entered on the register at the Companies Registry, and thereby comes into existence as a separate LEGAL PERSON. The certificate states the company's registered name, its date of incorporation and the number with which it was registered at Companies House. [JW]

certification mark A trade mark which distinguishes goods or services which have been examined, tested, inspected or in some way checked by an independent organization; for example, the 'Pure Wool' mark is a certification mark. [US]

certification officer (CO) An official appointed by the Secretary of State with various administrative, regulatory, investigative and quasi-judicial functions in relation to TRADE UNIONS. Responsibilities include: maintaining a list of trade unions and EMPLOYERS' ASSOCIATIONS; certifying INDEPENDENT TRADE UNIONS; ensuring trade union and employers' association compliance with statutory requirements; and determining complaints with respect to trade unions. By the Employment Relations Act 1999, the role of the CO was expanded to include handling claims for financial assistance from individuals seeking to exercise the 'citizen's right' to sue a trade union for losses caused by unlawful industrial action. [MJ]

certiorari (obsolete) One of the 'prerogative writs' by which the courts controlled the exercise of powers by public authorities. Now known as PREROGATIVE ORDERS. [MS]

cessate A cessate grant of PROBATE or **letters of administration** is a grant which is limited in time as to its duration; for instance, where a child is the sole EXECUTOR named in a WILL, a grant of letters of administration may be granted to someone else, limited until such time as the named executor reaches his or her majority. A cessate grant automatically expires when the limitation period expires. [CM]
  See also GRANT OF REPRESENTATION.

cession The transfer, by agreement, of TITLE over land territory by one STATE to another. Such transfer is achieved by a TREATY of cession between the intending grantor and the grantee. The grantor state can only transfer such title or interests that it possesses. The new title based on the treaty of cession, provided that it is not subject to any limitations, is itself assignable, in that the grantee can pass on its title to or interests in the territory to another entity. [IB]
  See also DERIVATIVE TITLE.

CET *See* COMMON EXTERNAL TARIFF.

CFI *See* COURT OF FIRST INSTANCE.

CFP *See* COMMON FISHERIES POLICY.

Ch The standard abbreviation for the Law Reports: Chancery cases, published by the INCORPORATED COUNCIL OF LAW REPORTING. [JW]
See also LAW REPORTS.

chain of representation It can often cause inconvenience if the EXECUTOR of an ESTATE dies without having completed the administration, and it might be necessary for another grant to be obtained to enable the administration to be completed. To minimize this inconvenience, the Administration of Estates Act 1925, s. 7, provides: 'An executor of a sole or last surviving executor of a TESTATOR is the executor of the testator.' Thus if A dies, leaving B as his executor, and B dies without completing the administration of A's estate but appoints C to be his (B's) executor, then C can become A's executor also, thus creating a chain of representation. This chain can extend indefinitely, so long as the statutory requirements are met. It applies only to executors, not ADMINISTRATORS, and only to executors who have obtained a grant of PROBATE. The chain will therefore be broken if no executor has been appointed, or if an executor dies without obtaining probate. [CM]
See also GRANT OF REPRESENTATION.

chamber A panel of judges appointed to hear a case in preference to a **full court** comprising the maximum number of judges entitled to sit. The term is used chiefly in the context of certain international tribunals. Thus, the EUROPEAN COURT OF JUSTICE (ECJ) and the COURT OF FIRST INSTANCE (CFI) can sit in chambers, or in **Grand Chamber**, as well as in full court formation. Chambers of three or five judges are common for both the ECJ and the CFI, with a chamber of one judge being possible for the CFI. Three or five judges are considered the norm at the ECJ, with three judges being the norm at the CFI. Both courts retain the option to sit in Grand Chamber (for both courts 13 judges) or in full court (27 judges) if the case is sufficiently complex or important. The ECJ is required to sit in Grand Chamber if a MEMBER STATE so requests it, and is required to sit in full court for particular types of cases. The INTERNATIONAL COURT OF JUSTICE can also sit as a three-judge chamber as an alternative to the 15-member full court. Hearing by a chamber of the court thus has a different connotation to the English concept of a hearing 'in chambers', which is used primarily for interlocutory or IN CAMERA proceedings. [MON & JW]

champerty The act of supporting or assisting another financially in bringing litigation in exchange for a share of the proceeds of the action. Champertous agreements were long considered as a means of encouraging litigation, and therefore contrary to public policy. Up until 1967, they could be sued as crimes or in TORT; today they may still be regarded as VOID CONTRACTS for that reason. Champerty may arise in two situations, though in both of these there is evidence of a trend towards liberalizing the law. The first situation arises where a (potential) litigant seeks to assign (see ASSIGNMENT) their rights to a cause of action to a third party. This has tended to be treated as champerty or **maintenance** where the assignee has had no personal interest in the litigation before the assignment. However, in *Massai Aviation Services* v. *The Attorney General* [2007] UKPC 12, the PRIVY COUNCIL held that an assignment of a company's causes of action to its sole shareholder was not void on the grounds of champerty. This is the first such case to recognize the validity of an assignment to a shareholder who is not also a creditor of the company, i.e. to someone whose interest in the litigation is really quite marginal.

Secondly, modern contingency or CONDITIONAL FEE AGREEMENTS also come very close to the line of champerty and it is in this context that most of the recent case law has developed. In *R (Factortame)* v. *Secretary of State for Transport (No. 8)* [2003] QB 381, it was decided that such an arrangement was not necessarily champertous, and detailed guidance was given on the criteria to apply in deciding whether it was. Nevertheless, there are still circumstances in which a non-party who funds litigation can be liable for the COSTS of the opposing party, to the extent of the funding they provided, should the action fail (see *Arkin* v. *Borchard* [2005] EWCA Civ 655).   [JW]

Chancery Division The Chancery Division is one of the three Divisions of the HIGH COURT. It is based in the Royal Courts of Justice in London, but also conducts work in eight Chancery District Registries, in Birmingham, Bristol, Cardiff, Leeds, Liverpool, Manchester, Newcastle-upon-Tyne and Preston. The Division undertakes a wide range of work in relation to BANKRUPTCY and INSOLVENCY (though outside London, it is the COUNTY COURT, not the Chancery District Registry, that has exclusive jurisdiction over bankruptcies), other company law and partnership matters, commercial disputes, disputes over land, tax, TRUSTS, and contentious PROBATE. Although listed separately, proceedings in the PATENTS COURT are also issued in the Chancery Registry and dealt with by Chancery Judges and Masters nominated to do so. Trials of claims in London are heard by High Court judges assigned to the Division, as are most interim applications involving INJUNCTIONS. Most other work, including procedural work and most post-trial work, is conducted by the six judges designated as **Chancery Masters**. In addition, in the Royal Courts of Justice in London, there are another six judges who are referred to as **Bankruptcy Registrars** (one of whom is designated Chief Registrar). Outside London, cases are dealt with by High Court and designated CIRCUIT JUDGES, with the work of the Chancery Masters being undertaken by designated DISTRICT JUDGES. The head of the Chancery Division is called the **Chancellor of the High Court**.   [JW]

See also FAMILY DIVISION; QUEEN'S BENCH DIVISION.

change of name In England and Wales, anyone over the age of 18 years may change their first or last name simply by using the new name. No legal formality is involved; however, evidence of the change may be required for some purposes. In such cases, the person may wish to make a public announcement of the change by notice in a newspaper or by providing a letter from a responsible person confirming the other's

identity and name change. For other purposes, such as passport applications, more formal evidence may be required, and the person may execute a statutory declaration or prepare a DEED poll confirming the name change. A BIRTH CERTIFICATE may only be changed in exceptional circumstances. A CHILD's name may be changed if all those with PARENTAL RESPONSIBILITY agree to the change, although in some cases, an unmarried father without parental responsibility may need to be consulted about the proposed change. Any dispute over such a proposed change will be decided by the court or the basis of the BEST INTERESTS of the child.   [AD]

See also UNMARRIED PARENTS.

Chapter VII The UN CHARTER is divided into thematic chapters. Chapter VII concerns action with respect to threats to the peace, breaches of the peace and acts of aggression. That part of Chapter VII encompassing the powers of the SECURITY COUNCIL in dealing with threats and breaches of the peace, as well as acts of aggression, is one of the cornerstones of the UN Charter. When the Security Council determines that any of these three situations has arisen, it may either order provisional measures under Article 40 (never used), take any action short of the use of armed force (Article 41 measures), or, where the above measures prove to be inadequate, it may authorize the use of armed force to restore international peace and security (Article 42 measures). Examples of Article 41 measures include the adoption of the International Criminal Tribunals for the former Yugoslavia and Rwanda on the basis of Resolutions 827 (1993) and 955 (1994) respectively. Examples of Article 42 measures include Resolution 678 (1990) relating to the use of force against Iraqi forces that had invaded Kuwait. Chapter VII also contains in Article 51 the requirements for self-defence in case of an armed attack.   [IB]

See also COLLECTIVE SECURITY; USE OF FORCE.

character evidence EVIDENCE of, or of a disposition towards, good conduct or bad conduct. In criminal proceedings the

ADMISSIBILITY of bad character evidence is governed by the Criminal Justice Act 2003, which provides seven gateways for the admission of such evidence. These are listed in s. 101 of the 2003 Act and admit evidence of the defendant's bad character where (a) all parties to the proceedings agree to the evidence being admissible; (b) the evidence is given by the defendant, or is elicited from him in cross-examination; (c) it is important explanatory evidence; (d) it is relevant to an important matter at issue between the defendant and the prosecution; (e) it has substantial probative value in relation to an important matter at issue between the defendant and a co-defendant; (f) it is evidence to correct false impression given by the defendant; or (g) the defendant has attacked another person's character. Evidence of a non-defendant's bad character can, under s. 100, only be given with the court's permission, and if (i) it is important explanatory evidence; (ii) it has substantial probative value in relation to a matter in issue, or it is of substantial importance in the context of the case, or (iii) all parties agree the evidence being admissible. [ALTC]

character merchandising The adaptation of the essential personality features (such as the name, image or appearance) of a fictional character or a real person in relation to various goods and/or services with a view to creating in prospective customers a desire to acquire those goods or to use those services because of the customers' affinity with that character or personality. There is, as yet, no *sui generis* right to regulate character merchandising, and owners of the character/personality must rely on existing INTELLECTUAL PROPERTY rights to protect the different types of merchandising. Only the person or legal entity that owns the rights in a character is entitled to exploit the character/personality, or to authorize others to do so. [US]

charge The formal accusation of a criminal offence made by a police officer following the conclusion of an interview with a suspect. [SN]

charge bargaining *See* PLEA BARGAINING.

charge by way of legal mortgage A form of MORTGAGE created by deed, where the borrower states that he is charging his property by way of legal mortgage as security for a loan or the payment of a debt. The charge by way of legal mortgage was introduced by the Law of Property Act 1925, s. 85 (1), and is now the most common method of creating a mortgage. It is the only way to create a legal mortgage over REGISTERED LAND (Land Registration Act 2002, s. 23(1)(a)). The main advantage of a charge by way of legal mortgage is simplicity, since although the lender is treated as though a long lease or sublease has been granted, the lease or sublease does not actually need to be created. [DR]

charge sheet The document prepared by a police officer to record the accusation against a suspect. The charge sheet contains the suspect's name and the details of any complainant and is signed by the suspect. [SN]

chargeable asset Any form of property which is not exempted from CAPITAL GAINS TAX (CGT), including land, buildings, company shares, investment debts, options, know-how, goodwill, domain names, foreign currency, rights under contracts, interests under settlements, and damages. Property which is created by a taxpayer, such as a house or a painting, is also an asset for CGT purposes. Broadly speaking, anything which can be owned in law and has a value (regardless of availability of a market in the property) is an asset. If something has no value, no calculation of tax by reference to the rate of CGT can be performed.

There is a substantial range of exemptions, including those for sterling currency, most motor vehicles, National Savings Certificates, most UK government securities, and some chattels. [RE]

chargeable gain The increase in value of an ASSET which is realized, or which is treated as being realized by a taxpayer during a year of assessment after taking account of any available exemptions and reliefs for CAPITAL GAINS TAX purposes.   [RE]

charges register In REGISTERED LAND, the part of a Land Register entry showing any MORTGAGES, RESTRICTIVE COVENANTS and other ENCUMBRANCES affecting the land.   [DR]

charging clause A provision in a trust entitling TRUSTEES to charge for their services. Although it might appear such a right is at variance with the FIDUCIARY nature of trusteeship, it is critical to allow for such payments; otherwise professional trustees, in particular, would have no incentive to assume the onerous duties of trusteeship. Thus even in the absence of express provision, the Trustee Act 2000, s. 29 allows for the reasonable remuneration of professional trustees with the exception of sole and charitable trustees or where a contrary intention is expressed in the trust deed. [PK]

charitable housing trust A HOUSING TRUST defined under s. 6 of the Housing Act 1985 which also conforms with the meaning of charity under s. 5(2) of the Charities Act 1993. TENANTS with LONG LEASES of flats belonging to a charitable housing trust are excluded from the right to collectively acquire the FREEHOLD of the building within which the flats are located.   [HC& DR]

charitable trust A purpose TRUST whose objects are deemed by the law to be so beneficial to the public interest that it is afforded extensive fiscal and legal advantages over private trusts. Charitable trusts are consequently exempt from many (although not all) forms of taxation and can claim back the tax paid by donors on their donations by way of 'gift aid'. They are also exempt from the beneficiary principle, with the Attorney General having *locus standi* to apply to court to enforce charitable trustees' duties, and the rule against PERPETUAL TRUSTS, which limits the duration of **private trusts** to the PERPETUITY PERIOD. Not every purpose that appears to be in the public interest will necessarily be charitable as the range of charitable objects has evolved over the years in parallel with previously recognized charitable purposes. In *Commissioners for Special Purposes of Income Tax* v.

Pemsel [1891] AC 531, Lord Macnaghten held that there were four heads under which charitable purposes might fall: (a) the relief of poverty; (b) the advancement of education; (c) the advancement of religion; and (d) other purposes beneficial to the community. In addition to coming within one of these four heads, to be charitable a trust had to be for the public benefit. This requirement was presumed under the first three *Pemsel* categories while, in respect of trusts for the relief of poverty, it has atrophied over the years, almost to vanishing point.

The Charities Act 2006, s. 2(2), has provided a statutory framework for charitable trusts by clarifying the types of purpose capable of being charitable. It has done so by listing twelve specific categories of charitable purpose, the first three *Pemsel* categories (although now including the *prevention* as well as the *relief* of poverty) and nine further heads which are, in effect, an elaboration of the existing case law concerning the different types of purpose held to be charitable under Lord Macnaghten's fourth category (along with a final catch-all category intended to include any other trusts previously held to be charitable). The Act has also removed the presumption of public benefit under the first three heads but (probably) not altered the minimal public benefit requirement in respect of trusts for the relief (and prevention) of poverty.

Although historically charities fell within the jurisdiction of the old COURT OF CHANCERY and now the HIGH COURT, the law of charities has for many years developed largely outside these confines as a result of the work of the CHARITY COMMISSION, with whom nearly all charities are required to register. This provides a cost-effective means of ensuring that the law and practice of charities remains relevant to the needs of the time and is likely to become more pertinent in the wake of the Charities Act 2006, s. 2A, which allows for the introduction of a Charity Tribunal to hear appeals from determinations of the Charity Commissioners into issues such as the refusal of charitable status (with a further appeal to the High Court on points of law). The term 'public trust' is synonymous with 'charitable trust' and any trust which is not charitable might correctly be described as private. [PK]

charity A body, with or without corporate status, formed to carry out purposes deemed to be charitable (see CHARITABLE TRUST). Charities are ultimately subject to the jurisdiction of the HIGH COURT, although in practice it is the CHARITY COMMISSION, with whom most charities are required to register, that supervises them and determines both the practice and increasingly the law of charities. [PK]

Charity Commission A statutory body, now governed by the Charities Act 2006, responsible for the administration of charities. The Commissioners are responsible for registering most charitable trusts, monitoring their accounts, promoting the effective use of charitable resources, encouraging best practice in the administration of charities, providing information and advice to charitable trustees, and checking and investigating abuses of charitable status. The Commission produces an annual report, detailing how the Commissioners operate and how the law of charity is developing, along with ad hoc reports on particular issues, and maintains a detailed and informative website at http://www.charitycommission.gov.uk. [PK]

chastisement Punishment through the infliction of physical pain. In earlier centuries, husbands were entitled to subject their wives to reasonable chastisement but legislation was introduced in the 19th century to punish wife-beating. 'Chastisement' is now usually used in connection with the physical punishment of children in order to discipline them. PARENTS are permitted to administer moderate and reasonable chastisement to their children. However, this would be no defence to a charge of WOUNDING WITH INTENT, causing GRIEVOUS BODILY HARM, assault occasioning ACTUAL BODILY HARM, or cruelty to a person under 16 (see the Children Act 2004, s. 58(1)–(2)). Nor can BATTERY causing actual bodily harm to a CHILD be

justified in civil proceedings as being reasonable chastisement (see s. 58(3)). CORPORAL PUNISHMENT is not permitted in schools (Education Act 1996, s. 548). [FK]

chattel Any tangible property other than a FREEHOLD interest in land. Chattels may be divided into **chattels real** (essentially LEASEHOLD interests in land) and **chattels personal**, which incorporate all other forms of tangible property. PERSONAL CHATTELS are extensively defined by the Administration of Estates Act 1925. [JW]
See also REAL PROPERTY.

cheating the public revenue Where a taxpayer performs, or attempts to perform, any kind of deliberate step with intent to defraud HM REVENUE AND CUSTOMS (the Revenue) and which denies the Revenue, or risks denying the Revenue the tax or duty to which it is entitled. It is a COMMON LAW offence preserved by the Theft Act 1968, s. 32(1)(a). There is also now a separate offence of fraudulent evasion of income tax contrary to the Finance Act 2000, s. 144(1). [RE]

check-off A system whereby employers deduct trade union dues before paying their workers and then pass the money to the union. For the statutory power which controls the amount of deduction, see the Trade Union and Labour Relations (Consolidation) Act 1992, s. 68. [MJ]

Chicago School The most prominent movement within the field of free market economics, named after the Department of Economics at the University of Chicago. The influence of the department also spread to Chicago's Graduate School of Business and to its Law School where much of the most important work in the ECONOMIC ANALYSIS OF LAW has been done. The leading figure in this last regard is Richard Posner, whose influence is based not only on the fact that he is an academic but also on his position as a judge who has been able to put his ideas into practice. [JP]

child For most purposes, a person under the age of 18 (see, for example, the Children Act 1989, s. 105, but compare the

Child Support Act 1991, s. 55). Different statutes specify different age limits.   [FK]

See also MINOR.

child abduction An offence under the Child Abduction Act 1984, defined as taking or detaining a CHILD under the age of 16, without lawful authority or reasonable excuse, so as to remove that child from the lawful control of any person having it, or so as to keep him or her out of the lawful control of any person entitled to have it (s. 2). This offence does not extend to PARENTS who were married to each other at the time of the child's birth, or to the mother of a child who was not married to the father; these persons cannot commit this offence. In addition, a father who has not been married to the mother can raise the fact that he is the father as a defence.

There is, however, another type of offence of ABDUCTION under the Act and this can be committed by a parent. It is an offence if a person connected with a child takes or sends a child out of the United Kingdom without the appropriate consent (s. 1), which includes that of any parent with PARENTAL RESPONSIBILITY. The category of persons 'connected with' the child who can potentially be held liable includes parents and GUARDIANS.   [FK]

See also INTERNATIONAL CHILD ABDUCTION.

child abuse Maltreatment of a CHILD by individual(s), whether they are adults or children, including maltreatment in an institutional setting. Child abuse may take the form of a harmful act or, in some circumstances, a failure to act to prevent harm. It is a criminal offence for a person who is 16 or over, and who has responsibility for a child or young person under 16, to, among other things, wilfully assault or ill-treat or cause or procure that child or young person to be assaulted or ill-treated in a manner likely to cause unnecessary suffering or injury to health (see the Children and Young Persons Act 1933, s. 1).

According to the statutory guidance issued by the government for use by professionals engaged in child protection work, there are four main categories of abuse: **physical abuse**, NEGLECT, **emotional abuse**

or **sexual abuse** (HM Government, *Working Together to Safeguard Children. A Guide to Inter-Agency Working to Safeguard and Promote the Welfare of Children* (London: TSO, 2006), para 1.29). Physical abuse includes cases where illness is fabricated or induced by a carer, and 'hitting, shaking, throwing, poisoning, burning or scalding, drowning, suffocating, or otherwise causing physical harm to a child' (para 1.30). Emotional abuse is the 'persistent emotional maltreatment of a child such as to cause severe and persistent adverse effects on the child's emotional development' (para 1.31). Sexual abuse 'involves forcing or enticing a child or young person to take part in sexual activities, including prostitution, whether or not the child is aware of what is happening' (para 1.32). If any of these kinds of abuse reach the threshold criteria of 'significant harm' or likelihood of significant harm laid down in the Children Act 1989, a local authority is permitted to seek a court order to afford protection to the child concerned.   [FK]

See also CARE ORDER; CHILD PROTECTION CONFERENCE; EMERGENCY PROTECTION ORDER; WILFUL NEGLECT.

child assessment order An order that allows an assessment of a CHILD's health and development to be carried out by a LOCAL AUTHORITY, in circumstances where that assessment has been denied (Children Act 1989, s. 43). The order may be made on the application of a local authority if the court is satisfied that the local authority has reasonable cause to suspect that a child is suffering, or likely to suffer, significant harm; that an assessment of the child's health, development or the way the child is being treated is necessary to determine whether the child is suffering or likely to suffer significant harm; and that such an assessment will not be made or will be unsatisfactory unless the court makes an order. The order is designed to deal with situations such as one where PARENTS refuse to cooperate with local authority inquiries and refuse access to the child. If there are concerns about the child's safety but the situation is not considered urgent enough to warrant emergency protection measures, this order is appropriate (HM Government, *Working Together to Safeguard Children. A Guide to Inter-agency Working to Safeguard and Promote the Welfare of Children* (London: TSO, 2006), para 5.68). The court may order parents/caregivers to produce the child and to comply with its directions concerning the assessment. If the child is of sufficient understanding to make an informed decision, he or she can refuse to submit to a medical or psychiatric examination or other assessment. The order can be made to have effect for a maximum of seven days. [FK]

See also CARE ORDER; EMERGENCY PROTECTION; THRESHOLD CRITERIA.

child destruction The offence known as child destruction is set out in the Infant Life (Preservation) Act 1929, s. 1. It is committed by a person who intentionally destroys the life of a child capable of being born alive before it has an existence independent of its mother. It is not an offence under this provision if the act which kills the child is done in good faith for the purpose only of preserving the life of the mother. Section 1 (2) states that evidence that a woman has been pregnant for 28 weeks or more is *prima facie* proof that the child in question was capable of being born alive. [BF]

See also ABORTION.

child employment Current law relating to the employment of children under the school-leaving age is based on the Children (Protection at Work) Regulations 1998 (SI 1998/274) as amended by the 2000 Regulations (SI 2000/1333), which implement the European Directive on the Protection of Young People at Work 94/33/EC. These Regulations in turn amend earlier law, in England and Wales, particularly the Children and Young Persons Acts 1933 and 1969. The general law is that children under 14 may not be employed, except occasionally to help with their parents' or guardians' light agricultural or horticultural work. However, depending on local authority BYELAWS, children over 13 may be employed on 'light work', which is defined as work which does not jeopardize

a child's heath, safety and development and his or her school attendance, or work experience. Work experience is permitted from the start of the school term preceding the child's leaving school: see Education (Work Experience) Act 1973 as amended. Children are also subject to various prohibitions in relation to particular types of work: see, for example, the Mines and Quarries Act 1954, s. 124 (no child is allowed underground in a mine or quarry unless undertaking prescribed training). 'Young people' under 18 years of age also receive additional protection from the Management of Health and Safety at Work Regulations 2006 (SI 2006/438) (risk assessment of premises and other dangers). [MJ]

See also YOUNG WORKERS.

child of the family A CHILD of both parties to a MARRIAGE or CIVIL PARTNERSHIP (which would include an adopted child). The term also refers to a child, other than a child who is a FOSTER CHILD, who has been treated by both spouses/partners as the child of both of them (see, for examples, the Children Act 1989, s. 105; the Matrimonial Causes Act 1973, s. 52). [FK]

See also ADOPTION.

child pornography Possession of, or participation in acts associated with the obtaining, producing or distributing of child pornography may involve a number of offences, including: (a) taking or making an indecent photograph or other image derived from a photograph of a child or young person under the age of 18, and distributing or showing such images are offences under the Protection of Children Act 1978, s. 1(1), as amended; (b) possessing an indecent photograph of a child under 16 is an offence under the Criminal Justice Act 1988 Act, s. 160; (c) possessing an indecent photograph or pseudo photograph is also an offence under the Protection of Children Act 1978, s. 1(a)(c), as amended; (d) causing or inciting child pornography, controlling a child involved in pornography, and arranging or facilitating child pornography are all offences under the Sexual Offences Act 2003, ss. 48–50. (These offences also trigger extended investigatory and asset recovery powers contained in the Serious Crime Act 2007.) [JW]

See also EXTREME PORNOGRAPHY; OBSCENE PUBLICATIONS; SERIOUS ORGANISED CRIME AGENCY.

child protection conference A meeting of professionals and FAMILY members, held in cases where a LOCAL AUTHORITY enquiry conducted under the Children Act 1989, s. 47, gives rise to concerns about the well-being or safety of a CHILD. The purpose of the conference is to consider the child's needs and the PARENTS' capacity to meet these needs, to assess any evidence as to the risk of significant harm and to decide how the child should be protected. Participants might include the child (where appropriate), family members, local authority social care staff who have been dealing with the family, medical professionals who have been involved with the family, the police and the local authority legal services representative. A local authority or NSPCC social worker, with the assistance of a core group of parents and professionals, may be expected to draw up a child protection plan to ensure that the child is protected in the future.

There is no statutory basis for the child protection conference but such conferences are required in terms of *Working Together to Safeguard Children. A Guide to Inter-agency Working to Safeguard and Promote the Welfare of Children* (London: TSO, 2006). [FK]

See also CARE ORDER; CARE PLAN; EMERGENCY PROTECTION ORDER; THRESHOLD CRITERIA.

child safety order An order under the Crime and Disorder Act 1998, s. 11, which empowers a magistrates' court to place a CHILD under the supervision, for up to 12 months, of a LOCAL AUTHORITY social worker or a member of a youth offending team. A child safety order may only be made in relation to children under the age of 10. The grounds for making an order are that the child has committed an act which, had he or she been aged 10 or over, would have constituted an offence; that the order is necessary to prevent the

child from committing such an act; that the child has contravened a ban imposed by a curfew notice; and that the child has acted in a way that caused or was likely to cause 'harassment, alarm or distress' to someone outside the child's household. The order may specify requirements with which the child is obliged to comply, the purpose of which is to ensure that the child receives appropriate care and is placed under control or to prevent a repetition of the kind of behaviour that led to the making of the order. Breach of an order can lead to CARE PROCEEDINGS being instituted. [FK]

See also CARE ORDER.

child witness In criminal proceedings, a witness, other than the defendant, who is under 17 at the time of the hearing (or, where the ADMISSIBILITY of a video recording is at issue, under 17 when the recording was made): see Youth Justice and Criminal Evidence Act 1999, s. 21. In civil proceedings, a witness who is under the age of 18. [ALTC]

Children and Family Court Advisory and Support Service (Cafcass) Established by the Criminal Justice and Court Services Act 2000. In any FAMILY PROCEEDINGS in which the welfare of a CHILD is or may be in question, s. 12(1) of the Act states the principal functions of Cafcass are to: (a) safeguard and promote the welfare of children; (b) give advice to any court about any application made to it in such proceedings; (c) make provision for the children to be represented in such proceedings; and (d) provide information, advice and other support for the children and their families. Cafcass brings together the services previously provided by the Family Court Welfare Service, the Guardian ad Litem Service and the Children's Division of the Official Solicitor. [AD]

See also ADOPTION SERVICE; CHILDREN'S GUARDIAN; WELFARE PRINCIPLE.

children in need Those children designated in terms of the Children Act 1989, s. 17 as being in need of services. These services, which must be provided by the LOCAL AUTHORITY in the area in which the CHILD lives, can take various forms, including accommodation, services in kind or, in exceptional circumstances, cash. A child is taken to be in need if he or she is disabled, is unlikely to have a reasonable standard of health, or is unlikely to attain or maintain a reasonable level of development unless the services are provided. Significant impairment of health or development unless services are made available can also render a child in need in terms of the statute. [FK]

children's contracts A child under the age of 18 is termed a MINOR and, as a general rule, minors do not possess full contractual capacity and so may not be bound by CONTRACTS that they enter into, although the other party will be bound. However, the minor will be bound in relation to contracts for NECESSARIES, for which a reasonable sum is payable; CONTRACTS OF EMPLOYMENT and apprenticeship contracts unless they are more burdensome than beneficial to the minor; certain contracts (e.g. tenancy agreements, partnership agreements and SHARE agreements) which may become binding unless repudiated when the minor reaches 18; and for any contract expressly ratified (see RATIFICATION) by the minor on reaching 18. In addition, a court may order the minor to return property acquired under a contract which is not binding on the minor where 'it is just and equitable to do so' (Minors' Contracts Act 1987, s. 3(1)). [JPL]

See also CAPACITY TO CONTRACT.

children's guardian An officer of CAFCASS. The Children Act 1989, s. 41(1), stipulates that in specified proceedings the court is obliged to appoint an officer of the service unless satisfied that it is not necessary to do so in order to safeguard the CHILD'S interests. The proceedings specified include applications for, and to discharge, CARE ORDERS or SUPERVISION ORDERS, and proceedings under Part V. In all these public law cases, the officer who must be appointed is the children's guardian. The GUARDIAN would normally be a qualified and experienced social worker and he or she is under a duty to safeguard the interests of the child and to represent the child. Usually, the child's solicitor is appointed and instructed by the guardian.

In care and supervision proceedings, the guardian will normally be asked to prepare a report for the court. [FK]

Chiltern Hundreds, stewardship of the Steward and Bailiff of Her Majesty's Three Chiltern Hundreds of Stoke, Desborough and Burnham in the county of Buckingham is one of two nominal offices under the Crown (the other is Crown Steward and Bailiff of the Manor of Northstead) which are taken by MPs who wish to leave the HOUSE OF COMMONS. The procedure dates back to 1623 when the House resolved that a Member could not directly resign his seat. A Member wishing to leave the Commons applies to the Chancellor of the Exchequer who grants whichever of the two offices is currently vacant. After leaving the Commons, the former MP also resigns the stewardship, in order to leave the post vacant for the next Member who wishes to resign. Other offices which are incompatible with membership of the Commons are listed in the House of Commons Disqualification Act 1975. [MS]

See also MEMBER OF PARLIAMENT.

Chinese wall *See* CONFLICT OF INTEREST.

choice-based lettings These provide an alternative way for a LOCAL HOUSING AUTHORITY to allocate its housing. Local housing authorities advertise the properties they have available. The advertisements set out the qualifying conditions, such as household size and the rules for applying, along with a reply coupon. Households express interest in a property by sending a reply coupon to the LANDLORD. Households are ranked according to transparent and objective criteria like age, length of residence, waiting time, or combinations of these factors. The property is offered to the household rated highest on the criteria. [HC & DR]

See also ALLOCATION OF COUNCIL HOUSING.

choice of jurisdiction clause A clause in a contract or other document or instrument, by which the parties indicate their consent to the submission of any disputes to the courts of an expressly identified COUNTRY. The requirements for these agreements are found in the BRUSSELS CONVENTION 1968 or Council Regulation 44/2001 EC. [RE]

choice of law A procedural stage in the litigation of a case involving the conflict of laws to determine what is the substantive law that will govern the agreement or dispute. This is often referred to as the LEX CAUSAE (law for the cause), i.e. the law applicable to the merits of the dispute. The choice of law can be established by agreement or by adjudication.

Agreement between the parties may be express, as in the case of contract, for example, where the parties choose the APPLICABLE LAW of the intended contract and expressly state that choice in their written agreement, or implied from the terms of the agreement and all relevant facts. This applies equally in respect of other deliberate relationships, such as settlements, wills, or a company's MEMORANDUM OF ASSOCIATION.

In adjudication, the choice of law rules of the LEX FORI or the LEX ARBITRI of the seat of arbitration will first be applied by the judge or arbitrator in order to determine what, if any, GOVERNING LAW the parties have chosen expressly or by implication. Where the judge or arbitrator determines that the parties have chosen their governing law, that choice will normally be applied. But where the judge or arbitrator determines that the parties have failed to choose the governing law, the judge or arbitrator will then use the choice of law rules of the *lex fori* or the *lex arbitri* in order to identify the governing law which is the most appropriate in the circumstances.

The European Commission is currently engaged in reviewing harmonization in relation to choice of law issues. [RE]

See also ARBITRATION AGREEMENT; PROPER LAW OF THE CONTRACT.

choice of law clause A provision in an agreement, or other written document or instrument, which expresses the parties' wishes as to the choice of substantive law to be applied by courts or arbitral tribunals to the merits of disputes arising out of the agreement or other legal instrument. [RE]

See also CHOICE OF LAW; CONFLICT OF LAWS; GOVERNING LAW; *LEX CAUSAE*; PROPER LAW OF THE CONTRACT.

chose in action An intangible property right (from the French, *chose* = thing). A personal right, such as to recover a debt, which has no tangible existence other than its recognition in law. [JW]

chose in possession A tangible item of personal property such as a book or table. The term denotes not just the thing itself, but also the associated rights of the owner to use and enjoy the thing. [JW]

Church Commissioners The Commissioners manage the CHURCH OF ENGLAND'S assets, invested in stock market shares and property, to generate income to support the ministry, and to help maintain the fabric of church buildings. The Church Commissioners cover about 18 per cent of the Church's total running costs. They also operate the central clergy payroll, administer the legal framework for parish reorganization, and determine the future use of redundant churches. There are 33 Commissioners in total, including the Archbishops of Canterbury and York. The Commissioners are represented on the General Synod by three of their number – the Estates Commissioners. The Commissioners as a body are answerable to the Synod and to Parliament and annual reports are submitted to both. The Commissioners' work is regulated by the Church Commissioners Measure 1947 (as amended). [JW]

Church of England The Church of England is the established Church in England, which means it is strongly integrated into the political structure of the country. This is reflected in the fact that the reigning monarch has the constitutional title of Supreme Governor of the Church of England, and that the Archbishops of Canterbury and York and senior bishops have seats in the House of Lords.

The Church is governed by its national assembly called the **General Synod**. The latter came into being in 1970 under the Synodical Government Measure 1969, replacing a previous body known as the Church Assembly. The General Synod comprises

467 members who sit in three 'Houses' – of clergy, bishops and laity. The House of Laity is the only House comprising unordained members of the Church.

Among its many functions, the General Synod has a legislative role regarding matters of Church governance, procedures and ministry. The Synod may legislate by **Measure** or **Canon**. A Measure is legislation that has received final approval from the General Synod and on which a resolution to present for ROYAL ASSENT has been passed in both Houses of Parliament and to which royal assent has been given. Under the Church of England (Assembly) Powers Act 1919, a Measure has the full force and effect of a STATUTE. Measures tend to include matters such as Church law governing ordination, the management and control of Church property, and the payment of stipends ('salaries' to the clergy) and pensions. Canons are promulgated by the General Synod alone and tend to be more in the way of guidelines and advice concerning the practices and ministry of the Church.   [JW]

See also ECCLESIASTICAL COURTS.

c.i.f. contract c.i.f. stands for cost, insurance, freight. It is a CONTRACT for the international sale of goods by which the seller agrees to supply the goods, to make a contract of carriage with a sea carrier, to deliver them to the agreed port of destination, and to insure the goods while they are in transit. The seller performs his contract by delivering the goods to the vessel and the relevant documents (invoice, bill of lading, insurance policy, etc.) to the buyer. Risk of accidental loss or damage passes to the buyer on shipment. The c.i.f. form imposes greater burdens on the seller than an F.O.B. CONTRACT but is nevertheless regarded as more convenient today than the f.o.b., and a far larger tonnage of cargo is carried c.i.f.   [JW]

circuit judge A judge who sits in the CROWN COURT.   [SN]

circumstantial evidence EVIDENCE from which a FACT IN ISSUE may be inferred. Circumstantial evidence is therefore evidence of a RELEVANT FACT as opposed to evidence of a fact in issue. Circumstantial evidence is to be distinguished from DIRECT EVIDENCE. [ALTC]

citizen's arrest A semi-vernacular term, denoting the power of persons other than police officers, or other persons with a statutory power of arrest, to make arrests. It is set out in the Police and Criminal Evidence Act 1984, s. 24A. A person other than a constable may arrest without a warrant anyone who is committing an INDICTABLE OFFENCE; anyone whom he has reasonable grounds for suspecting to be committing an indictable offence; anyone who is guilty of an indictable offence which has been committed; anyone whom he has reasonable grounds for suspecting to be guilty of committing an indictable offence which has been committed. The powers are restricted in that the person making the arrest must have reasonable grounds for believing it to be necessary, and that it must appear to the person making the arrest that it is not reasonably practicable for a constable to make it instead. It can be 'necessary' to make an arrest to prevent the person arrested from: (a) causing physical injury to himself or another; (b) suffering physical injury; (c) causing loss of or damage to property; or (d) making off before a constable can assume responsibility for him.   [BF]

See also BREACH OF THE PEACE.

Citizens of the United Kingdom and Colonies (CUKCs) (obsolete) The status in law of the nationals of the United Kingdom and those places that were still British colonies on 1 January 1949, when the British Nationality Act 1948 came into force. The category of CUKC was abolished by the British Nationality Act 1981.   [JW]

See also BRITISH CITIZENSHIP.

civil law **1**. In COMMON LAW countries, that part of the law that is concerned with the private interests and obligations of individuals and corporate bodies, such as TORT, CONTRACT and TRUSTS. It is synonymous with **private law** (which is the less ambiguous term) and contrasts with PUBLIC LAW, military law and ECCLESIASTICAL LAW or CANON LAW.

2. In COMPARATIVE LAW, it describes those legal systems that have evolved from, albeit in rather different ways, or been substantially influenced by Roman Law. In this context, then, civil law functions as a broad classification of a legal family or tradition comparable to the common law or ISLAMIC LAW traditions. Civil law countries include European countries like France, Germany, Italy and Spain, and other countries, most notably in Latin America and Africa, that were shaped by civil law influences during the colonial period.

3. Also sometimes used by lawyers to describe Roman law itself; see CORPUS JURIS CIVILIS.   [JW]

Civil List The sum made available out of the CONSOLIDATED FUND to support the royal household and certain members of the royal family.   [JW]

civil partnership A legal relationship created by the Civil Partnership Act 2004 entered into by two people of the same sex. The Act is intended to provide equality between same sex and opposite sex couples and a registered civil partnership will be treated for most legal purposes as broadly equivalent to civil MARRIAGE. Couples who enter into a registered civil partnership under the Act attract obligations and rights of support as between themselves and also legal recognition of their relationship for public law purposes such as immigration, employment and pension provision. A registered civil partnership, like a marriage, may only be dissolved by an order of the court, on the sole ground of IRRETRIEVABLE BREAKDOWN. The court, on making an order of DISSOLUTION, can make most of the same orders for ANCILLARY RELIEF as it does on issuing a DECREE NISI in DIVORCE proceedings. [AD]

Civil Procedure Rules (CPR) The new procedural code that was introduced in 1998 as part of the reforms to civil justice initiated by Lord Woolf's review, *Access to Justice* (1996). The new Rules provide a more uniform procedure for civil cases, in the COUNTY COURT, HIGH COURT and COURT OF APPEAL. They

do not apply to non-contentious proceedings for PROBATE, which are still governed by the Non-Contentious Probate Rules 1987, as amended, and have limited application in family proceedings. The CPR have sought to increase access to the courts by simplifying both the process of litigation and the language used by the courts (for example a WRIT is now called a CLAIM FORM). Another of Lord Woolf's objectives was to encourage early settlement and, where appropriate, the diversion of disputes away from the courts. Research to date seems to indicate that the Rules have had some impact in this respect. In particular, the volume of civil litigation has fallen since the introduction of the Rules, notably in the number of cases heard by the High Court. During 1999, for example, the number of claims issued by the QUEEN'S BENCH DIVISION fell by 37 per cent from 1998; in 2000 that figure fell by a further 63 per cent to a total of 26,876. In 2006 only 18,364 proceedings were issued (data derived from the official Judicial Statistics 1999, 2000 and Judicial and Court Statistics 2006). The Rules were also intended to reduce the costs of litigation, but, in this regard, research data are more equivocal. There is evidence that the costs of litigation in some cases have gone up, not least because the Rules have frontloaded legal costs, relative to the old regime, by increasing the amount of work that lawyers have to do in the early stages of case preparation. [JW]

See also ALLOCATION; ALTERNATIVE DISPUTE RESOLUTION; CASE MANAGEMENT; PRACTICE DIRECTION; PRE-ACTION PROTOCOL.

Civil Procedure Rules Committee Established under the authority of the Civil Procedure Act 1997, this is the body responsible for making, updating and revising the CIVIL PROCEDURE RULES. The Committee has 16 members, made up predominantly of HIGH COURT and COUNTY COURT judges, solicitors and barristers, together with the MASTER OF THE ROLLS and Deputy Head of Civil Justice, both of whom sit ex officio. The Committee has two non-lawyer members: a consumer affairs member and a lay advice member.   [JW]

civil restraint order A court order that can be made in civil, administrative, and some family proceedings to restrain a person from making a further claim or application in litigation. Courts have a general duty in civil proceedings under CPR Practice Direction 3C to consider making a civil restraint order whenever a statement of case or application is struck out or dismissed as totally without merit (see CPR Rules 3.3 (7), 3.4 (6) and 23.12), or when permission to appeal is denied, a notice of appeal is struck out, or a substantive appeal is dismissed on such grounds (CPR Rule 52.10 (6)).

The aim of a civil restraint order is to prevent VEXATIOUS LITIGATION. The courts' power to impose restraint orders involves a fine line between two potentially conflicting interests: the public interest in protecting citizens – and the courts – from unmeritorious litigation and the individual's interest in exercising their right of access to the courts; see *Bhamjee* v. *Forsdick* [2003] EWCA Civ 1113. In seeking to balance these interests the rules governing restraint orders require, as a basic condition of any order, that the person against whom the order is sought has persisted in making claims or applications which are wholly without legal merit. The rules also require that the extent of any restraint is proportionate. This is achieved (in theory) by the creation of three levels of order under CPR Rule 2.3(1): a **limited civil restraint order**, which prevents a party from making any further applications in the current proceedings; an **extended order**, restraining a party from issuing certain claims or making certain applications in specified courts; and the widest, a **general order**, which prevents that person from issuing any claim or making any application in specified courts. Under Practice Direction 3C, para. 4 (1), a general order can only be made in circumstances where an extended order is not deemed sufficient or appropriate. [JW]

See also GREPE V. LOAM ORDER; PROPORTIONALITY; STRIKING OUT.

Civil Service The administrative arm of government. Civil servants are employees of the CROWN, paid out of money voted annually by Parliament for that purpose. They are employed in central government departments (e.g. the Treasury, Ministry of Defence, etc.) and EXECUTIVE AGENCIES, but not in local government. Civil servants are required to abstain from overt political activity, and to serve whichever government comes into power. Their work is governed by the Civil Service Code which sets standards of conduct, including loyalty and confidentiality. The Code is sometimes criticized for placing civil servants' loyalty to the current administration above any constitutional duty to act in the PUBLIC INTEREST. Conventionally ministers accept public and parliamentary responsibility for the work of their departments, and for failings arising from the proper activities of individual civil servants within those departments. [JW]

See also MINISTERIAL RESPONSIBILITY.

civil trial centre A COUNTY COURT designated for the purposes of hearing cases allocated to the multi-track under CIVIL PROCEDURE RULES, Part 26. [JW]

See also ALLOCATION.

CJEC *See* COURT OF JUSTICE OF THE EUROPEAN COMMUNITIES.

claim *See also* CAUSE OF ACTION.

claim form The court form which must be completed by the person who is suing another for injury, loss or damage in a civil matter. The claim form will contain details of the **claimant** (the person suing), the **defendant** (the person being sued) and the remedy being sought (CPR Rule 16.2). It may include brief details of the circumstances of the claim, or these may be attached as separate Particulars of Claim (Rule 16.4). The claim form must be submitted to the court and served on the defendant or defendants (see SERVICE). [JW]

Claim Production Centre (CPC) Established in January 1990 in Northampton, the CPC centrally processes claim requests from major claimants, such as banks, credit card and finance companies, who routinely issue more than 1,000 claims annually. The

CPC can issue proceedings in the name of any county court in England and Wales. In 2005 the CPC issued 938,571 claims, representing 59 per cent of the total default claims issued in that year. Once issued and served, the case is managed by the local court in the usual way.   [JW]

claimant A person (a) who commences a claim in civil proceedings or (b). claims social security benefits.   [JW]

class gift A gift given to persons who come within a particular description (e.g. 'to my daughters') rather than to named individuals (e.g. 'to Bethany and Saskia').   [PK]

clausula si omnes (Lat.) Literally, an 'if all' clause. In INTERNATIONAL LAW, a clause binding on one party, or group of parties, only if the party or parties on the other side of the agreement or conflict are also bound by the same obligations. It is also known as a GENERAL PARTICIPATION CLAUSE.   [IB]

clean break The phrase used to describe a cessation of financial responsibility between spouses or civil partners on their separation, DIVORCE, DISSOLUTION of CIVIL PARTNERSHIP or ANNULMENT. The Matrimonial Causes Act 1973 and the Civil Partnership Act 2004 impose a duty on the court, when it decides to make an order for ANCILLARY RELIEF, to 'consider whether it would be appropriate so to exercise those powers that the financial obligations of each party towards the other will be terminated as soon after the grant of the decree as the court considers just and reasonable'. If appropriate, the court may make an order in effect imposing a clean break between the parties by setting a date at which MAINTENANCE payments will end or by prohibiting a party from making further applications to the court to continue payments. A clean break is not normally imposed on a party who is unable to become financially independent of the other, and the courts have consistently held that a clean break may not be made from a party's financial responsibilities for their child.   [AD]

See also LUMP SUM AWARD.

clean hands A shorthand term, referring to the equitable maxim 'he who comes to EQUITY must come with clean hands'. The phrase encapsulates the discretionary nature of equitable relief, which may be withheld when a party has, in the eyes of the court, acted inequitably. Thus a party seeking specific performance in respect of an agreement must not be in breach of it themselves; see, in particular, *Tinsley* v. *Milligan* [1994] 1 AC 340.   [PK]

clearance area An area of land which, following declaration of its status by the local housing authority, is to be cleared of all buildings. It is a remedy that has been available to local housing authorities since the 1930s in order to promote slum clearance.

Following the implementation of the HOUSING HEALTH AND SAFETY RATING SYSTEM in the Housing Act 2004 a clearance area may be declared in three different circumstances: (a) where each of the residential buildings in the area contain a Category 1 hazard and any other buildings in the area are dangerous or harmful to the health or safety of the inhabitants of the area; (b) if the authority is satisfied that both the residential buildings in the area, as a result of their bad arrangement or the narrowness or bad arrangement of the streets, and any other buildings are dangerous or harmful to the health or safety of the inhabitants; (c) where each of the residential buildings in the area contains a Category 2 hazard and any other buildings are dangerous or harmful to the health or safety of the inhabitants in circumstances specified by an order made by the Secretary of State.

In addition the local authority must be satisfied that there will be suitable residential accommodation available to the people who will be displaced from their homes as a result of the declaration, and that it has sufficient resources to carry out the clearance.   [HC & DR]

clerk to the justices A legally qualified person who provides MAGISTRATES with advice about law, procedure and practice.
                                            [SN]

click-wrap licence A click-wrap agreement is the electronic version of the SHRINK-WRAP LICENCE, and is often found in SOFTWARE licences (especially in relation to installation software) and/or internet websites. The end user is invited to click on the 'I accept the terms and conditions' or 'Agree' or 'OK' button to signify that he or she is bound by the terms of the agreement. Other terms which describe a similar sort of licence agreement are 'web-wrap' and 'browse-wrap' in relation to software which is used or downloaded over the internet. Click-wrap licences rest on stronger contractual foundations than shrink-wrap licences and end-users must expressly indicate their consent to the terms and conditions of the contract. Moreover, unlike shrink-wrap licences, the terms and conditions of a click-wrap licence are often displayed at the very start of the installation or downloading stage, which is a pre-contractual stage.

[US]

close An enclosed area of land. [DR]
See also BREACH OF CLOSE.

close company A UK company subject to special tax provisions. It is a company controlled by five or fewer **participators** (individuals or bodies corporate), or exclusively by participators (however many there are) who are directors. A participator is anyone who possesses or is entitled to acquire share capital or voting rights in the company, including a loan creditor.

A company is not close if it is controlled exclusively by a company which is not a close company, or by two or more companies none of which is itself a close company. [RE]

closed shop *See* UNION MEMBERSHIP AGREEMENT.

closed-shop agreement A closed shop exists where there is an agreement between management and unions to employ only union members. One result of COLLECTIVE BARGAINING may be an agreement that workers would – either before or after taking up employment – become union members. The distinction in time was replicated by the names for such agreements, as 'pre-entry' and 'post-entry' closed shops. Unions saw such agreements as protecting their membership base; others viewed the closed shop as holding back British industry. During the Thatcher government various legislative underpinnings for the closed shop were withdrawn and by 1990 there was no legal protection, the Employment Act of that year stipulating that it was unlawful to refuse employment to a person because he or she was not a member of a union. The Trade Union and Labour Relations (Consolidation) Act 1992, s. 152 provides that a non-union member may not be fairly dismissed for not belonging to a union, whether that union is independent or not. Section 152 has a long and varied pedigree, beginning as the law protecting a worker's freedom to join independent unions. As foreshadowed in Tony Blair's foreword to the White Paper, *Fairness at Work,* 1999, the closed-shop provisions found in Conservative anti-union laws have not been repealed. [MJ]

closing order (obsolete) Orders made under the Housing Act 1985 which enabled a LOCAL AUTHORITY to serve a notice prohibiting use of premises for any purpose not approved by the local authority. The Housing Act 2004 deleted all references to closing orders from the Housing Act 1985. Their function has now been replaced by PROHIBITION ORDERS and Emergency Prohibition Orders. [HC & DR]

CLS *See* CRITICAL LEGAL STUDIES.

Cm. *See* COMMAND PAPERS.

Cmd. *See* COMMAND PAPERS.

Cmnd. *See* COMMAND PAPERS.

co-decision procedure A legislative procedure, operating only within the EUROPEAN COMMUNITY (EC), set out in Article 251 EC Treaty. Under this procedure, the EUROPEAN PARLIAMENT, together with the COUNCIL OF MINISTERS, passes laws. Reflecting the increasing allocation of competence to the European Parliament, this procedure was introduced

into the EC by the TREATY ON EUROPEAN UNION.
[MON]

See also ASSENT PROCEDURE; COOPERATION PRO-
CEDURE; TREATY OF ROME.

co-imperium The exercise of government
or administration-like competencies over
part or the entirety of a territory by two
or more STATES, or by a group of states
under the aegis of an international organization. Unlike a CONDOMINIUM, a co-imperium does not involve the exercise of full
SOVEREIGNTY over the territory concerned.
For example, the administration of territories by United Nations Interim Administration in East Timor, Cambodia and Kosovo,
each constituted a co-imperium, because in
none of these territories did absolute sovereignty pass to the United Nations or any of
its members. The existence of a co-imperium is a matter of fact.   [IB]

co-operative housing association   A
FULLY MUTUAL HOUSING ASSOCIATION which is
registered as a co-operative under the
Industrial and Provident Societies Act
1965.   [HC & DR]

co-respondent   In DIVORCE proceedings
based on the fact of ADULTERY, the person
named by the PETITIONER as the alleged sexual partner of the respondent. Under the
Matrimonial Causes Act 1857, the petitioner was required to name the person
with whom the adultery was alleged to
have occurred. If the adultery was proved,
the court had the power to order the co-
respondent to pay the costs of the divorce
and, sometimes, damages to the aggrieved
husband. The award of damages is no
longer available, but a petitioner under
the Matrimonial Causes Act 1973 may
still name a co-respondent, and he or she
is still potentially liable for costs. In practice, however, petitions based on adultery
today rarely name a co-respondent. In recognition of this, and to discourage further
the culture of blame and fault in divorce,
the government is considering reform
which would ban petitioners from naming
co-respondents in the future.   [AD]

coaching a witness   The process of requiring or enabling a witness to rehearse or

practise their evidence before a court
appearance, particularly where the aim is
to encourage the witness to adapt or
improve their testimony in a way that
would benefit the witness or the party calling the witness. Coaching a witness is contrary to the professional codes of conduct:
see para. 705 of the Code of Conduct of the
Bar of England and Wales.   [JW]

Coase theorem   The theorem postulated
by the economist Ronald Coase (b. 1910)
which holds that where transaction costs
are zero, the efficient solution to a problem
will emerge irrespective of the legal rule
chosen to address the problem. This has
relevance, for example, in contemporary
discussions about the appropriate response
to carbon emissions: should there be a right
to pollute, as proposed by defenders of market-based solutions, or a right to clean air,
as proposed by defenders of solutions
linked to notions of environmental justice?
Hypothetical calculations may be carried
out in an attempt to answer such questions,
but the decision as to whether one or
another party bears transaction costs and
how such costs should be calculated will
still be open to debate.   [JP]

See also ECONOMIC ANALYSIS OF LAW.

Further reading: Ronald H. Coase, 'The
Problem of Social Cost', *Journal of Law and
Economics* (1960), 3(1), 1–44.

Code for Crown Prosecutors   A public
document, issued by the DIRECTOR OF PUBLIC
PROSECUTIONS, that sets out the general principles CROWN PROSECUTORS should follow
when they make decisions on cases:
http://www.cps.gov.uk/victims_witnesses/
code.html   [ALTC]

codicil   A testamentary document which is
ancillary to a WILL. It must be executed with
the same formalities as a will, and is frequently used when it is desired to make a
small alteration to an existing will, rather
than to prepare a new will entirely, for
example to change an EXECUTOR, or to alter
the amount of a LEGACY.   [CM]

See also TESTAMENT.

codifying statute   A STATUTE that brings

together and restates the existing statutory provisions and common law on a particular area of law. Such legislation is relatively rare; however, a classic example is the Sale of Goods Act 1893 (now 1979). [AF]

See also CONSOLIDATING LEGISLATION; STATUTORY INTERPRETATION.

coercion A rather anachronistic defence set out in the Criminal Justice Act 1925, s. 47. It is available (only) to a wife who commits an offence (other than MURDER or TREASON) in the presence of and under the coercion of her husband. The concept of coercion is broader than the type of threats required to establish a defence of DURESS. It must be shown that the wife's will was overborne by the wishes of her husband, but this might be on the basis of moral or emotional as well as physical pressure (see *R* v. *Cairns* [2003] 1 Cr App R 662).

The burden of proving coercion lies on the accused, and it must be demonstrated on the BALANCE OF PROBABILITIES. [BF]

cohabitation Living with another person, usually in a conjugal relationship. When partners live together without MARRIAGE or registering a CIVIL PARTNERSHIP they are said colloquially to be cohabiting. There is no formal definition of cohabitation for all legal purposes. In some situations, such as claims for protected tenancies or claims for protection against DOMESTIC VIOLENCE, cohabitation 'as husband and wife' (or civil partners) or over a specified period of time attracts legal consequences, but in many others it does not. For example, there is no legal obligation to support a cohabitant or former cohabitant, nor are there legal consequences attached to property-sharing or occupation by virtue of cohabitation. In England and Wales, unlike in other jurisdictions, cohabitation without marriage or civil partnership is regulated only on an ad hoc basis. [AD]

Coke, Sir Edward (c.1552–1634) A distinguished English judge and jurist, Coke (pronounced 'cook') held successive appointments as Chief Justice of the COURT OF COMMON PLEAS and of the **King's Bench**. He is remembered as a strong defender of the COMMON LAW against encroachments from the established Church and the Crown. A number of his judgments remain seminal early statements of common law, including *Dr Bonham's Case* (1610) 8 Co. Rep. 107a, which is often credited with founding the court's jurisdiction over JUDICIAL REVIEW of legislative action, and *Darcy* v. *Allein*, 77 Eng. Rep. 1260 (1606) (also known as *The Case of Monopolies*), which established the impropriety of allowing any individual to exercise a monopoly over a trade.

Coke's legal writings included his famous book on property, *The First Institute of the Laws of England, or a Commentary on Littleton*, which Thomas Jefferson, one of the framers of the US Constitution, reputedly found so tedious that he wrote to a friend, 'I do wish the Devil has old Cooke [*sic*], for I am sure I never was so tired of an old dull scoundrel in my life', and the *Prohibitions del Roi* in which he persuaded a reluctant King James I that the law must be left to lawyers to determine, and was not a matter for the Crown. [JW]

collateral contract A subsidiary CONTRACT based on a promise or contractual statement which provides the CONSIDERATION for, and is the reason why, the main contract is entered into. For example, in *Shanklin Pier* v. *Detel Products* [1951] 2 KB 854, contractors purchased paint for a pier from the defendant company because they were instructed to do so under the terms of their contract with the plaintiffs, the owners of the pier. The defendants had stated that two coats of their paint would last seven years and it was for this reason that the plaintiffs had instructed the contractors to use it. The paint proved defective but the plaintiffs, who suffered the loss, had not made the contract to purchase the paint. The court decided that there was a collateral contract between the plaintiffs and defendants on the basis of the statement about the paint and that this provided the consideration for the making of the contract to purchase it. [JPL]

collateral warranty A term in a CONTRACT which contains a qualified undertaking that reasonable care and skill has been used in making the statement in question, rather than a GUARANTEE that the statement is true. The collateral warranty device was frequently employed in order to award DAMAGES for a non-fraudulent FALSE STATEMENT when such damages were unavailable, unless there had been a breach of a term or a fraudulent MISREPRESENTATION, e.g. *Dick Bentley Productions Ltd* v. *Harold Smith (Motors) Ltd* [1965] 1 WLR 623. Since such a statement was interpreted as a term (qualified promise) in the contract, damages were available for its breach.   [JPL]

collecting societies Organizations that collectively manage COPYRIGHTS on behalf of their members; also called rights management organizations. The copyrightholder must expressly mandate an organization to administer his exploitation rights. This may entail authorization to licence the work, and/or to collect and distribute any remuneration due. The society will often charge a nominal membership fee and claim commission on any royalties collected. An example of a collecting society in the UK is the Authors Licensing and Collecting Society Ltd: http://www.alcs.co.uk.   [US]

collective agreement An agreement between employers (or an association of them) and a union (or two or more unions). It is not legally binding unless the parties agree differently, though it may be considered morally binding. The fact that the collective agreement is not legally binding does not affect the INCORPORATION OF TERMS from that agreement into the legally binding contract of employment or for services. For example, if the non-binding agreement specifies that a worker is to receive 20 pence more per hour, that agreement will become part of the worker's contract; that contract remains in force even though the collective agreement has been abrogated.   [MJ]

collective bargaining The bargaining process which leads to COLLECTIVE AGREEMENTS. Items covered may include pay, other terms and conditions of employment and termination (including REDUNDANCY).

The law largely abstains from intervention but there is provision for the DISCLOSURE OF INFORMATION for collective bargaining purposes found in the Trade Union and Labour Relations (Consolidation) Act 1992, s. 181.   [MJ]

collective mark A registered TRADE MARK which shows that goods or services have been provided by a person or organization which is a member of an association, and the mark is owned by the association for the benefit of all its members.   [US]

collective redundancy The proposal by an employer to dismiss 20 or more employees within a 90-day period (also called **mass redundancy**). UK law, found in s. 188 of the Trade Union and Labour Relations (Consolidation) Act 1992, as amended, is based on the Collective Redundancies Directive 1975 75/129/EEC (amended and consolidated in Directive 98/59/EC), which provides that if employers are contemplating mass redundancies, they must consult with representatives of employees.

Dismissal for redundancy in this context does not bear its normal meaning (as in the Employment Rights Act 1996, s. 139; see REDUNDANCY) but has a specific and wider definition: provided that the reason for dismissal is not related to an individual, the dismissal for this purpose is on grounds of 'redundancy'. The employers must consult with representatives of all affected employees (not just those to be dismissed) and consultation must begin at least 90 days before the dismissals take effect if there are 100 or more to be dismissed, and at least 30 days before the dismissals if more than 20 but fewer than 100 are to be dismissed.

Employee representatives must be union representatives if there is an independent union in the workplace representing the affected employees. The purpose of consultation is stated to be: avoidance of dismissals; reduction in the number to be dismissed; and mitigating the consequences of dismissal. Employers must act with a view to reaching agreement but they need not actually agree to what the representatives have put forward. The remedy for breach of the provisions is a PROTECT-

IVE AWARD of up to 90 days' pay. Unusually there is no financial cap to the amount of the week's pay recoverable. The award is punitive, not compensatory, and depends on the gravity of the employers' failure: see *Susie Radin Ltd* v. *GMB* [2004] IRLR 400 and *Smith* v. *Cherry Lewis Ltd* [2005] IRLR 86. [MJ]

collective responsibility *See* MINISTERIAL RESPONSIBILITY.

collective security A term of art describing the functions of the SECURITY COUNCIL in its role of maintaining international peace and security under CHAPTER VII of the UN CHARTER. In this role and in light of the powers granted to the Security Council by the UN Charter, the Council may, after securing the necessary votes, authorize the use of armed force against a STATE, or a non-state belligerent entity. When doing so, the Council would have already been given notice that a coalition force has been formed and is willing to undertake this task and hence the Council also authorizes that particular coalition to undertake the task. It is not clear from the wording of the Charter – and there is little practice in this regard – whether the Council may, when authorizing force against an aggressor state, also prohibit the victim state from using force to defend itself. [IB]

See also USE OF FORCE.

collusion (obsolete) Where there was evidence of an agreement between the parties, either to put forward a false case in order to obtain their divorce, or to suppress evidence of a defence to the divorce petition, or to create or organize the grounds for the divorce, or agree post-divorce arrangements, this constituted collusion under the Matrimonial Causes Act 1857 and was, until the passing of the Divorce Reform Act 1969, an absolute bar to divorce. [AD]

colony A territory under the direct control of another STATE, over which the latter exercises all the rights of SOVEREIGNTY. The process of colonialism began in the 15th century by European states under the rule of CONQUEST. The process of decolonization that took place in the 1960s through the UN General Assembly resulted in the liberation of former colonial territories in Africa and Asia from colonial rule to self-government and statehood. Some colonies, however, still remain, such as Gibraltar. The term 'colony' has no normative significance in international law, but it may do so in the context of domestic law, as was the case with designated British Crown colonies and the legal effects under UK law of such designation. Colonies can exist today to the extent that they do not violate people's right of SELF-DETERMINATION. [IB]

comitology The process whereby committees (i.e. advisory, management, regulatory or regulatory committees with scrutiny) are used to assist the EUROPEAN COMMISSION in the passing of implementing EC legislation. It follows the procedures set out in Decision 1999/468/EC, OJ 1999, L184//23, as amended. [MON]

See also DECISION; DIRECTIVE; OFFICIAL JOURNAL; REGULATION (EC LEGISLATION).

comity A unilateral act of a STATE, whereby certain courtesies are afforded to another state with the expectation of, or on the basis of, RECIPROCITY. Acts of comity encompass particularly the validation and recognition of executive, legislative and judicial acts of other states in the domestic legal system of the receiving state. An act of comity is in itself non-binding and unenforceable, except that it is possible for such acts, over time, to develop into rules of CUSTOMARY LAW. [IB]

Command papers Command papers are presented to the HOUSE OF COMMONS 'by command of Her Majesty', usually by a Minister. They include 'Blue Books' and 'White Papers'. Each paper is numbered in series, as follows: C. 1–9550, for papers published between 1833 and 1899; Cd. 1–9239 (1890–1918); Cmd. 1–9889 (1919–55); Cmnd. 1–9927 (1956–86); and Cm. 1986 to date. [MS]

See also PARLIAMENTARY PAPERS.

command theory The descriptive legal positivist position, developed by JEREMY BENTHAM but popularized by JOHN AUSTIN, which defines law as the command of a sovereign backed by a sanction. Austin's more unsophisticated version of command theory was influential in the teaching of jurisprudence in English universities until well into the 20th century. H.L.A. HART's modern version of LEGAL POSITIVISM is built upon his critique of Austin's account of command theory. [JP]

commercial agent A self-employed intermediary used by a business to sell its goods or services. Commercial agents now have a number of terms implied into their contracts, and are entitled to compensation and statutory notice of up to three months when the contract is terminated: see the Commercial Agents (Council Directive) Regulations 1993. The regulations do not apply to commercial agents that trade as a limited company. [JW]

commercial arbitration Arbitral proceedings in which the dispute between the parties has arisen out of a business relationship rather than out of, say, a domestic, consumer, or trustee relationship. It is ARBITRATION between business entities (such as traders and companies) in respect of commercial relationships, property and events. The *LEX ARBITRI* of some legal systems prohibits arbitration except in relation to commercial disputes, or has restrictions which do not apply to commercial arbitration. The distinction can also be important for the purposes of the New York Convention 1958. [RE]

See also DOMESTIC ARBITRATION.

Commercial Court Part of the QUEEN'S BENCH DIVISION of the HIGH COURT. Based in the Royal Courts of Justice in London, the Commercial Court deals with complex cases arising out of business disputes, both national and international, with particular emphasis on international trade, banking, commodity and ARBITRATION disputes. It also deals with shipping matters not handled by the COURT OF ADMIRALTY. The court is served by up to 15 Queen's Bench PUISNE JUDGES with specialist experience in commercial law. [AF]

Commission for Local Administration *See* LOCAL GOVERNMENT OMBUDSMEN.

Commission of the European Communities The more formal name for the European Commission, governed by Articles 211 to 219 EC Treaty. The Commission is a very powerful body in the EUROPEAN COMMUNITY (EC), passing laws pursuant to Article 249 EC Treaty. It comprises 20 Commissioners who are required to be independent and operate in the general interests of the EC. The individual Commissioners act as if they were Ministers in a government, each implementing a particular portfolio of policies. The Commission acts as an institution, implementing the Commissioners' policies in **Directorate Generals** (DGs) which closely resemble government departments. The Commission operates under the guidance of the President of the Commission, with the general policy framework being set out by the EUROPEAN COUNCIL and the COUNCIL OF MINISTERS. The Commission has a different role in Pillars II and III of the EUROPEAN UNION, in which it operates only in a support capacity to the European Council and the Council of Ministers. [MON]

Commissioners of Revenue and Customs A body of individuals appointed by the Queen who are responsible for the collection and management of taxes, customs and excise duties, and for the payment and management of tax credits. They do not have responsibility for prosecutions. Their appointment is in accordance with the provisions of the Commissioners for Revenue and Customs Act 2005, and they exercise their authority on behalf of the Crown.

Although the 2005 Act created a single new department, combining the former Inland Revenue and Customs and Excise, the process of integrating the two departments into one effective whole is yet to be completed. The Commissioners are engaged on a review of their responsibilities and powers in order to determine the next stages of the integration process. [RE]

See also HM REVENUE AND CUSTOMS.

committal The process of sending someone to a court or to prison. [SN]

committal for contempt *See* CONTEMPT OF COURT.

committal for sentence The procedure whereby a person convicted in a magistrates' court is sent to the CROWN COURT for SENTENCE when the sentencing powers of the lower court are considered insufficient. [SN]

committal proceedings A preliminary hearing in a magistrates' court in either way cases before the case is sent for trial before a JURY in the CROWN COURT. [SN]

Committee of the Regions One of the supporting institutions of the EUROPEAN COMMUNITY (EC), provided for by Articles 263 to 265 EC Treaty. Along with the Economic and Social Committee, it advises the COUNCIL OF MINISTERS and the EUROPEAN COMMISSION on the impact of legislative and policy changes in areas within its sphere of competence. The Committee of the Regions focuses on the impact of COMMUNITY LAW and policy on the various regions of the EC. It has a particular interest in the EC regional policy, the operation of the STRUCTURAL FUNDS, and the operation in practice of the concept of SUBSIDIARITY throughout the EC. [MON]
See also EUROPEAN SOCIAL FUND; REGIONALISM.

Committee of the whole House At the committee stage in the passage of a Bill through Parliament, the Bill may be referred to a committee at which all members of the HOUSE OF COMMONS or HOUSE OF LORDS may be present. This is called a Committee of the whole House and the discussion of the Bill takes place in the debating chamber ('on the floor of the House') rather than in a separate committee room. In the House of Commons, this procedure is fairly exceptional and tends to be used when the proposed legislation is of constitutional or other great importance. Bills may also be divided at the committee stage, so that some provisions are considered on the floor of the House of Commons and others by a Public Bill Committee. This is common practice for the finance Bills that follow the Budget. In the Lords, all public Bills are referred to a Committee of the whole House. [JW]

common *See* RIGHT OF COMMON.

Common Agricultural Policy (CAP) One of the key policies of the EUROPEAN COMMUNITY (EC), the CAP is based on Articles 32 to 38 EC. The CAP is said to be 'multi-functional', meaning that its core provisions, as set out in Article 33 EC, have many, often competing, objectives. Until the recent 'mid-term review', pursuant to Council Regulation (EC) No. 1782/2003, the CAP had been a highly centralized policy of the EC, but recent reforms allow for the devolution of some of its provisions back to national and sub-national government. [MON]

common assault An umbrella term covering both ASSAULT and BATTERY. The Criminal Justice Act 1988, s. 39, makes common assault a SUMMARY OFFENCE. An allegation in an INFORMATION should not allege assault and battery as that would be bad for duplicity. [BF]

Common Budget The budget of the EUROPEAN UNION (EU) is provided for under Articles 268 to 280 EC. It is comprised of revenue obtained from customs duties, charged under the COMMON EXTERNAL TARIFF; a share of the Value Added Tax revenue of each MEMBER STATE of the EUROPEAN COMMUNITY (EC); and a direct contribution from each Member State, calculated on the basis of that state's gross national income. The budget is set for a financial year, from 1 January to 31 December of each year, and is not allowed to go into deficit. Expenditure is used to finance all of the EC policy areas, together with some EU policy areas. The greater amount of the budget funds are used to finance the COMMON AGRICULTURAL POLICY and the EC's STRUCTURAL FUNDS. All expenditure on the Common Budget is subject to audit by the COURT OF AUDITORS. [MON]

common design *See* JOINT ENTERPRISE.

Common External Tariff (CET) A unified system of customs duties and charges having equivalent effect for goods being imported into the EUROPEAN COMMUNITY (EC), irrespective of the point of entry into the EC. Under international trade law, the EC is classified as a CUSTOMS UNION. Under this framework, the EC has, since 1 July 1968, operated a Common External Tariff (CET), also known as a Common Customs Tariff. Customs duties and charges having equivalent effect for trade in goods between MEMBER STATES were abolished in the setting up of the single market. [MON]

Common Fisheries Policy (CFP) The EUROPEAN UNION's instrument for the management of fisheries and aquaculture. The legal basis of the CFP is found within the COMMON AGRICULTURAL POLICY provisions of the EUROPEAN COMMUNITY TREATY, specifically Article 33 EC, although the two policy areas are treated and managed differently. The CFP focuses on four main areas: (a) the conservation of maritime resources; (b) controlling production through the Common Market organization of fishery and aquaculture products; (c) relations with international organizations and non-EUROPEAN COMMUNITY Member States; and (d) the structural reorganization of the EC's fishing industry. [MON]

common heritage of mankind This consists of particular locations over which no country may exercise any SOVEREIGNTY and whose resources shall not be alienated, but should be vested for the benefit of mankind as a whole. There are only two legally defined spaces designated as common heritages of mankind: (a) the sea-bed beneath the high seas and its subsoil (Article 136 UNCLOS); and (b) the moon and other celestial bodies in outer space (1979 Moon Treaty). [IB]
See also INTERNATIONAL SEA-BED AUTHORITY.

common land Land that is subject to RIGHTS OF COMMON. Since 1970, all common land has been registered on the REGISTER OF COMMONS, and the fact of registration is conclusive that such land is common land. The Commons Act 2006 (CA 2006) reformed the law relating to common land in England and Wales and will gradually replace the Commons Registration Act 1965 as it is implemented over the next few years.

The carrying out of works on common land has been regulated by a number of Acts since the 19th century, including the Inclosure Acts 1845 to 1882, the Commons Acts 1876 and 1899 and Law of Property Act 1925, ss. 193–194. When the CA 2006 comes into force, the older provisions will be replaced by a general prohibition on the carrying out of works on common land without the consent of the Secretary of State (or in Wales, the National Assembly for Wales), if those works have the effect of preventing or impeding access to or over common land, or of resurfacing common land (CA 2006, s. 38(2)). In particular, this will include the erection of fencing, the construction of buildings and other structures, and the digging of ditches and trenches and the building of embankments (CA 2006, s. 38(3)).

Four per cent of all the land in England and Wales is common land. The Countryside and Rights of Way Act 2000, s. 2, granted public rights of access over all registered common land for the purposes of open-air recreation. [DR]

common law 1. A term used to identify one of the world's leading legal 'families' or traditions, which exists alongside other major traditions such as the CIVIL LAW and ISLAMIC LAW. Common law is thus used in this way to describe any legal system or group of legal systems that has emerged from the system of laws that developed in England after the Norman Conquest. The common law tradition today includes the legal systems of England and Wales, the Republic of Ireland, the USA and members of the Commonwealth.
2. A means of distinguishing between institutional sources of law within the common law tradition. Thus legal principles that have been developed by the domestic (i.e. national) courts through the operation of PRECEDENT are referred to as common law rules or principles to distinguish them from rules formulated by STATUTE, DELEGATED LEGISLATION, European or INTERNATIONAL LAW norms.
3. Within the English legal system, a distinction is made between the historical sources of common law and EQUITY. By about the late 13th century, following the

increasing centralization and formalization of judicial authority in the royal courts, the practice developed whereby claimants who were prohibited from obtaining a remedy from the royal courts (which came to be called the COMMON LAW COURTS) petitioned the sovereign directly for relief. As the number of such petitions increased, the work was delegated to the LORD CHANCELLOR (usually at that time a senior churchman), who acted as the King's conscience in deciding such matters. Eventually this system also became formalized into equity – a parallel system of rules, procedures and remedies that operated out of the COURT OF CHANCERY – and sought to ameliorate some of the limitations of the common law. The division between the common law courts and the courts of equity continued until their jurisdictions were merged by the Judicature Acts 1873–75, giving all courts the power to apply both common law and equitable principles and remedies. One practical distinction remains from this historical division: while common law remedies are granted by the courts as of right when a claim is successful, equitable remedies are always at the discretion of the court, and the court will take into account the conduct of the claimant in deciding whether to grant equitable relief (see *D & C Builders* v. *Rees* [1965] 3 All ER 837). [JW]

See also ADVERSARIAL SYSTEM; COMPARATIVE LAW; CONFLICT OF LAWS; INQUISITORIAL SYSTEM; MAXIMS OF EQUITY.

common law courts Following the Conquest in 1066, one of the ways in which the new Norman rulers of England sought to assert their authority was through an increasingly uniform and standardized system of law – the COMMON LAW. Central to this process was the development of a distinct system of royal courts, which emerged from the 12th century out of the ROYAL COUNCIL or *Curia Regis*. The three superior common law courts were (in order of their founding) the COURT OF EXCHEQUER, the COURT OF COMMON PLEAS and the COURT OF KING'S BENCH. All three were seated at Westminster Hall, in London. The jurisdictional distinctions

between these courts were complex and arcane, and there was, because of their ad hoc development and the fees that they generated for the judges, a degree of competition between them. [JW]

See also EQUITY.

common-law marriage In some jurisdictions, after a heterosexual couple cohabit for a period of time and hold themselves out publicly as husband and wife, they are said to be living in a common-law MARRIAGE. Such a 'marriage' is informal, requiring no ceremony or registration, and may attract some legal consequences, such as the obligation to support. While the phrase is often used in common parlance in the UK, it is misleading to do so. This type of common-law marriage has not existed in England and Wales since 1753, or in Scotland since 2006. Although research suggests many people in England and Wales believe they are protected legally or are 'as good as married' if they live with their partners for a period of time, this is in fact not the case. [AD]

See also COHABITATION.

Common Market Not a strict legal concept, the term was used until 1992 to refer to the 'four freedoms' of the EUROPEAN COMMUNITY: FREE MOVEMENT OF GOODS, FREE MOVEMENT OF PERSONS, of services and of capital. With the SINGLE EUROPEAN ACT of 1986, and the further regulation and the development of a higher degree of market integration, the terms 'internal market' or single market are now used for the policy areas referred to as the 'four freedoms'. [MON]

See also RIGHT OF ESTABLISHMENT.

common mistake A situation in which both parties enter into a CONTRACT on the same fundamental mistaken basis. The mistake will nullify consent and the contract will therefore be VOID when the mistake makes the contract impossible to perform; for example, if it was unknown to the parties that the subject matter did not exist, or if performance would be essentially different from the performance contemplated by the parties (*Bell* v. *Lever Brothers Ltd* [1932] AC 161; *Great Peace Shipping Ltd* v. *Tsavliris*

(International) Ltd [2002] EWCA Civ 1407, [2003] QB 679). [JPL]

commorientes Strictly speaking this expression, derived from Roman law, means 'people who die together'. This obviously raises difficulties in deciding questions of inheritance, but it should be noted that it is not only when people die together, for example, in the same accident, that these problems arise. People who are far apart may die in entirely unrelated incidents but it may still be uncertain which one died first. To deal with this difficulty, the Law of Property Act 1925, s. 184, provides that where the order of death is uncertain, then for all purposes affecting the title to property, the younger shall be deemed to have survived the elder. This provision was subsequently amended as between spouses, and the current position between spouses is that a person cannot take on the INTESTACY of his spouse unless he survives the intestate for a period of 28 days (see Law Reform (Succession) Act 1995 s. 1 (1)). [CM]

community charge (poll tax) (obsolete) A local tax, imposed in 1988 by the Conservative government under Prime Minister Margaret Thatcher, which replaced domestic property rates. Although there was a lower level of tax for students and the unemployed, the tax was seen as falling disproportionately on poor people and was widely resented. Its enforcement led to rioting, and the largest riot in London on 31 March 1990 contributed to Mrs Thatcher's forced resignation in November that year. Her successor John Major replaced the poll tax with a community charge based on property values. [MS]
See also COUNCIL TAX.

Community design right EC design law defines 'design' as follows: 'the appearance of the whole or a part of a product resulting from the features of, in particular, the lines, contours, colours, shape, texture and/or materials of the product itself and/or its ornamentation' (see Council Regulation (EC) No. 6/2002, Article 3, and Directive 98/71/EC, Article 1). To qualify for registra-

tion, the design must also 'be considered to be new and to have individual character'. Features of the design which are 'solely dictated by its technical function' or permit the product to be mechanically connected to another product will be excluded from registered design protection.

Directive 98/71/EC on the legal protection of designs [OJ L 289/98], and Council Regulation (EC) No. 6/2002 on Community designs [OJ L 3/1] have harmonized all the substantive aspects of REGISTERED DESIGN law in all the EU Member States; the UNREGISTERED DESIGN RIGHT is at present still unharmonized.

Community design law offers the design creator a two-tier system of rights: (a) a three-year period of quasi-copyright protection under the Unregistered Community Design Right which is available automatically upon the first marketing of his/her design (Council Regulation, Article 11) ; or (b) a 25-year period of exclusive protection under the Registered Community Design Right, which is available upon registration of the design with the Community Design Office (Article 12).

Alternative means of protecting designs include national registered design protection; UK national unregistered design right; national COPYRIGHT protection, and Community or national TRADE MARK protection. [US]

Community dimension The term has a precise legal meaning in the context of the EUROPEAN COMMUNITY (EC) Merger Regulation, which is part of EC competition law. The EC Merger Regulation (ECMR, Council Regulation (EC) No. 139 2004 d, 20 January 2004 OJ 24, 29.01.2004) applies to CONCENTRATIONS having a Community dimension. A concentration has a Community dimension, under Article 1.2 of the ECMR, when: 'a) the combined aggregate worldwide turnover of all the undertakings concerned is more than EUR 5,000 million; and b) the aggregate Community-wide turnover of each of at least two of the undertakings concerned is more than EUR 250 million, unless each of the undertakings concerned achieves more than two-thirds of its aggregate Community-wide turnover within one and the same MEMBER STATE'. [MON]

community home A children's home run by a LOCAL AUTHORITY or a voluntary organization for children who are being 'looked after' – in care or on remand. The Children Act 1989 s. 53 places an obligation on local authorities to make arrangements for ensuring that community homes are available for the care and accommodation of children who are looked after and also, more generally, for purposes connected with the welfare of children in the area, whether they are looked after or not. Where the community home is run by a voluntary organization, the local authority has to bear responsibility for its equipment, maintenance and, normally, management.

[FK]

See also LOOKED AFTER CHILD.

community impact statement An oral or written statement to a court describing the anti-social behaviour problems in an area so that the court can contextualize the impact that a defendant's anti-social behaviour has had on the community. A community impact statement is commonly made by a local police or housing officer who can describe both from first-hand evidence and by presenting data or information from other agencies what the effects of the anti-social behaviour have been. [JW]

community land trust Devices to enable community OWNERSHIP of LAND as opposed to traditional private or public ownership. The legal forms are most developed in Scotland where the Land Reform (Scotland) Act 2003 introduced a community right to buy and a crofting community right to buy. In England there is no distinct right for the community to acquire land. Community land trusts are not-for-profit organizations which raise money to acquire land which is then used for purposes which serve the community, for instance affordable housing, community facilities, and affordable workshops and retail units. The most common legal forms of association for a community land trust are the industrial and

provident society or company limited by guarantee. [HC & DR]

Community law The body of law which emanates from the EUROPEAN COMMUNITY (EC). Its primary legislation is the TREATY OF ROME, as amended. SECONDARY LEGISLATION includes REGULATIONS, DIRECTIVES and DECISIONS. Also included are the rulings of the EUROPEAN COURT OF JUSTICE, the COURT OF FIRST INSTANCE and ancillary tribunals. Community law is said to be supreme over national law; that is, if there is a conflict between EC law and national law, then the EC law will prevail (see, for example, Case 26/62 *Van Gend en Loos* v. *Nederlandse Administratie der Belastingen* [1963] ECR 1). EC law is also said to have DIRECT EFFECT. [MON]

Community Legal Advice *See* LEGAL AID.

Community Legal Service That part of the LEGAL SERVICES COMMISSION (LSC) that provides legal advice and representation for people involved in civil cases through a network of LSC-funded advice providers.

[JW]

See also LEGAL AID.

community of assets In some jurisdictions, all property acquired or income earned by spouses after the MARRIAGE becomes jointly owned. This means that neither spouse can sell or otherwise dispose of the property without the permission of the other, and that on SEPARATION or DIVORCE the value of the jointly held assets is divided between them equally. This form of marital property regime, 'community of assets', is thought to reflect the joint and equal partnership of the spouses in the marital enterprise. Matrimonial property law in England and Wales, however, is based upon the separate ownership of spouses' income and property. Since the Married Women's Property Acts of the 19th century, spouses hold all their income and property, whether acquired before or after the marriage, separately and neither one is entitled to share the income or property of the other during the marriage or on separation, otherwise than under statutory provisions, especially the provisions of the Matrimonial Causes Act 1973. Most 'community property' jurisdictions allow for opting out of the community of assets regime, and PRE-NUPTIAL or SEPARATION AGREEMENTS may reflect this with respect to all or particular assets. As a result of recent court judgments, the Matrimonial Causes Act 1973 (and, implicitly, the Civil Partnership Act 2004) has been interpreted to require parties to try to achieve 'fairness', measured by a 'yardstick of equality' in the allocation of their property on divorce, or dissolution, and some suggest that this may, by default, move the law of England and Wales closer to a type of community of assets regime.   [AD]

See also ANTE-NUPTIAL SETTLEMENT; FAMILY ASSETS.

community penalty A sentence of the court which deals with the offender in the community rather than in prison. Community penalties include COMMUNITY PUNISHMENT ORDERS, COMMUNITY REHABILITATION ORDERS and DRUG TREATMENT AND TESTING ORDERS.
[JW]

community punishment and rehabilitation order An order requiring an offender to undertake a specified number of hours of unpaid work for the community with a programme of work designed to deal with the offending behaviour and encourage personal improvement supervised by the PROBATION SERVICE.   [SN]

community punishment order (formerly a community service order) A court order requiring an offender to undertake unpaid work for a specified number of hours. [SN]

community rehabilitation order (formerly a probation order) A community sentence which involves regular contact with the PROBATION SERVICE. It can also include attending an OFFENDING BEHAVIOUR PROGRAMME to address the reasons why the crime was committed.   [SN]

commutative contract Also known as a contract of exchange (or swap). The CONTRACT provides for property to be transferred from one party to the other in return for other property, but without any payment of money. Such a contract is a barter rather than a sale and so is not governed by the Sale of Goods Act 1979.   [JPL]

Companies Registry The home of the Registrar of Companies and site of the companies register, which is the official list of companies with a registered office in the UK. Companies must lodge certain documents with the Companies Registry, including the current address of the registered office, the articles and memorandum of association, annual accounts and particulars of the directors and Company Secretary.

Companies with a registered office in England and Wales use the Companies Registry in Cardiff; those registered in Scotland use the Edinburgh registry. Northern Ireland companies are served by another registry in Belfast, which is part of the Northern Ireland Department for Enterprise, Trade and Investment (DETI).   [JW]

See also CERTIFICATE OF INCORPORATION.

company A business association which is usually incorporated and therefore enjoys a separate legal personality from its members. Incorporation is normally by registration with Companies House under the terms of the Companies Act 2006, though incorporation may also be by royal charter or STATUTE.

Companies can take one of three main forms: a (private) limited company; a public limited company; and an unlimited company. In a **limited company**, its members' liability is limited in one of two ways. Where, as is most common, it is a company limited by SHARES, capital is raised by allotting shares to members, and their liability is restricted to the values of those shares. Alternatively a company may be limited by guarantee, in which case, should the company be wound up, the members must pay the agreed (nominal) amount which they guaranteed to pay on becoming members. A **public limited company (plc)** is also a company limited by shares, except that its shares can be offered to the public on the stock exchange, and it must have a minimum authorized capital of £50,000. An **unlimited company** is less common, and may be deemed less attractive, since its members carry unlimited liability should the company be wound up. However, an unlimited company does have other advantages in that it has greater freedom to raise and deal with capital than a limited company, and does not have to deliver its accounts to Companies House. A **community interest company** (CIC) is a company limited by shares or by guarantee and not having a share capital, with the specific aim of providing benefit to a community. CICs must be registered at Companies House, but are independently regulated by the CIC Regulator.   [JW]

See also CORPORATION TAX; LIQUIDATION.

comparative law The theoretical study of legal traditions or legal families (such as COMMON LAW, ISLAMIC LAW, etc.); the method of studying the tools and concepts of two or more legal systems by comparison with each other.   [JW]

compellable witness A WITNESS who may be forced to testify even if he or she does not wish to do so. Any person competent to testify (see COMPETENCE) is considered, as a general rule, to be compellable to do so. There are a number of exceptions to this (for example, specific provisions relating to the compellability of the spouse or civil partner of an accused are contained in legislation: see Police and Criminal Evidence Act 1984 (PACE), s. 80; Civil Partnership Act 2004, s. 84).   [ALTC]

compensation A monetary payment to compensate for injury, loss or damage. Compensation payments may be obtained by a variety of means other than traditional civil or criminal court proceedings. These include the following.

1. Awards of compensation by tribunals, most notably the EMPLOYMENT TRIBUNALS. An employment tribunal award for unfair dismissal may comprise two elements, a **basic award** equivalent to the amount of statutory redundancy payment the former employee would have been entitled to, and a **compensatory award** representing loss of earnings and other benefits of employment. Specific compensation principles apply to awards in cases of DISCRIM-

INATION, and where dismissal was either for trade union activities, or for refusal to enter into a CLOSED-SHOP AGREEMENT.

2. Statutory compensation schemes may exist to make one-off compensation payments in respect of harms for which it would not be reasonable, or in some cases possible, for individuals to pursue private claims. For example, victims of violent crime can claim under the CRIMINAL INJURIES COMPENSATION SCHEME, and the **Motor Insurers' Bureau** scheme can compensate the victims of road accidents caused by uninsured and untraced drivers.

3. Welfare benefit schemes may sometimes serve a compensatory function. **Industrial Injuries Disablement Benefit** thus makes weekly payments to individuals who have suffered a serious injury at work or contracted a defined industrial disease. One-off **Vaccine Damage Payments** are paid to individuals who suffer severe disability as a reaction to their own childhood vaccination against certain diseases or, in some cases, their mother's vaccination while pregnant.

4. '**Claims handling agreements**' may be agreed to deal with mass torts: once liability has been established by a TEST CASE or series of test cases, an agreement may be created to deal with all future claims outside the courts, but still under the nominal supervision of a judge or judges. The agreement will define how claims will be dealt with by claimants' solicitors, the defendant's claims handlers, and medical assessors. Victims who establish entitlement may, depending on the terms of the scheme, either receive a flat payment, or each claim will be treated on its merits, with compensation comparable to that awarded by a court.   [JW]

See also COMPENSATION ORDER; DAMAGES.

compensation order An order requiring a convicted person to pay compensation for loss or damage caused by the offending behaviour.   [SN]

compensatory award *See* COMPENSATION.

competence The ability of a person to testify if he or she wishes to do so. The general rule is that any person is competent to testify. In criminal proceedings, a person is not competent to testify 'if it appears to the court that he is not a person who is able to – (a) understand questions put to him as a witness, and (b) give answers to them which can be understood', and is not competent to testify for the prosecution unless he or she 'is not, or is no longer, liable to be convicted of any offence in the proceedings (whether as a result of pleading guilty or for any other reason)': see the Youth Justice and Criminal Evidence Act 1999, s. 53.

[ALTC]

competence competence *See* KOMPETENZ-KOMPETENZ.

Competition Commission An independent public body that replaced the Monopolies and Mergers Commission in 1999, following the passing of the Competition Act 1998. The Commission's powers were increased by the Enterprise Act 2002, which introduced a new regime for the regulation and assessment of mergers and market behaviour in the UK. The Commission's legal role is primarily to undertake merger and market investigations following a referral from a sector or industry regulator, the Office of Fair Trading or the Secretary of State. Following an investigation, the Commission has extensive powers, including the power to block a merger. In both merger and market investigations, it can direct companies, or the industry as a whole, to take a wide variety of steps to improve or safeguard competition. For example, as a result of its 2006 investigation of the home credit market, the Commission required all lenders to publish information on the price of loans on a website, to make it easier for customers to compare offers, and to change the early settlement rebate to give a fairer deal to customers who settle loans early. [JW]
See also COMPETITION LAW.

competition law The law regulating the competitive behaviour of business entities and markets. It has three main elements: (a) prohibiting agreements or practices that restrict free trade and competition between businesses, in particular the control of CARTELS; (b) banning behaviours that constitute an ABUSE OF DOMINANT POSITION within the market, or are anti-competitive practices that are intended to create a dominant position for a particular entity; and (c) supervising the mergers and acquisitions of larger corporations when these would lead to companies gaining more than a 25 per cent market share.

In English law, competition is largely regulated by the Fair Trading Act 1973, the Competition Act 1998 and the Enterprise Act 2002. Businesses are supervised by two main bodies in this field: the Office of Fair Trading and the COMPETITION COMMISSION. Under COMMUNITY LAW, Articles 81 and 82 of the EUROPEAN COMMUNITY TREATY provides the basis for EC competition law, with an extensive body of regulations now also made under the authority of those provisions. [JW]

competitive tendering A term used to refer to the competitive process employed to determine the award of CONTRACTS to provide goods and services in the public sector, e.g. for local and health authorities. [JPL]
See also PUBLIC PROCUREMENT.

complainant A person who makes a formal complaint. In relation to an offence of RAPE or other sexual offences, the complainant is the person against whom the offence is alleged to have been committed. [SN]

complaint The document used to start certain types of proceedings in a magistrates' court; the process of using such a document to start proceedings. [SN]

completely constituted trust A declaration of TRUST is completely constituted when the legal title to the trust property is vested in the hands of the TRUSTEE. Where a SETTLOR declares himself trustee on behalf of another, the title is already in the hands of the intended trustee and thus the trust becomes fully constituted the moment the trust is declared. In contrast, a trust in which a settlor intends trust property to be held on trust by another on behalf of the declared BENEFICIARY will only be completely constituted once the legal title has been transferred to the intended trustee. [PK]

completion In conveyancing, the moment at which the purchase price is paid by the buyer to the seller, in exchange ultimately for the LEGAL ESTATE in the land. In REGISTERED LAND, although the keys are handed over on completion, title to the legal estate only passes when the buyer is registered as the proprietor of the land at HM Land Registry. In UNREGISTERED LAND, the conveyance and TITLE DEEDS are passed to the purchaser on completion, and legal title passes at that moment. [DR]

compound settlement A type of settlement under the 1925 Settled Land Act comprising a number of settlements, often granted over a long period of time. Compound settlements can constitute an extremely complicated set of documents, but the classic example is where a settlement is created by a father, X, granting himself a life interest with the remainder to his son, Y, as an entailed interest. Once Y reaches adulthood, he can 'bar' the entail, thus giving himself the fee simple absolute in possession. At this point, Y is free to create another settlement giving himself a life interest, with the remainder to his son, Z. In this example the compound settlement will comprise of the original deeds of settlement, a deed of disentailment (the deed that bars the entailed interest), followed by further deeds of resettlement. By virtue of the Settled Land Act 1925, s. 1(1), all of these deeds can be read as forming one settlement. [DR]

compromis d'arbitrage (Fr. agreement to arbitrate) An agreement in which the parties are exclusively STATE entities, or a mixture of state and private entities (usually foreign corporations), and upon the basis of which the parties agree to submit a dispute to ARBITRATION. The *compromis* is an autonomous agreement to arbitrate, unlike an ARBITRATION CLAUSE, that has the same function but is incorporated in a more general contract between the parties. It is typically concluded after a dispute has arisen and most commonly in the absence of an

arbitration clause in the contract, or where the arbitration clause lacks detail. The *compromis* will provide agreement on the arbitral tribunal, the selection of arbitrators and the APPLICABLE LAW that will govern the dispute. It does not have the power to designate the PROCEDURAL LAW, as this is not only determined by the inherent jurisdiction of a judicial institution, but also by the internal procedure of the arbitral tribunal as well as the procedural law of the forum state. Inter-state disputes are referred to international courts and tribunals (such as the INTERNATIONAL COURT OF JUSTICE) or arbitral institutions on the basis of a *compromis* agreement between the parties. In the case of international tribunals, this is called a SPECIAL AGREEMENT. [IB]

compromise The outcome of a process of negotiation (whether or not prior to or concurrently with litigation or ARBITRATION, or assisted by a mediator or conciliator) in which each party will often make one or more concessions to the other to achieve consensus in order to settle a dispute. The terms of the settlement will normally be expressed in writing and take effect as a contract. However, where a compromise is reached while litigation or arbitration is in progress, the terms of the settlement can, sometimes, be incorporated into an agreed judgment or an agreed AWARD. A compromise recorded in writing should have a dispute resolution provision, such as an ARBITRATION CLAUSE.

Compromise should be distinguished from the term 'compromis' as in COMPROMIS D'ARBITRAGE. [RE]

compulsory purchase The process under which land is acquired for public use, with or without the consent of the owner, in exchange for compensation.

Compulsory purchase is started when an 'acquiring authority' (usually a public authority) issues a compulsory purchase order, identifying the land and stating the purpose for its acquisition. A public inquiry or written representation procedure is then held, during which interested parties (usually current owners of the land) may communicate their objections. The 'confirming authority' (usually a Secretary of State) must consider those objections before deciding whether or not to confirm the order. Once a confirmation notice has been served, aggrieved persons have a six-week period in which to challenge that notice in the High Court. If the confirmation notice is not successfully challenged, the acquiring authority has three years within which to serve a NOTICE TO TREAT or execute a general vesting declaration. Once the acquiring authority has exercised this power, it may take possession of the land and ultimately acquire ownership, with compensation either to be negotiated between the parties or, if no agreement can be reached, decided by the Lands Tribunal.

The law on compulsory purchase is complex and found within various Acts, most importantly the Compulsory Purchase Act 1965 and the Acquisition of Land Act 1981. In 2004 the Law Commission made detailed recommendations for the simplification and consolidation of compulsory purchase law, but these have yet to be acted upon.   [DR]

computer documents Documents produced by a computer. There are no longer any specific requirements to be satisfied for the ADMISSIBILITY of such documents.   [ALTC]

computer misuse When used in the context of the Computer Misuse Act 1990, the term can be taken to refer, broadly speaking, to behaviour amounting to HACKING. A person commits an offence under s. 1 of the 1990 Act where he or she causes a computer to perform any function with intent to secure access to any program or data held in any computer; and he or she knows that they have no authority to secure that access. A person's intent need not be directed at any particular program or data, or kind of program or data. Where a person has authorization to secure access, but does so for an unauthorized purpose, the offence is not committed. Thus, in *DPP* v. *Bignell* [1998] 1 Cr App R 1, a police officer who accessed the police national computer (authorized access) to obtain information on the ownership of a vehicle for a personal

(unauthorized) purpose did not commit an offence under s. 1 of the 1990 Act.

When the term 'computer misuse' is used in contexts other than the 1990 Act, it might be taken to refer more generally to illicit behaviour involving computers, or to CYBERCRIME.   [BF]

concealment of birth An offence under the Offences against the Person Act 1861, s. 60. It is committed by someone who endeavours to conceal the birth of a child by making a 'secret disposition' of the child's dead body. It is immaterial whether the child died before, at, or after its birth. Whether a disposition is 'secret' appears to depend on the probability that the body will be found. It was suggested in *R* v. *Brown* (1870) LR 1 CCR 244 that a secret disposition would occur 'if the body were placed in the middle of a moor in the winter, or on the top of a mountain, or in any secluded place, where the body would not be likely to be found'. In *R* v. *Berriman* (1854) 6 Cox CC 388, it was stated that the child must have 'arrived at that stage of maturity at the time of birth that it might have been a living child'. Thus the concealment of a non-viable foetus would not be an offence under this provision. Conviction can mean up to two years in prison, but there are very few convictions for this offence.   [BF]

concentration A term used in the context of EUROPEAN COMMUNITY (EC) merger control, part of the EC COMPETITION LAW framework. The current EC Merger REGULATION, Regulation 139/2004, states that it is for the purpose of 'the control of concentrations between undertakings', with concentrations being defined in Article 3 of that Regulation. Article 3.1 of Regulation 139/2004 provides that 'a concentration shall be deemed to arise where a change of control on a lasting basis results from: (a) the merger of two or more previously independent undertakings or parts of undertakings, or (b) the acquisition, by one or more persons already controlling at least one undertaking, or by one or more undertakings, whether by purchase of securities or assets, by contract or by any other means, of direct or indirect control of the whole or parts of one or more other undertakings'.

[MON]

See also COMMUNITY DIMENSION.

conciliation One of the processes used, particularly in employment law, as an ALTERNATIVE DISPUTE RESOLUTION strategy. Conciliation has no formal legal definition but occurs where a neutral third party seeks to bring the parties in dispute together to resolve their problems. The conciliator does not act as a judge but seeks to encourage the parties to reach their own settlement. [MJ]

See also ADVISORY CONCILIATION AND ARBITRATION SERVICE (ACAS).

conciliation officer An ACAS-appointed official who provides CONCILIATION in disputes both between employees and employers ('individual conciliation') and between unions and management ('collective conciliation'). The numbers of collective conciliations do not vary much, there being some 1,300 per year; individual conciliation varies depending on the number of claims brought before employment tribunals, and the number of these fluctuates year by year. Much ACAS conciliation is done nowadays by telephone. [MJ]

conclusive evidence EVIDENCE that is not permitted to be contradicted. [ALTC]

concurrent interests Two or more INTERESTS IN LAND which exist at the same time, such as JOINT TENANCIES and TENANCIES IN COMMON. [HC & DR]

concurrent lease A LEASE granted by a LANDLORD which runs for the same period and for the same premises as another (original) lease. The effect is that the concurrent leaseholder acquires the rights and obligations of the landlord in respect of the original lease. [HC & DR]

concurrent planning Planning for very young children (generally 0–2 years) who are removed by the LOCAL AUTHORITY from their birth PARENT(s) and placed with foster carers who are also approved as potential adopters. While the CHILD remains with the foster carers, efforts are made by social services, with the cooperation of the foster carers, to help the birth family and to reunite the parents with their child. If these efforts fail, then the child is adopted by the foster carers. Concurrent planning is intended to reduce the period of time children spend in foster care and also to limit the number of times that a child is moved from one family to another. [FK]

See also ADOPTION; FOSTER PARENT.

concurrent sentence Where a defendant has been sentenced to more than one term of imprisonment or community penalty, the court can order that the sentences are served at the same time. There is a general principle that concurrent sentences will be given if the offences form part of the same transaction. [SN]

condition An important term of the CONTRACT which can be said to 'go to the root' (or essence) of the contract. A breach of condition is a repudiatory breach (see REPUDIATION), so that for every breach of condition the injured party has the option to terminate or affirm the contract, in addition to claiming DAMAGES. By comparison, a WARRANTY is not an important term and its breach gives rise to the remedy of damages only. [JPL]

See also INNOMINATE TERM.

condition precedent A contingent CONDITION that suspends the CONTRACT until the particular event (condition) has occurred, e.g. a CONTRACT OF SALE will come into effect if, and when, a particular export licence is obtained. [JPL]

condition subsequent A contingent CONDITION which provides that the CONTRACT will come to an end if the specified event (condition) occurs, e.g. providing for a continuing supply contract to terminate when the market price reaches a stated figure. [JPL]

conditional acceptance Since an ACCEPTANCE must be unconditional, an acceptance 'subject to contract' (i.e. subject to further formalities) is not a valid acceptance. [JPL]

conditional admissibility Evidence may be admitted on condition that the judge's decision to admit may be reversed if facts emerge later in the proceedings that render the decision no longer appropriate. [ALTC]

conditional discharge A discharge of a convicted defendant which does not impose any immediate punishment, subject to the condition that they do not commit any further offences within a specified period. [SN]

conditional fee agreement (CFA) A written agreement between lawyer and client making the client's liability to pay the lawyer's fees conditional on whether or not the claim succeeds – often referred to as 'no win, no fee'. Conditional fee agreements can be made in respect of any litigation except family or criminal proceedings.

Under a CFA the client's lawyers build a **success fee** into the agreement, which pays a percentage uplift of the agreed fees should the action succeed. Should the client win the action, this uplift will normally be paid by the other side in addition to any DAMAGES and COSTS at the end of the case. The costs of the action will normally be underwritten by the client taking out insurance. In complex, high-value cases, these premiums may be substantial, but it is permissible to defer payment of the premium until the end of the case. If the client wins, the cost of the premium may be recovered from the other side as part of the costs. The client may still be liable for disbursements (legal expenses) incurred by their lawyers, e.g., fees for expert reports, company searches, travel expenses, etc., though these will also usually be recoverable from the other side. If the case is lost, the insurers will pay the other side's costs, as agreed or ordered by the court, and disbursements incurred by the client's own lawyers after the date of the CFA. [JW]

conditional interest An interest in LAND which may be terminated early or forfeited if or when a specified future event occurs. This could be the non-payment of rent, or a marriage of which the grantor disapproves. Conditional interests can be distinguished from determinable interests by the language that is used in the grant. An interest which is granted 'on the proviso that…' or 'on condition that…' something does not happen is a conditional interest. An interest which is to be 'enjoyed until …' or 'during …' is a determinable interest. [HC & DR]

conditional revocation Usually, when a TESTATOR revokes his WILL, he intends the revocation to take effect immediately, and it will do so. However, it may be his intention that the revocation will only take place if some condition is satisfied and then the revocation will not take place unless and until the condition is satisfied. A typical example would be where a testator, thinking he had correctly executed a new will, then destroyed a previous one, intending to revoke it. If it subsequently turned out the later will was invalid, it could be argued that the intention to revoke earlier was conditional upon the later will being valid. The name given to this concept used to be **dependent relative revocation** but this cumbersome expression has now been replaced by the simpler 'conditional revocation'. [CM]

See also REVOCATION OF WILL.

condominium A territory over which two or more countries exercise conjoint SOVEREIGNTY. Although the countries participating in the condominium exercise sovereignty, the territory itself is usually run by an autonomous local administration whose relationship to the sovereign powers is more akin to that of an agent. The UK and Egypt held a condominium over Sudan until 1956 and France and the UK held a condominium in the New Hebrides, which became independent under the name of Vanuatu in 1980. [IB]

condonation When a MATRIMONIAL OFFENCE such as ADULTERY is seen as condoned, i.e. ignored or forgiven, by the wronged party. Under the Matrimonial Causes Act 1857, a husband was conclusively deemed to have condoned his wife's adultery if he had sexual intercourse with her once after knowledge of her adultery, unless she induced him in this act by making a fraudulent statement of fact. A wife was presumed to have condoned her husband's matrimonial offence if she had sexual intercourse with him with that knowledge. The Act made condonation an absolute bar to DIVORCE. Condonation as a bar to divorce became problematic when the law began to encourage RECONCILIATION between the parties. Parties may now (under the terms of the Divorce Reform Act 1969) resume cohabitation for a period of up to six months after an allegation of adultery (allowed either as one continuous period or as several periods adding up to no more than six months in total) without that attempt at reconciliation constituting condonation of the offence. [AD]

See also COLLUSION; CONNIVANCE.

conduct money Money paid to a WITNESS in advance of the hearing of a case as compensation for the time taken to attend court. [SN]

confederation A STATE that is comprised of associated entities, but unlike the legal structure of a FEDERAL STATE, it is endowed with a weaker central authority and the possibility of dissolution is higher. The existence of a confederation is both a matter of law and fact. Thus, while the USA was first conceived as a confederation under its Articles of Confederation, it later became a federation after constitutional approval in 1789. On the other hand, the entities forming the unified Federal Republic of Yugoslavia prior to its dissolution comprised a federation on account of the single constitution and the strong central government. A confederation may also be established on the basis of a TREATY between states for the purpose of a common defence, financial and other common policies. Much like the case of the EUROPEAN COMMUNITIES, Member States retain their sovereignty but transfer some of their functions to prescribed common institutions. [IB]

See also SELF-DETERMINATION; STATE RESPONSIBILITY.

conference A meeting or interview between a barrister and his or her lay client, often accompanied by the client's solicitor or other representative. [JW]

confession Defined in the Police and Criminal Evidence Act (PACE), 1984,

s. 82(1), as including 'any statement wholly or partly adverse to the person who made it, whether made to a person in authority or not and whether made in words or otherwise'. The ADMISSIBILITY of confession EVIDENCE is governed by PACE, s. 76. [ALTC]

confidential communication A communication made in the course of a relationship – such as that between doctor and patient, priest and penitent, banker and customer, or journalist and source – that is carried on with the expectation that it is a confidential relationship. [ALTC]

See also BREACH OF CONFIDENCE; CONFIDENTIALITY; PRIVILEGE.

confidentiality The law on confidentiality is piecemeal and complex. The closest that English law comes to establishing a general right to confidentiality is through the TORT of BREACH OF CONFIDENCE. To obtain protection, information must be confidential in quality, it must be imparted in circumstances that create an obligation of confidence, and there must be a use of that information that is unauthorized by and detrimental to the claimant. The protection is not absolute and will not apply to information that is already in the public domain, or where the PUBLIC INTEREST in disclosure overrides the public interest in maintaining confidentiality – *Attorney General* v. *Observer Newspapers Ltd* [1990] 1 AC 109.

Specific duties of confidentiality may also be imposed by contract (usually between an employer and employee, in order to protect the employer's TRADE SECRETS) or by virtue of a special relationship, such as doctor and patient or lawyer and client. In both of these relationships, duties of confidentiality form part of the ethics of the profession, and breaches of confidentiality may potentially expose the doctor or lawyer to disciplinary as well as legal proceedings. The principle of lawyer–client confidentiality incorporates but is also wider than LEGAL PROFESSIONAL PRIVILEGE, and extends to bind the lawyer's employees and agents. The lawyer's duty of confidentiality may be overridden in

111 conflict of laws

cases where the lawyer–client relationship is being used to facilitate crime or fraud, or where the lawyer suspects that a crime likely to result in serious bodily harm to a person may be committed.

Various professionals, including lawyers, estate agents, and financial advisers are required by anti-terrorism and MONEY LAUNDERING legislation to report any suspicious activity (i.e. transactions which may involve money from the proceeds of crime, or money being used to finance terrorism) to the SERIOUS ORGANISED CRIME AGENCY.

[JW]

See also DOCTOR–PATIENT CONFIDENTIALITY; PRIVACY.

confiscation order An order that private property can be taken into possession by the state. The order, which is made following conviction, requires the defendant to pay an amount equal to the amount obtained from the crime. The purpose of this order is to deprive the defendant of the benefit obtained from crime. The prosecutor can take steps to preserve assets so that they are available to pay the order. If the order is not paid voluntarily then either the magistrates' court enforces the order as if it were a fine or the prosecutor may apply to the HIGH COURT to appoint a RECEIVER. [SN]

conflict of interest **1**. A situation in which a public official, professional person (such as a doctor or lawyer) or an employee has a private or personal interest which influences or has the capacity to influence the performance of his or her proper duties. There is no general legal rule that governs all conflicts of interest, so that situations tend to be dealt with in one of three ways: (a) through specific rules which have developed, for example, to require individuals elected or appointed to public office to disclose personal interests that may conflict with their public duties, and/or in some cases to exclude themselves from the decision-making process whenever there is an actual, or possibly even potential, conflict; (b) by professional ethics rules which may make acting in a conflict situation a disciplinary offence under the regulations of the appropriate

professional body; (c) under employment law, as acting in conflict situations may breach an employee's general duty of fidelity to their employer and, where it involves disclosure of business secrets, it may also breach express or implied terms in the CONTRACT OF EMPLOYMENT protecting the confidentiality of commercially sensitive information.

2. A situation in which a FIDUCIARY, such as a bank, TRUSTEE, SOLICITOR or BARRISTER, seeks to act for clients or beneficiaries whose interests are opposed. Strictly this is better seen as a conflict of duties for the fiduciary (see *Clark Boyce* v. *Mouat* [1993] 4 All ER 268), even though it is commonly referred to as a conflict of interests. Fiduciaries owe duties of loyalty and confidentiality to every client or BENEFICIARY (see, for example, *Longstaff* v. *Birtles* [2001] EWCA Civ 1219; *Royal Brunei Airlines Sdn Bhd* v. *Tan* [1995] 2 AC 378). A conflict thus places the fiduciary in a position in which loyalty to one client might necessarily undermine their loyalty (and perhaps obligation of confidentiality) to the other. Some such problems may be resolvable by the creation of information barriers – sometimes called **Chinese walls** – which are intended to prevent confidential or prejudicial information passing between individuals and/or teams that are or were involved in conflicting transactions. [JW]

conflict of laws One of two labels (the other being **private international law**), neither of which is wholly apt, to denote the procedural rules of law of a legal system which are applied by judges in order to determine certain issues between the parties to actions which are not entirely domestic in nature. The three main sets of issues which fall within the ambit of conflict of laws are: (a) jurisdiction of the court, where, for example, the respondent party is not present in the FORUM; (b) identification of the GOVERNING LAW which is appropriate to the merits of the claim; and (c) the recognition and enforcement of judgments made by foreign courts.

Much of the English conflict of laws is still COMMON LAW, but there are important statutory provisions, such as: the Civil Jurisdiction and Judgments Act 1982; the Recognition of Trusts Act 1987; the Contracts (Applicable Law) Act 1990; and Part III of the Private International Law (Miscellaneous Provisions) Act 1995.   [RE]

Further reading: Sir Lawrence Collins, *et al.*, *Dicey, Morris and Collins on the Conflict of Laws*, 14th edn (Sweet & Maxwell, 2006, with 1st Supplement, 2007); James Fawcett, and Janeen Carruthers, *Cheshire, North and Fawcett: Private International Law*, 14th edn, (Oxford University Press, 2008).

conjugal rights (obsolete) An archaic term referring to 'the comfort and companionship of MARRIAGE', it has meant the right to sexual relations or, in English law, the right to enforce a spouse's obligation to cohabit. Marriage historically included a legal duty to cohabit as husband and wife, and when one spouse abandoned or neglected this duty, the other could petition the court for a DECREE of **restitution of conjugal rights**, in effect ordering the errant spouse to return to the MATRIMONIAL HOME and take up his or her proper spousal role. Restitution of conjugal rights was abolished as a MATRIMONIAL CAUSE by the Matrimonial Proceedings and Property Act 1970.   [AD]

connivance (obsolete) Broadly, the consent or feigned ignorance of one party to their spouse's improper conduct or MATRIMONIAL OFFENCE (such as ADULTERY). The Matrimonial Causes Act 1857 made connivance, along with CONDONATION and COLLUSION, absolute bars to DIVORCE. Connivance was removed as a bar to divorce in England and Wales by the Divorce Reform Act 1969.   [AD]

conquest The acquisition of SOVEREIGNTY over territory by force of arms. Conquest is usually followed by a unilateral act of ANNEXATION of the territory under conquest. Conquest provided a lawful title to territory prior to the dawn of the 20th century, but it is unlikely that a conquest that is followed by annexation will have any legal effect in contemporary international law.   [IB]

See also USE OF FORCE.

consanguineous marriage A MARRIAGE between parties who are related by blood. A marriage (and now CIVIL PARTNERSHIP) between people of too close a consanguineous relationship is void. A list of relationships in which marriage is prohibited in England and Wales is found in the Marriage Act 1949 and includes relationships of lineal consanguinity (e.g. parents and children, grandparents and grandchildren) and collateral consanguinity (such as brother and sister, aunt and uncle). A similar list of prohibited consanguineous relationships is found in the Civil Partnership Act 2004. A number of non-blood relationships, e.g. adoptive relations and certain relations by marriage, are also incorporated within the PROHIBITED DEGREES OF RELATIONSHIP.   [AD]

See also VOID MARRIAGE.

consanguinity Relationship to another by blood, that is, by descent from a common ancestor.   [AD]

See also PROHIBITED DEGREES OF RELATIONSHIP.

consecutive sentences An order for a subsequent sentence of imprisonment or COMMUNITY PENALTY to commence as soon as a previous sentence expires. As a general principle, consecutive sentences should not be imposed for offences arising out of the same incident.   [SN]

consensual theory Consensual theory (or voluntarism) in international law claims that since all STATES are juridically equal and thus international law-making is premised on a horizontal system of authority, the legal basis of international obligation can only be derived from the consent of states. Such consent is manifested in the ratification of treaties, acquiescence or protest to an emerging customary rule or unilateral act. Consensual theory is predicated on the autonomy of each state. State autonomy suggests that a state is not subject to any external authority unless it has voluntarily consented to such authority. States therefore possess a 'will' that determines whether or not they want to be bound by a rule. The logical extension of consensual theory to new states (whether through

SECESSION or decolonization) suggests that they assume only those rights and obligations they consent to after coming into existence. [IB]

consensus ad idem (Lat. in agreement about the same thing) This agreement must be an objective agreement, evidenced by external words or actions. Subjective consensus ad idem, or a subjective meeting of minds, cannot suffice as agreement in law. [JPL]

consent to harm It is a requirement of all offences against the person that the conduct of the defendant be 'unlawful'. That which would otherwise be unlawful could be rendered lawful through the consent of the person 'against' whom the defendant's conduct takes place. Such consent may be express or implied by virtue of the surrounding circumstances. Thus, if a person touches another person while squeezing past them on a crowded railway station platform, this will not constitute a BATTERY, because the person touched is taken to consent to such trivial touchings by being in that situation.

While that person may consent to such touchings, the law does not permit them to give effective consent to any harm of the magnitude of ACTUAL BODILY HARM or greater, other than in specified exceptional circumstances (see *Attorney General's Reference No. 2 of 1980* [1981] 6 QB 715). Thus, where someone inflicts actual bodily harm on another with that person's consent, their conduct will none the less be unlawful and they will commit the offence of assault occasioning actual bodily harm. Similarly, where someone wounds another with that person's consent, a wounding offence will none the less have been committed.

The exceptional situations in which the recipient may give effective consent to such harms are situations which the law deems to be of appropriate social utility, and include medical procedures, contact sports and tattooing, but will not include consensual sado-masochistic sexual behaviour (see *R* v. *Brown* [1994] 1 AC 212). [BF]

consent to treatment The legal expression of the ethical principle of self-determination and respect for individual AUTONOMY (see *Schloendorff* v. *Society of New York Hospitals* 211 NY 125 (1914)). Any non-consensual touching may amount to the tort of BATTERY or a criminal offence. The consent of the patient to a proposed treatment is of the highest importance in preserving the automony of the patient and protecting the medical practitioner from legal action. (see *Malette* v. *Shulman* (1990) 67 DLR (4th) 321). The validity of consent turns on three points: (a) that the patient has the necessary capacity to consent; (b) that sufficient information has been provided to enable the patient to make a decision; and (c) that the consent has been given voluntarily and that there has been no undue influence or coercion. [HJ]

See also BEST INTERESTS; MENTAL CAPACITY; THERAPEUTIC PRIVILEGE.

conservation area An area designated as being of special architectural or historical interest, the character or appearance of which it is desirable to preserve or enhance (see the Planning (Listed Buildings and Conservation Areas) Act 1990, s. 69 (1)). The designation of a conservation area gives the local planning authority additional powers and duties in relation to the development and use of land in that area, including the following: (a) local planning authorities have a duty to publish proposals for the preservation and enhancement of the conservation area (s. 71); (b) in exercising its planning functions the local planning authority must pay special attention to the desirability of preserving or enhancing the character or appearance of that area (s. 72); (c) greater publicity is required for applications for planning permission where the development would affect the character or appearance of a conservation area (s. 73); (d) a building in a conservation area may not be demolished without the consent of the appropriate planning authority (s. 74); (e) the local planning authority may make grants and loans where such expenditure has or will make a significant contribution towards the preservation and enhancement of a conservation area (s. 77).

Conservation areas were first introduced in 1967 and there are now more than 8,000 in England and over 600 in Scotland. [DR]

See also BUILDING PRESERVATION NOTICE; LISTED BUILDING.

consideration Since English law enforces only bargains, in order to be legally enforceable a contractual promise which is not contained in a DEED must be supported by consideration, i.e. some act, forbearance or promise of value given in exchange for the promise. Thus, consideration can be defined as the price for which the other's promise is bought (*Dunlop* v. *Selfridge* [1915] AC 847). Consideration need not be **adequate** or equivalent to the value of the promise but it must constitute something of value in the eyes of the law (a **valuable consideration**). [JPL]

Consolidated Fund A bank account held at the Bank of England, called the Account of Her Majesty's Exchequer, through which all state revenue is channelled. By law, the Fund is used for payments to the European Union, judges' salaries, CIVIL LIST payments and the expenses of election returning officers; other expenditure will be authorized by annual Consolidated Fund Acts. [MS]

consolidating legislation A STATUE that brings together all the existing legisation on a subject. It achieves this by a process of repeal (i.e. removal of all the earlier provisions in force) and re-enactment. The aim of consolidating legistion is to tidy up the statute book and make it easier to find the law on a subject. A consolidation Act in the strict sense of the term does not change the existing law, nor does it convert COMMON LAW rules into legislation (see CODIFYING STATUTE). Where an Act consolidates and amends the law, this will be expressly state in its long title. [JW]

consolidation of mortgages The doctrine under which a lender, who has entered into two or more mortgages with the same borrower, can force the borrower who seeks to redeem one mortgage, to redeem both mortgages at once or none at all. In order for the right of consolidation of mortgages to exist, the mortgage deed must expressly provide for it (Law of Property Act 1925, s. 93). The right is equitable and therefore can only be exercised by the lender once the legal date of REDEMPTION in the mortgage has passed. [DR]

See also MORTGAGE.

conspiracy An INCHOATE offence, the essence of conspiracy is an agreement to commit a further offence. Conspiracy is principally a statutory offence, under the Criminal Law Act 1977, s. 1, as amended. It is committed when someone agrees with any other person or persons that a course of conduct will be pursued, which, if the agreement is carried out in accordance with their intentions, will amount to the commission of a further offence by one of the conspirators. The offence of conspiracy is complete at the moment of agreement; it is immaterial that the further offence is not committed. As with ATTEMPT, it is no defence that facts exist which render the commission of the further offence impossible (such as where A and B conspire to murder C, who, unknown to them, is already dead).

A number of forms of conspiracy continue to exist at COMMON LAW: conspiracy to corrupt public morals; conspiracy to defraud; and conspiracy to outrage public decency. [BF]

See also CORRUPTION OF PUBLIC MORALS.

constituency England, Wales, Scotland and Northern Ireland are divided into constituencies, generally based on whole or part local authorities, each returning one Member to the House of Commons on a first-past-the-post basis. At the May 2005 election there were 529 English constituencies, 59 in Scotland, 40 in Wales and 18 in Northern Ireland, making a total of 646. The constituency boundaries are set by the BOUNDARY COMMISSIONS.

Elections for the EUROPEAN PARLIAMENT are on a different basis. Here, the UK is divided into 12 regions, each region electing between three and ten Members of the European Parliament (MEPs). Each MEP represents all the members in his constituency. [MS]

constituency members There is a well-established convention that the interests of electors in a particular constituency should be represented only by the Member of Parliament for that constituency. The constituency member is thus the first port of call for any elector with a grievance. This may pose problems, for example, if an elector registered in one constituency wishes to complain about the closure of their workplace in another constituency. In these circumstances, they should contact their own MP, who may or may not choose to pass the complaint on to the MP representing the constituency where the elector works. Prisoners and people living abroad who wish to contact an MP are recommended to contact the MP for the constituency where they last appeared on the electoral register. Prisoners are allowed to correspond freely with an MP who is acting in a 'constituency capacity', and so must demonstrate a constituency connection with the MP before being allowed to conduct privileged correspondence with him.   [MS]

constitution The rules, principles and conventions of a self-governing institution, often in the form of a written document. In law, the term 'constitution' is most commonly associated with the legal framework for the governance of a nation-state. However, certain UNINCORPORATED ASSOCIATIONS at one extreme, and supranational organizations at the other, may also be governed by a constitution that has legal effect.   [JW]

See also CONSTITUTIONALISM.

constitutional convention One of a set of unwritten rules observed by organs of government. These are a true miscellany, including non-binding pledges made by past ministers or acknowledged in Parliament, self-denying conventions adopted by the Lords to accommodate the rise of democracy, and principles which have been advanced by constitutional theorists to explain the way things are done. Conventions do not have legal force, but are none the less unlikely to be broken without

very good cause. They include conventions on keeping Parliament informed of the content of TREATIES, which are ratified by the government under the ROYAL PREROGATIVE; the principle that the monarch will accept and act on the advice of her ministers; conventions about the monarch's choice of Prime Minister, or about the circumstances in which Parliament can be dissolved. It is by convention that the monarch grants ROYAL ASSENT to all legislation, and that Parliament will not debate the monarchy without the monarch's prior consent. The Prime Minister, by convention, has been drawn since 1963 only from the HOUSE OF COMMONS. The HOUSE OF LORDS should not reject a budget passed by the House of Commons. Failure to observe this convention in 1909 led to the passage of the Parliament Act 1911. It has been a convention that major parties will not stand against a Speaker seeking re-election, but it is not observed by the Scottish National Party. It is also a convention that the House of Lords does not veto legislation from the House of Commons that forms part of the government's election manifesto.   [MS]

constitutionalism The idea that the powers of government can and should be legally limited, and that governments derive their authority from observing such constraints. The notion of constitutionalism is commonly, but not necessarily associated with legal systems having a written CONSTITUTION. Constitutionalism seeks to distinguish adequately between two key concepts: SOVEREIGNTY and government. Sovereign power is often seen in legal theory as logically illimitable. If this is so it creates an obvious problem: how can a government be controlled by any constitutional restrictions on its powers, since a sovereign government, by definition, must be able to remove any such restraints? An answer lies in JOHN LOCKE's version of the SOCIAL CONTRACT, which can be interpreted to suggest that sovereignty ultimately resides *outside* government. Unlimited sovereignty is vested in the people themselves, who have the normative power to restrain or even remove their government if it acts beyond its constitutional limits. [JW]

constitutive theory In international law, the proposition that formal or implied recognition by other states is the determinative element which gives rise to a new STATE. This is not the dominant view and its opposing theory, the DECLARATORY THEORY, holds greater sway in the relevant jurisprudence. Proponents of the constitutive theory nevertheless point to the fact that all new states vigorously seek international recognition by other states and membership of the United Nations, irrespective of whether they already satisfy the four criteria for statehood in the 1933 MONTEVIDEO CONVENTION on the Rights and Duties of States. [IB]

construction of statutes *See* STATUTORY INTERPRETATION.

constructive desertion *See* DESERTION.

constructive dismissal Conduct by the employer contractually entitling the employee to leave, with or without giving notice. It is used in the context of the statutory claims for UNFAIR DISMISSAL and REDUNDANCY payments. For the purposes of the common law claim of WRONGFUL DISMISSAL, the same concept is properly called 'repudiation', though in modern usage this type of dismissal is also known as 'constructive'. The principal case remains *Western Excavating (ECC) Ltd* v. *Sharp* [1978] QB 761 (CA). The growth of implied terms in employment contracts, particularly of trust and confidence, has extended the scope of constructive dismissal in recent years. [MJ]

constructive fraud Types of MISREPRESENTATION which are unintentional as opposed to fraudulent. Constructive fraud also refers to conduct against which EQUITY will act to set aside the CONTRACT on grounds of unconscionability, i.e. abuse of confidence, UNDUE INFLUENCE or UNCONSCIONABLE BARGAINS. [JPL]

constructive knowledge A form of criminal negligence, relevant as a species of MENS REA in certain criminal offences, in which the defendant's blameworthiness arises from their failure to make the enquiries

that a reasonable person would have made; for example, this concept is used in the definition of the key HARASSMENT offences, which are committed by a person who knew or ought to have known that particular circumstances existed. [BF]

See also NEGLIGENCE (IN CRIMINAL LAW); STALKING.

constructive notice The equitable doctrine that treats a purchaser of LAND as if he or she has made a full investigation of TITLE and thereby binds the purchaser in respect of any EQUITABLE INTERESTS of which he or she had actual notice or should have discovered if he or she had carried out all the usual and proper inquiries.

[HC & DR]

constructive trust A TRUST that arises by operation of law, rather than via the express wishes of the SETTLOR, in circumstances where it would be unconscionable for the legal owner to retain beneficial ownership. The term is often misused to include situations where someone is made personally liable by assisting in a breach of trust (see KNOWING ASSISTANCE) or having received trust property which was then dissipated (see KNOWING RECEIPT). However the term should only be used in a proprietary context where actual property in the hands of the CONSTRUCTIVE TRUSTEE is held on constructive trust. Constructive trusts may be divided into **institutional constructive trusts** and **remedial constructive trusts.** In jurisdictions (such as England and Wales) which recognize the former, constructive trusts only arise in certain fact scenarios, as for example when a FIDUCIARY makes an unauthorized profit or accepts a bribe. In other jurisdictions (such as the United States) which recognize the latter, the constructive trust is used as a discretionary remedy to reverse UNJUST ENRICHMENT generally. As noted in *Westdeutsche Landesbank Girozentrale* v. *Islington London Borough Council* [1996] AC 669, 'English law has not been prepared to accept the remedial constructive trust', preferring instead to utilize the wider range of remedies available via the discretionary doctrine of PROPRIETARY ESTOPPEL. Despite this, and admittedly still within the confines of the institutional constructive trust, English law is arguably adopting a more remedial approach to the constructive trust. This is particularly evident in the context of the family home where in *Stack* v. *Dowden* [2007] UKHL 17 the HOUSE OF LORDS utilized the constructive trust in seeking to fashion an equitable remedy based upon the whole course of dealings between the parties rather than the particular factual matrix required under their previous decision in *Lloyds Bank* v. *Rosset* [1991] 1 AC 107.   [PK]

constructive trustee A legal owner who is deprived of the beneficial ownership of some property by the operation of the law. The term is often misused to refer to persons who are made personally liable for meddling with trust property (see KNOWING ASSISTANCE and KNOWING RECEIPT) although such people are not properly described as constructive trustees unless they retain legal title to property (or its traceable equivalent) subject to a CONSTRUCTIVE TRUST.
                                                  [PK]

consul An official representative of the government of one STATE in the territory of another. Article 1(2) of the 1963 Vienna Convention on Consular Relations provides for two categories of consular officers: career consular officers and honorary consular officers. Article 9 divides heads of consular posts into four classes: consuls-general, consuls, vice-consuls and consular agents. Unlike DIPLOMATIC AGENTS, under Article 41 of the 1963 Convention, consular agents do not enjoy absolute immunity from the criminal jurisdiction of the receiving state. However, under Article 43 they are entitled to immunity in respect of acts performed in the exercise of their consular functions.   [IB]
  See also STATE IMMUNITY.

consumer A person who enters into a CONTRACT other than in the course of a business, trade or profession.   [JW]

consumer credit agreement An agreement between an individual ('the debtor') and any other person ('the creditor') by which the creditor provides the debtor

with credit of any amount. An agreement providing credit exceeding £25,000 that is entered into by the debtor wholly or predominantly for the purposes of his business is exempted from protection as a consumer credit agreement. See the Consumer Credit Act 1974, as amended by the Consumer Credit Act 2006, ss. 8(1) and 16B(1).   [JW]

consumer hire agreement An agreement made by a person with an individual (the 'hirer') for the BAILMENT of goods to the hirer, which is not a HIRE-PURCHASE agreement, and is capable of subsisting for more than three months (see the Consumer Credit Act 1974, as amended by the Consumer Credit Act 2006, s. 15).   [JW]

consummation of marriage Ecclesiastical laws governing valid MARRIAGES included the requirement that the parties be physically able to consummate the marriage, and discovery at the time of the marriage of an inability to consummate was a ground for ANNULMENT. This ground for annulment continued when jurisdiction over marriage moved to secular jurisdiction in the Matrimonial Causes Act 1857, as marriage was said to presuppose the ability to have sexual intercourse (which became defined in later cases as penetration of the vagina by the penis). The Matrimonial Causes Act 1973 now provides that inability to consummate (s. 12 (a)) and WILFUL REFUSAL TO CONSUMMATE (s. 12 (b)) remain grounds for annulment of a marriage; they render a marriage voidable. The decree of nullity of marriage may be barred if the petitioner knew of the other's inability or intention to refuse to have sexual intercourse but led the respondent to believe that he or she would not seek to have the marriage annulled on this ground and that it would be unjust to grant the decree (s. 13 (1)). Non-consummation is not a ground for nullity in CIVIL PARTNERSHIPS.   [AD]
  See also IMPOTENCE; VOIDABLE MARRIAGE.

contact order 'An order requiring the person with whom a CHILD lives, or is to live, to allow the child to visit or stay with the person named in the order, or for that person and the child otherwise to have contact with each other' (Children Act 1989, s. 8). In English law, the concept of contact replaces the concepts of 'access' to and 'visitation' with children. Some parties, such as biological fathers, have standing as of right to make an application to the court for a contact order. Others, such as grandparents, require the leave of the court to make applications. In some circumstances, the child concerned may also apply. A contact order may be phrased generally (e.g. allowing the applicant and the person with whom the child lives to arrange contact as they see fit) or it might be specific (e.g. prescribing times, days and places for contact to take place). The court can make a contact order following the consent of the parties; by incorporating an agreement reached by mediation or negotiation; after contested proceedings; on its own motion in any FAMILY PROCEEDINGS; or on an interim or ex parte basis. Contact orders can only be made concerning children under 16 years of age and may not be made in respect of children who are in LOCAL AUTHORITY care. [AD]

See also CARE CONTACT ORDER; PROHIBITED STEPS ORDER; RESIDENCE ORDER; SPECIFIC ISSUE ORDER.

contaminated land Land which, due to substances on, under or in it, is causing harm to human health, property or the environment, or is giving rise to a risk of such harm being caused. Under the Environmental Protection Act 1990 (EPA 1990), contaminated land is 'any land which appears to the local authority in whose area it is situated to be in such a condition, by reason of substances in, on or under land, that: (a) significant harm is being caused or there is a significant possibility of such harm being caused; or (b) pollution of controlled waters is being, used or is likely to be, caused' (EPA 1990, s. 78A(2)).

Harm is defined as meaning 'harm to the health of living organisms or other interference with the ecological systems of which they form part and, in the case of man, includes harm to his property' (EPA 1990, s. 78A(4)). The Act set up a complex regulatory framework relating to contaminated land, based on the principle that the pol-

luter pays. There are around 100,000 identified areas of contaminated land in the UK and clean-up costs are notoriously high.

[DR]

contempt of court All courts have powers, either under statute or their inherent jurisdiction, to deal with actions by a person which obstruct the proper administration of justice or constitute disobedience of a court order or process. The law technically distinguishes between civil contempt and criminal contempt. **Criminal contempt** includes behaviour which is, though not in breach of a specific order or direction of the court, intended to interfere with the administration of justice in the proceedings, e.g. by attempting to intimidate or bribe a witness, interrupting or disrupting proceedings, or, as a juror, disclosing information about the jury deliberations. **Civil contempt** normally involves non-compliance with a court order or an undertaking given to the court.

The distinction between a civil and criminal contempt turns on the nature of the contempt, not the nature of the proceedings. Thus, a breach of undertaking given to a criminal court is still a civil contempt, and attempting to bribe a witness, even in civil proceedings, is a criminal contempt. In all cases, however, the contempt must be proved to the criminal standard, i.e., beyond reasonable doubt. Proceedings for contempt may potentially be brought against anyone – a lawyer, party, witness, or member of the public attending a trial.

Under the Contempt of Court Act 1981, a person may commit what is called 'strict liability contempt', by publishing any report of current court proceedings, addressed to the public at large or any section of the public, which creates a substantial risk that the course of justice will be seriously prejudiced. It is the absence of any requirement to prove an intention to interfere with the course of justice that distinguishes this form of statutory contempt from the COMMON LAW form. [JW]

contempt of Parliament Any action which obstructs or impedes either House of Parliament in the performance of its functions, or its Members or staff in the performance of their duties. Examples of contempt include speaking or writing critically about the House or the SPEAKER, giving false evidence to a parliamentary committee or bribing a MEMBER OF PARLIAMENT. A person accused of contempt can be summoned to appear at the Bar of House to be punished. MPs who commit contempt of the House can be suspended or expelled from Parliament. [MS]

contemptuous damages Damages that are awarded most frequently in DEFAMATION cases, where, even though the claimant has been technically successful in his action, the court seeks to express its disapproval of his conduct by awarding only a very small sum, conventionally the smallest coin of the realm. Additionally, no award of COSTS will be made to the claimant in such a case. [HJ]

See also DAMAGES.

contiguous zone In international law, an area of sea beginning where the TERRITORIAL WATERS ends and extending no more than 24 nautical miles from the baselines from which the breadth of the territorial sea is measured: see Article 33 of the United Nations Law of the Sea Convention (UNCLOS). The purpose of the contiguous zone is to allow the coastal state to exercise the control necessary to prevent infringement of its customs, fiscal, immigration or sanitary laws and regulations within its territory or territorial sea, and/or to punish infringement of the above laws and regulations committed within its territory or territorial sea. [IB]

See also FLAG STATE JURISDICTION.

continental margin 'The submerged prolongation of the land mass of the coastal STATE [which] consists of the sea-bed and subsoil of the shelf, the slope and the rise. It does not include the deep ocean floor with its oceanic ridges or the subsoil thereof' (Article 76(3) of the UN Law of the Sea Convention (UNCLOS)). [IB]

See also CONTINENTAL SHELF; TERRITORIAL WATERS.

continental shelf 'The sea-bed and sub-soil of the submarine areas that extend beyond [a coastal STATE'S] TERRITORIAL WATERS throughout the natural prolongation of its land territory to the outer edge of its CONTINENTAL MARGIN, or to a distance of 200 nautical miles from the BASELINES from which the breadth of the territorial sea is measured where the outer edge of the continental margin does not extend up to that distance' (Article 76 of the UN Law of the Sea Convention (UNCLOS)). In all cases, the outer limit of the continental shelf shall not exceed 350 nautical miles from the baselines used to measure the breadth of the territorial sea. The coastal state enjoys exclusive rights with regard to the exploration and exploitation of the continental shelf's natural resources. These resources consist of the mineral and other non-living resources, as well as all kinds of living organisms. [IB]

contingent gift A TESTATOR may provide that a GIFT made in his WILL shall be contingent or conditional upon a certain event, which may be prior or subsequent to the gift taking effect. An example of prior condition would be 'to A if she shall attain the age of 30 years'. Clearly, the gift does not take effect unless A does attain that age, and if she does not, the gift fails. An example of a subsequent condition would be 'to A provided he does not become a barrister', in which case the gift takes effect immediately, but will fail if A becomes a barrister at some future date, in which case the gift would have to be repaid. [CM]

contingent remainder *See* REMAINDER.

continuity of employment A statutory concept, now found in the Employment Rights Act 1996, used for the purposes of calculating qualifying periods for various employment law rights such as UNFAIR DISMISSAL, and for calculating compensation. For example, the qualifying period for an ordinary unfair dismissal claim is one year's continuous employment. It is possible to add together periods of employment broken by absences from work which have occurred by arrangement or custom in order to attain that one-year qualifying period. These weeks of absence count towards the period and do not break continuity of employment. Time on strike does not break continuity, but such an absence does not count towards the qualifying period. [MJ]

contra proferentem (Lat. against the person putting it forth) A principle of interpretation applicable to contracts and other documents, which provides that any ambiguity shall be construed against the drafter of the CONTRACT or document, or the person putting it forward. The court will adopt the meaning least favourable to that party. Contra proferentem is expressly incorporated into the Unfair Terms in Consumer Contracts Regulations (UTCCR) 1999, Reg. 7(2), providing for the interpretation most favourable to the CONSUMER to prevail where there is doubt concerning the meaning of a term. [JPL]

contract A legally binding agreement. In English law, a contract results where there is an OFFER and matching ACCEPTANCE (agreement), by parties having CAPACITY TO CONTRACT, as well as CONSIDERATION (unless the promises are contained in a DEED), compliance with any necessary formality requirements (e.g. writing is required for a contract for the sale of land) and an intention to be legally bound – so that domestic or social agreements are generally not contracts. The contract must not be VOID as a result of uncertainty of terms or fundamental MISTAKE and must not be affected by illegality. [JPL]

contract for personal services A CONTRACT under which services are to be performed by a specific individual or individuals. The performance by that individual is therefore an essential element of the contractual performance so that that person's death subsequent to the making of the contract amounts to an impossibility which will, in the absence of an express allocation of the risk, frustrate the contract. The person's unavailability may also frustrate the contract, depending on the likely length and nature of the interruption. Given the personal nature of the perform-

ance, a court is unlikely to order SPECIFIC PERFORMANCE of a contract for personal services because it would force one person to work for another in situations of loss of mutual trust and confidence (see *Page One Records v. Britton* [1968] 1 WLR 157). [JPL]

See also FRUSTRATION.

contract for sale In conveyancing, the document containing each parties' agreed rights and obligations when buying or selling an interest in land. Under the Law of Property (Miscellaneous Provisions) Act 1989, s. 2, a contract for sale of land must be in writing, contain all the terms agreed by the parties and be signed by each of the parties. For example, in an ordinary conveyancing transaction, the contract for sale contains the names of the parties, a description of the property, the TITLE of the property, the date for COMPLETION, the price, the Law Society's STANDARD CONDITIONS OF SALE and any special conditions of sale. [DR]

See also OPEN CONTRACT.

contract for services A contract for services is a contract between an 'employer' and a worker who is not an employee or an apprentice. [MJ]

See also CONTRACT OF SERVICE; WORKER.

contract of employment In general usage, this is the modern name for a CONTRACT OF SERVICE. It is the contract which regulates the relationship between an employer and an EMPLOYEE. There is no statutory definition. It is also used sometimes in statute as a subset of a contract of service along with a contract of apprenticeship. [MJ]

contract of sale A CONTRACT governed by the Sale of Goods Act 1979, which by s. 2(1) is defined as 'a contract by which the seller transfers or agrees to transfer the property in GOODS to the buyer for a money CONSIDERATION, called the price'. [JW]

contract of service The Trade Union and Labour Relations (Consolidation) Act 1992, s. 295, and the Employment Rights Act 1996, s. 230, simply state that a contract of service is a CONTRACT OF EMPLOYMENT or apprenticeship, but there is no statutory definition of a contract of employment. The primary purpose of the term is to distinguish between those who work under a contract of service (EMPLOYEES) and those who work under a CONTRACT FOR SERVICES (the self-employed, or independent contractors). [MJ]

contractarianism The philosophical movement which holds that political authority must be grounded in an agreement between the governed and the government. Contractarians are accordingly sceptical of alternative accounts that, for example, trace political authority back to God.

Traditional versions of this approach to the notion of a SOCIAL CONTRACT are to be found in the work of THOMAS HOBBES, JOHN LOCKE and JEAN-JACQUES ROUSSEAU. The most important recent example of a contractarian approach is to be found in JOHN RAWLS' *Theory of Justice*. [JP]

contributory negligence In TORT, the principle that where the claimant is partly responsible for any loss or damage suffered, the damages recoverable in respect of any claim for NEGLIGENCE or breach of statutory duty 'shall be reduced to such extent as the court thinks just and equitable having regard to the [claimant's] share in the responsibility for the damage' – s. 1, Law Reform (Contributory Negligence) Act 1945. [HJ]

controlled trust A TRUST solely controlled by one or more solicitors (and/or their employees) and subject to special accounting rules under the Solicitors Act 1974. [PK]

convention *See* TREATY.

convergence criteria Also known as 'Maastricht criteria', they are the financial and economic standards that must be met by MEMBER STATES of the EUROPEAN COMMUNITY (EC) in order to qualify for membership of the EC's single monetary policy, and its associated single currency, the EURO. These financial and economic standards include price stability, interest rate convergence,

public finance discipline and exchange rate stability. [MON]

See also EUROPEAN MONETARY UNION; MAASTRICHT TREATY.

conversion 1. An intentional TORT under the Torts (Interference with Goods) Act 1977. It is committed by a defendant who wrongfully takes possession of or deals with the claimant's goods in a manner inconsistent with the claimant's rights over them. Conversion can overlap with the crime of THEFT, but the civil action does not require proof of dishonesty.

2. In EQUITY, a legal fiction, applied to a contract for the sale of land where there was a duty to convert the property (i.e. to sell it and realize the proceeds of sale for a beneficiary). This would treat the buyer's interest as the real property interest even though the seller still held legal TITLE, and convert the seller's interest into a security interest (i.e. a personal property interest) in respect of the prospective proceeds of sale. The doctrine of conversion was abolished from 1 January 1997 by the Trusts of Land and Appointment of Trustees Act 1996. [JW]

converted tenancy A controlled tenancy which was converted by statute, primarily the Rent Act 1968, into a regulated tenancy. The Rent Act 1977 provides particular protections, for instance from the low rent exclusions from statutory security, and preserves particular rights, for instance the right to deduct overpayment of rent from current rent, for converted tenancies.

[HC & DR]

conveyance 1. For the purposes of the offence under the Theft Act 1968, s. 12 (taking a MOTOR VEHICLE or other conveyance without authority, sometimes known as TWOC), a conveyance is something constructed or adapted for the carriage of a person or persons, but the definition does not include conveyances which are controllable only remotely (see Theft Act 1968, s. 12(7)); see also AGGRAVATED VEHICLE TAKING.

2. A document other than a WILL transferring an interest in land; see also CONTRACT FOR SALE; CONVEYANCING. [BF]

conveyancing The process by which ownership of land is transferred from one person to another. Conveyancing is usually carried out by solicitors (though it may be carried out by a licensed conveyancer who is not a fully qualified solicitor), one of whom acts on behalf of the buyer, one on behalf of the seller. In an ordinary domestic conveyancing transaction for the sale of a FREEHOLD, carried out according to the Law Society's National Conveyancing Protocol, the process is as follows.

(a) After taking initial instructions from the client, the seller's solicitor prepares a draft contract package. This includes a draft CONTRACT FOR SALE, a SELLER'S PROPERTY INFORMATION FORM and a 'Fixtures and Fittings form' (the latter two are filled out by the seller). If the property is REGISTERED LAND, the seller's solicitor also obtains OFFICIAL COPIES of the Land Register entries for the property. If it is UNREGISTERED LAND, the solicitor will request the TITLE DEEDS from the seller and prepare an EPITOME OF TITLE.

(b) Once a buyer is found, the seller's solicitor sends the draft contract package to the buyer's solicitor. At this point the buyer's solicitor makes all relevant pre-contract SEARCHES, PRELIMINARY ENQUIRIES and investigates the seller's TITLE, by inspecting either the official copies or the epitome of title. If there are any uncertainties regarding the seller's title, the buyer's solicitor will raise any necessary REQUISITIONS ON TITLE in order to satisfy those uncertainties.

(c) If the buyer is using a MORTGAGE to contribute to the purchase price, this must now be arranged. The buyer's solicitor will ensure that the buyer has enough available funds to go ahead with the purchase.

(d) Both solicitors agree any necessary amendments to the draft contract, arrange a suitable date for completion between the clients and then go ahead with the exchange of contracts. At this point, the buyer pays the deposit (usually 10 per cent of the purchase price) and both parties become legally bound to complete the transaction.

(e) The buyer's solicitor raises any further requisitions on title that could not be raised prior to exchange, drafts the purchase deed (usually a deed of TRANSFER), drafts a mortgage deed if required, carries out pre-completion searches (for registered land, a Land Registry search; for unregistered land, a Land Charges Department search) and ensures that the sum required for completion will be available from the buyer.

(f) On the agreed date for COMPLETION, the buyer pays the balance of the purchase price, the seller's solicitor completes the transfer deed and authorizes the estate agent to release the keys to the buyer. The seller's solicitor will then discharge any mortgages the seller had on the property, pay the estate agent's commission if so authorized and account to the seller for the balance of the sale proceeds. The buyer's solicitor will pay any Stamp Duty Land Tax payable and send the necessary forms to the Land Registry so that the buyer is registered as the new legal owner of the property. Only once the buyer is registered does he become the legal owner of the property.

The timescale for a conveyancing transaction, at its quickest, can be four to six weeks from the solicitor taking initial instructions to exchange of contracts, with a further two to three weeks until completion. However, delays can and do often occur for a variety of reasons. The law relating to conveyancing and registered land was substantially reformed by the Land Registration Act 2002, which provided the necessary legal framework for the introduction of e-conveyancing. This will vastly simplify the process of conveyancing by bringing it up to date with the digital age and it is hoped that it will be fully introduced by 2009–10. [DR]

Further reading: Robert Abbey and Mark Richards, *A Practical Approach to Conveyancing*, 8th edn (Oxford: Oxford University Press, 2006).

conviction When an offender has pleaded or been found guilty of an offence by a court, he or she has been convicted of a criminal offence. This conviction appears on the offender's criminal record. [SN]

cooperation procedure A legislative procedure that operates within the EUROPEAN COMMUNITY (EC). The procedure was introduced by the SINGLE EUROPEAN ACT and is provided for in Article 252 EC. It is only used in the EUROPEAN MONETARY UNION. The procedure begins with a proposal by the COMMISSION OF THE EUROPEAN COMMUNITIES on which the EUROPEAN PARLIAMENT gives an opinion. On the basis of this opinion the COUNCIL OF MINISTERS formulates what is called a **common position**, indicating how the Council would like to decide. The common position is then sent to the Parliament for a second reading. If it adopts the common position, the Council will convert the common position into a DECISION, but if the Parliament rejects the Council's position, the measure can only be passed by a unanimous vote in the Council.   [MON]

See also ASSENT PROCEDURE; CO-DECISION PROCEDURE.

copyhold (obsolete) A form of FEUDAL TENURE, abolished by the Law of Property Act 1922, which converted all existing copyholds into FREEHOLDS. A copyhold was a legal estate in land, granted where that land formed part of a manor and evidenced by a copy of the court roll of the manor. Tenants under such an arrangement became known as 'tenants by copy of court roll' and the interest became known as copyhold. By the early 20th century it had become analogous to freehold and was therefore abolished.   [DR]

copyright A set of exclusive rights to reproduce protected works or authorize others to do certain acts with respect to such works for a limited period of time. Protected works are original LITERARY, dramatic, musical or ARTISTIC WORKS, sound recordings, films, broadcasts, and the TYPOGRAPHICAL ARRANGEMENT of published editions (see Copyright, Designs and Patents Act 1988, s. 1(1)). Subject to some exceptions, the Copyright, Designs and Patents Act 1988 declares that the author of a work is deemed to be the first owner of any copyright in it – see FIRST OWNERSHIP. Where two or more authors contribute to a work, they will be entitled to joint ownership of the copyright. Since copyright does not need to be

registered, it can be difficult to find out who is the current copyright owner.

The period of protection depends on the nature of the work. For literary, dramatic, musical and artistic works, it is from the time of creation until 70 years after the death of the author. This is irrespective of the OWNERSHIP of the work. The formula for film copyright is slightly different as authorship of film is a disputed concept. Thus, the duration of protection is 70 years after the death of the last surviving person in the following list: principal director, screenplay author, dialogue author or composer of the music for the film. This is also irrespective of authorship or ownership of the film. Sound recordings and broadcasts are protected for 50 years following the making or release of the recording/broadcast. Published editions are protected only for 25 years from the first publication of a new typographical setting of the work (irrespective of whether the work itself is protected by copyright).

Unlike PATENTS and TRADE MARKS, copyright does not need to be applied for and once a work is created it is generally protected automatically almost everywhere in the world without the need for any formalities, under the TRIPS Agreement and other WIPO international copyright conventions.

There is no European Community copyright law, though there are seven EC Directives which are slowly harmonizing the following substantive aspects of copyright law in all EU Member States: exclusive rights, duration of protection, RENTAL RIGHT, defences, SOFTWARE protection, RESALE ROYALTY RIGHT, DATABASE and satellite broadcasting/cable retransmission.   [US]

See also ORIGINALITY; INFRINGEMENT ACTION.

copyright tribunal An independent body established under the Copyright, Designs and Patents Act 1988. Anyone who has unreasonably been refused a licence by COLLECTING SOCIETIES or considers the terms of an offered licence to be unreasonable may refer the matter to the tribunal.

Specifically, the tribunal adjudicates when the parties cannot agree between themselves on the terms and conditions of licences or licensing schemes operated by collecting societies in the COPYRIGHT and related rights area. It has the statutory task of establishing conclusively the facts of a case and of coming to a decision which is reasonable in the light of those facts. Its decisions are appealable to the HIGH COURT only on points of law. [US]

coregulation An approach to REGULATION which seeks to involve all of the key stakeholders in a given sector of society in the process of regulation. Coregulation may go so far as to allow overall regulatory objectives to be set by the stakeholders or it may be restricted to allowing them to work out how pre-established legislative objectives are to be met. Involving stakeholders in this way is seen to produce a number of benefits, including the availability of a wider pool of expertise, as well as improved legitimacy and compliance.

The idea has gained some currency at the European level since the publication of the European Commission's White Paper on GOVERNANCE in 2001, which considered the advantages of alternatives to traditional regulation. The White Paper was clear in its preference for a more restricted understanding of coregulation, stressing that it was appropriate only where legislative objectives already existed and where fundamental rights or major political choices are not involved. Issues involving RISK may be seen as particularly appropriate to a coregulatory approach. [JP]

Further reading: European Commission, *European Governance: A White Paper*, COM (2001) 428 final.

coroner An officer of the CROWN with judicial and ministerial duties, responsible for investigating deaths that are reported to him or her as possibly occurring in unnatural or violent circumstances. Investigations can occur through a post-mortem examination of the body or INQUEST. If initial or post-mortem investigations reveal a natural cause of death, the death will be duly registered with the Registrar of Births and Deaths. If the death is found to be not due to a natural cause, or if it occurred in certain other circumstances (for example, in prison custody), the coroner will hold an inquest. Coroners are appointed from BARRISTERS, SOLICITORS and qualified medical practitioners with at least five years' standing (Coroners Act 1988, s. 2(1), as amended). [AF]

corporal punishment Physical punishment such as beating. Corporal punishment is not permitted in schools (Education Act 1996, s. 548). [FK]

See also CHASTISEMENT.

corporate governance *See* GOVERNANCE.

corporation An entity, often but not exclusively created for the purposes of industry or commerce, having an independent legal personality from its members (i.e., owners) and employees. Most corporations are **corporations aggregate**, possessing a number of members, but some artificial legal persons, such as the CROWN, comprise a single member and are defined as **corporations sole**. [JW]

See also COMPANY.

corporation tax A charge on the income and capital profits accruing to a company resident in the UK from its worldwide business ventures, and on any non-business benefits accruing to it, but excluding distributions received from other UK resident companies. Assessment of a corporate taxpayer's income profits is on the basis of income tax principles for the FISCAL YEAR in which a company's accounting period ends. Assessment of a corporate taxpayer's capital gains is on the basis of capital gains tax principles for the financial year in which gains are made.

CAPITAL ALLOWANCES are deductible for corporation tax purposes, and income losses from the trade can be set off in the year that they are incurred against profits from other sources, but if that claim is not made, then against profits in the trade in future years. Charges on profits are allowed against the profits of the year in which they are incurred. The totals of income profits and capital gains profits for an accounting period are added together and, subject to the provisions of the corporation tax legislation, the combined total is taxed at standard or small companies rates of tax for the appropriate financial year or years.

Where a company has foreign income or capital gains (or both), there may be DOUBLE TAXATION of those profits. Where there is a double taxation agreement between the UK and the state in which the profits were made, there may be DOUBLE TAXATION RELIEF available. This will usually take the form of a credit of foreign tax against UK tax. Where there is no double taxation agreement, there may be unilateral relief of an amount calculated by reference to the foreign tax paid.

Where a company resident in the UK has a subsidiary in a foreign STATE or country, the profits of that subsidiary do not form part of the worldwide profits of the UK resident company and, in consequence, are not brought into charge to corporation tax. If dividends are paid by the foreign subsidiary, those dividends are brought into charge to corporation tax, but there will usually be a withholding tax credit to set off against UK tax, either under a double taxation agreement or under UK unilateral tax relief provisions. Where a company does not receive dividends from its foreign subsidiary, the UK resident company might still be charged to corporation tax by reference to the profits of the overseas subsidiary under the controlled foreign companies (CFC) provisions of the Income and Corporation Taxes Act 1988 where there has not been an acceptable distribution policy in the circumstances of the particular foreign subsidiary.

UK resident companies are responsible for self-assessment of their tax liability for each accounting period. When submitting its TAX RETURN, a company must draw to the attention of HM REVENUE AND CUSTOMS (the Revenue) any CFC, and some other tax avoidance issues. [RE]

corporeal hereditaments Physical objects of property forming part of an ESTATE which, historically, could be inherited. Examples include LAND itself, and the buildings and trees attached to land. [DR]

See also HEREDITAMENTS; INCORPOREAL HEREDITAMENTS.

corpus juris civilis (Lat. the body of civil law) The modern name for the collection of Roman law sources compiled chiefly from 529 to 534 CE by order of Emperor Justinian I. Although of limited application in the disintegrating Roman Empire of its time, its rediscovery in the late 11th century, and gradual reception across Europe, made it a highly influential source of Western law. The four parts of Justinian's code are:

(a) The *Institutes*, which set out the basic elements of Roman jurisprudence. It is thought to have been written later than the *Codex*, primarily as the student textbook of its day. Its relative brevity and systematic treatment of laws under three categories – those relating to persons, things and obligations – made it highly influential as both a substantive source and conceptual structure for later codifications.

(b) The *Digest* or *Pandects* contained various rules derived from various legal sources and opinions mostly dating back to the second and third centuries CE. These became an important source of law and authority in the Middle Ages.

(c) The *Codex Justinianis*, the earliest part of the code to be completed, brought together a number of earlier imperial codes, from the time of the Emperor Hadrian (ruled 117–138 CE) up to and including laws promulgated by Justinian himself. Much of the *Codex* was concerned to secure the status of Christianity as the official religion of the empire, and link citizenship rights to profession of the Christian religion.

(d) The *Novels* (*Novellae Constitutiones*) were the last part to be added to the *corpus juris*, comprising about 168 'books' of laws that were introduced after 534 CE, and were placed into one volume by a later compiler. [JW]

corroboration 'Independent testimony which affects the accused by connecting or tending to connect him with the crime. In other words, it must be EVIDENCE which implicates him, that is, which confirms in some material particular not only the evidence that the crime has been committed, but also that the prisoner committed it': *R v. Baskerville* [1916] 2 KB 658, 667. There now remain only a few situations in which corroboration of prosecution evidence is a requirement for conviction: for example (a) a person may not be convicted of an offence of SPEEDING on the uncorroborated opinion of a WITNESS that the person prosecuted was driving the vehicle at a speed exceeding the limit: see Road Traffic Regulation Act 1984, s. 89(2); (b) a person charged with an offence of PERJURY may not be convicted on the uncorroborated evidence of a witness 'as to the falsity of any statement alleged to be false': see Perjury Act 1911, s. 13. [ALTC]

corrupt practices *See* ELECTION OFFENCES.

corruption Behaviour involving the abuse of power for gain, and linked principally to financial impropriety. Corruption offences are set out in the Prevention of Corruption Acts 1889 to 1916. See also the Anti-Terrorism, Crime and Security Act 2001, Part 12. [BF]

See also BRIBERY.

corruption of public morals It is not clear whether corruption of public morals is, of itself, an offence. However, CONSPIRACY to corrupt public morals is a (controversial and seldom prosecuted) offence at COMMON LAW (see *Shaw* v. *DPP* [1962] AC 220; *Knuller (Publishing, Printing and Promotions) Ltd* v. *DPP* [1973] AC 435; cases involving, respectively, the publication of a directory of prostitutes, and the publication of homosexual contact advertisements). Corrupting public morals is a forceful term, denoting conduct which, according to Lord Simon, 'a jury might find to be destructive of the very fabric of society' (see *Knuller* (above), at pp. 490–91). [BF]

cost of cure DAMAGES for BREACH OF CONTRACT are compensatory and COMPENSATION for loss of the contractual expectation is generally awarded in the form of damages represent-ing the difference in value between what was promised and what was received. However, such damages may fail to fully compensate when the term broken was a promise to construct a building or similar, particularly where the aim of the performance was to fulfil a subjective preference. In such circumstances there may be little difference in value between the property with the construction and without it and the claimant's purpose in contracting will not be fulfilled unless the failure or defect is remedied by cure or reinstatement. Therefore, in some circumstances it may be possible to recover the cost of cure (or repair) instead of the difference in value in order to ensure that the claimant's contractual expectation is fulfilled.

Cost of cure damages will be awarded only where such damages are reasonable, i.e. the cost of cure must not be out of all proportion to the benefit to be obtained and the rebuilding must either have been completed or an undertaking must be given to use the damages for this purpose (*Ruxley Electronics & Construction Ltd* v. *Forsyth* [1996] 1 AC 344). [JPL]

costs In civil litigation the court has powers to make a wide range of orders in respect of the costs of litigation. Nevertheless, the general underlying principle is that the winner can normally expect to recover costs from the loser (this used to be known as the principle of 'costs following the event'). This principle may not apply where the claimant's DAMAGES fail to exceed an amount previously offered or paid into court by the defendant.

In all cases costs must be **assessed** (see Part 47 of the CIVIL PROCEDURE RULES). This replaces the process of what used to be called 'taxation of costs'. Assessment may be on a **standard basis** or **indemnity basis**. Where costs are awarded on an indemnity basis, the winner will recover all costs incurred except those that are unreasonably incurred (e.g. if the judge determines that the winner's conduct in some way exacerbated the dispute by an unreasonable refusal to mediate or otherwise settle the action), or of an excessive amount (CPR

Part 44). Most costs, however, are awarded on the **standard basis**, i.e., payment of a reasonable amount in respect of costs reasonably incurred.

Judges will normally seek to assess costs on a **summary assessment** at the conclusion of the trial, though in more complex cases, or where the costs are substantially disputed, there may be a **detailed assessment** at a later stage by a **costs officer** (a costs judge of the Supreme Court, a district judge, or other authorized court officer).

[JW]

See also PART 36 OFFER.

council housing Residential rented housing provided under a general statutory duty by LOCAL AUTHORITIES. The roots of council housing lie in the 19th century when the problems of insanitary and overcrowded working-class housing stimulated both statutory and voluntary responses. For a variety of reasons, including the predominance of laissez-faire economic rationalities and a reluctance to accept state responsibility for the provision of services, direct provision of housing was limited to relatively small-scale projects initiated by 'model dwelling' companies, the forerunners of the HOUSING ASSOCIATION movement. Council housing only became possible on any significant scale following the creation of the London County Council in 1888 and its subsequent lobbying for the Housing of the Working-Classes Act 1890. This enabled local authorities to borrow money to buy land and build working-class housing. The First World War and the rhetoric of 'homes fit for heroes' gave a new and nationwide impetus to municipal housing because of the failure of private enterprise to respond to the housing crisis after the war.

A series of Housing Acts during the interwar years enhanced the role of municipal housing: for instance, the Housing Act of 1919 required local authorities to assess the requirements for working-class housing and submit schemes for meeting those needs, and the Housing Act 1930 imposed duties on local authorities to clear slums and prevent the deterioration of other areas, as well as dealing with individual unfit properties and rehousing displaced persons. By 1938 the London County Council had provided 60,800 cottages and 25,900 flats. However it was during the period following the Second World War that the provision of council housing became part of the comprehensive programme of social reform crafted by Beveridge's report, *Social Insurance and Allied Services* (1942). In 1945, 1.3 million properties were rented from local authorities; by 1975 that figure was 5.2 million.

The image of council housing became tarnished for a variety of reasons. Local government bureaucracy treated its tenants as second class. Not only did council tenants have no legal rights prior to the Housing Act 1980, the tenancy agreements they signed contained patronizing and punitive clauses. Housing provision by local authorities was often severely constrained by available resources and was therefore of poor quality. Tower blocks in particular were disliked by tenants. In many cases estates were considered to be as squalid as the slums they had replaced. This was demonstrated not only in the Ronan Point disaster of 1968, when a gas explosion led to the collapse of one corner of a tower block and the deaths of three people, but in the multiplicity of tenants' actions in connection with disrepair and squalor in their homes. The growing attractiveness and availability of owner occupation, the introduction of a right to buy, and, under the Housing Act 1988, the possibility for tenants to request the transfer of council housing to the private rented sector have all been part of the decline of council housing.

[HC & DR]

Further reading: D. Cowan and M. McDermont, *Regulating Social Housing: Governing Decline* (London: Routledge-Cavendish, 2006).

Council of Europe A European inter-governmental organization that was set up in 1949 and which is wholly distinct from the EUROPEAN COMMUNITY. It was set up as a peaceful association of democratic states which proclaimed their faith in the RULE OF LAW, democracy and HUMAN RIGHTS. These elements constitute criteria for membership. The most significant achievement of the Council of Europe has been the establishment of the EUROPEAN COURT OF HUMAN RIGHTS. The Council has also been active in promoting more than 200 TREATIES in different fields, from extradition to biotechnology – some with more success than others. It has also been engaged since the end of the Cold War in establishing democratization and rule of law mechanisms in new democracies. [IB]

Council of Ministers A law-making body, passing laws pursuant to Article 249 EC. Composed of government ministers from the various MEMBER STATES of the EUROPEAN UNION (EU), it is the most powerful of the EUROPEAN COMMUNITY (EC) institutions. It is also known as the **Council of the European Union**, or 'the Council'. It is subject to the guidance of, but should not be confused with, the EUROPEAN COUNCIL, which is an EU institution. It should also not be confused with the COUNCIL OF EUROPE, which is the human rights organization based in Strasbourg. The Council of Ministers is supported in its work by the EUROPEAN COMMISSION. The Council also operates within Pillars II and III of the EU, in a support capacity to the European Council. The institutions in Pillars II and III are, with the exception of the European Council, EC institutions which are also utilized by the EU. The EC institutions, when utilized, operate in different ways in the three different pillars of the EU. (Note that the TREATY OF LISBON will abolish the Pillar structure and unite institutions under the European Union.) The presidency of the Council of Ministers alternates from one country to another every six months. [MON]

See also EUROPEAN COMMUNITY TREATY; TREATY ON EUROPEAN UNION.

Council on Tribunals (obsolete) An advisory non-departmental public body sponsored by the Ministry of Justice. Its function was to keep under review and report on the structure and work of tribunals under its supervision and to consider and report on the administrative proced-ures of statutory INQUIRIES. The Council on Tribunals was established in 1958 following the recommendations of the Franks Report on Administrative Tribunals and Enquiries. It was abolished in November 2007 by s. 45 of the Tribunals, Courts and Enforcement Act 2007 and replaced by the ADMINISTRATIVE JUSTICE AND TRIBUNALS COUNCIL.

[JW]

council tax A charge on domestic premises or 'dwellings' situated in the area of a billing authority (i.e. a LOCAL AUTHORITY). Council tax was introduced, with effect from 1 April 1993, by the Local Government Finance Act 1992, as a replacement for the COMMUNITY CHARGE. The tax is payable by liable persons (usually, but not always, owner-occupiers) to the authority in respect of all dwellings which are not exempt. Dwellings are allocated to one of eight value bands, A to H. The difference between the bands is based on the following progressive proportional values: 6: 7: 8: 9: 11: 13: 15: 18, where band A equates to 6, and band H equates to 18 (see s. 5 of the 1992 Act). The bands are based on values as at 1 April 1991. Band A applies to dwellings up to £40,000 in value as at that date. Band H applies to dwellings over £320,000 in value as at that date. Bands B to G are for dwellings ranging in value between £40,000 and £320,000. See http://www.direct.gov.uk/MoneyTaxAndBenefits/CouncilTax/. [RE]

councillor An elected local government representative. Councillors are elected to represent an individual geographical area on the council, normally called a ward or division. To stand for election to a council a person must be over 18 years of age, on the electoral register for the council area, or have worked in that area for the preceding 12 months. Persons who are BANKRUPT, or have served a prison sentence of three months or longer in the last five years cannot stand for election. A council employee is also ineligible to be elected to the council that employs him or her. [JW]

See also LOCAL AUTHORITY.

counsel *See* BARRISTER.

Counsellors of State Persons appointed under the Regency Acts 1937–53 to undertake the duties of the sovereign while she or he is temporarily abroad or incapacitated by short-term illness or injury. The Counsellors of State are the husband or wife of the sovereign and the next four members of the royal family in line to the throne. [MS]

count A paragraph in the INDICTMENT, describing the charge against the defendant. [SN]

counterclaim A claim brought by a defendant in civil proceedings, in response to the claimant's claim. It will normally be issued by the defendant at the same time as any defence. A counterclaim is not the same as a defence, since it asserts an independent action against the claimant, rather than simply rebutting the claimant's own claim. It is thus possible in one action for both claim and counterclaim to succeed, either wholly or in part. [JW]

counterfeiting Under the Forgery and Counterfeiting 1981 Act, s. 14, it is an offence for a person to make a counterfeit of a currency note or of a protected coin, intending that he or another shall pass or tender it as genuine; or to make a counterfeit of a currency note or of a protected coin without lawful authority or excuse. [BF]

countermeasures See SANCTIONS.

country A term used for the purposes of referring to a territory which has its own, distinctive legal system, irrespective of whether the territory concerned is the whole or only a part of a sovereign STATE recognized in INTERNATIONAL LAW. The term 'country' is particularly important in the CONFLICT OF LAWS; for example, the sovereign state of the United Kingdom comprises three separate legal systems, namely England and Wales, Scotland and Northern Ireland: each is a country for the purposes of the conflict of laws. Other examples of countries in this sense are Jersey, Hong Kong, Louisiana, New South Wales and Quebec. However, larger units can also be treated as countries: for example, the United States has also been recognized as

a country for conflict of laws purposes (see *Adams* v. *Cape Industries plc* [1990] Ch 433). [RE]

county council A 'first tier' local government unit in England. [JW]
    See also LOCAL AUTHORITY.

county A geographical region in the UK and 'first tier' local government unit in England. The origins of the county and shire systems in the UK pre-date the arrival of the Normans. Various political and social changes including expansion of the franchise, increased urbanization and shifts in population density in the 19th and 20th centuries led to a number of administrative reorganizations in 1844 and (across the whole of the UK) in 1889, followed by a further major restructuring in 1974. The Local Government Act 1972 divided England into six metropolitan and 39 non-metropolitan counties and Wales into eight counties (the historic 13 counties of Wales had been defined by statute in 1539). The 34 Scottish county councils were also abolished by the Local Government (Scotland) Act 1973, and replaced by a system of regions, districts and island council areas. The English metropolitan counties were never entirely popular and were themselves abolished in 1985 and replaced mostly by DISTRICT COUNCILS. A number of new UNITARY AUTHORITIES subsequently replaced some county councils in 1992. In Wales and Scotland new unitary authorities were introduced across both nations in 1996. [JW]
    See also BOUNDARY COMMISSIONS; LOCAL AUTHORITY.

county court In the English legal system, the court that deals with all civil matters that, under the CIVIL PROCEDURE RULES, do not commence in the HIGH COURT, including claims for debt repayment, personal injury, BREACH OF CONTRACT concerning goods or property, family issues such as DIVORCE or ADOPTION, housing disputes, PROBATE, BANKRUPTCY and INSOLVENCY. Established originally by the County Courts Act 1846, now the County Courts Act 1984 (as amended), there are approximately 218 county courts throughout England and Wales, served by

CIRCUIT JUDGES and DISTRICT JUDGES. In addition, the county court has exclusive jurisdiction over small claims. The limit on small claims actions is £5,000, with personal injury claims carrying a £1,000 limit. With respect to remedies, the county court cannot grant search orders or FREEZING ORDERS.   [AF]

court appointed assessor A person with specialist technical knowledge appointed to assist the court in making a decision. The COURT OF APPEAL and HIGH COURT have wide powers to appoint assessors in civil proceedings. An assessor is not the same as an expert witness, since the former's function is purely to advise the judge(s) and an assessor may not be examined or cross-examined by the parties.   [JW]

Court for Crown Cases Reserved (obsolete) The predecessor to the COURT OF CRIMINAL APPEAL.   [ALTC]

Court of Admiralty The original Court of Admiralty dated back to at least the mid 14th century as the Court of the Lord High Admiral of England. As such, it derived its authority from the general jurisdiction of the ROYAL COUNCIL. It heard cases arising out of naval warfare and, increasingly, mercantile cases involving sea trade. It was also distinctive as a court using largely CIVIL LAW rather than COMMON LAW. As part of the reforms introduced by the Judicature Acts 1873–5, it became part of the Probate, Divorce and Admiralty Division of the HIGH COURT where it remained until 1971. Today it forms part of the QUEEN'S BENCH DIVISION of the High Court. It has jurisdiction over a wide range of civil matters relating to shipping, including actions concerning collisions at sea, loss of or damage to cargo and salvage. All admiralty cases are allocated to the **multi-track** under the CIVIL PROCEDURES RULES. A separate Admiralty Court also evolved in Scotland and by the 17th century was the principle mercantile court in that country. Its jurisdiction was ultimately absorbed into the modern COURT OF SESSION.   [JW]
    See also ALLOCATION.

Court of Appeal Established by the Judicature Act 1873, the Court of Appeal forms part of the SENIOR COURTS OF ENGLAND AND WALES (previously the Supreme Court of Judicature prior to the Constitutional Reform Act 2005). The Court of Appeal exercises appellate jurisdiction over all judgments and orders of the HIGH COURT and most judgments of the COUNTY COURTS.

The court is divided into two Divisions, Civil and Criminal. The **Civil Division** is presided over by the MASTER OF THE ROLLS and hears appeals on civil matters from the High Court, county courts and certain TRIBUNALS such as the EMPLOYMENT APPEAL TRIBUNAL and ASYLUM AND IMMIGRATION TRIBUNAL. The **Criminal Division** is presided over by the LORD CHIEF JUSTICE (LCG) and hears appeals from the CROWN COURT. This Division of the Court of Appeal was established in 1966, replacing the Court of Criminal Appeal.

The Court of Appeal is served by senior judges termed Lord Justices of Appeal. The PRESIDENT OF THE FAMILY DIVISION of the High Court, the Vice Chancellor of the CHANCERY DIVISION and High Court Judges can also sit. In both Divisions, single judges usually consider applications for LEAVE TO APPEAL and act as a 'filter' by carrying out certain specified functions of the full court. In the Civil Division, generally three judges will sit to hear an appeal, although as many as five may sit for important cases. In the interests of expediency, some civil matters may be heard by two judges. In cases of great urgency, the Court of Appeal is often de facto the final court of appeal (for example in *C* v. *S and Others* [1987] 2 FLR 505, concerning a putative father's right to prevent a prospective mother from having an abortion). In the Criminal Division, the court usually sits with three judges (either the LCJ or a Lord Justice of Appeal with two QUEEN'S BENCH DIVISION judges). Appeals against either sentence or conviction can only be made with the permission of the court.   [AF]
    See also HOUSE OF LORDS.

Court of Arbitration for Sport An INSTITUTIONAL ARBITRATION and mediation centre for sports-related disputes of all kinds which was originated by the International

Olympic Committee (IOC) in 1983 and – with the agreement of international and national sporting organizations and federations – was taken over and revised by the International Council of Arbitration for Sport (ICAS) in 1994. It provides ARBITRATION and mediation facilities in respect of financial disputes; and arbitration facilities (but not mediation facilities) in respect of disciplinary and similar disputes. It also provides facilities in respect of arbitration appeals from international sports organizations and from national sports federations. Subsidiary offices have been founded in Sydney and New York, and ad hoc provisions are made for large-scale sporting events, such as Olympic and Commonwealth Games, so that very fast-track arbitration awards (usually within 24 hours) can be issued during those events.

As the seat of arbitration of ICAS is in Lausanne, Switzerland, there is a limited right under the Swiss Federal Code on Private International Law to challenge ICAS awards in the courts of Switzerland. Subject to any such challenge, awards can be submitted to the Swiss courts for enforcement, and they can also be submitted to many foreign courts for recognition and enforcement pursuant to the New York Convention 1958.   [RE]

See also AD HOC ARBITRATION; AWARD.

Court of Auditors One of the supporting institutions of the EUROPEAN COMMUNITY (EC), provided for in Articles 246 to 248 EC Treaty. Its role is to carry out audits on accounts 'of all revenue and expenditure of all bodies set up by the Community' (Article 248 (1) EC). The Court of Auditors draws up a report at the end of each financial year, which is forwarded to the other institutions of the EC, and it publishes this report in the OFFICIAL JOURNAL of the EUROPEAN UNION.   [MON]

Court of Chancery The original court of EQUITY, historically presided over by the LORD CHANCELLOR. By the Judicature Acts 1873–5 its jurisdiction was merged with the HIGH COURT to create the CHANCERY DIVISION.   [AF]

Court of Common Pleas One of the com-

mon law courts established in England after the Norman Conquest. Under MAGNA CARTA it attained separate civil jurisdiction from the Court of **King's** (or **Queen's**) **Bench**. Between the 15th and 19th centuries, the jurisdictional distinctions between Common Pleas and the other common law courts (of King's Bench and Exchequer) became increasingly complex, and the Court of Common Pleas was finally abolished as part of the wide-ranging reforms to the court system introduced by the Judicature Acts 1873–75.

Although the term is now obsolete in English legal usage, Courts of Common Pleas still exist in the USA where, in some states, they are trial courts exercising civil and family jurisdiction.   [JW]

See also HIGH COURT.

Court of Criminal Appeal (obsolete) A court established by the Criminal Appeal Act 1907 which heard appeals from lower courts. It was abolished by the Criminal Appeal Act 1966 and replaced by the Criminal Division of the COURT OF APPEAL.   [SN]

Court of Exchequer (obsolete) A COMMON LAW court hearing matters relating to the CROWN itself and actions by private persons who had the right to sue in the Exchequer. The judges of the Court of Exchequer were known as barons, headed by the Lord Chief Baron of the Exchequer. By the Judicature Acts 1873–5 its jurisdiction was merged with the HIGH COURT to become the Exchequer Division. This Division was merged with the QUEEN'S BENCH DIVISION of the High Court in 1880.   [AF]

Court of First Instance (CFI) Created in 1989 with a view to reducing the workload of the EUROPEAN COURT OF JUSTICE (ECJ). Since then there has been an increasing delegation of responsibility from the ECJ to the CFI. The current main areas of operation of the CFI are direct actions brought by natural or legal persons against the EUROPEAN COMMUNITY institutions; actions brought by a MEMBER STATE against the EUROPEAN COMMISSION; cases brought by Member States against the COUNCIL OF MINISTERS in STATE AID and dumping cases; staff action against the EC institutions for compensaion for damage; cummunity TRADE MARK actions; and appeals on a point of law from the EUROPEAN CIVIL SERVICE TRIBUNAL. The CFI may sit in a CHAMBER formation, or as a fully court. [MON]

See also COURT OF JUSTICE OF THE EUROPEAN COMMUNITIES.

court of first instance There are two related meanings: **1**. any court in which proceedings commence; **2**. a trial court as opposed to an APPELLATE COURT. [AF]

Court of Justice of the European Communities The court structure of the EUROPEAN COMMUNITY (EC). It is comprised of three courts: the EUROPEAN COURT OF JUSTICE (ECJ), the COURT OF FIRST INSTANCE (CFI) and the EUROPEAN CIVIL SERVICE TRIBUNAL. The main tasks of these courts are to ensure the uniform interpretation and application of COMMUNITY LAW. The ECJ and the CFI are legislated for in the EUROPEAN COMMUNITY TREATY at Articles 220 to 245 EC, with the detail of their operation being set out in the Statute of the Court of Justice 2001. The rulings of the Court of Justice of the European Communities are legally binding on all of the EC, and form part of the *ACQUIS COMMUNAUTAIRE*, with the case law of the courts being referred to as *ACQUIS JURISPRUDENTIAL*. The Court of Justice of the European Communities is physically located in Luxembourg. The Court of Justice, through the ECJ, also has a (more limited) role in Pillar III of the EUROPEAN UNION (EU), Police and Judicial Cooperation in Criminal Matters (PJCCM), but has no role in Pillar II, the Common Foreign and Security Policy (CFSP). [MON]

Court of King's Bench (or Queen's Bench during the reign of a female monarch) This was the most senior of the ancient COMMON LAW courts of England, and originated with the jurisdiction '*coram ipso rege*' – cases that were heard before the king himself, though by the early 13th century the jurisdiction had been largely delegated to a senior judge, the LORD CHIEF JUSTICE, and a group of lesser (**puisne**) judges. The King's Bench was the principal court of

criminal jurisdiction, though in practice most of this caseload was heard locally at ASSIZES rather than at the King's Bench in Westminster Hall, The court of Westminster, by contrast, took responsibility for issuing the PREROGATIVE WRITS, and the writ of HABEAS CORPUS, and for a range of civil matters. Although the King's Bench initially had only a limited number of causes of action in TORT, by the 18th century, its jurisdiction, which it had managed to acquire at the expense of the COURT OF COMMON PLEAS, extended to most civil matters not involving real property. The Court of Queen's Bench was abolished in 1875 by the Supreme Court of Judicature Act 1873, and its jurisdiction transferred to the new High Court and specifically to the QUEEN'S BENCH DIVISION of that court. [AF]

court of record A court whose judicial proceedings, acts and decisions are retained on permanent record and which has the power to punish for CONTEMPT OF COURT. The HOUSE OF LORDS, COURT OF APPEAL, HIGH COURT and CROWN COURT are superior courts of record. The COUNTY COURT is an inferior court of record. [AF]

Court of Session The highest civil court located in Scotland, it has its origins in the informal King's Council dating back to the 15th century. This Council, among other things, advised the king on petitions addressed to him by his subjects. As the number of such petitions increased, some of the Council's members began to specialize in dealing with them, becoming de facto judges.

A court distinct from the King's Council, the College of Justice was established in 1532. It was staffed by 15 judges, led by the Lord President, who were collectively known as the Lords of Council and Session. This became the most important civil court and was the direct forerunner of the modern Court of Session. Originally, individual judges were deputed to hear evidence in the Outer House of the Court. The entire Court in the Inner House would then make decisions. By the 19th century some judges were sitting permanently in the Outer House and were able to decide cases there. In due course the Inner House became a court of appeal for cases decided in the Outer House.

The Court today is located in Parliament House in Edinburgh and currently has 34 permanent judges, still known formally as Senators of the College of Justice. There are also many temporary judges (drawn from the Scottish Bar and from among the ranks of SHERIFFS) as and when required by weight of business. The Inner House is divided into two equal divisions. The first has four judges and is presided over by the Lord President. The second has five judges and is presided over by the Lord Justice-Clerk. Extra divisions may also be created when required. The Outer House now has 25 judges, each sitting alone or in rare cases with a civil jury.

A particular feature of the Court of Session is its adaptability to the needs of modern society while maintaining tradition. Thus, while the judges still wear robes and wigs, recent times have seen the introduction of special arrangements to deal efficiently with commercial actions. These involve three specialist judges and more flexible procedures, including informal preliminary stages and a less rigid approach to pleading. Ongoing consultation with the business community seeks to ensure that these arrangements operate effectively.

While the Court of Session is the highest civil court located in Scotland, appeals from the Inner House currently lie to the HOUSE OF LORDS in London and will in future lie to the SUPREME COURT.   [JP]

court of summary jurisdiction (obsolete) Now known as the magistrates' court. [SN]

covenant A promise made by one person for the benefit of another, contained in a deed. The person making the promise is the **covenantor** and takes the burden under the covenant. The person to whom the promise is made is the **covenantee** and takes the benefit under the covenant.

In LEASES, covenants are commonly used to regulate the way in which the tenant may use the premises (e.g. a covenant not to assign or sublet the premises without the written consent of the landlord). On the sale of part of FREEHOLD land, the seller often requires the purchaser to enter into covenants for the benefit of the land being retained by the seller (e.g. a covenant to maintain a shared driveway).   [DR]

See also RESTRICTIVE COVENANT; USUAL COVENANTS.

coverture At common law, on MARRIAGE, the husband and wife became one in law. This doctrine of unity of spouses has been described most famously by Blackstone: 'the very being or legal existence of the woman is suspended during the marriage, or at least is incorporated and consolidated into that of the husband; under whose wing, protection and cover she performs every thing … and her condition during her marriage is called her coverture' (see *Commentaries on the Laws of England*, 4th edn (1770). The wife's coverture meant that she lost all legal personality. The doctrine of unity of spouses began to be dismantled in the 19th century by the Courts of Equity and later by statutory intervention regarding married women's property; however, it was not until the 20th century that the last legacies of the doctrine were removed from law.   [AD]

See also FEME COVERT; FEME SOLE.

CPR *See* CIVIL PROCEDURE RULES.

CPS *See* CROWN PROSECUTION SERVICE.

CPS Direct An out-of-hours telephone service provided by the DUTY PROSECUTOR for the purpose of providing charging decisions.
[SN]

'cracked' trial On the date set down for trial, the defendant offers acceptable PLEAS or the prosecution offers no evidence. [SN]

Creative Commons Creative Commons (CC) is a not-for-profit US-based organization, which operates a licensing platform which encourages the free use of creative works while preserving some rights of the creator, especially the MORAL RIGHT of attribution and the right of the author to receive remuneration for commercial usage of the work. Authors, by choosing the type of CC licence they wish to attach to their work, can offer and distribute their works without an intermediary for non-commercial use. All but one of the CC licences build upon the 'all rights reserved' concept of traditional COPYRIGHT, and instead offer a voluntary 'some rights reserved' approach. If a choice of reserved rights is made, the author has the option of tagging his work with the chosen form of CC licence: see http://creativecommons. org/. [US]

crime against peace *See* AGGRESSION.

crime prevention The taking of measures which seek to prevent the commission of crimes, or to reduce the adverse effects of criminal behaviour. Some crime prevention measures are **situational**, involving techniques which reduce the opportunity for potential offenders to commit crimes, for example, by way of the deployment of closed-circuit television (CCTV) surveillance, or other target-hardening measures such as more effective locks on property. Other crime prevention measures are **social**, in that they seek to address the motivations of potential offenders and to direct them away from offending behaviour. [BF]

crimes against humanity First formulated as an international offence in Article 6(c) of the 1945 Nuremberg Statute (see INTERNATIONAL MILITARY TRIBUNAL), the definition of the offence has since been significantly refined, particularly through CUSTOMARY LAW and following the Statutes of the ad hoc INTERNATIONAL CRIMINAL TRIBUNAL FOR YUGOSLAVIA (ICTY, Article 5) and INTERNATIONAL CRIMINAL TRIBUNAL FOR RWANDA (ICTR, Article 3).

The following elements are considered to have attained a customary status: (a) the existence of an overall **attack**, typically composed of other offences, such as rapes, killings, etc.; (b) an attack which has been directed against any civilian population; (c) the attack itself must be either widespread or systematic. Whereas the 'widespread' element refers to a multiplicity of crimes or victims, the 'systematic' element concerns proof of policy. A pros-

ecutor must prove either one of the two, not both, elements; (d) the appropriate *mens rea* for the crime should encompass knowledge of the overall attack and an intent to participate either at the policy level or in the perpetration of the various offences.

Slight differences exist, however, among the existing international tribunals. Under the ICTY Statute, a nexus is required between the crime and an armed conflict – whether domestic or international – whereas in the ICTR Statute the overall attack must encompass an act of **persecution** on the basis of national, political, ethnic, racial or religious grounds. Article 7 of the INTERNATIONAL CRIMINAL COURT Statute, while following the customary law definition, requires that the particular crimes that make up the overall attack be perpetrated on a widespread or systematic scale in order for the Court to exercise jurisdiction. [IB]

criminal case management framework A guide for practitioners providing information on how cases might be managed most effectively and efficiently from pre-charge through to conclusion. It describes CASE MANAGEMENT procedures and the roles and responsibilities of administrative staff operating those procedures. It also sets out the expectations of the judiciary. It was first introduced in April 2004 and is aligned to the CRIMINAL PROCEDURE RULES on case management that were introduced on 4 April 2005. [SN]

Criminal Cases Review Commission The independent public body responsible for investigating alleged miscarriages of justice in England, Wales and Northern Ireland. On an application, the Commission will consider whether there is fresh evidence or argument that may cast doubt on the safety of an original conviction. If it determines that there is, it can refer the case back to the appropriate appeal court for re-consideration, see http://www.ccrc.gov.uk/index.htm. Cases in Scotland are referred to the separate Scottish Criminal Cases Review Commission, see http://www.sccrc.org.uk/home.aspx. [SN]

criminal conviction certificate A certificate issued under the Police Act 1997 that provides details of the applicant's criminal CONVICTIONS or a statement that the applicant has no convictions recorded. [SN]

criminal damage Criminal damage is an offence under the Criminal Damage Act 1971, s. 1(1). It is committed where a person intentionally or recklessly, and without lawful excuse, destroys or damages any property belonging to another.

Aggravated criminal damage is an offence under s. 1(2) of the Act. This is committed where a person intentionally or recklessly destroys or damages any property, belonging to himself or another, intending thereby to endanger the life of another or being reckless as to whether the life of another would thereby be endangered.

Until the decision of the House of Lords in *R* v. *G* [2003] UKHL 50, the meaning of RECKLESSNESS in criminal damage was governed by the definition in *R* v. *Caldwell* [1982] AC 341. According to Lord Bingham in *R* v. *G*: 'A person acts recklessly within the meaning of section 1 of the Criminal Damage Act 1971 with respect to (i) a circumstance when he is aware of a risk that it exists or will exist; (ii) a result when he is aware of a risk that it will occur; and it is, in the circumstances known to him, unreasonable to take the risk.' [BF]

See also ARSON.

Criminal Defence Service That part of the LEGAL SERVICES COMMISSION (LSC) that provides legal advice and representation for people who are under police investigation or have been charged with a criminal offence. Services funded by the Criminal Defence Service include the duty solicitor scheme, which provides 24-hour access to legal advice to persons held in police custody, and the **Public Defender Service**, which provides, in some areas of England and Wales, access to legal advice and assistance from LSC-employed solicitors. [JW]

See also LEGAL AID.

Criminal Injuries Compensation Authority A government agency with the power to award damages to people who have been victims of violent crimes or those injured trying to apprehend criminals or prevent a crime. [SN]

See also COMPENSATION.

Criminal Injuries Compensation Scheme The Criminal Injuries Compensation Scheme is administered by the CRIMINAL INJURIES COMPENSATION AUTHORITY. The scheme exists to compensate innocent victims of violent crime, through the distribution of public money. Certain secondary victims, that is to say those in certain relationships to a victim of violent crime who has since died, may also be eligible for compensation. Historically, the level of compensation for which an applicant was eligible was determined by reference to the amount which would have been recovered in a notional civil action against the offender. Now, the amount of compensation is determined by reference to a statutory tariff. [BF]

criminal libel At common law, there were four types of criminal libel. One was BLASPHEMY, the others carried the labels defamatory, seditious and obscene. They all persist in some form.

Defamatory libel differs in some respects from the TORT of DEFAMATION. The level of alleged defamation required to merit the intervention of the criminal law must be serious. The defences based on PRIVILEGE are available in crime as well as in tort, but while truth is a complete defence in tort it may not be so in crime, where it must also be in the PUBLIC INTEREST for the libel to be published. In crime, it is sufficient to publish to the person defamed, while in tort a third party recipient is required. **Seditious libel** refers to the publication of material which, in the words of Sir James Fitzjames Stephen (see L.F. Sturge, *A Digest of the Criminal Law*, 9th edn (London: Sweet and Maxwell, 1950), at Article 114), is accompanied by, for example, 'an intention to bring into hatred or contempt, or to excite disaffection against' the sovereign or the institutions of government. What was known as **obscene libel** is now regulated, principally, by the Obscene Publications Acts. [BF]

See also OBSCENE PUBLICATIONS; TREASON.

criminal organization In INTERNATIONAL LAW this concept derives from Article 2(a) of the 2000 UN Convention against Transnational Organized Crime (CATOC). An **organized criminal group** is defined as 'a structured group of three or more persons, existing for a period of time and acting with the aim of committing one or more serious crimes or offences established in accordance with the Convention [i.e. participation in an organized criminal group, corruption, money-laundering, obstruction of justice], in order to obtain, directly or indirectly, a financial or other material benefit.'

Besides CATOC, international law recognizes the closely related concepts of **conspiracy** and **joint criminal enterprise** (JCE) as particular forms of individual criminal responsibility. The former, in accordance with Article 25(3)(d) of the INTERNATIONAL CRIMINAL COURT Statute, consists in contributing to the commission or attempted commission of a crime by a group of persons acting with a common purpose with the aim of either furthering the criminal activity or purpose of the group, or in the knowledge of the intention of the group to commit the crime. JCE was developed in the INTERNATIONAL CRIMINAL TRIBUNAL FOR YUGOSLAVIA, and consists of a plurality of persons, the existence of a common plan, design or purpose which amounts to or involves the commission of a crime and participation of the accused in the common design. [IB]

Criminal Procedure Rules The rules which provide the court with powers to actively manage the preparation of criminal cases waiting to be heard; to get rid of unfair and avoidable delays; and to promote certainty about what is happening for the benefit of everyone involved. The objective of these rules is that everyone involved in a criminal case must deal with the case justly. See http://www.justice.gov.uk/criminal/procrules_fin/index.htm. [SN]

See also OVERRIDING OBJECTIVE.

criminal record A record of CONVICTIONS held on the Police National Computer for individuals convicted of crimes. [SN]

criminal record certificate A certificate issued under the Police Act 1997 providing details of relevant matters recorded in central records which relate to the applicant. The application for a certificate should be accompanied by a statement that it is required for the purposes of an exempted question, which is a question relating to the Rehabilitation of Offenders Act 1974. [SN]

See also SPENT CONVICTIONS.

Criminal Records Bureau An agency of the HOME OFFICE set up to allow registered organizations such as schools access to criminal record information to assist them in making recruitment decisions. See http://www.crb.gov.uk. [SN]

Critical Legal Studies A movement that emerged in American legal thinking in the 1970s which shares the scepticism of AMERICAN REALISM and the view of law as an instrument of power held by MARXIST JURISPRUDENCE.

For the adherents of Critical Legal Studies (known as **Crits**) law is not a science or a rational means for reaching substantive outcomes in the case of disputes, but rather a mechanism for providing rationalizations of outcomes determined by existing power structures, whether these are economic, sexual, racial and so on.

While American Realism seeks a better understanding of what is actually happening in judicial decision-making as a means to improving the operation of law, CLS denies that this is possible as there is nothing distinctive about law at all. For the Crits, law is simply the exercise of power, hence the common shorthand definition of the movement's key message: law is politics. Nor is this observation confined to a few areas of law: adherents of CLS claim to have revealed law's role in the oppressive nature of society across the board.

Insofar as CLS denies that there is anything particular about law and legal reasoning, it draws inspiration from the full range of social science and humanities. Where defenders of CLS see its profound scepticism as an opportunity to connect law with broader political and moral argument, its opponents see it as lacking in anything constructive to say once the political dimension of law has been exposed. Others go so far as to suggest that teaching law students about CLS is dangerous as it seems to risk sending the message that winning cases is about the exercise of power rather than the exercise of legal reason according to ethical rules.

During the 1970s and 1980s CLS was at the cutting edge, but its mantle of the most radical movement in legal theory has now been taken over by POSTMODERN JURISPRUDENCE. [JP]

Further reading: David Kairys (ed.), *The Politics of Law: A Progressive Critique* (New York: Pantheon Books, 1982).

cross-appeal This occurs in civil proceedings, when the RESPONDENT to an APPEAL also decides to challenge some aspect of the decision of the lower court; for example, in a personal injury action, the appellant may appeal against the lower court's finding of liability. The respondent could not only contest the appeal, but could cross-appeal by claiming that the trial court erred in its assessment of the quantum or amount of damages. A respondent must obtain permission to cross-appeal from the appropriate appeal court, and, under CPR 52.5, this process is commenced by filing a respondent's notice of appeal. [JW]

cross-border services Commercial or professional services provided by a self-employed person or business entity across national borders. Where such activity is conducted within the EC internal or single market, it will be covered by the EUROPEAN COMMUNITY (EC) principle of **free movement of services**. Free movement of services is, along with FREE MOVEMENT OF GOODS, PERSONS and capital, one of the 'four freedoms' of the EC. The 'four freedoms' are core policy areas of the EC, which form the basis of the internal market. The principle of free movement of services is enshrined in Articles 49 to 55 EC, and has been elaborated on by a great deal of case law at the EUROPEAN COURT OF JUSTICE (ECJ). [MON]
See also RIGHT OF ESTABLISHMENT.

cross-examination The process of questioning a WITNESS called by another party. The purpose of cross-examination is twofold: first, to elicit EVIDENCE supporting the cross-examining party's version of the facts, and secondly, to discredit the evidence of the witness. [ALTC]

Crown The office of sovereign, which exists independently of the individual person who is monarch for the time being. The Crown has its own distinct LEGAL PERSON as a CORPORATION sole. Succession to the Crown is hereditary and governed by the Act of Settlement 1701, as amended, which secured the succession to legitimate descendants of Sophia, Electress of Hanover, granddaughter of King James I, so long as they are not, or are not married to, a Roman Catholic. A number of Private Members Bills have been put forward in recent years to amend the rules of succession by removing the principle of male **primogeniture**, which gives male heirs priority in the line of succession, and removing the bar to Catholic succession. None have succeeded in becoming law.

Today most of the powers of the Crown are exercised by Ministers under statutory authority. The Crown owns lands, employs staff and enters into contracts in its own name. It also enjoys IMMUNITY FROM PROSECUTION, although civil proceedings against the Crown may be brought under the Crown Proceedings Act 1947. It is still the case that a STATUTE will only bind the Crown by express words or necessary implication (see *Lord Advocate* v. *Strathclyde Regional Council* (1990) SLT 158). [JW]
See also CROWN PROCEEDINGS; DEMISE OF THE CROWN; ROYAL PREROGATIVE.

Crown Court A superior COURT OF RECORD created by the Courts Act 1971. The Crown Court deals with all crime committed or sent for trial by magistrates' courts. Cases for trial are heard before a judge and JURY. The Crown Court also acts as an appeal court for cases heard and dealt with by the magistrates. [SN]

Crown Court Rule Committee An advisory non-departmental public body created by the Supreme Court Act 1981, s. 86, which confers the power to make CROWN COURT RULES for the purpose of regulating and prescribing the practice and procedure to be followed by the Crown Court. The function of the Crown Court Rule Committee is to examine any proposed amendments to those Rules. The Committee is usually made up of three ex officio members, two judges of the Supreme Court, two circuit judges, a justice of the peace, two practising barristers and two practising solicitors. [SN]

Crown Court Rules A body of rules regulating the practice and procedure to be followed in proceedings in the CROWN COURT. Now largely superceded by the CRIMINAL PROCEDURE RULES. [SN]

Crown Office (obsolete) Now known as the Administrative Court Office. [JW]

Crown Office List (obsolete) *See* ADMINISTRATIVE COURT.

Crown proceedings Civil actions brought by and, more especially, against the CROWN. The Crown Proceedings Act 1947 overturned the convention that the Crown could only be sued by petition of right and made the Crown liable for torts committed by any CROWN SERVANT or agent in the course of their employment, for any breach of its obligations as a landowner or occupier of property, and its duties as an 'employer' (though note that employees of the Crown have a distinctive employment status). The right to sue the Crown in TORT was further extended to members of the armed and reserve forces by the Crown Proceedings (Armed Forces) Act 1987. Special provisions relating to civil proceedings by or against the Crown are contained in Part 66 of the CPR. [JW]

See also CIVIL SERVICE; ROYAL PREROGATIVE.

Crown Prosecution Service (CPS) The government agency responsible for prosecuting criminal cases investigated by the police in England and Wales. The CPS provides the police with advice on matters relating to a criminal prosecution, including the decision whether to prosecute. Guidelines issued to the CPS require that cases should be prosecuted firmly, fairly and effectively when there is sufficient evidence to provide a realistic prospect of CONVICTION, and when it is in the public interest to do so. The CPS is also responsible for determining the appropriate charge and preparing and presenting the case at court. See http://www.cps.gov.uk/about/index.html. [SN]

Crown prosecutor A lawyer with responsibility for reviewing and, where appropriate, prosecuting criminal cases following investigation by the police. Crown prosecutors also advise the police on matters relating to criminal investigations. The prosecutor should consider whether there is sufficient evidence to pass the evidential test and, if so, whether the public interest requires a prosecution. Although Crown prosecutors work closely with the police, they are responsible to the CROWN PROSECUTION SERVICE, an independent governmental organization. [SN]

Crown servant A person in the employment of the CROWN. Crown servants are not employed on a CONTRACT OF SERVICE within the strict meaning of that term, and are not employees as defined in the Employment Rights Act 1996 (as amended). In theory, then, they are employed only 'during the good pleasure of the Crown' and may be dismissed at will. However, much of the existing employment protection legislation has been expressly extended to Crown employees by s. 191 of the 1996 Act.

The title 'Crown servant' is still used in some formal and legislative contexts, but it has largely been replaced in everyday usage by the analogous term **civil servant**. [JW]

See also CIVIL SERVICE.

cruelty (obsolete) Grounds in the ECCLESIASTICAL COURTS for a DIVORCE *a mensa et thoro*. After the Matrimonial Causes Act 1857, it became grounds for a JUDICIAL SEPARATION ORDER and one of the aggravating factors a wife could allege in her petition for divorce from her husband on the grounds of his ADULTERY. It became grounds for divorce on its own in 1937. Originally, the respondent's behaviour had to be 'grave and weighty' and intentional; cruelty was a MATRIMONIAL OFFENCE and so implied a degree of culpability. In the Divorce Reform Act 1969, cruelty was replaced by 'behaviour' as one of the five facts establishing grounds for divorce. [AD]

cruelty to animals There are various offences involving cruelty to animals, conviction of which may lead, as part of a sentence, to disqualification from keeping particular animals. The offences are set out in the Protection of Animals Act 1911 and related legislation. [BF]

cum testamento annexo (Lat. with the will annexed) A type of grant of LETTERS OF ADMINISTRATION where a TESTATOR has left a valid WILL, but no EXECUTOR is applying for a grant of PROBATE. It may be that the testator did not name an executor in his will, or the named executor may have died or for some other reason be unable to apply for a grant. Some other person would then have to administer the estate, but since probate can be granted only to an executor, the grant made in this case would be a grant of Letters of Administration *cum testamento annexo*. [CM]

cur. adv. vult *See* CURIA ADVISARI VULT.

curator bonis SCOTS LAW term meaning 'one who has a care of goods' and referring to a person appointed by the court to act on behalf of an individual who otherwise lacks capacity, for example, because of their age.

Traditionally, a *curator bonis* could also be appointed where a person lacked capacity because of insanity, but this is no longer possible following the Adults with Incapacity (Scotland) Act 2000. Under the 2000 Act, a guardian or intervener may be appointed depending on whether long-term management of a person's affairs or short-term help is required in the event of

mental disorder or an inability to communicate. [JP]

See also ALIMENT.

curfew (from Old Fr. *cuevrefeu,* a rule requiring fires to be put out or covered at a certain time) A legal order requiring a person or persons to remain in their homes between specified hours. Curfews may be introduced in times of national emergency, or more generally as part of a variety of measures designed to preserve public order. In particular, they have recently been adopted as part of the government's policy to clamp down on young offenders and the perceived causes of young offending. Current provisions include: (a) Crime and Disorder Act 1998, s. 14, which empowers a local authority to apply to the Home Office to create local child curfew schemes which are intended to prevent children under the age of 10 from being allowed to wander the streets unsupervised during any specified hours between 9 p.m. and 6 a.m; (b) the Powers of Criminal Courts (Sentencing) Act 2000 (as amended), which enables a criminal court to impose a CURFEW ORDER on a young person under the age of 16 as part of a community sentence. [JW]

See also EMERGENCY POWERS.

curfew order An order requiring an offender to remain at a particular place at a specified time over a specified period. The order should name the person responsible for monitoring the offender during the CURFEW period. A curfew order may include the requirement for ELECTRONIC MONITORING. [SN]

curia advisari vult (Lat. the court wishes to be advised) Seen in abbreviated form in law reports as *cur. adv. vult* (c.a.v.), indicating that the judgment of the court was not delivered immediately at the end of the hearing but was reserved for consideration and delivered at a later date. [AF]

Curia Regis (Lat. the king's court) *See* ROYAL COUNCIL.

curtain principle The principle, under Settled Land Act (SLA) 1925, s. 110 (2), that a prospective purchaser of SETTLED

LAND is neither bound nor entitled to see the trust instrument under which the identities and interests of the beneficiaries under the SETTLEMENT are set out. In a settlement, it is the VESTING DEED that contains all the public information that a prospective purchaser of settled land needs to know. That information is sufficient for a purchaser to over-reach the interests of any beneficiaries under the settlement, therefore the identities and interests of those beneficiaries remain private, veiled behind the 'curtain' constructed by SLA 1925, s. 110 (2). [DR]

See also OVERREACHING.

custodian trustee A trustee who (in contrast to a MANAGING TRUSTEE) is charged with protecting, rather than managing, the TRUST property. [PK]

custody Superseded term for the rights and responsibilities of PARENTS over their children. Custody encompassed the right to physical control or possession of a CHILD as well as the power to make decisions about the child's upbringing. Prior to the coming into force of the Children Act 1989, parents who divorced might be awarded joint custody or one might retain custody while the other was given CARE AND CONTROL. The term is no longer of legal significance in this context; it has been replaced by the notions of PARENTAL RESPONSIBILITY, residence and contact. [FK]

See also CONTACT ORDER; RESIDENCE ORDER.

custody time limit The maximum period for which a person may be kept in custody before being brought to trial. [SN]

custom 1. A practice that has been followed as a matter of habit or tradition in a given locality. In certain circumstances, custom may harden into a source of law called CUSTOMARY LAW.

2. The established practice of a particular trade, industry or market sector, called a TRADE CUSTOM, or usage, which may be taken into consideration when interpreting contractual terms within that trade, etc. [JW]

customary international law One of the four sources of international law recog-nized by the Statute of the International Court of Justice and, historically, the main source of international law. It com-prises both objective and subjective elem-ents. The objective element is known as **state practice** and consists of all action undertaken by a STATE and its agents, either unilaterally (e.g. through the adoption of domestic laws, presidential or ministerial statements, etc.) or in the context of col-lective decisions or mechanisms (e.g. vot-ing in the UN General Assembly or other inter-governmental organizations). This state practice crystallizes into law when it is concise, consistent and exercised for a significant period of time.

The subjective element is known as *OPINIO JURIS SIVE NECESSITATIS*, which is when a state practice is undertaken in the conviction that it conforms either to a pre-existing legal obligation, or to a new obligation which the state is willing to accept. It is essentially, therefore, the *opinio juris* that renders state practice binding on the indi-vidual practising state and, when a number of states act consistently in the same way, their collective practice may give rise to a rule of customary international law. [IB]

customary law 1. In English law, a CUSTOM or practice that has been followed continu-ously, as if it were a legal right, in a particu-lar locality since **time immemorial**. Time immemorial, by convention, refers to the time before the accession of Richard I in 1189, which is regarded in English law as the beginning of legal memory – see *Moun-sey* v. *Ismay* (1863) 1 H & C 729. In practice, however, proof that the custom has been practiced uninterrupted throughout living memory is sufficient to raise the presump-tion that the custom has force of law in that locality. New customary laws are rarely rec-ognized today.

2. In colonial legal systems, the formal legal system was usually dominated by the 'received' rules, practices and institu-tions of the colonial power. In many such systems however, indigenous laws and cus-toms might be retained to govern the indi-genous peoples in respect of certain matters, for example, rules of marriage and succession, or intra-tribal land transfer. The colonial state normally retained exclusive jurisdiction over other matters, such as serious crime, and property matters affecting settlers. Matters of customary law were usually dealt with by customary methods, but sometimes with a right of appeal to a 'native court' (as it was often called), usually staffed by colonial magistrates. Some post-colonial countries have retained a plural legal system (see LEGAL PLURALISM) in which customary law remains a significant source of law.

3. A source of INTERNATIONAL LAW, properly called CUSTOMARY INTERNATIONAL LAW.   [JW]

customs duties Indirect taxes levied on the value of various goods imported into and exported from the UK and administered by HM REVENUE AND CUSTOMS (formerly by HM Customs and Excise). They originated in England during medieval times to raise revenue for the king in order to pay for the protection of shipping, but came to be used in the UK for the protection of domestic industries, giving preference to imports from particular foreign countries, and the raising of revenue for general purposes.

When the UK joined the EUROPEAN ECONOMIC COMMUNITY, many of the protective aspects of customs duties had to be repealed in order to remove barriers to trade within the Community as required by the EUROPEAN COMMUNITY TREATY. The UK is, therefore, unable to impose customs duties in relation to MEMBER STATES of the Community, or measures with the equivalent effect of customs duties, contrary to European Community legislation. Instead, there is now the COMMON EXTERNAL TARIFF which is applied by the UK and other member states.   [RE]

customs union An agreement between nations which provides for the abolition of customs duties between members and the establishment of a COMMON EXTERNAL TARIFF (CET), whereby the same customs duties and import quotas are applied to all goods entering the area. It is the operation of the CET that distinguishes a customs union from the looser structure of a **free trade area**, in which each member imposes its own external tariffs on goods from non-

member STATES. The best known customs union is probably the EUROPEAN UNION, though the oldest such organization in the world is the Southern African Customs Union (SACU) between South Africa, Botswana, Lesotho, Namibia and Swaziland, which has its origins in the Customs Union Agreement of 1910. The current SACU is governed by the Southern Africa Customs Union Agreement of 2002.   [JW]
See also CUSTOMS DUTIES.

cut-throat defence An attempt by a defendant in criminal proceedings to cast blame on a CO-DEFENDANT.   [ALTC]

cy-près doctrine (Old Fr. *cy*, here; *près*, near – 'as near as possible') A mechanism that provides a means of saving gifts to CHARITY that would otherwise fail, by allowing them to be used for a related charitable purpose. The doctrine can be used in respect of both initial failure (e.g. when the specified charity does not exist) and subsequent failure (e.g. when the specified purpose has already been achieved or becomes impracticable or impossible) and is governed by ss. 13 and 14 of the Charities Act 1993, as amended by the Charities Act 2006. The 2006 Act has also introduced a more flexible cy-près regime, enabling the CHARITY COMMISSION to take account of, not only the original intention that lay behind the gift, but also the social and economic circumstances prevailing at the time of the proposed alteration of the original purposes.   [PK]

cyber-squatting A legal concept under United States federal law, which means registering, trafficking in, or using a DOMAIN NAME with bad-faith intent to profit from the goodwill of a TRADE MARK belonging to someone else. UK registered trade mark and PASSING-OFF laws regulate cyber-squatting.   [US]

cybercrime An umbrella term, lacking any specific legal meaning, referring to crime committed via the medium of a computer network, typically the internet.   [BF]
See also COMPUTER MISUSE; HACKING.

D

damages A money payment awarded by a court as compensation in a civil action. Damages are a COMMON LAW remedy, and are normally awarded as of right to the victim of a TORT or BREACH OF CONTRACT. Damages for breach of contract may be **liquidated**, that is, a fixed amount agreed in advance as a term of the contract; awards in other contexts tend to be for an **unliquidated** sum, i.e. an amount to be determined by the court.

Damages are generally awarded on the principle that the award should, so far as possible, restore the claimant to the position he would have been in but for the defendant's breach. In some cases, however, a court may award NOMINAL DAMAGES to signify the infringement of the claimant's rights even though no real loss or damage has been suffered, or AGGRAVATED DAMAGES where some uplift of the award is merited to reflect the circumstances in which the wrong was committed. Damages may sometimes be awarded in JUDICIAL REVIEW proceedings, and in respect of a claim under the Human Rights Act 1998 (HRA). Damages are awarded under the HRA only as a remedy of last resort, and the basis upon which the award is calculated is less generous than is the norm in English law, reflecting the practice of the EUROPEAN COURT OF HUMAN RIGHTS – see *R (Greenfield)* v. *Secre-tary of State for the Home Department* [2005] UKHL 14. [JW]

See also EXEMPLARY DAMAGES; GENERAL DAMAGES; LIQUIDATED DAMAGES CLAUSE; SPECIAL DAMAGES.

dangerous dogs The Dangerous Dogs Act 1991 defines them as dogs of a type bred for fighting (s. 1), or dogs of any type which, in the opinion of the Secretary of State, present a serious danger to the public (s. 2). Under s. 1 it is an offence for someone to have in their possession or custody, other than in accordance with a scheme of exemption, a dog of the types known as the Pit Bull Terrier, the Japanese Tosa, the Dogo Argentino and the Fila Braziliero. The section also makes it an offence for a person to breed, or breed from, sell or exchange such a dog or to offer, advertise or expose such a dog for sale or exchange; to make or offer to make a gift of such a dog or advertise or expose such a dog as a gift; or to abandon such a dog; or allow it to stray. All such dogs must be muzzled and kept on a lead while in a public place. Section 3 of the 1991 Act also created a new offence of being an owner of a dog of any type or breed which is dangerously out of control in a public place or a non-public place in which it is not permitted to be. [BF]

dangerous driving Under the Road Traffic Act 1988 (as amended), s. 2, it is an offence to drive a mechanically propelled vehicle dangerously on a road or other public place. A person's driving will be regarded as dangerous if it falls far below what would be expected of a competent and careful driver and if it would have been obvious to the competent and careful driver that the driving created a danger of injury to any person or of serious damage to property (see Road Traffic Act 1988, s. 2A). [BF]

See also CAUSING DEATH BY DANGEROUS DRIVING.

dangerous instruments For the purposes of the Criminal Justice and Public Order Act 1994, s. 60 dangerous instruments are instruments which have a blade or are sharply pointed (s. 60(11)). Section 60(1) states that if a police officer of inspector rank or above reasonably suspects that persons in a relevant locality are carrying offensive weapons or dangerous instruments without good reason, he may authorize enhanced powers of stop and search in respect of such articles for up to 24 hours. [BF]

See also OFFENSIVE WEAPON.

dangerous machinery Machinery that is used in a factory must be shown to be dangerous before it needs to be enclosed or 'fenced' (Factories Act 1961, s. 14(1)). However, prime movers, e.g. engines (s. 12) and transmission machinery (s. 13), must be fenced, whether dangerous or not. [MJ]

dangerous offender One who has been convicted of a sexual or violent offence specified in the Criminal Justice Act 2003 Schedule 15, and whom the court considers to present a 'significant risk to members of the public of serious harm'. The majority of sexual and violent offences are listed in Schedule 15. Conviction as a dangerous offender has implications for sentencing and PAROLE.

Where the offence carries a maximum term of imprisonment of 10 years or more, a dangerous offender will be sentenced to an **indeterminate sentence of imprisonment for public protection** (IPP). The court will specify a minimum term (the 'tariff'), after which the offender will only be released if the **Parole Board** is satisfied that it is safe to do so. On release, offenders with an IPP sentence are subject to supervision on licence, and if, while on licence, they are considered to constitute an unacceptable risk to the public, they can be recalled to prison to continue serving their sentence. All recalled licensees are entitled to make representations to the Parole Board at an oral hearing.

Those convicted of a Schedule 15 offence carrying a maximum penalty of less than 10 years, will receive an **extended sentence for public protection** (EPP). This comprises two parts: a custodial sentence of at least 12 months; and an extended licence period. Release is at the discretion of the Parole Board at any time between the halfway point of the custodial period and the end date of the sentence. The licence can extend beyond the custodial sentence for up to five years for violent and eight years for sexual offences, provided that the combined period of custody and licence does not exceed the maximum penalty for the offence. [JW]

See also SEXUAL OFFENCE.

database A 'collection of independent works, data or other materials which are arranged in a systematic or methodical way and are individually accessible by electronic or other means' – see Council Directive 96/9/EC on the legal protection of databases and the Copyright, Designs and Patents Act 1988, s. 3A. [US]

See also DATABASE RIGHT.

database right A newly created right which exists independently of COPYRIGHT protection of a DATABASE. The right came into being on 1 January 1998 with the Copyright and Rights in Databases Regulations 1997 (SI 1997/3032), which implemented Council Directive 96/9/EC on the legal protection of databases. A database owner therefore has two potential means of protecting his product: through copyright and the *sui generis* database right. To gain copyright protection, a database will be considered original if and only if, by reason of the selection or arrangement of the contents of the database, the database constitutes the author's own intellectual creation. Protection under the database right will only be granted if there is substantial investment in obtaining, verifying or presenting the contents of the database.

The owner of the database right is the maker of the database, i.e. the person who takes the initiative in obtaining, verifying or presenting the contents of the database and assumes any investment risk involved. If such a person is an employee who does it in the course of his employment, the database right will vest in the employer, unless there is agreement to the contrary.

The database right is infringed if any unauthorized person 'extracts or re-utilises' all or a substantial part of the contents of the database (i.e. makes those contents available to the public). The database right lasts for a period of 15 years from the year in which it was completed or from the date it is made available to the public. The duration of the database protection can be extended further if any substantial change is made to the contents of the database. [US]

See also INFRINGEMENT ACTION.

de bene esse (Lat. of well-being) A phrase applied to a proceeding or action that is the best that can be done in the present circumstances or in anticipation of a future circumstance. It commonly relates to matters of EVIDENCE, for example, obtaining a DEPOSITION from a witness where it is likely that he or she will be unable to attend court. [AF]

de bonis non administratis (Lat. regarding goods not administered) A type of grant of LETTERS OF ADMINISTRATION where a previous grant to the ESTATE has been made, but where the PERSONAL REPRESENTATIVE has not completed the administration, leaving some assets to be dealt with. This could be due to the death or incapacity of the previous personal representative (but see CHAIN OF REPRESENTATION), or if the previous grant has been revoked. There will be a new grant, limited to the assets still to be dealt with. [CM]

de minimis non curat lex (Lat. the law is not concerned with 'trifles' (minimal things)) The law will not sit in judgment on minor or trivial transgressions of the law; for example, the law will not award damages for a 'trifling' nuisance. The rule is not restricted to the COMMON LAW; it applies, for example, in EUROPEAN COMMUNITY competition law (see Commission Notice on agreements of minor importance which do not appreciably restrict competition under Article 81(1) of the Treaty establishing the European Community 2001/C 368/07). [AF]

de Vattel, Emerich (1714–67) A Swiss jurist: his leading work was published in 1758, entitled *Le Droit des gens; ou, Principes de la loi naturelle appliqués à la conduite et aux affaires des nations et des souverains (The Law of Nations or the Principles of Natural Law Applied to the Conduct and to the Affairs of Nations and of Sovereigns)*. Although the book was greatly influenced by the writings of Christian von Wolff, and gave support to the view that INTERNATIONAL LAW be based on NATURAL LAW because of its superiority over POSITIVE LAW, de Vattel does not propose the abolition of the latter, but sees the peaceful coexistence of both. This is no more evident than in his exposition of self-defence as a natural right of STATES, but with the force used and its consequences being premised on positive law. [IB]

See also JUST WAR; USE OF FORCE.

death duties (obsolete) The general name applied to probate duty, account duty, legacy duty and succession duty. The first three of these duties were replaced by ESTATE DUTY in the Finance Act 1894, and the term 'death duties' continued to be used after 1894 in respect of succession duty and estate duty. Succession duty was discontinued in 1949, and the term 'death duty' remained in accepted use at least until estate duty was replaced in 1975 by CAPITAL TRANSFER TAX in the Finance Act (No. 2) 1975. Even then, the term 'death duty' continued to be used by some professionals and many members of the public. The term is still sometimes used in respect of inheritance tax, which replaced capital transfer tax in

1986, although inheritance tax is more often colloquially referred to as **gift tax**.

[RE]

death penalty *See* CAPITAL PUNISHMENT.

debenture Where a company borrows or owes money, the lender or creditor may secure the loan or debt by taking out a charge on the company's assets. This is recorded in a legal document called a debenture and is registered with the COMPANIES REGISTRY. The lender or creditor becomes a secured creditor of the COMPANY and is known as a **debenture holder**. [JW]

deceit A TORT which occurs when the defendant makes a statement of fact to the claimant, either knowing it to be false, or being reckless (careless) as to its truth, with the intention that the claimant will act on it, and the claimant acts upon the statement and suffers harm as a consequence (see *Derry* v. *Peek* (1889) 14 App Cas 337). [HJ]

See also PASSING OFF.

Decent Homes standard LOCAL HOUSING AUTHORITIES and registered social landlords are required by government to ensure that their housing stock reaches the Decent Homes standard by 2010. There are four criteria in defining a decent home. First, the dwelling must meet the current statutory minimum standard for housing and therefore should not pose a Category 1 hazard under the HOUSING HEALTH AND SAFETY RATING SYSTEM. Second, the dwelling must be in a reasonable state of REPAIR. Third, it must have reasonably modern facilities and services. A dwelling does not have reasonably modern facilities if it lacks three or more of the following: a reasonably modern kitchen (20 years old or less); a kitchen with adequate space and layout; a reasonably modern bathroom (30 years old or less); an appropriately located bathroom and WC; adequate insulation against external noise; an adequate size and layout of common areas for blocks of flats. Finally, the dwelling must provide a reasonable degree of thermal comfort. [HC & DR]

Decision 1. EUROPEAN COMMUNITY (EC) deci-sions, which are a form of SECONDARY LEGISLATION, created along with REGULATIONS and DIRECTIVES by Article 249 EC. Decisions are legally binding on the parties to whom they are addressed, and are binding once published in the OFFICIAL JOURNAL of the EC. They are most often used by the EUROPEAN COMMISSION, when acting in its quasi-judicial capacity in EC COMPETITION LAW cases, which regulate the market behaviour of large companies and other business undertakings.

2. EUROPEAN UNION (EU) secondary legislation in the context of Pillar III of the EU, which deals with Police and Judicial Cooperation in Criminal Matters (PJCCM). The legal tools in this Pillar are provided for in Article 34 EU, and are common positions, framework decisions, decisions and conventions (international treaties). These decisions, adopted by the COUNCIL OF MINISTERS only, are legally binding; however, along with the other Pillar III legal instruments, they do not have DIRECT EFFECT. [MON]

See also COMMUNITY LAW.

declaration 1. An out-of-court oral or written statement not made on OATH which may be admissible in court proceedings as an exception to the hearsay rule.

2. A discretionary remedy of the court, also called a **declaratory judgment**, available in both private and PUBLIC LAW matters, which clarifies an individual's legal status, rights or obligations. A declaration cannot be directly enforced, since it is merely a statement of existing rights rather than a requirement to do anything; its value lies in its ability to resolve the respective rights of the parties, and to provide a basis for further action if one of the parties were to continue to act contrary to the declaration. [JW]

Declaration of Delhi (1959) *See* RULE OF LAW.

Declaration of Geneva The WORLD MEDICAL ASSOCIATION International Code of Medical Ethics, first adopted by the General Assembly of the Association in Geneva in 1948. The document, which has since been amended on a number of occasions, is the modern version of the HIPPOCRATIC OATH and is a statement of the commitment of physicians to the humanitarian goals of medicine. [HJ]

See also DOCTOR–PATIENT CONFIDENTIALITY.

Declaration of Helsinki A statement of ethical principles developed by the WORLD MEDICAL ASSOCIATION to provide guidance to physicians and others involved in medical research on human subjects. [HJ]

See also NON-THERAPEUTIC RESEARCH; THERAPEUTIC RESEARCH.

declaration of incompatibility A declaration issued by judges under the Human Rights Act 1998, s. 4, stating that a provision or provisions of a STATUTE are incompatible with Convention rights. The declaration does not affect the validity of the statute in question, but places the onus on government to introduce changes that will bring it into line with the UK human rights obligations. The declaration of incompatibility has been described as a measure of last resort, as the judiciary is also under a statutory obligation, under s. 3(1) of the Human Rights Act, to interpret primary legislation as compatible wherever it is possible to do so: see *per* Lord Steyn in *R* v. *A* [2002] 1 AC 45. [JW]

See also EUROPEAN CONVENTION ON HUMAN RIGHTS; SOVEREIGNTY OF PARLIAMENT.

declaration of trust A statement by which a SETTLOR creates a TRUST. No particular formalities are required to create a trust, although a trust of property that includes land can only be enforced if the declaration is evidenced in writing and signed under the Law of Property Act 1925, s. 53(1)(b). This does not, of course, preclude an effective oral declaration of a trust of property including land, but any subsequent enforcement before the courts would require written evidence, signed by the settlor, confirming that such an oral declaration had taken place. [PK]

declaratory judgment See DECLARATION.

declaratory theory **1.** In INTERNATIONAL LAW, one of two theories that seeks to determine the legal effect of RECOGNITION of new

STATES or governments by established states. Declaratory theory proposes that statehood is established as soon as the new state exists objectively as a matter of fact. These objective elements of statehood are found in CUSTOMARY INTERNATIONAL LAW, as enunciated in Article 3 of the 1933 Montevideo Convention on the Rights and Duties of States. They consist of: the existence of territory, a permanent population, an effective government and the capacity to enter into relations with other states (independence). According to declaratory theory, therefore, the legal effects of recognition are limited and certainly not determinative of the existence of statehood. See also CONSTITUTIVE THEORY.

2. In the English COMMON LAW tradition, declaratory theory describes the idea put forward by writers such as BLACKSTONE, that judges do not, when exercising their powers to develop the common law through case law, make 'new' law, they merely explain or develop existing common law principles. The fiction that judges never engage in law-making, even in the context of ground-breaking cases like *Donoghue* v. *Stevenson* [1932] AC 562, which provided much of the groundwork for the development of common law liability in NEGLIGENCE, has been generally discredited in practice. (Though a more sophisticated version of declaratory theory arguably emerges in DWORKIN's celebrated essay on 'hard cases', and is later elaborated on in his book *Law's Empire* (1986).) However, declaratory theory has recently regained some practical importance following the case of *Kleinwort Benson Limited* v. *Lincoln City Council* [1999] 2 AC 349 in which the House of Lords used the theory to allow RESTITUTION (repayment) to a party to a CONTRACT for a MISTAKE of law that made the contract legally unenforceable. The logic of the House of Lords' approach was that, when a judge states what the law is in a case, his decision must have some retrospective effect, i.e. he is declaring what the law has always been, and this will have implications for a variety of arrangements that were (apparently) settled on a previous understanding of the law that is now shown to be wrong. This ruling, which has been quite widely criticized, has significant implications for a range of agreements, including contracts and CONSENT orders approved by the courts. A number of subsequent decisions have sought to restrict its scope to situations where there was an unequivocal mistake of law that left the agreement incapable of performance: see *Great Peace Shipping* v. *Tsavliris (International) Ltd* [2002] 2 Lloyd's Rep 653; *Brennan* v. *Bolt Burden* [2004] EWCA Civ 1017.

[IB & JW]

See also OVERRULING.

decompilation In computing, the process of converting an executable or 'ready to run' program code into a higher level programming language so that it can be read by a person. Under COPYRIGHT law, decompilation by a lawful user is generally permitted, and may, for example, be necessary to update, disinfect or debug a program. However, decompiling may also be used illegally in order to reproduce source code for use without the consent of the copyright owner. [US]

See also SOFTWARE.

decree Originally the judgment or statement of a Court of EQUITY, decrees were also made by ADMIRALTY Courts and Probate Courts. Decrees are still granted by the DIVORCE courts, and include decrees of divorce, ANNULMENT, judicial separation and PRESUMPTION OF DEATH. [AD]

decree absolute The second of the two-part termination of MARRIAGE, granted in DIVORCE, ANNULMENT or PRESUMPTION OF DEATH proceedings. In divorce, if there are no objections to the DECREE NISI, the court will automatically grant the decree absolute of divorce on the petitioner's application, which may be made after six weeks (or more) have elapsed since the pronouncement of the decree nisi. It is only the decree absolute that terminates the marriage. If the petitioner fails to apply for the decree absolute of divorce, the respondent may apply for it after three months have elapsed from the earliest date on which the petitioner could have applied for it. [AD]

decree nisi The first of the two-part termination of MARRIAGE. It is a conditional decree only, of DIVORCE, ANNULMENT or PRESUMPTION OF DEATH. In divorce, for example, if the petitioner has proved the ground for divorce (IRRETRIEVABLE BREAKDOWN) and one or more of the five facts required in the Matrimonial Causes Act 1973, and all other legal requirements for divorce are satisfied, the divorce court will pronounce a decree nisi of divorce. The decree nisi means the divorce is not final; it will not take effect until some later event, in this case, on grant of the DECREE ABSOLUTE. Decrees nisi must be pronounced in open court. [AD]

deductions from wages Whether an EMPLOYER may deduct payments from a worker's WAGES depends on the provisions of ss. 13–27 of the Employment Rights Act 1996, formerly the Wages Act 1986. The basic rules are that no deductions may be made except for those made under or authorized by statute (e.g. tax); those authorized by a provision in the CONTRACT OF EMPLOYMENT; and those agreed by the worker in advance (e.g. payment for private telephone calls). Special rules apply to those in retail employment and to deductions on account of INDUSTRIAL ACTION. [MJ]

deductive reasoning A process of reasoning by which a conclusion is drawn from a set of propositions in a way that is logically valid. In legal reasoning, the process of deduction requires that we start with a rule of law. This may be from a STATUTE or STATUTORY INSTRUMENT, a TREATY, or some other form of binding legislation, or from a clearly applicable (case law) principle of the COMMON LAW. The rule is then applied to a set of facts. If the facts meet all the conditions required by the rule, then, logically, we can assert that the rule applies. Thus, to provide a simple example:

Rule: Carrying a concealed weapon in a public place is a criminal offence.

Facts: Jill was carrying a concealed pistol in a public place.

This must lead us to

Conclusion: Jill has committed a criminal offence.

Pure deductive reasoning of this kind,

however, can only be used when applying clear rules to specific factual situations. Where the meaning or scope of a rule is unclear, the courts will often have to engage in a rather different process of INDUCTIVE REASONING, involving argument by analogy or comparison with other statutory sources (see *IN PARI MATERIAL*), or the evaluation of competing authorities as to the meaning of certain words.   [JW]

See also PRECEDENT.

deed A formal written document that makes clear on its face that it is intended to take effect as a deed and is validly witnessed as required under the Law of Property (Miscellaneous Provisions) Act 1989, s. 1(3) and delivered as specified by common law and statute (e.g. Law of Property Act 1925 s. 196). Prior to 1990 there was also a requirement that a seal be attached (hence the phrase signed, sealed and delivered) but this is no longer required. A deed executed since that date by an individual requires only that it be signed by the maker in the presence of a witness, or at the maker's direction in the presence of two witnesses, who must themselves sign the document. The document must then be delivered either actually by handing it to the recipient or constructively (e.g. by delivering it to their last place of abode). If a deed is executed by a company it must, prior to delivery, be signed by two directors, or the director and the secretary; alternatively, if the company has a seal, the deed may be executed by affixing the company seal to the document.   [PK]

deed of covenant A deed containing an undertaking to perform a specific task, for example to pay a certain amount of money over a fixed period of time.   [DR]

deed of gift A formal means of making a gift of personalty (personal property or CHATTELS) that precludes the need for delivery. PERSONAL PROPERTY can be transferred gratuitously either by words of gift coupled with delivery or a deed of gift.   [PK]

deep sea-bed An area consisting of the sea-bed and subsoil, situated beneath the water mass of the high seas. No STATE possesses SOVEREIGNTY or sovereign rights over the deep sea-bed, since this area and its resources have been designated in the UNITED NATIONS LAW OF THE SEA CONVENTION as 'COMMON HERITAGE OF MANKIND' (Article 136). This means that all rights in the resources in the area are vested in mankind as a whole, including land-locked states.   [IB]

See also CONTINENTAL SHELF; CONTINENTAL MARGIN; INTERNATIONAL SEA-BED AUTHORITY.

defamation The collective name for the TORTS of LIBEL and SLANDER. Defamation requires the publication of a false statement about another person that has the effect of discrediting that person's character or reputation. To constitute an actionable defamation, the statement must be communicated to a third party. If the defamatory statement is in permanent form (e.g. in writing, or a cartoon or recorded image), it will constitute a libel; if it is in non-permanent form (e.g. spoken), it constitutes a slander.

Any person who publishes or repeats the defamation will also be liable for that act independently of the original publisher of the statement. A distributor of books or newspapers may be able to escape liability if they can show that they had no knowledge of the offending material – the defence of **innocent dissemination**. More general defences are **justification**, which requires the defendant to prove that the statement was true, and **fair comment**, which requires proof that the statement complained of was an honest and fair statement of opinion, based on true facts, on a matter of public interest. A defendant may also avoid further liability by making an **offer of amends**, involving a statement of apology and/or correction and payment of compensation.

Actions in defamation are unusual in English civil procedure in that they are normally heard before a JURY. However, a summary procedure was introduced by the Defamation Act 1996, whereby claims for less than £10,000 may be heard by a judge alone. The normal remedies for defamation are DAMAGES, which may be substantial, and

INJUNCTION. There is no LEGAL AID to bring or defend actions in defamation. [HJ & JW]

See also MALICIOUS FALSEHOOD.

default judgment Under the CIVIL PROCEDURE RULES, Rule 12.1, a claimant may seek judgement in default, that is, without a trial where the defendant has either failed to file an ACKNOWLEDGEMENT OF SERVICE, or failed to file a DEFENCE to the claim. [JW]

defective equipment The Employers' Liability (Defective Equipment) Act 1969, s. 1(1), provides that an EMPLOYER is liable for any personal injury to an EMPLOYEE sustained in the course of employment 'in consequence of a defect in equipment provided by his employer for the purposes of the employer's business' and if 'the defect is attributable wholly or mainly to the fault of a third party (whether identified or not)'. [MJ]

defence In procedural terms, the defence can refer to the entire conduct of the defendant's case at trial.

It also has a more substantive usage, to refer to specific issues recognized by the criminal law as leading to the avoidance of criminal liability. Thus, where D pleads a defence successfully, he incurs no liability in respect of the alleged crime.

The criminal law recognizes different types of defence. Those which apply in respect of (broadly speaking) all offences are known as GENERAL DEFENCES. These include INSANITY. Those which apply only in respect of specific offences are known as SPECIAL DEFENCES. For example, PROVOCATION is only a defence to MURDER. Moreover, a defence such as provocation, which leads not to a complete avoidance of liability but to liability for a lesser offence (MANSLAUGHTER), is known as a partial defence.

Some defences, such as a plea of SELF-DEFENCE, involve the defendant pleading that their conduct was in fact the right thing to do under the circumstances. These are known as JUSTIFICATION defences. Other defences, such as DURESS, acknowledge the wrongfulness of the defendant's conduct, but suggest that the circumstances were such that it would be unfair

to impose on them the full weight of the law. These defences are known as EXCUSES.

Procedurally, it is normally necessary for a defendant to raise evidence that a particular defence is made out, whereafter the prosecution must disprove the defence beyond reasonable doubt. This is not the case for INSANITY or DIMINISHED RESPONSIBILITY, both of which a defendant must prove on the balance of probabilities. [BF]

See also BURDEN OF PROOF.

defence statement In criminal proceedings, 'a defence statement is a written statement – (a) setting out the nature of the accused's defence, including any particular defences on which he intends to rely, (b) indicating the matters of fact on which he takes issue with the prosecution, (c) setting out, in the case of each such matter, why he takes issue with the prosecution, and (d) indicating any point of law (including any point as to the admissibility of evidence or an abuse of process) which he wishes to take, and any authority on which he intends to rely for that purpose': Criminal Procedure and Investigations Act 1996, s. 6A(1). In cases which are to be tried on INDICTMENT, where the prosecution complies with its disclosure obligation, the accused must give a defence statement to the court and the prosecution. [ALTC]

See also ALIBI.

deferred sentence A SENTENCE which is determined after a delay to allow the court to assess any change in the person's conduct or circumstances after his or her conviction. [SN]

degrading treatment (degrading punishment) A concept of CUSTOMARY INTERNATIONAL LAW premised on the dignity of the human person and encountered in both international humanitarian law (e.g. Common Article 3 of the 1949 GENEVA CONVENTIONS), as well as in HUMAN RIGHTS treaties, particularly Article 7 of the INTERNATIONAL COVENANT ON CIVIL AND POLITICAL RIGHTS and Article 16 of the 1984 UN Convention against Torture and other Cruel, Inhuman, Degrading Treatment or Punishment. The latter does not positively define the nature of degrading treatment, but stipulates that it does not have to amount to an act of TOR-TURE. Inflicting degrading treatment or punishment is an international crime subject to the same jurisdictional and extradition provisions as the crime of torture. The EURO-PEAN COURT OF HUMAN RIGHTS has found degrading treatment to exist where it grossly humiliates a person or drives the victim to act against their will and conscience. This is also the case when it arouses in the person feelings of fear, anguish and inferiority, capable of humiliating and debasing them and possibly breaking their physical or moral resistance. In all cases, the test for degrading treatment or punishment will be based on a 'minimum level of severity'. [IB]

See also INHUMAN OR DEGRADING TREATMENT.

delegated legislation Laws made under the authority of STATUTE (referred to as the **parent** or **enabling Act**) or some other form of primary legislation. The main forms of delegated legislation in the UK are: statutory instruments (made by the UK Parliament); Scottish Statutory Instruments; Welsh Statutory Instruments; Statutory Rules of Northern Ireland; BYELAWS; and Church Instruments (part of ECCLESIASTICAL LAW).

Delegated legislation is widely used to fill in the regulatory detail necessary to complete the implementation of statutory powers, and to give effect to European DIR-ECTIVES. Much of this detail is highly technical and uncontroversial, but there are some concerns that governments may use their powers of delegation as a way of side-stepping parliamentary scrutiny of legislation. Delegated legislation is also referred to as secondary or **subordinate** legislation. [JW]

delegatus non potest delegare (Lat. a delegate cannot delegate) A principle of ADMIN-ISTRATIVE LAW that a person to whom legal authority or decision-making power has been delegated from a higher authority cannot then delegate that power to another, unless the original delegation so authorizes. See, for example, *Allingham* v. *Minister of Agriculture* [1948] 1 All ER 780. [JW]

delict Scottish law term for a civil wrong and thus broadly equivalent to a TORT in English law. [JP]

delivery up order An order to the infringer of INTELLECTUAL PROPERTY rights to deliver any infringing articles or devices used for making the infringing articles to the relevant intellectual property owner. The infringer must have such articles or devices in his custody or control in the course of a business, and must know or have reason to believe that it has been or is to be used to make infringing copies. A delivery up order can be made in relation to infringing copies of a COPYRIGHT work or infringing articles made to a REGISTERED DESIGN or illicit recordings of performances. [US]

demand with menaces An element of the offence of BLACKMAIL. [BF]

demise In land law, the granting of property on a LEASE. A subdemise is the granting of property on a sublease. [DR]

demise of the Crown At the end of a monarch's reign the succession passes immediately to the successor without any break or interregnum. The succession is formally confirmed by the PRIVY COUNCIL, sitting together with the Lord Mayor and Aldermen of London. They arrange for proclamation of the successor at certain traditional sites, including Charing Cross. The requirement that Parliament be dissolved on the death of the monarch was abolished in 1867 and the custom of sacking and rehiring civil servants at the death of the monarch was ended in 1901. At the first meeting of Parliament after the death of the monarch, members take an oath of allegiance to the incoming monarch. [MS]

demolition order When a LOCAL HOUSING AUTHORITY considers that a Category 1 or Category 2 hazard exists in relation to particular premises, an order requiring demolition of the premises is one of the options that are available to it. [HC & DR]

See also HOUSING HEALTH AND SAFETY RATING SYSTEM.

demonstrative legacy See LEGACY.

demoted tenancy Local authority landlords of SECURE TENANCIES and registered SOCIAL LANDLORDS of ASSURED TENANCIES can apply to court for a DEMOTION ORDER which operates to create a new and temporary tenancy with reduced SECURITY OF TENURE and reduced rights. Such tenancies are termed demoted tenancies. The grounds for demotion are that the TENANT, or another resident of, or visitor to, the tenant's home, has used the premises for illegal purposes, or has behaved in a way which is capable of causing nuisance or annoyance to any other person. The court must also be satisfied that it is reasonable to make the order. Demoted tenancies last for one year, during which time the tenant can be evicted without the need for the landlord to prove grounds for EVICTION. The period also offers the tenant the opportunity to improve their behaviour, because at the end of the year, if the landlord has taken no action, the tenancy will be promoted to a secure or assured tenancy once more.   [HC & DR]

See also INTRODUCTORY TENANCY.

demotion order An order of the COUNTY COURT that terminates a SECURE or ASSURED TENANCY and replaces it with a DEMOTED or demoted ASSURED SHORTHOLD TENANCY.   [HC]

dependent Relying on another for aid or (usually) financial support. In families, children are usually (financially) dependent upon adults, but others may also be dependent on a wage-earning or property-owning FAMILY member. The law does not require an individual to support all those who might be dependent on them, only their spouse, civil partner and children. In some circumstances, they and other dependants can make a claim for financial provision on the death of someone who was supporting them during his or her lifetime.   [AD]

See also FINANCIAL PROVISION ORDER; REASONABLE FINANCIAL PROVISION.

dependent relative revocation See CONDITIONAL REVOCATION.

dependent state A dependent STATE differs from a DEPENDENT TERRITORY in so far as the latter does not possess full SOVEREIGNTY and political independence. A dependent state, on the other hand, has achieved all the criteria for statehood, but on account of its finances, and usually its small size, it is unable to perform certain functions pertinent to its international relations, such as diplomatic representation through embassies and consuls abroad, as is the case with Liechtenstein and Switzerland, or Monaco with France, or the conduct of its self-defence.   [IB]

dependent territory A (land) area that does not possess full SOVEREIGNTY or political independence, but is instead ruled by another STATE. There are various degrees in the status of dependency, including self-governing territories endowed with a relative amount of autonomy (such as Greenland vis-à-vis Denmark), and those that are non-self-governing territories (e.g. the Cayman and British Virgin islands). In most cases, dependent territories possess a legal and monetary system that differs from that of the mother state, elect their own representatives and are not included in the territorial scope of inter-governmental organizations (such as the EUROPEAN COMMUNITY) to which the mother state is a party, such as the UK Crown Dependencies of Jersey and Guernsey.   [IB]

See also DEPENDENT STATE; MONTEVIDEO CONVENTION.

deposit See TENANCY DEPOSIT.

deposition A statement made on oath in civil proceedings before a judge or examiner of the court. A deposition is recorded in writing and may subsequently be used as evidence, provided notice of its intended use is given to all other parties to the proceedings by the party seeking to rely on it. Where a deposition is given in evidence at trial, it must be made available for inspection under CPR Rule 32.13.   [JW]

derecognition An EMPLOYER'S refusal to continue RECOGNITION of a TRADE UNION. [MJ]

deregulation The process of diminishing the role of the state in controlling particular sectors of the economy with a view to allowing competition to operate. The deregulation movement is associated in particular with liberal market political ideologies, which hold that greater efficiency will be achieved if the burden of REGULATION is lifted from business.

The most thoroughgoing variety of deregulation may be said to be the PRIVATIZATION of former state monopolies, especially utilities. Paradoxically, however, this process necessitates further regulation (albeit transitionally) in order to ensure the emergence of a market in a sector where none existed previously. [JP]

derivative deed A deed issued by reference to a previous deed either altering, confirming or supplementing its provisions. [PK]

derivative title A mode of acquisition of territory in international law. Common usage differentiates between two modes of acquisition; original and through derivative title. The former refers to acquisition through occupation and ACCRETION, since territory is acquired without the existence of a prior TITLE which the grantor passes on to the new grantee. Derivative title, however, concerns acquisition of territory through an act of CESSION, given effect through an agreement of cession, whereby territory is given by the grantor to the grantee. This distinction has little, if any, practical effect, and the rights associated with a derivative title will depend on the rights of the grantor and the cession agreement itself, which may provide for partial or complete cession of the grantor's rights. [IB]

derivative trust *See* SUB-TRUST.

derogation A means whereby a STATE may restrict or avoid, whether wholly or in part, a legal obligation. **1**. International human rights treaties commonly contain a clause which allows member states to derogate from specific TREATY obligations when particular circumstances arise. These circumstances are more or less standardized. Thus, Article 15 of the EUROPEAN CONVENTION ON HUMAN RIGHTS, for example, allows for derogation 'in time of war or other public emergency threatening the life of the nation'. However, this right of derogation is qualified in that it is only permitted to the 'extent strictly required by the exigencies of the situation, provided that such measures are not inconsistent with [the state's] other obligations under international law' (Article 15(1)). Moreover, not all rights are amenable to derogation, particularly *jus cogens* norms, such as the right to life (except in respect of deaths resulting from lawful acts of war), or the prohibition of torture and slavery. Human rights treaties also specify that when a participating state takes the decision to derogate particular rights, it is under an obligation to bring this clearly within the public domain and duly inform the depository or other member states.

2. In EC LAW, an exemption that allows a Member State to delay the implementation of an element of an EU legislative act into their legal system over a given timescale, or to avoid a certain REGULATION or DIRECTIVE entirely. [IB & JW]

desert theory One of the rationales underpinning sentencing, according to which an offender deserves to be punished on the basis of having committed an offence. Desert theory is itself underpinned by the notion of proportionality. The degree of punishment imposed should be in proportion to the seriousness of the offence. The Criminal Justice Act 2003, s. 142, designates punishment as one of the purposes of sentencing and requires a sentencing court to have regard to it and other purposes. [BF]

See also DETERRENCE THEORY; REHABILITATION; RETRIBUTION; RETRIBUTIVISM.

desertion One of the five facts a petitioner or applicant may use to establish the ground of IRRETRIEVABLE BREAKDOWN of the MARRIAGE or CIVIL PARTNERSHIP. It occurs where the respondent has deserted the petitioner or applicant for a continuous period of at least two years immediately preceding the presentation of the petition (Matrimonial Causes Act 1973, s. 1(2)(c)). Desertion includes a separation of households (which may include separate households under the same roof); an intention on the part of the deserter to remain permanently apart for the two years; there must be no consent to the desertion by the applicant; and there must be no justification for the desertion. **Constructive desertion** may arise if one partner's behaviour is so serious that the other is forced to leave the home. In this case, the fact of desertion can be established if the partner who stays can be shown to have the requisite intent.   [AD]

design There are several legal definitions of the term 'design' which reflect the different meanings within the various different intellectual property categories. Designs can be protected under COPYRIGHT law, REGIS-TERED DESIGN law, and as an UNREGISTERED DESIGN RIGHT, as well as under a COMMUNITY DESIGN RIGHT.

Under the **registered design law**, a design is 'the appearance of the whole or a part of a product resulting from the features of, in particular, the lines, contours, colours, shape, texture or materials of the product itself or its ornamentation' (Registered Designs Act 1949, s. 1(2)).

The definition of design is anchored to the appearance of the whole or part of the product. There is no specific indication that the design must be visible to the naked eye. A design need not have an 'aesthetic quality' to qualify for protection. Functional designs are also eligible for protection, barring such features which are dictated solely by a technical function or 'interface features'. Design of internal mechanisms (such as the 'under the bonnet' parts of motor vehicles) or other features which are irrelevant to the visual appearance of the product will qualify as designs.   [US]

See also COMMUNITY DESIGN RIGHT; ARTISTIC WORK.

designated caseworker A non-lawyer appointed by the DIRECTOR OF PUBLIC PROSECU-TIONS who is permitted to undertake specific casework and advocacy in the magistrates' court.   [SN]

designated family judge After implementation of the Children Act 1989, spe-cialized hearing centres were created in the COUNTY COURTS. FAMILY HEARING CENTRES were created to hear private law applications under the Children Act 1989 and CARE CENTRES were created to hear both private law cases and public law cases relating to children. CHILD law cases at these centres are heard by judges who have received special-ist training in child and family law matters and who will be able to deal with cases sen-sitively and expeditiously. These judges are called 'designated family judges' and 'nom-inated care judges'.   [AD]

destruction of will The Wills Act 1833, s. 20 provides that a WILL may be revoked by 'burning, tearing, or otherwise destroying the same by the TESTATOR, or by some person in his presence and by his direction, with the intention of revoking the same'. It will be noted from the above that the destruc-tion of the will with nothing further is not sufficient to revoke the will: there must be a specific intention to do so. Where a will has been damaged in some way, even where it is clear that it has been damaged by the testator himself, two questions have to be resolved, and many court cases have resulted from this. First, does the damage caused amount to 'destruction'; and sec-ond, if it does, was it caused with the inten-tion of revoking the will?   [CM]

See also REVOCATION OF WILL.

deterrence theory One of the rationales underpinning sentencing, according to which the proper sentence to be imposed is that which reduces the likelihood of fur-ther offending. Deterrence may be **individ-ual**, insofar as it relates to the likelihood of the particular offender himself offending again, or it may be **general**, insofar as it relates to the likelihood of others being deterred from offending by the sentence imposed on the particular offender. Section 142 (1)(b) of the Criminal Justice Act 2003 designates the reduction of crime, includ-ing by way of deterrence, as a purpose of sentencing and requires a sentencing court to have regard to it and other purposes. [BF]

See also DESERT THEORY; REHABILITATION; RETRI-BUTION; RETRIBUTIVISM.

detriment The term occurs in two contexts: **1**. in relation to DISCRIMINATION claims, it means 'putting at a disadvantage'; **2**. in the phrase 'detriment short of dismissal', it means unfair action or inaction by an EMPLOYER against a worker during employment. This phrase replaced 'action short of dismissal' in the Employment Relations Act 1996 because 'action' connoted a 'doing', an act, and did not include omissions. 'Detriment' is now used to cover both action and inaction.   [MJ]

devastavit (Lat. he has wasted) A claim made against a PERSONAL REPRESENTATIVE for a breach of duty which has caused a loss of ASSETS in the estate. This could be because he or she has given away assets, sold them at an undervalue, or for any other reason failed to collect and maintain them as he or she should. Any BENEFICIARY or creditor who has suffered loss in this way can bring an action.   [CM]

development A fundamental concept in planning law with two meanings (Town and Country Planning Act 1990 (TCPA 1990), s. 55(1)): (a) the carrying out of building, engineering, mining or other operations in, on, over or under land (**operational development**); (b) the making of any **material change of use** of any buildings or other land.

Operational development includes the demolition of buildings, rebuilding, structural alterations of or additions to buildings as well as any other operations normally undertaken by a builder (TCPA 1990, s. 55 (1A)); for example, extending a house or making an access way from a house. However, operational development specifically does not include the carrying out of improvements to a building if they affect only the interior of the building or do not materially affect the external appearance of the building (TCPA 1990, s. 55(2)).

A **material change of use** means a material change in the character of the use of buildings or land. This is a question of fact and degree in each case for the local planning authority to decide and the courts will only reverse such a finding if it is unreasonable. An example of a material change

of use is the conversion of a single dwellinghouse into two dwellinghouses (TCPA 1990, s. 55(3)(a)). A change of use within a use class does not constitute development. If DEVELOPMENT is carried out without PLANNING PERMISSION it is unlawful and may be subject to enforcement action by the local planning authority.   [DR]

See also DEVELOPMENT LAND; DEVELOPMENT PLAN; ENFORCEMENT NOTICE; STOP NOTICE; USE CLASSES.

development land Where the Secretary of State directs a local authority to do so, it must make an assessment of land which is in its area and which is, in its opinion, available and suitable for development for residential purposes (Local Government Planning and Land Act 1980, s. 116(1)). The local authority must comply with any directions the Secretary of State may give in relation to that assessment, in particular regarding the way in which consultation is carried out prior to the assessment.   [DR]

See also DEVELOPMENT.

development plan A collection of documents produced by a local planning authority, which set out the policy framework within which DEVELOPMENT in an area is to be controlled. The Planning and Compulsory Purchase Act 2004 (PCP 2004) introduced major changes to the documents that are to be included in a plan. Prior to the PCP 2004, the plan consisted of a STRUCTURE PLAN, a local plan, a local waste plan, a local mineral plan or – in unitary authorities – a unitary development plan only. For areas other than Greater London, the PCP 2004 replaces all of these plans with regional spatial strategies and local development plan documents (PCP 2004, s. 38(3)). For Greater London, the PCP 2004 replaces the plans with spatial development strategies and local development plan documents (s. 38(2)).

The PCP 2004 contained transitional provisions for new development plans to replace the old ones over a period of three years from 28 September 2004, the date when most parts of the Act came into force. In dealing with applications for PLAN-

NING PERMISSION, the local planning authority must have regard to the provisions of the development plan (Town and Country Planning Act 1990, s. 70(2)).   [DR]

devise A GIFT of REAL PROPERTY contained in a will. The word can also be used as a verb, for example, 'I devise all my property to X'. Although the meaning is very well established, it is not necessary to use it in a will, since the wording 'I give all my real property' is equally effective.   [CM]

devisee The recipient of a gift of REAL PROPERTY in a WILL.   [CM]

devolution The process of transferring political and legislative power from central government to regional or local units. In the UK system, devolved administrations have been created for Scotland, Wales and Northern Ireland. Each of these is created by a STATUTE passed by the UK Parliament: see the Scotland Act 1998, the Government of Wales Acts 1998 and 2006, and the Northern Ireland Act 1998 respectively. This reflects the core distinction between a system of devolved government and a federal system of government (such as that of the US), since devolution, in theory, leaves the SOVEREIGNTY OF PARLIAMENT intact. The devolution Acts are, technically, reversible and the devolved institutions remain constitutionally subordinate to the UK Parliament.

The UK has developed what is called an **asymmetric** system of devolution. This means that there is no single, common model of devolved administration. Thus, Scotland has a Parliament and separate executive, developed along the lines of the UK Parliament, and the Scottish institutions can create both primary and DELEGATED LEGISLATION within the devolved areas. Although the Westminster Parliament can still legislate on devolved matters, it will not do so, under the terms of the SEWEL CONVENTION, unless asked by the Scottish Parliament. By contrast, in Wales, devolved powers were granted initially by the Government of Wales Act 1998 to the NATIONAL ASSEMBLY FOR WALES as a corporate body. However, while arrangements

for Wales still differ from those in place in Scotland, the scope of devolved power has been substantially increased, and a formal separation created between legislature and executive by the Government of Wales Act 2006, which came into operation after the May 2007 elections.   [JW]

DG *See* DIRECTORATE GENERAL.

difference principle *See* DISTRIBUTIVE JUSTICE.

dilapidation A state of disrepair arising from use, generally used in connection with the disrepair recorded at the end of a TENANCY for which the TENANT is liable.

[HC & DR]

diminished responsibility A special defence to MURDER, which, if successfully pleaded, reduces the offence to MANSLAUGHTER. The defence of diminished responsibility is set out in the Homicide Act 1957, s. 2. The operation of the defence presupposes that a defendant has killed with the MENS REA for murder – manslaughter on the grounds of diminished responsibility is thus a form of so-called **voluntary manslaughter**. It requires that the defendant be suffering from an abnormality of mind that has substantially impaired his or her mental responsibility for his or her conduct in the killing. The notion of 'abnormality of mind' is potentially very broad. In *R* v. *Byrne* [1960] 3 All ER 1 it was suggested that it means 'a state of mind so different from that of ordinary human beings that the reasonable man would term it abnormal'. The aetiology of the defendant's condition is important and appropriate medical evidence will be required to show that it arises from one of the causes specified in the statute.

The Homicide Act 1957, s. 2(2) imposes a BURDEN OF PROOF on a defendant to establish diminished responsibility on the balance of probabilities. Whether this responsibility was 'substantially' impaired is a question of fact. If a defendant raises the defence of diminished responsibility, then the prosecution may adduce evidence that the proper defence is INSANITY (see Criminal Procedure (Insanity) Act 1964, s. 6).   [BF]

diplomatic agent A head of a DIPLOMATIC MISSION or a member of the diplomatic staff of the mission – see Article 1(e) of the 1961 Vienna Convention on Diplomatic Relations. All other persons employed by a diplomatic mission, such as administrative, technical and service staff of the mission, do not qualify as diplomatic agents and consequently do not benefit from the immunities and privileges enjoyed by them.   [IB]

See also DIPLOMATIC IMMUNITY.

diplomatic immunity DIPLOMATIC AGENTS and their families enjoy absolute immunity from criminal prosecution in the receiving STATE. Their immunity from civil and administrative jurisdiction, however, is not absolute and is removed in the following cases, in accordance with Article 31 (1) (a)–(c) 1961 Vienna Convention on Diplomatic Relations: (a) where an action relating to private immovable property situated in the territory of the receiving state is concerned, unless the agent holds it on behalf of the sending state for the purposes of the mission; (b) where an action relating to SUCCESSION in which the diplomatic agent is involved as EXECUTOR, ADMINISTRATOR, HEIR or LEGATEE as a private person and not on behalf of the sending state; (c) where it concerns an action relating to any professional or commercial activity exercised by the diplomatic agent in the receiving state outside his or her official functions.   [IB]

diplomatic mission A diplomatic mission is composed of its personnel, classified as either DIPLOMATIC AGENTS or other non-diplomatic staff, and its premises. The person of the diplomatic agent (see DIPLOMATIC IMMUNITY) and the premises are inviolable. In accordance with Article 3(a)–(e) of the Vienna Convention on Diplomatic Relations, the functions of a diplomatic mission include: (a) representing the sending STATE in the receiving state; (b) protecting in the receiving state the interests of the sending state and of its nationals, within the limits permitted by INTERNATIONAL LAW; (c) negotiating with the government of the receiving state; (d) ascertaining by all lawful means conditions and developments in the receiv-

ing state, and reporting on those to the government of the sending state; and (e) promoting friendly relations between the sending state and the receiving state, and developing their economic, cultural and scientific relations.   [IB]

direct applicability *See* DIRECTLY APPLICABLE LAW.

direct effect A principle of EUROPEAN COMMUNITY (EC) law which determines whether a provision of EC legislation is enforceable by the citizens of a MEMBER STATE, and against whom. The concept was originally developed by the EUROPEAN COURT OF JUSTICE (ECJ) in Case 26/62 *Van Gend en Loos* v. *Nederlandse Administratie der Belastingen* [1963] ECR 1. Direct effect may be **vertical**, i.e. effective in cases brought against a Member State, and/or **horizontal**, i.e. effective against other private parties. The provisions of the EUROPEAN COMMUNITY TREATY itself benefit from the principles of both horizontal and vertical direct effect (Case 43/75 *Defrenne* v. *Sabena* [1976] ECR 455), as do EC REGULATIONS. DIRECTIVES are said to have vertical direct effect if they are not implemented, not implemented correctly, or not implemented on time.

The concept of ESTOPPEL was used by the ECJ to further develop the concept of direct effect in Case 148/78, *Pubblico Ministero* v. *Ratti* [1979] ECR 1629. The argument in *Ratti* is premised on the duty on Member States to implement a Directive. If the Member State does not implement or incorrectly implements a Directive, it cannot subsequently rely, in any action brought against it by a legal or natural person, on its own wrongdoing to avoid being bound by the contents of that Directive. Directives do not have horizontal effect and so cannot be relied upon in actions against another private person. The effects of this rule have been mitigated by the development of the FRANCOVICH PRINCIPLE which established state liability in damages for non-implementation of Directives.   [MON]

See also DIRECTLY APPLICABLE LAW; INDIRECT EFFECT.

direct evidence The testimony of a witness concerning matters personally perceived by the witness, which, if believed, would be sufficient to prove a FACT IN ISSUE without further EVIDENCE or the need for INFERENCE. Direct evidence is to be distinguished from CIRCUMSTANTIAL EVIDENCE. [ALTC]

Direct Labour Organization (DLO) A body formed by a LOCAL AUTHORITY to bid for services previously carried out by that authority (e.g. the provision of school dinners and the refuse collection service). [MJ]

direction to jury An instruction to the JURY given by the trial judge, for example in the course of SUMMING UP. A large collection of specimen directions is provided by the Judicial Studies Board: see http://www.jsboard.co.uk/criminal_law/index.htm. [ALTC]

directions The pre-trial instructions given to the parties in civil proceedings by the court. **Allocation directions** are issued early in the proceedings, but thereafter procedure varies depending on whether a case is listed on the fast track or multi-track (see ALLOCATION). In all cases, allocation directions tend to focus on setting the timetable for any remaining disclosure of documents, for exchange of witness statements, and for submitting listing questionnaires. The scope of, or necessity for, expert evidence will also be considered, and directions given for joint or party-appointed experts as required. In fast track cases these are likely to be the only directions issued, until final directions for trial are issued after the filing of the listing questionnaire. In most fast track cases, directions are issued without a hearing.

In multi-track cases this second set of directions are called **case management directions** and may be issued with, or, in straightforward cases, without a further hearing. In many of the latter cases such directions are agreed and put forward by the parties themselves, and approved by the court. This will not be the case in complex high-value cases where the pre-trial process may be managed through a series of hearings at which additional directions may be given, or existing ones varied. [JW]

See also CASE MANAGEMENT CONFERENCE; PRE-TRIAL REVIEW.

Directive A form of EUROPEAN COMMUNITY (EC) legislation, along with REGULATIONS and DECISIONS. It is part of the *ACQUIS COMMUNAUTAIRE*, and is used for the purpose of the harmonization of laws across the EC. It is, as provided for by Article 249 EC, binding 'as to the results to be achieved'; however, that leaves to each MEMBER STATE of the EC the 'choice of form and method'. In the event that the Directive is not implemented correctly, not implemented at all, or is late in being implemented by a particular Member State, then the contents of the Directive have DIRECT EFFECT and may be enforceable against the relevant state. As with all EC SECONDARY LEGISLATION, Directives are in force once published in the OFFICIAL JOURNAL. [MON]

See also FRANCOVICH PRINCIPLE.

directly applicable law Any provision of COMMUNITY LAW that is automatically part of the law of each MEMBER STATE. EUROPEAN COMMUNITY TREATY provisions and REGULATIONS are directly applicable, DIRECTIVES are not. Once they are published in the OFFICIAL JOURNAL of the EUROPEAN COMMUNITY (EC), directly applicable laws must be applied by all of the courts and tribunals in the Member States. [MON]

See also DIRECT EFFECT; INDIRECT EFFECT.

directly effective law *See* DIRECT EFFECT.

director A person appointed to the board of directors of a COMPANY under procedures contained in the ARTICLES OF ASSOCIATION. Every registered company must have at least one director. An employee whose job title describes them as a 'director' but who is not a member of the board is not to be treated as a director in the proper sense of the term, although they may have ostensible authority (see AGENCY) to bind the company as if they were.

There are no formal legal requirements to be a director; however, a person must not have been disqualified by a court from acting as a company director, unless he or she has been given leave (permission) by a court to act for a specific company. An undischarged bankrupt also cannot hold a directorship except with leave of the court.

[JW]

Director of Public Prosecutions (DPP) The head of the CROWN PROSECUTION SERVICE, who must be a legal practitioner of at least ten years' standing. The DPP is appointed by the ATTORNEY GENERAL. A number of offences require the consent of the DPP to initiate a prosecution. [BF]

Directorate General *See* COMMISSION OF THE EUROPEAN COMMUNITIES.

directors' duties Directors act as AGENTS of the COMPANY and therefore owe the company (and its employees) a range of FIDU-CIARY and COMMON LAW obligations. These were codified by the Companies Act 2006, ss. 170–181, as the general duties of directors: to act within their powers; to promote the success of the company for the benefit of its members; to exercise independent judgement; to exercise reasonable care, skill and diligence; to avoid a CONFLICT OF INTERESTS; not to accept benefits from third parties; and to declare any interest in a proposed contract with the company. [JW]

disability discrimination DISCRIMINATION on the ground of disability is forbidden by the Disability Discrimination Act 1995. A disability is 'a physical or mental impairment which has a substantial and long-term adverse effect on [the claimant's] ability to carry out normal day-to-day activities'. Following amendment to the definition of disability in 2005, the mental impairment need not be clinically recognized and HIV-Aids, multiple sclerosis and some forms of cancer are now covered from the point of diagnosis. The coverage of the law has been substantially extended over recent years and discrimination is now forbidden if it is comprised of direct discrimination, disability-related discrimination (a version of indirect discrimination), a failure to make REASONABLE ADJUSTMENTS, HARASSMENT, and or victimization. [MJ]

See also DISABLED PERSON.

disabled person One protected by the Disability Discrimination Act 1995 as amended. He or she must have a 'physical or mental impairment which has a substantial and long-term adverse effect on his [or her] ability to carry out normal day-to-day activities' (s. 1(1)): 'substantial' means 'more than trivial'; 'long term' means lasting for, or expected to last, at least 12 months; 'normal day-to-day activities' are those everyday activities (e.g. eating, washing) which, when performed, affect one or more of the 'capacities' specified in the Act, e.g. mobility and manual dexterity. The definition of disability was amended in 2005, removing the requirement that the mental impairment be clinically recognized. [MJ]

See also DISABILITY DISCRIMINATION.

disapplying an Act of Parliament Membership of the EUROPEAN UNION carries with it an obligation to apply directly enforceable EC law within the UK. But if there is a conflict between European and DOMESTIC LAW, which prevails? The short answer is that EC law must prevail. This is a clear and direct legal consequence of the UK's accession to membership by virtue of the European Communities Act 1972. In practice, in most situations, such conflict may be resolved by creative interpretation, i.e. the court finds a way to interpret the relevant domestic legislation so as to comply with European law. However, in some instances, this is not possible. Where there is a direct and irresolvable conflict, it was established by the House of Lords in *R* v. *Secretary of State for Transport ex parte Factortame (No. 2)* [1991] 1 All ER 70, that the court must override or 'disapply' the offending STATUTE provision. This may seem to run counter to the SOVEREIGNTY OF PARLIAMENT as traditionally understood, but was justified by the court (*per* Lord Bridge at 108) on the basis that the supremacy of EC law 'was certainly well established in the jurisprudence of the [EUROPEAN] COURT OF JUSTICE long before the United Kingdom joined the Community. Thus whatever limitation of its sovereignty Parliament accepted when it enacted the European

Communities Act 1972 was entirely voluntary.'   [JW]

See also DIRECTLY APPLICABLE LAW; IMPLIED REPEAL.

disclosure and inspection of documents in civil cases This is governed by Part 31 of the CIVIL PROCEDURE RULES. Disclosure of a document by a party is achieved 'by stating that the document exists or has existed': CPR Rule 31.2. A party to whom a document has been disclosed has a general right to inspect it.   [ALTC]

disclosure of evidence in criminal cases This has a number of aspects. First, the prosecution has a duty in certain cases to disclose its case. Secondly, the Criminal Procedure and Investigations Act 1996 contains detailed provisions on prosecution disclosure of **unused material**. In general terms, under s. 3(1)(a), the prosecution must disclose to the accused any prosecution material which might reasonably be considered capable of undermining the case for the prosecution or of assisting the case for the accused. Thirdly, the Act also contains detailed provisions on **defence disclosure**.

Where one of a number of specified failures in relation to disclosure by the accused has occurred, or where the accused at trial acts inconsistently in some way with the defence disclosure, the court or the other side may 'make such comment as appears appropriate' (s. 11(5)(a)), and the court or JURY may draw appropriate INFERENCES in deciding whether or not the accused is guilty of the offence (s. 11(5)(b)). However, the accused cannot be convicted solely on such an inference: see s. 11(10).   [ALTC]

disclosure of information The Trade Union and Labour Relations (Consolidation) Act 1992, s. 181, provides that EMPLOYERS must give information for COLLECTIVE BARGAINING purposes to recognized INDEPENDENT TRADE UNIONS on their request. Two principal exceptions to this duty include information received in confidence and information relating to an individual where he or she has not given consent to the disclosure. The CENTRAL ARBITRATION COMMITTEE deals with complaints of breaches of s. 181.   [MJ]

disclosure of interest The duty of LOCAL AUTHORITY members to disclose (in advance or at the time of the meeting) any direct or indirect financial interest they have in a matter to be discussed at a council meeting. Failure to disclose an interest is a criminal offence.   [JW]

discontinuance A decision by the CROWN PROSECUTION SERVICE not to continue with a case.   [SN]

discretion 1. Legal discretion in general may be defined as 'the extent to which officials, whether they be judicial or administrative, make decisions in the absence of previously fixed, relatively clear, and binding legal standards' (D. Galligan, *Discretionary Powers* (Oxford: Clarendon Press, 1986), p. 1). The relationship between legal rules and discretion is an extremely important one and a growing body of empirical research into the operation of official discretion has emphasized the following key features of the relationship: (a) specific rules are invariably, in H.L.A. HART's phrase, 'open textured' and thus contain spaces within which discretion is either expressly permitted (e.g. the discretion of trustees in respect of their powers to invest trust capital), and/or cannot effectively be excluded (e.g. the discretion exercised by police officers on the street); (b) any system of rules is likely to be of limited effectiveness in restricting discretion across a whole decision-making process. If we constrain it at one point in the process, it will likely re-emerge somewhere else; (c) the absence of legal rules does not mean that decision-making is necessarily less normative – a range of organizational, political and economic norms and values will still shape how decisions are made. Consequently, the legal constraints on official decision-making should be viewed as only part of the normative context in which those decisions are made.

2. Legal discretion specifically as **judicial discretion** refers to the inherent power of judges to exercise discretion in decision-

making. In the sense that a judge may decide a case within a range of legitimate outcomes, discretion is a necessary part of judging and, under the doctrine of SEPAR-ATION OF POWERS, the lack of political or other constraints on this kind of judicial discretion is an important feature of judicial independence. Equally, the same doctrine also sets constraints on judicial discretion, in that it is often asserted that judges should avoid expansive uses of discretion that constitute a kind of judicial law-making, rather than the interpretation of existing norms. The rationale for this reflects two arguments: first, the need for legal certainty, that is, the idea that too much discretion is a bad thing precisely because it reduces the certainty, predictability and consistency of legal decision-making; and secondly, an invocation of the 'democratic deficit' of judicial bodies, that is, the idea that in the UK and many other legal systems, judges are not elected and so have no public mandate to make law. [JW]

discretion to exclude evidence The power of a court to exclude admissible EVI-DENCE. Such a power is provided, for example, by the Police and Criminal Evidence Act 1984 (PACE), s. 78(1): 'In any proceedings the court may refuse to allow evidence on which the prosecution proposes to rely to be given if it appears to the court that, having regard to all the circumstances, including the circumstances in which the evidence was obtained, the admission of the evidence would have such an adverse effect on the fairness of the proceedings that the court ought not to admit it.' In civil proceedings, CPR Rule 32.1 provides:

'1. The court may control the evidence by giving directions as to – (a) the issues on which it requires evidence; (b) the nature of the evidence which it requires to decide those issues; and (c) the way in which the evidence is to be placed before the court.

2. The court may use its power under this rule to exclude evidence that would otherwise be admissible.' [ALTC]

discretionary trust A trust where the TRUSTEES have a discretion as to who, among a class of beneficiaries, should benefit from the trust fund and in what proportions. Discretionary trusts can be either exhaustive, requiring the trustees to distribute the entire trust fund, or non-exhaustive, in which case an express **power of accumulation** entitles the trustees to accumulate some or all of the property in favour of accumulation beneficiaries. A member of the class has no vested property interest in the trust fund until the discretion is exercised in that person's favour, although such persons do have a right to be considered and *locus standi* to apply to court in respect of the trustees' exercise of their duties. The class also have the right, provided they are all *sui iuris* and act unanimously, to direct the trustees, under the RULE IN *SAUNDERS* V. *VAUTIER*, to terminate the trust or dictate how the discretion might be exercised. In *McPhail* v. *Doulton* [1971] AC 424, it was held that it was not necessary to list all the potential beneficiaries, provided the class among whom the discretion is to be exercised is defined with sufficient conceptual certainty. This provides the trustees with a clear criterion to apply in assessing whether someone comes within the class and the courts with the means to judge whether or not the trustees are acting within their discretion. Clearly, most words have a penumbra of ambiguity but trustees and the courts will only be defeated by terms that are inherently ambiguous – the classic example being 'friends', on the basis that different people mean different things by this term. [PK]

discrimination The less favourable treatment of another on the basis of some personal characteristic such as age, disability, gender, race or sexual orientation. Protection from discrimination is provided by both national and EUROPEAN COMMUNITY law, prohibiting discrimination in the workplace (including decisions on selection for employment, terms and conditions of employment, including pay, promotion, REDUNDANCY and DISMISSAL) and in the supply of or access to goods and services, including education, housing and social security benefits.

Article 14 of the EUROPEAN CONVENTION ON HUMAN RIGHTS also provides that the enjoyment of Convention rights must be secured to citizens without discrimination. Article 14 sets its protection widely, including discrimination 'on any ground such as sex, race, colour, language, religion, political or other opinion, national or social origin, association with a national minority, property, birth or other status'. The article not only provides a substantive ground for a claim, but can be used more broadly as a guiding principle when the EUROPEAN COURT OF HUMAN RIGHTS is considering the legality of any restrictions on a Convention right.

However, the impact of the Article is significantly restricted by the fact that it does not provide a free-standing and independent right of non-discrimination. A complainant can only bring a case if he or she is able to raise an issue in respect of another Convention right. Thus, in *Choudhury* v. *United Kingdom* (1991) 12 HRLJ 172, the applicant's claim under Articles 9 and 14 was declared inadmissible by the (then) EUROPEAN COMMISSION ON HUMAN RIGHTS. The Commission found that the failure of the UK to extend its BLASPHEMY laws to include non-Christian faiths was not actionable under Article 9 (freedom of religion) since this did not impose any positive obligation on the STATE to protect religious sentiments by effective blasphemy laws. Consequently, since there was no possible obligation on the state under Article 9, an action under Article 14 could not be sustained. Discrimination can also be justified under the Convention provided the distinction is reasonable, and justifiable on objective grounds, and the difference in treatment is proportionate (see PROPORTIONALITY) to the aim it is seeking to achieve.   [JW]

See also AGE DISCRIMINATION; DISABILITY DISCRIMINATION; EQUAL PAY; EQUAL TREATMENT; RACIAL DISCRIMINATION; SEX DISCRIMINATION; SEXUAL ORIENTATION DISCRIMINATION.

dishonest assistance *See* KNOWING ASSISTANCE.

dismissal In employment law, the termination by the employer of an employee's contract of employment. At COMMON LAW there are two main types of dismissal. The first type is sometimes known as 'direct', 'actual' or 'express' dismissal, and covers the situation where the employer dismisses (i.e. sacks) the worker, for example by expressly saying so. This is not necessarily unlawful, e.g. where dismissal follows a requisite period of notice, or where the employee's breach of contract gives grounds for summary dismissal, but if it is not in accordance with the contract, a dismissal may ground a common law action for WRONGFUL DISMISSAL.

The second type is called 'repudiation' and is sometimes known as **constructive dismissal**. This occurs where the employers have acted so badly that the employee is contractually entitled to leave (e.g. the employers have refused to pay any salary). These two varieties of dismissal are also reflected in the principles underlying statutory claims for UNFAIR DISMISSAL and REDUNDANCY PAYMENTS, which have largely superseded the action for wrongful dismissal. There is also a third type of dismissal, arising out of the expiry without renewal of a limited-term (previously called a fixed-term) contract of employment. [MJ]

disorderly house 'A house conducted contrary to law and good order in that matters are performed or exhibited of such a character that their performance or exhibition in a place of common resort (a) amounts to an outrage of public decency or (b) tends to corrupt or deprave or (c) is otherwise calculated to injure the public interest so as to call for condemnation and punishment (see *R* v. *Quinn* and *R* v. *Bloom* [1962] 2 QB 245 at 255, *per* Ashworth J).

It is an offence at common law to keep a disorderly house. The offence can, in theory, be committed by a single prostitute working in a private house (see *R* v. *Tan* [1983] QB 1053, and contrast the definition of BROTHEL, which requires more than one person offering services), although this would depend on the nature of the services offered. It is also a requirement that the house is open, though not necessarily to the general public. 'Keeping' requires an element of habitual or persistent behaviour. Thus, in *Moores* v. *DPP* (1992) 94 Cr App R 173, a single indecent performance by a male exotic dancer did not suffice. The Disorderly Houses Act 1751, s. 8, allows for the prosecution of those who appear, act or behave as keeper, even if they are not the actual keeper. [BF]

disposition A transfer of property either absolutely or via a trust as a result of a gift, sale, exchange or the grant of a security interest. [PK]

Dispute Settlement Body (DSB) *See* WORLD TRADE ORGANIZATION.

disqualification For the purposes of the criminal law, disqualification denotes a form of penalty imposed on commission of an offence, and consisting, in essence, in an order that the offender not take part, for a specified period, in a defined activity. Thus one may be disqualified from driving on commission of certain road traffic offences. Moreover, it is an offence to drive while so disqualified. One may also be disqualified from acting as a company director on conviction for various offences relating to the functioning of a COMPANY. It is an offence to act in contravention of such a disqualification order (see Company Directors Disqualification Act 1986, s. 13). [BF]

See also DRIVING WHILE DISQUALIFIED.

dissolution A registered CIVIL PARTNERSHIP may only be dissolved by order of the court. The Civil Partnership Act 2004 provides that there is only one ground for dissolution of civil partnerships: IRRETRIEVABLE BREAKDOWN. The Act further provides that the court must not hold the civil partnership to have broken down irretrievably unless the applicant satisfies the court of one or more of four facts: UNREASONABLE BEHAVIOUR, a two-year SEPARATION with consent of the respondent, separation for a period of five years, and DESERTION. A dissolution order is conditional only; after six weeks have elapsed from its making, the applicant may apply to the court to have it made final. It is only on the making of the final order that the civil partnership is dissolved and the parties become free to register new civil partnerships or MARRIAGES. [AD]

dissolution of Parliament Under the Parliament Act 1911, a Parliament can last for up to a maximum of five years, although the Prime Minister may choose to call a general election before the expiry of the full term. In either case, the monarch must issue a Royal Proclamation dissolving Parliament and requiring the **writs of election** to be sent out. A writ of election is an order, sent to each constituency, requiring an election to be held. At the same time, a general election timetable is put in place, leading to **polling day** (the day on which votes are actually cast), 18 days after dissolution. [JW]

distress for rent A COMMON LAW remedy for unpaid RENT which permits a LANDLORD in person or a certificated bailiff to enter tenanted property and seize goods until the rent is paid. The remedy is restricted to arrears of rent, although LEASES can define rent broadly, to include, for example, service charges. The landlord cannot use force to enter the premises. The goods may be sold five days after taking possession of them. The landlord must get the best price for the goods and must hand back any surplus monies to the TENANT, following the deduction of bailiff fees and the arrears. The tenant has a number of remedies in cases where the distress has been illegal, irregular or excessive.

Distress for rent applies to both residential and commercial premises although there are statutory safeguards in both the Rent Act 1977 and the Housing Act 1988 which restrict its use in residential cases. In practice it is rarely used within the residential sector. [HC & DR]

distribution right The exclusive right of a copyright owner under Council Directive 2001/29/EC on the harmonization of certain aspects of copyright and related rights in the information society to authorize or prohibit the circulation of physical copies of the work in which copyright resides. [US]

See also RENTAL RIGHT.

distributive justice On what basis can we say that the spread or distribution of social or material 'goods' – such as property, welfare, wealth, rights – is fair or proper? This difficult question lies at the heart of concerns with distributive justice. Principles of distributive justice are thus normative principles (SEE NORM) intended to guide decisions about the allocation of such goods.

The simplest and also potentially one of the most radical perspectives on distributive justice is **egalitarianism**. In its strict form, egalitarianism argues that every person should possess the same *level* of goods and services. A more moderated egalitarianism, by contrast, might say only that persons are entitled to equal *access* to social and material goods or resources. This is one basis, for example, on which discrimination is deemed to be wrong and unlawful – it undermines the principle of EQUAL TREATMENT, which is itself built on the belief that all persons are equally deserving of respect. Egalitarianism itself raises important questions about how we should measure the goods to be distributed, about the reasons that might justify a departure from equality and about the role of the state in fixing the distribution or redistribution of such goods. In one of the major contributions to 20th-century political and legal theory, JOHN RAWLS attempts to address these questions.

Drawing on the principle of equal respect, Rawls constructs what has become known as the '**difference principle**' as a way of determining what justifications there are for inequality. He argues that, subject to certain underlying constraints, social benefits and burdens should be distributed in such a way as to operate to the greatest benefit of the least advantaged members of society. This means that the difference principle actually *prescribes* inequality up to the point where the material position of the least advantaged can no longer be raised, but advocates strict equality in situations where the benefits to the least advantaged

are already maximized. At no point can the difference principle be used to justify materially disadvantaging the least advantaged group. The difference principle has been highly influential, but has also attracted widespread criticism, from strict egalitarians who see Rawls's favouring of the least advantaged as permitting too much inequality elsewhere in the system, from neo-liberals such as Nozick who are critical of its anti-libertarian and redistributive effects, and from UTILITARIANISM, which questions its failure to ensure utility maximization.   [JW]

Further reading: John Rawls, *A Theory of Justice,* revised edn (Cambridge, MA: Belknap Press, 1999).

district council A local authority area in England with responsibility for a part of a COUNTY, called a **district.** District councils have exclusive responsibility for a limited range of services, including local amenities, housing and planning, and share other local government responsibilities (such as education and social care) with the COUNTY COUNCILS.   [JW]

district court The local criminal court in Scotland, the jurisdiction of which coincides with the boundaries of the local authority. Presided over either by a stipendiary magistrate or a justice of the peace, the former has the power to imprison for a maximum of three months, the latter for a maximum of 60 days. The court deals with minor criminal offences. Prosecutions are brought by the PROCURATOR FISCAL. Appeal against conviction lies to the HIGH COURT OF JUSTICIARY.   [JP]

See also SHERIFF COURT.

district judge Formerly known as a county court **Registrar**; a salaried (full-time) judge who deals with the majority of cases coming before the county courts. The part-time judicial equivalent is called a **deputy district judge.** Under the Tribunals, Courts and Enforcement Act 2007, solicitors or barristers with at least five years' relevant experience may be appointed to sit as a district or deputy district judge.

[JW]

district judge (magistrates' court) Professional salaried members of the judiciary, they are appointed on the recommendation of the LORD CHANCELLOR and are barristers or solicitors of at least seven years' standing (previously known as stipendiary magistrates). A district judge can sit alone to try cases in the magistrates' court. [SN]

disturbance An interference with another's rights. The term is used most commonly in connection with possession of LAND or premises. If a LANDLORD breaches the TENANT's right to quiet enjoyment, for example, then that breach is a disturbance and the tenant is entitled to compensation. LOCAL HOUSING AUTHORITIES frequently pay disturbance allowances when tenants have had to move in order for works to be carried out to the property. [HC & DR]

dividend The distribution of part of a company's profits to shareholders. It may be paid once or, more often, twice a year. If an interim dividend is declared, it will be paid by a COMPANY midway through its financial year and the final dividend will be paid at the end. The company directors have discretion as to how much, if any, of a dividend to declare in any given year, and the distribution of the payment will depend on the terms of the share CONTRACT. Dividends are quoted in the amount paid per SHARE. [JW]

divisible contract A contract in which the parties' obligations are independent of each other so that a breach by party A will not entitle party B to cease performance of party B's obligations under the contract. Such contracts are rare and most contracts are indivisible, i.e. the parties' obligations are inter-dependent. [JPL]

division Both the HOUSE OF COMMONS and the HOUSE OF LORDS vote on important matters by a process of division, that is by a rising vote, whereby members of the House split into two groups, indicating a vote in favour of or in opposition to a motion from the floor. The vote is counted manually by tellers who count the members entering the appropriate **division lobby.** There are two lobbies in each House, one for those supporting and the other for those opposing a motion. The total votes in each lobby are written on a card, which is read by the SPEAKER, or the LORD SPEAKER, who then announces the final result. [JW]

Divisional Court A hearing conducted before a panel of two or sometimes three judges in one of the divisions of the HIGH COURT. [JW]

divorce The legal dissolution of a MARRIAGE, usually requiring an order of the court. Before 1857, judicial divorce was not available in England and Wales. The ECCLESIASTICAL COURTS could pronounce only decrees of nullity of marriage and divorces a *mensa et thoro* ('from board and bed'), what we would know now as judicial separation. Only Parliament could dissolve a marriage. Even after the Matrimonial Causes Act 1857 divorce was difficult to obtain; it was only available from the High Court in London and it could only be granted on very restricted grounds which required culpability on the part of a guilty spouse, the respondent, and complete innocence on the part of the wronged spouse, the petitioner. A limited number of matrimonial offences were sufficiently serious to justify the termination of a marriage.

Divorce law has gone through a number of reforms since then and each time reformers have debated whether, in the interests of promoting marriage, divorce ought to be made 'easier' or more 'difficult' in law. Reform initiatives in the 1960s, in particular, were concerned with the degree to which divorce ought to remain based upon fault – the matrimonial offence. It was questioned, for example, whether marriage breakdown could ever be fairly attributed to the 'fault' of one spouse only and the idea of the matrimonial offence was also said to increase hostility and acrimony between the parties; reformers explored seriously the idea of no-fault divorce by consent. The resulting Divorce Reform Act 1969 created a basis for divorce in England and Wales that was a compromise between matrimonial fault and no-fault approaches.

The 1969 Act is now incorporated with other legislation into the Matrimonial Causes Act 1973. It states that there is only one ground for divorce: IRRETRIEVABLE BREAKDOWN, of the marriage, but that a court may not find that a marriage has broken down unless one or more of five facts are proved: (a) that the respondent has committed ADULTERY and the petitioner finds it intolerable to continue to live with the respondent; (b) that the respondent has behaved in such a way that the petitioner cannot reasonably be expected to live with the respondent; (c) that the parties have lived separately for a continuous period of two years and the respondent consents to the divorce; (d) that the parties have lived separately for a continuous period of five years; or (e) that the respondent has deserted the petitioner for a continuous period of two years. If the court is satisfied as to one or more of these facts and as to the irretrievable breakdown of the marriage, it must grant a DECREE NISI of divorce. After a further six weeks, the petitioner is entitled to apply to the court for the DECREE ABSOLUTE of divorce. Only on the grant of the decree absolute is the marriage dissolved and the parties become free once again to marry or register a CIVIL PARTNERSHIP with another person. On granting a decree nisi, the court acquires the jurisdiction to reallocate the former spouses' finances between them: see ANCILLARY RELIEF.   [AD]

See also ANNULMENT; BREAKDOWN OF MARRIAGE; DESERTION; EXTRAJUDICIAL DIVORCE; GET; SEPARATION; UNREASONABLE BEHAVIOUR.

divorce registry The Central Index of Decrees Absolute and of Final Orders for the Dissolution or Annulment of Civil Partnerships keeps records of all DIVORCES and dissolutions granted in England and Wales from 1858 to the present day and is part of the PRINCIPAL REGISTRY OF THE FAMILY DIVISION, located in London. They are public records and, for a fee, staff will search them on request.   [AD]

See also FAMILY COUNTY COURTS.

DLO See DIRECT LABOUR ORGANIZATION.

dock An enclosed place in a criminal court

where the defendant is held during the trial.   [SN]

doctor–patient confidentiality The duty of a doctor to respect a patient's right to privacy is central to the doctor–patient relationship. Information regarding a person's health is by nature essentially private and a patient may be unwilling to disclose sensitive information that may affect his treatment if he believes it likely that it will be disclosed to others not involved in his care and treatment. The duty is expressed both in the HIPPOCRATIC OATH: 'Whatsoever things I see or hear concerning the life of men, in my attendance on the sick or even apart therefrom, which ought not to be noised abroad, I will keep silence thereon, counting such things to be as sacred secrets…' and in the DECLARATION OF GENEVA: '*I will respect the secrets that are confided in me, even after the patient has died.*'

A doctor's obligation of confidentiality extends to all patients regardless of age, but is not absolute; it must be balanced against society's interests in protecting vulnerable people from serious harm. Consequently, where a doctor believes that there is a serious risk of the patient's actions causing harm to himself or to a third party, and he cannot persuade the patient to make a voluntary disclosure, a doctor may be justified in breaching confidentiality. Communications between a doctor and patient enjoy some legal protections, chiefly: (a) although doctor–patient confidentiality does not attract any evidential PRIVILEGE (see *R* v. *Kingston (Duchess of)* (1776) 20 State Trials 619), the court has a discretion to uphold a refusal to disclose where it is satisfied that it is in the public interest to do so: *D* v. *NSPCC* [1978] AC 171; (b) doctors may only provide medical reports to third parties for insurance or employment purposes after obtaining the written consent of the patient under the Access to Medical Reports Act 1988. Patients may also exercise certain rights of access to their health records under the Data Protection Act 1998.   [HJ]

documentary evidence EVIDENCE contained in a document. Documentary evidence constitutes a major category of REAL EVIDENCE. Its ADMISSIBILITY depends on proof of its authenticity, and consideration of the purpose for which it is being admitted. For example, if a document is offered in evidence to prove the truth of a statement it contains, then its admission must not offend the rule against HEARSAY. There are also specific rules regulating the use of certain kinds of documents in evidence: see, for example, the Criminal Justice Act 2003, s. 117, concerning documents created or received in the course of employment or a similar context. [ALTC]

See also PUBLIC DOCUMENTS.

doli incapax (Lat. incapable of crime) A child under the age of 10 is conclusively deemed to be *doli incapax*, and therefore may not be charged with and convicted of a criminal offence. The rebuttable presumption that a child between 10 and 14 was not capable of committing a criminal offence was abolished by the Crime and Disorder Act 1998. [JW]

dolus specialis (Lat. special or specific deceit) In legal terms, this translates to the notion of SPECIFIC INTENT. The term *dolus specialis* tends to be used in CIVIL LAW and INTERNATIONAL LAW contexts, but not in the COMMON LAW tradition. International law recognizes a number of specific intent crimes, the most significant of which is GENOCIDE. In prosecuting for genocide, the prosecutor must demonstrate that the perpetrator intended to destroy a particular group in whole or in part. This (whole or in part destruction) constitutes the specific intent for the crime of genocide and it is this which differentiates genocide from CRIMES AGAINST HUMANITY. [IB]

domain name The unique identifier required of every website. Domain names consist of a second-level domain – a chosen word or series of words (e.g. 'penguin') – followed by a top-level domain (TLD), many of which describe the nature of the enterprise (e.g. .com, .edu, .org). Sometimes this is followed by an internet country code top-level domain (ccTLD) such as .uk. To obtain a domain name it is neces-sary to register it with a domain registry. A registered domain name is distinct from the BUSINESS NAME and is not subject to the same legal conditions as apply to business names. A domain name cannot be registered as a TRADE MARK, unless the business trades in that name in goods or services.

There is no accepted international legal treaty on domain names, though the WORLD INTELLECTUAL PROPERTY ORGANIZATION is currently attempting to draft a harmonized approach to domain name registration (see their Guide to Uniform Domain Name Dispute Resolution Policy (UDRP)). A ccTLD is an internet top-level domain generally used or reserved for a country or a dependent territory. The domain registry is typically controlled by the government of that country. Other domain names are regulated by the Internet Corporation for Assigned Names and Numbers (ICANN) Board. ICANN provides an administrative procedure for disputes concerning an alleged abusive registration of a domain name. The procedure is administered by the WIPO Arbitration and Mediation Centre (WIPO Centre). See http://arbiter. wipo.int/domains/decisions/index.html. [US]

See also CYBER-SQUATTING; PASSING OFF.

domestic arbitration An arbitral process between parties who are resident, domiciled or otherwise settled in the territory of the seat of arbitration. It is important to make a distinction between domestic and INTERNATIONAL ARBITRATION, and also international commercial arbitration. The distinction is important in relation to those jurisdictions which have restrictions on domestic arbitration proceedings, but have no restrictions in relation to international commercial arbitral proceedings.

A domestic arbitration can be one which is concerned with a commercial claim between business entities, or with a non-commercial claim such as between neigh-bouring property owners. [RE]

See also ARBITRATOR; COMMERCIAL ARBITRATION.

domestic law The laws of an individual STATE, as contrasted with INTERNATIONAL LAW. [JW]

domestic tribunal A body that exercises disciplinary or similar powers over the members of a profession or association – e.g. the Solicitors' Disciplinary Tribunal. The jurisdiction of a tribunal may be established by STATUTE, or by contract between members of the association. Decisions of a domestic tribunal may be subject to JUDICIAL REVIEW by the courts. Rights of appeal from a domestic tribunal may also lie to a court, but only where this is provided for by statute. [JW]

See also ADMINISTRATIVE TRIBUNAL; TRIBUNAL.

domestic violence Abuse of a FAMILY member. It can take the form of violence against children or elderly relatives, but most often occurs between intimate partners. While at one time concern about domestic violence focused on wife-beating, it is now accepted that domestic violence can take many forms, both physical and non-physical. While there is evidence that domestic violence can occur in same-sex relationships, or by women against men, the available research suggests that it is overwhelmingly directed by men against women. There is no specific offence in criminal law of domestic violence, but many of the physical acts constitute criminal assaults and other acts can constitute offences under the Protection from Harassment Act 1997. According to the HOME OFFICE, domestic violence accounts for a quarter of all recorded crimes in England and Wales and an average of two women per week are killed by their partners or former partners. Victims of domestic violence may also use the CIVIL LAW to protect themselves. The Family Law Act 1996 provides for those experiencing domestic violence to seek NON-MOLESTATION ORDERS or to have the abuser removed from the home. [AD]

See also CHILD ABUSE; OCCUPATION ORDER; RESTRAINING ORDER.

domicile A factor connecting a person to a particular legal system. For the purposes of conflicts of law, an individual's law of the domicile – *lex domicilii* – is their personal law, and as such it may be of considerable importance in determining both the juris-diction of a country's courts and various matters of legal status, capacity or right, such as capacity to marry, tax status and the basis upon which a person's property may be distributed after death.

Domicile is not capable of simple definition. It is often defined as the law of the COUNTRY in which a person makes their permanent home, but this is an oversimplification. It is possible to live for many years in a country without it becoming one's domicile – see, e.g., *Winans* v. *Attorney General* [1904] AC 287. Domicile may take one of three forms. First, everyone is born with a **domicile of origin**. This is determined at birth; where a child is born legitimate, it is the domicile of their father at the time; if illegitimate, the domicile of the mother. This remains, as it were, the default domicile. Second, a child under the age of 16 or a mentally disordered person may acquire a **domicile of dependency** where the domicile of the person on whom they are legally dependent changes. Lastly, an adult of full LEGAL CAPACITY may take a new **domicile of choice**. This requires evidence of both residence in the country of the new domicile, and an intention to reside there permanently or indefinitely. The burden of proving a change of domicile lies on the person who asserts it. The change of a domicile of origin must be proved beyond reasonable doubt, while the change of a domicile of choice needs only to be proved on a balance of probabilities. Even after a domicile of choice has been established, it may be lost as soon as either the fact of residence or the intention permanently to reside changes. At this point, the domicile of origin revives, unless a new domicile of choice can be established.

No one can at the same time and for the same purpose have more than one domicile. However, in a FEDERAL STATE (i.e. one comprising several different jurisdictions), the law may create different domiciles for different purposes. For example, in Australia, s. 39(3)(b) of the Family Law Act 1975 (Commonwealth) creates a unified Australian domicile for the purpose of DIVORCE jurisdiction, and separate from the domicile a citizen may have in one of the various states, such as New South Wales, or Victoria, for other purposes.

The rules for determining domicile may differ as between countries. In England, for CHOICE OF LAW purposes, the question where a person is domiciled must be determined according to English law – *Re Annesley* [1926] Ch 692. [JW]

dominant tenement A piece of land that is benefited by an EASEMENT or a profit appurtenant to land, that is, a benefit annexed or incident to ownership of the land, such as a right to graze animals on adjacent common land. [DR]

See also PROFIT À PRENDRE; SERVIENT TENEMENT.

dominion (obsolete) Originally used to refer to overseas CROWN territories, by the mid-1800s, the term was confined to wholly or virtually self-governing territories of the British Empire, particularly Canada, Australia and New Zealand. Thus a dominion was seen as evolving from the status of a dependent territory or that of a colony. By the 20th century, dominions were deemed to exercise full SOVEREIGNTY and this became clear with the passing of the Statute of Westminster in 1931. Dominion is also reserved to describe self-governing countries within the Commonwealth of Nations, other than the United Kingdom, where the British monarch remains head of state. Today, the former dominions of the Empire (including the UK) are known as Realms of the Commonwealth. [IB]

donatio mortis causa (Lat. a gift on account of death) A strange concept based on Roman law, which enables someone to make a GIFT of property to be effective on his death without observing the formal requirements of the Wills Act 1837. The justification for it appears to be that there may be a situation where someone wishes to make a testamentary disposition but is not in a position to make a WILL. Nevertheless, courts have criticized the doctrine as anomalous.

The requirements for a valid *donatio* are: (a) the gift must be made in contemplation of impending death; (b) it must be made on the condition that it will be absolute and perfected only on the donor's death; and (c) there must be a delivery of the subject matter of the gift amounting to a parting with ownership or title and not mere physical possession of the subject matter of the gift. The third requirement may be met by handing over something establishing title to the subject matter rather than the object itself.

A typical example of how this arises would be a situation where someone is seriously ill in hospital, and does not expect to recover, and hands some jewellery to a friend saying: 'If I don't recover I want you to have this.' It would be the same if the donor handed over the keys and registration document of a motor car rather than the car itself. [CM]

double criminality A principle entrenched in the law of EXTRADITION, whereby the requested state will proceed with extradition only where the alleged conduct of the accused amounts to a crime in both the requesting and the requested state.

Two types of extradition treaties have been devised in order to comply with this requirement. The first involves the inclusion of a list of crimes, common to all state parties (these are usually bilateral treaties). The disadvantage with the list-type of treaties is that they have to be updated regularly to take into account new crimes and developments.

The second is found in most modern treaties which adopt the practice of defining extradition offences by reference to a minimum level of punishment, thus avoiding the need for a list that can easily become outdated. In the context of the EUROPEAN ARREST WARRANT, where any of the following crimes are punished by a custodial sentence of at least three years, the double criminality rule does not apply: terrorism, trafficking in human beings, corruption, participation in a CRIMINAL ORGANIZATION, counterfeiting currency, MURDER, racism and xenophobia, RAPE, trafficking in stolen vehicles, fraud, including that

affecting the financial interests of the EU.
[IB]

double effect A principle invoked to explain why an effect that would be morally, and often legally, wrong if caused deliberately, is permissible as a side effect of an act that is in itself morally good (or at least not morally bad) and is justifiable in the circumstances as outweighing the bad effect. It refers most frequently to the situation in which a doctor administers drugs, often diamorphine, with the primary purpose of relieving pain, notwithstanding that as a secondary and not necessarily unforeseen consequence the life of the patient will be shortened. The intention is to relieve pain; the death of the patient – while not unforeseen – is unintended (see *Re J (Wardship: Medical treatment)* [1991] 2 WLR 140; *Airedale NHS Trust* v. *Bland* [1993] AC 789). [HJ]

See also ADVANCE DECISION; ASSISTED SUICIDE; EUTHANASIA.

double jeopardy 1. In English law, a defence to prosecution of a crime which has already been tried. If brought to trial, a defendant may plead *autrefois acquit* or *autrefois convict*, meaning that she or he has previously been acquitted or convicted of the same offence. If the plea is successful, it will bar any further proceedings on the INDICTMENT. Exceptionally, under the Criminal Justice Act 2003, a new trial will be permitted where the accused has been acquitted of a serious offence in court, but compelling new evidence has since come to light which indicates that he or she was guilty.
2. A principle of EXTRADITION law, whereby persons who have already been tried and discharged or convicted and punished in another STATE are exempt from extradition proceedings for the same OFFENCE. The principle may be subject to certain exceptions, particularly where the criminal proceedings were designed to shield the accused, or where an AMNESTY was granted in respect of a serious international offence which other states refuse to recognize. None the less, Article 2 of the 1975 Additional Protocol to the European Convention on Extradition prohibits extradition where an amnesty or pardon has been granted.
[JW & IB]

See also DOUBLE CRIMINALITY.

double probate When a WILL appoints two EXECUTORS, but only one of them applies for a GRANT OF PROBATE, the grant will normally be made with power to be reserved to the non-proving executor (i.e. the one who did not apply for the grant). This means that the non-proving executor is not precluded from applying for probate at a later date. Until then, the proving executor has full power to act alone, but if the second executor does apply, then the grant to him will be a double probate. This situation could arise, for example, if the second executor has not attained the age of 18 when the first grant is made. [CM]

double taxation Assessment to the same tax on the same source, on more than one occasion in the same time period, and payable either by the same person or by different persons.

In the domestic domain, the same income might be taxed twice in the same tax year where, for example, the income is taxed in the hands of a personal representative and then again in the hands of the same individual as beneficiary. In this situation, the same person (but in different capacities) is charged the same tax on different occasions in respect of the same income. Where the taxed income of a company is distributed to a shareholder who is charged tax on that income, different persons will be taxed in respect of the same value.

In the international domain, double taxation is, usually, created by different legal systems using different connecting factors and different tax jurisdictional bases in the context of cross-border business enterprise. The UK taxes individuals and companies on the basis of their residence. A taxpayer who is resident in the UK will be taxed on their income obtained from all sources, whether domestic or foreign (the **world-wide basis**). But another state might tax income on the basis of where the income is generated (the **source basis**). Thus, where a cross-border enterprise earns income in a state which uses the source basis, and the enterprise is resident in a state which uses the worldwide basis, there will be double taxation. [RE]

See also DOUBLE TAXATION RELIEF.

double taxation relief The reduction of a taxpayer's UK tax liability by reference to the tax paid by them in a foreign COUNTRY on value which is brought into charge to tax on the taxpayer in that other country as well as in the UK. The extent of the reduction is determined by UK tax law; and the amount of the reduction does not necessarily eliminate double taxation completely. Where there is a treaty between the UK and the foreign country, the reduction is referred to as double taxation relief (or double tax relief); but where there is no treaty, the reduction (if any) is referred to as unilateral tax relief. There are different forms of relief. The usual form of double taxation relief in the UK is a credit against UK tax. The UK has about 100 double tax treaties, but usually not with TAX HAVENS. Most of the double taxation treaties entered into by the UK are based on the Model Convention on Income and Capital (MTC) produced by the Organization for Economic Cooperation and Development. [RE]

DPP *See* DIRECTOR OF PUBLIC PROSECUTIONS.

drink-driving *See* DRUNKEN DRIVING.

driver For the purposes of the Road Traffic Act 1988, 'driver' includes any person engaged in the driving of a motor vehicle (see Road Traffic Act 1988, s. 192). [BF]

driving licence An official authorization to drive or ride a VEHICLE or motorcycle. Vehicles are divided into different categories and it is necessary to hold the appropriate licence for the type of vehicle being driven. Additionally, drivers must meet minimum age requirements for the vehicle, and satisfy the legal eyesight standards. A full licence is only issued after passing the appropriate driving test. A learner driver must be in possession of a provisional licence before driving on a public road or HIGHWAY. A full driving licence may serve as a provisional licence for categories of vehicle not covered by the full licence. Driving without a valid licence, or while disqualified, is a criminal offence. [BF]

See also DRIVING WHILE DISQUALIFIED; DRIVING WITHOUT A LICENCE.

driving while disqualified Under the Road Traffic Act 1988, s. 103, it is an offence to obtain a DRIVING LICENCE or to drive a motor vehicle on a road while disqualified from holding or obtaining a licence. [BF]

driving while unfit Under the Road Traffic Act 1988 (as amended), s. 4, it is an offence to drive or attempt to drive a mechanically propelled vehicle on a road or other public place when unfit through drink or drugs. [BF]

driving without a licence Under the Road Traffic Act 1988, s. 87, it is an offence to drive a motor vehicle on a road, or to cause or permit a motor vehicle to be driven on a road, otherwise than in accordance with a licence authorizing the driver to drive the class of vehicle in question. [BF]

driving without insurance Under the Road Traffic Act 1988, s. 143, it is an offence to use a vehicle, or to cause or permit a vehicle to be used, on a road or other public place, without a recognized policy of insurance. [BF]

droite de suite The French term for RESALE ROYALTY RIGHT whereby charges are collected on the resale of any COPYRIGHT protected ARTISTIC WORK. [US]

drug treatment and testing order A SENTENCE handed down by the court which aims to provide an offender with fast access to a drug treatment programme with the goal of reducing drug-related offending. Offenders agree their treatment plan with the probation and treatment services. The plan will set out the level of treatment and testing and what is required at each stage of the order. This type of sentence is appropriate for problem drug users aged over 16 who commit crime to fund their drug habit and show a willingness to cooperate with treatment. [SN]

drunken driving Under of the Road Traffic Act 1988, s. 5, it is an offence to drive or attempt to drive a motor vehicle on a road or other public place, or to be in charge of a motor vehicle on a road or other public place, with a concentration of alcohol in one's blood, breath or urine above the prescribed limit. [BF]

drunkenness See INTOXICATION.

DSB The WTO's Dispute Settlement Body. See WORLD TRADE ORGANIZATION. [JW]

dualism In INTERNATIONAL LAW theory, dualism represents a rejection of the argument that international and DOMESTIC LAW operate within the same sphere, even though they may in fact regulate the same subject matter. It is argued that because international law regulates inter-state relationships, whereas domestic law regulates those of natural or legal persons within STATES, the two systems are mutually exclusive and it is impossible for them to come into conflict with one another. [IB]

See also INCORPORATION DOCTRINE; MONISM; TRANSFORMATION DOCTRINE.

due diligence The performance of a check into the background of a party to a commercial transaction in order to ensure that they are able to meet their obligations and that they have accurately and fairly represented their position. The check may focus on a range of factors including solvency and compliance with regulatory requirements. [JP]

dum casta vixerit (From the Lat. *dum sola et casta vixerit,* while she lives unmarried and chaste) Historically, men's responsibilities to support their ex-wives were limited in this way. Obligations to support still continue until the remarriage of the recipient ex-spouse. [AD]

durante absentia (Lat. during the absence) Prior to the passing of the Supreme Court Act 1981, a grant of LETTERS OF ADMINISTRATION *durante absentia* could be made if the person entitled to a grant was outside the jurisdiction. However, that Act gave the court a general discretion to appoint an adminis-

trator by reason of any circumstance where it appears to be necessary or expedient to do so, which will normally cover this situation. [CM]

duress 1. A DEFENCE to a criminal charge in which the defendant admits that they fulfilled all the requirements of the offence in question, but suggests that they did so because their will was overborne by what they reasonably believed to be threats of death or serious physical injury, and that a sober person of reasonable firmness would have responded to the threat in a similar fashion (see *R* v. *Graham* (1982) 74 Cr App R 235). Duress is not a defence to a charge of MURDER or attempted murder (see *R* v. *Howe* [1987] 1 AC 417; *R* v. *Gotts* [1992] 2 AC 412). Special considerations apply to those who voluntarily expose themselves to the risk of being subjected to threats, by, for example, associating themselves with criminal gangs: in *R* v. *Hasan* [2005] 2 AC 467, the House of Lords took the view that the defence would not be available to defendant who foresaw or ought to have foreseen the possibility of being threatened in the requisite manner if they did not commit any type of crime.

Although duress developed initially to accommodate the situation of a defendant who was threatened by another, a further form of the defence has emerged in relatively recent years where the threat to the defendant comes not from another person but from the situation in which they find themselves. The requirements for so-called 'duress of circumstances' mirror those for the orthodox form of the defence in all other respects (see also NECESSITY).

2. In CIVIL LAW matters, acts carried out under duress are usually of limited or no legal effect, for example, a CONTRACT entered into under duress is VOIDABLE at the suit of the victim. It has also been held that excessively hard bargaining in negotiations establishing a settlement agreement might itself constitute a form of ECONOMIC DURESS, making the settlement voidable (see *Capital Structures plc* v. *Time & Tide Construction Ltd* [2006] CILL 2345 (TCC)). In the civil context, duress must be distinguished

both from UNDUE INFLUENCE and from NECES-
SITY. [BF & JW]

duty A moral or legal obligation, often
understood to exist as the correlative of a
RIGHT. [JP]
See also HOHFELD, WESLEY NEWCOMB; INTEREST
THEORY; WILL THEORY.

duty of care *See* NEGLIGENCE.

duty prosecutor A CROWN PROSECUTOR who
attends police stations to provide guidance
and advice to investigators and make charging decisions. [SN]

Dworkin, Ronald (b. 1931) Successor to H.
L.A. HART as Professor of Jurisprudence at
Oxford; currently holds positions at University College London and New York University.

Dworkin is among the sternest critics of
legal positivism, with Hart as his primary
target. His two principal objections to
Hart's account of the legal system are that
(a) it leaves no room for the operation of
principles as opposed to rules; and (b) it
wrongly characterizes the nature and
extent of judicial discretion.

As regards his first objection, Dworkin
contends that when lawyers reason about
rights and obligations they make use of
standards other than rules and in particular
they make use of principles. A principle, for
Dworkin, is a standard to be observed
because it is a requirement of JUSTICE or fairness or some other dimension of morality.
Principles differ substantially from legal
rules in Dworkin's account. Whereas legal
rules are applicable in an all-or-nothing
fashion (that is, if the circumstances mentioned by the rule have arisen, then the rule
must be applied, and if the circumstances
do not obtain, then there is no place for the
rule); principles, in contrast, merely state
reasons that argue in one direction or
another. Principles, accordingly, argue in
favour of a decision, but they do not
impose a decision in the way that an applicable rule does. Principles are thus considerations that judges must take into account
when deciding cases, but they may be outweighed by other principles. Equally, they
are outweighed by rules that directly contradict them. It is, however, possible for a
principle to prevail over a rule.

As regards Dworkin's second objection,
he believes that Hart's account allows
judges a strong DISCRETION in HARD CASES
that is at odds with their role in constitutional democracies. Hart distinguishes
clear cases and hard cases. The former are
cases in which some clear legal rule is obviously applicable to the facts at hand and
where, since it appears as if the judge
simply has to apply the rule to the fact,
the judge has no discretion. Hard cases,
on the other hand, are those in which
there is no clear rule that is obviously
applicable, and where, as a consequence,
the judge has an entirely free hand. The
judge, therefore, has discretion in a strong
sense because, in the absence of an applicable rule, he or she must create a new rule
by him- or herself. Presumably, judges must
do this by appealing to standards that are
more general than rules. Since these cannot
by Hart's definition be identified by the rule
of recognition, it follows that they must be
non-legal. Dworkin rejects this possibility.
For him, judges do not have discretion in
this strong sense, to appeal to non-legal
standards selected only according to their
own preference. For him, judges have only
a weak discretion in a hard case, that is, to
appeal to legal principles.

Dworkin postulates a hypothetical super-
human judge, Hercules, to carry forward
his consideration of a hard case. This
judge has the task of constructing a scheme
of principles that provides a coherent justification for COMMON LAW precedents. Dworkin understands the legal system as a
seamless web and thus Hercules is guided
by a concern with consistency and integrity
as he goes about his task. This approach
also leads Dworkin to propose his ONE
RIGHT ANSWER THESIS, in other words, the
notion that the answer to any legal question posed to Hercules will be the right one.
Lawyers seem to agree with this approach
insofar as they routinely operate on the
basis that a position is legal or illegal,
valid or invalid and accept that the judicial
determination of a case provides the final
answer.

Permeating Dworkin's extensive work is a particular liberal conception of law that finds its clearest expression in his RIGHTS THESIS, that is, the proposition that the government must treat people as equals. By this Dworkin intends that the government should not take any action with regard to an individual that he or she could only accept by abandoning his or her sense of equal worth. This can also be read positively to mean that the government has a duty to relieve individuals of burdens they would otherwise have to bear as a consequence purely of bad luck. Most controversially, Dworkin extrapolates from this to criticize the market insofar as it operates to reward individuals not simply because they have chosen to perform roles or tasks that are useful, but also because they happen by luck to possess the requisite skills or talents.   [JP]

Further reading: Ronald Dworkin, *Taking Rights Seriously* (London: Duckworth, 1978); *Law's Empire* (Cambridge, MA: Belknap Press, 1986); *Sovereign Virtue* (Cambridge, MA: Harvard University Press, 2000).

E

easement A right that an owner of land has over neighbouring land. For an easement to exist, it must have certain essential **characteristics** (*Re Ellenborough Park* [1956] Ch 131): (a) there must be a DOMINANT TENEMENT and a SERVIENT TENEMENT; (b) the owners of the dominant and servient tenements must be different persons; (c) the easement must accommodate the dominant tenement; (d) the right claimed must LIE IN GRANT.

Points (a) and (b) mean that there must be two separate pieces of land, owned by different people. Point (c) means that the dominant tenement must benefit from the right over the servient tenement. Point (d) means that the right must be specific and definable, and that both the person granting and the person receiving the benefit of the easement must have legal capacity to do so.

If these characteristics are met, a person wishing to rely on an easement must also be able to show that it has been **acquired**. Easements may be acquired by GRANT or reservation, express or implied, or by PRESCRIPTION.

Types of easement include rights of way, ancient lights, rights of support, rights of water and rights to air. [DR]

See also EASEMENT OF NECESSITY; EQUITABLE EASEMENT; LEGAL EASEMENT.

easement of necessity An EASEMENT that is so essential to the enjoyment of land that the land cannot be enjoyed without it. An easement of necessity may be acquired on the transfer of land, on the basis of the presumed intention of the parties to that transaction.

For example, Andrew sells a plot of land to Brian, in order for Brian to build a house on that land. If Brian's land is completely inaccessible, except for a path through Andrew's land, then an easement of necessity may be implied into that conveyance. However, the requirement for necessity is very strictly interpreted by the courts; for example, if the only right of access to land is over water, an easement of necessity will not exist (*Manjang* v. *Drammeh* (1991) 61 P&CR 194). [DR]

EAT *See* EMPLOYMENT APPEAL TRIBUNAL.

EC *See* EUROPEAN COMMUNITY.

ECB *See* EUROPEAN CENTRAL BANK.

Ecclesiastical Courts Courts created under the laws of the CHURCH OF ENGLAND with jurisdiction over ecclesiastical and disciplinary offences committed by the clergy of the Church.

The current system of Ecclesiastical Courts is laid down by the Ecclesiastical Jurisdiction Measure 1963 and Clergy Discipline Measure 2003. Each diocese of the Church has both a Consistory court for all faculty causes and for the trial of other offences not involving matters of Church doctrine, ritual or ceremonial, and a **bishop's disciplinary tribunal** for the hearing of disciplinary proceedings against a priest or deacon. The **Vicar-General's court** hears disciplinary proceedings against a bishop or an archbishop not involving matters of doctrine, ritual or ceremonial. The trial of all remaining offences against the laws ecclesiastical involving doctrine, ritual or ceremonial is the function of the **Court of Ecclesiastical Causes Reserved**. The court also has appellate jurisdiction in faculty causes involving doctrine, ritual or ceremonial. Other appeals from a Consistory Court, bishop's disciplinary tribunal or the Vicar-General's court go to the relevant archbishop's court for each of the provinces of Canterbury and York. These are the COURT OF ARCHES of Canterbury and the **Chancery Court** of York respectively. A right of appeal from the Court of Arches or the Chancery Court exists in faculty causes not involving matters of doctrine, ritual or ceremonial, and these will be heard by the PRIVY COUNCIL. A Commission of Review may be appointed by the Queen to review any finding of them Court of Ecclesiastical Causes Reserved. [JW]

ecclesiastical law Church law. Commonly used to describe the laws of the CHURCH OF ENGLAND and other Anglican communions.   [JW]

See also CANON LAW.

ECHR *See* EUROPEAN CONVENTION ON HUMAN RIGHTS.

ECJ *See* EUROPEAN COURT OF JUSTICE.

economic analysis of law The application of economic theory to legal questions associated particularly with the work of Richard Posner (both an academic and a judge) and other members of the CHICAGO SCHOOL. Posner claims to have developed a moral theory that surpasses UTILITARIANISM by substituting the criterion of **wealth maximization** for the maximization of happiness. Actions or social institutions are regarded as just or good on the basis of

whether they serve to maximize the wealth of society.

As applied to law, economic analysis on the one hand allows judges in individual cases to reach decisions on the basis of the most efficient outcome, and on the other provides policy-makers with a means of testing the likely effects of alternative legislative programmes, in both cases by applying the criterion of wealth maximization.

Posner claims that, whether they realize it or not, the judges who have shaped the common law have done so precisely by applying this sort of test. For him, as a consequence, economic analysis provides both a description of the law as well as a normative basis for its development and application.

Economic analysis has been most influential in the US, where judges and policy-makers make explicit reference to it. While it has had less impact in the UK, it is possible to detect the sorts of issues Posner refers to in judicial decisions. Equally, the advent of regulatory impact assessments reveals the increasing use of economic measures as part of the policy process.

The movement has, however, attracted criticism, notably from RONALD DWORKIN. Among the critics' concerns is whether wealth maximization is really an adequate measure: does the fact that an action increases social wealth necessarily make it desirable? Economic analysts of law are not absolutist in their application of the measure, but the question still poses problems for them outside of clear cases. Critics are also sceptical of the neutrality of the position adopted by economic analysis: does it not simply reflect a preference for free-market capitalism? There is also concern about the ability of the approach to deal with the justice or injustice of existing wealth distributions: no one could credibly claim that the existing distribution of wealth is no more than the efficient result of the operation of the market.   [JP]

See also COASE THEOREM.

Further reading: Richard A. Posner, *The Eco-*

nomic Analysis of Law, 7th edn (London: Wolters Kluwer Law & Business, 2007).

Economic and Social Council (of the UN) (ECOSOC) One of the primary organs of the UNITED NATIONS. Under Article 61(1) of the UN CHARTER, it must be composed of 54 UN members, elected by the General Assembly. Its functions include the initiation of studies and reports with respect to international economic, social, cultural, educational, health and related matters, and it has the right to make recommendations to the General Assembly, UN members and specialized agencies. It may also, within its fields of competence, prepare draft conventions, enter into agreements with specialized agencies and set up commissions in the economic and social fields and for the promotion of human rights and such other commissions as may be necessary for the performance of its functions (Articles 62–68 UN Charter). Since the adoption of the UN Charter in 1945, ECOSOC has established a large number of bodies to deal with specialized issues falling within its mandate. Among the more important are its human rights bodies, now under the aegis of the office of the High Commissioner for Human Rights.

[IB]

economic duress Threats or pressures affecting a person's financial or business interests so that he has no real choice other than to contract or to contract on the proposed terms. The effect of economic duress is to render a contract **voidable**. The threats or pressures must be illegitimate, e.g. a threat to breach the contract, and must be 'distinguished from the rough and tumble of the pressures of normal commercial bargaining' (*per* Dyson J in *DSND Subsea Ltd* v. *Petroleum Geo-Services ASA* [2000] BLR 530). Lawful demands can amount to illegitimate pressure if used to achieve an illegitimate purpose, e.g. BLACKMAIL, but lawful demands made in GOOD FAITH in arm's-length dealing between commercial concerns will not normally constitute duress.

[JPL]

economic loss DAMAGES for economic loss will be recoverable in NEGLIGENCE where such loss is a foreseeable consequence of other injury or damage. By contrast, though the position is complicated by some limited exceptions, **pure economic loss**, unaccompanied by damage or injury, cannot generally form the basis of a negligence claim (see *Cattle* v. *Stockton Waterworks Co.* (1875) LR 10). There are said to be various policy grounds for such a rule, concerns that it would open the floodgates to litigation; that the limits of liability would be difficult to establish; and that, ultimately, it is 'too great an interference for the state, through the courts, to seek to regulate economic welfare and redistribute economic losses by the law of negligence' – *per* Toulson J in *Lee* v. *Taunton and Somerset NHS Trust* [2001] FLR 419.

[HJ]

See also REMOTENESS OF DAMAGE.

economic sanctions Measures of an economic nature that are imposed against a STATE, either unilaterally by another state, or by an international organization. Their imposition by the UN SECURITY COUNCIL is possible under CHAPTER VII of the UN CHARTER. When the Security Council adopts economic sanctions it most typically establishes a Sanctions Committee to monitor the progress and implementation of the measures by UN member states.

States acting unilaterally can themselves impose economic sanctions against other states, but these will affect only the bilateral economic relations between the states involved. Although they are not expressly prohibited in the UN Charter, they may under certain circumstances be viewed as violating the principles of SELF-DETERMINATION or the prohibition against interference in the domestic affairs of other states.

[IB]

See also EMBARGO.

ECSC *See* EUROPEAN COAL AND STEEL COMMUNITY.

EEA *See* EUROPEAN ECONOMIC AREA.

effective date of termination If notice of dismissal is given, the effective date of termination (EDT) is the date on which the notice expires. When no notice is given, it is the date when termination takes effect. Where there is a limited-term contract which expires without being renewed, the EDT is the date when termination takes effect. When referring to REDUNDANCY PAYMENTS, the phrase used is not EDT but 'relevant date'.   [MJ]

effective remedy The obligation on a STATE, contained in Article 13 of the EUROPEAN CONVENTION ON HUMAN RIGHTS, to provide citizens with the means of determining claims and obtaining effective redress for violations of their rights under the Convention. It is not enough that the state provides a remedy, it must also be effective; so, for example, excessive delays in bringing cases to court could constitute a breach of Article 13. The right overlaps with, but is wider than, the right to a FAIR TRIAL guaranteed by Article 6, and should be determined separately from any alleged violation of Article 6 (see *Kudła* v. *Poland*, No. 30210/96, ECHR 2000-XI). Article 13 has not been incorporated into UK law by the Human Rights Act 1998, Schedule 1. The effect of this on the power of the UK courts to grant remedies for a breach of a Convention right is presently unclear. A corresponding obligation to Article 13 is also contained in Article 47 of the EU Charter of FUNDAMENTAL RIGHTS. [JW]

EFTA *See* EUROPEAN FREE TRADE ASSOCIATION.

egg shell skull rule A principle in criminal law that a defendant may not rely in his or her defence on the latent characteristic of their victim, if that characteristic means that the victim suffers greater harm as a consequence of the defendant's actions than would otherwise have been the case. Thus, where a person wounds a victim who has haemophilia, and the victim bleeds to death, it is no defence to a charge of murder for the defendant to claim, however correctly, that the wound would not have been fatal to a victim not suffering from haemophilia. Thus, in *R* v. *Blaue* [1975] 3 All ER 446, the defendant stabbed the victim, who was a Jehovah's witness. In accordance with her beliefs, the victim refused a blood transfusion. When she died, the defendant was not able to rely on her refusal of treatment in his defence to a charge of manslaughter. The principle applies also to tortfeasors in civil matters. The egg shell skull rule is thus a general expression of the notion that one takes one's victim as one finds them.   [BF]

EHCR *See* EQUALITY AND HUMAN RIGHTS COMMISSION.

eiusdem generis (Lat. of the same kind) A secondary aid to STATUTORY INTERPRETATION. Legislation may contain a non-exhaustive list using both specific and non-specific words. *Eiusdem generis* is used to argue that the non-specific words in the list should be interpreted to incorporate only things that are of the same kind or *genus* as the specific words. Thus it could be said (unless the context in which the words are used indicates a contrary intention) that the phrase 'rats, squirrels, rabbits, *and other animals*' should be read as restricted to animals that are rodents. [JW]

election The option given to the injured party to accept a BREACH OF CONTRACT as terminating the contract, or to affirm the contract.

Where the breach is **repudiatory** (on or after the time set for performance), in addition to the right to claim damages, the injured party can elect to accept the repudiatory breach as terminating the contract. This discharges the contract so that both parties' future obligations are cancelled.

Where the breach is **anticipatory**, the injured party has the option of either claiming damages immediately, or affirming and awaiting performance on the date set by the contract for performance. However, in this case, the ability to elect to affirm the contract is limited in that the affirming party must have 'a legitimate interest, financial or otherwise, in performing the contract rather than claiming damages' (*per* Lord Reid, *White & Carter (Councils) Ltd* v. *McGregor* [1962] AC 413). The election to affirm is generally irrevocable, i.e. the injured party cannot then change its mind before the contractual date set for performance.   [JPL]

election court A court comprising two

HIGH COURT judges with jurisdiction over cases alleging irregularities in the conduct of an election, or the commission of ELECTION OFFENCES.   [JW]

election offences A number of offences have been established under the Representation of the People Acts 1983 and 1985 and the Political Parties, Elections and Referendums Act 2000 to protect the integrity and fairness of the electoral process. Election (or 'electoral') offences fall broadly into three categories: corrupt practices, including intimidation, bribery, personation and unauthorized use of election expenses, are the most serious offences and are triable either way; illegal practices, such as a candidate exceeding the limit on allowed election expenses, or conducting an 'improper campaign'; and various miscellaneous offences, including illegal canvassing, tampering with nomination papers or ballot boxes. These last two categories involve offences that are only triable summarily.

While some election offences may only be committed by the candidate or his agent, others – such as bribery, intimidation, personation and tampering – may be committed by any person. Where a candidate who has been elected is reported by an ELECTION COURT to be guilty (either in person or by his agents) of any corrupt or illegal practice, his election shall be void. He will also be precluded from registering as an elector and of voting at any parliamentary, local or European election in the UK for five years.   [JW]

See also OFFENCE TRIABLE EITHER WAY; SUMMARY OFFENCE.

election petition An election can be challenged on the grounds of irregularity by the issue of an election petition by anyone who has the right to vote in that election, or by an unsuccessful or alleged candidate. A petition normally has to be made within 21 days of the return of the writ, with the name of the successful candidate, to the clerk of the CROWN; this period may be extended where the petitioner challenges the election on the grounds of corrupt or illegal practices. The petition will be heard by an ELECTION COURT.   [JW]

See also ELECTION OFFENCES.

Electoral Commission An independent public body created by the Political Parties, Elections and Referendums Act 2000. Its responsibilities include the registration of political parties, setting standards for and reporting on the conduct of local government, devolved legislature, UK parliamentary and EUROPEAN PARLIAMENT elections and all referendums in the UK, and, through the BOUNDARY COMMITTEE FOR ENGLAND, overseeing boundary arrangements for local government in England.   [JW]

electoral register The electoral register lists the name and address of everyone who has registered to vote in a given CONSTITUENCY. The register is a public document, and, by law, each local electoral registration office has to make the register available for anyone to look at. Since 2002 two versions of the register have been published. The **full register** contains the names and addresses of every person registered to vote and is updated on a monthly basis. It can be viewed at local council offices, but copies can only be supplied for limited purposes, such as elections and law enforcement. Credit reference agencies are allowed to use the full register, but only to check the accuracy of personal details, not for commercial purposes. The **edited register** is more widely available and can bought by any person, company or organization for commercial and other purposes, including marketing, mass mailing and identity checking. When registering to vote, individuals can opt to exclude their details from the edited register.   [JW]

electoral roll *See* ELECTORAL REGISTER.

electronic monitoring An offender or a person on BAIL or under a CURFEW ORDER may have an electronic tag worn on the ankle or wrist. This tag notifies monitoring services if the offender is absent during the curfew hours.   [SN]

eligibility for assistance A duty is owed by a LOCAL HOUSING AUTHORITY under the homelessness provisions of the Housing Act 1996 to persons eligible for assistance. This removes the right to housing assistance from anyone whose immigration status is restricted. There is one exception: a duty is owed to a person seeking ASYLUM, but whose status as an asylum seeker has not yet been determined by the Home Office. However, no duty will be owed if that person has any accommodation, including hostel accommodation, but excluding totally unsuitable accommodation.   [HC & DR]

embargo The prohibition or restriction of trade and commerce with a particular country, or with respect to particular products of that country. An embargo may be instituted and enforced unilaterally (e.g. by the USA against Cuba) or by a group of STATES, or imposed by the UN SECURITY COUNCIL acting under Article 41 of the UN CHARTER. The imposition of an embargo involves the adoption of domestic legislation providing for penalties, civil and criminal, for those who are found to have breached it. Moreover, it requires the establishment of a monitoring and implementation mechanism, whether the embargo is imposed by states or by the United Nations. Embargos imposed by states would not violate the non-intervention principle as long as a breach of an international obligation is involved, in which case the embargo would be tantamount to lawful COUNTERMEASURES.   [IB]

See also SANCTIONS.

embezzlement (obsolete)   An offence under the Larceny Act 1916, which was repealed in its entirety in England and Wales by the Theft Act 1968. Embezzlement was committed by a servant who kept for himself funds which had been given to him by a third party for transmission to his master. Such behaviour would now constitute THEFT.   [BF]

emblements The common law right of a former tenant to re-enter land, after the end of a tenancy, at harvest time to cut and carry away crops that he has sown. The right of emblements only arises where the tenancy is for an uncertain term (e.g. a TEN-

ANCY AT WILL, or a LIFE INTEREST under a Settled Land Act 1925 SETTLEMENT) and it does not come to an end as a result of the tenant's own actions. Only one crop can be taken and the right is only enforceable with regard to crops that normally repay the labour by which they are produced within a year.

With regard to AGRICULTURAL HOLDINGS, the right to emblements has been replaced by a statutory right of occupation. Under the Agricultural Holdings Act 1986, s. 21, a tenant at a RACK RENT, whose term ends by the death or ending of the estate of a landlord entitled only to an uncertain interest, has the right to hold and occupy the holding until the occupation is ended by a 12-month notice to quit, expiring at the end of a year of the tenancy.   [DR]

EMEA The European Medicines Evaluation Agency.

See also LICENSING OF MEDICINES.

emergency The Civil Contingencies Act 2004, s. 1 defines an emergency as an event or situation which threatens serious damage to human welfare or the environment in a place in the United Kingdom, or war or terrorism that threatens the security of the UK. A **state of emergency** may be declared by Royal Proclamation under the Emergency Powers Act 1964.   [JW]

emergency powers Powers granted by legislation to regulate activities in a state of EMERGENCY. Much of the current framework for instituting emergency powers is laid out in the Civil Contingencies Act 2004. Emergency powers are distinctive in enabling Ministers or other specified persons to undertake acts that would otherwise be unlawful under most normal social conditions, including authorizing the confiscation or destruction of private property, imposing broad restrictions on the movement of goods or persons, and powers to disapply or modify specified enactments and regulations. Emergency regulations may be issued by an Order in Council or, in cases of extreme urgency, by a senior government Minister.   [JW]

emergency protection order An order

made under the terms of the Children Act 1989, s. 44, as an emergency measure to protect a CHILD where there is reasonable cause to believe that they will suffer significant harm if they are not removed to a safe place or, conversely, to prevent them from being taken from a safe place. An order can also be made if the LOCAL AUTHORITY or NSPCC is attempting to make enquiries about a child who, it is suspected, is suffering or likely to suffer significant harm and those enquiries are frustrated by unreasonable refusal of access to the child and there is reason to believe that access is urgently needed. The order operates as a direction to the child's carer to produce the child and authorizes removal of the child to safe accommodation or it can prohibit the removal of the child from a safe place, such as a hospital. There is a presumption of reasonable access between the child and parents while the order is in force. The court can give directions relating to the examination or assessment of the child, but the child, if of sufficient understanding to make an informed decision, can refuse to submit.

An emergency protection order gives the local authority or NSPCC PARENTAL RESPONSIBILITY for the child, and this is shared with the other holders of parental responsibility, such as a parent. Parental responsibility should be exercised by the local authority or NSPCC only where this is necessary to safeguard or promote the child's welfare. The order lasts a maximum of eight days and can be extended only for a further seven days. If concerns about the child persist, it may be necessary to apply for a CARE ORDER on expiry of the EPO. [FK]

See also SECTION 47 ENQUIRY; THRESHOLD CRITERIA.

Emergency Remedial Action When a LOCAL HOUSING AUTHORITY is satisfied that a Category 1 hazard exists in relation to particular premises and that the hazard involves an imminent risk of serious harm to the health or safety of any of the occupiers of those or any other residential premises, the authority is entitled to take emergency remedial action under s. 40 of the Housing Act 2004. The action it may take is limited to what is immediately necessary to remove the imminent risk. A person who is served with notice of emergency remedial action can appeal to the RESIDENTIAL PROPERTY TRIBUNAL against the housing authority's decision. [HC & DR]

See also HOUSING HEALTH AND SAFETY RATING SYSTEM.

empanel To select from the JURY PANEL summoned to attend the CROWN COURT for jury service on a particular day the 12 men and women who will form the JURY to try the case. The procedure is also known as swearing-in. [SN]

employee A person working under a CONTRACT OF EMPLOYMENT (sometimes called a contract of service). He or she is the WORKER who is most protected by employment law. While some employment legislation, e.g. discrimination law, extends beyond employees, some of the major rights are restricted to employees, e.g. UNFAIR DISMISSAL, REDUNDANCY PAYMENTS. Usually it is easy to determine who is an employee, but where it is not, the most used test is that stated in *Ready Mixed Concrete (South East) Ltd* v. *Minister of Pensions and National Insurance* [1968] 2 QB 497 (MacKenna J): has the worker agreed to provide his or her own skill in return for pay?; if so, is there some element of control by the employers over what the worker does?; and, if so, are the other terms of the contract consistent with there being a contract of employment? If these conditions are satisfied, the worker is an employee. [MJ]

employees' inventions The law on INVENTIONS by EMPLOYEES is contained within the Patents Act 1977. By s. 39 an invention by an employee belongs to the EMPLOYER if it was made in the course of the normal duties of the employee or if the work was specifically assigned to him or her, provided in both cases that an invention might reasonably be expected to result from the work, or that the employee had special duties under contract to further the employer's interests. Any other invention belongs to the employee, even if the CONTRACT OF EMPLOY-MENT provides otherwise. [MJ]

employees' share scheme Some EMPLOY-EES may receive shares in the company for which they work as part of their WAGES. This system of payment is known as an employees' share scheme. The shares may be traded in the usual fashion; therefore, the value of the shares varies over time. [MJ]

employer Any natural person, company, partnership or unincorporated association which employs workers. [MJ]

See also LEGAL PERSON.

employers' association An organization which consists either wholly or mainly of EMPLOYERS, including individual owners, the principal purpose of which is the regulation of relations between employers and WORKERS or TRADE UNIONS or wholly or mainly of constituent or affiliated organizations which have such a principal purpose: see s. 122 of the Trade Union and Labour Relations (Consolidation) Act 1992. The association may be a company but it may be unincorporated. The CERTIFICATION OFFICER maintains a list of such organizations, but not all employers' organizations feature on the list. [MJ]

Employment Appeal Tribunal A superior COURT OF RECORD, which may sit anywhere but usually sits in London and Edinburgh. Judges in England and Wales are appointed by the JUDICIAL APPOINTMENTS COMMISSION on the recommendation of the LORD CHANCEL-LOR. Judges sit with lay members (normally two but up to four) who must have specialist knowledge of industrial relations either from the perspective of EMPLOYERS or EMPLOY-EES. The principal jurisdiction of the Employment Appeal Tribunal (EAT) consists in appeals from the EMPLOYMENT TRIBU-NALS and from the CERTIFICATION OFFICER. Created by STATUTE, the EAT's jurisdiction is restricted to matters given to it by Parliament. Appeals lie to the COURT OF APPEAL and thence to the HOUSE OF LORDS. [MJ]

employment conciliation *See* CONCILI-ATION.

employment tribunals Previously called industrial tribunals, employment tribunals were created in 1964 to deal with industrial training levies. Their jurisdiction has expanded over time and now consists of some 70 different areas, including REDUN-DANCY PAYMENTS (jurisdiction first given in 1965), EQUAL PAY (1970), UNFAIR DISMISSAL (1971), and the various DISCRIMINATION laws (1975–). Created by STATUTE, employment tribunals may act only as Parliament has ordained. The panel normally consists of a BARRISTER or SOLICITOR together with two wing members, both experienced in industrial relations, one on behalf of the EMPLOY-ERS, the other on behalf of the EMPLOYEES. Procedure is governed by the Employment Tribunals (Constitution and Rules of Procedure) Regulations 2004 (SI 2004/1861). There is no LEGAL AID available. Appeal generally lies to the EMPLOYMENT APPEAL TRIBUNAL. [MJ]

Empty Dwelling Management Order (EDMO) An order allowing a LOCAL HOUSING AUTHORITY to 'step into the shoes' of the owner of a privately owned unoccupied dwelling and secure its occupation and proper management. The ownership of the property is not transferred to the local housing authority, which meets its management costs from the income produced by letting out the dwelling. There are two forms of order, the interim EDMO and the final EDMO. Interim orders last for a maximum of 12 months. They can only be made with the authorization of the RESIDEN-TIAL PROPERTY TRIBUNAL, and letting requires the owner's consent. Final orders last for a maximum of seven years, do not require the authorization of the Tribunal, and allow the authority to let the property without the owner's consent. [HC & DR]

EMS *See* EUROPEAN MONETARY SYSTEM.

EMU *See* EUROPEAN MONETARY UNION.

en banc (Fr. on the bench) This term refers to a case that is heard before a full appellate court rather than the normal number of judges. The power to sit *en banc* is used sparingly for cases that are unusually complex, or raise particularly important points of principle, where the court may wish its decision to be particularly authoritative. In civil law systems the equivalent is usually a hearing before a *plenum* or plenary chamber. [JW]

enabling Act A STATUTE empowering some body or person to take certain action or actions. [JW]

enacting formula Words in a STATUTE that demonstrate it has the force of law. The normal enacting formula in the UK appears after the long title and states: 'BE IT ENACTED by the Queen's [King's] most Excellent Majesty, by and with the advice and consent of the Lords Spiritual and Temporal, and Commons, in this present Parliament assembled, and by the authority of the same, as follows…'

Scottish legislation does not use a traditional enacting formula, but states 'The Bill for this Act of the Scottish Parliament was passed by the Parliament on [date] and received Royal Assent on [date]'. [JW]

enactment A STATUTE (Act of Parliament) or Measure of the General Synod (see CHURCH OF ENGLAND). [JW]

encroachment The unlawful taking over of the land of another. In FREEHOLD property, a person encroaching on the land of a third party may establish ownership of that land under the law of adverse possession if his possession is unchallenged for a period of either 10 or 12 years.

In LEASEHOLD property, if a tenant encroaches upon the land of a third party, that land is added to the land under the lease until the expiration of the term of that lease. If that encroached-upon land is acquired by adverse possession, the third party's ownership of the land is extinguished and on expiry of the lease that land must be given up to the landlord, together with the land under the lease (*Smirk* v. *Lyndale Developments Ltd* [1975] Ch 317). A presumption therefore exists that the encroachment of the tenant is for the benefit of the landlord, a presumption that can only be rebutted by the conduct of the parties (e.g. if the tenant sells the encroached-upon land to a third party after giving notice to the landlord). [DR]

encumbrance (or incumbrance) An interest in or right over land owned by a person who is not the owner of the land. LEASES, EASEMENTS, RESTRICTIVE COVENANTS, MORTGAGES and adverse possession rights are all types of encumbrance. Encumbrances can reduce the value of an estate significantly, because if they are registered they are binding on subsequent purchasers.

In REGISTERED LAND, where a person purchases land with absolute title, he takes the land free of all encumbrances, except for interests recorded on the CHARGES REGISTER, OVERRIDING INTERESTS, adverse possession rights of which the proprietor has notice, and beneficiaries' rights where the proprietor is a trustee (Land Registration Act 2002, s. 11(4) and (5)). In UNREGISTERED LAND, an encumbrance will only be binding on subsequent purchasers if it is a registered LAND CHARGE or an OVERRIDING INTEREST. In a conveyancing transaction, the seller has a duty to disclose all latent encumbrances (i.e. those which are not apparent from an inspection of the property) to a prospective buyer. [DR]

endorsement A note on an offender's driving licence recording the details of a driving offence. Offences carrying an endorsement are listed in Schedule 2 to the Road Traffic Offences Act 1988. [SN]

endowment 1. The provision of a fixed income.

2. Property belonging to a charity. [PK]

enduring power of attorney *See* LASTING POWER OF ATTORNEY.

enforcement action *See* USE OF FORCE.

enforcement notice A notice issued by the local planning authority where it appears to them that: (a) there has been a breach of planning control (i.e. DEVELOPMENT has been carried out without PLANNING PERMISSION, or there has been a failure to comply with any condition or limitation subject to which planning permission was granted (Town and Country Planning Act 1990 (TCPA 1990), s. 171A)); and (b) it is expedient to issue the notice, having regard to the DEVELOPMENT PLAN and any other material considerations (TCPA 1990, s. 172 (1)).

An enforcement notice must state the matters which appear to constitute the breach of planning control, as well as specifying the necessary steps to be taken to remedy the breach. An enforcement notice may require the alteration or removal of any building or works within a certain time period. Alternatively, it may specify an activity not to be carried on except to the extent specified by the notice.

Time limits are crucial in relation to enforcement notices. Regarding operational development (or a change of use from any use to use as a dwellinghouse), no enforcement action can be taken after four years have passed from the date on which the development was substantially completed. Regarding other material changes of use, no enforcement action can be taken after ten years from the date of the breach. Breach of an enforcement notice is a criminal offence, carrying a potential fine of up to £20,000.   [DR]

See also STOP NOTICE.

enfranchised land LAND converted by the Law of Property Act 1922 from COPYHOLD (land held from TIME IMMEMORIAL to which rights had been acquired through CUSTOM and usage) to FREEHOLD. There are very few TITLES to land today which commence with an enfranchisement under the 1922 Act as a result of both the passage of time and compulsory registration.   [HC & DR]

See also REGISTERED LAND.

enfranchisement Giving the vote to a class or group of people. In the UK, changes to the FRANCHISE require legislation, thus women in the UK finally obtained equal voting rights to men by virtue of the Representation of the People (Equal Franchise) Act 1928.   [JW]

See also ENFRANCHISEMENT OF TENANCY.

enfranchisement of tenancy The statutory right of a TENANT either to buy the FREEHOLD or to extend the LEASE, originating with the Leasehold Reform Act 1967. The most recent amendments to the right are contained in the Commonhold and Leasehold Reform Act 2002. The right only applies to long leases – leases for which the original term was 21 years or more, or where there is a shorter lease but with a perpetual right of renewal – or shared ownership leases where the leasehold tenant now has a 100% share of the property. The Leasehold Reform Housing and Urban Development Act 1993 also provides a collective right of enfranchisement for a group of leaseholders, who represent at least half of the flats in a building, to purchase the freehold of that building.   [HC & DR]

engagement to marry At common law, engagements or promises to marry were treated as enforceable contracts and breach of a promise to marry was an actionable claim. These actions were abolished in 1970. Engagement is not a legal status and brings with it no special treatment or rights between the parties, except that, contrary to the property rules governing gifts, gifts exchanged between the engaged parties (including the engagement ring) may be given on the condition that they be returned if the MARRIAGE does not take place. There are also special rules regarding property ownership of the intended MATRIMONIAL HOME that may apply if the engagement is broken off.   [AD]

engross The preparation of an accurate copy of a deed or other legal document prior to execution by the parties.   [PK]

enlargement In land law, the expansion of a person's INTEREST IN LAND. There are particular types of enlargement available to persons with specific interests in land; for example, under the Fines and Recoveries Act 1833, ss. 15, 40, a TENANT IN TAIL in possession may execute a deed of disentailment, thereby enlarging his ENTAILED INTEREST into a FEE SIMPLE ABSOLUTE IN POSSESSION. Under the Law of Property Act 1925, s. 153, a lease may also be enlarged into a fee simple, if the following conditions are met: (a) the lease was originally created for at least 300 years and there are at least 200 years left to run; (b) there is no trust or right of redemption existing in favour of the reversioner; (c) there is no rent of any value payable on the lease; and (d) the lease is not liable for determination by re-entry for condition broken. [DR]

enslavement In international criminal legal parlance, enslavement is akin to its human rights counterpart, save for the ambit of the crime and the liability of the perpetrator, which are not mentioned in the human rights treaties. Article 7(2)(c) of the INTERNATIONAL CRIMINAL COURT (ICC) Statute defines enslavement as 'the exercise of any or all of the powers attaching to the right of ownership over a person and includes the exercise of such power in the course of trafficking in persons, in particular women and children'. This definition is not only wider than that contained in the 1927 Slavery Convention and the INTERNATIONAL COVENANT ON CIVIL AND POLITICAL RIGHTS, it is also situated in Article 7 of the ICC Statute, which refers to CRIMES AGAINST HUMANITY. Thus enslavement, under the appropriate circumstances may amount to a crime against humanity. This was also confirmed in the jurisprudence of the INTERNATIONAL CRIMINAL TRIBUNAL FOR YUGOSLAVIA (ICTY). In *ICTY Prosecutor* v. *Kunarac et al.* [Trial Chamber Judgment of 22 February 2001], the tribunal pointed to certain factors that determine enslavement, particularly control of someone's movement, control of their physical environment, psychological control, measures taken to prevent or deter escape, force, threat of force or coercion, duration, assertion or exclusivity, subjection to cruel treatment and abuse, control of sexuality and forced labour. The same principles apply to **sexual slavery**. [IB]

entailed interest An EQUITABLE INTEREST in land, inheritable only by a descendant of the person to whom the interest was granted. Prior to 1 January 1997, entailed interests were created where land was granted, for example, 'to X and the heirs of his body' or 'to X in tail'. This would create a succession of interests, entitlement to which would pass on the death of the previous TENANT IN TAIL under the pre-1926 rules on descendancy. If there was no one

alive who could trace their bloodline back to the person who originally granted the entailed interest, the property would revert back to that person or his or her successors. There are various types of entailed interest, including TAIL GENERAL, TAIL MALE, TAIL FEMALE and TAIL SPECIAL.

Under the Trusts of Land and Appointment of Trustees Act 1996, Schedule 1 para. 5, it is no longer possible to create entailed interests, although those existing prior to 1 January 1997 continue to have effect. Under the Fines and Recoveries Act 1833, s. 15 entailed interests may be barred by the tenant in tail, thereby enlarging the estate into a FEE SIMPLE ABSOLUTE IN POSSESSION. [DR]

See also HEIR; WORDS OF PROCREATION.

entire agreement clause A contractual clause which states that the document is intended and agreed to contain the entirety of the CONTRACT between the parties, and each party acknowledges that it has not relied on any promise or undertaking in entering into the agreement which is not expressly contained in the written document. Entire agreement clauses are often employed to ensure the application of the PAROL EVIDENCE RULE by making it clear that the parties consider the written document to contain all of the terms of their agreement. Entire agreement clauses deprive arguments based on collateral terms of any effect (*Inntrepreneur Pub Co.* v. *East Crown Ltd* [2000] 2 Lloyd's Rep 611). [JPL]

See also ENTIRE CONTRACT.

entire contract A contract (also called an **indivisible contract**) that is not divisible into separate obligations; for example, a lump sum contract for the construction of a wall, so that complete and precise performance by one party is required before the other party's obligation to perform will arise. It follows that a failure to completely and precisely perform will result in the other party being unable to recover payment for the work. The harshness of this position has been mitigated in practice by the doctrine of SUBSTANTIAL PERFORMANCE and also by the ability to recover on a QUANTUM MERUIT, independent of the contract, for performance which has been voluntarily accepted by the other party. [JPL]

See also DIVISIBLE CONTRACT.

entrapment 'Entrapment occurs when an agent of the state – usually a law enforcement officer or a controlled informer – causes someone to commit an offence in order that he should be prosecuted': *R* v. *Looseley* [2001] UKHL 53 at [36]. Entrapment may lead to the proceedings against the defendant being stayed as an ABUSE OF PROCESS. [ALTC]

entry as a trespasser An element in the offences of BURGLARY and AGGRAVATED BURGLARY. [BF]

entry into possession The exercise of the right by a LANDLORD or MORTGAGE lender to enter into possession of a property when a particular condition of a LEASE or mortgage has been breached by the person in possession. Whilst many DEEDS assert this right, statutory provisions require in most cases that a court order is obtained before any entry into possession. [HC & DR]

environmental search When buying residential or commercial property, an environmental search is one of several SEARCHES carried out by the solicitor acting for the buyer prior to the exchange of contracts. It involves making enquiries to various bodies (e.g. the Environment Agency and the Department for Environment, Food and Rural Affairs) in order to find out whether the land is contaminated, how the land has been used historically, whether there are any nearby contaminating or polluting processes, whether the area is radon-affected and whether there is a risk of subsidence or flooding. An environmental search should be carried out prior to most residential and commercial conveyancing transactions. [DR]

See also CONTAMINATED LAND; LOCAL SEARCHES.

epitome of title In the CONVEYANCING OF UNREGISTERED LAND, the epitome of title provides a summary of the ownership of the property. It must trace ownership for a minimum continuous period of 15 years from an original title document (the ROOT OF TITLE) to the present owner. It is normally produced before completion by the vendor delivering to the purchaser a set of copies of original documents, each marked as examine against original. The epitome will also contain a record of any **encumbrances**, covenants or other matters that will affect its ownership. [DR]

See also ABSTRACT OF TITLE.

Equal Opportunities Commission (EOC) (obsolete) Established by the Sex Discrimination Act 1975, the EOC was empowered to work towards the elimination of DISCRIMINATION on the ground of sex (including gender reassignment), to promote equality of opportunity between men and women, and to review the Equal Pay Act 1970 and the Sex Discrimination Act 1975. It issued two Codes of Practice: one on EQUAL PAY and one on SEX DISCRIMINATION. The EOC became part of the Commission for Equality and Human Rights in 2007. [MJ]

equal pay The Equal Pay Act 1970 makes it unlawful for a member of one sex to be paid less than a member of the opposite sex for doing the same job or a job of equal value. The Act is not confined to 'pay', but covers all contractual terms (non-contractual terms are governed by the Sex Discrimination Act 1975). The EMPLOYMENT TRIBUNAL can only award equal pay, i.e. it cannot award pay above that of the comparator. There are three modes of acquiring equal pay: (a) for 'like work' (i.e. the same work or work where there is no practical difference between the claimant's and the comparator's jobs); (b) 'work rated as equivalent' (i.e. two jobs have been ranked equally by a job evaluation survey); and (c) and WORK OF EQUAL VALUE. The EMPLOYER has a defence if they prove there was a genuine material difference between the jobs being compared: s. 1(3) of the Act. [MJ]

See also EQUALITY CLAUSE.

equal treatment The principle of equal treatment applies to all aspects of EUROPEAN COMMUNITY (EC) law. It applies to both the supply of goods and services and the treatment of persons, in particular the mobility of WORKERS between MEMBER STATES. The principle of equal treatment also underpins rights not to be discriminated against in terms of pay, tax and social security benefits. Equal treatment can also apply to non-EUROPEAN UNION nationals under Directive 2003/109/EC, the Long-term Residents Directive. [MON]

See also DISCRIMINATION; FREE MOVEMENT OF GOODS; FREE MOVEMENT OF PERSONS; MIGRANT WORKER; RIGHT OF ESTABLISHMENT.

Equality and Human Rights Commission (EHRC) Established under the Equality Act 2006, the EHRC came into being on 1 October 2007. It is a non-departmental public body that brings together the work of the three previous equality commissions (the EQUAL OPPORTUNITIES COMMISSION, the Commission for Racial Equality, and the Disability Rights Commission) and also takes on responsibility for all other areas of equality (e.g. age, sexual orientation, religion or belief and human rights). See http:// www.equalityhumanrights.com. [AF]

equality before the law *See* EQUALITY OF ARMS.

equality clause If a person wins an EQUAL PAY claim, an equality clause is inserted into their contract to bring the contested term into line with that in the comparator's contract: Equal Pay Act 1970, s. 1(1). [MJ]

equality is equity An equitable maxim that encapsulates the notion that, where there is no other basis for distribution, equity favours equal distribution between parties entitled to some property. [PK]

equality of arms The principle that the parties to legal proceedings are entitled to be treated as equal before the law. The principle is extremely wide and has implications for the whole litigation process before civil and criminal courts, DOMESTIC TRIBUNALS, and international courts and tribunals as well. At a minimum it means that parties must be afforded a reasonable opportunity to present their case, and to respond to that of their opponent. So far as possible, parties should not be procedu-

rally advantaged or disadvantaged as against the other (or as against the STATE). Equality of arms is a key feature of the right to a FAIR TRIAL, a fundamental human right, protected by the EUROPEAN CONVENTION ON HUMAN RIGHTS, Article 6, and the INTERNATIONAL COVENANT ON CIVIL AND POLITICAL RIGHTS. [JW]

equality of states A principle of CUSTOMARY INTERNATIONAL LAW enshrined in Article 1 (2) of the UN CHARTER. It means that, in principle, in the fields of treaty-making all participating STATES have the same rights and obligations, and in the context of international organizations, they all have equal rights of voting before particular bodies. Moreover, the established rules of international law apply to all states, irrespective of their financial or military power. [IB]

equitable 1. Just, fair and reasonable.
2. An interest recognized by the rules of equity and used to distinguish concepts that are recognized both at law and in equity, including EASEMENTS, LEASES and MORTGAGES, all of which have both a legal and equitable form.
3. An interest historically recognized only by the COURT OF CHANCERY, having no legal counterpart, such as RESTRICTIVE COVENANTS. [PK]

equitable assignment *See* ASSIGNMENT.

equitable charge A charge whereby property or an interest in property is made liable to the discharge of a debt or some other obligation. This differs from an EQUITABLE MORTGAGE, in that the interest in the property does not pass to the lender and the lender has no right of possession or FORECLOSURE. All that the lender does have is the right to apply for a court order for sale or the appointment of a receiver. For example, if Arthur enters into a contract to charge his car with the payment of £500 to Brian, an equitable charge would be created. If Arthur fails to pay, Brian must apply for a court order for sale of the car in order to realize his security. [DR]

See also GENERAL EQUITABLE CHARGE.

equitable easement An EASEMENT that

does not meet the formalities of a LEGAL EASE-MENT. This means an easement that is not created by deed, statute or PRESCRIPTION, will not last either forever or for a fixed period of time, or is not registered at the LAND REGISTRY. For example, the grant of a RIGHT OF WAY 'until such time as the road is adopted by the local authority' would be the grant of an equitable easement, since it will not last either forever or for a fixed period. Similarly, a contract for an easement that does not meet the formalities of a deed would be a contract for an equitable easement.

Prior to the Land Registration Act 2002 (LRA 2002), an openly enjoyed equitable easement could be an OVERRIDING INTEREST and therefore binding on a subsequent purchaser (*Celsteel Ltd* v. *Alton Housing Holdings Ltd* [1985] 1 WLR 204). However, since the LRA 2002 equitable easements are not binding on a purchaser of REGISTERED LAND and are only binding on a purchaser of UNREGISTERED LAND if they are registered as a Class D (iii) land charge under the Land Charges Act 1972. [DR]

equitable estate (obsolete) Prior to the Law of Property Act 1925 (LPA 1925), a right to hold property recognized in equity by the Court of Chancery. Under the LPA 1925, the term EQUITABLE INTEREST replaced equitable estate, which is now no longer legally accurate. Equitable estates were similar in nature to LEGAL ESTATES under the COMMON LAW system, but the equitable rules developed by the COURT OF CHANCERY were more flexible, in order to meet the needs of landowning families and wealthy industrialists. [DR]

See also ESTATE.

equitable estoppel A doctrine developed by EQUITY with the aim of preventing the injustice that can arise through the strict application of the CONSIDERATION requirement in the context of promises made to forgo rights under existing CONTRACTS. Thus, if one party agrees to forgo or suspend its rights under that existing contract, and the other party relies on that inducement, equity will intervene to prevent the inducing party from enforcing its strict legal rights. The scope of this equitable estoppel

was extended to cover promises relating to future conduct (see PROMISSORY ESTOPPEL) in *Central London Property Trust Ltd* v. *High Trees House Ltd* [1947] KB 130. [JPL]

See also DETRIMENT.

equitable interests In land law, an INTEREST IN LAND that is not recognized by law as a LEGAL ESTATE. Under the Law of Property Act 1925, s. 1, only a specified list of estates, interests and charges in or over land are recognized as legal estates, whereas all other estates, interests and charges take effect as equitable interests. Examples of equitable interests include the interests of a beneficiary under a trust (e.g. a TENANT FOR LIFE), future interests (e.g. an interest under an OPTION TO PURCHASE agreement) and interests which are not legal due to a failure to meet the formal requirements (e.g. an EQUITABLE LEASE created orally).

Equitable interests were developed by the Court of Chancery to mitigate the hardship caused by inflexible common law rules administered by the common law courts. However, whereas legal interests are enforceable against the world, equitable interests cannot be enforced against a person who buys the legal estate subject to those interests, if the purchaser has no knowledge of those interests (a bona fide purchaser for value without notice, or EQUITY'S DARLING). Nevertheless, equitable interests in REGISTERED LAND may be protected against third parties using notices and cautions and, in UNREGISTERED LAND, by registering the interest as a LAND CHARGE. [DR]

See also BENEFICIAL INTEREST.

equitable lease A LEASE which does not comply with the formalities required to create a legal interest in the LAND. For example, to create a legal interest, leases of three years or more must be created in writing by DEED. An equitable lease creates a very similar relationship between the LANDLORD and the TENANT as a legal lease. However, equitable leases may not be protected against third parties who acquire the landlord's interest. In REGISTERED LAND, only equitable tenants who are in actual occupation of the land are protected. In UNREGISTERED LAND, an equitable lease requires REGISTRA-

TION under the Land Charges Act 1972 as a Class C (iv) contract. [HC & DR]

equitable mortgage A MORTGAGE under which the lender only acquires an equitable interest in the property mortgaged. The following are types of equitable mortgage. (a) A CONTRACT to create a LEGAL MORTGAGE. This will be effective to create an equitable mortgage from the date of the contract, as long as the contract is in writing and incorporates all the expressly agreed terms. (b) A mortgage of an equitable interest, for example a LIFE INTEREST. (c) A mortgage that fails to meet the formalities for creating a legal mortgage, for example where a mortgage deed is signed but not witnessed.

It is no longer possible to create a mortgage by depositing the TITLE DEEDS with the lender, unless there is also an agreement in writing incorporating all the expressly agreed terms (Law of Property (Miscellaneous Provisions) Act 1989, s. 2). [DR]

See also EQUITABLE CHARGE.

equitable presumptions Certain assumptions made by EQUITY in the absence of evidence to the contrary; for example, equity assumes a bargain rather than a GIFT. This is expressed in the form of a **presumption of resulting trust** which assumes property purchased for or transferred to another is held by that other on a RESULTING TRUST. A countervailing **presumption of advancement** has been said to exist in certain special relationships (gifts from a father to a child, and from husband to wife, but not vice versa) whereby the donor will be presumed to intend that transfer as an absolute gift. Whether advancement now operates as a separate presumption is doubtful in the light of a number of judicial pronouncements which suggest that it is better regarded as 'no more than a circumstance of evidence which may rebut the presumption of resulting trust' (*per* Lord Upjohn in *Pettit* v. *Pettit* [1970] AC 777 at 814). Ultimately, of course, all presumptions are devices used to assign the BURDEN OF PROOF and may be rebutted by evidence to the contrary, on a balance of probabilities. Thus, for example,

evidence of words of gift would doubtless be enough to rebut the presumption of resulting trust if Paul gave Samantha an engagement ring. [PK]

equitable remedies The means equity developed to address wrongs in response to the extremely limited range of remedies available from the medieval common law courts. Today, the most important equitable remedies are SPECIFIC PERFORMANCE, RESCISSION, cancellation, RECTIFICATION, ACCOUNT, INJUNCTION and the appointment of a RECEIVER. Until the passing of the Judicature Acts 1873–5, equitable remedies were only available in the Courts of Chancery. Although now available in every division of the High Court (and, in certain instances, the county court), they necessarily retain their discretionary status (although mostly exercised on established lines) in deference to their equitable origins where the conduct of the claimant was a critical factor in whether or not equitable relief would be granted (see CLEAN HANDS). [PK]

equitable waste An unconscionable or unreasonable use of SETTLED LAND by a TENANT FOR LIFE, causing destruction to the land. Examples of acts of equitable waste leading to liability include pulling down a house, cutting underwood or saplings at unreasonable times and felling timber planted for the ornament or shelter of the PRINCIPAL MANSION HOUSE. Under the Law of Property Act 1925, s. 135, a tenant for life is never entitled to commit equitable waste unless expressly authorized by the terms of the SETTLEMENT. Where an act of equitable waste has been committed, a person with an interest in the REMAINDER or REVERSION of the land may bring a claim for an injunction or damages. [DR]

See also WASTE.

equity 1. An area of English law originally under the jurisdiction of the LORD CHANCELLOR, and later the COURT OF CHANCERY, historically quite distinct from the COMMON LAW administered by the king's courts. During the Middle Ages those who could not gain redress from the king's courts had the right to petition the king. As the common law forms of action were limited during this period to the existing forms of action and its primary remedy was monetary compensation in the form of damages, this became an increasingly important device to deal with new and novel claims.

As these involved issues of justice, the king sought advice from his primary spiritual adviser, the Lord Chancellor, normally an ecclesiastic, sometimes referred to as 'the keeper of the King's conscience'. In time, petitions from disappointed litigants went straight to the Lord Chancellor, who decided such matters on the basis of conscience, leading the jurist John Seldon to remark caustically that 'Equity varies with the length of the Lord Chancellor's foot'. Later a Court of Chancery developed to deal with the increasing number of petitions and, while the existence of this alternative form of redress was successful in coping with weaknesses in the common law, it inevitably led to conflict with the common law courts. This reached a head in the 17th century when James I resolved that in any dispute the views of the Lord Chancellor would prevail.

Over the next couple of centuries the rules of equity began to stabilize, with the setting out of maxims which articulated the basis of equitable intervention and the principles the Court of Chancery sought to apply via precedents that brought a measure of consistency to its adjudications. With the establishment of the High Court of Justice under the Judicature Acts 1873–5, the administration of equity and the common law was fused to enable litigants to obtain both common law and equitable remedies in the same court. However, it is important to avoid the so-called fusion fallacy, for it was only the administration of the two systems that was fused and not their practice. Thus common law and equity continue as two separate systems of law administered by the one court.

2. An equitable right or claim.

3. A share in a limited company.   [PK]

equity of redemption The bundle of equitable rights that an individual owns in a property that is subject to a MORTGAGE, the most important being the equitable right to REDEMPTION. The equity of redemption is an equitable interest in land that is dealt with like any other equitable interest.
                                                          [DR]
See also EQUITABLE INTERESTS.

equity's darling A term sometimes used to describe a bona fide (good faith) purchaser of a legal INTEREST in land for value without notice. A person who pays money or other valuable CONSIDERATION for property takes it free of any attached equitable interests if he can show that he had no notice of them. In such a case, the equitable interests will be extinguished. Certain interests may be entered on the LAND CHARGES REGISTER and, where they are, they will bind a purchaser with or without notice.   [DR]

erga omnes obligations (Lat. in relation to everyone) There are two broad types of international STATE obligations: those owed to other contracting parties (obligations *erga omnes partes*), and those owed to all states irrespective of any contractual commitment (obligations *erga omnes*). The latter exist as part of CUSTOMARY INTERNATIONAL LAW. The International Court of Justice, in its judgments in *Barcelona Traction Light & Power Co. Ltd* (*Belgium* v. *Spain*) [1970] ICJ Rep 3, and the *Genocide* cases (*Bosnia and Herzegovina* v. *Yugoslavia*) [1996] ICJ Rep 595 and *Bosnia and Herzegovina* v. *Serbia and Montenegro* ICJ 140 (26 February 2007) reiterated that some international crimes are so odious, such as GENOCIDE, slavery and others, that they create obligations on all states to prevent, prosecute and punish, irrespective of whether such crimes occurred on that state's territory or against its nationals. A state that is wholly unaffected by a grave or mass violation of human rights would also be entitled to sue a complicit state before international judicial bodies without having to demonstrate any other legal interest.   [IB]

See also UNIVERSAL JURISDICTION.

ERM *See* EXCHANGE RATE MECHANISM.

escheat In feudal land law, the return or

forfeiture to the lord of land held by his tenant. Generally, land would escheat under two conditions: the death of the tenant without HEIR or the tenant's conviction for FELONY. The escheat of lands for felony was abolished by statute in England in 1870; and, under the Law of Property Act 1925, land will not escheat purely for failure of heirs. Very exceptionally, escheat can still occur where a person is made bankrupt or a company is liquidated, and property is **disclaimed** by the Official Receiver or trustee in bankruptcy dealing with their affairs, causing the TITLE to revert to the CROWN. [JW]

See also BONA VACANTIA.

escrow A deed which has been delivered but which does not become operative until a future date or until some condition has been fulfilled. [PK]

espousal of claim The capacity of an entity under INTERNATIONAL LAW, whether that is a STATE, an international organization or an individual, to bring a claim before an authorized judicial or quasi-judicial body. That body's constitutional instrument will define the entities that possess legal capacity to make claims before it. [IB]

See also INTERNATIONAL LEGAL PERSONALITY.

estate In land law, a right to hold land for a period of time. The estate in FEE SIMPLE ABSOLUTE IN POSSESSION is the best type of estate that can be owned and in practice denotes complete ownership of the land.

The concept of the estate was developed as a response to the system of FEUDAL TENURE, under which all land was owned by the Crown. Since it was not possible for a person to own the land itself, a person was said to own an estate in land, classified with reference to the duration of his entitlement to hold the land. Various different types of estate came into existence and these can be broken down into inheritable FREEHOLD estates (e.g. a fee simple or FEE TAIL), non-inheritable freehold estates (e.g. a LIFE ESTATE) and LEASEHOLD estates (e.g. a TERM OF YEARS).

Under the Law of Property Act 1925, s. 1

(1), the only two LEGAL ESTATES in land are the fee simple absolute in possession (freehold) and the term of years absolute (leasehold). Estates which previously existed in law now have effect only as EQUITABLE INTERESTS. [DR]

See also EQUITABLE ESTATE.

estate contract In UNREGISTERED LAND, a contract to convey or create a legal estate, to confer an OPTION TO PURCHASE, a right of PRE-EMPTION (i.e. right of first refusal) or other similar right in respect of a legal estate (see Land Charges Act 1972, s. 2(4)(iv)). If an estate contract is registered as a Class C (iv) LAND CHARGE, it will be binding on a subsequent third party purchaser of the legal estate to which it relates.

In REGISTERED LAND, an estate contract may be protected by entering a notice in the Register of the registered proprietor's TITLE at the LAND REGISTRY. [DR]

estate duty (obsolete) A tax at graduated rates on the whole value of the ESTATE of an individual passing on his death. It was originally a 'voluntary duty' because lifetime gifts could be made in such a way as to avoid the duty. In 1975, estate duty was replaced by CAPITAL TRANSFER TAX, and then in 1986 capital transfer tax was amended and renamed inheritance tax. Some of the estate duty case law continues to be relevant for inheritance tax (see, for example *Ingram* v. *IRC* [1999] 1 All ER 297 [1999] STC 37, HL). [RE]

estate for years *See* TERM OF YEARS.

estate *pur autre vie* (obsolete) Prior to 1926, an estate that persisted for the duration of the life of another. For example, if X granted a LIFE ESTATE to Y, for the duration of Z's life, Y would be the owner of an estate *pur autre vie*.

Since the Law of Property Act 1925 abolished the life estate at law, it has no longer been possible to create a LEGAL ESTATE *pur autre vie*. However, it remains possible to create an EQUITABLE INTEREST *pur autre vie*. For example, where property is held on trust for X for the life of Y, X is the owner of an equitable interest *pur autre vie;* X is the TENANT *PUR AUTRE VIE*. [DR]

estate rentcharge A type of RENTCHARGE, most often reserved by a developer selling various plots of land, in order to maintain common parts and services on the estate. For a rentcharge to be valid, it must be created for the purpose of: (a) making COVENANTS to be performed by the individual plot owners, enforceable by the developer; or (b) contributing towards the cost of maintenance, repairs, insurance or other payments made by the developer for the benefit of the individual plots.

Where a rentcharge provides for contributions by plot owners, it is not valid unless the charge is reasonable in relation to the developer's obligations under that charge. Common examples of estate rentcharges are those charged for the maintenance of a private road or private sewage systems (see *Orchard Trading Estate Management Ltd* v. *Johnson Security Ltd* [2002] All ER 413). [DR]

estate subsisting at law *See* LEGAL ESTATE.

estoppel 1. A rule of evidence preventing a person from denying in court the truth of an admission or the existence of a fact that they have already alleged. There are three forms of evidentiary estoppel: (a) **Estoppel by deed**, which prevents a person who has executed a DEED from denying the facts as stated, usually in the recital to that deed. (b) **Estoppel by record**, or **issue estoppel**, which prevents a person from re-opening issues that are settled (RES JUDICATA), or part of a process previously adjudicated by the court. This prevents not just the reopening of a cause of action that has previously been litigated, but also (i) an attempt to reopen issues between the same parties via a different cause of action (see *Arnold* v. *National Westminster Bank plc* [1991] 2 AC 93), and (ii) situations where one party (whether in proceedings against the original other or a new party) seeks to argue a point which should have been brought forward in earlier proceedings, and to do so now would be an abuse of process (see ABUSE OF PROCESS ESTOPPEL). (c) **Estoppel by conduct**, also known as **estoppel by representation of fact**, whereby one party, who has made a representation in words or by conduct, or by silence or inaction (if under a duty to the other to speak or act), will be prevented from denying the truth of that representation, provided that it was made with the intention and the effect of inducing the other to change their position to their detriment.

2. A rule of substantive law preventing a person from enforcing certain rights where the other party has acted in reliance on some promise or forbearance by the former. This is sometimes referred to as **reliance-based estoppel**. There are essentially two types: the doctrine of PROPRIETARY ESTOPPEL which operates in respect of rights over land, and of PROMISSORY ESTOPPEL which affects contractual relationships. Both operate in EQUITY to override COMMON LAW rights. Some authorities argue that estoppel by representation of fact also operates as a general rule of law, not just as a rule of evidence, though this view remains contentious. [JW]

estovers A type of PROFIT A PRENDRE or RIGHT OF COMMON that entitles the owner of the right to take wood for domestic or agricultural purposes (e.g. as fuel, to build a fence, or to make animal bedding). [DR]

Estrada doctrine The view, adopted by the UK and many other states, that RECOGNITION of governments should not take place because it is an insulting practice that offends against the SOVEREIGNTY of other nations. Named after the Mexican Foreign Minister Don Genaro Estrada, who developed the doctrine in 1930, it enables governments to have dealings with more than one regime in the same STATE without having to express approval or disapproval of any of them. However, decision to avoid recognition or non-recognition of a government, as distinct from the recognition of states, remains a political act whose legal effects are uncertain. [IB]

See also CONSENSUAL THEORY; GOVERNMENT-IN-EXILE.

ethnic cleansing This concept was first used in the context of the Yugoslav civil war, 1992–95, with the purpose of emphasizing the policy of eradicating entire ethnic or religious groups, or forcing such groups to move from a particular geographical region. The term, however, has no legal significance, even though it was employed by the UN SECURITY COUNCIL in its Resolution 827 (1993) to establish the INTERNATIONAL CRIMINAL TRIBUNAL FOR YUGOSLAVIA. The practice of ethnic cleansing could, depending on the particular elements of the offence and the intent of the perpetrators, either constitute a CRIME AGAINST HUMANITY or GENOCIDE.

[IB]

EU *See* EUROPEAN UNION.

eugenics (from the Gr. *eugenes*, of good stock) The hereditary improvement of the human race through the practice of controlled selective breeding. This may be either negative selection: discouraging or preventing those with hereditary traits or features considered undesirable from breeding; or positive selection, whereby those possessing hereditary traits thought to be desirable are encouraged to produce offspring. The question of eugenics poses serious ethical and regulatory dilemmas in a number of areas, not least in the fields of embryo research, assisted conception and ABORTION. [HJ]

euro The single currency of 15 MEMBER STATES of the EUROPEAN UNION (EU) since its introduction in 1999. As a banking concept it replaced the notional European Currency Unit (ECU) which had been used to calculate EUROPEAN COMMUNITY (EC) payments since the creation of the EUROPEAN MONETARY SYSTEM (EMS) in 1979. The ECU was converted to the euro at a one for one exchange rate on 1 January 1999. Euro banknotes and coins started circulation on 1 January 2002. Two Member States of the EC, the UK and Denmark, maintain an opt-out provision for the euro. The remaining Member States are required to meet the CONVERGENCE CRITERIA before being permitted to join the **euro zone**. The euro and the euro zone, which comprises the Member States of the EC who have adopted the euro as their currency, are subject to control by the EUROPEAN CENTRAL BANK. [MON]

European Arrest Warrant Created to facilitate EXTRADITION requests among EU MEMBER STATES without procedural or governmental hurdles, the warrant is premised on the principle of **mutual recognition** of criminal judgments across the EU. A Member State court may issue a warrant for surrender where a final sentence of imprisonment or a detention order has been imposed for a period of at least four months, or with regard to alleged offences punishable by imprisonment or a detention order for a minimum period of at least one year. The DOUBLE CRIMINALITY rule is also abolished in respect of a range of serious offences punishable by a custodial sentence of at least three years. Following the issuing of a warrant, the issuing authority transmits it directly to the executing judicial authority. This must contain the following: information on the identity of the person concerned, the issuing judicial authority, the final judgment, the offence itself and the applicable penalty. The executing judicial authority must make a final determination no later than 60 days after the arrest. The grounds for refusing to execute a warrant is very limited; namely, applicability of the DOUBLE JEOPARDY principle, the offence is covered by an AMNESTY, or the person concerned may not be held criminally liable owing to his or her age. The Extradition Act 2003 gives force to the warrant in the UK with effect from 1 January 2004; however, the UK is one of a number of European states allowing retrospective applications in respect of offences committed before that date. [IB]

European Bank for Reconstruction and Development An international investment bank owned by 61 countries and two institutions, the EUROPEAN COMMUNITY (EC) and the European Investment Bank (EIB), which functions within the EC framework. The bank operates on the basis of funds subscribed by its members, and borrows on the international financial markets. The bank headquarters are in London. Its investments are in countries in transition, focusing on East European and western Asian economies. [MON]

European Central Bank (ECB) A EUROPEAN

COMMUNITY (EC) institution created by the EUROPEAN COMMUNITY TREATY as amended by the MAASTRICHT TREATY in 1992. It operates on the basis of the Protocol on the Statute of the European System of Central Banks and of the European Central Bank, which was attached to the EC Treaty by the Maastricht Treaty. The ECB is based in Frankfurt, Germany, along with the European System of Central Banks (ESCB), and operates the central banking system for the EURO zone.

[MON]

See also EUROPEAN MONETARY UNION.

European Civil Service Tribunal Created in 2004 pursuant to Council Decision 2004/752/EC, Euratom (2 November 2004), OJ L 333/7, it exercises authority, delegated from the EUROPEAN COURT OF JUSTICE, to adjudicate in any 'dispute between the Community and its servants within the limits and under the conditions laid down in the Staff Regulations or the Conditions of employment' (see Article 236 EC). The detail of its operation is set out in an Annex to the Statute of the European Court of Justice. Appeals from the European Civil Service Tribunal may be made to the COURT OF FIRST INSTANCE. [MON]

See also COURT OF JUSTICE OF THE EUROPEAN COMMUNITIES.

European Coal and Steel Community (ECSC) (obsolete) The first community set up by the original six MEMBER STATES of the EUROPEAN ECONOMIC COMMUNITY (EEC). It was set up by the Treaty of Paris in 1951, for 50 years. Its institutions were merged with those of Euratom and the EEC under the Treaty of Brussels (the 'Merger Treaty') in 1965, although all three organizations continued to maintain distinct legal systems and policy areas. While both Euratom and the EEC, now renamed the EUROPEAN COMMUNITY (EC), continue to exist, the ECSC came to an end after 50 years, with the subject matter of its provisions having been absorbed into the EC. [MON]

See also TREATY OF PARIS.

European Commission *See* COMMISSION OF THE EUROPEAN COMMUNITIES.

European Community (EC) A political and economic association of European STATES created by the TREATY OF ROME in 1957 (in force in 1958). Today it forms Pillar I of the EUROPEAN UNION (EU), which itself came into being pursuant to the Maastricht Treaty 1992 (otherwise known as the TREATY ON EUROPEAN UNION). The main focus of the EC has been the development of the COMMON MARKET, based on the 'four freedoms': FREE MOVEMENT OF GOODS, FREE MOVEMENT OF PERSONS, services and capital. In addition, EC Competition Policy, the COMMON AGRICULTURAL POLICY (CAP) and the COMMON FISHERIES POLICY (CFP) are all seen as being principal policy areas of the EC. COMMUNITY LAW is supreme over the national law of MEMBER STATES. [MON]

See also EUROPEAN ECONOMIC COMMUNITY.

European Community Treaty *See* TREATY OF ROME.

European Convention on Human Rights An international treaty, originally signed in Rome on 4 November 1950, committing members of the COUNCIL OF EUROPE to respect certain fundamental rights derived from the UNIVERSAL DECLARATION OF HUMAN RIGHTS (1948). The fundamental rights and freedoms protected by the Convention include: the right to life (Article 2); the prohibition of TORTURE (Article 3); the right to liberty and security of person (Article 5); the right to a FAIR TRIAL (Article 6); the right to PRIVACY (Article 8); and the FREEDOM OF THOUGHT (Article 9) and FREEDOM OF EXPRESSION (Article 10). The Convention also established the EUROPEAN COURT OF HUMAN RIGHTS in Strasbourg, France.

A distinctive feature of the Convention is that individual persons who feel their rights under the Convention have been violated by a STATE party can, in certain circumstances, take a case to the Court (see VICTIM). The decisions of the Court are legally binding, and the Court has the power to award COMPENSATION.

As an international treaty, the Convention is not part of the national law of any signatory state unless it has been expressly incorporated into national law. A large number of signatory states have taken this step, thereby making the Convention directly enforceable by domestic (i.e. national) courts. Where countries have a written CONSTITUTION, this has normally been achieved by incorporating the Convention within that constitution. In the UK, because there is no written constitution, the Convention was, after much debate, incorporated into law by the Human Rights Act 1998.   [JW]

European Council The most senior institution in the EUROPEAN UNION (EU) institutional hierarchy. It is provided for in Article 4 EU Treaty, and is composed of Presidents or Prime Ministers from each of the MEMBER STATES of the EU, the Ministers for Foreign Affairs, and the President of the EUROPEAN COMMISSION. The Council meets at least twice a year and its role is to 'provide the Union with the necessary impetus for its development and [to] define the general political guidelines thereof'. It is then for the COUNCIL OF MINISTERS, supported by the European Commission, to legislate and implement the policies in Pillar I of the EUROPEAN COMMUNITY (EC), and the Council of Ministers, with very limited support from the Commission, to legislate for and implement policies in Pillars II EU, Common Foreign and Security Policy (CFSP) and Pillar III EU, Police and Judicial Cooperation in Criminal Matters (PJCCM).

[MON]

See also TREATY ON EUROPEAN UNION.

European Court of Human Rights Established in Strasbourg under the auspices of the EUROPEAN CONVENTION ON HUMAN RIGHTS, the Court has the power to hear complaints (called **petitions**) from contracting parties to the Convention, and, in certain circumstances, from individuals or non-governmental organizations who can establish that they are VICTIMS within the terms of the Convention. It is not possible for one private individual to 'sue' another before the Court for breach of a Convention right. There are two significant barriers to individual complaints. First, an individual can only complain if the respondent country has recognized the right of individual petition. This is not a condition for ratifying the Convention. For example, the UK

was an original signatory to the Convention, but did not agree to the right of individual petition until 1966. Secondly, where the individual right of petition is recognized, the individual must still be able to demonstrate that they have exhausted all DOMESTIC LAW remedies before petitioning the Court.

Cases commence with a preliminary hearing before three judges of the Court who will determine if the petition should go to a full hearing. A case will only proceed if they are unanimous that it should do so. The full hearing will normally be before a **chamber** of seven judges, though the Court also has the power to sit as a **Grand Chamber** of 17 judges. This power tends to be exercised only where the petition raises a particularly important question of law. The Court's ruling is binding on the parties, and in some circumstances the Court may award COMPENSATION under Article 41 of the Convention.   [JW]

European Court of Justice (ECJ) The most senior court in the EUROPEAN COMMUNITY'S (EC) court structure, known as the COURT OF JUSTICE OF THE EUROPEAN COMMUNITIES. For a long time the ECJ was the only court of the EC. It is legislated for, along with the COURT OF FIRST INSTANCE (CFI), in the EUROPEAN COMMUNITY TREATY at Articles 220 to 245 EC. The details of the operation of the ECJ are set out in the Statute for the Court of Justice. The rulings of both the ECJ and the CFI are legally binding on all of the EC, and form part of the *ACQUIS COMMUNAUTAIRE*, with the case law of the courts being referred to as *ACQUIS JURISPRUDENTIAL*. Decisions from the CFI have a right of appeal to the ECJ. The ECJ also has a (more limited) role in Pillar III EUROPEAN UNION (EU), Police and Judicial Cooperation in Criminal Matters (PJCCM), but has no role in Pillar II EU, the Common Foreign and Security Policy (CFSP). The three-pillar structure of the EU, as set out in the current TREATY ON EUROPEAN UNION, is subject to review in the TREATY OF LISBON 2007.   [MON]

European Economic Area (EEA) A free trade area comprised of the EUROPEAN COMMUNITY, which is itself a CUSTOMS UNION oper-

ating a COMMON EXTERNAL TARIFF, and the EURO-
PEAN FREE TRADE ASSOCIATION states, excluding
Switzerland.   [MON]

European Economic Community (EEC)
(obsolete) The original name for what is
now known as the EUROPEAN COMMUNITY
(EC). The term 'European Communities'
was used for a time to refer to the EEC,
the now defunct EUROPEAN COAL AND STEEL
COMMUNITY and Euratom. The term 'European Community' was then increasingly
used to refer to the EEC, or what became
known, after the TREATY ON EUROPEAN UNION
(1992), as Pillar I of the EUROPEAN UNION.
                                                [MON]

European Free Trade Association (EFTA)
A free trade area now comprising Norway,
Iceland, Switzerland and Liechtenstein. It is
a separate organization from the EUROPEAN
COMMUNITY (EC) and EUROPEAN UNION (EU).
The EC, unlike EFTA, is recognized under
international trade law as being a CUSTOMS
UNION and involves a greater degree of inte-
gration and the development of suprana-
tional COMMUNITY LAW. The EFTA states are
closely allied with the EC and have,
together with the EC, created the EUROPEAN
ECONOMIC AREA. In addition, they have, to a
greater or lesser extent, become involved in
developments in Pillar III EU, Police and
Judicial Cooperation in Criminal Matters
(PJCCM), particularly through the SCHEN-
GEN AGREEMENT.   [MON]
    See also COMMON EXTERNAL TARIFF.

European Medicines Evaluation Agency
See LICENSING OF MEDICINES.

European Monetary System (EMS) (obsolete) Established in 1979, with the creation
of the European Currency Unit (ECU), a
notional currency used for the calculation
of payments made by the EUROPEAN COMMU-
NITY (EC). It operated by way of the European EXCHANGE RATE MECHANISM (ERM),
whereby national currencies had to maintain their currency fluctuating on the international currency markets within a narrow
percentage rate band from the ECU. The
ECU was calculated on the basis of a
weighted average of EC MEMBER STATE currencies. Both the EMS and the ECU were

replaced by the more tightly controlled
EUROPEAN MONETARY UNION (EMU) and, for
those countries who met the CONVERGENCE
CRITERIA, the single monetary policy and
the single currency, the EURO, from 1992.
                                                [MON]

European Monetary Union (EMU) Building on the single market created by the
EUROPEAN COMMUNITY (EC), and the EUROPEAN
MONETARY SYSTEM (EMS), MEMBER STATES have,
since 1992, engaged in close coordination
of economic and fiscal policies through the
European Monetary Union (EMU). For EC
Member States who have met the high
standards of the CONVERGENCE CRITERIA, a single monetary policy and a single currency,
the EURO, have been adopted. Two Member
States of the EC maintain an opt-out provision for the euro, the UK and Denmark. The
EMU is managed by the EUROPEAN CENTRAL
BANK in conjunction with the European System of Central Banks. EMU, as a legal
framework, was inserted into the EUROPEAN
COMMUNITY TREATY by the TREATY ON EUROPEAN
UNION.   [MON]

European Parliament One of the main
institutions of the EUROPEAN COMMUNITY
(EC), composed of directly elected representatives of the peoples of the EC MEMBER
STATES, elected for a term of five years. Governed by Articles 189 to 201 of the EUROPEAN
COMMUNITY TREATY, the European Parliament
has been increasing its powers since the
founding of the EC, when it was called
the **Assembly** of the EC. Within the EC
legal structure, the European Parliament
is less powerful than either the COUNCIL OF
MINISTERS or the COMMISSION OF THE EUROPEAN
COMMUNITIES; however, it does have law-
making powers which it exercises jointly
with the Council of Ministers pursuant to
Article 249 EC.   [MON]
    See also MEMBER OF THE EUROPEAN PARLIAMENT.

European patent Inventors and corporations can make a single application to the
European Patent Office (EPO) and request
patent protection in up to 37 countries who
are all signatories of the **European Patent
Convention (EPC).** The EPO is part of the
European Patent Organization which is an

inter-governmental, non-EU organization. The European Patent Office only determines the question of whether an invention is patentable or not. Where infringement of a European patent has occurred, patent owners must commence proceedings in the relevant national courts. All the contracting states (including the UK) are bound by the provisions of the EPC, including Article 69 which directs how the scope of protection conferred by patent claims is to be determined.   [US]

European Social Fund (ESF) Along with the European Regional Development Fund (ERDF) and the Cohesion Fund, the ESF is one of the STRUCTURAL FUNDS of the EUROPEAN COMMUNITY. Its purpose is to improve and develop employment levels throughout the EUROPEAN UNION. This includes encouraging workers to adapt to changing employment conditions, improving social integration and developing workers' abilities through training and education.
[MON]

European Union (EU) **1**. Under the TREATY ON EUROPEAN UNION (1992), the present three-pillar structure of the EU was created, encompassing the pre-existing EUROPEAN COMMUNITY (EC), set up under the EUROPEAN COMMUNITY TREATY as Pillar I, with Pillar II, the Common Foreign and Security Policy (CFSP) and Pillar III, the Justice and Home Affairs pillar (JHA), renamed Police and Judicial Cooperation in Criminal Matters (PJCCM).

2. Under the TREATY OF LISBON (2007), it is proposed to create a new one-pillar 'EU', which will encompass the aforementioned three-pillar policy areas.   [MON]

European Works Council (EWC) A consultative body operating at European level and consisting of both management and EMPLOYEE representatives within a Community-scale company or group of companies. The requirement to create an EWC is found in the Transnational Information and Consultation of Employees Regulations 1999 (SI 1999/3323) which implement the European Works Council Directive 94/45/EC in UK employment law. The Regulations gov-

ern companies or groups of undertakings which have over 1,000 employees across Member States, with at least 150 or more employees in two or more of those Member States. There is no obligation for a company to establish an EWC unless either management decide to do so, or employees or their representatives request it. A special negotiating body (SNB) must be established to determine the composition, functions and terms of office of members of an EWC or, alternatively, propose arrangements for an information and consultation procedure. Complaints about the process of establishing an SNB or EWC go to the CENTRAL ARBITRATION COMMITTEE. Complaints about the failure by employers to establish an EWC or information and consultation procedure go directly to the EMPLOYMENT APPEAL TRIBUNAL, which may impose a fine of up to £75,000.   [MJ]

eurotort A term that has been developed by some English-speaking EUROPEAN UNION legal academics to refer to what is more widely known as state liability for non-implementation of DIRECTIVES, or the FRANCOVICH PRINCIPLE.   [MON]

euthanasia (Gr. a good death) The deliberate killing of an individual, usually someone who is terminally ill or in unbearable pain, for the benefit of that individual. A moral distinction is often made between **active euthanasia**, when a positive act is committed with the intention of terminating life, such as the giving of a lethal injection and **passive euthanasia**, when treatment is withheld and the patient is allowed to die. The active/passive distinction is not, however, of great legal significance, as both forms of euthanasia may, in certain circumstances, constitute an unlawful act. Indeed, in the UK, the starting assumption is that euthanasia is against the law. Neither motive nor the consent of the patient provide a legitimate defence and a doctor who deliberately ends the life of a patient may find that he satisfies both the MENS REA and the ACTUS REUS of the crime of MURDER (see *Re A (Children) (Conjoined Twins: Surgical Separation)* [2000] 4 All ER 961). The doctor is also unable to rely on the fact that his or her actions have merely brought forward an otherwise inevitable event – any hastening of death may be regarded as murder. However, there may be difficulties in establishing CAUSATION. In such circumstances a charge of attempted murder is possible (see *R* v. *Cox* (1992) 12 BMLR 38). A more compassionate approach in cases where family or friends have acted to take the life of someone in unbearable agony is likely and a reduced charge of manslaughter may be possible giving greater discretion in sentencing. Palliative care (e.g. pain relief using powerful opiates) which might incidentally shorten the lifespan of a terminally ill patient is generally not considered to be euthanasia in the strict sense of the term and would not normally constitute homicide, provided that there is no intention to kill or cause serious bodily harm. The use of what are called 'extraordinary measures' – generally defined as medical interventions which are likely to be disproportionately burdensome (in terms of pain and suffering or loss of quality of life) relative to any potential benefit to the patient – also raises difficult legal issues. While the decision not to use extraordinary measures is unlikely to lead to criminal charges, it may have civil law implications, including allegations of medical negligence. Issues will also arise where patients are not competent to decide on treatment for themselves and the courts may be asked to adjudicate as to future treatment. The key issue to be determined in such cases is whether to continue existing treatment or commence a new treatment is in the BEST INTERESTS of the patient.

Two other definitions also arise in both moral and legal debate about euthanasia. (a) **Voluntary euthanasia** refers to situations where an individual having the capacity to do so expresses a wish to die. This will include *inter alia* cases where life-saving medical treatment is refused, requests for treatment to be stopped (see *Re B (Adult: refusal of treatment)* [2002] 2 All ER 449) and requests for ASSISTED SUICIDE. (b) **Non-voluntary euthanasia** relates to cases where, for example, a decision may be taken to stop life-supporting treatment in circum-

stances where the person is unable to make decisions for themselves. Such cases might include someone in a persistent vegetative state (see *Airedale NHS Trust* v. *Bland* [1993] AC 789), someone with severe learning difficulties, the very young or someone very old suffering from dementia.
[HJ]

See also ADVANCE DECISION; DOUBLE EFFECT; EUGENICS; NECESSITY.

evidence The information with which the matters requiring proof in a trial are proved. [ALTC]

See also ADMISSIBILITY; CHARACTER EVIDENCE; CIRCUMSTANTIAL EVIDENCE; DIRECT EVIDENCE; DOCUMENTARY EVIDENCE; EXPERT OPINION EVIDENCE; EXTRINSIC EVIDENCE; HEARSAY EVIDENCE; IDENTIFICATION EVIDENCE; ORAL EVIDENCE; ORIGINAL EVIDENCE; *PRIMA FACIE* EVIDENCE; REAL EVIDENCE; SECONDARY EVIDENCE; SIMILAR FACT EVIDENCE.

evidence in rebuttal Evidence that a cross-examining party is permitted to call to rebut answers given by a witness under CROSS-EXAMINATION. [ALTC]

evidence of disposition *See* CHARACTER EVIDENCE.

evidence of identity *See* IDENTIFICATION EVIDENCE.

evidence of user Evidence of the way in which the contractual parties have acted. It is admissible in limited circumstances, for example, to provide evidence to establish a waiver of obligations, and is useful for clarifying the meaning of terms in the context of EXECUTED contracts. [JPL]

EWC *See* EUROPEAN WORKS COUNCIL.

ex aequo et bono (Lat. according to what is right and good) The capacity of an international court or arbitral tribunal, when deciding the merits of a case, to give legal effect to notions of EQUITY, in the sense of what is fair, reasonable and just in the case at hand, rather than by reliance on what established law provides. Article 38(2) of the INTERNATIONAL COURT OF JUSTICE's Statute allows the Court to decide cases *ex aequo et bono* if the parties expressly agree to this. To date, no cases have been decided on this basis, as parties have never agreed to such a determination.   [IB]

ex nudo pacto non oritur action (Lat. a right of action does not arise out of a naked agreement) The principle that a contractual promise that is not supported by CONSIDERATION cannot be enforced.   [JPL]

ex parte (Lat. by or for one side) **1**. a hearing where only one party is given notice to attend. In civil proceedings the term *ex parte* is no longer used and has been replaced by the English 'without notice'.

2. In applications for JUDICIAL REVIEW, the case is nominally brought by the CROWN on behalf of the applicant and this is reflected in the case title as it appears in the LAW REPORTS. Conventionally this relationship used to be indicated by the use of *ex parte*, (often abbreviated to *ex p*) as in *R* v. *Ministry of Defence ex parte Smith*. The use of *ex parte* has been discontinued in this context also, having been replaced by 'on the application of'. This is written as *R (on the application of Greenfield)* v. *Secretary of State for the Home Department,* or simply, *R (Greenfield)* v. *Secretary of State for the Home Department.*   [JW]

ex post facto (Lat. after the fact) A description of any legal act, such as a STATUTE or PRECEDENT, having RETROSPECTIVE EFFECT.   [JW]

ex turpi causa non oritur actio (Lat. an action will not arise from a bad cause) A general principle of English law to the effect that the law will not assist in the promotion of illegal activities. See, e.g. *Gordon* v. *Metropolitan Police Commissioner* [1910] 1 KB 1098, where the court prevented the plaintiff from suing the police for recovery of the proceeds of illegal street gambling.   [JW]

examination The process of questioning a witness.   [ALTC]

See also CROSS-EXAMINATION; EXAMINATION-IN-CHIEF.

examination-in-chief The process of questioning one's own witness in court.   [ALTC]

examining justices Magistrates carrying

out the function of checking that the prosecution case papers justify the committal of an accused for trial in the CROWN COURT.   [SN]

Exchange Rate Mechanism (ERM) (obsolete) The ERM operated from 1979 to 1992 as a feature of the EUROPEAN MONETARY SYSTEM (EMS). The EMS consisted of an innovative coordination of monetary policies of the Member States of the EUROPEAN COMMUNITY (EC), which has led, since 1992, to the single monetary policy, and the single currency, the EURO, for participating countries. The EC operated a notional currency, the European Currency Unit (ECU), which was calculated against a weighted average of MEMBER STATE currencies. The ERM required participating national governments to maintain their currencies within a narrow percentage rate band from the ECU. This whole system operated on the basis of COMMUNITY LAW. The EMS was replaced by the EUROPEAN MONETARY UNION (EMU) in 1992. A modified ERM II currently operates as a preparatory phase for currencies about to adopt the euro.   [MON]

Exchequer Chamber (obsolete) An appellate court for COMMON LAW civil actions. The Court heard matters from the COURT OF KING'S BENCH, the COURT OF EXCHEQUER and the COURT OF COMMON PLEAS. It had four divisions: Court of Error for the Exchequer; the Court of Equity for the Exchequer; the Court of Errors in the King's Bench; and the Court of Exchequer Chamber (an assembly of all the exchequer judges for considering questions of law). Following the reforms of the Judicature Acts 1873–5, the Court of Exchequer Chamber was replaced by the COURT OF APPEAL of England and Wales.   [AF]

exclusion clause A contractual clause which purports to exclude all liability or the remedies that would usually arise in the event of BREACH OF CONTRACT or MISREPRESENTATION. The scope for parties to exclude their legal liability has been restricted by law, particularly in respect of business liability to consumers: see the Unfair Contract Terms Act 1977 and Unfair Terms in Consumer Contracts Regulations 1999. In cases where any such clause is ambiguous, the courts will interpret it narrowly. [JPL]

See also EXEMPTION CLAUSE; LIMITATION CLAUSE.

exclusion requirement A provision that can be included in an interim CARE ORDER (Children Act 1989, s. 38A) or an EMERGENCY PROTECTION ORDER (EPO) (Children Act 1989, s. 44A) to remove a possible threat to a CHILD. The provision can be included when there is reasonable cause to believe that, if a particular person is removed from the home, the child will cease to suffer, or cease to be likely to suffer, significant harm. Also, in the case of an EPO, an exclusion requirement can be included if the removal of the person will remove the obstacle to a SECTION 47 ENQUIRY.

The exclusion requirement can take the form of a provision requiring the person to leave the home; prohibiting the person from entering the home; or excluding the person from a defined area in which the home is situated. The court is empowered to attach a power of arrest, authorizing the police to arrest without a warrant in the event of a breach. An exclusion requirement can be made only if there is someone else living in the house, whether that person is a PARENT or not, who is able and willing to provide adequate care for the child. The carer must also have consented to the inclusion of the exclusion requirement. An exclusion requirement could be used, for instance, to remove a suspected child abuser or a violent parent from the home. [FK]

See also CHILD ABUSE; THRESHOLD CRITERIA.

exclusionary discretion *See* DISCRETION TO EXCLUDE EVIDENCE.

exclusionary rule A rule that provides that EVIDENCE must be excluded even if relevant; for example, the Criminal Justice Act 2003, Part II, Chapter 1, prescribes exclusionary rules relating to evidence of bad character (see CHARACTER EVIDENCE) and HEARSAY EVIDENCE. [ALTC]

exclusive economic zone A maritime belt beyond and adjacent to the TERRITORIAL WATERS, whose breadth shall not extend beyond 200 nautical miles from the BASE-

LINES used to measure the breadth of the territorial sea (see the UNITED NATIONS CONVENTION ON THE LAW OF THE SEA Article 57). The coastal STATE possesses sovereign rights in the EEZ 'for the purpose of exploring, exploiting and conserving and managing the natural resources, whether living or non-living, of the waters super-adjacent to the seabed and of the seabed and its subsoil, and with regard to other activities for the economic exploitation and exploration of the zone, such as the production of energy from the water, currents and winds' (Article 56). Since the coastal state only possesses sovereign rights and not SOVEREIGNTY over the EEZ, other states enjoy particular rights, such as the freedom of navigation and over-flight and of laying submarine cables and other internationally lawful uses of the sea related to these freedoms. [IB]

excuse *See* DEFENCE.

executed In contract law, 'executed' means 'already performed'. In determining whether an agreement is binding, where one party performs an act in response to a promise (as in a UNILATERAL CONTRACT), the performance of that act is said to be executed CONSIDERATION to support the promise and renders it binding. [JPL]

executed trust (perfect trust) A TRUST in which each beneficiary's interest has been set out and clearly defined by the SETTLOR. A fixed trust is an executed trust. [PK]

execution of will The process by which a valid WILL is made. With the exception of a PRIVILEGED WILL, a will has to be executed with certain formalities. The Wills Act 1837, s. 9, provides that no will is valid unless: '(a) it is in writing, and signed by the testator, or by some person in his presence and by his direction; and (b) it appears that the testator intended by his signature to give effect to the will; and (c) the signature is made or acknowledged by the testator in the presence of two or more witnesses present at the same time; and (d) each witness either signs the will or acknowledges his signature in the presence of the testator (but not necessarily in the presence of any other witness), but no form of ATTESTATION is necessary.'

The justification for these requirements is that they are necessary to ensure that the will does in fact represent the true wishes of the testator. A witness might be called upon to give evidence not only that the testator did indeed sign the will in his presence, but that he did so of his own free will, and not under DURESS. [CM]

executive agency A semi-autonomous body responsible for delivering services on behalf of a sponsoring central government department. The impetus came from the Ibbs Report in 1988 (*Improving Management in Government: the Next Steps*), which proposed splitting the core policy-making and service delivery functions of government departments in this way. It was followed by a Treasury requirement that all departments review their organizational structure and identify functions that could be abolished, contracted out to the private sector, managed under agency status, or retained as part of the status quo. This had a rapid and significant impact on operational structures; for example, the then Department of Social Security moved about 97 per cent of its staff into five executive agencies.

Executive agencies do not have a separate legal status from their sponsoring departments; however, they are managed by their own chief executives, have their own budgets and business plans, and are responsible for their own staff and staffing structure. Permanent staff remain members of the CIVIL SERVICE, but conditions of service and pay scales may vary between executive agencies, even within the same department. [JW]

executor *See* PERSONAL REPRESENTATIVE.

executor de son tort (Fr. executor in his own wrong) An expression used to describe someone who, without authority, has intermeddled with the property of a deceased person, with the result that he or she may become liable to the creditors or beneficiaries. The expression is an old one and the position is now governed by the Intestates' Estates Act 1952, which provides in effect that if a person receives any of the ASSETS of the ESTATE, without giving full consideration, he or she will be charged as executor in his own wrong to the extent of the estate coming into his hands. [CM]

executory In contract law, 'executory' means 'yet to happen'. In determining whether an agreement is binding, where there is an exchange of promises to perform in the future (as in a BILATERAL CONTRACT), each promise is binding, and liability exists, from the moment of the exchange of promises. The CONSIDERATION to support the promises is said to be **executory consideration**. [JPL]

executory trust (imperfect trust) A TRUST in which the general intentions of the SETTLOR have been revealed but not the specific terms. A DISCRETIONARY TRUST is an executory trust. [PK]

exemplary damages Exceptionally a court will seek to express its disapproval of the defendant's conduct by awarding exemplary (or **punitive**) DAMAGES. The point here is that the defendant's behaviour is regarded by the court as being so reprehensible that he must be punished and made an example of. The principles for such an award were laid down in *Rookes* v. *Barnard* [1964] AC 1129. This has subsequently been restricted to two categories of case: (a) where the defendant's conduct is calculated to make a profit; more often than not this will be a DEFAMATION (see *Cassell & Co.* v. *Broome* [1972] AC 1027); or (b) where there has been oppressive conduct by government servants, including police officers (see *AB* v. *South West Water Services Ltd* [1993] 1 All ER 609). Exemplary damages cannot be awarded for BREACH OF CONTRACT. [HJ]

exempt income Value acquired by a taxpayer in a period of assessment which would be classified as chargeable to income tax for that period but which is excluded from charge by the legislation or by application of one of the EXTRA-STATUTORY CONCESSIONS. Examples include income earned on individual savings accounts, interest earned on compensation for personal injury, and charitable donations. [RE]

See also GIFT AID.

exempt supply Provision of goods or services in respect of which Value Added Tax (VAT) must not be charged by any person, on the grounds that the goods or services fall within one of the categories which are not liable to output VAT. In such cases, a taxable person is also prohibited from recovering input tax (VAT) on the acquisition of goods or services necessary to enable him or her to make the supply of exempt goods and services. Examples of exempt supplies are land (an exempt good), education and health (exempt services). For some exemptions, such as education and health, the supply is only exempt if the person who makes the supply is a body or an individual identified as a supplier in the legislation (for example, a school, or a medical practitioner). [RE]

See also TAXABLE SUPPLY; ZERO-RATED SUPPLY.

exemption clause A generic term for terms or notices which either exclude (see EXCLUSION CLAUSE) or limit (see LIMITATION CLAUSE) the liability or remedies that would otherwise follow for BREACH OF CONTRACT or MISREPRESENTATION. The Unfair Contract Terms Act 1977 also prevents businesses from excluding or limiting their liability for death or injury resulting from NEGLIGENCE. Any attempt to exclude or limit liability in negligence for other loss or damage will only be permitted under s. 2(2) if the relevant contractual term or notice satisfies the requirement of reasonableness laid down by s. 11 of the 1977 Act. [JPL]

exequatur An authorization by which the receiving STATE grants permission to the establishment of a head of a consular post on its territory. [IB]

See also CONSUL; LETTER OF CREDENCE.

exhaustion of local remedies A well-recognized principle of INTERNATIONAL LAW, restricting the admissibility of petitions or applications lodged before international judicial or quasi-judicial institutions to matters which have already exhausted all, or all effective, remedies at the national level. The principle is embedded in both the 1966 INTERNATIONAL COVENANT ON CIVIL AND POLITICAL RIGHTS (ICCPR) and the EUROPEAN CONVENTION ON HUMAN RIGHTS (ECHR). Article 35 of the ECHR thus restricts individual applications to cases where the applicant has exhausted all possible judicial and other available remedies under the domestic law of their country. Such human rights courts are, therefore, meant to be courts of the very last resort. In some instances, however, where the internal judicial mechanisms are overly cumbersome and the exercise of remedies is unduly prolonged or ineffective (the 'effectiveness test'), human rights courts may accept the application even if the applicant has not exhausted all local remedies available to him or her. The effectiveness test has been upheld by the case law of the EUROPEAN COURT OF HUMAN RIGHTS on a number of occasions and is also spelled out in Article 41(1)(c) of the ICCPR. [IB]

exhaustion of rights Part of the EUROPEAN COMMUNITY'S (EC) approach to INTELLECTUAL PROPERTY law: there is an inherent tension between intellectual property law on the one hand, and EC COMPETITION LAW and EC FREE MOVEMENT OF GOODS laws on the other. The doctrine of exhaustion of rights is one of the ways that COMMUNITY LAW tries to reconcile this tension. The right's holder of intellectual property has control over goods protected by that intellectual property, until such time as he has sold the goods. Once the goods protected by the intellectual property right have been sold in the European Union, then the original owner has exhausted his intellectual property rights, and can no longer control what happens to that product. [MON]

exhibit EVIDENCE consisting of a material object that is produced for inspection in court. [ALTC]

expectation damages DAMAGES for BREACH OF CONTRACT aim to compensate the claimant by putting them into the position that they would have been in had the contract been properly performed (*Robinson* v. *Harman* (1848) 1 Ex 850). One of the roles of damages in contract law is therefore to compensate the claimant for any loss of expectation they would have received had the breach not occurred – hence expectation damages. Compensation for lost profit is compensation for an expectation of interest, as is payment of damages for the cost of substitute performance. Loss of expectation is normally calculated as the difference in value between what the claimant expected to receive under the contract and what it actually received, but in some cases the COST OF CURE or repair may be the only way to compensate for the lost expectation and can be awarded if it is reasonable to do so. [JPL]

expert opinion evidence EVIDENCE of an opinion, as opposed to evidence of a fact, given by a WITNESS qualified as an expert. The ADMISSIBILITY in certain circumstances of expert opinion evidence constitutes an important exception to the general rule which prohibits the admission of evidence of a witness's opinion and allows only the admission of evidence of facts perceived by a witness. [ALTC]

explosion Under the Explosive Substances Act 1883, as amended, s. 2, it is an offence for a person, unlawfully and maliciously, to cause, by any explosive substance, an explosion of a nature likely to endanger life or to cause serious injury to property. 'Maliciously' means intentionally or recklessly. The offence is made out whether or not any injury to person or property is actually caused, and is punishable by life imprisonment. [BF]

See also INTENTION; RECKLESSNESS.

exposure An offence created by the Sexual Offences Act 2003, s. 66, which is committed by a person who intentionally exposes his or her genitals and intends that someone will see them and be caused alarm or distress thereby. [BF]

express term A contractual term (or promise) explicitly agreed by the parties, either orally or in writing. It may be a CONDITION, a WARRANTY or an INNOMINATE TERM. [JPL]

express trust A TRUST that arises by reason

of the express wishes of the SETTLOR. To be valid, the THREE CERTAINTIES must be present, although no particular formalities are required to create an express trust. [PK]

See DECLARATION OF TRUST.

expropriation The taking of private property by the STATE, usually without compensation. [JW]

extempore **judgment** (Lat. without a time gap, or 'off the cuff') A judgment given orally at the conclusion of proceedings, as contrasted to a reserved judgment. Judges will generally try to avoid reserving judgment at first instance as this adds to the delay and expense of the case. In civil proceedings, in FAST TRACK cases, judgment will normally be *extempore*. In multi-track cases, when there are, for example, complex issues of law, a judgment is more likely to be reserved. APPELLATE COURT decisions in both civil and criminal matters will commonly be reserved. [JW]

extortion (obsolete) An offence at COMMON LAW, abolished by the Theft Act 1968, s. 32. It was replaced by the offence of BLACKMAIL. [BF]

See also BRIBERY; CORRUPTION.

Extra-statutory Concessions A collection of non-binding statements, which have been drafted by HM REVENUE AND CUSTOMS (the Revenue) or its predecessors and are intended to indicate the extent to which, and the occasions on which, the Revenue will disregard the strict requirements of UK tax law in respect of a limited number of statutory provisions. The concessions are neither primary nor secondary legislation because the Revenue has no authority to legislate. Therefore, they are not binding in any way or on any person.

Current Extra-statutory Concessions (ESCs) are published in the Revenue's booklet A104. A taxpayer can ask the Revenue to apply one or other of the ESCs to his tax circumstances, and the Revenue will usually accede to the request where it is appropriate to do so and where to refuse would result in an unfair result causing hardship to the taxpayer. However, the Revenue will not accede, or will withdraw a concession, where it considers that the concession will be used or has been used to further the tax avoidance or tax evasion plans of the taxpayer.

ESCs have been justified on the basis that it is the Revenue's duty to manage the tax system in the UK in an efficient manner and that it is reasonable for the Revenue to reduce the severity of the statutory provisions, in a few appropriate cases.   [RE]

extradition A process whereby a state requests another state (the requested state) to surrender a person in its hands and within its territory to the requesting state. The legal basis for an extradition request is the prior existence of a bilateral or multilateral extradition treaty, which typically contains a list of extraditable offences; a DOUBLE CRIMINALITY requirement, i.e. that the offence be a crime in both the requesting and requested states; the **speciality rule**, whereby the accused can only be tried for the specific offence for which extradition was sought and no other; a political OFFENCE exception, i.e. despite the existence of an extradition treaty, the requested state is under no obligation to extradite where there is reason to believe that the offence is actually of a political nature; the principle of DOUBLE JEOPARDY, whereby a person will not be surrendered if previously tried for the same offence.

Although extradition proceedings involve significant judicial determination as to the *prima facie* guilt of the accused, the final decision usually involves governmental approval, most typically from the Minister of Justice. The EUROPEAN ARREST WARRANT, where it applies, has abolished the need to enquire into the above procedures and principles.   [IB]

See also FAIR TRIAL.

extradition treaty Normally a bilateral inter-STATE agreement by which the contracting parties agree the range of offences that give rise to requests for EXTRADITION (either on the basis of a specific list of offences, or the minimum length of the prescribed custodial penalty) as well as the conditions that limit or prevent its implementation.

Although the vast majority of multilateral treaties dealing with transnational or international crimes contain extradition provisions, the enforcement of the latter depends on the existence of bilateral extradition treaties. However, in the EUROPEAN UNION, since 2002 the EUROPEAN ARREST WARRANT has come into operation. It is not based on a TREATY, but on a Framework Decision under Pillar III EU, and it overcomes many of the limitations of bilateral treaties.   [IB]

extrajudicial divorce DISSOLUTION of a MARRIAGE without court proceedings. An extrajudicial divorce cannot be obtained in England and Wales, but in some jurisdictions such a divorce is a valid termination of the marriage. A TALAQ, for example, may be a valid divorce if it was obtained according to law in a jurisdiction that recognizes it as such.   [AD]

See also GET.

extraterritoriality The place where a criminal offence was committed, when this is outside the land or maritime territory of the prosecuting STATE. In such cases, states may exercise extraterritorial jurisdiction on the basis of certain principles: UNIVERSAL JURISDICTION, nationality, passive personality and the protective principle. These principles may be enshrined either in domestic criminal law, international treaties or customary international law.   [IB]

extreme pornography An image constitutes extreme pornography under the Criminal Justice and Immigration Act 2008, s. 63 when it portrays, in an explicit and realistic way, either an act which threatens a person's life, or an act which results, or is likely to result, in serious injury to a person's anus, breasts or genitals, or an act which involves sexual interference with a human corpse, or a person performing a sex act with an animal, and the image is of such a nature that it is reasonable to assume that it has been produced principally or solely for the purpose of sexual arousal. 'Image' includes both still and moving images, or electronic data which are capable of conversion into an image. Sections 63–71 of the 2008 Act came into force on 26 January 2009 (SI 2009/2993). Since January 2009, possession of an extreme pornographic image becomes a criminal offence, triable either way. Following conviction on INDICTMENT it will carry, by virtue of s. 67(2) and (3), a normal maximum penalty of imprisonment for a term not exceeding three years. [JW]

See also OBSCENE PUBLICATIONS.

extrinsic evidence EVIDENCE derived from an external source, whether oral or written, which is used to add to, vary, or contradict a written document. In a number of legal contexts, the use of extrinsic evidence as an aid to the interpretation of a document is barred or restricted. For example, the Administration of Justice Act 1982, s. 21, provides that extrinsic evidence, including evidence of the TESTATOR's intention, may be admitted to assist in the interpretation of a WILL only where the language of any part of the will is meaningless, or creates an ambiguity on the face of the will, or where evidence, other than evidence of the testator's intention, shows that the language used in any part of the will is ambiguous in the light of surrounding circumstances.

[JW & ALTC]

See also PAROL EVIDENCE RULE.

F

facility and circumvention One of the reasons in SCOTS LAW that a contract or a will is VOIDABLE, that is, valid but subject to successful challenge.

'Facility' refers to a weakened state of mind short of insanity, e.g. as a result of illness, old age or indeed a general disposition whereby a person is unable to resist the suggestions of others. 'Circumvention' relates to pressure by another to influence the terms of the contract or will, albeit short of fraud. Where both facility and circumvention are present, the contract or will may be challenged and set aside by the court.

Note that where an insane person purports to enter into a contract or to make a will, the absence of true consent (in the case of a contract) or soundness of mind (in the case of a will) means that the documents in each case are VOID. [JP]

See also UNDUE INFLUENCE.

fact in issue A fact that must be proved by a party in a case in order for that party to succeed in the action; for example, in a MURDER case, the prosecution must, in order to succeed, prove that (a) the defendant caused the victim's death, and that (b) the defendant did so with the necessary MENS REA (that is, with the intention of causing death or really serious bodily harm). Thus (a) and (b) constitute the facts in issue in the case. [ALTC]

fact scepticism One of the two principal strands of AMERICAN REALISM whose adherents are not only sceptical of the role played by rules in judicial decision-making (as is the case with RULE SCEPTICISM), but also about the ability of judges to find the facts of a case to which rules are then applied. The main representative of this strand of thinking is JEROME FRANK whose view was that judges are essentially witnesses to witnesses. Accordingly, the judge's decision on which witness to believe is subject to his or her prejudices and emotional reactions. Fact sceptics therefore reject any idea of the judge as an objective fact-finder. [JP]

Further reading: Jerome Frank, *Law and the Modern Mind* (New York: Brentano's, 1930).

factum probandum (Lat. the fact to be proved) A fact in issue. [ALTC]

factum probans (Lat. the fact that proves) A RELEVANT FACT. [ALTC]

failure to maintain At common law, a husband used to have the duty to maintain his wife. That duty is now reciprocal between spouses and civil partners under the terms of the Domestic Proceedings and Magistrates' Courts Act 1978 and Matrimonial Causes Act 1973 for spouses, and in the Civil Partnership Act 2004 for registered civil partners. Each of these statutes provides that an application for financial provision may be made to the relevant court on the grounds that the respondent has failed to provide reasonable MAINTEN-ANCE for the applicant or a CHILD of the FAM-ILY. These applications may be made during the marriage or civil partnership while the parties are LIVING TOGETHER or after separation. The courts can order the spouse or civil partner to make periodic payments or lump sum payments to the other.   [AD]

See also MAINTENANCE ORDER; REASONABLE FINANCIAL PROVISION.

fair comment See DEFAMATION.

fair dealing A circumscribed defence allowing a person to use a COPYRIGHT work for the purposes of private study, research, criticism, review and reporting of current events. Fair dealing is not statutorily defined but is referred to under permitted acts: see Copyright, Designs and Patents Act 1988, ss. 29, 30.   [US]

See also INFRINGEMENT ACTION; SOFTWARE.

fair dismissal A DISMISSAL which is for a lawful reason (such as misconduct, REDUN-DANCY or that it would be illegal to continue employing the EMPLOYEE) and is not an UNFAIR DISMISSAL.   [MJ]

fair trial An international HUMAN RIGHT con-tained in Article 6(1) of the EUROPEAN CON-VENTION ON HUMAN RIGHTS, which states that 'everyone is entitled to a fair and public hearing within a reasonable time by an independent and impartial tribunal estab-lished by law'. (See also Article 14 of the INTERNATIONAL COVENANT ON CIVIL AND POLITICAL RIGHTS (ICCPR), which expresses the prin-ciple in similar terms.) The right to a fair trial is seen as a fundamental means of pro-tecting individuals from the unlawful deprivation of other basic rights such as the right to life and liberty of the person.

The guarantees afforded by Article 6 cover not only the court proceedings them-selves, but also pre-trial and post-trial stages. Additional measures protecting those charged with criminal offences are contained in Article 6(2) (the PRESUMPTION OF INNOCENCE) and Article 6(3), which speci-fies a number of minimum rights (such as access to legal advice) which should be

afforded to the accused. Moreover, the con-cept of a criminal charge is itself interpreted widely to encompass, for example, court martial proceedings, prison disciplinary proceedings, and some COMPETITION LAW and tax matters. Article 6 also closely inter-relates with a number of other Convention provisions, notably Article 3 (the prohib-ition on TORTURE, etc.) and Article 5, which affirms the principles of access to justice which also underpin Article 6. Article 6 is also an ABSOLUTE RIGHT under the ECHR, a point reaffirmed in a number of UK deci-sions under the Human Rights Act 1998.

[JW]

false imprisonment A TORT of strict liabil-ity, involving the direct and unlawful detention of an individual in such a way as to restrict his freedom of movement from a particular place. Incarceration is not necessary; it may be possible to restrict freedom of movement by threatening someone with the use of a firearm, for instance. It is simply necessary that the restraint is total and unlawful. False impris-onment can occur no matter how short the period of detention. It is also not necessary that the claimant be aware of his detention (see Murray v. Ministry of Defence [1988] 1 WLR 692).   [HJ]

See also ASSAULT; BATTERY.

false instrument See FORGERY.

false statement A requirement in estab-lishing an actionable MISREPRESENTATION. A false statement can include conduct which misleads or conveys a false impres-sion. As a general rule there is no duty of disclosure in contractual negotiations, so that silence cannot satisfy the false state-ment requirement. However, there are exceptions where silence can found liabil-ity in misrepresentation because there is a duty to speak so as to avoid presenting a misleading impression, e.g. correcting statements where circumstances have changed. There are also some relationships based on trust where there is a duty to speak, i.e. FIDUCIARY relationships and rela-tionships in contracts *uberrimae fidei* (of utmost good faith), such as insurance contracts. [JPL]

See also PERJURY.

Fam The standard abbreviation for the Law Reports: Family cases, published by the INCORPORATED COUNCIL OF LAW REPORTING. [JW]

See also LAW REPORTS.

familial homicide The unofficial label which has been attached to the offence of causing or allowing the death of a child or vulnerable adult under the Domestic Violence, Crime and Victims Act 2004, s. 5.

D commits this offence when (a) a child or vulnerable adult (V) dies as a result of the unlawful act of a person who was a member of the same household as V, and had frequent contact with V; and (b) D was such a person at the time of that act; and (c) at that time there was a significant risk of serious physical harm being caused to V by the unlawful act of such a person; and (d) either D was the person whose act caused V's death or, (i) D was, or ought to have been, aware of the risk mentioned in (c) above, and (ii) D failed to take such steps as he could reasonably have been expected to take to protect V from the risk, and (iii) the act occurred in circumstances of the kind that D foresaw or ought to have foreseen. The prosecution does not have to prove whether it was the first alternative in (d) above (i.e. D caused the death) or the second (the conditions in (i) to (iii) above) which applies.

The offence was created in response to concerns regarding the difficulty of proving which one of two carers was responsible for the death of a person in their care, when it was known that it must have been one of them, but it is not clear which one. In the absence of such clarity, it could prove impossible to convict either of them of MURDER or MANSLAUGHTER. See the Law Commission, *Children: Their Non-accidental Death or Serious Injury (Criminal Trials)* (Law Com No. 282, 2003). [BF]

See also OMISSION.

familial sexual offences *See* INCEST.

family A group of people connected in some way by a close relationship. There is no one legal definition of family for all purposes, but it usually includes people connected by BLOOD RELATIONSHIP, MARRIAGE, ADOPTION, CIVIL PARTNERSHIP, and cohabitants in a long, stable relationship. Not all family members have legal obligations or responsibilities to each other; those responsibilities vary with the nature of the relationship and the nature of the obligation, both in private law matters such as MAINTENANCE and in public law matters such as immigration. [AD]

See also AFFINITY; CONSANGUINITY.

family assets Categorization of assets as 'FAMILY assets' has significance in those jurisdictions subject to community property regimes, but has less significance in England and Wales where distribution of property on SEPARATION, ANNULMENT, DIVORCE or DISSOLUTION is governed by a separate property regime. It is, however, a term which could become more important in England and Wales since the House of Lords decision in *Miller* v. *Miller; McFarlane* v. *McFarlane* [2006] UKHL 24. In that case, Baroness Hale used the term 'family assets' to describe those assets acquired for the use and benefit of the whole family, including family businesses or joint ventures in which both the husband and wife (or civil partners) work. Although the Matrimonial Causes Act 1973 makes no distinction between the nature of the assets owned by the parties jointly or by either of them, which are subject to sharing on nullity, separation, dissolution or divorce, Baroness Hale suggested that there may be situations in which family assets could be treated differently from business or investment assets which have been generated solely or mainly by one party, or from property which either of them has brought into the MARRIAGE or CIVIL PARTNERSHIP by way of inheritance or gift. [AD]

See also ANCILLARY RELIEF; COMMUNITY OF ASSETS; PROPERTY ADJUSTMENT ORDER.

family assistance order An order made under the terms of the Children Act 1989, s. 16, requiring that a CAFCASS officer be available to advise, assist and befriend a person named in the order. Those who can be named in this way include a PARENT, a GUARDIAN and the CHILD. Where the court has the power to make an order concerning a child in the course of family proceedings under Part II of the Act (e.g. a SECTION 8 ORDER), irrespective of whether it actually makes that order, it can make a family assistance order. The consent must be obtained from any named person, other than the child, before an order can be made. An order could previously be made only in exceptional circumstances and could not exceed six months in duration. But following the enactment of the Children and Adoption Act 2006, the order is no longer seen as exceptional and it is possible to make an order for up to 12 months. [FK]

family county courts Specialist divisions of the COUNTY COURTS staffed by circuit judges who have received specialist training in family law matters. The County Courts hear the majority of family law cases in England and Wales: all matrimonial cases must be started in the 'DIVORCE county court', which is a county court specially designated as such, or in the PRINCIPAL REGISTRY OF THE FAMILY DIVISION in London, which is a divorce county court for this purpose. The equivalent county courts have been designated to deal with CIVIL PARTNERSHIP cases. The majority of cases under the 1989 Children Act are heard in county courts designated as either FAMILY HEARING CENTRES or CARE CENTRES, and in the Principal Registry in London. [AD]

See also DESIGNATED FAMILY JUDGE; FAMILY PROCEEDINGS.

Family Division A division of the HIGH COURT, created by the Administration of Justice Act 1970. Based at the Royal Courts of Justice in London, the Division deals with all matrimonial matters, both at first instance and on appeal; matters relating to MINORS and proceedings under the Children Act 1989; and judgments on behalf of those who are unable to make decisions for themselves, such as persistent vegetative state victims. The Family Division also deals with undisputed matters of PROBATE in the Probate Registry of the Family Division in

London, and the 11 probate registries in England and Wales. The Division consists of approximately 15–19 High Court judges and is headed by the PRESIDENT OF THE FAMILY DIVISION, now also the 'Head of Family Justice'. [AF]

See also CHANCERY DIVISION; QUEEN'S BENCH DIVISION.

family group conferencing A group meeting where family members and agencies are invited to come together with the aim of resolving conflict with – or antisocial or offending behaviour by – a child or young person. It is one of a number of RESTORATIVE JUSTICE strategies being developed in the social welfare and criminal justice systems. A family group conference will involve members of the extended family and representatives of social and educational agencies involved with the family. Where the conference has been set up in the context of specific anti-social or offending behaviour, the victim and a supporter will normally be invited to attend. The aim of a conference is to establish and agree an action plan for the young person involved, including proposals for reparation if appropriate. [JW]

family hearing centres Specialist COUNTY COURTS designated as competent to hear private law applications under the Children Act 1989. These are applications for PARENTAL RESPONSIBILITY, GUARDIANSHIP ORDERS, RESIDENCE ORDERS, CONTACT ORDERS, PROHIBITED STEPS ORDERS, SPECIFIC ISSUES ORDERS, Special Guardianship, or FAMILY ASSISTANCE ORDERS. They are staffed by DESIGNATED FAMILY JUDGES who have received specialist training in child law matters. [AD]

See also CARE CENTRE; FAMILY COUNTY COURTS.

family home Formerly referred to as the 'matrimonial home'. The dwelling house which the spouses or civil partners occupy, or intend to occupy, as their family home. Ownership of the family home while the MARRIAGE or CIVIL PARTNERSHIP persists is subject to the general law of property, but its occupation is subject to special rules. A nonowning spouse or civil partner has 'home rights' in the family home owned by the other partner which prevent that non-owning spouse or civil partner from being excluded from it without an order of the court. This right to occupy is a charge on the property and may be registered as such under the Land Registration Act 2002. If registered, the charge is binding upon third parties.

Without a court order extending them, home rights come to an end on the death of the owner, the DISSOLUTION of the marriage or civil partnership, or the disposition by the owning spouse of the property, unless the rights were registered and are binding on the purchaser. The family home also has a special status when it forms a part of a bankrupt's or intestate's estate. The occupation rights of (e.g.) a bankrupt's spouse in the family home are protected in many cases. While home rights only apply to married or civil registered partners, the right to occupy the family home, in cases of unmarried or unregistered partners, is also protected in some circumstances in cases of domestic violence. On divorce or dissolution of a civil partnership, the court has wide-ranging jurisdiction to transfer, sell or settle the family home as part of an order for ANCILLARY RELIEF.   [AD]

family life The right to family life as a HUMAN RIGHT has two elements: first, it is protected by Article 8 of the EUROPEAN CONVENTION ON HUMAN RIGHTS, as part of the general right to PRIVACY and a private life; secondly, the specific right to marry and found a family (sometimes called the **right to procreation**) is separately protected by Article 12. The right to family life has been extended to de facto relationships outside of MARRIAGE; it has thus been used to establish the rights of post-operative transsexuals to marry (*Goodwin* v. *United Kingdom* (2002) 35 EHRR 18) and of same-sex partners to succeed to certain property on the same terms as married couples (*Karner* v. *Austria* (2004) 38 EHRR 24; *Ghaidan* v. *Godin-Mendoza* [2004] UKHL 30 – see also CIVIL PARTNERSHIP).   [JW]

family mediation A process, ideally entered into voluntarily by the parties, intended to assist them to make joint decisions about their SEPARATION, children, finances and/or property. An impartial third person, a mediator who has no stake in the dispute and who is not an advocate for either side, facilitates communication between the parties to help them arrive at their own decisions. It is not intended to be family counselling, although it is hoped that mediation will also assist the parties to learn communication skills for the future.

Mediation was initially concerned with issues about children, but now includes all issues related to family separation. Along with negotiation and other collaborative processes aimed at diverting disputants from litigation, mediation is thought to be appropriate to family disputes because it can minimize conflict between separating parties, which is particularly important when the welfare of children is concerned. Solicitors and judges are encouraged to refer clients to mediation before court proceedings are begun, and in some cases an appointment with a mediator is required before one can have access to public funding for family-related disputes. Where appropriate, public funding can be obtained for mediation sessions; otherwise, mediation must be privately financed.   [AD]

family proceedings A specialist term used in reference to the court's jurisdiction to make SECTION 8 ORDERS under the Children Act 1989. 'Family proceedings' is defined by s. 8(3) of that Act, as amended, to mean any proceedings under the inherent jurisdiction of the High Court relating to children, and any proceedings under a list of nine statutes that encompass most causes concerning children, including the Matrimonial Causes Act 1973, the Adoption and Children Act 2002, the Crime and Disorder Act 1998 and the Family Law Act 1996. Relevant proceedings at any level of court may qualify as family proceedings.   [AD]

fast track *See* ALLOCATION.

father's rights The rights a father has in relation to his CHILD. Every father married to the mother of his child has PARENTAL RESPONSIBILITY in relation to that child. Unmarried fathers do not automatically have parental responsibility but can acquire it under the Children Act 1989, s. 4. A father can do this by entering into a PARENTAL RESPONSIBILITY AGREEMENT with the mother, if she is amenable, or seek a PARENTAL RESPONSIBILITY ORDER from the court, if she is not. These orders have been readily granted where the father has been able to show attachment and commitment to the child, provided his motives are not impugned (*Re S (Parental Responsibility)* [1995] 2 FLR 648). Since the end of 2003, unmarried fathers have been able to acquire parental responsibility by registering as the child's father in terms of the Births and Deaths Registration Act 1953 as permitted by the Children Act 1989 (s. 4 (1)(a)), amended by the Adoption and Children Act 2002. This provision is not retrospective.

Where a child is being placed for ADOPTION, even fathers without parental responsibility should be consulted. All fathers have a right to rely on the presumption in favour of reasonable contact with any of their children looked after by a LOCAL AUTHORITY. In private law proceedings, they have a right to apply to the court for a SECTION 8 ORDER under the Children Act 1989 without the leave of the court.

In the colloquial sense deployed by fathers' rights groups, a father's rights have been seen to encompass matters such as residence and contact as well as parental responsibility. [FK]

See also CONTACT ORDERS; RESIDENCE ORDERS.

federal state Also called a federation, a federal state is constituted on the basis of agreement between a number of territorial entities, whether states or otherwise, under a single, strong and unified central authority or government. The agreement, most typically translated into a constitutional instrument, will define the superiority of the central government and will provide for the dissolution of the federation under very strict and exceptional circumstances. A federal STATE evolves from a CONFEDERATION, which possesses a much weaker

central authority. Examples of federal states are the Federal Republic of Germany, the United States of America and Canada. The individual entities comprising the federation do not generally possess distinct international legal personality from the central federal state, unless the federal constitution and other states deem otherwise. The responsibility of the central federal state extends to cover acts of the federal entities. [IB]

See also STATE RESPONSIBILITY.

fee An inheritable legal interest in land. Under the system of FEUDAL TENURE, a tenant swore fealty (loyalty) to his lord and provided services, in exchange for the right to hold his lord's land. It became increasingly common for the lord to recognize the right of a tenant's HEIRS to inherit such an interest and such an inheritable interest became known as a fee.

Prior to 1926, there were several different types of fee, including the FEE SIMPLE ABSOLUTE IN POSSESSION, base fee, FEE TAIL and FEE FARM RENT. However, since the Law of Property Act 1925, the only type of fee that can exist at law is the fee simple absolute in possession. [DR]

fee farm rent A term dating from feudal times, meaning a perpetual rent payable on freehold land, reserved by the lord when the land was granted to the feudal tenant. A fee farm was similar in nature to a LEASEHOLD interest and the fee farm rent was the rent payable in exchange for possession of the land. Under the Law of Property Act 1925, s. 205(1)(xxiii), a fee farm rent is a type of RENTCHARGE. Most rentcharges have now been abolished by the Rentcharges Act 1977, which provided for their gradual extinction over a 60-year period. [DR]

See also FEE.

fee simple absolute in possession For practical purposes, ownership of a fee simple absolute in possession denotes complete ownership of land and is the best type of ownership available. The rights under a fee simple absolute in possession may be transferred or disposed of almost without limitation. In the REGISTERED LAND system, the fee simple absolute in possession is known as a FREEHOLD title with one of three classes: absolute TITLE, QUALIFIED TITLE or POSSESSORY TITLE.

'FEE' means an inheritable interest in land, 'simple' means that the estate is capable of being inherited by the 'general HEIRS' (although this no longer has any practical significance), 'absolute' means that it is owned without limitation and 'in possession' means that the estate is current.

Under the Law of Property Act 1925 (LPA 1925), the fee simple absolute in possession is one of only two LEGAL ESTATES in land that can exist, the other being the 'TERM OF YEARS absolute', also known as the LEASEHOLD estate (LPA 1925, s. 1(1)). Theoretically, the holder of a fee simple absolute in possession holds the estate as a tenant-in-chief of the Crown, but in reality the holder's rights continue indefinitely, unless the owner dies leaving no will and nobody who can succeed to the estate under the rules of intestacy, in which case the title will revert to the Crown through the process of ESCHEAT.   [DR]

fee tail (obsolete) Prior to 1926, the fee tail was one of the three principal LEGAL ESTATES in land that could be created, along with the FEE SIMPLE ABSOLUTE IN POSSESSION and the LIFE ESTATE. A fee tail existed for as long as the person to whom it was granted, or any of his blood descendants, remained alive. It was usually created where X granted property 'to Y and the heirs of his body' or 'to Y in tail'. The effect of this was to create a succession of estates until there was no one alive who could trace their bloodline back to Y, at which point the property would revert back to X or his successors in title.

The fee tail was developed in order to keep land within landed families for future generations. However, from the 15th century onwards, methods were devised so that the TENANT IN TAIL in possession of the land could use a TRUST INSTRUMENT to 'bar' the fee tail, converting it into a form of fee simple, thus frustrating the purpose of the original grantor. Under the Law of Property Act 1925, ss. 1, 130, the fee tail was abol-

ished as a legal estate, fee tails were converted into ENTAILED INTERESTS and attempts to create fee tails had the effect of creating entailed interests. Under the Trusts of Land and Appointment of Trustees Act 1996, Schedule 1, para. 5, it is no longer possible to create entailed interests either.   [DR]

felony (obsolete) The COMMON LAW classified each crime as a TREASON, a felony or a MISDEMEANOUR. This classification corresponded broadly to the seriousness of the crime and to the powers of ARREST attendant on its commission. The distinctions between felony and misdemeanour were abolished by the Criminal Law Act 1967, s. 1. It is acceptable now to refer to all crimes as offences.   [BF]

female genital mutilation (FGM) Also referred to as female circumcision or female genital cutting. The World Health Organization defines FGM as practices involving the partial or complete removal of the female external genitalia, or other injury to the female genitals for cultural or other non-therapeutic purposes. FGM is considered to be a violation of women's HUMAN RIGHTS and an act of violence under the 1979 Convention on the Elimination of All Forms of Discrimination Against Women (CEDAW). It is arguable (though there is no case law) that FGM is contrary to both the right to PRIVACY under Article 8 of the EUROPEAN CONVENTION ON HUMAN RIGHTS, which includes the right to protection of an individual's physical and emotional integrity, and the right to health in Article 12 of the INTERNATIONAL COVENANT ON ECONOMIC, SOCIAL AND CULTURAL RIGHTS. In English law, performing, assisting in or procuring most forms of FGM, including clitoridectomy, excision and infibulation (but excluding piercing and tattooing) would constitute a criminal offence under the Female Genital Mutilation Act of 2003. FGM performed on a MINOR would also constitute child abuse under English law and a child at risk of cutting could be made the subject of child protection measures under the Children Act 1989.   [JW]

feme covert (obsolete; Old Fr.) A married woman.   [AD]

See also COVERTURE.

feme sole (obsolete; Old Fr. a single woman) A woman who has never been married, is widowed or divorced.   [AD]

See also COVERTURE.

feminist jurisprudence A movement in legal theory applying the insights of feminism to law. Emergent especially since the 1970s and 1980s and associated particularly with CRITICAL LEGAL STUDIES (CLS), its origins can be traced back to the beginnings of feminism itself with Mary Wollstonecraft's *A Vindication of the Rights of Woman* (1792).

There are distinct strands within feminist jurisprudence, but they share basic feminist insights such as the fact that society has traditionally been *patriarchal*, that is, ordered according to male standards, where the male is regarded as the norm and the female as the exception, as well as a concern to expose the role that law has played in shaping such a society. In this latter regard, feminist jurists point out that law has been written and written about by a relatively small and unrepresentative group of men – white, middle-aged or elderly, privileged and wealthy. The language and voice of the law is accordingly male, with alternative voices going unheard. The absence of challenge encourages a male belief that law is in fact objective and neutral, rather than the reflection of a privileged minority. Feminist jurists thus do not only concentrate on the maleness of law, but also acknowledge the extent to which other minority voices are silenced.

Feminist jurisprudence shares concerns with CLS, but has also been critical of the apparent disengagement by CLS from social action. By contrast, feminist jurists are primarily concerned with what needs to be done in order to redress the injustices of a patriarchal society.

The key debate within feminist jurisprudence has been between liberals and radicals. Liberalism, with its emphasis on equality and rights, looks at first sight like a natural home for feminist jurists, but some perceive severe shortcomings in this position. For example, there is concern that to focus on giving people rights is to ignore the obstacles there may be to enforcing them. Radicals ask why the onus should be put on the individual to enforce what liberals already concede they should have. At an even deeper level, radicals believe that liberalism itself may actually be tainted by a male view of the world, which focuses on the individual rather than the collective and the cooperative. Finally, radicals are concerned that it may not always be appropriate to focus on the similarity between men and women: there may be times when it is more appropriate to stress the differences.

While radicals are enthusiastic about an approach that acknowledges difference and treats difference justly (e.g. in relation to pregnancy), liberals are concerned that this may actually serve to bolster the patriarchal notion that the male is the norm and the female the exception.

Radical feminists (such as Robin West) have themselves been challenged by cultural feminists (such as Carol Gilligan). Cultural feminists contend that radicals focus on the difference between male and female in a negative way (e.g. seeing sexual intimacy, pregnancy and childbirth as violations), whereas these differences should really be celebrated (e.g. the female's focus on nurture, care and cooperation).

[JP]

Further reading: Ann C. Scales, 'The Emergence of Feminist Jurisprudence: An Essay', *Yale Law Journal* (1986), 95 pp. 1373–1403.

feu duty In Scots law, a payment due periodically by the owner of a property (**vassal**) to their feudal **superior**. The Land Tenure Reform (Scotland) Act 1974 prohibited the creation of new feu duties and allowed most vassals to redeem their feu duty. Redemption took place automatically on the sale of a property, but could also be effected at any time upon payment of a sum, roughly 20 times the value of the feu duty.

All remaining feu duties were abolished with the end of the system of FEUDAL TENURE in Scotland under the Abolition of Feudal Tenure etc. (Scotland) Act 2000. [JP]

feudal tenure The economic system dating from the Norman Conquest in the 11th century, under which a tenant held the land of his lord. Under the original system of feudal tenure, all land was owned by the Crown and the land that the king did not keep possession of was granted to his tenants-in-chief to hold in return for services. By a process of SUBINFEUDATION, a tenant-in-chief could then grant parts of that land to himself as lord, to be held by his own tenants, which over time created various forms of tenure.

The main forms of tenure were knight's service (where land was held in return for military services), frankalmoign or divine service (religious services) and free or villein socage (agricultural services). Although originally the relationship of tenure was a personal one, the system evolved so that socage became the main form of free tenure and it became freely alienable (transferable) and inheritable by the tenant's heirs. The services were gradually reduced to money payments and the Tenures Abolition Act 1660 reduced the forms of tenure to socage (FREEHOLD) and COPYHOLD. Copyhold was eventually abolished by the Law of Property Act 1922.

Although strictly speaking all land is still owned by the Crown, this is no longer practically significant since any person can own an ESTATE in land, which in practice equates to ownership of the land itself. The land registration system of state-guaranteed ownership marks a further break with feudal tenure. [DR]

FGM See FEMALE GENITAL MUTILATION.

fi fa See FIERI FACIAS.

fiduciary 'Someone who has undertaken to act for and on behalf of another in a particular matter in circumstances which give rise to a relationship of trust and confidence' – per Millett LJ in *Bristol and West Building Society* v. *Mothew* [1998] Ch 1 [18]. Persons such as company DIRECTORS, SOLICITORS and TRUSTEES are common examples of those who act in a fiduciary capacity.

Where a **fiduciary relationship** exists, the fiduciary will owe certain duties to the other party in that relationship (the principal). These tend to be obligations based upon loyalty, confidentiality and good faith dealing. Not every breach by a fiduciary is a breach of fiduciary duty; for example, breach of the duty of care and skill that a fiduciary will normally owe the principal is not a breach of fiduciary duty as such. This is because the duty to use care and skill does not flow from the fiduciary nature of the relationship: a fiduciary may perform incompetently and negligently without being any the less loyal, and without acting in bad faith. In such cases, however, the standard of care expected of a fiduciary may sometimes be higher than in comparable non-fiduciary actions for NEGLIGENCE: see *Henderson* v. *Merrett Syndicates Ltd* [1995] 2 AC 145 [205].

As regards remedies, transactions in which fiduciaries have a personal interest may be set aside or held unenforceable; they may be required to account for profits to clients for any secret profit or third party commission obtained out of the transaction, and any losses attributable to negligent or wrongful steps taken by them while acting in a fiduciary situation may be recoverable by the principal by way of a claim for RESTITUTION or equitable COMPENSATION. [JW]

See also AGENCY; CONFLICT OF INTEREST; DIRECTORS' DUTIES.

fieri facias (Lat. you should cause to be done) A WRIT of the HIGH COURT authorizing a High Court Enforcement Officer to seize sufficient goods from a judgment debtor to sell and pay off the judgment debt and the cost of enforcement. [JW]

See also WARRANT OF EXECUTION.

FII See FRANKED INVESTMENT INCOME.

filing In civil proceedings, the delivery of a document by post or otherwise to the court office: CPR Rule 2.3. [JW]

Final Act The text of a TREATY that is incorporated in the body of the final document of the diplomatic conference adopting that treaty. In the event that the text contained in the Final Act is different from that which the state representatives have signed, then the signed text has authority and is endowed with legal force. Where the signed or initialled text cannot be reproduced, then, in accordance with Article 10(b) of the 1969 Vienna Convention on the Law of Treaties, the Final Act of the conference incorporating the text may serve as the authentic text. [IB]

financial provision order An order for periodical payments or a lump sum intended to adjust the financial position of the parties and any children of the FAMILY. The order can be made on DIVORCE, SEPARATION, ANNULMENT or DISSOLUTION of CIVIL PARTNERSHIP or on application for FAILURE TO MAINTAIN. It can be made in conjunction with other orders for ANCILLARY RELIEF, such as PROPERTY ADJUSTMENT ORDERS. In determining whether a financial provision order is appropriate and, if so, what order to make, the court must first give consideration to the welfare of any CHILD of the family; it must consider whether a CLEAN BREAK is appropriate, and, since the House of Lords decision in *White* v. *White* [2000] UKHL 54, it must try to achieve a fair outcome and not discriminate between husbands and wives and the respective roles they undertook in the family. The Matrimonial Causes Act 1973 and the Civil Partnership Act 2004 provide a list of factors for the court to consider in determining applications. [AD]

See also REASONABLE FINANCIAL PROVISION.

financial relief An order or orders adjusting the financial circumstances of spouses, civil partners or former spouses or civil partners. Orders for financial relief may also be made in favour of children. Financial relief orders include orders for MAINTENANCE PENDING SUIT, FINANCIAL PROVISION ORDERS, PROPERTY ADJUSTMENT ORDERS, PENSION SHARING ORDERS, or for the variation of any of these orders. The Matrimonial Causes Act 1973 contains provisions permitting the court to set aside or prevent property transactions made by a spouse if it can be shown that the transaction was made with the intention of defeating or minimizing the other spouse's claim for financial relief. [AD]

See also ANCILLARY RELIEF; FAILURE TO MAINTAIN.

Financial Services Authority (FSA) A statutory body set up to authorize and regulate providers of financial services, including stockbroking, investment advice, banking services and consumer financial services such as advice on and sale of MORTGAGES, private pension products and insurance. The Financial Services and Markets Act 2000 makes it a criminal offence for a person to undertake any regulated activity without FSA authorization. The FSA also has various powers under the Act to investigate the conduct of authorized persons, and to investigate allegations of market abuse and a range of financial crimes, including insider dealing and MONEY-LAUNDERING. [JW]

fine A financial penalty imposed as a sentence, and payable to the court. [BF]

Finnis, John (b. 1940) Australian natural lawyer, teaching at both Oxford University and Notre Dame University (USA), he is best known for *Natural Law and Natural Rights* (1980), which represents a major restatement of NATURAL LAW, drawing inspiration from Aristotle and especially AQUINAS. Although avowedly a Catholic, Finnis's approach to natural law does not depend on Christianity, but rather upon **practical reasonableness**. Natural law for him thus represents the set of principles of practical reasonableness that allow human life to be ordered. In this way, Finnis hopes to avoid the **naturalistic fallacy** pointed out by DAVID HUME.

It is necessary to know first of all what it is that humans pursue. Finnis proposes that they pursue those things that are objectively good for them, that is, things which are good in themselves and not simply because they are desired. He lists seven such '**basic goods**': life, knowledge, play, aesthetic experience, sociability or friendship, practical reasonableness and religion. Because these are all described as basic goods, there is no hierarchy among them; all must be regarded as equal. The basic goods are described as 'pre-moral' as it would be impossible to disagree with their value for human life without being unreasonable. Finnis seeks in this way to avoid the naturalistic fallacy which is commonly attributed to natural law theories and according to which they illegitimately derive a normative conclusion (an 'ought') from any purely factual premises (or 'is' statements). In so far as he is not grounding his explanation of natural law in any account of how humans live, he is able to claim that the basic goods are 'self-evident'.

With a clear statement of what it is that humans pursue in order to lead a good life, Finnis moves on to consider how they should go about doing that. This will require the exercise of practical reason and he lists nine tests of practical reasonableness or 'ought' statements, which tell humans what they should and should not do: (a) one should form a rational plan of life, in the form of a set of coherent intentions and commitments, which should provide a reference for the way in which one lives one's life; (b) there should be no arbitrary preferences among the basic goods; (c) there should be no arbitrary preferences among persons; (d) one should have a proper sense of detachment; (e) one should have a proper sense of commitment; (f) efficiency is to be pursued within reasonable limits, but is not itself to be a treated as a central principle; (g) there should be respect for every basic good in every action, such that no choice would contravene any basic good; (h) there should be consideration for the common good; (i) one should follow one's conscience, even where this is (in good faith) in error.

These statements form the natural law in Finnis's account and neither an individual nor the state could act contrary to them without contravening the natural law. Most importantly, Finnis argues that it is possible to ground FUNDAMENTAL RIGHTS in practical reason and specifically in the seventh test. He argues that an action that is manifestly at odds with one or other of the basic goods could never be justified. Thus the state could not execute an individual without disregarding the basic good of life, nor lie to citizens without disregarding the basic good of knowledge. As there is an absolute bar to this sort of behaviour by the state, it is possible to claim – on the basis of practical reason – that individuals have rights in those regards.   [JP]

Further reading: John Finnis, *Natural Law and Natural Rights* (Oxford: Oxford University Press, 1980).

firm offer A particular type of contractual OFFER which is expressed to be 'open' and available for ACCEPTANCE for a given period of time. The offer cannot be accepted once that period has elapsed. Unless the promise to keep the offer open for the stated period of time is supported by CONSIDERATION, the offeror is free to revoke the offer despite the fact that the period has not elapsed (see *Routledge* v. *Grant* (1828) 4 Bing 653).   [JPL]
      See also OPTION.

first offender A term used principally in the law of sentencing to denote an offender not previously convicted of an offence. [BF]
      See also PERSISTENT OFFENDER; REPEAT OFFENDER.

first ownership In relation to COPYRIGHT law, the AUTHOR of a work is the first owner of any copyright in it. The exception is if the work is a LITERARY, dramatic, musical or ARTISTIC WORK, or a film, and is made by an employee in the course of his employment. In that case the employer is the first owner of any copyright in the work, subject to any agreement to the contrary.   [US]

fiscal year The 12-month period starting on 6 April in one calendar year and ending on 5 April in the following calendar year. For the purposes of tax and taxation, this period is nowadays more usually referred to as the tax year.   [RE]

fitness for purpose GOODS supplied in the course of a business must be reasonably fit for any purpose which the buyer expressly or impliedly made known to the seller (Sale of Goods Act 1979, s. 14(3)), which need not be limited to the purpose for which such goods are generally supplied. The exception is where the circumstances show that the buyer does not rely, or it is unreasonable for the buyer to rely, on the seller's skill or judgement. Although this term is a CONDITION (s. 14(6)), s. 15A provides for a modification of the usual remedy if the buyer is not a CONSUMER and the breach is so slight that it would be unreasonable for the buyer to reject the goods. In these circumstances, the breach will not be a breach of condition but may be treated as a breach of WARRANTY so that the remedy is limited to DAMAGES for the BREACH OF CONTRACT.   [JPL]

fixed charge   An INTEREST or 'charge' secured by a creditor over a specific company ASSET or assets (such as the business premises, plant or machinery). The COMPANY cannot sell the asset without the consent of the secured creditor or by repaying the amount secured by the charge. Fixed charges take priority over other secured and unsecured debts should the company become insolvent.   [JW]

See also FLOATING CHARGE.

fixed penalty notice   A notice providing an opportunity to pay a fixed amount in order to discharge liability for conviction of an offence to which the notice relates. Used widely for offences under the Road Traffic Offences Act 1988, a fixed penalty notice can now also be issued to ANTI-SOCIAL BEHAVIOUR offenders and for certain environmental offences. See, variously, the Environmental Protection Act 1990, the Anti-social Behaviour Act 2003 and the Clean Neighbourhoods and Environment Act 2005. They can be issued by the police, by local authority officers and police community support officers to anyone over 10 years old.   [SN]

fixed term tenancy   If a TENANCY agreement states that it lasts for a set period of time, such as six months or one year, then it is a fixed term tenancy. The LANDLORD and the TENANT are bound by the contractual agreement to let for that fixed period. If the tenant wishes to leave during that period he or she can only do so with the agreement of the landlord. If the tenant leaves without the landlord's agreement

he or she may be liable for damages for breach of contract. Although in theory the tenancy automatically terminates at the end of the fixed term, in practice most occupiers have some degree of legal protection following the expiry of the fixed term.   [HC & DR]

fixture   An item that is annexed to land or to a building on land so that it forms part of the land itself. Whether or not an item has become a fixture of the land is a question of both the **degree** of physical annexation and the **object** of annexation.

Regarding **degree**, the general rule is that an item is not a fixture unless it is attached or fastened to the land or building; for example, a greenhouse and a free-standing statue have both been held by the courts not to be a fixture. However, the overriding factor is the **object** of annexation. Where the object of annexation is for the item to be permanent and make a lasting improvement to the land, rather than a temporary attachment necessary for the enjoyment of the item, that item will be considered to be a fixture. Therefore, a chalet placed on concrete blocks that were not fixed to the land, but could not be removed except by destruction, has been held by the court to be a fixture. Conversely, a tapestry stretc. hed across wood blocks, nailed to the walls with two-inch nails, has been held not to be a fixture.

When land is sold, all fixtures are sold with the land unless the parties contract otherwise. With regard to leases, at the end of a tenancy the tenant has certain limited rights to remove trade fixtures, ornamental and domestic fixtures and agricultural fixtures.   [DR]

flag state jurisdiction   The principle that competence to enforce a country's laws, judicial system and police powers over a merchant or public vessel on the high seas is vested in the country where the vessel is registered (the flag state), with the exception of acts of piracy, where jurisdiction is universal. Where a merchant vessel is in the INTERNAL WATERS of the coastal STATE, the latter enjoys normal territorial jurisdiction. Public vessels and foreign warships are always subject to flag state jurisdiction. [IB]

flexible working Certain categories of employee have the right to request a change in their working hours or conditions (including the possibility of working from home) to accommodate their responsibilities as carers. There is no right to flexible working as such, only a right to request flexible working under the Employment Relations Act 1996, ss. 80F–I. The Act applies to 'qualifying' employees, i.e. those who have been continuously employed for at least 26 weeks, and are the mother, father, guardian, adopter, or foster parent of a child under six or disabled child under 18 (or are married to or a partner of such person), and have or expect to have parental responsibility for that child.

The Work and Families Act 2006 extends this right to employees who look after sick or elderly relatives, or other adults who live with them. Such an employee may, in writing, request flexible working (flexible in terms of length of hours, place of work and times of work, or any other term). The employers are under a duty to consider the request within 28 days of its receipt. If they grant it, the change to the contract is a permanent one; if they refuse, the employee has a right of internal appeal which the employers must hear. If the employers still refuse, and the matter cannot be resolved internally, the employee can complain to the EMPLOYMENT TRIBUNALS, but only on limited procedural grounds. Alternatively, the ACAS arbitration scheme for flexible working may be used.   [MJ]

floating charge An INTEREST in – called a charge over – the general ASSETS of a COMPANY held by a secured creditor. The assets to which the charge attaches tend to change (because they are general assets such as cash or stock in trade) and the company can use those assets without the consent of the creditor until the charge 'crystallizes'. **Crystallization** occurs on the appointment of a RECEIVER, on the presentation of a winding-up petition, or as otherwise provided for in the document creating the charge. Under the Insolvency Act 1986, where a company is insolvent, the repayment of fixed charges has priority over floating charges. Floating charges, however, take priority over any unsecured debts.   [JW]

See also FIXED CHARGE; LIQUIDATION; RECEIVERSHIP.

f.o.b. contract Stands for free on board. It is a CONTRACT for the international sale of goods by which the seller agrees to deliver the goods to the ship, where both property in the goods and consequently risk for loss or damage passes from seller to buyer. The ship is, in effect, treated as the buyer's floating warehouse (see *Cowas-Jee* v. *Thompson* (1845) 18 ER 560). Insurance and freight costs are borne by the buyer.   [JW]

See also C.I.F. CONTRACT.

force and fear One of the reasons in SCOTS LAW for which a contract may be void. Where a contract has apparently been entered into, but one party has been forced or is in fear of the consequences of refusal, then there is no true consent and the contract is void.

Threats made against the reluctant party may be physical or psychological and may equally be made against a member of that party's family.

Where the threat relates to something that the other party may legitimately do, such as enforcing a debt, then there is no force and fear.   [JP]

force majeure (Fr. superior, or greater, force) The 'occurrence of an irresistible force or of an unforeseen event, beyond the control of the STATE, making it materially impossible in the circumstances to perform the obligation': see Article 23(1) of the 2001 International Law Commission Draft Articles on Responsibility of States for internationally wrongful acts. Therefore, it acts as a defence to non-fulfilment of an international obligation or the commission of an international wrong; but where the situation giving rise to *force majeure* is due, either alone or in combination with other factors, to the conduct of the state invoking it, or where the state has assumed the risk of that situation occurring, the wrongfulness of the defaulting state remains (Article 23 (2) of the 2001 Draft Articles). [IB]

See also REBUS SIC STANTIBUS; STATE RESPONSIBILITY; TREATY.

force majeure clause (Fr. irresistible compulsion or coercion) A contractual clause which involves an express ALLOCATION OF RISK should certain specified events arise without the fault of the parties, and which might make the contract impossible to perform, so that the contract would be discharged if those events were to occur. The events are usually listed in full and include strike, riots, flood, fire and other ACTS OF GOD. The clause generally places the risk of such events on the other party. If such a clause covers the event in question, it will therefore operate as an excuse for the performing party, and the other party will be unable to escape the contract by reliance on the FRUSTRATION doctrine, or to seek remedies for the failure to perform. [JPL]

forced marriage 'A person ("A") is forced into a MARRIAGE if another person ("B") forces A to enter into a marriage (whether with B or another person) without A's free and full consent' (see the Family Law Act 1996, s. 63A(4) as introduced by the Forced Marriage (Civil Protection) Act 2007). Force includes not just physical force but coercion by threats, whether against A, or any other person, including B ('I will kill myself if you don't marry him!') or other psychological means (see s. 63A(6)).

The aim of the 2007 Act is both symbolic – to send out the message that forced marriage is socially and morally unacceptable in UK society – and practical, by creating new civil remedies called **forced marriage protection orders**. These are akin to the existing orders under Part 4 of the 1996 Act which offer some protection from DOMESTIC VIOLENCE. Forced marriage protection orders will be available both to those at risk of forced marriage, and for those who have already been forced into marriage. Although civil remedies, the orders may carry a power of arrest where there is significant risk of harm to the intended victim, or to somebody else in connection with the marriage/intended marriage.

Breach of an order will be treated as a CONTEMPT OF COURT. The orders came into operation on 25 November 2008. [JW]

forcible entry Under the Criminal Law Act 1977, s. 6, it is an offence for a person, without lawful authority, to use or threaten violence for the purpose of securing entry into any premises for himself or for any other person, provided that there is someone present on those premises at the time who is opposed to the entry which the violence is intended to secure; and the person knows that that is the case.

Section 6(1A) of the 1977 Act exempts from the offence a displaced residential occupier or a protected intending occupier (a term defined in s. 12A of the 1977 Act) or somebody acting on behalf of such an occupier. The person must adduce sufficient evidence that he or she is such an exempt person, and the prosecution must prove that he or she is not. This exemption is intended to apply to those seeking to remove squatters from their premises. [BF]

foreclosure A legal remedy by which a borrower's property is vested in the lender in full settlement of the debt due under a MORTGAGE (Law of Property Act 1925, s. 88(2) and 89 (2)). Foreclosure becomes available to a lender after the contractual date of REDEMPTION specified in the mortgage has passed.

In order to foreclose, the lender must first apply to the court for an order of **foreclosure nisi**, under which the court will order the borrower to pay off the mortgage debt by a certain date. If the borrower fails to pay off the debt by that date, the lender is entitled to apply for an order of **foreclosure absolute**, under which the property will be vested in the lender.

The consequences of foreclosure are severe for a borrower, because if the property is sold for a sum that is greater than the mortgage debt, the lender can keep the excess money. However, the lender does have a right to ask the court for an order of sale instead of foreclosure. Furthermore, once an order of foreclosure absolute is made, the borrower may still apply to court to allow him to redeem the property after all. For these reasons, it is far more common for a lender to exercise a POWER OF SALE than to seek foreclosure.   [DR]

forest law (obsolete) A system of law outside of the COMMON LAW, introduced following the Norman Conquest to restrict use of and access to lands designated as royal forest. The forest laws created a number of offences of **trespass against the vert** (restricting public use of the land and vegetation of the forest) and **trespass against the venison** (effectively reserving certain animals and game birds within the forest precincts, such as deer, partridge and even rabbits, for hunting by the aristocracy). Offences against forest law were dealt with in special courts of local jurisdiction – referred to as courts of attachment or the 40-day court of Woodmote, Sweinmote (Swainmote) and Eyre or Justice-Seat. Although various tracts of land are still designated as royal forest, the forest laws and their courts were largely obsolete by the late 17th century.   [JW]

forfeiture Loss of TITLE to assets resulting from a breach or non-performance of a legal obligation or the commission of a crime.   [SN]

forfeiture of lease Ending the LEASE prematurely by RE-ENTRY of the LANDLORD onto the premises. Forfeiture is only relevant for commercial leases and long residential leases since the termination of short residential leases is covered by statute. Most long leases contain a clause entitling the landlord to forfeiture of the lease if the tenant breaches any of the conditions. There has been extensive statutory intervention to protect the residential TENANT from arbitrary or excessive forfeiture – most recently in the Commonhold and Leasehold Reform Act 2002. The landlord must inform the tenant that a breach has taken place and give the tenant an opportunity to remedy the breach. If the tenant fails to put the breach right, then the landlord must go to the LEASEHOLD VALUATION TRIBUNAL for a determination that a breach has occurred. It is only after such a determination that

the landlord can issue proceedings for forfeiture in the COUNTY COURT.   [HC & DR]
    See also RELIEF FROM FORFEITURE.

forfeiture order An order depriving the defendant of TITLE to his or her assets.   [SN]

forfeiture rule A COMMON LAW rule which provides that a person cannot inherit property from someone whom he or she has unlawfully killed.   [SN]

forgery Under the Forgery and Counterfeiting Act 1981, s. 1, the offence of forgery is committed by a person who makes a false instrument, with the intention that he or another shall use it to induce somebody to accept it as genuine, and by reason of so accepting it to do or not to do some act to his own or any other person's prejudice.
    The 1981 Act, s. 8, states that an 'instrument' is (a) any document, whether of a formal or informal character; (b) a stamp issued or sold by a postal operator; (c) an Inland Revenue (now HM REVENUE AND CUSTOMS) stamp; (d) any disc, tape, soundtrack or other device on or in which information is recorded or stored by mechanical, electronic or other means. The 1981 Act also sets out offences of copying (s. 2), using (s. 3) and using a copy of (s. 4), a false instrument.
    Currency notes do not count as 'instruments' for the purposes of the above offences. However, they do form the subject matter of the related offences of COUNTERFEITING.   [BF]

formal admission An acknowledgement by a party of the existence of a particular fact that absolves the party who would otherwise bear the burden of proving that fact from the responsibility of doing so. The position in criminal proceedings is governed by the Criminal Justice Act 1967, s. 10, and the position in civil cases by Part 14 of the CIVIL PROCEDURE RULES.   [ALTC]

formal investigations The EQUALITY AND HUMAN RIGHTS COMMISSION may carry out formal investigations, either on its own initiative or at the instigation of the Secretary of State for Trade and Industry, into a practice of any individual or organization. If the investigation concerns a certain individual or body, that party must be allowed to make representations. A report may be issued. If it is found that a person or body has acted unlawfully, a NON-DISCRIMINATION NOTICE may be issued. [MJ]

formal justice Also called by John RAWLS 'justice as regularity'. It is one component of the RULE OF LAW and can be characterized simply by the notion that like cases are to be treated alike. While this can rightly be considered an important basic guarantee, and one that underpins notions such as **equal treatment**, many theorists argue that formal justice does not go far enough. As Rawls also observes, treating like cases alike does not guarantee SUBSTANTIVE JUSTICE. This, he argues, will depend on the principles in accordance with which the basic legal structure is designed. Scholars from within the counter-tradition of CRITICAL LEGAL STUDIES tend to go further in arguing that formal justice hides deep social inequalities, and isolates legal discourse from political and moral discourses that could provide external criteria for evaluating the quality of JUSTICE delivered by law. [JW]

See also PROCEDURAL JUSTICE.

forms of action In the history of the COMMON LAW, an action was the means by which a complainant could obtain a remedy for injury or loss. The forms of action were specific 'WRITS', originally an instruction from the king to a royal official, usually the **sheriff**, to take certain steps in investigating a dispute; for example, requiring a person to appear before a court, or allowing property to be seized unless the defendant could justify retaining possession. By the 13th century about 50 such writs had become established, including the great writs of **trespass**, **debt** and **covenant**, and these largely set the parameters for legal proceedings. If the complaint could not be made to fit one of these established writs, there could be no remedy and no cause of action. As F.W. Maitland observed in *The Forms of Action at Common Law*, 'where there is no remedy there is no wrong'. The forms of action thus played a fundamental role in

shaping not just court procedure, but also the substantive common law. They were finally abolished by the Judicature Acts 1873–5. [JW]

forum The COUNTRY in which one or more elements of a dispute are being (or have already been) litigated. So, for example, where action is commenced in the HIGH COURT in England and Wales, the forum is England and Wales. Where a claimant applies to the High Court for one or more PROVISIONAL MEASURES, the forum in respect of that application is England and Wales, even though the litigation of the action may be taking place in Scotland or some other foreign country (i.e. in a foreign forum). In relation to ARBITRATION, the forum in which the arbitral proceedings are juridically located is always referred to as the seat of arbitration. [RE]

forum prorogatum (Lat. literally 'prorogated' or deferred jurisdiction) The practice of the INTERNATIONAL COURT OF JUSTICE (ICJ) in assuming jurisdiction over a dispute in the absence of a SPECIAL AGREEMENT between the parties, or even of a declaration under the OPTIONAL CLAUSE of its Statute, by inferring the consent of the state concerned (see the *Corfu Channel Case* (*United Kingdom* v. *Albania*) (Merits) [1949] ICJ Reps 4). [IB]

forum rei (Lat. the FORUM of the thing (in dispute)) The territory of a STATE or COUNTRY in which a thing is situated and in respect of which the courts of that territory have actual or potential jurisdiction. [RE]

See also LEX LOCI ACTUS; LEX LOCI SITUS.

foster child A CHILD who is in the long-term or short-term care of adults other than his or her biological PARENTS. This may be in terms of a voluntary arrangement whereby the child is being accommodated by the LOCAL AUTHORITY as a child in need, or the child is being looked after by the local authority pursuant to a CARE ORDER. Alternatively, it may be that the arrangement is a private one. In some cases, foster children are ultimately adopted by their foster parents. [FK]

See also FOSTER PARENT.

foster parent An adult other than the biological or adoptive PARENT of a CHILD who takes care of that child. Foster carers look after children in their own homes on a long-term or short-term basis. This may be in terms of a voluntary arrangement whereby the child is being accommodated by the LOCAL AUTHORITY as a child in need, or the child is being looked after by the local authority pursuant to a CARE ORDER, or the arrangement may be a private one. Foster care is often used by local authorities as an alternative to institutional care. A person with whom a child is placed by a local authority is referred to as a local authority foster parent unless that person is a parent of the child; or that person is not the child's parent but has PARENTAL RESPONSIBILITY for the child; or the child is in care and there was a RESIDENCE ORDER in force in favour of that person immediately before the care order was made (Children Act 1989, s. 23(3)–(4)). A private foster parent is someone other than a parent, a person with parental responsibility or a relative who takes a child into their own home and takes care of that child (Children Act 1989, s. 66).

Local authority foster parents must be approved and monitored by the local authority (see Care Standards Act 2000, Part III). They also receive payment. Private fostering arrangements are regulated under Part IX of the Children Act 1989. Foster parents do not obtain parental responsibility for children in their care unless they acquire it by court order. This may be by means of a residence order (Children Act 1989, s. 12) or a SPECIAL GUARDIANSHIP ORDER (Children Act 1989, ss. 14A–G).   [FK]

See also FOSTER CHILD.

Foucault, Michel (1926–84) Michel Foucault defies academic categorization. His work embraces – at least – history, philosophy, sociology and linguistics, and touches on themes and issues relevant to law and criminology.

A key theme in Foucault's work is a scepticism towards the professedly rational values of the Enlightenment, which in his view could be and were harnessed to legitimize oppressive practices towards margin-alized groups. Thus his historical engagement with psychiatry, *Madness and Civilization,* suggests that rather than being an impetus for the enhancement of freedom or for improvements in care, the Enlightenment led to the repression of those with what would now (still) be termed mental health problems, by subsuming the specificity of their personal experiences within analytic categories deployed by clinicians.

Foucault's most explicitly law-related work is *Discipline and Punish,* which begins with a vivid and disturbing account of the torturing to death in 1757 of Damiens the regicide. This is juxtaposed with an account of the seemingly mundane but tightly controlled daily timetable at a prison for young offenders in Paris 80 years later. Foucault disputes the claim that the demise of spectacular and horrific public punishments is attributable simply to the advancement of humanity, but suggests that the newer, less physically severe forms of punishment are different expressions of political power. In his exploration of this idea, Foucault's analysis of incarceration drew on BENTHAM's principle of **panopticism**: in Bentham's panoptical prison, the architecture would be such that the governor figure would be able to see all the inmates in their cells at all times, but the inmates would not be able to see whether they were being observed at any particular point. For Foucault, the relentless and minute monitoring of inmates' lives and routines constituted a particularly effective form of surveillance and REGULATION which facilitated the identification of even the most minor infractions, and which legitimated intervention for the purpose of control. This model of social organization, labelled 'disciplinary' by Foucault, could be extrapolated from the prison to the productive sites of capitalism, such as factories, where a 'disciplined' labour force would be an effective one. To a limited extent, Foucault's acknowledgement that power was a factor in social relations under capitalism was in line with the thinking of Marx, but Foucault rejected as reductive the Marxian emphasis on the state as a conduit of power. Rather, Foucault saw power as 'something which circulates … [It] is employed and exercised through a net-like organization' (see Gordon (1980) at p. 98). Power could be observed impacting on (disciplined) bodies; hence Foucault's reference to 'bio' power.

Although Foucault's notions of power and discipline could appear presumptively repressive, they contained within them the tools for their own disruption. The meaning of 'power' is thus given greater substance by a coexisting concept of resistance. It is put succinctly by McNay, who suggests (see McNay (1994) at pp. 6–7): 'Domination and resistance are no longer conceived of as ontologically different but as opposing effects of the same power relations. Thus the labelling of certain groups of individuals as "deviant" provides those groups with a coherent identity from which resistant counter-identities may be formulated …'

Governmentality was another significant concept for Foucault, through which he sought to explore how both official state institutions and other agencies directed the conduct of people through processes of inspection and through the gathering and deployment of data. [BF]

Further reading: Michel Foucault, *Madness and Civilisation: A History of Insanity in the Age of Reason* (Histoire de la folie a l'age classique), trans. Richard Howard (London: Routledge, 1984); Michel Foucault, *Discipline and Punish: The Birth of the Prison* (Surveiller et punir: Naissance de la prison), trans. Alan Sheridan (London: Penguin, 1977); Colin Gordon (ed.), *Power/Knowledge: Selected Interviews and Other Writings, 1972–77* (Brighton: Harvester, 1980); Alan Hunt and Gary Wickham, *Foucault and Law: Towards a Sociology of Law as Governance* (London: Pluto Press, 1994); Lois McNay, *Foucault: A Critical Introduction* (Cambridge: Polity, 1994).

franchise 1. The right to vote, which is controlled by various Representation of the People Acts, the most recent of which was passed in 2000. This provides that every British citizen is entitled to vote, provided they are 18 years of age or over; resident in the United Kingdom; not subject to any other legal disqualification (prisoners, some patients in mental hospitals, and hereditary peers are disqualified); and registered on the electoral register for the constituency in which they live. Commonwealth citizens and citizens of the Irish Republic resident in the UK may also vote in UK elections, provided they also satisfy these other criteria. Resident EU citizens may vote in EUROPEAN PARLIAMENT, devolved government and council elections but not in elections to the UK Parliament.

2. A commercial relationship based on a written CONTRACT (the **franchise agreement**), giving the franchisee a licence to manufacture, distribute or sell a branded product in a defined area or location for a stated period of time. Franchises are common in certain industries, particularly cleaning, fast food and certain retail activities. There is relatively little legal regulation specific to franchising, though franchise agreements within the EU must all comply with Regulation 2790/99 which outlaws some contract terms as anti-competitive (see COMPETITION LAW). The terms of the franchise agreement are critical. Most franchise agreements are granted on standard terms by the franchisor. Their provisions will therefore tend to be construed narrowly against the franchisor if there is any ambiguity or uncertainty as regards their scope or effects. A franchise agreement should identify in detail the duties and obligations of the parties, including issues such as the extent of the provision of business equipment, staff training, marketing and management systems by the franchisor, and the responsibilities of the franchisee in respect of the GOODS, services and equipment supplied, the franchisor's goodwill and INTELLECTUAL PROPERTY, and any rights of resale during the term of the franchise. It should also deal with the payment of franchise fees and set out the means by which the agreement may be renewed or terminated, and the consequences of such termination. [JW]

Francovich principle Named after Case

C6/90, *Francovich* v. *Italian State Republic* and Case C 9/90, *Bonifaci* v. *Belgian State* [1991] ECR I-5357, before the EUROPEAN COURT OF JUSTICE. This decision built on the pre-existing concept of DIRECT EFFECT of DIRECTIVES, and developed the basis on which a Member State might be held liable to an individual for its non-implementation of a Directive. Under *Francovich,* state liability is governed by three main principles: (a) the Directive must have been intended to confer rights on the individual; (b) the failure to implement must be 'sufficiently serious' to justify imposing liability (depending on factors such as the intention of the Member State, the clarity and precision of the obligations in the Directive, and whether there was an excusable error of law by the Member State); and (c) there must be a causal link between the state's breach of its obligation and the damage suffered by the individual.

The Francovich principle, together with the principles of direct effect and INDIRECT EFFECT, are the three main ways to implement COMMUNITY LAW through national courts. [MON]

See also EUROTORT.

Frank, Jerome (1889–1957) American jurist, Court of Appeals judge and key figure in the AMERICAN REALISM movement. His work forms the foundation of FACT SCEPTICISM. [JP]

See also RULE SCEPTICISM.

Franked Investment Income (FII) The gross value received by a UK resident company by way of income distribution from another UK resident company, comprising the actual income distribution, such as a DIVIDEND, and its associated tax credit. This gross value is the Franked Investment Income (FII) received.

When a UK resident company makes an income distribution to its shareholders, it must include an income tax credit calculated to amount to 10% of the gross distribution (i.e. the actual value of the income distribution is grossed up to 10%). Where the shareholder is another UK resident company, the recipient company includes the FII in its CORPORATION TAX computation in order to determine whether or not it is a small company for corporation tax purposes. The FII is then excluded in the calculation of the corporation tax payable, but the tax credit element of the FII can be used to frank (to treat as paid) the whole or part of the corporation tax payable, so that the receiving company pays the balance (if any) between its liability to corporation tax and the FII tax credit. Where the FII tax credit exceeds the amount of corporation tax payable by the receiving company, the FII tax credit cannot be refunded to the company. [RE]

Fraser guidelines The five criteria set down by Lord Fraser in *Gillick* v. *West Norfolk and Wisbech AHA* [1986] AC 112 (a case which related to the provision of contraceptive treatment and advice), by which the capacity of a minor to CONSENT TO TREATMENT is determined, enabling a doctor to treat the minor without parental knowledge or consent. They are (a) that the minor understands the advice given by the doctor; (b) that the doctor is unable to persuade the minor to inform her parents or to allow the doctor to do so; (c) that the minor is likely to begin or to continue to have sexual intercourse with or without contraceptive treatment; (d) that without advice or treatment the minor's physical or mental health or both are likely to suffer; (e) that the best interests of the minor require the doctor to give advice, treatment or both without parental consent. [HJ]

See also GILLICK COMPETENCE; MENTAL CAPACITY.

fraud on a power A POWER OF APPOINTMENT in a TRUST which is misused. Although ostensibly exercised correctly to make an appointment from within the class of objects, a fraud on the power occurs when this takes place in a way that renders it void. For example, a donee of a power who exercised it in favour of those objects who promised to pay or sleep with the donee would have committed a fraud on the power. This equitable jurisdiction applies to all powers so that even donees of a bare POWER are under a duty not to commit a fraud on the power. [PK]

fraudulent misrepresentation A false

statement of fact inducing a CONTRACT which is made either knowing that it is false, or without belief in its truth, or recklessly not caring whether it is true or false (*Derry* v. *Peek* (1889) 14 App Cas 337) and which renders the contract VOIDABLE. DAMAGES are also available for fraudulent misrepresentation in the TORT of DECEIT. [JPL]

free movement of goods Along with FREE MOVEMENT OF PERSONS, services and capital, it is one of the '**four freedoms**' of the EUROPEAN COMMUNITY (EC). The 'four freedoms' are core policy areas of the EC, which form the basis of the internal or single market. The principle of free movement of goods is enshrined in Articles 23 to 30 EC Treaty, and has been elaborated on by a high volume of case law at the EUROPEAN COURT OF JUSTICE (ECJ). Quantitative and qualitative restrictions on trade between MEMBER STATES of the EC have been abolished, as have customs duties and charges having equivalent effect, with internal trade barriers within the EC having been removed. [MON]
See also COMMUNITY LAW; CROSS-BORDER SERVICES.

free movement of persons More correctly, free movement of workers (who are EUROPEAN UNION (EU) nationals) is, along with FREE MOVEMENT OF GOODS, services and capital, one of the '**four freedoms**' of the EUROPEAN COMMUNITY (EC). The 'four freedoms' are core policy areas of the EC, which form the basis of the internal or single market. The principle of free movement of persons is enshrined in Articles 39 to 42 EC Treaty, and has been elaborated on by a high volume of case law at the EUROPEAN COURT OF JUSTICE (ECJ). In addition to the right of workers to move across EC borders, the EUROPEAN COMMUNITY TREATY provides for the RIGHT OF ESTABLISHMENT, which deals with the movement of individuals across borders as self-employed persons, or for undertakings (companies or other business legal entities) to be established in another MEMBER STATE.

More recently, since the TREATY OF AMSTERDAM (1997), provisions on the free movement of third country nationals throughout the EU have been inserted into the EC Treaty, having originally been provisions in the post-MAASTRICHT TREATY Pillar III EU, Justice and Home Affairs, and in the SCHENGEN AGREEMENT. These are now part of Title IV, visas, asylum, immigration and other policies related to free movement of persons, Articles 61 to 69 EC Treaty. The latter provisions are subject to two different opt-out provisions, the first on the part of the UK and Ireland, and the second, on the part of Denmark. [MON]
See also COMMUNITY LAW; CROSS-BORDER SERVICES; TREATY ON EUROPEAN UNION.

free trade area *See* CUSTOMS UNION.

freedom from discrimination *See* DISCRIMINATION.

freedom of association The right to associate with others and to assemble for peaceful purposes. It is protected under Article 11 of the EUROPEAN CONVENTION ON HUMAN RIGHTS and, in the UK, under the Human Rights Act 1998, s. 1 and Schedule 1. Article 11 expressly includes within its ambit the right to form and join TRADE UNIONS, and also extends to protect the right of political association (*United Communist Party of Turkey* v. *Turkey* (1998) 26 EHRR 121) and the freedom to engage in peaceful protest more generally. It is, however, a QUALIFIED RIGHT, and can be limited in the public interest; for example, in *Ahmed* v. *United Kingdom* [1999] IRLR 188, it was held that prohibiting certain LOCAL AUTHORITY officers from holding political appointments was proportionate to the aim of securing public confidence in the holders of public office. Public order laws similarly will not be regarded as an unlawful interference with the freedom to protest, provided that they do not constitute a disproportionate interference with that right – see *Steel* v. *United Kingdom* (1999) 28 EHRR 603. [JW]
See also PROPORTIONALITY.

freedom of expression A right set out in Article 10 of the EUROPEAN CONVENTION ON HUMAN RIGHTS and Schedule 1 of the Human Rights Act 1998. Freedom of expression (or **freedom of speech**) is an important right that has generated considerable case law under the Convention. It serves to protect a very wide range of expression, including political speech, the freedom of the press, commercial speech (*Autronic AG* v. *Switzerland* (1990) 12 EHRR 485) and even offensive, blasphemous or obscene communications (e.g. *Otto-Preminger Institut* v. *Austria* (1994) 18 EHRR 34). Freedom of expression can readily conflict with other human rights, notably the right to PRIVACY, the right to a FAIR TRIAL, and freedom of conscience (for example, where religious hatred laws might arguably provide legitimate constraints on free speech). The Strasbourg jurisprudence acknowledges that freedom of expression must be balanced against such other rights. Nevertheless, in *Sunday Times* v. *United Kingdom* (1979) 2 EHRR 245, the EUROPEAN COURT OF HUMAN RIGHTS indicated that any exceptions to freedom of speech must be restrictively construed, thereby perhaps allotting it a more foundational role in democratic society (for a similar approach in English law following the Human Rights Act, see *A* v. *B and C* [2002] EWCA Civ 337). Despite its importance, freedom of expression is a QUALIFIED RIGHT and so can be limited in the public interest, provided that the principles of legality, necessity and PROPORTIONALITY contained in Article 10(2) are strictly applied. [JW]

See also BLASPHEMY.

freedom of information The Freedom of Information Act 2000 came into force in January 2005 and gives an individual a legal right of access to information which is held by a public body, including central and local government, the police, the health service, schools and universities.

A freedom of information request must be submitted in writing to the holder of the information, giving the name and a return address of the person requesting the information, and clearly describing what is being requested. The organization approached is normally obliged to confirm whether or not it holds that information and, unless the information is exempt, provide it within 20 working days. A wide range of information is exempt, including **personal information** about a living person,

information that is already within the public domain, information related to matters of defence or national security, and information that attracts legal protection as confidential or subject to LEGAL PROFESSIONAL PRIVILEGE. Not all exemptions under the Act are absolute.

If a request is rejected, it is possible to complain to the body involved, which must then carry out an internal review of its decision. If this complaint in turn is rejected, there is an appeal to the Information Commissioner who has legal power to force disclosure, and a further right of appeal from the decision of the Commissioner to an independent **Information Tribunal**. [JW]

freedom of testation *See* TESTAMENTARY FREEDOM.

freedom of thought, conscience and religion Set out in Article 9 of the EUROPEAN CONVENTION ON HUMAN RIGHTS and Schedule 1 of the Human Rights Act 1998, this has two elements. First, individuals have an ABSOLUTE RIGHT to enjoy the basic freedoms of thought, conscience or religion – which, of course, implies the right to hold *any* religious or *no* religious belief (*Kokkinakis* v. *Greece* (1993) 17 EHRR 397). Secondly, Article 9 creates a separate QUALIFIED RIGHT to express or observe one's beliefs through teaching, practice and worship. The latter is expressed only as a qualified right in recognition of the problem that an absolute right to manifest one's beliefs might easily be incompatible with the equivalent rights of others; for example, if A's system of beliefs tells him to kill everyone who does not share his belief system, this is incompatible with the democratic and pluralist ideals upon which the Convention is founded. Thus, while no one should be able to punish A simply for holding to that belief, A could not argue that any legal prohibitions that prevented him from putting that belief into practice were an unlawful interference with his freedom of conscience. The EUROPEAN COURT OF HUMAN RIGHTS has also, in *Kokkinakis*, treated the right to proselytize (i.e. to seek to convert others to one's opinion or beliefs) as a necessary corollary of freedom of thought and religion, provided that it does not involve exerting undue pressure, violence or 'brainwashing'. [JW]

freedom under the law *See* RULE OF LAW.

freehold *See* FEE SIMPLE ABSOLUTE IN POSSESSION.

freeing order A court order under s. 18 of the Adoption Act 1976, reflecting the unconditional agreement of the PARENT to a CHILD'S adoption. This Act was repealed by the Adoption and Children Act 2002, but existing freeing orders are unaffected by the repeal. An existing freeing order is taken to satisfy the third condition for ADOPTION under s. 47(6) of the Adoption and Children Act 2002 (Schedule 4, para. 7). [FK]

freezing order An interim order of the court in civil proceedings intended to prevent the defendant from disposing of, diminishing, or moving assets out of the jurisdiction of the court; sometimes also called a **freezing injunction.** A freezing order may be obtained under Part 25 of the CIVIL PROCEDURE RULES (CPR). Any breach of the order, whether by the defendant or a third party holding those assets who has notice of the order, may be treated as a CONTEMPT OF COURT.

Until the introduction of the CPR, freezing orders were known as **Mareva injunctions,** from the case *Mareva Compania Naviera SA* v. *International Bulkcarriers SA* [1975] 2 Lloyd's Rep 509. [JW]

frustration A legal doctrine which provides an excuse for non-performance when, after a CONTRACT has been made, and without the fault of either party, an event occurs (known as a frustrating event) which has not been provided for by the parties and which renders further performance of the contract impossible, or illegal, or destroys the common purpose of both parties in contracting.

Frustration of contract discharges the contract so that both parties' future performance obligations no longer need to be performed. The pre-frustration obligations and positions of the parties will be determined in accordance with either COMMON LAW rules or the principles contained in the Law Reform (Frustrated Contracts) Act 1943. [JPL]

See also FORCE MAJEURE CLAUSE.

FSA *See* FINANCIAL SERVICES AUTHORITY.

fugitive offender A term used in the law of EXTRADITION to refer to a person in STATE A, whose presence is sought by State B, in order to face trial for a suspected offence, or to receive sentence for an offence in respect of which a conviction has been entered. [BF]

full powers The capacity of an individual to represent a STATE in the negotiation, signing or ratification of a TREATY. It is defined in the preamble to the 1969 Vienna Convention on the Law of Treaties as 'a document emanating from the competent authority of a State designating a person or persons to represent the State for negotiating, adopting or authenticating the text of a treaty, for expressing the consent of the State to be bound by a treaty, or for accomplishing any other act with respect to a treaty'. The possession of full powers has the purpose of expressing the consent of the state to be bound by the treaty through the act of the person possessing such powers. The following persons, on the basis of their functions, are not required to produce full powers under Article 7: a) Heads of State, Heads of Government and Ministers for Foreign Affairs, for the purpose of performing all acts relating to the conclusion of a treaty; b) heads of diplomatic missions, for the purpose of adopting the text of a treaty between the accrediting State and the State to which they are accredited; c) representatives accredited by States to an international conference or to an international organization or one of its organs, for the purpose of adopting the text of a treaty in that conference, organization or organ. [IB]

See also DIPLOMATIC MISSION.

fully mutual housing association A HOUSING ASSOCIATION which restricts membership to TENANTS or prospective tenants of the association, and which precludes the granting or assignment of tenancies to persons other than members. Tenants of fully mutual housing associations are COMMON LAW tenants as their landlord is excluded from the SECURITY OF TENURE provisions of the Housing Act 1988. A particularly well-known example of a fully mutual housing association is the Coin Street Cooperative on London's South Bank which uses the revenue generated by the Oxo Tower restaurant to fund its housing activities. [HC & DR]

See also CO-OPERATIVE HOUSING ASSOCIATION.

functus officio (Lat. having discharged the duty) The point at which a judge or official has completed their responsibility for a particular act or decision, after which they may be prevented from taking the matter further because of limitation by regulations. For example, in *R* v. *Special Immigration Adjudicator ex parte Bashir* [2002] Imm AR 1, it was held that, under the rules then in force, a special adjudicator was not *functus officio* until after the written determination was delivered. [JW]

fundamental breach (of contract) A term may be described as fundamental if it goes to the root of the CONTRACT. Where such a term is breached, this is sometimes referred to as a fundamental breach. An EXEMPTION CLAUSE may be effective to exclude or limit liability for such a fundamental breach if it covers the loss that has occurred (see *Photo Production Ltd* v. *Securicor Transport Ltd* [1980] AC 827). [JPL]

fundamental rights Moral and/or legal rights attaching universally to every human being. The term is most commonly used in the context of those HUMAN RIGHTS contained in the UNIVERSAL DECLARATION OF HUMAN RIGHTS, such as the right to life, freedom from torture, etc.

The extent to which some rights might be more fundamental than others is a moot point within the philosophy of human rights, and is also not just an abstract theoretical problem. There is concern in some quarters at the extent to which human rights discourses are expanding and developing to encompass new substantive rights. This process of 'human rights inflation' is seen by some commentators as devaluing and diluting the impact of human rights laws, and possibly lies behind some of the perceived political backlash against human rights protection. In this context, the characterization of some rights as fundamental may have both political and jurisprudential value. Nevertheless, most approaches that seek to define fundamental rights have their problems. For example, a NATURAL LAW approach to human rights will treat as fundamental those rights which are innate to our human beingness – they are quite literally the God-given natural rights with which we are born. Aside from the practical problems associated with competing theologies and the rise of secularism in most modern societies, one difficulty with this approach is that they may narrow the field too much, by giving us a very narrow conception of fundamental rights. Those rights plausibly attributable to the divine law will tend to be the most general, traditional and abstract (e.g. the basic rights to life and liberty). Many modern and, some would say, important, rights will sit very uneasily with a natural law approach; for example, the right to freedom of conscience and religion itself will be difficult to square with any theistic tradition that is intolerant of other religions, or of secularism. Rights to a private and family life (e.g. in the context of the abortion debate), or to non-discrimination on grounds of gender, or, even more controversially, sexual orientation, are also likely to run into major difficulties within a theist conception of fundamental rights. Similarly, JOHN RAWLS's attempt to define human rights as those norms that set the bounds of toleration also has the effect of restricting human rights to only a few fundamental rights. Rawls himself suggests the following make the grade: 'the right to life (to the means of subsistence and security); to liberty (to freedom from slavery, serfdom, and forced occupation, and to a sufficient measure of liberty of conscience to ensure freedom of religion and thought); to property (personal property); and to formal equality as pressed by the rules of NATURAL

JUSTICE (that is, that similar cases be treated similarly)' (*The Law of Peoples*, p. 65). Again, the objection can be raised that this rather risks throwing the baby out with the bathwater.

A more pragmatic approach might be to specify that a range of justificatory tests should be satisfied before we can properly talk of a right as a fundamental human right; for example, it might be proposed that a fundamental human right must not only deal with an extremely important human good, but should also respond to a common and substantial threat to that good, and impose burdens on others to protect that right that are justifiable, and achievable in most of the world's countries (see Nickel, *Making Sense of Human Rights*). This of course still does not address another concern, namely that our tendency to equate fundamental rights with *human* rights prioritizes such human goods over others, such as the rights of animals and of the environment itself, which perhaps ought to be regarded as equally fundamental. [JW]

Further reading: Patrick Hayden (ed.), *The Philosophy of Human Rights: Readings in Context* (St Paul, MN: Paragon Press, 2001); James Nickel, *Making Sense of Human Rights*, 2nd edn (Oxford: Blackwell, 2006); John Rawls, *The Law of Peoples* (Cambridge, MA: Harvard University Press, 1999).

funeral expenses In the administration of an ESTATE, the debts of the deceased have to be paid. The order in which debts are paid is important, because if the estate proves to be insolvent, some creditors will not be paid in full, and may not be paid at all. The priority of the debts is set down by STATUTE, which provides that funeral, testamentary and administration expenses have priority over most over debts. This means that whoever actually pays the undertaker can claim on the estate for repayment before ordinary creditors are paid. There may be dispute over the amount of funeral expenses claimed, and the law says that they must be reasonable, having regard to 'the station in life, the occupation and the creed' of the deceased. [CM]

See also TESTAMENTARY EXPENSES.

G

gambling The Gambling Act 2005, s. 3, defines gambling as including gaming, betting and participation in a lottery. **Gaming** is itself defined in s. 6 as playing a game of chance for a prize; games of chance can include games that involve an element of skill, but exclude sports.

Gambling in the UK is regulated and, subject to certain exceptions, betting and gaming are restricted to games on licensed premises. There are further restrictions on gambling on Sundays, and MINORS (under 18) must generally be excluded from premises, whether licensed or not, when gambling takes place. [JPL & JW]

See also GAMING CONTRACT; WAGERING CONTRACT.

gaming contract A contract that involves playing a game of chance for a prize. The Gambling Act 2005, ss. 334 and 335, reverse s. 18 of the Gaming Act 1845, which had provided that such contracts were null and VOID so that there could be no action in the courts to enforce the prize. Since 1 September 2007, the fact that a contract relates to gambling will not prevent its enforcement. [JPL]

See also WAGERING CONTRACT.

garden leave clause A contractual clause permitting an EMPLOYER to send an EMPLOYEE who has been given notice of DISMISSAL (or given notice to quit) on 'garden leave'; that is, the employee continues to be paid a normal salary but does not come into work. The aim is to deter the 'poaching' of clients and other staff by the employee on notice by breaking contact between the employee and clients/staff. [MJ]

GATS *See* GENERAL AGREEMENT ON TRADE IN SERVICES.

GATT *See* GENERAL AGREEMENT ON TARIFFS AND TRADE.

gazumping In conveyancing, the practice whereby a seller, who has already accepted an offer from a first buyer, goes on to accept a higher offer from a second buyer. This leaves the first buyer with no remedy, even though he may have already spent money on SEARCHES and surveys.

Gazumping can occur because although the seller has accepted the first buyer's offer, either party is free to withdraw from negotiations until the exchange of contracts. It is made more likely because the estate agent is legally bound to inform the seller of all offers made on his property. Therefore, the seller's estate agent is bound to pass on the second buyer's higher offer, and the seller is free to accept that offer and withdraw from negotiations with the first buyer. In Scotland, gazumping cannot occur, since the buyer and seller are legally bound to complete when an offer is accepted. [DR]

See also GAZUNDERING.

gazundering In conveyancing, the practice whereby a seller accepts a buyer's offer, but the buyer subsequently lowers his offer in between acceptance of the prior offer and the exchange of contracts. Gazundering is rarer in practice than GAZUMPING as it usually occurs only when property prices are falling. In Scotland, gazundering cannot occur, since the buyer and seller are legally bound to complete under the terms of the offer that has been accepted. [DR]

GBH *See* GRIEVOUS BODILY HARM.

gender reassignment Transgendered or transsexual persons may live as a member of their acquired gender, and some undergo hormonal treatment and/or surgery to modify their physical characteristics. The law will recognize for all purposes a person's acquired gender if a gender recognition certificate is issued to him or her. Medical gender reassignment steps are not required for the certificate to be issued. The Gender Recognition Act 2004 states that the Gender Recognition Panel must be satisfied that the person has or has had gender dysphoria (a medical condition to be attested to by two medical or mental health professionals), and that he or she has lived in the acquired gender for the preceding two years and intends to continue to live in the acquired gender permanently, before it can issue the certificate. The certificate entitles the transgendered person to a new BIRTH CERTIFICATE. [AD]

general act Another name sometimes used for a TREATY. [JW]

general action programmes A policy term rather than a legal concept, it refers to a programme of action, involving both policy and legal actions taken by the EUROPEAN COMMUNITY or EUROPEAN UNION institutions, in order to achieve a particular objective. Activity is normally set out for a defined time period. [MON]

General Agreement on Tariffs and Trade (GATT) A multilateral international agreement first signed in 1947 following the Bretton Woods Conference, which sought to establish an international trade organization in the wake of the Second World War. The GATT provides an international forum to encourage free trade between member STATES by regulating and reducing tariffs on traded goods and by providing a mechanism for resolving international trade disputes between states. The agreement itself is really a bundle of linked agreements that have been amended and extended over the years as a result of various 'rounds' of negotiation. The duration and complexity of these rounds has increased substantially as moves have been made to extend the scope and effectiveness of the agreement – the Tokyo Round (1973–79) lasted 72 months, and the last completed round, the Uruguay Round (1986–94), took 87 months, nearly twice as long as originally scheduled. The Uruguay Round extended the agreement fully to new areas such as intellectual property, services, capital and agriculture, and saw the creation of the WORLD TRADE ORGANIZATION (WTO) as a successor organization to GATT.

A new GATT was signed by 123 member states in Marrakesh in April 1994. The General Agreement serves now as the WTO's umbrella treaty for trade in goods. WTO law technically still distinguishes between GATT 1994, the updated parts of GATT, and GATT 1947, the original agreement which remains the authoritative source for much of GATT 1994. A further round of negotiations – the Doha Round – commenced in November 2001, focusing particularly on problems raised by developing countries concerning the implementation of the Uruguay Round Agreements. [JW]

Further reading: John H. Jackson, *The World Trading System: Law and Policy of International Economic Relations* 2nd revised edn (Cambridge, MA: MIT Press, 1997); Mitsuo Matsushita, Thomas J. Schoenbaum and Petros C. Mavroidis, *The World Trade Organisation: Law, Practice and Policy*, 2nd edn (Oxford: Oxford University Press, 2006).

General Agreement on Trade in Services (GATS) A multilateral international agreement which came into force in 1995 and constitutes the legal framework through which the WORLD TRADE ORGANIZATION (WTO) seeks progressively to liberalize trade in services. The agreement covers four different 'modes' of trade in services: Mode 1 – cross-border supply; Mode 2 – consumption abroad; Mode 3 – foreign commercial presence, and Mode 4 – movement of natural persons (i.e. individuals rather than companies). WTO members can decide where to liberalize sector by sector, including which specific mode of supply they want to cover for a given sector.

GATS represents an important and controversial new focus in international trade and WTO law. Before GATS services were very much treated as domestic activities that were not easy to trade across borders, and in some cases as activities that, because of their social and strategic importance, needed to be regulated closely by government and not exposed to the vagaries of the market; for example, essential services and social goods, such as the provision of water and electricity, sanitation, health and education. Liberalization of trade in services, it has been argued, is necessary because such trade has been limited by natural and artificial monopolies, and by anti-competitive practices which are not market efficient, and may not be in the interests of consumers. On the other hand, concerns are expressed by opponents of GATS that turning social goods into commodities that can be traded for profit like any other carries with it significant risks, especially for the poor and those in less developed economies.   [JW]

Further reading: Mitsuo Matsushita, Thomas J. Schoenbaum and Petros C. Mavroidis, *The World Trade Organisation: Law, Practice and Policy*, 2nd edn (Oxford: Oxford University Press, 2006); Jane Kelsey, *Serving Whose Interests? The Political Economy of Trade in Services Agreements* (London: Routledge-Cavendish, 2008).

General Commissioners A body of individuals, appointed by the LORD CHANCELLOR, to form a permanent legal tribunal for a district to which appeals are made by taxpayers against the decisions of HM REVENUE AND CUSTOMS in direct tax disputes. Appeals are to the General Commissioners unless there is an effective election to appeal to the SPECIAL COMMISSIONERS. The General Commissioners for each district are laypersons who, guided by a legally qualified and experienced clerk, bring business and local knowledge to bear on appeals in their district. The General Commissioners (Jurisdiction and Procedure) Regulations (SI 1994/1812) apply. Hearings are now usually in public, but decisions are not reported. Appeals from the General Commissioners are to the CHANCERY DIVISION of the HIGH COURT on points of law – not on the facts; and from there appeals are to the COURT OF APPEAL and then to the HOUSE OF LORDS, in each case on a point of law only.
                                                          [RE]

See also COMMISSIONERS OF REVENUE AND CUSTOMS.

general damages An award of damages in TORT covering non-monetary losses. The most common claims relate, in NEGLIGENCE, to the pain, suffering and loss of amenity (i.e. loss of enjoyment of life) caused by physical and psychological injuries, or the value attached to loss of reputation in DEFAMATION.   [HJ]

See also SPECIAL DAMAGES.

general defences Defences which are of general application and not specific to designated offences. Thus INSANITY and SELF-DEFENCE are general defences, while PROVOCATION and DIMINISHED RESPONSIBILITY are defences special to MURDER.   [BF]

general equitable charge An EQUITABLE CHARGE over land which is not secured by a deposit of documents relating to the LEGAL ESTATE affected; does not arise or affect an interest arising under a trust of land or a SETTLEMENT; is not a charge given by way of indemnity against rents; and is not included in any other class of land charge (Land Charges Act 1972, s. 2(4)(iii)).

In UNREGISTERED LAND, a general equitable

charge is a Class C (iii) LAND CHARGE and must be registered in order to be binding on future purchasers. An example of a general equitable charge is a RENTCHARGE payable under a LIFE INTEREST.   [DR]

See also EQUITABLE MORTGAGE.

general legacy See LEGACY.

General Medical Council (GMC) The body responsible for registering doctors to practise medicine in the UK. The GMC has four main functions set out in the Medical Act 1983, not least of which is the discipline of doctors failing to meet the expected professional standard. In the most serious cases this will result in a doctor being removed from the register and thus unable to continue practising in the UK. The four main functions are: (a) keeping up-to-date registers of qualified doctors; (b) fostering good medical practice; (c) promoting high standards of medical education; and (d) dealing firmly and fairly with doctors whose fitness to practise is in doubt.   [HJ]

general participation clause A provision in a TREATY (also referred to as a *clausula si omnes*) whereby parties agree that the treaty, or parts thereof, are inapplicable among themselves in circumstances where a third STATE – not being a party to that treaty – contracts with one or more parties to the treaty. The adverse impact of general participation clauses on humanitarian law treaties, as opposed to their effects on commercial treaties, was great. Consequently they are no longer employed in human rights or humanitarian law conventions, having been replaced by the THIRD PARTY RULE.   [IB]

general power of investment A power introduced under the Trustee Act 2000 allowing TRUSTEES to make most kinds of investment that they would be able to make if they were absolutely entitled to the TRUST fund. This is in marked contrast to the previous regime under which they were only permitted to make certain 'AUTHORIZED INVESTMENTS', although it does not extend to the purchase of land in foreign jurisdictions and may be excluded by express provision in the TRUST INSTRUMENT.

Trustees are also under a duty when exercising the general power to consider criteria relating to the suitability of the proposed investment and the need for diversification within the context of the particular trust they are managing. They are also required to obtain and consider proper advice, unless they reasonably consider it unnecessary or inappropriate to do so, and review periodically the investments made by reference to the same initial criteria.   [PK]

general principles of law The fundamental rights and principles that are said to underpin the operation of a legal system, and operate as a background source of law. The idea of general principles as an autonomous source of law has its origins in the CIVIL LAW tradition where unwritten general principles have been used to fill in the gaps left by legislation. Given the unwritten character of general principles, their scope remains uncertain. They tend to include broad concepts such as certainty, due process, equality (or NON-DISCRIMINATION), equity, ESTOPPEL (note that the latter two terms do not carry the technical connotations that they have under English law), good faith and PROPORTIONALITY. General principles tend to be significant in two main contexts.

1. General principles are an important historical source of INTERNATIONAL LAW and HUMAN RIGHTS. However, as international law has developed, many such principles have become codified into treaties or recognized as CUSTOMARY INTERNATIONAL LAW, and so the explicit reference to general principles has consequently declined. Nevertheless, they are still recognized as a legitimate source of international law and human rights in their own right; see, for example, Article 38(1) of the Statute of the INTERNATIONAL COURT OF JUSTICE and Article 1 of the First Protocol to the EUROPEAN CONVENTION ON HUMAN RIGHTS (ECHR). Following incorporation of the ECHR into UK law by the Human Rights Act 1998, reference to general principles may be made by UK courts in interpreting the scope of Convention rights.

2. In EUROPEAN COMMUNITY (EC) law, the

EUROPEAN COURT OF JUSTICE (ECJ) has developed a doctrine, based on Article 220 EC, that rules of COMMUNITY LAW may be derived from general principles in addition to the treaties and EC legislation. Using the methods of comparative law, much of the court's practice has particularly reflected the development of general principles in French and German law. Moreover, there is also an established line of cases indicating that the ECJ regards fundamental human rights, particularly as developed through the ECHR, as a further source of general principles (see Case 44/79 *Hauer v. Land Rheinland-Pfalz* (1979) ECR 3727). Again, this style of case law reasoning has had an impact on UK practice in cases having an EC dimension.   [JW]

General Synod *See* CHURCH OF ENGLAND.

Geneva Conventions The four 1949 Geneva Conventions deal with four distinct topics, yet are interlinked with a common theme: the protection of civilians and those no longer taking part in hostilities from the calamities of armed conflict. Their most immediate predecessors were the three 1929 Geneva Conventions, which were applicable during the Second World War. The first Geneva Convention of 1949 deals with the Amelioration of the Condition of the Wounded and Sick in Armed Forces in the Field; the second with the Amelioration of the Condition of the Wounded, Sick and Shipwrecked Members of Armed Forces at Sea; the third with the Treatment of Prisoners of War; and the fourth with the Protection of Civilian Persons in Time of War. Articles 2 and 3 of the Conventions are common to all of them. Article 2 describes the conditions for triggering the commencement of an international armed conflict so that the full range of humanitarian law protections can come into operation, while the common Article 3 was the first ever provision to deal with the protection of persons taking part in a non-international armed conflict. Each Convention contains a 'grave breaches' provision, detailing the most serious infractions that are subject to UNIVERSAL JURISDICTION and severe penalties.   [IB]

genocide The term was given normative substance for the first time in the 1948 Genocide Convention. The definition contained in Article 2 of the Convention is beyond any doubt part of CUSTOMARY INTERNATIONAL LAW as it has been included verbatim in all subsequent instruments, such as the Statutes for the INTERNATIONAL CRIMINAL TRIBUNAL FOR YUGOSLAVIA (ICTY), INTERNATIONAL CRIMINAL TRIBUNAL FOR RWANDA (ICTR) and the INTERNATIONAL CRIMINAL COURT (ICC).

Genocide is defined as the commission of any serious act with intent to destroy, in whole or in part, a (a) national, (b) ethnic, (c) racial or (d) religious group, as such. This could include killing group members, causing them serious mental harm, inflicting conditions of life calculated to bring about its destruction, imposing measures intended to prevent births and forcibly transferring children of the group to another group.

What distinguishes genocide from CRIMES AGAINST HUMANITY is the SPECIFIC INTENT (*DOLUS SPECIALIS*) of the perpetrator to destroy the group in whole or in part. The ICTR's jurisprudence is divided on whether the grounds for PERSECUTION are exhaustive and are not merely illustrative of stable groups, as opposed to temporary groups, such as political parties. Problems of this nature arise where genocide is committed against members of a group, identified as distinct by the perpetrators, but which does not fall within the four enumerated groups found in the Genocide Convention.   [IB]

See also ETHNIC CLEANSING.

Gentili, Alberico (1552–1608) An Italian jurist who inspired the work of GROTIUS and was the first to set the boundaries of natural law, by separating secular law from Roman Catholic theology and CANON LAW. Much of this also had to do with the fact that he was exiled from Italy on account of his Protestantism, finding refuge at Oxford where he became Regius Professor of Law. In 1588 Gentili published *De Jure Belli Commentatio Prima* ('First Commentary on the Law of War'), the first of a three-volume series, followed in 1598 by *De Jure Belli Libri Tres*. In his view, international law should comprise the actual practices of civilized nations, tempered by moral (but not specifically religious) considerations. Although he rejected the authority of the Church, he used the reasoning of the canon law as well as the civil law whenever it suited his purpose. [IB]

geographical indications A geographical indication is a sign used on goods that have a specific geographical origin and possess qualities or a reputation that are due to that place of origin – such as climate or soil. Agricultural products such as cheese, wine and olive oil are the typical products to which geographical indications are attached as they have qualities that derive from their place of production and are influenced by specific local factors, such as climate and soil. The TRIPS Agreement also sets out a higher level of protection for geographical indications on wines and spirits. Geographical indications can also indicate products that are made according to a specific, localized, manufacturing skill or tradition.

All WTO member states must provide legal means to prevent the use of geographical indications that suggest that a good originates in a geographical area other than its true place of origin, in a manner which misleads the public as to its geographical origin or which constitutes an act of UNFAIR COMPETITION. Under the UK law, TRADE MARKS that consist exclusively of signs or designations which serve to indicate geographical origin cannot be registered (see Trade Mark Act 1994, s. 3(1)(c)), but the law allows the registration of geographical names as what are called **certification** and **collective marks.** [US]

See also PASSING OFF; WORLD TRADE ORGANIZATION.

get In Jewish law, only a husband can DIVORCE a wife; this is referred to as 'giving her a get'. While a get is not, on its own, a valid divorce in English law, it is required in order for people of the Jewish faith to remarry in the eyes of their religion. The Matrimonial Causes Act 1973 permits the court to order that a DECREE NISI of divorce not be made absolute until parties married

according to the Jewish faith (or other prescribed religions) cooperate to dissolve the marriage according to that faith. This provision is intended to protect Jewish women and women of other religions who are dependent on their husbands to initiate or give them a divorce. [AD]

See also DECREE ABSOLUTE; TALAQ.

gift A gratuitous transfer or grant of property where the donor intends to pass the beneficial ownership to the recipient. Gifts may take place either in life or on death via a WILL which only takes effect on the death of the TESTATOR. The formalities necessary to make a gift vary by reference to the subject matter of the gift: for example a gift of personalty requires words of gift and delivery, or a deed of gift; a gift of land requires a DEED. If the formalities are not complied with, the legal title to the property will not pass and although equity could have saved such incomplete gifts by treating ineffective transfers as effective declarations of TRUST, it chose not to do so. The general rule is encapsulated in the maxim 'Equity will not perfect an imperfect gift', on the basis that an incomplete gift can always be perfected by the donor by subsequently complying with the formalities, and until this occurs it is wrong to impose the onerous duties of trusteeship on the would-be donor. Despite the general rule, there are a large number of both common law and equitable exceptions including PROPRIETARY ESTOPPEL, the RULE IN *STRONG V. BIRD*, *DONATIO MORTIS CAUSA*, etc. In recent years, the entire basis of the rule has been thrown into question as a result of a number of hard cases, where the higher courts have in effect saved incomplete gifts no longer capable of being perfected by the donor as effective declarations of trusts. [PK]

gift aid A scheme to increase the value of gifts made to charity by some taxpayers by adding income tax at the basic rate to those gifts. It is a relatively complex approach to charitable giving which allows charities to recover the basic rate tax which participating donor taxpayers pay to HM REVENUE AND CUSTOMS. The main conditions are that

(a) gifts must be money gifts made by United Kingdom taxpayers who pay basic rate tax (or make chargeable gains) in a tax year; (b) the gift is not deductible under the PAYROLL GIVING SCHEME; and (c) the taxpayer must sign a declaration (in the form prescribed by law) authorizing recovery of tax by the charity.

It the conditions are met, the effect is that the donor taxpayer's gift to charity, for example £80 in a tax year, is treated as a gift net of basic rate tax. As the gift is EXEMPT INCOME in the hands of the charity, it is entitled to recover the tax from the Revenue. In the example, that would be £20, giving the charity £100 instead of £80.
[RE]

Gillick competence Named after the case of *Gillick* v. *West Norfolk and Wisbech AHA* [1986] AC 112, which determined that a minor under the age of 16, deemed to have reached sufficient maturity and understanding, will have the MENTAL CAPACITY to CONSENT TO TREATMENT. The five criteria for establishing the existence of the necessary capacity are set out in the judgment of Lord Fraser and are known as the FRASER GUIDELINES. The decision in the case, which related to the provision of contraceptive treatment and advice, has enabled MATURE MINORS to make their own decisions not only in such cases but in respect of medical treatment generally and also in other areas of family proceedings.   [HJ]
See also AUTONOMY; BEST INTERESTS.

Glanvill (or Glanville), Ranulph de (d. 1190) Reputed author of the first major treatise on English law, the *Tractatus de Legibus et Consuetudinibus Angliæ* ('Treatise on the Laws and Customs of England'). [JW]

globalization of law A contested concept that defies easy definition. Discussions about globalization and law tend to focus either on the ways in which law is used as a tool to support or effect economic and political globalization (for example, the argument that transnational and international legal organizations like the UNITED NATIONS, the WORLD TRADE ORGANIZATION (WTO) and the World Bank have developed legal regimes

that are closely linked to the political economy of world markets), or to explore the ways in which globalization has challenged traditional forms of legal regulation. But this tends to say more about the role of law in globalization than about the globalization *of* law and legal culture itself.

In so far as it makes sense to talk about the globalization of law, it needs to be distinguished from the internationalization of law. INTERNATIONAL LAW is based on the SOVEREIGNTY of nation-states, whereas the globalization of law not only sits, at least to a degree, outside of that relationship, but may be eroding state sovereignty by locating greater legal authority in non-state actors and forms of law that are independent of state authority. The evidence for that is controversial (for example, consider debates about the nature of international human rights law) and, some academics suggest, still fairly scant. Most commentators seem to suggest that transnational commercial and trade law – where the growth in private ordering (see *LEX MERCATORIA*), private dispute resolution processes, such as international commercial arbitration and transnational MEDIATION, and the emergence of more distinctively transnational systems of law, such as WTO law – provide the strongest evidence for the emergence of any (semi-)autonomous global legal order.   [JW]
See also REGIONALISM; SOFT LAW; WORLD TRADE ORGANIZATION.

Further reading: A. Gearey, *Globalization and Law* (Lanham, MD: Rowman & Littlefield, 2005); T. Halliday and P. Osinsky, 'Globalization of Law', *Annual Review of Sociology* (2006), 32(1), pp. 447–70; M. Likosky (ed.) *Transnational Legal Processes – Globalisation and Power Disparities* (London: Butterworths, 2002).

GMC *See* GENERAL MEDICAL COUNCIL.

golden handcuffs An EMPLOYEE is given a financial incentive while working for an EMPLOYER but in return signs up to a restrictive CONTRACT OF EMPLOYMENT.   [MJ]

golden handshake An ex-gratia payment made to an EMPLOYEE on termination of employment, often with restrictive terms attached. [MJ]

golden hello A sum of money or other remuneration offered by an EMPLOYER as an inducement to an EMPLOYEE to work for that employer. [MJ]

golden rule *See* STATUTORY INTERPRETATION.

good behaviour The Magistrates' Courts Act 1980 provided MAGISTRATES with the power to require a person to enter into a RECOGNIZANCE, with or without a SURETY, to keep the peace or to be of good behaviour. [SN]

good consideration CONSIDERATION which the law recognizes as sufficient to support a PROMISE and render it binding; for example, if an act has been performed before there is any promise to make payment, that act may be regarded as **past consideration** and past consideration is not a good (or sufficient) consideration. Good consideration need not be adequate, i.e. it need not be the monetary equivalent of what has been promised in return, as long as it has some value in the eyes of the law (it is a **valuable consideration**). [JPL]

good faith The principle of good faith in contracting presupposes that negotiations and contractual dealings will be carried out with fairness and honesty and with no intention of seeking an unfair advantage or of deliberately acting to the detriment of the other party. Its operation is limited in English contract law. There is generally no obligation to negotiate in good faith but the courts accept that other principles may operate to achieve the same objective of fairness and honesty in contractual dealings. A specific requirement of good faith has been recognized in a number of contexts including (a) in setting standards of disclosure and other obligations around performance in contracts *uberrimae fidei* (of the utmost good faith) such as commercial agency and insurance contracts; and (b) in the consumer context, in relation to the definition of UNFAIR CONTRACT TERMS which are VOIDABLE at the option of the CONSUMER. By virtue of the Unfair Terms in Con-

sumer Contracts Regulations (UTCCR) 1999, a term is unfair where it has not been individually negotiated and, contrary to the requirements of good faith, causes a significant imbalance, to the detriment of the consumer, in the parties' rights and obligations under the contract (reg. 5(1)). In this context, good faith has been interpreted as requiring fair and open dealing and as having both a procedural aspect, i.e. avoidance of unfair surprise, and a substantive aspect, i.e. where the content is unbalanced (see *Director General of Fair Trading* v. *First National Bank plc* [2001] UKHL 52). [JPL]

good leasehold title The second-best class of TITLE to LEASEHOLD land recognized by the Land Registry the best class being absolute TITLE. It is awarded when the title is one that a willing buyer would be advised by a competent professional adviser to accept, but where the registrar has not seen and approved the FREEHOLD title.

Good leasehold title will be awarded by the Land Registry if the freehold estate is unregistered and the tenant is unable to investigate the freehold title. It has the same effect as registration with absolute title, except, importantly, it does not effect the enforcement of any right or interest affecting the title of the landlord who granted the lease. [DR]

good offices A type of international MEDIATION employed particularly by successive Secretary-Generals of the UNITED NATIONS. It involves putting to use the prestige and world authority represented by the office of the Secretary-General by mediating between parties to a dispute that is likely or close to significant escalation and possible use of armed force. Thus, good offices were used by Kofi Annan in 1998 in respect of the crisis between the USA and Iraq over the latter's refusal to cooperate with the weapons inspection regime set up by the SECURITY COUNCIL. The Secretary-General may, and has, delegated his good offices role to other diplomats, and this function has also been employed by individual STATES as well as other inter-governmental organizations. Good offices are voluntary and

their decisions non-binding on the parties.
        [IB]

goods Personal **chattels** which are physical items that can be touched and which are moveable, i.e. items of property. The definition excludes land, and the definition in the Sale of Goods Act 1979, s. 61, also excludes money and CHOSES IN ACTION (i.e. intangible property such as company shares, patents or cheques).   [JPL]

governance Rules, processes, systems and behaviours directed towards the achievement of the overall objectives of an organization and concerned in particular with the way in which power is exercised to that end in terms of transparency, participation and accountability.

Examples of the use of the term may be found in relation to the activities of the EUROPEAN UNION and in the context of corporations. The EUROPEAN COMMISSION responded to the perceived alienation of citizens from the institutions of the European Union by publishing a White Paper on European Governance in 2001. This set out ways in which the EU could operate more inclusively and accountably, in closer connection with citizens and with a view to producing more effective policies. To this end, alternatives to or enhancements of traditional modes of REGULATION were discussed, including the provision of better information, improved partnerships in the policy process, a focus on policy coherence, engagement with civil society, developing a culture of consultation and dialogue, reducing the complexity of European law and allowing more flexibility with regard to implementation by Member States, the use of COREGULATION, an improved culture of evaluation and feedback.

As regards **corporate governance**, the key concern is to determine in whose interests companies should be run and thus who will enjoy strong rights in the decision-making processes that affect their direction. On one hand, there are those who argue that companies are essentially run in the interests of shareholders and thus corporate governance must concern itself with ensuring that the shareholders can be satisfied that

their investment is protected. This view of corporate governance accordingly focuses on the information that is available to the market and on ensuring that those entrusted with managing the shareholders' investment cannot abuse their power. On the other hand, there are those who contend that companies must be run in the interests of a much broader range of stakeholders, including employees and suppliers. This view focuses on the fact that other stakeholders also make firm-specific investments that they may not be able to protect by contractual means and are thus also entitled to rights within corporate governance arrangements. This view of corporate governance seeks to propose models which would allow other stakeholders either to be directly involved in decision-making or at least to have their interests taken explicitly into account when decisions are made.   [JP]

Further reading: European Commission, *European Governance: A White Paper*, COM (2001) 428 final; Jill Solomon, *Corporate Governance and Accountability*, 2nd edn (Chichester: John Wiley, 2007).

governing law A general term used in CONFLICT OF LAWS to indicate the law which applies to a legal relationship (such as one based on a TORT) or to a legal issue (such as the capacity to enter into a CONTRACT). The governing law is the law to be applied in order to determine a legal question or issue – whether procedural (*LEX FORI* or *LEX ARBITRI*) or substantive (*LEX CAUSAE*) in nature. It is usually national law, but could be *LEX MERCATORIA*, which governs some or all of the issues arising for determination in an international legal dispute.   [RE]
    See also ARBITRATION; CHOICE OF LAW.

government-in-exile A governmental entity that has been driven out of its territory of authority and replaced by a new government. There is no concrete rule under INTERNATIONAL LAW definitively prohibiting such assumptions of power, nor any rule that grants authority to the exiled government. The matter is resolved on a unilateral, case-by-case basis by states, who may take no action in respect of recognizing the new government or not (see ESTRADA DOCTRINE), or may recognize the new government, or recognize the government-in-exile. Such a unilateral act has no legal effect, except in so far as the recognizing STATE may be deemed to breach the non-intervention principle (i.e. that intervention in the domestic affairs of other states is prohibited). In practice, where an enemy state has facilitated the displacement of a friendly government, the latter's allies will continue to recognize its authority, as was the case with the Kuwaiti government-in-exile following the 1990 Iraqi invasion. [IB]

See also RECOGNITION.

governmentality A term coined by the French historian and philosopher Michel Foucault (1926–84) in his effort to trace the emergence of the modern state. The term encompasses both the idea of government as well as that of thought and is thus intended to convey the message that it is not possible to consider the evolution of the state without considering the concomitant evolution of political rationality. His conclusion is that the emergence of the modern state and of the autonomous individual are inextricably linked, even to the extent that each determines the emergence of the other. [JP]

Further reading: Michel Foucault, 'Governmentality' in Graham Burchell, Colin Gordon and Peter Miller (eds), *The Foucault Effect: Studies in Governmentality* (Hemel Hempstead: Harvester Wheatsheaf, 1991), pp. 87–104.

grant In land law, the transfer or creation of ownership of property by an instrument in writing. Under the Law of Property Act 1925, s. 51(2), the actual use of the word grant is not necessary to create or transfer an interest in land. [DR]

See also LIE IN GRANT.

grant of representation A grant that is obtained from the court and is evidence of the authority of the PERSONAL REPRESENTATIVE to administer the estate of a deceased person. It will be either a grant of PROBATE, which will be made to an EXECUTOR named in the WILL, or a grant of **letters of administration** made to an **administrator** when either there is no will, or where the will does not appoint an executor.

An executor's authority derives from the will itself, but an executor will normally find it necessary to obtain a grant as evidence of his authority when he collects the assets. An administrator has no authority at all until such time as the grant is made. [CM]

grants in aid Payments from central government towards local authority expenditure. [JW]

gratuitous contract The possibility in Scots law for a contract to be formed in the absence of consideration.

Whereas in England the general position is that a contract is not enforceable if there is no consideration (that is, there is no reciprocity), the influence of CANON LAW on SCOTS LAW from the 12th century means that this is not the case in Scotland.

More recently, the passing of the Requirements of Writing (Scotland) Act 1995 means that a 'gratuitous unilateral obligation', except in the course of business, has to be in writing as opposed to being simply verbal. Whether a gratuitous unilateral obligation is the same as a gratuitous contract, however, is a moot point. [JP]

grave hardship The respondent to a DIVORCE petition or to an application for DISSOLUTION of a CIVIL PARTNERSHIP may, based on the fact of a five-year separation, oppose the divorce or dissolution on the grounds that the divorce or dissolution would cause him or her grave financial or other hardship and that it would be wrong in all the circumstances to dissolve the marriage or civil partnership. This provision was first enacted to protect 'innocent' spouses from being divorced against their will and suffering hardship as a result and has been extended to the Civil Partnership Act 2004. While the law speaks of financial or other hardship, successful claims reported in the case law have been of grave financial hardship only, and even these claims are rarely successful.

The term 'grave hardship' is also used in the context of publicly funded legal help, known as LEGAL AID. Funds are available for, among other things, legal help with disputes over FINANCIAL RELIEF on divorce or dissolution, but in some cases a deduction to recover some of the solicitor's costs, called the statutory charge, is made from the proceeds of those awards.   [AD]

green paper A government discussion document, officially published as a COMMAND PAPER.   [MS]

See also WHITE PAPER.

Grepe v. *Loam* **order** An order made under the inherent jurisdiction of the civil courts, barring a litigant from making any further applications in a matter without first obtaining the consent of the court. The power of a court to make a *Grepe* v. *Loam* order has been superseded by the introduction of CIVIL RESTRAINT ORDERS under CPR Rule 3.11 and Practice Direction 3C.   [JW]

grievous bodily harm 'Grievous' should be given its natural meaning of 'really serious' (see *DPP* v. *Smith* [1961] AC 290). 'Bodily harm' may include clinically recognizable psychological injuries, but not mere emotional upset (see *R* v. *Ireland* [1998] AC 147). It is an offence under the Offences against the Person Act 1861, s. 20, punishable by up to five years' imprisonment, to inflict grievous bodily harm, having intended or foreseen the infliction of (at least) some physical harm (*R* v. *Mowatt* [1968] 1 QB 421). Section 18 of the same Act makes it an offence, punishable by life imprisonment, to cause grievous bodily harm with intent to do so, or to cause grievous bodily harm with intent to resist or prevent a lawful arrest or detention. The concept of grievous bodily harm also has a significant role to play in the law of homicide. A person commits MURDER if he or she causes the death of a person, having intended either to kill or to cause grievous bodily harm.   [BF]

See also ACTUAL BODILY HARM.

gross negligence One of the alternative

mental elements of the offence of involuntary MANSLAUGHTER. Gross negligence was characterized as follows in *R* v. *Bateman* (1925) 19 Cr App Rep 8: 'in order to establish criminal liability the facts must be such that, in the opinion of the jury, the negligence of the accused went beyond a mere matter of compensation between subjects and showed such disregard for the life and safety of others as to amount to a crime against the state and conduct deserving punishment'.

In *Andrews* v. *DPP* [1937] AC 576, it was suggested: 'Simple lack of care such as will constitute civil liability is not enough. For the purposes of the criminal law there are degrees of negligence: and a very high degree of negligence is required to be proved before the [offence] is established.'

The test for gross negligence appears to be circular, and without reference to external criteria. The requisite degree of 'grossness' is simply that deemed by the jury as appropriate for the imposition of criminal liability.   [BF]

Grotius, Hugo (1583–1645) A Dutch jurist who became a lawyer at the age of 15 and wrote his first major work at 19. His greatest work is considered the *De Jure Belli ac Pacis Libri Tres* ('On the Laws of War and Peace'), written in 1625 and usually referred to as the first definitive text on INTERNATIONAL LAW. Using as his sources classical historical evidence and biblical exegesis, Grotius formulates a hybrid NATURAL LAW theory that prescribes normative behaviour for both STATES and individuals. He was much inspired by the work of GENTILI and, although he was deeply religious, he did not entrench himself in the rigid natural law of his generation and in the absence of sufficient TREATY and customary law he balanced natural law and political pragmatism, thus making law more scientific and less religious. In this way he refined the JUST WAR doctrine, the freedom of the high seas and other areas of international law. In *De Jure Belli ac Pacis* he also places great emphasis on the humanization of warfare.   [IB]

ground rent A special form of RENT which

is paid by the builder or owner of a building to the owner of the land for the use of the land to build on. The amount and due date for the payment of ground rent is specified in the lease. The Commonhold and Leasehold Reform Act 2002, s. 166, provides that a long leaseholder is not liable to pay ground rent to the LANDLORD unless the landlord has given notice that payment is due. The notice must conform to the statutory requirements amplified by the Landlord and Tenant (Notice of Rent) (England) Regulations 2004. [HC & DR]

group litigation A civil action or series of civil actions involving multi-party litigation. Unlike a REPRESENTATIVE ACTION, it does not require the claimants to demonstrate that they share a common interest, provided there are related issues of fact and law. The group litigation process provides special case management rules to expedite proceedings, cost-sharing orders, and the possibility for defendants to settle all claims by making a single, global payment to the group, leaving the issue of distribution between claimants to be resolved by the court, or the group's legal advisers. Group litigation can only be commenced with the consent of a senior judge who will issue a group litigation order under the CIVIL PROCEDURE RULES, Rule 19.11. [JW]

Grundnorm (Ger. basic norm) A key component in HANS KELSEN's analysis of the nature of legal validity. For Kelsen, a norm is valid in so far as that validity is conferred by another higher norm. That view, however, is destined to produce an infinite regress unless something intervenes to stop it. Thus the search for the reason for the validity of a legal system's norms ends with a norm whose validity, as the highest and the last of the system, is presupposed. It must be presupposed, because if it were not, then another source for its validity – another higher norm – would have to be found. This final norm is the *Grundnorm* and is the common source for the validity of all the norms belonging to a legal system. The structure of the legal order is accordingly for Kelsen hierarchical,

a pyramidal form, with the *Grundnorm* at the top.

The identification of the *Grundnorm* depends upon efficacy. The validity of the basic norm can be presupposed only if the legal order as a whole is effective – in other words, if legal officials are able to maintain law and order. Kelsen's ideas in this regard have been influential with courts in revolutionary situations. [JP]

guarantee 1. An agreement secondary to the main debt agreement by which the guarantor accepts liability for the debt of the person primarily liable on the debt in the event that the principal debtor defaults. It must be evidenced in writing (see Statute of Frauds 1677, s. 4) and requires independent CONSIDERATION. A guarantee must be distinguished from an INDEMNITY, which is a primary obligation to compensate for the loss suffered by another.

2. A manufacturer's guarantee, which refers to an undertaking by the manufacturer to repair or replace goods sold by retailers. Such guarantees are often given voluntarily and in that situation are not part of the CONTRACT OF SALE and so may not be enforceable at law, unless the buyer can show that the guarantee was a specific reason for purchasing that particular product. In practice, unenforceability tends not to cause widespread problems as most manufacturers will honour their guarantees, not least because of the reputational risks involved in not doing so. [JPL]

guarantee payment The Employment Relations Act 1996, s. 28, provides that an EMPLOYEE with more than one month's continuous service is to be made a guarantee payment if he or she has been absent from work for a whole day or more if there is no work because: (a) there has been a diminution of the type of work which the employee is employed to do; or (b) there has been some occurrence which has affected the employer's business which has led to the diminution in that type of work. INDUSTRIAL ACTION is deemed not to be such an occurrence. [MJ]

guard dog Under the Guard Dogs Act

1975, s. 7, a guard dog is a dog which is being used to protect premises, property kept on premises, or a person guarding the premises or such property. It is a SUMMARY OFFENCE under the same Act to use a guard dog, or allow its use, unless it is secured or under the control of a handler. [BF]

guardian A non-parent or non-parents appointed to step into the shoes of a deceased PARENT. A guardian has PARENTAL RESPONSIBILITY for the child and is obliged to ensure that the child is cared for and educated. However, the guardian has no duty to support the child financially and a FINANCIAL PROVISION ORDER cannot be made against a guardian. A guardian can only be appointed in accordance with the provisions of s. 5 of the Children Act 1989. A court can appoint a guardian where the child has no parent with parental responsibility; where a parent, guardian or special guardian in whose favour a RESIDENCE ORDER has been made dies; or the child's only or surviving special guardian dies. Alternatively, a guardian may be appointed without court involvement by any parent with parental responsibility, any guardian or any special guardian. The appointment must be in writing and signed. It may be incorporated in a WILL. An appointment normally takes effect after the death of any surviving parent with parental responsibility, though in some defined circumstances it may take effect immediately on the death of the person making the appointment. [FK]

See also GUARDIANSHIP ORDER; SPECIAL GUARDIANSHIP ORDER.

guardian ad litem Now known as children's guardian. [FK]

guardianship order **1**. An order made under the Mental Health Act 1983 in respect of someone who is 16 years old or over, and is suffering from a mental illness, disorder or impairment. A guardianship order must be shown to be necessary for the patient's welfare or the protection of others.

2. An order for the appointment of a GUARDIAN of a CHILD made under s. 5(1) of the Children Act 1989. [FK]

guillotine procedure A means of speeding up the legislative process in the HOUSE OF COMMONS. The government allocates a set number of days for the Committee and Report stages of a BILL; the total time available is then allocated between the different parts of the Bill. When the time limit for debate has been reached, all remaining votes on that part of the Bill must be taken without further discussion. Guillotines tend to be unpopular with the Opposition as they are sometimes seen as a way of controlling debate on controversial or potentially damaging matters for the government. The alternative view is that, in a crowded legislative schedule, they may be necessary if the government is to deliver on the commitments made in the Queen's speech. [JW]

guilt The assessment of the defendant's guilt is the ultimate object of the criminal trial. In order to achieve this end, the trial addresses a particular question, namely, has the prosecution proved, to the required standard, that the defendant committed the OFFENCE charged? Accordingly, the two verdicts possible at the end of a trial are 'guilty' and 'not guilty', the latter denoting that the prosecution has not reached the required standard of proof. There is no verdict of 'innocent'. [BF]

See also BURDEN OF PROOF; STANDARD OF PROOF.

guilty mind *See* MENS REA.

guilty plea By entering a plea of guilty the defendant waives the right to trial. It is a well-established principle that a guilty plea will result in a lighter sentence than a conviction following a not guilty plea. In accordance with the provisions of the Criminal Justice Act 2003, s. 170, the Sentencing Guidelines Council issued guidelines establishing the basis of the reduction in sentence following a guilty plea. [SN]

H

habeas corpus (Lat. you may have his body) One of the ancient PREROGATIVE WRITS enshrined in the Habeas Corpus Act of 1679, though its origins are believed to pre-date MAGNA CARTA (1215). It is used to challenge the legality of a person's detention in custody, whether by the STATE or a private person. An application for habeas corpus does not determine the detainee's guilt or innocence, but if there is an arguable case that the detention is unlawful, the custodian must appear before the court to justify its continuation, otherwise the detainee must be released. Since most of the state's powers of detention today are statutory, and therefore open to challenge by JUDICIAL REVIEW, habeas corpus is now rarely used in practice. [JW]

Habermas, Jürgen (b. 1929) The most influential contemporary German social theorist whose work has ranged across a variety of disciplines. As regards the law, the impact of Habermas's thinking emerges from his analysis of the modern capitalist state. For him, this process is characterized by a progressive encroachment of the state upon the 'lifeworld'. The latter is the sphere of lived existence within which individuals are able to realize themselves on the basis of common norms and understandings. The lifeworld accordingly offers the resources by which individuals may communicate

with each other in a way that is oriented towards understanding. Habermas refers to such communication as **communicative action** and it in turn allows the reproduction of the lifeworld. The modern state, however, threatens the lifeworld in a variety of ways. Habermas suggests that the systems associated with the modern state (economy, administration, law) essentially **colonize** the lifeworld and thus reduce the extent to which individuals are able to engage in self-determination, in turn threatening the reproduction of the lifeworld. Habermas also speaks in terms of the **juridification** of social relations, that is, the process by which such relationships become the concern of the state rather than remaining solely a matter for those directly involved to work out. Juridification may be carried out with the best of intentions (for example, the welfare state's aim to tackle inequalities), but may nevertheless have negative consequences for self-determination.

Law for Habermas has a dual quality, operating both as *medium* and as *institution*. Law as medium is that law which is part of the system, providing rules for the operation of the other systems. Law as institution, by contrast, is located within the lifeworld and is essentially the formal embodiment of a society's shared norms, values and understandings. Law as institution thus has the potential to bridge the gap between lifeworld and system, and indeed to alter law as medium on the basis of the discursive processes that characterize the lifeworld. In this way, the legitimacy of the law, for Habermas, is dependent upon the quality of the lifeworld's discursive processes.

Habermas's focus upon communicative action (communication oriented towards understanding) renders his an optimistic social theory whose normative demands, aimed as they are at supporting free speech, are widely attractive. Critics, however, are sometimes sceptical as to whether communication has the qualities that Habermas suggests, while others are doubtful that law as institution can play the role he envisages. Among Habermas's most important critics is NIKLAS LUHMANN. [JP]

Further reading: Jürgen Habermas, *The Theory of Communicative Action*, 2 vols (Cambridge: Polity Press, 1986 and 1989); *Between Facts and Norms* (Cambridge: Polity Press, 1997).

hacking Breaking computer security and corrupting or denying access to data on a system. The main anti-hacking laws in the UK are contained in the Computer Misuse Act 1990 which makes the following activities criminal offences: causing a computer to perform any function with an intent to secure unauthorized access to any program or data held in any computer; any act which causes an unauthorized modification of the contents of any computer with the requisite intent and the requisite knowledge; the distribution of hacking tools (including programs or data held in electronic form) if the supplier believes that it is likely to be used to commit, or to assist in the commission of a hacking offence.

Under the Terrorism Act 2000, s. 1(2)(e), the threat or use of computer hacking can also be a potential act of terrorism, where the use or threat of an action is 'designed seriously to interfere with or seriously to disrupt an electronic system', provided such acts are designed to influence the government or to intimidate the public or a section of the public, and made for the pur-

pose of advancing a political, religious or ideological cause. [US]

Hadley **v.** *Baxendale,* **rule in** *See* REMOTE-NESS OF DAMAGE.

Hague Conventions The Hague conferences of 1899 and 1907 had a twofold objective: (a) the conclusion of agreements relating to the peaceful settlement of disputes on an institutional basis and within a definite regulatory regime; and, since the use of armed force was not prohibited, (b) to adopt treaties that would regulate the conduct of hostilities between the belligerents. A large number of treaties and declarations were adopted as a result on both these fronts. ARBITRATION and MEDIATION processes were formalized; the conduct of warfare on land and war was codified in some detail; the treatment of neutral shipping and their rights on high seas were also codified; the use of particular weapons such as expanding bullets and asphyxiating gases was restricted or prohibited altogether. Some Hague Conventions finally fell into disuse, but those dealing with prohibited weapons and the rights and duties of belligerents during the conduct of hostilities were confirmed by the Nuremberg INTERNATIONAL MILITARY TRIBUNAL as being declaratory of CUSTOMARY INTERNATIONAL LAW. [IB]

half-secret trust *See* SECRET TRUSTS.

handling stolen goods An offence under the Theft Act 1968, s. 22. A person handles stolen goods if, otherwise than in the course of stealing, and knowing or believing the goods to be stolen, he dishonestly receives them, or dishonestly undertakes or assists in their retention, removal, disposal or realization by or for the benefit of another person, or if he arranges to do so.

The maximum penalty for handling is 14 years' imprisonment, in contrast to a maximum of seven years for theft. [BF]

Hansard The name by which the official reports of debates in Parliament are commonly known. The reports were originally published by the Hansard family in the 19th century, before reporting was taken over by the government in 1908. Hansard today is published in separate parts for the HOUSE OF COMMONS and HOUSE OF LORDS by the Stationery Office (TSO) and online at http://www.parliament.uk.

In 1992, after a period of many years during which the courts were not formally permitted to look at Hansard when seeking to understand the legislative intent behind a STATUTE, the House of Lords finally decided, by a 6–1 majority, to permit reference to parliamentary material. This may only be done where (a) the legislation in question is ambiguous, obscure, or appears to lead to an absurdity, and (b). the material relied on consists of statements by a minister or other promoter of the relevant BILL, together with any other material necessary to understand such statements and their effect, and (c) the statements relied on are clear (see *Pepper* v. *Hart* [1993] AC 593). [JW]

harassment Under the Protection from Harassment Act 1997, s. 1, it is a SUMMARY OFFENCE for a person to pursue a course of conduct which amounts to the harassment of another and which he or she knows, or ought to know, amounts to such. It is also an offence for someone to pursue a course of conduct which involves the harassment of two or more persons and which he or she knows, or ought to know, amounts to such, where their intention is to persuade any person not to do something which they are legally entitled or required to do, or to do something which they are not under any obligation to do. It is a defence for a person to show that the course of conduct was reasonable in the circumstances.

A course of conduct, in the context of harassment of a single person, must involve conduct on at least two occasions in relation to that person; and in the context of harassment of two or more persons, conduct on at least one occasion in relation to each of them.

The actual or potential victim of harassment may seek protection (through an injunction) and damages by way of civil proceedings (see Protection from Harassment Act 1997, s. 3).

References to harassment include the causing of alarm or distress. The causing of harassment, alarm or distress is also an element of the offences under the Public Order Act 1986, ss. 4A and 5. According to *Chambers and Edwards* v. *DPP* [1995] Crim LR 896, harassment does not require the causing of apprehension for one's personal safety. [BF]

See also STALKING.

harbouring an offender Under the Criminal Justice Act 1961, s. 22(2), it is an offence, triable either way, for a person to knowingly harbour (i.e. give shelter to, or hide) a person who has escaped from a prison or other relevant institution, or who, having been sentenced in the United Kingdom, Channel Islands or Isle of Man to imprisonment or detention, is unlawfully at large. It is also an offence to give to such a person any assistance with intent to prevent, hinder or interfere with their being taken into custody. [BF]

See also ASSISTING AN OFFENDER; PERVERTING THE COURSE OF JUSTICE.

hard case A case before a judge in which there is no clear rule that is obviously applicable. It can be contrasted with a clear case in which some well-defined legal rule is obviously applicable to the facts at hand.

The hard case is a core concern in theories of ADJUDICATION where differing views arise as to the appropriate role of the judge. RONALD DWORKIN, for example, has criticized H.L.A. HART on the grounds that his LEGAL POSITIVIST account of law, focusing as it does entirely on RULES, necessitates judges having a strong DISCRETION in such cases, which Dworkin regards as being at odds with the judicial function in a constitutional democracy. Dworkin contends that law is also composed of **principles**, standards of justice or fairness, to which judges must refer in the resolution of hard cases. [JP]

Hart, H.L.A. (1907–92) Professor of Jurisprudence at Oxford and the most influential POSITIVIST in the English-speaking world in the 20th century.

Hart is looking for 'an improved analysis of the distinctive structure of a municipal legal system' as well as a better understanding of what law, morality and coercion have in common and what differentiates them. Hart dismisses both NATURAL LAW and positivism in its classical form as adequate accounts. As regards the latter, he criticizes JOHN AUSTIN'S COMMAND THEORY on the ground that it could not differentiate between law and any order backed by threats, even those issued by a gang of robbers. Hart is thus interested in **obligation** as much as in correction. For him, the essential element in RULES is their **obligatoriness.** When social rules are broken, not only does this divergence arouse criticism, but such divergence from the rule is universally regarded as good reason for criticism. The criticism and the demands for future compliance are regarded as legitimate both by those who make the rules and those to whom they are addressed.

Among the social rules there are some whose importance is so great and obvious that people are thought to be under an obligation to observe them – these are called rules of obligation. The rules of obligation impose those duties that are normally called moral duties, e.g. not to kill or steal and so on. These are for Hart the **primary** rules of any system. In the primitive stages in the historical development of society the general body of rules that governs society cannot be separated into legal and moral. In such circumstances, however, difficulties are bound to arise as regards: (a) the content of the rules; (b) their inability to keep up with changes in society; and (c) the settlement of disputes. These difficulties can only be remedied through the introduction of what Hart calls **secondary** rules. These determine: (a) which are the primary rules in society; (b) who can change the primary rules either by repealing them, amending them or by enacting new ones; and (c) who can adjudicate in any dispute about primary rules. The development of secondary rules in Hart's terms marks the transition from a pre-legal to a legal society.

There are three types of secondary rules: (a) RULES OF RECOGNITION, which specify the feature or features that will conclusively identify a rule as a primary rule in a given system; (b) rules of change, which empower the introduction of new primary rules or the repeal or amendment of existing ones; and (c) rules of adjudication, which confer judicial powers on certain people, both with regard to the interpretation of rules and the imposition of penalties.

A legal system emerges, in Hart's view, when such a union of primary and secondary rules exists. [JP]

Further reading: H.L.A. Hart, *The Concept of Law*, 2nd edn (Oxford: Clarendon Press, 1994).

Hayek, Friedrich August von (1889–1992) Austrian economist who in the early part of his career offered a liberal, laissez-faire alternative to the more interventionist theory of J.M. Keynes. The preference of the economic world for Keynes' approach led Hayek to turn his attention to political theory, where he again defended laissez-faire policies, and to psychology, where he attacked the behaviourists. Permeating his work was the notion of 'spontaneous order', that is, the idea that social order emerges not from directed, centralized state action, but rather from the self-interested actions of dispersed individuals operating on the basis of limited knowledge. Similar themes are evident in his later work devoted to law where he suggested that law's sole purpose is to provide the basic rules and structures that allow citizens to pursue their individual goals. Law is accordingly not an instrument for social change deployed purposively by the state, but rather the minimal framework backed by the state within which citizens may negotiate and contract. [JP]

See also ECONOMIC ANALYSIS OF LAW.

Further reading: Friedrich August von Hayek, *Law, Legislation and Liberty: A New Statement of the Liberal Principles of Justice and Political Economy* (London: Routledge, 1982).

headnote The first part of a case report published in the LAW REPORTS. It contains a summary of the material facts, legal issues and decision of the court. It is written by the reporter or editor of the report, not the judge, and so is not strictly authoritative.

[JW]

Health and Safety Commission (HSC) Established by the Health and Safety at Work etc. Act 1974 to oversee health and safety matters in the workplace, the HSC has a Chair and a tripartite committee structure: three members representing TRADE UNIONS, three representing employers and three independent members. Day-to-day enforcement lies with the **Health and Safety Executive**, which acts on behalf of the HSC and carries out its functions. The HSC may direct the Executive to hold an inquiry or investigation into any accident or any other occurrence. See http://www. hse.gov.uk. [MJ]

Hearing Officer An official who operates within the EUROPEAN COMMUNITY (EC) legal framework in COMPETITION LAW cases. As the EUROPEAN COMMISSION acts as both prosecutor and in a quasi-judicial capacity in competition cases, the position of Hearing Officer was established in 1982 in order to ensure that competition law proceedings before the Commission were conducted impartially and objectively. The position was strengthened in 2001 in order to enhance 'the objectivity and quality of the Commission's competition proceedings and resulting decisions'. See http://ec.europa.eu/ comm/competition/hearing_officers/hearing_officers.html. [MON]

hearsay evidence An oral or written statement made by a person who is not called as a WITNESS in the case, which is presented in court as EVIDENCE of the truth of a matter contained in the statement. The question of purpose is critical to establishing whether or not a statement is hearsay. If it is admitted as proof that a particular statement was made at a given time or place, there is no question of hearsay arising: the document itself is proof of that fact. But the actual truth or falsity of anything it contains cannot be established by the document – it would require other evidence to confirm that, and so the contents of the document in this respect are hearsay. As a general principle, hearsay evidence is inadmissible. However, there are numerous and important exceptions to the rule. The position of hearsay evidence in civil proceedings is governed by the Civil Evidence Act 1995, which gives the courts a wide DISCRETION to admit out of court statements that would otherwise be hearsay. In criminal proceedings, the Criminal Justice Act 2003 allows, among other things, for the admission of statements by unavailable witnesses and sets down rules governing the ADMISSIBILITY of previous inconsistent statements. [ALTC]

See also CONFESSION; *RES GESTAE*.

hedge *See* HEDGEROW, HIGH HEDGES.

hedgerow A row of bushes, shrubs or trees forming a hedge. Most countryside hedgerows in England and Wales are protected by the Hedgerows Regulations 1997, (SI 1997/ 1160), which control the removal of hedgerows by a system of notification, administered by local planning authorities. A person wishing to remove a hedgerow must give a 'hedgerow removal notice' to the local planning authority, who will either give notice that the hedgerow may be removed or will issue a 'hedgerow retention notice', prohibiting the removal of the hedgerow. If a hedgerow is designated as an 'important hedgerow', on the basis of detailed criteria relating to archaeology, history, protected or threatened wildlife, its removal will be prohibited. [DR]

Hegel, Georg W. F. (1770–1831) Hegel's contribution to political philosophy was immense, and his direct treatment of law forms a relatively small part of his work, principally as a component of the *Philosophy of Right*. Hegel is perhaps best known for his intellectual method – dialectical reasoning (itself deployed, with radically different results, by Marx) – characterized as the positing of an argument in the form of a thesis, which itself was responded to by a counter-argument, an antithesis; thesis and antithesis were resolved by the reaching of a synthesis, which then itself became a new thesis, continuing the dialectical process.

The breadth of Hegel's work has caused disagreements at fundamental levels over his positions in the jurisprudential and political spectrums. For some, he is a natural lawyer, for others a positivist, for others, neither in their pure forms. In politics he has been deployed by proponents of both left and right. There is disagreement over whether his work countenances the possibility of justified civil disobedience.

In the *Philosophy of Right,* Hegel expounds a theory which promotes the actualization of the human spirit through the exercise of will ('the system of right is the realm of actualized freedom', at paragraph 4 (Wood, 1991)). The freedom to which Hegel refers is not limited to a negative liberal idea of being free from interference, but it encompasses a more positive concept of active self-determination. As Wood suggests (see Further reading: Wood at p. xi), 'freedom is really a kind of *action* ...'

A key element in self-actualization is property. Indeed, for Hegel, at the abstract level, the essence of property is in making the individual owner visible to others through that owner's interaction with objects in the external world. Thus one acquires property in something, not by desiring to have it, but by taking possession of it and thereby giving manifest existence to one's will.

Thus (see Wood at paragraph 51): 'My *inner* idea [*Vorstellung*] and will that something should be *mine* is not enough to constitute property, which is the *existence* [*Dasein*] of personality; on the contrary, this requires that I should *take possession* of it. The *existence* which my willing thereby attains includes its ability to be recognized by others.'

Property is inextricably linked with freedom, in that it gives one a yardstick by which to measure oneself – by which to gauge one's efforts at self-determination. Its visibility also endorses our individuality in a public domain by sending out a message: '*this* is *mine*'.

If property is a medium used by Hegel for an exploration of right and rights, then his approach to criminal law might be seen as its complement. He asserts that a crime is a negation of the rights of the victim. On the basis that rights are universal, crime is also a negation of the rights of all, including those of the offender himself. The vindication of rights requires that crime be annulled (an inexact translation from the verb *aufheben*, used by Hegel in various contexts). Indeed, the crime itself is, for Hegel, a conceptually null act, in that while it negates right, right persists and is beyond destruction. The annulment of crime is made manifest by the imposition of proper punishment, which involves due interference with the will (in the Hegelian sense) of the offender, thereby negating the offender's original negation of right by their criminal act. The fundamental justification for punishment is therefore retributive, rather than rehabilitative or deterrent; it seeks to make good that which has been damaged. Offenders should be punished on the basis of equivalence with the severity of their negation of rights. This is not a crude *lex talionis* (an eye for an eye, etc.), but a recognition that it is both feasible and proper to interfere with different rights of offenders (e.g. a fine interferes with property; a custodial penalty with liberty) to different degrees. Hegel suggests that his retributive approach is respectful of the personhood of the offender. The offender's punishment is not only just, but it is his right. As a rational being who has denied rights, both to others and to himself, his punishment is simultaneously not only a vindication of the rights of others, but also of *his* rights. [BF]

See also LEGAL POSITIVISM; NATURAL LAW; RETRIBUTIVISM.

Further reading: *Hegel's Philosophy of Right,* trans. with notes T.M. Knox (Oxford: Clarendon Press, 1942); Dudley Knowles, *Routledge Philosophy GuideBook to Hegel and the Philosophy of Right* (London: Routledge, 2002); Michael Salter (ed.), *Hegel and Law* (Aldershot: Ashgate, 2003); Allen W. Wood (ed.), *G.W.F. Hegel: Elements of the Philosophy of Right,* trans. H.B. Nisbet (Cambridge: Cambridge University Press, 1991).

heir (obsolete) Before 1926, a person who was entitled to succeed to the estate of his deceased ancestor under the rules of INTESTACY. Particular aspects of the old rules on descent were that male issue took priority over female issue, the eldest only of two male heirs inherited (though if the heirs were female they inherited together) and the heir took the same interest in the land that the ancestor had previously held. These rules were varied by certain local tenures, for example **gavelkind**, where all sons inherited equally, or **borough English**, where land devolved to the youngest son to the exclusion of any older brothers. The rules on descent and the concept of heirship were abolished by the Administration of Estates Act 1925.   [DR]
    See also HEIR APPARENT; HEIR PRESUMPTIVE; HEIRS OF THE BODY.

heir apparent (obsolete) Under the rules on INTESTACY applying prior to the Administration of Estates Act 1925, a person whose right to succeed to property cannot be defeated as long as he does not die before the person from whom he stands to inherit and is not excluded by a valid WILL.   [DR]
    See also HEIR.

heir presumptive (obsolete) Under the rules on INTESTACY applying prior to the Administration of Estates Act 1925, a person with a right to succeed to property whose right may be defeated by the birth of an heir closer in blood to the ancestor. For example, if X has a brother, Y, but no children, Y is an heir presumptive, because he currently stands to inherit X's property, but his right would be defeated if X has a child.   [DR]
    See also HEIR.

heirs of the body A restricted class of heirs, including only the lineal descendants of a person's bloodline (i.e. children), governed by the rules on intestacy applying prior to the Administration of Estates Act 1925. In land law, the expression is most commonly used in relation to an ENTAILED INTEREST, where land is granted 'to X and the heirs of his body', in order to ensure that an estate remains in the immediate

family. Entailed interests were abolished by the Trusts of Land and Appointment of Trustees Act 1996, Schedule 1, para. 5, although pre-existing entailed interests continue to have effect.   [DR]
    See also FEE TAIL; HEIR.

Henry VIII clause A provision in a STATUTE which enables that piece of legislation subsequently to be repealed or amended by DELEGATED LEGISLATION. This has the effect of reducing the scope for parliamentary scrutiny of any such changes or repeal. Such clauses acquired their name by association with the Statute of Proclamations 1539, which gave King Henry VIII wide powers to legislate by Royal Proclamation.   [JW]

hereditaments Interests in land comprising part of an ESTATE which, historically, could be inherited. Hereditaments are categorized as either CORPOREAL HEREDITAMENTS or INCORPOREAL HEREDITAMENTS and together make up the interests known as REAL PROPERTY (or REALTY).   [DR]

heritable property In SCOTS LAW, broadly speaking, land and buildings as well as things attached to them, as opposed to MOVEABLE PROPERTY, which is the term used to describe all other property.
    The distinction between heritable and moveable property dates back to the law of intestate succession (that is, inheritance in the absence of a will) prior to the Succession (Scotland) Act 1964 when different rules applied to different forms of property. Under the old law, the principle of **primogeniture** meant that the heritable property would go to the eldest son. While primogeniture was abolished by the 1964 Act, the distinction between heritable and moveable property remains significant with respect to legal rights, that is, the rights of the spouse and children under the Act to the estate in the event of intestacy.   [JP]

HFEA *See* HUMAN FERTILISATION AND EMBRYOLOGY AUTHORITY.

HHSRS *See* HOUSING HEALTH AND SAFETY RATING SYSTEM.

High Contracting Parties A term of art employed most commonly in pre-Second

World War international treaties, with the intention of giving a sense of prestige to the member STATES participating in a TREATY. It has no normative significance and is now replaced by the terms 'contracting parties', 'parties', 'member states' and others.   [IB]

High Court The High Court of Justice is a court created by the Judicature Act 1873 as part of the Supreme Court of Judicature (now known as the SENIOR COURTS OF ENGLAND AND WALES following the Constitutional Reform Act 2005). Based at the Royal Courts of Justice in London, the court also sits as District Registries throughout England and Wales. Almost all proceedings may be heard in any of those registries. The High Court consists of three divisions: the QUEEN'S BENCH DIVISION, FAMILY DIVISION and CHANCERY DIVISION. The High Court hears important civil matters at first instance, and has a supervisory jurisdiction over all subordinate courts and tribunals (including criminal appeals from the magistrates' court by way of CASE STATED). The High Court judiciary consists of the LORD CHIEF JUSTICE, the Vice Chancellor, the Head of the Family Division, the Head of the Queen's Bench Division, the Senior Presiding Judge and PUISNE JUDGES. Others, such as former High Court and COURT OF APPEAL judges, or former CIRCUIT JUDGES or Recorders, may be requested to sit as judges in the High Court. Proceedings are generally heard by a single judge; however, certain kinds of proceedings are assigned to a **Divisional Court** to be heard by a bench of two or more judges.   [AF]

High Court of Justiciary The highest criminal court in Scotland, the origins of which lie in the two royal justices who, from the 12th century, toured the country dealing with both civil and criminal cases. By the 16th century there was only one such justice, known as the Justice-General, dealing exclusively with criminal matters. During the 17th century, a second justice, the Justice Clerk, was once again involved. The Justiciary Court was established in Edinburgh in 1672, while judges were drawn from the COURT OF SESSION for circuit work.

The present court consists of 34 permanent judges presided over by the Lord Justice-General (who is also the Lord President of the Court of Session) and the Lord Justice Clerk. All are Senators of the College of Justice and thus also staff the Court of Session. When sitting in the High Court, the judges are known as Lord Commissioners of Justiciary. Retired judges and temporary judges (drawn from the Scottish Bar and from among the ranks of SHERIFFS) are also utilized when required by the weight of business.

A single judge sitting with a jury of 15 hears cases in the High Court. While its jurisdiction is unlimited, in practice it deals only with the most serious crimes. The SHERIFF COURT and the DISTRICT COURT deal with less serious crimes.

The High Court sits permanently in dedicated buildings in both Edinburgh and Glasgow and also has a permanent presence in the Sheriff Court building in Aberdeen. When on circuit to other centres in Scotland it sits in the local Sheriff Court.

In 1926, the Court of Criminal Appeal was formed within the High Court to hear appeals from there and from the Sheriff Court and District Court. When exercising this appellate jurisdiction it sits only in Edinburgh. At least three judges hear appeals against conviction and at least two hear appeals against sentence. More judges may be involved in particularly important or complex cases.

Significant reform of the court emerged from a Report in 2002 by Lord Bonomy and was given effect by the Criminal Procedure (Amendment) (Scotland) Act 2004. Innovations include a new preliminary hearing (since April 2005) at which the judge ensures that the case is sufficiently well prepared for a date for trial to be set. The aim is to minimize the inconvenience especially to jurors and witnesses of late trial adjournments.   [JP]

See also SCOTS LAW.

high hedges Hedges forming a barrier to light or access formed wholly or predominantly by a line of two or more evergreens, rising to a height of more than two metres above ground level (Anti-social Behaviour Act 2003, s. 66).

The 2003 Act gives an owner or occupier of domestic property the right to complain to his local authority if the height of a high hedge is adversely affecting the reasonable enjoyment of his property. If the local authority considers that the complaint is justified, it may issue a remedial notice to the owner of the hedge, setting out what he must do to remedy the problem. Failure to take action required by a remedial notice is an offence which, on prosecution, could lead to a fine of up to £1,000. [DR]

See also HEDGEROW.

highway Any route over which the public has a right to pass and repass, including a footpath, bridleway, carriageway, footway or cycle track, but not including a ferryway, railway or waterway. [JW]

See also ROAD.

hijacking The colloquial term for the offence committed by a person on board an aircraft in flight who 'unlawfully, by force or threat thereof, or by any other form of intimidation, seizes, or exercises control of, that aircraft, or attempts to perform any such act, or commits any of these acts as an accomplice' (see the Hague Convention for the Suppression of Unlawful Seizure of Aircraft 1971 (the Hijacking Convention)). The term may also be applied to similar acts on board vessels on the high seas, other than piracy which involves an attacking and a victim vessel. Such acts constitute an international offence under the 1988 International Maritime Organization Convention on the Suppression of Unlawful Acts Against the Safety of Maritime Navigation. [IB]

HIP *See* HOME INFORMATION PACK.

Hippocratic Oath Believed to have been written by the Greek physician Hippocrates in the 4th century BC, the Hippocratic Oath is one of the earliest codes of medical ethics. Its principles, which include promises that the physician will do no harm and will treat patients to the best of his or her ability, form the basis of modern codes, including the DECLARATION OF GENEVA. [HJ]

See also DOCTOR–PATIENT CONFIDENTIALITY.

hire purchase An agreement whereby a CONSUMER takes possession of goods on payment of a deposit and agrees to pay a further fixed number of instalments, at the end of which he may exercise an option to purchase the goods. Hire purchase agreements differ from ordinary credit agreements because the purchaser is treated as merely a bailee of the goods (i.e., he does not own the goods) until the agreement is paid off.

A hire purchase agreement normally involves three parties: the seller, the buyer and a creditor – usually a finance company. The seller will normally sell the goods to the finance company, which then enters into a hire-purchase agreement with the buyer. Consequently there is no contractual relationship between buyer and seller, and any dispute over quality of the goods, etc., must be addressed by the buyer to the creditor. Similarly, because the buyer possesses the goods merely as a bailee, he may not be able to dispose of them while the agreement subsists without the prior consent of the finance company. If the buyer is unable to keep up payments on the goods, then the creditor may be able to repossess them. However, where at least one third of the total amount payable has been paid, the goods become protected goods and the creditor must, unless the buyer agrees to return the goods, obtain a court order for possession (see Consumer Credit Act 1974, ss. 90–91). [JW]

See also BAILMENT.

historic building *See* LISTED BUILDING.

HL *See* HOUSE OF LORDS.

HM Customs and Excise (obsolete) *See* HM REVENUE AND CUSTOMS.

HM Inland Revenue (obsolete) *See* HM REVENUE AND CUSTOMS.

HMO *See* HOUSE IN MULTIPLE OCCUPATION.

HM Revenue and Customs (HMRC) The government department which has responsibility for the care and management of direct and indirect taxes in the United Kingdom. The department was created by the Commissioners for Revenue and Customs Act 2005 (the 2005 Act). The Department is the responsibility of Her Majesty's Commissioners for Revenue and Customs (the Commissioners), combining the responsibilities and operations of the former departments INLAND REVENUE and Customs and Excise. The Commissioners are responsible for the collection and management of revenue of those former departments and the payment and management of tax credits formerly the responsibility of the Inland Revenue (2005 Act, s. 5).

The operations of HMRC are supervised by the National Audit Office, the Revenue Adjudicato, and the Parliamentary Commissioner for Administration; and also by the Public Accounts Committee, and the Select Committee on the Treasury and the Civil Service of the Westminster Parliament. The Commissioners report to the Chancellor of the Exchequer, but must also provide a daily financial report to the Comptroller and Auditor General.

The Commissioners are responsible for the operations of the various offices which constitute much of the structure of the department. These offices include: Taxpayer Service Offices, Taxpayer District Offices, the Capital Taxes Office and VAT Offices. Criminal investigations into tax evasion are now conducted by the Revenue and Customs Prosecution Office (s. 34 of the 2005 Act).   [RE]

Hobbes, Thomas (1588–1679) English writer who produced the first fully developed version of SOCIAL CONTRACT theory in *Leviathan* (1651).

Hobbes lived through a period of extraordinary upheaval in the history of England marked by the execution of Charles I, the Civil War, the Commonwealth under Cromwell and the Restoration of the monarchy under Charles II. The trauma these events caused to the nation explains his preoccupation in this book with the establishment of stable and enduring government. His experiences also influenced his attitude to the emerging focus on individualism at this time, and his concern for the negative effects this could have on society.

It is certainly possible to envisage a time when individualism reigned, a period Hobbes terms the **state of nature**. This state is described as 'a war of every Man against every Man', where life is 'solitary, poor, nasty, brutish and short' and where individuals exist in a state of continual fear of violence and death.

Faced with such conditions, Hobbes argues, individuals naturally seek to achieve greater security and realize that they can only do so by establishing some form of government. Further, in order that the pre-existing conditions do not recur, each individual must surrender absolutely and unconditionally to the sovereign. The first principle of natural law for Hobbes is, then, self-preservation. Recognizing this fundamental need leads individuals to strive for society and in particular to accept absolute government.

Hobbes also mentions a second principle of natural law – namely, that having entered into society in this form, each individual must then be satisfied with as much freedom as he or she allows others – although this is not developed to the same extent as the first principle.

In so far as this is a theory of absolute government, the opportunities for citizens to question the rule of the sovereign are severely constrained. This is due to the nature of the social contract that Hobbes envisages. It is a contract among individuals, not a contract between individuals and the sovereign. Citizens therefore have no contractual rights to enforce against the sovereign. It does appear, however, that Hobbes recognizes what may be called an implied contract with the sovereign, albeit a fairly limited one: namely, that the sovereign will maintain peace and order. While any government would represent an advance over the anarchy of the state of nature, it is possible to see that a wide variety of regimes of greater or lesser liberality or tyranny could all be said to be fulfilling that implied contract. Hobbes does, therefore, concede that a failure to maintain peace and order would allow citizens to disobey the sovereign, but every other act or omission of the sovereign would have to be acquiesced to.

Having started from a state of nature and even from two principles of natural law, Hobbes reaches a conclusion where human law, the law of the sovereign, is paramount in practically all situations. Natural law reappears in the form of the instinct for self-preservation only when the sovereign fails to maintain peace and order. Otherwise, human or positive law must be obeyed. Thus, Hobbes, while usually described as a natural lawyer, might with equal justification be described as a normative positivist.

The apparent extremism, even desperation evident in Hobbes's view can be understood by recalling the events that he had witnessed: the violent overthrow of one monarchical government, a bloody civil war and the establishment of a wholly different republican order. In such a period of upheaval, almost any government was better than none and to look beyond the maintenance of peace and order would have appeared to be worrying about things in the wrong order. It was not long, after all, before the republican Commonwealth was gone and had been replaced by another monarchy – this time somewhat more constrained by Parliament. As Hobbes himself put it, those who worried about the problems that absolute government could cause were forgetting what civil war and anarchy were like.   [JP]

See also LEGAL POSITIVISM; LOCKE, JOHN; ROUSSEAU, JEAN-JACQUES.

Further reading: Thomas Hobbes, *Leviathan*, edited with an introduction by C.B. Macpherson (Harmondsworth: Penguin, 1981).

Hohfeld, Wesley Newcomb (1879–1918) American legal theorist best known for his influential analysis of rights. The starting point for Hohfeld's analysis is his desire to obtain clarity about what it means to say that 'A has the right to do R'. He demonstrates that this statement has no fewer than four meanings. First, that a specified other, B, has a correlative duty. For example, A has a claim right to prevent trespass on his or her property, which means that B has a correlative duty to keep off A's

land. Second, that A can choose whether or not to do R (that is, A has a privilege or liberty to do R). For example, A has the liberty to enter his or her own land and B has a no-right to prevent them. Third, A has the power to do R even though no particular right or privilege has been conferred. For example, B offers to sell A some additional land; A has the power to accept the offer and if he or she does so then B is under a correlative liability to A to sell it. Fourth, that A has an immunity from action by B in doing R. For example, absent any NUISANCE, A has an immunity to cultivate a garden on his or her land and B has a disability to prevent it.

Hohfeld's scheme of **jural relations** has allowed greater clarity in considering statements made about rights. This can be in relation to classical accounts such as that of THOMAS HOBBES (where references to rights turn out to be references to liberties) and JOHN LOCKE (where such references turn out to be references to claim rights) or to the increasing number of claims for the existence of rights in modern times. Hohfeld's scheme also encourages a more sophisticated analysis of rights in terms of relationships between individuals rather than simply as 'things' to be possessed.

The fourfold scheme does, however, have limitations. For example, not all duties appear to confer correlative rights. Equally, the inability of children to enforce rights would, on Hohfeld's analysis, indicate that they had none.   [JP]

Further reading: Wesley Newcomb Hohfeld, 'Fundamental Legal Conceptions as Applied in Judicial Reasoning', *Yale Law Journal* (1913), 23, p. 16; (1917), 26, p. 710.

holding out See AGENCY.

holding over The status of a TENANT who remains in possession after the expiry of a FIXED TERM TENANCY. The LANDLORD is entitled to payment for this period, described as mesne profits calculated at the open market value of the TENANCY. If the landlord accepts payment of RENT then a new tenancy is brought into effect.   [HC & DR]

Holmes, Oliver Wendell (1844–1935) An

eminent Justice of the US Supreme Court, regarded as one of the founders of AMERICAN REALISM.

His 1897 article, 'The Path of Law', *Harvard Law Review*, 10, pp. 457–78, is a foundational text for the movement with its insistence that the answer to the fundamental question 'What constitutes the law?' is 'The prophecies of what the courts will do in fact, and nothing more pretentious'. He thus replaced a lawyer's view of law – concerned with legal reasoning, deduction and axioms – with the so-called 'BAD MAN PERSPECTIVE' – concerned simply to know in what circumstances and with what degree of risk he will be subject to the imposition of the will of the state via the mechanism of the courts.

Holmes's views in this regard have been seen by some as more of a contribution to legal education than to legal theory, inasmuch as his seminal article was written at a time when American law schools taught that law was an exact science based on written materials and immune from social fluctuations.

Holmes is also seen as the founder of the strand of RULE SCEPTICISM within American Realism. [JP]

Further reading: William Twining, 'Other People's Power: The Bad Man and English Positivism', in *Globalisation and Legal Theory* (Cambridge: Cambridge University Press, 2000).

holograph will A WILL written by hand by the TESTATOR. Although the Wills Act 1837 provides that a will must be in writing, 'writing' is used in a wide sense and is not confined to handwriting. It therefore includes a will which is typewritten or printed on a word-processor, so that although a holograph will is perfectly acceptable, it is certainly not usual. [CM]

Home Condition Report A report produced by a licensed Home Inspector following a detailed inspection of a residential property. It is a voluntary component of a HOME INFORMATION PACK. It is designed to enable the homeowner and any prospective buyer to become aware of defects in the property that will influence their decisions in the selling or buying process. [HC & DR]

Home Information Pack A collection of documents which, since 14 December 2007, have been legally required to be prepared by a vendor in respect of any property which is available for sale. The Pack must contain basic information on the property (in the form of a **sale statement**), an Energy Performance Certificate, standard SEARCHES and evidence of TITLE. The Pack may, if a seller wishes, include a HOME CONDITION REPORT. [HC & DR]

home-loss payment Compensation which is payable to a person displaced from their home as a result of the compulsory acquisition of the dwelling as long as it has been their only or main residence for a period of at least one year. Particular statutory conditions are set out in the Land Compensation Act 1973. [HC & DR]

See also COMPULSORY PURCHASE.

Home Office Originally established in 1782, it has become one of the major departments of state. It is overseen by the **Home Secretary**, a minister of senior Cabinet rank. The Home Office has traditionally had a complex and wide-ranging set of responsibilities, but was reorganized in March 2007, after a number of well-publicized difficulties. As a consequence, the Home Office now has primary responsibility for three areas of government: counter-terrorism and intelligence, security (including policing), and immigration. Its former responsibilities for prisons, the probation services and policy relating to re-offending were transferred to the Ministry of Justice at the same time. [JW]

homeless person A person is homeless if he or she, together with any person he or she can reasonably be expected to live with, has no accommodation which they are entitled to occupy, and which it would be reasonable for them to continue to occupy (Housing Act 1996, s.175). Accommodation for this purpose includes accommodation overseas. A person is entitled to occupy a place he or she owns, or has a TENANCY or licence of, or a right to occupy by marriage.

A person may be homeless if he or she has rights over property which cannot be exercised: for instance, where the landlord has changed the lock to his or her flat or the person has nowhere to park his or her caravan. A person does not have to be actually homeless to qualify under the Act, provided he or she is likely to become homeless within the next 28 days. [HC & DR]

See also SUITABLE ACCOMMODATION.

homeworking Those who undertake work at home for payment. The employment status of such workers is often unclear. A homeworker who is not an EMPLOYEE will be regarded as self-employed and not entitled to rights and protection under employment legislation. Homeworkers are entitled to receive the MINIMUM WAGE unless the supplier of homework can demonstrate that they are clearly self-employed – s.35 of the National Minimum Wage Act 1998. For further information see http:// www.ngh.org.uk (National Group on Homeworking). [MJ]

homosexual conduct Consensual BUGGERY and consensual gross indecency between men remained offences until partial decriminalization in the Sexual Offences Act 1967. Of themselves, and subject to the ages of the participants, these behaviours are no longer offences in English law. [BF]

honour clause A clause in an agreement stating that the parties have agreed to be bound in honour only so that there is no INTENTION TO CREATE LEGAL RELATIONS (to be legally bound). This means that the normal presumption of an intention to create legal relations in a commercial contract will be rebutted (*Rose & Frank Co.* v. *J.R. Crompton & Bros Ltd* [1925] AC 445). [JPL]

hors de combat (Fr. outside the fight) In international humanitarian law, combatants are said to be *'hors de combat'* when, owing to the circumstances of the armed conflict, they have laid down their arms, are in detention, or are incapacitated from taking further part in hostilities either through wounds or sickness. The term is applicable to former combatants on land

and at sea and its principal purpose is to shield all such persons from further calamities of war, particularly by prohibiting making them military objects of attack, as well as by imposing an obligation on the capturing state to treat them humanely and address their medical needs. The legal basis for *hors de combat* protection lies in CUSTOMARY INTERNATIONAL LAW, as well as in the first and second 1949 GENEVA CONVENTIONS. [IB]

hostage Under the Taking of Hostages Act 1982, s. 1, it is an offence for a person to detain another person, and to threaten to kill, injure or continue to detain that person, in order to compel a state, international governmental organization or a person to do or to abstain from doing any act. The offence is committed irrespective of where in the world the detention takes place, and regardless of the perpetrator's nationality. [BF]

hostile witness A WITNESS who shows no desire to tell the truth. Hostility 'may be demonstrated by the witness's manner and demeanour alone. Thus a witness who declines to answer questions at all, or repeatedly says "I can't remember" … may be treated as hostile … On the other hand, the hostility may be demonstrated by inconsistency between the witness's evidence and a prior statement … The inconsistency need not take the form of a flat contradiction': *R* v. *Jobe* [2004] EWCA Crim 3155, [66]. [ALTC]

hot pursuit The right to pursue a foreign private ship 'when the competent authorities of the coastal STATE have good reason to believe that the ship has violated the laws and regulations of that State' (UNITED NATIONS CONVENTION ON THE LAW OF THE SEA, Article 111 (1)). Such pursuit must be commenced when the foreign ship or one of its boats is within the INTERNAL WATERS, the TERRITORIAL WATERS, or the CONTIGUOUS ZONE of the pursuing state and may only be continued outside the territorial sea or the contiguous zone – essentially all the way to the high seas – if the pursuit has not been interrupted. The right of hot pursuit ceases as soon as the ship pursued enters the territorial sea of its own state or of a third state. [IB]

hotchpot The bringing into account, on an INTESTACY, of certain benefits separately accrued to a beneficiary. The principle behind this concept was that originally a child of the deceased (but later a surviving spouse as well) should not benefit from the will or intestacy of the deceased, to the extent that they had already received a substantial benefit from the deceased. In other words, they should not benefit more than once, since this would be unfair on the other children of the deceased. Applying the rule gave rise to many problems and the rule was abolished in 1995 in respect of deaths after 1 January 1996. It is now of minor importance, and as each year passes it is less and less likely to arise.

The rules relating to hotchpot were complicated, and applied in three separate situations. (a) Upon an intestacy, any property which had been given by the deceased prior to his death to a child of his by way of advancement had to be brought into account by that child against his share of the estate. A gift by way of advancement is one intended to set up the child in life. (b) Upon a partial intestacy, any issue of the deceased acquiring a benefit under the will had to bring it into account in the distribution on intestacy. (c) Upon a partial intestacy, any spouse who acquires an interest under the will (apart from the gift of PERSONAL CHATTELS) has to bring it into account against the statutory legacy arising in the intestacy. [CM]

See also RULE AGAINST DOUBLE PORTIONS.

house in multiple occupation (HMO) A house or flat which is occupied by people who do not form a single household, such as people who live in a hostel or in bedsitters which have shared amenities. The general view is that HMOs contain some of the worst physical housing conditions and practices of housing management. On the other hand HMOs also provide an affordable and sometimes the only housing option for people on low incomes, such as benefit claimants, refugees and students. HMOs are subject to more regulation than

houses or flats containing a single household. The definition of an HMO has been revisited and expanded in the Housing Act 2004 because of the introduction both of the HOUSING HEALTH AND SAFETY RATING SYSTEM and new licensing of HMOs. The new definition is complex. An HMO is a building or part of a building which satisfies one of three statutory tests: (a) the standard test (designed to cater for most HMOs), (b) the self-contained flat test or (c) the converted building test.

Larger HMOs will require licensing by local authorities in order to operate. Other HMOs may be subject to additional licensing if the LOCAL HOUSING AUTHORITY so chooses. [HC & DR]

House of Commons The representative chamber of the UK Parliament comprising a total of 659 elected MEMBERS OF PARLIAMENT (MPs) – 529 representing constituencies in England, 72 from Scotland, 40 from Wales and 18 from Northern Ireland. Its composition will change at least once every five years as the result of a general election. Seats that fall vacant during a Parliament because a Member dies in office or resigns will be filled following a by-election in that Member's constituency.

The House of Commons has three main functions: (a) to scrutinize proposed legislation brought before it by government ministers, private Members and other bodies; (b) to examine the work of government ministers, departments and other public bodies; and (c) to provide external scrutiny of government expenditure and the public accounts. The business of the House is managed according to rules and procedures laid down in Standing Orders. It is presided over by the **Speaker**, who is elected by all Members from among their number. The Speaker is responsible for procedure and discipline in debates, and must act with complete impartiality. The government tends to define the business of the House, as Standing Order 14 (1) states: 'Save as provided in this order, government business shall have precedence at every sitting,' and it is the responsibility of the **Leader of the House** (a government minister) to arrange business in consultation with the opposition. [JW]

House of Lords 1. The second chamber of the UK Parliament, comprising predominantly individuals who have received titles as LIFE PEERS for political or public service, or services to industry and commerce. They are sometimes referred to as 'working peers' and are distinguished from hereditary peers whose titles are inherited. The House of Lords Act 1999 reformed the composition of the House by removing from hereditary peers their automatic right to sit in the House of Lords. As a transitional position, 92 hereditary peers have retained seats in the House, having been elected by their political parties or by cross-bench support. A further 26 seats are reserved for bishops of the CHURCH OF ENGLAND, comprising the Archbishops of Canterbury and York, the Bishops of Durham, London and Winchester, who sit as of right, and 21 other bishops who are selected by the seniority of their appointment. Further reforms of the House have been proposed since the 1999 Act, but have so far failed to progress to legislation. The latest government White Paper, *The House of Lords: Reform* (Cm. 7027), published in February 2007, proposes further reducing the numbers in the House of Lords to 540 seats (from around 740 now), with an equal division between appointed and elected representatives. It also recommends a free vote in the HOUSE OF COMMONS on the proposed reforms.

2. The highest court in the United Kingdom. Its proper title is the **Appellate Committee of the House of Lords**. It serves as the final court of appeal in both civil and criminal matters, and tends to hear in the region of 100 cases a year. Appeals to the House of Lords normally require permission ('**leave to appeal**') from the COURT OF APPEAL in England and Wales or Northern Ireland, from the Inner House of the COURT OF SESSION in Scotland, or from the Appellate Committee itself (but see also leapfrog appeal). The judicial House of Lords comprises a total of 12 judges who are elevated to the peerage as life peers and appointed to the Appellate Committee, normally from the Court of Appeal or one of the superior courts in Scotland or Northern Ireland. On appointment they receive the title **Lord of Appeal in Ordinary**, but are more commonly known as the 'law lords'. The law lords are entitled to sit in the House of Lords in its legislative capacity, but do so relatively rarely. By convention, they sit as cross-benchers and tend to avoid debates where their participation might be seen to have party political connotations. Nevertheless, some law lords have been vocal critics of government policy on specific matters of legal and judicial reform. Currently retired law lords can continue to sit in the House as life peers, but not on the Appellate Committee. Under the Constitutional Reform Act 2005, the judicial functions of the House of Lords are due to be transferred to a new SUPREME COURT of the United Kingdom, which will function wholly independently of the legislative House of Lords. [JW]

House of Lords Appointments Commission Following the recommendations of the 1999 White Paper on reform of the HOUSE OF LORDS, the House of Lords Appointments Commission was established on a non-statutory basis in May 2000. The Commission is an independent non-departmental public body that recommends to the Queen people to be appointed on merit as non-party-political LIFE PEERS. [JW]

housing association A society, company or body of trustees which (a) is established for the purpose of providing, constructing, improving or managing, or facilitating the construction or improvement of housing; and (b) does not trade for profit: see the Housing Associations Act 1985.

Housing associations are of increasing significance in the provision of social housing, providing accommodation for homeless people, low income groups and key workers both to rent and to buy and contributing to local housing authorities strategic work on homelessness anti-social behaviour and housing support. They generally let their accommodation on assured or assured shorthold tenancies. [HC & DR]

See also FULLY MUTUAL HOUSING ASSOCIATION;

HOUSING TRUST; HOUSING ASSOCIATION TENANCY; PUBLIC AUTHORITY; REGISTERED SOCIAL LANDLORDS.

housing association tenancy A residential TENANCY made between a HOUSING ASSOCIATION, a HOUSING TRUST or the Housing Corporation and a TENANT. The tenancy must have commenced prior to 15 January 1989. It cannot be a protected TENANCY because it is expressly excluded from statutory protection. [HC & DR]

Housing Health and Safety Rating System (HHSRS) A method introduced by the Housing Act 2004 for identifying faults in residential premises and evaluating the potential effect of those faults on the health and safety of the occupiers or visitors. It replaces the fitness for human habitation provisions of the Housing Act 1985 which have been repealed along with CLOSING ORDERS and repairs notices.

The HHSRS is a **risk assessment** process which enables local authorities to make informed decisions about enforcement action in relation to any risk to health disclosed by an inspection of property. It identifies potential housing hazards – to date 29 have been identified – including structural collapse, entry by intruders, and risks to the water supply. The risks posed by these hazards are then assessed on the basis of the likelihood of an occurrence within the next 12 months that could cause harm and the probable severity of the outcome, if it did happen. The probable severity of harm is classified as either 'extreme' (e.g. death), 'severe' (e.g. asthma, 'serious' (chronic severe stress, etc.) or 'moderate' (e.g. severe bruising), and weighted accordingly. The hazard score is then calculated and categorized as either a **category 1 hazard** or a **category 2 hazard**. The local housing authority must take appropriate enforcement action if it considers that a category 1 hazard exists in any premises. Where a category 2 hazard exists, no statutory duty is imposed on the housing authority, but they have the power to take action.

[HC & DR]

See also CLEARANCE AREA; DEMOLITION ORDER; EMERGENCY REMEDIAL ACTION; RESIDENTIAL PROPERTY TRIBUNAL.

housing trust A corporation or body of persons which is required by its constitution either to use the whole of its funds for providing housing accommodation, or to devote its funds to charitable purposes and use a substantial part of those funds for the provision of housing accommodation: see the Housing Act 1985, s. 6. [HC & DR]

See also CHARITABLE HOUSING TRUST.

HSC *See* HEALTH AND SAFETY COMMISSION.

human dignity In HUMAN RIGHTS discourse, human dignity is seen by some as a FUNDAMENTAL RIGHT that attaches to all persons automatically by virtue of their status as human beings, i.e. it is a reflection of each person's intrinsic worth. This perspective on human dignity draws heavily on KANT's moral view that human beings should never be used as objects, as the means to others' ends. An interesting example of the use of human dignity is the 2000 European Charter of FUNDAMENTAL RIGHTS, which not only states that human dignity is 'inviolable' (Article 1), but is structured in such a way as to treat human dignity as foundational. Part I of the Charter, entitled 'Dignity', thus treats a range of other rights and freedoms (the right to life and integrity of the person and freedoms from TORTURE and slavery) as derivative from human dignity. However, the elevation of human dignity to such a foundational status is contested by a number of writers, who observe both its elusive nature and resistance to precise definition, and suggest that it actually risks competing with and potentially restricting more established conceptions of human rights. [JW]

Human Fertilisation and Embryology Authority The government body responsible for the licensing and monitoring of all clinics and centres involved in fertility treatment, including human embryo research and the storage of human sperm, eggs and embryos. The Authority is responsible for ensuring that the principles of the Human Fertilisation and Embryology Act 1990 are adhered to. The following mechanisms exist to ensure that this is achieved: (a) a code of practice which gives clear operational guidelines to fertility clinics; (b) a register of patients and the result of treatments they received, the details of any donor involved and the children who are born; (c) the provision of information and advice for patients, donors and clinics about fertility treatments and the issues they raise; (d) up-to-date knowledge of developments in the field of embryo and reproductive research that will ensure that progress made is in everyone's best interests before it is adopted. [HJ]

Human Genetics Commission The UK government's advisory body on new developments in human genetics. The Commission focuses particularly on the social, ethical and legal implications of developments and seeks to promote public debate and take account of opinions expressed. The Commission was established in 1999, subsuming the role and function of its predecessors the Advisory Committee on Genetic Testing the Advisory Group on Scientific Advances on Genetics and the Human Genetics Advisory Commission. It is made up of 22 experts from the fields of genetics, law, ethics and consumer affairs and also has a consultative panel of people who have experience of living with genetic disorders. [HJ]

human rights Primarily those rights and freedoms that are deemed essential to individual freedom and dignity, including the rights to life, liberty and property, the freedoms of association, religion and expression, etc. Human rights can be conceptualized or classified in many different ways. One way is to view them historically, as developing through three phases. (a) **First generation** civil and political rights, which developed largely out of the 17th and 18th centuries, are conceptualized primarily as **negative rights** or **civil liberties** which require the protection of the STATE; for example, the right to private property, and freedoms from slavery and ARBITRARY DETENTION. (b) **Second generation** social, economic and cultural rights, which emerged primarily in the 20th century and constitute positive rights granted to individuals by the state, such as rights to

gender equality, minimum standards of education, housing, health and welfare, the right to a basic standard of living, and the individual protection of MINORITY RIGHTS. (c) Lastly there are **third generation rights**, which remain the least well developed and legally protected to date. These encompass collective, sometimes referred to as **solidarity rights**, such as rights to social, economic and technological development, to the enjoyment of natural resources, and to benefit from a healthy and sustainable environment.

Another approach is to classify them by reference to the kind of interest they protect. Thus it is possible to identify seven categories of interest that human rights law seeks to protect: **security rights** that protect people against individual crimes such as murder, torture and enslavement; **liberty rights** that protect the fundamental freedoms of thought, expression, association and movement; **due process rights** that protect against abuses of the legal process, such as imprisonment without trial, denial of access to legal advice, or use of excessive penalties; **equality rights** that guarantee equal citizenship and protect against discrimination; **political rights** that support political participation and the democratic process, including the right to vote, and freedom to protest; **social rights** to education and basic standards of welfare and housing; and **group (collective) rights**, including the right to self-determination, the protection of ethnic groups from genocide, and access to natural resources.

INTERNATIONAL LAW attempts to distinguish between these kinds of rights and generally provides different mechanisms for their recognition, protection and (sometimes) enforcement. The basis for most modern human rights protection stems from TREATY law, starting with the 1948 UNIVERSAL DECLARATION OF HUMAN RIGHTS, though that in itself lacks any binding force. Two international covenants were subsequently ratified with binding force on the contracting parties: the 1966 INTERNATIONAL COVENANT ON CIVIL AND POLITICAL RIGHTS and the 1976 INTERNATIONAL COVENANT ON ECONOMIC, SOCIAL AND CULTURAL RIGHTS. As its title suggests, the latter is primarily concerned with second generation rights and relies largely on the contracting parties themselves to undertake SELF-REGULATION and monitoring of standards. More effective at the individual level have been a number of regional human rights conventions, which have established procedures for hearing individual complaints, such as the EUROPEAN CONVENTION ON HUMAN RIGHTS and the **Inter-American Convention on Human Rights**, though these have tended to retain a stronger focus on the protection and adjudication of first and second generation rights, for example to security, liberty, due process and education.

The future of human rights continues to be hotly debated. While many argue that modern human rights law has made considerable progress, and achieved a remarkable consensus over the conditions necessary for human flourishing, others question just how much difference all this law has really made. Others still suggest that modern rights discourse imposes its own social costs, given a conception of human rights that still tends to prioritize individual over collective rights, and is seen by much of the developing world as highly Westernized and neo-colonial in its orientation and effect. [JW]

See also FUNDAMENTAL RIGHTS.

Further reading: James Nickel, *Making Sense of Human Rights,* 2nd edn (Oxford: Blackwell, 2006); Upendra Baxi, *The Future of Human Rights,* 2nd edn (New Delhi: Oxford University Press, 2005).

humanitarian intervention A supposed right under CUSTOMARY INTERNATIONAL LAW by which a STATE may exceptionally violate the territorial integrity of another state in order to prevent and put an end to ongoing mass HUMAN RIGHTS violations. The legal basis of this claim is at best tenuous, and even in cases where it is deemed to have been employed, none of the intervening states has expressly claimed to be acting on this ground. Moreover, none of the relevant resolutions of the UN SECURITY COUNCIL refer to humanitarian intervention in cases where force was authorized prior to the intervention, or subsequently. Some authors claim that humanitarian intervention precedes the UN Charter and was not extinguished when the latter came into force. Despite these academic arguments, it is hard to reconcile a right of humanitarian intervention in light of Chapter VII on collective security and the limitations placed on the USE OF FORCE through Articles 2(4) and 51 of the UN Charter. [IB]

See also UNITED NATIONS.

Hume, David (1711–76) Scottish philosopher and a key figure in the Enlightenment. He is best known within the law for his acute criticism of NATURAL LAW in which he demonstrated that its adherents were guilty of illogicality insofar as they derived value statements from statements of fact – the so-called **naturalistic fallacy**. [JP]

hunting with dogs Under the Hunting Act 2004, s. 1, it is an offence to hunt a wild mammal with a dog, unless the hunting is of a type exempted by Schedule 1 to the Act, or the defendant reasonably believes it to be exempt. For the purposes of the Act, the word 'hunting' bears its ordinary English meaning. Exempt hunting must take place on land which either belongs to the hunter or which the hunter has been given permission to use for that purpose by the occupier or owner. Permission may also be given by a constable where dogs are being used to recapture or rescue a wild mammal. [BF]

hybrid Bill *See* BILL.

hybrid power A power of appointment in respect of a class of objects defined by reference to the entire world, with the exception of a specified class and/or named individuals; for example, a power to appoint anyone with the exception of residents of Twin Peaks. [PK]

IAT *See* IMMIGRATION APPEAL TRIBUNAL.

IBRD *See* INTERNATIONAL BANK FOR RECONSTRUCTION AND DEVELOPMENT.

ICC *See* INTERNATIONAL CHAMBER OF COMMERCE; INTERNATIONAL CRIMINAL COURT.

ICCPR *See* INTERNATIONAL COVENANT ON CIVIL AND POLITICAL RIGHTS.

ICJ *See* INTERNATIONAL COMMISSION OF JURISTS; INTERNATIONAL COURT OF JUSTICE.

ICTR *See* INTERNATIONAL CRIMINAL TRIBUNAL FOR RWANDA.

ICTY *See* INTERNATIONAL CRIMINAL TRIBUNAL FOR THE FORMER YUGOSLAVIA.

identification evidence EVIDENCE identifying the defendant as the perpetrator of a criminal offence. Procedures for video identification, IDENTIFICATION PARADES and identification by means of evidence such as fingerprints, footwear impressions or DNA material are all governed by the Police and Criminal Evidence Act 1984 (PACE), Code D. Where a prosecution rests substantially on the correctness of eyewitness identification evidence, the judge is obliged to warn the jury of the special need for caution before convicting on that evidence (see *R* v. *Turnbull* [1977] QB 244).   [ALTC]

identification parade A procedure designed to test the ability of the WITNESS of a crime to identify its perpetrator. 'An "identification parade" is when the witness sees the suspect in a line of others who resemble the suspect': see Police and Criminal Evidence Act 1984 (PACE) Code D, para. 3.7. Identification parades are to be conducted in accordance with Annex B to Code D.   [ALTC]

identity, mistake of When a person claims to have a different identity in order to persuade another to enter into a CONTRACT, there will be a mistake as to identity. Mistake as to identity is a UNILATERAL MISTAKE (by the purchaser), but the mistake is induced by the other party (generally known as 'the rogue'). Usually, if there is a written contract naming the parties, the rogue cannot claim that the OFFER was intended for him or her (a different person to that named) and so cannot purport to accept it (*Shogun Finance Ltd* v. *Hudson* [2003] UKHL 62 [2004] 1 AC 919), so any resulting 'contract' is VOID, and any subsequent purchaser from the rogue cannot acquire a good TITLE. The mistaken party can recover the goods from him or her, or DAMAGES in the TORT of CONVERSION.

On the other hand, if the contract is made face to face, there is a presumption that the mistaken party intends to contract with the person who is physically present, i.e. the rogue. Therefore the contract is not void for mistake but will be VOIDABLE due to the rogue's FRAUDULENT MISREPRESENTATION as to identity. However, an innocent subsequent purchaser who acquires the goods from the rogue under the voidable title acquires a good title and can retain the goods.   [JPL]

ignoring traffic signals Under the Road Traffic Act 1988, s. 36, it is an offence for a person, driving or propelling a VEHICLE, to fail to comply with the indication given by a lawfully placed traffic sign.   [BF]

See also CARELESS DRIVING; DANGEROUS DRIVING.

ILC *See* INTERNATIONAL LAW COMMISSION.

illegal contract A CONTRACT that is either prohibited by STATUTE or at COMMON LAW as being contrary to public policy or is a contract that is performed in an illegal manner. An illegal contract is VOID and, generally, neither party can recover any money paid or transferred under it unless one party is innocent of the illegality. Related transactions may also be tainted with the illegality.   [JPL]

See also EX TURPI CAUSA NON ORITUR ACTION; IMMORAL CONTRACT.

illegal practices *See* ELECTION OFFENCES.

illegal trust An attempt to create a TRUST which is contrary to statute, morality or public policy and is therefore VOID.   [PK]

illegally obtained evidence EVIDENCE that has been obtained unlawfully or otherwise improperly. Evidence obtained by TORTURE is automatically inadmissible. Other illegally obtained evidence is ADMISSIBLE but may be excluded at the discretion of the judge, for example under the Police and Criminal Evidence Act 1984, s. 78(1).   [ALTC]

illegitimacy The legal status of a CHILD who was not born or conceived in wedlock and has not been subsequently legitimated according to law. At common law, illegitimate children had no legal relationship with their PARENTS, fewer legal rights than legitimate children and were subject to social ostracism. While the social importance of one's parents' marital status has almost disappeared and the legal conse-

quences of a child's status as legitimate or illegitimate have largely been removed by statute, the status itself still exists in law. In certain circumstances, a child may bring an application to the court, seeking a declaration that he or she is the legitimate child of his or her parents. The remaining legal consequences of the status of illegitimacy include disentitlement of such children from succeeding to dignities or titles of honour, and disentitlement of the fathers of such children from automatic PARENTAL RESPONSIBILITY. In circumstances where it is important to note the marital status of a child's parents, the preferred terms today are marital and non-marital children. [AD]

See also LEGITIMACY; LEGITIMATION; PRESUMPTION OF LEGITIMACY; UNMARRIED PARENTS.

illusory trust An arrangement that gives the outward impression of being a TRUST but is not in fact so because the apparent trustee has no power to deal with the trust property as authority to do so has been retained by the SETTLOR.   [PK]

Immigration Appeal Tribunal (obsolete) One of the two tiers of the former Immigration Appellate Authority (IAA), replaced by the single-tier structure of the ASYLUM AND IMMIGRATION TRIBUNAL (AIT) in 2005. The Immigration Appeal Tribunal heard applications for leave to appeal and appeals against decisions made by the Immigration Adjudicators (the first tier of the IAA). The main hearing centre was in Central London. The Immigration Appeal Tribunal, Immigration Adjudicators and IAA were abolished by the Asylum and Immigration (Treatment of Claimants, etc.) Act 2004 and members of the Tribunal became members of the new AIT.   [AF]

See also SPECIAL IMMIGRATION APPEALS COMMISSION.

immoral contract A CONTRACT involving sexual immorality, e.g. a contract to secure services of prostitution, is illegal, and therefore a VOID CONTRACT, since it contravenes public policy. Equally, contracts ancillary to immoral purposes are also regarded as contrary to public policy (see *Pearce* v. *Brooks* (1866) LR 1 Ex 213). However, it has been held that there is nothing *per se* contrary to public policy in a cohabitation agreement defining the property relationship between adults who intend to cohabit for the purposes of enjoying a sexual relationship (see *Sutton* v. *Mishcon de Reya* [2004] 1 FLR 837). [JPL]

immunity from prosecution 1. Exemption from criminal jurisdiction, allowing the person to avoid a criminal prosecution. The Queen and children aged less than ten are immune from prosecution. The State Immunity Act 1978 provides heads of state, their families and private staff with immunity from prosecution. Members of staff of a diplomatic mission have immunity in respect of acts performed in the course of their duty.

2. An undertaking to a witness not to prosecute on public interest grounds; for example, it may be in the public interest to use an accomplice as a prosecution witness rather than to prosecute them. If an accomplice indicates that they will only give evidence in return for immunity from prosecution, the matter must be referred to the DIRECTOR OF PUBLIC PROSECUTIONS. [SN]

See also WITNESS IMMUNITY.

immunity from suit Exemption or protection from being sued in civil proceedings. A range of persons enjoy immunity by virtue of their office, notably, the sovereign in person; members of the HOUSE OF COMMONS and HOUSE OF LORDS in respect of comments which attract PARLIAMENTARY PRIVILEGE; diplomats protected by DIPLOMATIC IMMUNITY; and judges insofar as they are protected by JUDICIAL IMMUNITY. Until 2000 advocates enjoyed immunity from being sued in NEGLIGENCE for work done in court in both civil and criminal proceedings; however, that immunity appears to have been removed entirely by the decision of the House of Lords in *Arthur J. S. Hall & Co.* v. *Simons* [2000] 3 All ER 673. Statements made by advocates in court proceedings still attract ABSOLUTE PRIVILEGE and may not be used as the basis for a DEFAMATION claim. [JW]

See also IMMUNITY FROM PROSECUTION; ROYAL PREROGATIVE.

impeachment (obsolete) A collective privilege of the HOUSE OF COMMONS to summon any person for trial for certain 'high crimes and misdemeanours', including TREASON, before both Houses of PARLIAMENT. The last resolution for impeachment carried in the House of Commons was against Lord Melville in 1806, for misappropriating public funds, a charge on which he was acquitted. Although it has never been formally abandoned, a move that would require legislation, the procedure is now deemed to be obsolete in English law. The power of impeachment still exists in some other jurisdictions, notably in the USA, where President Bill Clinton was impeached by the House of Representatives in December 1998 on charges of PERJURY and obstruction of justice, though subsequently acquitted on both charges by the US Senate. [JW]

See also PARLIAMENTARY PRIVILEGE.

impeding apprehension or prosecution *See* ASSISTING AN OFFENDER.

imperfect trust *See* EXECUTORY TRUST.

impersonation Under the Police Act 1996, s. 90, it is an offence for a person, with intent to deceive, to impersonate a member of a police force or special constable, or to make any statement or do any act calculated falsely to suggest that he is such. It is also an offence under this section for anyone who is not a constable to wear any article of police uniform in circumstances where it gives them an appearance so nearly resembling that of a member of a police force as to be calculated to deceive. It is also an offence under that section for someone who is not a member of a police force or a special constable to have in their possession any article of police uniform, unless they can prove that they obtained that article lawfully and have possession of it for a lawful purpose. Other statutory provisions relate to the impersonation of other law enforcement officers (e.g. Commissioners for Revenue and Customs Act 2005, s. 30). [BF]

implied authority *See* AGENCY.

implied condition The Sale of Goods Act 1979 provides that IMPLIED TERMS as to TITLE, description, satisfactory quality, fitness for purpose and correspondence with sample (ss. 12–15) are implied conditions, e.g. s. 14 (6). It does not follow, however, that where the buyer is not a CONSUMER, that breach of one of those conditions will be a repudiatory BREACH OF CONTRACT giving the injured party an option to terminate or affirm the CONTRACT, unless the term broken is the implied term as to title in s. 12(1). Section 15A, which applies unless a contrary intention appears from the contract, provides that if the breach is so slight that it would be unreasonable for the non-consumer buyer to reject the goods (i.e. terminate the contract) for a breach of the terms as to description, satisfactory quality, fitness for purpose or correspondence with sample, the breach is not to be treated as a breach of CONDITION but may be treated as a breach of WARRANTY, giving a remedy limited to DAMAGES only.

These implied conditions cannot be excluded or limited in a consumer CONTRACT and may be excluded or limited against a non-consumer only where the exemption is shown to be reasonable: see Unfair Contract Terms Act (UCTA) 1977, ss. 6(2) and (3). [JPL]

implied contract A CONTRACT that is not created or evidenced by express words of AGREEMENT but is inferred by the courts from the conduct of the parties or the nature of their relationship. It is difficult to establish the existence of such a contract. It is necessary to affirmatively establish the existence of an intention to be legally bound and this is linked to the question of whether the terms of the alleged agreement are sufficiently certain: see *Baird Textiles Holdings Ltd* v. *Marks & Spencer plc* [2001] EWCA Civ 274. [JPL]

See also INTENTION TO CREATE LEGAL RELATIONS; UNCERTAINTY OF CONTRACT TERMS.

implied malice A term used in the context of the *MENS REA* for MURDER, which, at COMMON LAW, had been described as MALICE AFORE-THOUGHT. The Homicide Act 1957, s. 1, acknowledged that such malice could be express or implied. This tends to be interpreted so that implied malice means an intention to do GRIEVOUS BODILY HARM, with express malice denoting an intention to kill. Both such intentions are sufficient to establish the *mens rea* for murder. [BF]

implied repeal A COMMON LAW doctrine which holds that where a later STATUTE is inconsistent with an earlier one, the earlier of the two must be treated as repealed or amended by implication. See, for example, the *dicta* of Lord Langdale in *Dean of Ely* v. *Bliss* (1842) 5 Beau 574 at 582: 'If two inconsistent Acts be passed at different times, the last must be obeyed, and if obedience cannot be observed without derogating from the first, it is the first which must give way … [the] operation … [of a statute] is not to be impeded by the mere fact that it is inconsistent with previous enactments.' The doctrine of implied repeal is seen as a necessary corollary to the SOVEREIGNTY OF PARLIAMENT: even Parliament cannot bind its own successors, since that would itself operate as a constraint on the sovereignty of the later Parliament. [JW]

implied term In CONTRACT law in general, a term that has not been expressly agreed by the parties but which becomes a term of their contract because the courts are required by STATUTE to apply it (e.g. the implied terms in the Sale of Goods Act 1979) or are otherwise prepared to recognize such a term. The courts will recognize terms, other than those expressly agreed, where they represent established customary practice or are strictly necessary to give effect to the presumed intentions of the parties (**terms implied in fact**) or are regarded for policy reasons as necessary in view of the subject matter of the contract (**terms implied in law**). An implied term may be a CONDITION, a WARRANTY or an INNOMINATE TERM and, although a term cannot normally be implied if it conflicts with an EXPRESS TERM, the statutory implied terms in the sales legislation either cannot be excluded or limited by an express term (in CONSUMER contracts) or can only be excluded or limited if shown to be reasonable (in non-consumer contracts).

In the CONTRACT OF EMPLOYMENT implied terms are terms which form part of the contract but were not expressly agreed between the EMPLOYER and the EMPLOYEE. These terms may be implied as a matter of law into every employment contract, e.g. each employee is entitled to be paid; or they may arise on the facts of an individual contract, e.g. these employers are entitled to transfer this employee to a different job (a **flexibility clause**) or to a different part of the UK (a **mobility clause**). Terms may also be implied from COLLECTIVE AGREEMENTS. Contractual terms which Parliament imposes are also sometimes called implied terms: the principal example is the EQUALITY CLAUSE imposed by the Equal Pay Act 1970, s. 1(1). [JPL & MJ]

See also IMPLIED CONDITION; TRADE CUSTOM.

implied trust A TRUST that arises either under an equitable presumption or by operation of law. Both RESULTING and CONSTRUCTIVE TRUSTS are implied trusts and a trust that is not implied is an EXPRESS TRUST. [PK]

impossibility of performance A CONTRACT may, unknown to the parties, be impossible to perform from its inception, e.g. because the subject matter does not exist (**initial impossibility**); or it may become impossible to perform, without the fault of either party, after the contract is made (**subsequent impossibility**). In the absence of a contractual provision allocating the risk of impossibility to one of the parties, the contract will be void for COMMON MISTAKE in cases of initial impossibility. In the case of subsequent impossibility, the contract will be discharged by virtue of the doctrine of FRUSTRATION. [JPL]

See also ALLOCATION OF RISK; TRANSFER OF RISK; VOID CONTRACT.

impotence The inability of a party as a result of physical or mental incapacity to have sexual intercourse with another person. The traditional heterosexual sex act is important in MARRIAGE, and sexual impotence may give rise to a petition for an ANNULMENT. A marriage in England and Wales is voidable if it has not been consummated owing to the incapacity of either party to consummate it: see Matrimonial Causes Act 1973, s. 12(a). [AD]

See also CONSUMMATION OF MARRIAGE; VOIDABLE MARRIAGE.

imprisonment The most severe sentencing option, for adult offenders. Whether imprisonment is available in respect of any given offender depends on the maximum sentence specified in the law governing the offence for which they have been convicted. According to the Criminal Justice Act 2003, s. 152, where a discretionary custodial sentence is an available option, it must not be used unless the court is of the view that the offence, or the combination of the offence and one or more offences associated with it, was so serious that neither a fine alone nor a community sentence can be justified for the offence. [BF]

improvement In the context of rented property, something which TENANTS do to improve (from their point of view) the premises. A tenant may need the landlord's permission before carrying out improvements. If this is the case, then the permission cannot be withheld unreasonably. A tenant may be entitled under some statutory schemes to compensation for improvements to the premises. [HC & DR]

impunity Exemption or freedom from punishment. The concept is particularly used in the context of INTERNATIONAL LAW and international humanitarian law where it describes the failure of the STATE to investigate human rights violations, to bring to justice and punish perpetrators, or to provide victims with effective remedies. Impunity is also used in the sense of **sovereign impunity** to describe the traditional immunity from prosecution enjoyed by heads of state, though the scope of such immunity has been reduced, not least by the creation of the INTERNATIONAL CRIMINAL COURT. [JW]

See also UNIVERSAL JURISDICTION.

imputation An assertion by the defendant in criminal proceedings to the effect that a person 'has committed an offence' or 'has behaved, or is disposed to behave, in a reprehensible way': see the Criminal Justice Act 2003, s. 106(2).   [ALTC]

imputation system An approach to the double charge to tax arising where the profits of a COMPANY are taxed in the hands of the company and also in the hands of its shareholders. A company resident in the UK pays CORPORATION TAX on its profits, and the shareholders can then be required to pay income tax on the proportion of those profits which are distributed to them.

In the UK, a company is regarded in law as a person, separate from the association of members who own the SHARES in the company, as a result of which the company is liable in its own separate capacity to pay corporation tax on its taxable profits, even though the members, as shareholders, can be liable to pay income tax on those same profits if distributed to them. To avoid this potential DOUBLE TAXATION, UK companies are required, when making a distribution, such as a dividend, to provide shareholders with tax credits at the designated income tax rate. A proportion of the corporation tax paid by the company is treated as the deduction of income tax at source on the distributed profits and, in this way, the tax credits represent the proportion of the corporation tax payable by the company. This is a form of imputation.

Until 5 April 1999, companies making distributions to shareholders were required to pay ADVANCE CORPORATION TAX to ensure that the tax credits were backed by actual payment of tax to the Inland Revenue. [RE]

See also FRANKED INVESTMENT INCOME; HM REVENUE AND CUSTOMS.

in camera (Lat. in chamber) The hearing of a case before a court sitting in private. The normal presumption is that judicial proceedings will take place in open court, unless an application is accepted for proceedings to be heard *in camera*. Such hearings may take place in a courtroom from which the public have been barred or removed, or in the judge's private office (chambers). The procedural rules for *in camera* hearings are contained in the CIVIL PROCEDURE RULES Part 39, Rule 39.2 and the CRIMINAL PROCEDURE RULES Part 16, Rules 16.9–16.11.   [JW]

in curia (Lat. in (open) court) The hearing of a case before a court sitting in public. Most judicial proceedings will take place in open court unless an application is made for proceedings to be heard *IN CAMERA*, i.e. in private.   [JW]

in gross In land law, a right in gross denotes a right that may be held independently of the ownership of land. The term is most commonly used with regard to EASEMENTS and PROFITS À PRENDRE. An easement in gross cannot exist, since it is an essential characteristic of an easement that it benefits a particular piece of land, the DOMINANT TENEMENT. However, a profit à prendre in gross can exist, and may be dealt with according to the ordinary rules on property (e.g. *Bettison* v. *Langton* [2001] 3 All ER 417).   [DR]

in loco parentis (Lat.) Used colloquially to describe someone acting in place of a PARENT, such as a relative or teacher. It has no legal significance.   [FK]

in pari materia (Lat. upon the same matter) A principle of STATUTORY INTERPRETATION which provides that where the meaning of a word or phrase is unclear, it should be construed consistently with the meaning to be found in another STATUTE (or statutes) on the same subject.   [JW]

in personam (Lat. against the person) Describes or indicates, for example, proceedings taken against some specific person or a right affecting a particular person or group of people (*actio in personam*).   [AF]

See also IN REM.

in re (Lat. in the matter of) Concerning; a phrase seen in the headings of law reports along with the name of the party involved or what the case is about. It may indicate that the judicial proceeding is uncontested or does not have designated adverse parties; for example, a case in which a WILL is being interpreted.   [AF]

See also LAW REPORTS.

in rem (Lat. against the thing) Describes or

indicates, for example, an action to assert a right of property 'against the world', that is, against no specific person (compare *IN PERSONAM*). A **judgment in rem** refers to a judgment of a court 'determining the status of a person or thing, or the disposition of a thing' (see *Lazarus-Barlow* v. *Regent Estates Co. Ltd* [1949] 2 KB 465); for example, a DECREE of nullity of DIVORCE. [AF]

inadmissible evidence EVIDENCE that does not satisfy the test of RELEVANCE or, even though relevant, is excluded by an exclusionary rule. [ALTC]

inadmissible reason When an EMPLOYER defends a claim for UNFAIR DISMISSAL, they may provide an 'inadmissible reason', that is, one which makes the dismissal automatically unfair, and in that case, the claimant does not have to prove that it is unfair. There is a growing list of such inadmissible reasons, which at present includes: dismissals for pregnancy, maternity, health and safety reasons, and making a protected disclosure (SEE WHISTLE-BLOWING). [MJ]

inalienability Property is inalienable if the current owner cannot dispose of it. Restrictions can be placed upon LAND and other property, for instance by a TESTATOR, which prevent subsequent owners from disposing of it as they wish. Inalienability is counter-intuitive to English property law, which seeks to uphold commercial freedom to engage in property transactions. One particular COMMON LAW rule, the rule against inalienability, operates to restrict the ability of testators to set up perpetual trusts, confining them to the PERPETUITY PERIOD. [HC]

See also RULE AGAINST PERPETUITIES.

incapacity Certain persons, such as the mentally disordered and MINORS, are considered to be incapable of making CONTRACTS and are sometimes referred to as persons acting under a disability. [JP]

See also CAPACITY TO CONTRACT; CHILDREN'S CONTRACTS.

incest Sexual behaviour between designated family members. For legal purposes only, the term 'incest' is obsolete. Formerly regulated by the Sexual Offences Act 1956, the offences in the 1956 Act have been replaced by a wider range of **familial sexual offences** in the Sexual Offences Act 2003.

Sections 25 and 26 of the 2003 Act create offences of, respectively, sexual activity with a child family member, and inciting a child family member to engage in sexual activity. The prohibited behaviour is sexual touching (which may of course include sexual intercourse) of or by a family member under the age of 18. The extent of the 'family' for these purposes extends beyond blood linkage to particular adoptive, step- and foster-relationships, and certain intra-household relationships of care, regardless of strict 'family' linkage (see Sexual Offences Act 2003, s. 27).

Sections 64 and 65 of the 2003 Act create offences of sex with an adult relative, which require vaginal or anal penetration by part of the adult's body or anything else, or penile–oral penetration. The list of prohibited relationships for these offences is narrower than in s. 27, and covers only certain blood relationships. The perpetrator must, for the purpose of these offences, be at least 16 years old, and the other party to the activity in question must be at least 18 years old. [BF]

inchoate Incomplete. In criminal law, an inchoate offence is one where the accused has taken sufficient steps towards the commission of the complete offence for that conduct in itself to warrant prosecution. Examples of inchoate offences include ATTEMPT and CONSPIRACY to commit an offence, such as attempted theft, or conspiracy to murder. [JW]

incitement to racial hatred Part III of the Public Order Act 1986 sets out a number of offences involving RACIAL HATRED. The basic offence, in s. 18, is committed by a person who uses any threatening, abusive or insulting words or behaviour, or who displays any threatening, abusive or insulting written material, intending to stir up racial hatred, or in circumstances where the stirring up of racial hatred is likely. [BF]

Incorporated Council of Law Reporting

(ICLR) Established in 1865 as the 'Council for Law Reporting' by the INNS OF COURT and LAW SOCIETY, it was incorporated in 1870 with the object of 'the preparation and publication, in a convenient form, at a moderate price, and under gratuitous Professional control, of [The Law] Reports of Judicial Decisions of the Superior and Appellate Courts in England'. Reports produced by the Council are fully authorized and judgments reported by the Council should normally be cited in preference to any other series (see *Practice Direction (Judgments: Form and Citation) (Supreme Court)* [2001] 1 WLR 194). There are three main reporting series operated by the Incorporated Council: the *Law Reports*, the *Weekly Law Reports* and the *Industrial Cases Reports*. The Council is comprised of members nominated by each of the four Inns of Court and by the General Council of the Bar. The ATTORNEY GENERAL and the SOLICITOR-GENERAL and the President of the Law Society are ex officio members. An executive committee sits once or twice a year and the full council meets only once a year. For further information see the ICLR website http://www. lawreports.co.uk/index.htm.   [AF]

incorporation doctrine   A doctrine which states that provisions of INTERNATIONAL LAW are automatically adopted and enforceable in a state in so far as they are consistent with the provisions of its domestic (i.e. national) law. The incorporation doctrine is the counterpart of a monist theory of international law. English law, by contrast, tends to operate according to an assumption of DUALISM.   [IB]

See also MONISM; TRANSFORMATION DOCTRINE.

incorporation of terms   Terms must have been incorporated into the CONTRACT in order to give rise to binding contractual obligations. Terms may be incorporated as a result of signature on a written document containing them; where reasonable notice of the existence of the term was given before or at the time of contracting; where the term formed part of a previous consistent course of dealing between the parties; or on the basis of the common understanding of the parties. Where notice

is relied on as the means of incorporating the term, the requirement is generally that reasonable notice must be given of the existence of the term to people in general. However, if the term is an ONEROUS OR UNUSUAL CLAUSE, a higher standard of incorporation is required and the term must fairly and reasonably be brought to the other party's attention.   [JPL]

incorporeal hereditaments   Intangible rights relating to property forming part of an ESTATE which, historically, could be inherited. Examples include EASEMENTS, PROFITS À PRENDRE and RENTCHARGES.   [DR]

See also CORPOREAL HEREDITAMENTS; HEREDITAMENTS.

incriminate   To make it appear more likely that a person has committed an offence; properly used in respect of a piece of EVIDENCE, whether in the form of WITNESS testimony, an object, or other item of admissible evidence which has that effect.   [BF]

See also ADMISSIBILITY; PRIVILEGE AGAINST SELF-INCRIMINATION.

indecency   An element in a number of SEXUAL OFFENCES (e.g. INDECENT ASSAULT). It is not, however, an element of the sexual offences now contained in the Sexual Offences Act 2003, which require that behaviour be 'sexual' rather than indecent. For the purposes of a number of offences under the law prior to the 2003 Act, indecency had to be 'gross'. It is not absolutely clear where the boundary between indecency and gross indecency was to be drawn, but it has been suggested that the location of the boundary would depend in part on the social mores of the day (see J.C. Smith, *Smith and Hogan, Criminal Law*, 9th edn (London: Butterworths, 1999), at p. 484).

Indecency remains an element of a number of offences, including those relating to indecent photographs and pseudo-photographs under the Protection of Children Act 1978, s. 1, and under the Criminal Justice Act 1988, s. 160.   [BF]

indecent assault (obsolete)   The Sexual Offences Act 1956, ss. 14 and 15, set out, respectively, offences of indecent assault on a woman, and indecent assault on a man. According to the House of Lords in *R* v. *Court* [1989] AC 28, an assault was indecent if (a) it was unambiguously indecent, regardless of the purpose of the defendant, or (b) in cases where the circumstances of the assault were ambiguous, if the defendant had an indecent purpose. The offences of indecent assault have been replaced by offences under the Sexual Offences Act 2003, including the offence of SEXUAL ASSAULT. [BF]

indecent exposure (obsolete) The term was commonly used in the context of two statutory offences: under the Vagrancy Act 1824, s. 4 (now replaced), which 'deemed a rogue and vagabond' a defendant who 'wilfully, openly, lewdly and obscenely expos-[ed] his person with intent to insult any female'; also under the Town Police Clauses Act 1847, s. 28, it was an offence for someone to 'wilfully and indecently expose his person' ('person' in these contexts meant 'penis'). A new gender-neutral offence of **exposure** (without the use of the label 'indecent') has been created by the Sexual Offences Act 2003, s. 66, and is committed by a person who intentionally exposes his or her genitals and intends that someone will see them and be caused alarm or distress. [BF]

See also VOYEURISM.

indemnity 1. An agreement by one party to pay another for any loss which that other party may suffer during the performance of a CONTRACT. Such an obligation may be incorporated into a written contract in the form of an **indemnity clause**. As a matter of general practice, there is no legal objection to the use of such clauses, though for public policy reasons the courts will tend to interpret them narrowly, in much the same way as EXEMPTION CLAUSES (see *Smith* v. *South Wales Switchgear Ltd* [1978] 1 WLR 165). Under the Unfair Contract Terms Act 1977, s. 4, a consumer cannot be made to indemnify another for their breach of contract or negligence if this would be unreasonable.

2. An order of RESCISSION may be accompanied by an indemnity. The aim of an indemnity is to restore the parties to their pre-contractual positions by requiring the misrepresentor to cover expenses incurred by the misrepresentee as a result of the obligations created by the contract which was induced by the MISREPRESENTATION (*Whittington* v. *Seale-Hayne* (1900) 82 LT 49). An indemnity is different to a DAMAGES award. It is most likely to be of relevance where damages are not available, for example because the court refused to exercise its discretion to award damages in the place of rescission under the Misrepresentation Act 1967, s. 2(2) despite the fact it was an INNOCENT MISREPRESENTATION. Normally such expenses would be recoverable as part of a damages award. [JPL]

indemnity basis *See* COSTS.

indemnity costs *See* COSTS.

indenture A DEED made between at least two living parties, usually used to transfer an ESTATE in land. Indentures are very rarely used in CONVEYANCING practice today. An indenture between two parties is written in duplicate on the same paper, then divided in two so that the ends of the documents are uniquely indented and can be fitted together to form a whole, thereby proving their authenticity. Under the Law of Property Act 1925, ss. 56 (2), 57, a deed does not need to be an indenture in order to have effect. [DR]

independence of the judiciary *See* JUDICIAL INDEPENDENCE.

independent advice A presumption of UNDUE INFLUENCE will arise where a transaction or gift raises the suspicion of undue influence in circumstances where either the transaction was between parties in a protected relationship, e.g. PARENT and CHILD or SOLICITOR and client, or between parties in an actual relationship of trust and confidence. The fact that the person who has contracted or the donor of the gift received the advice of an independent third party before deciding to CONTRACT or make the gift may rebut the presumption of undue influence by showing that the donor was not induced to contract as a result of the other's undue influence, but rather entered into it quite freely and with full knowledge of the nature of the transaction.

A lender (of a MORTGAGE) will also avoid being fixed with CONSTRUCTIVE NOTICE of the undue influence of a third party on the surety, and so lose its security, if the lender can establish that the surety received legal advice on the practical implications of the proposed transaction. In view of the cost implications, this advice does not need to be given by a different solicitor to that representing the third party (*Royal Bank of Scotland* v. *Etridge (No. 2)* [2002] 2 AC 773). [JPL]

independent contractor A WORKER who is not an EMPLOYEE and may be self-employed. [MJ]

See also CONTRACT OF EMPLOYMENT.

Independent Police Complaints Commission (IPCC) An independent, non-departmental public body, funded by the HOME OFFICE, which oversees the police complaints system. It was created by the Police Reform Act 2002 and became operational in April 2004; see http://www.ipcc.gov.uk. [SN]

independent trade union A TRADE UNION on the list maintained by the CERTIFICATION OFFICER may apply to that official for a certificate that it is independent. 'Independent' means not subject to the control of, or vulnerable to interference from, the employers, a group of employers or an employers' association: see the Trade Union and Labour Relations (Consolidation) Act 1992, s. 5. The certificate is, for all purposes, conclusive evidence of independence. Appeals lie to the EMPLOYMENT APPEAL TRIBUNAL against the grant, refusal to grant, or withdrawal of a certificate of independence. [MJ]

indictable offence Those offences which may be tried on INDICTMENT in the CROWN COURT. They are consequently more serious than SUMMARY OFFENCES. The category of indictable offences may be divided into offences triable on indictment only, and offences triable either way. Offences triable on indictment only are the most serious

offences, such as MURDER or RAPE, and must be tried in the Crown Court. Offences triable either way are in the middle of the range of seriousness, and include CRIMINAL DAMAGE up to a designated value, and ASSAULT occasioning ACTUAL BODILY HARM. These may be tried summarily or on indictment, depending on whether the magistrates accept jurisdiction to hear a case summarily, and on whether a defendant elects to be tried in the Crown Court. [BF]

indictment The document containing the formal charges against the accused on which he or she is to be arraigned at the beginning of a CROWN COURT trial. [SN]

indigenous peoples There is no legally binding definition of indigenous peoples in INTERNATIONAL LAW. In practical terms, the term typically encompasses communities with a deep historical continuity vis-à-vis particular territory which they inhabited well before colonization or invasion by other peoples. Indigenous peoples should, for all practical legal purposes, be distinguished from minorities, since they are treated distinctly in relevant legal instruments, particularly Article 27 of the INTERNATIONAL COVENANT ON CIVIL AND POLITICAL RIGHTS. Two binding instruments relating to indigenous peoples exist, though without defining their status. ILO Convention No. 107 is concerned with the protection and integration of indigenous peoples in the countries where they live; however, its strong integrationist stance has been criticized as paternalistic. ILO Convention 169, which partially revises Convention No. 107, imposes obligations on states to protect the recognized rights of indigenous peoples and to protect their social, cultural, religious and spiritual values. The UN General Assembly voted on 13 September to adopt the UN Declaration on the Rights of Indigenous Peoples. The Declaration is not a legally binding act, but sets standards for the treatment of indigenous people. It emphasizes the right of indigenous people to self-determination as well as outlining their rights to culture, language, health, education, employment and, more controversially, access to land and natural resources. [IB]

See also MINORITY RIGHTS.

indirect effect Also known as the duty of consistent interpretation. The principle of indirect effect was originally explained by the EUROPEAN COURT OF JUSTICE in Case 14/83 *Von Colson and Kamann* v. *Land Nordrhein-Westfalen* [1984] ECR 1891, and developed by Case C-106/89 *Marleasing SA* v. *La Comercial Internacional de Alimentacion SA* [1990] ECR I-4135. Under this doctrine, MEMBER STATE courts, where there is a possibility of a variety of interpretations and applications, are required to interpret and apply national laws in conformity with COMMUNITY LAW, even in circumstances where EUROPEAN COMMUNITY (EC) law is not directly effective (see DIRECT EFFECT). Indirect effect, direct effect and the FRANCOVICH PRINCIPLE are thus the three main ways of enforcing EC law through national courts. However, although these are all EC law concepts, unlike direct effect or the Francovich principle, the principle of indirect effect has also been extended to include matters under Pillar III EU, Police and Judicial Cooperation in Criminal Matters, by Case C-105/03, *Pupino* [2005] ECR I-5285. [MON]

See also DIRECTIVE; EUROPEAN UNION.

indirect evidence See CIRCUMSTANTIAL EVIDENCE.

individual responsibility See MINISTERIAL RESPONSIBILITY.

indivisible contract A CONTRACT where the parties' obligations are interdependent so that one party's complete and precise performance of its obligations must occur in order for the other's obligation to arise. For example, where construction work is to be performed for a lump sum payment on completion, the contractor will not be paid unless and until the work is completed. This strict principle has been mitigated by the doctrine of SUBSTANTIAL PERFORMANCE and by the fact that a recipient of a benefit of performance of the contract who voluntarily accepted that performance may be required to make a reasonable pay-ment for the value of that on the basis of a *QUANTUM MERUIT*. An indivisible contract is also sometimes called an **entire contract**. [JPL]

See also DIVISIBLE CONTRACT.

inductive reasoning A form of reasoning that takes us, by a process of INFERENCE, from a specific example or set of examples to a general conclusion. Inductive reasoning lies at the heart of the doctrine of PRECEDENT.

To give an example: in case (1) an oral conveyance of land from A to B was held to be invalid; in case (2) an oral conveyance of land from C to D was held to be invalid; in case (3) an oral conveyance of land from E to F was held to be invalid. So, it follows in case 4, other things being equal, that an oral conveyance of land from G to H will also be held invalid. The proviso here is important. Inductive reasoning can only ever give us a probable solution, not one that is logically inevitable. The closer the fit between the facts of case (4) and the earlier cases, the more confident we can be; likewise, the more cases we have that have been decided the same way, the more confident we can be. Indeed, this last point helps demonstrate that there are in fact two things going on when a court reasons inductively. One is widely referred to as **reasoning by analogy**, i.e. arguing that one situation is so like another that the same outcome should follow. Thus we might have a precedent in case 1, where the facts are A, B and C, and the court decides X. If we reason by analogy, we would say that in case 2, if the facts are again A, B and C, the court should decide X. Of course, if we were to have ten cases that showed the courts deciding X on facts A, B and C, then we would be a lot more confident that our conclusion X is 'correct' in the eleventh case (using 'correct' here in the sense of demonstrating consistency of reasoning). However, in this situation, we could actually go further and say that these ten cases do not just provide a high degree of confidence that case (11) should be decided the same way, they provide evidence for us to infer that *all* such cases should have the outcome X. In other words, more examples enable us to posit that a principle is being established (e.g. that all oral conveyances of land having certain characteristics are invalid). This is a process of what is properly called **ampliative induction** (i.e. it enables us to amplify the scope of our conclusion beyond the immediate case or situation). Moreover, once we have a sufficiently authoritative statement that a general rule has indeed been established, then the nature of the reasoning process changes again. Future applications of the rule, at least in clear cases, will involve DEDUCTIVE REASONING, not inductive. We are no longer making a fact-based analogy, but applying a clear rule to a known set of facts.

These distinctions are important in understanding the development of legal rules and principles. As the courts build up a body of case law over time, we see a set of increasingly refined principles and exceptions emerging through processes of applying, distinguishing and OVERRULING precedents. Thus, a case may come up where the facts are not A, B and C, but A, B and D, and the court decides that fact D makes a sufficient (in legal terms **material**) difference, so that the decision is Y, not X. This new decision therefore must modify our understanding of the principle involved; for example, the original principle that all oral conveyances of land are invalid may now have to be qualified in the light of a new case, e.g. to state that all oral conveyances of land are invalid, *except* those where the oral agreement is evidenced by the parties in writing.　　[JW]

industrial action This is the term used to denote STRIKES and action short of a strike such as sit-ins and go-slows. At COMMON LAW industrial action will amount to a BREACH OF CONTRACT, entitling the employers to dismiss for gross misconduct. However, those dismissed for taking part in lawful, official industrial action are protected in accordance with the Trade Union and Labour Relations (Consolidation) Act 1992, as amended, s. 238A.

The TRADE UNION and its individual members who take part in lawful industrial action are also protected from any action in TORT brought by the employers on the ground that it induces or threatens a breach of contract or interferes with the performance of a contract. However, **secondary industrial action** against an employer who is neither a party to the dispute, nor a supplier or customer of the employer in dispute, may be unlawful.　　[MJ]

industrial dispute *See* TRADE DISPUTE.

industrial tribunal (obsolete) *See* EMPLOYMENT TRIBUNALS.

ineffective trial On the trial date, if expected progress is not made because of action or inaction by one or more of the prosecution, the defence or the court, a further listing for trial is required.　　[SN]

inequality of bargaining power One party to a CONTRACT may have a dominant bargaining position over the other. Although this is not in itself a reason for setting aside a contract, it may lead to behaviour which amounts to taking advantage of that position so that the contract may be set aside for DURESS or UNDUE INFLUENCE. In a consumer CONTRACT, a term will be unfair if, contrary to the requirement of GOOD FAITH, it causes a significant imbalance in the parties' rights and obligations under the contract to the detriment of the consumer.　　[JPL]

infant In common usage, a baby or a young CHILD. While in some jurisdictions 'infant' is a legal term used to describe a person under the age of majority, in the UK the term 'child' is used for this purpose.　　[AD]

infanticide Under the Infanticide Act 1938, s. 1, where a woman, by any wilful act or omission, causes the death of her child under the age of 12 months, in circumstances which would normally amount to MURDER, but at the time of the killing the balance of her mind was disturbed by reason of the after-effects of giving birth, or by reason of the effect of lactation following the birth of the child, then she may raise infanticide as a defence to a charge of murder, or she may be tried directly for infanticide. A conviction for infanticide is treated as a conviction for MANSLAUGHTER, thus leaving the full range of sentencing options available. There are very few convictions for this offence. [BF]

inference The process of reaching a conclusion by reasoning from EVIDENCE. [ALTC]

inferences from accused's silence INFERENCES that the accused in a criminal case is guilty which may be drawn, in appropriate circumstances, from: (a) the accused's failure to mention facts when questioned or charged; (b) the accused's failure or refusal to account for objects, substances or marks; (c) the accused's failure or refusal to account for presence at a particular place; (d) one of a number of specified failures in relation to disclosure of evidence by the accused, or the fact that the accused at trial acts inconsistently in some way with the defence disclosure; or (e) the accused's silence at trial. [ALTC]

See also DISCLOSURE OF EVIDENCE IN CRIMINAL CASES.

informal admission An acknowledgement by a party of the existence of a particular fact that another party is asserting. Whereas a FORMAL ADMISSION abrogates the need for EVIDENCE to be introduced, an informal admission constitutes evidence which is introduced to prove a particular fact. [ALTC]

information The statement by which a MAGISTRATE is informed of the offence for which a SUMMONS or warrant is required. [SN]

Information Tribunal *See* FREEDOM OF INFORMATION.

infringement action In INTELLECTUAL PROPERTY matters, legal action taken to prevent unauthorized interference with the rights of the author, patentee, etc.

The basis on which an infringement action can be brought will depend on the nature of the right infringed. Broadly speaking, an infringement of a PATENT will occur when the subject matter claimed in a patent has been used, sold or disposed of without the owner's approval, or contrary to the terms of use. For COPYRIGHT or an unregistered DESIGN, infringement occurs if someone knowingly reproduces the writing, picture, or photograph, design etc. As regards a TRADE MARK, the registered owner may prohibit the unauthorized use of an identical or similar mark by another 'in the course of trade'. [US]

infringement proceedings A sub-group of ANNULMENT PROCEEDINGS under EUROPEAN COMMUNITY (EC) law. It is possible under Article 230 EC for a MEMBER STATE, the EUROPEAN PARLIAMENT, the COUNCIL OF MINISTERS or the **European Commission** to bring an action before the EUROPEAN COURT OF JUSTICE for SECONDARY LEGISLATION to be annulled or cancelled. Two of these causes of action are based on infringement, i.e. 'infringement of an essential procedural requirement' and 'infringement of this Treaty or of any rule of law relating to its application' (Article 230 EC). The COURT OF AUDITORS and the EUROPEAN CENTRAL BANK have limited rights to bring such actions, as does any individual or corporate body. [MON]

inhibition In the REGISTERED LAND system, an inhibition is an entry in the proprietorship section of the Land Register which prevents any dealings with the property, either generally or until the occurrence of a specified event. The Land Registration Act 2002 abolished inhibitions on 13 October 2003, although pre-existing inhibitions continue to have effect. Under the old system, governed by the Land Registration Act 1925, inhibitions were entered on the register by a court order or by a registrar at the Land Registry and were commonly used to prevent a bankrupt proprietor from disposing of his property in order to defraud his creditors. Since 13 October 2003, the purpose of an inhibition is achieved by the use of a RESTRICTION. [DR]

inhuman or degrading treatment Article 3 of the European Convention on Human Rights prohibits inhuman or degrading treatment or punishment. The rights protected by Article 3 are absolute. The distinction between torture and inhuman or degrading treatment lies primarily in the intensity and severity of the acts, and possibly also the intention of the perpetrator. To constitute inhuman treatment, the acts may be less severe than torture, but must still constitute a sufficiently serious attack on the physical, mental or psychological well-being of the victim. The boundaries of degrading treatment are probably the most significant in practice, and the most difficult to draw with any certainty, as actions complained of here may involve a more transitory effect on the victim, or constitute an affront to dignity rather than a more substantial attack on physical or psychological well-being. The jurisprudence of the European Court of Human Rights indicates that, while any form of arrest or detention may involve some element of humiliation, there is a threshold of unacceptable behaviour that must be crossed for Article 3 to apply. Handcuffing of prisoners, for example, is not, by itself, a violation of the Convention (see *Raninen* v. *Finland* (1998) 26 EHRR 563), whereas strip-searching, under certain conditions, may well constitute degrading treatment (see *Frerot* v. *France* [2007] ECHR Application No. 70204/01 (12 June 2007)). Whether or not an act is degrading will usually depend on all the circumstances of the case, including the nature and duration of the acts complained of, and the level of suffering of the individual victim. However, the Court may treat certain actions as fundamentally degrading in all their forms, and hence unlawful *per se*, in which case such boundary questions will not arise. Thus in *Tyrer* v. *United Kingdom* (1978) 2 EHRR 1, the judicial use of corporal punishment was regarded as a form of institutionalized violence and inherently in breach of Article 3.   [JW]

injunction An equitable remedy granted by a court in order to restrain a claimant from either doing or continuing an act complained of, or to prevent him continuing an omission. There are a number of different types of injunction: **prohibitory**, to prevent the continuation of a wrongful act or omission; **mandatory**, compelling the defendant to complete or carry out some

act; **interlocutory**, granted to maintain the status quo before a trial can take place; **interim**, to restrain the defendant from continuing his act or omission until a specific date; **perpetual**, granted to a successful claimant at completion of proceedings; *quia timet* (Lat. because he fears), granted when the claimant fears some very substantial or irreparable harm is about to befall him.   [HJ]

Inland Revenue (obsolete) The former government department, correctly known as Her Majesty's Commissioners of Inland Revenue, which had responsibility for the care and management of direct taxes in the United Kingdom, mainly comprising income tax, CAPITAL GAINS TAX and inheritance tax. The responsibilities of the department were, among many others, to assess and collect the direct taxes and to counteract attempts at evasion and avoidance of those taxes, for example, by taxpayers operating in the hidden, or black economy. The department operated through local offices dealing with income tax and capital gains tax returns, and through specialist offices such as the Shares Valuation Division and the Capital Taxes Office. All the functions of the department are now vested in HM REVENUE AND CUSTOMS.   [RE]

Inland Revenue Commissioners *See* COMMISSIONERS OF REVENUE AND CUSTOMS.

Inner London Family Proceedings Court A magistrates' court which operates as a specialist family court.   [FK]
   See also CARE CENTRE.

innocent dissemination *See* DEFAMATION.

innocent misrepresentation A false statement of fact which induces a CONTRACT but which was made honestly and with reasonable grounds for believing the statement to be true. RESCISSION may be too drastic a remedy in the case of innocent misrepresentation, so the court may decide to exercise its discretion under the Misrepresentation Act 1967, s. 2(2), and award DAMAGES instead of rescission. If a contract is rescinded for innocent misrepresentation, the court may also order an INDEMNITY as damages will not be available. [JPL]

innocent passage The right of navigation through another state's TERRITORIAL WATERS for the purpose of traversing that sea without entering INTERNAL WATERS or calling at a road or port facility outside internal waters. Passage is deemed to be innocent where it is not prejudicial to the peace, good order or security of the coastal STATE. Passage must always be continuous and expeditious, although a ship may stop and anchor in so far as this is incidental to its ordinary navigation, or if forced to do so as a matter of FORCE MAJEURE, or distress, or for the purpose of rendering assistance to other ships, aircraft or persons under distress (UNITED NATIONS CONVENTION ON THE LAWS OF THE SEA (UNCLOS), Article 18(2)). The regime of innocent passage also applies to passage through international straits (UNCLOS, Article 45). [IB]

innominate term A contractual term which is neither a CONDITION nor a WARRANTY. It is a type of term which is capable of being broken in many different ways, not all of which may be serious (*Hong Kong Fir Shipping Co. Ltd* v. *Kawasaki Kisen Kaisha Ltd* [1962] 2 QB 26). Consequently, the legal implications of a breach of an innominate term are determined by how serious the effects of the breach are. Where the consequences of the breach are serious, in that they deprive the injured party of substantially the whole benefit of the CONTRACT, it will be treated as a repudiatory breach (see REPUDIATION). If this is the case, the injured party will have the option to terminate or affirm the contract, in addition to the right to claim DAMAGES. If the effects of the breach are not serious, the injured party will be limited to a remedy in damages only. Innominate terms are also known as **intermediate terms** to indicate that they fall somewhere between the condition and the warranty in terms of seriousness and effect. [JPL]

Inns of Chancery (obsolete) Unincorporated societies of lawyers, smaller than the INNS OF COURT, whose origins probably lay in the households of the medieval Masters in Chancery. As the Inns of Court became more exclusively the preserve of the Bar during the 17th century, the Inns of Chancery became the home of attorneys and solicitors. However, unlike the Inns of Court, membership of these Inns did not provide their apprentices with a licence to practice and by the end of the 17th century, their educational role had largely ceased. The last surviving Inn of Chancery (Clifford's Inn) was abolished in 1903. [JW]

Inns of Court Unincorporated associations of lawyers established in London in the mid-14th century. Historically the Inns provided both accommodation and legal training for all lawyers, but from the 16th century they began to exclude attorneys and solicitors, becoming exclusively responsible for the training and discipline of barristers. The four Inns of Court are: Lincoln's Inn, Inner Temple, Middle Temple and Gray's Inn. The Inns still call qualified members to the Bar, and organize continuing education and social activities for their members. [JW]

inquest A formal inquiry, conducted by a CORONER, into the facts surrounding a death, the cause of which is unknown. An inquest will be held where the deceased has died suddenly or unnaturally, violently, in prison, or under suspicious circumstances. It is not a criminal trial to determine who is to blame for the death, but an investigation to determine 'who has died and how, when and where they came by their death, together with information needed by the registrar of deaths, so that the death can be registered'. (A leaflet is available from the DirectGov website at http://www.direct.gov.uk/en/Governmentcitizensand rights/Death/WhatToDoAfterADeath/ D6_066713.) If a person is charged with causing the death of the deceased or criminal proceedings are likely, the inquest will be adjourned until the person's trial is over. The Coroner will, before adjourning, find out who the deceased was and how he or she died in order to allow the death to be registered. Any other court proceedings will normally follow the inquest. Most inquests are held without a jury; however, under the Coroners Act 1988, s. 8(2), a coroner has the duty to summon a jury of 7 to 11 persons if the death occurred in prison or in police custody or if the death resulted from an incident at work. If a jury is called, it is the jury who make the final decision. During the inquest, the Coroner can call on all witnesses he or she thinks have relevant information pertaining to the inquiry. The Coroner is the first to question the witnesses, and anyone who has 'a proper interest' (e.g. a parent, sibling, spouse, insurer or beneficiary of a life insurance policy) may question the witnesses afterwards. Reforms to the inquest procedure are anticipated in the Coroners and Justice Bill (2008–09). [AF]

inquiry 1. In English law, the term inquiry refers to a range of activities. It is commonly used to refer to a **public inquiry**, usually set up by a Minister to examine some matter of public concern. These may take a number of forms. Ministers may use their executive powers to establish an ad hoc non-statutory inquiry, without formal powers, for example the Hutton Inquiry into the death of government weapons' expert Dr David Kelly. These in turn may sometimes be referred to as judicial inquiries where a senior judge is appointed to lead the inquiry, but that term is purely descriptive and has no special legal status or significance.

An inquiry may also be established and conducted by a committee of Privy Councillors. The 2004 Butler Inquiry which reviewed the controversial intelligence on weapons of mass destruction in Iraq was of this type. Other public inquiries with full powers to hear evidence and call witnesses may be established under general statutory authority, now contained in the Inquiries Act 2005, which consolidated and updated inquiries legislation, and came into force on 7 June 2005. It is notable, however, that the majority of public inquiries since 1900 have been ad hoc rather than statutory. The term inquiry is also widely used to describe other statutory or regulatory procedures which are not public inquiries in the same sense, such as planning inquiries,

or inquiries into accidents by regulatory bodies such as the Health and Safety Executive or the Civil Aviation Authority.

2. In INTERNATIONAL LAW, inquiry refers to the establishment of an impartial and independent commission of inquiry which, without possessing a judicial character, acts as a fact-finding mission that can represent its findings to the parties to a dispute. Examples of treaties providing for commissions of inquiry include the Taft treaties which the USA concluded in the 1900s with Britain and France, and the 1914 Bryan treaties that created permanent commissions of inquiry between the USA and Central and South American states.

[JW & IB]

See also CONCILIATION; HEALTH AND SAFETY COMMISSION; INQUIRY PANEL; PRIVY COUNCIL; TREATY.

inquiry panel A formal independent panel appointed to undertake an INQUIRY under the Inquiries Act 2005. By s. 3 of the 2005 Act, a panel may comprise a single chairman, or a chairman appointed with another member, or members. [JW]

inquisitorial procedure In COMMON LAW legal systems this term is often used to describe the adoption by a court or, more commonly, by a TRIBUNAL of a style of proceeding similar to that used in an INQUISITORIAL SYSTEM. Examples within the English legal system would be the procedure commonly employed in respect of small claims in the COUNTY COURT, or the relatively informal process adopted in hearing certain social security appeals. [JW]

inquisitorial system A legal system where the court is actively involved in determining the facts of the case, as opposed to an ADVERSARIAL SYSTEM where the role of the court is primarily to be a neutral umpire between the parties. The presiding judge, or sometimes a separate investigating judge, in an inquisitorial process is responsible for supervising the search for and gathering of evidence necessary to resolve the case, and will question witnesses directly. Advocates by contrast tend to have a less active role in the process than in an adversarial system. The adoption of an inquisitorial approach is commonly a feature of countries within the CIVIL LAW traditions of Western Europe and Latin America. [JW]

See also COMMON LAW; INQUISITORIAL PROCEDURE.

insanity A GENERAL DEFENCE, which is set out in the so-called **M'Naghten Rules** (see *M'Naghten* [1843–60] All ER Rep 229). The rules require that the defendant, at the time of committing the act in question, was 'labouring under such a defect of reason, from disease of the mind, as not to know the nature and quality of the act he was doing; or, if he did know it, that he did not know he was doing what was wrong'.

A disease of the mind has been interpreted to mean a disease which affects the functioning of the mind, and which can include, for example, diabetes and epilepsy (see *R* v. *Hennessy* (1989) 89 Cr App Rep 10; *R* v. *Sullivan* [1984] AC 156). A defendant who is deemed to meet the *M'Naghten* criteria will receive a special verdict of not guilty by reason of insanity and may be subject to compulsory detention. Accordingly, a defendant may attempt to plead AUTOMATISM instead, which will lead to a complete acquittal. The cause of the defendant's condition is thus crucial. If the cause is external, for example, a blow to the head, rather than a disease of the mind, then the proper defence will be automatism. The definition of insanity is not a medical one, and there may be an issue of compatibility with Article 5 of the EUROPEAN CONVENTION ON HUMAN RIGHTS (the RIGHT TO LIBERTY), which, according to *Winterwerp* v. *Netherlands* (1979) 2 EHRR 387, requires 'objective medical expertise' before those of unsound mind can be lawfully detained. [BF]

See also PRESUMPTION OF SANITY.

insider dealing Where a person uses unpublished price-sensitive information, which they have obtained by virtue of their access as an 'insider' in a business, for purposes of gain. Insider dealing constitutes a criminal offence under Part V of the Criminal Justice Act 1993, where the person who has information obtained as an insider (a) deals in price-sensitive securities; or (b) encourages another to deal in price-sensitive securities; or (c) discloses inside information to another. [JW]

insolvency An umbrella term that is used to encompass the law on individual voluntary arrangements, BANKRUPTCY (called **individual insolvency** in Scotland) and company LIQUIDATION and receivership. [JW]

institutional arbitration Also called administered arbitration, it requires a supervising institution, of a permanent character, which provides its own rules for the resolution of disputes and exerts a high level of administrative and quality control over the arbitral process. It is distinguished from AD HOC ARBITRATION, which is largely managed by the parties to the individual dispute.

In institutional arbitration, the arbitral institution does not involve itself in the arbitration process; that remains a matter for the ARBITRATOR, operating within the rules of the institution (for this reason it is not appropriate to refer to these bodies as *arbitration* institutions). The arbitrator will normally be appointed by the parties from a panel of institutionally recognized arbitrators, though it is also possible for the parties to request that the institution itself selects an arbitrator or arbitrators.

Arbitral institutions will charge fees for their services and facilities; this can make institutional arbitration more expensive than ad hoc arbitration in some, but by no means all cases. This may be considered justified by the level of support that good arbitral institutions can provide, and the fact that they tend to have a proven track record of arbitrations. There are, however, numerous national and international arbitral institutions, of varying quality, and care needs to be taken in the selection.

Well-established institutions include the International Court of Arbitration, operated by the INTERNATIONAL CHAMBER OF COMMERCE in Paris, the LONDON COURT OF INTERNATIONAL ARBITRATION and the national arbitration forum in the USA. [JW]

institutional constructive trust *See* CON-STRUCTIVE TRUST.

institutional writings The name given to certain texts by Scottish legal writers, which may be regarded as influential by the Scottish courts and even as potential sources of law in certain circumstances.

The diversity of, and lack of uniformity among, sources of law in Scotland up to the mid-17th century prompted some writers to attempt a more systematic approach inspired by the codification of Roman law. In the absence of any more authoritative statement of the law on a given issue, the Scottish courts came to accord these institutional writings the status of sources of law. Among the principal institutional writings are James Dalrymple, Viscount of Stair's *Institutions of the Laws of Scotland,* published in 1681, and David Hume's *Commentaries on the Law of Scotland Respecting Crimes,* published in 1797.

The status of institutional writing depends upon judicial recognition as such. While there is sometimes reference to institutional *writers,* it is important to recognize that not every text by such a writer enjoys institutional status.   [JP]

See also SCOTS LAW.

insulting behaviour Insulting behaviour is an element of the offences under s. 4 (causing fear of or provoking violence), s. 4A (intentionally causing harassment, alarm or distress) and s. 5 (causing harassment, alarm or distress) of the Public Order Act 1986. Whether behaviour is insulting is a question of fact. Thus, Lord Kilbrandon suggested in *Brutus* v. *Cozens* [1973] AC 854, at 866–867, that 'It would be unwise, in my opinion, to attempt to lay down any positive rules for the recognition of insulting behaviour as such, since the circumstances in which the application of the rules would be called for are almost infinitely variable; the most that can be done is to lay down limits … in order to ensure that the statute is not interpreted more widely than its terms will bear.'   [BF]

intellectual property Intellectual property encompasses four main types of rights:

(a) PATENT law, which gives temporary protection to technological inventions; (b) DESIGN rights, which protect the appearance of mass-produced goods; (c) COPYRIGHT, which gives rights in literary, dramatic, artistic and musical creations, as well as film, satellite, broadcast and sound recordings; and (d) TRADE MARK law, which protects any signs used in trade. It is intangible property, with no physical existence, but none the less with a separate and distinct existence from the physical goods within which the intellectual property resides. More than one type of intellectual property right may reside in the same creation or product.
                                                                                   [US]

Further reading: William R. Cornish, *Intellectual Property: Omnipresent, Distracting, Irrelevant?* (Oxford: Oxford University Press, 2004).

intention The most blameworthy form of MENS REA: criminal law recognizes two forms of intention. The first corresponds to the everyday usage of the term, and relates to the defendant's purpose or MOTIVE when acting: this is referred to as **direct** intention. The second refers to what the defendant understands will follow from his or her actions and is known as **oblique** or **indirect** intention.

Generally, the law does not differentiate between these forms of intention, so that if the definition of a crime requires that a person intends a particular consequence, proof of either direct or oblique intention will be acceptable. However, there are some crimes where only the purposive, direct form of intention will suffice. Thus, in *R* v. *Steane* [1947] KB 997, the defendant was charged with an offence under wartime regulations of 'doing an act likely to assist the enemy with intent to assist the enemy'. He had broadcast propaganda messages for Germany during the Second World War, under threats to himself and his family. It was held that he lacked the necessary intention for the offence. He must have known that his actions would have assisted the enemy and accordingly he would have had an oblique intention so to do. The success of his appeal demonstrates that only proof of direct intention would support a finding that that particular offence had been committed. (A competing interpretation of the decision in *Steane* is that it should have been held that he did intend to assist the enemy, but that he should have been able to benefit from the DEFENCE of DURESS.)

The development of the law on oblique or indirect intention has been closely linked with the development of the law on homicide, particularly the offence of MURDER, although, as noted above, this form of intention can be taken, by and large, to apply across the full range of relevant offences. If X's purpose is to shoot Y who, as X can see, is standing behind a window, then X's direct intention is to shoot Y. However, we may also say that he has an oblique intention to break the window, because he knows that this will happen as a consequence of his actions. In *R* v. *Moloney* [1985] AC 905, Lord Bridge gave the following helpful illustration (at 926): 'A man who, at London Airport, boards a plane which he knows to be bound for Manchester, clearly intends to travel to Manchester, even though Manchester is the last place he wants to be and his motive for boarding the plane is simply to escape pursuit.'

The courts have been keen to distinguish between the substantive concepts of foresight and intention. However, the approach that has been developed has been to use foresight as evidence of the existence of oblique intention. The key question has therefore been the degree of probability with which a consequence must be foreseen before it is legitimate to infer the existence of oblique intention. This issue was considered in *Moloney* (above); *R* v. *Hancock and Shankland* [1986] 1 All ER 641; *R* v. *Nedrick* (1986) 83 Cr App R 267; and more recently by the House of Lords in *R* v. *Woollin* [1999] 1 Cr App R 8, in which Lord Steyn (at 20) broadly endorsed the position taken in *Nedrick*: 'Where the charge is murder and in the rare cases where the simple direction [on the meaning of direct intention] is not enough, the jury should be directed that

they are not entitled to infer the necessary intention, unless they feel sure that death or serious bodily harm was a virtual certainty (barring some unforeseen intervention) as a result of the defendant's actions and that the defendant appreciated that such was the case.'

Lord Steyn took the view that 'find' was a more appropriate verb than 'infer'. Accordingly, a jury may not find the existence of intention to bring about consequence X unless they take the view that the defendant appreciated that consequence X was a virtually certain to follow his or her actions.

It appears to follow, curiously, that *oblique intention*, one of the most fundamental concepts in criminal law, has only an evidential, rather than a substantive definition. There is no articulation in the law of what an oblique intention is; rather, there is merely guidance as to the type of evidence which needs to exist before a court can find, from that evidence, the existence of such an intention, a position which was reinforced in *R* v. *Matthews and Alleyne* [2003] 2 Cr App R 30.   [BF]

See also BASIC INTENT; RECKLESSNESS; SPECIFIC INTENT; ULTERIOR INTENT.

Further reading: R. Antony Duff, *Intention, Agency and Criminal Liability: Philosophy of Action and the Criminal Law* (Oxford: Blackwell, 1990); Antje Pedain, 'Intention and the Terrorist Example', (2003), *Crim. L.R.*, pp. 579–593; Andrew Simester, 'Moral Certainty and the Boundaries of Intention', *Oxford Journal of Legal Studies* (1996), 16, pp. 445–469.

intention of the testator *See* ANIMUS TESTANDI.

intention to create legal relations An intention to be legally bound by an AGREEMENT so that its PROMISES are enforceable before the courts. It is a requirement for the legal enforceability of any agreement. There is a presumption that those making domestic or social agreements have no intention to be legally bound and that, by comparison, those entering into commercial agreements do intend to be legally bound. It is possible to rebut both presumptions by establishing clear evidence to the contrary, e.g. if the agreement contains an HONOUR CLAUSE stating that the parties intend to be bound in honour only and that the agreement is not to be enforceable in the courts. [JPL]

intentionality Under the Housing Act 1996, LOCAL HOUSING AUTHORITIES do not have to provide accommodation to HOMELESS PERSONS who have become homeless intentionally. The definition of intentionality is complex and has led to extensive litigation. It requires that the applicant has had accommodation which it would have been reasonable to continue to occupy, and by some deliberate act has lost it. The same criteria apply to threatened homelessness. The key to understanding intentionality is that the homelessness must result from a deliberate act of the applicant. So, for instance, a person in rent or mortgage arrears as a result of their careless financial management, who then loses their home, is homeless intentionally, whereas the person whose arrears arose from genuine and unforeseen difficulties will be unintentionally homeless. It can be a fine dividing line: in *R* v. *Exeter City Council, ex parte Trankle* (1993) 26 HLR 244, the applicants had lost their home by securing a loan to run a pub. It was held that they had acted unwisely, but in good faith, so their homelessness was not intentional. It is the housing department, subject to review and appeals procedures, which makes the decisions. It should give applicants an opportunity to explain their behaviour. [HC & DR]

See also LOCAL CONNECTION.

interdict A remedy in SCOTS LAW whereby one party seeks to prevent the other from doing something; for example, in breach of contract a pursuer may seek to enforce a negative obligation, that is, to prevent the defender from doing something that he or she agreed not to do. Where a decree of interdict is awarded, any wilful breach of its terms constitutes contempt of court. Due to the nature of the cases where an interdict may be sought (for example, in a family law context), it is possible for one to be awarded very rapidly by the court on an interim basis. [JP]

See also SPECIFIC IMPLEMENT.

interest 1. An entitlement or expectation based upon a legal (including equitable) right.

2. An amount to be paid as a charge for borrowing an initial sum of money (called the principal, or principal debt). Where the rate of interest on a debt is excessive, this may constitute evidence of an UNFAIR RELATIONSHIP between the creditor and the debtor.

3. An additional amount that may be claimed on both 'post-judgment' and 'pre-judgment' debts or damages as part of civil proceedings. Pre-judgment here refers to the interest awarded from the day payment fell due until judgment is entered or payment made (whichever is the earlier event). The rules on payment of interest pre-judgment are relatively complex and vary between CONSUMER and commercial debts and personal injury claims. Recommendations to simplify the system were put forward by the Law Commission in their report, *Pre-Judgment Interest on Debts and Damages* (Law Commission No. 287), 2004. Interest on consumer claims is currently at a set rate of 8%, calculated as simple rather than compound interest. Commercial claims are governed by the statutory rules on LATE PAYMENT COMPENSATION, which operates a variable but higher rate of interest. For personal injury claims, GENERAL DAMAGES attract 2% simple interest from the date that the claim is served; pecuniary damages carry simple interest at a variable rate, and no interest can be claimed on future losses. Different interest rates may also apply where the CONTRACT specifies the rate of interest, for example for a loan, credit card debt or MORTGAGE, and most such agreements compound the interest. Interest may also be claimed in respect of periods for which a sum remains outstanding after judgment. The rules on calculating post-judgment interest are contained in the Judgments Act 1838, s. 17. [JW]

interest in expectancy A future interest in property. [DR]

interest in land A right in, over or relating to land. Under the Law of Property Act 1925, s. 1(1)–(3), interests in land are divided into LEGAL ESTATES, legal interests and EQUITABLE INTERESTS; for example, where a FREEHOLD property is owned by X and Y, on trust for Y and Z as tenants in common, all three individuals have different interests in the land. X is the co-owner of the legal estate and a TRUSTEE of the land. Y is the co-owner of the legal estate, a trustee of the land and as one of the tenants in common is the owner of an equitable interest in the property. Z is one of the tenants in common and owns an equitable interest in the property. If a MORTGAGE was used to raise funds to buy the property, the mortgage lender will also have a legal interest in the land. [DR]

See also TENANCY IN COMMON.

interest theory One of the two principal theories of rights (the other being WILL THEORY) which claims that the statement 'A has the right to do R' means that certain *interests* of A as the rights holder are protected by law. This contrasts with will theory, in which what is protected is A's *choice* whether or not to do R. Associated in particular with Neil MacCormick, interest theory is critical of will theory on two main grounds. First of all, it is concerned with will theory's position that the essence of A's right is his ability to waive B's correlative duty: it is an observable fact that in certain cases (for example, in contract law) the law prohibits A's waiver of B's duties without thereby removing A's rights. Secondly, complications arise for will theory in cases such as children's rights where someone other than the rights holder exercises the right: applying will theory's analysis, the fact that the parent can choose whether or not to exercise the right would essentially deprive the child of any rights. [JP]

interfering with motor vehicles It is an offence under the Criminal Attempts Act 1981, s. 9, for a person to interfere with a MOTOR VEHICLE or trailer or with anything carried in or on it, with the intention of committing the offence of THEFT of the vehicle, theft of anything carried in or on the vehicle, or taking a CONVEYANCE without authority.

Under the Road Traffic Act 1988, s. 22A, it is an offence for a person, intentionally and without lawful authority or reasonable cause, to interfere with a motor vehicle, trailer or cycle, to interfere with traffic equipment (signs, barriers, lights etc.) or to cause anything to be on or over a road, in circumstances where it would be obvious to a reasonable person that to do so would be dangerous. 'Dangerous' refers to the danger of injury to any person on or near a road, or serious damage to property on or near a road. [BF]

See also TAKING WITHOUT CONSENT.

interim accommodation Interim accommodation is accommodation offered by a LOCAL HOUSING AUTHORITY to a statutorily HOMELESS PERSON pending an offer of permanent accommodation. There is no right to review the suitability of interim accommodation. [HC & DR]

interim application *See* APPLICATION.

interim injunction *See* INJUNCTION.

interim measures *See* PROVISIONAL MEASURES.

interim relief A temporary order granted by a court to preserve the status quo until a civil or PUBLIC LAW matter can come to trial. The following orders can be made on an interim basis: a DECLARATION, an INJUNCTION, and a STAY of proceedings. [JW]

interim rent Following the amendment of the Landlord and Tenant Act 1954 by the Regulatory Reform (Business Tenancies) (England and Wales) Order 2003, either a LANDLORD or a TENANT of business PREMISES can apply to the court to fix an interim rent which is payable pending either the termination of the LEASE following service of a notice to quit or the agreement of a new TENANCY. The tenant is most likely to apply when the commercial market is falling; the landlord when it is rising. [HC & DR]

interlocutory injunction *See* INJUNCTION.

internal waters All waters on the landward side of the BASELINE of the TERRITORIAL

WATERS. This includes river mouths, deltas, sea areas behind the baselines and others. Coastal STATES enjoy absolute criminal jurisdiction in internal waters, unlike the territorial sea. Equally, the right of INNOCENT PASSAGE does not generally extend to internal waters, except that where the establishment of a straight baseline has the effect of enclosing as internal waters areas which had not previously been considered as such, a right of innocent passage shall exist in those waters (UN Convention on the Law of the Sea, Article 8).   [IB]

international arbitration   An arbitral process in which the disputing parties are sovereign STATES or other subjects of INTERNATIONAL LAW. It is an arbitral process which is neither a DOMESTIC ARBITRATION, nor a COMMERCIAL ARBITRATION, nor an international commercial arbitration.   [RE]

See also ARBITRATION; PERMANENT COURT OF ARBITRATION.

International Bank for Reconstruction and Development (IBRD)   Also known as the World Bank, the IBRD was established in 1944 through a multilateral treaty. Membership requires membership of the International Monetary Fund (IMF). According to Article I of its Articles of Agreement, the World Bank's purpose is to assist in the reconstruction and development of countries by facilitating the investment of capital for productive purposes; to promote foreign direct investment through guarantees or participation in loans; to supplement private investment; to promote growth of international trade and foreign investment; to arrange loans, facilitate them or guarantee them. Since 1944 the World Bank has established new institutions under its auspices, all of which are now part of the World Bank Group, sharing objectives, policies and personnel: the International Finance Corporation (IFC), the International Development Association (IDA), the International Centre for the Settlement of Investment Disputes (ICSID) and the Multilateral Investment Guarantee Agency (MIGA). The Bank is also a trustee and administrator of trust funds established by states or international organizations to deal with development, reconstruction, health and other issues.

[IB]

International Chamber of Commerce   A non-profit-making, private association founded in France in 1919 by French, Belgian, American and British businessmen with a view to facilitating a process of harmonization of international trade and commerce. It has been responsible for a wide range of commercial innovations such as the Incoterms rules; the ATA Carnet customs clearance system; and codes of conduct for multinational corporations, for example in relation to environmental and taxation issues. It has members in over 150 countries, and there are national committees in over 60 of these countries. The principal governing organ is the ICC Council, the members of which are elected by the national committees. The Secretariat is based in Paris, and there is also an office of the Secretariat in Hong Kong.

Its work in relation to important issues in international trade and commerce is augmented by cooperating with the UNITED NATIONS and other international bodies. In particular, it has been a major player in the development of modern international commercial arbitration. It was involved in the early stages of the Geneva Protocol on Arbitration Clauses 1923, and the Geneva Convention on the Execution of Foreign Arbitral Awards 1927. Its 1953 Report and Preliminary Draft Convention on international arbitral awards prompted the ECONOMIC AND SOCIAL COUNCIL of the United Nations to draft its own convention on arbitration agreements and awards. The two draft conventions were considered at the conference in New York in 1958 at which a compromise third draft convention was agreed and adopted as the New York Convention 1958.   [RE]

See also ARBITRATION; ARBITRATION AGREEMENT; AWARD.

international child abduction   The taking of a CHILD from one jurisdiction to another and keeping it there without the consent of, and in contravention of the rights of, the person(s) with CUSTODY and

ACCESS. It is defined as the wrongful removal or retention of a child (Hague Convention on Civil Aspects of International Child Abduction 1980, Articles 1 and 3). In addition to the Hague Convention, there are other international conventions designed to secure the return of the child.

It is also an offence under the law of England and Wales for a person connected with a child, such as a PARENT or GUARDIAN, to take or send the child out of the United Kingdom without the appropriate consent (the Child Abduction Act 1984, s. 1).   [FK]

See also ABDUCTION; CHILD ABDUCTION.

International Commission of Jurists An international, non-governmental, human rights organization founded in 1952. The Commission comprises a standing group of 60 eminent jurists, appointed from prominent academics, practising lawyers and judges to reflect the diversity of world legal traditions. Commissioners are elected for a renewable period of five years, and are responsible for the governance of the organization, defining Commission policy and assisting in programme implementation. They are supported by an International Secretariat based in Geneva, Switzerland, and staffed by lawyers drawn from a wide range of jurisdictions. The Commission is a not-for-profit organization and therefore relies heavily on volunteer activists. The Commission undertakes advocacy and policy work aimed at strengthening the role of lawyers and judges in protecting and promoting human rights and the rule of law. It was responsible in 1959 for sponsoring the **Declaration of Delhi** on the Rule of Law, and has subsequently been instrumental in a range of other soft law measures shaping international human rights law and practice, including the formulation and adoption of both the UN Basic Principles on the Independence of the Judiciary (1985) and the Basic Principles on the Role of Lawyers (1990), as well as the Limburg Principles (1996), which guide international law in the area of economic, social and cultural rights. At national level, it operates through 'sections' (e.g. JUSTICE in the UK) and affiliates in over 70 countries. It currently runs a number of regional and thematic programmes; see http://www.icj.org/sommaire.php3?lang=en.   [JW]

International Court of Arbitration An organization created in 1923 by the INTERNATIONAL CHAMBER OF COMMERCE (ICC) as a permanent organ of the ICC, based in Paris. It is designed to foster and facilitate the settlement by arbitration of international commercial disputes between private parties and between states and private parties. It is not a national court, and does not conduct arbitrations itself. The members of the Court are professionals drawn from some 50 or so countries who, sitting as the Court and assisted by the ICC Secretariat, consider a wide range of issues arising in respect of ARBITRATION proceedings conducted or intended to be conducted pursuant to the ICC's arbitration rules. These issues include the following: acceptance or rejection of applications for ICC arbitration; identification of suitable arbitrators; setting the place of arbitration (i.e. the seat of arbitration); ruling on allegations made against sitting arbitrators (for example, for failing to behave impartially); and reviewing the terms of reference for arbitration submitted by each ARBITRAL TRIBUNAL. In particular, the Court reviews every proposed AWARD before it is released to the parties by the arbitral tribunal. By supervising and supporting arbitration proceedings conducted pursuant to its own arbitration rules, the Court endeavours to provide parties and arbitral tribunals with a self-contained procedure which can resolve all of the usual problems arising during an arbitration without reference to national courts, thereby reducing cost and delay. The functions of the Court also help to provide the parties with awards which might be regarded by national courts – on applications for recognition and enforcement – as being more likely to be procedurally sound than awards emanating from ad hoc arbitrations. The Court is also responsible for keeping the ICC arbitration rules under review, and for drafting new rules from time to time for submission to, and adoption by, the ICC.   [RE]

See also AD HOC ARBITRATION.

International Court of Justice (ICJ) A principal organ of the UNITED NATIONS, responsible for resolving legal disputes between STATES (contentious jurisdiction) as well as providing advisory opinions on matters arising from the mandate of inter-governmental organizations. The ICJ's contentious jurisdiction is triggered by lodging declarations under the Court's OPTIONAL CLAUSE mechanism, as well as by the conclusion of SPECIAL AGREEMENTS between two or more parties to bring a case before the Court. Judgments of the ICJ are binding only on the parties to the case and they are final, not subject to appeal. Where a case has commenced and there is some urgency about a particular aspect of the situation involved, the ICJ may grant provisional (i.e. interim) measures. When states trigger the Court's jurisdiction, they may limit the scope of INTERNATIONAL LAW, which it can apply in any given case; for example, they may exclude from its ambit the application of multilateral treaties (as has been the case with the USA). The judgments of the ICJ, although only binding on the specific parties to a dispute, are authoritative and persuasive and are treated generally as a valid expression of current international law.   [IB]

See also PERSUASIVE AUTHORITY; TREATY.

International Covenant on Civil and Political Rights (ICCPR) An international TREATY, the first major HUMAN RIGHTS treaty, that was adopted in 1966 and which eventually came into force in 1976. The ICCPR contains provisions on all major civil and political rights, both individual and collective. Significantly, it extends recognition to the right of SELF-DETERMINATION as a collective right. The ICCPR is also endowed with a quasi-judicial mechanism, the Human Rights Committee, which has competence to hear cases alleging violations of the rights of the Covenant. However, its jurisdiction is limited to violations alleged by nationals of a member STATE and then only if such states have ratified the ICCPR's

First Optional Protocol, which allows individual petitions. The Human Rights Committee has produced very significant jurisprudence that has received recognition in both domestic and international courts.   [IB]

International Covenant on Economic, Social and Cultural Rights (ICESCR) A TREATY adopted in 1966, at the same time as the INTERNATIONAL COVENANT ON CIVIL AND POLITICAL RIGHTS (ICCPR), it came into force in 1976. As its title suggests, the range of rights protected includes among others the right to housing, education, healthcare and food, and in this sense the ICESCR encompasses positive rights (i.e. rights which states must realize for their people). Some of the rights contained therein are also described as progressive rights, in that it was not possible to oblige Member States to realize all of them in a short space of time, particularly where some states were seriously underdeveloped. Therefore, Member States have undertaken to realize these rights fully when their financial situation and levels of development have improved.   [IB]

International Criminal Court (ICC) A permanent international court, established in 2002 to try persons accused of the most serious international crimes – GENOCIDE, CRIMES AGAINST HUMANITY and WAR CRIMES. The ICC is based on a TREATY, the Rome Statute, currently joined by 108 countries; a further 40 have signed but not ratified the treaty. The permanent seat of the Court is in the Netherlands, at The Hague.

The ICC can exercise jurisdiction only in cases where the accused is a national of a STATE party, or the alleged crime took place on the territory of a state party, or otherwise where a matter is referred to the Court by the UN SECURITY COUNCIL (this was the only way in which the Court was able to commence prosecutions with respect to the situation in Darfur, as Sudan is not a state party). In other regards, although it works closely with the UN, the ICC is functionally and legally independent. It is a court of last resort, and will not act if a case is being investigated or prosecuted by a national judicial system, unless it believes that the national proceedings are not genuine, for example where formal proceedings were commenced to shield a person from the ICC. [IB]

International Criminal Tribunal for Rwanda (ICTR) By Resolution 955 of 8 November 1994, the UN SECURITY COUNCIL established an ad hoc international tribunal to prosecute persons responsible for serious violations of international humanitarian law during the Rwandan genocide between 1 January 1994 and 31 December 1994. The Tribunal is based in Arusha, Tanzania, and comprises three Trial Chambers and an Appeals Chamber, which is shared with the INTERNATIONAL CRIMINAL TRIBUNAL FOR THE FORMER YUGOSLAVIA. The ICTR has its own staff, prosecutors and detention facilities for those awaiting trial. The 16 full-time and up to 12 part-time or *ad litem* judges are elected by the UN General Assembly from a list drawn up by the Security Council derived from a list of nominees submitted by UN MEMBER STATES. The judges are elected to the Tribunal for a term of four years, and are eligible for re-election. No country may have more than one judge sitting on the Tribunal at any one time.

The first trial commenced in January 1997 and the work of the Tribunal is scheduled to be wound up in 2010, with any outstanding cases transferred to competent national jurisdictions. By August 2008, 35 accused had been tried before the ICTR, with another 30 trials ongoing and seven defendants awaiting trial. [JW]

International Criminal Tribunal for the Former Yugoslavia (ICTY) An ad hoc international tribunal established by SECURITY COUNCIL Resolution 827, passed on 25 May 1993. ICTY was established to prosecute serious violations of international humanitarian law committed in the territory of the former Yugoslavia from 1991. The Tribunal has indicted 161 persons in total, with 46 proceedings ongoing in August 2008. The Tribunal's last indictments were issued in 2004 in line with its completion strategy, which sees the work

of the Tribunal being wound up by the end of 2010. Outstanding cases since 2004 have been referred to competent national jurisdictions within the former Yugoslavia.

The Tribunal is based at The Hague in the Netherlands and comprises three Trial Chambers and an Appeals Chamber, which is shared with the INTERNATIONAL CRIMINAL TRIBUNAL FOR RWANDA. The Chambers consist of 16 permanent judges and a normal maximum of 12 *ad litem* judges. A temporary increase in the number of *ad litem* judges to a maximum of 16 was approved by the UN Security Council in February 2008. All judges are elected by the UN General Assembly for a term of four years, and can be re-elected. [JW]

international law A body of rules that regulates the relations between sovereign states. What constitutes a binding rule of international law is an evolving and elusive process, but at the very least this includes treaties, custom and general principles of the laws of nations. In the 20th century, other non-binding forms of regulation have come to some prominence, such as resolutions of international organizations, usually referred to as SOFT LAW, as well as decisions of international tribunals as well as domestic (i.e. national) courts. These have had persuasive value on the conduct of international relations. Since states are the primary actors in the international field, it is they who create other entities and endow them with some degree of INTERNATIONAL LEGAL PERSONALITY. Thus legal personality has been transferred to international governmental organizations and individuals. Some theoreticians have cast doubt on whether international law is really 'law' in the sense of domestic binding rules. The reason behind this dilemma lies in the fact that, apart from a few exceptions, international law is a horizontal system of law-making where all parties are equal, rather than a vertical system, such as in the domestic sphere, where STATE authorities are supreme and impose the law on the governed. Despite these theoretical inquiries, the majority opinion is that, even as a matter of theory, international law is really law, but in a different sense from that of domestic law.   [IB]

International Law Commission (ILC) A subsidiary body of the UN General Assembly (established in 1948), it is composed of eminent international jurists and its mandate is to consolidate into TREATY form existing CUSTOMARY INTERNATIONAL LAW; that is, to codify the many fields comprising international law. The ILC has been responsible, among others, for the codification of the 1969 Vienna Convention on the Law of Treaties and the 2001 Articles on State Responsibility. In agreeing to study a particular topic, the ILC appoints a Rapporteur, who then proceeds to study customary law and receive the views of states. When an initial text has been drafted, depending on its reception by the community of states, the ILC may bring it before an international conference for possible adoption. All of the ILC's codification efforts have taken decades to conclude and some, such as the 2001 Articles on State Responsibility and the Draft Code of Crimes against the Peace and Security of Mankind, ultimately failed to become treaties.   [IB]

international legal personality The capacity of an entity to possess rights and duties under INTERNATIONAL LAW and a capacity to enforce these before a dispute settlement body of a judicial or other nature. STATES enjoy unlimited personality and can confer international legal personality on other entities, such as international organizations and individuals. The legal capacity of international organizations is defined by their founding instrument, and by the need to imply certain other capacities necessary to achieve their assigned functions (see implied powers doctrine).

International personality may be conferred on individuals by TREATY and custom and this is evident particularly in HUMAN RIGHTS treaties, which grant rights susceptible to individual enforcement.   [IB]

International Military Tribunal A special court established to try alleged Nazi perpetrators of WAR CRIMES and CRIMES AGAINST

HUMANITY. The tribunal was established by the Allied powers in the London Agreement of 8 August 1945, which provided the basis of the Tribunal's Charter. Proceedings in the first trial of 24 Nazi leaders were formally commenced in Nuremberg, Germany, on 20 November 1945, before a court which was composed of one member from each of the four Allied countries: France, the Union of Soviet Socialist Republics, the United Kingdom and the United States of America. The first trial ended on 1 October 1946, with 12 of the 24 being sentenced to death. A number of lesser trials followed, with over 200 German war crimes defendants being tried by the end of proceedings in 1949.

The Nuremberg trials had a significant influence on the development of international criminal law. The modern definition of war crimes has its basis in the **Nuremberg Principles** that were originally set down by Article 6 of the Charter and the judgment of the Tribunal, as developed by the INTERNATIONAL LAW COMMISSION in its report on the *Principles of International Law Recognized in the Charter of the Nüremberg Tribunal and in the Judgment of the Tribunal* (Yearbook of the International Law Commission, 1950, vol. II). The medical experiments conducted by Nazi doctors and prosecuted in the so-called 'Doctors' Trial' also led to the creation of the Nuremberg Code of medical research ethics. A separate International Military Tribunal for the Far East was also convened in Tokyo from 3 May 1946 to 12 November 1948 to deal with war crimes following secession of hostilities in the war against Japan.   [JW]

international minimum standards Typically SOFT LAW instruments in the form of UN General Assembly or UN Economic and Social Council (ECOSOC) resolutions, aiming to set out non-binding fundamental standards which states should try to achieve in particular fields of HUMAN RIGHTS where no TREATY exists. Examples of such instruments include the 1985 Standard Minimum Rules for Administration of Juvenile Justice (General Assembly), the 1977 Standard Minimum Rules for Treatment of Prisoners (ECOSOC) and the 1990 Standard Minimum Rules for Non-Custodial Measures (General Assembly). The term 'international minimum standards' is purely functional and has no normative significance.   [IB]

International Sea-bed Authority Established by the 1982 UNITED NATIONS CONVENTION ON THE LAW OF THE SEA (UNCLOS) and by the 1994 Agreement Relating to the Implementation of Part XI of UNCLOS. It possesses legal personality under the two instruments and its function is to manage the resources of the international sea-bed and to commission their exploration and exploitation by private investors for the benefit of mankind.   [IB]

See also COMMON HERITAGE OF MANKIND; INTERNATIONAL LEGAL PERSONALITY.

International Tribunal for the Law of the Sea (ITLOS) An international court established by the 1982 UNITED NATIONS CONVENTION ON THE LAW OF THE SEA (UNCLOS). ITLOS possesses jurisdiction to hear legal disputes arising from the interpretation of UNCLOS between state parties to UNCLOS, or between non-parties who submit a dispute to ITLOS. The court's jurisdiction may be triggered either by a SPECIAL AGREEMENT between states (setting out the dispute and the law to be applied), or by lodging declarations regarding the court's jurisdiction in future cases and the topics susceptible to judicial determination. Finally, it may be triggered by accession to multilateral treaties that provide for the court's jurisdiction as a means of particular dispute settlement. A Special Chamber of ITLOS has been devoted to legal disputes concerning the international sea-bed, the so-called International Sea-bed Disputes Chamber. The latter, unlike ITLOS which is composed of 21 judges, is composed of 11 judges, selected by a majority of the elected members of ITLOS from among themselves. [IB]

interpretation of wills This operates on the presumption that the role of the court is, so far as possible, to give effect to the TESTATOR's intention. By the time a WILL comes before the court to decide what it

means, the testator is not available to say what he meant and the court often has difficulty in deciding. This difficulty can arise for various reasons. Perhaps the testator has not expressed himself clearly, and it is not only in a 'home-made' will that this happens. There may be an ambiguity, and some words are capable of having a different meaning depending on the context in which they are used, e.g. 'money'.

To assist the court, various principles have been adopted, some of which have been given the title 'rule', although they are not treated as rules, but more as guidelines. For instance, 'the **dictionary rule**' says that if a testator has indicated in his will what meaning he attaches to a particular word, the court will give that meaning to it. 'The **technical words rule**' says that technical words in a will shall be given their technical meaning: this often refers to a technical legal expression, but not exclusively. 'The **golden rule**' states that a will is to be construed so as to avoid an INTESTACY, on the grounds that it is unlikely a testator would go to the trouble of making a will if he did not intend to deal with all his property.   [CM]

intervener A non-party who is allowed to join an ongoing court action, with the consent of the court, on the basis that they have a legitimate interest in or may be affected by the outcome of the case. An intervener must be distinguished from an *amicus curiae*, who may be invited by the court to assist it on a technical point of law. For example, in 1998, in the case before the House of Lords to determine whether General Pinochet should be extradited from the UK for alleged human rights abuses in Chile, Amnesty International was allowed to join the action as an intervener and was represented in court by a team of counsel led by Professor Ian Brownlie QC. At the same time, the court also appointed David Lloyd Jones QC as *amicus curiae* to advise their lordships on the issue of diplomatic immunity.   [JW]

intervening act See NOVUS ACTUS INTERVENIENS.

interview 'An interview is the questioning of a person regarding their involvement or suspected involvement in a criminal offence or offences which … must be carried out under CAUTION': see the Police and Criminal Evidence Act 1984 (PACE) Code C, para. 11.1A. Specific provisions governing the conduct of interviews are contained in Code C.   [ALTC]

intestacy Where the ASSETS of a deceased person are not disposed of by WILL. If no assets are disposed of by will the result will be a **total intestacy**, but if some assets are disposed of by will and some are not, then there is said to be a **partial intestacy**. Obviously when there is no will, there will be always be a total intestacy, but this could still be the case where the deceased leaves a will, but the will is not effective to dispose of any property.   [CM]

intimidation A variety of criminal offences have intimidation as one of their elements, or as one way of committing the ACTUS REUS.

1. The (virtually defunct) COMMON LAW offence of **embracery** (seeking to influence jurors). Today, behaviour constituting embracery is more likely to be charged as PERVERTING THE COURSE OF JUSTICE or the statutory offence of intimidating jurors under the Criminal Justice and Public Order Act 1994, s. 51. Section 51 requires that a person: (a) does an act which intimidates, and is intended to intimidate, another person; (b) knows or believes that the victim is, *inter alia*, a juror or potential juror; (c) intends by his act to cause the investigation or the course of justice to be obstructed, perverted or interfered with. If criteria (a) and (b) are proved against the defendant, he is presumed to be acting with the intent in criterion (c), unless he can prove to the contrary on the balance of probabilities (see s. 51(7) of the 1994 Act and *Attorney General's Reference (No. 1 of 2004)* [2004] EWCA Crim 1025).

2. An offence under the Trade Union and Labour Relations (Consolidation) Act 1992, s. 241, for a person, *inter alia*, wrongfully and without legal authority, to use violence to intimidate a person or his spouse or civil partner or children, or to injure his property, with a view to compelling that person to abstain from doing or to do any act which that person has a legal right to do or abstain from doing.

3. Intimidation also has procedural significance. The Criminal Procedure and Investigations Act 1996, ss. 54 and 55, set out a procedure for dealing with so-called 'tainted acquittals', where D has been acquitted; and another person P has been convicted, for example, of an offence involving intimidation of a juror or a witness in proceedings which led to the acquittal; and where it appears to the court in which P was convicted that there was a real possibility that without the intimidation D would not have been acquitted. In such cases, an application may be made to the HIGH COURT to quash D's acquittal. Intimidation or potential intimidation of jurors is also one of the factors which may trigger the 'jury tampering' powers of a court under the Criminal Justice Act 2003 to hear a trial on indictment without a JURY.   [BF]

See also PERJURY; THREAT; WITNESS INTIMIDATION.

intoxicating liquor (obsolete) A term used in the Licensing Act 1964 to identify alcohol-containing products subject to statutory regimes for sale and taxation. Intoxicating liquor was to be distinguished from other products containing alcohol which were to be used for purposes other than consumption. The Licensing Act 2003, which supersedes the 1964 Act, refers to 'ALCOHOL' rather than intoxicating liquor. A significant change brought about by the 2003 Act is that licences to sell alcohol are now granted by the local authority rather than by licensing justices.   [BF]

intoxication Generally speaking, the mere fact that a defendant is intoxicated at the time of committing an offence has no bearing on his or her criminal liability. Depending on the circumstances of the case, intoxication may operate as an aggravating or a mitigating factor in sentencing. However, in rare cases, a defendant may be so intoxicated that they are incapable of forming the MENS REA for a given offence. In these circumstances, the defendant's intoxication may be relevant to liability. Under such circumstances, if the defendant's intoxication is **involuntary**, he will not be liable, regardless of the nature of the offence. If the defendant's intoxication is **voluntary**, then whether and to what extent he is liable depends on the nature of the offence with which he is charged.

The law distinguishes between offences of SPECIFIC INTENT and BASIC INTENT. Broadly speaking, the former are offences requiring a *mens rea* of intention; the latter require something less serious than intention. Thus murder is an offence of specific intent, but manslaughter is an offence of basic intent. If the defendant is so intoxicated as to be incapable of forming the *mens rea* of an offence of basic intent, they will none the less be liable for that offence; but if they are so intoxicated as to be incapable of forming the *mens rea* of an offence of specific intent, they will not be liable for that offence, but may still be liable for a corresponding offence of basic intent. For discussion, see *DPP* v. *Majewski* [1977] AC 443. [BF]
See also MITIGATION.

intra vires (Lat. within the powers) *See* ULTRA VIRES.

intractable contact dispute A term often used by courts, by professionals such as lawyers, and also by commentators to describe long-running disputes between PARENTS regarding contact by the NON-RESIDENT PARENT with their children. These disputes arise on SEPARATION or DIVORCE. While many parents settle arrangements for contact amicably, intractable contact disputes are difficult to resolve and generally involve a number of applications to court. [FK]
See also CONTACT ORDER; RESIDENCE ORDER.

introductory tenancy A tenancy granted by a LOCAL HOUSING AUTHORITY that is not a SECURE TENANCY for at least the first 12 months of its operation. An introductory tenancy scheme can be introduced by local housing authorities under ss. 124 to 143 of the Housing Act 1996 (as amended by the Housing Act 2004). The great advantage to the landlord is that it is much easier to terminate the introductory tenancy in contrast to the secure tenancy. Whilst the possession procedure in the Housing Act 1985 requires notice, grounds and a court order, with the court retaining a discretion as to whether to order possession or not, the procedure in the 1996 Act significantly reduces the role of the court. If the LANDLORD has given notice in the proper form, and confirms the decision to evict, if the case proceeds to court, the court has no alternative other than to grant possession. The eviction procedure was unsuccessfully challenged on the grounds that it was inconsistent with Article 6 ECHR rights to a fair trial in *R (McLellan)* v. *Bracknell Forest BC; Reigate & Banstead BC* v. *Benfield and Forrest* [2001] EWCA Civ 1510.

Where the local authority landlord has continuing concerns about the behaviour of a tenant it can extend the 12-month 'probationary' period of the introductory tenancy by an additional six months. At the end of the 12-month or 18-month period the tenancy ceases to be an introductory tenancy and becomes a secure tenancy. [HC & DR]
See also DEMOTED TENANCY.

invention A PATENT is granted for inventions that are novel, involve an INVENTIVE STEP, and are capable of industrial application. British and European legislation do not define what is meant by 'invention'; however, both offer a negative definition by containing a non-exhaustive list of things which are not regarded as inventions (see the Patents Act 1977, ss. 1, 4 and the EUROPEAN PATENT Convention, Articles 52–57). According to this list, and to the case law, it is generally accepted that an invention is not an abstract, non-technical idea; rather, it is an idea which can be put into practice, or a solution to a specific problem, and is both of a concrete and technical character in any field of technology (see *VICOM/Computer-related invention* (T208/84) [1987] EPOR 74; *Genentech Inc.* v. *Wellcome* (1989) RPC 147). [US]

inventive step A condition of patentability. An invention shall be considered as involving an inventive step if, having regard to the state of the art, it is not obvious to a person skilled in the art (Patents Act 1977, ss. 1(1), 3; EUROPEAN PATENT Convention, Articles 52, 56).

There are four steps for determining whether an invention is obvious or not, as set out in *Windsurfing International* v. *Tabur Marine* (1985) RPC 59: (a) identify the inventive concept; (b) assume the mantle of a normally skilled but unimaginative addressee and impute to him what was, at that date, common general knowledge in the art in question; (c) identify what, if any, differences existed between the cited prior art and the alleged invention; and (d) determine whether, viewed without any knowledge of the alleged invention, those differences constituted steps which would have been obvious to a skilled man or whether they required any degree of invention.

The rationale for this condition is that the public should not be prevented from doing anything which is merely an obvious extension or a workshop variation on what is already in the public domain. [US]

See also PATENT.

inventor For the purposes of PATENT law, an inventor is the 'actual deviser of the invention' (Patents Act 1977, s. 11). Although inventors have a right to be named in the patent application, any person can apply for a patent registration if they can prove, under British, international or foreign law, that they are entitled to the property interest in the invention. Indeed, case law has also confirmed that the statutory provision defining inventors does not create an entitlement claim – see *Markem Corp.* v. *Zipher Ltd* [2005] EWCA Civ 267. [US]

inventory A list of property or assets. If ordered to do so by the court, the PERSONAL REPRESENTATIVE of a deceased person is under a statutory duty to exhibit on OATH in court a full inventory of the ESTATE, and any person interested in the estate may apply for such an order. [CM]

invitation to treat A statement made during the negotiation process for a CONTRACT which falls short of an OFFER and is no more than a statement indicating a willingness to receive offers from others. As such the response to an invitation to treat can at best be an offer and cannot result in AGREEMENT between the parties. Advertisements, circulars, price lists and displays in shop windows or on supermarket shelves are generally regarded as no more than invitations to treat. Equally, advertisements of auctions with no reserve and requests for TENDERS are also generally classified as invitations to treat. [JPL]

invitee An invitee, as opposed to a trespasser or a licensee, is a person who is invited onto PREMISES in order to carry out a particular purpose, for instance repairing the central heating boiler. The proprietor of the premises owes the invitee certain duties in TORT which arise from that status.

[HC & DR]

involuntary manslaughter *See* MANSLAUGHTER.

IPCC *See* INDEPENDENT POLICE COMPLAINTS COMMISSION.

irrationality *See* JUDICIAL REVIEW.

irrebuttable presumption A presumption that is conclusive and cannot be rebutted. An irrebuttable presumption is thus in reality a rule of law. For example, the Children and Young Persons Act 1933, s. 50, provides: 'It shall be conclusively presumed that no child under the age of ten years can be guilty of any offence.' [ALTC]

irresistible impulse The mere fact that a defendant finds it difficult to control his or her actions does not amount to a defence. The question, for the defence of INSANITY, is whether the defendant meets the requirements of the M'NAGHTEN RULES. For the purposes of AUTOMATISM, the defendant's conduct must be involuntary, a concept which is construed restrictively. In cases of unlawful homicide, depending on why the defendant finds it difficult to control his or her actions, the factor of an irresistible impulse impelling the defendant's actions may contribute to a finding of an abnormality of mind for the purposes of the defence of DIMINISHED RESPONSIBILITY. [BF]

irretrievable breakdown Irretrievable breakdown of MARRIAGE or CIVIL PARTNERSHIP is the only ground for DIVORCE or DISSOLUTION in England and Wales. For divorce, in order to establish that the marriage has broken down irretrievably, the petitioner must prove one or more of five facts: ADULTERY, DESERTION, two-year SEPARATION with consent of the respondent, separation for five years, or UNREASONABLE BEHAVIOUR. For dissolution of a civil partnership, the claimant must prove one or more of the last four facts above to establish the irretrievable breakdown of the partnership; the adultery fact is not available. If the court is satisfied as to one or more of these facts and of the irretrievable breakdown of the marriage or civil partnership, it must grant a DECREE NISI of divorce or a conditional dissolution order.
[AD]

See also BREAKDOWN OF MARRIAGE.

Islamic law The totality of Islamic law is known as the *Shari'a*, meaning the way or path to follow. This in itself emphasizes the extent to which Islam as a faith and as a system of personal law are largely indivisible.

At the top of the pyramid of sources of Islamic law is the Koran *(Qur'an)* itself, the word of God as revealed to the Prophet Muhammad, though only about 500 of over 6,000 verses are considered to form the basis of *Shari'a*. Below the Koran is the *Sunna* of the Prophet, literally the path taken by Muhammad in living and explaining the Koran. The *Sunna* comprises numerous *Hadith*, statements passed on from the Prophet through each generation to the present day. The legitimacy of each *Hadith* lies in its reliability, that is, in the strength of the chain *(isnad)* of authority connecting it to the words of the Prophet.

In addition to the primary sources of the *Shari'a*, there are a number of secondary sources, including *Ijma*, *Qiyas* and *Ijtihad*. There is some disagreement among scholars as to whether these are all secondary sources; in particular it is argued by some that *Ijtihad* is a technique rather

than a source of Islamic law. All of them are important in filling the many gaps left by the rather fragmentary nature of the primary sources. The *Ijma* represents the historical consensus of the community and is used as a way of avoiding conflict and contradiction within Islamic jurisprudence. *Qiyas* means application by analogy. In the absence of clearly applicable answers from the primary sources, jurists would look for an analogous situation in which a decision had been made. *Ijtihad* or *Istinbat* appears to be a similar, though perhaps narrower practice, and indeed *Ijtihad* and *Qiyas* are sometimes used as equivalents. The essence of *Ijtihad* is the exercise of independent legal reasoning in search of a solution to a new situation. It remains a somewhat controversial practice, but is seen by some scholars as critical in bringing new ideas and concepts into the tradition of Islamic jurisprudence. [JW]

Further reading: W.B. Hallaq, *Authority, Continuity and Change in Islamic Law* (Cambridge: Cambridge University Press, 2001); R. Kusha, *The Sacred Law of Islam* (Aldershot: Ashgate, 2002); J. Schacht, *An Introduction to Islamic Law* (Oxford: Clarendon Press, 1964).

issue estoppel *See* ESTOPPEL.

itemized pay statement A written statement of gross and net pay and the amount of deductions (including the reason for the deductions) that an EMPLOYER must give an EMPLOYEE: see the Employment Rights Act 1996, s. 8. The remedy is to complain to an EMPLOYMENT TRIBUNAL, which will award a declaration if the complaint is upheld; payment to the employee of any deductions which have not been notified may be ordered. [MJ]

See also DEDUCTIONS FROM WAGES.

ITLOS *See* INTERNATIONAL TRIBUNAL FOR THE LAW OF THE SEA.

ius ad bellum *See* USE OF FORCE; WAR.

ius civile (Lat. the citizens' law) Or *jus civile*, the law governing those possessing the status of citizens in the ancient Roman Empire. As such it was distinguishable from the *ius gentium* (the law of the people; compare the modern usage of *jus gentium*) which were the laws governing all other peoples in the Empire who were not citizens.   [JW]

ius cogens *See JUS COGENS.*

ius commune (Lat. common law) Or *jus commune,* the combination of CANON LAW and Roman law which formed the basis of a common system of legal thought in Western Europe. The *ius commune* was the product primarily of the universities following the rediscovery of Roman law in Europe in the 12th century. It provided primarily an intellectual rather than a practical model of law, but was nevertheless influential in shaping the law across Europe. Its relevance declined from the 16th century as a result of three key trends: the growth of NATURAL LAW theory; the emergence of the codification movement in continental Europe; and the abandonment of Latin in university teaching.

The institutional texts of the *ius commune,* written by medieval jurists, are still regarded as a historical source of law within the CIVIL LAW tradition, and may, very exceptionally, be referred to as a source of doctrinal authority. While the *ius commune* was undoubtedly influential on medieval English law, it is primarily a civil law construct and must be distinguished from the modern Anglo-American conception of the COMMON LAW.   [JW]

ius gentium or **jus gentium** *See IUS CIVILE; LAW OF NATIONS.*

J

J Mr (or Mrs) Justice.
See PUISNE JUDGE.

jactitation of marriage A false assertion that one is married to another person. Such a claim was actionable in England and Wales until 1986. [AD]

joinder of charges A rule that allows several counts against the person accused to be put in one indictment. Charges for any offences may be joined in the same INDICTMENT if founded on the same facts, or form or are part of a series of offences of the same or a similar character. [SN]

joinder of parties In civil proceedings, the bringing together of two or more claimants or defendants within a single action. Under Part 19 of the CIVIL PROCEDURE RULES there is no limit to the number of parties that can be joined in an action. [JW]
See also GROUP LITIGATION; REPRESENTATIVE ACTION.

joint and several liability Where two or more persons enter into a legal relationship which carries joint and several liability it means that they are all jointly liable *and* liable individually. This means, for example, that an action can properly be brought against only one of them in respect of a wrongful act committed by any one of the group, or by the group as a whole. Similarly, a debt owed by all might be enforced against all, or against any one. This may be advantageous to a claimant where, for example, one of the group becomes insolvent. Certain legal relationships, such as a partnership, normally carry joint and several liability. [JW]

Joint Committee on Statutory Instruments A committee of both Houses of Parliament responsible for the scrutiny of DELEGATED LEGISLATION. The Committee comprises 14 members, seven from each House. [JW]

joint enterprise Where A and B set off together to commit crime X, they are both liable for all the consequences flowing from conduct which they foresee has a real risk of occurring in furtherance of their plan to commit crime X. Thus, where A and B agree to burgle V's house and, during the BURGLARY, V returns home and is killed by A, with the *MENS REA* for MURDER, the question of whether B is also liable in respect of V's death depends on whether B foresaw a real risk that, if disturbed during the burglary, A would respond with violence sufficiently serious to constitute the *mens rea* of murder. The legal rules governing this type of situation are sometimes referred to as the doctrine of joint enterprise. B's foresight of risk would be determined by evidence of, for example, his knowledge of A's propensity (if any) for violence, and his knowledge (if any) that A was carrying a weapon apt for use in a homicidal manner.

If A commits an act which B does not foresee at all, then B will not be liable in respect of the consequences of that act. Thus, where A and B agree only to burgle V's house, and to take specific items from therein, if A spray-paints the walls with graffiti, then, unless B has foreseen this possibility, he will not be liable in respect of the CRIMINAL DAMAGE committed by A.

For discussion of the principles, see for example, *R* v. *Anderson and Morris* [1966] 2 QB 110; *R* v. *Chan Wing-Siu* [1985] AC 168; *R* v. *English* [1997] 4 All ER 545.   [BF]

See also ACCOMPLICE; AID AND ABET; PRINCIPAL; SECONDARY PARTY.

joint wills One WILL made by two persons. It is not to be confused with the doctrine of MUTUAL WILLS. Joint wills are very uncommon, and perhaps the only time they occur is when two people have been given a joint POWER OF APPOINTMENT to be exercised by will.   [CM]

joyriding Colloquial term denoting the unauthorized taking of a vehicle for recreational purposes.   [BF]

See also AGGRAVATED VEHICLE TAKING; TAKING WITHOUT CONSENT.

judgment in default *See* DEFAULT JUDGMENT.

Judges' Rules (Obsolete) Guidance regulating police powers and procedures in criminal investigation that were superseded by the PACE CODES OF PRACTICE.   [ALTC]

judicial accountability The principle that judges should be answerable to some other authority for actions taken in a judicial, or in some circumstances, personal, capacity.

A meaningful concept of judicial accountability is a relatively recent innovation in the English legal system, not least because of potential tensions between accountability – notably to the Executive or Parliament – and the necessary safeguarding of JUDICIAL INDEPENDENCE. Nevertheless, the modern legal system ensures an element of both **individual** and **institutional** judicial accountability.

Judges are individually accountable in a disciplinary sense, in that, since the Act of Settlement 1701, judges of the superior courts have held office only 'during good behaviour', subject to a power of removal by the Queen on a joint address by both Houses of Parliament (see the Supreme Court Act 1981, s. 11(3) (COURT OF APPEAL and HIGH COURT) and the Appellate Jurisdiction Act 1876, s. 6 (HOUSE OF LORDS)). No judge of the superior courts has been dismissed since 1701, though a small number have resigned in circumstances where there has been serious criticism of their judicial conduct. Other 'judicial office holders' (including CIRCUIT and DISTRICT JUDGES and CORONERS) may be removed for misconduct by the LORD CHANCELLOR under the Judicial Discipline (Prescribed Procedures) Regulations 2006. In addition, the LORD CHIEF JUSTICE has statutory powers to give 'formal advice' or a 'formal warning' or 'reprimand' to a judge in any court below the SUPREME COURT of the United Kingdom and may, in certain circumstances, suspend a judge from office (Constitutional Reform Act 2005, ss. 108–109). Complaints against any member of the judiciary must be made to the **Office for Judicial Complaints** (**OJC**), which was also created by the 2006 Regulations. The OJC has the power to screen complaints and may dismiss those which involve complaints about the judge's decision rather than his or her conduct, or which concern matters in a judge's private life which have no bearing on their fitness to hold judicial office. Any complaint which is not dismissed by the OJC will be considered further by a judge who must submit a report to the Lord Chief Justice or Lord Chancellor. In the first year of the new system, disciplinary action was taken against 32 judicial office holders, including the reprimand of two judges and the removal of 15 Justices of the Peace (OJC *Annual Report 2006–2007*).

Representatives of the senior judiciary and judges responsible for particular jurisdictions may be called to give evidence before Parliamentary Select Committees on aspects of the administration of justice. This provides a limited form of institutional accountability, but in an explanatory rather than a disciplinary sense. [JW]

See also JUDICIAL APPOINTMENTS AND CONDUCT OMBUDSMAN; JUDICIAL IMMUNITY.

Judicial Appointments and Conduct Ombudsman Created by the Constitutional Reform Act 2005, s. 62, the Judicial Ombudsman investigates complaints about the judicial appointments process and the handling of matters involving judicial discipline or conduct. The Ombudsman does not deal with substantive allegations of misconduct against judges as such, but acts as a check on maladministration by those bodies that are set up to deal with judicial appointments (notably the JUDICIAL APPOINTMENTS COMMISSION) or complaints about the personal conduct of judges, MAGISTRATES and TRIBUNAL members (that is, the **Office of Judicial Complaints**, tribunal Presidents and Magistrates Advisory Committees). The Ombudsman can make recommendations to the relevant body to make changes to their work or procedures, or recommend a decision be reviewed, or set aside the decision of the relevant body, and make an award of compensation to the complainant in respect of any maladministration. He has no power to intervene in any judicial decision, since that would undermine the principle of JUDICIAL INDEPENDENCE. [JW]

See also JUDICIAL ACCOUNTABILITY.

Judicial Appointments Commission An independent body set up by the Constitutional Reform Act 2005, s. 61, to appoint individuals to a range of judicial offices, including TRIBUNAL members. The Commission commenced operation in April 2006. It comprises a lay (i.e. not legally qualified) Chairman and 14 other Commissioners, the majority of whom are legally qualified, and five of whom must be sitting judges. Its statutory responsibilities in making appointments are: to select candidates solely on merit; to select people of good character; and to have regard to the need to encourage applications from a wider range of candidates. [JW]

Judicial Committee of the Privy Council Also commonly referred to as the Privy Council. Historically, it has acted as the final court of appeal for British colonies and dependent territories. The Privy Council sits in London and normally comprises the Lords of Appeal in Ordinary and sometimes senior members of the judiciary from Commonwealth countries who are also Privy Counsellors. It will normally sit as a bench of five judges, though seven or nine may sit on particularly important appeals (such as *Holley*, below). Decisions of the Privy Council create binding PRECEDENT for the law of the jurisdiction from which the case came. They are not strictly binding on English courts, though they may be treated as strongly persuasive authority in English law. This reflects the fact that most of the judges on the Privy Council also sit in the HOUSE OF LORDS, and so one can reasonably expect that, if the same issue were to come before the House of Lords, it would be decided in the same way. This theory was put to the test in a very unusual way following the Privy Council's decision on the defence of PROVOCATION in *Attorney General for Jersey* v. *Holley* [2005] 2 AC 580. A majority of the nine Law Lords sitting declared that the House of Lords' decision in *R* v. *Smith* [2001] AC 146 was wrong. When the same issue arose in *R* v. *Mohammed* [2005] EWCA Crim 1880, the English COURT OF APPEAL then refused to follow *Smith*, arguing that, as Jersey law on this subject was the same as English law, the position in English law was now as advanced by the majority in *Holley*. This approach was followed again by the Court of Appeal, in *R* v. *Shickle* [2005] EWCA Crim 1881, and in *R* v. *James* [2006] EWCA Crim 14, where Lord Phillips CJ accepted that, in this exceptional situation, for practical purposes the Privy Council decision had indeed 'overruled' the House of Lords.

In practice, despite decisions like *Holley*, the Privy Council is of declining significance. Most independent Commonwealth countries have now excluded the court's jurisdiction, though it still acts as the final appeal court for much of the Commonwealth Caribbean. It also has a limited domestic (UK) jurisdiction in respect of some devolution matters, though this will be transferred to the UK SUPREME COURT when that commences operation.   [JW]

See also PRIVY COUNCIL; *STARE DECISIS*.

judicial immunity The protection of holders of judicial office from personal liability (e.g. liability in TORT for NEGLIGENCE or DEFAMATION) for things said or done in good faith and within the proper scope of that office.   [JW]

See also IMMUNITY FROM SUIT.

judicial independence The constitutional principle that judges must be able to act free from political or other interference. Despite the absence of a written constitution containing a formal guarantee of judicial independence, the British constitution seeks to safeguard judicial independence primarily in three ways: (a) judges are appointed, not elected, and are individually and institutionally independent of the executive and the legislature (though note the exceptional position of judges in the HOUSE OF LORDS); (b) since the Act of Settlement of 1701, judges can only be removed from office for 'good cause'. Moreover, judges of the HIGH COURT and above cannot be removed without an address passed by both Houses of Parliament; (c) judges enjoy extensive immunity from being sued or prosecuted for what they do in their judicial capacity.

The Constitutional Reform Act 2005, s. 3, imposes a statutory obligation on the LORD CHANCELLOR and all government Ministers to uphold the continued independence of the judiciary. An equivalent obligation extends to the First Minister and other Ministers of the NORTHERN IRELAND ASSEMBLY under s. 4. [JW]

See also JUDICIAL ACCOUNTABILITY; JUDICIAL APPOINTMENTS COMMISSION; JUDICIAL IMMUNITY.

judicial notice The means by which a judge can act on certain facts without hearing EVIDENCE to prove them. Judicial notice may be had either of well-known matters about which the judge can draw from his general knowledge, or of other facts on which he can properly make inquiries from appropriate sources: see *Commonwealth Shipping*

Representative v. *P & O Branch Service* [1923] AC 191 at 212.   [ALTC]

judicial review 1. The process by which judicial supervision of the decisions of public bodies, including inferior courts and TRIBUNALS, is conducted by the ADMINISTRATIVE COURT. At COMMON LAW, a claim for judicial review may be based on the ground of **illegality**, **irrationality** or **procedural impropriety** by the body concerned (see *Council of Civil Service Unions* v. *Minister for the Civil Service* [1985] AC 374). The boundaries of these concepts can be problematic, but, in straightforward terms, it means that the claimant must be able to show that the body either (a) made a decision which it was not lawfully entitled to make, or (b) behaved in a way that no such reasonable or rational body should have behaved, or (c) failed to behave in accordance with standards of procedural fairness and NATURAL JUSTICE. Judicial review may also be used to challenge the consistency of a PUBLIC AUTHORITY's actions with its responsibilities under the Human Rights Act 1998. A claim for judicial review must be commenced under the special procedure contained in the CPR Part 54 where the claimant is seeking one of the PREROGATIVE ORDERS, and it remains the preferred procedure where the matter is exclusively a public law dispute, even if an alternative remedy is being sought (see *O'Reilly* v. *Mackman* [1983] 2 AC 237 and *Clark* v. *University of Lincolnshire and Humberside* [2000] 3 All ER 752). In addition, or alternatively to the prerogative orders, a claimant may seek a DECLARATION or INJUNCTION (both at the discretion of the court) and may include a claim for DAMAGES, though it is not permissible to seek damages alone (CPR Rule 54.3).

2. Under Article 230 of the EC Treaty, the EUROPEAN COURT OF JUSTICE has the power to hear challenges against legally binding acts of Community institutions by way of judicial review. Such acts may be challenged on the grounds of (a) a lack of competence; (b) infringement of an essential procedural requirement; or (c) an infringement of the Treaty or other legal rule governing the use of its powers. Actions are generally brought by another Community institution or a MEMBER STATE, but in very limited circumstances may be commenced by an individual. [JW]

judicial separation order Under the Matrimonial Causes Act 1973, s. 18, the court may grant a decree of judicial separation if the petitioner can prove one of the five facts necessary for a DIVORCE. The effect of a decree of separation is to relieve the petitioner of the obligation to cohabit with the respondent, and on granting the decree the court may make orders for ANCILLARY RELIEF. A spouse does not require such a decree to be 'legally' separated, but the existence of a decree may be proof of one or more of the five facts, should the parties later seek a divorce. Petitions for these decrees are not common. A civil partner may also be granted a judicial separation order if he or she can prove one or more of the four facts available for DISSOLUTION of the CIVIL PARTNERSHIP. The effect of a separation order in this context is the same as in the marital context, except for removing the obligation of the partners to cohabit, given that civil partnerships create no obligation to cohabit in the first place. [AD]

See also ADULTERY; DESERTION; IRRETRIEVABLE BREAKDOWN; SEPARATION; UNREASONABLE BEHAVIOUR.

juridical Of or relating to the law. [JP]

jurisprudence 1. Sometimes defined as synonymous with legal theory or legal philosophy, jurisprudence may best be described as that intellectual discipline which concerns itself not with the *content* of law but rather the *nature* of law – in what it is that makes law *law*.

Within that broad definition the scope of jurisprudence is immense. The principal schools of thought most readily identified are LEGAL POSITIVISM and NATURAL LAW, but jurisprudence encompasses many other movements including those concerned with JUSTICE and RIGHTS, the SOCIOLOGY OF LAW, Realism (American and Scandinavian), CRITICAL LEGAL STUDIES and ADJUDICATION THEORY, among many others.

Within British law schools, the study of jurisprudence as a compulsory course is sometimes under threat as pressure grows in the curriculum to include more obviously practical subjects. Defenders of jurisprudence are concerned by what they see as the emergence of an instrumental – even technocratic – approach to legal education and emphasize the opportunity that this course offers with regard to the development of critical analytical skills in law students. They equally stress the important contribution that the study of jurisprudence can make to the development of lawyers who are reflective about their practice rather than uncritical functionaries of the legal system.

2. Most commonly in the context of European Union law and cases from within the CIVIL LAW tradition, the term 'jurisprudence' is sometimes used in English to refer to the reasoning or principles derived from case law, as in the phrase, 'the jurisprudence of the Court of Justice shows …' [JP]

jurisprudence constante (Fr. established precedent) A legal doctrine within the CIVIL LAW tradition according to which a series of previous decisions consistently applying the same reasoning on a point of law carries significant weight and may be determinative in later cases. It is different from the COMMON LAW principle of STARE DECISIS in two ways. First, *stare decisis* can create a binding principle out of a single precedent, whereas *jurisprudence constante* requires a consistent line of reasoning through a long sequence of cases; secondly, even though *jurisprudence constante* operates with 'considerable persuasive authority' (see the decision of the Supreme Court of Louisiana in *Doerr* v. *Mobil Oil Corporation* 774 So.2d 119 (2000)) it still lacks the strictly binding authority of common law precedent; in theory at least, the court can always change its mind. [JW]

jurist An expert in the law, especially a legal scholar. [JP]

juror A person who has been summoned by a court to serve as a member of a JURY.

Jurors are selected at random from the electoral roll. Subject to a limited number of exceptions, everyone aged 18 to 70 who is registered as an elector is eligible for jury service provided he or she has been resident in the United Kingdom for a period of five years since attaining the age of 13. A person who is summoned for jury service is under a duty to attend. [SN]

juror intimidation See PERVERTING THE COURSE OF JUSTICE; WITNESS INTIMIDATION.

jury The body of persons summoned to attend for jury service in the CROWN COURT. The role of the jury is to consider evidence and then reach a verdict of 'guilty' or 'not guilty'. [SN]

jury bundle A set of itemized documents constituting evidence prepared for the jury at a criminal trial or inquest. In criminal trials the jury bundle is submitted by the prosecution. It may also be supplemented by a separate **defence bundle** prepared by the accused's lawyers. [JW]

jury directions See DIRECTION TO JURY.

jury panel Persons summoned to attend the CROWN COURT for jury service. Also known as the jury in waiting. [SN]

jury tampering See INTIMIDATION.

jus ad bellum See USE OF FORCE; WAR.

jus civile See IUS CIVILE.

jus cogens (Lat. coercive law) Peremptory rules of INTERNATIONAL LAW that lie at the apex of all rules of international law and are binding on all STATES without exception. *Jus cogens* norms, although usually derived from CUSTOM, override customary rules, as well as any conflicting TREATY rules. A *jus cogens* rule cannot be derogated by agreement (Vienna Convention on the Law of Treaties, 1969, Article 64). It is widely agreed that GENOCIDE, CRIMES AGAINST HUMANITY and fundamental human rights, such as the right to life constitute *jus cogens* norms. [IB]

See also ERGA OMNES OBLIGATIONS.

jus gentium See LAW OF NATIONS.

jus in bello See WAR.

jus in re aliena A Latin phrase meaning a right – such as an EASEMENT – in someone else's property, as distinct from a right to one's own property – *jus in re propria*. [HC & DR]

just war A theory seeking to define the conditions under which the use of armed force could be justified. Just war theory emerged from the early fathers of the Christian Church, but was first formulated by Thomas AQUINAS in his *Summa Theologica*. He took a moral, rather than a legal, approach to justifying armed force, by arguing in favour of three conditions: (a) proper authority, i.e. that a war could only be initiated under the authority of a sovereign; (b) a just cause; and (c) right intention, i.e. a war should not be premised on greed, malice or revenge. During the medieval period, the just war doctrine was refined by Francisco de Vitoria and Francisco Suarez to encompass an additional element of PROPORTIONALITY. None the less, the doctrine did not move away from a purely moralistic and NATURAL LAW basis until such time as it was reformulated by Hugo GROTIUS in his *De Jure Belli ac Pacis*. For Grotius, a just war certainly had to be undertaken under official authority, but was warranted only where an injury had been inflicted, or where the injury was imminent. The just war doctrine survived in some form or another until the end of the 19th century and is now replaced by the UNITED NATIONS Charter framework regulating the USE OF FORCE. [IB]

justice 1. A standard of treatment that is fair, reasonable and impartial; a moral and political ideal. Western conceptions of justice originate in the writings of Plato and Aristotle. Aristotle defined justice as the greatest of the great or 'cardinal' virtues along with prudence (i.e. wisdom), courage and temperance. Justice is the greatest because, unlike the other three, it is the only virtue that is a good *in itself*. Prudence, courage and temperance are good only when they are used to pursue other virtues, and individuals may use them to bad ends.

Justice by comparison can never be used to do harm, because then it will simply become injustice.

2. The condition of conformity with the law. Just conduct can be defined as conduct (whether by the state or a citizen) that is consistent with the obligations laid down by law. This of course begs the question whether there can be *unjust* laws. If there cannot, then, as Pascal observed, 'justice is what is established; and thus all our established laws will necessarily be regarded as just without examination, since they are established'. To try and avoid this circularity, philosophers have sought to define the (ideal) conditions under which law could be seen as just. For example, Kant described just laws as the law freedom would give itself if it could remove itself from the inclination of pleasure and its desires. More recently, JOHN RAWLS has argued that a just institution (including the law) would be one that reasonable and dispassionate individuals would choose if they could make their decision under conditions of fairness, which he in turn characterized as conditions of 'maximum equal liberty'. Recent discussions of justice have tended to focus on Rawls's contribution and criticisms thereof, notably in the work of the libertarian Robert Nozick and in the so-called 'communitarian critique' developed by writers such as Michael Sandel and Charles Taylor.

3. A synonym for part of the legal or judicial process when used in phrases such as 'criminal justice', or 'the civil justice system'.   [JW]

See also ADMINISTRATION OF JUSTICE; DISTRIBUTIVE JUSTICE; FORMAL JUSTICE; PROCEDURAL JUSTICE; SUBSTANTIVE JUSTICE.

Further reading: Plato, *The Republic*; Aristotle, *Nichomachean Ethics*; Blaise Pascal, *Pensées*, Section 5, 'Justice and the Reason of Effects'; John Rawls, *A Theory of Justice*, revised edn (Cambridge, MA: Belknap Press, 1999); Robert Nozick, *Anarchy, State and Utopia* (New York: Basic Books, 1977); Stephen Mulhall and Adam Swift, *Liberals and Communitarians*, 2nd edn (Oxford: Blackwell, 1996).

justices' clerk *See* MAGISTRATES' CLERK.

justification **1**. A defence to DEFAMATION, asserting that the alleged defamatory words are true.

2. In criminal law, a category of defence, based on the assertion that the accused's actions are justified on the facts and therefore not culpable: see NECESSITY and SELF-DEFENCE.   [JW]

juvenile court A special type of magistrates' court which is used for the trial of juveniles. This court was renamed the YOUTH COURT under the Criminal Justice Act 1991, s. 70.   [SN]

juvenile offender A young person aged between 15 and 17 years of age who has been given a custodial sentence.   [SN]

K

Kant, Immanuel (1724–1804) German philosopher and the leading figure in the Enlightenment. His output was considerable and has influenced a wide range of disciplines. The most obvious influence on law and jurisprudence can be seen in his best-known contribution to moral philosophy: the *categorical imperative*. This holds that one should only act in accordance with a rule that one would agree to becoming a universal rule. The categorical imperative thus provides a measure by which putative moral principles may be tested.

As to where the motivation for moral action comes from, Kant is clear that this is DUTY. He dismisses any consequentialist alternatives and thus is said to propose a *deontological* as opposed to a *teleological* theory. The uncompromising nature of Kant's approach may be seen in his famous injunction that one should always tell the truth irrespective of the consequences. This in turn is a manifestation of his position that one should always treat other people as ends in themselves and not as means to one's own ends. In lying to someone, one contravenes this injunction and treats the interlocutor as a means to one's own ends.

This internally coherent, if rather demanding, approach to moral philosophy may give the impression that Kant's only contribution to law and jurisprudence was to NATURAL LAW or theories of JUSTICE. While it is true that he was influential in this regard, for example in the work of JOHN RAWLS, that by no means exhausts his impact on law. Kant's views on morality mean that he can also be described as a normative positivist. Insofar as morality requires us to ensure that justice always prevails (whatever the consequences may be), it is necessary to have arrangements in place that allow disputes to be settled impartially and without reference to self-interest. This in turn gives rise to the need for law as well as an obligation not to undermine its authority. In other words, there is a moral obligation to obey the law. It may be wondered how Kant will deal with laws which are themselves immoral. The answer is that he, in common with other normative positivists, treats the question of whether a given law is moral as distinct from the question of whether it must be obeyed. [JP]

See also LEGAL POSITIVISM.

Further reading: Immanuel Kant, *Critique of Practical Reason* (Cambridge: Cambridge University Press, 1997).

keeping the peace A core duty of a police officer. Courts also have a power to bind persons over to keep the peace. A defendant who fails to comply with the bind-over risks a custodial penalty. Being bound over to keep the peace may form part or all of the penalty imposed for the commission of a particular offence. A bind-over may also be imposed in response to a complaint of a BREACH OF THE PEACE. The relevant complaint must be proved beyond reasonable doubt (see *Percy* v. *DPP* [1995] 3 All ER 124).   [BF]

See also OBSTRUCTING A POLICE OFFICER; QUEEN'S PEACE; STANDARD OF PROOF.

Kelsen, Hans (1881–1973) Austrian jurist and one of the principal figures in the field of descriptive LEGAL POSITIVISM. Born in Vienna, Kelsen worked for a period in Germany. He was forced to leave for Geneva during the Nazi era because of his Jewish heritage and ultimately moved to California, where he worked until his death.

Kelsen's aim was to develop what he termed a PURE THEORY OF LAW. His use of the term 'pure' was intended to emphasize that jurisprudence should be concerned solely with the description and understanding of the operation of NORMS ('ought' statements) and that it should not concern itself either with the processes by which law emerged or with its effects.

Kelsen's analysis produced considerable clarity with regard to the operation of law. For example, he demonstrated that the way in which legal norms are expressed can mislead as to their nature. Thus, criminal norms are often expressed in a form such as 'A person who commits offence X shall be liable to a fine or imprisonment or both'. The expression 'shall be' is misleading because the legislator is not predicting future events, but rather is prescribing what ought to happen in that situation. The legal norm thus provides a command and not a prediction for the future; a command that is better expressed by the verb *ought to be*. The use of the word 'ought' within a legal norm does not have moral implications. It is only a functional connection between the two elements of the norm, the antecedent (for example, the offence) and the consequent (for example, the imposition of the sanction).

For Kelsen, the norm acts as a scheme of interpretation. In other words, the actions of people in society become legally relevant if they are interpreted with the help of legal

norms. Any set of social or moral norms – not only legal norms – can confer meaning on actions. There are, however, two essential differences between legal norms and any other set of norms. (a) Only legal norms have at their disposal a centralized apparatus of coercion to penalize transgressors. Moral and social norms also have sanctions, but they do not have a system of centralized coercion. (b) They have different kinds of addressees. Moral norms aim at creating a good community by imposing moral duties on each individual. For their part, legal norms seek to prevent crimes not by imposing duties on the citizen, but rather by commanding that law officials punish those who violate the law. The law is not addressed to citizens. When the law states that a person who commits a murder will be punished, it is only informing citizens about the circumstances that are the condition for a sanction. But the law does not impose on the citizen a duty to avoid the conduct that brings about this action. The law only imposes a duty on law officials, a duty to punish wrongdoers. Kelsen describes such norms as **primary norms**. What could, therefore, appear to be the primary norm (a norm imposing a duty on the citizen) is for Kelsen only a **secondary norm** that may be inferred from a primary one.

Kelsen's analysis also offers a particular account of the nature of legal validity. For him, a norm is valid insofar as that validity is conferred by another higher norm. That view, however, is destined to produce an infinite regress unless something intervenes to stop it. Accordingly, the search for the reason for the validity of a legal system's norms ends with a norm whose validity, as the highest and the last of the system, is presupposed. It must be presupposed, because if it were not, then another source for its validity – another higher norm – would have to be found. This final norm is the **basic norm** or GRUNDNORM postulated by Kelsen and is the common source for the validity of all the norms belonging to a legal system. The structure of the legal order is accordingly for Kelsen hierarchical, a pyramidal form, with the *Grundnorm* at the top.

The identification of the *Grundnorm* depends upon efficacy. Thus, the validity of the basic norm can be presupposed only if the legal order as a whole is effective – in other words, if legal officials are able to maintain law and order. Kelsen's ideas in this regard have accordingly been influential with courts in revolutionary situations. [JP]

Further reading: Hans Kelsen, *Pure Theory of Law* (Berkeley and Los Angeles: University of California Press, 1967).

kerb crawling A vernacular term referring to the offence under the Sexual Offences Act 1985, s. 1, whereby a person commits this offence if he or she solicits another person or different persons for the purpose of prostitution, from a MOTOR VEHICLE in a street or public place. The soliciting must be persistent or done in such a manner or in such circumstances as to be likely to cause annoyance to any of the persons solicited, or nuisance to other persons in the neighbourhood. The definition of the offence is such that it can be committed by prostitute and client alike. [BF]

See also SOLICITING; STREET OFFENCES.

knowhow Technical information about an INVENTION or other technological product or process which is not necessarily part of the PATENT (or UTILITY MODELS or REGISTERED DESIGN) grant. Very often, knowhow information is equated with TRADE SECRETS and confidential information, but secrecy is not a necessary element in knowhow. **Knowhow agreements** are ancillary to PATENT LICENCES and are governed by CONTRACT, CONFIDENTIALITY, trade secrecy or UNFAIR COMPETITION laws, rather than INTELLECTUAL PROPERTY laws. [US]

knowing assistance The phrase that, conventionally (if somewhat inaccurately), describes the personal liability of someone who helps a TRUSTEE commit a BREACH OF TRUST or fiduciary obligation, or procures such a breach. In recent years the term has fallen out of favour after a series of decisions in the higher courts, most notably the speech of Lord Nichols giving the judgment of the PRIVY COUNCIL in *Royal Brunei Airlines* v. *Tan* [1995], that have established the test of liability to be one of dishonesty rather than knowledge. The phrase **dishonest assistance** is consequently favoured today and, despite the occasional attempt to over-complicate what is meant by dishonesty, it is now clearly established that this is an objective standard albeit with a strong subjective element. Liability is consequently dependent upon whether the assister, in light of his subjective knowledge of the circumstances, has acted dishonestly by reference to what society regards as honest. It was also established in *Tan* that the assister may be liable even if the trustee who commits the breach of trust does so innocently, as might well occur where a trustee relies upon a dishonest assistant for advice and guidance. [PK]

See also KNOWING RECEIPT.

knowing receipt The personal liability of someone who receives TRUST property in breach of trust where it is either impossible or impractical to make a proprietary claim in respect of the trust property received. The liability most often occurs in situations where the recipient no longer has the trust property or its traceable equivalent because the property has been dissipated, lost or passed gratuitously to another. However, a claim may also be made in situations where it is deemed too impractical to make a proprietary claim because of the complicated dealings that have occurred in respect of the trust property. A still unresolved controversy surrounds the test of liability to be applied in such situations that reflects no great credit on the law of trusts. Over a large number of cases, differing gradations of knowledge have been articulated, with some judges holding that liability must necessarily involve some degree of dishonesty, others suggesting that it should be equated with the equitable doctrine of notice and still others arguing for a restitutionary approach (see RESTITUTION) to make the recipient strictly liable. Logically this latter approach has much to commend it, given that the recipient has been enriched at the expense of the trust and thus should be liable to the extent that the enrichment is unjust. It would also bring the equitable remedy into line with its common law counterpart, **money had and received**, where strict liability is the clearly established test of liability. However, at a practical level, such an approach is likely to prove unworkable as, with every receipt of trust property, the burden of proof would shift to the recipient who would need to establish a change of position defence to escape liability. Given how frequently trust funds are dealt with and traded, this would place an intolerable burden on recipients, and the courts have instead retreated into ever vaguer articulations of liability with 'unconscionability' being the current favourite. This is in effect strict liability, subject to a change of position defence, but with the practical advantage that the burden of proof remains with those bringing the claim to prove that the receipt was unconscionable because no such change of position occurred – although whether asking the claimant to prove such a negative is itself practicable is open to similar doubts.   [PK]

Kompetenz-Kompetenz An arbitral tribunal's jurisdictional competence to determine its own jurisdictional competence, subject to any right of the parties to the ARBITRATION to appeal to the courts of the seat of arbitration. It is the JURISDICTION of an ARBITRAL TRIBUNAL – perceived by some as a traditional, pragmatic, fictional power inhering in the arbitral process upon the appointment of the tribunal – to decide (a) whether or not the tribunal has jurisdiction based on the ARBITRATION AGREEMENT; and (b) whether or not individual members of the tribunal have personal jurisdiction in relation to the parties and the dispute.

[RE]

L

laches (Norman Fr. slackness, negligence) Unreasonable delay or neglect in bringing an equitable claim. The doctrine is embodied in the equitable maxims that 'equity will not help those who fail to help themselves' and 'equity aids the vigilant'. However its modern day importance should not be overstated as it is only operative in the absence of statutory limitation periods, as these enable claimants to bring a claim at any time up until the expiry of the period laid down by statute, irrespective of what equity might deem unreasonable delay or neglect. [PK]

See also MAXIMS OF EQUITY.

land In law, land means more than the physical asset; it includes the rights and responsibilities associated with it, as well as having a temporal dimension. The Law of Property Act 1925, s. 205, defines land broadly as including 'land of any TENURE, and mines and minerals, whether or not held apart from the surface, buildings or parts of buildings (whether the division is horizontal, vertical or made in any other way) also a manor, ADVOWSON, and a RENT and other INCORPOREAL HEREDITAMENTS, and an EASEMENT, right, privilege, or benefit in, over, or derived from land'. It also includes goods which are fixed to the land. [HC & DR]

land certificate A certificate formerly produced by the Land Registry, providing proof of TITLE to land. Before the Land Registration Act 2002 (LRA 2002), possession of a land certificate showing the owner of land as the registered proprietor constituted conclusive evidence of TITLE to REGISTERED LAND and was a crucial prerequisite of the ability to sell. Since the LRA 2002 came into force on 13 October 2003, the Land Registry are no longer producing land certificates. Although the Land Registry will provide a Title Information Document if requested, title to land is evidenced by the Land Register entries themselves or OFFICIAL COPIES of those entries. [DR]

See also TITLE DEEDS.

land charge In UNREGISTERED LAND, a charge on or obligation affecting land that may be registered in the LAND CHARGES REGISTER so that the interest is protected against a third party purchaser of that land. Land charges are divided by the Land Charges Act 1972 into six classes from A to F. The most common forms of land charge are RESTRICTIVE COVENANTS (Class D (ii)), EQUITABLE EASEMENTS (Class D (iii)), ESTATE CONTRACTS (Class C (iv)), PUISNE MORTGAGES (Class C (i)) and matrimonial home rights (Class F).

Generally speaking, if a land charge is not registered then it will not be possible to enforce it against a later purchaser for value of the land to which it relates. For example, where a father grants an OPTION

TO PURCHASE his house to his son, falling within the definition of an estate contract, that option to purchase is registrable as a Class C (iv) land charge. However, if the son fails to register it, there is nothing to stop the father selling the house to a third party, even if that property is sold for only £500 (*Midland Bank Trust Co. Ltd* v. *Green* [1981] AC 513). [DR]

Land Charges Register A register maintained by the Land Registry's Land Charges Department in Plymouth, which keeps a record of all registered land charges in relation to unregistered land. Land charges are registered against the name of the owner of the estate when the charge was created, not against the land itself.

When buying unregistered land, it is crucial for the buyer to carry out a land charges search against the person's full, correct name or the results of that search may not be safely conclusive (see *Oak Co-operative Building Society* v. *Blackburn* [1968] Ch 730). Similarly, the person registering the charge must make sure they do so against the estate owner's correct name, preferably the name on the title deeds. A charge registered against the incorrect name of an estate owner would not rank ahead of a subsequent charge registered correctly (*Diligent Finance Co. Ltd* v. *Alleyne* (1972) 23 P & CR 346).

In registered land, charges are registered against the subject property and are maintained on the charges register in the Land Register entries for that property. [DR]
See also CHARGES REGISTER.

landlord A landlord is a person or an organization which grants a TENANCY to someone. Landlords need not be freeholders of premises, but may hold a LEASE themselves. Landlords can be individuals, trustees, personal representatives, corporations, local authorities, HOUSING ASSOCIATIONS or HOUSING TRUSTS. The nature of the landlord partially determines the type of statutory protection that a tenant may have, so for instance only local authority landlords can offer a SECURE TENANCY. A landlord of residential premises is obliged to provide the tenant with his or her name

and an address for service of notices (see the Landlord and Tenant Act 1987, s. 48).
[HC & DR]

lapse A GIFT by WILL fails and is said to lapse if the BENEFICIARY predeceases the TESTATOR. A testator cannot exclude the doctrine of lapse, but he may provide in his will that if the named beneficiary fails to survive him then an alternative beneficiary shall take, otherwise the lapsed gift will fall into RESIDUE of the estate under the Wills Act 1837, s. 25.

There are two exceptions to the doctrine of lapse. First, if the gift by will is intended to discharge what the testator considers to be a moral obligation. Second, where the gift is to a child or remoter descendant of the testator and the beneficiary predeceases the testator, leaving issue who are living at the testator's death, then such issue can take, provided the will does not contain a contrary provision (Wills Act 1837, s. 33).
[CM]

lapse of offer An OFFER will end or lapse, so as to be unavailable for acceptance, in the event of death or when the time period during which the offer was available to be accepted has expired, or, if no such period has been specified, then after a reasonable time. Death of the offeror will cause the offer to lapse unless (a) the offer does not require the performance of a personal service by the offeror, and so could be performed by the offeror's personal representatives, and (b) the offer was accepted by the offeree before having notice of the offeror's death. Death of the offeree is generally supposed to cause the offer to lapse. [JPL]
See also ACCEPTANCE.

larceny (obsolete) Larceny was the name given to the offence most closely corresponding to that which is now known as THEFT. The COMMON LAW and the Larceny Act 1916 required that a person, by a trespass, took possession of goods from another without that person's consent, and carried them away. [BF]

lasting power of attorney The Mental Capacity Act 2005 enables individuals who have the MENTAL CAPACITY to do so to confer lasting power of attorney on someone chosen to act as decision-maker on their behalf in the event of loss of capacity at some future date. Lasting power of attorney replaces the former **enduring power of attorney** and is more extensive as it provides not only for the appointment of an attorney to manage property and affairs, but also confers powers enabling decisions about personal welfare, including healthcare, to be taken at a time when decision-making capacity may be lacking.   [HJ]

late payment compensation Statutory compensation that a creditor may legally claim in respect of late payment of a commercial debt under the Late Payment of Commercial Debts (Interest) Act 1998, as amended. The amount of compensation is fixed by law and presently stands at £40 for debts up to £999.99; £70 for debts between £1,000 and £9,999.99, and £100 for debts of £10,000 and over. The compensation cannot be claimed where one of the parties contracts as a CONSUMER.   [JW]

late payment demand A letter seeking payment of a business debt, together with a claim for interest and compensation under the terms of the Late Payment of Commercial Debts (Interest) Act 1998, as amended. A payment is late for this purpose once the agreed credit period has expired, or, in the absence of an agreed credit period, where more than 30 days have passed since performance of the agreed obligation, or the supplier's invoice, or other notice of the debt, was received by the purchaser.

The legislation entitles the creditor to claim, in addition to the principal sum owed: (a) interest calculated at a statutory reference rate, based on the Bank of England Base Rate, plus 8%; (b) the amount of LATE PAYMENT COMPENSATION fixed by statute; and (c) reasonable debt recovery costs. Each of these amounts should be calculated and specified within the demand. The creditor is entitled to these amounts as of right, and does not require a court order to collect. If the debtor disputes or does not pay the outstanding amount, it may be enforced through the courts. A claim for statutory interest and compensation may be made retrospectively, provided it is within six years (five years in Scotland) of the entitlement arising.   [JW]

law The system or body of RULES which imposes obligations on individuals and where non-compliance involves the threat that a sanction will be imposed by the state's centralized organs of coercion either directly or on the application of another individual to those organizations.

Within JURISPRUDENCE the principal debate has been whether law is simply what the lawmaker says it is, irrespective of any moral evaluation (LEGAL POSITIVISM), or whether a rule can only attain the status of law if it also passes a moral test (NATURAL LAW).   [JP]

Law Commission An independent body established by the Law Commissions Act 1965 and responsible for keeping the law of England and Wales under review and making recommendations to the government for its reform, repeal and codification. The Commission consists of a Chairman (usually a judge) and four Commissioners, who may be appointed from among judges, solicitors, barristers and academic lawyers. There is also a separate Scottish Law Commission.   [JW]

law-jobs A concept emerging in the later work of KARL LLEWELLYN as a further strand of thought within AMERICAN REALISM beyond RULE SCEPTICISM and FACT SCEPTICISM. Llewellyn suggests that law exists to perform certain basic functions that are necessary for the continuation of society: specifically those related to avoiding and resolving disputes and to allocating and implementing authority. As a consequence of the need for these jobs to be done, people develop particular skills, which Llewellyn describes as **law-crafts**. Llewellyn contends both that the law-jobs he lists are derived from the observation of society rather than being abstract constructs and that these law-jobs must be carried out in any society. In other words, law is a functional requirement of any and every society.   [JP]

Further reading: Karl Llewellyn, 'The Normative, the Legal and the Law-Jobs: The Problem of Juristic Method', *Yale Law Journal* (1940), 49, pp. 1355–1400.

Law Lords *See* HOUSE OF LORDS.

law merchant *See* LEX MERCATORIA.

law of nations (Lat. *jus gentium,* the law of peoples, or law of nations) The term employed prior to the crystallization of the term INTERNATIONAL LAW to denote the rules governing the relations between sovereign nations. This was also the term employed by the classical writers of international law at a time before international rules had been codified in TREATY form and those authors were forced to deduce the applicable rules from the practice of STATES and NATURAL LAW. [IB]

law of the sea The field of INTERNATIONAL LAW that deals with the regulation between STATES of maritime territories and delineates the rights and duties of states therein. The law of the sea has traditionally developed on the basis of customary law and it was only in the latter half of the 20th century that it was codified, initially through the three 1958 Geneva Conventions and later consolidated into one major instrument, the 1982 UNITED NATIONS CONVENTION ON THE LAW OF THE SEA. Other international agreements exist regulating more specialized topics, such as fisheries, pollution and others. [IB]

See also CUSTOMARY INTERNATIONAL LAW; EXCLUSIVE ECONOMIC ZONE; INTERNAL WATERS; TERRITORIAL WATERS.

Law Officers The ATTORNEY GENERAL and SOLICITOR-GENERAL, together with the Lord Advocate and Solicitor-General for Scotland, are known as the Law Officers. [MS]

See also SCOTTISH LAW OFFICERS.

law reports Written records of cases decided in the superior courts. Law reporting is practised, to varying degrees, in all legal systems, since the law relies on having an available written record of decided cases to support both doctrinal development and consistency of decision-making. The trad-

ition of law reporting is particularly strong in the COMMON LAW world because of the doctrine of binding PRECEDENT: the idea that lower courts are obliged to follow relevant decisions of higher courts. This system could not operate effectively without reliable law reports.

The earliest known law reports in England and Wales are the YEAR BOOKS, which were produced from the early 13th to mid-16th century, probably by student lawyers at the INNS OF COURT. They were replaced by numerous series of 'nominate reports' (so called because each series was named after its author or compiler) written by practising lawyers, and subsequently consolidated into a series called the *English Reports.* The quality of the nominate reports was highly variable, and steps were taken to standardize and improve the quality of reporting in the 19th century, culminating, in 1865, in the founding of the INCORPORATED COUNCIL OF LAW REPORTING, which still takes responsibility for publishing the main series of law reports today.

There are also other commercially published series of reports, such as the generalist All England Law Reports, though most other series focus on specialist areas of law, such as the European Law Reports, Housing Law Reports and so on. A growing number of law reports are available online, free of charge, through the work of the Free Access to Law Movement which supports services like BAILII (the British and Irish Legal Information Institute; see http://www.bailii. org/) and the WorldLII portal (available at http://www.worldlii.org/). [JW]

Law Society The representative body of the SOLICITORS' profession in England and Wales. In January 2007, the Law Society created a separate regulatory body called the **Solicitors Regulation Authority** (SRA). The SRA now takes responsibility for setting professional standards and guidance, for dealing with individual complaints and investigations into solicitors' firms, and for prosecuting serious malpractice before the (independent) **Solicitors Disciplinary Tribunal;** see http:/www.lawsociety.org. uk/home.law and http://www.sra.org.uk/

consumers/consumers.page and http://www.solicitorstribunal.org.uk/.   [JW]

laying an information The procedure by which the statement informing the MAGIS-TRATE of an offence is brought to the magistrate's attention.   [SN]

LCIA *See* LONDON COURT OF INTERNATIONAL ARBITRATION.

LCJ *See* LORD CHIEF JUSTICE.

Leader of the House *See* HOUSE OF COMMONS.

leading question A question to a WITNESS which directly or indirectly suggests to the witness the answer to be given. It is generally impermissible to ask leading questions when examining one's own witness. [ALTC]

lease An INTEREST in an identifiable plot of LAND that provides the holder, the TENANT, with exclusive possession of the land for a FIXED or PERIODIC TERM, generally, but not inevitably, in exchange for a payment of RENT or a premium. The term 'lease' is not defined in statute and therefore its scope is found in case law. The classic definition is provided by Lord Templeman in *Street* v. *Mountford* [1985] AC 809 when it was made clear that it was not the label put upon the arrangement by the parties that determined its nature, but the legal reality of the agreement.

A lease is no longer wholly synonymous with a TERM OF YEARS. A tenant may have the benefit of a lease even though he or she is not able to establish a proprietary title that is good against all of the world. Since *Bruton (AP)* v. *London and Quadrant Housing Trust* (1999) 31 HLR 902, the status of a lease can be established by ESTOPPEL and its contractual characteristics are becoming more significant than its proprietorial characteristics.   [HC & DR]
    See also EQUITABLE LEASE; SECURITY OF TENURE.

leasehold The way in which property is held when it is subject to a LEASE. [HC & DR]
    See also LANDLORD; TENANT.

Leasehold Valuation Tribunal A formal body which operates under the auspices of the RESIDENTIAL PROPERTY TRIBUNAL Service and adjudicates disputes in connection with LEASEHOLD premises. Leasehold Valuation Tribunals hear disputes in connection with a range of matters, including the price to be paid when a leaseholder wants to buy (enfranchise), extend or renew the LEASE of their home and the value cannot be agreed with the leaseholder; rights of first refusal to buy the freehold when the landlord wishes to sell it; and liability for payment of service charges.   [HC & DR]

leave to appeal The technical term for seeking permission from a court to mount an APPEAL.   [JW]

legacy A GIFT of personal property made by WILL; it has the same meaning as **bequest**. A pecuniary legacy is one that consists of money. All legacies fall into one of three types, i.e. specific, general or demonstrative, and the distinction is important since they are dealt with differently (for example, regarding ADEMPTION or payment of debts).

A **specific legacy** is one where the subject of the gift is identified by description and distinguished from the rest of the estate, e.g. 'my golf clubs'. If the property no longer forms part of the estate of the testator at his death, the gift is adeemed.

A **general legacy** is one that does not relate to a specific part of the testator's property, e.g. 'the sum of £100'. Since no specific item is identified, it cannot be adeemed.

A **demonstrative legacy** is similar to a general legacy, but a particular fund is indicated to satisfy it, e.g. 'the sum of £100 from my account at the Midshires Bank'. The court construes this as a direction to satisfy the legacy from that source if it can do so, but if that cannot be done, then the legacy is treated as a general one. It cannot be adeemed.   [CM]

legal aid A scheme funded by the state to provide financial assistance to individuals requiring legal advice and representation. The current operation of the scheme in England and Wales reflects the framework established by the Legal Aid Act 1988, as substantially revised by the Access to Justice Act 1999. The 1999 Act created a new body, the LEGAL SERVICES COMMISSION, to administer the scheme, which was re-branded into two new services: the Community Legal Service (CLS) and the Criminal Defence Service (CDS).

The CLS, which funds advice and/or representation on civil matters, must operate within an annual budget. Eligibility for the CLS scheme is thus determined by a mix of priority areas of work and exclusions. Thus claims in respect of negligently caused injury or death (with the exception of clinical negligence), DEFAMATION, boundary disputes, business disputes and non-contentious matters such as conveyancing and the drafting of WILLS, are generally excluded from the scheme. In addition applicants are also subjected to a financial eligibility, or 'means' test, and a 'merits' test which assesses the prospects of success relative to the cost of taking action. Unlike the civil scheme, the CDS is not a cash-limited service, but defendants facing prosecution in the magistrates' court are subject to means-testing.   [JW]

legal capacity The power provided by law to have or to be the subject of legal rights and duties. Legal capacity is presumed to exist as of right in any **natural person** (i.e. a human being), subject to any legal disabilities that may arise, for example because of their age or mental incapacity. **Juridical** (or **artificial**) persons, i.e. the STATE, and certain business entities, such as a COMPANY, or international legal organizations which have an independent legal capacity from their members (e.g. the EUROPEAN COMMUNITY), will also normally enjoy full legal capacity to enter into certain legal relationships, and can sue or be sued in their own name.   [JW]

See also COMPETENCE; *DOLI INCAPAX;* GILLICK COMPETENCE; LEGAL PERSON; MENTAL CAPACITY.

legal easement An EASEMENT that satisfies the following three requirements: (a) it is created by deed, statute or PRESCRIPTION; (b) it is 'equivalent to a fee simple absolute in possession or a term of years absolute' (Law of Property Act 1925 (LPA 1925), s. 1 (2)), meaning that it must either last forever or for a fixed period; (c) in the case of expressly created easements, it is registered at the Land Registry (unless created under LPA 1925, s. 62).

Most easements are legal easements. Prior to the introduction of the Land Registration Act 2002 (LRA 2002), legal easements were OVERRIDING INTERESTS and therefore binding upon subsequent purchasers. However, under the LRA 2002, legal easements will only be overriding interests on first registration of a disposition of land. On later dispositions of registered land, most legal easements will not be overriding interests (LRA 2002, Schedule 3 para. 3).   [DR]

See also EQUITABLE EASEMENT.

legal estate An ESTATE that is recognized by the common law and valid against the whole world, irrespective of notice. Under the Law of Property Act 1925, s. 1(1), the only legal estates in land that are capable of existing are the FEE SIMPLE ABSOLUTE IN POSSESSION (freehold estate) and the TERM OF YEARS absolute (LEASEHOLD estate). All other estates in land have effect as EQUITABLE INTERESTS. [DR]

legal ethics An area of applied ethics focusing on the moral principles, legal rules and standards of conduct that guide, or ought to guide, the work of both individual lawyers and the legal profession as a collective entity. Examples of the former include rules and principles governing the proper representation of clients, lawyer–client CONFIDENTIALITY, and CONFLICT OF INTERESTS. The latter tends to focus on matters such as the moral and legal accountability of the profession to the society it serves, the ethical principles that shape the regulation and governance of the profession, and the responsibilities of the profession (if any) to facilitate access to the courts and legal services.   [JW]

See also BAR COUNCIL; CAB RANK RULE; LAW SOCIETY; LEGAL PROFESSIONAL PRIVILEGE.

Further reading: A. Boon and J. Levin, *The Ethics and Conduct of Lawyers in England and Wales,* 2nd edn (Oxford: Hart Publishing, 2008); D. Nicolson and J. Webb, *Professional*

Legal Ethics: Critical Interrogations (Oxford: Oxford University Press, 1999).

legal lease A legal lease creates a TERM OF YEARS absolute, one of the two ESTATES in LAND recognized by the Law of Property Act 1925. Particular formalities are required for leases of three years or over which must be created by DEED and registered.

[HC & DR]

See also PAROL LEASE.

legal mortgage *See* MORTGAGE.

legal person A person or institution recognized as a person at law. All living human beings are legal persons (properly called natural persons). Some institutions created by law, such as companies or corporations sole, and certain governmental or international organizations, are treated as equivalent to natural persons, and are said to be juristic or artificial persons. In practical terms, legal personality primarily affects an institution's ability to enter into legal relations, for example to make contracts, and to sue or be sued, in its own name. A person or entity may possess legal personality but may still face certain legal constraints because it lacks full LEGAL CAPACITY. Thus, for example, a young child is a legal person, but will lack the capacity by reason of their age to bring a legal action other than via a responsible adult acting as LITIGATION FRIEND.   [JW]

legal pluralism Historically, the notion that in colonial settings the legal system could encompass a variety of normative orders, notably the law of the colonial power as well as elements of existing indigenous law. Contemporary legal pluralists would deny that the legal system, strictly speaking, could itself have this plural character, but would nevertheless accept that within the same geographical space a variety of normative orders may coexist, of which the state legal system is only one. Legal pluralists are interested in how these different normative orders mutually influence one another as well as the people who are subject to them.

Among the most influential legal pluralistic accounts is Boaventura De Sousa Santos's study of a Brazilian *favela* or shanty town in which he maps congruent official and unofficial legal systems. However, this study has been the focus of criticism from those, such as Brian Z. Tamanaha, who are concerned that legal pluralism risks diminishing the importance and indeed the power of law, by according the label 'law' too readily to unofficial normative orders.

[JP]

Further reading: Sally Engle Merry, 'Legal Pluralism', *Law & Society Review* (1988), 22, pp. 869–96. Boaventura De Sousa Santos, *Toward a New Common Sense*, 2nd edn (London: Butterworths, 2002).

legal positivism The term used to describe theories of law which share certain features, including the idea that legal science should only study law as it *is* as opposed to any ideal system of law or any idea of what law *ought to be*; the assertion that law can only exist when it has been deliberately laid down by a rational individual (or group of individuals) with political power as opposed to any idea that law could be given to man by God or derived from nature; and a primary concern with the analysis of basic legal concepts in legal systems that have been or are extant. Legal positivism (or positive law) is therefore strongly contrasted with NATURAL LAW.

Tracing its roots back to the wider movement of POSITIVISM in the Enlightenment (as exemplified by the work of Auguste Comte), legal positivism in the English-speaking world is generally regarded as emerging with the work of JEREMY BENTHAM and his influential disciple JOHN AUSTIN. Modern legal positivism is especially associated in the 20th century with the work of HANS KELSEN and H.L.A. HART.

Enjoying an ascendancy over natural law for much of the 19th and early 20th centuries, legal positivism came under pressure in the aftermath of the Second World War when it was perceived by some (notably Gustav Radbruch) to have contributed to the atrocities in totalitarian states by rendering lawyers unable to raise moral objections to laws which had been validly passed. The resurgence enjoyed by natural law in the succeeding years is best exemplified by the work of Lon Fuller and JOHN FINNIS. [JP]

legal professional privilege Under certain circumstances, communications between a lawyer and client are immune from disclosure to a third party, such as a court or the other party in litigation. Information properly protected by the privilege is also exempted from disclosure under the Freedom of Information Act 2000, s. 42 (see FREEDOM OF INFORMATION).

The privilege is wide and absolute. It can be claimed by artificial legal persons, such as companies, as well as individuals. It can only be waived by the client, not the lawyer. It exists in two forms. (a) A **legal advice privilege** protects all confidential communications between lawyers acting in their professional capacity and their clients, provided that the communication was made for the dominant purpose of giving or seeking advice in any legal context (see *Three Rivers District Council and Ors* v. *Governor of the Bank of England (No. 6)* [2004] UKHL 48). (b) A **litigation privilege** protects communications between lawyers and clients, or between lawyers and third parties, where there is 'a real likelihood' of litigation or litigation is ongoing, and the document or other communication is made for the dominant purpose of advancing the litigation, or of giving legal advice in connection with it.

For EC law purposes only, communications concerning legal advice between in-house lawyers and the companies that employ them are not privileged. This is because in-house lawyers have been held to lack the quality of independence enjoyed by their external counterparts (see case 155/79, *AM & S Europe Ltd* v. *Commission* (1982) ECR 1575). This approach was recently followed in September 2007 in joined cases T-125/03 and T-253/03, *Akzo Nobel Chemicals Ltd and Akcros Chemicals Ltd* v. *Commission,* where the COURT OF FIRST INSTANCE refused to treat such documents seized by the European Competition Commission on a 'dawn raid' investigating possible breaches of European competition

law as capable of attracting privilege. This has significant consequences in the English context. Thus, if the Office of Fair Trading (OFT) investigates a company under the Competition Act 1998, that company's in-house lawyers' work will attract privilege under English law. However, where the OFT investigates as agent for the Commission, privilege will not attach to such in-house work. An appeal in the *Akzo Nobel* decision is pending before the EUROPEAN COURT OF JUSTICE. [JW]

legal rights The notion that an individual possesses RIGHTS by virtue of the fact that these are laid down by law. Legal rights may be contrasted with NATURAL RIGHTS, where the proposition is that an individual possesses inalienable rights by virtue simply of being human and irrespective of what may or may not be laid down by law. [JP]

legal separation In England and Wales, when spouses or civil partners separate, or begin to live apart with the intention of living apart permanently, the time period for the (two-year or five-year) SEPARATION facts required for DIVORCE or DISSOLUTION begins to run. They do not require a court order for the separation to be 'legal' for this purpose. While a petitioner spouse or applicant civil partner may have the option of obtaining a JUDICIAL SEPARATION ORDER, these orders are rarely sought. Otherwise, the term 'legal separation' may refer to the parties completing a written SEPARATION AGREEMENT in which they agree to cease COHABITATION and further agree property, financial, CHILD care or other arrangements as a result. [AD]

Legal Services Board A regulatory body created by the Legal Services Act 2007 to oversee the regulation of the legal services market. The Board is not a 'frontline' regulator but will oversee and monitor the activities of frontline regulators such as the **Solicitors' Regulation Authority** and the **Bar Standards Board**. The Board is required to have a mix of lay members and members drawn from the legal profession. The Chair of the Board may not be a qualified legal practitioner. The Board is expected to commence its regulatory activities in Spring 2010.   [JW]

Legal Services Commission (LSC) A public body responsible for administering the LEGAL AID Scheme in England and Wales and, within a framework of priorities set by the LORD CHANCELLOR, making detailed decisions about the allocation of resources across the scheme. The LSC took over the administration of the Legal Aid Scheme from the former Legal Aid Board with effect from 1 April 2000.   [JW]

See also COMMUNITY LEGAL SERVICE; CRIMINAL DEFENCE SERVICE.

legal year The annual period, traditionally beginning in October, during which the courts in England and Wales sit for four terms (Michaelmas, Hilary, Easter and Trinity). The start of the legal year is marked by a procession of judges walking to Westminster Abbey from Temple Bar followed by a 'Breakfast' reception in Westminster Hall. The religious service dates back to the Middle Ages when judges prayed for guidance at the start of the legal term.   [AF]

legatee The recipient of a LEGACY in a WILL.
                                                      [CM]

legislative competence The authority and capacity of a body to make and enact binding rules for those it governs. The concept is most commonly used in the context of law-making by devolved and FEDERAL STATES and supra-national or international legal organizations. Legislative competence is significant because acts which fall outside of the competence of a given legislature will not be valid laws; for example, the Scotland Act 1998, s. 29(2) – an Act of the UK Parliament – makes it clear that a purported Act of the Scottish Parliament would not be valid law if any of its provisions falls outside the Parliament's legislative competence as defined by that section. Similarly, EC DIRECTIVES must have a demonstrably correct legal basis in the EC Treaty, and one which confers a law-making power on the Community (see, for example, case C-377/98, *Kingdom of the Netherlands* v.

European Parliament and Council of the European Union (2001) ECR 1-7079). While the legislative competence of a body is normally defined by a founding document (such as a TREATY, CONSTITUTION or STATUTE), the precise boundaries of that competence may often be difficult to determine. Consequently, it is often one of the functions of a competent court to resolve questions of legislative competence. In 'Westminster' constitutions, such as the UK and New Zealand, however, where there is no written constitution as such and a strong tradition of SOVEREIGNTY OF PARLIAMENT, the scope for questioning the legislative competence of Parliament remains very limited.   [JW]

Legislative Competence Order (LCO) A form of ORDER IN COUNCIL, created by the Government of Wales Act 2006, which may be used to extend the LEGISLATIVE COMPETENCE of the NATIONAL ASSEMBLY FOR WALES, by adding a matter or matters to Part 1 of Schedule 5. An LCO must be approved by the Assembly and by both Houses of Parliament before it can be recommended to the Queen for approval. LCOs have been introduced to facilitate the development of devolved government in Wales, by reducing the Assembly's need to wait for a suitable BILL in the UK government's legislative programme in which provisions adding to its legislative competence can be included.   [JW]

legislature A body having primary legislative (law-making) powers. For the UK as a whole this is the Westminster Parliament.
                                                      [JW]

legitimacy The legal status of a CHILD whose PARENTS were married to each other at the time of conception or birth (or both). Alternatively, children can be legitimated by the subsequent MARRIAGE of their parents to each other (Legitimacy Act 1976, s. 2). There is a PRESUMPTION OF LEGITIMACY that the mother's husband is the father of her child, which may be rebutted. A child born to a married woman as a result of artificial insemination with the semen of a donor other than her husband is treated as the legitimate child of the spouses unless it is proved that the husband did not consent to the insemination (Family Law Reform Act 1987, s. 27). The child of a VOID MARRIAGE is treated as the legitimate child of the parents if, at the time of conception or insemination, or at the time of the marriage, if later, both or either of the parties reasonably believed that the marriage was valid (Legitimacy Act 1976, s. 1(1)). There is a presumption in relation to a child born after April 1988 that one of the parties did so believe (s. 1(4)). The legitimacy of children born of a VOIDABLE MARRIAGE is preserved despite an ANNULMENT (see Matrimonial Causes Act 1973, s. 16). Since the enactment of the Family Law Reform Acts of 1969 and 1987, the terminology of legitimacy and ILLEGITIMACY has given way in legislation to references to 'a person whose mother and father were married to each other at the time of birth' (or not) (see e.g. the Family Law Reform Act 1987, s. 1). In the past, an illegitimate child had no legal relationship with his or her father and was even at one time regarded as having no legal relationship with either parent. Now, although the status of legitimacy survives in the law, the legal disabilities affecting children of UNMARRIED PARENTS have almost entirely been removed. They are still not permitted, at present, to succeed to titles of honour or to property that attaches to a title. In addition, an unmarried father does not automatically acquire PARENTAL RESPONSIBILITY for his child. [FK]

See also FATHER'S RIGHTS; LEGITIMATION.

legitimate expectation 1. An ADMINISTRATIVE LAW principle which has emerged in English law since the late 1970s as a means of promoting fairness in public administration. Legitimate expectations may be procedural or substantive. A **procedural legitimate expectation** arises where a public body has led a person to believe that they will be granted a hearing or that some other procedural process will be adopted before a decision is made that affects their interests. Any subsequent failure to act in accordance with that person's reasonable expectation will expose the authority to challenge by way of JUDICIAL REVIEW. The possibility of an action based

on a **substantive legitimate expectation** has been more controversial, though the matter seems to have been placed beyond doubt by the Court of Appeal in *R* v. *North and East Devon Health Authority ex parte Coughlan* [2001] QB 213. Consequently, if a public body induces a legitimate expectation of a substantive benefit (for example, in the *Coughlan* case, the residents' belief that they would be able to live in their home for the rest of their lives), to then frustrate that expectation might be so unfair as to amount to an abuse of power. In these circumstances the court has to decide whether there was a sufficient public interest to justify the authority's departure from what has been promised. If there is not, then the authority has acted contrary to the legitimate expectations it created and will be found to have acted ULTRA VIRES.

2. An EC law concept, similar to the English notion of a substantive legitimate expectation, and reflecting the European Court of Justice's concern that Community policy is implemented according to administrative standards of good faith and fair dealing (see, for example, the opinion of Advocate General Trabucchi in Case 5/75, *Deuka, Deutsche Kraftfutter GmbH. B.J. Stolp* v. *Einfuhr- und Vorratsstelle für Getreide and Futtermittel* [1975] ECR 759 at 777). [JW]

legitimation The process of rendering legitimate. An illegitimate person is legitimated if his or her PARENTS marry each other. As long as the father is domiciled in England or Wales, and as long as the illegitimate person is alive at the date of the parents' MARRIAGE, he or she is treated as the legitimate CHILD of his or her parents as from the date of the marriage (Legitimacy Act 1976, s. 2). [FK]

See also ILLEGITIMACY; LEGITIMACY; PARENTAL RESPONSIBILITY; UNMARRIED PARENTS.

less favourable treatment DISCRIMINATION law is built on several concepts, one of which is direct discrimination. This form of discrimination consists of one person treating another less favourably on a prohibited ground such as sex or race. Direct discrimination cannot be justified except when it is on the ground of age (see AGE DIS-

CRIMINATION) where less favourable treatment may be 'objectively justified' if it is to further a 'legitimate aim' of the business (for example, rewarding experience, or maintaining health and safety), provided that the means of pursuing this aim are 'proportionate'. [MJ]

lessee A person to whom a LEASE is granted. [HC & DR]
See also TENANT; LANDLORD.

letter before action A formal letter commonly used prior to the launch of civil proceedings in which a potential claimant advises the potential defendant of his intention to commence proceedings, unless the latter performs some obligation (e.g. pays a debt, or completes a contracted task), or ceases to interfere with the claimant's legal rights. A letter before action is often a very effective form of self-help, and enables many disputes to be resolved without the intervention of the courts. There is no required form of words, though the letter should always (a) specify the failure of obligation or interference complained of; (b) give a specific and reasonable period of time for performance (it could be as little as seven or ten days for a debt; longer for a more complex obligation); and (c) make it clear that legal action will follow continued non-performance. There is no strict requirement to issue a letter before action, though failure to do so may be taken into consideration by the judge in awarding COSTS. [JW]
See also LATE PAYMENT DEMAND.

letter of credence A formal letter sent by one head of state to another, in which the name of an individual to be accredited to the DIPLOMATIC MISSION of the sending STATE is duly communicated. [IB]
See also DIPLOMATIC AGENT; EXEQUATUR.

letter of intent A statement of AGREEMENT made in the negotiating period leading up to the making of the CONTRACT. However, it does not amount to a legally binding contract since there is no intention to be legally bound. It is therefore no more than a pre-liminary attempt to put an understanding into written form. [JPL]
See also INTENTION TO CREATE LEGAL RELATIONS.

letters of administration *See* GRANT OF REPRESENTATION.

lex arbitri (Lat. law of the arbitration) The procedural law of the ARBITRATION, as opposed to the substantive or proper law governing the dispute. The *lex arbitri* will normally determine such matters as whether the dispute can be referred to arbitration, the conduct of the arbitration and the powers of the arbitrators, and the form and finality of any AWARD. The choice of *lex arbitri* is therefore important because the laws governing these matters will vary between jurisdictions. The *lex arbitri* is usually determined by the seat of arbitration. The seat itself will be chosen either by the parties themselves, or by a person, arbitral institution, or ARBITRAL TRIBUNAL appointed by the parties to make that decision. [RE]
See also ARBITRATION AGREEMENT; ARBITRATION CLAUSE; *LEX CAUSAE*.

lex causae (Lat. the law for the cause) In CONFLICT OF LAWS, that part of the rules of law of a COUNTRY which is applicable to substantive legal issues, such as the relevant contract law, land law, company law, etc. This term can be used, for example, to indicate a substantive GOVERNING LAW, an applicable law, or the PROPER LAW OF THE CONTRACT. [RE]

lex domicilii (Lat. law of (the country) of domicile) The personal law of an individual, or of an artificial entity, such as a company, which attaches to him or her by virtue of factual connection to a particular legal system (such as England and Wales). It is the law of the COUNTRY of DOMICILE (not necessarily of a STATE) which governs some legal issues regardless of where in the world the individual goes. Examples of the legal issues which can be governed by the *lex domicilii* include: capacity to enter into contracts; entitlement to inherit property on the death of another individual; and liability to tax, such as UK inheritance tax. It seems that the law of domicile encompasses both the procedural and the substantive law of the legal system.　　[RE]

See also DOMICILE; GOVERNING LAW; *LEX CAUSAE*.

lex fori (Lat. the law of the FORUM)　The law of the STATE or jurisdiction in which an action will be heard, including the substantive law (see *LEX CAUSAE*). For most purposes, there is no separate Latin tag for those parts of the law of a country which are not the *lex causae*. For the special purposes of CONFLICT OF LAWS, however, the term *lex fori* can be used to signify that part of the law of a country which is not the *lex causae* – perhaps leaving no separate term in that context for the whole of the law of a country.　　[RE]

See also GOVERNING LAW; *LEX LOCI ACTUS*.

lex loci actus (Lat. law of the place where the act occurred)　The laws of a territory in which a legally significant act takes place; also abbreviated to *lex actus*. In CONFLICT OF LAWS, this governs, for example, certain questions concerning the transfer of property (such as when property passes in intangibles, such as a BILL OF EXCHANGE, or certain interests in a trust fund). Different questions will however be determined by different principles. Thus, by contrast, where there is a dispute about tangible property, while the law of the place in which the transfer takes place is the *lex loci actus*, the property itself might be in another COUNTRY, in which case the law of that country would be the *LEX LOCI SITUS*, and the latter would determine questions over TITLE or the right to possession.　　[RE]

See also CONFLICT OF LAWS; TREATY OF ROME.

lex loci celebrationis (Lat. law of the place of celebration)　In English law, a marriage is valid if it satisfies the formalities of marriage according to the law of the country in which it was celebrated, provided that it is not otherwise a VOID MARRIAGE.　　[AD]

lex loci delicti commissi (Lat. the law of the place in which the wrong was committed)　In most CIVIL LAW countries, this governs the approach to CONFLICT OF LAWS in TORT. There can be some confusion with the *LEX LOCI ACTUS*, which would also usually be where the DELICT (tort) is committed. The problem

becomes more obvious in a context such as product liability, where the *lex loci actus* could be the COUNTRY of manufacture, while the *lex loci delicti* could be where the injury occurred. Since this makes it more rather than less difficult to establish the APPLICABLE LAW, the law of England and Wales has not accepted the principle as part of its conflict of laws; see *George Munro Ltd* v. *American Cyanamid Corporation* [1944] KB 432.　　[JW]

lex loci situs (Lat. the law of the place in which something is situated)　In conflict of laws this will be relevant where it refers to the law of the country: (a) in which land is situated, and according to which ownership and other rights and obligations are determined; (b) in which immoveable things other than land are situated, and according to which rights and obligations can be determined; and (c) in which moveable things are situated and according to which rights and obligations are, usually, determined.　　[RE]

See also *LEX LOCI ACTUS*.

lex mercatoria (Lat. merchant(s') law)　**1.** The international trade practices and customs of medieval merchants that operated largely independently of local borders and laws. In the context of the developments of English law, elements of the *lex mercatoria* were to be found in the development of specialist local jurisdictions governing trade and commerce (see LOCAL COURTS) and an early influence on ADMIRALTY law. The medieval *lex mercatoria* is also widely referred to by its English synonym, the **law merchant**.
　2. The theory, which has gained ground since the early 1960s, that modern international business transactions are largely private, self-regulatory relationships governed by rules derived from their own formal sources, and with ARBITRATION as the preferred method of dispute settlement. The theory remains controversial, but it asserts that the new *lex mercatoria* thus constitutes an autonomous legal system, distinct from both national legal systems and the system of (public) INTERNATIONAL LAW. When used in this context, the term

lex mercatoria is also sometimes translated as 'law merchant' – though usually prefixed by the word 'new' or 'modern'. [JW]

Further reading: T.E. Carbonneau (ed.), *Lex Mercatoria and Arbitration: A Discussion of the New Law Merchant* (Cambridge, MA: Kluwer Law International, 1998); A. C. Cutler, *Private Power and Global Authority: Transnational Merchant Law in the Global Political Economy* (Cambridge: Cambridge University Press, 2003).

lex posterior derogat priori (Lat. a subsequent law implies the abolition of a previous one) The principle of IMPLIED REPEAL or **abrogation** of inconsistent legislation. [JW]

lex specialis derogat generali (Lat. specific law abrogates general law) A general principle that is applied to resolve conflicts between sources of INTERNATIONAL LAW, e.g. between customary and treaty law, between the general law and a local or regional variation (such as the former practice of the Nordic countries to use a four-mile limit to define the outer boundary of their TERRITORIAL WATERS, which was an accepted deviation from the normal three-mile rule) or between different treaty provisions. Whether or not abrogation from the general law is permitted is always a matter of interpretation. The following factors will be indicative of situations where *lex specialis* will not override the general law: where the general law is *JUS COGENS*; where the general law benefits third parties; and where non-derogation may be inferred from the terms of the general rule. [IB]

libel A defamatory tort where the statement defaming the claimant is published by the defendant in a permanent form, such as print, broadcast words or visual images. Libel is actionable *per se* and does not need proof of actual damage. [HJ]

See also DEFAMATION; SLANDER.

licensing of medicines All new medicines must be licensed. There are two routes by which a drug may be granted a product licence in the UK, via (a) the **European Medicines Evaluation Agency** (EMEA) or (b) the **Medicines and Healthcare Products Regulatory Agency** (MHRA). The two processes are designed to be equivalent. The EMEA process was originally set up in 1995 with the intention of harmonizing regulatory policy throughout the EU. The EMEA system is obligatory for certain products, including new cancer and AIDS drugs. The MHRA was formed in 2003 as a new UK regulatory body, following the merger of the Medicines Control Agency (MCA) and the Medical Devices Agency (MDA). It has authority to license new pharmaceuticals and other medical products for use in the UK only and on a European Union-wide basis under EU mutual recognition procedures. In order to obtain a licence, a drug has to have undergone an approved development process which includes a number of clinical trial stages that must be successfully completed, three of which will be conducted on humans. A licence will only be granted where the licensing authority believes the medicine is of acceptable quality, is safe and effective and is of overall therapeutic benefit to patients. [HJ & JW]

See also NON-THERAPEUTIC RESEARCH; THERAPEUTIC RESEARCH.

lie in grant To be capable of being created or transferred by written instrument, usually a deed. Under the Law of Property Act 1925, s. 51, all interests in land lie in GRANT, although use of the word grant is not necessary to create such interests. The concept is particularly important in relation to EASEMENTS, since it is a requirement that for an easement to exist, it must lie in grant. The requirement has two aspects: (a) the person granting and the person receiving the benefit of the right must have legal capacity to do so; (b) the right being claimed must be defined and definable, such that it could be described in a deed. In relation to easements, it has been held that a right to a fair view does not lie in grant, since it cannot be adequately defined (*William Aldred's Case* (1610) 9 Co Rep 57b). [DR]

See also LIE IN LIVERY.

lie in livery To be capable of being created or transferred by delivery. Until the land law reforms of the 19th and 20th centuries, land was deemed to lie in livery, meaning that a FREEHOLD estate could only be transferred by delivery of the land. Under the Real Property Act 1845, land and INTERESTS IN LAND were deemed to also LIE IN GRANT, meaning that they could be transferred by written instrument. Under the Law of Property Act 1925, s. 51(1), all land and interests in land lie in grant only and cannot be transferred by delivery. [DR]

lien The right of a person to retain possession of the owner's GOODS, CHATTELS or documents until the owner pays what he owes to the person in possession. Liens may be **general** or **particular**. A lien is general when the property is held as security for any or all of the owner's outstanding debts; it is particular when the right extends only to debts arising in relation to the specific property held. The nature of the lien may be determined by COMMON LAW, TRADE CUSTOM and usage, STATUTE, or by the terms of an individual CONTRACT. For example, a solicitor's general lien over documents in his possession is recognized as a common law right, based on implied agreement (see *Barratt* v. *Gough-Thomas* [1950] 2 All ER 1048), whereas an accountant customarily only has a particular lien over documents belonging to his client, and so could not assert a general lien against a client unless that right has been expressly incorporated into the contract with the client. Other common examples of liens include a **repairer's lien** over goods he has repaired and an **unpaid seller's lien** over goods sold until he receives the price agreed (see Sale of Goods Act 1979, s. 41). Most liens are **possessory**, that is, they require actual possession of the goods, etc., involved. However, where there is an **equitable lien**, the right exists independently of possession. Equitable liens tend to be regarded as exceptional *sui generis* rights and have been found to exist in respect of certain CHOSES IN ACTION, but have yet to be extended consistently to chattels. A common law lien only gives a passive right to retain; there is no power of sale at COMMON LAW, although some statutes have additionally conferred such a power, and it is possible to incorporate a power of sale by contract. [JW]

life estate (obsolete) Prior to 1926, the life estate was one of the three principal legal estates in land that could be created, along with the FEE SIMPLE ABSOLUTE IN POSSESSION and the FEE TAIL. A life estate was a legal estate in land that lasted until the death of the owner of that estate. For example, if X, the owner of the fee simple absolute in possession, granted a life estate to Y, Y had a legal estate in that land until his death. On Y's death, his estate came to an end, leaving X as the owner of the fee simple (known as the REVERSION).

Following the Law of Property Act 1925, the life estate was abolished at law and it is now only possible to create an equitable LIFE INTEREST under a trust of land. [DR]

See also REMAINDER.

life in being A life in being is used to calculate the PERPETUITY PERIOD which determines the validity of future gifts made, for instance, in a will or by deed. The purpose of the rule is to prevent settlements vesting at any time beyond the lives of the settlor, his or her children, and his or her grandchildren.

Every person alive at the effective date of the will or on the execution of the deed is a potential life in being. At common law, for this purpose, conception is treated as being equivalent to actual birth and therefore an unborn child is also considered to be a life in being and so any actual period of gestation is included in calculating the perpetuity period. The settlor or the testator is able to select the lives in being he or she wishes to be used to measure the perpetuity period, and there is no need for those lives in being to have any connection with the gift, provided it is reasonably practicable to ascertain the date of the death of the last survivor. If this is not possible then the gift will be void for uncertainty. Testators have commonly used the royal family for their lives in being, for instance in clauses such as 'the period ending at the expiry of 21 years from the death of the last survivor of all the lineal descendants of Her late Majesty Queen Victoria who shall be living at the time when the gift comes into effect'. In *Re Villar* [1928] Ch 471 the court accepted that a royal lives clause on these lines was sufficiently certain despite there being at that time about 120 relevant lives in being dispersed throughout Europe.

For settlements which postdate the Perpetuities and Accumulations Act 1964 and which do not specify a time period, there is now a statutory list of lives in being which are the lives of the settlor, the beneficiaries and certain family members.   [HC & DR]

See also RULE AGAINST PERPETUITIES.

life interest An EQUITABLE INTEREST in land, held under a trust, limited to the duration of the beneficiary's life. It is common for the LEGAL ESTATE to be granted to the TENANT FOR LIFE as well as the equitable life interest. For example, X may grant his land to Y and Z to hold on trust for Y, for the duration of Y's life. In this situation, Y is both a trustee and the tenant for life. Under a Settled Land Act SETTLEMENT, the legal estate must also be vested in the person receiving the benefit of a life interest (Settled Land Act 1925, s. 4 (2)).

Under the Law of Property Act 1925 it was possible to create a life interest under either a STRICT SETTLEMENT or a trust for sale. However, since the Trusts of Land and Appointment of Trustees Act 1996 came into force on 1 January 1997, it is only possible to create a life interest under a trust of land, as governed by the 1996 Act.   [DR]

See also LIFE ESTATE.

life peers The system of life peers was created by the Life Peerages Act 1958 in order to broaden the social and political basis of membership of the HOUSE OF LORDS which, up until that time, had been comprised entirely of hereditary peers. Life peers are appointed by the Queen, on the nomination of the Prime Minister, or, since May 2000, on the nomination of the HOUSE OF LORDS APPOINTMENTS COMMISSION. This reflects a new distinction within the category of life peers between those who are appointed from the political list compiled by the Prime Minister (by convention a number of these appointees will have been pro-posed by the Leader of the Opposition and other party leaders) and those appointed by the Commission on merit as non-party political peers. These two groups have become colloquially known as 'working peers' and 'people's peers'. Unlike hereditary peers, as the name suggests, life peers cannot pass their title on to their children or other lineal descendants.   [JW]

life sentence An indeterminate term of imprisonment followed by a period of **release on licence**, which will normally extend for the remainder of the offender's natural life. MURDER carries a mandatory life sentence for any offender aged over 21. Where the offender is aged between 10 and 18, the sentence is also mandatory, though young offenders are said to be 'detained at Her Majesty's pleasure'. Discretionary life sentences are available to the courts as the maximum sentence for certain offences, including ARSON, MANSLAUGHTER and RAPE.

All life prisoners must serve a minimum period of imprisonment to meet the needs of RETRIBUTION and deterrence. This minimum period is announced by the trial judge in open court and is known as the 'tariff' period. The offender will not be eligible for release until that term has been served. In mandatory cases, the judge may make a **whole life order** in which case the offender is ineligible for release on licence. In discretionary life cases, if the judge declines to set a minimum term, this has the same effect as a whole life order.

The category of 'automatic' life sentences under the Powers of Criminal Courts (Sentencing) Act 2000, s. 109, was replaced under the Criminal Justice Act 2003, s. 225, by the indeterminate sentence of **imprisonment for public protection** for offences committed on or after 4 April 2005; see DANGEROUS OFFENDER.   [JW]

See also PAROLE.

life tenant *See* TENANT FOR LIFE.

lifetime transfer A transfer of value (normally a GIFT) which reduces a person's ESTATE for inheritance tax (IHT) purposes and which is made by an individual (the transferor) before his death. Transfers may be exempt (for example, because they fall within the annual allowance of £3,000 of exempt transfers) or immediately chargeable (for example, a gift to a DISCRETIONARY TRUST), or potentially exempt (so long as the transferor survives for seven years, the gift will not become chargeable). In the case of a transfer which is immediately chargeable, any tax is paid either by the transferor or, where there is an agreement between them to do so, by the recipient (the transferee). In the case of a transfer which is potentially exempt, the transferee will pay tax if, and only if, the transfer becomes chargeable. Where a lifetime transfer is chargeable, the rate of tax can depend on the value of any previously made lifetime transfer or transfers made by the transferor to the same or different transferees.

Estate planning often involves using lifetime transfers to reduce IHT liability by utilizing exemptions and reliefs, or by maximizing any benefit from a lower rate of tax on such transfers. However, care needs to be taken to ensure that a gift that saves IHT does not unintentionally create a CAPITAL GAINS TAX (CGT) liability.   [RE]

Limburg Principles A set of non-binding principles formulated by the INTERNATIONAL COMMISSION OF JURISTS as a means of assisting STATES and international organizations in the development and application of the INTERNATIONAL COVENANT ON ECONOMIC, SOCIAL AND CULTURAL RIGHTS. The Principles were published as UN doc. E/CN.4/1987/17, Annex, and in the *Human Rights Quarterly*, Vol. 9 (1987), pp. 122–35. Although non-binding, the Principles are widely viewed as an authoritative interpretation of Covenant provisions. A further group convened by the Commission met in 1996 and adopted an additional set of policies, called the Maastricht guidelines (these are entirely unconnected to the Maastricht Treaty, which is a EUROPEAN UNION legislative instrument), to elaborate further upon the Limburg Principles.   [JW]

limitation clause An EXEMPTION CLAUSE which purports to limit the liability for BREACH OF CONTRACT to a specified sum, such as the PRICE payable under the CONTRACT. Limitation clauses are construed more favourably than total EXCLUSION CLAUSES. A limitation clause can be distinguished from a LIQUIDATED DAMAGES CLAUSE which specifies a liquidated damages sum payable irrespective of the actual loss. A limitation clause merely sets the upper limit of the COMPENSATION payable for breach; however, a party can recover no more than its actual loss up to that limit.   [JPL]

limitation period The time period within which civil proceedings must be brought. Most limitation periods are defined by the Limitation Act 1980, as amended. The time limit varies according to the nature of the claim. In simple CONTRACT and TORT claims, a claim must normally be brought within six years of the cause of action arising (i.e. within six years of the breach of contract). Personal injury claims arising out of NEGLIGENCE or BREACH OF STATUTORY DUTY must normally be brought within three years of the accident. Separate rules govern actions over land, JUDICIAL REVIEW and product liability claims, among others. Expiry of a limitation period constitutes a complete bar to bringing an action, though the courts have some discretion to extend the limitation period where appropriate. Limitation problems can generate litigation in their own right; for example, where a property defect is hidden, or only gradually becomes apparent, there may be a dispute about when time began to run against the claimant.   [JW]

limited company *See* COMPANY.

limited executor The grant to an EXECUTOR may be limited either by the TESTATOR or by the court. A testator may appoint an executor for a limited purpose (for example, a literary executor) or for a limited time (for example, until my son attains the age of 18 years). Under the Supreme Court Act 1981, the court has the power to make a grant limited in any way it sees fit.   [CM]

See also GRANT OF REPRESENTATION.

limited owner A person with an interest in property that is less than a fee simple absolute in possession; for example, a tenant for life under a settlement, a tenant for years under a lease, or a tenant in tail under an entailed interest. The significance of a limited owner is that in certain circumstances it is possible for him or her to acquire a limited owner's charge over his or her property which, if registered, is enforceable against a third party purchaser of the property.   [DR]

limited owner's charge A charge arising when a TENANT FOR LIFE or STATUTORY OWNER (under the provisions of the Settled Land Act 1925) has paid tax under the Inheritance Tax Act 1984, allowing that person to recover the tax by way of a charge against the land. A limited owner's charge is a Class C (ii) LAND CHARGE, which means that if it is properly registered it is enforceable against a third party purchaser of the land. For example, where X is the tenant for life under a Settled Land Act SETTLEMENT and paid inheritance tax when his interest arose, he may recover that money from the rents and profits of the land of which he is tenant for life. If X registers this charge as a Class C (ii) land charge, then subsequently sells the property to a third party, Y, X will remain entitled to money under the limited owner's charge until the sum due has been paid in full.   [DR]
See also LIMITED OWNER.

liquidated damages clause A provision in a CONTRACT whereby the DAMAGES payable in the event of BREACH OF CONTRACT are agreed in advance. Since a liquidated damages clause is a genuine pre-estimate, judged at the date of making the contract, of the loss likely to be suffered in the event of the breach and is therefore intended to compensate for that loss, it is valid and enforceable whether the actual loss suffered is higher or lower than the amount specified in the clause. A liquidated damages clause should be contrasted with a PENALTY CLAUSE, which is unenforceable. Guidelines for distinguishing liquidated damages and penalty clauses were formulated by Lord Dunedin in *Dunlop Pneumatic Tyre Co. Ltd v. New Garage and Motor Co. Ltd* [1915] AC 79. Use of the term 'penalty' or liquidated damages is not conclusive.   [JPL]

liquidation The realization and distribution of the ASSETS of a COMPANY and, usually, the closing down of the business; also called **winding up**. There are two broad categories of liquidation: compulsory and voluntary. **Compulsory liquidation** requires a petition to the court, usually by a creditor, on the grounds that the company cannot pay its debts, or that the court considers a just and equitable winding up to be in the best interests of the company. **Voluntary liquidation** does not involve the courts or the Official Receiver. There are two types of voluntary liquidation: members' voluntary liquidation for solvent businesses and creditors' voluntary liquidation for insolvent ones. A liquidator may be appointed by the company or the creditors to oversee the winding up. The powers of directors cease once a liquidator is appointed.   [JW]
See also RECEIVERSHIP.

Lisbon Treaty *See* TREATY OF LISBON.

listed building A building of special architectural or historic interest, contained on a list compiled by the Secretary of State for Culture, Media and Sport under the Planning (Listed Buildings and Conservation Areas) Act 1990. Buildings are listed following recommendations made by English Heritage, who assess them on the basis of four main criteria: (a) architectural interest; (b) historic interest; (c) close historic associations with nationally important people or events; and (d) group value, where buildings comprise an important architectural or historical unity or a fine example of planning (e.g. a square or terrace).

Listed buildings are subject to additional planning controls prohibiting demolition, alteration or extension without the express consent of the local planning authority or Secretary of State. There are more than 500,000 listed buildings in England and almost 50,000 in Scotland.   [DR]
See also BUILDING PRESERVATION NOTICE.

literal rule *See* STATUTORY INTERPRETATION.

literary merit An aspect of the 'public good' defence to a charge of making an obscene publication. It is a defence to a finding that an article is obscene for it to be shown that publication of the article would be for the public good in the interests of science, literature, art, learning or of other objects of general concern (see Obscene Publications Act 1959, s. 4). [BF]

See also OBSCENE PUBLICATIONS.

literary work The Copyright, Designs and Patents Act 1988 confers COPYRIGHT protection on original literary works. A literary work is defined in the Act (s. 3(1)) as 'any work, other than a dramatic or musical work, which is written, spoken or sung, and accordingly includes – (a) a table or compilation other than a database, (b) a computer program, (c) preparatory design material for a computer program, and (d) a DATABASE.'

'Writing' is further defined as 'any form of notation or code, whether by hand or otherwise and regardless of the method by which, or medium in or on which, it is recorded' (Copyright, Designs and Patents Act 1988, s. 178).

The quality or style of the work does not matter, as long as the work passes the threshold of ORIGINALITY. The concept of 'literary' works is wide enough to include not only traditional literature but also translations, codes, ciphers, titles and advertising jingles. Copyright protection will only be granted to such works that give 'information, pleasure and instruction'. Such a work must be more than a mere innovative word though this does not necessarily mean that single words have no copyright protection in them (see *Exxon Corp.* v. *Exxon Insurance Consultants* (1982) RPC 69 (CA)). Adaptations and historical works are also considered to be literary works capable of copyright protection, though the s. 3 copyright law allows a wider use of historical works than of fictional works because there is no monopoly in ideas or facts (see *Ravenscroft* v. *Herbert* (1980) RPC 193). [US]

litigation friend In civil proceedings, a person responsible under Part 21 of the CIVIL PROCEDURE RULES for the commencement and conduct of litigation on behalf of a child or mentally disordered person. [JW]

See also CHILDREN'S GUARDIAN.

littoral states Two or more STATES facing each other with their common border in whole or in part being a river or a lake. The delimitation of such watercourses is ideally premised on a TREATY, in the absence of which the littoral states, either acting in concert or by submitting their dispute to an arbitral or judicial forum, may eventually settle for one of the more usual methods employed to date. These are the THALWEG method, used to delimit river boundaries, or the median line, where the boundary is a lake. Equally, in cases of state succession, such as with the Soviet Union and the creation of new littoral states around the Caspian Sea, agreements reached must reflect the consensus of all littoral states, otherwise their legal effects will be problematic. [IB]

living apart *See* SEPARATION.

living off immoral earnings (obsolete) See now the gender-neutral offences under the Sexual Offences Act 2003, ss. 52, 53 of, respectively, causing or inciting prostitution for gain, and controlling prostitution for gain. [BF]

living together *See* COHABITATION; COMMON-LAW MARRIAGE.

living will *See* ADVANCE DIRECTIVE.

LJ Lord Justice of Appeal.
See COURT OF APPEAL.

Llewellyn, Karl (1893–1962) American jurist and key figure within AMERICAN REALISM. He is associated particularly with the concept of LAW-JOBS. [JP]

local authority A body elected by residents within a LOCAL GOVERNMENT AREA. Members of a local authority are called **councillors** and are elected for a four-year term of office. Local authority functions are largely prescribed by STATUTE, and include responsibility for a wide range of local services, which may include matters such as (depending on the tier or level of local authority responsibilities) education, social care, housing and highways. Local authorities also exercise certain delegated law-making powers within their area. [JW]

See also BYELAW; LOCAL HOUSING AUTHORITY.

local connection A LOCAL HOUSING AUTHORITY's obligations for housing the homeless under Part 7 of the Housing Act 1996 can be restricted to those who have a local connection. Under s. 199, a person will ordinarily have a local connection with a local authority housing area if they are normally resident, employed or have family connections in the area, or there are other special circumstances. Under s. 198, if neither the applicant nor a person who would reasonably be expected to live with them has a local connection with its area, but does have a local connection with another local authority's area, responsibility can be passed by notifying that other authority. In the interim, the first authority approached must provide temporary accommodation until accommodation is available in the area where the local connection applies. The local connection proviso will not be applied to an applicant if to do so would be to return them to the probability of violence, including domestic violence. [HC & DR]

See also HOMELESS PERSON.

local courts Until at least the 18th century most legal disputes would have been dealt with in a court that exercised a highly localized or special jurisdiction, of which there were many in the English legal system. Two significant examples are the **courts leet** and **courts of pie poudre**, both of which illustrate the historically slow and piecemeal process of reform to the administration of local justice in England that took place up until the 19th century.

The court leet was, in the Middle Ages, the main court of local criminal jurisdiction. It developed out of the authority of the lord of the manor to adjudicate on virtually all matters that occurred within his lands. This manorial court, referred to as the **court baron**, gained the name of 'leet' when exercising its criminal powers. The introduction of a royal warrant procedure in Edward I's reign formalized a sharp distinction between the jurisdiction of the court baron, exercising purely manorial rights, and the court leet, which relied on the royal franchise. The court leet itself started to decline in the later Middle Ages in the face of the growing authority of the Royal Justices of the Peace, though some courts leet became part of the new local government in expanding boroughs where these incorporated an existing manor. In this way, many courts leet operated until nearly the mid-19th century. Although they had long since ceased to function, they were only formally abolished in 1998.

The name pie poudre (sometimes also spelt as piepowder, pye-poulder and other variations) reputedly refers to the dusty feet (in Old Fr. *pieds pouldre*) of travellers to market. Organized by medieval boroughs, generally under the authority of a Royal Charter or Warrant, these courts were held on the occasion of each fair or market. They had wide jurisdiction over disputes within the confines of that market. Matters would commonly include disputes over the quality of goods, and weights and measures, but also acts of theft and violence that might otherwise get out of hand and disrupt the market by riot and civil disorder. The pie poudre courts also declined as the regular COUNTY COURT system was consolidated and made more efficient. They had effectively ceased to function by the late 19th century, though they did not have their jurisdiction formally removed until the Administration of Justice Act 1977. [JW]

local government *See* LOCAL AUTHORITY.

local government area The geographical area constituting a single unit for local government purposes. The areas reflect the division generally in England into county, district and parish tiers of government. The introduction of a single tier UNITARY AUTHORITY into England and Wales in the 1990s has resulted in some reorganization of local government areas. [JW]

See also COUNTY COUNCIL; DISTRICT COUNCIL; LOCAL AUTHORITY.

Local Government Ombudsmen Independent offices that investigate complaints of maladministration by local government and certain other public bodies. Such OMBUDSMAN services were set up in the UK in the late 1960s and early 1970s. Today there are separate ombudsmen for England, Wales, Scotland and Northern Ireland. The English service is properly called the **Commission for Local Administration in England**, though the Commissioners are still more commonly referred to as local government ombudsmen. The functions of the ombudsmen in Wales, Scotland and Northern Ireland tend to be broader than in England, reflecting both the greater extent of regional government in these devolved administrations, and also recent moves to rationalize the range of ombudsman services.

In Wales, the office of **Public Services Ombudsman for Wales** came into operation on 1 April 2006, replacing the former offices of the Local Government Ombudsman for Wales, the Health Service Ombudsman for Wales, the Welsh Administration Ombudsman and Social Housing Ombudsman for Wales.

The **Scottish Public Services Ombudsman** likewise was set up in 2002 to replace three previous offices: the Scottish Parliamentary and Health Service Ombudsman, the Local Government Ombudsman for Scotland and the Housing Association Ombudsman for Scotland.

In Northern Ireland, the Northern Ireland Ombudsman (as the post is popularly known) combines two roles: the **Assembly Ombudsman for Northern Ireland** and the **Northern Ireland Commissioner for Complaints**. [JW]

local housing authority A local government body which has responsibilities for housing and homelessness in an area and at a level that is designed to coincide with the structure and form of the local council: see the Housing Act 2004, s. 261. [HC & DR]
See also LOCAL AUTHORITY.

local justice area An area established for the purposes of the administration of magistrates' courts. [SN]

Local Safeguarding Children Boards Bodies that have to be established by each LOCAL AUTHORITY in order to fulfil their statutory obligation under the Children Act 2004, s. 13. The objectives of these Boards are set out in s. 14(1) as being to 'co-ordinate what is done by each person or body represented on the Board for the purposes of safeguarding and promoting the welfare of children in the area' and to 'ensure the effectiveness of what is done by each such person or body for those purposes'. Those bodies or services represented on a Board might include the police, probation services, health services, CAFCASS and youth offending teams. The function of safeguarding children includes protecting them from maltreatment and preventing impairment of their health and well-being. Boards are expected to achieve their statutory objectives by such means as developing mechanisms to identify children at risk; developing policies and procedures concerning the action to be taken where there are concerns about a CHILD'S safety; the setting of thresholds for intervention; and the monitoring of the effectiveness of interventions. LSCBs are also expected to recruit and train professionals working with children. [FK]
See also AREA CHILD PROTECTION COMMITTEE.

local searches In conveyancing, local searches are carried out by the solicitor acting for the buyer prior to the exchange of contracts. Local searches involve a search of the local Land Charges Register and the making of enquiries of the local authority. The search reveals information regarding any COMPULSORY PURCHASE orders on the property, as well as CONSERVATION AREAS, financial charges, LISTED BUILDING registrations, tree preservation orders and other planning entries affecting the property.

Standard enquiries of the local authority reveal information regarding any planning and building regulation issues, road maintenance issues, nearby transport schemes, CONTAMINATED LAND and radon gas issues.

There are also optional additional enquiries that may be made regarding, for example, noise abatement notices, public RIGHTS OF WAY or protected HEDGEROWS.

It is essential to carry out local searches prior to all conveyancing transactions, because issues covered by the local searches can drastically reduce the value of a particular property (e.g. if a house is shortly to be subject to compulsory purchase by the local authority). [DR]

See also SEARCHES.

local taxation Charges on land and buildings in the area of a LOCAL AUTHORITY and payable to the authority as its revenue for the provision of services in the authority's area. The sources of that revenue are the COUNCIL TAX and what is usually known as the UNIFORM BUSINESS RATE (UBR). The rate of council tax is set by each authority, but the UBR is set by the Secretary of State.

Council tax applies to all dwellings, including mobile homes and houseboats. The rules provide assistance for some categories of local residents: for example, exemptions for disabled people, rebates for single-person households and benefits for some households in which income levels are low.

The UBR incorporates a small business rate relief, and there are reliefs available in respect of empty properties and some rural villages. [RE]

lock-out One response of EMPLOYERS to the threat of INDUSTRIAL ACTION may be to prevent their WORKERS from obtaining access to the workplace by a lock-out, or by other means prevent them from working with a view to compelling them to accept certain terms and conditions. 'Lock-out' also covers, for example, the suspension of EMPLOYEES. [MJ]

lock-out agreement An agreement which prevents the prospective seller of property from engaging in the practice of GAZUMPING. Usually, once a prospective buyer has had an offer accepted on a property, both the prospective buyer and seller are free to withdraw from negotiations at any time prior to the exchange of contracts. Under a lock-out agreement, the seller agrees not to consider any other offers on the property for a specified period. Lock-out agreements were judicially approved in *Pitt* v. *PHH Asset Management Ltd* [1994] 1 WLR 327. Since they are not contracts for the sale of land, they are subject to the ordinary rules of offer and acceptance.

[DR]

Locke, John (1632–1704) English thinker influenced by THOMAS HOBBES but who developed a distinct account of the SOCIAL CONTRACT in his *Two Treatises of Government* (1690). In the same way that Hobbes was profoundly influenced by the political upheaval he witnessed during the 17th century, so Locke responded to the events that overtook English government during his lifetime. In particular, he was influenced by the Glorious Revolution of 1688, which had seen the last of the Stuart monarchs, James II, overthrown and replaced by William and Mary. This event also marked a profound shift in the theory of government. The Stuart monarchs maintained until the last the notion of the divine right of kings. For them, there was no need for any popular foundation for government. While others disagreed, the fact remained that deposing James II violated English law with regard to the royal succession. William and Mary were invited by Parliament to take his place, but a new settlement needed to be made to allow for this extraordinary state of affairs. Parliament responded with a very CONTRACTARIAN solution. In the resolution before the House of Commons, preceding the new settlement, it was stated that King James, 'Having endeavoured to subvert the constitution of the kingdom, by breaking the original contract between king and people … has abdicated the government; and … the throne is therefore vacant.'

This was a remarkable rewriting of history, but it served the purpose. And while some criticized this new approach, their criticism merely served as a starting point for Locke who was in due course to provide the intellectual foundation for the Revolution, and indeed to develop a version of the SOCIAL CONTRACT that directly influenced the drafters of the American Constitution as well as those involved in the French Revolution.

Like Hobbes, Locke postulated a precontractarian state of nature out of which the social contract eventually emerged. Whereas Hobbes described this as a period of brutality, Locke saw it instead as a golden age. The only problem was the fact that a man's property was not secure. Note that 'property' for Locke did not have the relatively restricted meaning it has today, but would also have included an individual's own skills, abilities and efforts as well as a right to physical subsistence. Locke's property rights, therefore, have much in common with what would now be called human rights. Whereas Hobbes was essentially pessimistic about men in a state of nature, Locke adopted an approach that shows the clear influence of AQUINAS. He does not deny that men can act like beasts but he focuses instead on what distinguishes them from beasts – their possession of reason. Locke believes that it is through the exercise of reason that men come to know what it is that God wills for them. God thus enters into Locke's contractarian approach in a way that he did not in Hobbes's. And, echoing Aquinas, Locke holds that what God wants from men is self-evident. They may act otherwise, but as humans they instinctively know what is required of them.

In Locke's state of nature, accordingly, each person had clear duties as contained in God's natural law. And where there are duties, there are corollary rights. It was open to each individual in the state of nature to seek recompense for any breach of rights by another. But enforcing these rights would be a very uncertain affair. As a consequence, government was required to secure these rights with the result that each individual's right to pursue any breach of duty on the part of another was transferred to the sovereign.

Locke, like Hobbes, rather glossed over the question of whether the state of nature and the transfer of sovereignty were historical facts, but there was a more pressing need for him to deal with the question of how contemporary individuals had consented to the fact that their ability to protect their natural rights had been transferred to the sovereign. His approach was to distinguish two varieties of consent: tacit and express. As regards tacit consent, Locke proposed that merely by remaining within the state and enjoying all the rights, privileges, benefits and protections, an individual must be understood to have consented to the power exercised by the sovereign. Crucially, however, only express consent, for Locke, could make an individual a full member of society and furnish them with all the rights enjoyed by a citizen. The fact that few if any actually then or now expressly consent to the transfer of power to the sovereign is a problem for Locke that he does not address, leaving more of a burden to be placed on tacit consent than he actually allows.

Furthermore, despite the fact that he discusses a social contract, its implications are discussed mainly in relation to the citizens, rather than the sovereign. In connection with the latter, Locke tends to speak instead about trust. In other words, whereas the relationship between the citizen and the sovereign is contractual, based especially on tacit consent, the relationship between sovereign and citizen is fiduciary, based on the trust which Locke holds that citizens place in him.

It is this trust relationship, rather than a contractual relationship, on which Locke bases his discussion of whether it is ever permissible for citizens to disobey the sovereign. The answer for Locke is an emphatic 'yes'. If a sovereign betrays the trust placed in him by the citizens, then he may in fact be overthrown. Such a sovereign has put himself in a state of war with his citizens, and just as any or all of them would be at liberty to fight and repel an aggressor, so may they deal with the untrustworthy sovereign.

This does not mean that when confronted with an unjust law the citizen could disobey or even revolt. The sovereign had to offend in this regard repeatedly before there could be any question of revolt. But should there be, as he put it, 'a long train of Actings' revealing such a breach of trust, then it would not be the citizens who would be disturbing government by resisting or revolting; rather the responsibility would be with the sovereign. The citizens, by contrast, would actually be acting so as to restore good government. The sovereign would be acting contrary to natural law, the citizens in accordance with it.

Locke has been immensely influential. His focus on property rights as natural rights means that he has been recruited by capitalist apologists, even if his discussion of the right to physical subsistence means that he would have found this absurd. More importantly, his ideas were extremely influential in the American War of Independence and for the drafters of the American Constitution. [JP]

Further reading: John Locke, *Two Treatises of Government* and *A Letter Concerning Toleration*, edited by Ian Shapiro (New Haven CN: Yale University Press, 2003).

locus standi (Lat. a place to stand) *See* STANDING.

lodger A lodger is an informal description of someone who pays RENT to live in the home of the LANDLORD. A lodger is usually a licensee rather than a TENANT and receives services such as breakfast and cleaning. [HC & DR]

loitering It is an offence under the Street Offences Act 1959, s. 1 for a common prostitute (male or female) to loiter or solicit in a street or public place for the purposes of prostitution. 'Loitering' is not itself defined in the Act. [BF]

See also SOLICITING; STREET OFFENCES.

London Court of International Arbitration (LCIA) An arbitral institution originally inaugurated in 1892 with the name of the City of London Chamber of Arbitration. It changed its name in 1903 to the London Court of Arbitration, and again, in 1981, to the London Court of International Arbitration. It is not a court in the normal sense of the word. It provides a comprehensive service in relation to international commercial disputes, including administering arbitrations pursuant to its own Arbitration Rules (currently the 1998 Rules) and, for AD HOC ARBITRATIONS, pursuant to the UNCITRAL ARBITRATION RULES 1976. It is also ready to assist with mediation (including assisting with the selection of mediators and overseeing the process) or other alternative dispute resolution processes. [RE]

See also INTERNATIONAL ARBITRATION.

long lease Long leases are LEASES which are more than 21 years in length. The term usually refers to long residential leases. Nearly all flats in England and some houses are held on long leases. At the expiry of the long lease the property will revert to the freeholder unless the lease is extended or the leaseholder acquires the freehold or rights to stay on as a periodic tenant are exercised. The relationship between the leaseholder and the freeholder is set out in the lease which will specify, among other things, the responsibilities for repair, the payment of GROUND RENT and the calculation of service charges for maintenance of the common parts and the exterior of the property. In recent years there has been extensive statutory intervention to extend the rights of the long leaseholder, most recently in the Commonhold and Leasehold Reform Act 2002. [HC & DR]

See also ENFRANCHISEMENT OF TENANCY; FORFEITURE OF LEASE.

look and feel test A term used in the software and website lexicon to describe the appearance of the program, especially the graphical user interface (GUI) of the program, including its design, colours, art works and the menu layout (such as windows, buttons, drop-down features, etc.). The term is sometimes employed to determine COPYRIGHT infringement of SOFTWARE as non-literal copying of a computer program can still result in a program which is similar in appearance and function to the copied program. The UK courts, however, are reluctant to allow copyright protection of the 'look and feel' of the program simply because it appears to be 'an unjustifiable extension of copyright protection' (see

Navitaire Inc. v. *easyJet Airline Co. Ltd* [2004] EWHC 1725 (Ch)). A more recent decision has further emphasized that under the EC Software Directive, 'ideas' are not protected, which is reinforced by the TRIPS Agreement. Moreover, even though a program emulates another, copying of general ideas is allowed under the law (see *Nova Productions Ltd* v. *Mazooma Games Ltd; Nova Productions Ltd* v. *Bell Fruit Games Ltd* [2007] EWCA Civ 219). [US]

looked after child A CHILD who is being accommodated on a voluntary basis under the Children Act 1989, s. 20, or in terms of a CARE ORDER under s. 31. The child must be accommodated and maintained (s. 23). It is the duty of the LOCAL AUTHORITY to safeguard and promote the welfare of any child being looked after (s. 22). Before making any decisions about the arrangements for the child, the local authority should ascertain, as far as practicable, the wishes of the child, the PARENTS and any other relevant persons. Wherever practicable, the child should be enabled to live with a FAMILY member. In any event, the accommodation must be near the child's home, provided that this is reasonably practicable, and siblings should be accommodated together. [FK]

See also FOSTER CHILD; FOSTER PARENT; PARENTAL RESPONSIBILITY; VOLUNTARY ACCOMMODATION.

Lord Advocate *See* SCOTTISH LAW OFFICERS.

Lord Chancellor Historically one of the great offices of state. Until 2006–07, the Lord Chancellor exercised three key functions: head of the judiciary in England and Wales; a Cabinet Minister with responsibility for what was, originally, the Lord Chancellor's Department (now the Ministry of Justice); and Speaker of the HOUSE OF LORDS. The constitutional position of the Lord Chancellor had been debated for a number of years, with concerns being expressed that the role violated the doctrine of SEPARATION OF POWERS. As part of a wider package of constitutional changes, the Constitutional Reform Act 2005 divested the Lord Chancellor of two of these potentially conflicting roles by creating a separate position of **Lord Speaker**, which is equivalent to the

role of Speaker of the HOUSE OF COMMONS, and transferring the Lord Chancellor's judicial responsibilities to the LORD CHIEF JUSTICE. In June 2007, the Rt. Hon. Jack Straw was appointed Secretary of State for Justice, and the first Lord Chancellor since the 17th century to sit in the House of Commons. [JW]

Lord Chief Justice (LCJ) Head of the judiciary of England and Wales and President of the Courts of England and Wales. Before the Constitutional Reform Act 2005 came into force on 3 April 2006, the role of head of the judiciary of England and Wales was held by the LORD CHANCELLOR. Under the 2005 Act, the LCJ, as President of the Courts of England and Wales, has approximately 400 statutory duties and his or her key responsibilities include representing the views of the judiciary to Parliament and government; giving judgments and laying down PRACTICE DIRECTIONS in many of the most important appeal cases; sharing responsibility with the Lord Chancellor for the Office for Judicial Complaints; and chairing the Sentencing Guidelines Committee and Judicial Executive Board and Judges' Council. He or she is entitled to sit in the COURT OF APPEAL, the HIGH COURT, the CROWN COURT, the COUNTY COURTS and magistrates' courts. The LCJ is the President of the Criminal Division of the Court of Appeal and under the 2005 Act this role acquired the title 'Head of Criminal Justice' (s. 8). In practice, appointments are generally made from among Appeal Court judges; however, the appointments may also be made from the Judicial Committee of the House of Lords. The Act also provides for a Deputy Head to be appointed (from among the Lord Justices of Appeal) in order to allow the LCJ to delegate some of his or her administrative authority (s. 8(4)(b)). Following the 2005 Act, Lord Chief Justices will now be appointed by a special panel convened by the Judicial Appointments Commission. [AF]

Lord Speaker *See* LORD CHANCELLOR.

loss of a chance Loss of expectation that cannot be affirmatively established to have been suffered, but which might have been suffered as a result of the BREACH OF CONTRACT; for example, in *Chaplin* v. *Hicks* [1911] 2 KB 746, the breach of contract meant that the plaintiff lost the opportunity to win a prize. There was no certainty that she would have been successful; however, it was established she had a 1 in 4 chance of success of which she had been deprived by the breach. DAMAGES for loss of a chance in contract are recoverable where there is a real or substantial chance of the loss occurring, e.g. an alleged loss of profit, as opposed to a purely speculative gain (see *Allied Maples Group Ltd* v. *Simmons & Simmons (a firm)* [1995] 1 WLR 1602). The amount of the damages award is discounted to reflect the percentage chance of the loss occurring.   [JPL]

loss of amenity Part of a GENERAL DAMAGES award that reflects the claimant's loss of the physical or mental capability to do things that they used to do as a result of personal injury by another's NEGLIGENCE. The value attached to such **amenities of life** as sports and hobbies is determined objectively by the court. Non-pecuniary loss of this kind is not normally compensated in damages for BREACH OF CONTRACT but there is an exception where a major or important object of the contract is to provide pleasure, relaxation, or freedom from molestation, so that it becomes part of the claimant's expectation under the contract, e.g. loss of enjoyment of the ability to dive into a swimming pool that had not been constructed to the required depth (see *Ruxley Electronics & Construction Ltd* v. *Forsyth* [1996] AC 344).   [JPL]

loss of expectation *See* EXPECTATION DAMAGES.

LSC *See* LEGAL SERVICES COMMISSION.

LSCB *See* LOCAL SAFEGUARDING CHILDREN BOARD.

Luhmann, Niklas (1927–98) Influential German social theorist whose most prominent contribution to the study of law has been through the application of AUTOPOIESIS theory to social systems, including the legal system.

For Luhmann, society is composed of normatively closed but cognitively open communicative social subsystems such as law, politics, economy, science and religion. Each subsystem of society operates on the basis of its unique and fixed binary code (legal/illegal in the case of law) and steers itself by means of variable programmes. Each subsystem also performs a particular function within society. In the case of law, this is to stabilize normative expectations – in other words, to provide ready answers to what is required in given situations so that we are not thrown back on cognitive learning every time we are confronted with a new situation.

In contrast to JÜRGEN HABERMAS, whose view of society places the emphasis on the importance of communicative action (communication oriented towards understanding) as the means by which individuals establish identities on the basis of common norms and understandings within the lifeworld, Luhmann's vision of society raises serious obstacles to communication understood in this way. Insofar as each social subsystem constructs its own environment on the basis of its own code – so that information is internally constructed rather than simply transferred – the sort of intersubjective understanding envisaged by communicative action appears impossible in Luhmann's account.

The deep division between Luhmann's and Habermas's views emerges from a profoundly different understanding of the nature of contemporary society. Whereas Habermas (for all his misgivings about the negative effects of the Enlightenment in terms of the colonization of the lifeworld by technocratic systems) remains committed to the spirit of the Enlightenment in terms of the possibility of progress and improvement on the basis of rational discursive processes, Luhmann's is an essentially post-Enlightenment theory. For Luhmann, the Enlightenment view is simply wrong. Society is not amenable to the sort of rational planning generally assumed by political, economic and even legal actors for the reason that it is, as far as he is concerned, composed of autopoietic systems.

Luhmann has accordingly been the subject of stern criticism on the grounds that his theory is fatalistic or even pessimistic. Supporters of Luhmann's approach, however, retort that his unblinking willingness to confront the harsh reality of contemporary society raises at the very least the possibility of a richer understanding even if, by definition, that understanding offers us little, if anything, by way of information that could be added to the policy process.   [JP]

Further reading: Niklas Luhmann, *Law as a Social System* (Oxford: Oxford University Press, 2004); Michael King and Chris Thornhill, *Niklas Luhmann's Theory of Politics and Law* (Basingstoke: Palgrave Macmillan, 2003).

lump sum award A one-off award of money which can be ordered to be paid in instalments. On DIVORCE or DISSOLUTION of a CIVIL PARTNERSHIP, lump sum awards are often used to effect a CLEAN BREAK between the parties. Lump sum orders (or clauses in agreements) can be used to allow one party to meet any expenses or liabilities incurred since the SEPARATION, to adjust the parties' capital assets, or as the capitalization of MAINTENANCE payments. Lump sum awards may be made in conjunction with other orders for FINANCIAL RELIEF. They may be made in favour of a spouse or for the benefit of a CHILD of the FAMILY under the Matrimonial Causes Act 1973 (in which they are included as FINANCIAL PROVISION ORDERS); under the Domestic Proceedings and Magistrates' Courts Act 1978; to or for the benefit of a child in certain circumstances under the Children Act 1989; and to a dependant out of a deceased's estate under the Inheritance (Provision for Family and Dependants) Act 1975.   [AD]

M

Maastricht Treaty *See* TREATY ON EUROPEAN UNION.

magistrate Someone who acts as a judge in the magistrates' court. Magistrates, also known as Justices of the Peace, are appointed by the Lord Chancellor and Secretary of State for Justice on the advice of local Advisory Committees to carry out judicial and administrative duties locally. A magistrate must normally live in or within 15 miles of the county for which he or she acts. Their original function was to assist in keeping the peace. They try less serious criminal offences, which involves considering the evidence in contested cases. Some magistrates are specially trained to deal with family cases. They are unpaid and normally sit as one of a 'BENCH' of three magistrates. They are not required to have formal or academic qualifications or knowledge of the law. Advice on law and procedure is provided by a qualified MAGISTRATES' CLERK. Magistrates are required to sit for a minimum of 26 half-days each year and to be available for full-day sittings. [SN]

magistrates' clerk A legally qualified person whose primary duty is to give advice to magistrates on law and procedure. [SN]

Magna Carta (Lat. the Great Paper or Great Charter) The original Magna Carta was acceded to by King John in 1215 at Runnymede, in the modern county of Surrey, following an armed rebellion by his barons. Magna Carta arguably laid a number of the foundations for modern constitutional government and civil liberties. It guaranteed the freedom of the Church, restricted the king's powers to raise taxes, and guaranteed certain minimum rights of due process. The Charter was frequently confirmed and renewed by successive monarchs during the Middle Ages, but tended to be regarded no differently from an ordinary STATUTE of the time. It was in fact of little real effect in constraining the powers of the CROWN. By the 16th century, for various political reasons, the Magna Carta came to be represented as a more significant source of constitutional legitimacy for both Crown and citizens, and the Charter later played a role in the political and legal power plays that marked the run-up to the English Civil War. Parts of the Charter continued to be renewed into the 18th century; however, with the rise of modern parliamentary democracy, the Charter became less relevant, and by the late 19th century most clauses had been repealed, so that the document today is primarily of cultural and historical relevance. [JW]

See also SOVEREIGNTY OF PARLIAMENT.

maintenance Payment of money from one spouse or civil partner (or former spouse or civil partner) to another for the benefit of the latter spouse or civil partner or a CHILD. Maintenance usually, but need not, represents a contribution to daily living expenses, and in some cases may be paid as a contribution towards future expenses or retirement. It is usually paid periodically, but can also be paid by way of a lump sum. Maintenance may be paid pursuant to a MAINTENANCE AGREEMENT between the parties or by order of the court, or, in the case of child maintenance, through the Child Support Agency. Maintenance pursuant to the Matrimonial Causes Act 1973 or the Civil Partnership Act 2004 is a FINANCIAL PROVISION ORDER. Maintenance may also be ordered by the court under the Domestic Proceedings and Magistrates' Courts Act 1978; for the benefit of a child in certain circumstances under the Children Act 1989; and, in some cases, financial provision orders may be made to provide 'reasonable' maintenance to be paid from a deceased's estate to some family members classed as dependants under the Inheritance (Provision for Family and Dependants) Act 1975. [AD]

See also FAILURE TO MAINTAIN; LUMP SUM AWARD; MAINTENANCE PENDING SUIT; REASONABLE FINANCIAL PROVISION.

maintenance agreement A written agreement between spouses or civil partners to pay MAINTENANCE to the other for his or her benefit or for the benefit of children. Agreements may be made before MARRIAGE or CIVIL PARTNERSHIP, during it, or after SEPARATION, and can relate to maintenance payable during COHABITATION or post-separation or DISSOLUTION. Parents of children may also make agreements for CHILD maintenance. Maintenance agreements are defined and regulated by statute. Parties are free to enter into maintenance agreements; however, such agreements are not, strictly speaking, enforceable and the court may make an order contrary to, or altering, the terms of the agreement or void any term which purports to prohibit a party from applying to the court for ANCILLARY RELIEF. [AD]

See also ANTE-NUPTIAL SETTLEMENT; PRE-NUPTIAL AGREEMENT; SEPARATION AGREEMENT.

maintenance order *See* FINANCIAL PROVISION ORDER.

maintenance pending suit Also known as an interim order; a court order for periodical payments intended to last only during the period between the initiation of proceedings for DIVORCE, judicial separation, DISSOLUTION of CIVIL PARTNERSHIP or ANNULMENT and the determination of the suit. The court has wide discretion to make a 'reasonable' order for the MAINTENANCE of a party in order to assist them while their case is being heard. [AD]

majority verdict *See* VERDICT.

making off without payment An offence under the Theft Act 1978, s. 3. It is committed when D, knowing that payment on the spot for any goods supplied or service done is required or expected from him, dishonestly makes off without having paid and with intent to avoid payment of the amount due.

The offence may be charged, for example, when D eats a meal at a restaurant, stays at a hotel, or fills a car with petrol at a garage, and leaves without paying. The offence of THEFT could be difficult to prosecute under such circumstances. If D only decided to avoid payment once the service had been conferred or the property obtained, then the service or property was not obtained by deception. Similarly, if property had been transferred before D became dishonest, then the property was not appropriated dishonestly for the purposes of theft. [BF]

malice aforethought A COMMON LAW expression denoting the MENS REA for MURDER. The term must now be understood as meaning an INTENTION to kill or to cause GRIEVOUS BODILY HARM. [BF]

malicious falsehood A TORT previously known as **slander of title**. Malicious falsehood involves the making of a false and malicious statement concerning a person's business or property interests to someone other than that person for a dishonest or improper motive. Three criteria must be satisfied: (a) a false statement of fact must be made; (b) there must be malice; and (c) the claimant must suffer damage. The tort protects individual economic interests as well as commercial interests (see *Kaye* v. *Robertson* [1991] 1 FSR 6; *Joyce* v. *Sengupta* [1993] 1 WLR 337). [H]

See also DECEIT; PASSING OFF.

malicious prosecution An intentional TORT; the claimant must have been the subject of a criminal prosecution which eventually terminated in his favour. To succeed in his claim, he must prove that the prosecution was initiated by the defendant; that the defendant acted in the absence of facts justifying the prosecution, and without believing honestly that the facts justified the prosecution; and that the defendant's actions were activated by malice. The tort does not extend to civil proceedings in general, nor to any disciplinary proceedings (e.g. by a LOCAL AUTHORITY), even if those are of a quasi-criminal nature (see *Gregory* v. *Portsmouth City Council* [2000] 1 AC 419). [JW]

See also ABUSE OF PROCESS.

malicious wounding One of the offences under the Offences against the Person Act 1861, s. 20, punishable by up to five years' imprisonment. A person commits this offence if he or she wounds another, having intended or foreseen the causing of some physical harm (see *R* v. *Mowatt* [1968] 1 QB 421). Thus, in order to commit the offence, it is not necessary that the person foresees the actual WOUND. [BF]

See also GRIEVOUS BODILY HARM.

management order An order which requires the LOCAL HOUSING AUTHORITY to step into the shoes of the LANDLORD of a HOUSE IN MULTIPLE OCCUPATION when they are unable to license the property. Management orders may also be used where it is necessary to manage other problematic properties. The latter orders require the approval of the RESIDENTIAL PROPERTY TRIBUNAL, unlike the mandatory orders made in connection with houses in multiple occupation. [HC & DR]

See also EMPTY DWELLING MANAGEMENT ORDER.

managing trustee A TRUSTEE who has day-to-day control of the TRUST property. [PK]

See also CUSTODIAN TRUSTEE.

mandamus (obsolete; Lat. we command) One of the 'prerogative writs' by which the courts controlled the exercise of powers by public authorities. Now known as prerogative orders. [MS]

mandate (obsolete) In INTERNATIONAL LAW it refers specifically to a territory established as a League of Nations mandate under Article 22 of the Covenant of the League of Nations. All mandated territories were previously administered by states defeated in the First World War, namely Germany and the Ottoman Empire. The mandate entailed an obligation by the mandatory (supervising) power to both the local population and the League. The amount of control and the nature of administration of each mandatory power was decided on an individual basis by the League of Nations. Despite this, mandates were largely seen as de facto colonies of the empires of the mandatory powers. With the adoption of the UN Charter the mandate system was replaced by the trusteeship system until the era of decolonization. [IB]

See also COLONY; TRUST TERRITORY; TRUSTEESHIP COUNCIL.

mandatory order A court order compelling a public body to fulfil its legal obligations, for example requiring an authority to assess a disabled person's needs, or obliging an inferior court to hear a claim which it alleged that it had no STANDING to hear. Failure to comply is punishable as a CONTEMPT OF COURT. A mandatory order may be made in conjunction with a QUASHING ORDER, for example where a LOCAL AUTHORITY's decision is quashed because the decision was *ULTRA VIRES*, the court may simultaneously quash the original decision, and order the authority to review the decision in a way that is within its powers. [JW]

Manila Declaration The Manila Declaration on the Peaceful Settlement of International Disputes was appended to UN General Assembly Resolution 37/10, adopted in 1982. This reiterates the principles found in the Assembly's 1970 Declaration on Friendly Relations, which was part of CUSTOMARY INTERNATIONAL LAW. Part II of the Manila Declaration urges states in cases of dispute to consider submitting them to the INTERNATIONAL COURT OF JUSTICE, or the General Assembly or the SECURITY COUNCIL, irrespective of the fact that the latter two are not judicial entities. The Declaration, being a General Assembly resolution, is a non-binding instrument. [IB]

See also SOFT LAW; USE OF FORCE.

Manor of Northstead Crown Steward and Bailiff of the Manor of Northstead is one of two nominal offices under the CROWN (the other is Steward and Bailiff of the Chiltern Hundreds) which are taken by MPs who wish to leave the HOUSE OF COMMONS. The procedure dates back to 1623 when the House resolved that a Member could not directly resign his seat. A Member wishing to leave the Commons applies to the Chancellor of the Exchequer, who grants whichever of the two offices is currently vacant. After leaving the Commons, the former MP also resigns the stewardship, in order to leave the post vacant for the next Member who wishes to resign. Other offices which are incompatible with membership of the Commons are listed in the House of Commons Disqualification Act 1975. [MS]

See also MEMBER OF PARLIAMENT.

manslaughter The name given to various forms of unlawful homicide. Broadly speaking, for analytical purposes, there are two types of manslaughter. **Voluntary manslaughter** refers to killings which are accompanied by the MENS REA for MURDER, but where a legally recognized mitigating factor is present, for example where a defendant pleads DIMINISHED RESPONSIBILITY or PROVOCATION, or SUICIDE pact, defences which are addressed in the Homicide Act 1957, ss. 2, 3 and 4, respectively. **Involuntary manslaughter** refers to killings in which the *mens rea* for murder is absent. Involuntary manslaughter is itself divided into two types: manslaughter by GROSS NEGLIGENCE and manslaughter by an unlawful and dangerous act. The former is committed where a person owed a duty of care to the deceased victim, in circumstances in which there was a risk of death, and that duty was breached in a manner that makes it proper for the criminal law to intervene. Unlawful and dangerous act manslaughter is committed by someone who commits a crime, as a result of which the victim dies. Thus, where D assaults V, who as a result, falls and strikes his head on a kerb, and dies, D may have committed manslaughter. D's initial crime must be 'dangerous', that is to say that '… all sober and reasonable people would inevitably recognize [that it] must subject the other person to, at least, the risk of some harm … albeit not serious harm …' (see *R* v. *Church* [1966] 1 QB 59, at p. 70).

A judge sentencing for manslaughter has the full range of options available, from absolute discharge to life imprisonment. [BF]

marginal rate of tax An expression used to indicate the rate at which a direct tax would be charged if the taxpayer were to receive one additional unit of value of the direct tax base, usually in situations where the tax is charged at varying rates on bands of value. So, for example, in the case of an income tax which is charged on a progressive basis, a taxpayer whose top rate of tax is 20% (basic rate), and whose income does not exceed the basic rate band, would have a marginal rate of tax of 20%, being the rate at which one more pound sterling of general income would be taxed. If, however, the taxpayer had used the full basic rate band of value, the marginal rate on the next pound would be 40%, that being the next rate which would be applied to that additional pound received by the taxpayer. Where the taxpayer knows their marginal rate of tax, they can, in some circumstances, consider whether or not to receive more of the value which will be taxed. This could also be the case where a taxpayer's marginal rate is 40% for income tax purposes and they are considering whether or not to realize a capital gain for the tax year. [RE]

See also CAPITAL GAINS TAX; CORPORATION TAX.

mariner's will *See* PRIVILEGED WILL.

marital breakdown Marital breakdown, if it is irretrievable, is the only ground for DIVORCE in England and Wales.   [AD]
See also BREAKDOWN OF MARRIAGE; IRRETRIEVABLE BREAKDOWN.

marital immunity *See* RAPE.

marital rape *See* RAPE.

marriage An agreement entered into between a man and a woman, formalized by certain legal rules and procedures, which creates and imposes rights and obligations between them relating to matters such as finances, property, inheritance, pensions and children. Marriage also confers a legal status on the parties. The classic definition of marriage in English law comes from the case of *Hyde* v. *Hyde* (1866) LR 1 P and D 130 at 133: 'the voluntary union for life of one man and one woman to the exclusion of all others'. This means that marriage (a) must be voluntarily entered into; (b) is for life; (c) must be heterosexual; and (d) must be monogamous. The legal rules for contracting a valid marriage are set out in the Matrimonial Causes Act 1973, s. 11, and the Marriage Act 1949 (as amended) sets out the formalities for solemnization and REGISTRATION OF MARRIAGES. Same sex partners are prohibited from marrying and are limited to registering their CIVIL PARTNERSHIP under the Civil Partnership Act 2004.   [AD]
See also ANNULMENT; BIGAMY; DIVORCE; RIGHT TO MARRY; VOID MARRIAGE; VOIDABLE MARRIAGE.

marriage by certificate A MARRIAGE to be solemnized outside the Church of England, either according to other religious rites or civilly, may not proceed without either a Superintendent Registrar's certificate or a Registrar General's licence. Applying for the certificate provides notice in the district in which the marriage is to be solemnized of the parties' intention to marry and evidence of their declaration of consent and capacity to marry. If no impediment is shown during the 15-day waiting period,

the certificate must be issued and the marriage can proceed.   [AD]
See also BANNS; MARRIAGE BY REGISTRAR GENERAL'S LICENCE; MARRIAGE BY RELIGIOUS LICENCE; MARRIAGE CEREMONY.

marriage by Registrar General's licence A MARRIAGE to be solemnized outside the Church of England, either according to other religious rites or civilly, may not proceed without either a Superintendent Registrar's certificate or a Registrar General's licence. While marriages may be solemnized only in certain approved premises, the Registrar General may issue a licence for a marriage to be solemnized elsewhere, for example where one party is house-bound or detained in prison.   [AD]
See also MARRIAGE BY CERTIFICATE; MARRIAGE BY RELIGIOUS LICENCE; MARRIAGE CEREMONY.

marriage by religious licence A MARRIAGE to be solemnized in the Church of England must be preceded by public notice of the intention to marry, either by the publication of BANNS or by the issuing of a licence. A common licence may be issued by the archbishop of the diocese in which the marriage is intended to be solemnized and a special licence may only be granted by the Archbishop of Canterbury. A special licence may permit the parties to marry at any time and in any place.   [AD]
See also MARRIAGE BY CERTIFICATE; MARRIAGE BY REGISTRAR GENERAL'S LICENCE; MARRIAGE CEREMONY.

marriage ceremony The formalities of the MARRIAGE ceremony differ according to whether or not the marriage is solemnized according to the rites of the Church of England. They are contained in the Marriage Act 1949, as amended. Marriages solemnized in the Church of England must be presided over by a member of the clergy and (except where a special licence has been granted) in the presence of two witnesses between the hours of 8 a.m. and 6 p.m. Marriages solemnized according to other religious rites must take place in a registered building, in the presence of at least two witnesses. **Civil marriages** may be solemnized in a register office or other approved premises by a register of mar-

riages in the presence of two witnesses. A specific form of words is required for the parties' declaration or vows. Failure to comply with the formal requirements of the marriage ceremony, including the preliminaries, if both parties were aware of the failure, can render the marriage void. [AD]
See also VOID MARRIAGE.

marriage certificate See REGISTRATION OF MARRIAGE.

marriage of convenience Known in UK immigration law as a 'sham MARRIAGE', this is a marriage where the parties have no intention of LIVING TOGETHER as husband and wife, but go through a MARRIAGE CEREMONY in order to avoid the effect of immigration law or rules. These marriages are valid assuming they were entered into by consent, but do not give a non-national the right to reside in the country; regulations specifically exclude such a party from being a spouse for that purpose. In order to clamp down on marriages of convenience, a person who comes to the UK from overseas to get married or to register a CIVIL PARTNERSHIP must have a designated visa in their passport for that purpose. A person already in the UK but who is subject to immigration control must obtain a certificate of approval from the Home Office. Immigration and Home Office authorities must satisfy themselves that the proposed marriage is genuine before the visa or certificate will be issued. Notice of intention to marry must then be given to a designated registrar. If a registrar to whom notice to marry has been given, or a registrar who has performed or is intending to perform a marriage ceremony, has reasonable grounds to suspect that the marriage is not a genuine marriage, he or she must report it to the Home Office. [AD]

marriage settlement An ANTE-NUPTIAL or POST-NUPTIAL SETTLEMENT of property made on either or both of the parties to a MARRIAGE, including by will. The Matrimonial Causes Act 1973, s. 24(i)(c), gives the court, as part of its jurisdiction in ANCILLARY RELIEF claims, the power to vary any such marriage settlement or extinguish any interest under it, and the Civil Partnership Act 2004 gives the court the same powers over such 'relevant settlements'. [AD]

Martens clause Contained in the preamble to the 1907 Hague Convention No. IV, on the regulation of warfare on land, the clause was inserted at the instigation of Fyodor Martens, then Russian Foreign Minister to the 1907 Hague Conventions, and its purpose was to provide general guidance where humanitarian law was silent or underdeveloped. It provided that, in those circumstances, STATES and their armies should be guided by the dictates of public conscience and the principles of humanity. The Martens clause is now viewed as expressing CUSTOMARY INTERNATIONAL LAW, and armed forces on the battlefield, as well as those with authority to adopt military decisions, are expected always to bear in mind the consequences of their actions on civilians and those who are wounded or are rendered HORS DE COMBAT. These principles have found application more recently in the decisions of the INTERNATIONAL CRIMINAL TRIBUNAL FOR THE FORMER YUGOSLAVIA (ICTY). [IB]

martial law An act of domestic (i.e. national) law, not of INTERNATIONAL LAW, where governance over territory is transferred to military authorities in the case of invasion, civil war or other major insurrection. It is imposed by the authorities of a STATE, either in the entirety of the state's territory, or across parts of it. The imposition of martial law may be unconstitutional, but may also be legitimate where the situation requires extreme measures. When it is imposed, the legal instrument employed to give it effect must become public, with information as to restrictions and its possible duration. Moreover, since martial law involves DEROGATION from human rights instruments, other member states to such instruments must be duly notified. In time of armed conflict, and where territory is occupied, the occupying power may under the same circumstances declare the imposition of martial law, so long as this contributes to the safety and peace of the occupied territory. [IB]

Marxist jurisprudence An understanding of law emerging from the thinking of Karl Marx (1818–83). Marx understood history as an inevitable and inexorable progression towards the emergence of a communist society via the intermediate steps of primitive communalism, slavery, feudalism and capitalism.

As far as law is concerned, while Marx saw it as the means by which the ruling class dominated the working class, it is actually less important in his account than economic relations, which he regards as the motive force behind the progress of history. Indeed, insofar as law exists simply to preserve economic inequalities, there is no need for it in a communist society and Marx's account sees it, together with the state, withering away.

Law is accordingly part of the **superstructure** in Marxist analysis, as opposed to part of the **base**. That is to say, it is not understood to be part of society's foundations, where Marx places the conditions of production and economic relations, but rather part of the arrangements that emerge and operate so as to preserve the status quo of the base.

This analysis of law's position has given rise to criticism of Marxist jurisprudence on the basis that it appears counterintuitive to view law only in this way. While it is not unreasonable to see law as part of the superstructure in the way Marxists contend, it seems unrealistic to deny that it also plays a role in the basic fabric of any of the precommunist societies Marx refers to. Critics contend, for example, that legal relations may actually constitute economic relations. If that is conceded, then the distinction between base and superstructure may collapse.

Marxist jurisprudence has suffered with other aspects of Marxism in the wake of the collapse of the Soviet Union. Prior to that, it influenced others such as KARL RENNER in Austria and played a role in the emergence of the CRITICAL LEGAL STUDIES movement in the US. [JP]

Further reading: Hugh Collins, *Marxism and Law* (Oxford: Oxford University Press, 1982).

mass redundancy *See* COLLECTIVE REDUNDANCY.

Master of the Rolls (MR) The judge who, along with the Senior LAW LORD, ranks joint second in the judicial hierarchy under the LORD CHIEF JUSTICE and is traditionally the head of the COURT OF APPEAL (Civil Division). By the Courts Act 2003, the Master of the Rolls was given the statutory post of the 'Head of Civil Justice' (s. 62(1)). As a Head of Division and Member of the PRIVY COUNCIL, the Master of the Rolls is given the title 'Right Honourable'. The 'Rolls' to which the title refers is the Roll of Solicitors of which, ceremonially, the Master of the Rolls is custodian. The title also derives from the fact that, historically, the postholder was responsible for keeping important public records. He or she still maintains responsibility for documents of national importance and is the Chairman of the Advisory Council on Public Records and the Chairman of the Royal Commission on Historical Manuscripts. The Master of the Rolls also officially authorizes SOLICITORS to practise and, in a broader sense, is consulted on matters affecting the civil justice system and RIGHTS OF AUDIENCE. Under the 2003 Act, a Deputy Head of Civil Justice may be appointed in order to assist the Master of Rolls in his or her work. [AF]

maternity leave Leave for pregnancy and/or childbirth. Under current law, which changed on 1 October 2006 as a result of the Work and Families Act 2006, there are three periods of leave for a mother. Compulsory maternity leave lasts for the two weeks immediately after the birth of her child (Employment Rights Act 1996, s. 72) or for four weeks if the mother was engaged in factory work (Public Health Act 1936, s. 205, and Factories Act 1961, Sched. 5). It is unlawful to permit a woman to work in breach of these laws. Ordinary maternity leave (OML) is a 26-week period available to all pregnant WORKERS and is not compulsory. Additional maternity leave (AML) is an additional 26-week period of unpaid leave which begins at the end of OML. [MJ]

maternity pay Pay during MATERNITY LEAVE

may be contractual, in which case the contract of employment is the source, or statutory. By the Work and Families Act 2006 the length of the period during which a mother may receive maternity pay has been extended from 26 weeks to 39 weeks from 1 April 2007. If a woman who works does not qualify for SMP, she may be entitled to a maternity allowance. The government aims to increase this by 2010 so that the entire 12 months' leave is paid. [MJ]

maternity rights This term does not have a set meaning but covers those rights available to women before and after childbirth, including MATERNITY LEAVE, MATERNITY PAY and health and safety rights (such as in respect of breastfeeding). [MJ]

matrimonial causes Proceedings for DIVORCE, ANNULMENT or JUDICIAL SEPARATION; alternatively, an archaic phrase for those matters related to the law of MARRIAGE and divorce. With more and more FAMILIES living in arrangements outside of formal marriage, the law governing members' rights and obligations to each other is better described now as 'family law'. The phrase retains currency, however, in the Matrimonial Causes Act 1973, the principal law governing divorce and ANCILLARY RELIEF in England and Wales. [AD]
    See also FAMILY PROCEEDINGS.

matrimonial home Now known as the FAMILY HOME. [AD]

matrimonial offence Before the reform of DIVORCE law in England and Wales, a divorce could only be obtained on grounds which required culpability on the part of a guilty spouse, the respondent, and complete innocence on the part of the wronged spouse, the petitioner. These matrimonial offences were said to violate the very purpose of MARRIAGE. Only a limited number of matrimonial offences were sufficiently serious to justify the termination of a marriage. Divorce law has gone through a number of reforms from the first statute in 1857 and reform initiatives in the 1960s in particular were concerned with the degree to which divorce ought to remain based on fault or the matrimonial

offence. Current law does not adopt the language of 'matrimonial offence' and the only ground for divorce is IRRETRIEVABLE BREAK-DOWN of the marriage. Three of the five facts required to prove irretrievable breakdown, however, (UNREASONABLE BEHAVIOUR, ADULTERY and DESERTION) retain elements of the old matrimonial offences from which they derived. [AD]

matrimonial proceedings *See* MATRIMO-NIAL CAUSES. [AD]

mature minor A MINOR under the age of 16 deemed to have reached sufficient maturity and understanding to have the MENTAL CAP-ACITY to consent to medical treatment. [HJ]
    See also GILLICK COMPETENCE.

maxims of equity A series of statements said to embody the basic principles that underpin the development of the law of EQUITY. Important as they are historically, it is necessary to view them within their legal context for they do not exist in isolation and can easily mislead if viewed as absolute statements of principle. They are often contradictory and invariably subject to exception and are often used as little more than pegs on which to hang the robes of judicial intervention and/or invention. The most important equitable maxims are:

Equity acts *in personam.*
Equity acts on the conscience.
Equity aids the vigilant.
Equity follows the law.
Equity is equality.
Equity looks on that as done which ought to be done.
Equity will not assist a volunteer.
Equity will not suffer a wrong without a remedy.
Equity looks to the intent rather than the form.
He who comes into equity must come with clean hands.
He who seeks equity must do equity.
Where the equities are equal, the first in time shall prevail. [PK]

McKenzie friend A non-legally qualified person who sits with an unrepresented party during a court hearing, to offer advice and assistance. The term comes originally from a divorce case, *McKenzie* v. *McKenzie* [1971] P 33, though the concept itself is far older.

It is well established that a McKenzie friend may act as moral support, take notes or offer whispered advice during the hearing. The presumption in favour of allowing such assistance is strong, and a refusal could arguably now be challenged under the Human Rights Act 1998, Schedule 1, Part 1, Article 6. However, the right to a McKenzie friend is never absolute (see *R* v. *Leicester City Justices, ex p Barrow* [1991] QB 260) – and so may be refused if a particular McKenzie friend is considered potentially disruptive or inappropriate, or if it is considered that assistance may impede the OVERRIDING OBJECTIVE of litigation. So far as it exists, the right to assistance vests in the party, not in the McKenzie friend him- or herself (i.e. it is the litigant's right to assistance, not the particular friend's right to assist), and so any refusal needs to be challenged by the litigant in person, though the purported McKenzie friend should normally be permitted to assist in that challenge.

A McKenzie friend has absolutely no right to act as an advocate, but may, exceptionally, and with the express consent of the court, be permitted so to act in a specific case. This reflects the court's discretion under the Courts and Legal Services Act 1990, ss. 27 and 28, to grant an otherwise unqualified person a right of audience or a right to conduct litigation in relation to particular proceedings. Consent must be sought as it is a criminal offence and also a CONTEMPT OF COURT to do any act in the purported exercise of such a right where none has been conferred.

McKenzie friends may not charge fees, but may be entitled to recover out-of-pocket expenses for travel, etc. They may be held liable in NEGLIGENCE for any misleading legal advice given to the litigant in person. [JW]

See also LITIGATION FRIEND.

mechanically propelled vehicle *See* MOTOR VEHICLE.

mediation A method of ALTERNATIVE DISPUTE RESOLUTION in which a neutral third party (a **mediator**) works with the parties to a dispute to achieve a mutually acceptable solution or settlement. Mediation is increasingly used as an adjunct to court processes in a range of general civil and family law matters. It is also used to resolve employment and neighbour disputes. It has a long tradition in INTERNATIONAL LAW where it is used to resolve disputes and conflicts between states (see GOOD OFFICES).

Mediation is commonly thought of as a process of 'facilitated negotiation', in which the introduction of the third party itself changes the process of negotiation and, in theory at least, increases the likelihood of settlement without recourse to the courts. Other advantages claimed for mediation are that it can produce a wider range of outcomes than litigation, and that it is less expensive than pursuing a claim through the courts. The mediator's role is to manage the mediation process. The outcome remains with the parties, and a mediator has no power or authority to impose a settlement on the parties (unlike an ARBITRATOR). Mediators may but need not be qualified lawyers, or they may have other specialist expertise, e.g. in engineering, social work, surveying, etc., relevant to the nature of the dispute. Most mediators today have also undertaken specialist training in mediation skills. [JW]

See also ADR ORDER; CONCILIATION; FAMILY MEDIATION.

Medicines and Healthcare Products Regulatory Agency *See* LICENSING OF MEDICINES.

Member of Parliament A person elected to a seat in the HOUSE OF COMMONS. Members of Parliament are elected on a first-past-the-post system in 659 geographical constituencies, covering England, Scotland, Wales and Northern Ireland, whose boundaries are set by BOUNDARY COMMISSIONS.

An individual who wishes to stand as a Member of Parliament must be eligible to do so: she or he must be 21 years of age or over, and must not be a Member of the HOUSE OF LORDS, suffering from mental illness, an undischarged BANKRUPT, or a person convicted of certain criminal offences. Historically, members of the Anglican and Roman Catholic clergy had also been ineligible, but their disqualification was removed by the House of Commons (Removal of Clergy Disqualification) Act 2001.

Various enactments also allow for the disqualification of an individual from parliamentary candidacy. The most important of these is the House of Commons Disqualification Act 1975 (as amended), which identifies six classes of office-holder who are disqualified: (a) holders of certain judicial offices including HIGH COURT, COURT OF APPEAL and SUPREME COURT judges; (b) Civil Servants, whether full time or part time; (c) members of the regular armed forces; (d) full-time police officers; (e) members of the legislature of any non-Commonwealth country; and (f) holders of any other offices expressly listed in the Act. On the passing of the 2001 Act, above, bishops of the CHURCH OF ENGLAND were expressly added to the list of such offices.

[MS & JW]

Member of the European Parliament (MEP) A directly elected representative from a MEMBER STATE of the EUROPEAN COMMUNITY. Elections to the EUROPEAN PARLIAMENT are held once every five years. MEPs sit in the Parliament in cross-EUROPEAN UNION political groupings. [MON]

Member State A country which has applied for, and has been accepted as, a member of the EUROPEAN COMMUNITY (EC), having met all of the accession criteria of the EC, and has adopted the *ACQUIS* COMMUNAUTAIRE of the EC and *acquis union* of the EUROPEAN UNION. [MON]

memorandum in writing In land law, under the Law of Property Act 1925, s. 40, an oral contract relating to land made prior to 27 September 1989 is enforceable if it is evidenced by a memorandum in writing. Such a memorandum must contain the names of the parties, a description of the property and the consideration and be signed by the party against whom it is to be enforced.

For contracts made on or after 27 September 1989, an oral agreement evidenced by a memorandum in writing is no longer sufficient for a contract relating to land to exist. This is because s. 40 of the Law of Property Act 1925 was repealed by the Law of Property (Miscellaneous Provisions) Act 1989 (LPMPA 1989). Under LPMPA 1989, s. 2, a contract relating to land must be in writing, incorporate all terms which the parties have expressly agreed and be signed by both parties. This has reduced the possibility of individuals reaching informal agreements concerning land. [DR]

memorandum of association One of a number of documents necessary to incorporate a UK company. It will include the following clauses: the company's registered name; the location of its registered office; the company's purpose and objectives (called the **objects clause**); its share capital and share value; and, usually, the names of the first members (called **subscribers**) and their shareholdings.

The memorandum acts as the primary 'constitutional' or governing document of a company. Historically, the objects clause was thought to be critical in determining the scope of what the company could do, and so has usually been drafted widely, since activities falling outside the clause would be strictly beyond its powers (*ULTRA VIRES*). The effects of the *ultra vires* doctrine have, however, been abolished by the Companies Act 2006. [JW]

mens rea (Lat. a guilty mind) The state of mind required for the commission of an offence. Thus, in general terms, a crime comprises the combination of *ACTUS REUS* and *mens rea*. *Mens rea* is sometimes referred to as the mental element or internal element of a crime. Thus the *mens rea* for MURDER is an INTENTION to kill or to do GRIEVOUS BODILY HARM. The *mens rea* for CRIMINAL DAMAGE is intention or RECKLESSNESS that the damage in question be caused. While these forms of *mens rea* are defined by the defendant's actual state of mind, other forms of *mens rea*, most particularly GROSS NEGLIGENCE and NEGLIGENCE, are defined by reference to the defendant's failure to exhibit the level of care that would be taken by a notional reasonable person.

All criminal offences are capable of being analytically broken down into their constituent elements of *actus reus* and *mens rea*. Of course, what constitutes those elements differs from crime to crime, but the general formula of 'crime = *actus reus* + *mens rea*' is valid.   [BF]

mental capacity The consent of a patient to proposed medical treatment will only be valid where the patient has the capacity to give such consent. There is a presumption that adult patients have the capacity to give such consent. Lack of capacity may exist in a number of situations: emergency situations where the patient temporarily lacks capacity (see *Re F (Mental Patient: Sterilization)* [1990] 2 AC 1); where the patient belongs to a class often or normally lacking capacity, such as children (see *Gillick* v. *West Norfolk and Wisbech AHA* [1986] AC 112) or the mentally ill.

The Mental Capacity Act 2005 governs decision-making on behalf of adults, in circumstances in which they lose mental capacity at some point in their lives, for example as a result of mental illness, brain injury or dementia, and where the incapacity has been present since birth. Mental illness or disability does not automatically rebut the presumption of capacity (see *Re C (Adult Refusal of Treatment)* [1994] 1 WLR 290). This is given legislative force by Part 1 of the 2005 Act which sets out criteria for determining a lack of capacity in adult patients, based on patients' ability to understand and use the information necessary to make a decision for themselves. The Act also establishes a system for providing **independent mental capacity advocates** for particularly vulnerable people.   [HJ]

See also CONSENT TO TREATMENT; FRASER GUIDE-LINES; GILLICK COMPETENCE.

Mental Health Act Commission (MHAC) Established in 1983, the Commission acts as a monitoring body to safeguard the interests of those compulsorily detained under the provisions of the Mental Health Act 1983. The Commission's primary concerns relate to the legality of detention and the protection of human rights. The Commission lists its functions as follows: 'to keep under review the operation of the Mental Health Act 1983 in respect of patients detained or liable to be detained under that Act; to visit and interview, in private, patients detained under the Mental Health Act in hospitals and mental nursing homes; to consider the investigation of complaints where these fall within the Commission's remit; to review decisions to withhold the mail of patients detained in the High Security Hospitals; to appoint registered medical practitioners and others to give second opinions in cases where this is required by the Mental Health Act; to publish and lay before Parliament a report every two years; and to monitor the implementation of the Code of Practice and propose amendments to Ministers.'   [HJ]

MEP *See* MEMBER OF THE EUROPEAN PARLIAMENT.

merchantable quality The Sale and Supply of Goods Act 1994, s. 1, introduced the standard of SATISFACTORY QUALITY (Sale of Goods Act 1979, s. 14(2)) to replace the now obsolete obligation to supply goods of 'merchantable quality'.   [JPL]

mercy killing *See* ASSISTED SUICIDE; EUTHANASIA.

mere equity A right affecting property such as a right to rectify a defective conveyance. Mere equities are neither legal interests that bind the world, nor equitable interests which (historically at least) bind the world with the exception of EQUITY'S DARLING. A mere equity binds the parties to the transaction and anyone apart from a *bona fide* (good faith) purchaser for value of any interest in the property (be it legal or equitable) without notice of the equity.   [PK]

Meroni doctrine Based on the decision in Case 9/56, *Meroni* v. *High Authority* [1957–58] ECR 133, at 151, with regard to the TREATY OF PARIS, this principle now applies to all EUROPEAN COMMUNITY (EC) treaties. The doctrine was recently restated by the EUROPEAN COURT OF JUSTICE (ECJ) in Grand

CHAMBER, in joined Cases C-154/04 and C-155/04, *R, on the application of Alliance for Natural Health and Nutri-Link Ltd* v. *Secretary of State for Health* and *R, on the application of National Association of Health Stores and Health Food Manufacturers Ltd* v. *Secretary of State for Health and National Assembly for Wales* [2005] ECR I-06451 at para. 90. The ECJ held that when the Community legislature 'wishes to delegate its powers' with regard to amending legislation, 'it must ensure that the power is clearly defined and that the exercise of the power is subject to strict review in light of objective criteria'. Failure to do so might result in the delegation of a discretion which might 'be capable of impeding, excessively and without transparency' a key EC principle (e.g. in the case of *Nutri-Link* it was the FREE MOVEMENT OF GOODS). [MON]

messuage (obsolete) A term for a house and its associated LAND, orchards and outbuildings [HC & DR]

MFN *See* MOST-FAVOURED-NATION TREATMENT.

MHAC *See* MENTAL HEALTH ACT COMMISSION.

MHRA The Medicines and Healthcare Products Regulatory Agency. [HJ & JW]
See LICENSING OF MEDICINES.

micro-state A STATE entity that occupies either a small amount of territory or possesses a small population. The criteria established under the 1933 Montevideo Convention on the rights and duties of states and CUSTOMARY INTERNATIONAL LAW are objective and, as long as they are satisfied, the entity concerned attains statehood irrespective of territorial or population size. Obviously, some practical restrictions apply to such states. It may become financially onerous for them to pay arrears for membership to international organizations, or assume the responsibilities that flow from such membership. This is a requirement contained in Article 4 of the UN CHARTER, and as a result some micro-states have declined from applying for membership. [IB]

migrant worker A person who moves from one country to another for the purpose of finding employment. The rights of the worker who moves from one EUROPEAN COMMUNITY (EC) MEMBER STATE to another are protected under the FREE MOVEMENT OF PERSONS (workers) provisions. The protection of the migrant worker is part of EC social policy, which is set out in the SOCIAL CHAPTER. Rights of a migrant worker include the right to EQUAL TREATMENT for nationals of the host Member State, and the right of NON-DISCRIMINATION on the basis of nationality. [MON]

military testament *See* PRIVILEGED WILL.

minimum wage The national minimum wage (NMW) was introduced by the National Minimum Wage Act 1999 and is overseen by the Low Pay Commission. It provides a legal guarantee of minimum wages on a national basis. It comprises three basic rates: one for those aged over 22, one for those aged 18–21 (inclusive) and (since 2004) one for those aged 16–17, with special provisions for apprentices. [MJ]

See also WAGES COUNCILS.

ministerial responsibility By CONSTITUTIONAL CONVENTION, government Ministers share **collective responsibility** for government policy and **individual responsibility** for their own actions and the actions of the government department that they oversee. Collective responsibility is defined by two key principles. First, that once a decision has been made by Cabinet, all Ministers (whether in Cabinet-level posts or not) are bound by it. Consequently, any Minister who is unable to stand by a Cabinet decision must resign his post. A relatively recent example was Robin Cook's decision in March 2003 to resign as leader of the House of Commons over the UK government's decision to participate in military action against Iraq. Secondly, collective responsibility also means that all Cabinet discussion should remain confidential, and any divisions between Ministers remain a private matter within Cabinet and ministerial committees. Although more information is now given to the public about the operation of Cabinet than used to be the case, the convention of confidentiality is mostly observed, as otherwise it tends to undermine the authority of the government as a whole (as happened in the later years of John Major's administration in 1992–97).

The scope of the convention of individual responsibility is rather less certain. Ministers are formally responsible for the conduct and administration of their portion of government. They are not personally responsible for actions within their departments which are contrary to instructions and undertaken without their knowledge, though they are constitutionally obliged to explain what has gone wrong. While there is a perception that Ministers have become less willing to resign over significant mistakes in the delivery and implementation of policy, this may not be entirely accurate, as resignation has long been the exception rather than the rule, and has tended to depend as much on the Minister's level of support in the Cabinet and the governing party as on any shared notion of the boundaries of ministerial responsibility. This aspect of ministerial responsibility is perceived to be evolving into a more fluid concept of **ministerial accountability**, whereby Ministers are expected to give an account of their actions to Parliament and the public, and in this regard the onus on Ministers to answer to criticism has probably increased rather than decreased in recent years. This does not, however, mean that Ministers are necessarily sanctioned for their perceived failures with any greater frequency. The second arm of individual responsibility is generally less controversial and of less constitutional significance. Ministers, and Members of Parliament in general, are supposed to operate according to high standards of personal conduct. Sexual impropriety, the taking of bribes and financial misdealing are not generally seen as consistent with high public office, and so will tend to be resignation matters. [JW]

minor A person who is not of full age (s. 12 Family Law Reform Act 1969). A person becomes of full age when he or she attains the age of 18 (s. 1). Minors are sometimes referred to as INFANTS. [FK]

See also CHILD.

minor interests A term used by the Land Registration Act 1925 (LRA 1925), s. 3(xv) to describe certain interests in land which were not OVERRIDING INTERESTS and were not capable of being disposed of or created by a registered disposition. The Land Registration Act 2002 (LRA 2002) repealed the LRA 1925 and does not use the term 'minor interest'. Nevertheless, it is still used as a term of art to describe the residual category of interests under the LRA 2002 which may only be protected against a third party purchaser by entering a RESTRICTION or notice on the Land Register. Common examples of these interests include EASEMENTS and RESTRICTIVE COVENANTS, both of which can be protected in the REGISTERED LAND system by a notice on the CHARGES REGISTER against the registered estate. [DR]

minority rights A set of international human rights applying specifically to ethnic, religious or linguistic minorities and indigenous peoples. Following the creation of the UN after the Second World War, the vulnerability of minorities was recognized by the establishment, first, of a Sub-Commission on the Prevention of Discrimination and the Protection of Minorities, followed by the introduction of Article 27 of the INTERNATIONAL COVENANT ON CIVIL AND POLITICAL RIGHTS. The latter affords minority members with an individual RIGHT to enjoy, in community with the other members of the group, their culture, language, religion and practices. Other international initiatives have followed, notably the Declaration on the Rights of Persons Belonging to National or Ethnic, Religious and Linguistic Minorities, the Declaration on the Rights of Indigenous Peoples and two Council of Europe treaties, the Framework Convention for the Protection of National Minorities and the European Charter for Regional or Minority Languages. [IB]

See also SELF-DETERMINATION.

mischief rule *See* STATUTORY INTERPRETATION.

misdemeanour (obsolete) A term of historical significance, denoting – broadly speaking – less serious criminal offences. [BF]

See also FELONY; TREASON.

misdescription In CONVEYANCING, an error in the description of the extent or quality of the property to be sold, made either in the CONTRACT FOR SALE or by a representation of fact by the seller. If the misdescription is material and substantial, affecting the subject matter of the contract to the extent that it may reasonably be supposed that, but for such misdescription, the buyer would not have entered the contract at all, the contract may be rescinded by the buyer, who cannot be compelled to go ahead with the purchase (*Flight* v. *Booth*[1834] 1 Bing NC 370, at 377 *per* Tindall CJ). If, on the other hand, the misdescription is trivial, the contract may not be rescinded, and only compensation may be claimed (*Jacobs* v. *Revell* [1900] 2 Ch 858, at 865 *per* Buckley J). An example of substantial misdescription allowing rescission would be where the size of a property is overstated by around 40% (*Watson* v. *Burton* [1957] 1 WLR 19). Often misdescription will lead to a potential cause of action under the Misrepresentation Act 1967. [DR]

misdirection An erroneous direction given by the judge to the JURY in a criminal trial. In such circumstances, the Court of Appeal may quash the conviction. [ALTC]

misprision The concealment or a failure to report a matter to a relevant person in authority. Until the Criminal Law Act 1967 abolished the distinction between FELONY and MISDEMEANOUR, **misprision of felony** was an offence at COMMON LAW. Misprision of TREASON remains a common law offence. [BF]

misrepresentation A false statement of fact or conduct made by a misrepresentor that conveys a false impression and which induces the other (the misrepresentee) to enter a CONTRACT. It renders the contract voidable, i.e. liable to be set aside at the option of the misrepresentee by means of RESCISSION. A misrepresentation may be fraudulent, negligent or innocent and the type of misrepresentation affects the remedies available, particularly the ability to recover DAMAGES and the measure of those damages. [JPL]

See also FRAUDULENT MISREPRESENTATION; INNOCENT MISREPRESENTATION; NEGLIGENT MISREPRESENTATION.

mistake A misunderstanding or erroneous belief, at the time of contracting, concerning the basis on which the parties contracted. A mistake may negate or nullify consent where the nature of the mistake prevents the parties from ever reaching agreement. There are three types of mistake at common law: COMMON MISTAKE, MUTUAL MISTAKE and UNILATERAL MISTAKE. A document that, as a result of a mistake, does not correctly record what the parties intended may be rectified by the courts. [JPL]

See also IDENTITY, MISTAKE OF; NON EST FACTUM; OPERATIVE MISTAKE.

mistrial A trial that is so tainted by irregularity that it constitutes a nullity. 'To constitute a mistrial the proceedings must have been abortive from beginning to end': see *R* v. *Middlesex Quarter Sessions (Chairman), ex p DPP* [1952] 2 QB 758, 769. [ALTC]

mitigation The explanation for the offence given on behalf of a guilty party in order to excuse or partly excuse the offence committed in an attempt to minimize the sentence. Before sentencing, the court must take into account matters relating to both the offence and the offender's personal circumstances. The Powers of Criminal Courts (Sentencing) Act 2000, s. 158, provides that the court should not be prevented 'from mitigating an offender's sentence by taking into account any such matters as, in the opinion of the court, are relevant in mitigation'. Changes to the Bar Council Code of Conduct prevent defence counsel from making any derogatory or defamatory comments during a plea in mitigation relating to the conduct of any other person unless such allegations go to a matter in issue which is material to the case, and which appear to be supported by reasonable grounds. Defence counsel is now under an obligation to notify prosecution counsel, in advance, of their intention to use defamatory mitigation. Where defence counsel persists, prosecuting counsel should invite the court to determine the issue by calling evidence in the form of a NEWTON HEARING. [SN]

mitigation of loss The injured party must take reasonable steps to minimize the loss resulting from the other party's TORT or BREACH OF CONTRACT; if they do not, they will be unable to recover for any loss attributable to this failure to minimize (or mitigate). [JPL]

mixed fund A collection of both PERSONAL PROPERTY and REAL PROPERTY interests combined together; for example, where a person leaves both money investments and INTERESTS IN LAND to his children under a will. [DR]

mixed legal system A concept used in COMPARATIVE LAW to describe a legal system that draws substantially on more than one legal 'family' or tradition. Examples of mixed legal systems include Scotland, which is unusual, historically, in combining COMMON LAW and elements of the uncodified IUS COMMUNE of Roman law; the US State of Louisiana, which is heavily influenced by CIVIL LAW, though operating within a common law federal system; and perhaps Japan and South Korea, which are sufficiently influenced by German civil law for some commentators to suggest that they are better regarded as mixed rather than East Asian systems. Many former European colonies in Africa, South-East Asia and the Middle East also retain features of different traditions, including elements of CUSTOMARY LAW and sometimes a mix of received traditions from Islam and the Western European traditions. Looked at in this way there are relatively few 'pure' legal systems in the world, and the influences of globalization are arguably increasing moves to harmonize and approximate laws in ways that further blur traditional differences. [JW]

See also APPROXIMATION OF LAWS; GLOBALIZATION OF LAW; LEGAL PLURALISM.

mixed property Property that has aspects of both REAL PROPERTY and PERSONAL PROPERTY, so that it cannot be accurately described as either; for example, the right to EMBLEMENTS is considered to be personal property and on death passes as personal estate, despite the fact that it possesses the characteristics of an INTEREST IN LAND. Other examples include heirlooms and TITLE DEEDS, both of which are items of personal property, despite the fact that on death they devolve with the land. [DR]

M'Naghten rules *See* INSANITY; PRESUMPTION OF SANITY.

molestation Under the Family Law Act 1996, parties can obtain a NON-MOLESTATION ORDER against a person associated with them, who has acted violently against them, or who has pestered, harassed, intimidated or threatened them. Molestation is not defined in the Act, but case law has suggested that it covers interference 'sufficiently serious to warrant intervention by the court'. Molestation is therefore a form of DOMESTIC VIOLENCE that can be prohibited by the court. [AD]

Money Claim Online (MCOL) Launched in February 2002 by Her Majesty's Courts Service, MCOL enables claimants to issue claims over the internet to recover money owed. The progress of the CLAIM can be viewed online and, although the whole proceedings cannot yet be managed electronically, a number of other key stages, such as requests by claimants for entry of judgment can also be conducted online. All MCOL proceedings are issued in the name of Northampton County Court, and MCOL now issues more claims than any individual COUNTY COURT in England and Wales. The MCOL service can be accessed at http://www.moneyclaim.gov.uk. [JW]

See also DEFAULT JUDGMENT.

money-laundering The practice of disguising illegally obtained money or other economic goods by distributing it through normal business channels, or converting it into other goods or property. The Money Laundering Regulations 2007 (SI 2007/2157) implement the EC Third Money Laundering Directive in the UK. The regulations impose a number of duties on regulated businesses, including obligations to put anti-money-laundering systems in place and to report any 'suspicious activity' (transactions) to the appropriate authorities. Regulated businesses include most UK financial and credit businesses, such as banks, building societies, pawnbrokers, savings and investment firms, as well as legal practitioners in private practices (when undertaking certain financial and property transactions), accountants, tax advisers, insolvency practitioners, estate agents, trust or company service providers, and casinos. [JW]

monism Legal theorists have long argued as to whether international or domestic law should prevail one over the other. According to the monist theory, international and domestic law comprise particular manifestations of a single entity called law. But, although they operate within the same discipline or field, conflicts between the two are inevitable. Monists argue that international law prevails and several theories have been propounded to support this position; for example Hans KELSEN offered a monist-positivist approach that premised itself on the existence of a GRUNDNORM, the highest norm from which all others thereafter derive their validity. To Kelsen, international law represents a higher legal order because it is generally derived from the practice of STATES, whereas domestic law is predicated on states as entities that have already been established in international law. By contrast, a monist-naturalist position sees the supremacy of international law only through the prism of NATURAL LAW. Consequently, the validity of international law is measured only against natural law, which is supreme, and is applicable only where it conforms to natural law. [IB]

See also DUALISM; INCORPORATION DOCTRINE; TRANSFORMATION DOCTRINE.

Monroe doctrine The Monroe doctrine was put forward unilaterally in 1823 by then US President James Monroe, with significant input from John Quincy Adams. The doctrine contained four significant elements: recognition that South American states were no longer colonies but had

attained full SOVEREIGNTY; they were, moreover, republics in their constitutional nature rather than monarchies; future European intervention in their affairs would be viewed as a threat to the USA; and the USA pledged in turn that she would remain neutral in European affairs, and in relations between European states and their existing colonies in the Americas. The Monroe doctrine became a long-standing tenet of American foreign policy and in the Cold War was used to justify US intervention in Latin America where it was deemed that Soviet intervention existed, even if the latter followed an invitation from the governments concerned. [IB]

Montevideo Convention A regional treaty that was adopted by South American countries in 1933. It has subsequently entered the realm of CUSTOMARY INTERNATIONAL LAW, as regards its enumeration of four criteria that are constitutive of statehood. In accordance with Article 1 of the Convention, these are: the defined territory, a permanent population, an effective government and the capacity to enter into relations with other states (independence). Academic opinion is split on whether other criteria have developed as essential prerequisites of statehood, particularly recognition by other states, as well as democratic governance. The majority view appears to be that the creation of statehood is an objective fact encapsulated in the four criteria and no recognition is necessary. [IB]

See also CONSTITUTIVE THEORY; DECLARATORY THEORY; STATE.

month Under the Interpretation Act 1978, unless expressly defined otherwise, a month for the purposes of an Act of Parliament means a calendar month. The same presumption operates for deeds and other written documents by virtue of the Law of Property Act 1925 and for the purposes of court proceedings under the CIVIL PROCEDURE RULES, Rule 2.10. [JW]

moral law A synonym for NATURAL LAW insofar as this term is used to denote the notion that it is possible to say what is right and wrong, what ought to be done and what ought not to be done, without reference to human or positive law. [JP]

moral rights The rights of authors of artistic, dramatic, musical and literary works, and of film directors to be identified as the author of their work, to uphold its integrity (in the sense of completeness), and to object to false attribution (Copyright, Design and Patents Act 1988, ss. 77–84). The final moral right is a limited right of privacy which does not actually benefit the author of a work, but belongs to the commissioner of photographs and films, commissioned for private and domestic purposes.

Moral rights are not assignable but can be waived by the author. Moral rights generally cease on expiry of the COPYRIGHT protection of the work (i.e. life of the author plus 70 years), with the exception of the right against false attribution, which expires 20 years after the author's life.

The right of attribution and the right of integrity are recognized international moral rights (see Article *6bis* of the Berne Convention for the Protection of Literary and Artistic Works). They are also recognized under the national copyright laws of all the European Union MEMBER STATES, though there is as yet no EU DIRECTIVE which recognizes these rights. [US]

mortgage The transfer of an interest in land or personal property as security for a loan or the payment of a debt. Mortgages are most commonly used in the purchase of a house. Under a mortgage, the lender is granted various rights over the borrower's property, subject to the provision that those rights are terminable on the repayment of the loan according to the terms of the mortgage. The borrower is the **mortgagor**, since it is the borrower that grants the rights under the mortgage. The lender is the **mortgagee**, since it is the lender that receives the benefit of the security.

A **legal mortgage** may be created by either of the following methods (Law of Property Act 1925, ss. 85–87): (a) a DEMISE or sub-demise, subject to a provision for cesser on REDEMPTION. This means a mortgage on freehold or leasehold property, created by granting a lease or sublease to the lender, subject to a provision that it is terminable on the repayment of the loan; or (b) a deed of CHARGE BY WAY OF LEGAL MORTGAGE. In registered land, a charge by way of legal mortgage is the only way to create a legal mortgage and it must be registered to take effect (Land Registration Act 2002, ss. 23(1) (a), 27(2)(f)). A mortgage created in any other way can only be an EQUITABLE MORTGAGE.

The main right of the borrower under a mortgage is the equitable right of redemption, under which the mortgage is discharged as long as the loan and any interest due has been paid. The lender has the right to possession of the land (though this is usually restricted by a condition in the mortgage that possession will not be taken as long as the borrower makes regular payments), the right of insurance of the property at the borrower's expense, the right to grant leases once in possession of the property and the right of CONSOLIDATION OF MORTGAGES. If a borrower defaults on his mortgage obligations, remedies available to the lender include FORECLOSURE, possession, exercise of the POWER OF SALE and the appointment of a RECEIVER. [DR]

See also EQUITY OF REDEMPTION; MORTGAGE ACTION; PRIORITY OF MORTGAGES; PUISNE MORTGAGE; REGULATED MORTGAGE; SUB-MORTGAGE.

Further reading: Judith-Anne Mackenzie and Mary Phillips, *Textbook on Land Law*, 11th edn (Oxford: Oxford University Press, 2006); Edward Hector Burn and John Cartwright, *Cheshire and Burn's Modern Law of Real Property*, 17th edn (Oxford: Oxford University Press, 2006).

mortgage action An action brought by the lender on a MORTGAGE following the default of the borrower in making repayments under the terms of the mortgage. A mortgage action may be an action for possession or a debt action for repayment of sums owed to the lender. [DR]

mortgagee A person who lends money under a MORTGAGE. The lender is the mortgagee because it is the lender that receives the benefit of the security in exchange for the loan. [DR]

mortgagor A person who borrows money under a MORTGAGE. The borrower is the mortgagor because he or she grants the rights under the mortgage as security for the loan. [DR]

Most-Favoured-Nation (MFN) Treatment Where a STATE agrees to deal with a partner state on the most favourable terms available for trade in goods and/or services. Although MFN arrangements can be agreed bilaterally between individual states, together with the adoption of NATIONAL TREATMENT STANDARDS, MFN has also become one of the guiding principles of WORLD TRADE ORGANIZATION (WTO) trade law. It thus constitutes Article 1 of the General Agreement on Tariffs and Trade (GATT), and is also contained in Article II of the General Agreement on Trade in Services (GATS), and Article 4 of the Agreement on Trade-Related Aspects of Intellectual Property Rights (TRIPS). Consequently WTO members must, as a condition of membership, grant MFN status to each other. In this way MFN has become a principle for ensuring equality of treatment among members. Exceptions exist whereby preferential treatment may be granted to developing countries, and within regional free trade areas and CUSTOMS UNIONS. [JW]

motive The purpose or purposes behind a person's conduct, or the desire or desires which inform it. For the purposes of establishing MENS REA, and hence criminal liability, a person's motive is not generally relevant, although it may provide strong evidence of their direct INTENTION. [BF]

motor vehicle Defined by the Road Traffic Act 1988, s. 185(1)(c), as 'a **mechanically propelled vehicle** intended or adapted for use on roads'. It follows that there are kinds of mechanically propelled vehicle which are not motor vehicles and therefore cannot lawfully be used on roads – these will include vehicles such as go-karts, unregistered or unlicensed scramblers and quad bikes. It is also a criminal offence to drive any mechanically propelled vehicle

(whether intended or adapted for use on roads or not) on any common land, moorland, footpath, bridleway or restricted byway (see Road Traffic Act 1988, s. 734, as amended). [JW]

motoring offences A term used to denote a broad range of offences committed in situations involving the use of motor vehicles. For the purposes of recording crime data, motoring offences are broken down into a variety of sub-categories, relating, for example, to the manner of driving, to compliance with vehicle testing and documentation requirements, and to obstructing, waiting and parking. [BF]

See also CARELESS DRIVING; CAUSING DEATH BY DANGEROUS DRIVING; DANGEROUS DRIVING; DRIVING WHILE DISQUALIFIED; DRIVING WHILE UNFIT; DRIVING WITHOUT A LICENCE; DRIVING WITHOUT INSURANCE; DRUNKEN DRIVING; PRESCRIBED LIMIT (BLOOD ALCOHOL).

moveable property In SCOTS LAW, all property other than HERITABLE PROPERTY. Broadly speaking, all property that it is possible to move, other than land, buildings and things attached to them. [JP]

MP *See* MEMBER OF PARLIAMENT.

MR *See* MASTER OF THE ROLLS.

multiple admissibility A somewhat misleading term, describing the situation in which an item of evidence is held to be ADMISSIBLE for one purpose, but not for others. [ALTC]

murder The unlawful killing of another human being, committed MALICE AFORETHOUGHT, i.e., with an intention to kill or to cause grievous (meaning really serious) bodily harm. There are a number of special defences to a charge of murder, namely DIMINISHED RESPONSIBILITY, PROVOCATION and SUICIDE pact. Where any of these is pleaded successfully, it will reduce the conviction from one of murder to voluntary MANSLAUGHTER. A conviction for murder carries a mandatory life sentence. [BF]

music piracy Piracy is wilful COPYRIGHT infringement, i.e. copying a copyright work without permission from the owner of the intellectual property (under the Copyright, Designs and Patents Act 1988, s. 16). There are various infringing activities set out in the CDPA 1988 in relation to recorded music, including distributing, selling, hiring out, or offering for sale or hire, unauthorized copies of CDs, or possessing such unauthorized copies with a view to distributing, etc., these to other people; distributing such unauthorized copies on such a scale as to have an impact on the copyright owner's business; playing or showing in public a sound recording, if the person knew or had reason to believe that copyright would be infringed (see ss. 18–26).

Some of these acts constitute criminal offences (CDPA 1988, s. 107) and the offender can be liable on summary conviction to imprisonment for a maximum term of six months or on conviction to a maximum term of ten years.   [US]

muteness   Failure or inability of the accused to answer directly to the INDICT-MENT. If the accused chooses to remain silent, the court may order a NOT GUILTY PLEA to be entered on their behalf. Where muteness is voluntary, the accused is considered to be 'mute of malice'.   [SN]

mutual mistake   A situation in which both parties are mistaken about a fundamental matter affecting the operation of the CONTRACT but they make different mistakes; sometimes known as a 'cross-purpose mistake' and the mistake prevents the parties reaching AGREEMENT so that the alleged contract is VOID. However, if it is possible to say either that party A's interpretation is more reasonable than party B's or that party B provoked A's mistake, there will be a contract on the basis of A's interpretation.   [JPL]

See also COMMON MISTAKE; IDENTITY, MISTAKE OF; OPERATIVE MISTAKE; UNILATERAL MISTAKE.

mutual wills   The doctrine of mutual wills arises when two (or possibly more) people agree to make wills in similar form, the intention being that the survivor will dispose of his estate in a particular manner; for instance, a husband and wife might agree to leave everything to the survivor of them and, on the death of both of them, to their daughter. The problem here is that a WILL is always revocable, so that after the first one dies, there is nothing to stop the survivor from changing his or her will, and this could be considered a FRAUD on the other. To deal with this situation, the courts have said that on the death of the first one, a CONSTRUCTIVE TRUST is imposed upon the survivor in favour of the intended BENEFICIARY of the original will. Although the doctrine has been established for many years, it still presents problems, for instance in identifying precisely what property is subject to the trust. Also, since the obligation of the survivor is to leave property in his or her will, what is to stop him or her dissipating it in his or her lifetime? It appears that the survivor must avoid transactions 'calculated to defeat the intention of the agreement', such as making *inter vivos* gifts of large amounts, but the position is far from clear.
                                                                    [CM]

N

National Assembly for Wales The legislative body of the devolved Welsh government. The reformed Assembly was established under the Government of Wales Act 2006. The Act extends the LEGISLATIVE COMPETENCE of the Assembly beyond that contained in the first devolution Act, the Government of Wales Act 1998. Schedule 5 of the 2006 Act defines 20 **fields**, or areas of activity, in which the Assembly has devolved law-making powers. In these fields, new Welsh laws, called **Assembly Measures**, can make any provision that could be made by an Act of the UK PARLIAMENT. Additional devolved power can be granted to the Assembly on a case-by-case basis by LEGISLATIVE COMPETENCE ORDER – a type of ORDER IN COUNCIL which needs to be passed by the UK Parliament. The 2006 Act also converts the **Welsh Assembly Government** from a committee of the National Assembly to being a separate executive body, comprising up to 14 Welsh Ministers, and makes future provision for a referendum on increasing the Assembly's legislative powers to the level of the SCOTTISH PARLIAMENT. [JW]

National Conditions of Sale *See* STANDARD CONDITIONS OF SALE. [DR]

National Industrial Relations Court (obsolete) Part of the fundamentally revised law laid down by Edward Heath's government in the Industrial Relations Act 1971. Its President was Sir John Donaldson, later MASTER OF THE ROLLS. The refusal by TRADE UNIONS to comply with the Act and their view that the Court was biased against them led to its abolition by the Trade Union and Labour Relations Act 1974. [MJ]

National Institute for Health and Clinical Excellence (NICE) An independent body with national responsibility for the provision of guidance on the promotion of good health and the prevention and treatment of ill-health. Guidance is given across three broad areas: (a) public health – guidance on the promotion of good health and the prevention of ill-health for those working in the National Health Service (NHS), local authorities and the wider public and voluntary sector; (b) health technologies – guidance on the use of new and existing medicines, treatments and procedures within the NHS; and (c) clinical practice – guidance on the appropriate treatment and care of people with specific diseases and conditions within the NHS. [HJ]

national treatment standard A principle adopted by many states, whereby an ALIEN on the territory of a foreign state can expect equality of treatment under that state's national law, subject to certain exceptions; for example, the state of residency is not compelled to provide more favourable financial or other conditions, nor employment in the public sector, nor access to legal aid and other rights and benefits reserved for nationals. The various standards of treatment will vary in accordance with the national constitution, as well as on the basis of agreements between the host state and that of the alien's nationality. Such agreements may provide for RECIPROCITY, open door, preferential treatment, MOST-FAVOURED-NATION TREATMENT and others. A particular manifestation of such agreements is the bilateral investment treaty, which provides a standard of treatment for investors in other states. The adoption of national treatment standards is also one of the cornerstones of WORLD TRADE ORGANIZATION (WTO) trade law. [IB]

natural child A biological CHILD as opposed to, for example, an adopted child or child born as a result of certain methods of assisted reproduction. The scope accorded to the term 'natural PARENT' was discussed in *Re G (Children)* [2006] UKHL 43; [2006] 2 FLR 629. Baroness Hale drew a distinction between legal and natural parents. Natural parents, she said, include genetic parents, who provide the gametes which produce the child, as well as gestational parents, who 'conceive and bear' the child in a surrogacy arrangement. However, the judge seemed also to include 'social and psychological' parenthood in the category of natural parenthood and this would make adoptive parents 'natural parents'. [FK]

natural justice Principles of procedural fairness closely associated with the RULE OF LAW. At COMMON LAW, natural justice is encapsulated in two principles: (a) that public bodies, judges and TRIBUNALS have a duty to act fairly and without self-interest or BIAS, encapsulated in the notion *NEMO JUDEX IN CAUSA SUA* (no one may be judge in their own cause); and (b) that individuals are entitled to the opportunity to present their case, again often expressed by the Latin tag *AUDI ALTERAM PARTEM* (let the other side be heard). Breach of the principles of

natural justice may provide grounds for JUDICIAL REVIEW. The principles are also bolstered by the right to FAIR TRIAL contained in Article 6 of the EUROPEAN CONVENTION ON HUMAN RIGHTS, which is now incorporated into UK law by the Human Rights Act 1998. [JW]

natural law The stream of legal theoretical thinking which holds that there is a necessary connection between law and morality. Thus, for something to count as law it must comply with criteria other than those internal to the legal system itself. Natural law is usually contrasted with positive law or LEGAL POSITIVISM, which holds that there is no necessary connection between law and morality and in some cases that any reliance on morality to determine legal status is dangerous.

Natural law thinking may be traced back to the ancient Greeks. Plato, for example, proposed that human law was in accordance with natural law insofar as it matched the ideal of law. While this judgement was amenable to human reason, it could only be made by specially trained philosopher kings. Aristotle, on the other hand, believed that human law was in accord with natural law insofar as it helped individuals attain their natural goal or *telos*: to live as social beings in the setting of the city-state.

The influence of the ancient Greeks is clear in the major Christian contributions to natural law thinking. Writing at a time when Aristotle's writings had been lost, St Augustine reveals a Platonic influence when he identifies the ideal law against which the justice of human law may be measured as God's law. Writing much later, when Aristotle's works were once again known within Christendom, AQUINAS proposed that human law was in accord with natural law insofar as it supported individuals in fulfilling their earthly goal of living as social beings in specifically Christian communities.

Natural law accordingly developed a specifically Christian character, albeit that the role of human reason, traceable back to the ancient Greeks, had never disappeared.

This latter fact perhaps allowed the easy secularization of natural law in the aftermath of the Reformation when the rejection of Catholicism forced Protestant thinkers to look elsewhere for inspiration than the then-dominant work of Aquinas. Most prominent in this regard was Hugo de Groot (GROTIUS) who took as his starting point the Greek observation that individuals naturally wanted to live in well-ordered societies. For Grotius, reason demanded this and accordingly reason could be the source of natural law even if God did not exist.

Natural thinking was also advanced by the work of those writers working in the SOCIAL CONTRACT tradition: THOMAS HOBBES, JOHN LOCKE and JEAN-JACQUES ROUSSEAU.

The long dominance of natural law was finally ended with the acute criticism levelled against it by DAVID HUME. He demonstrated that natural law proceeded on the basis of a fallacy: namely that it is possible to derive an 'ought' proposition from an 'is' proposition or, in other words, a value statement from a statement of fact. The lack of logic at the heart of the naturalistic fallacy presented a serious problem for natural law and provided the platform for the emergence of positivism.

The subsequent dominance of positivism has not gone unchallenged, as natural lawyers have sought, especially in the period since the Second World War, to circumvent Hume's objections. Most notable in this regard have been Lon Fuller with his PROCEDURAL NATURALISM and JOHN FINNIS, who has attempted a full-scale reconstruction of natural law based on the notion of the self-evidence of certain basic human goods.
[JP]

natural rights The notion that an individual possesses inalienable rights by virtue of being human. Some variants of this approach trace the origin of these rights back to God, others to nature. In either case the effect is to establish a formidable barrier to any attempt by the state to encroach upon the integrity and liberty of the individual.

Now more likely to be discussed under the rubric of human rights, the idea of natural rights found one of its earliest and clearest expressions in the work of JOHN LOCKE. His *Two Treatises of Government* (1690) influenced the key figures in the American Revolution, such as Thomas Jefferson and Thomas Paine, and thus in turn the drafting of the American Constitution itself.

Among other important statements of natural or human rights may be listed the Declaration of the Rights of Man and the Citizen following the French Revolution (1789) and the United Nations' Universal Declaration of Human Rights (1948). The most recent influential theoretical statement of natural rights is to be found in the work of JOHN FINNIS. [JP]

naturalization A legal process by which a person obtains a new nationality. In the UK, BRITISH CITIZENSHIP may be acquired by naturalization after a specified period of legal residence in the UK, provided that the applicant has 'indefinite leave to remain' in the UK or an equivalent immigration status for this purpose, and can meet certain standards of language competence and of knowledge of life in the UK. Naturalization is at the discretion of the relevant Secretary of State, but is normally granted if the legal requirements are met.
[JW]

ne bis in idem (Lat. not twice for the same) The rule against DOUBLE JEOPARDY. [ALTC]

necessaries A MINOR or mentally disordered person will be bound in relation to CONTRACTS for necessaries, for which a reasonable sum is payable. Necessaries are defined by the Sale of Goods Act 1979, s. 3(3), as 'goods suitable to the condition in life of the minor ... and to his actual requirements at the time of the sale'. This was interpreted in *Nash* v. *Inman* [1908] 2 KB 1 to exclude 11 fancy waistcoats on the basis that the minor already had a suitable supply of clothing to meet his 'condition in life'. [JPL]
See also CHILDREN'S CONTRACTS.

necessity 1. There is some controversy as to whether a defence of necessity, strictly so-called, is recognized in criminal law. In *R v. Dudley and Stephens* (1884) 14 QBD 273, the two defendants were in a shipwreck and had to take to a lifeboat. Also in the lifeboat was the ship's cabin boy. After a lengthy period at sea without food, they killed the cabin boy and sustained themselves with his flesh and blood. The jury originally declined to convict and the case was remitted to the QUEEN'S BENCH DIVISION by a special procedure. That court convicted the defendants of MURDER. They could not avail themselves of a defence of necessity, even in such trying circumstances. There was no acceptable reason to justify the selection of the cabin boy to be killed; rather he had been chosen because he was the weakest. However, the court declined to enforce the DEATH PENALTY against the defendants and imposed short prison sentences instead. It is not clear whether *Dudley and Stephens* is authority for the suggestion that (a) there is no defence of necessity known to the criminal law; (b) there is no defence of necessity available on a charge of murder; or (c) that even if there is a defence of necessity, it was not made out in these facts.

The reluctance of the courts since *Dudley and Stephens* to articulate a general defence of necessity is in part due to caution about allowing citizens to weigh and balance the values of different human lives, even when faced with tragic choices. However, traces of the defence have been spotted in cases where the party faced with the difficult choice is a medical practitioner; for discussion, see *R v. Bourne* [1938] 3 All ER 615; *Gillick v. West Norfolk and Wisbech AHA* [1986] AC 112; *Re F (Mental Patient: Sterilization)* [1990] 2 AC 1; and, more recently, *Re A (Children) (Conjoined Twins: Medical Treatment) (No. 1)* [2000] 4 All ER 961. In *Re A*, the Court of Appeal had to rule on the lawfulness of an operation to separate conjoined twins, in circumstances in which it was known that one of the twins would die, but as a result of which it was hoped to provide the stronger twin with a chance of long-term survival. The prognosis was that if the surgery was not performed, both twins would die within months. The Court of Appeal ruled that the operation could be lawfully performed. Part of the reasoning of the court concerned the defence of necessity, which could, it was suggested, be more appropriately applied where there was no dispute (in contrast with *Dudley and Stephens*) as to who was the appropriate victim of the tragic choice – the weaker twin would have died in any event; the stronger twin had the chance of survival following the operation. Brooke LJ drew on the work of Sir James Fitzjames Stephen (see L.F. Sturge, *A Digest of the Criminal Law*, 9th edn (Sweet & Maxwell, 1950)): thus, the defence might apply where the act (i.e. the surgery) is needed to avoid inevitable and irreparable harm; and where the act is no more than is reasonably necessary for the purpose to be achieved; and where the harm caused is not disproportionate to the harm avoided.

While there has been controversy about the existence of a general defence of necessity, as above, that has been limited to the idea of necessity operating as a JUSTIFICATION for taking particular action. More established, however, is a form of necessity which operates as an EXCUSE, and which has become known as 'DURESS of circumstances'. This defence operates in a similar fashion to the more conventional duress by threats, and accordingly, is available to a person whose will is overborne by circumstances, where a sober person of reasonable firmness would have responded in the same way. As with duress by threats, the defence is not available to a charge of murder or attempted murder. For discussion, see *R v. Graham* [1982] 1 All ER 801; *R v. Willer* (1986) 83 Cr App R 225; *R v. Conway* [1989] QB 290.

2. Necessity may, in limited circumstances, act as a civil law defence against certain intentional TORTS (such as CONVERSION), and in cases of **medical necessity**, where it will provide a defence to trespasses against the person, whether BATTERY or FALSE IMPRISONMENT; see *Re L (By his Next Friend GE)* [1998] 3 All ER 289. Medical necessity will arise in circumstances in which it is necessary to administer urgent medical treatment to a patient temporarily lacking the

MENTAL CAPACITY to consent on his or her own behalf. Such a situation may arise when a patient is brought into hospital in an unconscious state following an accident, or perhaps during an operation when something serious but unexpected needs urgent attention. The doctrine is set out in detail in *Re F* [1990] 2 AC 1. Treatment administered in such circumstances must be no more than is reasonably required, in the best interests of the patient, before he or she regains consciousness and the ability to give consent. [BF & HJ]

See also SELF-DEFENCE.

necrophilia Until the Sexual Offences Act 2003, necrophilia was not a distinct offence. Now s. 70 of the 2003 Act creates an offence of sexual penetration of a corpse, by a person who intentionally penetrates, with part of his body or anything else, part of the body of a dead person, when he knows that, or is reckless as to whether that is what is penetrated, and the penetration is sexual. [BF]

neglect 1. A criminal offence where a person who is 16 or over, and who has responsibility for a CHILD or young person under 16, among other things, wilfully neglects or causes or procures that child or young person to be neglected in a manner likely to cause unnecessary suffering or injury to health: see the Children and Young Persons Act 1933, s. 1.

2. A category of child maltreatment justifying intervention in the FAMILY and, if necessary, the taking of a child into care. Statutory guidance issued by the government, for use by professionals engaged in child protection work, defines neglect as 'the persistent failure to meet a child's basic physical and/or psychological needs, likely to result in the serious impairment of the child's health or development' (HM Government, *Working Together to Safeguard Children. A guide to inter-agency working to safeguard and promote the welfare of children*, London: TSO, 2006). If the neglect reaches the threshold criteria of 'significant harm' or likelihood of significant harm laid down in the Children Act 1989, the LOCAL AUTHOR-

ITY is empowered to seek a court order to afford the child protection. [FK]

See also CARE ORDER; CHILD ABUSE; EMERGENCY PROTECTION ORDER; WILFUL NEGLECT.

negligence A TORT, requiring the proof of four elements: (a) that the defendant owes the claimant a duty of care; (b) that he has acted in breach of that duty; (c) that he has caused harm or loss to the claimant; (d) and that the damage is not too remote. The **duty of care** is not a limitless concept. The defendant will only owe a duty of care to one 'so closely and directly affected by [his] act that [he] ought reasonably to have them in contemplation when directing [his] mind to the acts or omissions which are called in question', *per* Lord Atkin in *Donoghue* v. *Stevenson* (1932) AC 562. A **breach of duty** is constituted by an 'omission to do something which a reasonable man, guided upon those considerations which ordinarily regulate the conduct of human affairs, would do, or doing something which a prudent and reasonable man would not do' (*Blyth* v. *Birmingham Waterworks Co.* (1856) 11 Ex 781). In most cases, **causation** will be established by the so-called **'but for' test**, i.e. on the BALANCE OF PROBABILITIES, the harm suffered would not have occurred 'but for' the defendant's negligent action (*Barnett* v. *Chelsea and Kensington HMC* [1969] 1 QB 428). However, where harm arises as a cumulative result of a single ongoing process, which may be only partly attributable to the defendant's negligence, the court will seek to establish whether his actions contributed materially to the risk of harm (*McGhee* v. *National Coal Board* [1973] 1 WLR 1). Once negligence is established the defendant will be liable for all direct losses (**damage**) flowing from his actions, unless it can be established that any loss is too remote (SEE REMOTENESS OF DAMAGE). [HJ]

negligence (in criminal law) A form of MENS REA which corresponds to a failure to measure up to the standards of the reasonable person. Criminal offences rarely specify negligence as explicitly the form of *mens rea*, but will instead utilize some concept of reasonable behaviour.

Thus, the offence of CARELESS DRIVING in the Road Traffic Act 1988, s. 3, refers to 'due care and attention' and 'reasonable consideration' for other road users as indicators of a negligence offence. In *McCrone* v. *Riding* [1938] 1 All ER 157, this was held to be an objective test which was not qualified by the actual experience of the driver. Lord Hewart CJ suggested (at 158): 'That standard is an objective standard, impersonal and universal, fixed in relation to the safety of other users of the highway. It is in no way related to the degree of proficiency or degree of experience attained by the individual driver.' [BF]

See also GROSS NEGLIGENCE; INTENTION; MANSLAUGHTER; RECKLESSNESS.

negligent misrepresentation A false statement of fact made honestly by one person to another, but without exercising reasonable care to ensure its truth, in order to induce that person to enter a CONTRACT. A negligent misrepresentation renders the contract VOIDABLE so that the remedy of RESCISSION will be available in principle and also the possibility of DAMAGES under the Misrepresentation Act 1967, s. 2(1), if the misrepresentor is unable to prove that he had reasonable grounds to believe, and did believe up to the time the contract was made, that the facts represented were true. [JPL]

See also NEGLIGENT MISSTATEMENT; INNOCENT MISREPRESENTATION; FRAUDULENT MISREPRESENTATION.

negligent misstatement A false statement made honestly but carelessly, i.e. without exercising reasonable care to ensure it was true, in breach of a DUTY OF CARE in TORT. The duty of care will arise only where there is an assumption of responsibility for the giving of the advice or the making of the statement. A contractual link between the person making the statement and the person to whom the statement was made is not required (see *Hedley Byrne & Co. Ltd* v. *Heller & Partners Ltd* [1964] AC 465: the misstatement led to a CONTRACT with a third party which resulted in loss). DAMAGES are available for losses suffered if the elements of this tort can be established. The key distinction between NEGLIGENT MISREPRESENTATION and negligent misstatement is that the basis of liability for the former is contractual misrepresentation whereas liability for the latter depends on establishing the existence of a tort. [JPL]

nemo dat quod non habet (Lat. no one gives who possesses not) In CONTRACT law, this translates to the general rule (Sale of Goods Act 1979, s. 21(1)) that a person who does not have TITLE of property, e.g. a thief, cannot transfer any title to another. However, there are important exceptions to the *nemo dat* rule in which title to goods can be passed by a person who is not the owner; for example, the true owner may be prevented ('estopped') by his conduct from denying the SELLER's authority to sell, and sales under a VOIDABLE title to a purchaser in good faith and without notice are specifically excluded (s. 23). Other exceptions occur in the case of sales by a seller in possession after a sale (s. 24), sales by a buyer in possession after a sale (s. 25) and sales of motor vehicles obtained on hire purchase (Hire Purchase Act 1964, s. 27). [JPL]

See also ESTOPPEL; PURCHASER FOR VALUE WITHOUT NOTICE.

nemo judex in causa sua (Lat. no one may be judge in their own cause) The rule against BIAS. Sometimes alternatively written as *nemo debet esse judex in propria causa*. [JW]

nervous shock *See* PSYCHIATRIC HARM.

neutral citation A unique reference number given to a case which is the official number attributed to that judgment. The citation has three elements: the date, the court code and the case number, which is assigned sequentially by the relevant courts in order of its appearance in that court; for example, the 67th case to be heard in the QUEEN'S BENCH DIVISION of the HIGH COURT during the year 2007 would be written as: [2007] EWHC 67 (QB). Each judgment is prepared and issued as approved with single spacing, paragraph numbering (in the margins), and no page numbers. Where there is more than one judgment, the paragraph numbering carries on sequentially. Neutral citations have been applied to every judgment of the COURT OF APPEAL and of the Divisional Court of the Queen's Bench Division (*Practice Direction (Judgments: Form and Citation)* [2001] 1 WLR 194) since January 2001, with the system extended to every judgment of the High Court in 2002 (*Practice Direction (Judgments: Neutral Citations) (Supreme Court)* [2002] 1 WLR 346). They have also been adopted for the HOUSE OF LORDS and the PRIVY COUNCIL. The full list of neutral citations is as follows:

UKHL – House of Lords

UKPC – Judicial Committee of the Privy Council

EWCA Civ – Court of Appeal, Civil Division

EWCA Crim – Criminal Division

EWHC (Admin) High Court, Administrative Court

   (Admlty) Admiralty Court

   (Ch) Chancery Division

   (Comm) Commercial Court

   (Fam) Family Division

   (Pat) Patents Court

   (QB) Queen's Bench Division

   (TCC) Technology and Construction Court   [AF]

neutrality The status of a STATE during an armed conflict between other nations in which the neutral state takes no part, direct or indirect, in the hostilities and does not allow the use of its territory for the benefit of either party. Where the neutral state engages in action that may be deemed to benefit one of the parties to the armed conflict, it may lose its neutrality and suffer consequences commensurate to its level of participation. The duties of neutral states include the following: if members of the armed forces of the warring parties are found on neutral territory, the latter has an obligation to detain them until the end of the war; the neutral state must take all possible measures in order to prevent its nationals from entering the armed conflict on either side; it must not allow its ports to be used by the warships or cargo vessels of the warring parties, unless they

are in distress; and in the latter circumstance it must not allow any repairs to be made, except in so far as is necessary for the basic seaworthiness of the vessel.   [IB]

neutralization The demilitarizing of land or maritime territory which may be agreed in time of armed conflict or peace. Neutralization may be achieved through a treaty between the parties concerned, or be ordered by the UN Security Council, acting under CHAPTER VII (Article 41) of the UN CHARTER. Where neutralization is agreed or ordered, it produces the legal effect of restricting use of territory, but in no way affects territorial SOVEREIGNTY. One prominent example is the demilitarization of Antarctica. More specialized forms of neutralization are the designation by the Council or by agreement of no-fly zones or SAFE HAVENS.   [IB]

***Newton* hearing** From the case *R* v. *Newton* (1983) 77 C App R 13. A hearing held when a defendant admits guilt but disputes the prosecution's version of events and the court needs to determine the basis on which the defendant is to be sentenced. If the factual dispute between the prosecution and defence versions is so different that it affects the appropriate sentence in the case, the court must hear evidence on the disputed points. These hearings are similar in form to a mini trial. The prosecution are first required to call evidence in relation to the matters in dispute, and the defence will then call evidence to support their version of the facts. The BURDEN OF PROOF lies upon the prosecution, who must prove their assertions of fact beyond reasonable doubt.   [SN]

See also MITIGATION.

next of kin This is a frequently used term but has no statutory or formal definition. One is often asked to designate a 'next of kin' on admission to hospital, for example, which simply means that the person so designated would be contacted in case of emergency. In practice, hospitals and police have tended to regard spouses and close blood relatives as next of kin, but there are no rules concerning who one can designate. A person's designated next of kin does not acquire any legal right to consent to medical treatment on their behalf, does not acquire any inheritance rights, or any legal liabilities. He or she is merely someone who is notified about the emergency and who may be asked for guidance about the patient's wishes if they are unable to express them.   [AD]

NGO *See* NON-GOVERNMENTAL ORGANIZATION.

NIRC *See* NATIONAL INDUSTRIAL RELATIONS COURT.

no case to answer In criminal proceedings, a submission that can be made by the defence after the closure of the case for the prosecution and before the defence has started to call its WITNESSES. If the submission of no case to answer is successful, the case will be withdrawn from the JURY and an acquittal directed. It will only succeed if the court accepts that there is no EVIDENCE on which to convict the accused, or that, if left to a properly directed jury, the prosecution evidence taken at its highest is insufficient to ground a conviction. The relevant principles to be applied in considering a no case submission were clarified by the Court of Appeal in *R* v. *Galbraith* [1981] 1 WLR 1039 at 1042.

In civil proceedings, the defendant similarly can make a submission that the claimant has no real prospect of success. If the submission is successful, the judge must give judgment to the defendant.

[ALTC & JW]

nolle prosequi (Lat. to be unwilling to pursue) A procedure to terminate proceedings on INDICTMENT against an accused. Whilst all prosecutors have powers to discontinue or offer no evidence in a case, only the ATTORNEY GENERAL may enter a *nolle* by submitting a statement to the court that proceedings should be discontinued. The Attorney General's DISCRETION is wide, and no reasons need to be given. Once entered, a *nolle prosequi* does not operate as a discharge or acquittal and the defendant remains liable to be re-indicted. It is most commonly used in situations where it is deemed not to be in the public interest to proceed, for example

where the defendant is experiencing serious health problems.   [JW]

nominal damages Awarded in cases where, even though the defendant has committed a TORT or BREACH OF CONTRACT, the claimant, while having had his or her rights infringed, has suffered no compensatable loss.   [HJ]

nominated care judges *See* DESIGNATED FAMILY JUDGE.

non-cohabitation order *See* JUDICIAL SEPARATION ORDER.

non-discrimination The prohibition on DISCRIMINATION is a cross-cutting theme in COMMUNITY LAW, applying to persons, goods, services and the RIGHT OF ESTABLISHMENT. It is more developed as a concept in EUROPEAN COMMUNITY (EC) social policy, where it includes the prohibition on discrimination in the workplace, and principles of access to social security. There is extensively developed case law on non-discrimination on the basis of sex or sexual orientation.   [MON]

See also FREE MOVEMENT OF GOODS; FREE MOVEMENT OF PERSONS; MIGRANT WORKER.

non-discrimination notice If during a FORMAL INVESTIGATION the EQUALITY AND HUMAN RIGHTS COMMISSION concludes that the person or organization subject to the investigation is acting contrary to the relevant anti-discrimination statute, it may issue a non-discrimination notice, which (a) forbids that organization from committing any more discriminatory acts; (b) makes it inform the Commission of changes it proposes to make to prevent further discriminatory behaviour; and (c) makes it inform the party allegedly discriminated against of such changes. Before issuing such a notice the Commission must inform the organization or person of its conclusions and offer them the opportunity to make representations. Appeals against the issuance of such a notice are to the EMPLOYMENT APPEAL TRIBUNAL.

[MJ]

non est factum (from Lat. *non est factum suum*: this is not my deed) In CONTRACT law, the plea of *non est factum* may provide a defence to a party against whom a claim is brought in reliance on a signed written agreement. A person will generally be bound by the terms of any document they have signed and cannot plead that they did not read or understand the document. However, the plea of *non est factum* may be available where the party signing is able to show they were unaware of the true meaning of the document when signing and so could not be taken to have given consent. *Saunders* v. *Anglia Building Society* [1971] AC 1004 established that it will be rare for such a plea to succeed since the party signing needs to establish that they were not careless but that the document actually signed as a result of such a mistake was very different to what was intended.

[JPL]

non-governmental organization (NGO) The name typically afforded in international legal parlance to certain private entities, which are legal persons and registered under the law of a particular country. NGOs are established to pursue policies, and often to take actions, at the national and international level to advance certain causes such as HUMAN RIGHTS (e.g. Amnesty International and Human Rights Watch), the environment (e.g. Greenpeace) and others. NGOs have very limited INTERNATIONAL LEGAL PERSONALITY, which in most cases is conferred upon them on a case-by-case basis. Thus, NGOs may attain observer status at those inter-governmental organizations whose statute permits such status and in some cases it is permitted for the prosecutor or judges of international tribunals to seek evidence from them, such as in the Statute of the INTERNATIONAL CRIMINAL COURT. In the practice of the ad hoc tribunals for Yugoslavia and Rwanda, NGOs were allowed to submit *amici* briefs in order to clarify the law in certain areas. Multinational corporations are not usually referred to as NGOs and may possess a larger degree of international legal personality on account of bilateral investment treaties and contracts signed with state entities. The International Committee of the Red Cross is an NGO, whose competence in the international legal field, however, is more akin to that of an international organization. [IB]

See also INTERNATIONAL CRIMINAL TRIBUNAL FOR RWANDA; INTERNATIONAL CRIMINAL TRIBUNAL FOR THE FORMER YUGOSLAVIA.

non-jury list A list in the QUEEN'S BENCH DIVISION of cases to be tried by a judge sitting alone or with COURT APPOINTED ASSESSORS. [SN]

non-molestation order Under the Family Law Act 1996, s. 42, parties can obtain non-MOLESTATION orders against a person associated with them, who has acted violently against them, or who has pestered, harassed, intimidated or threatened them. The Act defines 'associated person' to include spouses, civil partners, cohabitants, people who were formerly in those relationships with each other, and others who have had an intimate personal relationship with each other but who have not cohabited. The order prohibits the respondent from molesting another person or a relevant CHILD. It can refer to molestation in general or to specific acts and it may last for a specified period or until further order of the court. In urgent circumstances, the order may be made without notice to the respondent, but the court will consider, among other things, the risk of significant harm to the applicant or a relevant child if the order is not made immediately. Breach of a non-molestation order is a criminal offence.

[AD]

See also RESTRAINING ORDER.

non-resident parent When the legal parents of a CHILD do not reside together, either because of SEPARATION, DIVORCE, DISSOLUTION of CIVIL PARTNERSHIP or because they have never lived together, the parent with whom the child lives is the resident parent and the other parent is the non-resident parent. Additionally, the term has statutory meaning under the Child Support Act 1991. For the purposes of that legislation: 'the parent of any child is a "non-resident parent", in relation to him, if (a) that parent is not living in the same household with the child and (b) the child has his home with a person who is, in relation to him, a person with care' (s. 3(2)). Non-resident parents are liable for child support for a qualifying child whether or not they have PARENTAL RESPONSIBILITY for that child. [AD]

non-therapeutic research All new medicines must be licensed. In order to obtain a licence there are a number of clinical trial stages that must be successfully completed, three of which will be conducted on humans. Non-therapeutic research conducted on healthy volunteers takes place at Phase I. There is no therapeutic (i.e. healing) benefit to the participants, as researchers are usually seeking to measure toxicity and absorption. Phases II and III will normally involve THERAPEUTIC RESEARCH. [HJ]

See also DECLARATION OF HELSINKI; LICENSING OF MEDICINES.

non-user Failure to use or exercise a right over land, mainly in relation to EASEMENTS, PROFITS A PRENDRE and RIGHTS OF COMMON. Where non-use is coupled with an intention to abandon a right, that right may be extinguished. However, mere non-use of a right is not sufficient for a person to lose their entitlement to that right, even if non-use has occurred for an extremely long period (see *Benn* v. *Hardinge* (1992) 66 P&CR 246, where a RIGHT OF WAY had not been used for 175 years). [DR]

norm A principle of right action which is binding upon, or treated as binding, by, the members of a group or society at large and which serves to guide, control or regulate behaviour. Norms may be permissive, enabling one to act, as well as prescriptive, i.e. requiring one to act or not act. Laws properly so-called are sometimes referred to as **legal norms** to distinguish them from other 'social' norms and values. [JW]

normative jurisprudence The theoretical investigation of law on the basis of any approach which seeks to describe it *as it ought to be* on the basis of some external measure, for example NATURAL LAW theories which insist upon the necessary connection between law and morality. Normative jurisprudence may be contrasted with ANALYTICAL JURISPRUDENCE. [JP]

Northern Ireland Assembly Part of the UK's devolved system of government. It is constituted by a single-chamber, democratically elected body comprising 108 members, known as Members of the Legislative Assembly (MLAs).

The obligation to create a devolved Northern Ireland Assembly arose out of the Belfast Agreement (also known as the 'Good Friday' Agreement) of 10 April 1998, which established an accord intended to bring to an end over 30 years of conflict within Northern Ireland. The Agreement was endorsed by referendum in May 1998 and given legal effect by the Northern Ireland Act 1998, which constructed a framework of interrelated bodies, including the Northern Ireland Assembly. Under the Act the Assembly has legislative and executive authority for **transferred matters**. These are only negatively defined in that they constitute all matters which are not **excepted** or **reserved** to the Westminster Parliament. Excepted matters remain the indefinite responsibility of the UK Parliament, while reserved matters are those that will continue to be dealt with by Westminster unless and until the Secretary of State for Northern Ireland has determined that they will be devolved to the Assembly. Excepted and reserved matters are defined in the Schedules to the Northern Ireland Act.

The Assembly's legislative acts are called **Acts of the Northern Ireland Assembly**. They must receive the ROYAL ASSENT, which means that they must first be approved by the Secretary of State for Northern Ireland. They are also subject to JUDICIAL REVIEW and may be struck down if they exceed the powers of the Assembly, or violate EC law or the EUROPEAN CONVENTION ON HUMAN RIGHTS, or if they are found to discriminate against individuals on grounds of political opinion or religious belief.

The Assembly also appoints Members to the **Northern Ireland Executive** as Ministers. The structure of the Executive is determined under a power-sharing arrangement. First and Deputy First Ministers are appointed as leaders of the largest and second largest Assembly 'bloc' (based on 'Unionist', 'Nationalist' and 'Other' alliances in the Assembly). All parties with a significant number of seats are entitled to at least one Minister, and ministerial portfolios are divided among the parties in proportion to their strength in the Assembly. Attempts to maintain the Assembly's operation on a permanent basis have been frustrated by disagreements between the main political parties, the Democratic Unionist Party (DUP), the Ulster Unionist Party (UUP) and Sinn Fein. As a consequence, the operation of the Assembly has been suspended four times between February 2000 and May 2007, including a lengthy period of suspension from 2003 to 2007. [JW]

See also DEVOLUTION.

Northern Ireland Ombudsman *See* LOCAL GOVERNMENT OMBUDSMEN.

noscitur a sociis (Lat. known by their associates) A secondary principle of construction which makes the logical and rather obvious point that words must be understood with reference to the surrounding words in the statute or document being interpreted. [JW]

See also EIUSDEM GENERIS.

not guilty plea A denial of guilt by the accused to the charge brought by the prosecution. [SN]

not proven The third verdict possible in a Scottish criminal trial in addition to 'guilty' and 'not guilty', which arises when the court is not convinced that the accused is innocent but the required standard of proof (beyond reasonable doubt) has not been met. While a person whose case is found not proven is free from any future prosecution for the same offence, there are periodic calls for the abolition of the verdict because of the stigma attaching to a person who has been discharged but not found not guilty of the offence charged. [JP]

notice of intended prosecution A formal notice issued under the Road Traffic Offenders Act 1988 which is sent to the registered keeper of a vehicle warning that they may be prosecuted for a road traffic offence. This notice, which is frequently used in speeding cases, is usually sent with a request to name the driver of the vehicle. Failure to supply the information without reasonable excuse can result in a penalty similar to the one that would have been imposed for the original offence. [SN]

notice of transfer The procedure used in cases of serious and complex fraud whereby the prosecution can have the case sent direct to the CROWN COURT without the need to have the accused committed for trial. [SN]

See also COMMITTAL PROCEEDINGS.

notice to treat In COMPULSORY PURCHASE, a notice given by the acquiring authority (usually a public authority) when it wishes to purchase land that is subject to a compulsory purchase order. A notice to treat must be served on 'all the persons interested in, or having power to sell and convey or release, the land, so far as known to the acquiring authority after making diligent inquiry' (Compulsory Purchase Act 1965 (CPA 1965), s. 5(1)). Furthermore, the notice must: (a) give particulars of the land to which the notice relates; (b) demand particulars of the recipient's estate and interest, and of the claim made by him in respect of the land; and (c) state that the acquiring authority is willing to treat for the purchase of the land and for compensation payable for the damage which may be sustained by reason of the execution of the works (CPA 1965, s. 5(2)).

After a notice to treat has been served, it is valid for three years and is similar to a draft CONTRACT FOR SALE between the parties, with only the compensation to be agreed. Once compensation is agreed, it has the full effect of a contract for sale, though if the sum is disputed the issue may be referred to the Lands Tribunal. [DR]

notifiable offence A criminal offence that is serious enough to be recorded by the police and entered into UK national crime statistics, known collectively as 'recorded crime': see http://www.homeoffice.gov.uk/rds/recordedcrime1.html. Most either way and INDICTABLE OFFENCES are notifiable. [SN]

nova causa interveniens *See* NOVUS ACTUS INTERVENIENS.

novation An agreement between at least three persons, involving the release of an existing CONTRACT between two of the parties and the substitution of a new contract with a third party. It can be used for restructuring debts or partnerships. For example, A owes B £1,000; under the terms of the novation agreement B agrees to release A from the obligation and to substitute C as the debtor of this sum. As novation involves a new agreement, it is distinguishable from the ASSIGNMENT of a contractual benefit.   [JPL]

novus actus interveniens (Lat. a new intervening act) A general defence in TORT whereby the defendant is able to rely on the subsequent act of a third party that, intervening between the original act and the damage, is the direct cause of that damage, that is, it breaks the causal connection between the defendant's wrongful act and the harm suffered by the claimant. Also referred to as a *nova causa interveniens* – a new intervening cause.   [HJ]

 See also CAUSATION.

nuclear testing The INTERNATIONAL COURT OF JUSTICE has never pronounced nuclear testing *per se* an unlawful activity. In the absence of a TREATY or customary rule prohibiting nuclear testing, one has to examine general INTERNATIONAL LAW to determine to what extent such tests constitute lawful acts. Nuclear testing cannot take place on the high seas because it is designated as *RES COMMUNIS* and reserved only for peaceful purposes. Equally, the sea-bed and subsoil thereof is out of bounds, being covered by the special regime of COMMON HERITAGE OF MANKIND. It is possible, therefore, for nuclear testing to take place on the land or maritime territory of the testing STATE, in accordance with the following limitations: (a) observance of environmental rules relating to trans-boundary pollution; (b) obser-

vance of the PRECAUTIONARY PRINCIPLE; (c) any harm, whether environmental, health-related or other, caused against another state would render the testing state liable to make REPARATION.   [IB]

nuisance *See* PRIVATE NUISANCE; PUBLIC NUISANCE; STATUTORY NUISANCE.

nuisance neighbours A term used to refer to inhabitants of a property whose anti-social behaviour has an adverse impact on the quality of life of the inhabitants of other properties in the locality. Among the possible legal responses to the behaviour of nuisance neighbours is the application, by the police, local authority or a social landlord, for ANTI-SOCIAL BEHAVIOUR ORDERS to regulate the future conduct of those in question.   [BF]

nulla poena sine lege (Lat. no punishment without law) The phrase articulates an aspect of the constitutional principle of the RULE OF LAW, that nobody shall be subjected to any punishment unless they have breached a specific rule of criminal law. The principle requires that the law be sufficiently certain, and that it be applied prospectively but not retrospectively, in order to determine whether a breach has occurred, so that citizens can regulate their own conduct according to what the law is at the time of their actions. As well as being a part of the common law, the principle finds expression in, for example, Article 7 of the EUROPEAN CONVENTION ON HUMAN RIGHTS.   [BF]

nullity of marriage *See* ANNULMENT; VOID MARRIAGE; VOIDABLE MARRIAGE.

nuncupative will A WILL declared orally, rather than in writing, which will be valid only if the TESTATOR is able to make a PRIVILEGED WILL.   [CM]

O

oath An undertaking given by a WITNESS to tell the truth in court. An oath may be taken by holding a holy book in an uplifted hand and saying: 'I swear by Almighty God that the evidence which I shall give shall be the truth, the whole truth, and nothing but the truth.' [ALTC]

obiter dictum (Lat. a saying by the way) Comments made in passing by a judge on a legal point, but not forming part of the *RATIO DECIDENDI* of the case. *Obiter* comments cannot be binding on later courts, but may constitute PERSUASIVE AUTHORITY. [JW]

   See also STARE DECISIS.

objects clause *See* MEMORANDUM OF ASSOCIATION.

objects of a power Those persons in whose favour a POWER OF APPOINTMENT might be exercised. Until the power is exercised in their favour the objects of a power have no rights in the property to which the power relates and cannot compel the donee of the power to exercise it as it is a purely permissive right. However, the objects of a power do have *LOCUS STANDI* to apply to court if an alleged fraud on the power has occurred, while objects of a fiduciary power do, by dint of the fiduciary duty owed to them, have additional rights, including the right to be fairly considered alongside their fellow objects. [PK]

obscene publications Under the Obscene Publications Act 1959, s. 2, it is an offence for a person, whether or not for gain, to publish an obscene article or to have an obscene article for publication for gain (to himself or another). Under s. 1 of the 1959 Act, an article is anything containing or embodying matter to be read, looked at, listened to, etc., and an article is obscene if its effect is such as to tend to deprave and corrupt persons who are likely, having regard to all relevant circumstances, to read, see or hear the matter contained or embodied in it. [BF]

obscene telephone calls The making of obscene telephone calls is covered by the law relating to malicious communications, and also by the offence of improper use of a public electronic communications network, under the Communications Act 2003, s. 127. Under this provision, a person commits an offence if he or she sends or causes to be sent by means of a public electronic communications network a message that is grossly offensive or of an indecent, obscene or menacing character. It is not necessary for the purposes of s. 127 that the message actually be received by anybody.

   Making multiple obscene telephone calls to multiple recipients may also constitute a PUBLIC NUISANCE at COMMON LAW. [BF]

obstructing a police officer Under the Police Act 1996, s. 89, it is an offence to resist or to wilfully obstruct a constable in the execution of his duty, or a person assisting a constable in the execution of his duty. Under the same section, it is also an offence to ASSAULT a constable in the execution of his duty, or a person assisting a constable in the execution of his duty.   [BF]

occupation (of land) LAND is occupied by someone if that person has a physical presence upon the land and physical control over it. Actual occupation of land, which may have arisen informally, is protected from the impact of land registration because it counts as an OVERRIDING INTEREST in land. This means that a person's occupation will bind the purchaser of the land unless he or she makes inquiries, and the rights are not disclosed, or the occupation is not reasonably discoverable upon inspection.   [HC & DR]
See also OCCUPIER.

occupation order An order under the Family Law Act 1996 which may declare or regulate the right to occupy the FAMILY HOME. Occupation orders are used to assist victims of DOMESTIC VIOLENCE to re-enter their home if they have fled violence or to exclude an abuser from the home, or from part of the home, if the victim wishes to remain in it. An occupation order is intended to be a temporary rather than a permanent order; it is considered by the courts to be a serious matter, and therefore courts will require cogent evidence that it is necessary. It may be granted in conjunction with a NON-MOLESTATION ORDER in order to offer further protection. A power of arrest may also be attached to the order. The criteria for granting orders vary depending on whether the applicant is otherwise entitled to occupy the home, whether by virtue of home rights or some form of legal or beneficial ownership. [AD]

occupier A person who is in occupation of LAND. The occupier may be there lawfully (for instance as a TENANT or an OWNER-OCCU-PIER) or unlawfully as a trespasser. In English law, occupiers may gain some very limited rights simply by their presence on the land if a purchaser fails to inspect the land or make reasonable inquiries.   [HC & DR]
See also RESIDENTIAL OCCUPIER.

offence A term denoting behaviour proscribed by the criminal law.   [BF]

offence triable either way An offence which can be tried either in the magistrates' court or in the CROWN COURT.   [SN]
See also INDICTABLE OFFENCE; SUMMARY OFFENCE.

offence triable only on indictment An offence which can only be tried in the CROWN COURT.   [SN]
See also OFFENCE TRIABLE EITHER WAY; INDICTABLE OFFENCE; INDICTMENT.

offence triable summarily An offence which can only be tried in a magistrates' court.   [SN]
See also OFFENCE TRIABLE EITHER WAY; SUMMARY OFFENCE.

offences against the person An umbrella term with various possible meanings. It can be taken to refer to unlawful homicides and non-fatal offences against the person including SEXUAL OFFENCES. It might also be used to refer to assaults and to the principal non-fatal, non-sexual offences under the Offences against the Person Act 1861. The term is often used by way of contradistinction with offences against property.   [BF]

offences against the state An umbrella term for offences committed against institutions of the STATE. The term can refer, for example, to offences relating to TREASON, SEDITION, terrorism and OFFICIAL SECRETS. [BF]

offending behaviour programme A programme of work undertaken by an offender as part of a COMMUNITY PENALTY, which is intended to address the reasons or behaviour underlying a person's offending. Examples include: substance-related offending; aggression replacement therapy training; sex offender treatment; and integrated domestic abuse programmes. [SN]

offensive weapon Under the Prevention of Crime Act 1953, s. 1, it is an offence for a person, without lawful authority or reasonable excuse, to have with him in any public place any offensive weapon. It is for the person to prove that he or she had lawful authority or reasonable excuse. An offensive weapon is any article made or adapted for use for causing injury to the person, or intended by the person having it with them for such use. [BF]

See also PROHIBITED WEAPON.

offer A statement of willingness to CONTRACT on the terms proposed without further negotiation and with the intention that the offer will form a binding contract if it is accepted. An offer must therefore be (a) clear and complete; (b) certain as to its terms; and (c) communicated. The person making the offer is known as the **offeror** and the person or persons to whom the offer is made is known as the **offeree**. An offer must be distinguished from all prior statements made in the course of negotiations towards a contract, known as INVITATIONS TO TREAT, since only an offer is capable of immediate translation into a contract by the fact of ACCEPTANCE. [JPL]

See also UNCERTAINTY OF CONTRACT TERMS.

offer of amends *See* DEFAMATION.

office copy *See* OFFICIAL COPIES.

Office for Judicial Complaints *See* JUDICIAL ACCOUNTABILITY; JUDICIAL APPOINTMENTS AND CONDUCT OMBUDSMAN.

official copies A copy of an official document which is sealed by the office that issues it. In REGISTERED LAND, official copies of the REGISTER OF TITLE relating to a particular property are admissible in evidence to the same extent as the original. [DR]

Official Custodian for Charities A post created by the Charities Act 1960 to provide charities with a means of holding land that avoids many practical problems that might otherwise arise. The Official Custodian, as the post holder is normally known, is today appointed by the CHARITY COMMISSION under Charities Act 1993, s. 2(2), and is normally a member of the Commission's staff. The role is particularly useful to unincorporated charities as the vesting of the legal TITLE to

land in the Official Custodian avoids the need to change the details of ownership whenever there is a change of TRUSTEE. Incorporated charities such as charitable companies have no need to use this device as the land can be vested in the name of the CHARITY itself rather than its individual trustees. [PK]

Official Journal (OJ) The official publication of the EUROPEAN COMMUNITY (EC) and EUROPEAN UNION (EU). According to the Europa website, the Official Journal is 'published daily in more than 21 languages'. It is published in three series, with the **L series** focusing on EU legislation, the **C series** on EU information and notices, and the **S series** being a supplement to the OJ. An electronic-only version of the C series is known as OJ C E. See http://publications.europa. eu/official/index_en.htm. [MON]

official secrets Information that is protected because it constitutes sensitive security, intelligence or defence information, or certain information about international relations or law enforcement, or secrets belonging to foreign governments or international organizations. Civil servants, members of government, members of the armed forces, police and government contractors may all be under various duties not to disclose information under the Official Secrets Acts 1911–1989 and the Acts create various offences associated with the unauthorized disclosure of such information. They also create a number of offences concerning spying or espionage activities. [MS]

Ogden Tables Actuarial tables produced by the government's Actuary Department for calculating future pecuniary loss in personal injury cases. The tables are ADMISSIBLE as EVIDENCE for this purpose in accordance with the Civil Evidence Act 1995, s. 10. [HJ]

See also DAMAGES.

Old Bailey *See* CENTRAL CRIMINAL COURT.

Olivecrona, Karl (1897–1980) *See* SCANDINAVIAN REALISM.

ombudsman (Old Sw. *umbuðsmann*, representative) An independent official, normally appointed by the state to oversee the investigation of complaints by citizens of misconduct or maladministration by state, regulatory and sometimes industry bodies. Ombudsmen generally have powers to investigate and report on cases of maladministration; they may have powers to require the body being investigated to take steps to rectify the complaint, and in some cases they may have powers to order payment of compensation. Examples of ombudsmen schemes in the UK include the various LOCAL GOVERNMENT OMBUDSMEN, the Legal Services Ombudsman (who oversees complaints handling by the legal professional bodies) and the Financial Ombudsman Service, which deals with complaints between consumers and businesses providing financial services.   [JW]

See also PARLIAMENTARY AND HEALTH SERVICE OMBUDSMAN.

omission In general terms, criminal liability does not come about on the basis of an omission or failure to act. The criminal law usually requires a person to commit a positive act before liability can arise.

However, there are occasions where an omission can constitute the *ACTUS REUS* of an offence. Thus a statute may prescribe liability on the basis of a failure to perform a particular task: for example, under the Road Traffic Act 1988, s. 170, it is an offence for a driver to fail to stop if involved in an accident.

There are also other situations in which the criminal law imposes a duty to act and a failure to discharge such a duty may contribute to the formation of the *actus reus* of an offence. If someone is in a particular form of special relationship with a potential victim of harm they must take appropriate steps to try to prevent the potential victim from coming to that harm; for example, if a person saw their child drowning in a shallow pool of water, he or she would be under a duty to take steps to try to assist the child (see *R* v. *Gibbins and Proctor* (1918) 13 Cr App R 134). A duty to act may also arise under a contract, where the nature of the contract is to create obligations towards persons other than parties

to the contract; for example, if a person is employed as a swimming pool lifeguard, and someone appears to be drowning in the pool, the lifeguard would be under a duty to take steps to try to assist that person (see *R* v. *Pittwood* (1902) 19 TLR 37). A duty to act may also arise where a person voluntarily assumes a moral obligation to assist another party; for example, if a member of the public notices a person in difficulty in the sea, and begins to swim out to assist them, he or she then comes under a legal duty to take steps to try to assist that person (see *Gibbins and Proctor*, above).   [BF]

one right answer thesis The proposition made by RONALD DWORKIN that there is one right answer to any legal question, including a HARD CASE. He is able to make this claim as a result of his contention that the legal system is composed of more than just RULES (as he understands H. L. A. HART to say) and in particular also encompasses principles to form a 'seamless web'. Insofar as a judge is constrained to look to principles when confronted with a hard case (and is not, therefore, able to look where he or she pleases) then the answer is to be found within the legal system. Furthermore, as the judge must consider the coherence and fit of his or her answer with the legal system, they will be guided towards the right answer to the question before them.
[JP]

onerous or unusual clause A contract term imposing a burden that is not usually found in a contract of that kind, or which imposes a significantly higher burden than normal on the other contracting party; for example in terms of fees or penalties charged under the contract. Where a contractual provision is onerous or unusual, it can be incorporated as a term only if fairly and reasonably drawn to the other party's attention (see *Interfoto Picture Library Ltd* v. *Stiletto Visual Programmes Ltd* [1989] QB 433). It is the particular clause that must be onerous or unusual rather than the type of clause.   [JPL]

See also INCORPORATION OF TERMS; UNFAIR CONTRACT TERMS.

onus of proof *See* BURDEN OF PROOF.

open contract In CONVEYANCING, a contract for the sale of land which does not expressly state all of the necessary terms of the contract is said to be an open contract. Rules of open contract have been developed by the courts over time, which, if not otherwise agreed by the parties to a contract, are presumed to apply. For example, if the CONTRACT FOR SALE does not include a term stipulating the quality of TITLE to be transferred, open contract rules presume an agreement by the seller to give good, marketable title.

In an ordinary conveyancing transaction, most terms of the contract are expressly provided for. This means that the open contract rules, which are generally quite strict on the seller, have only residual importance. Nevertheless, certain rules remain important, such as the obligation on the seller of full and frank disclosure in the contract of all latent ENCUMBRANCES and known defects in title.

[DR]

open procedure One of three alternative procedures set out in the EC Public Procurement Directives governing the inviting and awarding of CONTRACTS for the supply of goods and services in the public sector and utilities contracts. If the value of the contract is over a specified minimum, the public procurement process is activated and the contract is required to be advertised in the OFFICIAL JOURNAL of the EU, inviting all suppliers in the EU who are able to comply with the TENDER specification to put in tenders or bids. The procedure sets out a process for determining the award of the contract and there is a right to claim DAMAGES in the event that the correct procedure is not followed. [JPL]

See also PUBLIC PROCUREMENT.

open space For planning purposes, local authorities are expected to audit and assess the local need for and provision of open space. The audit is designed to support a planning strategy which enables the local authority to make effective planning decisions balancing the needs of competing groups. Government Planning Policy Guidance (PPG17, para. 10) explains that 'Existing open space, sports and recreational buildings and land should not be built on unless an assessment has been undertaken which has clearly shown the open space or the buildings and land to be surplus to requirements. For open space, "surplus to requirements" should include consideration of all the functions that open space can perform.' [HC & DR]

opening speech 1. In a criminal trial, a speech made by prosecution counsel. It provides an overview of the case against the defendant and a summary of the prosecution evidence. Defence counsel may also make an opening speech outlining the defence case and criticizing the evidence produced by the prosecution, in addition to providing evidence on behalf of the accused.

2. In a civil trial, the speech made by counsel for the claimant at the commencement of the hearing. [SN]

operative mistake A MISTAKE which is recognized by law as having an effect on the CONTRACT, i.e. rendering it void, because it is regarded as sufficiently fundamental. [JPL]

See also COMMON MISTAKE; IDENTITY, MISTAKE OF; MUTUAL MISTAKE; UNILATERAL MISTAKE.

operative words Words contained in a DEED which have the effect of transferring the interest that is the subject matter of the deed. In a conveyance of UNREGISTERED LAND, the operative words normally used are that the seller 'hereby conveys' the property to the buyer. In REGISTERED LAND, the Land Registry's standard forms use the sentence 'the transferor transfers the property to the transferee'. [DR]

opinio juris sive necessitatis (Lat. an opinion of law or necessity) The term is usually abbreviated to *opinio juris* and describes the subjective element comprising CUSTOMARY INTERNATIONAL LAW. The existence of customary law is manifested where a STATE practice is accompanied by the belief on the part of the state concerned that such practice conforms to a legal, rather than a moral, obligation. Obviously, it is not always easy to detect this element of custom and so courts and tribunals that investigate the existence of a customary rule tend to infer *opinio juris* from evidence of a consistent practice over a period of time. There is also a trend in INTERNATIONAL LAW claiming that, since in some fields it is difficult, if not impossible, for certain states to exhibit actual practice (for example, with regard to outer space for those countries that do not possess the necessary technology, or with regard to the law of the sea for land-locked states), customary law should require only *opinio juris*. [IB]

oppression Defined in the Police and Criminal Evidence Act 1984 (PACE), s. 76 (8), as including 'TORTURE, inhuman or degrading treatment, and the use or threat of violence (whether or not amounting to torture).' A CONFESSION obtained by oppression of the person making it is not ADMISSIBLE in evidence against him or her: see PACE, s. 76(2)(a). [ALTC]

option A right to choose to purchase specified property within a stated period of time, which is granted by agreement. In order to be legally binding, the option PROMISE must be supported by CONSIDERATION, unless contained in a DEED. Where an option is stated to be exercisable by notice in writing, it is not validly exercised until the written notice is actually communicated (see *Holwell Securities Ltd* v. *Hughes* [1974] 1 WLR 155). [JPL]

option to purchase In CONVEYANCING, a contract under which the prospective buyer can serve notice on the prospective seller, requiring him or her to sell the land to the buyer.

An option to purchase is a contract for the sale of land. Therefore, under the Law of Property (Miscellaneous Provisions) Act 1989, s. 2, it must be in writing, incorporate all the agreed terms and be signed by both parties. Furthermore, the option must have a time limit of less than 21 years and has effect as an EQUITABLE INTEREST only. In order for the option to be binding on third parties it must be registered, either as a notice in the case of REGISTERED LAND, or as a Class C (iv)

LAND CHARGE in the case of UNREGISTERED LAND. [DR]

See also ESTATE CONTRACT; PRE-EMPTION.

optional clause Under Article 36(2) of the Statute of the INTERNATIONAL COURT OF JUSTICE, a STATE may unilaterally declare (an 'optional clause declaration') that it recognizes the jurisdiction of the Court as compulsory in relation to any other state accepting the same obligation. Such declarations are of a contractual nature, and therefore binding upon the parties that make them. The consent of a state to submit a case to the ICJ may be inferred from its conduct (*Nicaragua* v. *United States*, Jurisdiction Phase [1984] ICJ Reports 392, 27 June 1986). Since declarations under the optional clause are contractual in nature, states may append reservations to them in order to exclude particular types of disputes or specific states. [IB]

See also RESERVATION.

oral agreement An agreement made by word of mouth rather than in writing, e.g. purchasing a newspaper at the newsagent's shop. Unless a CONTRACT is required to be in writing, or evidenced in writing, an oral agreement is normally sufficient to form the basis of a valid contract. [JPL]

oral evidence Evidence given orally in court; also referred to as **testimony**. Oral evidence may be distinguished from REAL EVIDENCE. [ALTC]

Order in Council A type of legislation that may take one of two different forms. **1**. UK primary legislation (i.e. equivalent to an Act of Parliament) made under the powers of the ROYAL PREROGATIVE. This type of Order in Council is now relatively unusual, but is still used to make certain political appointments and appointments in the CHURCH OF ENGLAND, in the governance of British Overseas Territories, and in exercising other prerogative powers with regard to international relations. These Prerogative Orders in Council should not be confused with the PREROGATIVE ORDERS issued by the courts.

2. A form of UK DELEGATED LEGISLATION governed by the Statutory Instruments Act

1946, but subject to a greater level of formality than ordinary statutory instruments. The Orders are made under the authority of a parent statute (for example under EMERGENCY POWERS legislation). The use of Orders in Council has increased by virtue of the fact that they are now sometimes used to implement European Directives, and play an important part in the devolution of legislative authority to Scotland, Wales and Northern Ireland (for example, Northern Ireland Orders in Council are UK Statutory Instruments, but have the status of primary legislation within Northern Ireland under the Northern Ireland Acts 1974–2000).

See also LEGISLATIVE COMPETENCE ORDER. [JW]

order of committal An order sending a person to prison for CONTEMPT OF COURT. [SN]

original evidence Evidence that is not HEARSAY. [ALTC]

originality COPYRIGHT law will protect literary, dramatic, musical and artistic works if such works are original. There is no definition of the term 'originality' in the Copyright, Designs and Patents Act 1988, s. 1(1) (a), save in respect of DATABASES (s. 3A (2)). The term 'original' does not mean that the work must be the expression of original or inventive thought; instead, originality is proved if the following elements are present in the work: (a) the work originates from the author; (b) it is not copied from another work; (c) it is not insubstantial or commonplace; and (d) labour, skill and capital or judgement have been expended in creating the work.

The criterion of originality relates to the principle that ideas are not protected, but the expression of an idea is. The original elements in the plot of a play or a novel can constitute a substantial part of a work so that copyright may be infringed by a work that does not reproduce a single sentence of the original, but nevertheless borrows heavily from the prior work. However, this is only possible in cases where the expression of the idea in the claimant's work is sufficiently clear (see *Baigent and*

Leigh v. *The Random House Group Ltd* (*Da Vinci case*) [2007] EWCA Civ 247). [US]

ostensible authority *See* AGENCY.

ouster In land law, the dispossession of a person from his property, resulting in a requirement to pay compensation, possibly by payment of rent. Ouster can refer to FREEHOLD or LEASEHOLD property, though under a lease the term 'eviction' is more commonly used. Ouster is primarily of modern relevance in matrimonial home disputes where one person is forced to leave their home. [DR]

outer space The precise upward limit of airspace and the beginning of outer space are not defined in INTERNATIONAL LAW, with the result that several theories are claimed in relation to this matter. The most acceptable and sensible one is that which takes into account the lowest limit that permits free orbit of spacecraft, which stands at 100 miles from the surface of the sea. Outer space encompasses, therefore, any space above 100 miles, as well as all celestial bodies and the Moon. These are treated by CUSTOMARY INTERNATIONAL LAW (UN General Assembly Resolution of 1963 on Outer Space), as well as the 1967 Treaty on Principles Governing the Activities of States in the Exploration and Use of Outer Space, as *RES COMMUNIS* and part of the COMMON HERITAGE OF MANKIND. They are to be used for peaceful and scientific purposes and no STATE may claim SOVEREIGNTY over them. States are responsible for any harm caused as a result of their activities in outer space. [IB]

outsourcing When work previously done in-house is transferred to another organization. Outsourcing is commonly used as a money-saving strategy by COMPANIES. Common services outsourced include answering telephones and office cleaning. Employment protection on the TRANSFER OF UNDERTAKINGS (TUPE) may apply to outsourcing, transferring the work between entities, and bringing work back in-house. [MJ]

overreaching In land law, the process by

which a person purchases land that is the subject of a TRUST, free of the EQUITABLE INTERESTS of the beneficiaries under that trust, provided statutory conditions are met, particularly the Law of Property Act 1925, ss. 2 and 27. The most important rights which can be overreached are equitable rights to occupy a property under a trust. The effect of overreaching is that the beneficiaries' interests in the land are removed from the land and attached to the proceeds of sale, for the trustees to either distribute the money to the beneficiaries or invest it so as to provide income for them, depending on the terms of the trust. The statutory conditions for overreaching differ depending on whether the land is sold by trustees under a trust of land, by SETTLED LAND ACT TRUSTEES, by a MORTGAGE lender exercising a POWER OF SALE, by personal representatives or by a court order.

Where land is sold by the trustees of a trust of land, CAPITAL MONEY (normally the purchase price) must be paid to at least two trustees or a trust corporation, in order for the beneficiaries' interests to be overreached. Under a Settled Land Act SETTLEMENT, in addition to the requirement that capital money must be paid to at least two trustees or a trust corporation, the sale must also be within the powers of the TENANT FOR LIFE. Furthermore, the Settled Land Act 1925, s. 72(2), sets out a list of interests that cannot be overreached in relation to SETTLED LAND. [DR]

overriding interests In the REGISTERED LAND system, an INTEREST IN LAND that overrides a registered disposition of land. In practice, this means that when a person acquires a registered property, he takes that property subject to any overriding interests, whether or not those interests are registered. The Land Registration Act 2002 (LRA 2002) considerably reduced the number of interests that could be overriding interests, establishing a multi-tiered system comprised of: (a) interests which override first registration, contained in LRA 2002, Schedule 1, including most LEASES granted for a term of less than seven years, interests belonging to a person in actual occupation of the property (e.g. a person with a LIFE INTEREST), LEGAL EASEMENTS, PROFITS À PRENDRE and local LAND CHARGES; and (b) interests which override a registered disposition (i.e. dealings subsequent to first registration), contained in LRA 2002, Schedule 3, including the same interests as above but with modifications relating to leases, interests of persons in actual occupation, easements and profits.

Since overriding interests do not need to be registered to be binding on third parties, it is fundamentally important for a prospective buyer to carry out all necessary SEARCHES and inspections in order to discover any overriding interests affecting a property. For example, if there is an occupier with a life interest under a trust, the buyer must be satisfied that the occupier will release such rights in order for the buyer to take the property free of those rights. [DR]

overriding objective The principle contained in both Part 1 of the CIVIL PROCEDURE RULES and Part 1 of the CRIMINAL PROCEDURE RULES, that the primary objective of the Rules is to enable the court to deal justly with cases. This is defined differently in the civil rules and the criminal rules. Thus, in civil cases the objective includes ensuring that cases are dealt with efficiently and expeditiously, and that the parties are on an equal footing; in criminal cases, though efficiency is also stressed, it includes recognizing the rights of a defendant, and respecting the interests of witnesses, victims and jurors. When the courts exercise any of their powers they must consider whether this will further the overriding objective. Moreover the parties (or participants in a criminal case) are also under certain duties to support the overriding objective. [JW]

overruling The process whereby the decision of a court is subsequently annulled by a court of higher authority determining that the earlier case was wrongly decided. Where a case is overruled it is no longer of binding authority. [JW]

See also PRECEDENT.

owner occupier 1. A person who owns the FREEHOLD or a LONG LEASE of the property which is their only or main residence.

2. For the purposes of the Rent Act 1977, a person who owns the house in which he lived prior to letting it out on a regulated tenancy or a restricted contract. Under these tenancies, an owner-occupier can regain possession of the house in order to live there, if the correct notices have been given to the tenant. [DR]

ownership The right to hold, use and dispose of property subject only to another's superior rights, or other restrictions entered into by agreement with a third party or by operation of law. For example, a long leaseholder is entitled to use and sell his or her LONG LEASE and is described as an OWNER-OCCUPIER, but his rights of ownership are limited by the (superior) rights of the LANDLORD. The landlord in turn owns the FREEHOLD, but that ownership is subject to those rights he or she has sold to the long leaseholder. Ownership may be of a **corporeal** (tangible or material) thing, which may also be defined as either MOVEABLE or immoveable property, or it may be of an **incorporeal** (intangible) thing, such as a PATENT.

Ownership may be divided into legal and equitable (beneficial) interests, as in the situation where a TRUSTEE holds the legal interest in land for the benefit of another under the terms of a TRUST. Ownership must also be distinguished legally from lesser forms of OCCUPATION, possession or use of property. [HC, DR & JW]

P

P *See* PRESIDENT OF THE FAMILY DIVISION.

PACE Codes of Practice The Codes of Practice (A–H) which are issued under the authority of the Police and Criminal Evidence Act 1984 (PACE), Part VI, s. 66, and regulate police powers and procedures in criminal investigation. See http://police.homeoffice.gov.uk/operational-policing/powers-pace-codes/pace-code-intro/. [ALTC]

pacta sunt servanda (Lat. agreements must be kept) A basic principle of CIVIL LAW and of INTERNATIONAL LAW. In international law it is encapsulated in Article 26 of the 1969 Vienna Convention on the Law of Treaties which states 'every TREATY in force is binding upon the parties to it and must be performed by them in good faith'. There exists a small number of exceptions to the *pacta sunt servanda* rule which will avoid the party breaking the agreement from incurring STATE RESPONSIBILITY. These include situations where a treaty is void as a result of fraud, corruption and coercion; supervening impossibility of performance; a fundamental change of circumstances (see *REBUS SIC STANTIBUS*); or the emergence of a new *JUS COGENS* norm that is in conflict with treaty provisions. [IB]

pacta tertiis nec nocent nec prosunt A principle of CIVIL LAW which means that an agreement, or in INTERNATIONAL LAW, a TREATY, can create neither rights nor obligations for a third party without their consent. [IB]
See THIRD PARTY RULE.

parcel In land law, a plot or portion of land. [DR]
See also PARCELS CLAUSE.

parcels clause In the CONVEYANCING of UNREGISTERED LAND, the part of the deed that describes the extent and boundaries of the property to be transferred. [DR]

parent A mother or a father of a CHILD. The term is used in relation to, but not confined to, biological parents who have conceived the child without technological intervention. In *Re G (Children)* [2006] UKHL 43, the House of Lords drew a distinction between legal parents and natural parents. They are not mutually exclusive categories, since in most, but not all, cases the natural parent will also be a legal parent. As an exception, for example, the artificial insemination donor is the 'natural progenitor' of the child but is not a legal parent. Only legal parents have STANDING to bring and defend legal proceedings about a child. Natural parenthood includes genetic parenthood (where the parent provides the gametes that create the child) and also gestational parenthood (where a SURROGATE MOTHER carries and bears a child). It also includes, according to the court, social and psychological parenthood and, by extension, adoptive parenthood.

All parents who are married to each other have PARENTAL RESPONSIBILITY automatically. All mothers, whether married or not, have parental responsibility automatically. Unmarried fathers are not vested with parental responsibility automatically but they can acquire it through registering the birth, through agreement with the mother or through a court order (Children Act 1989, s. 4, as amended). [FK]

See also NATURAL CHILD; UNMARRIED PARENTS.

parental responsibility 'All the rights, duties, powers, responsibilities and authority' which a PARENT has by law in relation to his or her CHILD and that child's property (Children Act 1989, s. 3(1)). It also includes certain rights which would have been held by a GUARDIAN of the child's ESTATE (s. 3(2)). Parental responsibility encompasses physical possession, contact and protection; the authority to name the child; the authority to determine education, religion, discipline, medical treatment, travel and education; and the administration of the child's legal, contractual and proprietary affairs.

Parental responsibility can be held by a number of persons; the fact that one person (or LOCAL AUTHORITY) acquires parental responsibility does not mean that any other person with parental responsibility loses it. If parental responsibility is held by a mother or by married parents jointly, it cannot be lost except by ADOPTION or when the child reaches the age of 18. Parental responsibility cannot be transferred or abandoned, although it is possible to arrange for some or all of it to be exercised by a person or agency acting on behalf of the person with parental responsibility (s. 2 (9)). Parental responsibility can vest by law in persons other than biological parents, such as guardians, special guardians and adoptive parents. If more than one person has parental responsibility, generally speaking each can exercise it independently of the other. There are, however, certain decisions which require consultation and some, such as marriage or adoption of the child, which require the consent of all persons with parental responsibility. Where a CARE ORDER or an EMERGENCY PROTECTION ORDER is in force, parents' exercise of parental responsibility may be limited to some extent. [FK]

See also PARENTAL RESPONSIBILITY AGREEMENT; PARENTAL RESPONSIBILITY ORDER; PARENTAL RIGHTS; REGISTRATION OF BIRTH; UNMARRIED PARENTS.

parental responsibility agreement An agreement between UNMARRIED PARENTS which enables the father to have PARENTAL RESPONSIBILITY for their CHILD (Children Act 1989, s. 4 as amended). Alternatively an agreement between a parent who has parental responsibility for the child and the child's STEP-PARENT, whether through CIVIL PARTNERSHIP or MARRIAGE, that the step-parent will have parental responsibility for that child. If both of the child's parents have parental responsibility, both must agree in order for the step-parent to acquire parental responsibility (s. 4A). Parental responsibility agreements must be made in the prescribed form (see the Parental Responsibility Agreement Regulations 1991, as amended by the Parental Responsibility Agreement (Amendment) Regulations 2005). A parental responsibility agreement may only be brought to an end by order of court. [FK]

See also FATHER'S RIGHTS; PARENTAL RESPONSIBILITY ORDER; PARENTAL RIGHTS.

parental responsibility order An order of court awarding PARENTAL RESPONSIBILITY. Such an order can be made to give parental responsibility to an unmarried father (Children Act 1989, s. 4, as amended) or a STEP-PARENT (s. 4A). A person who has acquired parental responsibility by an order of court only ceases to have parental responsibility if a court so orders. Where a court makes a RESIDENCE ORDER in favour of the father of a CHILD, then it must – if the father would not otherwise have parental responsibility – make a parental responsibility order (s. 12 (1)). An order made in terms of s. 12 cannot be brought to an end while the residence order remains in force (s. 12(4)). In deciding whether to make a parental responsibility order, the court has to accord paramount importance to the welfare of the child (*Re G (A Minor)(Parental Responsibility Order)* [1994] 1 FLR 504) and it must be shown in terms of s. 1(5) that there is some advantage to the child in making the order (*Re P (Parental Responsibility)* [1998] 2 FLR 96). Courts are generally willing to make a parental responsibility order in favour of an unmarried father provided he passes what has been called the CAR test: that he has shown a degree of commitment to the child, that he has a good relationship (indicating attachment) with the child and that he has genuine and sound reasons for applying for parental responsibility (*Re P* (above); *Re H (Illegitimate Children: Father: Parental Rights)(No. 2)* [1991] 1 FLR 214; *Re S (Parental Responsibility)* [1995] 2 FLR 648).

[FK]

See also FATHER'S RIGHTS; PARENTAL RESPONSIBILITY AGREEMENT; PARENTAL RIGHTS; REGISTRATION OF BIRTH; UNMARRIED PARENTS; WELFARE PRINCIPLE.

parental rights The rights a PARENT has in relation to his or her CHILD, including the right to physical possession of the child and the right to make decisions concerning the child's upbringing, residence, education, religion and medical treatment. Parents also have the right to deal with the child's financial and property interests, and the right to engage in litigation concerning the child's interests. Whereas in past centuries fathers had very extensive rights over their children, these rights have been gradually eroded and supplanted by the WELFARE PRINCIPLE, and this in turn was accompanied by greater parity in the status of mothers and fathers. The notion of parental rights was subsumed in the concept of PARENTAL RESPONSIBILITY when the Children Act 1989 was passed. Parental rights exist, not for the benefit of the parent, but for the benefit of the child. They are justified only in so far as they enable parents to perform parental duties. Parents' rights decline as children grow older and become more capable of making independent decisions (see *Gillick v. West Norfolk and Wisbech Area Health Authority* [1986] AC 112). [FK]

See also FATHER'S RIGHTS; PARENTAL RESPONSIBILITY AGREEMENT; PARENTAL RESPONSIBILITY ORDER.

Parenting Order Parenting Orders are governed by the Crime and Disorder Act 1998 and the Anti-Social Behaviour Act 2003, and can be deployed when a child is, for example, involved in anti-social behaviour or crime. They can consist of a parenting programme, through which parents are helped to develop skills in order to meet the needs of the child, and also of designated ways in which parents are required to exercise parental responsibility over the child. When a Parenting Order is given by a court, it is subsequently administered by a YOUTH OFFENDING TEAM. The Order may be free-standing or may form part of a set of interventions. Analogous arrangements may be entered into voluntarily between parents and Youth Offending Teams, and these are known as **Parenting Contracts**. [BF]

Parliamentary and Health Service Ombudsman Originally established under the Parliamentary Commissioner Act 1967 as the Parliamentary Commissioner for Administration, the roles of Parliamentary Commissioner and Health Service Ombudsman were effectively combined in 1973. Today the OMBUDSMAN has powers to investigate complaints of maladministration by government departments, a range of other public bodies in the UK, and the NHS in England. [MS]

parliamentary papers Papers laid before Parliament and printed. They include BILLS, reports and proceedings of Parliamentary Committees and COMMAND PAPERS. Both the HOUSE OF COMMONS and the HOUSE OF LORDS issue series of parliamentary papers. [MS]

parliamentary privilege '[T]he sum of the peculiar rights enjoyed by each House collectively as a constituent part of the High Court of Parliament, and by Members of each House individually, without which they could not discharge their functions, and which exceed those possessed by other bodies or individuals. Because neither House could perform its functions without the unimpeded services of its Members, privileges are required by each House for the protection of its Members and for the vindication of its own authority and dignity' (Memorandum by the Clerk of the House of Commons to the Report by the Select Committee on Parliamentary Privilege, HC 34, 1966–67).

The HOUSE OF COMMONS enjoys five main privileges (the privileges of the HOUSE OF LORDS are similar): (a) individual freedom of speech (members cannot be sued for libel or face criminal proceedings for statements made on the floor of the House); (b) freedom from civil (but not criminal) arrest while Parliament is in session; (c) collective access to the CROWN through the Speaker; (d) the collective right to control its own proceedings; and (e) the collective right to punish for **breach of privilege** or **contempt of Parliament**.

Privilege is enforced in the Commons by a Committee on Standards and Privileges, established in 1995. Whether or not any behaviour constitutes a contempt is a matter for the Committee, but examples could include disrupting proceedings in Parliament, refusing to give evidence before a select committee, or seeking to bribe or otherwise improperly influence a Member. Members may be punished for contempt by removal from the House, suspension or imprisonment; others may be reprimanded or imprisoned. [MS]

parliamentary sovereignty *See* SOVEREIGNTY OF PARLIAMENT.

parliamentary supremacy *See* SOVEREIGNTY OF PARLIAMENT.

parol evidence rule The general rule that EXTRINSIC EVIDENCE that adds to, varies or contradicts a written document is inadmissible. [ALTC]

See also ENTIRE AGREEMENT CLAUSE.

parol lease A LEASE which does not require the formalities of creation by deed in order to be enforceable. Leases which are for a term of less than three years, which are to come into effect immediately, do not need to be created by deed. A parol lease may be oral or written. [HC & DR]

See also LEGAL LEASE.

parole The system by which prisoners can be conditionally released from prison

before the end of their sentence. Under the Criminal Justice Act 2003, any person sentenced to more than 12 months' imprisonment must be **released on licence** after serving half of their sentence, unless they are deemed to be DANGEROUS OFFENDERS. The decision whether to grant parole in the latter case is taken by the **Parole Board**, who take into account reports from, primarily, the prison service and probation service, but may also hear evidence or receive a statement from the victim. The key factor determining whether an applicant for parole will be released is the level of risk they pose to the public. If a parole application is turned down, the offender's case will be reviewed on an annual basis. An offender released on licence may be required to complete the remainder of the term if they offend within the remaining period of their sentence. [BF]

See also ANTI-SOCIAL BEHAVIOUR CONTRACT; ANTI-SOCIAL BEHAVIOUR ORDER.

Part 8 claim Generally, non-hostile civil proceedings commenced under the CIVIL PROCEDURE RULES Part 8 and used to resolve questions of law or the interpretation of legal documents. A Part 8 claim is commenced using form 'N208', which should identify the parties, the question for the court and the remedy being sought. [JW]

Part 36 offer An offer to settle proceedings made at any time after those proceedings have commenced; so called because such offers are made within the regime laid down by the CIVIL PROCEDURE RULES Part 36. The advantage of a Part 36 offer is that it will normally provide the offeror with protection from liability for COSTS should the matter go to trial and subsequently settle for or deliver at judgment an amount less than that offered. To obtain protection, defendants' offers normally have to be backed up by an actual payment of money into court, which the claimant may then accept in full and final settlement of the claim. These are conventionally known as **Part 36 payments**. Offers made before commencement of proceedings can also be brought within the protection of Part 36 payments if they were made on equivalent terms to a Part 36 offer and the offeror makes a payment into court after commencement. Other offers to settle are also generally referred to as Part 36 offers and cover all offers by a claimant (e.g. an offer to settle for a lesser amount than that originally claimed) and those offers by a defendant which are identified in Part 36 as not requiring payment into court. The law on this topic is made more complex by the fact that CPR Part 36 does not constitute a complete code on offers to settle and offers can also be made, in certain circumstances, outside of these rules.   [JW]

See also CALDERBANK LETTER.

part performance Prior to the Law of Property (Miscellaneous Provisions) Act 1989, CONTRACTS for the sale or disposition of an interest in land were required to be evidenced in writing and signed in accordance with the Law of Property Act 1925, s. 40. However, the equitable doctrine of part performance recognized that if there was such written evidence it might not be properly signed and therefore permitted a court to order SPECIFIC PERFORMANCE of an oral contract for the sale of land which had been partly performed in the expectation that the other party would perform his obligations (s. 40(2)). The acts of part performance needed to point to the existence of a contract and needed to be acts done by the person seeking to enforce the contract.

The Law of Property (Miscellaneous Provisions) Act 1989, s. 2, now requires that contracts for the sale or disposition of an interest in land, made on or after 27 September 1989, must be in writing; consequently the doctrine of part performance has been superseded for all such contracts made after this date.   [JPL]

partition 1. In land law, the ending of co-ownership of land by division of the land into separate parts. Partition is effected by deed, transferring each part to be solely owned by one of the former co-owners. Since 1926, partition can only be carried out with the agreement of the co-owners. Provision for compensation may be included in order to achieve equality of partition.

2. In international law, see SECESSION. [DR]

party wall The wall of a building standing partly on the land of one owner and partly on the land of another, or a wall separating buildings in different ownership. The law relating to the construction and repair of party walls is governed by the Party Wall etc. Act 1996.

A party wall is not the same as a **party fence wall**, which is a wall that sits astride a boundary and does not form part of a building.   [DR]

See also RIGHT TO SUPPORT.

passing off A COMMON LAW cause of action, which will lie where a business leads prospective customers or consumers to think that its goods are those of another trader, in a manner calculated to injure the business or goodwill of that other (in the sense that this is a reasonably foreseeable consequence). The claimant must also be able to show that the passing off causes actual damage to their business or its goodwill (see *Erven Warnink BV* v. *J. Townsend & Sons (Hull) Ltd* [1979] AC 731). Common methods of passing off include using a name or a TRADE MARK that is very similar to the claimant's, and imitating the appearance of their goods.

The normal remedy is DAMAGES, though it is also possible to obtain an INJUNCTION (in a *quia timet* action) to halt continuing infringement. The action coexists with registered trade mark protection.   [US & HJ]

passive euthanasia *See* EUTHANASIA.

past consideration If the CONSIDERATION alleged to support a PROMISE, and to render it enforceable, pre-dates the promise it will be past consideration and invalid as such (see *Re McArdle* [1951] Ch 669). For example, a promise of a reward made after a passer-by has rescued the PROMISOR from drowning in a lake would not be a promise given in exchange for the act of rescue. However, if a promise of reward is made for finding and returning a lost cat, that act can constitute good consideration to support the earlier promise.   [JPL]

patent A legal TITLE, for a maximum term

of 20 years, which grants to its holder the right to exclude third parties from making or using the INVENTION which is the subject of the patent. A patent is only granted to an invention which is new (the test of **novelty**) and involves an INVENTIVE STEP (i.e. a non-obvious development from a previous technology or practice), and which is capable of industrial applicability (see the Patents Act 1977, ss. 1 and 4). An invention shall be considered capable of industrial application if it can be made or used in any kind of industry, including agriculture.

Even if an invention fulfils all three conditions, patent law specifically excludes inventions from registration where their commercial exploitation would be contrary to public policy or morality; they are plant or animal varieties or essentially biological processes for producing plants or animals; or they are methods of treatment of the human or animal body by surgery or therapy or of diagnosis practised on the human or animal body.

The patent itself comprises a description of the invention (a PATENT SPECIFICATION) and an explanation as to which of its features are novel and inventive (the **claims**). Registration is a compulsory requirement. All patent rights are territorial in nature, and an infringement is actionable only if the act takes place in the UK. [US]

See also BIOTECHNOLOGICAL INVENTIONS; EUROPEAN PATENT; INFRINGEMENT ACTION.

patent agent A professional who has expertise in the field of PATENTS. Patent agents normally have a scientific or technical background, coupled with the ability to draft and analyse legal documents; they work either in patent departments of large industrial organizations, in private firms of patent agents, or in government departments, and their work focuses on obtaining and enforcing intellectual property rights with regard to patents. Patent agents have the right to argue cases in the PATENTS COUNTY COURT and some patent agents also have the right of audience in the PATENTS COURT in appeals from the UK INTELLECTUAL PROPERTY OFFICE.

The profession is governed by the **Char-**tered Institute of Patent Attorneys and there is a professional qualification and examination run by the Institute, together with the Institute of Trade Mark Attorneys. These examinations lead to an entry on both the Register of Patent Agents and the Register of Trade Mark Agents. [US]

See also TRADE MARK ATTORNEY.

patent licence A patent licence is granted on any PATENT or any application to work an INVENTION which is the subject matter of the patent. A patent licence may often give only a very basic permission to manufacture under the patent without any further technological KNOWHOW or TRADE SECRET information or other expertise which is necessary to work the invention efficiently. Some patents are endorsed in the Register of Patents with a licence of right which allows anyone a right to a licence under the patent.

Patent licences, just like other INTELLECTUAL PROPERTY licensing arrangements, can be subject to COMPETITION LAW scrutiny, especially if the patent licence is worded so as to deter other competitors by tying the patent to other products, or by unfair pricing behaviour. [US]

See also ASSIGNMENT.

patent specifications A PATENT application comprises two parts. The first is an abstract consisting of a title and a brief summary of the invention; the second is the patent specification. The specification is made up of a description, which is likely to contain both text and diagrams or drawings, and one or more claims which specify the scope of protection.

Where a EUROPEAN PATENT is concerned, the description part of the specification tends first to explain the background to the invention and the prior art. It then presents the problem which the invention addresses and the solution being offered. After this, it explains how to carry out the invention. This must all be done in a way that supports the validity of the claims and be sufficiently clear and descriptive for a person of normal skill in the relevant technical field to be able to repeat the invention. [US]

Patents County Court (PCC) An alternative venue to the PATENTS COURT for all INTELLECTUAL PROPERTY litigation at county court level, established under the Copyright, Designs and Patents Act 1988. There is no limit to the level of DAMAGES and COSTS it can award nor any limitation on the jurisdiction of the PCC by virtue of the complexity of the case. Cases can be, and have been, sent to and from the Patents Court. The judge of the PCC usually has specific and additional jurisdiction to sit in the Patents Court. BARRISTERS, qualified SOLICITORS and PATENT AGENTS are entitled to initiate and prosecute cases in the PCC. The PCC works to the same rules as the Patents Court. The SMALL CLAIMS TRACK is not available where intellectual property litigation is concerned. [US]

Patents Court Part of the CHANCERY DIVISION of the HIGH COURT, the Patents Court only deals with matters concerning PATENTS, REGISTERED DESIGNS and appeals against the decision of the Comptroller General of Patents. It also has the power to transfer cases commenced in the High Court to the PATENTS COUNTY COURT. See CPR, Part 52 and Rule 63.17. [US]

paternity leave STATUTE provides for paternity leave and paternity pay. Paternity leave is available to an EMPLOYEE who has been continuously employed for at least 26 weeks preceding the 14th week before the expected week of childbirth (this is matched for adoption). It should be noted that leave is not restricted to biological fathers but may extend to male or female partners of the mother who have or are expected to have responsibility for the child's upbringing. The duration is for one or two weeks after birth and if two weeks are taken, the weeks must be consecutive. Leave must be taken within 56 days of the birth. If an employee qualifies for paternity leave, gives the required notice and provides evidence of the birth and the relationship with the child's mother, he or she is also entitled to either **statutory paternity pay** or 90% of normal weekly earnings for the week(s) chosen.

Note also that the Work and Families Act

2006 makes provision for up to 26 weeks additional paternity leave. This right will be dealt with in separate regulations, and the government has said it intends to introduce it at the same time as it extends the period of maternity pay to 12 months. The date of introduction is not yet certain, but is likely to be in 2010. [MJ]

Pay As You Earn A statutory scheme for the deduction of income tax at source from wages, salaries and pensions in which employers and pension fund trustees are obliged by statute to account to HM REVENUE AND CUSTOMS (the Revenue) for the tax deducted, and to provide employees and pensioners with certificates of deduction to prove the amount of tax paid by them for the tax year.

The amount of income tax deducted is indicated in Pay As You Earn (PAYE) tables which are issued to employers and pension trustees by the Revenue, and which are used in conjunction with the tax codes issued by the Revenue to employers and pension trustees for each employee and pensioner. The employer or trustee must account to the Revenue, usually each month, for the amount of tax deducted or the amount which should have been deducted in the month.

If an employee or pensioner (the taxpayer) prepares his or her TAX RETURN and assesses the tax payable, allowance must be made for the tax already paid under the PAYE scheme. The information received by the Revenue in a taxpayer's tax return is used by the Revenue to formulate the tax code for the taxpayer concerned. [RE]

payroll giving scheme A procedure for the payment of charitable donations which employees wish to have paid directly from their wages or salaries before tax is calculated and accounted for to HM REVENUE AND CUSTOMS under the Pay As You Earn scheme. [RE]

See also GIFT AID.

PC *See* PRIVY COUNCIL.

pecuniary legacy *See* LEGACY.

peer-to-peer copying Sharing and downloading material from the internet using specialist peer-to-peer (P2P) SOFTWARE. P2P systems usually lack dedicated, centralized infrastructures, but depend on the voluntary participation of peers to contribute resources (i.e. music, text, image or film files) out of which the infrastructure is constructed. In a P2P distribution network, the information available for access does not reside on a central server or one computer; rather, each computer makes information available to every other computer in the dynamic network. At any given moment, the network consists of other users of similar or the same software being online at that time. Because the information is decentralized in a P2P network, the software provides a method of cataloguing and indexing all the available information and files so that users may access and download. Critically, the contents of all files are held at all times on the users' computers, and what P2P essentially does is to hold a database of file names and, if requested, the ISP address information of each user.

Problems arise when the material flowing through networks of this sort is COPYRIGHT-protected and is reproduced without the permission of the copyright owners. It is an infringement of copyright in the work to download music, films, books and any other copyright-protected works from the internet using P2P file-sharing software without the authorization of the copyright owner. It is of no avail that the downloader was not aware that the work was a copyright-protected work. It is also an infringement of copyright in the work for third parties to sell and market P2P software, and decisions in Australia and the United States have held such parties guilty of copyright infringement by virtue of authorization of infringement, or vicarious and contributory infringement or of inducing infringement (see *A&M Records Inc.* v. *Napster Inc.*, 239 F.3d 1004 (2001); *MGM Studios, Inc.* v. *Grokster Ltd* 545 U.S. 913 (2005); *Universal Music Australia Pty Ltd* v. *Sharman License Holdings Ltd* [2005] FCA 1242). Unauthorized P2P file-sharing of copyrighted materials is extremely difficult to police as the structure of P2P systems makes it hard for copyright owners to track the movement of copyright materials as they pass from user to user. [US]
See also INFRINGEMENT ACTION.

penalty clause A provision in a CONTRACT whereby the DAMAGES payable in the event of BREACH OF CONTRACT are agreed in advance. A penalty clause is designed as a threat to compel the other party to perform and is therefore punitive rather than a genuine pre-estimate of the likely loss resulting from the breach. A penalty clause is therefore unenforceable and the injured party will only be able to recover for actual loss, subject to the usual limitations (see REMOTENESS OF DAMAGE and MITIGATION OF LOSS).

A penalty clause can be compared with a LIQUIDATED DAMAGES CLAUSE, which is an enforceable agreed damages provision. Guidelines for distinguishing liquidated damages and penalty clauses were formulated by Lord Dunedin in *Dunlop Pneumatic Tyre Co. Ltd* v. *New Garage and Motor Co. Ltd* [1915] AC 79. Use of the term 'penalty' or liquidated damages is not conclusive. [JPL]

penalty points In addition to paying a fine or fixed penalty, persons convicted of a road traffic offence can have their driving licence endorsed with a penalty ranging from 3 to 11 points or a period of disqualification, depending on the seriousness of the offence. If a person incurs 12 or more penalty points within a period of three years they will be liable to be disqualified under the 'TOTTING-UP' system. [SN]
See also ENDORSEMENT.

pendente lite (Lat. pending suit) A type of grant of LETTERS OF ADMINISTRATION of the ESTATE of a deceased when a PROBATE claim has begun. The reason for this is that there may be action which has to be taken right away and cannot wait until the action has been completed, for example, where assets have to be collected and safeguarded. When the action is completed, the grant terminates. An administrator *pendente lite* cannot distribute any of the estate without the court's consent (see Supreme Court Act 1981, s. 117). [CM]

pending action An unresolved legal action or proceedings in court. In land law, a pending action may be registered at the Land Charges Department on the Register of Pending Actions, so that the outcome of that legal action will bind a purchaser for value of the land to which it relates. Once registered, it remains effective for five years and may be renewed at five-yearly intervals. Examples of pending actions which are commonly registered are boundary disputes and claims for a property transfer by a spouse in divorce proceedings.   [DR]

penetration Defined as a key constituent of the 'relevant act' for the offence of RAPE (Sexual Offences Act 2003, s. 1) and assault by penetration (s. 2). To constitute rape, penetration must be with the penis; whereas, under s. 2, the penetration may involve another part of the body, or any object, provided that the penetration is sexual in nature. Penetration is, according to s. 79 of the 2003 Act, 'a continuing act from entry to withdrawal'.   [BF]

See also SEXUAL ASSAULT.

pension earmarking One of the FINANCIAL PROVISION ORDERS available to the court under the Matrimonial Causes Act 1973 and the Civil Partnership Act 2004. On ANNULMENT, DIVORCE or DISSOLUTION of a CIVIL PARTNERSHIP an occupational pension becomes a part of the pool of assets to be considered for adjustment between the parties. The court can order the trustees or managers of the spouse's or civil partner's pension fund to earmark for the benefit of the non-pensioned spouse or civil partner a percentage of the pension and to make payments to him or her when the pension is available for payment to the pensioned spouse or civil partner. The percentage to be earmarked is determined according to the exercise of the court's discretion under the relevant Act. Earmarking orders are not often made because of the difficulties associated with the delay in their execution. In most cases, a PENSION SHARING ORDER is preferred.   [AD]

pension sharing order One of the FINANCIAL PROVISION ORDERS available to the court

under the Matrimonial Causes Act 1973 and the Civil Partnership Act 2004. On ANNULMENT, DIVORCE or DISSOLUTION of a CIVIL PARTNERSHIP an occupational pension becomes a part of the pool of assets to be considered for adjustment between the parties. A pension sharing order is an order splitting one party's pension between both parties so that each has his or her own pension and each operates independently of the other on annulment, divorce or dissolution of a civil partnership. The order will specify the percentage of the split which is determined according to exercise of the court's discretion under the relevant Act. The newly created pension may be kept with the old pension administrator or transferred to another administrator if the (former) spouse or civil partner wishes. Each party is then responsible for making payments into his or her pension.   [AD]

See also PENSION EARMARKING.

peppercorn rent A small token payment of RENT which demonstrates that the agreement is for rent to be paid, and therefore is legally recognizable as a LEASE as opposed to a licence.   [HC & DR]

per incuriam (Lat. through insufficient care) Where a court's decision is made in ignorance of a key legislative provision, or a PRECEDENT that would have made a material difference to the decision, that case is said to have been decided *per incuriam*. This provides one of the few situations, under the principle in *Young* v. *Bristol Aeroplane Co. Ltd* [1944] KB 718, in which the COURT OF APPEAL can overrule its own earlier decision. In practice, however, very few errors are actually serious enough to justify a ruling of *per incuriam*.   [JW]

per my et per tout (Fr. by the part and the whole) Describes the unity of possession which is a fundamental characteristic of joint ownership of land.   [HC & DR]

per stirpes (Lat. through the stems or through the branches) A method of distribution according to descent when issue are claiming following the death of a parent; it can be contrasted with the alternative method which is known as ***per capita***.

Suppose that X dies intestate, leaving no surviving spouse, and that his son A predeceased him, leaving two sons A1 and A2 surviving, and that his daughter B also predeceased X, leaving three daughters B1, B2, B3 surviving. X's estate then falls to be divided among his grandchildren, who total five in number. If the beneficiaries were entitled *per capita* they would receive one-fifth part each. However, if they are entitled *per stirpes* (which in fact they are in this example) then A's branch of the family would take one half, and A1 and A2 would share that equally, while B's branch of the family takes one half and B1, B2, B3 share that equally. [CM]

See also INTESTACY.

peremptory challenge (obsolete) A right to challenge a juror without cause. The right was abolished by the Criminal Justice Act 1988, s. 118. [SN]

peremptory norm *See* JUS COGENS.

perfect trust *See* EXECUTED TRUST.

performance of a contract When each party carries out its obligations under the CONTRACT. On full performance by each party the contract will be discharged. The specified contractual obligations may amount to a guarantee of performance (strict contractual obligations), or the standard of performance required may be a qualified standard, i.e. to exercise reasonable care and skill in performing. If the required standard of performance is not met, a BREACH OF CONTRACT will occur. [JPL]

performer's rights Rights given to performers in order to protect their performances, which remain independent of any COPYRIGHT in, or MORAL RIGHTS relating to, the work or the recording or broadcast of the performance. A 'performance' is a live performance of a dramatic performance (which includes dance and mime), a musical performance, a reading or recitation of a LITERARY WORK, or a performance of a variety act or any similar presentation. No other type of performances will qualify for protection.

A performer's rights are infringed, for example, by a person who, without the performer's consent, makes a recording of the performance, rents or lends to the public copies of a recording of the performance, or issues to the public copies of a recording of the performance, prior to its being placed in circulation in the EUROPEAN ECONOMIC AREA. A performer's rights are also infringed by a person who, without his consent, shows, plays in public, or communicates to the public, or imports or deals with an illicit recording of the performance (i.e. a bootleg recording). Performers' rights expire 50 years from the year in which the performance takes place, or 50 years from the year in which a recording of the performance is released (if one was made). [US]

Further reading: Richard Arnold, *Performers' Rights*, 3rd edn (London: Sweet and Maxwell, 2004).

perished goods For the purposes of the Sale of Goods Act 1979, goods under a CONTRACT of sale that have been totally destroyed or damaged to such an extent that they no longer fit their contract description. The Sale of Goods Act 1979, s. 6, provides that where a contract is for the sale of specific goods which, unknown to the SELLER, have perished by the time the contract is made, the contract is VOID. If the goods perish after the making of the contract, but before the risk has passed to the buyer, and in the absence of an express allocation of the risk, the doctrine of FRUSTRATION will discharge the parties from performance of future obligations under the contract, e.g. delivery and payment. [JPL]

See also TRANSFER OF RISK; VOID CONTRACT.

perjury Under the Perjury Act 1911, s. 1, it is an offence for a person, lawfully sworn as a witness or interpreter in judicial proceedings, wilfully to make a statement material to those proceedings, which he knows to be false or does not believe to be true. Section 13 of the 1911 Act states that a conviction for perjury requires more evidence than merely that of a single witness. Perjury is viewed as a serious offence on the basis that it subverts the administration of justice. [BF]

Permanent Court of Arbitration (PCA) A public international institution which was created by the 1899 HAGUE CONVENTIONS for the Pacific Statement of International Disputes to provide a panel of arbitrators (nominated by contracting STATE parties to those Hague Conventions) to deal with disputes between states arising out of international treaties (including bilateral and multilateral investment treaties), and other agreements to arbitrate.

The seat of the court is at the Peace Palace, in The Hague, Netherlands. Its facilities are available to states for ad hoc arbitrations (such as the one formed for the case of *New Zealand* v. *France* in 1990 (the *Rainbow Warrior*). Moreover, since 1935, the PCA has provided services for the resolution of disputes involving mixed claims between states, state entities, inter-governmental organizations and private parties. [RE]

See also AD HOC ARBITRATION; ARBITRATOR; INSTITUTIONAL ARBITRATION; INTERNATIONAL LAW.

permissive waste *See* WASTE.

perpetual trusts A TRUST that can last in perpetuity, such as a charitable trust, because it is not bound by the rule against perpetual trusts. Because of the fear of property being locked in trusts for too long, the COMMON LAW developed the RULE AGAINST PERPETUITIES, one aspect of which limited the maximum duration of most trusts to what is known as the PERPETUITY PERIOD. [PK]

perpetuity period A total period equivalent to a LIFE IN BEING, plus 21 years, or, for dispositions following the Perpetuities and Accumulations Act 1964, a period of 80 years may be substituted. [HC & DR]

See also RULE AGAINST PERPETUITIES.

persecution *See* CRIMES AGAINST HUMANITY.

persistent offender For the purposes of evaluating performance and developing best practice, criminal justice agencies have used a definition of persistent offender which refers to '[s]omeone who is 18 years or over and has been convicted

of six or more recordable offences in the last 12 months' (see HMIC et al., *Joint Inspection Report into Persistent and Prolific Offenders*, Home Office Communications Directorate, 2004).

The significance of persistent offenders lies in the high proportion of crime which is committed by a relatively small number of offenders. Thus, appropriate interventions on persistent offending are viewed as integral to successful crime reduction strategies. [BF]

See also REPEAT OFFENDER.

persona non grata (Lat. an unwelcome person) The term concerns the designation of the head of a DIPLOMATIC MISSION or any member of the diplomatic or non-diplomatic staff of the mission of a sending STATE as not acceptable by the receiving state, at any time and without having to explain its decision (see Article 9 of the 1961 Vienna Convention on Diplomatic Relations and Optional Protocols). The sending state must be notified before expulsion takes place. In such cases, the sending state shall, as appropriate, either recall the person concerned or terminate his function with the mission. It is possible for a person to be declared *non grata* before arriving in the territory of the receiving state. If the sending state fails to remove the person declared as not acceptable within a reasonable time, the receiving state may refuse to recognize that person as part of the mission, with the consequence that the person would not enjoy DIPLOMATIC IMMUNITY. [IB]

personal allowance An amount of value which is excluded during the process of assessing a taxpayer's liability to income tax for a tax year. The allowance is personal to the taxpayer. It cannot be transferred to any other individual or person. Every taxpayer who is resident in the United Kingdom is entitled to a new allowance each tax year. The amount of the allowance increases each year in line with inflation.

If the taxpayer has insufficient income to absorb the allowance, the unused element cannot be carried forwards or backwards to any other tax year and the allowance is wasted. The allowance is specific to income tax and cannot be transferred for use in the context of any other direct or indirect tax.

There are chiefly two kinds of personal allowance. The standard allowance is an amount which is set against the taxpayer's total income for a tax year: it reduces the amount or value of income which is brought into charge to tax. The higher personal allowances (also referred to as age allowances) for taxpayers over the age of 64 are amounts which are set against the tax charged on the income brought into charge to tax: i.e. the higher allowances reduce tax, not income.

For CAPITAL GAINS TAX and inheritance tax, there are annual exemptions, which have a similar function. [RE]

personal chattels The Administration of Estates Act 1925 provides that on INTESTACY a surviving spouse is entitled, among other benefits, to the personal chattels of the deceased, and defines them as follows: 'carriages, horses, stable furniture and effects (not used for business purposes), motor cars and accessories (not used for business purposes), garden effects, domestic animals, plate, plated articles, linen, china, glass, books, pictures, prints, furniture, jewellery, articles of household or personal use or ornament, musical or scientific instruments and apparatus, wines, liquors and consumable stores, but … not … any chattels used at the death of the intestate for business purposes nor money or securities for money' (s. 55(x)).

This definition has frequently been criticized by judges, and indeed it has been found difficult to apply in many cases. However, the expression is found frequently in professionally drawn wills, which make a specific bequest of personal chattels 'as defined in' the Act. [CM]

Personal Equity Plan A scheme which was intended to generate savings by the grant of tax exemptions to UK tax-resident individuals in respect of qualifying savings accounts (plans) created between 1987 and 1999. The scheme ended on 5 April 1999 and no new plans were permitted after that date. Plans existing on that date continue

to have the exemptions originally granted. [RE]

See also EXEMPT INCOME.

personal property Moveable assets and goods; essentially all forms of property which are not REAL PROPERTY, INCORPOREAL HEREDITAMENTS (i.e. intangible rights over land such as an EASEMENT, or PROFITS À PRENDRE), or CHOSES IN ACTION (such as money and investments). Also called **personalty**.

See also CHATTEL.

personal representative Someone who undertakes the administration of the ESTATE of a deceased person. This expression includes both an EXECUTOR and an ADMINISTRATOR. The personal representative is responsible for collecting the ASSETS, paying the debts and distributing the estate to the beneficiaries. [CM]

personal services *See* CONTRACT FOR PERSONAL SERVICES.

personality rights There is no personality right as such in the UK. This is in contrast to the development law on personality rights in the US and in other EU Member States. Personality rights can be loosely defined as the right of an individual (especially a celebrity) to control all aspects of his or her own personality, i.e. use of one's name, image and likeness. There are two aspects of such control: the right to stop commercial usage of such features, and the right to stop intrusion into one's private sphere.

What is available under UK law is a piecemeal type of protection under TRADE MARK, REGISTERED DESIGN, COPYRIGHT, PASSING OFF and DEFAMATION laws. Under trade mark law, it is difficult to register an image of a personality as a trade mark as such images do not show distinctiveness in the traditional sense but instead detract consumers from the source of the product to the personality of the celebrity. It is also difficult to protect names or faces under copyright law.

In relation to the private sphere of an individual, the only traditional route to protection was through the law on CONFIDENTIALITY. The Human Rights Act 1988 and the recent development of the law on

PRIVACY now offer a more robust form of protection. [US]

Further reading: H. Beverley-Smith, *The Commercial Appropriation of Personality* (Cambridge: Cambridge University Press, 2002).

persuasive authority Where a PRECEDENT is not binding on a court, that decision may nevertheless be regarded as influential, and may be applied, if there is no stronger binding authority on the court. In the English legal system, the following are examples of persuasive authority: decisions of courts lower in the hierarchy than the court presently hearing the case; decisions from courts in other, generally COMMON LAW, countries; decisions of the JUDICIAL COMMITTEE OF THE PRIVY COUNCIL. [JW]

See also STARE DECISIS.

perverse verdict A term principally used in the context of JURY trials to refer to a VERDICT which appears to go against the evidence. [BF]

perverting the course of justice A COMMON LAW offence, which is committed when a person does an act, or a series of acts, which has the tendency to and is intended to pervert the course of justice. It is not necessary that the course of justice actually be perverted, and sometimes the offence is known as attempting to pervert the course of justice. The offence may be committed in various ways, for example by fabricating evidence, or seeking to persuade a WITNESS to change their evidence, or by seeking to influence a verdict by intimidating jurors. [BF]

See also CONTEMPT OF COURT; WASTING POLICE TIME; WITNESS INTIMIDATION.

petty patent A petty patent system often provides for fast-track, no-examination registration whereby an applicant may obtain a short-term PATENT. It is closely related to UTILITY MODELS. There is no harmonized European petty patent regime, nor is there any petty patent protection in the UK, though a number of individual states, including Germany, Iceland, Japan, China and Taiwan, all offer petty patents, or, as in

the case of Australia's 'innovation patent', similar regimes. [US]

petty sessions (obsolete) A court of summary jurisdiction, now known as the magistrates' court. [SN]

philanthropic purpose A purpose within a TRUST INSTRUMENT that is regarded as being for the public good, although not necessarily charitable. The term is often used as a synonym for benevolent purposes, although it is sometimes regarded as having a somewhat narrower ambit. It is likely that, as the range of benevolent purposes that are not also charitable reduces in the wake of the Charities Act 2006, the separate ambit of philanthropic purposes (such as it is) will reduce to vanishing point. [PK]

picketing A person may, in contemplation or furtherance of a TRADE DISPUTE, attend at or near their place of work or, if they are a TRADE UNION OFFICIAL, at or near the place of work of a member of the TRADE UNION whom they represent and whom they are accompanying, provided that the person is attending for the purpose only of peacefully communicating or obtaining information or of peacefully persuading any person not to work or to work. A person who has been dismissed (see DISMISSAL) may picket at their former workplace. For the purposes of the Trade Union and Labour Relations (Consolidation) Act 1992, s. 220, the place of work is any premises from which the person works or from which the work is administered. Picketing beyond the protection given by s. 220 is unlawful and gives rise to various TORTS and crimes, e.g. obstruction, public and private nuisance, breach of the peace, intimidation. There is no right to stop traffic. Picketing other than at one's place of work ('flying pickets') is therefore illegal, as is mass picketing if a tort or crime occurs (see *Thomas* v. *National Union of Mineworkers (South Wales Area)* [1986] Ch 20).

See also s. 219(3) of the Act, which provides that if a person is picketing but that conduct does not fall within s. 220, there is no defence to any action such as inducing a breach of contract, which occurs when they persuade employees to stop work in breach of their contract of employment. If what the person did falls within s. 220, the union gains immunity from action. [M]

pie poudre *See* LOCAL COURTS.

piscary A type of PROFIT À PRENDRE or RIGHT OF COMMON that gives the owner the right to take fish from another person's land. [DR]

planning permission Formal permission of the local planning authority, which is required in order to carry out any DEVELOP-MENT of land. Planning permission is usually granted in one of three main ways.

(a) By a development order, which may be general, special or local. The Town and Country Planning (General Permitted Development) Order 1995 (SI 1995/418), allows a wide range of development, including development within the curtilage of a dwellinghouse (e.g. erecting a porch outside the front door of a house) and the construction of a fence or other means of enclosure.

(b) By a deemed grant of planning permission. Planning permission may be deemed to have been given when a public authority authorizes development to be carried out by a local authority or other body carrying out statutory functions (e.g. Network Rail).

(c) By an express grant of planning permission following individual application to the local planning authority. The local planning authority has a duty to publicize all applications for planning permission and for certain types of development has a duty to consult specialist bodies (e.g. local highway authorities). Decisions are usually made by the local authority's planning committee and must be made in accordance with the DEVELOPMENT PLAN unless material considerations indicate otherwise. Planning permission may be granted conditionally, subject to such conditions as the authority thinks fit, or refused. Most decisions of planning authorities may be appealed to the Secretary of State and subsequently to the High Court on a point of law. [DR]

See also ENFORCEMENT NOTICE; STOP NOTICE.

plea The reply by a defendant to a CHARGE put by a court. The defendant is asked to plead either guilty or not guilty. [SN]

See also MUTE; NOT PROVEN.

plea bargaining A process by which a defendant may enter a GUILTY PLEA in order to secure a concession in the way he is treated at the sentencing stage, which would not be available were he to enter a plea of not guilty and subsequently be convicted at a contested trial.

There are two forms of plea bargaining. The first is where the defendant, charged with crime X, agrees to plead guilty to lesser crime Y, rather than contest the original charge. This is sometimes referred to as **charge bargaining**. Thus, when charged with an offence of WOUNDING WITH INTENT under the Offences against the Person Act 1861, s. 18, a defendant might offer to plead guilty to the less serious offence of malicious wounding under s. 20 of that Act.

A defendant may also offer a guilty plea to the offence with which he is charged in order to secure a lower sentence than that which he would obtain if he contested the charge and was ultimately found guilty. The process of giving a lower sentence is sometimes referred to as a sentence discount. In the past, defendants would sometimes be given an indication of a likely sentence on a guilty plea by their legal representatives, after the latter had consulted, along with the prosecution representative, with the judge. Such informal bargaining was always problematic, because of the need for defendants to enter their pleas freely and voluntarily. A favourable indication of sentence could be construed as an incentive to plead guilty. None the less, it was universally acknowledged that an early plea of guilty would attract a lesser sentence than would be the case on conviction after a contested trial. The COURT OF APPEAL in *Goodyear* [2006] 1 Cr App R (S) 6 formalized the procedure for indication of sentence in the Crown Court. The defendant may seek such an indication in writing. The judge is not obliged to give an indication, but if he or she does so, it is binding. The indication lapses if the defendant proceeds to a contested trial. [BF]

plea before venue A procedure in the magistrates' court, introduced by the Criminal Procedure and Investigations Act 1996, which provides that for an OFFENCE TRIABLE EITHER WAY, a defendant is given the opportunity to indicate their likely plea. The accused is asked whether they intend to plead guilty or not guilty before the court determines whether the case will be dealt with summarily (by the Magistrates' Court) or on INDICTMENT by the CROWN COURT. [SN]

plea in mitigation *See* MITIGATION.

pleading guilty by post A procedure used in road traffic cases which gives the accused the opportunity – in non-serious cases – of pleading guilty by post. Originally introduced under the Magistrates' Courts Act 1980, s. 12. [SN]

See also FIXED ENALTY NOTICES.

pleadings *See* STATEMENTS OF CASE.

plene administravit (Lat. he has fully administered) A defence of a PERSONAL REPRESENTATIVE to an action brought by a creditor of the ESTATE. By entering this plea, he is saying that all ASSETS of the estate have been distributed. [CM]

police court A term used in some jurisdictions (no longer in England and Wales) to denote an inferior court having the power to prosecute minor criminal offences and to hold for trial persons charged with more serious offences. [SN]

police protection order If a police constable has reasonable cause to believe that a CHILD is at risk of significant harm, the officer may remove the child to a safe place or prevent the child from being removed from a safe place, such as a hospital (Children Act 1989, s. 46). Usually this is referred to simply as 'police protection' (s. 46(2)) but it can also be referred to as a 'police protection order'. As soon as is reasonably practicable, the constable must ensure the case is put in the hands of an officer designated

to inquire into such cases. The constable also has to inform the LOCAL AUTHORITY in whose area the child was found. The local authority children's services department will take steps to protect the child if necessary, for example by applying for an EMERGENCY PROTECTION ORDER. If necessary, the designated officer is permitted to apply on behalf of the local authority. Police protection cannot exceed 72 hours in duration and if, during that period, the inquiry is completed, the designated officer must release the child unless he or she still has reasonable cause to believe that the child will suffer significant harm if released. [FK]

See also THRESHOLD CRITERIA.

poll tax A flat-rate tax paid by every adult. It is derived from the colloquial English use of poll, meaning 'head'. [JW]

See also COMMUNITY CHARGE.

polluter pays *See* PRECAUTIONARY PRINCIPLE.

portion *See* RULE AGAINST DOUBLE PORTIONS.

positive action While POSITIVE DISCRIMINATION is generally unlawful, positive action is lawful. It consists of behaviour which seeks to make known, to people in categories which have been discriminated against in the past or which are poorly represented in the workforce, that jobs are available. However, the success of the application must not depend on the applicant being part of that category. For example, if a department store were to take steps to reach out to older workers by advertising in periodicals such as *The Oldie*, that is lawful. Appointing a person simply because he or she is older is unlawful discrimination against younger workers. [MJ]

positive discrimination Where members of a particular 'group' (e.g. of race, gender or sexual orientation) are treated more favourably because of their race, gender, etc. UK and EC law does not allow affirmative or positive DISCRIMINATION except in narrow circumstances (e.g. the Sex Discrimination Act 1975, ss. 47–48, permit single-sex training to change the balance of genders in jobs where there is an imbalance, but appointment to jobs must be made on merit, not on the grounds of sex). Similarly in EC law, POSITIVE ACTION to encourage women to apply for jobs and promotion is permitted; however positive discrimination, whereby women are preferred over men when both are equally ranked, is not permitted. [MJ]

See also EQUALITY AND HUMAN RIGHTS COMMISSION.

positive law Man-made law, especially law laid down by government or some other sovereign authority, and especially such law set down in written form whether as statute or code. The term is most often used in discussions of NATURAL LAW as a means of distinguishing man-made law from some version of moral law, which has its source either in scripture or in the exercise of human reason. [JP]

positivism The movement emerging from the profound changes in thinking brought about by the scientific revolution and the Enlightenment and associated in particular with the work of Auguste Comte (1798–1857). Comte held that only scientific knowledge could be regarded as sound knowledge in contrast to any purported knowledge deriving from other sources such as religion. This had implications for thinking about the relationship between humans and nature and about the nature of society.

Technocratic thinkers adopting this positivist approach maintained that since humans were now in a position to discover the truth about nature and society rather than being beholden to the revealed truth of sacred texts, decisions about how to control nature and order society could henceforth be taken on rational grounds. This ideal state of affairs would not emerge immediately but rather would occur after a series of historically inevitable transformations. For Comte, positivism was the third stage in mankind's attempt to account for the world, material and social, following on from theological and metaphysical efforts. This positivist approach influenced many fields of thought, including law. [JP]

See also LEGAL POSITIVISM.

Further reading: Auguste Comte, *The Positive Philosophy* (New York: AMS Press Inc., 1974).

possession claims online (PCOL) Under CIVIL PROCEDURE RULES, Rule 55.10A and PRACTICE DIRECTION 55B, possession claims for residential property for non-payment of rent or mortgage may be commenced electronically using the PCOL service. The project was piloted live in a number of south Wales county courts during 2006 and was being rolled out nationally in 2007. The PCOL service can be accessed at http://www.possessionclaim.gov.uk/pcol/. [JW]

possessory title One of the three classes of title to freehold land recognized by the Land Registry. It is awarded when the person applying for registration is in actual possession of the land, or if the person is in receipt of the rents and profits of the land, but cannot be registered with absolute title or QUALIFIED TITLE.

Possessory title will be registered in approximately 1% of cases, often where the person applying for registration has acquired their rights through adverse possession, or where the title deeds for the property have been lost. It has the same effect as registration with absolute title except, importantly, it is subject to any right or interest adverse to the proprietor's title that existed at the time of registration.

Possessory title may be upgraded to absolute title where the Registrar is satisfied as to the title of the estate (e.g. if missing title deeds are found) or where the possessory title has been registered for 12 years and the Registrar is satisfied that the proprietor is in possession of the land. [DR]

postal acceptance If an ACCEPTANCE of a CONTRACT is to be communicated by post, that acceptance takes effect when the letter of acceptance is posted. It is irrelevant to communication of the acceptance that the letter is never delivered. This rule of postal acceptance will, however, be overridden by the terms of the offer if they require actual receipt of the acceptance letter. [JPL]

postmodern jurisprudence The application of postmodern ideas, originally developed within art and architecture, to the field of law. Postmodernism is most simply defined as a rejection of grand narratives, of objectivity, of rationality, of progress – in short, of all those ideas and concepts that characterized the Enlightenment and which have been so influential in the formation of the modern world. Whereas the Enlightenment sought to replace God with Reason as the ultimate foundation for knowledge and society, postmodernism denies that any such ultimate foundation is possible.

The impact on law is profound: if there is no such ultimate foundation, ideas of truth, of democracy, of judgement, of regulation and so on, are all fatally undermined. This profoundly sceptical dimension in postmodernism has to some extent led to its replacing CRITICAL LEGAL STUDIES as the most radical movement in law schools and legal theory.

The methods by which postmodern jurisprudence achieves its ends are many and various, but among the most important are deconstruction, as developed especially by Jacques Derrida and those influenced by the psychoanalytical techniques of Jacques Lacan.

Postmodernism is a wide and varied movement but its adherents are united not only by their scepticism of grand narratives and universal values, but also by their concern with the stultifying effects of the modern state and its assault (albeit well-meaning) on the individual. To speak of the individual subject (in the terms employed by law, for example) is meaningless for postmodernism, insofar as the individual is now no more than the locus of a range of different subjectivities imposed by state, market, class and so on. In response, postmodernists call for more inclusion and participation in order that structures of domination and oppression may be undermined. Concerns such as these resonate with those interested in minority rights, among whom postmodernism has also had an impact.

The difficulty (indeed, the impenetrability) of some postmodern writing as well as the message it conveys (which can some-times border on, if not indeed fall squarely within, nihilism) means that it has attracted scathing criticism. There is no doubting the sincerity of many of its proponents, however, and their insights into law and its place in society serve as an important challenge to any too ready acceptance of the status quo.   [JP]

Further reading: Costas Douzinas and Ronnie Warrington, *Postmodern Jurisprudence* (London: Routledge, 1991).

post-nuptial settlement A settlement of property made after a MARRIAGE, on either or both of the parties to the marriage, including by will. The Matrimonial Causes Act 1973, s. 24(1)(c), gives the court, as part of its jurisdiction in ANCILLARY RELIEF claims, the power to vary any such MARRIAGE SETTLEMENT or extinguish any interest under it.
[AD]

See also ANTE-NUPTIAL SETTLEMENT.

potentially exempt transfer (PET) A LIFE-TIME TRANSFER of value made by an individual (the transferor) which reduces the value of the ESTATE of a person and which is chargeable to inheritance tax (IHT) unless the transferor lives for at least seven calendar years after making the transfer.

A potentially exempt transfer (PET) does not have to be reported unless it becomes actually chargeable. However, a record of all PETs must be kept so that the transferor's personal representatives can report relevant transfers. Where a PET becomes actually exempt, it is of no relevance: it does not affect the rate of IHT on any later lifetime transfers or the rate of IHT chargeable on the value of the transferor's estate on death. However, where a PET becomes actually chargeable, it must be reported to the Capital Taxes Office, the value enters the transferor's cumulative total, the donee is liable to pay any IHT, and the value can affect the rate of IHT payable on subsequent lifetime transfers made by the transferor, and the value of the deceased transferor's estate on death.   [RE]

power One of the four ways in which WESLEY NEWCOMB HOHFELD defines a RIGHT. Thus he notes that the phrase 'A has the right to do

R' can be understood to mean that A has the *power* to do R even though no particular right or privilege has been conferred. For example, B offers to sell A some additional land; A has the *power* to accept the offer and if he or she does so then B is under a correlative *liability* to A to sell it. [JP]

power in nature of a trust *See* TRUST POWER.

power of appointment A right to select who should benefit under a TRUST. The person with the right to choose is known as the donee of the power, while those in whose favour the right might be exercised are its objects. Powers may be: **special** – restricted to objects within a certain class; **hybrid** – open to everyone with the exception of a certain class; or **general** – subject to no limitations and consequently available to anyone, including even the donee of the power, and thus akin to full ownership. Powers, unlike trusts, are permissive not mandatory and the donee of a power is under no requirement to exercise it. This is unproblematic where the donee is a non-fiduciary, in which case the power is often referred to as a mere power and the donee only under a duty not to commit a FRAUD ON A POWER.

However, the conceptual distinction between trusts and powers is more troublesome in the context of FIDUCIARY powers, which are also permissive but where the donee of the power is still under a duty to consider exercising it: not because it is a power, but because he is a FIDUCIARY. As a consequence, fiduciary powers are very similar to (but not the same as) DISCRETIONARY TRUSTS, which is why in *McPhail* v. *Doulton* [1971] AC 424, the HOUSE OF LORDS applied the existing test for the validity of powers to such trusts. Under a power there is no need to compile a complete list of possible recipients, because all the donee needs, and likewise the courts to supervise, is a conceptually certain definition of the class of person capable of being chosen. This provides both the donee of the power and the courts with a clear test of eligibility. Both fiduciary and mere powers are consequently valid, in this respect, pro-

vided they contain an '*is or is not*' test, with the BURDEN OF PROOF borne by anyone arguing he *is* within the class, and with anyone who, either, *is not*, or cannot prove on the BALANCE OF PROBABILITIES that he *is*, excluded from consideration. [PK]

power of arrest The Police and Criminal Evidence Act 1984 (PACE), s. 24(1) (as amended by the Serious Organised Crime and Police Act 2005 (SOCA)) permits a constable to arrest without a warrant anyone who is about to commit an offence; anyone who is in the act of committing an offence; anyone whom he has reasonable grounds for suspecting to be about to commit an offence; anyone whom he has reasonable grounds for suspecting to be committing an offence. Section 24(2) permits a constable who has reasonable grounds for suspecting that an offence has been committed, to arrest without a warrant anyone whom he has reasonable grounds to suspect of being guilty of it. Section 24(3) permits a constable, where an offence has been committed, to arrest without warrant anyone who is guilty of the offence; or anyone whom he has reasonable grounds for suspecting to be guilty of it.

Under ss. 24(4) and 24(5), the power of arrest in ss. 24(1), (2) and (3) is only exercisable if the constable has reasonable grounds for believing the arrest to be necessary to enable the name or address of the person in question to be ascertained; to prevent the person in question causing physical injury to him- or herself or another, or suffering physical injury, or causing loss of or damage to property, or committing an offence against public decency, or causing an unlawful obstruction of the highway; to protect a child or other vulnerable person from the person in question; to allow the prompt and effective investigation of the alleged offence; or to prevent the hindering of any prosecution for the offence by the disappearance of the person in question. [BF]

See also CITIZEN'S ARREST.

power of attorney A DEED by which a person authorizes another to act on his behalf, or delegates some specific function to him.

A PERSONAL REPRESENTATIVE is entitled to delegate 'any of the trusts, powers and discretions vested in him' under the Trustee Delegation Act 1999.   [CM]

See also LASTING POWER OF ATTORNEY.

power of sale 1. A remedy available where a borrower has defaulted on his MORTGAGE repayments, allowing the lender to sell the property to settle the debt owed to him. A power of sale **exists** in all LEGAL MORTGAGES unless expressly excluded, **arises** after the legal date of redemption has passed (usually after the first six months), but only becomes **exercisable** if one of three statutory conditions is met (Law of Property Act 1925, s. 103): (a) a formal notice requiring payment of the mortgage money has not been complied with for three months; (b) interest on the mortgage has been unpaid for two months; or (c) the borrower has breached some other condition of the mortgage.

In practice these conditions are often replaced with more stringent conditions in the mortgage deed. When the lender exercises his power of sale, he has a duty to take reasonable precautions to secure a proper price. The lender becomes a trustee of the proceeds of sale and must put the money towards paying off any prior mortgages that the sale was not made subject to, expenses incurred in arranging the sale, the mortgage debt itself and, if there is any money left over, paying the balance to the borrower.

2. Under a Settled Land Act SETTLEMENT, a statutory power of the TENANT FOR LIFE to sell the settled land. Such a sale must be made for the best consideration in money that can reasonably be obtained (Settled Land Act 1925, ss. 38–39).   [DR]

See also EQUITY OF REDEMPTION; FORECLOSURE; REDEMPTION.

powers of investment   *See* AUTHORIZED INVESTMENTS.

Practice Directions   Statements of court practice and procedure which supplement and expand on the CIVIL or CRIMINAL PROCEDURE RULES. The purpose of Practice Directions is to provide additional guidance to court users and increase uniformity of practice between courts. Under the Constitutional Reform Act 2005, which amends the powers to make Practice Directions contained in the Civil Procedure Act 1997, s. 5, and the Courts Act 2003, s. 74, a general power to make Practice Directions is vested in the LORD CHIEF JUSTICE, subject to the agreement of the LORD CHANCELLOR in most instances. Under Part 1 of Schedule 2 of the Constitutional Reform Act, the Lord Chief Justice, with the agreement of the Lord Chancellor, can nominate another judicial office-holder to exercise these powers. For the civil courts, the Lord Chief Justice has nominated the MASTER OF THE ROLLS.   [JW]

praecipe (Lat. command)   Before a WRIT OF EXECUTION can be sealed for issue by the QUEEN'S BENCH DIVISION, a signed *praecipe*, a form on which the person seeking the writ writes out the particulars he wishes it to contain, must be filed with the court. [JW]

pre-action protocols   Procedural standards in civil litigation which outline the steps parties should take to exchange information with each other about a prospective claim. They are intended to improve communication between parties and facilitate either early settlement, or efficient resolution through the courts. Protocols have been devised so far to support general personal injury, clinical negligence, construction and engineering, DEFAMATION, disease and illness claims, housing disrepair, professional negligence and JUDICIAL REVIEW proceedings. Additional protocols are likely to be developed in the future.

The CIVIL PROCEDURE RULES (CPR) allow the court to take into account compliance or non-compliance with the applicable protocol when giving CASE MANAGEMENT directions (e.g. in considering whether to grant an extension of time), and when considering orders for costs under CPR Rule 44.3(1)(a).

[JW]

pre-contractual agreement   An agreement made in the negotiating period leading up to the making of the CONTRACT, such as a LETTER OF INTENT. This does not amount to a legally binding contract since there is no intention to be legally bound. It is therefore no more than an attempt to put a preliminary understanding into written form. As a general rule, English law does not recognize any liability between the parties prior to the making of a contract. However, such liability may arise through the use of a COLLATERAL CONTRACT (*Harvela Investments Ltd* v. *Royal Trust Co. of Canada (CI) Ltd* [1986] 1 AC 207); an IMPLIED CONTRACT (*Blackpool & Fylde Aero Club* v. *Blackpool Borough Council* [1990] 1 WLR 1195: obligation to consider conforming tenders); as a result of an express PROMISE to negotiate in GOOD FAITH; or as a result of the operation of an ESTOPPEL. In addition, pre-contractual expenses may be recoverable in RESTITUTION in some circumstances.   [JPL]

pre-emption In land law, a right of first refusal to buy land before it is sold to someone else. The position regarding protection of pre-emption rights against third parties is complex. In UNREGISTERED LAND, pre-emption rights are a type of ESTATE CONTRACT and registrable as a Class C (iv) LAND CHARGE (Land Charges Act 1972, s. 2(4)(iv)). However, a right of pre-emption may only be protected via registration as a land charge once the owner has declared his or her intention to sell the land (*Pritchard* v. *Briggs* [1980] Ch 338).

In registered land, the position is clearer, as pre-emption rights are considered proprietary regardless of whether the owner has declared an intention to sell (Land Registration Act 2002, s. 115). Therefore, once acquired, the right of pre-emption may be protected against third parties by placing a notice at the land registry against the registered title.   [DR]

See also OPTION TO PURCHASE.

pre-hearing assessment *See* PRE-HEARING REVIEW.

pre-hearing review (PHR) A hearing to deal with preliminary matters and issue interim orders and directions before a case comes before the EMPLOYMENT TRIBUNAL (see Rules 18 and 20 of the Employment Tribunals Regulations 2004) (Constitution and Rules of Procedure). The PHR must take place in public and each party must have the opportunity to put forward oral or written arguments, although no evidence is called. The Chair of the PHR must not be the Chair of the employment tribunal which hears and determines the case. At the PHR the Chair may order a party to pay a deposit not exceeding £500 if he or she considers that the contention put forward is arguable but has little chance of success. The Chair may also strike out a claim or defence if it is considered so weak as to be unarguable; and claims and responses may also be struck out or amended on the grounds that they, or the conduct of the proceedings, are vexatious or scandalous.   [MJ]

pre-sentence report A report prepared by the PROBATION SERVICE or the YOUTH OFFENDING TEAM to assist the court in determining the appropriate sentence to impose on an offender. A pre-sentence report is normally required if the court is considering imposing a custodial sentence or a COMMUNITY PENALTY with requirements. The report should include an assessment of the nature and seriousness of the offence, the offender's circumstances and his or her culpability.

[SN]

pre-trial review **1**. In criminal proceedings, a preliminary hearing at which the MAGISTRATE or DISTRICT JUDGE considers the issues before the court and fixes the timetable for the trial.

2. In civil cases, a final case management hearing that is sometimes used in complex multi-track cases. Where a pre-trial review is held, it will normally take place eight to ten days before trial.   [SN & JW]

See also CASE MANAGEMENT.

precatory trust *See* PRECATORY WORDS.

precatory words Words accompanying a GIFT of property, expressing the hope, faith, desire, request or confidence that the gift will be disposed of in a certain way. In such situations it is important to establish whether the donor intended to impose a legal obligation (by means of a precatory

TRUST) or only a moral obligation on the recipient. This is usually considered in the context of CERTAINTY OF INTENTION, where the courts were, until the mid-19th century, all too eager to impose a trust on LEGATEES, who were often widows whose husbands had expressed their confidence that the bequest would be used to support their children.

However, as noted in *Lambe* v. *Eames* (1870) LR 6 Ch App 597, imposing a trust in such situations was often 'a very cruel kindness indeed', reducing the widow to the role of a destitute TRUSTEE with no right to enjoy property whose beneficial ownership was thereby vested in the children. The courts consequently became reluctant to impose a trust unless it was clear that such a device had been intended, acknowledging that in many situations a donor trusts a donee, and thus has no desire to impose a trust upon her. This was in effect a retreat from formalism, in line with other developments such as the courts' current willingness to discover a trust in extremely informal circumstances, as occurred in *Paul* v. *Constance* [1977] 1 WLR 527 where, even though the parties did not actually know what a trust was, the court was satisfied that this was the type of property holding they had envisaged in their informal discussions.   [PK]

precautionary principle A moral, political and legal principle for managing the RISK of adverse effects of human activity on the environment, or human, animal or plant health under conditions of uncertainty. There is no single accepted definition of the precautionary principle, though the World Commission on the Ethics of Scientific Knowledge and Technology (COMEST) has produced the following 'working definition':

When human activities may lead to morally unacceptable harm that is scientifically plausible but uncertain, actions shall be taken to avoid or diminish that harm. Morally unacceptable harm refers to harm to humans or the environment that is

- threatening to human life or health, or
- serious and effectively irreversible, or

- inequitable to present or future generations, or
- imposed without adequate consideration of the human rights of those affected.

The principle marks a significant but controversial shift in perceptions about the proper role of law in contexts like environmental regulation, health and safety and food safety. Whereas the role of law was traditionally shaped around conventional, reactive, civil liability obligations, such as 'polluter pays', the precautionary principle operates on the assumption that, given the scope and scale of risks involved in many human activities, the law must have a much more strongly preventative function. In this way it is sometimes said that the precautionary principle represents the political and legal construction of a 'better safe than sorry' policy towards environmental and other risks.

The principle has become widely used in international laws and conventions. Within the UNITED NATIONS system, it is included in the 1992 Rio Declaration on Environment and Development, the UN Framework Convention on Climate Change and the Cartagena Protocol on Biosafety (2000). It is also included as Article 5.7 of the WORLD TRADE ORGANIZATION's Agreement on the Application of Sanitary and Phytosanitary Measures (SPS Agreement) of 1994.

Moreover, the precautionary principle forms a significant part of the EUROPEAN COMMUNITY's (EC) risk assessment (a scientific task) and risk management (a managerial and legal task) framework. In particular, it was established as a guiding principle of EC environmental law by the TREATY ON EUROPEAN UNION (1992). The EC's approach to the precautionary principle has been set out in a detailed European Commission Communication (COM (2000) I, 2 February 2000) which states that (para. 6), 'where action is deemed necessary, measures based on the precautionary principle should be: proportional to the chosen level of protection, non-discriminatory in their application, consistent with similar measures already taken, based on an examination of the potential benefits and costs of action or lack of action …, subject to review, in the light of new scientific data, and capable of assigning responsibility for producing the scientific evidence necessary for a more comprehensive risk assessment.'

Further guidance has also come from the COURT OF FIRST INSTANCE in Case T-13/99, *Pfizer Animal Heath SA* v. *Council of the European Union* [2002] ECR II-3305, which observed that, in light of the fact that 'neither the Treaty nor the SECONDARY LEGISLATION' provided a definition of the precautionary principle, risk assessment for the purposes of applying the principle must comprise a 'two-fold task'. This is, first, to determine 'what level of risk is deemed unacceptable' and secondly to conduct 'a scientific assessment of the risks'. Moreover the Court held that in this process the EC institutions enjoy 'a broad discretion, in particular when determining the level of risk deemed unacceptable for society'. [JW & MON]

See also NON-DISCRIMINATION; PROPORTIONALITY.

Further reading: COMEST, *The Precautionary Principle* (Paris: UNESCO, 2005); E. Fisher, J. Jones and R. von Schomberg (eds), *Implementing the Precautionary Principle: Perspectives and Prospects* (Cheltenham: Edward Elgar, 2006).

precedent 1. The system, especially in COMMON LAW countries, of treating decisions of higher COURTS OF RECORD as binding on lower courts in the same legal system, and sometimes on courts at the same level. In England, decisions of the HOUSE OF LORDS bind all courts below itself, but, by virtue of its own 1966 Practice Statement, the House cannot bind itself for the future. The decisions of the COURT OF APPEAL are, subject to certain limited exceptions, binding on itself, and on all lower courts.

2. The status of a single case as authority for a point of law. A distinctive feature of the COMMON LAW tradition is that a single decision of a superior court of record can and will have binding force on future courts. [AF]

See also PERSUASIVE AUTHORITY; *STARE DECISIS*.

predatory pricing The practice of pricing goods or services at such a low level that forces, or at least has the potential to force, smaller competitors out of the market. Where a **dominant business**, i.e. one that has a substantial or very substantial share of the market, engages in predatory pricing this will constitute an abuse of market position contrary to Article 82 of the EC Treaty and the Competition Act 1998. [JW]

predecessor in title A previous owner of an estate, right or interest. For example, if A sells 32 Fern Way to B, A is one of B's predecessors in title. [DR]

See also TITLE.

pregnancy *per alium* (Lat. pregnancy by another) One of the grounds on which a MARRIAGE is voidable is that, at the time of the marriage, the respondent was pregnant by some person other than the petitioner (Matrimonial Causes Act 1973, s. 12(f)). A petitioner may be barred, however, from relying on this ground if, at the time of the marriage, he knew about the pregnancy (s. 13(3)) or, if since discovering the circumstances of the pregnancy, knew he could apply to have the marriage ANNULLED but conducted himself so as to lead the respondent reasonably to believe that he would not do so and that it would be unjust to the respondent to grant the DECREE (s. 13 (1)). [AD]

See also VOIDABLE MARRIAGE.

preliminary enquiries In CONVEYANCING, enquiries made by the solicitor acting for the buyer prior to the exchange of contracts, in order to find out as much as possible from the seller about the property before the buyer enters into a legally binding CONTRACT FOR SALE.

Traditionally, preliminary enquiries were made by the buyer's solicitor on a wide range of issues, such as boundaries, disputes, notices affecting the property, services and guarantees affecting the property. However, under the National Conveyancing Protocol, introduced in 1990, the seller now fills in the SELLER'S PROPERTY INFORMATION FORM and Fixtures, Fittings and Contents form and provides these to the buyer's solicitor. It is then for the buyer's solicitor to raise any additional preliminary enquiries.

Preliminary enquiries are usually carried out at the same time as pre-contractual SEARCHES. It is crucial for the buyer's solicitor to obtain as much information about a property as possible, since the answer to a preliminary enquiry may drastically reduce the value of a property, e.g. by revealing the existence of a long-standing neighbour dispute that would seriously impair the prospective buyer's enjoyment of the property.   [DR]

preliminary measures   *See* PROVISIONAL MEASURES.

preliminary ruling A decision of the EURO-PEAN COURT OF JUSTICE pursuant to an ARTICLE 234 REFERENCE.   [JW]

pre-nuptial agreement An agreement between two parties, usually concluded in writing, made in advance of, and anticipation of, their MARRIAGE to each other. Such agreements may provide for how the parties wish to arrange their financial, care or other living arrangements during the time of their COHABITATION, or in the event of their SEPARATION or even DIVORCE. Pre-nuptial agreements are valid and enforceable in many countries, but are not strictly enforceable in England and Wales. Anticipating separation or divorce in an agreement made before marriage was thought to be contrary to public policy; however, recently the courts have considered such agreements in making orders for ANCILLARY RELIEF.   [AD]

See also ANTE-NUPTIAL SETTLEMENT; SEPARATION AGREEMENT.

preparatory hearing A pre-trial hearing which aims to facilitate the judicial management of cases heard in the CROWN COURT. The procedure was established by the Criminal Justice Act 1987, s. 7, for serious and complex frauds. The concept was extended by the Criminal Procedure and Investigations Act 1996, s. 29, to encompass any complex or lengthy case which a judge considers would substantially benefit from such a hearing. A range of matters can be dealt with, including ADMISSIBILITY issues, without requiring the JURY to attend.   [SN]

prerogative of mercy The prerogative of mercy is an aspect of the royal prerogative and consists of the powers to grant **pardons** and to enter a *NOLLE PROSEQUI*. A free pardon removes all the consequences of an offence, but not the conviction itself. A pardon may also take the form of a commutation of sentence, or a REMISSION or partial remission of sentence. A *nolle prosequi* has the effect of stopping legal proceedings.   [BF]

prerogative orders Formerly called 'prerogative writs', there are three prerogative orders available to the administrative court under rules now contained in CPR Part 54 and used to control the exercise of powers by public bodies. These are (a) A QUASHING ORDER (formerly *certiorari*), enabling the court to override or 'quash' decisions already taken; (b) A prohibiting order (formerly the writ of prohibition), preventing the body from taking a decision which, once taken, would be capable of being quashed; and (c) A MANDATORY ORDER (formerly *mandamus*), which compels the body to take a required action where not to do so would be unlawful. The principle on which these orders operate was set out by Lord Atkin in *R* v. *Electricity Commissioners, ex parte London Electricity Joint Committee Company* (1920) Ltd [1924] 1 KB 171: 'Whenever any body of persons having legal authority to determine questions affecting the rights of subjects, and having the duty to act judicially, act in excess of their legal authority, they are subject to the controlling jurisdiction of the [court] exercised in these writs.'   [MS]

prerogative writs (obsolete) *See* PREROGA-TIVE ORDERS.

prescribed limit (blood alcohol)   *See* DRUNKEN DRIVING.

prescription The acquisition of an EASE-MENT or PROFIT À PRENDRE, as a result of the uninterrupted use of land over a long period of time. Prescription is based on the fictional presumption that the right being claimed was expressly granted at some time in the past, as evidenced by the fact that there is a long-term user of the right. There are three methods of establishing the existence of an easement or profit by prescription: (a) common law prescription; (b) the doctrine of lost modern grant; and (c) the Prescription Act 1832.

Under each of the above, there are three general conditions that must be met in order to establish prescription: (a) the use must be 'as of right', meaning that the right must have been exercised openly, and must not have been exercised by force or with permission (otherwise it would be a licence); (b) the right must be acquired by a fee simple owner against a fee simple owner; and (c) the use must be continuous, i.e. the use must be regular enough for a reasonable person to know that a continuous right is being asserted (*Hollins* v. *Verney* (1884) 13 QBD 304).

The main difference between the methods relates to the length of time the claimant must establish he has been using the right for. Under **common law prescription**, the claimant must establish that he has been using the land since time immemorial, specifically since 1189. The courts have since adopted the rule that use for 20 years or more raises a presumption of use since 1189, but this presumption may be rebutted by evidence that at any time since 1189 the right could not or did not exist. Therefore, it is extremely difficult to establish common law prescription.

Under the doctrine of **lost modern grant**, the courts developed the rule that if the claimant can establish that he has been using the right for 20 years or more, the court will presume that the right was expressly granted by deed, but that this deed has been lost. This presumption cannot be rebutted by proving that no grant has been made, but it can be rebutted by proving that during the period in which it is alleged the grant was made, the grant could not legally have been made (e.g. if there was no person capable of making the grant, or if the two pieces of land were owned by the same person). Although once described as a 'revolting fiction' (*Angus & Co.* v. *Dalton* (1877) 3 QBD 85 at

94, *per* Lush J), this method has been used to establish the existence of an easement (*Bridle* v. *Ruby* [1989] QB 169).

Under the **Prescription Act 1832** (PA 1832), there is a short period and a long period of use which must be established, as well as separate rules relating to the right to light. The short period is 20 years for easements and 30 years for profits, minus periods during which the owner of the SERVIENT TENEMENT was an infant, a patient under the Mental Health Act 1983 or a TENANT FOR LIFE. The long period is 40 years for easements and 60 years for profits, minus periods during which the servient land was held by a tenant for life or a tenant under a lease for more than three years. The advantage of the long period is that a claim can only be defeated by evidence of written permission. In order to establish a right under the PA 1832, there are two further conditions in addition to the three general conditions listed above. First, the period of use must be the period 'next before action', meaning that if the use ceases before the claimant brings an action to rely on the right, the right will not be established. Secondly, the use must have been exercised without interruption. If the use has been interrupted and the owner of the DOMINANT TENEMENT has submitted to that interruption or failed to communicate discontent with that interruption for more than one year, the claim will fail (*Dance* v. *Triplow* (1991) 64 P & CR 1).

In 1966 the 14th Report of the Law Reform Committee (Cmnd 3100) recommended the abolition of prescription, to be replaced by a simpler method of a single period of 12 years' use. However, these proposals have not been implemented.   [DR]

Further reading: Judith-Anne Mackenzie and Mary Phillips, *Textbook on Land Law*, 11th edn (Oxford: Oxford University Press, 2006); Kevin Gray and Susan Francis Gray, *Elements of Land Law*, 5th edn (Oxford: Oxford University Press, 2008).

President of the Family Division The administrative head of the FAMILY DIVISION of the HIGH COURT. He or she also presides over panels in the COURT OF APPEAL. Following the Constitutional Reform Act 2005, the President of the Family Division also holds ex officio the post of 'Head of Family Justice' (s. 9) and under the same section, a Deputy Head may be appointed from among the Court of Appeal judges to assist the President with his or her duties. [AF]

See also PRESIDENT OF THE QUEEN'S BENCH DIVISION.

President of the Queen's Bench Division Head of the QUEEN'S BENCH DIVISION of the HIGH COURT, responsible for the work of the Division. Prior to the Constitutional Reform Act 2005, the LORD CHIEF JUSTICE held this role. The President of the Queen's Bench Division (as with other Heads of Division) is appointed by the Queen, on the recommendation of the Prime Minister on advice from the LORD CHANCELLOR. [AF]

See also MASTER OF THE ROLLS; PRESIDENT OF THE FAMILY DIVISION.

presiding judge A PUISNE JUDGE assigned to one of the six CROWN COURT circuits in England and Wales. Under the Courts and Legal Services Act 1990, each circuit operates under the administration of two Presiding Judges. In addition, a Senior Presiding Judge is appointed from the Lords Justices of Appeal. [AF]

See also COURT OF APPEAL.

presumption An assumption or supposition that the law requires. A presumption can generally be overridden or **rebutted** by evidence to the contrary (e.g. the PRESUMPTION OF DEATH can be rebutted by evidence that the person presumed dead is actually alive). Although the law sometimes refers to the existence of **irrebuttable presumptions** (see, for example, *DOLI INCAPAX*), the term is logically a misnomer and such presumptions are better understood as rules of law. [JW]

presumption of death The Matrimonial Causes Act 1973 (s. 19) permits a spouse (the Civil Partnership Act 2004 contains a similar provision for civil partners) to petition the court for a DECREE of presumption of death and DISSOLUTION of the MARRIAGE if he or she has reasonable grounds for supposing that the other spouse is dead. The fact

that for a period of seven years or more the spouse has been missing, and the petitioner has no reason to believe that the spouse is living, shall be evidence of death until the contrary is proved. A decree of presumption of death and dissolution of marriage means that the spouse will be able to contract a legally valid subsequent marriage, even if the other spouse later reappears. [AD]

presumption of due execution A presumption that a WILL has been made with the proper formalities, under the Wills Act 1837, s. 9. It may not be clear from the face of the will whether the correct formalities have been observed; for instance, the document may have the signature of the TESTATOR, and two other signatures, but no indication of whether these other signatures are those of attesting witnesses, or whether the testator signed in their presence. In this situation, the court may apply this presumption. It will not be applied if the circumstances show that the will was not duly executed. It will be applied where there is no proof one way or the other, but it seems more probable than not the correct formalities were observed. [CM]

See also ATTESTATION.

presumption of innocence The principle that the prosecution in a criminal case generally bears the burden of proving every issue. There are two broad exceptions to this. First, a defendant who raises INSANITY or insane AUTOMATISM as a defence, or who argues that they are UNFIT TO PLEAD, bears the burden of proving it. Secondly, a statutory provision may expressly or impliedly place the burden of proving a particular issue on the defendant. [ALTC]

presumption of legitimacy The presumption of paternity in favour of a married man whose wife gives birth to a child. That is, if a married woman gives birth, it is presumed in law that her husband is the father and therefore that the child is legitimate. The presumption can be rebutted by 'evidence which shows that it is more probable than not' that the husband is not the father (Family Law Reform Act 1969, s. 26). This can be circumstantial evidence; however, more often it is DNA or scientific tests. In any proceedings in which the parentage of a child is at issue, the court can order scientific (DNA) tests to be taken by the parties, and if a claimant who wishes to rely on a presumption of legitimacy fails to undertake those tests without reasonable cause, the court may dismiss the claim without evidence of rebuttal of the presumption. As the legal status of legitimacy has decreased significantly in importance, courts in recent cases have doubted the strength of the presumption in favour of determining scientifically the truth of the child's paternity. [AD]

See also ILLEGITIMACY; LEGITIMACY; LEGITIMATION.

presumption of sanity The criminal law operates a strong presumption of sanity, and so a defendant wishing to claim that they are insane bears the burden of proving so, on a balance of probabilities (see *M'Naghten* [1843–60] All ER Rep 229). [BF]

See also INSANITY.

presumption of survivorship *See* COMMORIENTES.

presumptive evidence *See* PRIMA FACIE EVIDENCE.

previous convictions CONVICTIONS for an earlier offence that may become relevant in later court hearings. Generally previous convictions are only admissible for the purpose of determining sentence; however, there are exceptions under the Criminal Justice Act 2003, whereby a defendant's convictions for previous offences may, under certain conditions, be admitted as evidence determining guilt. The 2003 Act also imposes a restriction on the ability of defence lawyers to CROSS-EXAMINE prosecution witnesses about their own previous convictions. [SN]

previous dealing A prior CONTRACT between the parties. A term, such as an EXEMPTION CLAUSE, may be incorporated into a contract on the basis that the parties had previously contracted on a consistent basis

including this term. In these circumstances the other side cannot claim that they have no notice of its existence. [JPL]

previous sexual experience The sexual experience of the complainant of a sexual offence on occasions other than that which is the subject of the present complaint. The ADMISSIBILITY of EVIDENCE of previous sexual experience is governed by the Youth Justice and Criminal Evidence Act 1999, s. 41, as applied in *R* v. *A* [2001] 2 AC 45. [ALTC]

previous statement A statement made by a witness on an earlier occasion. There are specific requirements, for example in the Criminal Justice Act 2003, governing the ADMISSIBILITY of such a statement. [ALTC]

price The monetary CONSIDERATION for the transfer of property. In a CONTRACT for the SALE OF GOODS where the price is not fixed in the contract and there is no contractual mechanism for fixing it, the court will imply a reasonable price (Sale of Goods Act 1979, s. 8). [JPL]

prima facie **case** A case that would, if uncontradicted, be sufficient for a judgment to be made in favour of the party presenting the case. If the prosecution in criminal proceedings fails to establish a *prima facie* case, the defence is entitled to a ruling of NO CASE TO ANSWER. [ALTC]

prima facie **evidence** EVIDENCE that would be sufficient to establish a fact unless contradicted. [ALTC]

primary disclosure (obsolete) An aspect of the superseded framework of prosecution disclosure. For the present framework, see DISCLOSURE OF EVIDENCE IN CRIMINAL CASES. [ALTC]

primary evidence EVIDENCE that, on its face, provides the best evidence available. For example, the original of a document rather than a copy of it. [ALTC]

See also BEST-EVIDENCE RULE.

primary facts 'Facts which are observed by witnesses and proved by [ORAL EVIDENCE] or facts proved by the production of a thing itself, such as an original document' (see *Metropolitan Borough of Battersea* v. *British*

Iron and Steel Research Association [1949] 1 KB 434, 436).   [ALTC]

principal **1**. In criminal law, the actual perpetrator of a crime, as contrasted with a **secondary party**, i.e. any person who aids or abets the principal in the commission of the offence.

2. In financial agreements, the original sum of money lent or invested, as distinguished from the interest to be paid.

3. In AGENCY, the person for whom an AGENT acts.   [JW]

principal mansion house The main house on land which is subject to a SETTLE-MENT, governed by the Settled Land Act 1925 (SLA 1925). Whether or not a house is a principal mansion house is a question of fact in each case, but SLA 1925, s. 65(2), states that a house is **not** a principal mansion house where it is occupied as a farmhouse, or the site of the house and its land does not exceed 25 acres. It is possible for one house to replace another as the principal mansion house on a settled estate, where that house has been adapted for such use by the tenant for life (see *Re Feversham Settled Estate* [1938] 2 All ER 210).

Under SLA 1925, s. 65(1), where a settlement came into operation prior to 1926, the TENANT FOR LIFE's power of sale may only be exercised in relation to a principal mansion house with the consent of the SET-TLED LAND ACT TRUSTEES, or the court. For post-1926 settlements, consent is required only if the terms of the settlement lay down such a requirement.   [DR]

Principal Registry of the Family Division Located in London, this 'family court' has the jurisdiction of a DIVORCE county court, a CARE CENTRE and a FAMILY HEARING CENTRE. This means that it can hear divorce matters, and both private and public law matters under the Children Act 1989.   [AD]

See also DESIGNATED FAMILY JUDGE; FAMILY COUNTY COURTS.

Principles of Better Regulation In 1997 the BETTER REGULATION TASK FORCE identified five principles which it proposed as a measure for judging and enhancing the quality of regulation. These principles of better regulation are **transparency**, **accountability**, PROPORTIONALITY, **consistency** and **targeting**. The continuing implementation of these principles in state legislation and the work of regulatory agencies is now overseen by the BETTER REGULATION EXECUTIVE. [JW]

priority notice In UNREGISTERED LAND, a notice given by a person to the Land Charges department, stating an intention to register an interest as a LAND CHARGE. A priority notice must be issued at least 15 days before the land charge is to be registered and has the effect that if the interest is duly registered within 30 days from the issue of the priority notice, the land charge will have effect as though registered on the date the interest was created (Land Charges Act, s. 11). For example, if X enters into negotiations with Y to acquire an ESTATE CONTRACT, X may issue a priority notice stating that he intends to register the interest as a Class C (iv) land charge. Once the estate contract is finalized, if X registers that interest within 30 days of the issue of the priority notice, the registration has effect from the date the estate contract was created.
                                                  [DR]

priority of mortgages Where there is more than one MORTGAGE on the same property, the priority of mortgages is the order in which the mortgages will be paid off on the sale of that property.

For REGISTERED LAND, the priority of mortgages runs in date order, so that the earliest registered mortgage has priority over later mortgages. However, if a mortgage is not registered, later registered mortgages will have priority over it.

For unregistered land, the lender on a first mortgage usually holds the title deeds and will therefore have priority over subsequent mortgages. Subsequent LEGAL MORTGAGES must be registered as a Class C (i) LAND CHARGE and subsequent EQUITABLE MORTGAGES must be protected as a Class C (iii) land charge. Registered mortgages take priority in date order and failure to register a mortgage means that later registered mortgages will take priority.

The priority of mortgages becomes

important if the proceeds on the sale of a property are less than the aggregate sum owed on each of the mortgages. In this situation, the last in the line of priorities will not be paid off in full and the lender will have to pursue the original borrower for the remainder of the debt due. [DR]

privacy The right to a private life, as set out in Article 8 of the EUROPEAN CONVENTION ON HUMAN RIGHTS (ECHR). The right is broad-ranging, but includes protecting the confidentiality of one's personal and business communications (letters, telephone calls, emails etc.), the quiet enjoyment of one's home or office, the right to a FAMILY LIFE, and the right to engage privately in consensual and non-violent sexual practices regardless of one's sexual orientation. In a recent extension, the right to privacy under the ECHR is now also said to encompass an individual's right to protection of his or her reputation; see *Pfeifer* v. *Austria* [2007] ECHR 12566/03 (15 November 2007). Under the Convention, privacy is a QUALIFIED RIGHT; consequently it is subject to a number of PUBLIC INTEREST justifications for interference.

Although the right to a private life is protected as a Convention right under the UK's Human Rights Act 1998, the UK courts have so far tended to be cautious in applying it beyond the established, piecemeal bounds of BREACH OF CONFIDENCE, DEFAMATION, statutory data protection and similar rights, and a number of English decisions have expressly rejected the arguments for a generic TORT of invasion of privacy; see *A* v. *B plc* [2002] 3 WLR 542, and the HOUSE OF LORDS' decision in *Wainwright* v. *The Home Office* [2003] 3 WLR 1137. Nevertheless, as the Strasbourg jurisprudence, in cases like *Peck* v. *UK* (2003) 36 EHRR 41 and *Von Hannover* v. *Germany* (2005) 40 EHRR 1, continues to extend privacy protection into settings outside the scope of existing English breach of confidence laws, this approach may prove harder to maintain. [JW]

private international law See CONFLICT OF LAWS.

private law That part of the law that deals with matters between private individuals, such as CONTRACT law, TORT, employment, etc. It may be contrasted with those parts of the law that concern the government and constitution or the legal relationship between citizens and the state, and are referred to as PUBLIC LAW. [JW]

private life See PRIVACY.

Private Member's Bill See BILL.

private nuisance An unlawful interference with a person's use or enjoyment of his LAND, or some right over or in connection with it. The claimant must either be in occupation of, or have some property right over the land affected by the nuisance in order to bring an action: see *Hunter* v. *Canary Wharf* [1997] 2 All ER 426. The main remedies for private nuisance are DAMAGES and/or an INJUNCTION. In some limited circumstances there may also be a right for the claimant to **abate** (i.e. remove) the nuisance. Where a statutory provision has been introduced to deal with activities that would otherwise constitute a private nuisance, the action should be brought under the STATUTE, not at COMMON LAW. [HJ]

See also PUBLIC NUISANCE; STATUTORY NUISANCE.

privatization The transfer of state-owned entities (for example, utilities) to private ownership. The process is usually associated with liberal market political ideologies, which hold that greater efficiency will be achieved when a business is subject to market pressures rather than protected by state subsidies. Other motivations towards privatization include the desire to allow a business improved access to finance and to free a business from political interference.

Privatization may be said to represent the most thoroughgoing example of DEREGULATION. In this regard, it is noteworthy that the privatization of former state-owned monopolies has (almost paradoxically) given rise to an exponential growth in REGULATION and regulatory agencies, which are required to ensure that a market emerges where none has existed previously. That said, however, the role of regulators in this regard is seen as a transitional arrangement until market forces are able to operate.   [JP]

privilege 'The right of a party to refuse to disclose a document or produce a document or to refuse to answer questions on the ground of some special interest recognized by law' (see Civil Procedure Rules, glossary). Generally, therefore, a person entitled to claim privilege is not required to disclose the privileged material or to give EVIDENCE of that material.   [ALTC]

See also DOCTOR–PATIENT CONFIDENTIALITY; LEGAL PROFESSIONAL PRIVILEGE; PARLIAMENTARY PRIVILEGE.

privilege against self-incrimination A proposition that a person cannot be coerced, with the threat of punishment, into giving evidence against him- or herself. Thus, when W testifies in D's trial, the privilege would allow W to refuse to answer questions which would incriminate him or her.

The privilege is not absolute. The Criminal Evidence Act 1898, s. 1(2), states that an accused who gives evidence in his own defence can be asked questions in CROSS-EXAMINATION regarding the offence with which he is charged. Moreover, certain statutes require parties to provide particular pieces of (possibly incriminating) information, with penalties for non-compliance. The Road Traffic Act 1988, s. 172, requires the keeper of a vehicle to provide evidence as to who was driving the vehicle, when it is alleged that the person driving has committed one of a range of driving offences. Non-compliance with this requirement is an offence. The PRIVY COUNCIL in *Brown* v. *Stott* [2001] 2 WLR 817 took the view that the use in evidence of the admission provided under s. 172 was not such as to make the trial unfair within the meaning of Article 6 of the EUROPEAN CONVENTION ON HUMAN RIGHTS. The relatively light penalties available under s. 172 (a FINE, ENDORSEMENT and possible DISQUALIFICATION) were a factor in the decision, and can be contrasted with *Heaney and McGuinness* v. *Ireland* [2001] Crim LR 481, a decision relating to the law on terrorism, in which there was the

possibility of imprisonment for non-compliance with the relevant information-seeking provision; the EUROPEAN COURT OF HUMAN RIGHTS found a violation of Article 6.
                                                       [BF]

See also RIGHT TO SILENCE.

privileged will A WILL made by one person in one of the following categories: (a) any soldier (which for this purpose includes a member of the RAF) being on actual military service; (b) Royal Naval personnel on actual military service; and (c) a mariner or seaman at sea. A person falling into one of these categories can make a will without any formalities at all, and the testator can be under the age of 18 years. The reason for the privilege is said to be that it would be unfair and unrealistic to require people in these situations to observe normal legal requirements, when they may not have access to legal advice for long periods.

Although no formalities have to be observed, the testator is still required to have ANIMUS TESTANDI and proving that may be a matter of considerable difficulty. [CM]

privity of contract The doctrine of privity of CONTRACT provides that a person who is not a party to a contract cannot acquire any rights under that contract or be subject to any of its burdens. It followes that only those who had provided CONSIDERATION for a PROMISE could enforce that promise, even if the third party was intended to benefit under the contract. Third parties could not derive rights from a contract between others. The privity doctrine remains the general rule in English law but the Contracts (Rights of Third Parties) Act 1999 allows third parties to enforce rights in their favour despite the fact that they are not parties to the contract and have not provided consideration. However, it is possible to expressly exclude the effect of the Act.   [JPL]

See also THIRD PARTY RIGHTS.

privity of estate The relationship between landlord and tenant, where the tenant holds land directly from the landlord, entitling each party to enforce their respective rights and obligations against one another; for example, if L grants a 21-year lease to T, the relationship between the parties is one of privity of estate (as well as PRIVITY OF CONTRACT) and both parties will be able to enforce the COVENANTS entered into under the lease against one another.

If L subsequently sells his REVERSION to L2 and T assigns his lease to T2, L2 and T2 will have privity of estate and will be able to enforce the covenants entered into under the original lease against each other, despite the fact that they were not the original parties to the lease. If T2 later assigns the lease to T3, privity of estate will then exist between L2 and T3. This process of transferral of the rights and obligations as landlord and tenant under the original lease can continue indefinitely until the term of the lease expires.

If, however, in the original example, T sublets part of the property to ST, a new relationship of privity of estate is created between T and ST, but there is no privity of estate between L and ST, because ST does not hold directly from L. This means that L can enforce covenants against T and T can enforce covenants against ST, but L cannot enforce covenants against ST. [DR]

Privy Council The modern Privy Council descends from the ancient Curia or Royal Council that gave advice to the monarch. Today it is the means by which interdepartmental agreement is reached on aspects of government business which, for historical or other reasons, are conducted by Ministers as Privy Counsellors rather than Departmental Ministers. This includes business conducted under powers of the ROYAL PREROGATIVE, and those areas where statute has given law-making powers to the Privy Council, to be exercised by ORDER IN COUNCIL.

The head of the Privy Council is the **Lord President of the Council**, who is one of the Great Officers of State of the UK. The Lord President will be a member of the Cabinet and, normally, the Leader of either the HOUSE OF LORDS or the HOUSE OF COMMONS. Appointment to the Privy Council is made by the SOVEREIGN on the advice of the Prime Minister. There is no limit to the number of Privy Counsellors holding office, and as the appointment is, in practice, for life, there are many more Privy Counsellors than actually take part in the activities of the Council. Most active members of the Council are senior politicians, including the Prime Minister, members of Cabinet, the Leader of the Opposition, and First Ministers of the devolved governments. Senior judges – Lords of Appeal in Ordinary, judges of the COURT OF APPEAL of England and Wales and of Northern Ireland, and judges of the Inner House of the COURT OF SESSION – are also nominated to the Privy Council, and may sit judicially as members of the JUDICIAL COMMITTEE OF THE PRIVY COUNCIL. [MS]

probate The grant made by the court to an EXECUTOR appointed by WILL. It comes in two forms, **common form** and **solemn form**. Common form, as the name implies, is the usual method of proceeding in the administration of the ESTATE. Although the authority of the executor stems from the will, he or she cannot commence court proceedings without obtaining a grant, and if, therefore, someone holding assets refused to pay them to the executor, he or she would have to obtain probate before they could force payment. It is routine for people holding assets, for example, banks or building societies, to require a grant to be obtained before they will pay over the money, unless the amount involved is small.

Probate in solemn form is much less frequent, and is normally sought only when there is some doubt as to the validity of the will, or where the executor anticipates that the will may be challenged. Upon the grant being obtained in solemn form, the will cannot afterwards be challenged by any party to the proceedings, nor by persons who knew of the proceedings but did not challenge them at the time. [CM]

probation hostels These are now known as **approved premises**. They are supervised by the National Probation Service, and house offenders who have been placed there by courts as a condition of a community order, or by the Parole Board on licence. Approved premises are intended to offer a structured regime for residents, including an overnight curfew, in order that they can be monitored more effectively. [BF]

probation officer A member of the PROBATION SERVICE; the person responsible for preparing PRE-SENTENCE REPORTS which assist the court in sentencing and for enforcing community orders made by the courts. [SN]

probation service The National Probation Service for England and Wales is a law enforcement agency and independent public authority under the supervision of the HOME OFFICE. It works with offenders and the court and supports MAGISTRATES and judges in their sentencing decisions by producing about 246,000 PRE-SENTENCE REPORTS and 20,000 BAIL information reports each year. It also provides supervision and assessment of offenders serving community sentences as well as those on early release from prison and on post-custody licences.

Following the Social Work (Scotland) Act 1968, the probation service in Scotland was merged with other LOCAL AUTHORITY welfare services, and is now designated as Criminal Justice Social Work Services. [JW]

procedural impropriety *See* JUDICIAL REVIEW.

procedural justice Making decisions according to fair and proper processes; thus a feature of – many would say a synonym for – FORMAL JUSTICE. Procedural justice must be contrasted with SUBSTANTIVE JUSTICE, since the difficult question for procedural justice is whether we are justified in considering ourselves bound by legitimate authority to comply with a judgment that we know or strongly believe to be in error as regards the substantive merits. As Fuller has argued, we tend to want a morally fair or just procedure and may consider the procedure justified only if it does tend to produce substantive justice. [JW]

procedural law *See* ADJECTIVE LAW; SUBSTANTIVE LAW.

procedural naturalism A variant of NATURAL LAW, associated particularly with Lon Fuller, that focuses not on law's substantive content but rather on the procedural requirements for a functioning legal system. While it is accordingly less contentious than substantive variants, it is open to the criticism that it is unable to deal with the problem of procedurally correct but nevertheless evil legal systems. [JP]

proces-verbale (Fr. the transactions or report of proceedings) The official record of meetings, usually of international conferences leading to the signing of a TREATY, which are maintained and compiled by the secretariat of the conference. These official records do not have any legal force *per se*, but they may be useful as supplementary means of treaty interpretation in accordance with Article 32 of the 1969 Vienna Convention on the Law of Treaties. There possibly exists an overlap between official records designated as *TRAVAUX PREPARATOIRES* and records classified as *proces-verbale* and treating these as the same type of document for the purpose of supplementary treaty interpretation avoids hair-splitting distinctions. [IB]

procreation *See* FAMILY LIFE.

Procurator Fiscal The public prosecutor in Scotland. There is a Procurator Fiscal (and deputies as appropriate) for every sheriffdom in Scotland. Reports of crimes are made by the police to the local Procurator Fiscal and to the Crown Office (that is, the office of the LORD ADVOCATE). A decision is then taken as to whether prosecution would be in the public interest. In most cases, the decision will be taken by the Procurator Fiscal, with only the more serious cases being discussed with the Crown Office.

Less serious crimes are dealt with under summary procedure or 'on complaint' in either the local DISTRICT COURT or SHERIFF COURT. More serious crimes are dealt with under solemn procedure or 'on indictment' in either the local sheriff court or the HIGH COURT OF JUSTICIARY. The Procurator Fiscal may appear in the district court and the sheriff court and will thus deal with cases under summary procedure and such cases under solemn procedure as are dealt with by the sheriff court. [JP]

procuring 'To produce by endeavour. You procure a thing by setting out to see that it happens and taking the appropriate steps to produce that happening' *per* Lord Widgery CJ in *Attorney General's Reference (No. 1 of 1975)* [1975] QB 773 at p. 779. Thus it denotes one form of behaviour constituting the ACTUS REUS of being an ACCESSORY.

A secondary party may procure the commission of an offence without the PRINCIPAL knowing about the procuring. If D spikes P's drink, knowing that P is about to drive, it can be said that D procures P's offence of driving with excess alcohol, even though P is not aware of the spiking. [BF]

See also AID AND ABET.

procuring breach of contract Intentionally inducing another to break a CONTRACT he has made with a third party. Procuring a breach of contract constitutes a TORT (knowing interference with contractual rights) which is actionable by the party who suffers loss due to the breach; for example, in *Lumley* v. *Gye* (1853) 2 E & B 216, a singer was induced to break her contract to perform at a theatre and the theatre owner was able to sue for DAMAGES. [JPL]

profit à prendre A right to enter another person's land to take a profit of the soil or a portion of the soil itself. Examples include: (a) the profit of pasture (the right to graze animals); (b) the profit of PISCARY (the right to take fish); (c) the profit of TURBARY (the right to cut turf or peat); (d) the profit of ESTOVERS (the right to take wood for use as fuel or for domestic or agricultural purposes).

A profit may be a **several profit** (enjoyed by a person to the exclusion of others) or a **profit in common** (enjoyed in common with others, see RIGHTS OF COMMON). Furthermore, a profit may be either a **profit appurtenant to land** or a **profit IN GROSS**.

A **profit appurtenant to land** is a profit that is attached to the ownership of land

and may be acquired by grant or by PRESCRIPTION. Profits appurtenant to land must possess the four characteristics of easements and are limited by reference to the needs of the DOMINANT TENEMENT; for example, if a person owns a profit of piscary appurtenant to land, the number of fish must be limited to the needs of the dominant tenement.

A **profit in gross** exists independently of land and can be exploited commercially, assigned and dealt with according to the ordinary rules of property; for example, a profit of piscary in gross would entitle the owner of that profit to take fish in order to sell them. [DR]

See also EASEMENT; SERVIENT TENEMENT.

prohibited degrees of relationship In English law, a MARRIAGE or CIVIL PARTNERSHIP between people closely related either by blood or marriage, that is, those prohibited degrees of relationship, is void. [AD]

See also CONSANGUINEOUS MARRIAGE; VOID MARRIAGE.

prohibited steps order An order made under the Children Act 1989 that no step that is specified in the order (e.g. removing the child from the country or making a unilateral decision about medical treatment for the child), and which a person with PARENTAL RESPONSIBILITY would normally be able to take, may be taken by any person without the consent of the court (s. 8). The order can be made against anyone, irrespective of whether they have parental responsibility for the child. The court will always decide these matters with the welfare of the child as its paramount consideration. [AD & FK]

See also CONTACT ORDER; RESIDENCE ORDER; SPECIFIC ISSUES ORDER; WELFARE PRINCIPLE.

prohibited weapon Prohibited weapons are a type of firearm. They may or may not be lethal, and are specified in the Firearms Act 1968, s. 5. It is an offence to possess, purchase, acquire, manufacture, sell or transfer prohibited weapons without the authority of the Secretary of State. [BF]

See also OFFENSIVE WEAPON.

prohibition (obsolete) One of the 'prerogative writs' by which the courts controlled the exercise of powers by public authorities. See PREROGATIVE ORDERS. [MS]

prohibition notice If a Health and Safety Executive inspector or LOCAL AUTHORITY Environmental Health Officer considers that activity at a workplace is being, or is likely to be, carried on in such a manner that may occasion serious personal injury, they may issue a prohibition notice, which directs the person on whom the notice is served to remedy the defect before the activity is recommenced; see the Health and Safety at Work etc. Act 1974, s. 22. Appeals against the issue of prohibition notices lie to the EMPLOYMENT TRIBUNALS; see the Health and Safety at Work etc. Act 1974, s. 24. [MJ]

prohibition order An order of the court preventing an inferior court or TRIBUNAL or other public body from acting beyond the scope of its powers (*ULTRA VIRES*). A prohibition order differs from a QUASHING ORDER in that it works prospectively, by requiring the relevant body not to do something it has in contemplation, whereas a quashing order invalidates a past unlawful action. [JW]

See also INJUNCTION.

promise An undertaking expressing an intention to perform or refrain from performing some act. A CONTRACT is traditionally alleged to be based on the binding nature of voluntarily assumed promises. In order to be legally enforceable, a promise must be supported by CONSIDERATION or be contained in a DEED. [JPL]

Further reading: C. Fried, *Contract as Promise: a theory of contractual obligation* (Cambridge MA: Harvard University Press, 1981).

promissory estoppel An equitable doctrine that enables a promise to alter future conduct in respect of a contractual obligation to have limited, defensive enforceability, despite the absence of CONSIDERATION to support it. The doctrine operates on the basis that the promisee has acted in reliance on the promise, so that it would be unfair for the promisor to go back on, or deny, the promise at this time. There is no require-

ment that the promisee must have acted to his or her detriment. Promissory estoppel applies only to promises made to alter the terms of existing CONTRACTS. In English law, it can be used only as a defence and not as the basis for a claim; its effect is to suspend rather than extinguish the right to revert to the position before the alteration promise was made. [JPL]

proof The process of establishing the truth of an assertion. [ALTC]

proper law of the contract The GOVERNING LAW of an agreement identified according to COMMON LAW rules. Courts in the United Kingdom are required by the terms of the Contracts (Applicable Law) Act 1990 to apply the provisions of the Rome Convention 1980, unless the relationship between the parties falls within one of the exclusions provided for in the Convention. Consequently the proper law is now largely redundant except in cases such as ARBITRATION and RESTITUTION. In those cases, the courts are looking for, in the absence of an acceptable CHOICE OF LAW by the parties, a close connection between the legal relationship and a legal system. [RE]

See also ARBITRATION AGREEMENT; *LEX CAUSAE*.

property adjustment order An order the court may make as ANCILLARY RELIEF on DIVORCE, DISSOLUTION of CIVIL PARTNERSHIP or ANNULMENT. Property adjustment orders include: (a) a transfer of property order (Matrimonial Causes Act 1973, s. 24(1)(a)) which directs one party to transfer specified property to the other party either for his or her benefit or for the benefit of a CHILD and is often made with regard to the FAMILY HOME; (b) a settlement of property order (MCA 1973, s. 24(1)(b)) which directs a party to settle property for the benefit of the other or a child; (c) an order varying a MARRIAGE SETTLEMENT (MCA 1973, s. 24(1)(c)); and (d) an order extinguishing rights under a marriage settlement (MCA 1973, s. 24(1)(d)). The Matrimonial Causes Act 1973 and the Civil Partnership Act 2004 provide a list of factors for the court to consider in determining applications. If the court makes a property adjustment order, it can also make an order for the sale of property, including a deferred sale, and for the division of the proceeds of sale between the parties. Property adjustment orders are often combined with FINANCIAL PROVISION ORDERS in order to achieve a fair division of assets between parties and to achieve a CLEAN BREAK. [AD]

proponent The party asserting a certain issue in a case. [ALTC]

proportionality 1. A GENERAL PRINCIPLE OF LAW, originating in German law, that has been adopted into COMMUNITY LAW. It means that the actions required by a piece of EUROPEAN COMMUNITY (EC) legislation must be proportionate to (i.e. must not go beyond the steps necessary to achieve) the objective that it pursues. Initially this concept developed through the case law of the EUROPEAN COURT OF JUSTICE. However, it is now defined and elaborated on in the 'Protocol on the application of the principles of SUBSIDIARITY and Proportionality', annexed to the TREATY OF AMSTERDAM.

2. Similarly, a central principle of the EUROPEAN CONVENTION ON HUMAN RIGHTS, particularly in respect of QUALIFIED RIGHTS. Whether or not such a right has been breached will depend on whether the actual interference with that right is proportionate to a legitimate aim of the STATE in imposing such interference. The test of proportionality is applied by British courts in the context of JUDICIAL REVIEW proceedings brought under the Human Rights Act 1998. Thus, in *A and Others* v. *Home Secretary* [2005] 2 AC 68, it was held that the administrative detention of foreign nationals under provisions of the Anti-terrorism, Crime and Security Act 2001 was a disproportionate response to the threat of terrorism, and contrary to Article 5 of the Convention.

3. As a consequence of the OVERRIDING OBJECTIVE of both the CIVIL PROCEDURE RULES and the CRIMINAL PROCEDURE RULES, the principle that the court must ensure that the process followed and resources allocated to a case are proportionate to that case's needs and fair to both parties. [MON & JW]

propounder The person seeking to have a WILL accepted as authentic, who will normally be the EXECUTOR named in the will, or someone seeking a grant of LETTERS OF ADMINISTRATION with the will annexed. [CM]

proprietary estoppel A means by which the courts both prevent a legal owner of LAND from insisting on their strict legal rights and recognize informal rights in land. It provides an equitable remedy where the owner has (a) made a representation to another person in connection with interests in land which that person (b) relies on (c) to their detriment. Examples of proprietary estoppel recognized by the courts include a man who carried out unpaid chores over many years for an elderly woman who had promised that 'she would see him right' (*Jennings* v. *Rice* [2003] EWCA Civ 159), and a man who gave up school to work for and eventually manage a farm on the understanding that he would inherit the business (*Gillett* v. *Holt* [2001] Ch 210). Courts can award claimants an interest in the land, a right to occupy the land, or monetary compensation when long-term occupation of the land is not an appropriate remedy. [HC & DR]

See also CONSTRUCTIVE TRUST.

proprietor The person with legal TITLE to property, i.e. the owner. [DR]

prosecution The institution or conduct of criminal proceedings against an accused person. A prosecution is commenced by laying an INFORMATION before a magistrate who issues a SUMMONS requiring the accused to appear before a MAGISTRATE to answer the allegation contained in the information. Alternatively, a prosecution is commenced when a suspect is charged with an offence. [SN]

prosecutor A lawyer appointed by the state to conduct the case against the accused. In England and Wales, the CROWN PROSECUTION SERVICE is responsible for prosecuting criminal cases investigated by the police. [SN]

protected child A CHILD who was being

cared for by carers who were not local authority FOSTER PARENTS and who had given notice under the Adoption Act 1976, s. 22, that they intended to apply for ADOPTION. This term is not used in the Adoption and Children Act 2002 which repealed the 1976 Act. [FK]

protected occupier The status of agricultural workers who fall within the scheme of protection of the Rent (Agriculture) Act 1976. No new protected occupancies can be created following the implementation of the Housing Act 1988. Protection extends to occupation of the house following cessation of employment as an agricultural worker, and the surviving spouse of a protected occupier succeeds to his or her status. [HC & DR]
See also ASSURED TENANCY.

protective award By the Trade Union and Labour Relations (Consolidation) Act 1992, s. 189, as amended, if EMPLOYERS fail to observe their duty to consult representatives in a COLLECTIVE REDUNDANCY situation or fail to follow the provisions of s. 188A in respect of elections for EMPLOYEE representatives, an EMPLOYMENT TRIBUNAL must grant a DECLARATION and may make a protective award. By s. 189(3) 'a protective award is an award in respect of one or more descriptions of employees ... ordering the employer to pay remuneration for the **protected period**' to all affected employees. The protected period is defined in s. 189 (4) as being 'of such length as the tribunal determines to be just and equitable in all the circumstances having regard to the seriousness of the employer's default', but must not exceed 90 days. Modern decisions stress that the protective award is punitive against the employer, not compensatory for the employees: see *Susie Radin Ltd* v. *GMB* [2004] ICR 893 (CA). [MJ]

protective trust (alimentary trust) A TRUST limited to the lifetime of the BENEFICIARY, used to avoid the consequences of subsequent events (most usually BANKRUPTCY). On the occurrence of the subsequent event the beneficiary's right to the income of the trust is terminated and a discretionary trust of the income arises in favour of a class normally including the beneficiary and his family. Protective trusts are governed by the Trustee Act 1925, s. 33. [PK]

proving a will *See* GRANT OF REPRESENTATION.

provisional measures A term used in INTERNATIONAL LAW and CONFLICT OF LAWS to describe procedural decisions of courts (orders) which relate to litigation between disputing parties but which are ancillary to the merits of the dispute, and the normal procedural issues arising in litigation. Orders can include the following kinds of INJUNCTIONS: (a) to protect the subject matter of the claim; (b) to preserve the evidence which might need to be submitted to the court; and (c) to prevent the removal or dissipation of the credit balance of a bank account from which damages and costs might be paid after the conclusion of the action. Orders can also be made in connection with obtaining evidence from abroad, and for providing security for costs in the event that the respondent party succeeds in defending the claim. Application for provisional measures can sometimes be advisable prior to commencement of ARBITRATION.

Some orders can be made where the action is being pursued in a foreign court. Thus, the courts in England and Wales can make appropriate orders even where the action is, for example, in the court of another European Community State. In these circumstances the provisions of the BRUSSELS CONVENTION 1968 (see Articles 24 to 26) or Council Regulation 44/2001 of 22 December 2000 (see Articles 31 to 33) apply. [RE]

provocation A partial defence to a charge of MURDER. When successfully argued, provocation reduces the offence from murder to MANSLAUGHTER. The requirements of provocation are set out in both the COMMON LAW and in STATUTE. Thus, Devlin J in *R* v. *Duffy* [1949] 1 All ER 932n stated that in order for a defendant to be eligible for the defence, he or she would have to suffer a 'sudden and temporary loss of self-control, rendering [him or her] so subject to passion as to make him or her for the moment not master of his mind', and also that which had caused the defendant to undergo such a loss of self-control would have a similar (notional) effect on a reasonable person. The test for provocation can therefore be said to have a subjective (how did the defendant react?) and an objective (how would the reasonable person have reacted?) element.

On the subjective element, the requirement of a sudden and temporary loss of self-control has been criticized as being too restrictive, in that it fails to accommodate the experiences of women who kill, having been the victims of sustained periods of abuse, typically in a domestic context, and who may exhibit a 'slow-burn' reaction to the abuse, rather than an obviously sudden loss of self-control. In *R* v. *Ahluwalia* [1992] 4 All ER 889, it was stated that a time lag between the final provoking event and the homicidal response was not an actual bar to the defence, but it did make it more difficult to establish.

On the objective element, the Homicide Act 1957, s. 3, states: 'the question whether the provocation was enough to make a reasonable man do as he did shall be left to be determined by the jury; and in determining that question the jury shall take into account everything both done and said according to the effect which, in their opinion, it would have on a reasonable man.' The Act makes clear that the defence leaves considerable scope for the jury to evaluate the defendant's conduct in comparison with that of the notional reasonable person. The key question on this aspect of the defence has been the extent to which the reasonable person can be taken to share the characteristics of the defendant. In *R* v. *Camplin* [1978] AC 705, Lord Diplock suggested (at p. 718): 'the reasonable man ... is a person having the power of self-control to be expected of an ordinary person of the sex and age of the accused, but in other respects sharing such of the accused's characteristics as they think would affect the gravity of the provocation to him'. The list of characteristics which affect the gravity of the

provocation is potentially limitless, and may include some which are morally problematic (see *R* v. *Morhall* [1995] 3 All ER 659, where the defendant was addicted to glue-sniffing and was taunted about his addiction). There has been significant controversy as to whether the only characteristics relevant to the power of self-control are sex and age: see *R* v. *Smith (Morgan)* [2001] 1 AC 146 and compare *Attorney General for Jersey* v. *Holley* [2005] UKPC 23.   [BF]

See also BATTERED WOMEN'S SYNDROME; SPECIAL DEFENCES.

PSR *See* PRE-SENTENCE REPORT.

psychiatric harm A defendant may incur liability for psychiatric harm suffered by someone who witnesses an incident in which a loved one (the primary victim) is injured as a result of the defendant's NEGLIGENCE. The harm suffered must be a recognizable psychiatric injury, as determined by medical evidence, rather than normal grief, shock or distress. There must be sufficiently close ties of love and affection between the claimant, as the secondary victim, and the primary victim for the risk of psychiatric harm to be reasonably foreseeable if they apprehended that the primary victim had been injured or might be injured. In addition, there must be proximity to the accident, or its immediate aftermath, in terms of time and space. The secondary victim must have seen or heard the accident or its immediate aftermath with their own senses (see *Alcock* v. *Chief Constable of South Yorkshire* [1991] 4 All ER 907).   [HJ]

public authority Under the Human Rights Act 1998, s. 6 (3), a public authority includes any court or TRIBUNAL or any 'person certain of whose functions are functions of a public nature'. Public authorities must refrain from breaching HUMAN RIGHTS protected by the 1998 Act. A VICTIM of any such breach may seek a remedy from the courts under s. 7. Where a body exercises both private and public functions, e.g. a HOUSING ASSOCIATION, it can be challenged under the Human Rights Act only in respect of its public functions (see *Poplar Housing and Regeneration Community Association Ltd* v. *Donoghue* (2001) 33 HLR 823). While LOCAL AUTHORITIES are public authorities for the purposes of the Act, these are not legal equivalents; 'public authority' has a significantly wider meaning.   [JW]

public company A registered COMPANY that can offer its shares to the public. Its MEMORANDUM OF ASSOCIATION must state that it is a public company, and it must possess an authorized share capital of at least the prescribed statutory minimum (currently £50,000 or €65,500) and it must end its name with the words 'Public Limited Company', or 'plc' or the Welsh equivalent. A newly formed public company cannot commence business activities or exercise any borrowing powers until the COMPANIES REGISTRY has issued a trading certificate under the Companies Act 2006, s. 761.
                                                                [JW]

public documents Documents such as public registers, and returns made under public authority with respect to matters of public interest. Public documents are admissible as EVIDENCE of facts stated in them: see Civil Evidence Act 1995, s. 7(2); Criminal Justice Act 2003, s. 118(1). [ALTC]

public inquiry *See* INQUIRY.

public interest Something that affects, or is of real and legitimate concern to, the public at large or a significant cross-section of the public; a matter of 'pressing social need' (*per* Laws LJ in *Ashworth Hospital* v. *MGN* [2001] 1 WLR 515 at [101]). The concept is widely used in public policy arguments, often in situations where the courts may have to balance competing interests, for example, between PRIVACY or a claim of QUALIFIED PRIVILEGE on one side, and freedom of the press, national security interests and other 'right to know' claims on the other. It is also sometimes used to describe generically, i.e. as 'public interest litigation', cases that are brought in the public interest, often by means of GROUP LITI-GATION.   [JW]

public law That part of the law that deals with matters relating to government, the constitution and ADMINISTRATIVE LAW. It may be contrasted with those parts of the law that concern the legal relationships between individual citizens, and are called private law.   [JW]

public lending right (PLR) A means by which authors are paid for loans of their books from public libraries. The scheme was set up by the Public Lending Right Act 1979 and is also supported by the EC Directive on RENTAL RIGHT and lending right. In the UK, payment is made from government funds to contributors whose books are borrowed from public libraries situated in the UK. A book is eligible for PLR registration provided that: it has an eligible contributor; it is printed and bound (paperbacks counting as bound); copies of it have been offered for sale; and that the authorship is personal and not a company or organization. Books that are wholly or mainly musical scores, newspapers, magazines and journals, and Crown Copyright publications, are not eligible for PLR.

To receive the PLR, the author should have their home or principal home in the UK or in any other EEA country. An eligible contributor is someone who is named on the title page or is entitled to a royalty payment from the publisher; they do not necessarily have to own the COPYRIGHT in the book. If two or more contributors are involved, the PLR must be divided between them after consultation.   [US]

public limited company *See* PUBLIC COM-PANY; COMPANY.

public nuisance An act committed without lawful authority, or a failure to discharge a legal duty, that interferes with the comfort, health or safety of the public. This is primarily a criminal offence but if a person suffers some special damage as a result, this can give rise to an action in TORT: see *Attorney General* v. *PYA Quarries* [1957] 2 QB 169. The question of whether a sufficient cross-section of the community has been affected to make the nuisance a public one is a question of fact in every case. The key test is whether, *per* Denning LJ in the *PYA Quarries* case (at 191), 'it was a nuisance which was so widespread in its range, or so indiscriminate in its effect, that it would not be reasonable to expect one person to take proceedings on his own responsibility to put a stop to it'.

Types of behaviour treated as a public nuisance have included the obstruction of roads and waterways, the emanation of soot or unpleasant fumes from a factory site, the organization of a 'rave', and the making of large numbers of nuisance telephone calls. Various of these activities are now covered by separate statutory offences and in *R* v. *Goldstein and Rimmington* [2005] UKHL 63, the House of Lords proposed that, as a matter of practice, an alleged offence falling within the remit of a STATUTE should be charged under that statute, and not as a public nuisance. It was accepted that, as a consequence, this would leave only a limited sphere of application to the COMMON LAW offence. [HJ]

See also PRIVATE NUISANCE; STATUTORY NUISANCE.

public procurement The process of obtaining goods or services for use in the public sector is known as public procurement and legislation originating from the EU ensures that set procedures are in place to award and administer CONTRACTS falling within its scope. In particular, public sector contracts need to be advised on an EU basis and need to be open to all who meet the criteria for performance, e.g. the Public Contracts Regulations 2006 and the Utilities Contracts Regulations 2006. These implement EU Directives which provide for alternative procedures for requesting and submitting TENDERS, for example the OPEN PROCEDURE. Where the correct procurement procedure has not been used, EU law provides for the ability to recover DAMAGES. [JPL]

Public Services Ombudsman for Wales
See LOCAL GOVERNMENT OMBUDSMEN.

public trust *See* CHARITABLE TRUST.

public trustee An officer appointed by the LORD CHANCELLOR under the Public Trustee Act 1906 to provide TRUSTS with a TRUSTEE

of last resort. The public trustee may be appointed to a trust in circumstances where no other suitable trustee can be appointed. The public trustee may act as executor when requested to do so, but may also act as ADMINISTRATOR of an estate of a deceased person (with or without a will), or as trustee of a trust whether as original or substitute trustee, usually only as a last resort, and in the interests of vulnerable individuals or persons under disability, or where there are differences between executors, trustees or beneficiaries. [PK]

Pufendorf, Samuel von (1632–94) A German jurist and statesman, best known for his contribution to INTERNATIONAL LAW theory, engaging with the work of both HUGO GROTIUS and THOMAS HOBBES. He asserted that the law of nations is a branch of NATURAL LAW, while taking the view also that natural law does not extend beyond the limits of this life. His conception of natural law was based on the notion of humans as social creatures, thereby positing a social contract theory ahead of ROUSSEAU. He disputed Hobbes's conception of the state of nature as being one of war, arguing instead that the natural relations of nations are peaceable, and war is justified only after attempts at peaceful redress have failed. He supported STATE power over claims by the Church to exercise secular authority, and his work on this subject became the basis of church–state relations in 18th-century Germany. He also took the view that international law is not restricted to the relations between Christian nations, but governs all nations because they form part of humanity. These views are developed in his *Elementa jurisprudentiae universalis* [Elements of Universal Jurisprudence] (1660), *De jure naturae et gentium* [On the Law of Nature and of Nations] (1672) and *De officio hominis et civis* [On the Duty of Man and Citizen] (1682). [IB]

***puisne* judge** (Old Fr. *puisne*; modern *puine*, later born, inferior) The formal name given to an ordinary judge of the HIGH COURT by the Supreme Court of Judicature Act 1877, commonly referred to in practice as 'High Court judges'. *Puisne* judges hold the title

'Honourable' while they hold that rank and are referred to as Mr or Mrs Justice – i.e. the 'Honourable Mr(s) Justice –'. On appointment, *puisne* judges are also knighted or made Dames. To qualify for appointment as a *puisne* judge, a person must have 10 years' qualification within the meaning of the Courts and Legal Services Act 1990, s. 71 (that is, someone who has had a general RIGHT OF AUDIENCE on all matters in that court for at least 10 years). [AF]

puisne mortgage In UNREGISTERED LAND, a LEGAL MORTGAGE which is not protected by a deposit of documents relating to the LEGAL ESTATE affected (Land Charges Act 1972, s. 2 (4)(i)). Puisne mortgages are registrable as a Class C (i) LAND CHARGE. [DR]
    See also MORTGAGE.

punishment One of the purposes of sentencing, most readily associated with DESERT THEORY and RETRIBUTIVISM. [BF]
    See also DETERRENCE THEORY; REHABILITATION.

punitive damages *See* EXEMPLARY DAMAGES.

purchaser In land law, a person to whom land is expressly transferred; for example, a person who buys land for money or other consideration, or is given land in a will, is a purchaser. [DR]
    See also VENDOR.

purchaser for value without notice In all of the exceptions to the *NEMO DAT QUOD NON HABET* rule, a good TITLE can only be passed by a SELLER who has no title if the buyer takes the goods for a VALUABLE CONSIDERATION, in good faith and without any knowledge of the fact that the seller's title was defective. For example, if the seller has a voidable title to the goods which has not been voided at the time of the sale, the buyer will acquire a good title provided the goods are purchased in good faith and without (actual) notice of the seller's defect in title (Sale of Goods Act 1979, s. 23). Equally, it is a fundamental principle of the law relating to negotiable instruments that the bona fide holder for value of a negotiable instrument is able to acquire a better title than his transferor. [JPL]

pure theory of law The POSITIVIST legal theory produced by HANS KELSEN. The term 'pure' was intended to emphasize that jurisprudence should be concerned solely with the description and understanding of the operation of NORMS ('oughts') and that it should not concern itself either with the processes by which law emerged or with its effects. [JP]

purpose trust A trust that defies the BENEFICIARY PRINCIPLE, having neither human nor legal personalities as objects of the TRUST. Purpose trusts may be either charitable or non-charitable, although the latter category are invariably VOID apart from a small category of anomalous private purpose trusts, including trusts for individual animals and trusts for the maintenance of monuments and graves. [PK]

Q

QB The standard abbreviation for the Law Reports: Queen's Bench cases, published by the INCORPORATED COUNCIL OF LAW REPORTING.

[JW]

See LAW REPORTS.

QBD *See* QUEEN'S BENCH DIVISION.

qualified privilege A statement (whether spoken or written) cannot be the basis for an action for DEFAMATION where it was made on a privileged occasion and certain other conditions were satisfied. There are three relatively distinct forms of qualified privilege. The first is sometimes called COMMON LAW privilege. This is difficult to define in general terms but broadly encompasses statements made under a social, moral or legal duty to a person who has a corresponding interest in receiving them; for example, a reference to a prospective employer will normally be protected by the privilege, provided it was not made maliciously or for an improper motive. The common law privilege has become less significant in the light of statutory amendments, most notably those contained in the Defamation Act 1996, Schedule 1, which protects two categories of publication. Part I of Schedule 1 covers fair and accurate reports of public proceedings in legislatures, courts, government-appointed public inquiries, and international organizations anywhere in the world, and authorized documents produced by those bodies. The defence in respect of Part I can only be defeated by evidence that publication was malicious.

Part II covers publications produced by a wide range of public bodies, including documents issued for the information of the public by the legislatures of EUROPEAN UNION (EU) MEMBER STATES, by EU institutions and other international organizations; statements made available by courts in Member States or the EUROPEAN COURT OF JUSTICE; and statements made in public proceedings of local authorities, proceedings at lawful public meetings and at general meetings of public companies. Part II privilege can be defeated not just by evidence of malice, but by a failure to give the claimant a right of reply.

Thirdly there is 'Reynolds-style qualified privilege', so called after the decision in *Reynolds* v. *Times Newspapers* [2001] 2 AC 127. This protects stories published in the media, providing publication was in the public interest, it was not malicious and it also met certain standards of responsible journalism. [JW]

See also ABSOLUTE PRIVILEGE; WAIVER OF PRIVILEGE.

qualified rights Under the EUROPEAN CONVENTION ON HUMAN RIGHTS, rights which require a balance to be struck between the rights of the individual and the needs or interests of the state or the wider community. Qualified rights include respect for family life (Article 8); the right to practise one's religion or beliefs (Article 9); freedom of expression (Article 10) and of association (Article 11); and the right to peaceful enjoyment of one's possessions (Protocol 1, Article 1). [JW]

See also ABSOLUTE RIGHTS; HUMAN RIGHTS.

qualified title The rarest of the classes of TITLE to land recognized by the Land Registry, awarded when the person applying for registration can only establish title for a limited period or where the title is defective. The details of the defect will be entered on the Register, and the qualified title will be subject to any right or interest arising from that defect.

Qualified title is registered in approximately 1 in 100,000 cases and may occur where, for example, the purchaser of an UNREGISTERED LAND has failed to investigate title for the previous 15 years. It may be upgraded to absolute TITLE if, at a later date, the registrar is satisfied as to the title of the estate. This may be the case if the defect in title is no longer a material concern. [DR]

See also GOOD LEASEHOLD TITLE; POSSESSORY TITLE.

qualifying law degree An undergraduate or **senior status** (i.e. postgraduate) law degree that satisfies the requirements of the legal professional regulators in England and Wales. A degree will constitute a qualifying law degree where a minimum of 180 credits (at least 50% of the degree) involves study of the seven 'Foundation' subjects, namely Contract, Criminal law, Equity and Trusts, European Union law, Land law, Public law, and Tort. A qualifying degree normally exempts the holder from the first stage of training as a SOLICITOR or BARRISTER. [JW]

quality of goods Where a SELLER sells goods in the course of a business there is an IMPLIED TERM in the sales CONTRACT that the goods are of satisfactory quality (Sale of Goods Act 1979, s. 14(2)). This relates to the need for the goods to be of a minimum state and condition and may not be excluded or limited in a consumer contract (Unfair Contract Terms Act 1977, s. 6(2)). However, a party may contract to obtain some specific quality in the goods, e.g. Royal Doulton china, to be supplied. If there is a contract term, for example part of the contract description (SGA 1979, s. 13) promising the existence of the quality, a claim will lie for BREACH OF CONTRACT in the event that the quality is absent. Equally, if there is a contractual MISREPRESENTATION that the goods possess a particular quality and this is untrue, a claim will lie in misrepresentation. However, it will be extremely difficult to avoid a contract on the basis of a MISTAKE as to a quality in the absence of a PROMISE or statement to this effect. This is because there is no mistake as to the subject matter of the sale contract (see *Smith* v. *Hughes* (1871) LR 6 QB 597; *Leaf* v. *International Galleries* [1950] 2 KB 86), only as to an attribute or 'collateral' matter. [JPL]

quantum meruit (Lat. as much as is observed) A claim for a reasonable value for the services performed. It is a remedy available in RESTITUTION on the basis of preventing UNJUST ENRICHMENT. Where a CONTRACT fails to materialize but one party has requested the other to perform the services covered by the contract and they have been performed, the performance may be remunerated on the basis of a *quantum meruit*. Similarly, if work has been performed and accepted under a VOID CONTRACT, a claim based on a *quantum meruit* will enable the performing party to recover for its reasonable value. If the obligation to perform is entire, i.e. a lump sum is payable on completion, but only part of the work is completed, it may be possible to recover for the value of that work on the basis of a *quantum meruit* where it has been voluntarily accepted by the other party. [JPL]

quantum valebat (Lat. as much as it is worth) A claim analogous to the *QUANTUM MERUIT*. It allows recovery based on market valuation where goods were sold on the basis of an implied PROMISE to pay their value rather than for a fixed PRICE. [JPL]

quarter days Traditionally, quarter days were the days when servants were hired, and RENTS and rates were due. The tradition still lingers on in determining the due date for the payment of rent in some LEASES. The quarter days, derived from religious festivals, and approximately three months apart, are Lady Day, 25 March; Midsummer Day, 24 June; Michaelmas Day, 29 September; and Christmas Day, 25 December.

[HC & DR]

Quarter Sessions (obsolete) Court sessions presided over by a Justice of the Peace which were held four times a year in each county and county borough. Quarter sessions, which were abolished by the Courts Act 1971 and replaced by the CROWN COURT, heard criminal charges and criminal and civil appeals. [SN]

quashing order A court order nullifying a decision made by a public body. Such an order is usually made where an authority has acted beyond its legal powers (*ULTRA VIRES*). Where the court makes a quashing order, it will normally send the case back to the original decision-maker, requiring it to revisit its decision in light of the court's findings, or, exceptionally, the court may take the decision itself. [JW]

quasi-contract *See* RESTITUTION.

quasi-easement A right exercised by a PROPRIETOR over his own land, which, if he did not own that land, would be capable of existing as an EASEMENT; for example, if the owner of Whiteacre and Blackacre uses a path across the back garden of Whiteacre to reach Blackacre, this is a quasi-easement (*Roe* v. *Siddons* (1888) 22 QBD 224). It is not a proper easement because the requirement that the pieces of land are owned by different people is not met. However, if that owner subsequently sold Blackacre, the right to use that path could be acquired by the new owner of Blackacre as an easement, either by express or implied GRANT.

[DR]

See also RIGHT OF WAY.

que **estate** (Norman Fr. whose estate) A claim to have established an EASEMENT or PROFIT À PRENDRE by PRESCRIPTION, based on the use of the land by the owner of the DOMINANT TENEMENT and those who owned it before him. Easements can only be prescribed in a *que estate*, since there must be a dominant and SERVIENT TENEMENT for an easement to exist. However, profits can also be prescribed IN GROSS, by a person and his ancestors, independent of the ownership of land. [DR]

Queen's Bench Division One of the three Divisions of the HIGH COURT. It is based in the Royal Courts of Justice in London, but work of the Queen's Bench Division is administered in provincial offices known as district registries. The Division deals primarily with the COMMON LAW matters of CONTRACT (except those specifically allocated to the CHANCERY DIVISION) and TORT. It also deals with applications for JUDICIAL REVIEW and appeals from magistrates' courts and inferior courts (by way of CASE STATED), where it sits as the ADMINISTRATIVE COURT, as well as appeals and applications under a variety of statutory provisions. Three specialist jurisdictions operate as part of this division: the COURT OF ADMIRALTY, the COMMERCIAL COURT and the Technology and Construction Court. The head of the Queen's Bench Division is called the PRESIDENT OF THE QUEEN'S BENCH DIVISION, a new post created by the Constitutional Reform Act 2005. The President is supported by 71 full-time High Court judges, who in turn are assisted by part-time Deputy High Court judges and CIRCUIT JUDGES sitting as High Court judges. The work of the central office in London is the responsibility of the Senior Master, acting under the authority of the President. Judges of the Queen's Bench Division also sit in the EMPLOYMENT APPEALS TRIBUNAL and COURT OF APPEAL. [AF]

See also FAMILY DIVISION; PUISNE JUDGE.

Queen's Council (QC) A barrister or solicitor-advocate with at least ten years' experience of practice who has been adjudged excellent in advocacy and appointed as 'one of Her Majesty's counsel learned in the law'. Since 2005 applicants have been required to apply to an independent selection panel. The decision to appoint is based on the candidate's application, which includes a 'self-assessment' of their skills against published competences, references from members of the judiciary before whom they have appeared recently, and from other practitioners and clients, and a formal interview before a selection panel. The final list of successful applicants is sent to the Secretary of State for Justice and thence to the Queen for the issue of the 'letters patent' which formally grant the appointment. Where the monarch is male, appointees are referred to as **King's Counsel** (KC).   [JW]

Queen's Peace The conditions in which society can function in a civilized fashion. Criminal offences are, by virtue of their status as offences against social norms in which there is a proper PUBLIC INTEREST, offences against the Queen's Peace. The offences of MURDER and MANSLAUGHTER make specific reference to the concept, in that the causing of death must take place under the Queen's Peace. It is the duty of a police constable to maintain the Queen's Peace. [BF]
    See also BREACH OF THE PEACE; KEEPING THE PEACE; POWER OF ARREST.

Queen's Regulations Regulations governing the armed services of the UK. There are separate sets of regulations for each of the armed services: army, navy and air force and they provide much of the detailed basis for military law and discipline. They are referred to as King's or Queen's Regulations depending on the reigning monarch.
                                                                        [JW]

queer theory A movement emerging from gay and lesbian studies in the early 1990s. Its starting point (which it shares with feminism and gay and lesbian studies) is a rejection of the idea that identity (and specifically sexual or gender identity) is determined by reference to the biological and an acceptance of the notion that it is instead socially constructed. Similarly, it notes those other movements' observations of social constructions of what counts as normal and deviant. Whereas gay and lesbian studies focuses on homosexuality in this last regard, queer theory has a broader

interest in all forms of sexuality which are routinely characterized as 'deviant' and as a consequence in those forms of 'normal' sexuality against which deviance is measured. Queer theory thus rejects any idea that sexuality and sexual behaviour can be defined by reference to biology or to ideas of morality and focuses on apparent disjunctions between sex, gender and sexuality. It accordingly calls into question some of the most basic categories and assumptions encountered in law, including man, woman, male and female. In terms of methodology, queer theory has drawn inspiration from deconstruction.   [JP]

Further reading: Annamarie Jagose, *Queer Theory* (Melbourne: University of Melbourne Press, 1996).

questioning of suspects The general rules relating to the questioning of suspects are contained in the Police and Criminal Evidence Act 1984 (PACE) and in the related Codes of Practice issued under PACE (especially *Code C: Code of Practice for the Detention, Treatment and Questioning of Persons by Police Officers*; *Code E: Code of Practice on Audio Recording Interviews with Suspects*; *Code F: Code of Practice on Visual Recording with Sound of Interviews with Suspects*).
    When a person is questioned about their involvement or suspected involvement in an offence, the questioning must take place under caution. The caution is a warning in the following terms: 'You do not have to say anything. But it may harm your defence if you do not mention when questioned something which you later rely on in court. Anything you do say may be given in evidence.'
    An interview must normally take place at a police station. A suspect is entitled to have a legal adviser present while being interviewed, other than in a limited range of circumstances where a sufficiently senior officer reasonably believes that particular specified adverse consequences might follow from the solicitor's presence (see PACE, s. 58).
    Interviews with persons cautioned on suspicion of involvement in an indictable

offence must be audio-recorded, and Code F under PACE makes provision for interviews which are visually recorded with sound.

Those conducting interviews need to be mindful of PACE, s. 76, which makes inadmissible any confession obtained by oppression or, broadly speaking, in circumstances which would render a confession unreliable. These criteria are intended to prevent confessions being procured either by threats or by inducements. Section 78 of PACE also permits a court to exclude prosecution evidence where to admit it would have a sufficiently serious adverse impact on the fairness of the proceedings.   [BF]

See also POWER OF ARREST; SEARCH AND SEIZURE.

quia emptores (Lat. whereas purchasers) A statute of 1290, the preamble to which begins with these words. The Statute of Quia Emptores prohibited SUBINFEUDATION so that no further relationships of lord and tenant could be created in relation to interests in land held under a FEE simple, except by the Crown. It established the principle that land could only be transferred by substitution, meaning that where a person sells his land to another, the purchaser of that land is placed in the same position the seller had previously been in. The Statute of Quia Emptores continues to be legally relevant and as recently as 1968 it was decided that it should remain in force.   [DR]

See also FEUDAL TENURE.

quia timet *See* INJUNCTION.

Quistclose trust A specialized form of TRUST that can sometimes arise, either expressly or impliedly, in the context of a commercial loan. The doctrinal basis of the *Quistclose* trust is still the subject of controversy as it appears to subvert the normal boundaries of contract and property by providing unsecured lenders with a beneficial interest in money lent for a particular purpose, up until that purpose is accomplished. Under a CONTRACT of loan, title to money borrowed in such circumstances usually vests in the borrower the moment it is received, with any misapplication of the funds giving

rise solely to a personal action for BREACH OF CONTRACT. In contrast, under a *Quistclose* trust, the lender either retains or acquires (depending upon the analysis adopted) a beneficial interest in the money lent, but not used, for a particular purpose. This enables a proprietary action to be maintained and ensures that the lender will be repaid any loan monies not used for the stated purpose (nor otherwise dissipated), even where the borrower is insolvent. The device first arose in *Barclays Bank* v. *Quistclose Developments* [1970] AC 567, where Lord Wilberforce based his analysis on the presence of two trusts, a primary trust to carry out a purpose, and a secondary trust on behalf of the lender which arises when the initial purpose fails. Such an analysis is open to the obvious objection that, as a purpose trust, the initial trust is VOID for contravening the BENEFICIARY PRINCIPLE, unless it falls within one of the rare anomalous exceptions or happens to be charitable. However, rather than sounding the death knell of the *Quistclose* trust, this critique has encouraged later judges and commentators to employ a variety of other rationalizations, on the dubious assumption that such trusts are commercially useful and should consequently be capable of doctrinal assimilation.

The *Quistclose* trust has consequently been reinterpreted in a variety of ways including: a BARE TRUST with the loan monies held by the borrower as TRUSTEE on behalf of the lender, subject to a mandate allowing the borrower to apply the monies for the particular purpose and so extinguish the trust; a RESULTING TRUST that arises when the purpose becomes impossible, prior to which the borrower holds the beneficial ownership subject to the lender's equitable right to prevent the money being used for any other purpose; and, occasionally, as a *Re Denley* [1968] Ch 373 type PURPOSE TRUST. More recently, in *Twinsectra* v. *Yardley* [2002] 2 AC 164, an attempt was made by the HOUSE OF LORDS to meld the first two post-Wilberforce justifications by characterizing the *Quistclose* trust as a resulting trust that arises by operation of law, from the outset, when the loan monies are transferred to the borrower subject to the lender's equitable right to prevent misuse. It is, however, unclear how such an analysis applies to expressly created *Quistclose* trusts nor, more generally, why the courts and most commentators are so keen on preserving a mechanism which is, in reality, a disguised form of security interest, not subject to the registration requirements that ensure that companies' secured debts are normally a matter of public record, consequently making the market less transparent.   [PK]

R

R (Lat. *Rex* or *Regina*, King or Queen) An abbreviation used in case citations, e.g. *R* v. *Smith* to indicate the role of the Crown as representing the state's interest in criminal or judicial review proceedings.   [JW]

racial discrimination Racial DISCRIMINATION, contrary to the Race Relations Act 1976, as amended, consists of direct discrimination, indirect discrimination, segregation, HARASSMENT and victimization. 'Race' covers not just 'race' but also nationality, national and ethnic origins and colour: see s. 3. Because the EC Race Directive 2000/43/EC does not apply to colour and nationality, there are two definitions of indirect discrimination in race discrimination law (Race Relations Act 1976, s. 1(1)(b) and s. 1(1A)) and there is a definition of harassment (s. 3A) which does not apply to discrimination on colour or nationality grounds. There are various exceptions, notably genuine occupational qualifications and requirements (e.g. requiring an actor to play a character of a particular colour). The Race Relations (Amendment) Act 2000 placed a duty on prescribed public authorities to promote racial equality. Members of some religions fall within the protection of the 1976 Act, e.g. Judaism, Sikhism, where there is a strong link between faith and ethnic origin and identity.   [MJ]

See also EQUALITY AND HUMAN RIGHTS COMMISSION.

racial hatred The Public Order Act 1986, s. 17, defines racial hatred as 'hatred against a group of persons ... defined by reference to colour, race, nationality (including citizenship) or ethnic or national origins.' [BF]

See also INCITEMENT TO RACIAL HATRED.

racist abuse There is no specific offence of racist abuse; however, such conduct may provide evidence of the commission of an offence under Part III of the Public Order Act 1986; of racial aggravation for the purposes of racially aggravated offences under the Crime and Disorder Act 1998; or of a BREACH OF THE PEACE.   [BF]

See also INCITEMENT TO RACIAL HATRED; RACIAL HATRED.

rack rent The best market RENT available for the LAND and buildings in question. It can be contrasted with a GROUND RENT, which is a rent calculated without taking the value of the buildings into account.

[HC & DR]

rape The intentional penetration of the vagina, anus or mouth of another person with the penis, when that other person does not consent to the penetration and the accused does not reasonably believe that the other person consents (Sexual Offences Act 2003, s. 1). Section 1(2) of the 2003 Act states that whether a belief is reasonable is to be determined having regard to all the circumstances, including any steps taken by the accused to ascertain whether the other person consents.

The definition of rape underwent significant change from the latter part of the 20th century onwards. The Sexual Offences Act 1956 merely declared that it was an offence for a man to rape a woman, without defining the elements of the offence. The offence was accordingly defined at COMMON LAW as unlawful sexual intercourse with a woman, without her consent, by force, fear or fraud. The first full statutory definition of the offence was set out in the Sexual Offences (Amendment) Act 1976, s. 1, which was passed following the recommendations of the Heilbron Committee. Rape was still predicated on the act of 'unlawful sexual intercourse with a woman who at the time … does not consent'.

In 1991, the House of Lords in *R* v. *R* [1992] 1 AC 599 decided that the so-called 'marital immunity', whereby a husband could not, at law, commit rape on his wife, could no longer stand. This anachronism was predicated on the fiction that, on marriage, a wife gave irrevocable consent to intercourse at any time of her husband's choosing. This was reflected in the Criminal Justice and Public Order Act 1994, s. 142, which removed the word 'unlawful' from the definition of the offence. Up until the decision in *R* (above), the word had been used to designate intercourse which took place outside marriage. Section 142, for the first English law, recognized male rape as an offence and also brought the non-consensual anal penetration of a woman within the definition of rape.

Under the 2003 Act, non-consensual penile-oral penetration is brought within the definition of rape for the first time; it is worthy of note that this has been the position in a number of other jurisdictions for some time. Section 74 of the 2003 Act sets out a definition of consent: 'a person consents if he agrees by choice, and has the freedom and capacity to make that choice'. Section 75 of the 2003 Act sets out a number of situations in which there is a rebuttable presumption that the complainant is not consenting, and that D has no reason-

able belief in consent. These situations include, among others, where violence is used against the complainant, where the complainant is unconscious or asleep, or where the complainant has, without her consent, been caused to take a stupefying substance. Section 76 of the Act sets out situations in which it is to be conclusively presumed that the complainant is not consenting, and that D has no reasonable belief in consent. These situations are where D intentionally deceives the complainant as to the nature or purpose of the act in question; and where D intentionally induces the complainant to consent by impersonating a person known personally to the complainant.

Section 5 of the 2003 Act makes a separate offence 'rape of a child under 13' and the definition of the act is the same as s. 1. However, the consent of that person is immaterial to the commission of the offence. It also does not appear on the face of the section to be a defence that D believes that person to be 13 or over. [BF]

Further reading: Peter Rook and Robert Ward, *Rook & Ward on Sexual Offences Law and Practice*, 3rd edn (London: Sweet and Maxwell, 2004); Jennifer Temkin, *Rape and the Legal Process*, 2nd edn (Oxford: Oxford University Press, 2002); Home Office, *Setting the Boundaries: Reforming the law on sex offences* (London: Home Office Communication Directorate, 2000).

ratification Refers to the adoption or affirmation of previously unauthorized actions. Once ratified, the authorization for the act is retrospective. An unauthorized CONTRACT entered into by a person without authority to act as AGENT for the PRINCIPAL may subsequently be ratified and therefore be treated as authorized and binding. A contract made with a MINOR may be enforceable against the minor if the minor chooses to ratify (adopt) it at the age of 18. [JPL]

See also CHILDREN'S CONTRACTS.

ratification of treaties An 'international act … whereby a STATE establishes on the international plane its consent to be bound by a TREATY' (Article 2(1)(b) of the 1969 Vienna Convention on the Law of Treaties). Consent to be bound is expressed through ratification when: (a) the treaty provides for consent to be expressed through ratification; (b) it is otherwise established that the negotiating states were agreed that ratification should be required; (c) the representative of the state has signed the treaty subject to ratification; or (d) the intention of the state to sign the treaty subject to ratification appears from the FULL POWERS of its representative or was expressed during the negotiation (Article 14, Vienna Convention). Typically, the process of ratification requires that national parliaments, depending on constitutional requirements, approve the text of the treaty, after which the treaty is passed into domestic law, usually through the adoption of a relevant law, and an instrument of ratification is drawn up which is forwarded to other state parties or the depository of the treaty, expressing the intention of the state to be bound by the treaty. [IB]

ratio decidendi (Lat., the reason for deciding) The statement of legal principle(s) upon which a specific case is decided; commonly referred to as 'the *ratio*'. The *ratio* of a case is an abstraction from what the judge says about the way in which the legal rules apply to the material facts of that case. Where there is more than one judge deciding the case, the *ratio* will reflect the points of agreement between the judges, or at least those that are in the majority. The *ratio* of the case is the only part that is capable of constituting a binding PRECEDENT. [JW]

See also OBITER DICTUM.

Rawls, John Bordley (1921–2002) American moral and political philosopher, regarded as among the most important of the 20th century, Rawls is best known for *A Theory of Justice* (1971) in which he is concerned to establish the principles of justice as fairness. He does this by constructing a thought-experiment, the Original Position, in which a group of rational individuals must agree on the fundamental principles of justice that will govern society, both its basic structure and its institutions. These individuals must act in their rational self-interest. They know that whatever principles they choose will be binding on them. They have no knowledge, however, of the features that distinguish them from other people, such as their sex, ethnicity, physical and mental abilities, cultural and religious identity. They know that they will hold a conception of the good (and that this may differ from that held by other people) but they do not know what it will be. The individuals in the 'original position' are thus said to be behind the 'veil of ignorance'. Rawls can accordingly claim that since the conditions in which the principles of justice are to be chosen are fair, so will those principles be just.

Rawls uses this device to mount an attack on his principal opponent, UTILITARIANISM. By conflating what is right with what is good, this approach falls foul of the rational self-interested decision-making of the individuals in the original position because they do not know what their conception of the good will turn out to be. What is right is thus shown to be logically prior to what is good.

Rawls believes that two principles of justice emerge from the original position. The first (the principle of greatest equal liberty) is that each person is entitled to the most extensive system of basic liberties that is compatible with a similar system for everyone else. The second is expressed in two parts: the first states that there must be fair equality of opportunity; the second (the difference principle) that social and economic inequalities are just only insofar as they work to the benefit of the least advantaged people in society.

Rawls goes on to check that the principles of justice emerging from this thought-experiment accord with our existing considered judgements. He thus engages in a process of working from both of these positions until a reflective equilibrium about our considered convictions of justice is reached. Rawls's aim is to persuade us that by engaging in this process we will modify our considered judgements about what is just on the basis of the original position – rather than the other way around.

For all of this to work, of course, it is necessary to assume that everyone is minded to adhere to this approach to justice. In a pluralist society, however, it is not possible to make this assumption. Rawls later realized that the ideas on stability and the well-ordered society, which he had expounded in *A Theory of Justice*, did not accord with the fact of pluralism. He addresses this problem in *Political Liberalism* (1993) where he replaces the idea that all will ultimately accept the principles of justice wholeheartedly following a process towards reflective equilibrium with the idea of an overlapping consensus. This holds that whichever conception of justice individuals adhere to in a pluralist society there is at least agreement on a core political conception of justice. This political conception is still moral, but is restricted to the basic structure of society rather than the more specific questions about which there may be disagreement.

Up to this point in his work, Rawls operated on the explicit assumption that he was describing a closed society. He drops this assumption in *The Law of Peoples* (1999) and considers the just foreign policy of a liberal democracy – the basic principles, the appropriate treatment of societies that are not liberal democracies, war and international distributive justice.   [JP]

See also JUSTICE.

Further reading: John Rawls, *A Theory of Justice*, revised edn (Harvard, MA: Harvard University Press, 2005); *Political Liberalism*, revised edn (New York: Columbia University Press, 2005); *The Law of Peoples*, new edn (Harvard: Harvard University Press, 2001).

re-engagement order An EMPLOYER may be ordered by an EMPLOYMENT TRIBUNAL to re-engage an employee where there has been an UNFAIR DISMISSAL of that employee. This order takes the form of obliging the employers, their successors or associated employers to put the employee in a job comparable to that which he or she held before DISMISSAL.   [MJ]

See also REINSTATEMENT ORDER.

re-examination The process of questioning one's own WITNESS after that witness has undergone CROSS-EXAMINATION. Questioning in re-examination is generally limited to matters arising from the EVIDENCE given by the witness in cross-examination.   [ALTC]

re-entry The process by which LANDLORDS repossess their LAND following a breach of condition of the LEASE by the TENANT which entitles the landlord to FORFEITURE. Forfeiture is seriously curtailed by statute and the courts. The standard process for re-entry for short residential leases and for other leases covered by statutory regimes is possession proceedings.   [HC & DR]

See also RELIEF FROM FORFIETURE.

real estate *See* REAL PROPERTY.

real evidence EVIDENCE which may be inspected by the TRIER OF FACT. Examples of real evidence are diverse and include the demeanour of a WITNESS, material objects such as the alleged murder weapon, evidence from out-of-court inspections of, for example, the scene of the crime ('views'), DOCUMENTARY EVIDENCE, and photographs and photographic images.   [ALTC]

real property LAND, physical objects attached to land and rights relating to land. Historically, real property meant property that would be protected by the courts by an action *in rem*, or a 'real action'. 'Real' derives from the Latin word *res*, meaning 'thing', and means that the court would restore to a dispossessed owner the thing itself instead of only giving compensation for the loss. Since the courts would only allow an action *in rem* in relation to a FREEHOLD interest, real property strictly speaking only includes freehold interests. LEASEHOLD interests are a hybrid of land and personal property, classified as chattels real.   [DR]

realty *See* REAL PROPERTY.

reasonable adjustments One form of

DISCRIMINATION in DISABILITY DISCRIMINATION law is that of failure by the EMPLOYER to make reasonable adjustments: see the Disability Discrimination Act 1995 as amended, s. 4A. The law applies where any physical feature of premises (as defined in s. 18D(2)) or a provision, practice or criterion (a phrase which includes 'arrangements': see s. 18D(2)) places a DISABLED PERSON at a substantial disadvantage in comparison with those who are not disabled. The Disability Discrimination Act 1995, s. 18B provides examples of reasonable adjustments, e.g. altering premises, reallocating work duties, altering hours of work, transferring the disabled person to an existing vacancy, allowing absence for rehabilitation. [MJ]

reasonable financial provision When the court makes a FINANCIAL PROVISION ORDER on DIVORCE, JUDICIAL SEPARATION, DISSOLUTION of CIVIL PARTNERSHIP or ANNULMENT, it must consider the overriding objective of fairness and the factors listed in the Matrimonial Causes Act 1973. When the court makes an order for MAINTENANCE PENDING SUIT, it is directed to make any order it thinks reasonable. The court must also consider reasonableness when it entertains an application by one party that the other has failed to provide reasonable MAINTENANCE for him or her or for the CHILD. The term reasonable financial provision is also used in legislation which permits the court to make an order in favour of specified surviving dependants of a deceased person (including civil partners, spouses, children and certain cohabitants) when the disposition of the deceased's estate does not provide them with reasonable financial provision. When the applicant is a surviving spouse or civil partner of the deceased, reasonable financial provision means such financial provision as it would be reasonable in all circumstances for them to receive, whether or not that provision is required for their maintenance. Reasonable financial provision for any other applicant is that amount which would be reasonable in all circumstances for their maintenance: see the Inheritance (Provision for Family and Dependants) Act 1975, s. 1(2)(b). [AD]

See also DEPENDENT; FAILURE TO MAINTAIN.

reasonable force A defendant acting in the prevention of crime under the Criminal Law Act 1967, s. 3, or in SELF-DEFENCE under the COMMON LAW, is entitled to use such force as is reasonable in the circumstances as he believes them to be. It was recognized in the PRIVY COUNCIL in *Palmer* v. *R* [1971] AC 814 that what constitutes reasonable force is not to be measured with excessive exactitude. As Lord Morris stated (at p. 832): 'a person defending himself cannot weigh to a nicety the exact measure of his necessary defensive action. If a jury thought that in a moment of unexpected anguish a person attacked had only done what he honestly and instinctively thought was necessary that would be most potent evidence that only reasonable defensive action had been taken.' [BF]

rebus sic stantibus (Lat. things standing thus) A fundamental change of circumstances unforeseen by the parties may not be invoked as a ground for terminating or withdrawing from a TREATY (Article 62(1) of the 1969 Vienna Convention on the Law of Treaties). A STATE is permitted to invoke *rebus sic stantibus* where: (a) the existence of those circumstances constituted an essential basis of the consent of the parties to be bound by the treaty; and (b) the effect of the change is radically to transform the extent of obligations still to be performed under the treaty. A fundamental change of circumstances may not be invoked as a ground for terminating or withdrawing from a treaty if: (a) the treaty establishes a boundary; or (b) the fundamental change is the result of a breach by the party invoking it either of an obligation under the treaty or of any other international obligation owed to any other party to the treaty. Where the invocation of *rebus sic stantibus* has the legal effect of terminating a treaty, it may alternatively suspend its operation (Article 62(3)). [IB]

receiver 1. A person appointed to manage

and/or realize the assets of an insolvent individual or business, or the property of an offender that represents the proceeds of crime.

2. A person appointed under Part 69 of the CIVIL PROCEDURE RULES to preserve property that is or may become the subject of litigation, or in order to enforce a judgment. [JW]

receiving *See* HANDLING STOLEN GOODS.

reciprocity In INTERNATIONAL LAW, reciprocity means that two or more STATES agree to act in a particular way that is favourable to one another, under the condition that the other state(s) will act in the same way. In this manner they establish reciprocal rights. The principle of reciprocity can emanate as a result of bilateral or multilateral TREATY arrangements, custom or, more unofficially, a unilateral act of one state that is premised on the belief that the other state to whom the favour is being made will act in a similar way. Before the emergence of the international system of human rights, the principle of reciprocity was employed to grant rights to and protect aliens. Currently, it is widely employed in the field of transnational commerce. [IB]

See also MOST-FAVOURED-NATION TREATMENT; NATIONAL TREATMENT STANDARD; STATE RESPONSIBILITY.

recklessness A form of MENS REA, less blameworthy than INTENTION, relating to the taking by a person of a risk that a prohibited circumstance will exist or a prohibited consequence may occur. Thus, for example, a person commits BATTERY, if he or she applies unlawful force to the victim, intending that or being reckless as to whether such force be applied.

The test for recklessness was set out in *R* v. *G* [2003] UKHL 50, a case of CRIMINAL DAMAGE (although the test appears to apply to virtually all offences of which recklessness is an element). Lord Bingham concluded (at 41): 'A person acts recklessly within the meaning of section 1 of the Criminal Damage Act 1971 with respect to – (i) a circumstance when he is aware of a risk that it exists or will exist; (ii) a result when he is

aware of a risk that it will occur; and it is, in the circumstances known to him, unreasonable to take the risk.'

In essence, being reckless amounts to consciously taking an unreasonable risk. The test for recklessness is subjective, in that a finding of recklessness depends on what the factfinder considers the defendant to have been aware of or to have foreseen. If a STATUTE contains the term 'maliciously' to denote a required *mens rea*, this amounts to a requirement of intention or recklessness (see *R* v. *Cunningham* [1957] 2 QB 396).

Prior to the decision in *R* v. *G*, there were two forms of recklessness known to criminal law. The subjective form of *mens rea* outlined above applied, broadly speaking, to OFFENCES AGAINST THE PERSON, and a different form applied in the context of criminal damage. The latter test was set out in the decision of the House of Lords in *R* v. *Caldwell* [1982] AC 341; to all intents and purposes this was overruled in *R* v. *G*. [BF]

recognition Where EMPLOYERS deal with TRADE UNIONS for one or more purposes, they are said to 'recognize' the union. In UK law, recognition may be **voluntary** or **statutory**, and there is also a third method, sometimes known as **semi-voluntary**. 'Voluntary' connotes that the employers, whether under pressure or not, have made a decision to recognize the union. Such recognition may be express or implied; however, recognition for the purposes of representing employees at disciplinary meetings does not entail recognition for all purposes of COLLECTIVE BARGAINING. 'Statutory' means that the provisions of Schedule A1 to the Trade Union and Labour Relations (Consolidation) Act 1992 have been complied with and a union or group of unions applies for recognition under statute by having recourse to the CENTRAL ARBITRATION COMMITTEE (CAC). Statutory recognition is only for the purposes of pay, hours and holidays (para. 3(3)); pensions are specifically excluded. A 'semi-voluntary' mode of acquiring recognition occurs when a union has applied to the CAC but recognition has not yet been granted, and the employers agree to recognition without the Schedule A1 procedures being followed. [MJ]

recognition of a state The legal effect of recognition of STATES, governments and situations of belligerency is premised on either the constitutive or declaratory theories. Recognition of one state by another, according to the more potent viewpoint, is not a necessary element of statehood. Recognition is either a unilateral act of one state, or a collective act by more than one. The latter takes place where an international organization, such as the UNITED NATIONS, accepts a state for membership. Where one state does not recognize another, as is the case with Arab states refusing to recognize Israel, it does not mean that that unrecognized entity does not exist under international law. The practical effect of such failure to recognize is that the concerned states do not enter into diplomatic or other relations. In the context of these situations it is very common for refusing states to enter into special declarations when signing a treaty in which the opposing state is also a party. These declarations reiterate that signature and ratification by the refusing state in no way implies recognition of the opposing state. [IB]

See also CONSTITUTIVE THEORY; DECLARATORY THEORY.

recognition procedure (obsolete) Under the Employment Protection Act 1975, ss. 11–16, an INDEPENDENT TRADE UNION could apply through ACAS for RECOGNITION. This recognition procedure was abolished by the Employment Act 1980, largely because of EMPLOYERS' non-cooperation with ACAS: see *Grunwick Processing Laboratories Ltd* v. *ACAS* [1978] AC 655 (HL). [MJ]

recognizance A formal undertaking to pay the CROWN a specified sum if an accused fails to surrender to custody. [SN]

reconciliation Both the Matrimonial Causes Act 1973 and the Civil Partnership Act 2004 encourage partners to make attempts at reconciliation before their claims of IRRETRIEVABLE BREAKDOWN of MARRIAGE or CIVIL PARTNERSHIP are heard by a court. The statutes provide that solicitors must discuss with the applicant or petitioner the possibility of reconciliation and refer him or her to resources such as counselling that may assist with reconciliation. The court also has the power to adjourn proceedings at any stage if it feels there is a reasonable possibility of reconciliation between the parties. The SEPARATION facts that may be relied upon to establish irretrievable breakdown also contain provisions encouraging parties to attempt reconciliation. [AD]

recreational charity A public TRUST that comes within the definition of a CHARITY under the Recreational Charities Act 1958. The Act was passed in response to case law that brought the previously considered charitable status of trusts to provide recreational facilities into doubt. The Act is of questionable usefulness as it provides a definition that is infamously convoluted, requiring that the facilities be provided in the interests of 'social welfare'. The term 'social welfare' is itself defined as requiring that the facilities be provided to improve the conditions of life of people generally or those who have need of them by reference to their youth, age, infirmity or disablement, poverty or social and economic circumstances. It is, perhaps, not surprising that the exact meaning of this term is the subject of continuing debate despite a number of inconsistent attempts to clarify the issue within the HOUSE OF LORDS. [PK]

rectification In general, the correction of a document where it does not accurately express the parties' common intention in entering into a CONTRACT, LEASE or CONVEYANCE. Parties to a contract may rectify their agreement by common consent, provided that any third party rights are not affected by the rectification.

In the context of REGISTERED LAND, it involves an alteration of the title register which: (a) involves the correction of a mistake; and (b) prejudicially affects the title of a registered proprietor (Land Registration Act 2002 (LRA 2002), Schedule 4, para. 1). A mistake may include an error made by a Land Registry official or an error made by the parties to the transaction themselves (e.g. where a TRANSFER is forged).

Both the courts and the Land Registry's Chief Land Registrar have the power to order rectification of the Register and in general where they have the power to order rectification they must do so, unless there are exceptional reasons for not doing so (LRA 2002, Schedule 4, paras 3(3), 6(3)). However, if a proprietor is in possession of the land, such rectification may not be made without the consent of the proprietor, unless he or she has by fraud or lack of proper care caused or substantially contributed to the mistake, or it would for any other reason be unjust for the alteration not to be made (LRA 2002, Schedule 4, paras 3(2), 6(2)). This means that where there is a boundary dispute between neighbouring proprietors, the register will usually be rectified in favour of the proprietor in possession of that land. When rectification occurs, innocent parties have a right to an indemnity from the Chief Land Registrar for any loss suffered.

Prior to the LRA 2002, rectification was a blanket term used to describe any alteration of the register.   [DR]

See also RECTIFICATION OF WILL.

rectification of will The power of the court to correct or rectify a WILL under the Administration of Justice Act 1982, s. 20. The court must be satisfied that the will is so expressed that it fails to carry out the TESTATOR's intentions, in consequence of (a) a clerical error, or (b) a failure to understand his or her instructions.

A clerical error means a mistake in recording the wishes of the testator when the will was drafted or transcribed, and could be made either by the testator himself or herself, or by someone preparing the will. A failure to understand instructions obviously implies that the testator has given instructions to another to prepare his or her will and that the instructions have not been followed accurately.   [CM]

reddendum (Lat. that which is given back or reserved) The clause in a LEASE which specifies the rent payable and the due dates. The clause often begins with the words 'the rent reserved is …'.   [HC & DR]

redemption Under a MORTGAGE, the right of redemption is the right to pay off the loan plus any interest provided for in the mortgage, so that the mortgage is discharged.

At law, the right is extremely limited since the borrower can only redeem on the date or dates specified in the mortgage deed. After that date the borrower loses his legal right to redemption. However, in equity the borrower has a general right to redeem at any time as long as the loan and any interest payable has been duly paid. As a result of the equitable principle that there should be no clogs on the EQUITY OF REDEMPTION, any provisions in a mortgage that would operate to prevent the borrower from redeeming will be void.

The legal date of redemption is usually specified in a mortgage deed to be a date within the first six months of the mortgage, so that the lender can exercise a POWER OF SALE if the borrower defaults on his mortgage repayments.   [DR]

redundancy This term is defined in the Employment Rights Act 1996, s. 139, for the purposes of both UNFAIR DISMISSAL and REDUNDANCY PAYMENTS as DISMISSAL attributable wholly or mainly to (a) the cessation of or the intention to cease carrying on the business for which the EMPLOYEE was employed; (b) the cessation of or intention to cease business in the place where the employee was employed; (c) the requirements of the business for employees to carry out work of a particular kind have ceased or diminished or are expected to cease or diminish. It should be noted that a different definition applies for the purposes of COLLECTIVE REDUNDANCY.   [MJ]

redundancy payment If an EMPLOYEE who has been continuously employed for at least two years is dismissed by reason of REDUNDANCY, they may be entitled to a redundancy payment under statute. The amount is calculated according to a maximum weekly sum, the number of years' continuous employment up to a maximum of 20 years, and a multiplier based on the age of the applicant. In addition to statutory redundancy payments there may be contractual or ex gratia payments.   [MJ]

refreshing memory A person giving oral EVIDENCE in criminal proceedings may, at any stage, refresh his memory of it from a document made or verified by him at an earlier time, provided that he states in his oral evidence that the document records his recollection at that earlier time, and that his recollection of the matter is likely to have been significantly better at that time than it is now.   [ALTC]

refugee A person who 'owing to well-founded fear of being persecuted for reasons of race, religion, nationality, membership of a particular social group or political opinion, is outside the country of his nationality and is unable or, owing to such fear, is unwilling to avail himself of the protection of that country; or who, not having a nationality and being outside the country of his former habitual residence as a result of such events, is unable or, owing to such fear, is unwilling to return to it' (Convention and Protocol Relating to the Status of Refugees 1951, Article 1). The test of 'well-founded fear' is objective (see *R* v. *Home Secretary ex p Sivakumaran* [1988] 2 WLR 92). See also *Islam* v. *Secretary of State for Home Department* (1999) 149 NLJ 528, which discusses the meaning of 'membership of a particular social group'. **Persecution** means the ill-treatment, based upon hostility to individuals or groups, arising generally from political or religious conflict or extremism (see *R* v. *Secretary of State for Home Department ex p Adan* (2000) *The Times*, 20 December).   [AF]

See also ASYLUM.

regionalism A term, along with regionalization, that can be used in two different contexts in law, one at an INTERNATIONAL LAW level and one at a COMMUNITY LAW level. At an international law level, regionalism means putting countries into groups, depending on which part of the world they are located. For example, the EUROPEAN COMMUNITY (EC) is defined in international trade law as being

a Regional Integration Association, as opposed to globalism, which is the grouping of all (or most) of the countries of the world into a global regulatory framework, for example in the WORLD TRADE ORGANIZATION.

Within the EC, regionalism or regionalization refers to the operation of the EC regional policy, the work of the COMMITTEE OF THE REGIONS, and the operation of the various STRUCTURAL FUNDS. Under these processes, the EC is divided into different areas depending on their location, wealth and structural economic problems, with various initiatives taken at EC level to assist weaker or less favoured regions.   [MON]

See also EUROPEAN SOCIAL FUND; GLOBALIZATION OF LAW.

register of commons A register kept by each commons registration authority (either the local county council, district council or London borough council) for its area, maintaining a record of land registered as COMMON LAND and RIGHTS OF COMMON. Each unit on the register contains the following: (a) a land section, identifying the common land; (b) a rights section, listing the nature of the rights of common and the people entitled to exercise them; and (c) an ownership section, showing the owner of the common land.

The register of commons is a public document and commons registration authorities carry out searches of the register for a small fee. In conveyancing, such searches are often carried out by the buyer's solicitor prior to the exchange of contracts, in order to reveal any rights of common which may adversely affect the value of a property. Once the Commons Act 2006 comes fully into force, it is intended that the register of commons will be available electronically.

[DR]

register of electors *See* ELECTORAL REGISTER.

register of title The public register maintained by the Land Registry evidencing ownership of TITLE TO REGISTERED LAND. For every registered property, entries on the register of title contain three parts: Part A: the Property Register, describing the land and estate that comprises the title (often with reference to the title plan); Part B: the Proprietorship Register, specifying the class of title identifying the owner and listing any RESTRICTIONS or notices (e.g. an option to purchase); Part C: the Charges Register, showing any MORTGAGES, RESTRICTIVE COVENANTS and other rights affecting the property.

OFFICIAL COPIES of the register of title for a particular property may be ordered from the Land Registry by any member of the public for a small fee and are admissible in evidence to the same extent as the original.   [DR]

registered design   INTELLECTUAL PROPERTY law offers the DESIGN proprietor the option of seeking an exclusive monopoly right (registered design) or an anti-copying right (UNREGISTERED DESIGN RIGHT). Registered design law is governed by the UK Registered Designs Act 1949 (as amended in 2006) and the Community Design Regulation and Directive, which provides protection across the EUROPEAN UNION. All substantive aspects of the UK registered design protection system conform to the Community Design system, and the design holder has the option to seek either UK-wide registration or Community-wide protection.

Registration is conferred on a design which can be shown to have **novelty** and **individual character**; that is, it must in some way be new and have features that give it an appearance of originality. Registration chiefly protects the outward appearance of objects, including matters of configuration, shape and ornamentation, such as the pattern on wallpaper, plates, or textiles, the shape of a car or a coffee pot. Registered design protection is not granted to features of appearance which are solely dictated by the product's technical function (the spout on a kettle cannot be protected, though an innovative and individual ornamentation on the spout could be), nor to designs which are contrary to public policy or to accepted principles of morality. Works of art, international emblems, flags, complex products, spare parts and printed material that is primarily of a literary character also cannot be registered.

The registered design scheme offers a maximum term of 25 years' protection from the date of filing the application for registration. The registration of a design gives the registered proprietor the exclusive right to authorize use of the design. There are several exempted acts which will not infringe the registered design right, including: acts done privately and for non-commercial purposes; acts done for experimental purposes; and acts of reproduction for teaching purposes or for the purpose of making citations.   [US]

See also COPYRIGHT.

registered land   Land, the TITLE to which is registered at the Land Registry. Under the Land Registration Act 2002 (LRA 2002), s. 4, which came into force on 13 October 2003, registration of title is compulsory on the occurrence of specified events, including, most importantly, the transfer of a FREEHOLD estate or a LEASEHOLD estate for a term of more than seven years, either for valuable consideration, by way of gift, pursuant to an order of court, or by means of an assent. In practice, this means that almost all transfers of land will give rise to compulsory registration.

The registered land system simplifies the process of CONVEYANCING compared to UNREGISTERED LAND because, apart from several notable exceptions (e.g. OVERRIDING INTERESTS), all proprietary interests affecting every registered title are recorded on the Land Registry's REGISTER OF TITLE. Inspection of OFFICIAL COPIES of the register against a particular title provides most of the information required by an intended purchaser of that land.

Registered land is guaranteed by the Land Registry, which means that if a person is registered as the proprietor of an estate, and this later proves to be wrong, any innocent party suffering loss will be compensated for that loss. Over 90% of the land in England and Wales is registered and the government's aim is for all land eventually to be registered.   [DR]

registered social landlord   A not-for-profit organization providing low-cost housing, usually a HOUSING ASSOCIATION, but also a HOUSING TRUST which is registered with the Housing Corporation.   [HC & DR]

registered trade mark Registered trade mark law is governed by the Trade Marks Act 1994 (for national trade marks), and the Council Directive 89/104/EEC for EU member States. The Community Trade Mark Regulations 2006 govern use of the Community trade mark in the UK.

Protection is available for any sign which can distinguish the goods and services of one trader from those of another. The law adopts a very expansive notion of sign; it is 'any sign capable of being represented graphically, particularly words, including personal names, designs, letters, numerals, the shape of goods or of their packaging, provided that such signs are capable of distinguishing the goods or services of one undertaking from those of other undertakings' (Article 2 of Council Directive 89/104/ EEC) to approximate to the laws of the MEMBER STATES relating to trade marks. In English law a sign can also be protected under the COMMON LAW action of PASSING OFF.

The main criterion of protection is **distinctiveness**, that is a capacity to distinguish the goods or services to which it is applied from the goods and services of other undertakings. Distinctiveness may be inherent in the mark itself or it may be acquired by association with a product over a period of time. Trade marks which are devoid of any distinctive character shall not be registered by virtue of s. 3(1)(b) of the 1994 Act. The law will also refuse to give protection to marks on various other absolute grounds (see the Trade Marks Act 1994, ss. 3, 4), irrespective of distinctiveness; for example, marks which comprise certain specially protected emblems, or shapes which result from the nature of the goods themselves, as well as marks which should be rejected on grounds of morality and public policy or those indicative of the characteristics of the goods or services.

Once a national or Community trade mark application is made, the application is either accepted, or objections are raised by the examiner. If accepted, the application is then published and third parties have the opportunity to oppose it. If no one opposes the application, the mark can be registered. A trade mark registration operates in perpetuity, as long as the registration is renewed every 10 years.   [US]

See also CERTIFICATION MARK; COLLECTIVE MARK; INFRINGEMENT ACTION.

Further reading: Jeremy Phillips, *Trade Mark Law: A Practical Anatomy* (Oxford: Oxford University Press, 2003).

Registrar of Friendly Societies (obsolete) *See* CERTIFICATION OFFICER.

registration of birth The entry in a register, made by the registrar of births and deaths for the sub-district in which a CHILD was born, of certain particulars concerning the birth (Births and Deaths Registration Act 1953, s. 1).

It is the duty of the mother and father to provide the necessary information and to sign the register within 42 days of the birth (s. 2). Although changes to the law are being debated, this duty does not at present extend to an unmarried father, nor does he have an independent right to register the birth. Since 2003, unmarried fathers may acquire PARENTAL RESPONSIBILITY by being registered as the father on the birth certificate (Children Act 1989, s. 4); that is, registration confers parental responsibility. Normally, an unmarried father can be registered as the father only if he and the mother attend to register together. If he attends alone to register, he must produce a **statutory declaration** of paternity, acknowledging that he is the father, together with a declaration signed by the mother. If the mother attends alone, she cannot register the father unless both he and she have signed a declaration acknowledging that he is the father. However, either the father or the mother can attend alone to register the father where a valid PARENTAL RESPONSIBILITY AGREEMENT or a relevant court order is produced along with a declaration that the agreement is valid or that the court order is in force. The relevant court orders include a PARENTAL RESPONSIBILITY ORDER and an order made under Schedule 1 of the Children Act 1989 requiring the father to make financial provision for the child (Births and Deaths Registration Act 1953, s. 10). The father's name can be entered at a later stage if the PARENTS jointly request this; if the necessary declarations are made; if there is a parental responsibility agreement; if there is a relevant order of court; or if the parents have married (ss. 10A and 14). If necessary, others can register a birth instead of the parents: the occupier of the house or hospital where the child was born; someone who was present at the birth; or someone who is responsible for the child (s. 1(2)). [FK]

See also FATHER'S RIGHTS; PARENTAL RIGHTS.

registration of marriage MARRIAGES lawfully solemnized, including meeting the preliminary requirements of obtaining the appropriate certificates or licences, are automatically registered. The parties will then receive a **marriage certificate** which details the date and place of marriage, the name, age and condition of the bride and groom, their occupation and usual address, the name and occupation of each person's father and the names of the witnesses and of the person who solemnized the marriage. Foreign marriages may not subsequently be registered in England and Wales, but there is provision for creating a record of a foreign marriage in the General Register Office. [AD]

See also MARRIAGE BY CERTIFICATE; MARRIAGE BY REGISTRAR GENERAL'S LICENCE; MARRIAGE BY RELIGIOUS LICENCE; MARRIAGE CEREMONY.

regulation The use of rules or other instruments by a public authority to ensure that resources or activities valued by society are controlled in accordance with agreed norms or standards whether by means of prohibition, instruction or enabling mechanisms. Beyond this general definition, there are accounts of regulation that emphasize narrower or broader understandings. Thus the term may be taken narrowly to refer simply to straightforward commands contained in legislative instruments. Alternatively, it may be used more broadly to encompass all aspects of the state's attempts to influence behaviour whether at the level of the individual or at that of the economy or society as a whole. This latter usage would include (in addition to commands) interventions based on incentives, disclosure of information and so on.

Regulation is most often deployed in circumstances where there is felt to be a failure of the market. Accordingly, it may be used to control monopolies where the absence of competition would allow the holder of the monopoly to abuse his or her dominant position. It may also be used to respond to negative externalities, that is, where costs associated with the production of an item are not reflected in the price, but rather are borne by third parties or by society as a whole (for example, the costs associated with cleaning up pollution caused by an industrial process). Markets may also be said to fail (and thus regulation may be felt to be required) when information required to make decisions about transactions is not available or where there is a significant imbalance in the bargaining positions of those involved in market transactions.

Regulation may also be deployed as a response to RISK. Examples include the risks associated with working in hazardous environments, the deployment of new technologies and exposure to harmful substances.

While regulation is most often identified as a state activity conducted in the general interest, the impetus to regulate may come from sources outside the state apparatus. Specific interest groups may instigate or at least try to influence the process. Examples include both non-governmental organizations and industry representative bodies. These groups may have relatively altruistic motives in bringing a particular problem to the attention of the state, but may equally seek to further private interests. Similarly, close relationships between regulators and regulated can be viewed positively as an indication that both are striving cooperatively for common objectives or negatively as a sign that the regulator has been 'captured' by the regulated. [JP]

See also COREGULATION; DEREGULATION; PRIVATIZATION; SELF-REGULATION.

Further reading: Robert Baldwin and Martin Cave, *Understanding Regulation: Theory, Strategy, and Practice* (Oxford: Oxford University Press, 1999).

Regulation (EC legislation) One of the legal instruments of the EUROPEAN COMMUNITY (EC). Forming part of the *ACQUIS* COMMUNAUTAIRE, Regulations, along with DIRECTIVES and DECISIONS, are the secondary forms of legislation in the EC. They are most often used for the purposes of harmonization of laws among the EC MEMBER STATES. Article 249 EC provides that 'a regulation shall have general application. It shall be binding in its entirety and directly applicable in all Member States.' A Regulation has effect as law once passed and published in the OFFICIAL JOURNAL of the EC, L series. [MON]

rehabilitation One of the rationales underpinning sentencing, the aim of which is to prevent the offenders from committing further crimes by addressing their individual propensity for offending, and by intervening in order to enable them to reform, so that they can cope effectively with the pressures that caused them to offend in the first place. Thus, rehabilitative interventions may be therapeutic in nature. The Criminal Justice Act 2003, s. 142, designates the reform and rehabilitation of offenders as one of the purposes of sentencing and requires a sentencing court to have regard to it and other purposes. [BF]

See also DESERT THEORY; DETERRENCE THEORY; RETRIBUTION; RETRIBUTIVISM.

rehabilitation period A set length of time after the date of conviction. Once a rehabilitation period has expired and no further offending has taken place, a conviction is considered to be 'spent'. [SN]

See also SPENT CONVICTION.

rehearing A subsequent hearing of a case that has already been adjudicated. Most APPEALS do not constitute a full rehearing of the evidence in the case. The exception to this rule in the criminal justice system is an appeal from the magistrates' court to the CROWN COURT, where the case is heard again by a judge sitting with two MAGISTRATES, and

at which both the original and additional evidence may be presented. In civil cases, the CIVIL PROCEDURE RULES Part 55 makes it clear that appeals are normally to involve only a review of the lower court's decision, unless the appeal court expressly determines that, in the circumstances of an individual case, it is in the interests of justice to hold a full rehearing. [JW]

See also RETRIAL.

reinstatement order An EMPLOYMENT TRIBUNAL may reinstate an EMPLOYEE into the post he or she held before an UNFAIR DISMISSAL. When considering a remedy for unfair dismissal, the tribunal must consider reinstatement first; then a RE-ENGAGEMENT ORDER; then COMPENSATION. Reinstatement and re-engagement are sometimes known as 're-employment'. The remedy of both reinstatement and re-engagement is discretionary, depending on the wishes of the employee, the practicability of the remedy, and, if the employee caused or contributed to the dismissal, whether it would be just and equitable to order re-employment. [MJ]

rejection of offer An OFFER may be refused or rejected by the offeree and, once rejected, it is no longer available to be accepted. Where the response to the offer is a counter-offer, this automatically rejects and destroys the offer (see *Hyde* v. *Wrench* (1840) 3 Beav 334). However, a request for further information does not amount to a rejection so that the offer remains open to be accepted. [JPL]

See also ACCEPTANCE.

release on licence *See* PAROLE.

relevance Having the tendency to render the fact to be proved more probable than it would be without that EVIDENCE. [ALTC]

relevant evidence EVIDENCE that satisfies the test of RELEVANCE. [ALTC]

relevant fact A fact that is not itself a FACT IN ISSUE but one that makes proof of a fact in issue more probable. [ALTC]

relevant transfer The Transfer of Undertakings (Protection of Employment) Regulations 2006 SI 2006/246 replace the 1981

Regulations of the same name. The common abbreviation is TUPE. They provide that on a 'relevant transfer', most contractual (e.g. WRONGFUL DISMISSAL) and statutory (e.g. SEX DISCRIMINATION) rights which the EMPLOYEE had against the transferor EMPLOYER are transferred to the transferee employer: see Reg. 4. The existence of a 'relevant transfer' depends on whether, at the time, there was the transfer of an **economic entity** which has kept its identity (Reg. 3(1)). An economic entity is an organized grouping of resources which pursues a commercial activity, whether or not that activity is central to the business as a whole (Reg. 3(2)). A 'service provision change' is deemed to be a 'relevant transfer' (Reg. 3(1)(b)); however the transfer of one task, the procurement or supply of goods and public administration changes are excluded.   [MJ]

See also ACQUIRED RIGHTS.

reliance theory Explains the source of contractual obligations as the fact of reliance on the PROMISE rather than the fact that the promise is made. This theory alleges that contractual obligations ensure that those who are induced to rely on promises in agreements are compensated for any loss they suffer as a result of that reliance. However, it is difficult to explain the fact that liability can rest on wholly EXECUTORY promises; or that PROMISSORY ESTOPPEL, which is based on reliance, cannot be seen as a source of contractual obligations.   [JPL]

Further reading: L.L. Fuller and William R. Perdue, 'The Reliance Interest in Contract Damages', *Yale Law Journal*, 46 (1936) p. 53; P.S. Atiyah, 'Contract promises and the law of obligations', *Law Quarterly Review*, 94 (1978), p. 193.

relief from forfeiture The courts have a discretionary power to protect a TENANT from FORFEITURE. The remedy is based on the disproportionate impact of forfeiture of a LEASE: for instance, a long leaseholder who has paid £300,000 for a property but has failed to get the landlord's consent to the assignment may have breached a covenant in the lease, but the penalty for breach – loss of his or her property – is dis-

proportionate. The landlord must follow a statutory procedure and apply to court in order to exercise the right to forfeiture and in practice relief will almost always be granted as long as the breach is remedied, e.g. by obtaining the necessary consents.
                                                                    [HC & DR]

religion *See* BLASPHEMY; CANON LAW; CHURCH OF ENGLAND; CONSCIENCE AND RELIGION; FREEDOM OF THOUGHT; ISLAMIC LAW; JEWISH LAW; RELIGIOUS HATRED.

religious hatred Defined as 'hatred against a group of persons defined by reference to religious belief or lack of religious belief' (see Public Order Act 1986, s. 29). The Racial and Religious Hatred Act 2006 amends the Public Order Act 1986 by inserting a new Part 3A into that Act, which outlaws incitement to religious hatred by the use of words or behaviour, the publication or distribution of written material, the public performance of a play, or by distributing or playing a recording or broadcasting a programme. No proceedings for an offence under Part 3A may be commenced without the consent of the ATTORNEY GENERAL.   [JW]

remainder An INTEREST IN LAND that will not take effect until the ending of a prior interest in possession; for example, where X gives land 'to Y for life and after his death to Z', Y has a LIFE INTEREST in possession and Z owns the remainder. Although Z will not be entitled to possession of the land until Y's death, Z's remainder is a current interest in land, which may be dealt with accordingly. On Y's death, Z's remainder will become a FEE SIMPLE ABSOLUTE IN POSSESSION. Under the Law of Property Act 1925, s. 1, a remainder can only be an EQUITABLE INTEREST.

A remainder may be either a **vested remainder** or a **contingent remainder**. A **vested remainder** is one where the REMAINDERMAN is ascertained and the interest is ready to take effect in possession, subject only to the determination of the prior interest. The example above is a vested remainder because Z is ascertainable and the interest is ready to take effect subject only to Y's death. A **contingent remainder** is one where the identity of the remainder-man is unascertainable, or the right of possession is dependent on an uncertain event. For example, where X gives land 'to Y for life and after his death to his eldest living child if he reaches the age of 21' there is a contingent remainder, since Y's eldest living child's entitlement to the estate is contingent upon an uncertain event, namely his reaching the age of 21. [DR]

remainderman A person entitled to an interest in land in REMAINDER; for example, where X gives his land 'to Y for life, remainder to Z', Z is the remainderman. [DR]

remand Between court appearances a defendant will be remanded, either on BAIL or in custody. It is common to speak of the defendant who is remanded on bail as being 'bailed' and the defendant who is remanded in custody as being 'remanded'. Defendants who have been remanded in custody pending the outcome of their trial are sometimes referred to, in the context of imprisonment, as being 'on remand'. [BF]

remedial constructive trust *See* CON-STRUCTIVE TRUST.

remedy The method of recovery, redress or protection flowing from the infringement of a legal right. Remedies include the award of DAMAGES or forms of equitable relief, such as an INJUNCTION or decree of SPECIFIC PERFORMANCE. Remedies are of fundamental practical and conceptual importance to the operation of law. They are the law's way of giving substance to the values expressed by legal rights; without the remedy, the right itself remains intangible. [JW]

See also UBI JUS, IBI REMEDIUM.

remission (obsolete) A reduction in sentence. It was routinely applied to custodial sentences – and would only be forfeited for poor behaviour in custody – until its abolition by the Criminal Justice Act 1991. Thus, until the 1991 Act, a person who was sentenced to three years' imprisonment could expect to have one year of the sentence deducted as remission. The use of remission

was criticized because it hindered transparency in sentencing. [BF]

See also RELEASE ON LICENCE.

remoteness of damage In order to recover DAMAGES in CONTRACT and TORT, the loss must not be too remote. However, different tests for remoteness apply.

1. In relation to a BREACH OF CONTRACT claim, the loss (or type of loss) must have been a natural consequence of the breach, or within the parties' contemplation as a serious possibility or probable result of its breach at the time of the contract (see *Hadley* v. *Baxendale* (1854) 9 Exch 341 and *Heron II* [1969] 1 AC 350). In practice this means that in order to be recoverable the loss must be either one that would arise in the ordinary course of events following such a breach, or if the loss was a consequence of special circumstances in that case, those circumstances must have been known to the defaulting party at the time the contract was entered into.

2. In tort, a distinction must be made between NEGLIGENCE and intentional torts (i.e. where there is some deliberate wrongdoing or intention to cause loss or harm, such as TRESPASS TO THE PERSON or DECEIT). In actions for negligence, losses will only be recoverable if they are a foreseeable consequence of the breach of duty (*The Wagon Mound (No. 1)* [1961] AC 388). That does not mean that the precise nature of the harm must have been foreseeable, but it must have been of a kind or type of loss that was. With regard to intentional torts, the defendant will be liable for all the direct consequences of his actions (see *Quinn* v. *Leathem* [1901] AC 495, 537; and *Doyle* v. *Olby (Ironmongers) Ltd* [1969] 2 QB 158). More recently, however, Lord Nicholls has indicated, in the context of an action for CONVERSION, that the courts should adopt a differentiated test, whereby the damage must be a direct consequence if the conversion is knowingly wrongful, but foreseeable if it is not (see *Kuwait Airways* v. *Iraqi Airways* [2002] 2 AC 883). It remains to be seen how far that approach will be extended to other torts that may be committed intentionally or otherwise. [JPL & JW]

removal of an arbitrator Where the *LEX ARBITRI* permits, the parties can agree the circumstances in which the arbitrator can be required to stand down; and the parties or one of them may apply to the courts of the seat of arbitration for the removal of an arbitrator. In England and Wales, the Arbitration Act 1996 provides for removal of an arbitrator by the court where, for example, the arbitrator: (a) is proved not to be impartial or there are justifiable doubts to that effect; (b) is alleged to be physically or mentally incapable; or (c) has demonstrated his failure to conduct the proceedings with 'reasonable despatch' or to make an award with reasonable despatch, and in either event 'substantial injustice has been or will be caused' to the party applying for the removal.   [RE]

remuneration certificate Where a client wishes to question how fair and reasonable a solicitor's charges are, they can apply to the Legal Complaints Service (see http:// www.legalcomplaints.org.uk/how-we-handle-complaints/about-your-solicitors-bill. page) for a remuneration certificate under the Solicitors' (Non-Contentious Business) Remuneration Order 1994. The process is free of charge, but applies only to non-contentious business, i.e. matters other than litigation. Litigation COSTS are assessed by the court.   [JW]

renewal of lease The grant of a new LEASE between the same parties on similar terms – other than RENT – and relating to the same property as a previous lease which has been terminated. The Landlord and Tenant Act 1954 contains a statutory framework for the renewal of commercial leases.

[HC & DR]

See also INTERIM RENT.

Renner, Karl (1870–1950) Austrian jurist and politician whose theory of law was influenced by Marxist sociology. Renner sought to demonstrate that although legal concepts such as property appear stable through time, the function they perform is subject to (possibly significant) change. His approach was to insist that an understanding of a legal concept depended on an understanding of its economic base. For example, in the earlier stages of economic development identified by Marx, such as feudalism, property and production would be co-located. Thus, a farm would be owned by the same person who was directly responsible for the production on that farm. Within capitalism, however, ownership and production are no longer co-located and the former becomes a means by which control may be exercised over the latter. Renner's point is that while the legal concept (property) has not changed, the social function it performs has been profoundly transformed.

Renner's insistence on the stability of legal concepts may appear to put him at odds with Marx, who held that law was part of the mutable superstructure rather than the unchanging base, but his subtle distinction between legal form and legal function is perhaps more realistic than Marx's approach.   [JP]

See also MARXIST JURISPRUDENCE.

Further reading: Karl Renner, *The Institutions of Private Law and their Social Functions* (London: Routledge and Kegan Paul, 1949).

rent The entire sum of money or the provision of goods and services which can be quantified in money which is payable by the TENANT to the LANDLORD. The payment of rent was suggested by the House of Lords in *Street* v. *Mountford* [1985] AC 809 as an essential characteristic of a tenancy. However, in *Ashburn Anstalt* v. *Arnold* [1989] Ch 1 the court accepted that while payment of rent was influential in the decision about whether an agreement was a LEASE or a licence it was not a prerequisite of a tenancy.   [HC & DR]

rent rebate A benefit paid by LOCAL AUTHORITIES to their own TENANTS who are eligible for housing benefit. It is paid into the rent accounts of tenants rather than directly to them.   [HC & DR]

rent registration Part of a statutory system of protection of regulated tenancies under the Rent Act 1977. Regulated tenants can apply to the rent service to have their rent registered as a fair rent. Only residential tenancies granted before 15 January 1989 benefit from rent registration.

[HC & DR]

rental right The right given to all COPYRIGHT owners (except broadcasters and publishers) to authorize or prohibit the rental of copies of the work. Rental for this purpose means making a copy of the work available for use, on terms that it will or may be returned, for direct or indirect economic or commercial advantage.

The rental right is affiliated to the PUBLIC LENDING RIGHT but it is different in that the lending right allows a copyright owner to control the use of the work through a public establishment, such as a lending library, for non-economic or non-commercial advantage. [US]

See also DISTRIBUTION RIGHT.

rentcharge A periodic payment in respect of land that does not refer to rent under a LEASE or a sum payable by way of interest. A rentcharge is similar to rent under a lease, except that a rentcharge can itself be owned and is a burden on the land itself, whereas rent under a lease is incidental to the relationship of landlord and tenant. A rentcharge payable on a FREEHOLD or LEASEHOLD interest is capable of existing as a LEGAL ESTATE. Otherwise it is an EQUITABLE INTEREST, which may be registered as a GENERAL EQUITABLE CHARGE (e.g. a rentcharge on a LIFE INTEREST). If a rentcharge is in arrears for over 40 days, the owner of the charge is entitled to take possession of land and take income from the land until the costs occasioned by non-payment of the rent are satisfied.

Prior to 1977, rentcharges were commonly used where a proprietor would sell his freehold for a lump sum plus a rentcharge to be paid annually. The Rentcharges Act 1977 abolished most types of rentcharges, providing that, subject to two exceptions, no further rentcharges could be created after 21 August 1977 and all existing rentcharges would be extinguished after 60 years. The two exceptions are: (a) rentcharges created under a trust of land where the land is charged either voluntarily, or in consideration of marriage or the formulation of a civil partnership, for the benefit of a specific person; and (b) ESTATE RENTCHARGES. [DR]

renunciation of probate A person who has been appointed EXECUTOR by the WILL of a TESTATOR is not obliged to accept the appointment. He may renounce at any time until he accepts office. Once he accepts office, he can no longer renounce. He will accept office either by taking PROBATE, or by doing an act in relation to the testator's ASSETS indicating an intention to act in the administration. The renunciation is made by a written document signed by the executor and filed in a Probate Registry. Once an executor has renounced, the renunciation may be retracted only with the permission of the court. [CM]

repairs Refers to a covenant in most leases which sets out the different obligations of landlord and tenant in connection with repairs. In short residential leases, statute has intervened to place the obligation firmly with the landlord. [HC & DR]

reparation The INTERNATIONAL LAW obligation on a STATE to make full reparation for injury caused by an internationally wrongful act, according to Article 31 of the INTERNATIONAL LAW COMMISSION's 2001 Articles on the Responsibility of States for Internationally Wrongful Acts. Full reparation shall take the form of restitution, compensation or satisfaction, whether singly or in combination. Restitution requires re-establishing the situation which existed before the wrongful act was committed, provided that restitution is not materially impossible and does not involve a burden out of all proportion to the benefit deriving from restitution instead of compensation (Article 35). Where restitution is not feasible, compensation shall cover any financially assessable damage, including loss of profits (Article 36). Satisfaction may consist of an acknowledgement of the breach, an expression of regret, a formal apology or another appropriate measure of this kind (see Article 37). Interest on any PRINCIPAL may also be payable when necessary in order to ensure full reparation (Article 38). [IB]

See also STATE RESPONSIBILITY.

reparation order An order made against a child or young person who has been convicted of an offence, requiring him or her to make specific reparations to the victim or to the community. [SN]

repeat offender A term used principally in the law of sentencing to denote an offender previously convicted of an offence or offences. [BF]
See also FIRST OFFENDER; PERSISTENT OFFENDER.

representation order An order authorizing payment of LEGAL AID for a defendant. [SN]

representative action A civil action in which one or a few members of a group or 'class' sue on behalf of themselves and other members of the same class under the CIVIL PROCEDURE RULES, Rule 19.6. No court permission is required to launch a representative action, though the court does retain powers to exclude a party from acting as a representative of the class. Any judgment given in a representative action is generally binding upon all those represented in the claim. [JW]
See also GROUP LITIGATION.

reprisal The limited use of armed force by one state in response to an act in breach of the laws of armed conflict by another. Under CUSTOMARY INTERNATIONAL LAW a right of reprisal exists, provided that such reprisal complies with four principles: (a) it must be an action of last resort; (b) notice of the planned action has been given to the other state; (c) the harm inflicted on the adversary is proportionate to that which they have caused; and (d) the reprisal is temporary, and will stop when the other party ceases its illegal behaviour. TREATY law has increasingly moved to outlaw reprisals. Article 51 of the UN CHARTER further limits the right of reprisal to instances of legitimate self-defence, and the 1949 GENEVA CONVENTIONS also prohibit reprisals against the persons or objects under their protection. [IB]
See also RETORSION; SANCTIONS; USE OF FORCE.

republication of will A WILL normally dates from the date it was executed. However, if it is republished, it is deemed to date from the date of republication. A will may be republished either by re-executing it or by reference to it in a subsequent CODICIL with the intention to republish it, for example by using an expression such as 'and in all other respect I confirm my said will'. This will does not, of course, take effect until the death of the testator, but the date of the will can have important consequences. If a will refers to a BENEFICIARY by description, then it will be the person who satisfies the description at the date of the will, and not at the date of death of the testator, who will benefit. [CM]
See also EXECUTION OF WILL.

repudiation **1**. In contract law, repudiation refers to a repudiatory BREACH OF CONTRACT, whereby one of the parties from whom performance is due makes it clear, either explicitly or impliedly, that they will not perform or continue to perform one or more of their obligations under the CONTRACT. Repudiation may involve renouncing the contract or the party may incapacitate itself from performing its obligations (e.g. by selling the property in question to another). Alternatively, it will occur when breaches of certain terms of the contract take place, such as breach of a CONDITION or breach of an INNOMINATE TERM.
2. In INTERNATIONAL LAW, an action or statement by a STATE, indicating that it will no longer be bound by a TREATY obligation. Such repudiation is contrary to international law, unless it can be justified on one of the grounds for securing release from such an obligation under Articles 46–53 of the Vienna Convention on the Law of Treaties. [JPL & IB]

requisition A document issued under the Criminal Justice Act 2003, s. 29, requiring a person to appear before a magistrates' court to answer a written charge. [SN]

requisitions on title In CONVEYANCING, formal written questions presented by the buyer's solicitor in order to investigate the seller's TITLE to land. Traditionally, requisitions on title were raised following the exchange of contracts. However, modern practice is to raise most requisitions before exchange, with only a limited number of standard requisitions raised after exchange and prior to COMPLETION.

Requisitions on title are most important in relation to UNREGISTERED LAND, where investigation of the ABSTRACT OF TITLE or EPITOME OF TITLE raises uncertainty regarding the seller's entitlement to land. Requisitions are commonly raised regarding any outstanding mortgages, restrictive covenants, grants of probate (where the property devolved on death), evidence of joint ownership and the stamping and execution of deeds. Unless the seller's solicitor provides adequate answers to these requisitions, the buyer may not be satisfied that the seller has good title to the land and may withdraw from the transaction. [DR]

res communis (Lat. a thing held in common) Property that is owned in common or by the community, so, for example, in some national legal systems, land owned by the STATE is technically *res communis*. In INTERNATIONAL LAW, it constitutes an area that is not subject to the legal title of any state, such as the high seas or OUTER SPACE. [JW]

res extincta (Lat. things that do not exist) It is applied as a contractual doctrine to COMMON MISTAKE so that where, unknown to both of the parties at the time the CONTRACT was made, the subject matter had been destroyed, or had never existed, the mistake will be so fundamental as to render the contract void for impossibility. [JPL]

See also VOID CONTRACT.

res gestae (Lat. things done; the transaction) The COMMON LAW recognizes a principle that evidence of out-of-court statements may be ADMISSIBLE as an exception to the hearsay rule, if these statements are so closely connected in time, place and circumstances with some transaction which is at issue that they can be said to form a part of that transaction. This principle has been preserved for criminal cases by the Criminal Justice Act 2003, s. 118(4) which states that evidence may be given of '(a) [a] statement … made by a person so emotionally overpowered by an event that

the possibility of concoction or distortion can be disregarded, (b) [a] statement accompany[ing] an act which can be properly evaluated as evidence only if considered in conjunction with the statement, or (c) [a] statement relat[ing] to a physical sensation or a mental state (such as intention or emotion)'. [ALTC]

res ipsa loquitur (Lat. the thing speaks for itself) In NEGLIGENCE, it is normally up to the claimant to demonstrate that, on the BALANCE OF PROBABILITIES, the defendant was in breach of his duty of care. However, in some cases the facts so strongly suggest negligence on the defendant's part that they may be said to 'speak for themselves'. In such cases a breach of duty will be presumed, unless the defendant can offer some alternative explanation (see *Scott* v. *London and St Katherine's Dock Company* (1865) 3 H & C 596). [HJ]

res judicata (Lat. a thing (already) judged) The inability, in law, of a party to litigation or ARBITRATION proceedings to pursue a claim (or a COUNTERCLAIM) on a CAUSE OF ACTION against the other party where the matter has already been determined between those same parties by the issue of a final and binding judgment in litigation or a final and binding award in arbitration. So, for example, where a court (including a foreign court) has issued a judgment in an action between A and B, neither A nor B may re-litigate or arbitrate that same cause of action in England, provided that there is no ground to condemn the judgment. An equivalent rule applies in respect of arbitral awards. [RE]

See also AWARD.

resale royalty right Under the Artist's Resale Right Regulations 2006, Reg. 3, the author of any picture, print, painting or other form of graphic art, or sculpture, ceramic, glassware or photograph in which COPYRIGHT subsists, has a right to a ROYALTY on any sale of such work which is a resale subsequent to the first transfer of ownership by the author. A copy of a work will not be protected unless it is one of a limited number which have been made by the author or under his or her authority. The resale right will last for as long as copyright subsists in the work.

The sale of an art work will not be regarded as a resale if the seller previously acquired the work directly from the author less than three years before the sale; and the sale price did not exceed 10,000 euros. The following persons may be liable to pay the resale royalty: the seller; the agent of the seller; the agent of the buyer; or the buyer. The resale right can only be exercised through a COLLECTING SOCIETY.   [US]

rescission An equitable remedy which may be exercised by the injured party to set aside a VOIDABLE CONTRACT with the aim of restoring the parties to their original pre-contract positions. It can be achieved by clearly indicating an intention no longer to be bound by the CONTRACT and communicating that to the other party. However, it may require the intervention of the court to confirm the right to rescind by court order. Rescission may be lost (barred) through affirmation, lapse of time, inability to restore the original positions (*RESTITUTIO IN INTEGRUM*) or where third parties have acquired rights in the goods or property to be restored. The Misrepresentation Act 1967, s. 2(2) allows the court to award DAMAGES, where it would be equitable to do so, in place of the remedy of rescission, which would otherwise be available, because rescission would be too drastic a remedy in the light of the nature of the misrepresentation and in the light of the loss to the misrepresentee if the contract could not be rescinded. Rescission has been held to be a total remedy so that partial rescission is not possible. It has the effect of treating the contract as if it had never existed, i.e. ending it retrospectively, and so must be distinguished from terminating a contract for repudiatory breach (sometimes confusingly termed 'rescission') which has the effect of discharging both parties' future obligations under a valid contract.   [JPL]

resealed grant The Colonial Probates Act 1892 provides that a GRANT OF REPRESENTATION made in any country to which the Act has been applied may be resealed in the HIGH COURT, and will then have the same effect as if the grant had been made in England and Wales. This now covers most Commonwealth countries. The situation this deals with is typically when the deceased dies abroad and a grant is made to his estate in that country, but it transpires that he has also left ASSETS in this country which also have to be dealt with. The Act removes the necessity of having to go through the formalities of applying for a further grant of representation here, and substitutes a quick and informal procedure.   [CM]

reservation Defined in Article 2(1)(d) of the 1969 Vienna Convention on the Law of Treaties as 'a unilateral statement, however phrased or named, made by a STATE when signing, ratifying, accepting, approving or acceding to a TREATY, whereby it purports to exclude or to modify the legal effect of certain provisions of the treaty in their application to that state'. Reservations are permitted as long as they are not expressly prohibited by the treaty itself, or by the treaty's object and purpose. Where the other parties to a treaty are silent as to a reservation, they are deemed to have accepted it and no other act of recognition is required. Where, however, parties do not accept the reservation, they can choose to modify their treaty relations with the reserving party with regard to the matter raised by the reservation only, or they can modify their relations with the reserving state completely. Since 1995, the practice of states with regard to HUMAN RIGHTS and humanitarian law-related treaties has been to prohibit any and all reservations.

[IB]

See also RATIFICATION OF TREATIES.

reserved legal activity Defined by the Legal Services Act 2007, s. 12, as work that involves the exercise of a RIGHT OF AUDIENCE; the conduct of litigation; 'reserved instrument' activities; PROBATE activities; notarial activities or the administration of oaths. Undertaking certain 'reserved' or protected legal work, notably obtaining probate or acting as an advocate for a fee, has long been unlawful under English law for anyone other than a SOLICITOR or BARRIS-

TER. The Legal Services Board, once fully operational from 2010, will have the power to extend the scope of reserved legal activity to other professional bodies operating under its umbrella. It will be a criminal offence to undertake a reserved legal activity unless one is authorized to do so by an approved regulatory body, or exempted by virtue of appearing in the list of exempted occupations contained in Schedule 3 of the 2007 Act. [JW]

See also MCKENZIE FRIEND.

residence order An order made under the Children Act 1989 which settles the practical details of where a CHILD will live. Residence replaces the old concept of custody and the order is intended to signify that both parents retain PARENTAL RESPONSIBILITY for the child even after they separate, and the issue is only with whom the child will live. A NON-RESIDENT PARENT will usually continue contact with the child, either by CONTACT ORDER or agreement. Residence orders may also be made in favour of non-parents such as grandparents (but not a LOCAL AUTHORITY), in which case parental responsibility will attach to the order. The residence order can be shared between two or more people who live separately and the court may impose conditions on it. The court will always decide these matters with the welfare of the child as its paramount consideration. [AD]

See also PROHIBITED STEPS ORDER; SPECIFIC ISSUES ORDER; WELFARE PRINCIPLE.

residential occupier A residential OCCUPIER is a person who lawfully occupies a property as a residence. 'Lawfully' here means as a result of a contract, or through the operation of statute or a rule of law. Therefore it would include a contractual TENANT, a licensee whose licence has not been lawfully terminated, a service occupier and a statutory tenant among others.

If a residential occupier is evicted other than in accordance with the law, then the person who evicts him commits a criminal offence. A criminal offence is also committed if someone harasses the residential occupier. Harassment includes acts likely to interfere with the peace or comfort of the residential occupier or the persistent withdrawal of services such as water and electricity. [HC & DR]

Residential Property Tribunal Part of the Residential Property Tribunal Service, it deals with a broad range of issues arising under the Housing Act 2004, including appeals in respect of the enforcement measures in the HOUSING HEALTH AND SAFETY RATING SYSTEM, the licensing of HOUSES IN MULTIPLE OCCUPATION and selective licensing. The statutory basis of a Residential Property Tribunal is as a Rent Assessment Committee (RAC), but when the RAC is constituted to exercise its 2004 Act jurisdiction it is known as a Residential Property Tribunal. Appeals from decisions of Residential Property Tribunals are made to the Lands Tribunal. [HC & DR]

residuary legatee *See* RESIDUE.

residue The 'residue of an ESTATE' is the expression given to whatever is left over after all specific, general and demonstrative GIFTS have been made. Most WILLS list any such gifts, and have a final clause leaving the residue, i.e. anything not already disposed of, to a residuary LEGATEE or residuary DEVISEE depending on the nature of the ASSETS. [CM]

See also LEGACY.

resisting arrest Under the Offences against the Person Act 1861, s. 38, it is an offence for someone to ASSAULT any person with intent to resist or prevent the lawful apprehension or detainer (in effect, the arrest) of himself or of any other person for any offence. Section 18 of the 1861 Act sets out offences of wounding or causing GRIEVOUS BODILY HARM with intent to resist arrest. [BF]

See also OBSTRUCTING A POLICE OFFICER; POWER OF ARREST; ULTERIOR INTENT.

respondent The opposing or defending party in an APPEAL or petition to the courts. [AF]

See also APPELLANT.

responsibility of states *See* STATE RESPONSIBILITY.

restitutio in integrum (Lat. to restore in its entirety (i.e. to its original state)) If it is not possible to restore the original position, for example by returning goods or property received in their original condition, the equitable remedy of RESCISSION is not available since the basis of rescission is that the contract is set aside and treated as if it had never existed. However, where the imperfections are minor, and particularly in the case of FRAUDULENT MISREPRESENTATIONS, equity will allow the remedy of rescission and may impose terms to achieve practical justice, for example, an ACCOUNT OF PROFITS can be made while holding the property or a financial allowance granted to cover their deterioration in the period prior to being returned (see *Erlanger* v. *New Sombrero Phosphate Co.* (1878) 3 App Cas 1218). [JPL]

restitution The return of property or goods to their owner or the person entitled to possession. If the recipient has received the money or property as a result of a MISTAKE or illegality, or has given nothing at all of the performance promised in exchange for it, he or she would be unjustly enriched if permitted to retain the money or property. An obligation therefore arises to return the property or goods. This obligation is said to be 'like contract' (**quasi-contract**) but it does not arise from a voluntary acceptance of the obligation but from operation of law. [JPL]

See also UNJUST ENRICHMENT.

restitution order An order restoring stolen goods (which includes goods obtained by deception or blackmail) to the owner. The Powers of Criminal Courts (Sentencing) Act 2000, s. 148, provides that the court may order anyone having possession or control of the goods to restore them to the person entitled to recover them. [SN]

restitutionary interest The interest of a party in recovering money or property transferred where the recipient would be unjustly enriched if permitted to retain it, for example where an advance payment has been made but there has been no performance of the other party's obligations under the CONTRACT. [JPL]

See also UNJUST ENRICHMENT.

restorative justice 1. A voluntary process within the criminal justice system that seeks to resolve conflict and repair or reduce the impact of offending on the victim and the community. Restorative justice operates through a number of diversionary mechanisms, including ANTI-SOCIAL BEHAVIOUR CONTRACTS, victim–offender MEDIATION and FAMILY GROUP CONFERENCING, and encourages informal reparation by offenders. It has also influenced a growing variety of COMMUNITY PENALTIES which stress reparation and are now available to the courts.

2. A broad theory of conflict resolution which extends beyond the criminal justice sphere. It encompasses a number of growing social movements to institutionalize community-based, reconciliatory and preventative approaches to conflict, including conflicts caused by violations of human and legal rights. These initiatives range from tribunals such as the TRUTH AND RECONCILIATION COMMISSIONS to local innovations in schools, social services and community organizations. [JW]

Further reading: D. Sullivan and L. Tifft, *The Handbook of Restorative Justice: A Global Perspective* (Abingdon: Routledge, 2006).

restraining order Under the Protection from Harassment Act 1997, s. 5, the court, on sentencing a person for any offence, has the power to make a restraining order prohibiting the defendant from doing anything which amounts to harassment or causes fear of violence to the victim or another person, such as the victim's CHILD. Conditions may be attached to the order and it may last for a definite or indefinite time. The court also has the power to make such an order when a defendant has been acquitted of an offence if the court thinks it is necessary to protect a person from harassment by the defendant. Breach of a restraining order is itself an offence. [AD]

restraint of trade A contractual term limiting a party's right to exercise his or her trade or carry on his or her business. Such terms are common in employment and partnership CONTRACTS and may seek to prohibit the employee or partner from engaging in a similar business in a particular geographical location for a specific period after the current relationship ends, or seek to protect TRADE SECRETS and confidential information. A restraint of trade provision will be void unless the party relying on it establishes that it does not infringe public policy and is reasonable as between the parties in terms of duration, scope and location (see *Nordenfelt* v. *Maxim Nordenfelt Guns and Ammunition Co. Ltd* [1894] AC 535 *per* Lord Macnaghten). [JPL]

restriction In the REGISTERED LAND system, an entry on the Land Register regulating the circumstances in which a disposition of a registered ESTATE or charge may be the subject of an entry in the Register (Land Registration Act 2002 (LRA 2002), s. 40 (1)). A restriction is entered on the Land Register against the registered estate to which it relates. Essentially, a restriction prevents a person from dealing with a registered estate, in order to protect the legitimate interest of a third party. Such a restriction may be indefinite, for a certain period, or until the occurrence of a specified event (LRA 2002, s. 40(2)(b)). Such a specified event may be the giving of notice, the obtaining of consent, or the making of an order by the court or by a Land Registry registrar (LRA 2002, s. 40(3)).

Persons who may apply for a restriction include the registered proprietor as well as persons with sufficient interest in making an entry (e.g. a person with an equitable interest in the land under a trust, where there is only one legal owner). If the application is not made by the PROPRIETOR, he must be notified and may object to the restriction being entered.

Restrictions are often used where LEASE-HOLD property is managed by a management company; for example, a restriction may be placed on the register stating that no registration of a disposition of the property shall be made without the consent of an officer of that management company. [DR]

restrictive covenant In land law, a promise made by deed under which one person (the **covenantor**) agrees to restrict the use of his land for the benefit of the land of another (the **covenantee**). Restrictive covenants are often used in the sale of a part of land, where the buyer promises, for example, not to use the premises as anything other than a dwellinghouse or not to block accessways.

Restrictive covenants are enforceable by and against not only the original parties to the covenant, but in certain circumstances by and against successors in TITLE to the land as well, where the benefit or burden 'runs with the land'. The benefit of a covenant will pass to the covenantee's successor in title, both in law and in equity, where: (a) the covenant 'touches and concerns' the land of the covenantee, meaning that the mode of occupation or value of the land itself must be affected, rather than the covenantee personally (*Rogers* v. *Hosegood* [1900] 2 Ch 388); (b) at the time the covenant was entered into, it was intended between the parties for the benefit of the covenant to run with the land (Law of Property Act 1925, s. 78 implies such an intention into all freehold covenants); (c) at the time the covenant was entered into, the covenantee owned the benefited land (*Webb* v. *Russell* (1789) 3 Term Rep 393); and (d) the successor claiming to enforce the covenant derives his title from or under the original covenantee (*Smith and Snipes Hall Farm Ltd* v. *River Douglas Catchment Board* [1949] 2 KB 500).

The burden of a restrictive covenant cannot run with the land in law, but it can in equity and will bind the covenantor's successor in title where: (a) the covenant is negative in nature, not requiring the expenditure of money (*Haywood* v. *Brunswick Permanent Benefit Building Society* (1881) 8 QBD 403); (b) the covenant 'touches and concerns' the land of the covenantee (as above); (c) at the time the covenant was entered into, the covenantee owned the benefited land (as above); (d) the parties intended the burden to run with the land (LPA 1925, s. 79 implies such an intention into all freehold covenants); and (e) the successor in title to the land has notice of the restrictive covenant. In UNREGISTERED LAND, for pre-1926 restrictive covenants, the purchaser must have actual, constructive or imputed knowledge of the covenant, whereas for post-1926 restrictive covenants, the interest must be registered as a Class D (ii) LAND CHARGE. In REGISTERED LAND, the restrictive covenant must be entered on the charges register for the land affected.

The law on restrictive covenants has been strongly criticized and subject to several proposed reforms, most recently in the Law Commission's report, *Transfer of Land: On the Law of Positive and Restrictive Covenants* (Law Com. No. 127, 1984), which proposed the abolition of the current law on covenants, to be replaced by 'land obligations'. The 1984 proposals will not now be implemented, although the Law Commission are currently planning a detailed consultation paper on the law of easements and covenants, which will revisit aspects of the 1984 report.   [DR]

See also COVENANT.

Further reading: Judith-Anne Mackenzie and Mary Phillips, *Textbook on Land Law*, 11th edn (Oxford: Oxford University Press, 2006); Edward Hector Burn and John Cartwright, *Cheshire and Burn's Modern Law of Real Property*, 17th edn (Oxford: Oxford University Press, 2006).

resulting trust (Lat. *resalire*, to jump back) A TRUST that arises in certain circumstances when the absolute owner of property transfers legal title to another but acquires a beneficial interest in the property, or its product, as a result of the equitable interest, supposedly, 'jumping back' to the transferor under a resulting trust. There are broadly three situations where resulting trusts arise: (a) the **voluntary conveyance** (or gratuitous transfer) resulting trust, which arises when a gratuitous *inter vivos* (i.e. lifetime) transfer is made from A to B, in the absence of any evidence suggesting that a GIFT was intended; and where B is

neither the wife nor child of a male transferor, in which case the countervailing presumption of advancement applies; (b) the **purchase money** resulting trust, which arises when A effects a gratuitous transfer to B, by making an *inter vivos* payment to C to convey rights to B subject to the same exclusionary conditions; and (c) the **failed trust** resulting trust, which arises whenever A transfers property to an intended TRUSTEE in circumstances where the trust either wholly or partly fails, with the effect that any undisposed portion of the equitable title returns to A on trust.

The term traditionally forms part of the threefold classification of trusts into express, constructive and resulting, although, unlike its counterparts, the definition does not refer to how the trust arose but only where the equitable TITLE went. Thus any trust, whether express or constructive, in which the beneficial interest returns to the transferor, can properly be described as a resulting trust. The traditional threefold classification is consequently flawed and of questionable analytical use, leading to a still unresolved debate concerning the doctrinal basis of resulting trusts. Lord Browne Wilkinson in *Girozentrale Westdeutche Landesbank* v. *Islington LBC* [1996] AC 669 rooted his analysis in the notion of implied intention, although it is unclear how this applies to failed trust resulting trusts which often arise quite contrary to the intention of the settlor and where there is no room for a presumption to operate as there is no evidential gap to fill.

Another approach has been based on the absence of intention to give beneficially (either implied or, in the case of failed trusts, explicit). However, it is difficult to see how the presumption in respect of **gratuitous transfer** resulting trusts is different to Browne-Wilkinson's approach as, in this context, there is no means of effecting a transfer that does not dispose of the entire interest except by means of a trust. Finally, there is the older, and probably more convincing analysis, adopted by the HOUSE OF LORDS in *Vandervell* v. *IRC* [1967] 2 AC 291, which suggested there are simply two quite different types of resulting trust: **presumed resulting trusts**, which rebuttably arise in respect of gratuitous transfers; and **automatic resulting trusts**, that arise by operation of law, in the wake of failed trusts; which, as later commentators have noted, are therefore a form of CONSTRUCTIVE TRUST. [PK]

resulting use Prior to 1926, a type of USE where legal title to property was transferred but there was no consideration, or the property was not stated to be held 'to the use of' a beneficiary, i.e. beneficial ownership did not transfer. In such a situation, beneficial ownership reverted, or resulted, back to the original owner and under the Statute of Uses 1535 the title was revested in the original owner. For example, where X conveyed his estate to Y, but X did not state for whose use the property was to be held, or Y did not give consideration for the estate, both the legal and equitable estate reverted back to X. [DR]

See also RESULTING TRUST.

retainer A CONTRACT FOR SERVICES existing between a solicitor and client. [JW]

retirement age Until 2006 the UK had no legal retirement age (by contrast with the statutory pensionable age). Following the Employment Equality (Age) Regulations 2006 (SI 2006/1031) the national 'default retirement age' for both men and women is set at 65. Mandatory retirement before that age is unlawful unless a lower age can be objectively justified. Retirement age can also be set higher than 65. [MJ]

See also AGE DISCRIMINATION.

retirement of trustees A TRUSTEE may retire from a TRUST under an express power in the trust instrument, under the Trustee Act 1925, s. 39, under an order of the court or by direction of the beneficiaries under the Trusts of Land and Appointment of Trustees Act 1996, s. 19. [PK]

retorsion (or retortion) Refers to an act of retaliation by a STATE, other than a REPRISAL involving the use of armed force, for a similar act committed by another state. The concept of retorsion itself is not an autono-

mous legal concept, but simply describes such acts of retaliation. Examples of retorsion include the declaration of diplomatic agents as *personae non grata* as a response to the same measure taken by the sending state. Where an act of retorsion does not constitute an internationally wrongful act that gives rise to STATE RESPONSIBILITY, the act itself carries merely political rather than legal implications. [IB]

See also PERSONA NON GRATA; SANCTIONS; USE OF FORCE.

retrial A new trial is permissible in cases of serious offences where there has been an acquittal in court, but compelling new evidence has subsequently come to light which indicates that an acquitted person was in fact guilty. This power was introduced by the Criminal Justice Act 2003 which reforms the law relating to DOUBLE JEOPARDY. The COURT OF APPEAL may also order a retrial where there has been a serious irregularity in procedure, such as to render the original trial a mistrial. A retrial may also be ordered where a JURY is unabled to reach a sufficient majority to return a verdict. [SN]

retribution *See* RETRIBUTIVISM.

retributivism A set of ideas about sentencing, corresponding, broadly speaking, to DESERT THEORY. Retributivism proceeds on the basis that offenders deserve to be punished for their behaviour, the punishment serving as retribution for the crime. [BF]

See also REHABILITATION.

retrospective effect A legal act that effects matters that have taken place before it came into operation. The issue of retrospectivity is relevant as regards both public legal acts, such as a STATUTE or PRECEDENT, and private acts initiated by CONTRACT or DEED. First, there is a general presumption against retrospectivity of statutes, unless it is clear from the drafting that such an effect is intended. By contrast, changes in the COMMON LAW as the result of a new precedent will have retrospective effect. This is by virtue of the fiction that the judges are not changing the law, merely rectifying an earlier error or uncertainty. The consequences can be substantial where a large number of transactions have proceeded on the assumption that the 'old' law was correct (see, for example, *Kleinwort Benson Ltd* v. *Lincoln City Council* [1999] 2 AC 349) and the judges may sometimes decide not to upset settled law for this reason. Where the law is changed in this way the principle of RES JUDICATA prevents cases already decided under the old law from being reopened.

Secondly, as regards contracts and deeds there is no legal principle preventing the parties from giving retrospective effect to certain terms, or to the entire agreement, if that is clearly their intention (see *Trollope & Colls* v. *Atomic Power Contractors* [1963] 1 WLR 333, where the backdating of agreed contract terms was permitted). Similarly in *Bradshaw* v. *Fawley* [1980] 1 WLR 10, the High Court held that the parties were able, in a deed, to backdate certain of their obligations to a time pre-dating the date of the deed. [JW]

reversion The interest in land retained by a person who has granted an interest which is less than his or her own to someone else; for example, the owner of a freehold estate grants a LEASE of 10 years to a TENANT. Upon expiry of the 10 years the property reverts – returns – to the owner. The freeholder retains an interest in the land, which is a **reversionary interest.** The reversion is itself an asset which can be bought and sold.
[HC & DR]

reversionary interest *See* REVERSION.

reversionary lease A LEASE which is granted with a commencement date in the future. The term should not be confused with a lease of the REVERSION.
[HC & DR]

reverter of sites The practice of reverting land donated for charitable purposes to the donor when the land ceases to be used for the purposes for which it was donated. This form of donation was encouraged by a number of 19th-century statutes including the School Sites Act 1841 and led to the establishment of voluntary schools and museums before such provision was made

by the state. The problem arises when the charitable purposes no longer apply but the original donor of the land cannot be traced. The Reverter of Sites Act 1987 abolished rights of reverter under these 19th-century statutes and replaced them with a trust for sale in favour of the persons who (but for the 1987 Act) would be entitled under the reverter, but without entitling them to occupation of the land. [HC & DR]

revival of will A WILL which has been revoked may be revived under the provisions of the Wills Act 1837, s. 22, which states that if a revoked will is re-executed, or if a CODICIL is executed showing an intention to revive the will, then the will may be revived. If it is revived, then it is deemed to have been made on the date it was revived, rather than the date on which it was originally executed. It appears that a will which has been revoked by its destruction by the TESTATOR cannot be revived, since it is no longer in existence. [CM]

See also DESTRUCTION OF WILL; EXECUTION OF WILL; REVOCATION OF WILL.

revocation of grant The court has a wide discretion to revoke a grant of PROBATE or letters of administration under the Supreme Court Act 1981, s. 121, which provides: 'Where it appears to the High Court that a grant either ought not to have been made or contains an error, the court may call in the grant and, if satisfied that it would be revoked at the instance of a party interested, may revoke it.' [CM]

See also GRANT OF REPRESENTATION.

revocation of offer An OFFER may be expressly terminated, cancelled or withdrawn by the offeror so that it can no longer be accepted. Alternatively, this revocation may occur by implication, for example where there is a second offer which automatically revokes the first by making it clear that the intention is to supersede it (see *Pickfords Ltd* v. *Celestica Ltd* [2003] EWCA Civ 1741). In general terms, an offer may be revoked at any time before ACCEPTANCE (see *Offord* v. *Davies* (1862) 12 CBNS 748), although not if there is a legally binding firm offer. In the case of revocation of unilateral offers this might operate harshly so that the courts may interpret the offer as preventing effective revocation once the offeree has started to perform (*Errington* v. *Errington & Woods* [1952] 1 KB 290; compare *Luxor (Eastbourne) Ltd* v. *Cooper* [1941] AC 108). Revocation is not effective until communicated to the offeree (see *Byrne & Co* v. *Van Tienhoven & Co* (1880) 5 CPD 344), although compare the position of revocation of a unilateral offer made to unidentified offerees. Revocation of an offer need not be communicated by the offeror; it is sufficient that revocation is communicated by a source that the offeree might reasonably believe (*Dickinson* v. *Dodds* (1876) 2 ChD 463). [JPL]

revocation of will A WILL does not take effect until the death of the TESTATOR, and can be revoked at any time during his lifetime. The law recognizes several methods for revocation: under the Wills Act 1837, s. 20, 'by the burning, tearing or otherwise destroying the same … with the intention of revoking the same', by 'another duly executed will or CODICIL', and 'by some writing or declaring an intention to revoke'; under s. 18 (1) of the same Act, a will is automatically revoked by the testator's later MARRIAGE. However, there is an exception in s. 18 (3), which applies to any will made after 1 January 1983, if 'it appears from the will that at the time it was made, the testator was expecting to be married to a particular person, and that he intended that the will should not be revoked by the marriage'. [CM]

right Something that may be claimed legally or morally. Agreement on this basic definition, however, masks deep-seated differences among jurists as to the nature of rights. The two principal competing schools of thought are INTEREST THEORY and WILL THEORY. The former emphasizes the *benefit* enjoyed by the individual who exercises a right, the latter stresses the *choice* possessed by the individual as to whether or not to exercise it. Among the most influential analyses of rights is that produced by WESLEY NEWCOMB HOHFELD. [JP]

See also DUTY.

right of abode *See* BRITISH CITIZENSHIP.

right of audience A right to appear and act as an ADVOCATE in legal proceedings. Historically, only BARRISTERS enjoyed rights of audience in every court in England and Wales (which they still retain) and until recently, were seen to hold exclusive rights to the CROWN COURT, HIGH COURT (in open session), the Divisional Courts, COURT OF APPEAL and HOUSE OF LORDS. SOLICITORS enjoy very limited rights of audience, generally restricted to lower courts (such as the magistrates' court and COUNTY COURT) and TRIBUNALS. However, they may be heard in certain preliminary matters and magistrates' court appeals in the Crown Court and in chambers in the High Court. They can gain higher rights of audience by taking additional training to become SOLICITOR-ADVOCATES. Many tribunals have no rules regarding rights of audience and representation can be made by any person chosen by a party. Rights of audience are now granted to a wider group of legal professionals and other specified persons under the Courts and Legal Services Act 1990, as amended by the Access to Justice Act 1999. Further powers to grant rights of audience have been created under the Legal Services Act 2007. [AF]

See also MCKENZIE FRIEND.

right of common A type of PROFIT À PRENDRE, entitling the owner of the right to take or use a part of any natural product of another person's land. Examples of rights of common are the right to graze animals (known as pasture), the right to take fish (PISCARY), the right to cut turf or peat (TURBARY) and the right to take wood for use as fuel or to build a fence (ESTOVERS).

The Commons Act 2006 (CA 2006) reformed the law on commons and town and village greens in England and Wales, and once fully in force will replace the Commons Registration Act 1965 (CRA 1965). At the time of writing, most provisions of the CA 2006 were not yet in force, though it is intended that they will be implemented in the next few years.

Rights of common can be acquired by express GRANT, operation of statute, or by

PRESCRIPTION (once the CA 2006 comes into force, it will not be possible to acquire rights of common by prescription). The existence of an entry on the REGISTER OF COMMONS is conclusive in determining whether or not such a right exists (CRA 1965, s. 10, CA 2006, s. 18), which means that a right of common must be registered to be enforceable. [DR]

See also COMMON LAND.

right of establishment In addition to the FREE MOVEMENT OF PERSONS (workers), the EUROPEAN COMMUNITY (EC) offers, to natural and legal persons, the right to move from one EC MEMBER STATE to another as self-employed persons, or as an undertaking (a COMPANY or other legal business entity). These rights are set out in Articles 43 to 48 EC, and have been further developed by EUROPEAN COURT OF JUSTICE case law. [MON]

right of re-entry *See* RE-ENTRY.

right of support A type of EASEMENT commonly involving the right to support of a building by adjoining buildings. Although there is a natural right to support of one's soil by the soil of a neighbour's land, there is no natural right of support of buildings. However, the right of support may be acquired by GRANT, express or implied, or by PRESCRIPTION.

Where a right of support has been acquired, the owner of the SERVIENT TENEMENT may not pull his wall down, although he may let it fall down by failing to repair it (*Jones* v. *Pritchard* [1908] 1 Ch 630). In such a situation, however, the owner may enter his neighbour's property in order to carry out repairs (*Bond* v. *Nottingham Corporation* [1940] Ch 429). [DR]

See also DOMINANT TENEMENT; PARTY WALL.

right of way A type of EASEMENT involving the right to pass over another person's land. A right of way may be public, acquired under the Highways Act 1980 or by the doctrine of dedication and acceptance; or private, acquired by the law on acquisition of easements. A right of way may also be general or limited, for example a footway.

A **general** right of way is one that the owner of the DOMINANT TENEMENT can use at any time and in any manner. A **limited** right of way is one that is restricted, as to either the time it is used (e.g. a right of way limited to daytime use) or the mode in which it is used (e.g. a right of way limited to foot passengers only). [DR]

right to air A type of EASEMENT relating to the flow of air through a defined channel. There is no natural right to the passage of air. However, rights to the passage of air through a defined channel may be acquired by GRANT or reservation, express or implied, or by PRESCRIPTION. An example of a right to air is where a restaurant has a right to ventilation through a ventilation duct situated on neighbouring premises (*Wong* v. *Beaumont Property Trust Ltd* [1965] 1 QB 173). [DR]

right to legal advice Everyone who is arrested or questioned by the police is normally entitled to free legal advice and representation. A suspect detained at a police station must be informed of the right to see a SOLICITOR. If the suspect chooses to have legal representation, the solicitor or legal representative will sit with them during the interview. There are limited exceptions where the police may delay access to legal advice, e.g. in drug-trafficking or suspected terrorist cases. [SN]

right to liberty A human right guaranteed under Article 5 of the EUROPEAN CONVENTION ON HUMAN RIGHTS (the right to liberty and security of the person). Article 5 has three elements. First, there is an exhaustive list of circumstances in which a person can lawfully be deprived of his liberty (see paragraphs 1 (a) to (f)). Second, in Article 5(2) there is a list of procedural safeguards which must also be met in the context of the permissible grounds, including the right of prompt access to judicial proceedings to determine the legality of one's arrest or detention, and to trial within a reasonable time. And, lastly, there is a right to compensation where a VICTIM can show that they were improperly deprived of liberty. [JW]

right to marry The right is enshrined in the European Convention on Human

Rights, Article 12 as follows: 'Men and women of marriageable age have the right to marry and to found a family, according to the national laws governing the exercise of this right'; this right has been incorporated into English law in the Human Rights Act 1998. Courts have interpreted this Article as one right – the right to marry and found a FAMILY. Unlike in other countries, the right has so far not extended in UK law to persons of the same sex, although it has been extended to TRANSSEXUAL PERSONS who obtain a Gender Recognition Certificate. [AD]

See also GENDER REASSIGNMENT; MARRIAGE.

right to silence The principle that, generally, it is legally permissible to remain silent in response to police questioning and as a defendant in court. Nevertheless there are specific statutory provisions (e.g. Road Traffic Act 1988, s. 172) that prescribe a criminal sanction for declining to provide information to the police. [ALTC]

See also INFERENCES FROM ACCUSED'S SILENCE.

rights of water A type of EASEMENT relating to water. There is no general right to water that percolates through soil since water cannot in general be the subject matter of property (*Race* v. *Ward* (1855) 4 E & B 702). Nevertheless, there are many different rights of water that may be acquired, either by GRANT or reservation, express or implied, or by PRESCRIPTION.

The most common example of a right of water is the right for a domestic property to receive water through the water pipes, as provided by the local water authority. This is known legally as the right to receive water through a pipe situated on the SERVIENT TENEMENT (*Rance* v. *Elvin* (1985) 50 P & CR 9). Other examples of rights of water include the right to receive an undiminished flow of water through a defined channel, the right to discharge water on to neighbouring land and the right to pollute the waters of a stream or river. [DR]

See also DOMINANT TENEMENT.

rights thesis The proposition in the work of RONALD DWORKIN that the government must treat people as equals. By this Dwor-

kin intends that the government should not take any action with regard to individuals that they could only accept by abandoning their sense of equal worth. This can also be read positively to mean that the government has a duty to relieve individuals of burdens they would otherwise have to bear as a consequence purely of bad luck. Most controversially, Dworkin extrapolates from this to criticize the market in so far as it operates to reward individuals not simply because they have chosen to perform roles or tasks that are useful, but also because they happen by luck to possess the requisite skills or talents. [JP]

riot An offence under the Public Order Act 1986, s. 1, triable on INDICTMENT only and punishable by ten years' imprisonment and/or an unlimited fine. A prosecution for riot requires the consent of the DIRECTOR OF PUBLIC PROSECUTIONS. It must be proved that 12 or more persons were present together using or threatening unlawful violence for a common purpose, and that their conduct (taken together) was such as would cause an (actual or notional) person of reasonable firmness present at the scene to fear for his or her personal safety. For a defendant to be guilty of the offence, they must actually use, rather than merely threaten, unlawful violence. The MENS REA of the offence is an intention to use violence or an awareness that one's conduct may be violent (see Public Order Act 1986, s. 6(1)). [BF]

See also AFFRAY; VIOLENT DISORDER.

risk The probability that a particular adverse event will occur during a defined period of time. Risk is one of the principal impetuses behind REGULATION: the assessment that a risk exists will prompt the state to take action to attempt to remove or at least minimize it. Examples include the risks associated with work in a hazardous environment, the deployment of new technologies or exposure to a harmful substance.

Responding to risk through regulation is, however, by no means a straightforward exercise. At the outset there may be disagreement as to whether a given risk actually exists. Even if there is agreement on this point, different assessments may exist as to its magnitude. There may also be difficulty in determining the source of the risk as well as disagreements about how to manage it.

Problems such as these may arise even among experts deploying technical methods in relation to the identification, assessment and management of risk. A further level of complexity emerges when differences exist between expert or technical approaches to risk on the one hand and the perceptions of risk held by the general public on the other. Such disagreements have traditionally been characterized as being between rational and irrational approaches to risk, but there is an increasing recognition that this oversimplifies the situation. More recently, there have been efforts to respond to risk by means of COREGULATION, that is, in ways that engage all of those concerned, and with an emphasis on establishing and maintaining trust between expert and lay actors.

One of the most influential contributions has been Ulrich Beck's *Risk Society*, in which the author suggests that contemporary society is characterized by a transition from an industrial society – in which the logic of wealth production dominates the logic of risk production – to a risk society where this relationship is reversed. Critics of this approach point out that it is simply not sophisticated enough to account for the variety of ways in which risks are regulated. It may nevertheless be the case that the normative dimension of Beck's account is more important than the descriptive. In other words, Beck's account may point towards a transformation that is still underway rather than one that is complete and thus may raise profound questions about the adequacy of many existing regulatory responses to risk.   [JP]

Further reading: Ulrich Beck, *Risk Society: Towards a new modernity* (London: Sage, 1992).

Risk and Regulation Advisory Council
Following publication in 2007 of the BETTER REGULATION COMMISSION's (BRC) report, 'Pub-

lic Risk – the Next Frontier for Better Regulation', the BRC was wound up and replaced by the Risk and Regulation Advisory Council. The Council commenced work in January 2008 and currently comprises seven members of the former BRC. Its primary functions are to work with ministers, senior civil servants and key stakeholders to develop a better understanding of public risk and of appropriate approaches to managing risk in regulation and policy-making.   [JW]

road 1. A definable right of way between two points (see *Oxford* v. *Austin* [1981] RTR 416).
2. For the purposes of traffic regulation, 'any length of HIGHWAY or of any other road to which the public has access and includ[ing] bridges over which a road passes' (see the Road Traffic Regulation Act 1984, s. 142).   [JW]

road rage A modern vernacular noun, referring to threatening or violent behaviour exhibited by a motorist. There is no specific road rage offence, though the behaviour may, in appropriate circumstances, lead to other charges, such as DANGEROUS DRIVING or ASSAULT.   [BF]

road traffic accident The Road Traffic Act 1988, s. 170, imposes a number of duties on drivers. Failure to comply with these duties is an offence. The section applies where an accident occurs on a road or other public place, owing to the presence of a mechanically propelled vehicle, and personal injury is caused to somebody other than the driver of that vehicle; or damage is caused to another vehicle, or to an animal (for these purposes an animal is a horse, cattle, ass, mule, sheep, pig, goat or dog) other than one in that vehicle, or to any other property on or adjacent to the road. The driver of the vehicle must stop and give – to any person with reasonable grounds for asking – his name and address, the name and address of the owner of the vehicle, and the identification marks of the vehicle. If the driver does not give his name and address, he must report the accident to the police as soon as is reasonably practicable or within 24 hours. Where personal injury occurs, the driver is also under a duty to provide details of insurance cover, either at the time to anybody with reasonable grounds for requiring them, or to a police station within seven days.   [BF]

robbery An offence under the Theft Act 1968, s. 8. It is committed when a person steals, and immediately before or at the time of doing so, and in order to do so, uses force on any person, or puts or seeks to put any person in fear of being then and there subjected to force. Robbery is triable on INDICTMENT, and is punishable with imprisonment for life.   [BF]

See also THEFT.

root of title In UNREGISTERED LAND, a document in the TITLE DEEDS that can form the basis of an ABSTRACT OF TITLE or an EPITOME OF TITLE, which proves that the owner of land has TITLE to that land. A good root of title (i.e. one that proves title to land) is a document that must: (a) deal with or show ownership of the whole legal and equitable interest in the property; (b) contain an adequate, identifiable description of the property; (c) cast no doubt on the validity of the title; and (d) be at least 15 years old (Law of Property Act 1969, s. 23).

The most common example of a good root of title is a conveyance on sale that is over 15 years old. If a buyer accepts a root of title that is less than 15 years old, he is bound by any ENCUMBRANCES that would have been discovered if he had investigated title for the full period of 15 years. It is also possible that he will only be granted QUALIFIED TITLE on first registration, thereby reducing the value of the property.   [DR]

Ross, Alf (1899–1979) A Danish international jurist and leading scholar of SCANDINAVIAN REALISM, very much influenced by Hans KELSEN. His fundamental premise was to dismiss the metaphysical basis of many of the concepts on which INTERNATIONAL LAW is based – such as state succession, the formation of custom, the debate between DUALISM and MONISM regarding the hierarchy of norms in internal legal orders – as being out of touch with reality and contributing only to hollow fictions. Among his most famous works are *A Textbook of International Law* (1947) and *Directives and Norms* (1968).
     [IB]

Rousseau, Jean-Jacques (1712–78) Swiss thinker and a key figure in the Enlightenment who is associated especially with France because of his influence on revolutionary thinking. He produced a version of SOCIAL CONTRACT theory distinct from the earlier English offerings of THOMAS HOBBES and JOHN LOCKE – and indeed perhaps the most developed variant before that of JOHN RAWLS in the 20th century.

In common with Hobbes and Locke, Rousseau postulates a pre-CONTRACTARIAN state of nature. In his account, the main feature of this situation is the fact that it prevents humans from achieving their natural moral potential. The social contract for Rousseau is thus the means by which individuals, recognizing the stifling constraints of the state of nature, agree to organize themselves in society; and society is the means by which the fulfilment of natural moral potential is achieved. There is a clear echo here of Aristotle.

Rousseau differs from Hobbes and Locke in as much as his social contract does not envisage that society will be ruled by a sovereign. Instead, the idea is that individuals will henceforth surrender to the **general will**. This aspect of Rousseau's work has given rise to a great deal of misunderstanding. It is a short step from the notion of a ruling general will to the tyranny of the majority – or worse, to the manipulative use of the notion of a general will by a tyrant or a totalitarian state. Rousseau intended no such thing. The general will was not for him some simplistic arithmetical sum of individual wills, but rather an appreciation of what was in the general interest. Such an appreciation would not emerge from popular votes based on gut reactions, but only from rational deliberation. Rousseau thus expresses concerns that motivate some of the most important contemporary legal and political theorists, such as JÜRGEN HABERMAS.

This need for rational deliberation also

led Rousseau to be sceptical of what would now be regarded as the standard model of representative democracy. The idea that one could vote once and issue a mandate to government for four or five years was, for Rousseau, absurd. As he put it, 'Every law the people has not ratified in person is null and void – is, in fact, not a law.'

This can appear extreme at first sight, and perhaps a further indication of the influence of Aristotle – an anachronistic reference to Athenian direct democracy – but modern practice may in fact be more supportive of Rousseau. As noted by adherents of proceduralization, there is a growing use of direct or participatory democratic techniques in a wide range of situations where governments face complex problems that appear to defy traditional approaches. [JP]

Further reading: Jean-Jacques Rousseau, *The Social Contract*, translated and introduced by Maurice Cranston (Harmondsworth: Penguin, 1968).

Royal Assent The final stage in the process by which a BILL becomes law. The Royal Assent is pronounced by the Clerk of Parliaments in formal session in the HOUSE OF LORDS. Once it has received the Royal Assent, a Bill becomes an **Act of Parliament** and, unless there is a provision to the contrary within the Act, it becomes law on that date. **Measures** of the CHURCH OF ENGLAND also become law on receiving the Royal Assent. [JW]

See also STATUTE.

Royal Council (obsolete) Originally called the *Curia Regis* (Lat. the king's court), this was the general council of the king. It originated with the Norman Conquest (1066) as the feudal assembly of all the king's chief lords and tenants. It developed during the reign of Henry I (1100–35) into a smaller body of advisers made up of officials of the royal household and other friends and supporters of the king. It assisted the king across the range of executive, legislative and judicial functions. The Council was thus the source from which the higher law courts, the Privy Council and the Cabinet were all ultimately to emerge, which

demonstrates how much less clearly differentiated these aspects of the state were than they are today. [JW]

Royal Prerogative 'The residue of discretionary or arbitrary authority which at any given time is legally left in the hands of the Crown' – A.V. Dicey, *An Introduction to the Study of the Law of the Constitution,* 10th edn (London: Macmillan, 1959). These powers are often sub-divided into three categories: (a) those which are technically the personal prerogatives of the sovereign – to appoint her Prime Minister, summon or dissolve Parliament, and assent to legislation (though note that these are circumscribed by conventions that actually give the sovereign little choice about any of them); (b) the legal prerogatives of the CROWN, notably Crown immunity, and the related principle that the Crown cannot be bound by STATUTE, except where expressly so stated (see *Lord Advocate* v. *Dumbarton District Council* [1990] 2 AC 580); and (c) the prerogatives of the executive arm of government – to make and ratify treaties, govern overseas territories, powers of political patronage, to grant pardons and to deploy the armed forces.

All prerogative powers are, to some degree, controversial because they are generally exercised by the executive, with relatively little democratic oversight from Parliament. The power of the courts to oversee prerogative power is, in some respects, of long standing (see the *Case of Proclamations* (1611) 12 Co Rep 74, which demonstrated the courts' authority to determine the existence and extent of the prerogative). But defining the scope for JUDICIAL REVIEW of the exercise of prerogative power has proved more problematic, though the courts today are tending to take a more robust approach following the landmark decision in *Council for Civil Service Unions* v. *Minister for Civil Service* [1985] AC 374 (the *GCHQ* case). [JW]

royalty A payment received by an INTELLECTUAL PROPERTY author or owner in a licensing arrangement, whereby the author or owner agrees that a third party can utilize their technology or COPYRIGHT work, DESIGN or

TRADE MARK. The amount of royalty to be paid is to be agreed between the two parties. In relation to PATENT LICENCES, the royalty rate often depends on a fixed percentage of sales volumes for products made under the technology licence. If a copyright work is being licensed from a COLLECTING SOCIETY, however, the rate of royalty payable is often set by the society.   [US]

RSC *See* RULES OF THE SUPREME COURT.

rule against double portions A GIFT made by a parent to a child to set the child up for life, or to make substantial provision for him or her. The type of gift would include, for example, providing the purchase money for a business.

The 'rule against double portions' is a rebuttable PRESUMPTION that if the parent makes a WILL containing a substantial legacy to a child, the legacy will be satisfied or adeemed by a subsequent substantial gift *inter vivos* to that child. The underlying basis of the rule is the assumption that a parent will wish to order equality among his or her children, and so will not wish to make provision twice for the same child. The presumption can be rebutted if the nature of the two gifts is different, or by extrinsic evidence of the testator's actual intention. Since the abolition of HOTCHPOT for deaths after 1 January 1996, it could be argued that this presumption is an outdated concept.   [CM]

rule against inalienability *See* RULE AGAINST PERPETUITIES.

rule against perpetual trusts *See* RULE AGAINST PERPETUITIES.

rule against perpetuities A rule designed to prevent LAND being tied up 'for perpetuity' in ways which prevent its development or enjoyment long into the future. The rule restricts future dispositions of property by prescribing a period of time, known as the PERPETUITY PERIOD, during which any such disposition must take effect. The Perpetuities and Accumulations Act 1964 has made any dispositions subsequent to the Act, which actually must vest or take effect (if at all) outside the perpetuity period, void. However this formulation has introduced an added complexity as it is necessary to 'wait and see', potentially for the whole perpetuity period, to determine whether the interest will be valid or not.

The rule has been shaped by public policy concerns, which are centuries old, that attempt to balance the freedoms inherent in property ownership, including the freedom to dispose of property after death, with the need to prevent attempts to control behaviour over generations. Perpetuity issues are technical, complex and incomprehensible to virtually all except specialist lawyers. The rules cause particular difficulties for commercial transactions. The LAW COMMISSION considered the rule in 1998 and has made various proposals for reform: see 'The Rule Against Perpetuities and Excessive Accumulations', Law Commission Report No. 251.   [HC & DR]

rule in *Strong* v. *Bird* An exception to the principle that 'EQUITY will not perfect an imperfect GIFT'. The rule in *Strong* v. *Bird* (1874) LR 18 Eq 318 states that if a would-be donor (A) expresses a present intention to make a gift of personal property to a potential donee (B), and that intention is unchanged until A's death, then, where B is made the executor of the will, he or she will be entitled to hold the property as beneficiary. The onus of proving that A had an intention to make the gift during their lifetime is on B. Where the donor expresses only an intention to make the gift at some future time, the rule will not be satisfied (see *Re Freeland* [1952] Ch 110). The rule can also operate to extinguish a debt, and to perfect an imperfectly constituted TRUST, that is, one where the settler has not delivered the trust property to trustees.   [JW]

rule of law The idea that no citizen is above the law, and that government should be conducted according to legal authority rather than a purely arbitrary exercise of power. For a STATE to operate according to the rule of law, the following conditions ought to apply: a presumption of equality before the law, in that all citizens (regardless of status) are subject to the ordinary law of the land administered by regular courts and TRIBUNALS; laws must be reasonably clear, accessible (i.e. published), mutually consistent and stable, so that citizens are able to conduct themselves, and plan their activities in accordance with the law; citizens should have ready access to a public court system with impartial judges; there must be a sufficient SEPARATION OF POWERS between the legislative, executive and judicial arms of the state to enable the legislature to restrict the exercise of executive discretion and to ensure that such discretion, where granted, is amenable to JUDICIAL REVIEW. A statement of the principles necessary for the rule of law was constructed by the INTERNATIONAL COMMISSION OF JURISTS and published as the **Declaration of Delhi** in 1959. This also stressed the importance of the rule of law in safeguarding fundamental HUMAN RIGHTS, and creating and maintaining the social, economic and political conditions that would uphold HUMAN DIGNITY.

In the UK system specifically, the doctrine of the rule of law is closely connected to two other fundamental principles: the SOVEREIGNTY OF PARLIAMENT and the INDEPENDENCE OF THE JUDICIARY. In theory, both the courts and Parliament act as a check on potential abuses of executive power, and they both derive their authority from the rule of law. Whether, in the absence of a written CONSTITUTION, this provides a sufficient check on government is a matter of debate, particularly given a context in which many commentators believe power has become increasingly diverted away from the courts and Parliament by the use of executive and administrative DISCRETION.   [JW]

rule of recognition The principal secondary rule in H.L.A. HART's legal positivist account of the legal system. The function of the rule of recognition is to specify the feature or features that will conclusively identify a rule as a **primary rule** (a rule of legal obligation) in a given system.

In its earliest form, the rule of recognition may simply be the acknowledgement that reference to a particular written list of rules (for example, the Twelve Tables) is the appropriate way to resolve any doubt as to which are a community's primary rules.

In a developed legal system, however, the rule of recognition is likely to be more complex, identifying the general characteristics possessed by primary rules. These may include the fact that a rule has been enacted by a specific body or the fact that it is related to a previous judicial decision. [JP]

rule scepticism One of the two principal strands of AMERICAN REALISM whose adherents are sceptical of the role played by rules in judicial decision-making. In contrast to traditional views, which see judges applying clearly defined rules to established facts in a syllogistic fashion in order to reach a determination, rule sceptics insist that other factors will often influence the decision, which the judge may or may not explicitly acknowledge. For example, a judge's own beliefs or emotional reaction to the facts of a case may actually determine the way he or she interprets the rule.   [JP]

See also FACT SCEPTICISM; HOLMES, OLIVER WENDELL.

Rules of the Supreme Court (RSC) (obsolete) The rules governing proceedings in the High Court and Court of Appeal made under the authority of the Senior Courts Act 1981. They have been almost entirely superseded by the CIVIL PROCEDURE RULES 1998 (CPR). As a general principle, judicial decisions on the RSC are of no relevance to the interpretation of the CPR; see *per* Lord Woolf in *Biguzzi* v. *Rank Leisure plc* [1999] 1 WLR 1926.   [JW]

rules Standards of behaviour that impose an obligation which individuals not only feel obliged to obey but where non-compliance will result in criticism from others. Rules can be contrasted with *habits*, which may be examples of convergent behaviour but where non-compliance will not provoke criticism from others. Legal rules (as opposed to moral or other social rules) are those where the obligation is imposed by law and where non-compliance will be a matter for the state's centralized organs of coercion.

H.L A. HART famously defined the legal system as a system of rules and thus provoked the criticism of DWORKIN who insisted that it must also encompass principles if judges are not to be allowed an undue degree of freedom when confronted with a HARD CASE in which no rule is readily applicable.   [JP]

running with the land *See* RESTRICTIVE COVENANT.

***Rylands* v. *Fletcher*, rule in** A rule of strict liability in TORT: 'the person who for his own purposes brings onto his lands and collects and keeps there anything likely to do mischief if it escapes must keep it in at his peril, and, if he does not do so, is *prima facie* liable for all the damage which is the natural consequence of its escape' (see *Rylands* v. *Fletcher* (1868) LR 1 Ex 265 at 279–80). The development of the rule has been controversial and liability is now restricted to NUISANCE cases where there has been an isolated escape and the harm suffered is reasonably foreseeable (see *Cambridge Water* v. *Eastern Counties Leather plc* [1994] 2 AC 264).   [HJ]

S

SAD *See* SINGLE ADMINISTRATIVE DOCUMENT.

sado-masochism *See* CONSENT TO HARM.

safe haven A demilitarized zone within sovereign territory designated by the UN Security Council or the warring parties as an area where civilians can take refuge, whether for a specific amount of time or indefinitely. Such safe havens were agreed between UN peace-keeping missions and the warring parties during the war in Bosnia. Another alternative to safe havens could be instituted through the designation of no-fly zones either by the Security Council acting under Chapter VII of the UN CHARTER or again by the warring parties. The Council instituted no-fly zones as part of its sanctions regime against Iraq, in an attempt to ensure that minority civilian populations were allowed to live without intimidation from Iraqi authorities. Safe havens do not possess an autonomous legal status or formal definition in INTERNATIONAL LAW. As there is no particular international rule regarding safe havens, there is no clear rule about attacking them. Analogies should be drawn from humanitarian law regarding the absolute prohibition of attacks on civilians that are taking no active part in hostilities and the equally absolute prohibition of attacks on undefended towns and localities. [IB]

safety committee A workplace committee responsible for monitoring accidents, and improving safety rules and systems of work. When at least two SAFETY REPRESENTATIVES request a safety committee, the EMPLOYER must establish one within three months of the request: see the Health and Safety at Work etc. Act 1974, s. 2. Safety committees are not restricted to safety but may cover the working environment as a whole: see the Health and Safety Commission's Code of Practice ('guidance notes') on Safety Committees, para. 2. [MJ]

safety representative Under the Health and Safety at Work etc. Act 1974, s. 2, an INDEPENDENT TRADE UNION which is recognized by the EMPLOYERS may appoint safety representatives from EMPLOYEES in respect of whom the union is recognized. Employers must consult with such representatives with a view to maintaining the health and safety of employees (s. 2(6)). The Act provides a long list of duties to be performed by the safety representatives including inspection of the premises at least once every three months. [MJ]

sale A transaction involving the transfer from one person (the SELLER) to another (the buyer) of property or a right to property, for example land or goods, in exchange for CONSIDERATION. [JPL]

sale by description Where a CONTRACT for the SALE OF GOODS identifies the goods or type of goods being sold and this identification was intended to be a term of the contract and amounts to a substantial ingredient in the identity of the goods being sold, the sale is a sale by description for the purposes of the Sale of Goods Act 1979, s. 13. The goods may be fully agreed upon at the time of the sale, e.g. a particular and identified piece of furniture, or a particular quantity of a described type of goods; in either case, if the contract contains words of description or identification the sale will be made by description. Section 13 provides that the goods delivered must match the contractual description or identification or there will be a BREACH OF CONTRACT by the SELLER. [JPL]

sale by sample Sale of Goods Act 1979, s. 15(1) provides that a CONTRACT of sale is a contract of sale by sample where there is an EXPRESS or IMPLIED TERM providing that it is; for example, if the SELLER submitted a sample to the buyer on which to base the decision to purchase. Where there is such a sale by sample, there is an implied term that (a) the goods will correspond with the quality of the sample; (b) the buyer will have a reasonable opportunity to compare the bulk with the sample; and (c) the goods will be free from any defect which would not be apparent on reasonable examination of the sample. [JPL]

sale of goods A CONTRACT for the sale of goods is a contract whereby the SELLER agrees to transfer or actually transfers the property (ownership) in goods to the buyer for a money CONSIDERATION known as the PRICE (Sale of Goods Act 1979, s. 2(1)). If the transfer of ownership of the goods is to take place in the future, or is subject to the fulfilment of some future CONDITION, the contract is termed an **agreement to sell**; see Sale of Goods Act 1979, s. 2(5).

Sale of goods contracts contain IMPLIED TERMS designed to protect the buyer (Sale of Goods Act 1979, ss. 12–15) by which the seller impliedly PROMISES that the seller has ownership in the goods to transfer to the buyer; that the goods correspond with the description under which they were sold; that they are of satisfactory quality; and are reasonably fit for the buyer's purpose. [JPL]

sale on approval A sale is made on approval where, under the terms of the CONTRACT, the goods are delivered on the basis that the recipient can retain possession of the goods for a set time before deciding whether or not to buy them. Sale on approval is sometimes known as 'sale or return'. If the prospective buyer decides not to buy the goods, property in the goods does not pass and the goods are returned, in their original state, to the SELLER. However, the Sale of Goods Act 1979, s. 18, Rule 4 provides that property (or ownership) of goods sold on approval passes when either (a) the buyer indicates his approval to the seller or does any act adopting the transaction, such as consuming the goods or reselling them; or (b) the buyer retains the goods for longer than the period fixed in the contract or, where there was no fixed period, retains them for longer than a reasonable period. [JPL]

salvage of trust property The court's inherent power to sanction a MORTGAGE or sale of part of an infant's beneficial interest for the benefit of the portion retained. The power can only be used in cases of extreme necessity, for example when expenditure is necessary to save buildings from collapse. An extension of this jurisdiction permits the courts to authorize TRUSTEES, in an emergency, to perform acts beyond the powers given to them under the TRUST instrument or statute generally, where it is in the best interests of the trust estate and the BENEFICIARIES' unanimous consent cannot be obtained because at least one is under a disability and/or does not yet exist. [PK]

sanctions Discriminatory measures, including counter-measures, that are imposed against a STATE, either unilaterally by another state, or by an international organization. Certain types of sanctions involve to some extent abrogation of the SOVEREIGNTY principle and can therefore be applied only under limited circumstances. Their imposition, other than financial sanctions, is possible only by the UN Security Council under CHAPTER VII of the UN CHAR-TER, and in particular Article 41 thereof. The sanctions provided therein are indicative and include complete or partial interruption of economic relations and of rail, sea, air, postal, telegraphic, radio and other means of communication and the severance of diplomatic relations. Where sanctions have been imposed by the Security Council under Article 41, all UN Member States are under an obligation to give effect to such sanctions.

Sanctions of a milder form, that do not involve abrogation of a state's sovereignty, may be imposed unilaterally by other states (counter-measures) or by international organizations within the scope of their mandate. Such sanctions may include the expulsion of a state from an organization, or its exclusion from participation in certain organs. Counter-measures are permitted, in accordance with the 2001 INTERNATIONAL LAW COMMISSION Articles on STATE RESPONSIBILITY, where a state has committed an internationally unlawful act and the injured state has called on the responsible state to cease the act and fulfil its obligations. The purpose of counter-measures is to force the responsible state to fulfil its obligations and thus where the dispute is pending before a judicial body or the obligation has been fulfilled, counter-measures must cease.   [IB]

See also ECONOMIC SANCTIONS; EMBARGO.

satisfactory quality An IMPLIED TERM in CONTRACTS for the SALE OF GOODS (Sale of Goods Act 1979 (SOGA), s. 14 (2)) and analogous contracts involving the transfer of ownership or possession of goods supplied in the course of a business, that the goods will be of satisfactory quality (Supply of Goods and Services Act 1982, s. 4(2) as amended).

By SOGA, s. 14(2A), goods will be of satisfactory quality if they meet the standard that a reasonable person would regard as satisfactory, taking account of any description of the goods, the PRICE (if relevant) and all the other relevant circumstances. In addition, s. 14(2B) states that the quality of goods includes their state and condition

and that aspects of quality may include (a) fitness for all the purposes for which goods of the kind in question are commonly supplied; (b) appearance and finish; (c) freedom from minor defects; (d) safety; and (e) durability. However, this obligation will not apply where the goods have been examined or the defects pointed out (s. 14 (2C)). If the goods supplied do not meet this standard, the SELLER will be in BREACH OF CONTRACT.

The Sale and Supply of Goods Act 1994 introduced the standard of 'satisfactory quality' to replace the now obsolete obligation to supply goods of 'merchantable quality'.   [JPL]

satisfied term When an INTEREST in LAND for a TERM OF YEARS is created for a specific purpose which is fulfilled, the expired period is described as the satisfied term. Any period of time which remains is known as the outstanding term.   [HC & DR]

Saunders v. *Vautier*, **rule in** A principle which enables any BENEFICIARY, who is *sui juris* (i.e. of full age and sound mind), to require the trustees to transfer to the beneficiary that portion of the TRUST property that represents the beneficiary's interest under the trust. The principle, in fact, predates the case by which it is known (*Saunders* v. *Vautier* (1841) 49 ER 282) and represents a significant limitation on the ambit of trusts which are, under this rule, always vulnerable to collapse if all the beneficiaries are *sui juris* and decide to exercise their right to terminate the trust even if, under the terms of the trust, the settlor has attempted to exclude the rule. From a policy perspective the principle represents a clear limitation on the rights of settlors to bind property by means of a trust by recognizing the individualistic autonomy of adult beneficiaries of sound mind. Doctrinally it encapsulates a liberal concept of ownership in which the ultimate owner of the trust property is the beneficiary, not the SETTLOR, whose interest terminates once the property has been settled on trust; nor the TRUSTEE, whose technical legal title is always subject to the beneficiary's substantive equitable interest.   [PK]

Scandinavian Realism The movement in legal theory inspired especially by the insights of the Swedish philosopher Axel Hägerström. He insisted that despite the fact that modern societies had thrown off beliefs in the supernatural and the magical, concepts used in pre-modern societies such as 'right' and 'duty' continued to exercise similar psychological effects in modern times as they had in pre-modern.

The principal representatives of the Scandinavian Realist movement include the Swedish jurist Karl Olivecrona (1897–1980) and the Danish jurist Alf Ross (1899–1979). Olivecrona's view is that it makes no sense to think of law in terms of the command either of an individual sovereign or of a collective state: the former involves an impossibility; the second an abstraction. Instead, he sees law's force emerging from an individual's psychological reaction to the formalities that attend it. People become used to the idea that the formalities of legislation and of judicial pronouncement imply certain consequences. Thus, even though rules and decisions are backed by force this rarely needs to be used because the consequences are internalized. Despite the fact that Olivecrona disagrees with HANS KELSEN in his insistence that law thus becomes a causal as opposed to a normative science, he has been criticized for not actually backing his theorizing with empirical observation.

Ross, though also influenced by Hägerström, shifted the attention from the psychology of individual citizens to that of judges. Thus for him, when legal theorists discuss law they are not referring to law as it is understood by citizens but rather to the concepts transmitted from law teachers to their students. These propositions about the nature of legal rules essentially provide future practitioners with a means of predicting how judges and other officials react when confronted with such rules. Ross accordingly shares the focus of AMERICAN REALISM on courts and judges, but differs from it in suggesting that legal rules do provide a means of predicting judicial behaviour. [JP]

Further reading: Karl Olivecrona, *Law as Fact* (London: Stevens, 1971); Alf Ross, *On Law and Justice* (London: Stevens, 1958).

Schengen Agreement An international convention, originally signed in 1985 between the states of the Benelux Economic Union, Germany and France. It is primarily concerned to abolish border controls among participating countries, to establish a common policy on the temporary entry of visitors (including the so-called 'Schengen Visa'), to harmonize external border controls, and to deal with matters of cross-border policing and judicial cooperation.

The Agreement was implemented pursuant to the Schengen Convention 1990, and was subsequently acceded to by most other MEMBER STATES of the EUROPEAN COMMUNITY and the EUROPEAN FREE TRADE ASSOCIATION (EFTA) states of Norway and Iceland. The UK and Ireland, however, maintained an opt-out of the Schengen Convention. The body of law associated with Schengen, known as the Schengen *acquis*, was subsequently incorporated into EUROPEAN UNION (EU) law by the TREATY OF AMSTERDAM in 1997. Those parts of the Schengen *acquis* which dealt with 'Visas, asylum, immigration and other matters dealing with the movement of persons' (third country nationals) were integrated into Pillar I EC (Title IV). The balance of the Schengen provisions dealing with cross-border policing and law enforcement cooperation, were integrated into the now renamed Pillar III EU, Police and Judicial Cooperation in Criminal Matters (PJCCM).

Currently, Norway and Iceland maintain their Schengen commitments as a matter of INTERNATIONAL LAW. Denmark maintains the Pillar I commitments as international law, but is fully involved in the Pillar III PJCCM Schengen provisions as EU law. The UK and Ireland have subsequently opted back into most of the Pillar III PJCCM provisions, but have maintained their opt-out status for the Pillar I provisions of Schengen. Switzerland, another EFTA state, has also signed up for some of the Schengen PJCCM provisions as part of its international law obligations. [MON]

See also TREATY ON EUROPEAN UNION.

Scots law Described as a mixed legal system in so far as it has drawn inspiration from a range of sources over a long period of time and does not fall squarely into either the COMMON LAW or CIVIL LAW categories.

Although Scotland was initially untouched by the Norman Conquest, the influence of the Normans was gradually felt and became much greater under David I who had spent many years at the English court prior to ascending to the Scottish throne in 1124. This influence was most obvious in the system of FEUDAL TENURE, which, with the Crown as the paramount superior, in turn allowed the king to spread the influence of royal justice throughout the land.

CANON LAW was also influential from the 12th century, with Church courts exercising a range of civil and criminal jurisdiction and in particular dealing with matters that would now be termed family law. The fact that there is no doctrine of CONSIDERATION in Scots contract law (and thus the possibility of a GRATUITOUS CONTRACT, in contrast to the position in England) is a consequence of the influence of canon law at this time.

Canon law is also the means by which the influence of Roman law first appeared in Scotland. Roman law exercised a strong attraction on Scottish lawyers at a time when their English counterparts were rapidly developing and expanding Norman law into a complex body of precedents. In contrast, Roman law was characterized by reasoning from general principles to their application in specific situations. The dominance of canon and Roman law over Norman alternatives grew during the period of tension between England and Scotland in the 13th and 14th centuries, but the damaging effects of warfare on Scotland generally meant that the development and implementation of law regressed.

Matters improved during the 15th century, as the Scottish Parliament developed a sizeable body of legislation, while the establishment of the College of Justice in 1532 meant that the country at last had a court staffed by a professional judiciary, trained in canon and civil (Roman) law.

The importance of Roman law at this stage probably explains why, despite the appearance of case reports at this time, a system of binding precedent did not emerge.

Again, given the importance of Roman law, the emerging legal profession had resort to French and Dutch universities for training at this time. While canon law did not survive the Reformation in the mid-16th century, except in so far as it was now part of Scots common law, Roman law did not suffer the same fate. Indeed, its influence extended from the 17th century through the INSTITUTIONAL WRITINGS.

Full union with England had been discussed since the Union of the Crowns in 1603 and had been mooted again during the Cromwellian occupation in the mid-17th century, but it was not until the early 18th century that it was finally achieved. Scotland's financial crisis at that time, due in no small measure to the failure of the scheme to occupy Darien in Panama, Central America as a colonial trading venture, and England's desire to secure its northern border during its ongoing war with France, brought the two countries together. The TREATY OF UNION of 1707 saw the end of the Scottish and English Parliaments and the emergence of a new Parliament for Great Britain at Westminster.

While the Scottish legal system was preserved 'in all time coming' by the Treaty, the application by the Scottish courts of legislation emerging from the new Parliament meant that gradually the influence of Roman law diminished as that of English law increased. Growing trade between the two countries also provided a route by which English influence permeated Scots law, and in time Scots lawyers increasingly cited English authority, albeit that the courts were selective in what they adopted.

The continuation of this process in the 19th century saw in due course the adoption from England of *stare decisis* or binding PRECEDENT, and thus marked a clear rupture between Scots law and the civil law world.

During the last century, precedent has increased in importance in Scots law, as has the influence of legislation. In common with England, Scots law has also had to come to terms with European Law since the accession of the United Kingdom to the European Communities in 1973. Most recently, Scots law has once again begun to emerge from the SCOTTISH PARLIAMENT following devolution.   [JP]

See also SCOTTISH GOVERNMENT.

Scottish Executive *See* SCOTTISH GOVERNMENT.

Scottish government From September 2007, the statutory term for the Ministers of the Scottish government exercising devolved powers under the Scotland Act 1998, previously known as the Scottish Executive. Also referred to as the **Scottish Ministers**, this body is composed of the First Minister, the SCOTTISH LAW OFFICERS (the Lord Advocate and the Solicitor-General for Scotland) and other Ministers appointed from among the ranks of MSPs by the First Minister. The Executive is drawn from the party or parties holding a majority in the SCOTTISH PARLIAMENT.

The First Minister, as head of the Scottish Executive, is the equivalent of the Prime Minister at Westminster. He or she is formally appointed by the sovereign on the basis of a nomination made by the Scottish Parliament.

The number and responsibilities of the Ministers appointed (beyond the Law Officers) is a matter for the First Minister. Junior Ministers may also be appointed to assist with ministerial business, but they are not members of the Scottish Executive. At present there are Ministers dealing with the following portfolios: Europe, External Affairs and Culture; Parliamentary Business; Finance and Sustainable Growth; Enterprise, Energy and Tourism; Transport, Infrastructure and Climate Change; Education and Lifelong Learning; Children and Early Years; Schools and Skills; Health and Wellbeing; Public Health; Communities and Sport; Justice; Community Safety; Rural Affairs and the Environment.   [JP]

Scottish law *See* SCOTS LAW.

Scottish Law Officers The collective title for the Crown's legal advisers in Scotland:

the **Lord Advocate** and the **Solicitor-General for Scotland**. They are appointed by the Queen on the recommendation of the First Minister, who in turn will have sought the approval of the SCOTTISH PARLIAMENT. They may be MSPs but this is not a requirement for appointment given that there may not be any suitably qualified lawyers in the Parliament at any given time. If a Law Officer is not a Member of the Scottish Parliament, they may still take part in its work but cannot vote. The Lord Advocate and the Solicitor-General are members of the SCOTTISH GOVERNMENT and represent it in court. The Lord Advocate is also in charge of the prosecution of crimes and the investigation of deaths in Scotland, thus overseeing the work of the PROCURATORS FISCAL.

A third Scottish Law Officer, the **Advocate General**, emerged with the creation of the Scottish Parliament and has the function of advising the UK government on SCOTS LAW and in particular on whether the Scottish Parliament is correctly exercising its powers. Where the Advocate General has concerns in this regard, he or she may prevent a Scottish Bill being sent for the Royal Assent and refer the issue to the Judicial Committee of the Privy Council.   [JP]

Scottish Parliament The legislature exercising the powers devolved from Westminster under the Scotland Act 1998. In contrast to Westminster, the Scottish Parliament is **unicameral** (that is, has one chamber and thus no upper house) with 129 elected Members (Members of the Scottish Parliament or MSPs). These Members elect a Presiding Officer (equivalent to the Speaker in the House of Commons) and two deputies, who hold office until the next election.

Election to the Parliament is via a combination of the 'first past the post' system (as used for election to the House of Commons) and a version of proportional representation known as the **Additional Member** system, based on party lists. Seventy-three MSPs are elected as constituency members, using the same constituencies as for Westminster. Fifty-six MSPs are elected as regional members, with seven representing each of eight regions, using the same boundaries as for elections to the European Parliament. Elections are normally held every four years, although extraordinary elections may be held in certain circumstances.

Membership of the House of Commons does not disqualify a person from being an MSP. While many of the same disqualifications as apply to the Commons also apply to the Scottish Parliament, there are exceptions including EU citizens resident in the UK, peers and ministers of religion, all of whom may be MSPs.

The party or parties holding a majority in the Scottish Parliament will form the SCOTTISH GOVERNMENT, that is the body constituted by the First Minister, the SCOTTISH LAW OFFICERS and the Scottish Ministers. [JP]

Scottish Public Services Ombudsman
See LOCAL GOVERNMENT OMBUDSMEN.

SEA *See* SINGLE EUROPEAN ACT.

seal A specific wax attachment (or, more recently, a paper sticker attachment) to a document in order to indicate its authenticity. A seal is no longer a requirement for the valid execution of an instrument by an individual as a DEED: Law of Property (Miscellaneous Provisions) Act 1989, s. 1 (in force 31 July 1990). Since the Companies Act 1989, companies are no longer required to execute documents by attaching the company seal (now Companies Act 2006, s. 45). However, if a company has a seal then it must comply with the requirements of s. 45(2) and having a common seal is a prerequisite to the company's ability to have an official seal for sealing securities (s. 50). [JPL]

search and seizure General police powers of entry, search and seizure are set out in Part II of the Police and Criminal Evidence Act 1984 (PACE) and the Code of Practice for Searches of Premises by Police Officers and the Seizure of Property Found by Police Officers on Persons or Premises (Code B).

Premises may be lawfully searched with the consent of the person entitled to grant entry, provided they are made aware of the purposes and extent of the search. Alternatively, a SEARCH WARRANT may be sought from a MAGISTRATE. Generally, an application for a warrant must be supported by authorization from an inspector. The application must satisfy the justice of the peace that there are reasonable grounds for believing that an indictable offence has been committed; and, broadly speaking, that there is material on the premises which is likely to be of substantial value to the investigation of the offence; and which is likely to be admissible at any trial. There are also limited powers of entry without a warrant, which apply mainly where it is sought to effect an arrest, or to save life or limb.

Provided that a constable is lawfully on any premises, he may seize anything which is on the premises if he has reasonable grounds for believing that it has been obtained in consequence of the commission of an offence; or that it is evidence in relation to an offence which he is investigating, or any other offence; and that it is necessary to seize it in order to prevent it being concealed, lost, etc. Property seized as a result of a search may be retained for as long as is necessary in all the circumstances; for example, for use as evidence, or for forensic examination in connection with an offence.

The officer in charge must make a record of the search, setting out prescribed details. [BF]

See also POWER OF ARREST.

search warrant A warrant issued by a judge or MAGISTRATE authorizing a police officer to enter premises and search for and seize evidence relating to a criminal offence. [SN]

searches When buying residential or commercial property, various searches must be made by the solicitor acting for the buyer in order to find out as much as possible about the property to be bought. Pre-contract searches are carried out prior to the exchange of contracts in order to reveal any issues and ENCUMBRANCES that may reduce the value of the subject property, before the buyer becomes legally bound to go ahead with the purchase. Pre-completion searches are carried out in between exchange of contracts and COMPLETION in order to ensure that the information obtained prior to exchange remains accurate and to protect the buyer's position from any undisclosed encumbrances.

Pre-contract searches that should be carried out in relation to all property include LOCAL SEARCHES, an ENVIRONMENTAL SEARCH and a physical inspection of the property. In relation to UNREGISTERED LAND, an Index Map search and a Central LAND CHARGES search should also be made. Some searches are advisable depending on the location of the property, such as a Commons Registration search or a Coal Mining search.

Pre-completion searches include official Land Registry searches (in relation to REGISTERED LAND), a Central Land Charges search (in relation to unregistered land), a bankruptcy search and a further physical inspection of the property. [DR]

secession Occurs when part of a STATE (whether a federated state or a COLONY) breaks away (secedes) from the whole. The act of secession itself is regulated by state practice and it is acceptable as long as the means to achieve it do not violate INTERNATIONAL LAW and where the principle of SELF-DETERMINATION is respected. The question remains, however, as to whether the rights and obligations of the old federal state are automatically transmitted to the new seceding state. The principle of nontransmissibility responds to this query in the negative, giving rise to the 'clean-slate theory' for new seceding states, subject to some notable limitations. New seceding states are always bound by pre-existing treaties and domestic administrative boundaries (*UTI POSSIDETIS*), as well as TREATY law relating to international crimes and fundamental HUMAN RIGHTS. [IB]

second opinion appointed doctor (SOAD) A doctor appointed by the Secretary of State (in practice the appointment is made by the MENTAL HEALTH ACT COMMISSION) to give a second opinion with regard to proposed treatment to be administered with or without the patient's consent under s. 57 or s. 58 of the Mental Health Act 1983. [HJ]

secondary disclosure (obsolete) An aspect of the superseded framework of prosecution disclosure. For the present framework, see DISCLOSURE OF EVIDENCE IN CRIMINAL CASES. [ALTC]

secondary evidence EVIDENCE that consists, for example, of a copy of a document rather than the original. [ALTC]

secondary legislation 1. DELEGATED LEGISLATION made under the authority of a STATUTE or some other form of primary legislation.

2. In EU law, all legislation that is not contained in the EU Treaties. Under Article 249 of the EC Treaty, the main instruments of secondary legislation are REGULATIONS, DIRECTIVES, DECISIONS, Recommendations and Opinions. [JW]

secondary party *See* ACCESSORY; PRINCIPAL.

secret trust A TRUST that arises in the context of testamentary dispositions and takes effect despite the will containing no mention of either the trust, or its terms, in seeming disregard of the Wills Act 1837, s. 9, which would normally require such details to be included on the face of the document. There are two forms of secret trust: **fully secret trusts**, in which not even the existence of the trust is mentioned in the will, with the secret TRUSTEE appearing to take absolutely; and **half secret** (or semi-secret) **trusts** in which the existence of the trust, but not its terms, are included in the document and where the legatee's status as trustee (but not the beneficial ownership) is apparent from the will. Secret trusts are a product of social convention and a means by which a TESTATOR can leave property on behalf of persons or causes with whom he does not want to be associated, even in death. The device consequently has tended to be used to benefit illegitimate children and secret lovers; or to support radical causes, although the latter is only possible provided it amounts to a valid PURPOSE TRUST. The terms of a secret trust have to be communicated to the intended trustee, at least, before the will takes effect (i.e. prior to the death of the testator), while it is often suggested that in respect of half secret trusts communication has to take place even earlier, before the will is even written. However, it can be plausibly argued that this represents an illogical distinction between the two types of secret trust, ignores the fact that prior to death a will has no effect on the testator's estate, and is based on a misreading of the leading case of *Blackwell* v. *Blackwell* [1929] AC 319.

The doctrinal basis of secret trusts is also a matter of debate with older authorities suggesting they are a CONSTRUCTIVE TRUST imposed to avoid the Wills Act being used as an instrument of fraud by enabling legatees to defraud the intended beneficiaries by taking the trust property absolutely. The problem with such a rationale is that it is impossible to justify giving effect to the terms of a half secret trust on such a basis, because there is no possibility of fraud in such situations as the legatee's status as trustee is apparent on the face of the document, and the court can simply rely upon the words in the will to require the legatee to hold on resulting trust for the residuary legatees. It was for this reason that half secret, unlike fully secret trusts, were not recognized until the HOUSE OF LORDS broadened the notion of fraud in *Blackwell* v. *Blackwell* [1929] to include fraud on the testator's intention. Such an approach is unconvincing and little more than a linguistic charade, which has led to renewed attempts to discover a unifying theory. Currently most courts and commentators appear to subscribe to the notion that secret trusts are not testamentary dispositions at all, but *inter vivos* trusts, declared during the lifetime of the testator and consequently not subject to the Wills Act 1937, that lie in suspense until the trust property vests in the trustee under the terms of the will. Whether this is any more convincing a theory is open to question and perhaps no justification is possible beyond the pragmatic one that secret trusts arguably provide a necessary counterweight to the otherwise onerous terms of the Wills Act 1837. [PK]

section 1 statement The Employment Rights Act 1996, s. 1, stipulates that an EMPLOYER must provide an EMPLOYEE with a written statement of the particulars of the CONTRACT OF EMPLOYMENT within two months of the commencement of employment. This statement is often known as the 's. 1 statement'. It merely evidences the contract of employment but is not the contract itself. [MJ]

section 8 orders Court orders made under the terms of the Children Act 1989, s. 8. There are four types of orders provided for under this section: RESIDENCE ORDERS, CONTACT ORDERS, SPECIFIC ISSUE ORDERS and PROHIBITED STEPS ORDERS. [FK]

section 37 investigation An investigation conducted under the Children Act 1989, s. 37. The section provides that where there are FAMILY PROCEEDINGS before a court, and a question arises regarding the welfare of the CHILD, which leads the court to think that a CARE ORDER or SUPERVISION ORDER might be warranted, the court may direct the appropriate LOCAL AUTHORITY to investigate the child's circumstances. The local authority conducting the investigation must consider whether it should apply for a care or supervision order, whether it should offer assistance or whether it should take any other action. If it decides not to apply for a care or supervision order, it must notify the court of its reasons and inform the court of any other action it is taking or planning to take. [FK]

See also WELFARE PRINCIPLE.

section 47 enquiry An enquiry conducted in terms of the Children Act 1989, s. 47, which provides that a LOCAL AUTHORITY has a duty to make enquiries if it is informed that a CHILD in its area is the subject of an EMERGENCY PROTECTION ORDER, is in police protection, has contravened a curfew, or there is reasonable cause to suspect that the child is suffering, or is likely to suffer, significant harm. The obligation also arises in cases where a local authority has itself obtained an emergency protection order with respect to a child. The enquiry is directed at determining whether any action is needed to safeguard or promote the welfare of the child and, in particular, whether the local authority should apply for a court order, such as an interim CARE ORDER.

The Framework for the Assessment of Children in Need and their Families (DoH, 2000) is used to collect and analyse information obtained in the course of s. 47 enquiries. Enquiries entail completing a core assessment and, normally, in the course of an enquiry, interviews are conducted with the child concerned, the PARENTS or caregivers and any professionals involved with the FAMILY. If after completion of the enquiry there are concerns that the child is at risk, a CHILD PROTECTION CONFERENCE is called. If concerns persist, the local authority may decide to apply for a care order or a SUPERVISION ORDER. See also *Working Together to Safeguard Children* (London: TSO, 2006), chapter 5. [FK]

See also POLICE PROTECTION ORDER; THRESHOLD CRITERIA.

sector principle A proposed method of territorial boundary delimitation in the Arctic and Antarctic regions by simply drawing straight lines of longitude from the Pole to the furthest point of the contiguous state's land mass to produce a sector of SOVEREIGNTY. Its application does not produce title, it is simply a method of delimitation. It is not universally recognized: in the Arctic region, sector claims have been made by Canada and Russia, but have been refused by the USA, Finland, Norway and Denmark. [IB]

secure accommodation order An order authorizing a LOCAL AUTHORITY to place, or keep, a CHILD in accommodation provided for the purposes of restricting the liberty of that child (Children Act 1989, s. 25). A secure accommodation order may be made in respect of a child who is being looked after by a local authority under a voluntary arrangement made with the parent(s) or under a CARE ORDER. However, it can only be made if the child has a history of absconding, or is likely to abscond, from other types of accommodation and, if he or she absconds, the child is likely to suffer significant harm. Alternatively, an order may be granted in circumstances where, if the child is kept in another type of accommodation, he or she is likely to injure him/herself or other persons. [FK]

See also LOOKED AFTER CHILD; THRESHOLD CRITERIA.

secure tenancy The most common form of TENANCY granted by local authorities. It provides the council tenant with strong SECURITY OF TENURE as well as a bundle of other rights collectively known as the Tenant's Charter. Before 15 January 1989, when the Housing Act 1988 was implemented, HOUSING ASSOCIATIONS were able to grant secure tenancies and any such tenancy retains its secure status.

The Housing Act 1985 sets out the statutory framework. A secure tenancy must comply with the **tenant condition** set out in s. 81 of the 1985 Act and the **landlord condition** set out in s. 80. The tenant condition requires that the tenant or the joint tenants are individuals (as opposed to companies or associations), and that the tenant (or where there are joint tenants, at least one of them) occupies the dwelling house as his or her only or principal home. If the tenant ceases to occupy the property, all the protections of the secure status are lost, and he or she can be evicted with limited formalities. The landlord condition lists the bodies able to grant secure tenancies. These are limited but include LOCAL AUTHORITIES, and urban development corporations.

The landlord cannot terminate the secure tenancy without a court order, and the court will not grant an order unless the landlord has first served on the tenant a notice of intention to seek possession that specifies the statutory ground upon which it is claiming possession. The grounds are set out in Schedule 2 to the 1985 Act. There are three sets of grounds: (a) those where the court can order possession if it considers it reasonable to do so (e.g. non-payment of rent or breach of obligation of the tenancy and anti-social behaviour by the tenant or someone residing with or visiting the tenant); (b) those where the court may order possession if suitable alternative accommodation is available, for instance where the property is overcrowded; and

(c) those where the court may order possession if it is both reasonable to do so and suitable alternative accommodation is available.

The court has extensive powers to adjourn possession proceedings or suspend possession orders. However Parliament has intervened to reduce that discretion in cases of anti-social behaviour when the court must consider the effect that the nuisance or annoyance has had and will have on the community if it is allowed to continue. [HC & DR]

secure training centre Centres for young offenders aged from 12 to 17 run by private operators contracted by the Home Office. Originally designed to accommodate offenders aged from 12 to 14 who received a SECURE TRAINING ORDER under the Criminal Justice and Public Order Act 1994, they are now used for offenders aged 12 to 17 who are serving a custodial sentence under the Powers of Criminal Courts (Sentencing) Act 2000, ss. 90, 91 and 100. Placement in a centre requires the consent of the Secretary of State. [SN]

secure training order (obsolete) An order made under the Criminal Justice and Public Order Act 1994 which provided that an offender aged between 12 and 14 should be subject to a period of detention in a SECURE TRAINING CENTRE, followed by a period of supervision. The secure training order was abolished by the Powers of Criminal Courts (Sentencing) Act 2000. [SN]

security Money deposited to ensure that the defendant in a criminal case attends court. [SN]

Security Council The principal organ of the UNITED NATIONS for the maintenance of international peace and security. Its function, composition and powers are regulated by the UN CHARTER. It is composed of five permanent members (USA, China, Russian Federation, UK and France) and ten rotating non-permanent members. Its resolutions are binding on all UN members, but in order for it to adopt one it is necessary that all five permanent members consent and that at least four of the non-permanent members do so too. It has been the practice of the Council since 1950 that abstentions count as positive votes and not as vetoes. The Council's strength lies in the fact that through its binding resolutions it can authorize the use of any measures falling below the use of armed force (Article 41 measures), as well as armed force itself when it deems this to be necessary (Article 42 measures). These COLLECTIVE SECURITY powers of the Council were dormant throughout the Cold War and were revived after the Soviet Union's collapse in 1990. The Council may and has in the past set up numerous subsidiary organs in order to assist it in the implementation of resolutions it has adopted. These subsidiary organs are endowed by the Council with binding powers, but are subject to the Council's overall control. [IB]

See also CHAPTER VII; USE OF FORCE.

security of tenure The extent to which an occupier of land is protected from eviction. Various statutory regimes give different levels of security to occupiers. For instance the Rent Act 1977 gives extensive security so that the TENANT can only be evicted following service of a notice, proof of statutory grounds and a court order. In contrast, an assured shorthold tenant can be evicted without proof of grounds simply on the basis of two months' notice and a court order. [HC & DR]

See also ASSURED TENANCY; SECURE TENANCY.

sedition Inciting by words or writing disaffection and public disorder towards Parliament, the STATE or sovereign authority, or seeking a change in the law by unlawful means. Sedition is a COMMON LAW offence; it is rarely used today. [MS]

See also TREASON.

self-incrimination A response to a question or producing a document that would have a tendency to incriminate the person providing the response or producing the document. The law recognizes a general PRIVILEGE or right against self-incrimination. See, however, the RIGHT TO SILENCE. [ALTC]

self-defence A defence to any charge of which the unlawful use or threat of force is an element. It is a JUSTIFICATION, and leads to a complete ACQUITTAL. A person may in fact use force in a variety of situations: in defence of himself or herself, in defence of another, in defence of property or in the prevention of crime. Where force is being used in the prevention of crime (or in effecting or assisting in an arrest), the relevant law is the Criminal Law Act 1967, s. 3. Where a person is using force other than in the prevention of crime, the situation is governed by COMMON LAW, but the parameters of the defence are the same: a person may use force that is reasonable in the circumstances that he or she believes them to be (see *R* v. *Gladstone Williams* (1984) 74 Cr App R 276). Thus, where someone is mistaken as to the need to use force, they may still benefit from the defence as long as their mistake is honest, and as long as the force used is not excessive in the circumstances that they believe them to be.

The common law and s. 3 of the 1967 Act overlap considerably. Thus, where someone uses force against V to prevent V from attacking E, this could be for the prevention of crime (s. 3) or for the defence of E (common law).

Even where someone successfully pleads self-defence to MURDER, the result is a complete acquittal, and not a finding of MANSLAUGHTER. This is because the person's conduct is *lawful* and consequently cannot constitute any offence against the person.

[BF]

See also NECESSITY; REASONABLE FORCE.

self-determination A collective right in INTERNATIONAL LAW whose origin may be found in the post-Second World War Declaration of US President Wilson and which has now become a positive right under TREATY (Articles 1(2) and 55 of the UN CHARTER and Article 1 of the 1966 INTERNATIONAL COVENANT ON CIVIL AND POLITICAL RIGHTS) and CUSTOMARY INTERNATIONAL LAW. It is granted only to the distinct legal category of 'peoples', which includes cohesive national groups, as opposed to minorities or indigenous groups who are not also peoples. The right encompasses both an internal and an external element. The internal element consists of the right to freely determine their political status and pursue their economic, social and cultural development. External self-determination consists of the right to choose the mode of statehood and to be independent from other STATES. Self-determination was recognized as a legal obligation in the decolonization era through seminal resolutions of the UN General Assembly and by the INTERNATIONAL COURT OF JUSTICE in its Advisory Opinion in the *Western Sahara* case [1975] ICJ Rep 12.

[IB]

See also INDIGENOUS PEOPLES; MINORITY RIGHTS; RECOGNITION OF A STATE.

self-regulation The situation where the REGULATION of a particular sector of society is at least to some extent a matter for that sector itself rather than for the STATE. The state may, nevertheless, have some role to play as the rules by which a particular body or group self-regulates may be laid down by STATUTE or in that the process of self-regulation may be overseen by some state agency. It is noteworthy also that self-regulation may arise as a result of the fear on the part of some sector of society that if it does not act, then regulation will be imposed on it by the state.

Self-regulation is prevalent in the professions, such as law and medicine, where professional bodies set and enforce standards for their members. It may equally appear, however, in industrial and business settings where a government agency may set broad parameters within which individual firms must regulate themselves.

Self-regulation is most often justified on the grounds that it allows those possessing the relevant expertise to be involved in regulation and thus produces a more efficient regulatory system than would be the case if it were in the hands of a government agency.

Critics of self-regulation are concerned that behaviour which an independent agency would censure will go unpunished in the self-regulatory setting because of self-interest. They are equally concerned that self-regulatory bodies lack the legitimacy enjoyed by a government agency as well as the transparency and accountability that permeates such agencies. Supporters respond that where a professional body plays an enforcement role, its concern with protecting the reputation of the profession as a whole will ensure that breaches of the regulations by individuals will indeed be punished and equally that a similar concern will ensure that transparency and accountability are achieved.   [JP]

Further reading: Anthony Ogus, 'Rethinking Self-Regulation', *Oxford Journal of Legal Studies* (1995), 15, 1997.

seller The party to a SALE OF GOODS contract who either transfers or agrees to transfer property (ownership) in the goods to the buyer in exchange for the agreed CONSIDER-ATION.   [JPL]

See also VENDOR.

Seller's Property Information Form A form that is filled out partly by the seller of property and partly by the seller's solicitor in order to anticipate any PRELIMINARY ENQUIRIES that the buyer may have and also to fulfil the seller's duty to disclose all latent ENCUMBRANCES and defects in title. The form provides information on issues such as boundaries and fences, neighbour disputes, exclusive or shared services and facilities, occupiers, use of the property for planning purposes and EASEMENTS.

Under the Law Society's National Conveyancing Protocol, the Seller's Property Information Form is part of the contract for sale, along with the contract itself and the Law Society's Fixtures, Fittings and Contents form. It is therefore crucial that the seller provides accurate information, since failure to do so could lead to the seller being found liable for the reduction in the value of the property attributable to, for example, an undisclosed neighbour dispute.   [DR]

sending for trial Procedure introduced by the Crime and Disorder Act 1998, s. 51, whereby INDICTABLE OFFENCES are transferred to the CROWN COURT without the need for a committal hearing in the magistrates' court.   [SN]

Senior Courts of England and Wales Under the Constitutional Reform Act 2005, in preparation for the creation of the new UK SUPREME COURT, the COURT OF APPEAL, HIGH COURT and CROWN COURT, which were collectively known as the **Supreme Court of Judicature,** have been renamed the Senior Courts of England and Wales. All legislative references to the 'old' Supreme Court have been changed retrospectively to Senior Courts, and the Supreme Court Act 1981 is now to be known as the Senior Courts Act 1981. [JW]

sentence The penalty ordered by a judge or MAGISTRATE following conviction by a court or a plea of guilty.   [SN]

See also CONCURRENT SENTENCE; CONSECUTIVE SENTENCES.

separate trials An order made in cases where the accused will be prejudiced by a single trial of all the COUNTS on the INDICT-MENT.   [SN]

separation The separation facts in the Matrimonial Causes Act 1973 and the Civil Partnership Act 2004 on which parties may rely to obtain a DIVORCE or DISSOLUTION order, require the parties to **live apart** for continuous periods of either two or five years. For both the five-year and the two-year separation facts, the words 'live apart' have specific meaning. First, to be living apart, the parties must live in separate households, but separate households may be established under the same roof if the parties live as two units rather than as one (for example by not sharing meals, sleeping arrangements or lives together); however, physical separation is not sufficient. Secondly, one or both of the parties must regard the MARRIAGE or CIVIL PARTNERSHIP as finished, therefore having the intention to end consortium with the other. Two years of living apart is evidence that the marriage or civil partnership has broken down irretrievably (see IRRETRIEVABLE BREAK-DOWN) if the respondent consents to the divorce or dissolution. Without consent, a five-year period of separation is required. If the parties resume cohabitation for longer than six months and then separate again, the two- or five-year period will be required to start again, this time from the later separation date. [AD]

See also JUDICIAL SEPARATION ORDER; LEGAL SEPARATION; SEPARATION AGREEMENT.

separation agreement A written agreement between spouses or civil partners about what is to happen to their property and finances on SEPARATION. While parties are free to enter into separation agreements, they may not oust the jurisdiction of the court to make an order contrary to the terms of the agreement. The court has the power to alter agreements in certain circumstances and any term which purports to prohibit a party from applying to the court for ANCILLARY RELIEF is void. While these agreements are not, strictly speaking, enforceable, courts have begun to give them more weight when determining applications for ancillary relief. [AD]

See also ANTE-NUPTIAL SETTLEMENT; MAINTENANCE AGREEMENT; PRE-NUPTIAL AGREEMENT.

separation of powers The principle, expounded by Montesquieu in *De l'Esprit des Lois* (1748) ('The Spirit of the Law') that the RULE OF LAW requires the three major functions of state – legislative, executive and judicial – to be exercised by independent bodies. Montesquieu's ideas have since been highly influential in shaping democratic constitutional arrangements in modern STATES. [JW]

separation order *See* JUDICIAL SEPARATION ORDER.

Serious Organised Crime Agency (SOCA) A national law enforcement agency created by the Serious Organised Crime and Policing Act 2005. It operates as an executive non-departmental public body sponsored by, but operationally independent of, the Home Office. It is an intelligence-led agency with law enforcement powers to deal with organized crime (e.g. trafficking of Class A drugs, organized immigration crime, organized vehicle crime, and fraud) and provides financial and operational intelligence to trace the proceeds of crime or suspected terrorist funding, and undertake asset recovery

resulting from serious crimes. It was formed as a result of the amalgamation of the National Crime Squad (NCS), the National Criminal Intelligence Service (NCIS), the UK Financial Intelligence Unit (UKFIU), the Assets Recovery Agency, and relevant parts of HM REVENUE AND CUSTOMS (HMRC) and the UK Immigration Service. [BF]

service The process of giving a legal document to another where that document forms the commencement or part of a legal process, especially court proceedings. The date of service is often significant as it may determine the date by which the recipient must respond to the person serving the document, or to the court. Where service of a document by post is permitted by STATUTE, it is 'deemed to be effected by properly addressing, pre-paying and posting a letter containing the document and, unless the contrary is proved, to have been effected at the time at which the letter would be delivered in the ordinary course of post' (see the Interpretation Act 1978, s. 7). [JW]

See also ADDRESS FOR SERVICE; ACKNOWLEDGEMENT OF SERVICE.

service occupancy Persons living in TIED ACCOMMODATION will not have a TENANCY if it is necessary for them to live in the premises in question in order to carry out their employment duties, or if occupying the premises is a requirement imposed for the better performance of their employment duties. Such occupancies are construed as service licences and are therefore excluded from the Housing Act 1988. They are also specifically excluded from the SECURE TENANCY regime in Schedule 1 to the Housing Act 1985. [HC & DR]

servient tenement A piece of land that is burdened by an EASEMENT or a profit appurtenant to land. [DR]

See also DOMINANT TENEMENT; PROFIT À PRENDRE.

servitude A right over another person's land; for example an EASEMENT or PROFIT À PRENDRE. [DR]

settled land Land that is the subject of a SETTLEMENT. [DR]

Settled Land Act trustees The trustees of a SETTLEMENT governed by the Settled Land Act 1925 (SLA 1925). Settled Land Act trustees have specific powers and duties that differ from those under a pre-1997 trust for sale or a post-1997 trust of land. The identity of the trustees is determined according to SLA 1925, s. 30(1), which essentially states, in order of priority, that the trustees will be the persons with power of sale of the SETTLED LAND, or the persons declared to be trustees of the settled land by the settlement, or the persons appointed as trustees by deed by the beneficiaries.

Settled Land Act trustees usually have fewer powers than trustees under a pre-1997 trust for sale or a post-1997 trust of land, because the TENANT FOR LIFE holds the legal estate and has extensive management powers. The main role of Settled Land Act trustees is to receive any capital money arising out of transactions relating to the settled land and to invest that money, as well as generally to 'conserve the settled property' by intervening if the tenant for life acts or intends to act beyond his powers. If there is no tenant for life, for example if the designated tenant for life is a minor, the trustees may become the statutory owner, exercising the powers of the tenant for life. [DR]

settlement In land law, a disposition – either made between living persons or contained in a will – creating a succession of limited interests in property. The interests may be limited, for example by way of succession (e.g. LIFE INTERESTS) or by way of conditions (e.g. on X's qualification as a doctor). There are different types of settlement, including COMPOUND SETTLEMENTS, STRICT SETTLEMENTS, marriage settlements (created before or at the time of marriage) and voluntary settlements (made by GIFT).

Following the 1925 property law reforms, settlements could only be created using a Settled Land Act TRUST, governed by the Settled Land Act 1925, or a TRUST FOR SALE, governed by the Law of Property Act 1925. Settled Land Act settlements and trusts for sale became increasingly outdated throughout the 20th century, eventually leading to their abolition by the Trusts of Land and Appointment of Trustees Act 1996 (TLATA 1996). Since 1 January 1997, settlements can only be created under a trust of land, governed by TLATA 1996. Pre-1997 trusts for sale converted automatically into trusts of land overnight, while pre-existing Settled Land Act settlements continue to have effect. [DR]

settlor A person who disposes of his property under a SETTLEMENT or TRUST. [DR]

sever an indictment An application made by the defence to a judge requesting that COUNTS in the INDICTMENT are tried separately. [SN]

severance 1. In contract law, where possible the courts will seek to save a contract that is illegal or defective in part by removing or 'severing' the VOID parts of the contract from the good parts. Severance is only possible where sufficient of the contract remains after severance to make sense of the parties' obligations. This is sometimes referred to as the **blue pencil test**.

2. Similarly, where a provision within a piece of DELEGATED LEGISLATION is *ULTRA VIRES*, the courts will, if possible, sever the offending provision, leaving the remainder of the instrument as valid law; see *DPP* v. *Hutchinson* [1990] 2 AC 783.

3. The conversion of an equitable joint TENANCY in land to a TENANCY IN COMMON as a consequence of one of the joint tenants' bankruptcy, the sale of an interest in the land, written notice from one of the tenants, or by mutual agreement of them all. [JW]

See also SEVER AN INDICTMENT; WORDS OF SEVERANCE.

severance pay Pay on leaving employment, particularly pay which is enhanced by contractual or ex gratia sums. [MJ]

Sewel Convention The UK government's policy that it will not legislate on a matter which has been devolved to the SCOTTISH PARLIAMENT, the Northern Ireland Assembly or the Welsh Assembly without the consent of those bodies. It is named after the Minister, Lord (John) Sewel, who outlined the policy during the passage of the Scotland Bill in the House of Lords in 1998 (see HANSARD HL (Debs) vol. 592, col. 791 (21 July 1998).

There is no reference to this matter in the Scotland Act 1998, although it is mentioned in the Memorandum of Understanding and Supplementary Agreements Between the United Kingdom Government, Scottish Ministers, the Cabinet of the National Assembly for Wales and the Northern Ireland Executive Committee, drawn up in 1999. This Memorandum is not legally binding, but the expectation is that the UK government will not act contrary to the Convention.

This position reflects the doctrine of parliamentary sovereignty. Thus, although power has been devolved, the Westminster Parliament has not prevented itself from legislating on such matters in future or indeed from repealing the legislation by which devolution was effected. [JP]

sex discrimination Sex DISCRIMINATION in employment is forbidden by the Sex Discrimination Act 1975, as amended. Discrimination under the Act applies to discrimination on the grounds of marital status and gender but not sexual orientation, for which separate provision is made (see SEXUAL ORIENTATION DISCRIMINATION). There are exemptions, in particular genuine occupational qualifications (e.g. modelling bikinis). The Equality Act 2006 now places a duty on public authorities to promote sexual equality. [MJ]

sex offenders' register The Sex Offenders Act 1997 introduced a requirement for sex offenders to let the police know if they changed name or address. The notification requirements are now set out in the Sexual Offences Act 2003. The 2003 Act requires those convicted of an offence specified in Schedule 3 to the Act to provide the police with various items of identifying information (see s. 83 of the 2003 Act). Subsequent changes to the information must also be notified within prescribed timescales (see s. 84). Offenders must also renotify the

police within specified periods, even if the information has not changed (see s. 85). The offences specified in Schedule 3 are all SEXUAL OFFENCES. The duration of the notification requirements depends on the severity of the sentence imposed upon conviction. It is an offence under s. 91 to fail, without reasonable excuse, to comply with a notification requirement. [BF]

sexual assault It is an offence under the Sexual Offences Act 2003, s. 3, for a person to intentionally touch another person, where the touching is sexual, where the other person does not consent to the touching, and where the person doing the touching does not reasonably believe that the other is consenting.

'Sexual' is defined in s. 78 of the 2003 Act, which provides that an activity is sexual if a reasonable person would consider that whatever its circumstances or any person's purpose in relation to it, it is because of its nature sexual; or if a reasonable person would consider that because of its nature it may be sexual, and because of its circumstances or the purpose of any person in relation to it (or both), it is sexual.

Section 79 of the 2003 Act provides that touching can be done with any part of the body, with anything else, and through anything. In *R* v. *H* [2005] 2 All ER 859, it was held by the Court of Appeal that the defendant's grabbing of the victim's tracksuit bottoms constituted touching the victim.

Section 2 of the 2003 Act provides for a more serious offence of assault by PENETRATION, to cover situations where the assault involves the intentional sexual penetration of the victim's vagina or anus. [BF]

See also RAPE; SEXUAL OFFENCE.

sexual offence An umbrella term referring to a broad range of offences against the sexual integrity of a victim. Sexual offences underwent a substantial codification and consolidation with the enactment of the Sexual Offences Act 2003, and that Act criminalizes a variety of behaviours which are wrongful on account, for example, of the actual lack of consent of the victim; or on the basis that the victim is, for a reason such as youth or lack of capacity, not equipped to give a proper consent to the conduct in question; or in the sense, in the context of offences involving, for example, BESTIALITY or NECROPHILIA, that the conduct is sufficiently morally problematic to merit the intervention of the criminal law. Schedule 3 to the Sexual Offences Act 2003 sets out a range of sexual offences, conviction for which triggers notification requirements (in effect, the requirement that the convicted defendant be placed on the SEX OFFENDERS' REGISTER). As well as many of the offences under the 2003 Act, Schedule 3 specifies, for example, offences relating to CHILD PORNOGRAPHY under the Protection of Children Act 1978, s. 1, and under the Criminal Justice Act 1988, s. 160. Some offences which may, indirectly, involve sexual behaviour, might be more properly categorized as public order offences. These would include offences relating to prostitution under the STREET OFFENCES Act 1959 and the Sexual Offences Act 1985.   [BF]

See also FAMILIAL SEXUAL OFFENCES; RAPE; SEXUAL ASSAULT.

sexual orientation discrimination The Employment Equality (Sexual Orientation) Regulations 2003 (SI 2003/1661), implementing the Equal Treatment Framework Directive 2003/78/EC, makes DISCRIMINATION based on sexual orientation unlawful. The regulations prohibit discrimination on the grounds of homosexuality, heterosexuality and bisexuality, but exclude sexual practices such as paedophilia from protection. Two exceptions are when being of a certain sexual orientation is a genuine and determining occupational requirement, and when being of a certain sexual orientation is required by the tenets of an organized religion (or a significant number of the adherents of that religion demand that the person be of a certain sexual orientation).   [MJ]

sexual slavery *See* ENSLAVEMENT.

share A unit of capital in a COMPANY, entitling the owner to a proportion of the distributed profit, known as a DIVIDEND. The size of shareholding defines the extent of the shareholder's interest and liability in respect of the company. Shares carry voting rights and also become tradeable commodities in their own right. Shares fall primarily into two categories. They may be **preference shares**; these have limited voting rights, but may provide a more secure investment than ordinary shares. This is because dividends on preference shares have to be paid before dividends on ordinary shares, and are fixed, so they do not reflect increases (or decreases) in profits in the way that ordinary shares do. Preference shareholders also have a higher priority than ordinary shareholders if the company is liquidated. **Ordinary shares** constitute the main equity capital in the company. This means that ordinary shareholders tend to carry the greatest risk (though their liability is restricted in a limited liability company to the paid-up value of their holding), but may also achieve the greatest profit when the company does well. Ordinary shareholders generally have full voting rights in the annual general meeting. Both preference and ordinary shares are subject to the same tax regime on dividends.   [JW]

See also LIQUIDATION.

share transfer A formal legal document transferring shares to a new owner. Transfer requires that the name of the new owner is disclosed and entered on the register of members of the company. This process can now be completed electronically using the Bank of England's electronic trading system (CREST).   [JW]

See also STAMP DUTY; STAMP DUTY RESERVE TAX.

sheriff *See* SHERIFF COURT.

sheriff court The local court in Scotland, tracing its origin to the 12th century when the sheriff (or shire reeve) was the royal officer for each local area or sheriffdom. The title of sheriff was often inherited and court work was actually done by sheriff deputes. In the 18th century, heritable sheriffs were abolished and sheriff deputes became sheriffs with sheriffs substitute working under them. Further reform in the 20th century saw sheriffs become sheriffs principal (with responsibility for an entire sheriffdom) and sheriffs substitute become sheriffs (with responsibility for a sheriff court district). There are now six sheriffdoms in Scotland with 49 sheriff courts.

The sheriff court deals with both civil and criminal business. There is no limit on the value of civil cases it may deal with, nor is there a limit on the fine that it may impose in criminal cases, although there is a limit of five years for custodial sentences. In civil cases, with the sheriff sitting alone, the court has wide jurisdiction with only a few exceptions, including nullity of marriage and nullification of documents. In criminal cases, where the judge may sit alone (under summary procedure) or with a jury of 15 (under solemn procedure), jurisdiction is again wide, although the sheriff court can not deal with murder or rape, which will be heard by the HIGH COURT OF JUS-TICIARY. While other more serious crimes may also be dealt with by the High Court, there is no requirement that this be the case. Thus, even though the sheriff court's sentencing powers are limited to a maximum of five years' imprisonment, cases may be dealt with by that court and remitted to the High Court for sentencing, following conviction, if a heavier sentence is thought appropriate.

Appeals from the sheriff court lie to the Sheriff Principal or to the Inner House of the COURT OF SESSION in civil cases and to the High Court of Justiciary in criminal cases.

[JP]

shifting use *See* USE.

shoplifting There is no separate offence of shoplifting. The term refers to the commission of the offence of THEFT from retail premises. Depending on whether the shoplifter enters the relevant building as a trespasser, he or she may also commit the offence of BURGLARY.   [BF]

short committal A procedure by which the defence can agree to the magistrates' court committing the accused for trial in the CROWN COURT without consideration of the evidence. This is the most commonly used form of COMMITTAL for trial.   [SN]

shrink-wrap licence Licence agreements which can only be read and accepted by the end-user or consumer by opening the shrink-wrap packaging containing the product, which is often a SOFTWARE package. There is no signature by the licensee. The purpose of such licences is often to restrict the use of the software, and limit the liability of software companies.

The validity of a shrink-wrap licence is dependent on the consumer, COPYRIGHT and CONTRACT laws of the country in which the product is consumed or purchased. The validity of such licences is unclear under English law as such licence agreements are only valid between the producer and the initial end-user, and not other parties such as the retailer or a subsequent lawful end-user. Moreover, it is doubtful whether adequate consideration has passed from the end-user to the software manufacturer. The issue of the validity and enforceability of shrink-wrap licences in the United States is also unresolved (see *ProCD, Inc.* v. *Zeidenberg*, 86 F. 3d 1447 (1996); *Specht* v. *Netscape Communications Corp.* 150 F. Supp. 2d 585 (2001)).

[US]

See also CLICK-WRAP LICENCE.

signature A traditional signature comprises a person's name, either in full or using one or more initials and a surname, written by that person. In CONTRACT law, it is used as an indicator of that person's agreement to a document and is taken as intent to be bound by its terms (see *L'Estrange* v. *Graucob* [1934] 2 KB 394). Alternatively, an illiterate person may indicate assent by marking the document with a cross.

Electronic signatures were given legal recognition by the Electronic Communications Act 2000, s. 7. An electronic signature covered by the certification procedures under the Act may therefore fulfil the same function as a handwritten signature in the context of electronic communications.   [JPL]

See also NON EST FACTUM.

signature of treaty The general rule is, unless otherwise stated, that signature of a TREATY has the effect of authenticating its text subsequent to its adoption by the treaty conference (Article 10(b) of the 1969 Vienna Convention on the Law of Treaties). None the less, a STATE may wish to be bound by a treaty on the basis of its signature, without protracting the process through an additional act of RATIFICATION. In such circumstances, the consent of a State to be bound by a treaty is expressed by the signature of its representative when: (a) the treaty provides that signature shall have that effect; (b) it is otherwise established that the negotiating States were agreed that signature should have that effect; or (c) the intention of the State to give that effect to the signature appears from the full powers of its representative, or was expressed during the negotiation (Article 12 of the Vienna Convention). Where a State has signed a treaty and has not expressed an intention to be bound, it is obliged to refrain from acts which would defeat the object and purpose of the treaty until it shall have made clear its intention not to become a party to the treaty.   [IB]

signature of will   For a WILL to be valid it must be signed by the testator, and it must appear that the testator intended by his signature to give effect to the will (see Wills Act 1837, s. 9). The requirement for a signature is satisfied if the TESTATOR signs his name or makes some mark that is intended to represent his name. Thus a cross or thumb-print have been accepted, as has the expression 'your loving mother'. The testator's signature need not necessarily be made by himself, as it can be made by some other person in his presence and by his direction.

Originally, the testator's signature had to be made at the 'the foot or end' of the will, but the interpretation of the expression by the court gave rise to many problems, so that precise requirement is no longer necessary. As a matter of fact, nearly all wills are signed 'at the foot or end thereof', but a signature anywhere else will suffice if it can be shown that it intended to give effect to the will.   [CM]

similar-fact evidence   EVIDENCE of a defendant's bad character that was excep-

tionally treated as admissible in criminal proceedings at COMMON LAW. The common law principles relating to the ADMISSIBILITY of such evidence have been superseded by the provisions of the Criminal Justice Act 2003, s. 101.   [ALTC]

simple contract   A CONTRACT that does not have to be in any particular form, that is it does not need to comply with any formal rules as to writing or attestation of SIGNATURE. A simple contract may therefore be made orally or in writing but will not be made by means of a DEED. Obligations in simple contracts need to be supported by CONSIDERATION in order to be enforceable.
       [JPL]

simple trust   *See* BARE TRUST.

sine die   (Lat. without a day)   A court hearing adjourned *sine die* is adjourned indefinitely without a further hearing date having been allocated.   [JW]

single administrative document (SAD)   A Revenue and Customs document also known as C88. It is used for declaring imports into the EUROPEAN COMMUNITY (EC). The same document, in a variety of languages, is used for this purpose throughout the EC.   [MON]

Single European Act (SEA)   A treaty signed by EUROPEAN COMMUNITY (EC) MEMBER STATES in 1986, and which came into force in 1987. The SEA was the first major reform of the TREATY OF ROME of 1957 in light of the increasing membership of the EC, and the need to complete the single market programme by 1992. The role of the EUROPEAN PARLIAMENT within the EC was increased, and first mention was made of a COURT OF FIRST INSTANCE. In addition, the EUROPEAN COUNCIL was formally recognized, and new policy areas were introduced to the existing policy and legal framework.   [MON]

single-union agreement   EMPLOYERS may refuse to recognize more than one TRADE UNION for COLLECTIVE BARGAINING purposes. Such recognition is called a 'single-union agreement'. Factories on greenfield sites (e.g. car assembly plants) often have such agreements.   [MJ]

skeleton argument A document prepared by a party or their legal representative, outlining and delineating for the parties and the court the points that are in issue, and the nature of the party's argument, with reference to legal authority where appropriate. The court can require that skeleton arguments are served on the court and the other party before trial. [JW]

slander A defamatory TORT where the statement defaming the claimant is published by the defendant in a non-permanent form; for example, the defamatory words are spoken rather than published in writing. In most circumstances, unlike the tort of LIBEL, proof of harm suffered must be shown by the claimant. [HJ]

See also DEFAMATION.

small claims track In civil litigation, the means for dealing with: personal injury claims where the total claim is for not more than £5,000 and the personal injury element is for not more than £1,000; housing disrepair claims by a TENANT involving not more than £1,000 for the cost of repair; and any other claim (e.g. in CONTRACT or as a debt) involving not more than £5,000.

Small claims are heard in the COUNTY COURT. Cases proceed according to a relatively simplified procedure, and, if the parties agree, a case may be dealt with by the judge purely on the papers and without an oral hearing. If there is a hearing it will be informal. The judge can proceed in any reasonable way, and this includes acting as an ARBITRATOR. See CIVIL PROCEDURE RULES, Parts 26 and 27. [JW]

smuggling Not defined in the Customs and Excise Management Act 1979, but according to the decision in *R* v. *Hussain* [1969] 2 QB 567 it refers to the importation of goods without paying the appropriate duty, or the importation of goods which it is prohibited to import. [BF]

SOCA *See* SERIOUS ORGANISED CRIME AGENCY.

social chapter The part of the EUROPEAN COMMUNITY TREATY – Articles 136 to 145 EC – which provides for EUROPEAN COMMUNITY (EC) social policy. This area was sub-stantially strengthened by the TREATY ON EUROPEAN UNION in 1992, with the UK maintaining an 'opt-out' provision, which it subsequently abandoned under the TREATY OF AMSTERDAM in 1997. The social chapter is not to be confused with the 'Social Charter', whose full name is the Community Charter of the Fundamental Social Rights of Workers, 1989, which is a European SOFT LAW document. [MON]

social contract The notion that the duties owed by an individual within society depend upon some form of real or putative agreement, either among citizens or between the citizen and the sovereign. The idea can be traced back to Socrates (470–388 BC) who explained his refusal to escape from prison on the grounds that a citizen is bound to obey even an unjust law because by remaining in a particular state they have entered into an implied contract to obey the laws of that state. The difficulties that this line of argument can produce are already evident at this early stage when Socrates elsewhere suggests that a citizen may disobey the law where it requires him or her to inflict an injustice on another.

The idea was taken up by THOMAS HOBBES and JOHN LOCKE in the 17th century and JEAN-JACQUES ROUSSEAU in the 18th and received renewed attention in more recent times as a result of the work of JOHN RAWLS. [JP]

See also CONTRACTARIANISM.

social landlord A term used to describe LOCAL HOUSING AUTHORITY and housing association LANDLORDS, who provide housing on social rather than market-based principles. [HC & DR]

See also COUNCIL HOUSING; REGISTERED SOCIAL LANDLORD.

sociology of law The application of sociological approaches and insights to law. Whereas lawyers tend to have a rather narrow positivistic perspective, which focuses first on what the law is, and then on its application to specific circumstances, the sociological perspective on law is as interested in where the law comes from (why the need has been felt for a particular law to be passed) and what actually happens once it has been passed (does it produce the intended effect?).

Legal sociologists justify their approach on the basis that sociology and law are both concerned with the totality of social relations. Sociology may thus offer a richer understanding of the law than a more narrowly based approach such as the ECONOMIC ANALYSIS OF LAW.

Motivations behind the deployment of a sociological approach to law may be purely scientific or more instrumental. The scientific approach sees a value in the simple extension of knowledge about the relationship between law and society. Among those whose theorizing has been influential in this way is MAX WEBER. The instrumental approach, by contrast, seeks this knowledge as a means of improving the ability of law to achieve desired societal effects.

While the sociology of law may be interested in a wider range of questions about law than lawyers themselves may habitually ask, it too has adherents who espouse an approach based upon POSITIVISM. Foremost among the proponents of this approach may be mentioned Emile Durkheim for whom social facts were to be treated as things in the same way as the objects studied by the natural sciences. Others, however, are sceptical of claims for the scientific rigour of sociological positivism, even if its tools and techniques do indeed seek to ensure a similar level of objectivity as the natural sciences. These sceptics highlight the fact that, as compared to the natural scientist, the social scientist is very much a part of the phenomenon he or she is studying, thus rendering claims to objectivity problematical.

Despite the seeming difficulty that this criticism raises for sociological positivism, an alternative view turns it into a virtue. Interpretive sociology notes that the very fact that social relations are more complex than the causal relations studied by the natural sciences means that the ability of the sociologist to empathize with those he or she is observing renders those observations more valuable. This approach to legal sociology, drawing on the classic work in this regard by Max Weber, seeks to understand how participants in a given social setting themselves understand that situation. Thus, instead of seeking an objective view based on social facts treated in the same way as natural facts, interpretive sociology strives to discover the subjective meaning individuals impose on social action and social contexts.   [JP]

Further reading: Roger Cotterrell, *The Sociology of Law: An Introduction*, 2nd edn (London: Butterworths, 1992).

soft law Instruments that do not produce a primary binding legal effect. The purpose of soft laws is to set standards that might not be politically achieved or expedient if implementation was sought through conventionally binding forms of law. Examples include UN General Assembly resolutions (as well as resolutions of all other international organizations, unless otherwise specified), multilateral declarations made at the conclusion of inter-state conferences (e.g. the 1992 Rio Declaration on Environment and Development), and draft treaties before being formalized or having never achieved that status. 'Codes of conduct', 'communications' and 'guidelines', etc. in the area of EUROPEAN COMMUNITY law are also described as soft law instruments. A good number of principles contained in soft law instruments, or the entire instrument itself, have eventually entered the realm of CUSTOMARY INTERNATIONAL LAW (e.g. the 1970 UN General Assembly Resolution on Principles of International Law Concerning Friendly Relations and Co-operation between States) and have achieved their standard-setting aim by preparing the ground for the adoption of binding treaties (e.g. the UNIVERSAL DECLARATION OF HUMAN RIGHTS with regard to the INTERNATIONAL COVENANT ON CIVIL AND POLITICAL RIGHTS and the INTERNATIONAL COVENANT ON ECONOMIC, SOCIAL AND CULTURAL RIGHTS).   [IB]

software Software packages face classification difficulties under both COPYRIGHT and PATENT law; for example, a software package may comprise the computer program, a built-in dictionary or thesaurus and technical documentation – all of which would ordinarily be classified as LITERARY WORKS. However, the package may also contain digital artwork, graphic icons or photographs – which would be categorized as ARTISTIC WORKS. If the package is available for downloading via the internet, there may be a broadcast involved as well. A further difficulty is that different rights and terms of protection arise for different types of works.

International copyright law, under the TRIPS AGREEMENT, states that computer programs are to be considered literary works and are to be protected under copyright law. As such, the law on literary works will ordinarily apply. However, Council Directive 91/250/EEC of 14 May 1991 on the legal protection of computer programs has introduced several special provisions, which have been incorporated within UK copyright law.

There is no definition of computer programs, either under the EC or UK copyright laws, though the term includes preparatory design material leading to the development of a computer program, provided that the nature of the preparatory work is such that a computer program can result from it at a later stage. Copyright protection will be granted to a computer program which is original. Copyright protection will only extend to the expression of a computer program, and ideas and principles which underlie any element of the computer program, including its interfaces, will be excluded from protection.

The general copyright provisions which permit a person to do certain acts in relation to a copyright work will apply equally to computer programs. In addition, the law accords the lawful user of a computer program the right to do the following activities: making necessary back-up copies of the program; copying or adapting the program if necessary, especially for corrections; and the DECOMPILATION of the computer program.

To a certain extent, software can be protected by patent law, subject to certain conditions. The patentability of inventions in the UK and in the EU is governed primarily by the Patents Act 1977 and the European Patent Convention (EPC) 1973, which states that certain types of INVENTIONS, including computer programs, are excluded 'as such' (Article 52). However, 'computer-implemented inventions' may be protected if the applicant can make the necessary claims for patentability, and demonstrate they are industrially applicable. [US]

soldier's will *See* PRIVILEGED WILL.

solemn form *See* PROBATE.

soliciting A common prostitute (male or female) who loiters or solicits in a street or public place for the purposes of prostitution commits an offence under the STREET OFFENCES Act 1959, s. 1. Soliciting does not require words; physical movements will suffice. It was suggested in *Weisz* v. *Monahan* [1962] 1 All ER 664, by Lord Parker CJ (at 665) that 'soliciting ... involves the physical presence of the prostitute and conduct on [their] part amounting to an importuning of prospective customers'. Therefore, a person who advertises his or her services by placing business cards in, for example, public telephone boxes, does not commit the offence of soliciting (although such behaviour may amount to an offence under the Criminal Justice and Police Act 2001, s. 46). [BF]

See also KERB CRAWLING; LOITERING.

solicitor A qualified legal practitioner admitted to the Roll of Solicitors in England and Wales under the terms of the Solicitors Act 1974. Solicitors are normally graduates who have satisfied the academic stage of training and then completed a vocational qualification called the Legal Practice Course. They must also undertake two years of work-based training as a trainee solicitor (the duration of the traineeship is currently under review). On qualification they are able to undertake any legal work for a fee, except that solicitors who wish to appear as advocates in the senior courts must obtain a further specialist advocacy qualification. Solicitors in practice must hold professional indemnity insurance, and have a current annual practising certificate. Their conduct is also regulated by the **Solicitors Regulation Authority**. [jw]

solicitor-advocate A solicitor who has obtained a senior courts advocacy qualification and thus may exercise a right of audience (i.e. a right to appear as an advocate) before any court in England and Wales. [jw]

Solicitor-General Deputy to the ATTORNEY GENERAL and one of the government LAW OFFICERS; usually a sitting Member of Parliament. Under the Law Officers Act 1997, the Solicitor General, as deputy, can discharge any of the functions of the Attorney General for England and Wales, and of the Attorney General for Northern Ireland. [MS]

solicitor's undertaking See UNDERTAKING.

sovereign immunity See STATE IMMUNITY.

sovereignty 1. In political and legal theory, the concept is used to describe the seat of supreme authority within the STATE. In practice the site of sovereign power will depend upon the political and legal organization of each state, often as defined by its constitution. Today most democracies subscribe to the doctrine of the SEPARATION OF POWERS, which seeks to maintain a system of checks and balances between executive, legislative and judicial authorities as a way of preventing one branch of government from becoming autocratic. Philosophically speaking, however, sovereignty remains a problematic concept. The modern conception of sovereignty is commonly traced to the French jurist and political philosopher, Jean Bodin (1530–96). In his 1576 treatise *Six Livres de la république*, ('On the Republic'), Bodin describes the **sovereign** as the supreme lawmaker; a ruler above human law and subject only to divine or natural law. More modern definitions of sovereignty have tended to locate the sovereign's authority in some human rather than divine agency. SOCIAL CONTRACT theories have thus sought to ground the sovereign's authority in the will of the people, and LEGAL POSITIVISM has similarly tended to

assert that sovereignty derives its authority from society's habit of obedience to a political superior. These approaches have provided an adequate description of sovereignty in fact, but seem to fall short philosophically in failing adequately to address the paradox of how the sovereign can at one and the same time be the final authority in the state and yet owe his or her position to some higher (human) authority within that same state. HOBBES's conclusion that true sovereign power must therefore be treated as totally absolute and authoritarian is an unpalatable one, not least to Hobbes himself, who therefore reserves to subjects certain fundamental rights of disobedience.

2. In INTERNATIONAL LAW, the legitimate exercise of power and legal authority over territory by a state. Norms of sovereignty today are enshrined in the UN CHARTER: Article 2(4) prohibits attacks on 'territorial integrity or political independence', and Article 2(7) sharply restricts intervention. At the same time, however, regionalism and globalization have weakened the absolute character of the nation-state's claim to exclusive sovereignty, particularly through the creation of regional blocs like the EUROPEAN UNION.

3. A further distinction may be made between *de jure* sovereignty, which is the legal right to exercise that authority, and *de facto* sovereignty, which reflects the factual ability to do so. Normally *de facto* and *de jure* sovereignty will be possessed by the same entity. Exceptionally, however, the distinction may be significant in both international and domestic law; for example where *de jure* sovereignty is contested (in respect of the People's Republic of China's claims over the territory of Tibet and Taiwan), or where there is an actual division of *de facto* and *de jure* sovereignty over certain territory (as in the case of Guantanamo Bay, where the majority of the US Supreme Court has held that the US, while lacking *de jure* sovereignty over the territory of the base, exercises sufficient *de facto* sovereignty to warrant extending HABEAS CORPUS rights to detainees); see *Boumediene* v. *Bush* (2008), available at http://

www.law.cornell.edu/supct/html/06-1195.ZS.html. [JW]

sovereignty of Parliament The constitutional doctrine, also known as the doctrine of **parliamentary supremacy**, which states that Parliament is the supreme lawmaker in the UK. This has three specific consequences: (a) the legislative power or competence of Parliament is unlimited – it can make or repeal any law that it chooses; (b) no other body – including the courts – may question the validity of a STATUTE (see *Pickin* v. *British Railways Board* [1974] AC 765, which held that any question as to the validity of an Act is a matter for Parliament itself); and (c) no Parliament can bind itself or its successors (see *Ellen Street Industries Ltd* v. *Minister of Health* [1934] 1 KB 590 – a section of a statute stipulating that all provisions that were inconsistent with it 'shall cease to have or shall not have effect' was held by the court to be ineffective; no Parliament can prevent a future Parliament from repealing legislation, either expressly or by implication).

The question has arisen whether parliamentary supremacy has been undermined by a number of more recent developments which have placed strong practical constraints on Parliament's legislative freedom; among these have been Britain's accession to the European Communities (now the EUROPEAN UNION), and its incorporation of the EUROPEAN CONVENTION ON HUMAN RIGHTS into English law. Membership of the EU has presented the greater challenge, since a condition of accession, enshrined in the European Communities Act 1972, has been that EC law must override contrary UK law. It has been held that a UK court may be required to 'disapply' any statute provision that is incompatible with EC law (see *R* v. *Secretary of State for Transport ex parte Factortame (No. 2)* [1991] 1 AC 603). This obviously gives the courts a degree of power over legislation that appears to be inconsistent with traditional notions of sovereignty, though the fact that the courts arguably derive such power from the European Communities Act itself is seen as some justification.

The UK's incorporation of the European Convention does not go as far. The Human Rights Act 1998 expressly stops short of enabling the courts to disapply statutes that are inconsistent with Convention rights, but it does place a very strong obligation on courts to interpret legislation in a manner consistent with the Act, and certainly makes it unlikely that a court would treat a later statute as impliedly repealing the 1998 Act or any part of it. Indeed, a number of commentators, and even some judges, are tending to the view that certain statutes, like the European Communities Act and the Human Rights Act, have a special constitutional status which protects them from IMPLIED REPEAL or amendment (see, for example, the dictum of Laws LJ in *Thoburn* v. *Sunderland City Council* [2003] QB 151 at [50]), though this position remains controversial. [JW]

See also DECLARATION OF INCOMPATIBILITY; DISAPPLYING AN ACT OF PARLIAMENT; HENRY VIII CLAUSE.

Speaker *See* HOUSE OF COMMONS.

special agreement or *compromis* An ad hoc agreement between two or more STATES with the intention of conferring jurisdiction on the INTERNATIONAL COURT OF JUSTICE in accordance with Article 36(2) of its Statute. The *compromis* will set out the parties' agreement as to the nature and extent of their legal dispute and the law which the Court is authorized to apply. It is possible, however, for the parties to offer very little information to the Court, in which case the Court will make its own determination as to the dispute and the APPLICABLE LAW. The special agreement is not constrained by any particular form and the ICJ has taken the view that it may consist of a unilateral application that is later followed by a separate act of consent by the opposing party, either by communication to the Court or by taking part in the proceedings. [IB]

See also COMPROMIS D'ARBITRAGE; OPTIONAL CLAUSE.

Special Commissioners Individuals, appointed by the LORD CHANCELLOR, who usually sit alone (but can sit in pairs) for the purpose of hearing appeals made by taxpayers against the decisions of HM REVENUE AND CUSTOMS (HMRC) in direct tax disputes. An appeal is to the Special Commissioners where the taxpayer makes an **effective election** to appeal to those Commissioners rather than to the GENERAL COMMISSIONERS. In most appeals this is entirely at the choice of the taxpayer, but it is important to note that, unlike the General Commissioners, the Special Commissioners can award limited COSTS if they believe the taxpayer or HMRC has acted unreasonably.

The Special Commissioners are legally qualified and experienced individuals who bring specialist tax knowledge (for example international tax expertise) to bear on the appeals made to them. The Special Commissioners (Jurisdiction and Procedure) Regulations 1994 (SI 1994/1811) apply. Hearings are now usually in public, and decisions are reported. Appeals from the Special Commissioners are to the CHANCERY DIVISION of the HIGH COURT on points of law – not on pure matters of fact – and, from there, appeal is (normally) to the COURT OF APPEAL but only with the permission of the Court of Appeal. From the Court of Appeal any further appeal is to the HOUSE OF LORDS but subject again to being granted permission to do so by either the Court of Appeal or House of Lords. [RE]

See also COMMISSIONERS OF REVENUE AND CUSTOMS.

special damages DAMAGES for loss of earnings, medical expenses and other incidentals. Losses under this head are not presumed to have been incurred unless they have been quantified or specifically proved. [HJ]

See also GENERAL DAMAGES.

special defences Defences which apply to specific offences, rather than to offences in general. Thus, PROVOCATION and DIMINISHED RESPONSIBILITY, as defences specific to a charge of MURDER, are special defences, whereas INSANITY and AUTOMATISM are GENERAL DEFENCES. [BF]

special guardianship order An order under the Children Act 1989, ss. 14A–G, as amended, appointing one or more persons to be a CHILD's special guardian(s). Those entitled to apply for an order include the child's GUARDIAN, a person with a RESIDENCE ORDER and the child's local authority FOSTER PARENT, provided the child has lived with that foster parent for the preceding year. A special guardian has PARENTAL RESPONSIBILITY for the child and is entitled to use it to the exclusion of any other person who has parental responsibility, apart from another special guardian. This can be a useful order where ADOPTION is not appropriate but the carer needs to be able to exercise parental responsibility. [FK]

See also FOSTER CHILD.

Special Immigration Appeals Commission (SIAC) A superior COURT OF RECORD that hears appeals against decisions made by the Secretary of State for the Home Department (Home Office) to deport, or exclude, someone from the UK on national security grounds, or for other public interest reasons. It also hears appeals against decisions to deprive persons of citizenship status. It is governed by the Special Immigration Appeals Commission Act 1997; see http://www.siac.tribunals.gov.uk [AF]

special measures Measures that are made available by the Youth Justice and Criminal Evidence Act 1999 to assist vulnerable and intimidated WITNESSES in criminal proceedings. Such measures include screens, live links, allowing evidence to be given in private, dispensing with the wearing of wigs or gowns, video-recorded evidence-in-chief, the use of intermediaries and the use of aids to communication. [ALTC]

special procedure The procedure designed to expedite an undefended DIVORCE or DISSOLUTION of CIVIL PARTNERSHIP. In these cases, one spouse or civil partner will complete the petition or application outlining the facts relied on to establish the ground for divorce or dissolution, provide written evidence of those facts and submit them to the appropriate court. If the other partner does not contest the application (or provides consent where required) and the court is satisfied that the facts have been made out and that the marriage or civil partnership has broken down irretrievably (see IRRETRIEVABLE BREAKDOWN), it will issue the DECREE NISI without requiring the parties to attend court. The parties must then wait the appropriate period before applying for the DECREE ABSOLUTE or final order. The majority of divorces in England and Wales adopt this 'special procedure'. Consultation is currently underway to consider applying the special procedure to ANNULMENT proceedings as well. [AD]

special procedure material Broadly, journalistic material, material held in confidence and material held subject to a restriction on disclosure or an obligation of secrecy. The procedure to be followed by the police in applying to a judge to obtain access to special procedure material is contained in the Police and Criminal Evidence Act 1984, s. 14 and Schedule 1. [ALTC]

special trust Any trust that is not a BARE TRUST. [PK]

special verdict A verdict that the defendant in a criminal case is not guilty by reason of INSANITY. A special verdict is not to be returned 'except on the written or oral EVIDENCE of two or more registered medical practitioners at least one of whom is duly approved': see the Criminal Procedure (Insanity and Unfitness to Plead) Act 1991, s. 1(1). [ALTC]

specific goods Goods which are identified and agreed upon by both parties, at the time the CONTRACT of sale is made, as the goods to be transferred under that contract, for example a named car with a given number plate (Sale of Goods Act 1979, s. 61(1)). If the contract is for the sale of specific goods, then the SELLER is obliged to deliver those goods or the seller will be in BREACH OF CONTRACT. Specific goods must be distinguished from unascertained goods, which are not so identified at the time of the sale contract. [JPL]

specific implement A remedy in Scots law where one party seeks to compel another to do something. For example, in breach of contract, a pursuer may seek to enforce a

positive obligation – to compel the defender to do something he or she has agreed to do.

Where specific implement is sought and the court awards a decree *ad factum praestandum* (for the performance of the act in question), any wilful breach of its terms will constitute contempt of court. As a consequence, specific implement is not as widely used in breach of contract cases as might be imagined: if it were used, for example, in every case of non-payment then any continuing debtor would be in contempt of court and thus subject to fine or imprisonment. [JP]

See also ACTION FOR PAYMENT; INTERDICT.

specific intent A term used in contrast to BASIC INTENT and of principal significance in the context of the defence of INTOXICATION. If a defendant is so intoxicated as to be unable to form the *mens rea* for an offence of specific intent, then he will not be liable for that offence. Offences of specific intent are, broadly speaking, those with a *mens rea* of intention. Thus, for example, murder, and causing grievous bodily harm with intent under the Offences against the Person Act 1861, s. 18, are offences of specific intent. Intoxication does not operate as a complete defence; instead, the defendant becomes liable for a corresponding offence of basic intent. Thus, if D is so intoxicated as to be incapable of forming an intention to kill or to do grievous bodily harm, he cannot be liable for murder but may none the less be liable for manslaughter, which is a crime of basic intent. For discussion, see *DPP* v. *Majewski* [1977] AC 443. [BF]

specific issue order An order made under the Children Act 1989, 'giving directions for the purpose of determining a specific question which has arisen or which may arise in connection with any aspect of PARENTAL RESPONSIBILITY for a CHILD' (s. 8). It has been used, for example, to obtain permission for a child to be sterilized, to allow a child to be brought up in a particular religion and to resolve a parental dispute about the child's education. The court will always decide these matters with the welfare of the child as its paramount consideration. [AD]

See also CONTACT ORDER; PROHIBITED STEPS ORDER; RESIDENCE ORDER; WELFARE PRINCIPLE.

specific legacy *See* LEGACY.

specific performance An order of the court instructing the party in BREACH OF CONTRACT to carry out its obligations under the CONTRACT. It is an equitable remedy and therefore discretionary. It will not be ordered if DAMAGES would be an adequate remedy. Damages are only likely to be an inadequate remedy if it would not be possible to purchase substitute goods (for example if the goods are unique, and in sales of land). Specific performance will not normally be granted to enforce contracts of PERSONAL SERVICE although in some circumstances a defendant may be restrained by INJUNCTION from breaching a negative stipulation in such a contract, for example an exclusive services obligation (see *Warner Brothers Pictures Incorporated* v. *Nelson* [1937] 1 KB 209). [JPL]

speculative loss Where the claimant is unable to establish its LOSS OF EXPECTATION because that loss is too speculative, it will be limited to making a claim for recovery of reliance loss or the contractual expenditure wasted as a result of the BREACH OF CONTRACT (see *McRae* v. *Commonwealth Disposals Commission* (1951) 84 CLR 377). [JPL]

See also LOSS OF A CHANCE.

speeding Under the Road Traffic Regulation Act 1984, s. 89, a person commits an offence if he or she drives a motor vehicle on a road at a speed exceeding a limit imposed by any relevant enactment. [BF]

spent conviction A conviction which an offender is not normally obliged to disclose when applying for employment. The Rehabilitation of Offenders Act 1974 enables many criminal convictions to become 'spent' after a REHABILITATION PERIOD, which is determined by the nature and length of the sentence. [SN]

split order (obsolete) An order that was formerly available on DIVORCE, giving legal CUSTODY to one PARENT and CARE AND CONTROL to the other. These orders were rendered defunct on the coming into force of the Children Act 1989 and have been replaced by orders relating to residence, contact and PARENTAL RESPONSIBILITY. [FK]

See also CONTACT ORDER; RESIDENCE ORDER.

squatter A person occupying land as a trespasser. [HC & DR]

stakeholder pension This form of pension is a government-created one for those who do not have an occupational pension. The principles are laid down in the Welfare Reform and Pensions Act 1999 and the Stakeholder Pension Scheme Regulations 2000 (SI 2000/1403) and include minimal management charges, low levels of minimum contribution, TRUSTEES or stakeholder managers to look after the interests of members, and a defined contribution arrangement. [MJ]

stalking A term used to describe behaviour whereby A, for example, repeatedly or persistently follows or surveils or contacts B, makes their presence known to B, when B does not wish to be followed, surveilled or contacted etc., in that fashion; and where A's purpose is to harass B or to persuade B to behave in a particular way. The principal law regulating stalking is the Protection from Harassment Act 1997; the offences were created under ss. 2 and 4. [BF]

See also HARASSMENT.

Stamp Duty A tax on some legal instruments. Subject to available exemptions, all instruments within the scope of the legislation must be stamped. The term 'instrument' includes 'every written document' (see the Stamp Act 1891, s. 122(1)).

The duty originated in the late 17th century, was augmented by STAMP DUTY RESERVE TAX with effect from 1986, and ceased to apply to transactions in land (save for transitional provisions) with effect from 1 December 2003 after the introduction of Stamp Duty Land Tax.

Stamp Duty remains a tax on instruments within the scope of the 1891 Act (as substantially amended by subsequent Finance Acts), predominantly on SHARE TRANSFERS, but including some others such as company securities transfers. It is the instrument itself which is charged to duty at a fixed rate of £5, or at 0.5% *ad valorem* (i. e. on the value of the underlying transaction).

Stamp Duty is payable on dutiable instruments executed in the United Kingdom, and dutiable instruments executed elsewhere but dealing with relevant property situated in or in relation to events occurring in the UK. Whether or not an instrument is executed in the UK or elsewhere, the duty is payable within 30 days of 'execution'. Execution is usually taken to mean 'signed' (see s. 122(1)). Failure to comply results in interest charges and penalties after the 30-day limit. The usual practice is not to date instruments until the latest possible time. [RE]

Stamp Duty Reserve Tax A direct tax payable in respect of UK-based stocks and shares which are traded on financial markets regardless of geographical location, but which does not apply, or ceases to apply, where STAMP DUTY is paid on a paper transfer document specific to the agreement for transfer.

It is a tax payable to HM REVENUE AND CUSTOMS by the transferee – usually at the rate of 0.5% – if there are no exemptions or reliefs, of the CONSIDERATION agreed for the transfer of ownership of stocks and shares (and other chargeable securities) of UK companies, and of any Societas Europaea, which has its registered office in the UK. The tax is secured automatically in financial market settlements through CREST, the electronic settlement system for UK and Irish securities. Where the tax has been paid, it can be reclaimed where a relevant share (or stock) transfer document is charged to Stamp Duty. The tax can also apply to certain non-market agreements. [RE]

Standard Conditions of Sale The set of Standard Conditions of Sale normally used in the sale of residential property and small business premises. The most recent version of the Standard Conditions of Sale is the 4th edition, representing the 24th edition of the National Conditions of Sale and the Law Society's Conditions of Sale 2003.

Incorporation of the Standard Conditions of Sale has the effect of avoiding the application of many of the OPEN CONTRACT rules, which are generally considered to be unfair on the seller. In an ordinary sale of residential property, the Standard Conditions of Sale are reproduced in full in the CONTRACT FOR SALE and may be varied with the agreement of the parties. [DR]

standard form contract A contractual set of terms and CONDITIONS that was not specifically negotiated to apply to the immediate transaction but was drawn up in advance to apply generally to the drafting party's transactions. Such CONTRACTS have cost savings for the parties but tend to favour the drafter of the terms and conditions and the other party may have no real option other than to agree. Standard form contracts are therefore sometimes referred to as 'contracts of adhesion'.

The content of standard form contracts may be subject to legislative and common law regulation in the form of the Unfair Contract Terms Act (UCTA) 1977, the Unfair Terms in Consumer Contracts Regulations (UTCCR) 1999 and the penalty rule. Under the UTCCR, in relation to consumer contracts, the control of UNFAIR CONTRACT TERMS applies to 'terms which have not been individually negotiated' and this will be presumed where the term 'has been drafted in advance and the consumer has therefore not been able to influence the substance of the term'. Further, a contract may be treated as a pre-formulated standard term contract despite the fact that there may have been some limited negotiation in relation to a term or terms. In relation to commercial contracts, a standard term may be subject to the reasonableness test under UCTA where one contracts 'on the other's written standard terms of business'. Although this is not defined in the legislation, there is a body of case law which assesses how much negotiation is possible before a set of terms cease to be 'standard'. [JPL]

standard of proof The standard to which

the party bearing the BURDEN OF PROOF in relation to a particular issue is required to discharge that burden. 'The function of a
standard of proof … is to "instruct the fact-
finder concerning the degree of confidence
our society thinks he should have in the
correctness of factual conclusions for a particular type of adjudication." … The standard serves to allocate the risk of error
between the litigants and to indicate the
relative importance attached to the ultimate decision' (see *Addington* v. *Texas* 441 US
418, 423 (1979), quoting from *In re Winship*
397 US 358, 370 (1970)). The two standards
of proof recognized in the law of England
and Wales are proof on the BALANCE OF PROB-
ABILITIES and proof BEYOND REASONABLE DOUBT.
[ALTC]

standard investment criteria The two
factors to which trustees must have regard,
under the Trustee Act 2000, s. 4 (3), when
exercising any statutory or express power
of investment, are: (a) the suitability to
the TRUST of both the type and specific
investment which is to be made or
retained; and (b) the need to diversify
investments of the trust as appropriate in
the circumstances.   [PK]

standing The right to be heard in court or
other proceedings. Also referred to as *locus
standi* (a place to stand). All court or tribunal proceedings are premised on the need
for the claimant to establish a CAUSE OF
ACTION, but in some civil proceedings a
claimant must go further to establish standing, i.e. to positively demonstrate that they
are eligible to bring or join proceedings. In
most private litigation this is not an issue,
but it may arise substantively in four contexts: (a) where a party is seeking to be
joined to an established action, or substitute themselves for another party;
(b) where a party is seeking to establish
that they have a sufficient interest to
bring JUDICIAL REVIEW proceedings; (c) where
parties seek to establish a common interest
in a REPRESENTATIVE ACTION; and (d) where a
large number of parties wish to be joined
in a **group litigation order**. In each of these
situations special procedural rules have

been created to determine whether or not
a party can be heard.   [JW]
See also GROUP LITIGATION; JOINDER OF PARTIES.

Star Chamber Historically, a civil and
criminal court, named after the star-
painted ceiling of the room in which it
was originally held in the Palace of Westminster, London. At its height, the jurisdiction of the Court of Star Chamber was
similar to that of the COURT OF CHANCERY in
principles and procedures and under its
criminal jurisdiction it was seen as a court
of 'criminal equity'. The Star Chamber
became very unpopular in the reigns of
the Stuarts, by reason of the tyrannical
exercise and often illegal widening of its
powers. The Star Chamber was abolished
in 1641. In modern times, the term has
been revived as a synonym for any tribunal
purporting to exercise its powers in an arbitrary or tyrannical manner.   [AF]

stare decisis (Lat. to stand by the decision)
The doctrine expresses the distinctively
binding nature of PRECEDENT in the COMMON
LAW tradition. In England and Wales this
means that, within the hierarchy of the
courts, a decision by a higher court will
generally be binding on and should be followed by lower courts. However, the process of interpreting and applying
precedents is not a mechanical one, and
there is scope for legitimate disagreement
about whether and how a precedent
applies.

The binding element of a judgment is the
ratio decidendi – the reasons for the decision.
Consequently, where a judge has to decide
a later case on similar facts, he must determine first, whether the precedent is potentially binding by virtue of the courts'
relative positions in the hierarchy (so the
COURT OF APPEAL, for example, is bound by the
HOUSE OF LORDS), and then whether there is
any reason, based on a material difference
between the facts of the cases, or possibly
on grounds of legal principle or public policy, for departing from or distinguishing
the reasoning in the earlier case. Where
the court is technically bound but finds reasons for not following or distinguishing the
precedent case, this does not affect the val-

idity of the original precedent, though the new decision does help redefine the scope of that precedent, and thus tells us something new about how it might be applied in the future. Only a court higher in the hierarchy can overrule a precedent so that that earlier decision becomes redundant.

It is said that the value of *stare decisis* is that it helps the law become more certain and predictable (though sometimes at the cost of rigidity, as common law principles can only be changed by overruling the now unhelpful precedent, or by legislative intervention from Parliament), while retaining some flexibility to respond to a changing social, economic and political environment through the possibility of review by higher courts.   [JW]

state A state comes into existence through objective means when certain criteria have been satisfied. These criteria are found in CUSTOMARY INTERNATIONAL LAW, as reflected in the 1933 Montevideo Convention on the Rights and Duties of States, and consist of a permanent population, defined territory, an effective government and the capacity to enter into relations with other states (independence). The cumulative existence of these elements gives rise to statehood. The legal consequence of statehood is legal personality, legal equality, as well as the assumption of rights and duties under INTERNATIONAL LAW towards not only other states, but one's own citizens (international human rights obligations) and territory (i.e. not to be used for terrorist purposes against other states).   [IB]

See also CONSTITUTIVE THEORY; DECLARATORY THEORY; MONTEVIDEO CONVENTION; RECOGNITION; SECESSION; STATE RESPONSIBILITY.

state aid Assistance, either by way of grants, tax rebates or other direct or indirect assistance, that countries traditionally gave to companies and other business undertakings within their STATE in order to assist their survival and development. The process of state aid has been severely curtailed and regulated by EUROPEAN COMMUNITY (EC) law, notably Articles 87 to 89 EC. Article 87 both prohibits state aid which distorts or threatens to distort competition,

and identifies what kinds of aid are compatible with the requirements of the EC Treaty. Article 88 establishes procedures for monitoring state aid, and Article 89 creates powers to make regulations for the application of Articles 87 and 88.   [MON]

state immunity STATE (or sovereign) immunity from suit is conferred under CUSTOMARY INTERNATIONAL LAW and is usually implemented by domestic immunity statutes.

Immunity from criminal prosecution does not extinguish the offence, it simply provides a procedural bar for the exercise of jurisdiction by criminal courts. It is of two types: (a) immunity *ratione personae* (by reason of the person), which is enjoyed by existing heads of state, foreign ministers and acting heads of government, and covers their person completely; and (b) immunity *ratione materiae* (by reason of the activity), which confers protection to acts conducted by the state as an international legal person, and therefore only incidentally confers protection on the state agents who carry out these acts. Immunity *ratione personae* ends when its beneficiaries are removed from their post and such persons can be tried for acts committed while they held their posts (see the *Belgian Arrest Warrant* case (*Democratic Republic of Congo* v. *Belgium*) [2002] ICJ Rep 1; *R* v. *Bow Street Metropolitan Stipendiary Magistrates, ex parte Pinochet Ugarte (No. 3)* [2000] 1 AC 147). As far as persons enjoying *ratione materiae* immunity are concerned, it has become commonplace, particularly in the USA and UK, for courts to deem the commission of crimes as incompatible with the functions of a state and therefore to remove the immunity of such persons.

The civil immunity of states is also regulated by customary law and regional conventions, which are again implemented by domestic STATUTE. In general terms, states (and their property) do not enjoy immunity from civil jurisdiction where the contested activity concerns a commercial transaction. The immunity afforded to DIPLOMATIC AGENTS is distinct from state immunity and, in any event, diplomatic property cannot be confiscated or seized.   [IB]

See also CRIMES AGAINST HUMANITY; DIPLOMATIC IMMUNITY; INTERNATIONAL LEGAL PERSONALITY.

state of emergency *See* EMERGENCY.

state responsibility Responsibility arises from every internationally wrongful act of a STATE. An internationally wrongful act consists of conduct (an action or omission) that is attributable to a state under INTERNATIONAL LAW (because it was perpetrated by an agent or representative of the state, or on behalf or through the acquiescence of the state) and constitutes a breach of an international obligation (e.g. non-fulfilment of a TREATY or contractual obligation, or breach of a customary rule).

The perpetration of an internationally wrongful act entails a number of consequences for the defaulting state: a duty of continued performance of the obligation breached, cessation and non-repetition of the wrongful act and REPARATION. These principles are part of CUSTOMARY INTERNATIONAL LAW and are contained in the INTERNATIONAL LAW COMMISSION's (ILC) 2001 Articles on Responsibility of States for Internationally Wrongful Acts. Note, also, that particular treaties can establish their own rules of responsibility which take precedence over these general principles (see, for example, the EUROPEAN CONVENTION ON HUMAN RIGHTS and the GENERAL AGREEMENT ON TARIFFS AND TRADE).
                                                                                                [IB]

statement of arrangements A statement specifying the arrangements proposed for the future of any children of the parties to DIVORCE proceedings or to the DISSOLUTION of a CIVIL PARTNERSHIP. A form delineating these arrangements must be completed if the petitioner or the respondent has any children under the age of 16, or over 16 but under 18 if they are in education or undertaking training. The form urges the parties to reach agreement; however, if they do not, separate forms may be submitted. The petitioner must file the completed form with the court when the petition is issued, whether or not the form is also signed by the respondent.   [FK]

See also CONTACT ORDER; RESIDENCE ORDER.

statute The primary form of legislation in the English legal system, also known as an **Act of Parliament**. To become a statute, a parliamentary BILL must normally obtain the consent of a majority of both Houses of Parliament, and of the sovereign – called the ROYAL ASSENT. Once it has received the Royal Assent it is, by virtue of the SOVEREIGNTY OF PARLIAMENT, the supreme form of English law and, traditionally, its validity cannot be challenged in any English court. This principle has been diluted by UK membership of the EUROPEAN UNION, which gives the courts a limited power to 'disapply' parts of an Act of Parliament that are inconsistent with European law (see *R* v. *Secretary of State for Transport ex parte Factortame (No. 2)* [1991] 1 AC 603).

The term **statute law** is used to refer to the whole body of laws enacted by statute.
                                                                                                [JW]

See also DECLARATION OF INCOMPATIBILITY.

Statute of Rome *See* INTERNATIONAL CRIMINAL COURT.

Statute of Uses *See* USE.

statutory demand A demand for payment in a specified form in respect of a debt of £750 or more. If the debt is not paid within 21 days, a statutory demand entitles the creditor to petition the court to wind up the company, or to make an individual bankrupt.   [JW]

See also BANKRUPTCY; LATE PAYMENT DEMAND; LIQUIDATION.

statutory instrument *See* DELEGATED LEGISLATION.

statutory interpretation The judicial process of establishing (formally called 'constructing'), with the aid of rules and principles, the true meaning of a STATUTE or SECONDARY LEGISLATION. The rules and principles of statutory interpretation are formally divided into **primary** and **secondary** aids to construction. The primary aids are conventionally characterized as three rules:

the Literal, Golden and Mischief Rules, though this is increasingly seen by the courts and legal scholars as a crude over-simplification of a much more complex process. The 'true' meaning of an Act of Parliament is not necessarily apparent from the words used; it may have to be constructed out of competing arguments about the intended purposes of the Act. Interpretation is thus not simply a matter of picking the 'right' rule and applying it. Nevertheless, judges still sometimes refer to these 'rules' as a justification for their approach, and so they cannot be disregarded.

The **literal rule** describes the common-sense starting point to interpretation: that the court should construe the Act according to the plain, literal, meaning of the words used.

Where the words are capable of bearing more than one meaning, and it is not clear which meaning was intended, or where the application of the literal rule would result in some anomaly or absurdity in the application of the Act, the court will adopt what is commonly called a **purposive approach** to interpretation: that is, an approach which will, so far as the language will allow, give effect to the intention or purpose of the legislation. The **golden rule** (see *Grey* v. *Pearson* (1857) 6 HL Cas 61) is seen as an early formulation of a purposive approach which allows the court to depart from the literal meaning in order to avoid a manifest absurdity in the application of legislation. The **mischief rule**, also called the rule in *Heydon's Case* (1584) 3 Co Rep 7a, is an older, and narrower, variant on this principle. Where an Act has been passed to remedy a wrong ('mischief') created or allowed by the COMMON LAW, the mischief rule allows the court to consider the nature of that wrong and determine what remedy Parliament intended to provide.

Although literalism still operates as the default position in statutory interpretation, commentators tend to agree that judges today are more ready to adopt a purposive approach than their predecessors. This culture change is, in part, attributed to the growing complexity of legislation and also, through the influence of EUROPEAN COMMUNITY law and the Human Rights Act 1998, to the greater exposure of English judges to the more purposive interpretative traditions of continental Europe.

Secondary aids to construction comprise a set of disparate rules and principles. Some are essentially rules of grammar such as *EIUSDEM GENERIS* and *NOSCITUR A SOCIIS*; others set out how different parts of the same Act should be read together, or define what extrinsic (external) aids to interpretation can legitimately be used.

The courts also apply a number of general presumptions to the interpretation of statutes, including (a) that they will not retrospectively effect substantive legal rights; (b) that 'penal' statutes (such as criminal or tax legislation) should, in cases of ambiguous application, be construed to the advantage of the subject; (c) that they will not seek to exclude the jurisdiction of the courts; and (d) that they will not derogate from fundamental rights and international law obligations. Such presumptions can be overridden ('rebutted') in a statute by the use of clear words or a necessary implication to the contrary.   [JW]

See also HANSARD; *TRAVAUX PRÉPARATOIRES*.

statutory maternity pay *See* MATERNITY PAY.

statutory nuisance Matters that are mainly of an environmental nature and enforceable by public bodies rather than the individuals affected. The Environmental Protection Act 1990 sets out a range of matters, such as the state of premises, smoke/fumes/gases from private dwellings, industrial pollution, and noise in the street that will be regarded as nuisances where they are prejudicial to health or otherwise constitute a nuisance.   [HJ]

See also PRIVATE NUISANCE; PUBLIC NUISANCE.

statutory owner Under the Settled Land Act 1925 (SLA 1925), a statutory owner is the owner of the LEGAL ESTATE under a SETTLEMENT where there is no TENANT FOR LIFE. The statutory owner is either the person upon whom the settlement confers the powers of the tenant for life; or in any other case, the trustees of the settlement (SLA 1925, s. 117 (1)(xxvi)).   [DR]

See also SETTLED LAND ACT TRUSTEES; VESTING DEED.

statutory trust 1. Until 1997, a TRUST created by STATUTE whenever land was co-owned (see TRUST FOR SALE). Since 1997 statutory trusts have been replaced by trusts of land governed by the Trusts of Land and Appointment of Trustees Act 1996 (TOLATA).

2. A trust that arises on INTESTACY whenever there are children of the deceased, under the age of 18, who are entitled to all or part of the estate. The terms of the trusts are set out under the Administration of Estates Act 1925, s. 47, which provides that the child's interest is held on trust until the age of 18.   [PK]

statutory will If a person becomes incapable of managing his or her affairs, he or she may be made subject to the control of the COURT OF PROTECTION, who may, unless there is a valid power of attorney in place, either make certain decisions for that person, or appoint a **deputy** to look after his or her interests. Under the Mental Capacity Act 2005, s. 18, a statutory will can be made for such a person, and the court will authorize someone (normally the deputy) to sign on the patient's behalf, and SEAL it with the official seal of the court. The contents of the will are decided by the court, and broadly speaking will be what the court thinks the patient would have decided for him or herself, had they been able to consider the matter and been advised by a competent SOLICITOR.   [CM]

stay To halt proceedings or the execution of a judgment. A stay remains in place unless and until lifted by order of the court. A **stay of proceedings** in civil matters may be exercised whenever the court considers it necessary or just. It is often used as a case management tool, e.g. to enable the parties to seek MEDIATION or to negotiate a settlement, or to prevent an ABUSE OF PROCESS. It must normally be ordered by the court (see Supreme Court Act 1981, s. 49 (3) and CPR Rule 3.3), but in some circum-

stances proceedings may be stayed without a court order. For example, under CPR Rule 15.11(1), where six months have elapsed since the end of the period in which a defendant should have filed a DEFENCE, ADMISSION or COUNTERCLAIM, and the claimant has not entered or applied for DEFAULT JUDGMENT, the proceedings are stayed automatically. A stay does not amount to a dismissal or discontinuance of the action; proceedings continue to exist, albeit in suspension, and may be revived where appropriate. Usually this will require the express permission of the court, or the meeting of some formal condition for continuance. The enforcement of a judgment may also be stayed in some circumstances, and this is properly called a **stay of execution pending appeal** (CPR Rule 52.7). Although the courts now have a wide jurisdiction to stay execution pending appeal – see *Hammond Suddard Solicitors* v. *Agrichem International Holdings Ltd* [2001] EWCA Civ 1915 – it should be noted that this power is exercised cautiously and as an exception to the general principle that judgment takes effect as soon as it is given.   [JW]

See also ADJOURNMENT; APPEAL.

step-parent One who is married to or is the civil partner of the mother or father who has PARENTAL RESPONSIBILITY for a CHILD. MARRIAGE or CIVIL PARTNERSHIP do not automatically give the step-parent parental responsibility for the child, but may create obligations to support the child if the child is treated as a 'child of the FAMILY'. A step-parent may acquire parental responsibility for a child by agreement with all others who have parental responsibility, by order of the court, or by adoption. A step-parent may, in certain circumstances, apply for SECTION 8 ORDERS (of the Children Act 1989) in respect of the child.   [AD]

See also CONTACT ORDER; PROHIBITED STEPS ORDER; RESIDENCE ORDER; SPECIFIC ISSUES ORDER.

Stockholm Declaration A non-binding instrument adopted by the UN Conference on the Human Environment in 1972, with the aim of setting out 'common principles to inspire and guide the peoples of the world in the preservation and enhancement of the human environment'. This was the first general environmental instrument to be adopted in the international context and despite its SOFT LAW character it has been the foundational basis for subsequent international environmental law developments. It sets out certain basic principles, in particular: the personal right to a clean environment; avoidance of depletion of natural resources for the benefit of future generations; putting in place mechanisms to avoid pollution for toxic gases, as well as pollution of common spaces, such as the high seas; lending of assistance to developing states to overcome that status, since under-development is a principal source of environmental degradation; SUSTAINABLE DEVELOPMENT; rationalization of domestic demographic policies; internationalization of environmental matters because of the effects of trans-boundary pollution beyond the immediate STATE. [IB]

See also COMMON HERITAGE OF MANKIND.

stop notice If a local planning authority has issued an ENFORCEMENT NOTICE, before the expiry of the period for compliance with that notice they may issue a stop notice, prohibiting the carrying out of the activity to which the enforcement notice relates (see Town and Country Planning Act 1990 (TCPA 1990), s. 183). A stop notice can be served on any person who is interested in the land or engaged in activity prohibited by the notice, and a further notice may be displayed on the site of the activity.

If a stop notice is withdrawn, or if the enforcement notice to which it relates is withdrawn, varied or quashed, the person occupying the land when the stop notice was issued has a qualified right to compensation in respect of any loss or damage directly attributable to the prohibition contained in the notice (TCPA 1990, s. 186). Contravention of a stop notice is a criminal offence carrying a potential fine of up to £20,000. [DR]

street offences The Street Offences Act 1959 was passed following the recommendations of the Wolfenden Committee, which reported in 1957, having considered the possibility of reform to the law govern-

ing prostitution. The theme which emerged from the Report was that while prostitution itself should not be criminalized, its potentially adverse public effects should be regulated. The principal offences created by the Act are those of LOITERING and SOLICITING. [BF]

See also KERB CRAWLING.

strict liability offences An offence is one of strict liability if no MENS REA is required in respect of one or more elements of the ACTUS REUS. Thus, for example, the offence of DRIVING WITHOUT INSURANCE is committed even where a person does not realize, and has no reason to realize, that he or she has no insurance.

When a STATUTE is silent on the issue of *mens rea*, the job of deciding whether it imposes strict liability falls to the courts. Lord Scarman in *Gammon Ltd* v. *A-G of Hong Kong* [1985] 1 AC 1, at 14B, set out five principles governing the imposition of strict liability: '(1) there is a presumption of law that *mens rea* is required before a person can be held guilty of a criminal offence; (2) the presumption is particularly strong where the offence is "truly criminal" in character; (3) the presumption applies to statutory offences, and can be displaced only if this is clearly or by necessary implication the effect of the statute; (4) the only situation in which the presumption can be displaced is where the statute is concerned with an issue of social concern, and public safety is such an issue; (5) even where a statute is concerned with such an issue, the presumption of *mens rea* stands unless it can also be shown that the creation of strict liability will be effective to promote the objects of the statute by encouraging greater vigilance to prevent the commission of the prohibited act.'

The strength of the presumption of *mens rea* is reiterated by Lord Nicholls in *B* v. *DPP* [2000] 2 AC 428, at 463H: 'The question, therefore, is whether, although not expressly negatived, the need for a mental element is negatived by necessary implication. "Necessary implication" connotes an implication which is compellingly clear. Such an implication may be found in the language used, the nature of the offence, the mischief sought to be prevented and any other circumstances which may assist in determining what intention is properly to be attributed to Parliament when creating the offence.'

There appears to be a greater willingness to impose strict liability in the context of so-called 'quasi-crimes', sometimes known as crimes which are *mala prohibita* (bad only in the sense that they are instances of prohibited behaviour), where the stigma attached to conviction is not as serious as in the case of a 'true crime' (or a crime which is *mala in se*, bad in itself). However, this is a problematic approach, because strict liability can be seen operating in the context of some very serious offences (see, for example, the offence of rape of a child under 13 under the Sexual Offences Act 2003, s. 5, where Parliament's clear intention is that the defendant's belief that the victim is 13 or over should be immaterial).

In terms of the language of the provision in question, the presumption of *mens rea* is sufficiently strong as to impose a fault requirement in a silent provision, even where an adjacent provision makes express provision for fault (compare *Sherras* v. *De Rutzen* [1895] 1 QB 918 with *Barnfather* v. *London Borough of Islington Education Authority, Secretary of State for Education and Skills* [2003] EWHC 418).   [BF]

See also INTENTION; RECKLESSNESS.

Further reading: Andrew Simester (ed.), *Appraising Strict Liability* (Oxford: Oxford University Press, 2005); Solomon Salako, 'Strict criminal liability: a violation of the Convention?' (2006), *Journal of Criminal Law*, 70, 531–549; Paul Roberts, 'Drug dealing and the presumption of innocence: the Human Rights Act (almost) bites' [2002], *International Journal of Evidence and Proof*, 17–37.

strict settlement An old form of SETTLE-MENT, developed in order to keep landed estates within the family. Prior to 1925, the classic example of a strict settlement was where X created a LIFE ESTATE for himself and granted a FEE TAIL to his son Y and his heirs. The effect of this was that it was not possible for Y, acting alone, to sell the property, making it less likely for the property to be lost to the family.

Following the Settled Land Act 1925, strict settlements had to be made under a trust and the TENANT FOR LIFE was given extensive powers to deal with the property, including the power of sale. For this reason, and also for tax reasons, strict settlements became substantially less popular than trusts for sale, often being created by mistake rather than by design.

In 1989 the Law Commission recommended their abolition, and since the Trusts of Land and Appointment of Trustees Act 1996 came into force on 1 January 1997 it is no longer possible to create new strict settlements, though pre-existing ones continue to have effect.   [DR]

strike In general there is no definition of 'strike' in employment law. However, the Trade Union and Labour Relations (Consolidation) Act 1992, s. 246, provides that, for the purposes of INDUSTRIAL ACTION law found in Part V of the Act, 'strike' means 'any concerted stoppage of work'.   [MJ]

striking out In civil proceedings, a court or tribunal may order a written document or part of a document to be deleted or 'struck out'. Such deleted material can no longer be relied upon in those proceedings. The power to strike out may vary according to the court or tribunal before which proceedings are commenced. In general civil litigation, however, striking out is largely governed by the CIVIL PROCEDURE RULES. In particular, a court may, on its own initiative or on application from a party to the proceedings, strike out any statement of case, or part of it. Under CPR Rule 3.4 there are three grounds for striking out a statement of case: (a) where it discloses no reasonable grounds for bringing or defending the claim; (b) where it is an abuse of process or otherwise is likely to obstruct the just disposal of the case; or (c) where there has been a (significant) failure to comply with a relevant rule, PRACTICE DIRECTION or court order. Where the court strikes out a statement of case it may then make any order for the other party which it considers appropriate; see CPR Rules 3.4(3) and 3.5. Thus, for example, where a defence is struck out in its entirety, the court may enter a DEFAULT JUDG-MENT in the claimant's favour. [JW]

See also ABUSE OF PROCESS; CIVIL RESTRAINT ORDER.

structural funds Part of the EUROPEAN COM-MUNITY (EC) **regional policy** and, along with the COMMON AGRICULTURAL POLICY, accounting for the biggest expenditure of EC revenue. Under the EC regional policy, the territory of the EC is divided into regions according to the wealth or economic structural problems of the region. Regions are then given additional funds from the EC budget in order to help them develop economically. The funds are designed for a specific funding period. In the funding period 2007–13 the funds available are the Cohesion Fund, the European Regional Development Fund (ERDF), the EUROPEAN SOCIAL FUND (ESF) and the Solidarity Fund. Major infrastructure projects, such as transport infrastructure, have been funded under the ERDF. [MON]

See also COMMITTEE OF THE REGIONS; REGIONAL-ISM.

structure plan A document produced by a local planning authority, formulating the authority's, general policies in respect of the DEVELOPMENT and use of land in their area (see Town and Country Planning Act 1990 (TCPA 1990), s. 31(2)). Structure plans were specifically required to include policies and proposals in respect of the conservation of natural beauty and amenity of the land, the improvement of the physical environment and the management of traffic (see TCPA 1990, s. 31(3)). The Planning and Compulsory Purchase Act 2004 (PCPA 2004) repealed TCPA 1990, s. 31 and provides for the gradual phasing out of structure plans, to be replaced by **regional spatial strategies**. Nevertheless, structure plans remain in force in a number of local planning authority areas pending the adoption of successor documents.

Prior to the PCPA 2004, in non-metropolitan non-unitary authorities, the structure plan constituted one part of a local planning authority's DEVELOPMENT PLAN. In formulating the plan, authorities were to have

regard to regional or strategic guidance given by the Secretary of State, current national policies, available resources, economic, environmental and social considerations and other specifically listed considerations (see TCPA 1990, s. 31(6) and the Town and Country Planning (Development Plan) (England) Regulations 1999, (SI 1999/3280)). [DR]

sub-mortgage A MORTGAGE of a mortgage. If the lender on a mortgage wishes to raise money, he may borrow money on the security of that mortgage, rather than transferring it. The lender on the original mortgage, who is now the borrower on the sub-mortgage, is called the sub-mortgagor. The lender under the sub-mortgage is called the sub-mortgagee.

If the borrower on a sub-mortgage defaults on his repayments, the lender may exercise a POWER OF SALE, but only in relation to the mortgage itself. This means that the mortgage may be sold, but the borrower on the original mortgage will retain the EQUITY OF REDEMPTION in the property. [DR]

sub-tenancy *See* SUBLEASE.

sub-trust A declaration of TRUST, on behalf of another, by a BENEFICIARY under a trust creates a sub-trust. The beneficiary as **sub-trustee** holds the equitable title on trust for the sub-beneficiary who assumes the beneficial ownership. The legal title remains throughout in the hands of the TRUSTEE under the primary trust, as the sub-trust is only concerned with the equitable interest. This results in the legal, equitable and beneficial title each being separately vested and a situation in which the BENEFICIAL OWNER is neither the legal nor equitable owner. As a declaration of trust, sub-trusts are subject to the Law of Property Act 1925 (LPA), s. 53 (1)(b), which requires no formalities to be complied with, apart from where the subject matter is land, in which case the declaration of sub-trust should be evidenced by signed writing. However, it is sometimes asserted that sub-trusts amount, in practice, to assignments of the equitable INTEREST, with the sub-trustee effectively disappearing from the picture. If this is correct, sub-trusts should be subject to the more exacting requirements of the LPA, s. 53 (1)(c), which requires that the assignment of an equitable interest, under a trust of *any* property, be *by* signed writing. Such an analysis, arguably, confuses equitable and beneficial ownership and should thus be questioned. Even the advocates of this approach concede it cannot apply in situations where the sub-trustee retains a role, such as that which occurs where a discretion as to who should benefit under the sub-trust is held by the sub-trustee. Thus a declaration of a sub-trust can only take effect as an assignment, if at all, under a bare sub-trust in which the sub-trustee retains no role in respect of either the equitable or beneficial title.   [PK]

subdemise *See* DEMISE.

subinfeudation In the system of FEUDAL TENURE, the process by which a tenant-in-chief of the Crown granted an interest in his land, known as a FEE, to a person who would hold that land as sub-tenant of the tenant-in-chief. This process could continue indefinitely; for example, X, a tenant-in-chief of the Crown, could grant a fee to Y, who could grant all or part of that land by fee to Z, who could then grant all or part of that land by fee to A. The effect of subinfeudation was that land ownership became gradually more complicated and the original lord of a manor found it increasingly difficult to prove his ownership and reap profits from the land. Subinfeudation was abolished in 1290 by the Statute of *QUIA EMPTORES*, confirming substitution as the only method for alienating fee simple interests in land.
                                                    [DR]

subject to contract A phrase used by conveyancers prior to the exchange of contracts in order to confirm that pre-exchange negotiations are not legally binding. Under the Law of Property Act 1925, s. 40, which applies only to contracts made prior to 27 September 1989, contracts for the sale of land could be created orally, and

were enforceable if there was a written memorandum or note of the agreement, or if there was part performance. The phrase 'subject to contract' was used to confirm that pre-exchange correspondence was not intended to be a memorandum of an oral contract.

For contracts made on or after 27 September 1989, the Law of Property (Miscellaneous Provisions) Act 1989, s. 2 lays down the requirement that contracts for the sale of land must be made in writing, contain all the terms agreed by the parties and be signed by each of the parties. Therefore, use of the phrase 'subject to contract' is no longer strictly necessary, although many conveyancers continue to use the phrase in order to avoid any misunderstanding.   [DR]

See also CONTRACT FOR SALE.

sublease A LEASE granted by a LESSEE which is for a term which must be less than the term the lessee has been granted by his or her LANDLORD. Subletting usually requires the consent of the landlord which cannot be unreasonably withheld. FORFEITURE of the lessee's lease terminates the sublease as do possession proceedings. However, surrender of the lease does not terminate the sublease.   [HC & DR]

subsidiarity A concept used in the context of EUROPEAN COMMUNITY (EC) law, set out in Article 5 EC Treaty and the Protocol on the principles of subsidiarity and PROPORTIONALITY attached to the EUROPEAN COMMUNITY TREATY. An exact legal definition of subsidiarity has been problematic since its insertion into the EC Treaty by the TREATY ON EUROPEAN UNION in 1992, with Jacques Delors, then President of the EUROPEAN COMMISSION, offering a prize to anyone who could adequately define it. It is understood that the prize has never been claimed. In relatively simple terms, the principle of subsidiarity means that, in areas of shared competence between the MEMBER STATES of the EC and the EC itself, decisions should be taken 'as close as possible to the citizen', unless 'by reason of the scale or effects of the proposed action' the objective would be better achieved at the EC level (see Article 5, above). One consequence of subsidiarity is that the EU should not legislate over matters that can be effectively addressed by legislation at national level. [MON]

substantial performance Where there has been substantial performance of the contractual obligation, i.e. where the obligation has been largely fulfilled and there are only a few minor deficiencies, the party can recover the contract PRICE, less a deduction to repair the minor deficiencies in performance (*Hoenig* v. *Isaacs* [1952] 2 All ER 176). Contractual obligations are generally indivisible or interdependent and the common law principle is that a contracting party must completely and precisely perform its obligations in order to be entitled to receive the other party's performance (for example, payment). It followed that performance which was short of this standard would be unremunerated. This position has been mitigated by the doctrine of substantial performance. [JPL]

substantive justice Justice that is concerned with ensuring that people get what they deserve. Of course, as the principle of redistribution 'from each according to his ability, to each according to his need' demonstrates, this may not necessarily equate to formal ideas of equality and JUSTICE. While substantive justice might seem like a useful corrective to formalism, its effect can be highly controversial, as two simple examples illustrate. Suppose, on the one hand, that two speeding drivers are stopped, and each is fined £50. One driver earns £10,000 a year, the other £100,000. Both may be equally culpable, but the real impact of the penalty is, although formally just, substantively unjust. To achieve a substantive equality of penalties, the second driver should arguably be fined £500.

Consider also a situation in which someone who commits a murder can be proven guilty only with illegally obtained evidence. Therefore they may have to go free according to the RULE OF LAW. In such a case, he or she would receive formal justice but not necessarily substantive justice. The critical question in such cases thus becomes

one chiefly of justification: as RAWLS formulates the question, what considerations are we justified in using to praise or condemn those social practices? [JW]

See also DISTRIBUTIVE JUSTICE; FORMAL JUSTICE; PROCEDURAL JUSTICE.

substantive law That part of the law that deals with rights, duties and obligations rather than the rules of EVIDENCE and court procedure. [JW]

See also ADJECTIVE LAW.

substitutional legacy It occasionally happens that a TESTATOR gives two general legacies of the same amount to the same BENEFICIARY. When this occurs, it has to be decided whether the legacies are cumulative (so that the beneficiary takes both), or whether they are substitutional (so that the beneficiary takes only one). If the legacies are contained in the same instrument, there is a PRESUMPTION that they are substitutional, but if they are contained in separate documents, for example a WILL and a subsequent CODICIL, then there is a rule of construction that the legacies are cumulative, unless they are expressed to be given for the same motive, in which case there is a presumption that they are substitutional. [CM]

See also LEGACY.

succession The area of law dealing with the manner in which property devolves following the death of the owner. It therefore covers the making of WILLS, the interpretation of wills by the courts, the distribution of ASSETS upon INTESTACY, the possible claims on an estate by family or dependants, inheritance tax, GRANTS OF REPRESENTATION and the administration of ESTATES. [CM]

suicide A criminal offence until it was decriminalized by the Suicide Act 1961, s. 1. However, under s. 2 of that Act, it remains an offence to aid, abet, counsel or procure another person's suicide or attempted suicide.

Suicide pacts are dealt with in the Homicide Act 1957, s. 4. In accordance with that provision, where A and B enter into and purport to carry out a suicide pact, as a result of which A dies but B unintentionally survives, B will not be guilty of the MURDER of A, but rather of VOLUNTARY MANSLAUGHTER.

[BF]

suitable accommodation The accommodation that a LOCAL HOUSING AUTHORITY makes available to **eligible applicants** under Part 7 of the Housing Act 1996 must, by s. 206, be suitable. This is interpreted to mean suitable not only for the applicant but also for all members of their household who normally reside with them, or who might reasonably be expected to reside with them. Account will therefore need to be taken of any medical, physical or social needs of the applicant and their household that might affect the suitability of accommodation. Any risk of violence or racial harassment must also be taken into account. Accommodation which is not affordable or is located at a distance from essential facilities may be found to be unsuitable.

If an applicant refuses an offer of suitable accommodation, then the local housing authority's duty to them under the legislation is discharged. An applicant has the right to an internal review of the suitability of an offer of accommodation other than INTERIM ACCOMMODATION. The application for internal review must be made within 21 days of the offer. If the applicant remains dissatisfied, then within 21 days he or she can appeal the decision on a point of law to the COUNTY COURT. [HC & DR]

See also ELIGIBILITY FOR ASSISTANCE; INTENTIONALITY; HOMELESS PERSON.

summary conviction Conviction following a trial in a magistrates' court. [SN]

summary offence A criminal offence that can only be tried summarily before magistrates. These include most road traffic offences, COMMON ASSAULT, BREACH OF THE PEACE and other lesser public order offences, as well as offences against local BYELAWS. [SN]

summing up A concluding summary of the case, provided by the judge to the JURY.

[ALTC]

summons An order to appear before a magistrates' court, setting out the basis of the accusation against the accused and the time and place when he or she must appear.

[SN]

See also WITNESS SUMMONS.

Sunday trading The Sunday Trading Act 1994, now part of the Employment Relations Act 1996, protects '**protected shop workers**' and '**opted-out shop workers**'. 'Protected shop workers' are those who were employed on the date the 1994 Act came into force (26 August 1994), who were not employed to work only on Sundays, and who since have been continuously employed as shop workers; and also includes those who cannot contractually be required to work on Sundays (whether the contract was entered into before or after 26 August 1994). 'Opted-out shop workers' are those who, by contract, may be required to work on Sundays, who are not employed to work only on Sundays and who have given their EMPLOYERS an opting-out notice. Members of both categories may opt in to Sunday working. It is automatically a case of UNFAIR DISMISSAL when employers dismiss protected and opted-out shop workers. Similar protection exists in respect of DETRIMENT. [MJ]

supervision order 1. An order in terms of the Children Act 1989, empowering a court to appoint a supervisor to take steps to give effect to the order and to 'advise, assist and befriend' (s. 35) the CHILD who is the subject of the order. The order does not give the supervisor, who is the LOCAL AUTHORITY, PARENTAL RESPONSIBILITY, but it may require the supervised child to comply with the directions of the supervisor specifying where the child should live, whom the child should see, what places the child should attend and what activities, such as education and training, the child should undertake. A supervision order lasts for up to one year initially but it can be extended on application by the supervisor for up to three years. There are no enforcement mechanisms and if the supervisor's directions are not complied with, the only step the supervisor can take is to seek a variation or discharge. In the event of a discharge, it may be appropriate for the local authority to seek a CARE ORDER instead.

The grounds for a supervision order are set out in s. 31 of the 1989 Act (THRESHOLD CRITERIA). The court is required to choose the least interventionist approach wherever possible and will make a supervision order rather than a care order, provided this does not jeopardize the child's safety (*Re W (A Minor)(Interim Care Order)* [1994] 2 FLR 892, 898).

2. A type of YOUTH COMMUNITY ORDER as defined in the Criminal Justice Act 2003, s. 147 (2). Where a person under 18 is convicted of a criminal offence, the court may make an order placing him or her under the supervision of a local authority, a PROBATION OFFICER or a member of a YOUTH OFFENDING TEAM (Powers of Criminal Courts (Sentencing) Act 2000, s. 63). [FK]

supremacy of parliament *See* SOVEREIGNTY OF PARLIAMENT.

Supreme Court The Constitutional Reform Act 2005 will replace the HOUSE OF LORDS as a judicial body with a new Supreme Court of the United Kingdom. The existing Law Lords will become the first **Justices of the Supreme Court**, with the senior judge taking the post of **President of the Supreme Court**. The Court will sit in London in the Middlesex Guildhall building, which is being refurbished for that purpose. It is anticipated that the new Supreme Court will commence work after completion of its building, due in October 2009.

The 2005 Act also makes provision for a new appointments process for Supreme Court Justices. A selection commission will be formed as vacancies arise. This will be composed of the President and Deputy President of the Supreme Court and a member of the Judicial Appointments Commission of England and Wales, the Judicial Appointments Board for Scotland and the Northern Ireland Judicial Appointments Commission. New Supreme Court judges will not be eligible to sit in the House of Lords and will not receive peerages. [JW]

Supreme Court of Judicature (obsolete) The collective name for the COURT OF APPEAL and the HIGH COURT in England and Wales. These courts became the Supreme Court of Judicature under the Judicature Act 1873, which removed the appellate function of the HOUSE OF LORDS. This reform was short-lived, however, as the House of Lords was restored as the final court of appeal by the Appellate Jurisdiction Act 1876. Confusingly, the title of Supreme Court of Judicature was nevertheless retained for the Court of Appeal and High Court, until finally removed by the Constitutional Reform Act 2005. Under the 2005 Act, the Court of Appeal and High Court are now collectively called the **Senior Courts of England and Wales**. [JW]

surety In criminal proceedings, a person who guarantees that a defendant will attend court. [SN]

surrogate mother A woman who carries a CHILD pursuant to a surrogacy arrangement: the Surrogacy Arrangements Act 1985, s. 1. [FK]

survivorship *See* COMMORIENTES.

suspended sentence A custodial sentence that takes effect only if the offender commits another offence within a specified period. If the later offence is non-imprisonable, sentencing guidelines indicate that it may be appropriate not to activate the suspended sentence. Under the Criminal Justice Act 2003, where the suspended sentence is subject to a specific requirement (such as an unpaid work requirement, a CURFEW requirement, or drug treatment requirement), the sentence can also be activated if the offender fails to comply with that requirement. [SN]

sustainable development May be defined as 'development that meets the needs of the present without compromising the ability of future generations to meet their own needs' (see Brundtland Report, *Our Common Future*, Oxford University Press, 1987). Sustainable development is a guiding principle found only in SOFT LAW instruments, particularly the Brundtland UN Commission Report and the 1993 Rio Declaration. Its existence only within the context of soft law makes its legal status problematic. Its implementation thus seems to depend on, or consist of, a number of other principles, such as the right to development, intergenerational equity, balancing of developmental needs with conservation of natural resources and others, many of which themselves are of dubious normative value. [IB]

See also STOCKHOLM DECLARATION.

sworn evidence EVIDENCE given after taking an OATH or making an AFFIRMATION. [ALTC]

T

tail *See* ENTAILED INTEREST.

tail female An ENTAILED INTEREST granted specifically 'to X and the heirs female of the body' or 'to X in tail female'. The effect of a tail female is to create a succession of entailed interests for as long as a female blood descendant of X exists.　　[DR]

See also TAIL GENERAL; TAIL MALE; TAIL SPECIAL.

tail general An ENTAILED INTEREST granted specifically 'to X and the heirs of the body' or 'to X in tail'. A tail general is so-called because on X's death his property will descend to X's general heirs, under the pre-1926 rules of descendancy.　　[DR]

See also FEE TAIL; HEIR; TAIL FEMALE; TAIL MALE; TAIL SPECIAL.

tail male An ENTAILED INTEREST granted specifically 'to X and the heirs male of his body' or 'to X in tail male'. The effect of a tail male is to create a succession of interests for as long as a male blood descendant of X exists.　　[DR]

See also FEE TAIL; TAIL FEMALE; TAIL GENERAL; TAIL SPECIAL.

tail special An ENTAILED INTEREST granted to the heirs of two specified persons, rather than the heirs of one; for example, where an entailed interest is granted specifically 'to X and the heirs begotten by him on the body of Y', it is only the heirs of X who are

also the issue of Y that may be entitled as a TENANT IN TAIL.　　[DR]

See also FEE TAIL; TAIL FEMALE; TAIL GENERAL; TAIL MALE.

tainted acquittal An acquittal affected by interference (such as threats or intimidation) with a WITNESS, potential witness or JUROR. The Criminal Procedure and Investigations Act 1996, ss. 54–57, enable the HIGH COURT to quash a tainted acquittal and order a retrial for the original offence.　　[SN]

taking without consent (TWOC) The offence of taking a motor vehicle or other CONVEYANCE without authority, under the Theft Act 1968, s. 12. It is committed by a person who makes unauthorized use of a conveyance – whether as driver or passenger – in circumstances which may or may not amount to THEFT. The offence was created in order to prosecute behaviour such as JOYRIDING, where the takers of the vehicle are acting principally for recreational purposes and may thus not have the intention to permanently deprive the owner of the vehicle – which would be necessary for an offence of theft. The offence is often abbreviated to TWOC, a term that is now a semi-official piece of law enforcement vernacular, with associated nouns such as 'twoccer' and 'twoccing'.　　[BF]

See also AGGRAVATED VEHICLE TAKING.

talaq In ISLAMIC LAW, a unilateral DIVORCE

where the husband can divorce the wife by uttering a form of words without the presence of witnesses or the wife's consent. A talaq divorce effected in England and Wales would not be a valid divorce, as only a court can dissolve a marriage. But the English court has the discretion to recognize a talaq divorce effected in a country which recognizes it as valid.   [AD]

See also DISSOLUTION.

tax haven A STATE or COUNTRY having different tax laws from the one in which a taxpayer is resident for tax purposes, and in which the taxpayer can protect his income and capital assets from the tax laws of his tax residence. The term has no formal legal definition but is used colloquially, and sometimes legislatively.

Any state or country can become a refuge jurisdiction in relation to another state or country, but there are certain states and countries, and even cities, which are regarded as being deliberate tax havens in order to attract value to their economies. Many residence jurisdictions have anti-avoidance legislation to counteract the operation of tax havens. A distinction can be made between tax havens and **offshore jurisdictions** more generally (though they are often the same countries), since the latter may provide the facilities for offshore financial centres without being in the full sense a tax haven.   [RE]

tax point The date of the supply of goods or of services by a person who is registered for Value Added Tax purposes, the date being whichever is the earlier of the date of payment, the invoice date, the date of delivery (goods) or the date of performance (services).   [RE]

tax return A communication in writing, or sometimes electronically, from a taxpayer to HM REVENUE AND CUSTOMS (the Revenue), by which the Revenue acquires the information that it needs in order to be able to perform an assessment or confirm the completeness and accuracy of a self-assessment. Tax returns are required for each tax, but they are not always known as 'returns'

(for example, the account to be submitted on death for inheritance tax purposes).

Annual returns are required from some taxpayers in respect of income tax and CAPITAL GAINS TAX, and from some companies in respect of CORPORATION TAX. In the case of inheritance tax, a return is required to report immediately any chargeable LIFETIME TRANSFER, and/or POTENTIALLY EXEMPT TRANSFER which becomes chargeable.

Value Added Tax returns are normally required every three months, but some taxpayers can make monthly returns, for example if they regularly recover input tax. Annual returns can be agreed for taxpayers with comparatively low turnovers, whereas taxpayers with very large turnovers can be required to make some monthly returns.

Instruments which are required to be stamped do not always require an accompanying return. But, for example, a transaction in land for consideration will require a return to the Stamp Office in form SDLT 1. Where there is an exemption from duty, as in the case of gifts, there is no return. Instead, the transferee will include a statement in the transfer document certifying that no duty is payable.

Failure to submit required returns can result in penalties.   [RE]

See also ANNUAL RETURN; STAMP DUTY; STAMP DUTY RESERVE TAX.

tax statute Primary legislation without which the CROWN is constitutionally and practically unable to collect taxes. There are two kinds of tax STATUTE: principal Acts (e.g. the Income and Corporation Taxes Act 1988) and Finance Acts.

Annual adjustments to tax law are effected by the Finance Act. Principal UK tax statutes have different functions, including: (a) to provide structure and institutions, such as the Commissioners for Revenue and Customs Act 2005; (b) to impose particular taxes, such the Value Added Tax Act 1994; (c) to provide for management and enforcement, such as the Taxes Management Act 1970; and (d) to provide supplementary provisions, such as the Provisional Collection of Taxes Act 1968.

The Tax Law Rewrite programme is producing redrafted tax legislation so as to provide more clearly expressed legislation, but without changing the effect of the law. The Capital Allowances Act 2001, the Income Tax (Earnings and Pensions) Act 2003, the Income Tax (Trading and Other Income) Act 2005 and the Income Tax Act 2007 have resulted from the programme. CORPORATION TAX law is yet to be rewritten, with one or more new Acts expected to come on to the statute book when it is.   [RE]

See also BUDGET.

taxable supply The provision by a business of goods or services for a CONSIDERATION, subject to available exemptions under the UK Value Added Tax (VAT) legislation. Where a taxable supply has been made by a taxable person acting 'in the course or furtherance of any business carried on by him' (see the Value Added Tax Act 1994, s. 4 (1)) the supply is chargeable to VAT.   [RE]

See also ASSET; EXEMPT SUPPLY; TAX POINT; ZERO-RATED SUPPLY.

taxation of costs (obsolete) *See* ASSESSMENT OF COSTS.

tenancy 1. Broadly, the holding of LAND by any TITLE; this is reflected in terms such as joint tenancy of a FREEHOLD, or TENANCY IN COMMON.

2. Specifically, and also the most generally understood meaning of tenancy is the holding of property on a LEASE. The House of Lords decided in *Street* v. *Mountford* [1985] AC 809 that a tenancy involved the exclusive possession of land, for a term, at a RENT. The most important characteristic of a tenancy is exclusive possession. Rent is not strictly necessary, but some form of CONSIDERATION is required. There are many different forms of tenancy, including commercial and residential tenancies. Many tenancies attract statutory protection.

[HC & DR]

See also SECURE TENANCY.

tenancy at sufferance TENANTS who, following the termination of a TENANCY, continue to occupy property without either statutory authority or the consent of the LANDLORD have a tenancy at sufferance.

They are therefore not tenants at will, since that would require the agreement of the landlord. Nor are they trespassers. However, if the tenants remain in possession despite positive objections from the landlord, then their status will change to that of trespasser, as the tenancy at sufferance is essentially a passive concept.   [HC & DR]

See also TENANCY AT WILL.

tenancy at will A TENANCY where the TENANT is in possession, which can be terminated by either the LANDLORD or the tenant at will, without prior notice. It can either be created expressly or by implication if no rent is paid. It is the non-payment of rent that distinguishes it from a periodic TENANCY. A tenancy at will is a personal as opposed to a property interest and therefore it does not survive the death of either of the parties or attempts at ASSIGNMENT. As a category, it overlaps with the licence, which has proved a useful concept in recent years; see *Binions* v. *Evans* [1972] Ch 359 where a widow who had been allowed to occupy a cottage 'as a tenant at will free of rent for the remainder of her life or until determined as hereinafter provided' was found to be a licensee and not a tenant at will.   [HC & DR]

tenancy by estoppel Where someone purports to grant a TENANCY but does not have the legal power to do so, he or she is prevented (estopped) from denying that a tenancy exists. A tenancy by ESTOPPEL is distinct from a legal tenancy because it only binds the grantor and the grantee, and not third parties. If the grantor subsequently becomes capable of granting a legal tenancy, then the status of the tenancy by estoppel changes and becomes a legal tenancy; see *Bruton* v. *London & Quadrant Housing Trust* [2000] 1 AC 406.   [HC & DR]

tenancy deposits Private LANDLORDS frequently require TENANTS to pay deposits to protect themselves from financial loss as a result of damage to the property or the tenant's failure to pay rent. The tenant does not forfeit the entire deposit as a result of breach of contract, only the amount necessary to reimburse the landlord for his or her loss.

Following extensive campaigning by Shelter and Citizens Advice, the government enacted a tenancy deposit scheme. The Housing Act 2004, ss. 212–215 and Schedule 10, require that at least one tenancy deposit scheme is set up. All landlords who take a deposit from an assured shorthold tenant must pay it into a scheme within 14 days. The government intends to set up a custodial scheme and possibly insurance schemes. If a landlord fails to pay a deposit into a scheme, the tenant can apply to the county court for an order either that the deposit is repaid or paid into the custodial scheme within 14 days. The court must also order the landlord to pay the tenant compensation of three times the deposit. The landlord will also be unable to serve a s. 21 notice upon the tenant to terminate the assured shorthold tenancy while he or she is failing to comply. The scheme applies to all deposits paid after 6 April 2007.   [HC & DR]

tenancy for years A FIXED TERM TENANCY.
                                                                  [HC & DR]

tenancy from year to year A periodic TENANCY that can be terminated by either party with one year's notice. It is not a tenancy that is renewed annually, but one continuous tenancy which may subsist for many years until notice is served. A tenancy from year to year is recognized by the annual period for the payment of RENT. The money may be paid more frequently than annually; what matters is whether the rent is expressed as a yearly rent or whether some other period is provided for. It may arise by express agreement, or be implied by law or by STATUTE. For instance, the Agricultural Holdings Act 1986 provides that an agreement to let agricultural land, which falls within the definition of AGRICULTURAL HOLDING under that Act, for a period of less than one year takes effect as a tenancy from year to year. The tenancy from year to year is most common for agricultural land, where a full year is required for the tenant to benefit from his or her work on the land.   [HC & DR]

tenancy in common A form of co-ownership of land, where two or more persons each have the right of possession and each owns a distinct share in the property. Under the Law of Property Act 1925, ss. 1 (6), 34, a tenancy in common can only exist as an EQUITABLE INTEREST under a trust. It is common for co-owners to own the LEGAL ESTATE as joint tenants and to own the equitable interest as tenants in common. Unlike a joint TENANCY, it is possible for tenants in common to own unequal shares in property, therefore it is often used where two or more persons buy a property together but contribute unequal shares. For example, where X and Y buy a property together, but X pays 70% of the purchase price and Y pays 30% of the purchase price, normally X and Y will jointly own the legal estate as joint tenants, holding the property on trust for themselves as tenants in common, with a share of 70% to X and 30% to Y.

A tenant in common is free to dispose of his equitable interest separately and may also apply to the court under the Trusts of Land and Appointment of Trustees Act 1996, s. 14, for an order of sale of the entire legal estate. On death, the equitable interest under a tenancy in common passes according to the terms of a person's will or the rules on intestacy, not under the principle of survivorship.   [DR]
See also UNDIVIDED SHARES.

tenant A person or organization that is granted a TENANCY or a LEASE.   [HC & DR]
See also LANDLORD.

tenant for life 1. Under the Settled Land Act 1925 (SLA 1925), a tenant for life is a person of full age who is entitled to an equitable LIFE INTEREST in SETTLED LAND under a SETTLEMENT. The tenant for life has extensive statutory powers (SLA 1925, ss. 38–72), including the power to sell the settled land, to grant leases, to mortgage the property, in addition to any other powers specifically provided for in the settlement. The tenant for life also holds the LEGAL ESTATE and is entitled to all income arising out of the settled land. However, CAPITAL MONEY arising out of the exercise of those powers must be paid to the SETTLED LAND ACT TRUSTEES.

2. More generally, a tenant for life (or life tenant) is a person with a life interest, whether or not that life interest is held under a settlement. [DR]

tenant in tail A person who is entitled to an ENTAILED INTEREST. A tenant in tail is commonly entitled either in possession or in remainder; for example, if X grants a SETTLE-MENT 'to Y and the heirs of his body', Y is the tenant in tail in possession and Y's successor is the tenant in tail in remainder. Under the Fines and Recoveries Act 1833, s. 15, a tenant in tail may bar the entail, thereby enlarging his interest into a legal FEE SIMPLE ABSOLUTE IN POSSESSION. [DR]

See also FEE TAIL.

tenant *pur autre vie* A person owning an interest under an ESTATE *PUR AUTRE VIE*. [DR]

tenant's fixtures Items installed in a property by the TENANT, which may be removed by the tenant during or at the end of the lease. Shop fittings are frequently installed in commercial LEASES on this basis. Curtains and blinds are the equivalent in residential leases. The significant characteristic is that they can be removed without damaging the LANDLORD's property. [HC & DR]

tenantable repair The obligation of a tenant in rented premises to maintain the property in a condition which would allow it to be rented out. [HC & DR]

See also REPAIRS.

tender 1. An OFFER to provide or purchase goods or services for a specified PRICE. By comparison, an invitation to others to tender is usually an INVITATION TO TREAT rather than an offer (*Spencer* v. *Harding* (1870) LR 5 CP 561). It follows that ACCEPTANCE of the tender must occur for there to be a CONTRACT between the parties. However, where the invitation to tender contains a PROMISE to accept the highest or lowest price, the tender will amount to acceptance of the unilateral offer containing that promise, so that in the event of its breach the tenderer will have a remedy in damages for breach of

the promise (*Harvela Investments Ltd* v. *Royal Trust Co of Canada (CI) Ltd* [1986] AC 207).

2. Also an offer (tender) of performance which requires the concurrence of the other party, for example, tendering delivery of goods being manufactured and supplied under a SALE OF GOODS contract where the BUYER must accept delivery. A tender of performance is the equivalent of performance so that in this example the seller has performed and if the buyer refuses to accept or rejects the goods the buyer will be in BREACH OF CONTRACT. [JPL]

tenure A term which derives from feudal times, relating to the relationship between the feudal lord and those to whom he granted LAND, and describing the way in which such land was held. It retains some meaning in the context of the remaining legal estates in land, as FREEHOLD or LEASEHOLD land. It is most commonly used in renting, for instance, in the phrase 'SECURITY OF TEN-URE' to describe the protection that a TENANT has from eviction. [HC & DR]

term of years A leasehold interest in LAND. It is distinct from FREEHOLD which is of potentially infinite duration because it is limited in time. A term of years is carved out of freehold estates. The term does not have to be in years; it can be in weeks or months. What is crucial is that the period is identifiable. [HC & DR]

See also LEASE.

terra *nullius* (Lat. land belonging to no one) Territory over which no STATE possesses SOVEREIGNTY. The discovery and effective occupation of *terra nullius* in the past gave rise to a good title of territorial acquisition even if the land was inhabited by indigenous people, but no such territories exist any longer under this designation. It may be said that if the concept refers to lack of sovereignty, then *terra nullii* could include the high seas. This assumption is, however, fallacious, since both the UNITED NATIONS CONVENTION ON THE LAW OF THE SEA and customary law expressly establish a special regime that prohibits acquisition by proclaiming a general freedom of the high seas. [IB]

See also COMMON HERITAGE OF MANKIND; CUSTOMARY INTERNATIONAL LAW.

territorial limits 1. In INTERNATIONAL LAW, the territorial limits as set by the regime of boundaries. In the case of maritime territory, such as the UK, the final boundary of the coastal STATE is the outermost end of the TERRITORIAL WATERS. As far as the airspace above land territory and the territorial sea is concerned, SOVEREIGNTY extends upwards until OUTER SPACE.

2. In English law, the geographical limits within which English or UK legislation will operate, properly called its **territorial extent**. [IB]

territorial waters The territorial waters (or territorial sea) of a state begin from the designated BASELINES for a distance not exceeding 12 nautical miles seawards. All water landwards from the baselines is termed 'internal waters'. For all legal purposes, the territorial sea is an extension of the coastal STATE's land into the sea, and with few exceptions relating to navigation, passage and FLAG STATE JURISDICTION, the coastal state enjoys full SOVEREIGNTY and not merely sovereign rights within the territorial sea. [IB]

See also TERRITORIAL LIMITS; UNITED NATIONS CONVENTION ON THE LAW OF THE SEA.

test case An action brought specifically to test the feasibility of a legal argument or to clarify the law on a specific point, on the basis that a significant number of other cases will turn on the result. Test cases are often, though not exclusively, brought by campaign groups or PUBLIC INTEREST law firms and may take the form of a REPRESENTATIVE ACTION or GROUP LITIGATION (as in the 'big tobacco' litigation) or, often by a government or regulatory agency, as an application for a DECLARATION. An example of the latter is the action launched in July 2007 in the High Court by the Office of Fair Trading, which confirmed that banks' unauthorized overdraft charges were subject to assessment as to fairness under the Unfair Terms in Consumer Contract Regulations 1999, Reg. 6(2) (see *Office of Fair Trading* v. *Abbey National plc and Others* [2008] EWHC 875 (Comm.)). [JW]

See also STANDING.

testament The expression of wishes as to how property is to be disposed of upon death. Originally, it was confined to an expression relating to PERSONAL PROPERTY only, and not to REAL PROPERTY, but that distinction has long since been abandoned, and the word is now synonymous with the word 'WILL'. It is in fact rarely used except in the expression 'last will and testament'. [CM]

testamentary capacity The legal capacity to make a valid will. There are two aspects to be considered, one as to age, and one as to mental competence.

So far as age is concerned, the Wills Act 1837, s. 7 (as amended) provides that 'no will made by any person under the age of 18 years shall be valid'. There is, however, an important exception to this, as a person entitled to make a PRIVILEGED WILL can do so even though he has not attained the age of 18 years. Since the position as to age is clear, the requirement has not given rise to much litigation.

As to mental capacity, the position is much less straightforward, and has given rise to many cases. The leading case of *Banks* v. *Goodfellow* (1870) LR 5 QB 549 lays down certain principles to guide a court in reaching its decision. These principles are in substance that the testator must at the time of making the will understand three things: (a) what will be the effect of his wishes being carried out at his death?; (b) the extent of the property of which he is disposing; and (c) the claims to which he ought to give effect.

It is important to note, therefore, that the question to be decided by the court is not whether the testator is mentally ill or disabled, but whether he is capable of comprehending the specific matters mentioned, and if he is suffering from an insane delusion, whether it affects the dispositions he makes. So that the fact that a testator firmly believed he was Julius Caesar would not by itself be relevant if the provisions of the will did not reflect his belief, but it would be relevant had he left property to finance an invasion of Britain by Roman soldiers. [CM]

testamentary expenses Although the expression 'testamentary and administration expense' appears in the Administration of Estates Act 1925, no statutory definition is given. It is clear from decided cases, however, that the expression refers to the expenses incurred in the proper performance of the duties of a PERSONAL REPRESENTATIVE in the administration of the estate, and includes, for example, the cost of legal advice, obtaining a GRANT OF REPRESENTATION, collecting and distributing the ASSETS of the deceased. Inheritance tax payable on an estate also ranks as an administration expense. [CM]

testamentary freedom The situation in which a TESTATOR is allowed to dispose of his entire ESTATE by his WILL; this contrasts with a situation where the law provides that some or all of the ASSETS of a deceased person are disposed of in a certain way, whether the testator agrees with it or not. For instance, a legal system might provide that all of a testator's land went to his heir, or that a substantial share went to his widow, even if he has left a will making other provisions. It is something of a semantic question whether English law at present acknowledges complete testamentary freedom or not. Whilst a joint tenant cannot deal in his will with his interest, in law he has no 'share' which is his; so that it could be said that testamentary freedom still exists. However, the provisions of the Inheritance (Provision for Family and Dependants) Act 1975, as amended, mean that certain categories of persons have the right to apply to court, asking for provision to be made for them from the estate of the deceased even where he has disposed of all his property by will, and the court has a discretion as to what order to make. Although a testator still has the ability to make a will disposing of all his estate, he cannot be sure that all his GIFTS will be effective. [CM]

testamentary guardian The GUARDIAN of a child, appointed by the WILL of a PARENT having PARENTAL RESPONSIBILITY for that child. The guardianship will only take effect on the death of the parent (see Children Act 1989, s. 5). [CM]

testamentary intention *See* ANIMUS TESTANDI.

testate A person is testate if they dispose of property by their WILL. If they do not dispose of any property by will, there is said to be a total INTESTACY, and if they dispose of some but not all of the property there is said to be a partial intestacy. In the unusual case, therefore, of someone executing a will but failing to dispose of any property, there will be a total intestacy. Someone who dies without making a will is always intestate. [CM]

testator The name given to a man who makes a WILL. The feminine form is 'testatrix'. [CM]

testimony *See* ORAL EVIDENCE.

Thalweg principle (From Ger. *Thalweg*, valley line) Determines the method of delimitation of rivers used as boundaries between STATES. The Thalweg is in most cases the middle (or central) line of the main navigable channel. In some cases, and in the context of particular agreements, it may have another meaning, i.e. the line of deepest soundings, but it is likely that the two methods usually coincide in practice. [IB]

See also ACCRETION; AVULSION.

theft A criminal offence requiring the dishonest appropriation of property belonging to another with the intention of permanently depriving the other of it: see Theft Act 1968, s. 1. The offence has five elements, all of which are defined in the Act and must be proved. These elements constitute the ACTUS REUS and MENS REA of the offence. Thus the unlawful act is the appropriation (s. 3) of property (s. 4) belonging to another (s. 5). Theft is drawn widely enough to encompass within 'appropriation' not just the conventional taking of property, but other acts (e.g. failing to return property) or omissions that

are inconsistent with another's ownership. Property for the purposes of the offence includes all forms of personal property and most intangibles, but not land. The *mens rea* of theft comprises the remaining two elements of the offence: first it must be shown that the appropriation was dishonest (s. 2), so a taking of property by mistake cannot be theft; and, secondly, that there was also an intention permanently to deprive the owner (s. 6). The latter focuses on intention at the time of the offence, so the fact that the taker subsequently changes their mind and returns the property does not prevent the original act from being theft. Theft is an OFFENCE TRIABLE EITHER WAY and carries a maximum sentence in the CROWN COURT of seven years' imprisonment.
[BF]

therapeutic privilege Doctors have a general duty to ensure that a competent patient is given enough information to enable them to exercise their AUTONOMY in decision-making. There are, however, circumstances in which a doctor may believe that the disclosure of information about risks of treatment and alternative procedures that should normally be disclosed would be harmful to the patient. In such instances the doctor may exercise so-called therapeutic privilege and withhold the information (see *Sidaway* v. *Board of Governors of Bethlem Royal Hospital and Maudsley Hospital* [1985] AC 871). [HJ]

See also BEST INTERESTS; CONSENT TO TREATMENT; MENTAL CAPACITY.

therapeutic research All new medicines must be licensed. In order to obtain a licence there are a number of clinical trial stages that must be successfully completed, three of which will be conducted on humans. NON-THERAPEUTIC RESEARCH conducted on healthy volunteers takes place at phase I. There is no therapeutic (i.e. healing) benefit to the participants, as researchers are usually seeking to measure toxicity and absorption. In phases II and III, the participants will be suffering from the condition that the medicine is seeking to treat and will be hoping to receive some thera-

peutic benefit from participation in the trial. [HJ]

See also DECLARATION OF HELSINKI; LICENSING OF MEDICINES.

third party rights The Contracts (Rights of Third Parties) Act 1999 allows third parties to enforce rights in their favour, despite the fact that they are not parties to the CONTRACT and have not provided CONSIDERATION. It thus forms an important exception to the doctrine of PRIVITY OF CONTRACT. However, the Act makes no provisions for third parties to be subject to burdens and it is possible to expressly exclude the effect of the Act. Most significantly, not all third party rights are made enforceable. Either the contract must expressly state that the third party is to have the right to enforce it or the third party must be expressly identified in the contract. The term must purport to confer a benefit on the third party and there must be nothing in the contract to indicate that the parties did not intend the term to be enforceable by the third party; see the Contracts (Rights of Third Parties) Act 1999, ss. 1(1) and (2). [JPL]

third party rule A principle of TREATY law whereby a treaty produces legal effects only on the parties to it. Treaties are, therefore, inapplicable to third parties. In accordance with Article 35 of the 1969 Vienna Convention on the Law of Treaties, 'an obligation arises for a third STATE from a provision of a treaty if the parties to the treaty intend the provision to be the means of establishing the obligation and the third state expressly accepts that obligation in writing'. Equally, where a treaty confers rights on a third state, those rights will be deemed to have legal effect, unless the third state expressly indicates otherwise (Article 36 of the Vienna Convention). Where a treaty provision has become part of CUSTOMARY INTERNATIONAL LAW or *JUS COGENS*, the third party will be bound by the rule, irrespective of whether it consents or not to be bound by the relevant treaty. [IB]

threat A variety of criminal offences have a threat as one of their elements, or as one way of committing the *ACTUS REUS*. These include the offence of threats to kill under the Offences against the Person Act 1861, s. 16; the (virtually defunct) COMMON LAW offence of embracery (seeking to influence jurors – behaviour which is now more likely to be charged as PERVERTING THE COURSE OF JUSTICE or the offence of intimidating jurors under the Criminal Justice and Public Order Act 1994, s. 51); the offence of INTIMIDATION under the Trade Union and Labour Relations (Consolidation) Act 1992, s. 241; and a range of terrorist offences (terrorism, at law, includes acting or threatening to act for designated purposes: see the Terrorism Act 2000 and subsequent legislation). [BF]

See also HARASSMENT; STALKING; THREATENING BEHAVIOUR.

threatening behaviour Threatening, abusive or insulting words or behaviour is an element of the offences under the Public Order Act 1986, s. 4 (causing fear of or provoking violence), s. 4A (intentionally causing harassment, alarm or distress) and s. 5 (causing harassment, alarm or distress). Whether behaviour is threatening is a question of fact.

Words or behaviour are not threatening, abusive or insulting simply because they give rise to a risk of fear or provocation of immediate violence; nor simply because they annoy or cause anger; nor simply because they are distasteful or rude (see e.g. *Brutus* v. *Cozens* [1973] AC 854; *Valentine* v. *Lilley* [1983] QB 92; *R* v. *Ambrose* (1973) 57 Cr App Rep 538). [BF]

See also INSULTING BEHAVIOUR.

three certainties A phrase that articulates the three basic requirements of a valid EXPRESS TRUST: **certainty of intention (or words)** – that there must be an intention to create a trust; **certainty of subject matter** – that it must relate to identifiable property; and **certainty of objects (or persons)** – that there must be identifiable beneficiaries. It is commonly stated that the three certainties are necessary requirements of a valid express trust. In reality this represents a statement of the obvious point that a trust cannot normally exist unless there is both property to be held subject to it and beneficiaries who can benefit under it pub-

lic trust, while, as an expressly created device, it cannot be created unintentionally (see RESULTING TRUST, CONSTRUCTIVE TRUST). Although the detailed application of these requirements is somewhat more complicated, it is important not to lose sight of their essentially simple and interrelated function in establishing whether an intentionally created trust exists.

In establishing **certainty of intention** no particular form of words is required, as demonstrated in the context of PRECATORY WORDS where the courts have demonstrated for over a century that they are concerned with substance, not form. Consequently, as established in *Paul* v. *Constance* [1977] 1 WLR 527, even those ignorant of the concept can create an express trust provided that was the type of institution envisaged.

Certainty of subject matter has two aspects requiring that both the property to be held on trust and the entitlement of each BENEFICIARY be sufficiently well identified. With regard to the former, the property to be held on trust must already exist. A trust of future property is no trust at all because there is currently nothing to which the trust can apply. Thus a trust of the £100 I expect to earn from next year's dividend of shares I currently own is not a trust, because the money has not yet come into existence. However a trust of 50% of next year's dividend on those shares would be valid, because I currently own the shares and thus the right to the dividend. It is also important to sufficiently segregate trust property from non-trust property to avoid the difficulties that might otherwise arise if something befalls a mixture of trust and non-trust property.

Finally, in respect of **certainty of objects**, the courts are concerned to establish that the beneficiaries are identified with sufficient certainty to ensure the trustees can carry out their duties to the beneficiaries, and that the court can supervise the trustees in this role. Thus under a fixed trust it must be possible to compile, on the balance of probabilities, a complete list of beneficiaries, for otherwise the trustees cannot distribute the correct share each is due. In contrast, under a DISCRETIONARY TRUST, the trustees are not required to distribute a share to each beneficiary but only to choose from among a class of potential recipients. It was decided by the HOUSE OF LORDS in *McPhail* v. *Doulton* [1971] AC 424, that, as with POWERS OF APPOINTMENT, it is not necessary to compile a complete list of beneficiaries under a discretionary trust. For all the trustees need to carry out their duties, and likewise the courts to supervise them, is a conceptually certain definition of the class of person capable of benefiting, providing both the trustees and the courts with a clear test of eligibility. [PK]

threshold criteria The criteria or conditions specified under the Children Act 1989, s. 31, for the granting of a CARE ORDER or SUPERVISION ORDER. The threshold criteria are that the CHILD is suffering, or is likely to suffer, significant harm. The harm, or likelihood of harm, must be attributable to the fact that the care being given to that child does not meet reasonable standards or, alternatively, to the fact that the child is beyond parental control. 'Harm' is defined as ill-treatment or impairment of health or development and includes harm caused by witnessing DOMESTIC VIOLENCE. The definition of 'ill-treatment' covers physical, sexual and emotional abuse. There must be proof of the threshold criteria; mere suspicion does not suffice (*Re H and Others (Minors)(Sexual Abuse: Standard of Proof)* [1996] 1 FLR 80); *In re B (Children) (Care Proceedings: Standard of Proof) (CAF-CASS Intervening)* [2008] UKHL 35). The concept of significant harm is also crucial to the grounds for granting emergency orders under the Children Act but the requirement for proof is less onerous. [FK]

See also CHILD ABUSE; EMERGENCY PROTECTION ORDER; NEGLECT; SECURE ACCOMMODATION ORDER; VOLUNTARY ACCOMMODATION.

tied accommodation If accommodation is linked with employment then it is described as 'tied'. Typical examples of tied accommodation are caretakers of schools who live on the premises, or agricultural workers who live in cottages on the farm where they work. The extent of security of tenure enjoyed by the employee living in tied accommodation depends upon whether the agreement is a service TENANCY or a SERVICE OCCUPANCY. Agricultural workers who live in tied cottages receive specific protections depending upon the date of commencement of their occupancy.

[HC & DR]

tied cottage *See* TIED ACCOMMODATION.

time immemorial *See* CUSTOMARY LAW.

time of the essence The use of the expression 'time is of the essence' in relation to a contractual obligation indicates that performance of that contractual obligation (for example, to deliver the goods or make a payment by the stipulated date for its performance) is a CONDITION of the CONTRACT so that any breach will give rise to the option for the injured party to terminate the contract without consideration of the effect or magnitude of the breach (*Hartley* v. *Hymans* [1920] 3 KB 475; *Lombard North Central plc* v. *Butterworth* [1987] 1 QB 527). Time will be of the essence where it is expressly stipulated in the contract, or if this intention can be inferred from the nature of the transaction or surrounding circumstances (see, for example, *Bunge Corporation* v. *Tradax Export SA* [1980] 1 Lloyd's Rep 294, *per* Megaw LJ at 306 in relation to time stipulations in mercantile contracts, although compare *Torvald Klaveness A/S* v. *Arni Maritime Corporation, The Gregos* [1994] 1 WLR 1465 where the House of Lords examined the impact of the breach in determining whether the breach of such a time stipulation amounted to REPUDIATION).

[JPL]

time off for public duties The Employment Rights Act 1996, s. 50 provides for unpaid **time off** for MAGISTRATES and members of various bodies (local authorities, tribunals, police authorities, boards of prison visitors, health authorities, education authorities, the Environment Agency, water authorities and the General Teaching Council). The amount of time off must be reasonable, and the EMPLOYERS must balance their requirements for the work to be done against the public need to perform the duties. 'Time off' means leave during the

EMPLOYEE's normal WORKING HOURS, therefore the rearrangement of working hours is not permitted. Complaints of breaches of s. 50 are made to the EMPLOYMENT TRIBUNALS within three months of the alleged breach and COMPENSATION may be awarded. [MJ]

title In land law, title is a person's right to property as well as evidence of that right. In REGISTERED LAND, the four classes of title are: (a) **absolute title** – property registered with absolute title is fully guaranteed against any third party interest in the land, except for interests that are also protected on the register or OVERRIDING INTERESTS; (b) **good leasehold title** – the LEASE itself is guaranteed to be valid but there is no guarantee that the freehold or superior interest that the lease was granted from is valid; (c) **qualified title** – guaranteed subject to any interests deriving from specified defects in title; and (d) **possessory title** – only guaranteed from the date of registration, meaning that it is subject to any right or interest subsisting at the time of registration. Title to registered land is evidenced by OFFICIAL COPIES of the Land Registry's REGISTER OF TITLE, showing the owner as the registered proprietor of the subject property.

In UNREGISTERED LAND, good title is proved by the production of the TITLE DEEDS, an ABSTRACT OF TITLE or an EPITOME OF TITLE, showing an unbroken chain of ownership for at least 15 years (Law of Property Act 1969, s. 23). [DR]

title deeds A collection of documents detailing the transfer of interests in a particular parcel of UNREGISTERED LAND, providing evidence of TITLE to that land. Title deeds commonly contain documents such as conveyances transferring the land from one person to another, deeds of gift, deeds detailing devolution on death (e.g. assents), deeds of mortgage and trust deeds. The owner of land is entitled to custody of the title deeds and ownership of the title deeds passes with ownership of the land. When mortgaging unregistered land, the title deeds are usually handed over to the mortgage lender, so that the borrower cannot sell the land without the consent of the mortgage lender.

Since title deeds can be a large collection of documents, title to unregistered land is usually proved by the production of an ABSTRACT OF TITLE or EPITOME OF TITLE showing an unbroken chain of ownership for at least 15 years. Title to REGISTERED LAND is evidenced by official copies of the REGISTER OF TITLE, maintained by the Land Registry. [DR]

See also ROOT OF TITLE.

title in goods Where a SELLER transfers title to goods to a buyer under a CONTRACT for the SALE OF GOODS, the seller has transferred its **property rights** in those goods. These property rights relate to the owner's enjoyment of the goods and the title provides evidence of that right. Title tends therefore to be equated with property and with ownership of the goods, and the expression 'good title' may be used to indicate that an owner of goods has good evidence of title or ownership.

The Sale of Goods Act 1979, s. 12, implies three terms relating to the title of goods : (a) the IMPLIED TERM that the seller has the right to sell the goods or, in the case of an agreement to sell, that the seller will have the right to sell at the time when the property in the goods is to pass; (b) a WARRANTY of quiet possession (that the buyer will not be prevented from enjoying the use of the goods transferred); and (c) a warranty of freedom from encumbrances, such as a LIEN, which may affect goods. [JPL]

Tobar doctrine The basis on which, in the early 1900s, a number of Latin American states entered into treaties that provided for the de-recognition of STATES in the event of an interruption of their constitutional order. This was adopted at a time when the influence of former European colonial powers and the USA was challenging the institutional and ideological status quo of the region. The application of the doctrine was short-lived and was succeeded by the more viable ESTRADA DOCTRINE in 1930 and in 1933 by the MONTEVIDEO CONVENTION on the Rights and Duties of States. Both of these set the legal framework for the existence of statehood without recourse to dubious political acts, such as the de-recognition advocated under the Tobar doctrine. [IB]

See also CONSTITUTIVE THEORY; DECLARATORY THEORY; MONROE DOCTRINE; RECOGNITION OF A STATE.

tolerated trespasser The legal status of a former secure or assured tenant against whom an immediate or suspended possession order has been made, who remains in possession of the property with the approval of the former LANDLORD despite (in the case of a suspended possession order) having breached the terms of the order. The status was the creation of Lord Browne-Wilkinson in *Burrows* v. *Brent LBC* (1996) 29 HLR 167, who wanted to avoid the practical difficulties inherent in LOCAL HOUSING AUTHORITIES either having to evict people they did not wish to evict or having to go to court to vary the terms of a possession order. In his opinion, the landlord did not necessarily have an intention to create a new licence or TENANCY when someone was allowed to remain in possession after the termination of the tenancy. Where no such intention existed, the former secure tenancy ceased to exist and the former TENANT could be characterized as a trespasser whose presence in the property was tolerated by the former landlord.

During the period of the tolerated trespass, the normal benefits of a secure tenancy such as succession rights and repairing obligations do not exist and the landlord is not entitled to RENT although they may collect mesne profits. The secure tenancy is capable of being revived by an application to the court to vary the order by changing the date for possession. Moreover, the former landlord can end the status of tolerated trespasser by granting a new tenancy. However, a long line of cases has emphasized the courts' reluctance to designate actions of local authority landlords – for instance, in writing letters referring to rent and conditions of tenancy – as the equivalent of a grant of a new tenancy.

The status of tolerated trespasser is unsatisfactory for a number of reasons. In particular, former tenants who pay off the arrears that triggered the possession proceedings are no longer in a position to apply to the court to vary the possession order and thus revive their former secure tenancy. The only way forward is for the former landlord to grant a new secure tenancy; however, this may trigger new rights, such as additional succession rights.

[HC & DR]

tort (Old Fr. wrong, or harm) That part of the law of civil obligations that does not arise from contractual duties or property rights as such. There are a number of different torts including BATTERY, DEFAMATION, NEGLIGENCE, NUISANCE and trespass. Some of these are intentional, such as defamation and battery, whereas others, such as negligence, are accidental wrongs. There are also a number of examples of strict liability in tort. Some torts, such as ASSAULT or battery, may also constitute crimes, and in some circumstances negligent acts or advice, or NEGLIGENT MISSTATEMENTS, may also provide the basis for an action for BREACH OF CONTRACT. Proof of tortious liability normally entitles the victim to redress in DAMAGES for harm suffered, or an INJUNCTION may be granted to prevent further or future harm occurring. [HJ]

torture 'Any act by which severe pain or suffering, whether physical or mental, is intentionally inflicted on a person for such purposes as obtaining from him or a third person information or a confession, punishing him for an act he or a third person has committed or is suspected of having committed, or intimidating or coercing him or a third person, or for any reason based on discrimination of any kind, when such pain or suffering is inflicted by or at the instigation of or with the consent or acquiescence of a public official or other person acting in an official capacity. It does not include pain or suffering arising only from, inherent in or incidental to lawful sanctions' (UN Convention against Torture, 1984, Article 1).

Torture is prohibited in a range of national laws and international conventions. Article 3 of the EUROPEAN CONVENTION ON HUMAN RIGHTS states that 'No one shall be subjected to torture or to inhuman or degrading treatment or punishment.' This is an ABSOLUTE RIGHT under the Convention and is now part of UK law following the Human Rights Act 1998. Under Article 7 of the Statute of the INTERNATIONAL CRIMINAL COURT, torture may also be considered a CRIME AGAINST HUMANITY 'when committed as part of a widespread or systematic attack directed against any civilian population, with knowledge of the attack', and so may be prosecuted accordingly. [JW]

totting up A colloquial term used to describe the procedure under the Road Traffic Offences Act 1988, s. 35, which provides for the disqualification of a licence holder where the total number of points on the licence add up to 12 or more. An offender who has acquired 12 or more points can avoid a 'totting-up' disqualification if the court is satisfied that there are sufficient mitigating circumstances. [SN]

See also PENALTY POINTS.

trade custom (or usage) A long-standing, clearly established and well-known practice within a particular trade or market sector. Where a CONTRACT is silent on the question, a term can be implied (and so incorporated) into the contract which reflects such a local custom or trade usage in the particular sector (see *Hutton* v. *Warren* (1836) 1 M & W 466; *British Crane Hire Corporation* v. *Ipswich Plant Hire Ltd* [1975] QB 303). Trade custom may also be employed in the contractual interpretation of contracts employed in a particular sector. [JPL]

See also IMPLIED TERM.

trade dispute For the purposes of the law of INDUSTRIAL ACTION, found in Part V of the Trade Union and Labour Relations (Consolidation) Act 1992, a 'trade dispute' is defined in s. 244(1) as a dispute between WORKERS and their EMPLOYERS which relates wholly or mainly to one or more of the following: (a) terms and conditions of employment, or the physical conditions in which any workers are required to work; (b) engagement or non-engagement, or termination or suspension of employment or the duties of employment, of one or more workers; (c) allocation of work or the duties of employment between workers or groups of workers; (d) matters of discipline; (e) a worker's membership or non-membership of a TRADE UNION; (f) facilities for officials of trade unions; and (g) machinery for negotiation or consultation and other procedures, relating to any of the above matters, including the RECOGNITION by employers or employers' associations of the right of a trade union to represent workers in such negotiation or consultation or in the carrying out of such procedures. [MJ]

trade fixture A fixture installed into rented commercial property by a tenant for the purpose of carrying out their business. These remain the property of the tenant and can be removed by them at any time. [HC & DR]

See also TENANT'S FIXTURES.

trade mark *See* REGISTERED TRADE MARK.

trade mark attorney A professional who has expertise in the field of INTELLECTUAL PROPERTY. Trade mark attorneys advise on a range of trade mark related issues, including all aspects of registration, use and infringement of trade marks, and file TRADE MARK applications worldwide as well as in the UK. Employment will normally be within a firm of trade mark attorneys, or a firm of patent agents with a department specializing in trade mark work. Trade mark attorneys are also employed in-house by a number of large companies.

The profession is governed by the **Institute of Trade Mark Attorneys** and there are professional qualifications and examinations run by the Institute. The Institute is authorized to grant rights of audience in the PATENTS COUNTY COURT and the HIGH COURT to suitably qualified members of the Institute who are also registered trade mark agents. [US]

See also PATENT AGENT.

trade secret A product or process that is not disclosed to the public, not patented and is kept secret will be considered to constitute a trade secret. Any use or performance of the invention by third parties without authorization may be illegal under the law of CONFIDENTIALITY. Trade secrets are strictly speaking not INTELLECTUAL PROPERTY as such though they encompass a lot of things which would constitute protected intellectual property but for the secrecy. Indeed, trade secrecy is used if it is difficult to obtain intellectual property protection because the latter requires disclosure to the public.

To keep trade secrets protected, the information must be confidential, and it is necessary to ensure that everyone who works with the secret or knows of it signs a confidentiality agreement.   [US]

See also PATENT.

trade union Under the Trade Union and Labour Relations (Consolidation) Act 1992, s. 1, a 'trade union' is 'an organization (whether temporary or permanent) –

(a) which consists wholly or mainly of WORKERS of one or more descriptions and whose principal purposes include the regulation of relations between workers of that description or those descriptions and EMPLOYERS or EMPLOYERS' ASSOCIATIONS or

(b) which consists wholly or mainly of –
(i) constituent or amalgamated organizations which fulfil the conditions in paragraph (a) (or themselves consist wholly or mainly of constituent or affiliated organisations which fulfil those conditions); or –
(ii) representatives of such constituent or affiliated organisations, and whose principal purposes include the regulation of relations between workers and employers or between workers and employers' associations, or the regulation of relations between its constituent or affiliated organisations.'   [MJ]

trade union official An officer of a TRADE UNION, union branch or sector, or someone appointed or elected in accordance with union rules to represent members or a group of members: see the Trade Union and Labour Relations (Consolidation) Act 1992, s. 119.   [MJ]

transfer To make over ownership of a right from one person to another.

In CONVEYANCING, a DEED of transfer must be used for the sale of all REGISTERED LAND. A deed of transfer is also commonly used for the sale of UNREGISTERED LAND if the title is required to be registered for the first time following completion (as is the case in most transactions).   [DR]

transfer of risk Risk refers to the possibility of accidental loss occurring through destruction of, or damage to, the goods. Under the Sale of Goods Act 1979 s. 20, unless otherwise agreed, the goods will normally remain at the SELLER's risk until the property (i.e. ownership or some proprietary interest) in the goods passes to the buyer. When the property in the goods is transferred to the buyer, which need not coincide with delivery of the goods to the buyer, the risk will then be transferred to the buyer. It follows that if specific goods are destroyed while at the seller's risk, the seller will be liable for failure to deliver. Equally, if the goods are destroyed while at the buyer's risk, the buyer would be liable to pay the PRICE and could not claim that the goods had not been delivered even if the destruction occurred prior to delivery to the buyer.   [JPL]

See also TITLE.

transfer of undertakings *See* ACQUIRED RIGHTS; RELEVANT TRANSFER.

transferred malice A doctrine of criminal law whereby A remains liable for a given offence, albeit that the actual victim of the offence differs from the intended victim. Consider the following: A fires a gun at B, intending to kill B. B ducks out of the way of the bullet, which hits C, who dies. A is liable for the murder of C, even though C was not the intended victim. In terms of the doctrine, A's malice is transferred from B to C. The outcome is also explicable in terms of basic criminal law concepts, without recourse to the notion of transferred malice. The *ACTUS REUS* of MURDER is the causing of death of a person in being. The *MENS REA* for murder is intention to kill or to do grievous bodily harm to a person in being. A clearly meets these criteria.

Transferred malice will not, of itself, render A liable for CRIMINAL DAMAGE where A intends to punch B, but misses and punches through a window. The *actus reus* was the causing of the damage to the window, but the *mens rea* was the intention to punch B, and they cannot be combined to create a composite offence (see *R* v. *Pembliton* (1874) LR 2 CCR 119). However, if it could be proved that A was reckless as to the possibility of causing damage to the window, he might be liable for criminal damage (see *R* v. *G* [2003] UKHL 50).   [BF]

transformation doctrine A doctrine which asserts that a provision of INTERNATIONAL LAW only becomes a part of domestic (i.e. national) law by a deliberate and specific act of integration, such as the promulgation of legislation, a decision in a court case, etc. The transformation doctrine is the practical counterpart of the theory of DUALISM.   [IB]

See also INCORPORATION DOCTRINE; MONISM.

transitional justice A framework of activities designed to confront past HUMAN RIGHTS abuse as part of a process of political transformation. Transitional justice initiatives generally involve a range of judicial and non-judicial strategies and institutional reforms to support and sustain a move to peaceful and/or democratic government in a country. These initiatives may include: the prosecution of leading perpetrators (either through domestic law, special tribunals, or, now, at the INTERNATIONAL CRIMINAL COURT); establishing TRUTH AND RECONCILIATION COMMISSIONS; memorializing the dead or disappeared; developing reparations packages for victims and others closely affected by the abuse; and reforming state institutions implicated in the abuse, such as the police, security services, military and/or judiciary.   [JW]

transsexual person A person with the outward appearance or anatomy of one sex but who feels psychologically, socially or emotionally that they are of the other sex. The medical term for this condition is 'gender dysphoria'. Many transsexual people opt to obtain treatment by seeking gender reassignment surgery and/or hormone treatment to establish the outward characteristics of their psychological sex. A person with gender dysphoria can legally change his or her sex by meeting the requirements of the Gender Recognition Act 2004, which will result in the issue of a Gender Recognition Certificate, the effect of which is that the person's gender becomes, for all purposes, his or her acquired gender.   [AD]

See also GENDER REASSIGNMENT.

travaux préparatoires (Fr. preparatory works) This term encompasses documentation employed by the parties when conferring or deliberating on the text of a TREATY, or which constitutes the preparatory or background papers to an item of domestic (i.e. national) legislation. In the treaty context, this may include the statements and declarations of STATE representatives, objections to the statements of other representatives, etc. Such *travaux préparatoires*, unless constituting a binding agreement in themselves, are not binding. None the less, to the extent that they clearly demonstrate the intention of the parties on particular aspects of the treaty, where interpretation of the agreed text is uncertain, they may be used in accordance with Article 32 of the 1969 Vienna Convention on the Law of Treaties as a supplementary means of treaty interpretation.

The approach to *travaux* in domestic systems varies, with CIVIL LAW jurisdictions historically being more liberal in their use than their COMMON LAW counterparts. The English legal system still takes one of the most restrictive approaches. Reference may be made to reports and working papers of law reform bodies (such as the LAW COMMISSION) in identifying the mischief behind legislation, but judicial opinion on the use of government WHITE PAPERS is divided. The bar on using HANSARD (the official report of parliamentary debates) was removed, subject to certain restrictions, in *Pepper* v. *Hart* [1992] 3 WLR 1032.   [IB & JW]

See also STATUTORY INTERPRETATION.

treason A variety of forms of conduct against the interests of the sovereign, undertaken by a person who owes allegiance to the sovereign. A number of examples of such conduct are set out in the Treason Act 1351, and include levying war against the monarch in the realm, and endeavouring to hinder the proper successor to the throne from succeeding. The Treason Felony Act 1848, which applies to a person who may or may not owe allegiance to the sovereign, designates as an offence a number of other forms of conduct. A person commits an offence under the 1848 Act, s. 3, if they evidence their intention to adversely interfere with the sovereign in the designated manner by publishing any printing or writing or by any overt act.   [BF]

See also MISPRISION.

treasure Under the Treasure Act 1996, an object is treasure where *either* it was found after 24 September 1997, and is at least 300 years old when found and (a) is not a coin but has metallic content of which at least 10% by weight is precious metal, or (b) is one of at least two coins in the same find which are at least 300 years old and at least 10% of precious metal, or (c) is one of at least ten coins in the same find which are at least 300 years old; *or*, if found after 1 January 2003, it is part of a group of two or more metallic objects of any composition that are of prehistoric date and come from the same find; *or*, it is an object which would have been TREASURE TROVE if found before the commencement of the Act.

All treasure vests in the CROWN, though the finder may be entitled to compensation based on the fair market value of the find. All finds of treasure must be reported to a CORONER for the district in which they are found within 14 days of their discovery, or within 14 days of the finder realizing that the find might constitute treasure.   [JW]

treasure trove (obsolete) Originally, items made substantially of gold and silver, hidden by an unknown owner. Before 1996 such objects vested in the CROWN by prerogative RIGHT, irrespective of the ownership of the land on which the TREASURE was found. The narrow definition of 'treasure' meant that many valuable objects, or objects with archaeological, historical or cultural significance were not preserved by the state. These difficulties led to the modernization of the law in the Treasure Act 1996, which has redefined 'treasure' to ensure that a much wider category of finds now vest in the Crown. The Act also creates a SUMMARY OFFENCE of failing to report the discovery of treasure.   [HC & DR]

Treasury Counsel A group of BARRISTERS appointed by the ATTORNEY GENERAL to advise on and, if necessary, conduct prosecutions of important and complex cases at the CENTRAL CRIMINAL COURT and other London courts on behalf of the CROWN PROSECUTION SERVICE. There are six Senior Counsel (who, despite the name, are not Queen's Counsel) and ten Junior Counsel.   [AF]

Treasury Solicitor Legal adviser to the Treasury and certain other government departments who do not have their own solicitor. The Treasury Solicitor is the head of the Treasury Solicitor's Department and, in addition to advising the Treasury, also instructs parliamentary counsel on BILLS, and instructs counsel to appear on behalf of the CROWN on Treasury matters. He or she is also Her Majesty's Procurator-General (who acts for the Crown in the Prize Court) and acts as Queen's Proctor (representing the Crown in probate, matrimonial and admiralty cases). The office of Treasury Solicitor was combined with the Director of Public Prosecutions between 1883 and 1908.   [AF]

treaty An agreement that is concluded between two or more STATES in written form and is governed by international law. Treaties can be bilateral (between two states), or multilateral (between multiple states) and in all circumstances are legally binding between the contracting parties. Some common principles have been shaped under CUSTOMARY INTERNATIONAL LAW relating to the legal effects of treaties. The most fundamental are: (a) upon ratification or signature, whatever the case may be, a state is bound by the terms of the treaty; (b) treaties do not, as a general rule, produce legal effects for third states (i.e. non-parties); (c) states may, if the treaty so provides, append RESERVATIONS with regard to particular provisions of the treaty, but in all cases such reservations may not offend the object and purpose of the treaty; (d) obligations assumed under a treaty must be fulfilled in good faith; (e) a treaty does not override rules of *JUS COGENS*; (f) a state may avoid its obligations under a treaty where there has been a fundamental change of circumstances (*REBUS SIC STANTIBUS*) and in certain cases of *FORCE MAJEURE*. Treaties may also commonly be designated as a Protocol, Charter, Covenant or CONVENTION.

[IB]

Treaty of Amsterdam Signed in 1997, it amended the three-pillar structure of the EUROPEAN UNION (EU) that was created by the TREATY ON EUROPEAN UNION (TEU) of 1992. The Amsterdam Treaty renumbered the articles in both the TREATY OF ROME (EC Treaty) and the TEU. It also transferred a large part of Pillar III Justice and Home Affairs (JHA) to Pillar I EUROPEAN COMMUNITY (EC), creating a new Part IV governing visas, ASYLUM, immigration and the free movement of third country nationals within the EC. Also transferred was judicial cooperation in civil matters. What was left in Pillar III became known as Police and Judicial Cooperation in Criminal Matters (PJCCM). The Amsterdam Treaty also integrated the **Schengen** *acquis* into the EU, putting those parts of the Schengen *acquis* that fit with Part IV EC into the first pillar, and the balance into the new PJCCM. With continuing opt-outs being maintained by the UK and Ireland from the Schengen *acquis* in Pillar I, but with both countries subsequently opting into most of the PJCCM provisions, the Amsterdam Treaty added further complexity to the already complex structure of the EU. [MON]

See also SCHENGEN AGREEMENT; TREATY OF LISBON.

Treaty of Lisbon Signed and adopted by the EUROPEAN UNION (EU) countries on 13 December 2007, it takes the form of an amending treaty that will reform the existing TREATY ON EUROPEAN UNION and the EURO-PEAN COMMUNITY TREATY, changing the latter into the Treaty on the Functioning of the EU. The Lisbon Treaty is currently subject to national ratification procedures which began in 2008. However, the rejection of the treaty by Ireland on 12 June 2008 has created uncertainty in this regard. Effects of the treaty, if ratified, will include removing the existing three-pillar structure established in 1992; the EU will gain legal personality; the Charter of Fundamental Rights will become legally binding (although not part of the treaty itself); national parliaments will have increased power in terms of input on legislative proposals; the EU's voting system will be simplified through more qualified majority voting; and the single position of the High Representative for the Union in Foreign Affairs and Security Policy (subsuming the current two posts in charge of external relations, and foreign and security policy) will be created. The UK has negotiated certain opt-outs including the Charter of Fundamental Rights and in the area of Freedom, Security and Justice and ratified on 19 June 2008. Poland has negotiated an opt-out of the qualified majority voting amendments until 31 March 2017. [AF]

See also TREATY OF NICE.

Treaty of Nice One of the treaties establishing the legal framework of the EUROPEAN UNION (EU), signed in 2001 and in force in 2003. It amended the post-Amsterdam framework of the Common Foreign and Security Policy (Pillar II of the EU). In addition, it made a number of substantial amendments to the EUROPEAN COMMUNITY (Pillar I of the EU), including altering the relationship between the EUROPEAN COURT OF JUSTICE (ECJ) and the COURT OF FIRST INSTANCE (CFI). [MON]

See also COURT OF JUSTICE OF THE EUROPEAN COMMUNITIES; TREATY OF AMSTERDAM.

Treaty of Paris The legal basis for the EUROPEAN COAL AND STEEL COMMUNITY (ECSC) in 1951. The ECSC was the first community set up by the original six MEMBER STATES of **Euratom**, the atomic energy community, and the better known EUROPEAN ECONOMIC COMMUNITY (EEC), now known as the EURO-PEAN COMMUNITY (EC). The ECSC was set up for a fixed period of 50 years. That time has now expired, and the ECSC has ceased to exist, with the EC taking over any ongoing coal and steel issues.   [MON]

Treaty of Rome Otherwise known as the European Community Treaty (EC Treaty) and formerly known as the European Economic Community Treaty, it is the legal basis of the EUROPEAN COMMUNITY (EC). It was signed in 1957 and came into force in 1958. It forms the primary law of the EC, being interpreted in a quasi-constitutional mode by the EUROPEAN COURT OF JUSTICE, with the secondary legal instruments of REGULATIONS, DIRECTIVES and DECISIONS of the EC institutions being used to develop the EC legal framework, or *ACQUIS COMMUNAUTAIRE*.

The Treaty of Rome has been amended many times, most recently by the SINGLE EUROPEAN ACT 1986, the TREATY ON EUROPEAN UNION (TEU or Maastricht Treaty 1992), when the two other pillars of the EUROPEAN UNION were created, the TREATY OF AMSTERDAM 1997 and the TREATY OF NICE 2001. The TREATY of LISBON of 2007 substantially reforms the EC Treaty and the current Treaty on European Union.   [MON]

See also EUROPEAN ECONOMIC COMMUNITY.

Treaty of Union The treaty effecting the union of England and Scotland in 1707 to form Great Britain. Such a union between England and Scotland had been discussed following the Union of the Crowns in 1603 and again under Cromwell in the mid-17th century, but had come to nothing. By the beginning of the 18th century, however, a number of factors conspired to make the idea more attractive to both parties. Scotland was in a dire financial position following the failure of its colonial venture in Central America (the so-called Darien Scheme). England, at war with France, was keen to secure its northern border, not least because of the 'Auld Alliance' between Scotland and France.

The Treaty saw the end of both the Scottish and English Parliaments and the establishment of the Parliament of Great Britain at Westminster, with Scotland having 45 representatives in the Commons and 16 in the Lords. While the Scottish legal system was explicitly retained by the Treaty,

this was with the exception that English law relating to trade and taxation would apply in Scotland after the Union. Furthermore, the Treaty allowed that Scots law could be altered by the new Parliament, without restriction as regards public matters, but only 'for the evident utility of the subjects within Scotland' as regards private matters.

The Scottish courts were explicitly retained with the same authority and privileges as before the Union. No mention was made in the Treaty of the judicial role of the House of Lords, although within a few years it had assumed jurisdiction to hear appeals from the COURT OF SESSION, thus becoming the ultimate court of appeal for civil matters in Scotland.   [JP]

See also SCOTS LAW.

Treaty on European Union Two different documents currently hold the title 'Treaty on European Union'. Currently in force is the Treaty on European Union, otherwise known as the **Maastricht Treaty** 1992, which brought into force the three-pillar structure of the EUROPEAN UNION: Pillar I, EUROPEAN COMMUNITY, which has its own LEGAL CAPACITY; Pillar II, Common Foreign and Security Policy (CFSP); and Pillar III, originally known as Justice and Home Affairs (JHA). Since the TREATY OF AMSTERDAM 1997, which moved part of Justice and Home Affairs to Pillar I EC, and integrated the Schengen *acquis* (the body of law based on the SCHENGEN AGREEMENT) into the three-pillar structure of the EU, Pillar III is now known as Police and Judicial Co-operation in Criminal Matters (PJCCM).

The TREATY OF LISBON 2007 proposes amendments to the existing Treaty on European Union, including the establishment of a new EU as a one-pillar structure, encompassing all of the previous three pillars, as well as giving the EU legal capacity.   [MON]

trespass to the person Unlawful interference with the person through the TORTS of ASSAULT, BATTERY or FALSE IMPRISONMENT.   [HJ]

trial bundle A paginated set of court papers, witness statements and any other

documents to be relied on by a party at trial.
[JW]

trial _in absentia_ A criminal trial conducted in the absence of the defendant.

1. In English law the Crown Court has a
discretion at COMMON LAW to proceed in the
absence of a defendant, though it is 'to be
exercised with great caution and with close
regard to the overall fairness of the proceedings' (see _R_ v. _Jones (Anthony)_ [2003] 1 AC 1
at [6]). In the case of proceedings before the
magistrates' court, there is an express statutory power to hear trials in the defendant's
absence under the Magistrates' Courts Act
1980, s. 11. Guidance on trials _in absentia_ is
contained in the Consolidated Criminal
Practice Direction, paras. I.13.17 – I.13.19,
available at http:/www.justice.gov.uk/
criminal/procrules_fin/contents/practice_
direction/pd_consolidated.htm.

2. In international criminal law there is
no general rule prohibiting trials _in absen-
tia_, although they are likely to compromise
the ability of an accused to exercise his or
her rights to a FAIR TRIAL. The INTERNATIONAL
CRIMINAL COURT (Article 63) and the Yugoslav
(Article 21(4)) and Rwanda (Article 20(4)
(d)) tribunals all explicitly prohibit trials
in absentia. In some instances, however,
they are permissible under the ICC Statute,
particularly where an accused refuses to
appear for trial, or where he or she disrupts
the proceedings. [ALTC & IB]

See also INTERNATIONAL CRIMINAL TRIBUNAL FOR
RWANDA; INTERNATIONAL CRIMINAL TRIBUNAL FOR
THE FORMER YUGOSLAVIA.

trial on indictment The trial of a person
charged with an INDICTABLE OFFENCE which
takes place in the CROWN COURT before a
judge and JURY. [SN]

tribunal 1. In domestic law, a body established to settle disputes that fall outside the
jurisdiction of the regular UK courts; for
examples, see the ASYLUM AND IMMIGRATION TRI-
BUNAL, or EMPLOYMENT TRIBUNALS.

2. In international law, a term commonly (but not necessarily) used to
describe an international judicial body
such as the INTERNATIONAL TRIBUNAL FOR THE
LAW OF THE SEA or the INTERNATIONAL CRIMINAL
TRIBUNAL FOR RWANDA.

3. In evidence and procedure, (or 'trier')
a distinction is made between the tribunal
of fact and tribunal of law to emphasize
that the determination of questions of
fact and law are functionally distinct activities, and may even be exercised by different persons; for example, in serious
criminal trials it is the JURY that sits as the
tribunal of fact. [JW]

See also ADMINISTRATIVE TRIBUNAL; DOMESTIC
TRIBUNAL.

tribunal-appointed expert An assessor,
legal adviser or technical adviser who is
appointed by an ARBITRAL TRIBUNAL to report
to the tribunal and to the parties (often
with the prior right for the parties to provide input to the report), in the interests of
efficiency and costs. Such an appointment
is authorized expressly by the parties in
their ARBITRATION AGREEMENT or in institutional rules incorporated into the arbitration agreement, or is authorized by the _LEX
ARBITRI_ of the seat of arbitration. The general
duty of the arbitral tribunal requires it to
afford each party an opportunity to comment on any information and opinions
expressed in a report, and to examine the
expert if the expert gives evidence.

A separate issue arises in the event that an
arbitral tribunal appoints an expert to give
advice to the tribunal alone, for example on
the duties of the ARBITRATOR or some other
issue in the _lex arbitri_ of the seat. In so far as
private advice may be authorized, it must
not result in the expert taking any decision
in respect of the substantive and procedural
rights of the parties: that is the duty of the
arbitral tribunal. [RE]

See also ARBITRATION; INSTITUTIONAL ARBITRA-
TION.

tribunal of inquiry (obsolete) _See_ INQUIRY.

trier of fact The individual or body with
the responsibility for determining questions of fact in proceedings. Questions of
fact include questions relating to the cred-
ibility of WITNESSES, the weight to be
accorded to EVIDENCE, and whether the
FACTS IN ISSUE have been proved. [ALTC]

TRIPS Agreement The Agreement on Trade-Related Aspects of Intellectual Property Rights (TRIPS) is found in Annex 1C of the Marrakesh Agreement Establishing the WORLD TRADE ORGANIZATION (WTO). It is a multilateral agreement on intellectual property rights, and it follows and supplements the existing international principles on intellectual property found in prior agreements and conventions governed by the WORLD INTELLECTUAL PROPERTY ORGANIZATION (WIPO). The Agreement covers a broad range of intellectual property rights and seeks to harmonize three main areas: (a) standards – the Agreement sets out the minimum standards of protection to be provided by each WTO Member, including compliance with the main Conventions of the WIPO, and also adds a substantial number of additional obligations on matters where the pre-existing Conventions are silent or were inadequate; (b) enforcement – this is a major part of the TRIPS Agreement as no prior international intellectual property agreement or Convention provided for domestic procedures and remedies for the enforcement of intellectual property rights; the Agreement also sets out rules on civil and administrative procedures and remedies, provisional measures, special requirements related to border measures and criminal procedures, which specify, in a certain amount of detail, the procedures and remedies that must be available so that rights-holders can effectively enforce their rights; (c) dispute settlement – since the Agreement is part of the WTO legal system, disputes between Members in relation to the implementation and obligations of the TRIPS Agreement is subject to the WTO dispute settlement process.   [US]

trust A property-holding device which separates the management of property from its enjoyment. The trust arose from the ashes of the medieval USE and is generally regarded as equity's greatest contribution to contemporary jurisprudence, providing an extremely flexible tool used extensively both in commercial and social settings: from investment vehicles to family homes; corporate structures to mem-

bers' clubs; tax havens to charities. Under a trust, legal title is vested in a TRUSTEE who is subject to a mixture of personal and proprietary obligations arising from a fiduciary duty imposed by equity which ensures the trustee cannot benefit personally from the position. The trustee is consequently not the BENEFICIAL OWNER and is subject to obligations enforced either by beneficiaries, in whom the equitable title is vested under a private trust, or, in the case of a public trust, by the ATTORNEY GENERAL, who is empowered to enforce valid charitable purposes.

Trusts may be created expressly, impliedly or by operation of law. The settlor, who creates the trust, normally relinquishes all rights in the trust property unless he becomes a trustee or BENEFICIARY under the trust or retains some interest by, for example, expressly reserving a power of appointment. A trust may be declared orally apart from when the subject matter includes land, in which case the declaration must be evidenced by signed writing as required under the Law of Property Act 1925, s. 53 (1)(b).   [PK]

trust corporation The public trustee, along with corporations either appointed by the court to act as trustees or entitled to do so because they are incorporated as such in the UK, are trust corporations. A trust corporation may exercise all the powers that would otherwise require two trustees, such as overreaching the beneficial interests on a sale of land when purchase money is paid to the corporation.
                                                     [PK]

trust for sale An arrangement whereby TRUSTEES are under an obligation to sell property and hold the proceeds of sale on TRUST for a BENEFICIARY or beneficiaries.   [DR]

trust instrument A document, usually in the form of a deed, setting out the terms of a TRUST.   [PK]

trust power 1. A power in the nature of a trust is a POWER OF APPOINTMENT held by trustees and thus subject to their fiduciary duty. Despite the non-obligatory nature of powers, trustees are required to consider their exercise because of the FIDUCIARY nature of trusteeship. As a consequence, the distinction between trust powers and non-exhaustive discretionary trusts is, at best, slight (see DISCRETIONARY TRUSTS). Trust powers are often referred to as fiduciary powers, a term broad enough to cover any FIDUCIARY in whom a power of appointment is vested, in contrast to bare powers, held by non-fiduciaries, where the donee of the power is under no such obligation.

2. The term is sometimes used (often with the addition of a hyphen) to refer to a specialized form of discretionary trust in which the trustees hold on a fixed trust, subject to a power to prefer particular beneficiaries from within that class.

3. An old term for a discretionary trust, best avoided due to the possibility of confusion with the previous two meanings. [PK]

trust property *See* TRUST.

trust territory A territory where an administering authority (a STATE) has been appointed to oversee its development into a well-functioning independent state. The trusteeship system is a follow-up to the MANDATE system adopted in the aftermath of the Second World War. At the close of the Second World War, the victorious states allocated among themselves trust territories throughout the world and the UN CHARTER established a principal organ, the TRUSTEESHIP COUNCIL, to oversee the pragmatics of administration of trust territories. It should be noted that the administering authority did not possess SOVEREIGNTY over the territory. However, since the trust territory itself was not an independent state, and its inhabitants were not citizens of the administering power, they were technically stateless. This issue remained problematic until the end of the decolonization era. Now there are no more trust territories.

[IB]

See also COLONY.

trustee The person(s) in whom the legal title is vested under a TRUST. The trustee owes a FIDUCIARY duty to the beneficiaries and is not permitted to benefit personally under the trust, nor to allow any conflict to arise between his self-interest and his duties under the trust. It is, however, quite usual for the trust instrument to authorize the remuneration of trustees, while, in the absence of express entitlement, professional trustees have a right to be remunerated under the Trustee Act 2000, Part V. Trustees include both individuals and corporate bodies (a TRUST CORPORATION) as well as specialist forms of trustee, including judicial trustees, CUSTODIAN TRUSTEES and the public trustee. An intended trustee may refuse the office and once appointed can retire or be removed, but remains liable for acts committed during the trusteeship. The beneficiaries or the fellow trustees usually have the power to appoint new trustees, although the court has a residual right to do so. Trustees have a wide range of powers and duties emanating from EQUITY, STATUTE and, if one exists, the TRUST INSTRUMENT, including a duty to act impartially between beneficiaries and the power to advance money.   [PK]

trustee investments *See* AUTHORIZED INVESTMENTS.

trustee *de son tort* (Fr. by his own wrong) When someone who is not a TRUSTEE intermeddles with the TRUST, albeit innocently, he may be made liable for any loss as a trustee *de son tort*. Such persons are subject to the same FIDUCIARY obligations as the other trustees and treated in every respect as if they had been similarly appointed under the terms of the trust. Recent judicial pronouncements (e.g. *Dubai Aluminium Co. Ltd* v. *Salaam* [2003] 2 AC 366) have suggested that the term *de facto* trustee might be a more apposite description because liability is strict, and not dependent upon dishonesty.   [PK]

Trusteeship Council One of the six principal organs of the UNITED NATIONS. Its functions, scope and voting procedures are delineated by Chapter XIII of the UN CHARTER. The purpose of the Council was to oversee the administration of trust territories that existed at the end of the Second World War. With the end of colonization in the early 1970s and following the release of the last held trust territory, the island of Nauru in the South Pacific, the Council has been left without an object. Calls for its dissolution, or an alteration of its mandate, have been widespread. [IB]

See also COLONY.

Truth and Reconciliation Commission A commission of inquiry, sometimes also called a **Truth Commission**, created to investigate past HUMAN RIGHTS abuses, usually following a period of civil unrest or sometimes the peaceful transition to democratic government in a country. The Truth and Reconciliation Commission established by President Nelson Mandela in South Africa after the collapse of apartheid is often considered a model of its kind and, since then, commissions have been established in many parts of the world, including East Timor, Ghana, Peru and Sierra Leone. The aim of a commission is to find out the truth about past abuses in order to give some sense of closure to victims and the families of victims and to enable the society as a whole to move forward from these events. Perpetrators are normally offered immunity from prosecution if they give evidence before such commissions, and for this reason they are sometimes considered controversial. [JW]

See also RESTORATIVE JUSTICE; TRANSITIONAL JUSTICE.

Further reading: David Dyzenhaus, *Judging the Judges, Judging Ourselves: Truth, Reconciliation and the Apartheid Legal Order* (Oxford: Hart Publishing, 1998); Priscilla Hayner, *Unspeakable Truths: Facing the Challenge of Truth Commissions* (NewYork: Routledge, 2002).

TUPE Common abbreviation for the Transfer of Undertakings (Protection of Employment) Regulations 2006 (SI 2006/246), which replaced the 1981 Regulations of the same name. [MJ]

See also ACQUIRED RIGHTS; RELEVANT TRANSFER.

turbary A type of PROFIT À PRENDRE or RIGHT OF COMMON that entitles the owner of the right to cut turf or peat from another person's land. [DR]

TWOC *See* TAKING WITHOUT CONSENT.

typographical arrangement The style, composition, layout and general appearance of a page of a published work. COPYRIGHT in the typographical arrangement of a published edition rests with the publisher of the work under the Copyright, Designs and Patents Act 1988, ss. 9(2)(d) and 11. [US]

U

ubi jus, ibi remedium (Lat. where there is a right, there is a REMEDY) One of the MAXIMS OF EQUITY – reflecting the approach of equity that no wrong should be left without a CAUSE OF ACTION – and codified into medieval Chancery practice by the Statute of Westminster II (13 Edw. 1 c.24). Historically remedies were critical to the development of English law, since they provided the foundation for the development of rights of action before the courts. This is exemplified by *Ashby* v. *White* (1703) 92 ER 126 which emphasized the reciprocal nature of the relationship between rights and remedies, and, by building on the principle *ubi jus, ibi remedium,* developed a broad FORM OF ACTION, known as **action on the case**, which in turn was fundamental to the development of modern TORT law. [JW]

UBR *See* UNIFORM BUSINESS RATE.

udal law A system of land-holding found in Orkney and Shetland and derived from ancient Norse law. As an allodial form of land-holding (where land is owned outright without being subject to any superior interest), there were significant differences from the rest of Scotland where FEUDAL TENURE held sway until its abolition in 2000.

Among other differences between udal and feudal tenure are the possibility for a udal title to include ownership of the foreshore and (historically) the possibility for

ownership in udal land to pass without a written document. This latter difference was removed with the extension of the Land Register to Orkney and Shetland in 2003, meaning that full ownership in udal land can now only be obtained upon registration. [JP]

UK Intellectual Property Office The body responsible for the governance, policy and implementation of INTELLECTUAL PROPERTY rights in the UK. It is an executive agency of the Department for Business, Innovation and Skills. Its primary task is to grant PATENT, DESIGN and TRADE MARK rights in the UK. It is also responsible for formulating and delivering UK policy on all aspects of intellectual property, including COPYRIGHT law, and is involved in awareness-raising activities. It was formerly called the **Patent Office.** [US]

ulterior intent A requirement in certain crimes to intend to bring about a consequence beyond or behind the criminal act itself. 'Ulterior' thus means 'existing in the background'; for example, one of the offences under the Offences against the Person Act 1861, s. 18, is maliciously causing grievous bodily harm with intent to resist arrest. The MENS REA for grievous bodily harm is denoted by the term 'maliciously'. The *mens rea* for resisting arrest is intentionality, and is an example of an ulterior intent, in that it defines the background against which the causing of grievous bodily harm occurs.   [BF]

ultra vires (Lat. beyond the powers) Where the actions of a public or other body exceed their formal powers, those actions may be unlawful and therefore void. The *ultra vires* concept arises in a wide variety of contexts. Government ministers, local councils, civil servants, companies, charities and inferior courts are all constrained by the terms of their legal authority, which, if exceeded, may be challenged as *ultra vires*.

DELEGATED LEGISLATION in particular is subject to control by the judicial review process, whereby judges can declare a piece of delegated legislation to be *ultra vires* its enabling Act. *Ultra vires* in this context may take one of two forms. It may be **procedural** where the enabling Act sets out procedural rules to be followed and the body which has been given the delegated power has not followed them. Alternatively, the *ultra vires* may be **substantive**, where, on the proper interpretation of the enabling Act, the body to which powers have been delegated has stepped outside of its lawful authority.   [JW]

See also PREROGATIVE ORDERS.

umpire An additional, initially passive ARBITRATOR, whose jurisdiction to make decisions in ARBITRATION only takes effect where the initially active arbitrators (usually two in number) cannot reach agreement on a dispute submitted to arbitration. The umpire becomes active if the original arbitrators fail to reach agreement, at which stage the umpire acts as if appointed as sole arbitrator and the other appointed arbitrators become FUNCTUS OFFICIO.

Where the LEX ARBITRI of the seat of arbitration permits, and the parties agree, the umpire can adjudicate on separate issues rather than the whole claim. In this way, the original arbitrators remain active save in respect of the deadlocked issues, over which the umpire takes active jurisdiction.   [RE]

UN *See* UNITED NATIONS.

uncertainty of contract terms An agreement may be too uncertain if important terms have not been agreed upon or an essential term is too vague to be capable of enforcement. In such circumstances the parties' apparent agreement will be void for uncertainty of terms unless the court is able to fill the gaps; for example executed agreements where the court has evidence of the meaning to be attached to vague terms, or reasonable implications in accordance with statute such as a reasonable PRICE where the CONTRACT is silent on this matter and there is no contractual mechanism for fixing the price (Sale of Goods Act 1979, s. 8).   [JPL]

See also VOID CONTRACT.

UN Charter The Charter of the UNITED NATIONS was signed in San Francisco on 26 June 1945, at the conclusion of the United Nations Conference on International Organization, and came into force on 24 October 1945. It is the constituent treaty of the United Nations, and one of the constitutional texts of the INTERNATIONAL COURT OF JUSTICE, which was itself created by the Charter.   [IB]

UNCITRAL Arbitration Rules Procedural rules prepared under the auspices of the UNITED NATIONS (UN) Commission on International Trade Law (UNCITRAL) for the conduct of AD HOC ARBITRATION proceedings. They were adopted by the United Nations General Assembly on 15 December 1976 and are respected internationally, providing an influential benchmark for arbitration rules in general; and they are acceptable for most kinds of arbitration proceedings in most countries. They can be used in relation to almost every aspect of ARBITRATION: they provide rules ranging from the composition of the tribunal, to the conduct of arbitral proceedings, to the making of awards – but without denying the parties flexibility in determining the course of their proceedings.   [RE]

See also AWARD; UNCITRAL MODEL LAW.

UNCITRAL Model Law An international document, with no legally binding effect, which is intended to influence governments and STATE or national legislatures to harmonize their ARBITRATION laws with those of other states as regards international commercial arbitration. It is to be used as a precedent or guide to the provisions that might be included in new arbitration legislation for the state or COUNTRY concerned, and can be adopted or adapted as required.

The central goals of the document are to persuade national legislatures to increase party and tribunal autonomy by minimizing state intervention in the arbitral process (usually through the activities of the state's courts), while at the same time providing a means whereby arbitration proceedings (whether ad hoc or institutional) can be supported by the state's courts, and whereby the conduct of arbitrators and parties can be supervised when essential.

The Model Law was approved during 1985 by the UNITED NATIONS Commission on International Trade Law (UNCITRAL) and then approved by the United Nations General Assembly. Over 30 legal systems have incorporated the Model to a greater or lesser extent. Within the UK, Scotland has adopted the terms of the Model without material change. In England and Wales and Northern Ireland, the Model has been augmented to a substantial extent, while at the same time keeping to the logical order of the Model and retaining much of the wording found in the Model (see http://www.un.or.at/uncitral/).   [RE]

See also AD HOC ARBITRATION; INSTITUTIONAL ARBITRATION.

UNCLOS *See* UNITED NATIONS CONVENTION ON THE LAW OF THE SEA.

unconscionable bargain Also known as a 'catching bargain', it implies an agreement where the terms reflect an abuse of position or a taking advantage; for example a CONTRACT where the terms are grossly unfair to one party. The recognition of unconscionable bargains in English law stems from the cases of the expectant heirs (see *Earl of Aylesford* v. *Morris* (1873) 8 Ch App 484, in which the heir borrowed at excessive interest against a future inheritance but equity intervened to set aside the transaction and *Fry* v. *Lane* (1888) 40 ChD 312, in which there was found to be protection for

'poor and ignorant' persons who transferred property at an undervalue without INDEPENDENT ADVICE). The mere fact of inequality of bargaining power is insufficient to establish an unconscionable bargain; there must be 'morally reprehensible' conduct on the part of the stronger party or evidence of unfair advantage being taken of that weaker position.

[JPL]

underlease *See* SUBLEASE.

undertaking 1. A promise made in legal proceedings to do a certain act; for example, as a condition for obtaining an interim INJUNCTION, the applicant may be required to give an undertaking to the court to pay any DAMAGES which the respondent sustains as a result of the order and which the court considers the applicant should pay. Breach of an undertaking may be treated as a CONTEMPT OF COURT.

2. An enforceable promise made by a SOLICITOR on behalf of his or her client. **Solicitor's undertakings** are used in a number of contexts; for example, in CONVEYANCING transactions, provided the proceeds of sale are sufficient, the seller's solicitor will commonly give an undertaking to the buyer's solicitor to pay off the MORTGAGE on the seller's property on completion of the sale. This provides the buyer with an important guarantee that their purchase will be free of the mortgage. An undertaking may also be sought as an alternative to court enforcement proceedings by a creditor where a debtor owns property which is for sale and the proceeds of sale would extinguish the debt. A solicitor's undertaking, once given, is binding on the solicitor, who can be sued if the actions are not carried out. Breach of undertaking is also a disciplinary offence under the LAW SOCIETY's professional conduct rules.

3. Under COMMUNITY LAW, an undertaking is a business such as a sole trader, COMPANY or partnership. Agreements between undertakings or associations of undertakings 'which have as their object or effect the prevention, restriction or distortion of competition within the common market' are unlawful by virtue of Article 81 of the EUROPEAN COMMUNITY TREATY.   [JW]

undisclosed principal *See* AGENT.

undivided shares The equitable interest owned by a co-owner of land under a TENANCY IN COMMON. Traditionally, to create a tenancy in common, land was granted to two persons 'to own in undivided shares'. Although other terms are now normally used to create tenancies in common (e.g. 'to own in equal shares'), the phrase 'undivided' shares is used in the Law of Property Act 1925, ss. 1(6), 34, establishing the rule that tenancies in common can only be created in equity.   [DR]

undue influence EQUITY will set aside an agreement or transfer of property where it has resulted from the exercise of influence that prevented the transferor or donor from exercising independent judgement in relation to that transaction and which enabled an unfair advantage to be received by the transferee or donee. Undue influence may be actual ('overt acts of improper pressure or coercion such as unlawful threats') and so akin to DURESS. Alternatively, the undue influence may be presumed to arise from the type of relationship between the parties, or from their actual relationship of trust and confidence where the transaction itself is suspicious in the sense that it suggests the other would not have entered into it unless 'his will was overborne'. However, the court will not set aside a transaction for undue influence where it can be shown that it was in fact the product of the exercise of free will, for example following INDEPENDENT ADVICE (*Royal Bank of Scotland* v. *Etridge (No. 2)* [2002] 2 AC 773).   [JPL]

unenforceable In CONTRACT law, a contract or PROMISE is said to be unenforceable if it cannot be sued upon or relied upon before the courts.   [JPL]

unenforceable contract A CONTRACT which is valid but UNENFORCEABLE because of a formalities failure, i.e. contracts of guarantee which, contrary to the Statute of Frauds 1677, s. 4, are not evidenced in writing.   [JPL]

unenforceable promises PROMISES that cannot be enforced (sued upon before the courts); for example, because they are not supported by good CONSIDERATION.   [JPL]

unenforceable trust A private TRUST which is valid but unenforceable because it lacks beneficiaries with *LOCUS STANDI* to enforce its terms. Although such trusts would, for this very reason, normally be void for contravening the BENEFICIARY PRINCIPLE, there are a small group of anomalous PURPOSE TRUSTS exempt from that requirement. These private purpose trusts are, as a consequence, neither void nor enforceable and are sometimes referred to as **trusts of imperfect obligation** because the trustees' duties are not matched by a corresponding right vested in anyone to enforce those obligations.   [PK]

unfair competition A generic term used to describe commercial practices that are anti-competitive, and may therefore involve a breach of COMPETITION LAW, such as an abuse of a dominant position, an agreement or decision of a group of companies or a trade association that prevents, restricts or distorts competition, or unjustified state aid to enterprises, or breaches of fair trading laws.

In addition to regulating competitive behaviour in the marketplace, unfair competition laws play an important role in supplementing INTELLECTUAL PROPERTY protection. The Paris Convention for the Protection of Industrial Property (Article 10*bis*) requires its member countries to provide protection of industrial property against unfair competition, i.e. acts of competition that are contrary to honest practices in industry or commerce. The Paris Convention then lists the following as acts of unfair competition in relation to industrial property: (a) all acts of such a nature as to create confusion with the establishment, the goods or the industrial or commercial activities of a competitor; (b) false allegations in the course of trade of such a nature as to discredit the establishment, the goods or the industrial or commercial activities of a competitor; (c) indications or allegations, the use of which in the course of trade are liable to mislead the public as to the characteristics of certain goods.

In most European CIVIL LAW jurisdictions there is a general law of unfair competition. This is not the case in the UK. Such practices in English law are dealt with via the COMMON LAW torts of PASSING OFF and MALICIOUS FALSEHOOD. The TORT of passing off is not concerned with copying or slavish imitation and these acts, *per se*, are not considered unlawful outside the recognized intellectual property laws. There is no tort of copying nor a general tort of unfair competition (see *Hodgkinson & Corby Ltd and Roho Inc.* v. *Wards Mobility Services Ltd* [1995] FSR 169). [US]

unfair contract terms Statute may regulate certain provisions in CONTRACTS on the basis of unfairness. This applies to both EXEMPTION CLAUSES (Unfair Contract Terms Act (UCTA) 1977) and, in the consumer context, unfair terms more generally (Unfair Terms in Consumer Contracts Regulations (UTCCR) 1999). This regulation renders such clauses either totally UNENFORCEABLE by the party seeking to rely on the clause or unenforceable unless reasonable; for example, UCTA 1977, s. 2(1), provides that a party may not exclude or limit its liability in NEGLIGENCE for causing death or personal injury. A party may not exclude or limit its liability for breach of the IMPLIED TERMS as to description, SATISFACTORY QUALITY, fitness for purpose or correspondence with sample, as against a consumer (see s. 6(2)), but may do so against a non-consumer (s. 6(3)), as long as the clause is shown to be reasonable.

The UTCCR 1999 apply to contracts between consumer and business SELLERS or suppliers and state that an unfair term will not be binding on the consumer. A term is unfair where it has not been individually negotiated and, contrary to the requirements of good faith, causes a significant imbalance, to the detriment of the consumer, in the parties' rights and obligations under the contract. [JPL]

unfair dismissal The law of unfair dismissal was laid down in the Industrial Relations Act 1971 and is now found in the Employment Rights Act 1996. For a 'normal' unfair dismissal complaint, which is made to the EMPLOYMENT TRIBUNALS within three months of the EFFECTIVE DATE OF TERMINATION, the EMPLOYEE must prove that he or she is qualified to bring the claim (e.g. has one year's continuous employment) and has been dismissed. The BURDEN OF PROOF then moves to the EMPLOYER to prove that they had a potentially fair reason to dismiss (e.g. capability, conduct, REDUNDANCY, breach of a statutory obligation, or 'some other substantial reason'). The tribunal decides whether the dismissal was fair or unfair, taking into account the employer's size, administrative resources and equity, and the substantial merits of the case. If the employee wins, the tribunal may award one remedy: reinstatement, re-engagement or COMPENSATION. [MJ]

unfair relationship The court may make various orders under the Consumer Credit Act 1974, s. 140B in relation to a CONSUMER CREDIT AGREEMENT if it determines that the relationship between the creditor and the debtor arising out of the agreement is unfair to the debtor. A relationship will be unfair under s. 140A of the 1974 Act because of one or more of the following: the terms of the agreement or of any related agreement; the way in which the creditor has exercised or enforced any of his rights under the agreement or a related agreement; and/or any other thing done by, or on behalf of, the creditor. [JW]

unfavourable witness A WITNESS who fails to meet the expectations of the party calling him or her, or who gives EVIDENCE which is unfavourable to the case of that party. If this has occurred, the party calling the witness may not bring evidence specifically to discredit the witness, but may assent evidence which is inconsistent with or which contradicts the evidence given by this witness. [ALTC]

unfit to plead Unfit by reason of mental state to be tried for a criminal offence. A finding of unfitness to plead is not to be made 'except on the written or oral evidence of two or more registered medical practitioners at least one of whom is duly approved': see Criminal Procedure (Insanity) Act 1964, s. 4(6), as amended.   [ALTC]

uniform business rate A charge on non-domestic property at the same rate throughout the United Kingdom. It is a tax on business premises at a rate set by the Secretary of State for Environment, Transport and the Regions. Local government taxation was last reformed substantially in 1988, in the Local Government Finance Act of that year. The previous system of general rates was terminated and the business rate was introduced with effect from 1 April 1990.

Where the premises are shown in a local non-domestic rating list which is in force, the occupier (the ratepayer) is liable to pay the business rate for every day that he or she is in occupation of the premises (s. 43 of the 1988 Act). Rating lists for non-domestic premises are compiled by the VALUATION OFFICER for each local authority on 1 April each year. The list must also show the rateable value of the premises. See http://www.mybusinesslink.gov.uk.   [RE]

unilateral contract A CONTRACT that involves a PROMISE or undertaking to perform an act and a response whereby the act is performed, e.g. reward cases (*Carlill* v. *Carbolic Smoke Ball Co.* [1893] 1 QB 256). The promisee cannot accept by promising to perform the act in question, so that 'unilateral' refers to the fact that only one party makes a promise. The performance of the act is the CONSIDERATION to support the offeror's promise, so that until performance of the act only the promisor is bound.   [JPL]

See also ACCEPTANCE.

unilateral discharge In cases of performance or partial performance by one party, the CONTRACT (and the other's obligations under it) can be discharged only if that other party purchases a unilateral (one-sided) discharge by providing fresh CONSIDERATION, or if the parties enter into a deed of discharge.

This process is sometimes known as **accord and satisfaction**, i.e. the other's obligation to perform is released as a result of a

fresh agreement (accord) for which fresh consideration (satisfaction) is provided. For example, A owes B £100 for installing a radiator which is payable by 30 September. B has installed the radiator in A's home, when on 28 September B agrees to accept £80 in full satisfaction and to release A from the previous obligation to pay the £20 balance.   [JPL]

See also BILATERAL DISCHARGE.

unilateral mistake Where one party to the CONTRACT acts on the basis of misunderstanding and the other knows or ought to have known that a MISTAKE was being made. Such a mistake will render the contract void only where it relates to a fundamental mistake, such as the subject matter of the contract, as opposed to some quality attaching to it (*Smith* v. *Hughes* (1871) LR 6 QB 597). There must be an absence of a coinciding OFFER and ACCEPTANCE due to the mistake. (In *Shogun Finance Ltd* v. *Hudson* [2003] UKHL 62, [2004] 1 AC 919, a mistake as to identity was made where the offer was actually made to a different person and so could not be accepted by the impostor.)   [JPL]

unincorporated association A body that lacks an independent legal personality in which the membership come together for a common purpose with an identifiable constitution or rules (which may be written or oral). An unincorporated association is easily set up and is often used for social purposes. There is nothing to prohibit its use for trading, though the inability of the association to own property in its own right can be problematic. For tax purposes it is potentially liable to CORPORATION TAX. Unlike a CORPORATION, an unincorporated association enjoys no rights or duties independently of its individual members, who must therefore carry the full risk of personal liability. If an unincorporated association has charitable objects (or aims), it can apply to the CHARITY COMMISSION for charitable status.   [JW]

union membership agreement (obsolete) This was a form of **closed shop** which was abolished in 1990.   [MJ]

See CLOSED SHOP AGREEMENT.

unit trust A TRUST which enables small investors to acquire interests in a range of companies and other investments and thereby spread their risk. The shares and investments are held by custodian trustees to the order of the managing trustee on behalf of the investors who acquire a share in the beneficial interest in proportion to their contribution.   [PK]

unitary authority A single-tier LOCAL AUTHORITY that is responsible for all local government functions within its geographical area. When COUNTY COUNCILS were first established in 1889, a type of metropolitan unitary authority was created, called a county borough, which was independent of county council administration. In 1974, county boroughs were abolished and a two-tier system of county and DISTRICT COUNCILS was introduced. By the early 1990s it was clear that the two-tier system itself was unduly complex, and in some places inefficient. Powers were therefore introduced to construct new unitary authorities, though their introduction has been gradual and incomplete in England, so that there remains a mixture of unitary and two-tier local government across the country. Both Wales and Scotland operate de facto unitary systems.   [JW]

United Nations (UN) An international organization that was founded in 1945 in the aftermath of the Second World War. The UN enjoys powers conferred on it by its founding treaty, the UN CHARTER, as well as 'implied powers' on the basis of its assigned functions. It consists of the following principal organs: the General Assembly, SECURITY COUNCIL, Secretariat of the Secretary General, ECONOMIC AND SOCIAL COUNCIL, the TRUSTEESHIP COUNCIL and the INTERNATIONAL COURT OF JUSTICE. Its membership extends to all peace-loving countries and is currently almost universal. Its most significant organ is the Security Council, whose resolutions are binding on all MEMBER STATES. The resolutions of all other organs do not have a binding effect – except in so far as they relate to the internal workings of the UN, such as its budget – but some resolutions adopted by the General Assembly have crystallized into CUSTOMARY INTERNATIONAL LAW. The principal organs of the UN may establish subsidiary bodies commensurate with their powers. A key aspect of the United Nations relates to Article 103 of its Charter, according to which the obligations under the Charter always take precedence whenever there is a conflict between an obligation assumed under the UN Charter and another treaty. This renders the UN Charter as a kind of constitutional instrument.   [IB]

United Nations Convention on the Law of the Sea (UNCLOS) Adopted in 1982, this TREATY is in large part premised on its three 1958 predecessor conventions and on CUSTOMARY INTERNATIONAL LAW. It deals comprehensively with all matters relating to the law of the sea, including topics such as the protection of the marine environment. It established an international judicial organ, the LAW OF THE SEA tribunal, dealing with disputes arising from the application of the Convention. Not all sea matters are dealt with exclusively or exhaustively by UNCLOS; for example, a few states have found it politically expedient to disagree on the scope of the CONTINENTAL SHELF and so decided to remain outside the ambit of UNCLOS altogether.   [IB]

See also INTERNATIONAL SEA-BED AUTHORITY.

unity of personality *See* COVERTURE.

unity of seisin Ownership of two different plots of LAND becomes united in one owner. It operates to extinguish rights which one of the plots had over the other. The most common example is of an EASEMENT, the burden of which affected one of the plots and benefited the other.   [HC & DR]

Universal Declaration of Human Rights (UDHR) Adopted in 1948 by the General Assembly of the UNITED NATIONS in the form of a resolution. The resolutions of the General Assembly are not legally binding and thus the UDHR has no binding force. None the less, the rights contained therein are now considered to have crystallized into CUSTOMARY INTERNATIONAL LAW and some of them into *JUS COGENS* (such as the right to life, freedom from torture and others). The adoption of the UDHR was meant to stimulate interest in the matter of human rights and to serve as a 'standard-setting' mechanism so that a second generation of rights could in the future be adopted. In this sense, the UDHR is the predecessor of the 1966 INTERNATIONAL COVENANT ON CIVIL AND POLITICAL RIGHTS and the COVENANT ON ECONOMIC, SOCIAL AND CULTURAL RIGHTS. A significant difference in premise in contrast with these covenants is that the UDHR was formulated around NATURAL LAW notions (see Article 1). Despite the fact that the UDHR has acquired customary recognition, at the time of its adoption the membership of the General Assembly was significantly smaller than its current composition and some developing countries claim that its values are reflective of Western civilization; for example, Saudi Arabia refused at the time to accept the right of freedom of religion. [IB]

universal jurisdiction A controversial concept in INTERNATIONAL LAW whereby states claim criminal jurisdiction over persons whose alleged crimes were committed outside the boundaries of the prosecuting STATE. It is also referred to as the **universality principle**. Jurisdiction is thus claimed solely on the basis of the serious nature of the crime under international law, without regard to where it was committed, the nationality of the alleged perpetrator, or of the victim. A serious crime for this purpose might include CRIMES AGAINST PEACE, CRIMES AGAINST HUMANITY, WAR CRIMES, GENOCIDE, and TORTURE.

The issue came to prominence with Belgium's introduction of a law of universal jurisdiction in 1993. This was repealed in 2003 following *Democratic Republic of the Congo* v. *Belgium*, a case before the INTERNATIONAL COURT OF JUSTICE, which held that the issue of an arrest warrant under Belgian law against the Congolese Minister of Foreign Affairs failed to respect his ministerial immunity from criminal jurisdiction. It was alleged by a number of human rights groups at the time that pressure from the US government had also played a part in the Belgian government's decision to repeal its law.

The creation of the INTERNATIONAL CRIMINAL COURT (ICC) in 2002 has, in the eyes of some commentators, reduced the case for domestic universal jurisdiction laws, although the ICC does not have jurisdiction over crimes committed before 2002. [IB]

universality principle *See* UNIVERSAL JURISDICTION.

unjust enrichment The law of RESTITUTION allows the recovery of gains where one party has been unjustly enriched at the expense of the other. This is sometimes referred to as 'quasi-contract', although less so of late since the obligation to make restitution may arise independently of any CONTRACT. For example, money may have been paid under a VOID CONTRACT, or services may have been supplied under the mistaken belief that there was an obligation to do so. In both cases, the recipient would be unjustly enriched if permitted to keep the money or benefit without having to pay for it. Therefore, the money paid may be recovered or a reasonable sum payable for services on the basis of a *QUANTUM MERUIT*. [JPL]

unlawful possession of drugs Under the Misuse of Drugs Act 1971, s. 5, it is an offence to unlawfully possess a controlled drug; it is also an offence to possess a controlled drug, unlawfully or lawfully, with intent to supply it to another. A person 'possesses' a controlled drug when it is in their physical control or custody, and they know that it is in their control or custody. Under s. 28 of the 1971 Act, it can be a defence for a person to raise evidence that they did not believe, suspect, or have reason to suspect that the substance was a controlled drug. [BF]

See also CANNABIS.

unlawful sexual intercourse (obsolete) There were two offences of unlawful sexual intercourse under the Sexual Offences Act 1956, ss. 5 and 6. The behaviours countenanced by these offences are now covered by various provisions of the Sexual Offences Act 2003. [BF]

See also AGE OF CONSENT; RAPE; SEXUAL ASSAULT.

unlawful trust *See* VOID TRUST.

unlawful wounding There are two principal statutory provisions dealing with unlawful wounding, namely the Offences against the Person Act 1861, s. 18, which sets out a number of offences of WOUNDING WITH INTENT, and s. 20 of the same Act, which contains the offence of MALICIOUS WOUNDING.

[BF]

See also WOUND.

unless order An order of the court, also called a **peremptory order**, directing a party to perform some step in proceedings or comply with the directions in the order, and specifying the consequences of default (see CIVIL PROCEDURE RULES, Rule 3.1(3)). [JW]

unlimited company *See* COMPANY.

unmarried parents PARENTS of a CHILD who are not, and have never been, married to each other. All mothers, whether married or not, have automatic PARENTAL RESPONSIBILITY for their children. Only fathers who were married to the mother at the time of birth, or who subsequently marry her or register themselves as the father automatically acquire parental responsibility. Otherwise they have to acquire it through mechanisms such as ADOPTION or under the Children Act 1989, s. 4. [FK]

See also FATHER'S RIGHTS; LEGITIMACY; LEGITIMATION.

unreasonable behaviour The colloquial term for one of the facts which may establish the IRRETRIEVABLE BREAKDOWN of a MARRIAGE or CIVIL PARTNERSHIP. The actual phrase is that the 'respondent has behaved in such a way that the petitioner [or applicant] cannot reasonably be expected to live with the respondent' (see Matrimonial Causes Act 1973, s. 1(2)(b)). It is, therefore, the expectation of continued COHABITATION which must be proved to be unreasonable, rather than the respondent's behaviour. The test is both objective in that the court must be satisfied that the petitioner or applicant cannot reasonably be expected to live with the respondent; and subjective in that the court will look at the effect of the behaviour on the particular applicant or petitioner. [AD]

unregistered company A body which is incorporated but not required to register. Certain foreign companies operating in the UK, or companies created by private statute or royal charter may be unregistered. Unregistered companies are governed by a number of specific provisions in the Companies Act 2006 and subsequent regulations. Special rules also apply to the winding-up of an unregistered company.

[JW]

unregistered design right A DESIGN can be protected by an unregistered design right. The UK right differs considerably from the unregistered COMMUNITY DESIGN RIGHT.

The UK unregistered design right is a hybrid intellectual property right which was introduced to fulfil a perceived need for an automatic, short-term, quasi-copyright protection for both functional and non-functional three-dimensional designs. The right is available for any 'design of any aspect of the shape or configuration whether internal or external of the whole or part of an article' (see Copyright, Designs and Patents Act 1988, s. 213). The design must be original, in the sense that it is not commonplace in the design field in question at the time of its creation (see *Farmer Build Ltd* v. *Carier Bulk Materials Handling Ltd and others* [1998] EWCA Civ 1900).

There are no formalities, and the unregistered design right comes into being automatically as soon as an original design is recorded in a design document or an article is made to such a design. The term of protection is 15 years from the end of the calendar year in which a design was first recorded or an article was made to the design. The owner of a national unregistered design right has the exclusive right to reproduce the design for commercial purposes by making articles to the design or making a design document for the pur-

pose of enabling such articles to be made.
[US]

See also ARTISTIC WORK; DESIGN; ORIGINALITY; REGISTERED DESIGN.

unregistered land Land, the title to which is not registered at the Land Registry. Less than 10% of the land in England and Wales remains unregistered, due to the requirement of compulsory registration on almost all transfers of FREEHOLD or LEASE-HOLD estates for a term of more than seven years. Proof of TITLE to land in the unregistered system is based on the production of TITLE DEEDS, an ABSTRACT OF TITLE, or an EPITOME OF TITLE and is notoriously complex and uncertain, compared to the relatively simple system of REGISTERED LAND. [DR]

unsworn evidence In criminal proceedings, a person who is under the age of 14, or who does not have 'a sufficient appreciation of the solemnity of the occasion and of the particular responsibility to tell the truth which is involved in taking an OATH', may not be sworn: see Youth Justice and Criminal Evidence Act 1999, s. 55(2). A person of whatever age who is competent to testify but may not be sworn is to give unsworn EVIDENCE, which has the same effect as SWORN EVIDENCE: see s. 56. In civil cases, a child (defined as someone under the age of 18) who understands the nature of an oath must give sworn evidence, but a child who does not understand the nature of an oath may give unsworn evidence if 'he understands that it is his duty to speak the truth' and 'has sufficient understanding to justify his evidence being heard': see Children Act 1989, s. 96(2).
[ALTC]

unsworn statement (obsolete) A statement made by an accused person not under oath from the DOCK; this was also known colloquially as a 'dock statement'. The right to make an unsworn statement was abolished by the Criminal Justice Act 1982. [SN]

use A forerunner of the TRUST, uses were a product of the COURT OF CHANCERY and enabled land to be conveyed to a legal owner for the use of another to overcome the restrictions placed on the legal ownership of land by the medieval COMMON LAW. The use's flexibility was soon employed to avoid the royal fees, called feudal incidents, that were associated with legal ownership and consequently deprived the Crown of much of its feudal revenue. In response, a cash-strapped Henry VIII passed the Statute of Uses 1535, which executed the use by converting the person on whose behalf the land was held into the legal owner, and thus still subject to these incidents. Against a backdrop of disquiet about what was described as Henry VIII's 'fiscal feudalism', the statute was easily overcome, by the device of a use upon a use, with Chancery declaring that the statute only executed the first and not the second use. Thus a legal conveyance of land to A, to the use of B, to the use of C resulted in B holding the legal title to the use of C, whose use was therefore still not subject to the restrictions and feudal incidents of legal ownership. It was this second use that, over the next couple of centuries, developed into what we today recognize as the trust. [PK]

use classes Generally speaking, a material change in the use of buildings or land constitutes development and requires PLANNING PERMISSION (Town and Country Planning Act 1990 (TCPA 1990), s. 55(1)). However, where a change in the use of land falls within the same specified class of use, it will not be taken to constitute DEVELOPMENT (TCPA 1990, s. 55(2)(f)). The different use classes are specified in the Town and Country Planning (Use Classes) Order 1987, (SI 1987/764), as amended.

Part A covers shopping area uses, including shops (A1), financial and professional services (A2), restaurants and cafés (A3), drinking establishments (A4) and hot food takeaways (A5). Part B covers other business and industrial uses, including business use (B1), general industrial (B2), special industrial groups (B3 to B7) and storage and distribution (B8). Part C covers residential uses, including hotels (C1), residential institutions (C2) and dwelling-houses (C3). Part D covers social and community uses of a non-residential kind, including non-residential institutions (D1) and assembly and leisure (D2).

Changes of use within a category do not constitute development. Furthermore, certain changes of use from one class to another are specified in the 1987 Order not to constitute development, for example changes from financial and professional services (A2) to shops (A1). Some classes of use are specifically listed as being outside the scope of the Order, for example use as a theatre, use for the sale of fuel or motor vehicles, or use as a casino. [DR]

use of force The employment of armed force between states. Its regulation is governed by CUSTOMARY INTERNATIONAL LAW and the UN CHARTER. Article 2(4) of the UN Charter prohibits any use of armed force, even the slightest. In order for the armed force to be illegal under Article 2(4) it is not necessary that it actually violates the territorial integrity or political independence of the victim STATE. Where a state is a victim of armed force that does not amount to an 'armed attack', it does not have the right to respond with armed force in self-defence. Rather, its only response is to claim compensation. Self-defence can only arise under Article 51 of the Charter where the force employed by the aggressor amounts to an armed attack. The UN Charter does not define what amounts to an armed attack, though the INTERNATIONAL COURT OF JUSTICE (ICJ) has held that an armed attack consists of a very significant use of armed force calculated on a scale and effects basis. More recently, however, the ICJ in the *Oil Platforms* case (*Islamic Republic of Iran* v. *USA* (1994) 94 ILR 478) seems to have decreased the gravity of the 'armed attack concept', by stating that even an attack against a warship can trigger the right of self-defence.

The SECURITY COUNCIL may, under Article 42 of the UN Charter, authorize the use of armed force. Such an authorization may not be made by any other regional organization (UN Charter Article 53). [IB]

See also COLLECTIVE SECURITY; WAR.

user The use or enjoyment of property; see

Oxfordshire County Council v. *Oxford City Council and another* [2006] UKHL 25 ('a right may be created by prescriptive user of the land'). [HC & DR]

usual authority *See* AGENCY.

usual covenants A phrase used to describe covenants which will be implied into any LEASE where it is preceded by a contractual agreement. The usual covenants always include the following: the tenant will pay rent; the tenant will pay his taxes and rates; the tenant will keep and deliver up the premises in repair; the tenant will allow the landlord to enter the property and view the state of repair; the landlord will allow the tenant quiet enjoyment and will not derogate from his grant; and the landlord will have a right to re-enter should the tenant fail to pay his rent.

This list is not exhaustive and the courts may find more covenants to be usual, depending on the particular circumstances in each case. [DR]

See also COVENANT.

uti possidetis (Lat. as you possess) Historically a principle in INTERNATIONAL LAW that territory remains with the STATE in possession at the end of a conflict, unless otherwise provided for by TREATY. Latterly it has been adopted as a principle of boundary demarcation for newly independent states. Its contemporary formulation, primarily in the African decolonization context, was premised on drawing (sometimes straight) lines along the former colonial divides on the basis that this was a good and equitable policy that would avoid friction. The sanctity of such boundaries was confirmed by the INTERNATIONAL COURT OF JUSTICE in the *Temple* case (*Cambodia* v. *Thailand*) [1962] ICJ Rep. 26 and by other international ARBITRAL TRIBUNALS (e.g. the *Rann of Kutch Arbitration* (*India* v. *Pakistan*) (1968) 50 ILR 2). The same principle was also employed after the break-up of the former Yugoslavia (Opinions No. 2 and 3 of the Badinter Arbitration Commission), on the basis of the internal administrative boundaries of the Yugoslav republics, and in the case of the USSR, on the basis of formal agreement

between Russia and the seceding republics.
[IB]

utilitarianism An approach to the problem of JUSTICE which proceeds from the moral premise that happiness (or some other good) should be maximized.

As discussed by lawyers, it is most associated with the work of JEREMY BENTHAM, whose version of utilitarianism is built on his observation that men and women are essentially in thrall to the dual masters, pleasure and pain.

Utilitarianism is a **teleological** or **consequentialist** approach to justice insofar as something is judged to be right or wrong on the basis of the consequences that ensue (as opposed to a **deontological** approach, which stipulates that certain things are right or wrong irrespective of the consequences).

Two broad versions of utilitarianism may be distinguished. **Act utilitarianism** focuses its attention on the consequences of individual actions: if they are good, then the action is good. **Rule utilitarianism** considers what the consequences would be if the rule was that everyone should act in the way in question in similar circumstances: thus, even if the consequences of the action in the immediate case were good, rule utilitarianism would disallow the action if the answer to its question indicated that the consequences of a general rule in such terms would be bad.

Despite its superficial appeal, utilitarianism is the subject of trenchant criticism from those such as JOHN RAWLS who adopt a deontological approach to the problem of justice. Among their concerns are: utilitarianism's apparent treatment of individuals merely as means to the ends of others rather than as ends in themselves; its apparent indifference to the question of how happiness (or some other good) is distributed, provided it is maximized; and the difficulty that exists in actually measuring happiness (or some other good). As a consequence, utilitarianism is less influential today than it was (especially in the 19th century), although it exists as a foundation for the modern movement known as the ECONOMIC ANALYSIS OF LAW.   [JP]

Further reading: J.J.C. Smart and Bernard Williams, *Utilitarianism: For and Against* (Cambridge: Cambridge University Press, 1973); John Rawls, *A Theory of Justice*, revised edn (Harvard, MA: Harvard University Press, 2005).

utility model Where technical designs cannot fulfil the strict PATENT criteria, protection is still available in some countries under either utility model or PETTY PATENT laws. However, there is no utility model law in the UK at the present time. This form of protection is available in the majority of EU MEMBER STATES, but the terms and conditions of protection vary markedly as there is no harmonized position on this area within the EUROPEAN UNION. Utility model or petty patent protection differs from that afforded under patent laws in that the conditions of protection are less onerous and protection can usually be obtained rapidly and cheaply.   [US]

See also UNREGISTERED DESIGN RIGHT.

Further reading: Uma Suthersanen, Graham Dutfield and Kit Boey Chow, *Innovation without Patents* (Cheltenham: Edward Elgar, 2007).

utter barrister (largely obsolete) The proper term for the degree of BARRISTER, it was derived from 'outer' or 'ouster' barrister as these lawyers (unlike King's or Queen's Counsel) were historically obliged to plead from outside or 'without' the bar that traditionally separated the judges from the floor of the court.   [JW]

V

vacant possession The obligation generally inserted into a contract of sale or LEASE that a VENDOR or a TENANT leave a property empty of goods and occupiers at the time of completion of the transaction or termination of the lease. [HC & DR]

vacated trial Where, prior to the trial, a request to give up the trial date is granted. A further listing for trial may or may not be required and the court time vacated may or may not be filled with another case. [SN]

valuable consideration In order to be an enforceable (good) CONSIDERATION to support a PROMISE, whatever is relied upon as the act, forbearance or promise must have some value in the eyes of the law, although the law is not concerned whether the value is adequate and does not interfere with the fairness of the parties' bargain. Consideration will only have value in the eyes of the law if it is capable of expression in economic terms. It follows that sentimental or other motives for promises are not a valuable consideration (*Thomas* v. *Thomas* (1842) 2 QB 851), nor is refraining from certain types of conduct which there was no right to engage in (*White* v. *Bluett* (1853) 23 LJ Ex 36). [JPL]

valuation officer One who values property for the purposes of business rating and COUNCIL TAX valuation in England and Wales, and compiles and maintains a rating list under a statutory duty imposed by the Local Government Finance Act 1988. Valuation officers work within the Valuation Office Agency (VOA), an executive agency of HM REVENUE AND CUSTOMS. [JW]

See also UNIFORM BUSINESS RATE.

value If a purchaser has acquired property 'for value', it means that VALUABLE CONSIDERATION has been supplied; however, that value need not be equivalent to the value transferred. For the purposes of becoming a 'holder for value' of a BILL OF EXCHANGE under the Bills of Exchange Act 1882, s. 27, 'valuable consideration' is defined as (a) any CONSIDERATION sufficient to support a simple CONTRACT and (b) any antecedent debt or liability, i.e. where a cheque is written to pay for goods or services already supplied. [JPL]

van Bynkershoek, Cornelius (1673–1743) A Dutch international jurist. He is best known for his contribution to the LAW OF THE SEA, particularly through his 1702 book, entitled *De Domino Maris* ('Of the Dominion of the Sea'; not to be confused with John Selden's *Mare Clausum,* which was translated into English in 1652 under the same title). Van Bynkershoek advocated a general right of navigation, trade and fishing on the high seas and examined the modalities of coastal state jurisdiction. He argued that in analogy to ownership over physical objects, which can only take place once the object is in the possession of a person, ownership of the sea, or part thereof, is only possible where a maritime area may be controlled from the adjacent land territory. He therefore advocated 'command and possession' in relation to the TERRITORIAL WATERS, setting as a suitable measurement the CANNON-SHOT RULE, although he did not actually create that rule in his writings.   [IB]

variation of contract A binding alteration of the original CONTRACT terms, i.e. an alteration that is supported by CONSIDERATION. This can be achieved by bilateral discharge or mutual release, by which each party supplies consideration for the other's PROMISE to release it from its existing obligations under an executory contract and replace it with the agreement on the new terms (release and replacement); or by accord and satisfaction (i.e. agreement and fresh consideration), where one party has performed its existing obligations and agrees to release the other from its obligations or to amend the other's contractual obligation in exchange for some fresh consideration, such as payment of a sum of money or some other fresh concession.   [JPL]

variation of trust A TRUSTEE is usually required to carry out the exact terms of the trust, and can be sued by the beneficiaries if he fails to do so. However, there are circumstances in which the court can sanction a variation of the terms, both under the inherent jurisdiction of the court and by STATUTE, most notably the Variation of Trusts Act 1958. This Act gives the court a wide discretion to vary the trust terms, provided, normally, this is in the interests of the beneficiaries.   [PK]

vehicle *See* CARRIAGE; MOTOR VEHICLE.

vendor The seller of property.   [DR]
See also PURCHASER.

venereal disease The intentional or reckless transmission of venereal disease to an unknowing sexual partner may constitute an offence of causing GRIEVOUS BODILY HARM

with intent under the Offences against the Person Act 1861, s. 18; or malicious infliction of grievous bodily harm under s. 20 of the same Act (see *R* v. *Dica* [2004] EWCA Crim 1103). It is none the less possible for a sexual partner to consent to the risk of contracting such a disease, thereby precluding liability, at least for the offence under s. 20 (see *R* v. *Konzani* [2005] EWCA Crim 706).   [BF]
See also CONSENT TO HARM.

venire de novo (Lat. to come anew) An order annulling the original trial and directing a new trial, after a mistrial involving a fundamental irregularity.   [SN]
See also RETRIAL.

Venne criteria Guidelines used for assigning cases in the magistrates' court, deriving from the recommendations of the Venne Committee's report, *The Role of the Stipendiary Magistrate* (Lord Chancellor's Department, 1996).   [SN]

verdict A finding of guilty or not guilty. A not guilty verdict means that the prosecution has failed to prove that the defendant committed the offence. JURY verdicts must be unanimous unless the judge allows a **majority verdict**. Under the Juries Act 1974, s. 17, a majority verdict cannot be accepted until the jury has deliberated for at least two hours, or such longer period as the judge sees fit, depending on the complexity of the case. A judge may accept the following majorities: from a jury of 12, a majority of 11–1 or 10–2; from a jury of 11, 10–1 and from a jury of 10, 9–1. A jury of 9 must return a unanimous verdict. MAGISTRATES' verdicts may be by majority.   [SN]

vested in interest A phrase used to signify that an INTEREST IN LAND is a right of future possession of an estate; for example, if X grants a LIFE INTEREST to Y, REMAINDER to Z, Z's interest is said to be vested in interest. Although Y has a current right of enjoyment of the estate, VESTED IN POSSESSION, Z's remainder is a right of future enjoyment.   [DR]

vested in possession A phrase used to

signify that an INTEREST IN LAND is an interest in possession, i.e. that there is a present right of enjoyment of the land; for example, if X grants a LIFE INTEREST to Y, vested in possession, Y has the right to live on that land for his lifetime. This may be contrasted with an interest in land that is VESTED IN INTEREST, which is a right to a future interest in possession.

[DR]

vested remainder *See* REMAINDER.

vesting assent Under the Settled Land Act 1925, the instrument whereby a personal representative, after the death of a TENANT FOR LIFE or a STATUTORY OWNER, vests settled land in a person entitled as tenant for life or statutory owner.

For example, X creates a succession of LIFE INTERESTS under a Settled Land Act SETTLE-MENT, to himself for his life, then to his wife Y for her life, REMAINDER to Y's children. When X dies, his personal representatives will execute a vesting assent, vesting the land in Y as the tenant for life. [DR]

See also VESTING DEED.

vesting declaration A statement in a DEED appointing new TRUSTEES in whom the trust property is to vest. [PK]

vesting deed One of two documents required by the Settled Land Act 1925 (SLA 1925) for the valid creation of a SETTLE-MENT made by one living person to another. The other document required is a trust instrument.

Under the SLA 1925, a **principal vesting deed** conveys the LEGAL ESTATE in the land to the TENANT FOR LIFE, or, if there is no tenant for life, to the STATUTORY OWNER. If the tenant for life is already the legal owner, it declares by way of confirmation that he is the legal owner. A principal vesting deed must contain the following: (a) a description, either specific or general, of the settled land; (b) a statement that the settled land is vested in the person or persons to whom it is conveyed or in whom it is declared to be vested, upon the trusts affecting the land; (c) the names of the trustees of the settlement; (d) any further powers conferred by the trust instrument, in addition to those available

to a tenant for life under the SLA 1925; and (e) the name of any person entitled to appoint new trustees (SLA 1925, s. 5(1)).

If additional land is later acquired using capital money arising out of the settlement, such land must be conveyed to the tenant for life using a **subsidiary vesting deed** (SLA 1925, s. 10). [DR]

See also CURTAIN PRINCIPLE; VESTING ASSENT; VESTING ORDER.

vesting order Under the Settled Land Act 1925 (SLA 1925), a court order having the same form and effect as a VESTING DEED or a VESTING ASSENT. A vesting order may be applied for where: any person who is bound under the SLA 1925 to execute a conveyance, vesting deed or vesting assent fails to do so within one month of a written demand to do so; any such person is outside the United Kingdom, or cannot be found, or it is not known whether he is alive or dead; or for any reason the court is satisfied that the conveyance, vesting deed or vesting assent cannot be executed, or cannot be executed without undue delay or expense.

[DR]

veto An express voting power granted to a STATE in the context of decision-making procedures established by a TREATY. The veto is a negative power, in the sense that, if exercised by a party, it serves to oppose the matter that is proposed. In the UN CHARTER, for example, the permanent members of the SECURITY COUNCIL may exercise their veto power in order to block the adoption of a resolution, since the adoption of resolutions by the Council requires the positive votes of all five permanent members. In the General Assembly, on the other hand, a state may offer a negative vote on a proposed resolution, but since Assembly resolutions are not binding, the negative vote does not have a legal effect for the resolution but serves only as a unilateral act. In the EUROPEAN COMMUNITIES and the EUROPEAN UNION, the right of effective veto has been conferred on state parties on important matters, such as the admission of new MEMBER STATES. [IB]

vexatious litigation The bringing of

actions and applications that are hopeless and without legal merit. Lord Bingham CJ, with whom Klevan J agreed, has characterized vexatious litigation (in *Attorney General* v. *Barker* [2000] 1 FLR 759 at para. 19) thus: 'it has little or no basis in law (or at least no discernible basis); that whatever the intention of the proceeding may be, its effect is to subject the defendant to inconvenience, harassment and expense out of all proportion to any gain likely to accrue to the claimant; and that it involves an abuse of the process of the court, meaning by that a use of the court process for a purpose or in a way which is significantly different from the ordinary and proper use of the court process.' [JW]

See also ABUSE OF PROCESS; CIVIL RESTRAINT ORDER; *GREPE* V. *LOAM* ORDER; STRIKING OUT.

vicarious liability A situation in which, based on the existence of a specific relationship between them, one party is responsible for harm caused as a result of the actions of another. The most common example is where an EMPLOYER is responsible for the negligent acts of his EMPLOYEE where those acts are committed during the course of his employment. [HJ]

victim 1. In general, a person who has made an allegation to the police, or has had an allegation made on his behalf, that he has been directly subjected to criminal conduct.

2. In human rights law, a person directly affected by an act or omission that contravenes the EUROPEAN CONVENTION ON HUMAN RIGHTS. Only victims have the right to commence proceedings under the Convention. [SN]

victim personal statement In homicide cases a statement drafted by a member or members of the deceased's immediate family (who are regarded as VICTIMS of the crime for this purpose). If it is to be used in proceedings the statement becomes part of the case papers and must be disclosed to the defence and to the court. Depending on the family's wishes, the statement may either be read privately by the judge or read out in open court by the prosecutor after conviction and before sentence is passed. The personal statement is not intended to change the way in which sentences are determined, but may help to provide a fuller understanding of the nature and impact of the crime when passing sentence. The court will not take into account a victim's views on what constitutes an appropriate sentence. [JW]

victimless crimes A term used to denote crimes in which there is no apparent VICTIM and no COMPLAINANT, in many cases because the behaviour constituting the crime is consensual, or because it is not directed at a particular individual or identifiable group: it might be argued that the private use of controlled drugs, prostitution and tax fraud are victimless crimes. The status of 'victimlessness' is controversial, because while there might not be an obvious victim there may be many individuals who are directly or indirectly harmed by the conduct. Thus, the private use of controlled drugs sustains an unregulated market in such drugs which fosters dependency among those with addiction and related healthcare problems, and brings attendant social problems to the locations in which the drugs are bought and sold. Prostitution is viewed by some as being characterized by relationships of dominance and exploitation. Tax fraud might not impact directly on given individuals, but it limits the capacity for government spending and hence arguably impacts on the life chances of citizens as a whole. [BF]

video evidence EVIDENCE contained in a video recording. Such evidence may consist, for example, of recordings made by closed-circuit television cameras, or of recordings of out-of-court interviews with child witnesses which it is sought to introduce in evidence under the Youth Justice and Criminal Evidence Act 1999. [ALTC]

video piracy A term employed by COPYRIGHT holders rather than a legal concept. It refers to the wilful and unauthorized reproduction, communication and distribution of films on video cassettes, or more recently, on DVDs. The response to these activities is that the industry has increased copy-protection measures to control the copying and uploading of DVD and video contents. Copyright laws in the UK, EU and internationally prevent anyone from tampering with or circumventing such copy-protection measures. It is also illegal to distribute devices (including SOFTWARE) which enable the circumvention of such copy-protection measures (see, for example, the Copyright, Designs and Patents Act 1988, ss. 296–296 ZB, as amended by the Copyright and Related Rights Regulations 2003).

[US]

See also COPYRIGHT INFRINGEMENT; MUSIC PIRACY.

vinculo matrimonii (Lat. the bond of marriage) *See A VINCULO MATRIMONII.*

violent disorder An offence under the Public Order Act 1986, s. 2, which is triable either way. It must be proved that there were three or more persons present together, using or threatening unlawful violence, such that their conduct (taken together) would cause an (actual or notional) person of reasonable firmness present at the scene to fear for their personal safety. The *MENS REA* of the offence is an intention to use or threaten violence or an awareness that one's conduct may be violent or threaten violence (see Public Order Act 1986, s. 6(2)). [BF]

See also AFFRAY; RIOT.

void Not valid or legally binding from the outset. [JW]

void contract A CONTRACT that was never valid. It is automatically of no effect from the very beginning and the parties acquire no rights or property under it. It also gives rise to no remedial consequences (although see *QUANTUM MERUIT*). A void contract will result in the event of a fundamental mistake or where there is UNCERTAINTY OF CONTRACTUAL TERMS. [JPL]

void marriage A MARRIAGE which never existed according to law. The grounds which render a marriage void are listed in the Matrimonial Causes Act 1973, s. 11 and include marriages within the PROHIBITED DEGREES OF RELATIONSHIP, marriage to someone not of the opposite sex, marriage to someone who is already lawfully married or civilly partnered, marriage to someone under the legal age and marriage without certainty of the formalities of ceremony or registration. A decree of nullity is not necessary; however, as the court has jurisdiction to make awards of ANCILLARY RELIEF on ANNULMENT, it is usually in the parties' interests to obtain one. Any person may seek a declaration that a marriage is void and there are no bars to granting the decree if one or more of the grounds is established. The Civil Partnership Act 2004 makes similar provisions for the validity and non-validity of CIVIL PARTNERSHIPS. [AD]

See also BIGAMY; CAPACITY TO MARRY; VOIDABLE MARRIAGE.

void trust A TRUST that is unlawful and against the policy of the court to either enforce or allow to take effect; for example, trusts that offend the RULE AGAINST PERPETUITIES, or are deemed to be for an immoral purpose are void. Property that is settled subject to a VOID trust is normally held on RESULTING TRUST for the settlor. [PK]

voidable Capable of being set aside as not valid or legally binding. [JW]

voidable contract A contract that is capable of being set aside via the remedy of RESCISSION. This means that it remains valid until the injured party takes steps to set it aside. However, once rescinded the contract is treated as void. The key distinction therefore is that a VOID CONTRACT is automatically of no effect from the very beginning, whereas a voidable contract requires the injured party to take steps to achieve this effect. MISREPRESENTATION, DURESS or UNDUE INFLUENCE will render a contract voidable. [JPL]

voidable marriage A MARRIAGE which exists unless and until it is ANNULLED. On granting a decree of nullity the court retains its power to make orders for ANCILLARY RELIEF. The grounds which render a marriage voidable are listed in the MATRIMONIAL CAUSES Act, s. 12. They include non-CONSUMMATION OF MARRIAGE, lack of consent and PREG-

NANCY *PER ALIUM*. Only the parties to a marriage can bring proceedings to annul their marriage. The Civil Partnership Act 2004 makes similar provisions for voidable CIVIL PARTNERSHIPS; however, it does not include grounds of non-consummation or venereal disease.   [AD]

voidable trust A TRUST which may be set aside at the behest of the settlor; for example, a trust that arises in the wake of DURESS or UNDUE INFLUENCE is voidable, as is a trust declared by a minor.   [PK]

voir dire (Old Fr. to tell the truth) An oath that is taken by a witness in a trial within a trial held for the purpose of establishing a fact, or facts, relevant to the determination of, for example, whether certain EVIDENCE should be admitted.   [ALTC]

volenti non fit injuria (Lat., that to which a man consents cannot be considered an injury) A defence to a claim in TORT is provided when the claimant voluntarily accepts a RISK. For instance, participants in a sporting event such as a boxing match consent to the risk of a particular type of harm resulting. For this defence to be successful, the claimant must have prior knowledge of the risk involved which is then voluntarily accepted freely and without coercion or undue influence. It is not possible to consent to harm that would otherwise constitute a criminal offence: (see *R* v. *Brown* [1994] 1 AC 212).   [HJ]

voluntary accommodation A term sometimes used to refer to accommodation provided by the LOCAL AUTHORITY under the Children Act 1989, s. 20. This can take the form of accommodation in an institutional setting or in a foster home. A CHILD can be accommodated provided those with PARENTAL RESPONSIBILITY consent or cooperate. There is no need for a court order and the arrangement, as well as the consequences, must be distinguished from the situation where the child is looked after in terms of a CARE ORDER. Children can be accommodated when PARENTS are unable to care for their children and need some respite. While this is generally a temporary measure, children can also be accommodated

long term. The local authority has a duty to accommodate children in need if there is no person with parental responsibility; if the child is lost or abandoned; or if the person caring for the child is prevented, whether permanently or otherwise, from providing suitable accommodation or care.

The local authority does not acquire parental responsibility. It cannot accommodate a child if someone with parental responsibility objects and is willing and able either to provide the child with accommodation or to arrange for it to be provided (s. 20(7)). Once the child is accommodated, any person with parental responsibility can remove the child at any time (s. 20(8)). [FK]

See also FOSTER CHILD; FOSTER PARENT; LOOKED AFTER CHILD.

voluntary bill procedure A procedure, used exceptionally, whereby the prosecution applies to a HIGH COURT judge for consent to prefer a BILL OF INDICTMENT without normal COMMITTAL proceedings. The voluntary bill procedure might be used, following the committal of one defendant, where the prosecution seeks to add more defendants to an indictment without having the delay of further committal proceedings because the date set for the trial of the original defendant is imminent. This procedure should not be used to deprive a defendant unjustifiably of the right to committal proceedings.   [SN]

voluntary disposition A transfer of land that is not made for valuable consideration. Common examples of voluntary dispositions include a gift, a disposition by will, or sale for a nominal fee, but not a transfer of land made in consideration of marriage or formation of a civil partnership. Under the Law of Property Act 1925, s. 173(1), a voluntary disposition of land made with intent to defraud a subsequent purchaser is voidable (i.e. it can be set aside) at the instance of the purchaser.   [DR]

voluntary euthanasia *See* EUTHANASIA.

voluntary manslaughter *See* MANSLAUGHTER.

voluntary settlement A TRUST made gratuitously, without valuable CONSIDERATION.

[PK]

voluntary waste *See* WASTE.

voyeurism Four offences of voyeurism are created by the Sexual Offences Act 2003, s. 67. A person commits the first offence if, for the purpose of obtaining sexual gratification, he observes another person doing a private act, knowing that the other person does not consent to being observed for his sexual gratification. A person commits the second offence by operating equipment with the intention of enabling another person to observe, for the purpose of obtaining sexual gratification, a third person doing a private act, knowing that the third person does not consent to his operating equipment with that intention. A person commits the third offence if he records another person doing a private act, with the intention that he or a third person will, for the purpose of obtaining sexual gratification, look at an image of that person doing the act, knowing that that person does not consent to his recording the act with that intention. A person commits the fourth offence if he installs equipment or constructs or adapts a structure with the intention of enabling himself or another person to commit the first offence outlined above.

[BF]

W

wagering contract A CONTRACT whereby each party stands to win or lose a sum of money or something of value, depending on which one has made a correct prediction of the outcome of a future event. It is a type of gambling contract within the definition in the Gambling Act 2005, s. 3, since it amounts to betting on an outcome. Section 9 of the Act defines betting as including making or accepting a bet on either the outcome of a race, competition or other event or process, or on the likelihood of something occurring or not occurring or on whether something is true or untrue.

The Gambling Act 2005, ss. 334 and 335, reversed the Gaming Act 1845, s. 18, which had provided that such contracts were null and void so that there could be no action in the courts to enforce any bet or alleged winnings. Since 1 September 2007, the fact that a contract relates to gambling does not prevent its enforcement.   [JPL]

See also GAMING CONTRACT.

wages Includes *inter alia* salary, commissions, holiday pay, statutory sick and MATERNITY PAY, and even money paid under a PROTECTIVE AWARD. EMPLOYERS and EMPLOYEES are free to contract on whatever pay terms they desire provided there is no illegality (such as an agreement to defraud HM Revenue and Customs), that the rules in relation to deductions of wages are complied with, and the amount is above the national MINIMUM WAGE.   [MJ]

wages councils (obsolete) From 1909 to 1993, England and Wales had, by STATUTE, Wages Councils in various industries where COLLECTIVE BARGAINING had not taken root, which provided a minimum wage. They were seen as auxiliary supports for collective bargaining and it was intended that they would be abolished once collective bargaining was in place. They were abolished on 30 August 1993 by the Trade Union Reform and Employment Rights Act 1993, s. 35.   [MJ]

See also MINIMUM WAGE.

wait and see principle *See* RULE AGAINST PERPETUITIES.

waiver (contractual) Occurs when one party voluntarily gives up its right to insist on the contracted-for performance or remedy. A waiver may be express or implied from conduct; for example acting in a way which is inconsistent with the existence of a right to performance.   [JPL]

waiver of privilege Has the effect of allowing evidence to be adduced in circumstances where it would otherwise be precluded by the operation of a PRIVILEGE. Waiver is of considerable practical importance in the context of LEGAL PROFESSIONAL PRIVILEGE. Here the privilege is that of the client, not the lawyer. Thus, only the client can waive it. A waiver may be express or implied from circumstances where the client does (or authorizes) something which is inconsistent with the confidentiality which the privilege is intended to protect. Considerable care therefore needs to be taken to ensure that the privilege is not lost accidentally. Thus, in *Brunel University* v. *Webster and Vaseghi* [2007] EWCA Civ 482, an implied bilateral waiver of privilege was held to have occurred when both the claimants and the university included without prejudice material in the TRIAL BUN-DLE for an EMPLOYMENT TRIBUNAL hearing. By contrast, in criminal proceedings it is accepted that a defendant who merely gives evidence that he made no comment during a police interview on the advice of his solicitor does not thereby waive his privilege (see *R* v. *Beckles* [2004] EWCA Crim 2766).

By the Defamation Act 1996, s. 13 , where the conduct of a person in or in relation to proceedings in Parliament is at issue in DEF-AMATION proceedings, he or she may waive for themselves the ABSOLUTE PRIVILEGE that attaches to statements made in Parliament, to enable such evidence to be adduced in the proceedings. [JW]

See also PARLIAMENTARY PRIVILEGE.

war A legal status that exists when parties use armed force to enforce rights or settle conflicts. International humanitarian law increasingly uses the term 'armed conflict', thereby significantly reducing the norma-tive significance of war as a concept. In the *Tadic Jurisdiction Decision,* Case No. IT-94-1-AR72 before the INTERNATIONAL CRIMINAL TRIBU-NAL FOR THE FORMER YUGOSLAVIA (ICTY), an armed conflict was said to exist (para. 70): 'whenever there is a resort to armed force between STATES or protracted armed vio-lence between governmental authorities and organized armed groups or between such groups within a State'. At COMMON LAW a state of war cannot exist without a formal declaration of war or commence-ment of hostilities by the CROWN.

In INTERNATIONAL LAW, the law of war can be divided into two elements: **jus ad bellum**, which concerns the legality of using armed force to resolve a conflict and **jus in bello**, which concerns the regulation and control of actual hostilities. The UN Charter requires all signatories to refrain from the threat or USE OF FORCE against the territorial integrity or political independence of another state, though this does not constitute a bar on the use of armed force in self-defence, or pos-sibly by way of REPRISAL against an act of aggression. The HAGUE CONVENTIONS and GEN-EVA CONVENTIONS provide a framework of rules governing the *jus in bello,* but never-theless do not cover all types of conflict, and many modern conflict situations, such as Afghanistan, may operate in a grey area where the status of the conflict and hence of combatants is contested and uncertain.

The term 'war' is also used by states as a form of defence against the fulfilment of pre-existing contractual obligations, such as when invoking FORCE MAJEURE or a funda-mental change of circumstances (*REBUS SIC STANTIBUS* rule, Article 62 of the 1969 Vienna Convention on the Law of Treaties). [IB]

war crimes In international humanitarian law, any violation of the laws of WAR that amounts to a criminal act. The modern concept of war crime was largely developed under the auspices of the Nuremberg Trials, based on the definition in the 1945 London Charter that established the trials. War crimes comprise the murder and ill-treat-ment of prisoners of war or civilian popu-lations, the use of civilians as slave labour, the killing of hostages, and the destruction of civilian property above and beyond any destruction justified by military necessity. [IB]

See also CRIMES AGAINST HUMANITY; INTER-NATIONAL CRIMINAL COURT; INTERNATIONAL MILI-TARY TRIBUNAL.

ward of court A MINOR under the court's protection. Legal control of the minor's person and property are under the control of the court. This does not mean that the CHILD is under the physical control of the court, but that those who have PARENTAL RESPONSIBILITY or de facto care of the child must seek the court's consent when it comes to making important decisions about the child's property or upbringing. The paramount concern of the court in exercising this jurisdiction is the welfare of the child. The powers of the court in relation to WARDSHIP have been circumscribed by the Children Act 1989; where possible, SECTION 8 ORDERS should be used in preference to the exercise of the wardship jurisdiction.

Any person with an interest in the child can apply to have the child made a ward of court. The child becomes a ward immediately an application for wardship is made, but ceases to be a ward unless an application is made within 21 days to hear the case. A child who is a ward of court remains a ward until attaining their majority unless the court makes an order to the contrary or a CARE ORDER is made. [FK]

See also WELFARE PRINCIPLE.

wardship Jurisdiction vested in the HIGH COURT to make a MINOR a WARD OF COURT. Wardship gives the court legal control of the child's person and property. [FK]

warned list *See* CAUSE LIST.

warrant backed for bail An ARREST WARRANT issued by a magistrate or a judge which has been endorsed with a direction to release the accused on bail immediately following arrest. [SN]

warrant of arrest An order of the court for the arrest of a person. A warrant is not required in respect of alleged INDICTABLE OFFENCES, and, under the Serious Organised Crime and Police Act 2005, the police possess extensive powers to arrest without a warrant where they have reason to consider it necessary to do so. [SN]

warrant of commitment An order of the court sending someone to prison. [SN]

warrant of execution An order of the COUNTY COURT, authorizing the appropriate court officer (a county court bailiff) to seize sufficient goods from a judgment debtor to sell and pay off the judgment debt and the cost of enforcement. [JW]

See also FIERI FACIAS.

warranty A promissory statement, i.e. a statement that the facts represented are true. It follows that such a statement amounts to a term and that if broken there is a BREACH OF CONTRACT. However, it is not regarded as an important term in the sense that it goes to the root of the CONTRACT, and a breach of warranty will not be a REPUDIATORY BREACH, entitling the injured party to elect to terminate or affirm the contract. Instead, compensatory DAMAGES are regarded as the appropriate remedy. Compare CONDITION and INNOMINATE TERM.

In insurance law, a warranty by the insured is a condition so that its breach is repudiatory and entitles the insurer to treat the insurance contract as terminated. Warranty is also used in some contexts, for example in SALES OF GOODS, to indicate that statements made, for example by the SELLER, have become terms of the contract because the seller was guaranteeing that reasonable care and skill had been taken in making those statements to ensure their accuracy. [JPL]

waste In land law, an act or omission by a tenant of land, causing a lasting alteration to the nature of the land in question. An action in tort may be brought by a person with an interest in the REVERSION or REMAINDER of the land, either for an injunction or damages.

Voluntary waste is the positive commission of an act which alters the nature of the land; for example pulling down a house, removing FIXTURES and fittings and, in certain circumstances, cutting timber. **Permissive waste** is an omission to act, such as allowing buildings to fall into disrepair. The rules on liability for waste depend on the type of tenancy. Generally, all tenants (except TENANTS FOR LIFE) are liable for voluntary waste, unless those acts amount to improvements of the land, in which case they are acts of **ameliorating waste**, for which there is no liability. Conversely, only a tenant for years has been held liable for permissive waste.

A tenant for life is only liable for voluntary waste if he is made **impeachable** for waste under the terms of the SETTLEMENT.

He is only liable for permissive waste if the SETTLOR has imposed on him an obligation to keep the property in repair. [DR]

See also EQUITABLE WASTE.

wasted costs order A court order made against the legal representative of a party to any legal proceedings disallowing certain costs, or requiring him or her personally to meet the whole or any part of the costs of an action. A wasted costs order will only be ordered when the court has determined that costs were incurred by the representative's improper, unreasonable or negligent actions. As advocates have a collective responsibility to ensure that a case is ready for any hearing, the court may in appropriate circumstances, and especially if the matter has been entirely funded at public expense, make an order against all the representatives involved (see for example, *Re G (children) (care proceedings: wasted costs)* [1999] Fam. 104). [JW]

wasting police time Under the Criminal Law Act 1967, s. 5(2), a person commits an offence if he or she causes wasteful employment of police time by knowingly making to any person a false report suggesting that an offence has been committed, or giving rise to apprehension for the safety of persons or property, or suggesting that he or she has information material to a police inquiry. This is a SUMMARY OFFENCE and the consent of the DIRECTOR OF PUBLIC PROSECUTIONS is required before proceedings are instituted (see Criminal Law Act 1967, s. 5(3)). [BF]

weapons of mass destruction (WMD) Weapons that have the potential for causing death and damage on a large scale. The term has no autonomous meaning in INTERNATIONAL LAW. International law prohibits the use of specific weapons on the basis of treaties, and CUSTOMARY INTERNATIONAL LAW regulates how lawful weapons are to be employed. A large range of weapons may be classified as WMD, such as chemical and biological weapons, nuclear weapons, ballistic missiles and others. Of the weapons just mentioned, only the chemical and biological ones are prohibited by TREATY and possibly by customary law. The use of nuclear weapons and ballistic missiles is not prohibited under international law (in cases of urgent self-defence in accordance with the INTERNATIONAL COURT OF JUSTICE's *Advisory Opinion on the Use of Nuclear Weapons*, 8 July 1996), since no practice or treaty law exists to this effect. The only limitations as to their use are prescribed under the general customary framework of humanitarian law; that is, that the weapon and its users must be able to discriminate between civilians and combatants and that it should not cause unnecessary suffering and superfluous injury. The second limitation stems from the power of the UN SECURITY COUNCIL to order states to destroy all weapons in their arsenal designated by the Council as WMD. The Council ordered Iraq to do so in its Resolution 687 (1991) and appointed an inspection committee to monitor such destruction. [IB]

See also USE OF FORCE.

Weber, Max (1864–1920) German sociologist (and lawyer) whose aim was to explain the nature of **capitalism**, its emergence uniquely in Western society and its consequences for other aspects of life. His major work *Economy and Society* includes his influential analysis of the role of law.

Weber's approach reflects his desire to understand **social action**, which for him was a matter of understanding the meaning which individual actors gave their actions within a social context. His analysis relies on two particular methods: the ideal type and varieties of rationality. His use of ideal types is not meant to indicate a rigid understanding of all social action – Weber was clear that an infinite variety existed – but rather serves as an aid to our understanding of any observed action on the basis of its relationship to one or other model of social action. Ideal types thus serve as a measure against which observed action may be gauged.

Weber proposed four ideal types of social action: action guided by emotion; action guided by tradition; value-rational action; and purpose-rational action. He uses these to trace the evolution of society from its most primitive forms through to the capitalism with which he is particularly concerned. For Weber, then, capitalism is characterized by the purpose-rational pursuit of profit within a free market.

Law, for Weber, plays a key role as a framework for economic purpose-rational action insofar as it provides rules, instruments, forms of business organization and enforcement mechanisms which support and guarantee economic transactions. Economic actors are accordingly able to plan with greater certainty and security than would otherwise be the case. Law's predictability and logic (not only in economic transactions but also more broadly) thus serve as the basis for its acceptance in modern society, rather than any traditional, religious or ideological foundation, as may have been the case in earlier societies.

The precise form of modern Western law is an important aspect of Weber's account. His discussion of varieties of rationality is important in this regard. In particular, he distinguishes between substantively rational and formally rational law. The former is dependent upon general rules that have as their basis some ideology, whether religious, political or otherwise. The latter is dependent on general rules without reference to any such ideology. Within formally rational law, Weber further distinguishes logically formal law, which he regards as the highest form. This relies on the logical analysis of meaning and the application of fixed legal rules. It is this last form that he understands to be characteristic of capitalist society and indeed to have allowed its development. More specifically, he regards logically formal law as capable of **systematization**, that is, the integration of all legal propositions to provide a clear, consistent, coherent and comprehensive system of rules within which all fact situations may be subsumed, such that law can offer the certainty required by modern economic and social life.

Weber was interested by the fact that England did not appear to fit his analysis. Law there had not been codified, as it had been in all of the other advanced capitalist countries he considered, and thus appeared to lack the rationalization he believed necessary for the emergence of capitalism. That said, however, Weber was not rigid in the application of his ideal types and did not believe that capitalism, as a particular stage in economic evolution, necessarily required a particular correlative development in law. Rather he believed that different solutions could emerge in different places in response to similar problems. Thus, it could be suggested that the English law's provision of clear procedures and guaranteed rights served the same purpose as codification in offering a framework for economic transactions.

The influence of Weber on the SOCIOLOGY OF LAW has been immense. Many works in this field draw inspiration from Weber or use his analysis as a starting point. While his influence has endured for practically a century, it is questionable whether his ideas about the legitimacy of law (based on its predictability and logic) are a sufficient explanation in contemporary conditions.   [JP]

Further reading: Max Weber, *Economy and Society* (Berkeley, CA: University of California Press, 1978).

weekly tenancy A tenancy which is not a FIXED TERM TENANCY, and for which the rent is payable on a weekly basis, is a weekly tenancy no matter how long it lasts. It does not expire at the end of the first week unless notice is given, nor is there a reletting in each new week. Instead, it is best understood as a continuing relationship between the LANDLORD and TENANT where the notice period is decided by the weekly requirement to pay rent.   [HC & DR]

See also TENANCY FROM YEAR TO YEAR.

welfare principle The principle whereby the welfare of the CHILD is a primary factor to be taken into account in decisions relating to children. This principle has long informed the COMMON LAW, such as the law on WARDSHIP. However, it also has statutory recognition. The Matrimonial Causes Act 1973, s. 25, for example, states that the welfare of the child must be the court's first consideration when deciding on the financial consequences of divorce. The most important of these statutory provisions is the Children Act 1989, s. 1, which states that the welfare of the child should be the court's paramount consideration when determining any question relating to the upbringing of a child or the administration of a child's property or finance. (See, similarly, the Adoption and Children Act 2002, s. 1(2), in relation to adoption decisions.) The notion of paramountcy dictates that, after all the relevant factors have been taken into account, the welfare (also referred to as the best interests) of the child must determine the outcome of the decision-making process (*J* v. *C* [1970] AC 668, 710). However, this well-established interpretation of the paramountcy principle, and even the legitimacy of the principle itself, is now being challenged by scholars in the light of the Human Rights Act 1998 and PARENTS' rights to their private and family life under Article 8 of the EUROPEAN CONVENTION ON HUMAN RIGHTS.   [FK]

See also SECTION 8 ORDERS.

Welsh Assembly *See* NATIONAL ASSEMBLY FOR WALES.

whistle-blowing The Public Interest Disclosure Act 1998 inserted various provisions into the Employment Rights Act 1996 aimed at protecting **whistle-blowers** from UNFAIR DISMISSAL and DETRIMENT. A whistle-blower may be described as a WORKER who discloses information in the public interest, i.e. information relating to crimes, breaches of a legal obligation, miscarriages of justice, dangers to health and safety or the environment and the deliberate concealing of evidence relating to any of these in respect of an organization. The law is complex, and the disclosure must be made in the right way to the right person to qualify as a 'protected disclosure': see the Employment Rights Act 1996, ss. 43A–L. Where an EMPLOYER dismisses a worker who is not an EMPLOYEE (e.g. an agency worker) for having made a protected disclosure, the DISMISSAL is taken to be a detriment within s. 47B of the 1996 Act. By s. 103A, a

dismissed employee who has made a protected disclosure is deemed to be automatically unfairly dismissed (see also INADMISSIBLE REASON).   [MJ]

White Paper '[A document] produced by the Government setting out details of future policy on a particular subject. A White Paper will often be the basis for a BILL to be put before Parliament. The White Paper allows the Government an opportunity to gather feedback before it formally presents the policies as a Bill.' (See 'Glossary – Parliamentary Jargon Explained' at http://www.parliament.uk/about/glossary.cfm?ref=whitepa_9927.)
          [JW]

See also PARLIAMENTARY PAPERS.

whole life order *See* LIFE SENTENCE.

wilful neglect An OFFENCE under the Children and Young Persons Act 1933, s. 1, as a form of 'cruelty to persons under sixteen'. A person who has attained the age of 16 and who has responsibility for a CHILD or young person under 16, commits a MISDEMEANOUR if he or she wilfully neglects that child in a manner likely to cause unnecessary suffering or injury to health, including mental health. Also included under the heading of cruelty are, among other things, wilful assault or ill-treatment of a child. A person who has responsibility for a child is defined to include a person who has PARENTAL RESPONSIBILITY and any person who has the care of the child (s. 17).   [FK]

See also CHILD ABUSE; NEGLECT.

wilful refusal to consummate One of the grounds which renders a marriage voidable. Wilful refusal is a settled and definite decision not to consummate the marriage, made without reasonable excuse. It must be distinguished from **inability to consummate**, which is an inability that may be either physical or psychological, but must be permanent and incurable. Petitioners may not rely on their own wilful refusal and may be barred if the petitioners knew that it was open to them to take proceedings, but led the respondent to believe that they would not take proceedings and that it would be unjust to the respondent to grant the DECREE on these grounds (Matrimonial Causes Act 1973, s. 13(1)). Non-consummation is not a ground for ANNULMENT in CIVIL PARTNERSHIPS.   [AD]

See also CONSUMMATION OF MARRIAGE; VOIDABLE MARRIAGE.

will An expression of wishes (frequently to do with the disposal of property) by a person known as the TESTATOR, which he or she intends to take effect only upon his or her death. A will may comprise either a single document, or the total of the testator's testamentary documents read together at the time of his or her death. A will must normally comply with the formalities prescribed by the Wills Act 1837, s. 9: it must be in writing, signed by or on behalf of the testator in the presence of two or more witnesses, who must sign and attest the will. The testator must have TESTAMENTARY CAPACITY at the time of signing, and the intention that this document shall constitute his or her will (*ANIMUS TESTANDI*). Once made, a will can be amended by a properly executed alteration, or a CODICIL. It can be revoked by its deliberate destruction, by the making of a later valid will, or by the subsequent MARRIAGE or entry into a CIVIL PARTNERSHIP by the testator.   [CM]

See also ATTESTATION; JOINT WILLS; MUTUAL WILLS; PRIVILEGED WILL; RECTIFICATION OF WILL; REVOCATION OF WILL; SIGNATURE OF WILL; STATUTORY WILL.

will theory 1. The basis of classical CONTRACT law originating in the 19th century was that contract was the binding nature of PROMISES and promissory obligations which had been voluntarily made and assumed. Contract was therefore seen as reflecting the 'will' or autonomy of the parties and contractual principle developed to give effect to this expressed 'will' or the assumed will of the parties. It followed that the courts would not interfere with party autonomy but merely assisted in giving effect to the parties' own intentions.

2. One of the two principal theories of rights (also known as **choice theory**), which holds that the statement that 'A has the right to do R' means that A's *choice* whether or not to do R is what is being pro-

tected. In other words, employing HOHFELD's scheme, the essence of A's right is his ability to waive B's correlative duty to him. Associated in particular with H.L.A. HART, the theory's foundation is a vision of law that lays stress on its role in promoting and protecting individual freedom.

See also INTEREST THEORY.

WIPO *See* WORLD INTELLECTUAL PROPERTY ORGANIZATION.

with notice *See* APPLICATION.

withdrawal of case from jury *See* NO CASE TO ANSWER.

without notice *See* APPLICATION.

without prejudice negotiations Negotiations, oral or written, that are genuinely aimed at the settlement of a case. Such negotiations are protected by PRIVILEGE and cannot be admitted as evidence.   [ALTC]

See also CALDERBANK LETTER; PART 36 OFFER.

witness 1. A person who gives evidence, either by way of a statement or orally in court. To be a witness, the person called must be competent to testify (see COMPETENCE). Most competent witnesses may be compelled to give evidence if they are reluctant to do so.

2. A person who observes the signing of a legal document and signs it themselves to attest to their presence at the act of signing. Witnesses provide an important guarantee of the authenticity of documents, and may be required as a legal formality for certain documents, such as a WILL.   [JW]

witness immunity A written agreement by the CROWN not to prosecute a person for a specific offence, or specific offences; or that a prosecution against a person will be terminated either in whole or in part. A witness immunity is absolute and not conditional. The immunity will apply regardless of whether other evidence is, or becomes, available. An immunity on behalf of the Crown is never granted prospectively. Thus, no immunity will be granted which condones, requires, or purports to authorize, or permits the commission of an offence in the future.   [SN]

witness intimidation It is a criminal offence for a person (a) to intimidate or intend to intimidate a witness or potential witness with the intention of perverting, obstructing or otherwise interfering with the course of justice, or (b) to harm, intend to harm, or threaten to harm that person because of what they know or believe (see the Criminal Justice and Public Order Act 1994, s. 51). The offence may be committed where the intimidation or harm, etc., is directed at a third party (a friend or relative of the witness). It is also an offence under s. 51 to intimidate a juror, potential juror, or any other person assisting in the investigation of an offence.   [JW]

See also PERVERTING THE COURSE OF JUSTICE.

witness summons A document served on a witness requiring him or her to attend court to give evidence.   [SN]

witness undertaking A written agreement by the CROWN to refrain from using in criminal proceedings certain specific information, documents or evidence provided by the witness. Sometimes referred to as a 'Salmon undertaking', it allows a person to waive the PRIVILEGE against self-incrimination without risk of prosecution. This form of undertaking does not prevent a witness from being prosecuted where other evidence which justifies a prosecution is, or becomes, available.   [SN]

Wittgenstein, Ludwig (1889–1951) Austrian philosopher ranking among the greatest of the 20th century, whose work has had an impact on a wide range of disciplines. In law, his later work has been influential in that it introduced the idea that meaning emerges from the *use* to which words are put. Wittgenstein discussed this phenomenon in terms of language games, that is the development of conventional uses of words within defined contexts. The possibility that law might constitute such a language game is immediately apparent. Foremost among the JURISTS influenced by Wittgenstein, albeit his earlier work, was H.L.A. HART.   [JP]

Further reading: Ludwig Wittgenstein, *Philosophical Investigations*, 2nd edn (Oxford: Blackwell, 1968).

WLR The standard abbreviation for the Weekly Law Reports, published by the INCORPORATED COUNCIL OF LAW REPORTING.   [JW]

See LAW REPORTS.

WMA *See* WORLD MEDICAL ASSOCIATION.

WMD *See* WEAPONS OF MASS DESTRUCTION.

words of limitation In a conveyance of UNREGISTERED LAND, the words that define the interest to be acquired by the purchaser of the land; for example, where land is conveyed by X 'to Y and his heirs' or 'to Y in fee simple', this denotes that a FEE SIMPLE ABSOLUTE IN POSSESSION is to be acquired. Words of limitation are no longer essential in conveyancing, because under the Law of Property Act 1925, s. 60(1), where no words of limitation are used this has the effect of transferring the fee simple, unless a contrary intention appears in the conveyance. Nevertheless, words of limitation are still used to create LIFE INTERESTS, ENTAILED INTERESTS and future interests; for example, in a gift of land 'to Y for life, remainder to Z', the words 'for life' are the words of limitation that create the life interest.   [DR]

See also WORDS OF PROCREATION; WORDS OF PURCHASE.

words of procreation Words in a deed that creates an ENTAILED INTEREST or, prior to 1926, a FEE TAIL or estate tail. Valid words of procreation under the common law were 'to X and the heirs of his body', or 'to X in tail'. To create a TAIL MALE, the words 'to X in tail male' or 'to X and the heirs male of the body' were valid. To create a TAIL FEMALE, the words 'to X in tail female' or 'to X and the heirs female of the body' were valid.

Under the Law of Property Act 1925, s. 130(1), entailed interests could only take effect as EQUITABLE INTERESTS, and only if the words of procreation used were those which prior to 1926 would have created an estate tail by deed. The effect of this was that after 1925, commonly used informal words of procreation such as 'to X and his issue', 'to X for life and his descendants', and 'to X and his children', could not be used to create entailed interests. Section 130 was repealed by the Trusts of Land and Appointment of Trustees Act 1996, s. 2, Schedule 1 para. 5; consequently, entailed interests can no longer be created at all. [DR]

See also WORDS OF LIMITATION.

words of purchase In a conveyance of UNREGISTERED LAND, the words that define the persons who are to acquire an INTEREST IN LAND; for example, if land is given 'to X and his heirs', the words 'to X' are words of purchase, since they define X as the purchaser of the land. Conversely, the words 'and his heirs' are WORDS OF LIMITATION, since they define the interest to be created, in this example a FEE SIMPLE ABSOLUTE IN POSSESSION.
[DR]

words of severance Words in a CONVEY-ANCE or transfer to two or more people that indicate an intention that the property is to be held by them as tenants in common rather than joint tenants. [HC & DR]

work of equal value Work performed by a man and a woman that is of equal value to the employer. Whether work is of equal value is determined by an independent expert whose name appears on a list kept by ACAS or by the EMPLOYMENT TRIBUNALS. The tasks performed by a man and a woman are ranked under headings such as effort, skill and decision-making to see whether the jobs are of equal value to the employer.
[MJ]

See also EQUAL PAY; EQUALITY CLAUSE.

work to rule A form of INDUSTRIAL ACTION whereby WORKERS abide closely by their CON-TRACT OF EMPLOYMENT, resulting in a slowing down of work. Lord Denning MR said that so doing was a breach of the duty of cooperation and accordingly a BREACH OF CONTRACT: see *Secretary of State for Employment* v. *ASLEF (No. 2)* [1972] 2 QB 443 (CA).
[MJ]

worker The main usage of this term is in the Employment Rights Act 1996, s. 230, where a 'worker' is defined – except in relation to a shop worker and a betting worker – as: 'an individual who has entered into or

works under (or, where the employment has ceased, worked under) – (a) a CONTRACT OF EMPLOYMENT, or (b) any contract, whether express or implied and (if it is express) whether oral or in writing, whereby the individual undertakes to do or perform personally any work or services for another party to the contract whose status is not by virtue of the contract that of client or customer of any profession or business undertaking carried on by the individual …'. [MJ]

See also EMPLOYEE.

working hours In general, the maximum number of hours of work per week must not exceed 48 (including overtime) averaged across a 17-week reference period. Time on call is classified as work if the WORKER is on call even if he or she is asleep. There are several exceptions including those who have signed an opt-out agreement and those with autonomous decision-making powers, e.g. a managing director. [MJ]

World Bank *See* INTERNATIONAL BANK FOR RECONSTRUCTION AND DEVELOPMENT.

World Court *See* INTERNATIONAL COURT OF JUSTICE.

World Intellectual Property Organization (WIPO) A Geneva-based agency of the UNITED NATIONS (UN) with the main task of helping to guarantee the protection of intellectual property rights worldwide. As of June 2007, 184 countries are members of WIPO. The agency administers 24 international treaties, a number of them of major significance in the field. Since 1996, WIPO has cooperated with the WORLD TRADE ORGANIZATION (WTO), which negotiated the agreement on Trade-Related Aspects of Intellectual Property Rights (TRIPS), in assisting with the implementation of the TRIPS AGREEMENT and to provide assistance for developing countries. [US]

World Medical Association Formed in 1947 in the aftermath of the Second World War, the Association was created to ensure the independence of physicians and the development of the highest ethical standards, professional competence and freedom. [HJ]

World Trade Organization (WTO) An international organization based in Geneva which deals with the rules of global trade between STATES. It administers and develops a framework of WTO law based around a core of multilateral trade treaties: the GENERAL AGREEMENT ON TARIFFS AND TRADE (GATT), the GENERAL AGREEMENT ON TRADE IN SERVICES (GATS) and the Agreement on Trade-Related Aspects of Intellectual Property Rights (TRIPS). Through its **Dispute Settlement Body**, it also provides a forum for the resolution of international trade disputes between members.

The WTO operates primarily through three tiers of governance and decision-making. Its top-level body is the **Ministerial Conference** which meets at least once every two years. Below that is the **General Council** which meets several times a year and mostly comprises ambassadors and heads of delegation in Geneva. The General Council also meets as the Trade Policy Review Body and the Dispute Settlement Body. At the next level are three specialist Councils which correspond to the three main WTO Agreements: the **Goods Council**, **Services Council** and **Intellectual Property (TRIPS) Council**. These in turn report to the General Council: see http://www.wto.org/. [JW]

wound A wound occurs, at law, when the continuity of the skin is broken. The whole skin, not just the cuticle or upper skin, must be broken. Internal bleeding does not constitute a wound. For discussion, see *C (a minor)* v. *Eisenhower* [1984] QB 331. [BF]

See also MALICIOUS WOUNDING; UNLAWFUL WOUNDING; WOUNDING WITH INTENT.

wounding with intent A shorthand term for a number of the offences under the Offences against the Person Act 1861, s. 18, most particularly the offence of malicious wounding with intent to do GRIEVOUS BODILY HARM, although the shorthand is equally valid if the defendant's ULTERIOR INTENT is to resist arrest or to prevent the lawful arrest or detention of another person. There is no specific offence limited to 'intentional wounding' without proof of ulterior intent. A defendant who did intentionally wound another would be guilty of the broader offence of MALICIOUS WOUNDING under s. 20 of the Offences against the Person Act 1861. [BF]

See also UNLAWFUL WOUNDING; WOUND.

writ An order issued by a court requiring the person or body named to do, or forbear from doing, some act. [JW]

writ of delivery A WRIT OF EXECUTION in civil proceedings requiring a HIGH COURT enforcement officer to seize goods and deliver them, or their assessed value, to the claimant. In the COUNTY COURT it is referred to as a **warrant of delivery** and is enforced by a county court bailiff. [JW]

writ of execution A WRIT used in civil proceedings to enforce a court judgment. Writs of execution include the writs of delivery, FIERI FACIAS, possession and sequestration, and may be issued by the COUNTY COURT or HIGH COURT. By virtue of Schedule 1 of the CIVIL PROCEDURE RULES, writs of execution in the QUEEN'S BENCH DIVISION are still issued under the authority of the RULES OF THE SUPREME COURT, Order 46. [JW]

See also PRAECIPE.

writ of possession A WRIT OF EXECUTION used in civil proceedings to enforce an order for the possession of LAND. It requires a HIGH COURT enforcement officer to enter the property in order to give VACANT POSSESSION to the claimant. The equivalent order in the COUNTY COURT is called a **warrant of possession**. [HC & DR]

writ of sequestration A WRIT OF EXECUTION in civil proceedings, issued in accordance with the CIVIL PROCEDURE RULES Part 23. Sequestration is normally only invoked after a serious case of CONTEMPT OF COURT has already arisen. It has the effect of binding and holding the defendant's property under the authority of sequestrators (individuals appointed by the court to carry out the sequestration) from the time it is issued until the defendant complies with the original court order. [JW]

written charge A document issued by a public prosecutor under the Criminal Justice Act 2003, s. 29, which institutes criminal proceedings by charging a person with an offence. [SN]

written statement of employment *See* SECTION 1 STATEMENT.

wrongful dismissal An EMPLOYER who dismisses an EMPLOYEE without notice, or less than the correct length of notice, is said to have wrongfully dismissed them unless the employer had **cause** (i.e. justification) to do as they did. 'Cause' may include gross misconduct and taking part in unlawful INDUSTRIAL ACTION. Wrongful dismissal is a contractual action, subject therefore to contractual principles. The sole remedy is damages, calculated according to the length of notice which should have been given. Claims may be brought in the ordinary courts within six years of dismissal or, if the claim is for £25,000 or less, in the EMPLOYMENT TRIBUNALS, with a LIMITATION PERIOD of three months. [MJ]

WTO *See* WORLD TRADE ORGANIZATION.

Y

Year Books The earliest series of LAW REPORTS in the English legal system, written during the period from approximately 1285 to 1535. They were derived largely from the notes taken by student advocates and are of primarily historical interest today. [JW]

year of assessment The statutory period of 12 months, ending on 5 April, which comprises the tax year in which income and capital gains arising to a taxpayer in that period are charged to tax. [RE]

See also CAPITAL GAINS TAX; TAX RETURN.

yearly tenancy *See* TENANCY FROM YEAR TO YEAR.

YOT *See* YOUTH OFFENDING TEAM.

young adult offender An offender who is aged between 18–20 years. [SN]

Young Offender Institutions Custodial facilities which can house offenders between the ages of 15 and 21 years. Offenders aged from 15 to 17 are housed separately from those aged 18 to 21. [BF]

young worker In employment law, a young WORKER is one who is over the compulsory school-leaving age but is not 18. See, for example, the Working Time Regulations 1998 (SI 1998/1833). [MJ]

youth community order The collective term introduced by the Criminal Justice Act 2003, s. 147(2), for a range of what had been called youth 'community sentences', i.e. the CURFEW ORDER, exclusion order, ATTENDANCE CENTRE ORDER, ACTION PLAN ORDER and SUPERVISION ORDER. [JW]

youth court A specialized form of magistrates' court exercising jurisdiction over offences committed by persons who have not yet attained the age of 18 and other matters related to children and young persons. Cases are heard by MAGISTRATES or by a DISTRICT JUDGE (MAGISTRATES' COURTS). The hearing is similar to proceedings in the magistrates' court, though the procedure is adapted to take account of the age of the defendant. The magistrates and judges who sit in the youth court have received specialist training on dealing with young people. The court is not open to the general public and only those directly involved in the case will normally be present. The press may attend and report the proceedings but will not usually be allowed to publish the defendant's name. The youth court can send a young person to the CROWN COURT if the offence is very serious and the sentencing powers of the youth court are thought to be insufficient. [SN]

Youth Offending Team (YOT) A team made up of representatives from the local police, social services, PROBATION SERVICE, health, education, drugs and alcohol misuse and housing officers. The YOT is charged with working with individual young offenders to evaluate the risks they may pose to others, and to identify suitable programmes to address their needs and prevent re-offending.   [SN]

See also ACTION PLAN ORDER.

Z

zero-rated supply The provision of goods and services, by a taxable person, the value of which is taxed at the Value Added Tax (VAT) rate of 0 per cent. Where a taxable supply is made of goods or services which are zero-rated, the supply is taxed, but at 0 per cent. A registered taxable person is entitled to recover the input VAT which relates to their 0 per cent supplies because the supplies have been taxed. Recovery against zero-rated supplies occurs in the same way as recovery of input tax against supplies made by them at the standard rate. This should be contrasted with recovery of input tax where the supplies are exempt. The goods and services which are taxable at 0 per cent include food, clothing and transport. (See Value Added Tax Act 1994, Schedule 8.)   [RE]

See also EXEMPT SUPPLY.

APPENDIX

The Court System in England and Wales

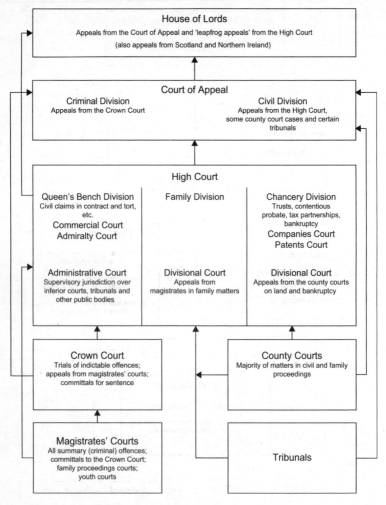

House of Lords
Appeals from the Court of Appeal and 'leapfrog appeals' from the High Court
(also appeals from Scotland and Northern Ireland)

Court of Appeal

Criminal Division
Appeals from the Crown Court

Civil Division
Appeals from the High Court,
some county court cases and certain
tribunals

High Court

Queen's Bench Division
Civil claims in contract and tort,
etc.
Commercial Court
Admiralty Court

Family Division

Chancery Division
Trusts, contentious
probate, tax partnerships,
bankruptcy
Companies Court
Patents Court

Administrative Court
Supervisory jurisdiction over
inferior courts, tribunals and
other public bodies

Divisional Court
Appeals from
magistrates in family matters

Divisional Court
Appeals from the county courts
on land and bankruptcy

Crown Court
Trials of indictable offences;
appeals from magistrates' courts;
committals for sentence

County Courts
Majority of matters in civil and family
proceedings

Magistrates' Courts
All summary (criminal) offences;
committals to the Crown Court;
family proceedings courts;
youth courts

Tribunals

Note: The House of Lords is due to be replaced by
the Supreme Court of the United Kingdom on
1 October 2009.

The Court System in Scotland

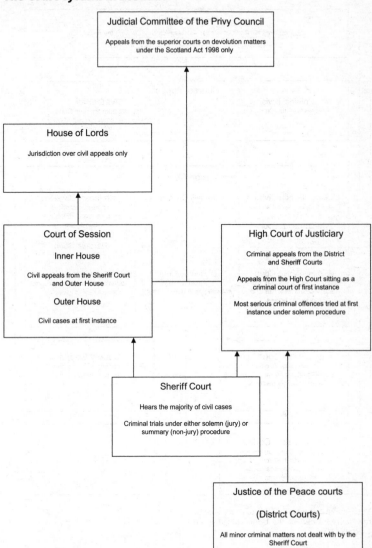

Judicial Committee of the Privy Council

Appeals from the superior courts on devolution matters under the Scotland Act 1998 only

House of Lords

Jurisdiction over civil appeals only

Court of Session

Inner House

Civil appeals from the Sheriff Court and Outer House

Outer House

Civil cases at first instance

High Court of Justiciary

Criminal appeals from the District and Sheriff Courts

Appeals from the High Court sitting as a criminal court of first instance

Most serious criminal offences tried at first instance under solemn procedure

Sheriff Court

Hears the majority of civil cases

Criminal trials under either solemn (jury) or summary (non-jury) procedure

Justice of the Peace courts

(District Courts)

All minor criminal matters not dealt with by the Sheriff Court

Note: The House of Lords is due to be replaced by the Supreme Court of the United Kingdom on 1 October 2009.

PENGUIN REFERENCE / LAW

MEDIA LAW
GEOFFREY ROBERTSON, QC
AND ANDREW NICOL, QC

'*Media Law* is a unique work. It should be read by media lawyers as well as lawyers with an interest in the media, journalists and publishers, and above all, those who doubt the extent of the media regulation in the UK'
New Law Journal

Media law is a minefield – but a minefield through which all working in the media must find their way if freedom of speech is to remain a reality in Britain.

This remarkable book provides practitioners with a thorough overview of the disparate laws that impinge upon journalists' and broadcasters' freedom to publish. The authors provide specialist analysis of case law wherever possible, as well as exhaustive coverage of all major areas of media law, detailing the up-to-date position on defamation, obscenity, official secrecy, copyright and confidentiality, contempt of court and protection of privacy.

Geoffrey Robertson, QC, and Andrew Nicol, QC, give an expert assessment of media law and offer wise counsel as to how its many uncertainties are likely to be resolved in practice.